ENCYCLOPEDIA OF SPECIAL EDUCATION

ENCYCLOPEDIA OF SPECIAL EDUCATION

A REFERENCE FOR THE EDUCATION
OF THE HANDICAPPED AND OTHER
EXCEPTIONAL CHILDREN AND ADULTS

VOLUME 2

EDITORS

CECIL R. REYNOLDS, Ph.D.
Texas A&M University

LESTER MANN, Ph.D.
Hunter College,
City University of New York

A WILEY-INTERSCIENCE PUBLICATION
JOHN WILEY & SONS
NEW YORK • CHICHESTER • BRISBANE • TORONTO • SINGAPORE

Library of Congress Cataloging-in-Publication Data

Encyclopedia of special education.

  "A Wiley–Interscience publication."
    1. Handicapped children—Education—United States—
Dictionaries. 2. Exceptional children—Education—
United States—Dictionaries. 3. Handicapped—Education—
United States—Dictionaries. I. Reynolds, Cecil R.,
1952–   . II. Mann, Lester.
LC4007.E53 1987   371.9′03′21   86-33975
ISBN 0471-63005-5 (Vol. 2)
ISBN 0471-82858-0 (Set)

Printed in the United States of America

10 9 8 7 6 5 4 3 2 1

EPICANTHIC FOLD

The epicanthic fold, also known as epicanthus, refers to the vertical fold of skin from the upper eyelid covering the lacrimal caruncle at the inner canthus of the eye (the point where the upper and lower eyelids meet). The expression of epicanthus may be extreme, covering the entire canthus, or mild. It is a normal feature in some ethnic groups, such as those of Asian descent. Epicanthus also is commonly seen in infants under approximately 3 years (Waldrop & Halverson, 1971).

In persons for whom there is no evidence of ethnic etiology, the presence of epicanthus may represent a congenital anomaly. Epicanthus is a physical anomaly that typically is observed in persons with Down's syndrome, for example (*Blakiston's*, 1979). Epicanthus also is one of several minor physical anomalies that has been associated with learning and behavior problems in children (Rosenberg & Weller, 1973; Waldrop & Halverson, 1971).

REFERENCES

Blakiston's Gould medical dictionary (4th ed.). (1979). New York: McGraw-Hill.

Rosenberg, J. B., & Weller, G. M. (1973). Minor physical anomalies and academic performance in young school children. *Developmental Medicine & Child Neurology, 15*, 131–135.

Waldrop, M. F., & Halverson, C. F. (1971). Minor physical anomalies and hyperactive behavior in young children. In J. Hellmuth (Ed.), *The exceptional infant* (Vol. 2, pp. 343–380). New York: Brunner/Mazel.

CATHY F. TELZROW
*Cuyahoga Special Education
Service Center, Maple
Heights, Ohio*

DYSMORPHIC FEATURES
MINOR PHYSICAL ANOMALIES

EPIDEMIOLOGY

Epidemiology is reviewed within two models: medical and psychological. Epidemiology is the study of specific medical disorders within communities to measure risk of attack and to uncover etiological clues and modes of spread. Reid (1960) defines epidemiological inquiry as "the study of the distribution of diseases in time and space, and of the factors that influence this distribution."

While elucidating etiology is a prime concern, collected data is used in planning services and devising treatment modes (Graham, 1979). Basic data includes (1) identification of a particular disorder in a defined population, (2) incidence rates, (3) prevalence rates, and (4) dynamic patterns of occurrence over time. In addition to identifying disease syndromes and origins, epidemiology serves to test the reliability of concepts derived solely from clinical studies, thus avoiding assumptions based on relationships that may be merely correlational rather than causative.

Epidemiology employed to study psychological disorders uncovers common underlying factors in nonmedical problems. The premise of both models remains unchanged: to complete the clinical picture (Morris, 1964). Neither model is used solely to collect information but to use data to further effective treatment and services for disordered populations.

One basic difference between medical and psychological epidemiology is that the former has definitive criteria for judging physical normalcy while the latter, focusing primarily on behavior, is left with a range of altering, social criteria that are difficult to quantify. Another difference between the models concerns the search for etiology that may or may not be relevant to nonmedical surveys, depending on the conceptual perspective of the researcher (e.g., psychoanalytic, behavioral systems theory). Nevertheless, a profitable psychological inquiry employs quantitative cutoff points, if defined arbitrarily, to identify deviations from the norm (Rutter et al., 1970). Epidemiologists who take behavior as the starting point define disorders according to social criteria, itemize behaviors, count behaviors empirically, and factor analyze data to examine the amount of variance explained by particular behavior dimensions for different populations (Rutter, 1977).

Methodological problems in the psychological approach include (1) whether the population is represented in sampling; (2) questionnaire reliability; (3) whether nonresponders represent an atypical group; and (4) whether observed behavior is related to events and people in a subject's life. Psychological epidemiology is the vehicle for a number of comprehensive studies along a wide range of topics: child abuse (Baldwin & Oliver, 1975; Light, 1973); specific reading retardation in relation to deviant behavior (Rutter & Yule, 1973); disorders of middle childhood (Pringle et al., 1966; Rutter et al., 1970); adolescent turmoil (Rutter et al., 1976); and autism (Folstein & Rutter, 1977).

REFERENCES

Baldwin, J. A., & Oliver, J. E. (1975). Epidemiology and family characteristics of severely abused children. *British Journal of Preventive & Social Medicine, 29*, 205–221.

Folstein, S., & Rutter, M. (1977). Generic influences and infantile autism. *Nature, 265*, 726–728.

Graham, P. (1979). Epidemiological studies. In H. C. Quay & J. S. Werry (Eds.), *Psychopathological disorders of childhood*. New York: Wiley.

Light, R. J. (1973). Abused and neglected children in America: A study of alternative policies. *Harvard Educational Review, 43*, 556.

Morris, J. N. (1964). *Uses of epidemiology*. Baltimore, MD: Williams & Wilkins.

Pringle, M. L. K., Butler, N. R., & Davie, R. (1966). *11,000 seven-year-olds*. London: Longmans.

Reid, D. D. (1960). *Epidemiological methods in the study of mental disorders*. Geneva, Switzerland: World Health Organization.

Rutter, M. (1977). Surveys to answer questions. In P. J. Graham (Ed.), *Epidemiological approaches in child psychiatry*. New York: Academic.

Rutter, M., Graham, P., Chadwick, O., & Yule, W. (1976). Adolescent turmoil: Fact or fiction. *Journal of Child Psychology & Psychiatry, 17*, 35–56.

Rutter, M., Tizard, J., & Whitmore, K. (Eds.). (1970). *Education, health and behavior*. London: Longmans.

Rutter, M., & Yule, W. (1973). Specific reading retardation. In L. Mann & D. Sabatino (Eds.), *The first review of special education*. Philadelphia: JSE.

C. MILDRED TASHMAN
College of Saint Rose

DIAGNOSIS IN SPECIAL EDUCATION
ETIOLOGY
RESEARCH IN SPECIAL EDUCATION

EPILEPSY

Epilepsy is the most common neurological disease. The term seizure disorder frequently is applied to the syndrome and often is used synonymously. Epilepsy generally connotes a tendency to have recurring seizures, together with periodic or permanent cerebral dysfunction. Epileptic seizures involve the abnormal electrical activity, or discharge, of cerebral neurons. In 1870, Hughlings Jackson defined epilepsy as a group of disorders with paroxysmal and excessive neuronal discharge that cause a sudden disturbance in neurologic function. Brain (1955) defined epilepsy as "a paroxysmal and transitory disturbance of the function of the brain which develops suddenly, ceases spontaneously, and exhibits a conspicuous tendency to recurrence" (p. 1093). Alter, Masland, Kurtzke, and Reed (1972) proposed the definition of a sudden change in intellectual, sensory, motor, autonomic, or emotional activity, limited in length (usually under 1 hour) and presumably associated with neuronal overactivity.

Many attempts have been made to classify the different epilepsies, but no classification is widely accepted. Over the past several years, an International classification of seizures has evolved that condenses the diverse manifestations of epileptic seizures into a concise scheme (Table 1). Terms other than the more commonly known grand mal, petit mal, psychomotor, and focal were required, as it became clear that most recurrent seizures begin in local areas of the cerebral cortex and present clinically as sequences of symptoms consequent to the spread of discharges to adjacent and distant regions of the brain. While

Table 1. International Classification of Epileptic Seizures[a]

Partial Seizures (beginning locally)
A. Simple partial seizures (consciousness not impaired)
1. With motor symptoms
2. With somatosensory or special sensory symptoms
3. With automatic symptoms
4. With psychic symptoms
B. Complex partial (psychomotor) seizures (with impaired consciousness)
1. Beginning as simple partial seizures and progressing to impairment of consciousness
2. With impairment of consciousness at onset
a. with impairment of consciousness only
b. with automatisms
C. Partial seizures secondarily generalized
a. secondary to simple partial seizures
b. secondary to complex partial seizures
II. Generalized Seizures (bilaterally symmetric and without local onset)
A. Absence seizure (petit mal)
B. Myoclonic seizures
C. Clonic seizures
D. Tonic seizures
E. Tonic-clonic seizures (grand mal)
F. Atonic seizures
III. Unclassified Epileptic Seizures (incomplete data)

[a] Modified from Proposal for Revised Clinical and Electroencephalographic Classification of Epileptic Seizures (1981).

this new classification scheme has improved professional communication and patient care (Goldensohn, Glaser, & Goldberg, 1984), it has not yet gained uniform acceptance by workers in the field.

Seizures are divided into two major categories: partial and generalized. Partial seizures begin in unilateral (focal or local) areas and may or may not spread bilaterally. Generalized seizures begin with immediate involvement of bilateral brain structures.

Partial seizures are divided into three types: (1) simple partial attacks that arise from a local area and do not impair consciousness: (2) complex partial seizures that begin in a local area but spread bilaterally and therefore impair consciousness; and (3) simple or complex partial seizures that may spread widely and secondarily evolve into generalized major motor seizures. Generalized seizures begin with immediate involvement of both hemispheres and are associated with either bilateral motor movements or changes in consciousness, or both. Generalized seizures are divided into six types: (1) short absence seizures with associated 3-Hz (cycles per second) generalized spike-and-wave discharges in the EEG (electroencephalogram); (2) atypical absence seizures; (3) myoclonic seizures; (4) clonic seizures; (5) tonic-clonic seizures; and

(6) atonic seizures. Seizures that cannot be classified because of incomplete data are listed simply as unclassified.

Partial seizures are the most common type of epileptic seizures. The first clinical and EEG features indicate that they begin in unilateral structures. Partial seizures are divided into two types that are based primarily on whether consciousness is affected. If consciousness is unimpaired during the attack, it is a simple partial type. If there is a degree of altered awareness or unresponsiveness, or both, it is a complex partial seizure.

Simple partial seizures often exhibit primary neurologic symptoms that indicate the site of origin. They are divided into four subtypes: partial motor attacks, autonomic attacks, somatosensory attacks, and special sensory attacks. Partial motor attacks involve motor activity from any portion of the body. They usually involve the limbs, face, or head, and sometimes cause speech arrest. If a partial motor seizure progresses with sequential involvement of parts of the body that are represented by contiguous cortical areas, it is known as a Jacksonian seizure. Localized paralysis or weakness that may last for minutes or days sometimes occurs and indicates an underlying structural lesion. Partial motor seizures also can be continuous for extended periods of time.

Autonomic symptoms (such as thirst or a desire to micturate) are rarely the sole manifestations of recurrent seizures. Somatosensory attacks usually are described as feelings of numbness, deadness, or "pins and needles." Special sensory seizures include simple visual, auditory, olfactory, gustatory, and vertiginous feelings such as seeing flashing lights, hearing buzzing, or smelling unpleasant odors. Nearly all special sensory seizures are, at one time or another, the aura or earliest symptoms of a complex partial or generalized tonic-clonic seizure. On occasion, these seizures may have what are referred to as psychic phenomena associated with them such as déjà vu, flashback experiences of previous events, or forced thinking. Affective symptoms such as fear or depression may be experienced.

Characteristically, complex partial seizures begin with emotional, psychic, illusory, hallucinatory, or special sensory symptoms. This is followed by clouding of consciousness with automatic behavior and amnesia. Sometimes, consciousness becomes impaired at the onset of the attack. Complex partial seizures occur in over 50% of adults with seizure disorders. After the aura, the individual becomes partially or completely unresponsive and may perform apparently purposeful activity. These automatisms are usually simple acts (e.g., picking at clothes, examining nearby objects, simply walking about), but more elaborate behavior may be seen during the period of impaired awareness. In the state of depressed awareness, patients may actively resist efforts to restrain them. A complete attack usually lasts between 1 and 3 minutes; on recovery, there is complete amnesia for the attack except for the aura or partial motor onset. Complex partial seizures usually begin in the temporal lobe but may originate from the frontal, parietal, or occipital regions. Attacks that begin with visual hallucinations, for example, frequently begin in the posterior portion of the temporal lobe but may originate in the occipital lobe. Attacks beginning with unpleasant odors uniformly begin in temporal structures, usually in the anterior medial portion. Automatic behavior (automatisms) that are an integral part of a complex partial seizure may occur after abnormal discharges have spread bilaterally.

Generalized seizures involve bilateral brain regions and are of six types. Absence seizures are short interruptions of consciousness that last from 3 to 15 seconds each. They are not associated with auras or other evidence of focal onset. Absence seizures begin and end abruptly and recur from a few to several hundred times per day. Ongoing behavior stops. While otherwise immobile, the individual may show inconspicuous flickering of the eyelids or eyebrows about three times per second; there may be simple automatic movements, such as rubbing the nose, putting a hand to the face, or chewing and swallowing. Falling or loss of muscle tone does not occur. Immediately following the short interruption of awareness, the individual is again mentally clear and fully capable of continuing previous activity. In patients with absence seizures of this type, there are bilaterally synchronous 3 Hz spike-and-wave discharges, usually occurring against an otherwise normal background activity. The age of onset of these short absence seizures is almost always after age $2\frac{1}{2}$; they almost never occur for the first time after age 20. Individuals with short absence seizures rarely have other neurological problems, but 40 to 50% of the patients have infrequent, easily controlled, generalized tonic-clonic seizures. Photic sensitivity is present in some cases.

Absences clinically similar to the type described may occur in brain-damaged patients (a condition known as the Lennox-Gastaut syndrome), but the episodes occur less frequently and are of longer duration, and the EEG includes slower (1.5–2 Hz spike-and-wave) discharges as well as continuous abnormalities in the background activity. Short periods of unresponsiveness, which also occur in individuals with complex partial seizures, are usually easily distinguished from the generalized absence seizures because complex partial seizures are preceded by auras or special sensory symptoms, last longer, and are followed by confusion or sleepiness. In complex partial seizures, the EEG typically shows focal interictal (that time between seizures) spikes, most often from the temporal lobe. Prolonged changes in behavior rarely continue for a day or more, although this is more likely to occur with absence seizures accompanied by continuous 3 Hz spike-and-wave discharges than with complex partial seizures. In either case, the patient performs activity in a confused manner with varying degrees of consciousness and amnesia.

Generalized tonic-clonic seizures occur at some time in most patients with epilepsy regardless of the individual's usual pattern. A tonic-clonic seizure is classified under generalized seizures if the attack itself, the neurological examination, and the EEG all indicate that bilateral cerebral structures are simultaneously involved at the onset. A tonic-clonic seizure is classified as a partial seizure evolving to a secondarily generalized one if the same criteria indicate that the attack began in one hemisphere and then spread to produce a major generalized attack.

Tonic-clonic convulsions usually last 3 to 5 minutes and are characterized by a complex loss of consciousness and falling. As the patient falls, the body stiffens because of generalized tonic contraction of the limb and axial muscles. The legs usually extend and the arms flex partially. After the tonic stage, which usually lasts less than 1 minute, jerking or clonic movements occur in all four limbs for about 1 minute. Next, a period of unconsciousness follows (about 1 minute) during which the patient appears more relaxed. Consciousness then is regained and the patient usually is confused, sleepy, and uncooperative for several minutes prior to full recovery.

Myoclonic seizures are involuntary contractions of the limb and truncal muscles that are sudden, brief, and recurrent. Slight bilateral symmetric myoclonic movements often occur in persons who have absence seizures with 3 Hz spike-and-wave complexes, but rarely are severe bilaterally symmetric myoclonic jerks the predominant symptoms of individuals with absence seizures.

Tonic spasms are sudden flexions of the body, waist, and neck. These attacks begin when the patient is between 2 and 6 months of age and do not persist after age 5. The infant often displays bilateral myoclonic jerks and abrupt head-drops. These spasms occur many times per day, usually in clusters, and are part of a syndrome called infantile spasms, in which the typical EEG pattern is known as hypsarrhythmia. Most infants with tonic spasms and hypsarrhythmia later are found to be mentally impaired.

Atonic or astatic seizures usually begin in childhood and are characterized by sudden loss of postural tone. Sometimes this causes the patient to drop abruptly to the ground. The episodes occur without warning, are extremely short, and frequently cause injury. Sometimes the decrease in muscle tone is less complete and causes only slumping or head-drop. If consciousness is lost, it is regained within a few moments of the loss of tone. The attacks often are seen in retarded children with other evidence of brain abnormality. Atonic seizures persist into adulthood and are particularly difficult to treat.

Status epilepticus is a condition in which there are persistent and repetitive tonic-clonic convulsions. It is considered a medical emergency that requires immediate and vigorous appropriate treatment, as lack of treatment or inappropriate treatment can result in severe brain damage or death.

Treatment for epilepsy generally consists of four parts: (1) identification and elimination of factors that cause or precipitate attacks; (2) sustaining of general mental and

Table 2. Commonly Used Anticonvulsant Medications

Generic Name	Common Trade Name	Seizure Type Controlled
Phenytoin	Dilantin	Partial
		Generalized tonic-clonic
Phenobarbital	—	Partial
		Generalized tonic-clonic
Primidone	Mysoline	(Same as phenobarbital)
Ethosuximide	Zarontin	Absence
		Atonic
Carbamazepine	Tegretol	Partial
		Generalized tonic-clonic
Clonazepam	Clonopin	Atypical absence
		Myoclonic
Valproic Acid	Depakene	Absence
		Myoclonic

physical health and social integration; (3) pharmacological therapy that raises the convulsive threshold to prevent attacks; and (4) surgical therapy for carefully selected patients with seizure of focal origin or for those for whom medication has proven completely ineffective. The basic principle of anticonvulsant (pharmacologic) therapy is to select an appropriate drug for the specific type of seizure until seizure control is achieved or until toxic side effects limit further increments. One of the major causes of failure of drug therapy is patient noncompliance in taking medication. This may occur because patients misunderstand directions or neglect to take all prescribed doses because of actual or imagined side effects or for psychological reasons. The common medications used for seizure control are listed in Table 2.

Whenever convulsive seizures are associated with a surgically removable space-occupying lesion of the brain (e.g., tumor, abscess), removal of the lesion often is performed. Surgical removal of portions of the brain for treatment of seizures often is a risky and imprecise procedure as certain cognitive functions may be disrupted by removal of brain tissue. In addition, the focus of the seizure disorder often is several centimeters away from the visible lesion. The anterior portion of the temporal lobe is the most frequent site of surgical excision in individuals with medically intractable seizures.

REFERENCES

Alter, M., Masland, R. L., Kurtzke, J. F., & Reed, D. M. (1972). Proposed definitions and classifications of epilepsy for epidemiological purposes. In M. Alter & W. A. Hauser (Eds.), *The epidemiology of epilepsy: A workshop* (pp. 101–110). National Institute of Neurological Disease and Stroke. Monograph No. 14. Washington, DC: U.S. Department of Health, Education, and Welfare.

Brain, W. R. (1955). *Diseases of the nervous system* (5th ed.). New York: Oxford University Press.

Goldensohn, E. S., Glaser, G. H., & Goldberg, M. A. (1984). Epilepsy. In L. P. Rowland (Ed.), *Merritt's textbook of neurology* (7th ed., pp. 629–650). Philadelphia: Lea & Febiger.

Proposal for revised clinical and electroencephalographic classification of epileptic seizures. (1981). *Epilepsia, 22*, 489–501.

RICHARD A. BERG
*West Virginia University
Medical Center, Charleston
Division*

ABSENCE SEIZURES
ANTICONVULSANTS
ELECTROENCEPHALOGRAPH
GRAND MAL SEIZURES

EPILEPSY FOUNDATION OF AMERICA (EFA)

The Epilepsy Foundation of America (EFA) is a nonprofit, voluntary health organization devoted to epilepsy care, treatment, research, and education. The national foundation, together with its numerous local chapters, provides information on a wide variety of issues related to epilepsy, including low-cost anticonvulsant medication, legal rights, and employment. The foundation provides a discount drug pharmacy service for its members.

Numerous excellent publications relevant to the school-age child with epilepsy are available from the foundation. These include pamphlets such as "What Everybody Should Know About Epilepsy," "Epilepsy: The Teacher's Role," and "Epilepsy School Alert." School Alert is one of two major annual educational programs sponsored by the foundation. In operation since 1972, the School Alert program was developed in conjunction with the Department of School Nurses and the National Education Association; it is designed for EFA chapter use with schools in the local chapter vicinity. Some state departments of education have officially endorsed the School Alert program.

The address for the Epilepsy Foundation of America is 1828 L Street, N.W., Washington, DC 20036.

REFERENCES

Epilepsy school alert. (1974). Washington, DC: Epilepsy Foundation of America.

Foster, J. C., Szoke, C. O., Kapisovsky, P. M., & Kriger, L. S. (1979). *Guidance, counseling, and support services for high school students with physical disabilities.* Cambridge, MA: Technical Education Research Centers.

CATHY F. TELZROW
*Cuyahoga Special Education
Service Center, Maple
Heights, Ohio*

EPINEPHRINE

Epinephrine is one of the naturally occurring catecholamines (together with norepinephrine and dopamine). Its action sites are mainly in the sympathetic nervous system (Katzung, 1982). Leavitt (1982) suggests wider involvement of epinephrine in autonomic processes owing to its presence in the hypothalamus. The gross actions of epinephrine are to relax bronchial muscles, constrict bronchial vasculature, and increase cardiac output, thus increasing overall oxygenation. Secondary central nervous system effects may occur through the overall increase in blood pressure and oxygen availability (McEvoy, 1984). Thus, the overall action of epinephrine is that of a mild stimulant. Because of its action as a bronchodilator, one of the chief uses of epinephrine is in providing symptomatic relief for sufferers of asthma and chronic obstructive pulmonary diseases.

Side effects of epinephrine overdosage or sensitivity are similar to those of other stimulants; i.e., fear, anxiety, tenseness, restlessness, sleeplessness, or excitability (Blum, 1984). More serious reactions appear similar to amphetamine toxicity and include psychomotor agitation, assaultiveness, disorientation, impaired memory, panic, hallucinations, and homicidal or suicidal ideation/tendencies (McEvoy, 1984). Toxicity is more likely to occur among persons who are hypertensive or hyperthyroid (McEvoy, 1984).

REFERENCES

Blum, K. (1984). *Handbook of abusable drugs.* New York: Gardner Press.

Katzung, B. G. (1982). *Basic and clinical pharmocology.* Los Altos, CA: Lange Medical.

Leavitt, F. (1982). *Drugs and behavior.* New York: Wiley.

McEvoy, G. K. (1984). *American hospital formulary service: Drug information 84.* Bethesda, MD: American Society of Hospital Pharmacists.

ROBERT F. SAWICKI
*Lake Erie Institute of
Rehabilitation, Lake Erie,
Pennsylvania*

CATECHOLAMINES
DOPAMINE

EQUAL EDUCATIONAL OPPORTUNITY

In its earliest form, equal educational opportunity referred to a belief that education would "close no entrance to the poorest, the weakest, the humblest. Say to ambition everywhere, the field is clear, the contest fair; come, and win your share if you can!" (Woodard & Watson, 1963). A number of judicial decisions have affirmed this basic premise that underlies equal educational opportunity (e.g., *Brown* v. *Board of Education*, 1954, 1955; *Lau* v. *Nichols*, 1974; *Regents of California* v. *Bakke*, 1978).

While there is general agreement on what constitutes equal educational opportunity, there is some uncertainty as to whether this implies equal access to education, the process of education, or the outcomes of education (Hyman & Schaaf, 1981). In the case of handicapped learners, the concept of equal opportunity has focused on equal access and equity in the process of education.

The first equal opportunity decision involving handicapped students (*PARC* v. *Commonwealth*, 1971) resulted in an order providing that the state of Pennsylvania could not postpone or deny handicapped children access to a publicly supported education. In addition, those school districts that provided education to preschool children were required to provide such education for handicapped children. A similar case in the District of Columbia (*Mills* v. *Board of Education*, 1972) resulted in a similar judicial order, with the court indicating that

> if sufficient funds are not available to finance all of the services and programs that are needed and desirable in the system, then the available funds must be expended equitably in such a manner that no child is entirely excluded from a publicly supported education consistent with his needs and ability to benefit therefrom.

Apart from protections afforded by the judiciary, attorney generals in a number of states interpreted state laws, regulations, and administrative guidelines to include the public education of handicapped children and youths (e.g., Arkansas, 1973; Wisconsin, 1973).

With the passage of PL 94-142, the Education of All Handicapped Children Act, the federal government extended the concept of equal educational opportunity to include the process by which education is delivered. Not only was access to education required, but it was to be provided, to the extent possible, with nonhandicapped students in regular education classrooms. Moreover, handicapped students were to receive specially designed instruction to meet their unique needs, as well as the related services (e.g., audiology, psychological services) required for handicapped students to benefit from special education.

REFERENCES

Hyman, J. B., & Schaaf, J. M. (1981). *Educational equity: Conceptual problems and prospects for theory.* Washington, DC: National Institute of Education.

U.S. Department of Education. (1985). *Seventh annual report to Congress on the implementation of the Education of the Handicapped Act.* Washington, DC: U.S. Department of Education.

Woodard, C. V., & Watson, T. (1963). *Agrarian rebel.* New York: Oxford University Press.

PATRICIA ANN ABRAMSON
*Hudson Public Schools,
Hudson, Wisconsin*

BROWN *v.* BOARD OF EDUCATION
MAINSTREAMING
MILLS *v.* BOARD OF EDUCATION
PENNSYLVANIA ASSOCIATION FOR RETARDED CITIZENS
   v. PENNSYLVANIA

EQUAL EMPLOYMENT OPPORTUNITY COMMISSION (EEOC)

The purposes of the Equal Employment Opportunity Commission (EEOC) are to eliminate discrimination based on race, color, religion, national origin, and age in hiring, promoting, firing, wages, testing, training, apprenticeship, and all other conditions of employment. The commission also promotes voluntary action programs by employers, unions, and community organizations to make equal employment opportunity an actuality. The EEOC also is responsible for all compliance and enforcement activities relating to equal employment among federal employees and applicants, including handicap discrimination (*Federal Register*, 1985, p. 398).

The EEOC was created under Title VII of the Civil Rights Act of 1964. Title VII was amended by the Equal Employment Opportunity Act of 1972 and the Pregnancy Discrimination Act of 1978. The commission consists of five commissioners appointed by the president with advice and consent of the Senate to five-year terms. The president designates a commissioner as chairperson and appoints a counsel general. The work of the commission has been credited with widespread banning of various forms of discrimination against a variety of groups. Reorganization Plan One of 1978 transferred to the EEOC Section 501 of the Rehabilitation Act of 1973, which pertains to employment discrimination against handicapped persons in the federal government.

The EEOC has field offices that receive written complaints against public or private employers, labor organizations, joint labor-management, and apprenticeship programs for charges of job discrimination or age discrimination. Charges of Title VII violations in private industry or state or local government must be filed with the commission within 180 days of the alleged violation. The commission has the authority to bring suit in federal district court if a negotiated settlement cannot be found. The commission encourages settlements prior to determination by the agency through fact-finding conferences and informal methods of conciliation, conference, and persuasion.

The EEOC has issued several guidelines on employment policies and practices, the most comprehensive of which are the Guidelines on Discrimination Because of Sex (April 5, 1972) and the Guidelines on Employee Selection Procedures (August 1, 1970). The commission is also a major publisher of employment data on minorities and women. For further information, contact the Director,

Office of Public Affairs, Equal Employment Opportunity Commission, Room 412, 2401 E. Street NW, Washington, DC 20507.

REFERENCES

Darby, M. (1983). Equal employment opportunity commission. In D. R. Whitman (Ed.), *Government agencies*. Westport, CT: Greenwood.

Equal Employment Opportunity Commission. (1983). 17th annual report. *American statistics index* (10th Suppl.).

Federal Register. *The United States government manual 1985–86*. Washington, DC: U.S. Government Printing Office.

DANIEL PAULSON
University of Wisconsin, Stout

CIVIL RIGHTS OF THE HANDICAPPED
EQUAL EDUCATION OPPORTUNITY

EQUAL PROTECTION

Equal protection is a term often applied to the need for due process in the differential treatment of any persons in society. In special education, equal protection applies to placement proceedings or any other action that might result in differential treatment of a child. The term is derived from the Fourteenth Amendment to the U.S. Constitution.

The Fourteenth Amendment equal protection clause provides, in a simple, straightforward statement, the far-reaching assertion that "no state shall . . . deny to any person within its jurisdiction the equal protection of the laws." The court system has interpreted this statement in numerous cases and generally holds that it does not require that all persons be treated equally under all laws at all times. According to Overcast and Sales (1982), the essence of the constitutional guarantee provided by the equal protection clause of the Fourteenth Amendment is that any classifications made in a rule or a law must be reasonable and not of an arbitrary nature. In determining the reasonableness of a classification, the courts normally look to see whether (1) the classification itself is a reasonable one, (2) the classification furthers an appropriate or legitimate government purpose, and, (3) the classification's subgroups, or classes, are treated equally (Overcast & Sales, 1982).

Whenever the classification affects a fundamental right or is related to suspect criteria (e.g., is statistically related to membership in a protected class such as race or handicap), the judiciary also will examine two additional criteria. The court wishes to determine in these circumstances, which circumstances are always extant in special education, whether the classification is necessary to promote some compelling state interest, and whether the classification represents the least burdensome alternative available or that can be designed. Suspect criteria that have been identified by the courts include race, religion, national origin, alien status, legitimacy, poverty, and sex. Discrimination related to these categories takes place almost daily in the schools, however, it must be based on a valid distinction among the groups.

The courts have held that they have the right to intervene in the actions of schools and others when any basic constitutional safeguard is violated, including the equal protection clause (e.g., *Epperson* v. *Arkansas*, 1968; *Ingraham* v. *Wright*, 1977). The equal protection clause has been used to protect students' right to an education on a number of occasions; this clause may be (and certainly has been) interpreted as granting the right to equal educational opportunity. School systems cannot discriminate among groups of people when providing an education unless there is a substantial and legitimate purpose for the discrimination (Bersoff, 1982). Prior to the passage of PL 94-142, the Education for All Handicapped Children Act of 1975, advocates fighting for the right of the handicapped to attend public schools, from which they were frequently excluded, relied heavily on the equal protection clause of the Fourteenth Amendment in winning their cases. The equal protection clause also has been invoked in favor of children classified as handicapped who have argued they are not handicapped and claimed that by placing them in special education programs, they have been denied equal protection through exclusion from access to regular education with normal children (Bersoff, 1982).

REFERENCES

Bersoff, D. N. (1982). The legal regulation of school psychology. In C. R. Reynolds & T. B. Gutkin (Eds.), *The handbook of school psychology*. New York: Wiley.

Overcast, T. D., & Sales, B. D. (1982). The legal rights of students in the elementary and secondary public schools. In C. R. Reynolds & T. B. Gutkin (Eds.), *The handbook of school psychology*. New York: Wiley.

CECIL R. REYNOLDS
Texas A&M University

EDUCATION FOR ALL HANDICAPPED CHILDREN ACT OF 1975
LARRY P.
MARSHALL v. GEORGIA
MATTY T. v. HOLLADAY

EQUINE THERAPY

Equine therapy refers to prescribed medical treatment that uses horsemanship to alleviate an extensive array of physical, psychological, cognitive, and social disabilities.

Brought to the United States from Europe, it has grown steadily in this country in popularity and credibility since 1970. Its effectiveness depends on the integration of services provided by a physician who prescribes treatment, a physical therapist who designs the therapeutic regimen, and an instructor who implements the program.

Kuprian (1981) distinguishes between hippotherapy, in which the horse's symmetrical rhythms are transferred to the rider's body passively, and riding therapy, in which the rider engages in active exercise (relaxation, stretching, strengthening). Still more advanced is vaulting, in which gymnastics are introduced (Kroger, 1981), and riding as sport, in which an individual competes against others, having accomplished a sufficient degree of fitness and skill (Heipertz, 1981). To the extent possible, grooming, tacking, and general horsemanship are added to each of these.

Among the benefits accredited to equine therapy by its proponents, riding skill notwithstanding, are improved physical mobility, stability, muscle tone, coordination, and balance; sensory integration; cognitive training and retraining; academic performance; emotional stability (self-esteem, accountability, diminished aggression); communication facility; and the ability to relate to others and function within a group (Brooke, 1976; Mason, 1980; Minner, Lawton, & Rusk, 1983; Stanford & Hawn, 1982). The fact that riding offers so many advantages to individuals of varying capacities is attributable, according to Rosenthal (1975), to its ability to satisfy the need inherent in all people for controlled risk activity. It is not recommended for all disabilities, however. Epilepsy characterized by seizures, for example, is considered too risky, as are bone and joint anomalies.

Additional information may be obtained from the Cheff Center for the Handicapped, Augusta, MI; the North American Riding for the Handicapped Association (NARHA), Ashburn, VA; and Winslow Therapeutic Riding Unlimited, Inc., Warwick, N.Y.

REFERENCES

Brooke, G. A. G. (1976). What riding offers the mentally handicapped. *Voice, 26*(2), 12–13.

Heipertz, W. (1981). Riding therapy for orthopaedic cases. In W. Heipertz (Ed.), *Therapeutic riding: Medicine, education, sports* (translated by M. Takeuchi) (pp. 55–66). Canada: National Printers, Inc.

Kroger, A. (1981). Vaulting as an educational aid in schools for behaviorally disturbed children. In W. Heipertz (Ed.), *Therapeutic riding: Medicine, education, sports* (translated by M. Takeuchi) (pp. 40–54). Canada: National Printers.

Kuprian, W. (1981). Hippotherapy and riding therapy as physiotherapeutic treatment methods. In W. Heipertz (Ed.), *Therapeutic riding: Medicine, education, sports* (translated by M. Takeuchi) (pp. 14–39). Canada: National Printers.

Mason, H. (1980). A ride to health. *Special Education in Canada, 54*(4), 28–29.

Minner, S., Lawton, S., & Rusk, P. (1983). Equine therapy for handicapped students. *Pointer, 27*(4), 41–43.

Rosenthal, S. R. (1975). Risk exercise and the physically handicapped. *Rehabilitation Literature, 36*(5), 144–149.

Stanford, E., & Hawn, P. (1982). *Equestrian therapy in the treatment of traumatic head injury patients.* Paper presented at the Fourth International Congress on Therapeutic Riding, Malvern, PA.

SUSAN SHANDELMIER
*Eastern Pennsylvania Special
Education Regional
Resources Center, King of
Prussia, Pennsylvania*

**OCCUPATIONAL THERAPY
PHYSICAL THERAPY**

ERRORLESS LEARNING

Errorless learning is the practice of structuring a task so that the learner is taught a skill or concept without having the opportunity to make errors. A detailed analysis of all subskills is made and then ordered into a task analysis. The presentation of the task by the teacher to the learner follows a paradigm that maximizes the probability of success. The plan calls for interrupting a response on the part of the learner if it appears that the wrong response will be given. The system uses a cuing system to maximize success. It also structures response options to maximize success. The first response would require no discrimination on the part of the learner but would consist merely of the model (correct response) presented to the learner. In a second stage, the correct response and a foil would be presented with a cue to the correct response. As the teaching progresses, the discriminations that must be made become more complex. The model has been used with the severely retarded and the young learner. The rationale for the model is that by structuring a task so that errors are not committed, the learning is more efficient. Learners do not commit errors and therefore do not waste time practicing errors.

ROBERT A. SEDLAK
University of Wisconsin, Stout

**DIRECT INSTRUCTION
LEARNED HELPLESSNESS
TASK ANALYSIS**

ERTL INDEX

The problem of cultural bias in traditional measures of intelligence has led to the development of alternative assessment strategies. One rather exotic strategy is the use of the Neural Efficiency Analyzer (NEA). Introduced by Ertl (1968), this instrument is purported to measure the reaction time of brain waves to 100 randomly presented flashes of light. Ertl argued that in contrast to traditional methods of intellectual assessment, the score obtained from the Neural Efficiency Analyzer (Ertl Index) was free of cultural influences and thus was appropriate for use with any ethnic group regardless of age.

The Ertl Index consists of the average time from the onset of the stimulus light to the appropriate brain wave change. Based on this average evoked potential, an estimate of the subject's performance on a more traditional measure of cognitive functioning (e.g., Wechsler Intelligence Scale for Children) is also calculated. In support of this proposed relationship between the Ertl Index and intellectual functioning, Ertl (1968) presented data suggesting a concomitant decrease in the neural efficiency score upon ingestion of chemicals known to impede cognitive functioning (e.g., alcohol). Moreover, Ertl found that when these chemicals were removed, the neural efficiency scores returned to normal limits.

Clinically, Ertl proposed that the Ertl Index would serve as a screening measure for cognitive difficulties. He argued that special educational placement based on culturally free measures such as the Ertl Index would eliminate the educational misclassification of culturally deprived children. Moreover, Ertl proposed that the Ertl Index "should permanently dispel the myth of racial inequality in the United States" (Tracy, 1972, p. 90). In support of this argument, Ertl (Tracy, 1972) presented data suggesting that there were no significant differences between the brain wave activities (Ertl Index) of blacks and whites.

While the Neural Efficiency Analyzer appeared to be an innovative attempt to minimize the cultural bias in intelligence testing, empirical evidence does not support the use of this measure on a clinical basis. Indeed, Evans, Martin, and Hatchette (1976) showed that the Ertl Index did not discriminate between children with learning problems and normal controls. Similarly, it was found that the Ertl Index did not significantly predict college grade point averages (Sturgis, Lemke, & Johnson, 1977).

REFERENCES

Ertl, J. (1968). Evoked potential and human intelligence. Final Report, USOE, Project No. 6–1454.

Evans, J. R., Martin, D., & Hatchette, R. (1976). Neural Efficiency Analyzer scores of reading disabled, normally reading and academically superior children. *Perceptual & Motor Skills, 43,* 1248–1250.

Sturgis, R., Lemke, E. A., & Johnson, J. J. (1977). A validity study of the Neural Efficiency Analyzer in relation to selected measures of intelligence. *Perceptual & Motor Skills, 45,* 475–478

Tracy, W. (1972). Goodbye IQ, Hello EI (Ertl Index). *Phi Delta Kappan, 54,* 89–94.

JEFFREY W. GRAY
Ball State University

RAYMOND S. DEAN
Ball State University
Indiana University School
of Medicine

INTELLIGENCE
INTELLIGENCE TESTING
NEURAL EFFICIENCY ANALYZER

ESQUIROL, JEAN E. (1722–1840)

Jean E. Esquirol, a French psychiatrist, studied under Phillipe Pinel in Paris, and succeeded him as resident physician at the Salpetriere. His exposure of inhumane practices in French institutions for the mentally ill contributed greatly to the development of properly run hospitals in France. Esquirol identified and described the main forms of mental illness, and in 1838 published *Des Maladies Mentales*, the first scientific treatment of the subject.

REFERENCE

Esquirol, J. E. (1838). *Des maladies mentales.* Paris: Bailliere.

PAUL IRVINE
Katonah, New York

ETHICS

Fischer (1978) has defined ethics as "the formal, well established standards that a profession follows in order to protect and promote the welfare of its clients and society" (p. 116). The prime responsibility of special educators lies in ensuring that the individuals they serve receive the services they need and are granted their educational rights (Paul, 1981).

Special education professionals such as special education teachers, social workers, counselors, psychologists, and researchers work with exceptional children and adults in a number of different settings. These special education professionals are guided by ethical standards that are published by different professional organizations. These standards are revised periodically to reflect current social changes and legal mandates (Mearig, 1978). For example, the American Psychological Association (1981) provides ethical guidelines for psychologists while the National Education Association (1985) provides a code of ethics for educators. These ethical standards dictate behaviors expected of professionals and provide guidelines for making professional decisions. Many of these organizations organize ethics committees in order to monitor the behavior of members of the profession.

For special educators working with exceptional children, a number of ethical issues are important. Special education professionals are responsible for knowing the ethical standards of the profession and must be knowledgeable about the rights of exceptional children and their parents. Parents of special education children need to be informed of these rights, including the granting of consent for evaluation, diagnosis, and education. The right to privacy of the individual youngster and the family must be protected and all records and pertinent information kept confidential. When delivering an intervention, special education professionals are mainly responsible for choosing an educational alternative that would not be harmful, physically or mentally, to the handicapped youngster.

For researchers working in the special education field, the American Psychological Association (1982) and others (Kimmel, 1981) offer behavioral standards. Subjects participating in special education studies must be informed of their rights. Informed consent must be obtained and confidentiality guaranteed.

However, these ethical guidelines are not all inclusive. Professionals will face situations not specifically addressed in ethical codes. For example, educators face a frequent ethical dilemma when the interests of the exceptional child are in conflict with the interests of the system (e.g., school, clinic). Although the primary responsibility is to the child, the professional is also expected to carry out requirements of the system that employs them (Weintraub & McCaffrey, 1976). Often, special education professionals are also faced with the dilemma of challenging the decision of a parent because that decision may not be in the child's interest. Because special education professionals often work within complicated contexts and are faced by conflicting forces, the answer to an ethical dilemma may not be found in the standards set forth by professional organizations. Under such circumstances, special education professionals may need to abide by their own individual decision processes, which should maintain as a priority the welfare of the handicapped child.

REFERENCES

American Psychological Association. (1981). *Ethical principles of psychologists*. Washington, DC: Author.

American Psychological Association. (1982). *Ethical principles in the conduct of research with human participants*. Washington, DC: Author.

Fischer, C. T. (1978). Dilemmas in standardized testing. In J. S. Mearig et al. (Eds.), *Working for children* (pp. 115–134). San Francisco: Jossey-Bass.

Kimmel, A. J. (Ed.). (1981). *Ethics of human subject research*. San Francisco: Jossey-Bass.

Mearig, J. S. (1978). Beyond guidelines: Opportunity and responsibility. In J. S. Mearig & Associates (Eds.), *Working for children* (pp. 296–325). San Francisco: Jossey-Bass.

National Education Association, (1985). *NEA Handbook: 1985–86*. Washington, DC: Author.

Paul, J. L. (1981). Service delivery models for special education. In J. M. Kauffman & D. P. Hallahan (Eds.), *Handbook of special education* (pp. 291–310). Englewood Cliffs, NJ: Prentice-Hall.

Weintraub, F. J., & McCaffrey, M. A. (1976). Professional rights and responsibilities. In F. J. Weintraub, A. Abeson, J. Ballard, & M. L. LaVor (Eds.), *Public policy and the education of exceptional children* (pp. 333–343). Reston, VA: Council for Exceptional Children.

EMILIA C. LOPEZ
Fordham University

SPECIAL EDUCATION, LEGAL REGULATION OF POLITICS AND SPECIAL EDUCATION SUPERVISION IN SPECIAL EDUCATION

ETIOLOGY

Etiology is the study of causes of diseases and impairments. When considering handicapped individuals, however, one needs to be concerned not only about specific causes but about the individual's developmental history. Only in the most severe cases is the relationship between cause and outcome one to one. For the most part, regardless of the initial cause, the ultimate outcome is a result of the child's interaction with his or her physical and social environment. Indeed, for most handicapping conditions, no specific cause can be identified. Sources of handicapping conditions are summarized in the Table.

Genetically Based Disorders

A variety of handicaps have their basis in specific chromosomal or single-gene disorders, or have a polygenic (many-gene) predisposition. Because of both basic principles of genetics and the complex interaction between genetic and environmental factors in development, the genotype, the individual's genetic makeup, rarely corresponds exactly to the phenotype, the individual's appearance and behavior (Vogel & Motulsky, 1979; Kopp, 1983).

Chromosomal Abnormalities. Normal humans have 23 pairs of chromosomes in their body cells—22 pairs of similar autosomes and one pair of sex chromosomes. Females have two relatively long X, whereas males have one X and one shorter Y, sex chromosomes. In the development of germ cells (meiosis), each pair normally splits such that each germ cell has 23 chromosomes. However, occasionally one chromosome does not split (nondisjunction), resulting in a double dose or absence of that chromosome, or a chromosome breaks and becomes partly attached to another (translocation). These, and other processes, can lead to chromosomal abnormalities.

Most such abnormalities lead to spontaneous abortion, but the incidence in live births is about 1 in 200. Involving large numbers of genes, these abnormalities have broad and typical physical and behavioral effects. They tend to produce general intellective deficiency, minor in some syndromes but severe in others.

Autosomal trisomies involve an extra autosomal chromosome; affected individuals have 47 chromosomes. Down's syndrome (trisomy 21) is the most common, but at

Source of Handicapping Conditions

Source	Example or Effect
Genetic	
Chromosomal	
Autosomal trisomies	Down's syndrome
Autosomal deletions and additions	Cri du chat
Sex-chromosome aneuploidies	Klinefelter's, Turner's, XYY syndromes
Constriction or weakness	Fragile X syndrome
Single-gene	
Dominant	Neurofibromatosis, tuberous sclerosis
Recessive	Inborn errors of metabolism (e.g., PKU, galactosemia, Tay Sachs)
Sex-linked	Lesch-Nyhan syndrome
Polygenic	Mild mental retardation, predisposition toward variety of impairments
Prenatal teratogens	
Radiation	Growth failure, major malformations
Maternal infections	
TORCH complex (toxoplasmosis, rubella, cytomegalovirus, herpes)	Growth retardation, visual and auditory impairments, mental retardation
Syphilis	Mental retardation, meningitis
Drugs and hormones	
Thalidomide	Limb, digit, external ear malformations
Alcohol	Fetal alcohol syndrome
Androgens	Masculinization of females
Antitumor agents	Major growth and central nervous system defects
Anticoagulants	Growth retardation, visual and auditory impairments
Anticonvulsants	Fetal hydantoin syndrome

Source of Handicapping Conditions (*continued*)

Source	Example or Effect
Perinatal factors	
Maternal infection	
Herpes	Same as TORCH complex above
Prematurity	Cerebral palsy, mental retardation
Low birth weight	Growth retardation, mental retardation, cerebral palsy
Asphyxia	Cerebral palsy, variety of other impairments
Postnatal chemical or traumatic factors	
Infection	
Encephalitis	Mental retardation
Toxins	
lead	Mental retardation, epilepsy, sensory impairments
Food additives	Attention deficit disorder
Accidents and child abuse	Brain damage (specific) leading to variety of impairments
Learning	
Conditioning (Pavlovian)	Phobias
Operant conditioning	Negative self-concept, avoidant disorders
Observational learning	Phobias, articulation disorders

least five others have been described. Virtually all increase in incidence with maternal age and result in growth failure and mental retardation.

Autosomal partial deletions and additions are low-incidence disorders that, except for 18 p-, which shows highly variable effects, generally result in severe mental retardation. The best known is 5 p-, cri du chat, so named because affected infants' cries sound like a cats meows.

Sex chromosome aneuplodies involve an added or missing sex chromosome. Klinefelter's (XXY) and XYY syndromes affect only males; Turner's syndrome (XO) affects only females. Intelligence of affected individuals averages about 90, but this is highly variable.

Chromosomal constriction or weakness can now be identified with improved test procedures. Fragile-X syndrome may be second only to Down's syndrome as a chromosomal basis of mental retardation.

Single-Gene Effects. Except for sex-linked recessive traits, individuals inherit a gene for each single-gene trait from each parent. Different forms (alleles) of a given gene can lead to different manifestations of a trait. Individuals are said to be homozygotic or heterozygotic for a given trait if they have inherited two similar or two different alleles, respectively. Single-gene traits follow Mendelian principles of inheritance: a dominant trait will be expressed if the individual has inherited at least one dominant gene for the trait, whereas a recessive trait will be expressed only if the individual inherits the recessive gene from both parents. An exception is sex-linked recessive traits, the genes for which are carried on the sex chromosomes. Such traits may be expressed if the recessive gene is inherited from one parent and no counterpart gene is inherited from the other parent to suppress its effects. In part because the Y-chromosome is shorter than the X and therefore carries fewer genes, such sex-linked traits appear much more commonly in males; these traits are transmitted by their mothers, who are carriers. Both X-linked dominant and X-linked recessive traits may appear. Other patterns of inheritance such as codominance and partial dominance complicate the notion of simple dominance-recessiveness relations, as do the phenomena of penetrance, pleiotropy, and variable expressivity (Thompson & Thompson, 1980).

Over 1300 dominant, recessive, and sex-linked single-gene disorders have been described (McKusick, 1978), and more are discovered regularly. They lead to a variety of deficits—over 100 are associated with hearing impairments, 15 with spinocerebellar ataxia, and over 200 with protein defects, many of which lead to mental retardation. Because of the number and variety of such traits, only a few can be described.

A child has a 50% chance of having a dominant trait manifested by one parent. Such traits may also arise through spontaneous mutation (Abuelo, 1983). Once the gene appears, it will be transmitted to succeeding generations unless the effects are so severe that affected individuals do not have children. Dominant gene syndromes are characterized by variable expressivity; effects may range from severe to virtually nonobservable. Indeed, some syndromes may appear to skip generations when effects in one generation are minimal (Thompson & Thompson, 1980). Pleiotropy, multiple effects of a single gene, in dominant gene syndromes involves skeletal, neuromuscular, cranial, ocular, and frequently intellective, defects.

Neurofibromatosis, a fairly common dominant-gene disorder, leads to the development of masses of neurofibromatomas, cafe-au-lait skin spots, skeletal deformities, and, less commonly, mild mental retardation. Joseph Merrick, "the Elephant Man," had an extraordinarily severe case of neurofibromatosis without apparent intellective impairment (Howell & Ford, 1980).

A child has a 25% chance of inheriting a recessive single-gene defect if both parents are heterozygotic (carriers) for the defect. Recessive single-gene defects may result in a variety of conditions, including sensory impairment, ataxia, and mental retardation.

In a large number of cases a defective gene results in impaired metabolism that in turn leads to the accumulation of some unmetabolized substance, which may be toxic. Among the more common and better understood of such inborn errors of metabolism or metabolic disorders are phenylketonuria, galactosemia, and Tay-Sachs disease. Some disorders can be detected through amniocentesis, and a few can be treated through dietary intervention.

A variety of single-gene-based defects that appear more commonly in males than females are sex-linked, frequently called X-linked. Among these are several forms of sensory impairments, the best known of which is red-green colorblindness. Lesch-Nyhan syndrome, which appears virtually solely in males, is an X-linked inborn error of metabolism that results in deterioration of motor coordination, mental retardation, and self-destructive behavior.

Higher incidence in males than females and familial patterns of incidence suggest that some types of attention deficit disorders and learning disabilities may have X-linked predisposition.

Polygenic Factors. Many human characteristics, particularly those that vary along a continuum, arise from polygenic factors interacting with environmental conditions. Two such traits are intelligence and height. Thus mental retardation, particularly of a mild degree, may result from the same basic complex of factors as does normal intelligence (Zigler, 1967). Polygenic predispositions may exist for a variety of impairments, including epilepsy, autism, childhood and adult schizophrenia, learning disabilities, neural tube defects, (spina bifida) and, controversially, criminality (Wilson & Herrnstein, 1985).

Prenatal Influences

Prenatal development is generally divided into three periods: germinal or ovum (weeks 0–2), embryonic (weeks 3–8), and fetal (weeks 9–birth). Major developments in each period are germinal—the ovum (fertilized egg) becomes implanted on the uterine wall and differentiates into placental and embryonic tissue; embryonic—characterized by major differentiation of all major organs and systems and external body features; and fetal—characterized by rapid growth and further differentiation of internal and external systems and features.

Although the embryo/fetus is generally well protected from environmental insult, a variety of chemicals, called teratogens, can cross the placenta and cause malformations (see Table). Teratogens have their major adverse impact during critical periods, times of most rapid tissue differentiations. There are less severe effects during sensitive periods. As shown in the Figure, systems have individual but overlapping critical periods, mainly around the time of the embryonic periods, and sensitive periods that extend into the fetal period. Sensitive periods for central nervous system, eyes, and external genitalia extend

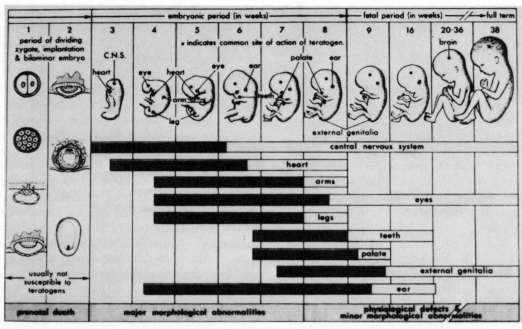

Critical (dark bars) and sensitive (light bars) periods for teratogenic action on various tissue systems. From Moore (1982).

well after birth, so these systems are unusually sensitive to later teratogenic influence. During the early germinal period, teratogens generally either have no effects or are lethal, although they may cause certain major malformations (Moore, 1982).

Radiation and a variety of drugs and maternal infections have teratogenic influences, as shown in Table 1. Effects shown are of severe manifestations and are highly variable; in many cases exposed infants will be asymptomatic. The action of teratogens can be summarized as follows (Brown, 1986).

1. No agent is 100% teratogenic; influence is affected by both maternal and embryonic factors.

2. Teratogens act in specific ways and have specific effects, but some have multiple effects and different teratogens may have similar effects (e.g., TORCH complex).

3. Organ systems have individual but largely overlapping critical and sensitive periods.

4. Major effects of teratogens are death, malformations, growth retardation, and functional deficits.

5. Adverse effects are dose dependent, increasing in frequency and severity with increased degree and duration of exposure to a teratogen.

6. Some agents that have major teratogenic influence on the embryo may have little adverse effect or even positive effect on the mother. TORCH complex is an example of the former, and thalidomide and dilantin are examples of the latter.

Perinatal Influences

No single definition of the perinatal period has been universally accepted; Freeman (1985a) defines the period as a few hours or days before birth, whenever in gestation that occurs, to a few hours or days after delivery. Since herpes is almost always transmitted to the newborn as it passes through the birth canal, it is, strictly speaking, a perinatal influence, although it is classified as a member of the TORCH complex.

The major perinatal concerns are prematurity and low birth weight (LBW): "Premature birth, defined as either low birth weight (LBW) or as birth prior to term gestation, remains the major contributing factor to neonatal morbidity and mortality" (Barden, 1983, p. 139). Overall incidence of low birth weight (<2500 gm), whether full-term or preterm, has remained roughly constant at about 8% in the United States in recent years, with incidence about 6% in middle and upper socioeconomic status (SES) groups and as high as 16% among low SES groups. Blacks are particularly at risk, largely because of their low SES overrepresentation. Of the about 250,000 premature or LBW infants born each year in the United States, some 40,000 to 45,000 die within a month of birth. This is a significant improvement in survival for all weight classes, especially in the 1000 to 2000 gm range. Unfortunately, some 60,000 of the survivors may be at risk for the development of serious disability (Behrman, 1983), although relatively few of those actually manifest any long-term sequelae (Kopp, 1983).

Until relatively recently, premature and LBW infants

were grouped together into a single class determined by low birth weight; some authorities still discuss them together. However, more accurate ways of assessing gestational age have revealed two overlapping but distinctive categories with their own characteristics and sequelae. Premature infants will, because of their early birth, generally be below average in weight and have immature organ systems, including the pulmonary, cardiovascular, and central nervous systems; this may lead to a variety of clinical problems. The LBW infants' low weight also may have interfered with the normal development of organ systems. Both show behavioral deficits, including poor reflex control, hypoactivity, lack of responsiveness, adnd irritating cries, that may interfere with normal parent-infant interactions.

The most important complication for both groups is asphyxia, particularly if the episode is severe enough to result in hypoxic ischemic encephalopathy (HIE), in which case a variety of handicapping conditions may result.

Infants with low birth weights, large heads, low 5-minute Apgar scores, apneic episodes, or abnormal tone are 10 to 30 times more likely then normal infants to develop cerebral palsy; neonatal seizures and low 10-minute Apgar scores increase the risk even more. However, 90% of infants suffering from these problems show no serious later deficits (Freeman, 1985b). At one time, researchers (Pasamanick & Knoblock, 1966) postulated a "continuum of reproductive casualty": a degree of perinatal problems directly related to a degree of later impairment. That is, a small degree of problem causes minor impairment, and a major degree causes major impairment. However, no such continuum operates. Instead, a threshold effect appears to occur, in which low degrees of asphyxia, for example, can be completely tolerated, whereas levels above threshold produce manifest damage (Freeman, 1985a). In addition, recovery from perinatal problems is influenced by caretaking behavior (Sameroff & Chandler, 1975) and other SES-related factors. The combined adverse effect of biologic brain injury and socioeconomic disadvantage is sometimes said to put affected children in double jeopardy (Avery, 1985).

Improvements in delivery room and neonatal intensive care unit procedures have significantly improved the prognosis for high-risk infants. Further improvements in combination with training programs in parenting behavior for high-risk groups should lead to even better prognosis.

Postnatal Chemical and Physical Effects

Birth is clearly a landmark, associated with adaptation to an external environment and self-breathing and feeding. But many developmental processes begun prenatally continue, including development of the central nervous system and vulnerability to insult.

Brain damage can, of course, lead to virtually all impairments, with type and degree a function of the area damaged, the extent of damage, and the age at which the damage occurred. Infections, high fever, malnutrition, and certain toxins can cause diffuse damage to major areas of the brain, whereas physical insult can result in focal lesions, damage to more limited areas. A major issue is the effect of age at time of injury on recovery from brain damage. The Kennard principle that recovery is easier the earlier the brain damage is no longer accepted. Relations appear to be complicated, involving, in addition to age and type of damage, the individual's prior experience.

Infants are at particular risk for infection, and diseases such as meningitis may result in seizures and brain damage that can lead to later mental retardation, cerebral palsy, epilepsy, or specific learning disabilities (Thompson & O'Quinn, 1979).

Because of their effects on developing central nervous system tissue, certain toxins pose considerable risk for children. Of particular concern is lead poisoning, which in severe doses can produce devastating brain damage in children, resulting in severe mental retardation, sensory impairment, and seizures. In lesser doses it may produce lowered intelligence, behavioral problems, and specific learning difficulties. The effects are dose dependent, and apparently no level of blood lead is safe.

Malnutrition in infancy, particularly when severe enough to lead to marasmus or kwaskiorkhor, is a potential cause of diffuse brain damage and resulting mental retardation. Of particular concern is severe malnutrition occurring early in infancy or lasting more than 4 months; this may result in later retardation regardless of the adequacy of subsequent diet (Cravioto & Delicardie, 1970). Early effective treatment of malnutrition leads to "catch-up growth," lessening long-term consequences (Brann & Schwartz, 1983). Failure to thrive resulting from either parental neglect or infant-based impairments may have long-term consequences.

Accidents, particularly automobile accidents, are a common cause of specific brain damage in children. Child abuse is increasingly seen as another important factor.

Role of Learning

Learning plays such a ubiquitous role in the development of normal human behavior that its role in causing or exacerbating impaired behavior is sometimes overlooked in discussing etiology. Learning processes can result in direct impairments or the indirect exacerbation of other impairments. For example, phobias can be acquired through Pavlovian (classical or respondent) conditioning, in which an initially neutral stimulus such as a dentist is paired with pain, or through observational learning (imitation), in which a child observes a parent's severe fear of dentists.

Operant conditioning, or learning by consequences such as reinforcement and punishment, has an important influence on the way in which children with impairments react to those impairments and to themselves. If, for example, a retarded child's attempt to solve problems meets with failure (and perhaps ridicule as well), then the child may develop fear of failure and a poor self-concept. Through respondent conditioning, the child may become highly anxious in subsequent problem-solving settings. Anxiety, in turn, can lead to avoiding problem settings and increasing dependency on others, further reducing the child's own competence. Zigler (1967) has described the negative role that a number of such learned motivational-emotional factors can have on children with mental retardation. Research indicates that these factors adversely affect children with other impairments as well (Brown & Reynolds, 1986).

If a child's responses have no contingent impact on the environment and the child has no control over what happens, then learned helplessness may result, leading to an expectation of failure and apathy.

Developmental Considerations

Temperament. Children's own characteristics influence their development and the way in which others behave toward them. In reports from the landmark New York Longitudinal Study, Thomas, Chess, Birch and their colleagues (e.g., Chess & Thomas, 1984) have documented the importance of temperament as a factor in children's development. Temperament is a relatively stable personality variable that affects such responses as adaptation to new situations and persistence. Children whose temperamental style is described as difficult are more likely to manifest behavior disorders than are other children.

Poverty. Poverty contributes to impairments both directly and indirectly and may be self-perpetuating. A number of factors that may lead to or exacerbate impairments are higher in low SES groups. These include poor prenatal care; obstetric and perinatal complications, especially prematurity and low birth weight; malnutrition; abusive parents; restricted verbal codes; and inadequate caretaking.

Birch and Gussow (1970) propose that a cycle of poverty acts to transmit poverty across generations. Risk factors associated with low-SES-based factors lead children to be more likely to suffer school failure. School failure leads to unemployment and underemployment which, in turn, maintain poverty conditions and thus perpetuate the cycle into another generation.

Inadequate caretaking behavior occurs in poorly trained parents, particularly under the stress of large families and low SES conditions. Such parents may be able to cope with a normal infant but be stretched beyond their limits in dealing with infants with pre- or perinatal complications. Such infants may, because of their behavioral characteristics, evoke inadequate and even abusive parenting behavior, exacerbating already present impairments and inducing them in infants who under more appropriate conditions would develop normally.

Interactions between infants and caretakers are crucial in the development of some impairments. Indeed, in a now classic review, Sameroff and Chandler (1975) found little evidence for a "continuum of reproductive casualty." Instead, the way in which caretakers could or could not adequately cope with their infants determined later impairments, resulting in what they termed a "continuum of caretaking casualty." Interactions between characteristics of infants and characteristics of caretakers are important factors in development.

Additionally, adequacy of therapy has obvious impact on the development of children with conditions that may lead to impairments. The more serious the condition, the more extreme and unusual will be the necessary treatment, resulting in a "continuum of therapeutic environment" (Brown, 1986). In some cases, treatment will be required that simply does not exist in the natural environment. Thus PKU is treated with a synthetic diet and newborns with perinatal complications or birth injuries are placed in increasingly sophisticated neonatal intensive care units.

Prevention of Impairments

Applications of present knowledge and techniques could significantly reduce incidence and severity of impairments (Brown, 1986). Some methods are (1) wider use of genetic screening and counseling; (2) more adequate prenatal care for at-risk pregnant women; (3) training in parenting skills for prospective parents; (4) wider dissemination of information, materials, and training on birth control to reduce family size in at-risk groups and early pregnancy in adolescents (school-based clinics should be considered); (5) provision of adequate postnatal nutrition, medical care, and psychological stimulation for at-risk infants. Prevention, although expensive, is both less costly and more humane than remediation.

REFERENCES

Abuelo, D. N. (1983). Genetic disorders. In J. L. Matson & J. A. Mulick (Eds.), *Handbook of mental retardation* (pp. 105–120). New York: Pergamon.

Avery, G. (1985). Effects of social, cultural and economic factors on brain development. In J. H. Freeman (Ed.), *Prenatal and perinatal factors associated with brain disorders* (Publication No. 85-1149, pp. 163–176). Bethesda, MD: National Institutes of Health.

Barden, T. P. (1983). Obstetric management of prematurity. Part 2. Premature labor. In A. A. Fanaroff & R. J. Martin (Eds.), *Behrman's neonatal-perinatal medicine* (3rd. ed., pp. 139–149). St. Louis: Mosby.

Behrman, R. E. (1983). The field of neonatal-perinatal medicine. In A. A. Fanaroff & R. J. Martin (Eds.), *Behrman's neonatal-perinatal medicine.* (3rd. ed., pp. 1–3). St. Louis: Mosby.

Birch, H. G., & Gussow, J. D. (1970). *Disadvantaged children: Health, nutrition, and school failure.* New York: Grune & Stratton.

Brann, A. W., Jr., & Schwartz, J. F. (1983). Central nervous system disturbances. In A. A. Fanaroff & R. J. Martin (Eds.), *Behrman's neonatal-perinatal medicine* (3rd ed., pp. 347–403). St. Louis: Mosby.

Brown, R. T. (1986). Etiology and development of exceptionality. In R. T. Brown & C. R. Reynolds (Eds.), *Psychological perspectives on childhood exceptionality: A handbook* (pp. 181–229). New York: Wiley.

Brown, R. T., & Reynolds, C. R. (Eds.). (1986). *Psychological perspectives on childhood exceptionality: A handbook*. New York: Wiley.

Chess, S., & Thomas, A. (1984). *Origins and evolution of behavior disorders*. New York: Brunner/Mazel.

Cravioto, J., & Delicardie, E. (1970). Mental performance in school-age children. *American Journal of Diseases in Children, 120*, 404–410.

Freeman, J. M. (1985a). Introduction. In J. M. Freeman (Ed.), *Prenatal and perinatal factors associated with brain disorders* (Publication No. 85-1149, pp. 1–11). Bethesda, MD: National Institutes of Health.

Freeman, J. M. (1985b). Summary. In J. M. Freeman (Ed.), *Prenatal and perinatal factors associated with brain disorders* (Publication No. 85-1149, pp. 13–32). Bethesda, MD: National Institutes of Health.

Howell, M., & Ford, P. (1980). *The true history of the elephant man*. New York: Penguin.

Kopp, C. B. (1983). Risk factors in development. In P. H. Mussen, M. M. Haith, & J. J. Campos (Eds.), *Handbook of child psychology* (4th ed., Vol. 2, pp. 1081–1188). New York: Wiley.

McKusick, V. A. (1978). *Mendelian inheritance in man* (5th ed.). Baltimore, MD: Johns Hopkins University Press.

Moore, K. L. (1982). *The developing human* (3rd ed.). Philadelphia: Saunders.

Pasamanick, B., & Knoblock, H. (1966). Retrospective studies on the epidemiology of reproductive casualty: Old and new. *Merrill-Palmer Quarterly, 12*, 7–26.

Sameroff, A. J., & Chandler, M. J. (1975). Reproductive risk and the continuum of caretaking casualty. In F. D. Horowitz, M. Hetherington, S. Scarr-Salapatek, & G. Siegel (Eds.), *Review of child development research* (Vol. 4, pp. 187–244). Chicago: University of Chicago Press.

Thompson, J. S., & Thompson, M. W. (1980). *Genetics in medicine* (3rd ed.). Philadelphia: Saunders.

Thompson, R. J., & O'Quinn, A. N. (1979). *Developmental disabilities*. New York: Oxford University Press.

Vogel, F., & Motulsky, A. G. (1979). *Human genetics*. Berlin: Springer-Verlag.

Wilson, J. Q., & Herrnstein, R. J. (1985). *Crime and human nature*. New York: Simon & Schuster.

Zigler, E. (1967). Familial mental retardation: A continuing dilemma. *Science, 155*, 292–298.

ROBERT T. BROWN
*University of North Carolina,
Wilmington*

AUTISM
BRAIN DAMAGE
CAFE AU LAIT SPOTS
CHILD ABUSE
CONDITIONING
EPILEPSY
INBORN ERRORS OF METABOLISM
LEAD POISONING
LEARNED HELPLESSNESS
LOW BIRTH WEIGHT INFANTS
MALNUTRITION
PREMATURITY/PRETERM
SPINA BIFIDA
TEMPERAMENT
TORCH COMPLEX

EUGENICS

The term eugenics refers to attempts to improve the hereditary characteristics of man. The idea of improving the human stock arose from the observation of the great diversity of human characteristics and abilities and the tendency for characteristics to run in families. Thus the human population might be improved by breeding from the best stock, as is commonly done with considerable success in plants and animals. This idea was expressed by the Greek poet Theognis as early as the sixth century BC, and various eugenics plans for the ideal state were included in the writings of Plato.

Although eugenics is an ancient idea, it gained intellectual credibility with the general acceptance of the Darwinian theory of evolution and the idea that man is a product of an evolutionary process that continues in the present and will extend into the future. The term eugenics was coined in 1883 by Francis Galton, who was greatly influenced by the work of his cousin Charles Darwin. Galton's eugenics proposals centered around providing scholarships and other inducements for superior young people to marry and raise large families, as well as assistance to those of low ability in limiting family size.

The modern history of eugenics can be divided into two contrasting periods (Haller, 1984). In the first part of the twentieth century, prior to World War II, there was widespread acceptance of the hereditary basis for human differences among scientists and the general public alike. The eugenics movement flourished, and in the United States was influential in the establishment of restrictive immigration and the passage of sterilization laws in a number of states. The second period, following the war, was characterized by the opposite trend. There was virtual consensus among behavioral scientists that the earlier conceptions were mistaken and there was a strong taboo inhibiting research and publication concerning the hereditary basis of human behavior. Eugenics became a bad word, and the term fell into disuse.

This massive swing of the pendulum appears to be purely ideological; it was not based on surprising new findings of any kind. No doubt the events of World War II, including the Holocaust and other excesses of the Nazis, created widespread revulsion toward attempts to change human populations. The civil rights movement and attempts to improve the lot of the disadvantaged probably also contributed to a new respect for human rights that seemed incompatible with many of the eugenics proposals of the earlier period.

Recent eugenics proposals have been modest in scope and entirely voluntary. Muller (1965) proposed that sperm from outstanding males be stored and made available to women who voluntarily choose to conceive a child with it. Although such sperm banks are now in existence, they have not yet gained the popularity that Muller invisioned. Shockley (1972) proposed that a bonus amounting to $1000 for each IQ point below 100 be offered for voluntary sterilization to nonpayers of income tax. It is interesting to note that both Muller and Shockley are winners of the Nobel Prize and that both used their prestige to urge public acceptance of the eugenics idea, but the climate was turning in the opposite direction.

It seems clear that a properly administered eugenics program could achieve considerable success over a period of time, but it is instructive to note that no such program has been properly administered for a long enough time to demonstrate success on even a small scale. To have any effect on the course of human evolution, a eugenics program would have to alter the relative fertility of substantial segments of the world population over a long period of time. The human population is now so large and so disorganized politically that it is difficult to imagine how any of the past eugenics proposals could have a significant impact. Human reproductive patterns appear to be governed by forces that are still beyond human control.

Homo sapiens evolved from a common ancestor with modern apes over a period of about a million years. Although little is known about the details of this process, the early humanoids probably lived dangerously as hunters and gatherers in small isolated groups dispersed over a wide area. There must have been extremely strong selection for intelligence, language usage, and cooperativeness, since evolution of these traits was rapid. It seems likely that favorable cultural adaptations were selected along with favorable genetic traits, so that human culture evolved along with human biology.

For the past 10,000 years, humans have lived as farmers in fixed abodes. Osborn (1968) has reviewed studies of the fertility of agrarian primitive peoples performed before they were subjected to modern influences. These studies show that the more successful farmers tended to have larger families than the less successful, and that their offspring tended to have a better chance for survival. Sta-

Family Income and Education of Women, 18–44 Years Old, Who Have Had a Child in 1984

Characteristic	Number of Women (thousands)	Total Births per 1000 Women
Family income		
Under $10,000	9,210	88.5
$10,000–14,999	6,408	70.8
15,000–19,999	6,097	69.7
20,000–24,999	5,314	67.6
25,000–29,999	4,806	58.8
30,000–34,999	4,392	64.8
35,000 and over	12,043	46.0
Years of school completed		
Less than high school	8,093	81.9
High school, 4 years	21,934	65.2
College, 1–3 years	11,428	54.8
College, 4 years	5,923	72.2
College, 5 or more years	2,926	55.9

Source: U.S. Bureau of the Census, *Statistical Abstract of the United States, 1986.*

tistics from the past century also tend to show that the more successful in terms of education and income tended to have more surviving children than did the less successful. Thus, during most of its history, humankind appears to have had a eugenic reproductive pattern. This is undoubtedly the basic cause of the current level of human achievement.

Recently, however, a dysgenic reproductive pattern has emerged worldwide. In the United States, for example, education and family income are now negatively related to births. The Table shows that the birth rate at the lowest income and educational levels is almost double that at the highest level. Van Court and Bean (1985) have shown a significant negative correlation between vocabulary test score and number of children in a large and representative sample of American adults. In the past, differences in survival contributed significantly to differential fertility, but infant mortality has declined to the point that it is no longer a significant factor. Differential birth rates are now the only source of reproductive advantage.

On a larger scale, the most successful national populations are growing at less than half the rate of the less successful. The industrial democracies (such as Canada, Denmark, France, Germany, Japan, the United Kingdom, and the United States) had between 60 and 72 births per 1000 women aged 15 to 49 in 1973, while virtually all less developed nations had in excess of 100 births per 1000 women. A number (such as Algeria, Kenya, Mexico, and Nicaragua) had more than 200 births per 1000 women. In aggregate, the less developed regions are increasing in population at 2.3% per year, while the developed regions are increasing at 0.9% per year.

These trends appear to be beyond rational control. Osborn (1968) attributed them to advances in birth-control technology, which provides effective methods that require information, foresight, planning, and money. Thus the most successful have been the first to take advantage of the enhanced ability to control reproduction. Osborn optimistically predicted that this effect is likely to be temporary, and that favorable birth differentials will return when the new technology has been completely assimilated and everyone has the number of children they desire and can support.

In fact, the future of human heredity is exceptionally difficult to forecast at this time because of the rapid advances that are being made in genetics and biology that will likely result in new technologies of reproduction. Already we have in vitro fertilization, which could be used to separate genetic selection from childbearing and child rearing. Perhaps the future will bring the ability to clone humans and to alter the human genetic code. With these possibilities on the horizon, and others that cannot be foreseen, the present may not be the opportune time to undertake the politically awesome task of reversing the current dysgenic reproductive trends.

REFERENCES

Bajema, C. J. (1976). *Eugenics then and now*. Stroudsburg, PA: Dowden, Hutchinson, & Ross.

Haller, M. H. (1984). *Eugenics*. New Brunswick, NJ: Rutgers University Press.

Muller, H. J. (1965). Means and aims in human genetic betterment. In T. M. Sonneborn (Ed.), *The control of human heredity and evolution*. New York: Macmillan.

Osborn, F. (1968). *The future of human heredity*. New York: Weybright & Talley.

Shockley, W. (1972). Dysgenics, geneticity, raceology: A challenge to the intellectual responsibility of educators. *Phi Delta Kappan, 53,* 297–312.

Van Court, M., & Bean, F. D. (1985). Intelligence and fertility in the United States: 1912–1982. *Intelligence, 9,* 23–32.

ROBERT C. NICHOLS
DIANE JARVIS
*State University of New York,
Buffalo*

GENETIC COUNSELING
GENETIC FACTORS IN BEHAVIOR
HEREDITY

EUSTIS, DOROTHY HARRISON (1886–1946)

Dorothy Harrison Eustis introduced the use of guide dogs for the blind in the United States. Born in Philadelphia,

Eustis established an experimental breeding kennel for dogs at her estate in Switzerland. With her husband, George Morris Eustis, and Elliott S. (Jack) Humphrey, an American horse breeder and trainer, she began a program of experimental breeding of dogs for police and army duty. She was also aware that trained guide dogs had been used successfully by the blind in Germany.

Convinced that guide dogs could make the difference between independent and dependent living for the blind, she wrote an article, "The Seeing Eye," for the *Saturday Evening Post*, urging the use of dogs as guides for the blind. The resulting deluge of mail from blind Americans led to the establishment, in 1929, of the United States' first guide-dog training school, in Nashville, Tennessee. Seventeen men and women and their dogs were trained the first year, after which the school was moved to Morristown, New Jersey, where it continues to the present day.

REFERENCES

Eustis, D. H. (1927, November 5). The seeing eye. *The Saturday Evening Post*, 43–46.

Putnam, P. B. (1979). *Love in the lead*. New York: Dutton.

PAUL IRVINE
Katonah, New York

EVALUATION

In the broadest sense, evaluation is concerned with the determination of worth or merit. It includes obtaining information for use in judging the value of a program, product, procedure, or objective. To the extent that such judgments are based on accurate information, and that that information was collected in a systematic manner, evaluation can be said to have taken place, since the real worth of alternatives can be determined.

Evaluation is thus a form of disciplined inquiry, but it should not be confused with research aimed at obtaining generalizable knowledge by testing claims about functional relationships among variables describing a phenomenon. Evaluation and research possess differences in their focus, generalizability, and value emphasis. The focus of evaluation is on decisions; research seeks conclusions. The generalizability of evaluation decisions is low, while research conclusions aim at high generalizability. The value of evaluation is on determining worth, while research seeks truth in the form of lawful relationships.

Although there is consensus about the nature of evaluation in general, a variety of models exist with respect to the specific nature of evaluation. For example, one model views evaluation as roughly synonymous with education measurement (e.g., Ebel, 1965), while another model bases evaluation on professional judgment (e.g.,

Eisner, 1975) and represents an alternative to precise measurement. This model often is used by accreditation agencies, where judgments are based on opinions of experts, whether or not the data and criteria used in making those judgments are clear. During the 1930s, Tyler (1942) introduced evaluation models based on an assessment of whether or not goals have been attained. Evaluation is viewed as a process of comparing performance data with clearly specified objectives and it may take any number of forms (e.g., Hammond, 1973; Metfessel & Michael, 1967; Popham, 1975).

The use of extrinsic criteria in evaluation was emphasized in other models (Cronbach, 1973). One model was elucidated by Scriven (1967, 1983), who described the formative-summative distinction (i.e., evaluators who formatively try to improve a still-under-development curriculum and evaluators who summatively assess the worth of a completed curriculum). He also described goal-free evaluation (i.e., focus on program outcomes both intended and unanticipated).

Stake (1967) developed the Countenance Model of evaluation, which emphasized two primary operations, descriptions and judgments that incorporate antecedent, transaction, and outcome phases of an educational program. Each of the primary operations is placed in a data matrix with intents and observations on the description side and standards and judgments on the judgment side. Based on the data matrices, it is possible to perform either relative comparisons (i.e., one program versus another), absolute comparisons (i.e., one program versus perceived standards of excellence), or both.

Another class of evaluation models is concerned not with the determination of worth per se but rather with the collection and presentation of data necessary to facilitate decisions (Alkin, 1969). An example is Stufflebeam's (1971) CIPP model, which represents four types of evaluation: context evaluation (a rationale for determining objectives); input evaluation (information on how to employ resources to achieve program objectives); process evaluation (identification of defects in the procedural design of the program); and product evaluation (measurement and interpretation of the attainments yielded by the program). These evaluations are performed in a context of delineating (i.e., focusing), obtaining (i.e., collecting, organizing, and analyzing), and providing (i.e., synthesizing) information. Another example is the Discrepancy Model (Provus, 1971), which is particularly concerned with the comparison between posited standards and actual performance. The comparison of performance with standards and resulting (if any) discrepancy leads to four alternatives: proceed unaltered, alter performance, alter standards, or terminate program.

For special education, evaluation is an important and necessary process. The variety of service delivery systems as well as the specialized curriculum, methods, and materials used need to be evaluated to determine their worth.

The efficacy of such procedures cannot be assumed. Evaluation in special education is also necessary on an individual level, as evidenced by the provision in PL 94-142 that the individual education plan (IEP) contain criteria and procedures for determining, at least on an annual basis, whether goals and objectives are being achieved. The evaluation schemes for an IEP are varied (Jenkins, Deno, & Mirkin, 1979; Maher & Barbrack, 1980), but all are conceptually related to the evaluation models previously described. The evaluation should be designed to determine the effective portions of the IEP so they may be continued or expanded, and the ineffective portions, which must be revised, deleted, or completely restructured when a change in procedure is indicated.

REFERENCES

Alkin, M. C. (1969). Evaluation theory development. *Evaluation Comment, 2*(1), 2–7.

Cronbach, L. J. (1973). Course improvement through evaluation. In B. R. Worthen & J. R. Sanders (Eds.), *Educational evaluation: Theory and practice.* Belmont, CA: Wadsworth.

Ebel, R. L. (1965). *Measuring educational achievement.* Englewood Cliffs, NJ: Prentice-Hall.

Eisner, E. W. (1975). *The perceptive eye: Toward the reformation of educational evaluation.* Palo Alto, CA: Stanford Evaluation Consortium.

Hammond, R. L. (1973). Evaluation at the local level. In B. R. Worthen, & J. R. Sanders (Eds.), *Educational evaluation: Theory and practice.* Belmont, CA: Wadsworth.

Jenkins, J. R., Deno, S. L., & Mirkin, P. K. (1979). Measuring pupil progress toward the least restrictive alternative. *Learning Disability Quarterly, 2,* 81–91.

Maher, C. A., & Barbrack, C. R. (1980). A framework for comprehensive evaluation of the individualized education program (IEP). *Learning Disability Quarterly, 3,* 49–55.

Metfessel, N. S., & Michael, W. B. (1967). A paradigm involving multiple criterion measures for the evaluation of the effectiveness of school programs. *Educational & Psychological Measurement, 27,* 931–943.

Popham, W. J. (1975). *Educational evaluation.* Englewood Cliffs, NJ: Prentice-Hall.

Provus, M. M. (1971). *Discrepancy evaluation.* Berkeley, CA: McCutchan.

Scriven, M. (1967). The methodology of evaluation. In R. E. Stake (Ed.), *Curriculum evaluation.* American Education Research Association Monograph Series on Evaluation No. 1. Chicago: Rand McNally.

Scriven, M. (1973). Goal-free evaluation. In E. R. House (Ed.), *School evaluation: The politics and process.* Berkeley, CA: McCutchan.

Stake, R. E. (1967). The countenance of educational evaluation. *Teachers College Record, 68,* 523–540.

Stufflebeam, D. L., Foley, W. J., Gephart, W. J., Guba, E. G., Hammond, R. L., Merriman, H. O., & Provus, M. M. (1971). *Educational evaluation and decision making.* Itasca, IL: Peacock.

Tyler, R. W. (1942). General statement on evaluation. *Journal of Educational Research, 35,* 492–501.

KENNETH A. KAVALE
University of Iowa

PROGRAM EVALUATION RESEARCH IN SPECIAL EDUCATION

EXCEPTIONAL CHILDREN

Exceptional Children (EC) is the official scholarly journal of the Council for Exceptional Children (CEC). It is published six times a year in September, October, November, January, February, and April. It has been published continuously since 1934. According to its current editor (Ysseldyke, 1984), the journal will solicit and publish the following types of articles: scholarly data-based research papers in the field of special education; papers that will have a broad base of interest among practitioners in special education; major research projects that are of specific interest; papers that integrate previously published research into a set of conclusions; illustrations of the applications of research to educational practice; policy analyses; major addresses presented at national or regional CEC meetings; comments or critiques directed at recent articles published by EC (subject to the same review process); and reviews of books, major legislation affecting special education, and governmental funding sources and recipients.

REFERENCE

Ysseldyke, J. E. (1984). *Exceptional children*: New directions. *Exceptional Children, 55,* 7–10.

THOMAS E. ALLEN
Gallaudet College

EXHIBITIONISM

Exhibitionism is the repeated exposure of the genitals to unwitting strangers to produce sexual excitement without attempts at further sexual activity (American Psychiatric Association, 1982). Convicted exhibitionists are almost exclusively male. Approximately one-third of all sex offenders are arrested for exhibitionism, making it the most common sexual crime in the United States (Rosenhan & Seligman, 1984).

Viewed from a psychoanalytical perspective, exhibitionism is considered a symptom of a more fundamental problem such as a defense against a fear of castration or a fixation at the phallic stage of development. Behavioral views are in stark contrast with this position. Although

there are numerous behavioral approaches, all place emphasis directly on the exhibitionistic behavior and the variables that promote or maintain it (Wilson & O'Leary, 1980). Behaviorally based treatments have received the most empirical scrutiny.

One of the earliest behavioral treatments of an exhibitionist was reported by Bond and Hutchison (1960). The systematic desensitization program used, however, proved only partially successful. Quirk (1974), reporting on a follow-up of the person treated by Bond and Hutchison, used a biofeedback desensitization method. For 1 year following treatment, there were no instances of exhibitionism. A single instance then occurred, at which time a reapplication of the treatment proved successful at a 2-year follow-up. Maletzky (1977) also found some individuals benefited from posttreatment "booster sessions" in an assisted covert sensitization treatment that used aversive imagery and noxious odors.

Hayes, Brownell, and Barlow (1978) found a self-administered covert sensitization technique in which realistic aversive scenes (e.g., being arrested) were used was effective. There is evidence that techniques that are effective with persons voluntarily seeking treatment are equally effective with persons who are treated involuntarily (Maletzky, 1980).

REFERENCES

American Psychiatric Association. (1982). *Desk reference to the diagnostic criteria from diagnostic and statistical manual of mental disorders* (3rd ed.). Washington, DC: Author.

Bond, I. K., & Hutchison, H. C. (1960). Application of reciprocal inhibition therapy to exhibitionism. *Canadian Medical Association Journal, 83,* 23–25.

Hayes, S. C., Brownell, K. D., & Barlow, D. H. (1978). The use of self-administered covert sensitization in the treatment of exhibitionism and sadism. *Behavior Therapy, 9,* 283–289.

Maletzky, B. M. (1977). "Booster" sessions in aversion therapy: The permanancy of treatment. *Behavior Therapy, 8,* 460–463.

Maletzky, B. M. (1980). Self-referred versus court-referred sexually deviant patients: Success with assisted covert sensitization. *Behavior Therapy, 11,* 306–314.

Quirk, D.A. (1974). A follow-up on the Bond-Hutchison case of systematic desensitization with an exhibitionist. *Behavior Therapy, 5,* 428–431.

Rosenhan, D. L., & Seligman, M. E. P. (1984). *Abnormal psychology.* New York: Norton.

Wilson, G. T., & O'Leary, K. D. (1980). *Principles of behavior therapy.* Englewood Cliffs, NJ: Prentice-Hall.

JAMES P. KROUSE
*Clarion University of
Pennsylvania*

EXPECTANCY AGE

Expectancy age refers to a method used to compare performance on an intelligence or scholastic aptitude measure with performance on an achievement measure. The practice most likely had its origins in the accomplishment ratio proposed by Raymond Franzen in 1920. Franzen advocated dividing a pupil's subject age, obtained from an achievement test, by his or her mental age, obtained from an intelligence test (Formula 1):

$$100 = \left(\frac{\text{Subject age}}{\text{Mental age}}\right) = \text{Subject ratio.}$$

Formula 1 was applied to each subject matter domain measured by a particular achievement test. Separate ratios were computed for reading, mathematics, and other subjects for which achievement test results were available. Subject ratios above 100 denoted performance greater than expected for the pupil's mental age, while subject ratios below 100 signified performance lower than expected for the pupil's mental age. The average of a pupil's subject ratios was termed the accomplishment quotient, an overall index of achievement in relation to mental age. A number of serious technical flaws resulted in the abandonment of the use of ratios in relating achievement to intellectual ability or capacity.

Present-day test developers and users, like their 1920 counterparts, continue to search for meaningful ways to relate intelligence and achievement test results. Government intervention in establishing procedures for identifying children with severe learning disabilities in connection with PL 94-142 has undoubtedly served to intensify pressures placed on test users. The proliferation of several discrepancy formulas that use age equivalents or grade equivalents has resulted in further confusion and inappropriate practices (Reynolds, 1981). For example, the use of a mental age, obtained either directly from an intelligence test or indirectly when only an IQ is available, to establish an expectancy age has sometimes occurred from solving for *MA* in Formula 2:

$$MA = \frac{(CA)(IQ)}{100}.$$

Age equivalents in various achievement domains (e.g., reading, mathematics, spelling) are then compared one by one with the expectancy age to identify discrepancies between intelligence and achievement. Such practices are technically indefensible for the following reasons.

Age equivalents constitute a scale of unequal units. The difference in performance between an age equivalent of 6-0 and 7-0 is, for example, much greater than the difference in performance between an age equivalent of 14-0 and 15-0 for both the intelligence and the various achievement domains. In fact, an age equivalent must be extrapolated after about age 16 for most traits because there is little real growth beyond this age. Both the unequal units of the age equivalent scale and their artificial extension, or ex-

trapolation, render them unsuitable for any sort of statistical manipulation. Thus the simple arithmetic operation of subtraction needed to search for discrepancies between ability and achievement is untenable.

Further difficulties with age equivalents result from their unequal variability, both at successive age levels within one subject matter domain as well as among different subject matter domains. The variability of age equivalents in arithmetic computation, for example, will be considerably smaller at a particular age level than that for reading comprehension. For this reason, there is no technically sound method to interpret discrepancies at different age levels within a single subject matter domain or across subject matter domains.

An added difficulty occurs when an attempt is made to compare age equivalents from tests having dissimilar norm groups. If the norming sample for an intelligence test differs from that for an achievement test, then observed discrepancies between age equivalents on the two measures may merely represent systematic differences between the two norm groups.

One other difficulty that must be mentioned in connection with such comparisons is the correlation between intelligence and achievement in various subject matter domains. Because the relationship between intelligence and reading comprehension, for example, differs from that for intelligence and arithmetic computation, the magnitude of observed discrepancies cannot be accepted at face value without taking into account the phenomenon known as regression to the mean. Interpretation of differences is thus difficult because the correlation between each intelligence-achievement pairing differs both within a single age level as well as across age levels. For these reasons, the practice of using an expectancy age as a benchmark for undertaking achievement test comparisons to identify pupils with suspected learning disabilities or atypical ability-achievement relationships cannot be recommended on technical or logical grounds.

REFERENCES

Franzen, R. (1920, November). The accomplishment quotient. *Teachers College Record,* 114–120.

Otis, A. S. (1925). *Statistical method in educational measurement.* New York: Harcourt Brace Jovanovich.

Reynolds, C. (1981). The fallacy of "two years below grade level for age" as a diagnostic criterion for reading disorders. *Journal of School Psychology, 19*(4), 350–358.

GARY J. ROBERTSON
American Guidance Service,
Circle Pines, Minnesota

GRADE EQUIVALENTS
SEVERE DISCREPANCY ANALYSIS

EXPRESSIVE DYSPHASIA

Expressive dysphasia is used in this discussion to refer to the problem of language production encountered by those who have experienced language dysfunctions as a result of central nervous system damage. Verbal expression difficulties may be placed on a continuum ranging from mild to severe.

Brookshire (1978) considers dysphasia to be a verbal information processing disorder affecting comprehension and production of words, whether they be in isolation, phrases, or sentences.

Reductions in available vocabulary, impairment of auditory retention span, and impairments in perception and production of messages are common characteristics of dysphasic individuals (Jenkins, et al., 1975).

Word-finding problems are common, and recall problems involving grammatical structures may be present, reducing the number of such structures available to express a message (Brookshire, 1978). A loss of grammatical forms is felt to be a more severe disruption of the language process than dysnomia (Jenkins et al., 1975).

Problems in using correct verb tenses may be noted, with the individual producing sentences such as "He run." Other grammatical problems such as pronoun confusion or difficulties using articles, prepositions, conjunctions, and demonstratives also have been noted (Brookshire, 1978). More complex sentence structures such as those containing dependent or relative clauses may be troublesome for the dysphasic individual to understand and use. Certain types of grammatical transformations such as questions, negations, and passive constructions also are likely to cause problems.

Speech may be fluent, except for pauses owed to word-finding difficulties. Grammar, articulation, and rhythm may be intact, but semantic problems result in speech that is devoid of meaning. This group of symptoms has been labeled Wernicke's aphasia (Brookshire, 1978). Speakers are unaware of their errors as a result of poor auditory comprehension and monitoring. The term Broca's aphasia has been used to characterize verbal expression that is labored, halting, misarticulated, and often telegraphic. In the absence of paralysis of the speech mechanism, these difficulties seem to be related to deficiencies in planning and executing voluntary motor movements required for speech production. Darley, Aronson, and Brown, cited in Brookshire (1978), argue that Broca's aphasia can be more accurately classified as apraxia of speech rather than a true aphasia.

Paraphasia also may be present. In this condition, a substitution for a target word is produced, which maintains some relationship to the word intended. The condition may take the form of reversing syllables within the same word (e.g., tevelison for television), telescoping elements of adjacent words together; omitting sounds; or substituting a word for another word with a similar sound structure. At times, a new word may be produced, called a neologism. Such errors generally are confined to specific naming attempts and may not be a part of habitual language usage (Eisenson, 1973).

REFERENCES

Brookshire, R. H. (1978). *An introduction to aphasia* (2nd ed.). Minneapolis, MN: BRK.

Eisenson, J. (1973). *Adult aphasia: Assessment and treatment.* New York: Appleton.

Jenkins, J. J., Jiménez-Pabón, E., Shaw, R. E., & Sefer, J. W. (1975). *Schuell's aphasia in adults: Diagnosis, prognosis and treatment.* Hagerstown, MD: Harper & Row.

K. SANDRA VANTA
*Cleveland Public Schools,
Cleveland, Ohio*

DYSNOMIA
DYSPHASIA

EXPRESSIVE LANGUAGE DISORDERS

Children who do not develop language normally are referred to as language disordered. Their most salient symptoms are problems in expression, but it is important to stress that many of these children also have some degree of receptive difficulties of various types. Children with language disorders are usually identified in preschool age by parents or health care unit staff who notice that the children appear to be late in developing speech and language skills.

Language disorders are heterogeneous with respect to etiology, nonlinguistic symptoms, severity, and linguistic characteristics. A disorder can occur as a relatively isolated defect in a child with no other obvious handicaps. Within such a specific language disorder, four degrees of impairment are differentiated: mild, moderate, severe, and very severe (Ingram, 1972). These categories also differ from one another qualitatively after a period of time (Nettelbladt, 1983).

However, language disorders also occur secondary to other types of primary handicaps such as mental retardation, hearing defects, acquired aphasia (i.e., cases where language has reached maturity prior to brain damage), adverse environmental factors, psychiatric disorders, dysarthria, and cleft palate (Fundudis, Kolvin, & Garside, 1979). Prevalence studies (e.g., Morley, 1972) report language disorders in 11 to 15% of 4 year olds, and 3 to 6% of 6 year olds; of the latter, 0.7 to 1.5% have severe language disorders.

Heredity is one of the more common anamnestic factors in the case histories of children with language disorders, but recently brain dysfunction has been claimed to be a major cause of some language disorders in children (Rapin & Wilson, 1978). In the severe group, various motor problems can be found such as verbal apraxia, clumsiness, and late attainment of motor milestones. Environmental and social factors appear to play an important secondary role in helping or hindering the child in compensating for the language handicap (Dalby, 1977).

Prognostically, research has shown a connection between onset and course of language development and later educational and occupational achievements (e.g., Klackenberg, 1980). Children with a specific language disorder at age three or four are likely to show general learning disabilities, reading and writing disabilities, and poor verbal expression in school.

In order to assess a child with a language disorder, it is important to have a thorough knowledge of normal language development. In the last two decades, a tremendous amount of research in this area has had a strong impact on clinical work with language disorders. This research has resulted in the construction of several new tests and a greater emphasis on qualitative descriptive methods (Muma, 1978). As a complement to quantitatively based norms, stage models for language development in different areas have been presented (Crystal, Fletcher, & Garman, 1976; Prutting, 1979; Stark, 1980; and Nettelbladt, 1983); they have been found useful in clinical work. By using these models, a particular child's linguistic accomplishments can be matched to a general outline of specific language behaviors. The most frequent linguistic symptoms in children with language disorders are phonological and articulatory problems (Nettelbladt, 1983), but syntactic and morphological problems are often found (Crystal et al., 1976). Recently, analysis of semantic and pragmatic, i.e., communicative, problems has been emphasized (Crystal, 1981; Gallagher & Prutting, 1983).

There are several educational consequences for children with language disorders. During the preschool period, it is important that the speech and language pathologist play an active role in carefully assessing the child's disorder, in counseling parents and the preschool teacher, and in giving the child either individual or group therapy. By school age, the specific speech and language therapy often has to be supplemented and gradually replaced by special education, especially in the areas of reading and writing.

REFERENCES

Crystal, D. (1981). *Clinical linguistics.* New York: Springer-Verlag.

Crystal, D., Fletcher, P., & Garman, M. (1976). *The grammatical analysis of language disability. A procedure for assessment and remediation.* London: Arnold.

Dalby, M. (1977). Aetiological studies in language retarded children. *Neuropädiatrie* (Suppl.), *8,* 499–500.

Fundudis, T., Kolvin, I., & Garside, R. (1979). *Speech retarded and deaf children: Their psychological development.* London: Academic.

Galagher, T., & Prutting, C. (Eds.) (1983). *Pragmatic assessment and intervention issues in language.* San Diego: College-Hill.

Ingram, T. T. S. (1972). The classification of speech and language disorders in young children. In M. Rutter & J. Martin (Eds.), *The child with delayed speech. Clinics in Developmental Medicine,* No. 43. London: Heinemann Medical.

Klackenberg, G. (1980). What happens to children with retarded speech at 3? Longitudinal study of a sample of normal infants up to 20 years of age. *Acta Paediatrics, 69,* 681–685.

Morley, M. (1972). *The development and disorders of speech in childhood.* Edinburgh: Churchill Livingstone.

Muma, J. (1978). *Language handbook. Concepts, assessment, intervention.* Englewood Cliffs, NJ: Prentice-Hall.

Nettelbladt, U. (1983). *Developmental studies of dysphonology in children.* Lund, Sweden: Gleerup.

Prutting, C. (1979). Process: The action of moving forward progressively from one point to another on the way to completion. *Journal of Speech & Hearing Disorders, 44,* 3–30.

Rapin, I., & Wilson, B. (1978). Children with developmental language disability: Neurological aspects and assessment. In M. Wyke (Ed.), *Developmental dysphasia.* New York: Academic.

Stark, R. (1980). Speech development in the first year. In G. Yeni-Komshian, J. Kavanagh, & C. Ferguson (Eds.), *Child phonology* (Vols. 1 & 2). New York: Academic.

ULRIKA NETTELBLADT
University of Lund, Sweden

LANGUAGE DEFICIENCIES AND DEFICITS
LANGUAGE DELAYS

EXTENDED SCHOOL YEAR FOR THE HANDICAPPED

Between 1977 and 1981, 46 cases were filed in state and federal courts to contest the unwillingness of local educational agencies to provide special education for a period beyond the traditional school year (Marvell, Galfo, & Rockwell, 1981). The issue in those cases was whether a state or local policy of refusing to consider or provide education beyond the regular school year (usually 180 days) for handicapped children violated mandates under Part B of the Education of the Handicapped Act (EHA).

In the leading case, *Battle* v. *Pennsylvania* (1980), a third circuit court of appeals held that Pennsylvania's inflexible application of a 180-day maximum school year prevented the proper formulation of appropriate educational goals and was, therefore, incompatible with the EHA's emphasis on the individual. Most of the courts that have considered limitations on the length of the school year, as applied to handicapped children, have invalidated them for essentially the reasons stated in the *Battle* decision.

The court decisions have provided some general guidelines, but controversial areas remain relative to the provision of extended-year services to the handicapped. One major issue relates to determining which handicapped children are eligible for extended-year services. Generally, the individual plaintiffs or class of plaintiffs involved in those lawsuits consisted of severely handicapped children, a term that generally is not confined to a separate and specific category but indicates a degree of disability that necessitates intensified services. Courts have made it clear that determination of whether a child will receive a program in excess of the traditional school year must be made on an individual basis. To prevail, an individual must demonstrate that such a program is required for a particular child to benefit from the education provided during the preceding school year, in accordance with the interpretation of "free appropriate public education" set forth by the U.S. Supreme Court in *Board of Education* v. *Rowley* (1982).

Courts generally have accepted the argument advanced in the *Battle* case that severely handicapped children, as compared with nonhandicapped children, have greater difficulty in acquiring and transferring skills, are more likely to lose a greater number of skills over time (or regress), and take a longer time to recoup those skills. There is disagreement, however, as to whether a continuous program of education, without extended breaks, would lessen the likelihood of regression in certain severely handicapped children. In accordance with the *Rowley* decision, courts have stressed the importance of the individualized education program (IEP) process in educational decision making regarding extended-year services (e.g., *Crawford* v. *Pittman*, 1983).

Another major area of controversy concerns the cost of extended-year services. Courts have rejected arguments by school officials that limited fiscal resources justify limitations on the services that may be provided for handicapped children. Since *Mills* v. *Board of Education* (1972), courts have almost uniformly held that lack of funds may not limit the availability of appropriate educational services for handicapped children more severely than for nonhandicapped children.

REFERENCE

Marvell, T., Galfo, A., & Rockwell, J. (1981). *Student litigation: A compilation and analysis of civil cases involving students, 1977–1981*. Williamsburg, VA: National Center for State Courts.

SHIRLEY A. JONES
*Virginia Polytechnic Institute
and State University*

**SPECIAL EDUCATION, LEGAL REGULATION OF
MILLS *v.* BOARD OF EDUCATION DISTRICT OF
COLUMBIA**

EXTINCTION

Extinction, also termed planned ignoring, is a behavior reductive procedure that occurs when a behavior that has been previously reinforced is no longer reinforced in order to reduce or eliminate the occurrence of that behavior (Sulzer-Azaroff & Mayer, 1986). Extinction has been used to effectively reduce a wide variety of inappropriate behaviors, usually those that are maintained by social attention (Spiegler, 1983).

The reductive effect on behavior is best demonstrated when extinction is effectively implemented as follows:

1. All sources of reinforcement to the behavior are identified and withheld.
2. Reinforcement of an alternative desirable behavior occurs along with extinction of the undesirable behavior.
3. Extinction is applied consistently following the emission of the response in question.
4. Extinction conditions are maintained for a sufficient period of trials until reduction in behavior is complete.

There are further considerations in the use of extinction. Extinction is a gradual behavior-reduction technique and does not work immediately. In addition, an immediate increase in the rate and intensity of the response under extinction conditions may occur temporarily before reduction in response. Extinction conditions of one behavior may initially induce aggression in other behaviors. Finally, behaviors reduced under extinction may be situation-specific and may not generalize to other conditions. Although extinction is an effective behavior-reduction technique, because of its limitations (considerations), it should not be used for the immediate reduction of severely abusive behaviors.

REFERENCES

Spiegler, M. D. (1983). *Contemporary behavioral therapy*. Palo Alto, CA: Mayfield.

Sulzer-Azaroff, B., & Mayer, G. R. (1986). *Achieving educational excellence using behavioral strategies*. New York: Holt, Rinehart, & Winston.

RHONDA HENNIS
LOUIS J. LANUNZIATA
*University of North Carolina,
Wilmington*

**AVERSIVE CONTROL
AVERSIVE STIMULUS
BEHAVIOR MODIFICATION
PUNISHMENT**

EYE-HAND COORDINATION

Eye-hand coordination refers to the ability of an individual to direct fine motor activities of the hand in response to directive input and feedback provided by the visual system. Eye-hand coordination is a subskill of the larger concept of visual-motor coordination. The latter concept refers to the role of vision in directing and controlling voluntary movements of the body.

A deficiency in eye-hand coordination can arise from many sources, including deficiency in visual perception, acuity, figure-ground distortion, and discrimination. Similarly, underdeveloped muscles of the hand or damage in the lower sensory-neural pathways can affect the outcome of eye-hand coordination efforts. However, excluding obvious visual defects and/or disturbance in the lower neural or musculature systems, eye-hand coordination difficulty is most likely traceable to disruption within the cerebellum.

The cerebellum is a small mass attached to the brain stem near the (dorsal, inferior) base of the cerebrum. According to Gaddes (1985), the cerebellum collects sensory inputs not only from haptic sensitivity (touch) but also from the perception of visual stimuli. The structure is apparently capable of rapid activity following relatively limited input. The cerebellum apparently "acts as a filter to smooth and coordinate muscular activity" (Gaddes, 1985, p. 53). Moreover, dysfunction in the mid-cerebellum may produce generalized motor clumsiness. If the clumsiness is manifested in a visual-motor disability, the result is a decrement in manual dexterity (apraxia). Perceptual activities, writing, and other fine motor activities are generally affected. Although such conditions do disrupt the development of school progress, Gaddes (1985) maintains that little empirical evidence specifically relates dysfunction of the cerebellum to the special education classification of learning disabilities. Exceptions to this view, however, have been offered (Ayres, 1972; Valk, 1974).

As noted, eye-hand coordination has generally been studied under the more comprehensive topic of visual- (or visuomotor) motor deficiency. Several academic and behavioral deficits have been associated with this problem, including speech and language problems as well as problems in reading, arithmetic, spelling, and handwriting. Additionally, elements of emotional disorders have been associated with visual-motor difficulties. These disorders appear to stem largely from the negative attitudes developed toward academics.

The importance of eye-hand coordination is apparent. However, central issues pertaining to assessment and training remain a source of empirical controversy. Informal assessment often proceeds from the observation of daily skills thought to be dependent on eye-hand coordination ability. Activities that might be used for informal diagnosis (and perhaps training) include tracing, scissor use, lacing, design copying, and other similar tasks (Lerner, 1981). More formal assessment might be approached through laboratory-derived procedures (e.g., use of the rotary pursuit) or published tests (e.g., the *Developmental Test of Visual-Motor Integration* [Beery, 1982]). It should be noted that a review of the formal tests associated with eye-hand coordination generally reveals a lack of evidence of appropriate development, reliability, and validity (Salvia & Ysseldyke, 1985).

A number of authors have argued strongly the importance of visual-motor activities as a basis for academic deficiency and as a trainable (remediable) skill. Among the more forceful proponents of this theory was Getman (1965), who emphasized the importance of visual training, a developmental model that employed the training of a visuomotor learning schema. In Getman's view failures in visuomotor activities, of which eye-hand coordination is an element, can result in behavioral, cognitive, and academic failure.

Despite Getman's (1965) and other theorists' models, the efficiency of visuo-training approaches is a controversial topic. This is particularly true where the purpose of the training program is to improve readiness skills, intelligence test scores, or academic achievement. Additionally, there may be doubt that the programs actually train the abilities in question. Somewhat countering the research base that suggests the ineffectiveness of past efforts, Hallahan and Cruickshank (1973) have suggested that the data are limited and often too flawed to provide an adequate assessment of the potential value of training programs.

REFERENCES

Ayres, A. J. (1972). *Sensory integration and learning disorders.* Los Angeles: Western Psychological Services.

Beery, K. E. (1982). *Revised administration, scoring and teaching manual for the developmental test of visual-motor integration.* Cleveland: Modern Curriculum Press.

Gaddes, W. H. (1985). *Learning disabilities and brain function: A neuropsychological approach* (2nd ed.). New York: Springer-Verlag.

Getman, G. N. (1965). The visuomotor complex in the acquisition of learning skills. In J. Hellmuth (Ed.), *Learning disorders* Vol. 1. Seattle, WA: Special Child Publications.

Hallahan, D. P., & Cruickshank, W. (1973). *Psychoeducational foundations of learning disabilities.* Englewood Cliffs, NJ: Prentice-Hall.

Lerner, J. (1981). *Learning disabilities: Theories, diagnosis and teaching strategies* (3rd ed.). Boston: Houghton Mifflin.

Salvia, J., & Ysseldyke, J. E. (1985). *Assessment in special and remedial education* (3rd ed.). Boston: Houghton Mifflin.

Valk, J. (1974). Neuroradiology and learning disabilities. *Tydschrift Voor Orthopedagogiek, 11,* 303–323.

TED L. MILLER
University of Tennessee,
Chattanooga

VISUAL-MOTOR AND VISUAL-PERCEPTUAL PROBLEMS
VISUAL PERCEPTION AND DISCRIMINATION

EYSENCK, HANS J. (1916–   )

Hans J. Eysenck was born and educated in Berlin, Germany; he moved to England in the late 1930s to oppose university admission requirements of Nazi party membership. He received his BA in 1938 and PhD in 1949 in psychology from the University of London. Eysenck then joined Maudsley Hospital and founded a department of psychology within the Institute of Psychiatry at Maudsley and its sister hospital Bethlem. He was appointed professor of psychology at the University of London in 1955.

Eysenck has been described as the gadfly of his profession: a persistent critic of psychoanalysis, psychotherapy, and projective assessment. He established clinical psychology as a profession and was the first to train clinical psychologists and develop behavior therapy (introducing theories from the Pavlovian school).

Eysenck applied methods in research that had traditionally been applied to the study of intelligence to the study of human personality as a whole. He used factor analysis and discriminant function analysis to search out major factors in personality; he then tried to develop hypotheses linking those factors to widely accepted psychological and physiological concepts. This approach to the treatment of scientific data has been a general theme throughout Eysenck's research; it reflects his view of humans as a biosocial organisms whose actions are determined equally by evolutionary and social factors. Eysenck's research has produced over 800 articles and 40 books in a vast array of subjects. His works include *Dimensions of Personality* (1947), *A Model for Intelligence* (1982), and books popularizing psychology such as *Check Your Own IQ* and *Psychology Is About People*. He also founded two journals, *Behavior Research and Therapy* and *Personality and Individual Differences*, and coedited the *Encyclopedia of Psychology* (1972).

REFERENCES

Eysenck, H. J. (1947). *Dimensions of personality*. London: Routledge & Kegan Paul.

Eysenck, H. J. (1966). *Check your own IQ*. Harmondsworth, England: Penguin.

Eysenck, H. J. (1972). *Psychology is about people*. New York: Library.

Eysenck, H. J. (1982). *A model for intelligence*. New York: Springer.

Eysenck, H. J., Arnold, W., & Meili, R. (Eds.). (1972). *Encyclopedia of psychology*. New York: Herder & Herder.

ELAINE FLETCHER-JANZEN
Texas A&M University

F

FACTOR ANALYSIS

Factor analysis is a statistical technique intended to reduce mathematically the interrelationships within a set of variables to a simpler structure. This structure is assumed to represent one or more variables not directly measurable; hence, they may be termed latent factors. Each observed variable in the original set is related mathematically to each of the latent factors. The relationship may be zero.

Factor analysis was developed from practical problems in psychology and the physical sciences. When scientists measured many different variables they were unable to discern patterns of relationships because of the sheer number of correlations. Because the information in some variables might be redundant, scientists sought a method to reduce the number of variables needed to describe things they observed. This method is termed dimensional reduction. Its initial solution, mathematically straightforward, is now called principal components analysis.

One of the limitations of principal components analysis is an assumption about the nature of the variables: that they have been measured without error. Psychologists rightly questioned this assumption for much of their data, and they developed new factor analysis models that incorporated error of measurement. These models can be termed common factor models, since they all assume that the latent factors of interest should be related to two or more of the observed variables. Single variable factors would usually be uninteresting even though they could be detected. Thus, the first major problem in the conduct of factor analysis is to decide whether principal components or common factor models are most appropriate.

The theoretical and practical problem resulting from common factor models is the determination of the percentage of variance for each variable that is shared with the common factors, termed communality, and often written h^2. The unshared variance, or $1-h^2$, is called uniqueness. It is decomposed into specific variance and error variance. Specific variance may be totally unrelated to other variables. It may be shared with variables or factors not measured and unrelated to those measured in the study. A common method to estimate communality is to use the squared multiple correlation between each variable and the other variables in the study. This has been shown to yield a lower bound for the number of factors.

A major problem of factor analysis is deciding how many latent factors there are. In principal components, the issue is one of parsimony: how few factors are needed to represent the set of observed variables? In common factors, the issue is usually theoretical: How many factors are needed to represent the observed variables? While a factor may have two or three variables with which a correlation exists, when measured with regression weights (termed factor loadings), such a factor may be discarded as theoretically uninteresting or isolated. A technical help in determining the number of factors is the magnitude of a factor's eigenvalue, the sum of the squared loadings of all variables for the factor. Eigenvalues below 1.0 indicate chance or spurious factors. A plot of the eigenvalues from largest to smallest, termed a scree plot, is also of assistance because sharp drops in the values often indicate the end of important factors.

Psychometricians distinguish between exploratory and confirmatory factor analysis. In the latter there is usually a theoretical basis for determining the number of factors. This basis is absent in exploratory factor analysis. Confirmatory factor analysis has been closely associated with the work of Karl Joreskog, who has applied the theory of linear structural relations (LISREL) to it. The method of maximum likelihood estimation is used to attempt to fit the observed correlation matrix to a theoretically specified pattern of factor loadings. Often, certain loadings are assumed to be zero, corresponding to independence of some variables from a given factor. Statistical chi square tests for fit allow comparison of various models in confirmatory factor analysis.

Once the number of factors has been decided, theoretically or experimentally, the next major problem is encountered: rotation for best interpretation. Since the initial solution to a factor analysis represents an arbitrary orientation of the factors in factor space, any other rotation in the space is mathematically correct. It is useful to view the factors in such a way that variables load highly on one factor and low on others, termed simple structure. There are two classes of rotations, rigid and oblique. Rigid rotations maintain all factors to be independent of one another, geometrically equivalent to axes in an euclidean geometric space being at 90 degrees to one another. Thus, rotations of the factor pattern result in a best fit to simple structure. Varimax is the commonest procedure used.

Oblique rotations are equivalent to allowing the axes

in the factor space to become nonorthogonal or at non-90-degree angles to each other. The result is that the correlation between the factors must be considered in interpreting loadings. There are two sets of numbers of interest, the factor pattern and the factor structure. The pattern is the matrix of regression weights of variables on the factors, while the structure is the matrix of correlations between variables and factors. The major methods for oblique rotation are oblimin, promax, and quartimax. The first two methods seem to have provided the most satisfactory results in simulation studies, although there remain difficulties in employing oblique methods in exploratory factor analysis.

In research on different groups, the question is occasionally raised concerning similarity of the factor patterns. Cattell (1978) discusses five different methods of examining congruity of factor patterns. The simplest is the congruence coefficient, computed much like a correlation coefficient. Another, the salient variable similarity index, is nonparametric and has better tables for significance tests than the congruence coefficient. Harman (1976) is a useful reference for all aspects of factor analysis.

REFERENCES

Cattell, R. B. (1978). *The scientific use of factor analysis in behavioral and life sciences*. New York: Plenum.

Harman, H. H. (1976). *Modern factor analysis* (3rd ed.). New York: Academic.

VICTOR L. WILLSON
Texas A&M University

DISCRIMINANT ANALYSIS
MULTIPLE REGRESSION

FAILURE TO THRIVE

Failure to thrive (FTT) is defined as "a progressive decline in responsiveness, accompanied by loss of weight and retardation in physical and emotional development among infants who have been neglected, ignored, or institutionalized" (Goldenson, 1984, p. 283). A common diagnostic criterion is that affected children are below the fifth percentile for height and weight (Committee on Nutrition, American Academy of Pediatrics, 1985). The incidence is greatest in infancy and early childhood. It can occur in children who were normal at birth although incidence is higher in premature infants (Kotelchuck, 1980). The low growth rate has no obvious organic basis and may occur even when affected children are provided with adequate food. Regardless of the definition, FTT "has become a catchall term for all growth failures of unknown origin in young children . . . [Its] cause has remained perplexing" (Kotelchuck, 1980, pp. 29–30).

In the 1950s, FTT and similar conditions came to be viewed psychodynamically as an outcome of maternal deprivation: the infant or young child reacted emotionally to the lack of maternal affection and contact (Bowlby, 1951). The nutritional and growth problems were said to result from the disturbed mother-infant interactions. However, the effects of maternal deprivation itself are not as great or persistent as originally reported (Rutter, 1972). Further, some studies report that mothers of FTT children, contrary to the maternal deprivation or neglect model, are not identifiably different from mothers of normal children (Kotelchuck, 1980). Affected children frequently have histories of infant feeding problems, including vomiting and poor appetite, suggesting that infants' own characteristics may be partly responsible for the condition (Pollitt & Eichler, 1976). Unfortunately, relatively few well-controlled studies of FTT and its correlates are available, resulting in uncertainty and contradictory conclusions (Kotelchuck, 1980).

Frequently associated with failure to thrive is deprivation dwarfism (Patton & Gardner, 1969). Indeed, the two may be different terms for the same basic condition (Pollitt & Eichler, 1976), since deprivation dwarfism is presumed also to result from psychosocial deprivation. In deprivation dwarfism, however, the child is stunted to the point of literally appearing dwarflike. Notable is the fact that when removed from the disturbed home setting and placed in a hospital or foster home, such children frequently show "catch-up growth" (Patton & Gardner, 1969), which tends to return them to their expected growth level.

Failure to thrive is best viewed as a heterogeneous disorder with multiple causes. Psychosocial neglect is clearly indicated as a potential issue, particularly when hospitalization is followed by catch-up growth, but it may account for only one-third of the cases. Organismically based factors associated with, among other things, feeding problems, general lack of responsiveness, hormonal disturbance, or prematurity, are more common likely causes (Kotelchuck, 1980). In cases resulting from neglect, "there is a fine line between failure to thrive and child abuse" (Committee on Nutrition, American Academy of Pediatrics, 1985, p. 199).

Regardless of uncertainty regarding FTT, educators and counselors should be sensitive to the possibility that extremely short and thin children may be suffering from psychosocial deprivation or neglect rather than from either primary malnutrition, an organically based growth disorder, or genetically determined smallness.

REFERENCES

Bowlby, J. (1951). Maternal care and mental health. *Bulletin of the World Health Organization, 3,* 355–534.

Committee on Nutrition, American Academy of Pediatrics.

(1985). *Pediatric nutrition handbook* (2nd ed.). Elk Grove Village, IL: American Academy of Pediatrics.

Goldenson, R. M. (Ed.). (1984). *Longman dictionary of psychology and psychiatry*. New York: Longman.

Kotelchuck, M. (1980). Nonorganic failure to thrive: The status of interactional and environmental etiologic theories. In B. W. Camp (Ed.), *Advances in behavioral pediatrics* (Vol. 1, pp. 29–51). Greenwich, CT: JAI Press.

Patton, R. G., & Gardner, L. I. (1969). Short stature associated with maternal deprivation syndrome: Disordered family environment as cause of so-called idiopathic hypopituitarism. In L. I. Gardner (Ed.), *Endocrine and genetic diseases of childhood* (pp. 77–89). Philadelphia: Saunders.

Pollitt, E., & Eichler, A. (1976). Behavioral disturbances among failure-to-thrive children. *American Journal of Diseases of Children, 130,* 24–29.

Rutter, M. (1972). *Maternal deprivation reassessed.* New York: Penguin.

ROBERT T. BROWN
ELLEN B. MARRIOTT
*University of North Carolina,
Wilmington*

DEPRIVATION, BIONEURAL RESULTS OF
DEVELOPMENTAL DELAY
MALNUTRITION

FALSE POSITIVE AND FALSE NEGATIVE

The term false positive, developed in the vocabulary of medicine, is often confusing when used in other circles. In medicine, a condition is reported as positive when the condition is present. When the condition is reported as negative it is in the normal or average range. Therefore, a false positive refers to a judgment about the presence of an exceptional attribute that is actually in the average range or a score or judgment that incorrectly indicates a diagnosis (or a classification) of an individual who has been diagnosed as brain injured when in fact he or she is only exhibiting reasonably normal developmental delays. A false negative, the opposite of a false positive, results when an individual is determined to be average when in fact the individual is exceptional. For example, occasionally a child with cerebral palsy (who by medical diagnosis and by definition is brain injured) will reproduce, almost perfectly, drawings of geometric figures from a test for brain injury. By the results of the drawing test, the individual is a false negative. Whereas a negative interpretation of a clinical test indicates that nothing unusual has been found, a positive interpretation indicates exceptionality or pathology.

Further confusion may result when terms used in personnel selection are mixed with clinical terminology. In personnel selection, false rejections corresponds to false positives in clinical terminology. In the language of personnel specialists, a false rejection is an individual who has a score on a selection instrument that is below the cutoff (e.g., too exceptional to be successful on the job) but who is eventually successful on the job. False acceptances are those individuals who have scores on the selection tests above the cutoff but who are failures on the job. Even though nonnumerical conditions may influence the cutoff score, or various conditions may determine success on the job, such individuals are known as false negatives.

One of the most crucial factors in determining the number of false negative and false positive decisions is the cutoff score (which many be multiple scores on many parts of an assessment) used to indicate the presence (positive) or absence (negative) of pathology or whatever exceptional attribute is being evaluated. Personnel using a suicide prediction scale would be inclined to use a cutoff score that would deliberately decrease the number of persons who would be considered to be in the normal range (i.e., false negative) so that adequate protection could be put in place. Where incorrectly diagnosing pathology has dire implications but the condition itself is mild, a cutoff score would be set to underdiagnose, that is, to increase the number of false negatives and reduce the number of false positives.

The following Figure gives an illustration of the concept of false negative and false positive as it has been used in the diagnosis of learning disabilities (Reynolds, 1984). Four cells are illustrated: students who are learning disabled and are so diagnosed are true positives; students who are learning disabled but are diagnosed as normal are false negatives; students who are not in fact learning disabled are false positives; students who are not learning disabled and are not diagnosed as learning disabled are true negatives. Frequently, in deciding on a diagnosis, assessment results are interpreted in a way to minimize either false negatives or false positives. In special education, learning disability diagnosis is best structured to minimize false negatives (Reynolds, 1984) while the di-

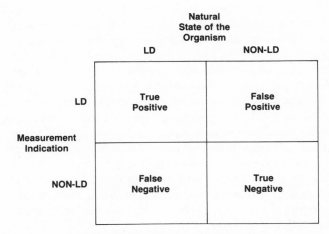

Concept of false negative and false positive.

agnosis of mental retardation is best designed to minimize false positives.

Authors and publishers of tests and other predictive devices should provide an indication of the predictive confidence associated with each score. For many predictions, locally developed tables will be better than national data. Such tables should be developed, if they are not provided, to indicate the efficiency of various cutoff scores. Data should be provided about the percentage of correct classifications, especially for scores close to the cutoff, and about the expected percentage of false positive and false negative classifications for each group being considered. Prediction is often improved when more than one score is used, as in a formula derived from multiple regression. Data of various kinds and types usually produce better predictive information than scores from similar instruments.

REFERENCE

Reynolds, C. R. (1984). Critical measurements issues in learning disabilities. *Journal of Special Education, 18,* 451–476.

JOSEPH L. FRENCH
Pennsylvania State University

LEARNING DISABILITIES, SEVERE DISCREPANCY ANALYSIS

FAMILIAL DYSAUTONOMIA

Familial dysautonomia was first identified as a synddrome by Riley and his associates in 1949; it was termed Riley-Day syndrome (Riley, Day, Greeley, & Langford, 1949). The symptomatology, which is extensive, results from involvement of the central (CNS) and peripheral nervous systems (PNS) and impacts on other developing systems of the body. Primarily found in Jews of eastern European extraction, dysautonomia is transmitted genetically, with the mode of inheritance believed to be autosomal recessive. The disorder is prominently marked by the individual's insensitivity to pain, absence of lacrimation, and absence of taste buds, in addition to many functional incapacities from birth. Dysautonomia is rarely diagnosed during the neonatal period (Perlman, Benady, & Sassi, 1979), although early identification is important to its management and to provision of appropriate treatment and educational services. The disorder is progressive, with those involved rarely living beyond the fourth decade of life. Exceptions have been noted, however, and since improvement can occur, an optimistic attitude may enhance the emotional relationship between family members (Meijer & Hovne, 1981).

Neonatal functioning, when identified, may be marked by unusual posture and limb movements as well as difficulties in swallowing (Perlman et al., 1979). The latter may be associated with other oropharyngeal deficits, may interfere with subsequent normative speech development, and may require the assistance of speech therapy. With regard to problems of swallowing, early identification and the provision of a feeding program would greatly assist the young child, as feeding problems have also been found in a large percentage of this population (Ganz, Levine, Axelrod, & Kahanovitz, 1983). As an adult, the dysautonomic may be dysarthric, resulting from involvement of the CNS. The presence of altered posture and limb movements may further interfere with the integration of more complex motor patterns, and delayed developmental milestones may also be noted (Ganz et al., 1983).

Orthopedic problems, including scoliosis and kyphosis, may also develop, thus requiring the use of adaptive aids for positioning and, in severe cases, to aid in locomotion. Physical therapy input would probably be indicated by this time, as might occupational therapy to assist the individual in maintaining range of motion. If the disorder progresses to the point where hospitalization becomes necessary, as much contact as possible should be maintained with the child or adolescent's educational placement and home setting by the hospital. "Hospitalization is indeed a disrupting and threatening experience even for the older, more experienced adult patient . . . and the younger child with more limited coping skills . . . is at particular psychological risk" (Barowsky, 1978, p. 48). Decreased vitality, resulting from compromised vital functions that may occur with severe scoliosis and kyphosis, as well as with cardiovascular and pulmonary problems associated with dysautonomia, may dictate adjustment of the individual's activity levels and routines. Additionally, the presence of ataxia (difficulties with balance and maintaining position in space) presents problems of both coordination and safety to the dysautonomic individual.

Since dysautonomia is generally not marked by a decrease in IQ, individuals can benefit from educational programming geared to the mainstream student. They may also take an active role in the treatment and educational process and thus feel more in control of the disorder that has altered their lives. The maintenance of maximal functional ability can best be attained by the active involvement of dysautonomics on their own behalf, rather than through their passive compliance, often ascribed to the old medical model of treatment. Thus, individuals with familial dysautonomia require specialized educational, medical, and psychological treatment through their lifespans: the absence of any of these components represents a marked deficit in the management process.

REFERENCES

Barowsky, E. I. (1978). Young children's perceptions and reactions to hospitalization. In E. Gellert (Ed.), *Psychosocial Aspects of Pediatric Care.* New York: Grune & Stratton.

Ganz, S. B., Levine, D. D., Axelrod, F. B., & Kahanovitz, N. (1983). Physical therapy management of familial dysautonomia. *Physical Therapy, 63*(7), 1121–1124.

Meijer, A., & Hovne, R. (1981). Child psychiatric problems in "autonomous dysfunction." *Child Psychiatry & Human Development, 12*(2), 96–105.

Perlman, M., Benady, S., & Sassi, E. (1979). Neonatal diagnosis of familial dysautonomia. *Pediatrics, 63*(2), 238–241.

Riley, C. M., Day, R. L., Greeley, D. M., & Langford, W. S. (1949). Central autonomic dysfunction with defective lacrimation. I. Report of five cases. *Pediatrics, 3,* 468–478.

ELLIS I. BAROWSKY
*Hunter College, City University
of New York*

CENTRAL NERVOUS SYSTEM ORTHOPEDIC IMPAIRMENTS

FAMILIAL RETARDATION

The term familial is used in the field of retardation as a synonym for cultural-familial retardation and also to refer to retardation associated with known heredity disorders. Discussions about whether retardation is inherited or owed to inappropriate environmental stimulation are a part of the debate on the basis of intelligence—the nature-nurture or heredity-environment controversy—that dates back to the 1930s. That debate is unresolved, but it is now abundantly clear that some medical disorders associated with mental retardation are transmitted genetically, whereas the etiology of others is uncertain (Westling, 1986).

Numerous studies have evidence suggesting hereditability in the cultural-familial group with mild, or educable, retardation. Reed and Reed (1965) provided extensive data on the issue. Of their 289 probands (initial cases), there were 55 who had the diagnosis of "cultural-familial, probably genetic" and had no other medical diagnosis associated with retardation. All of the 55 probands had at least one retarded primary family member, and retardation was found across two or three generations. The Reeds estimated that when both parents have cultural-familial retardation, the probability of retardation in a child born to them is about 40%, in contrast to a probability of about 1% if neither parent is retarded. The Reeds estimated that retardation incidence could be reduced by one-third to one-half if retarded couples chose not to have children. Analysis of the results of over 40 studies (excluding the challenged British studies) of identical and fraternal twins and other family relationships strongly suggests that hereditary factors are associated with intelligence, so the existence of a polygenic factor in cultural-familial retardation is credible. Consensus now seems to be that a polygenic pattern in combination with adverse environmental fac-

tors best explains retardation in the cultural-familial group.

Diagnosis of genetically based medical syndromes is more probable in cases where the degree of mental impairment is severe. Among the genetically determined disorders with which mental retardation is associated are metabolic disorders such as phenylketonuria (PKU) and chromosomal anomalies such as cri du chat (5p monosomy). Genetic defect may be inherited from the parents, or it may be due to a mutation caused by viruses, certain chemicals, or radiation. Mutant genes may be dominant or recessive, and inheritance thereafter follows normal Mendelian laws.

Since about 1950, a large number of chromosomal anomalies, many associated with retardation, have been described in the literature. The most common of these is Down's syndrome, which has an incidence of about 1 in 700 births. It occurs most often in births to mothers over 35 years old. About 95% of the cases are due to mutations; most of the others are inherited from a one parent who is a carrier of the gene. Males with Down's syndrome do not reproduce, but the rare females who have children will pass on the affected gene to all offspring. Most people with Down's syndrome have trisomy 21, meaning that they have three rather than two chromosomes at location 21. Translocations involve location of part or all of a chromosome in the wrong place and include D/G translocations involving chromosomes 13–15 with 21 and G/G translocations involving 21/22. The rare mosaic Down's cases result from trisomy that begins after cells have begun to multiply; incidence of mosaicism is about 1 in 3000 births overall, but about 1 in 10 if the mother shows a mosaic karyotype (a diagrammatic representation of form, size, and attachments of chromosomes). The retardation may be at any level, but IQ averages reported from surveys are around 35 to 50 for persons of school age or above. However, early reports on small numbers of children participating in two intensive early educational programs indicated that many of those children with Down's syndrome scored at or above the mild retardation level on language or intelligence tests when tested after the preschool program or in primary grades (Hayden & Haring, 1976; Rynders & Horrobin, 1975).

Nearly all abnormalities of amino acid metabolism are potential causes for mental retardation, but the likelihood of retardation varies greatly (Lee, 1980). The best known cause is phenylketonuria (PKU), which has an incidence of between 1 in 5000 and 1 in 20,000 in different countries. Fortunately, a simple blood screening test in the first week of life alerts physicians to the possibility of PKU and further diagnostic tests are easily made. Modification of diet beginning in infancy can prevent the extremely deleterious effects of PKU. However, women with hyperphenylalaniemia (silent PKU) are more likely than others to produce retarded children. Since inheritance follows the usual Mendelian laws for recessive genes, babies born to treated adults with PKU are at high risk for PKU or carrier status (Guthrie, 1972).

Other rare genetic metabolic disorders associated with retardation include histidinemia, hereditary fructose intolerance, Wilson disease (hepatolenticular degeneration), galactosemia, maple syrup urine disease, Hartnup syndrome, Hurler disease (lipochondrodystrophy or gargoylism), and several of the amaurotic familial idiocy group, including infantile Tay-Sachs disease. Adults who are carriers of some of these disorders (e.g., Tay-Sachs) can be identified and may choose not to have children. Early death is associated with some metabolic disorders, but for some others medical treatments may prevent the severe disability associated with the disorder (Grossman, 1983; Lee, 1980).

Approximately one-third of the cases of hypothyroidism (cretinism) are of the nonendemic familial type, which is hereditary. Untreated cretins have retardation, short stature, and other physical signs. Hypothyroidism is readily diagnosed in infancy and most cases respond readily to medical treatment. Among other rare inherited conditions associated with retardation are cri du chat, Patou, Edwards, Lesch-Nyhan, Hunter, Duchenne, Williams, and Lawrence-Moon-Biedl syndromes, and tuberous sclerosis, congenital ectodermoses, neurofibromatosis, and trigeminal cerebral angiomatosis. Retardation is also found with greater than expected frequency in the genetic disorders of Turner and Klinefelter syndromes, but the majority of those victims are not retarded (Feingold, 1980; Grossman, 1983; Sciorra, 1980).

In summary, heredity is clearly a factor in some disorders with retardation as a concomitant condition. However, those are the minority of retardation cases, usually associated with severe retardation, and found primarily in cases of chromosomal defects and endocrine dysfunction. In other disorders, genes are indicted, but the mechanism is unclear. It is probable that there is a hereditary component in cultural-familial retardation, but the mechanism and amount of genetic contribution is uncertain.

REFERENCES

Feingold, M. (1980). Delineation of human genetic syndromes with mental retardation. In M. M. McCormack (Ed.), *Prevention of mental retardation and other developmental disabilities.* New York: Marcel Dekker.

Grossman, H. J. (Ed.). (1983). *Classification in mental retardation.* Washington, DC: American Association on Mental Deficiency.

Guthrie, R. (1972). Mass screening for genetic disease. *Hospital Practice, 7,* 93–100.

Hayden, A. H., & Haring, N. G. (1976). Programs for Down's syndrome children at the University of Washington. In T. D. Tjossem (Ed.), *Intervention strategies for high risk infants and young children.* Baltimore, MD: University Park Press.

Lee, M-L. (1980). Aminoacidopathy and mental retardation. In M. M. McCormack (Ed.), *Prevention of mental retardation and other developmental disabilities.* New York: Marcel Dekker.

Reed, E. W., & Reed, S. C. (1965). *Mental retardation: A family study.* Philadelphia: Saunders.

Rynders, J. E., & Horrobin, J. M. (1975). Project EDGE: The University of Minnesota's communication simulation program for Down's syndrome infants. In B. Friedlander, G. Sterritt, & G. Kirk (Eds.), *Exceptional infant: Assessment and intervention* (Vol. 3). New York: Brunner/Mazel.

Sciorra, L. J. (1980). Chromosomal basis for developmental disability and mental retardation. In M. M. McCormack (Ed.), *Prevention of mental retardation and other developmental disabilities.* New York: Marcel Dekker.

Westling, D. L. (1986). *Introduction to mental retardation.* Englewood Cliffs, NJ: Prentice-Hall.

SUE ALLEN WARREN
Boston University

CONGENITAL DISORDERS
CRETINISM
CRI DU CHAT SYNDROME
DOWN'S SYNDROME
HEREDITY
PHENYLKETONURIA
TAY-SACHS DISEASE

FAMILY COUNSELING

Family counseling is an interactive process that aims to assist families in regaining a balance comfortable to all members (Perez, 1979). Family counseling is a therapeutic technique for exploring and alleviating the current interlocking emotional problems within a family system by helping family members to change dysfunctional transaction patterns together (Goldenberg & Goldenberg, 1985).

Family counseling is usually indicated when the family's ability to perform becomes inadequate. Unlike individual counseling, which focuses on the person's intrapsychic difficulties, family counseling emphasizes the relationships that transpire during therapeutic settings (Goldenberg & Goldenberg, 1983). Family counseling evolved from an extension of psychoanalytic treatment to coverage of a full range of emotional problems. The field includes work with families, the introduction of general systems theory, the evolution of child guidance and marital counseling, and an increased interest in new clinical techniques such as group therapy. It grew out of a need to expand traditional therapy from a linear approach to a multifactor systematic view of individuals and their families (Frank, 1984).

Goals of family counseling include (1) increasing each member's tolerance for each member's uniqueness; (2) increasing each member's tolerance for frustration when loss, conflict, and disappointment are encountered; (3) increasing the motivation of each member to support, encourage, and enhance each other member; and (4) increasing congruent perceptions of family members (Perez, 1979).

Families of children in special education require family counseling frequently simply because of the multiplicity of crises with which they are faced. Black (1982) indicates that the treatment of handicapped children and their families is as complex and diverse as are the disorders from which they suffer. The communication problems indigenous to handicapping conditions (sensory, affective, or cognitive) cause enormous problems of communication within the family. These problems can be mitigated through the use of family therapy. A frame of reference must be retained, however, in that the presence of a handicapped child does not presume family problems.

Through the use of family counseling, parents and other family members may alter their behavior patterns to produce positive changes in the behaviors of their children (Kozloff, 1979).

REFERENCES

Black, D. (1982). Handicap and family therapy. In A. Bentovin, G. Barnes, & A. Cooklin (Eds.), *Family therapy* (Vol. 2). New York: Grune & Stratton.

Frank, C. (1984). Contextual family therapy. *American Journal of Family Therapy, 12*(1), 3–12.

Goldenberg, I., & Goldenberg, H. (1983). Historical roots of contemporary family therapy. In B. B. Solman & G. Stricker (Eds.), *Handbook of family and marital therapy*. New York: Plenum.

Goldenberg, I., & Goldenberg, H. (1985). *Family therapy: An overview*. Monterey, CA: Brooks/Cole.

Kozloff, M. A. (1979). *A program for families of children with learning and behavior problems*. New York: Wiley.

Perez, J. (1979). *Family counseling: Theory and practice*. New York: Van Nostrand.

ANNE M. BAUER
University of Cincinnati

COUNSELING THE HANDICAPPED
FAMILY RESPONSE TO HANDICAP
FAMILY THERAPY

FAMILY EDUCATIONAL RIGHTS AND PRIVACY ACT

See BUCKLEY AMENDMENT.

FAMILY RESPONSE TO A HANDICAPPED CHILD

Handicapped youngsters have the potential to substantially alter the dynamics of family life (Knoblock, 1983).

Changes in the family structure typically start with the parents' reactions to the handicapped child. Initially there is the impact of a handicapped child on parental adjustment; then there is the combined influence of the handicapped child and the resulting parental reactions on other siblings in the family.

Parents are often slow to recognize that their child is not developing normally. Typically, someone outside of the family unit (e.g., pediatrician, teacher, psychologist, etc.) will make the initial diagnosis (Cartwright, Cartwright, & Ward, 1985). Once the parents acknowledge that a problem exists, they may be initially comforted in knowing that a more severe disorder is not present. For example, a husband and wife may be relieved that their child is learning disabled but not mentally retarded. They may also be initially consoled in the belief that the problem can be cured relatively quickly. Unfortunately, many handicapping conditions cannot be corrected. Others may require years of education or therapy before the child is no longer affected by the disorder. The parents' recognition that the problem will not go away easily may trigger a crisis reaction. This reaction has been described by Luterman (1979) with reference to deaf youngsters and Kubler-Ross (1969) with reference to the terminally ill.

A state of shock is typically the first reaction of parents to learning that their child is handicapped. This period often lasts from a couple of hours to a few days and is characterized by a calm detachment from the actual problem. Parents eventually become aware that a real problem exists. Their emotional reaction at this time is heightened. Typical emotional reactions include inadequacy when faced with the demands of raising a child with special needs, confusion in light of the vast amount of new and highly technical information offered by professionals about the disorder, anger that the child does not conform to the parents' expectations, and guilt that the parents could have avoided or prevented the disability.

As a defense against these strong emotions, many parents begin to deny the existence of a problem. This denial may take the form of seeking professional opinions that are overly optimistic, or becoming angry with professionals who present a modest prognosis for the child's development. When parents begin to accept that the child does have a handicap, they may discuss their child's problem with both professionals and casual acquaintances. Parents in this phase offer realistic statements regarding the prognosis for the child's overcoming the disorder. Acknowledgment clears the way for the final stage, in which the parents actually adapt to the demands of having a handicapped child.

Parents eventually become committed to providing the experiences and opportunities necessary to maximizing the child's potential. The acknowledgment and constructive action phases are likely to recur throughout the child's development. Each time a new stage is reached (e.g., adolescence, adult independence, etc.), the parents will again have to acknowledge the problem and initiate an appropriate course of action.

Parental reaction to the handicapped child may have an equally strong influence on siblings in the family (Wolfensberger, 1967). As parents progress through the preceding stages, their relationship with other children in the family is likely to change. In general, the more time parents spend in constructive action, the more favorable the influence of siblings. Parents who actively support the development of their handicapped child are likely to provide the siblings with numerous opportunities to observe and model positive attitudes and behaviors. Siblings able to benefit from these experiences are likely to develop a positive relationship with their handicapped brother or sister. Further, these experiences may result in the siblings' developing problem-solving skills that enhance their own adjustment.

Conversely, parents who fail to reach the stage of constructive action are likely to have an adverse influence on their other children. A parent's denial, for example, may involve the handicapped youngster in the sibling's social activities. This, of course, may cause the silbing to resent his or her handicapped brother or sister. Recognition of the problem without constructive action may cause a parent to have unrealistic expectations for the handicapped child's siblings. The nonhandicapped child's exceptional performance may be expected to offset the guilt and disappointment resulting from the handicapped child's limited performance.

The care and attention required by many handicapped children may substantially diminish the time available for nonhandicapped family members. When a parent spends an excessive amount of time with a handicapped youngster, it may deprive the other children of opportunities and experiences important for their own growth and development.

In conclusion, parents of handicapped children are likely to experience a crisis reaction. This reaction begins with the initial shock and ends in acknowledgment of the handicap and constructive action. The parents' ability to move quickly through the stages of the crisis reaction to the point of constructive action will, to a large extent, determine the overall adjustment of the family.

REFERENCES

Cartwright, G. P., Cartwright, C. A., & Ward, M. E. (1985). *Educating special learners* (2nd ed.). Belmont, CA: Wadsworth.

Knoblock, P. (1983). *Teaching emotionally disturbed children.* Boston: Houghton Mifflin.

Kubler-Ross, E. (1969). *On death and dying.* New York: Macmillan.

Luterman, D. (1979). *Counseling parents of hearing impaired children.* Boston: Little, Brown.

Wolfensberger, W. (1967). Counseling the parents of the retarded. In A. A. Baumeister (Ed.), *Mental retardation: Appraisal, education and rehabilitation.* Chicago: Aldine.

PATRICK J. SCHLOSS
Pennsylvania State University

PARENT COUNSELING
PARENT EFFECTIVENESS TRAINING

FAMILY SERVICES ASSOCIATION OF AMERICA (FSAA)

Founded in 1911 and known as the Family Welfare Association of America, the association is a federation of 270 local agencies located in over 200 localities. The local agencies provide a variety of services designed to resolve problems of family living. Family counseling, family life education, and family advocacy services are used in dealing with parent-child, marital, and mental health problems. The association assists in the development of local agencies.

Strong family life is promoted through contact with the media, government, business, and industry. The association compiles statistics, conducts research, sponsors competitions, and bestows awards. Publications include a journal and a directory of member agencies. Public information activities include the production and dissemination of manuals, pamphlets, brochures, and public service releases. Biennial meetings are held in odd-numbered years. The association maintains a library with primary holdings in social work, family life, psychology, and urban problems. A placement service is also available. Association offices are located at 44 East 23rd Street, New York, NY 10010. Telephone: (212) 674-6100.

PHILIP R. JONES
*Virginia Polytechnic Institute
and State University*

FAMILY THERAPY

The field of marriage and family therapy is frequently referred to as the fourth mental health discipline. The other three disciplines—psychiatry, psychology, and social work—are certainly older than the field of marriage and family therapy, but this new discipline has evolved rapidly to achieve a position of status in the mental health field. One reason for this occurrence is that the field was initially populated by members of the other three disciplines and so was able to advance based on the collective experiences of these contributors. Another reason is that these other disciplines all had acknowledged the role of the family in the development of human problems and in the treatment process. The profession of marriage and family discipline evolved as a profession wherein the collective body of knowledge regarding clinical implications of the family were gathered and developed. Also, two primary professional organizations evolved from the development of this shared body of knowledge and the resultant clinical focus, the American Association for Marriage and Family Therapy (AAMFT) and the American Family Therapy Association. From a review of the historical development of this field, one can appreciate the important roles played by members of each of the other three mental health disciplines in its evolution. There was a creative competition among the fields and a diversity of backgrounds that also contributed to the rapidity of the new field's growth. This is in contrast to psychoanalysis and other clinical schools of thought that had only the creative benefit of Sigmund Freud as a primary developer.

Therefore, while marriage and family therapy has a relatively short history, it does have a collectively long past. The earliest traces of the family as a significant treatment factor can be found in Freud's early works. He was convinced that human conflicts were spawned in early interactions between children and their families. While he acknowledged the importance of the family in this regard, he attempted to isolate the family from treatment in order to liberate his patients from the problems of the family. It was as though he viewed the family as an infectious disease to be kept out of the psychoanalytic operating room. Like Freud, most clinicians in the first half of the twentieth century acknowledged the family as an important variable in human problems and also continued to exclude the family from the treatment process.

It was not until the 1950s that the field of marriage and family therapy, as it is known today, began to emerge. About this time, early pioneers began to include family members in the process of helping to effect change. These practitioners were recognizing that it was as important to understand and treat what was happening between people as it was to focus on what was happening inside the individual. While clinical observation was demonstrating that it was productive to include family members in the change effort, a developing body of research findings were also substantiating this factor.

The decades of the 1960s and 1970s resulted in the firm acknowledgement of marriage and family therapy as the fourth mental health discipline. The primary professional association of marriage and family therapists is the American Association of Marriage and Family Therapy (AAMFT). This association is headquartered in Washington, DC, and has primary responsibility for the certification and endorsement of both training programs and individual practitioners. Individuals and training programs seeking the professional endorsement of this association must first meet the professional standards established and then demonstrate their professionalism by meeting ongoing education requirements and review of their currency

in the field. While the AAMFT has certain service functions it makes available to the professional membership, it continues to have as a primary function ensuring that quality services are available to American families. Consequently, the American public can be sure of the quality of an individual marriage and family therapist by determining whether he or she is a clinical member of the AAMFT. The current membership of AAMFT is approximately 12,000. References related to family therapy and handicapped children are listed below for further reading.

REFERENCES

Aponte, H. (1976). The family school intervention: An eco-structural approach. *Family Process, 15,* 303–311.

Dunlop, W. R., & Hollingsworth, J. S. (1977, July). How does a handicapped child affect the family? Implications for practicioners. *Family Coordinator*, pp. 286–293.

Foster, M., & Berger, M. (1985). Research with families with handicapped children: A multilevel systemic perspective. In L. L'Abate (Ed.), *Handbook of family psychology and therapy* (Vol. 2). Homewood, IL: Dorsey.

Strom, R., Rees, R., Slaughter, H., & Wurster, S. (1981). Child-rearing expectations of families with atypical children. *American Journal of Orthopsychiatry, 51,* 285–296.

Turnbull, H. R., & Turnbull, A. P. (1982). Parent involvement in the education of handicapped children: A critique. *Mental Retardation, 20*(3), 115–122.

CHARLES P. BARNARD
University of Wisconsin, Stout

PARENTAL COUNSELING

FARRELL, ELIZABETH E. (1870–1932)

Elizabeth E. Farrell, who began her teaching career in an ungraded rural school in upstate New York, accepted a position as an elementary teacher in New York City in 1900. Observing that some children were unable to make satisfactory progress in the elementary classes, Farrell, using her experience in the rural school in which she had taught all grades, formed an ungraded class for these children, the first special class in the public schools of New York City. In 1906 a Department of Ungraded Classes was formed with Farrell as director, a position she held until her death.

Farrell designed the nation's first training program for special class teachers in 1911 at the Maxwell Training School in New York City, and she taught the first university courses for special class teachers at the University of Pennsylvania in 1912. Largely through her efforts, a program to prepare special class teachers was established at the Oswego (New York) Normal School in 1916.

Farrell originated and edited *Ungraded*, the journal of

the Ungraded Class Teachers' Association. She was a founder of the Association of Consulting Psychologists. In 1922 she was one of 12 special educators who founded the International Council for Exceptional Children, and she served as its first president.

REFERENCE

Warner, M. L. (1944). Founders of the International Council for Exceptional Children. *Journal of Exceptional Children, 10,* 217–223.

PAUL IRVINE
Katonah, New York

FEARS

See PHOBIAS AND FEARS.

FEBRILE CONVULSIONS

Febrile convulsions are seizures associated with fevers or high body temperature in childhood. Single or multiple generalized seizures in infancy or early childhood may be associated only with fever in about 4% of the population. Typically, febrile convulsions occur soon after the onset of a fever-producing illness not directly affecting the central nervous system. Usually the seizure occurs 3 to 6 hours after the onset of the fever (Livingston, 1972), although such seizures can be seen during the second or third day of an illness (Lennox-Buchtal, 1973). When the seizure begins, body temperature is usually at its peak at 39 to 40 degrees C. Acute upper respiratory infection, tonsillitis, otitis media, and bronchial pneumonia are some common causes of febrile convulsions. The seizure is usually generalized and of short duration, although some may last as long as 20 minutes or more (Spreen, Tupper, Risser, Tuokko, & Edgell, 1984). The movements seen with these convulsions are bilateral but may show unilateral elements. Males have been found to be more susceptible to febrile seizures than females. Most investigators feel that there is an inherited susceptibility to seizure above a certain threshold of body temperature with autosomal dominant transmission (Brazier & Coceani, 1978).

Typically, this form of seizure activity is benign. Initially, it is difficult to separate these benign febrile convulsionss from seizures caused by brain damage owed to unrecognized meningitis or congenital brain defects. The signs of a benign prognosis include (1) onset of the convulsions between the ages of 6 months and 4 years; (2) a normal EEG within a week after the seizure; (3) the absence of clinical signs of brain damage; and (4) the lack

of atypical features or excessive duration of the attack. The chances of additional febrile seizures are about one in two if the first episode occurs before the age of 14 months, and much lower if the first attack occurs after 33 months of age. Few children have attacks later in life; however, it is not always possible to predict whether subsequent febrile or nonfebrile seizures will follow (Goldensohn, Glaser, & Goldberg, 1984).

Children who have a single febrile seizure have an excellent prognosis, as there appears to be little, if any, lasting neurological or mental deficit (National Institutes of Health, 1980). For those children who have a febrile convulsion in conjunction with afebrile seizures, preexisting central nervous system abnormalities, or a fever-inducing illness involving the central nervous system resulting in a convulsive episode, the prognosis is much less positive (Spreen et al., 1984).

REFERENCES

Brazier, M. A. B., & Coceani, F. (Eds.). (1978). *Brain dysfunction in infantile febrile convulsions.* International Brain Research Organization Monograph Series. New York: Raven.

Goldensohn, E. S., Glaser, G. H., Goldberg, M. A. (1984). Epilepsy. In L. P. Rowland (Ed.), *Merritt's textbook of neurology* (7th ed.) (pp. 629–650). Philadelphia: Lea & Febiger.

Lennox-Buchtal, M. (1973). Febrile convulsions: A reappraisal. *Electroencephalography & Clinical Neurophysiology, 32* (Suppl. 1).

Livingston, S. (1972). Epilepsy in infancy, childhood, and adolescence. In B. Wolman (Ed.), *Manual of child psychopathology* (pp. 45–69). New York: McGraw-Hill.

National Institutes of Health. (1980). Febrile seizures. A consensus of their significance, evaluation, and treatment. *Pediatrics, 66,* 1009–1030.

Spreen, O., Tupper, D., Risser, A., Tuokko, H., & Edgell, D. (1984). *Human developmental neuropsychology,* New York: Oxford University Press.

RICHARD A. BERG
West Virginia University Medical Center, Charleston Division

ABSENCE SEIZURES
EPILEPSY
GRAND MAL SEIZURES

FEDERAL IMPACT ON SPECIAL EDUCATION

See SPECIAL EDUCATION, FEDERAL IMPACT ON.

FEDERAL REGISTER (FR)

The *Federal Register* (*FR*) is a uniform system for publishing all executive orders and proclamations, proposed rules, regulations, and notices of agencies authorized by Congress or the president, documents required to be published by an act of Congress, and other documents deemed by the director of the *FR* to be of sufficient interest. It does not contain rules of Congress or of the courts. As such, it serves as formal notice to the public of legally significant actions and is typically the first place of public appearance of these documents (Cohen & Berring, 1984).

Since the *FR* publishes notices promulgated by federal agencies such as the U.S. Department of Education, it is an important source for laws pertaining to special education. The Education for All Handicapped Children Act (PL 94-142), for example, was first published here. Also, the *FR* is the primary source for the announcement of grant and contract competitions administered by special education programs. Guidelines and priorities for the spending of federal special education monies are contained therein as well.

The *FR* was established by the Federal Register Act of 1935 and is considered prima facie evidence of the filing and text of the original documents. It is issued each federal working day.

REFERENCE

Cohen, M. L., & Berring, R. C. (1984). *Finding the law*. St. Paul, MN: West.

DOUGLAS L. FRIEDMAN
Fordham University

FEEBLE-MINDED

Feeble-minded is the historical term applied to individuals of borderline or mild mental retardation. The term was used as early as the sixteenth century. The Swiss physician Aurealus Theophastus Bombastus von Hahenheim, better known as Paracelsus (1493–1541), used the term feeble-minded to describe individuals who act as "healthy animals."

J. Langdon Down (1826–1896) categorized distinct types of feeble-mindedness. Accidental feeble-mindedness resulted from trauma, inadequate prenatal care, prolonged delivery, inflammatory disease, or the unwise use of medication. Developmental feeble-mindedness resulted from disturbed mothers, parents inebriated at the time of conception, overexcitement during infancy through early childhood, or pressure from school at the time of second dentification or puberty. Although his patients were from poverty-stricken, urban neighborhoods, Down did not conceive of environmental factors as influencing development.

Edouard Sequin (1812–1880) offered yet another classification scheme: idiocy, or moderately to profoundly retarded; imbecility, or mildly retarded with defects in social development; backward or feeble-minded (enfant arriere); and simpleness or superficial retardation evidenced by the slowing down of development. The feeble-minded child was described by Sequin as a child who is retarded in development, and who has low muscle tone, uncoordinated use of the hands, and limited comprehension but no sensory deficits. Unlike Down, Sequin was sensitive to the fact that environmental factors and neglect could have a negative impact on development. Owing to the work of Samuel Gridley Howe (1801–1876) in the mid 1800s, it became more widely recognized that a percentage of feeble-minded children were the result of impoverished environments.

In the late 1800s, three broad categories of intellectual functioning appeared: idiot (severely and profoundly retarded); imbecile (moderately retarded); and feeble-minded (mildly retarded). With the introduction of standardized tests of intelligence in the United States, the Committee on Classification of Feeble-Minded of the American Association for the Study of the Feeble-Minded (now the American Association on Mental Deficiency) in 1910 issued a definition that set reasonable parameters on who could be classified as feeble-minded:

> The term feeble-minded is used generically to include all degrees of mental defect due to arrested or imperfect development as a result of which the person so affected is incapable of competing on equal terms with his normal fellows or managing himself or his affairs with ordinary prudence. The tripartite classification of mental retardation included: idiots (those so deeply defective that their mental development does not exceed that of a normal child of about 2 years); imbeciles (those whose mental development is higher than that of an idiot but does not exceed that of normal child of about 7 years); and moron (those whose mental development is above that of an imbecile but does not exceed that of a child of about 12 years). (p. 61)

In the 1930s feeble-mindedness was defined as retarded intelligence with social incompetence. During the 1940s the term mentally deficient replaced feeble-minded as a generic label.

REFERENCES

Committee on Classification of Feeble-minded. (1910). *Journal of Psycho-Asthenics, 15*, 61–67.

Kanner, L. (1967). Historical review of mental retardation (1800–1965). *American Journal of Mental Deficiency, 72*, 165–189.

Scheerenberger, R. C. (1983). *A history of mental retardation*. Baltimore, MD: Brookes.

Seguin, E. (1971). *Idiocy and its treatment by the physiological method*. New York: Kelly.

Sloan, W., & Stevens, H. (1976). *A century of concern: A history of the American Association on Mental Deficiency 1876–1976.* Washington, DC: American Association on Mental Deficiency.

CAROLE REITER GOTHELF
Hunter College, City University of New York

IDIOT
MENTAL RETARDATION

FEINGOLD DIET

One of the most widely acclaimed (particularly in the popular press) yet least empirically supported treatment modes for hyperactive children is the Feingold diet (Feingold, 1975, 1976). Specifically, Feingold (1975, 1976) has insisted that children with learning and behavioral disturbances have a natural toxic reaction to artificial food colors, flavorings, preservatives, and other substances that are added to foods to enhance their shelf life. The Feingold diet purports to be an additive-free dietary regimen that attempts to eliminate artificial flavorings, colorings, and even several nutritional fruits and vegetables containing salicylates. While the use of the Feingold diet has been frequently advocated in the therapeutic treatment of hyperactivity, learning disabilities, and other behavioral disorders, Feingold (1975) has claimed his additive-free diet to be effective in treating other handicapping conditions, including mental retardation, autism, and conduct disorders.

Feingold's unempirically substantiated claims have suggested that nearly 50% of hyperactive children in his clinical population have displayed marked improvements, and that in the majority of cases, the children have had a complete remission of symptoms as a result of the additive-free dietary regimen (Feingold, 1975, 1976). According to the Feingold group, these improvements have been demonstrated in both the social and cognitive domains. Feingold has even claimed striking academic improvements as a function of the additive-free diet, despite the fact that academic achievement has been an area little influenced by therapeutic efforts with this population (Barkley & Cunningham, 1978). Further, Feingold has insisted that the younger the child, the more expedient and pervasive the improvement that may be observed. For example, according to Feingold (1975), the efficacy of the additive-free diet in infants and toddlers may be documented in as little as 24 hours to one week. Feingold has noted that in adolescents, where improvement is predicted to be least successful, notable effects often take as long as several months to be seen.

The intense debate resulting from Feingold's claims has spawned a number of empirical studies supported by the federal government. A consensus of these studies (Conners, 1980; Spring & Sandoval, 1976) did not support Feingold's claims, and criticized Feingold's earlier work on the basis of its marginal research methodology, including poor placebo controls. Although Conners (1980) has accused Feingold of making "gross overstatements" (p. 109) regarding his diet, Conners does concede that a small number of hyperactive children (less than 5%) do respond favorably to the diet. Nonetheless, it is still unclear whether it is the Feingold diet that is responsible for the observed improvements in this small percentage of children or the regimen associated with the laborious preparations surrounding this special diet. For example, one research group (Harley & Matthews, 1980) has attributed any success of the Feingold diet to a placebo effect. They claim altered aspects of family dynamics often result from special procedures and efforts in implementing the Feingold diet. Others have attributed its effects to the familiar Hawthorne effect. Further, it must be cautioned that many practitioners have recognized that several of the foods Feingold has recommended for elimination from children's diets contain important nutrients necessary for their growth and development. Consequently, there has been concern in the pediatric community that the Feingold diet may not fulfill the nutritional needs of children treated with this approach.

Despite the frequent failures to corroborate Feingold's (1975, 1976) original claims (Conners, 1980; the Feingold diet continues to have loyal followers. Many parents have even formed a national association, frequently contacting food manufacturers to provide additive-free food products. Perhaps contributing to its widespread acceptance is the fact that the Feingold diet is commensurate with society's penchant for dieting, health food fads, and natural foods. Further, the Feingold diet offers an alternative to psychotropic medication, which many parents perceive as risky and having side effects, although this has not been verified in the research literature (Ross & Ross, 1982). Citing the etiology and treatment of hyperactivity as an allergic reaction to food may be more palatable to parents than neurological or psychogenic hypotheses, but it is almost certainly less valid.

REFERENCES

Barkley, R. A., & Cunningham, C. E. (1978). Do stimulant drugs improve the academic performance of hyperactive children? A review of outcome studies. *Clinical Pediatrics, 17,* 85–92.

Conners, C. K. (1980). *Food additives and hyperactive children.* New York: Plenum.

Feingold, B. F. (1975). *Why your child is hyperactive.* New York: Random House.

Feingold, B. F. (1976). Hyperkinesis and learning disabilities linked to the ingestion of artificial food colors and flavors. *Journal of Learning Disabilities, 9,* 551–559.

Harley, J. P., & Matthews, C. G. (1980). Food additives and hyperactivity in children. In R. M. Knights & D. J. Bakker (Eds.),

Treatment of hyperactive and learning disordered children. Baltimore, MD: University Park Press.

Ross, D. M., & Ross, S. A. (1982). *Hyperactivity: Current issues, research and theory* (2nd ed.). New York: Wiley-Interscience.

EMILY G. SUTTER
*University of Houston, Clear
Lake*

RONALD T. BROWN
*Emory University School
of Medicine*

HYPERACTIVITY
HYPERKINESIS
IMPULSE CONTROL

FELDHUSEN, JOHN F. (1926–   )

Toward Excellence in Gifted Education, the title of a 1985 book by John Feldhusen, is also the definitive theme of the work that has evolved from Feldhusen's first publications on comparisons of mental performance among children of low, average, and high intelligence to his present studies on giftedness. Feldhusen, born in Waukesha, Wisconsin, received his BA in 1949, his MS in 1955, and his PhD in 1958 from the University of Wisconsin, Madison. An interim period as counselor and teacher provided practical background for his early studies on such diverse topics as programmed instruction, testing and measurement, delinquency, and classroom behavior. His contributions to the field of educational psychology culminated in his presidency of Division 15 of the American Psychological Association in 1975.

Feldhusen has exhibited a continuing concern for instruction in creative thinking and problem solving, coau-thoring a practical handbook, *Creative Thinking and Problem Solving in Gifted Education* (1985). His primary interest in using research, theory, and evaluation to guide program and curriculum development in gifted education became the impetus for advocacy of professional training for teachers of the gifted, numerous cooperative efforts with public school personnel, and in-service training throughout Indiana. It also has resulted in a steady stream of publications and teacher-targeted presentations and workshops throughout the United States. Feldhusen became chairman of the Educational Psychology and Research Section of Purdue University in 1977 and director of the Purdue Gifted Education Resource Institute in 1978. He is also an active promoter of graduate programs in gifted education.

Feldhusen is committed to the concept that gifted and talented youths are individuals who need special services not only to achieve as highly as possible, but also to experience self-fulfillment as human beings. Thus he believes that identification of the gifted must focus on finding those who need services, rather than on labeling youths, and on guiding development of individualized programs, which he discusses in *Curriculum for the Gifted* (in press). Feldhusen's contributions to gifted education have been recognized by his election to the presidency of the National Association for Gifted Children in 1981. He was awarded the status of distinguished scholar in that organization in 1983, and was appointed editor of the association's journal, *Gifted Child Quarterly,* in 1984.

REFERENCES

Feldhusen, J. F. (Ed.). (1985). *Toward excellence in gifted education.* Denver: Love.

Feldhusen, J. F., & Treffinger, D. J. (1985). *Creative thinking and problem solving in gifted education.* Dubuque, IA: Kendall-Hunt.

VanTassel-Baska, J., & Feldhusen, J. F. (in press). *Curriculum for the gifted.* Newton, MA: Allyn & Bacon.

PATRICIA A. HAENSLY
Texas A&M University

FENICHEL, CARL (1905–1975)

Carl Fenichel was founder and director of the League School for Seriously Disturbed Children in Brooklyn, New York. At the school, Fenichel provided one of the early demonstrations that it is feasible to educate severely emotionally disturbed children in a day program when the parents are given intensive training in appropriate home management and care.

Educated at the City College of New York, the New School for Social Research, and Yeshiva University, where

John F. Feldhusen

he earned the doctorate in education, Fenichel began his professional career as a teacher and psychologist. During his years at the League School, he served as professor of education at Teachers College, Columbia University, and as a lecturer at the Downstate Medical College in Brooklyn. Fenichel's pioneering League School, which he founded in 1953, served as a model for many of the first day programs for severely emotionally handicapped children in the United States.

PAUL IRVINE
Katonah, New York

FERAL CHILDREN

Victor, the Wild Boy of Aveyron, and Caspar Hauser are perhaps the best known of numerous more or less well-documented "feral children." Such children have spent various periods of their childhood under wild or at least uncivilized conditions. They have long been of interest to philosophers, psychologists, anthropologists, and educators, who have looked to them for answers to questions about the nature of man, the permanence of early experience, and the efficacy of education in overcoming early deprivation.

For convenience, feral children may be divided into two basic groups: (1) those who have grown up in open "wild" settings such as jungles or forests, and (2) those who have grown up under extreme environmental and social deprivation. Victor and Caspar Hauser are examples of the two groups respectively. In addition, a subgroup of "wild" children has supposedly been raised by animals. Amala and Kamala, the wolf girls of Midnapore (Singh & Zingg, 1942), are but two recent examples. Such so-called wolf children continue to fascinate the public at large.

The antiquity of interest in using conditions of early rearing to learn of man's nature is indicated by King Psammitichus's experiment, as reported by Herodotus. To determine what language was the most ancient, the king ordered that two infants be nursed by goats and separated from all contact with humans. Supposedly the first word they said was Phrygian for bread, and the Egyptians yielded to the primacy of the Phrygians. Ireland (1898) indicated that similar experiments were conducted by Emperor Frederick II and James IV of Scotland. Interest in feral children peaked in the eighteenth century with scientific uncertainty about who are and are not humans (the word orangutan comes from Malaysian for wild man). There were attempts to discriminate between Descartes' endowment of humans with innate ideas and Locke's empiricist concept of the human mind as a blank slate. Feral children were studied as models of Rousseau's noble savage (Lane, 1986; Shattuck, 1980).

Craft's (1979) claim of "some 50 documented cases of animal-reared children . . ." (p. 139) not withstanding, no fully documented examples of children reared by wolves, bears, gazelles, baboons, or any nonhumans, exist. Singh's claim that Amala and Kamala were reared by wolves was accepted by Zingg (Singh & Zingg, 1942) and the famous pediatrician-psychologist Arnold Gesell (1941), but the claim was convincingly disputed by Ogburn and Bose (1941). Ogburn (1959) later detailed how a particular feral child falsely became converted into the "Wolf Boy of Agra," even though the child had not been with wild animals at all. Although Maclean (1977) claims evidence to support Amala and Kamala's wolf rearing, this is dubious and not subject to verification. We have no more hard evidence on the general subject than did Ireland (1898), who concluded that the notion of wolf children belonged with nursery myths.

Similar controversy exists over other questions asked about feral children. Arguments still rage over whether, as Pinel felt about Victor, all such children were retarded to begin with and thus abandoned (Dennis, 1951), or whether, as Itard felt about Victor, they had initially been essentially normal and behaved primitively because of severe deprivation (Lane, 1975, 1986), or whether they had become autistic because of uncaring mothers (Bettelheim, 1959).

Unfortunately, we probably will never have clear answers to any of the questions asked of feral children. Their stories have the shortcomings of all retrospective case histories—lack of complete information, potentially biased observers, the lack of repeatability and control, the impossibility of knowing how the children would have behaved if raised under normal conditions, and the virtual impossibility of empirical verification of events in the children's lives before their discovery. As one example, Dennis (1951) has pointed out that many of the children apparently did not disappear from their families until they were several years of age. How, then, can the supposed permanence of their primitive characteristics be attributed to their normal early experience? As another example, we do not know whether Genie, a contemporary deprived child, would have developed normal language under normal conditions. Given the limits of the data, the problem of direction of causality seems unsolvable. Attributing all behavioral deficits to these children's unnatural rearing environment is a clear case of illogical *post hoc ergo propter hoc* (after this, because of this) reasoning. Thus cases of feral children are almost inevitably open to alternative interpretations.

We do know from reports of numerous modern cases that considerable intellective, motor, social-emotional, and even language development can occur in formerly severely deprived, abused or neglected, and institutionalized children (Clarke & Clarke, 1976; Skuse, 1984). Early deprivation, if not extremely prolonged, can be overcome, particularly with special and intensive intervention. Early adverse learning experiences are not irreversible, a message of considerable optimism to those in special education.

REFERENCES

Bettelheim, B. (1959). Feral children and autistic children. *American Journal of Sociology, 64,* 455–467.

Clarke, A. M., & Clarke, A. D. B. (Eds.). (1976). *Early experience: Myth and evidence.* New York: Free Press.

Craft, M. (1979). The neurocytology of damaging environmental factors. In M. Craft (Ed.), *Tredgold's mental retardation* (12th ed., pp. 137–143). (Bailliere-Tindall.) Saunders.

Dennis, W. (1951). A further analysis of reports of wild children. *Child Development, 22,* 153–159.

Gesell, A. L. (1942). *Wolf child and human child.* New York: Harper.

Ireland, W. W. (1898). *Mental affections of children, idiocy, imbecility, and insanity.* London: J. & A. Churchill.

Lane, H. (1976). *The wild boy of Aveyron.* Cambridge, MA: Harvard University Press.

Lane, H. (1986). The wild boy of Aveyron and Itard. *History of Psychology, 18,* 3–16.

Maclean, C. (1977). *The wolf children.* New York: Hill & Wang.

Shattuck, R. (1980). *The forbidden experiment.* New York: Farrar Straus Giroux.

ROBERT T. BROWN
University of North Carolina, Wilmington

CASPAR HAUSER CHILDREN
EARLY EXPERIENCE AND CRITICAL PERIODS
GENIE
ITARD, JEAN M. G.
WILD BOY OF AVEYRON

FERNALD, GRACE MAXWELL (1879–1950)

Grace Maxwell Fernald received her PhD in psychology from the University of Chicago in 1907. In 1911 she became head of the psychology department and laboratory at the State Normal School at Los Angeles. The remainder of her career was spent at the Normal School and the University of California at Los Angeles.

Fernald's lasting contribution to the field of education is her method for teaching disabled readers, a method that uses not only visual and auditory approaches, but kinesthetic and tactile cues as well. In 1921, UCLA's Clinic School, later renamed the Fernald School, was founded by Grace Fernald.

REFERENCES

Fernald, G. (1943). *Remedial techniques in basic school subjects.* New York: McGraw-Hill.

Sullivan, E. B., Dorcus, R. V., Allen, R. M., Bennet, M., & Koontz, L. K. (1950). Grace Maxwell Fernald. *Psychological Review, 57,* 319–321.

PAUL IRVINE
Katonah, New York

FERNALD, WALTER E. (1859–1924)

Walter E. Fernald received his medical degree from the Medical School of Maine, served as assistant physician at the State Hospital in Minnesota, and then became the first resident superintendent of the Massachusetts School for the Feeble-Minded (later renamed the Walter E. Fernald State School). A leader in the movement for humane treatment of mentally retarded persons, he developed an educational plan that provided a 24-hour-a-day program for each child. He devised a system for diagnosing and classifying mentally retarded people on the basis of total development rather than test results alone. Under his leadership, the Massachusetts school became an international center for the training of workers in the field of mental retardation. Fernald was also influential in the develop-

Grace Maxwell Fernald

Walter E. Fernald

ment of federal and state legislation relating to mental retardation (Wallace, 1924).

REFERENCE

Wallace, G. L. (1924). In memoriam Walter E. Fernald. *American Journal of Mental Deficiency, 30,* 16–23.

PAUL IRVINE
Katonah, New York

FERNALD METHOD

Multisensory remedial reading methods, commonly used in remedial and special education, are based on the premise that some children learn best when material is presented in several modalities. Typically, kinesthetic and tactile stimulation are used along with visual and auditory modalities. The multisensory programs that feature tracing, hearing, writing, and seeing are often referred to as VAKT (visual-auditory-kinesthetic-tactile) (Hallahan, Kauffman, & Lloyd, 1985).

One of the most widely known and used multisensory approaches to teaching handicapped children to read is the Fernald method (Gearheart, 1985). The rationale for the Fernald Word Learning Approach, which is usually known as the VAKT approach, was described by Fernald in 1943; it is based on the belief that if a child learns to use all senses, the child will make use of these experiences in learning to read. If one modality is weak, the others will help to convey the information. In practice, the VAKT approach is not confined to reading, but includes spelling and writing instruction. In essence, it is a language experience and whole-word approach (Kirk & Chalfant, 1984).

Fernald believed that overcoming the emotional problems failing students have with reading would be easier if their reading material were of interest to them. Therefore, stories are written down as suggested by the students, with as much help from the teacher as needed, and then read. Also, a student selects words that he or she wishes to learn and works on them, repeatedly feeling, spacing, seeing, saying, and hearing a word until it can be written from memory. Words that have been mastered are kept in a file so that a student may refer back to them as needed. Fernald was opposed to having the student sound out words; she emphasized the reading and writing of words as a whole. Although the Fernald approach has strong advocates who can provide case studies documenting its successful use, research evidence does not reveal that it has been particularly successful (Myers, 1978).

REFERENCES

Fernald, G. (1943). *Remedial techniques in basic school subjects.* New York: McGraw-Hill.

Gearheart, B. R. (1985). *Learning Disabilities.* St. Louis: Times Mirror/Mosby.

Hallahan, D. P., Kauffman, J. M., & Lloyd, J. W. (1985). *Introduction to learning disabilities.* Englewood Cliffs, NJ: Prentice-Hall.

Kirk, S., & Chalfant, J. C. (1984). *Academic and developmental learning disabilities.* Denver: Love.

Myers, C. A. (1978). Reviewing the literature on Fernald's technique of remedial reading. *Reading Teacher, 31,* 614–619.

JOSEPH M. RUSSO
*Hunter College, City University
of New York*

**HEGGE-KIRK & KIRK APPROACH
ORTON-GILLINGHAM METHOD**

FETAL ALCOHOL SYNDROME (FAS)

Fetal alcohol syndrome (FAS) is a recently described complex of physical anomalies and behavioral deficits that may occur in offspring of heavy-drinking mothers. Less serious sequelae occasionally affecting offspring of drinking mothers are commonly termed fetal alcohol effects (FAE). The FAS is associated with three effects (the triad of the FAS; Rosett & Weiner, 1984, p. 43): (1) growth retardation, (2) characteristic facial anomalies, and (3) central nervous system dysfunction, generally involving mental retardation. With an estimated incidence of 1.1 per 1000 live births, FAS is among the most common preventable handicapping conditions. Incidence of FAS and FAE among alcohol-abusing mothers is much higher, at least 25 and 91, respectively, per 1000 births (Abel, 1984).

Since the first generally accepted descriptions in 1973 FAS has been the topic of thousands of reports of human cases and correlates and experimental animal models. The confounding effects of other factors such as maternal smoking, malnutrition, and other drug use, have made isolation of effects owed solely to alcohol difficult. Prospective research programs such as the Boston City Hospital Prenatal Study (Rosett & Weiner, 1984) and animal research have helped to identify effects owed to alcohol itself. Detailed summaries of reports on FAS and FAE are in Abel (1984) and Rosett and Weiner (1984).

The biochemical basis for the disorder is not known, and no one mechanism may be responsible. Alcohol-related maternal malnutrition does not appear to be the cause. Two possible mechanisms are alcohol-induced embryonic hypoxia (Abel, 1984) and zinc deficiency (Çavdar, 1984).

Historically, many authors have suggested that the potentially damaging effects of maternal alcohol consumption were known even in ancient times. However, in a thorough review, Abel (1984) claims that many citations of ancient concerns about alcohol are based on erroneous secondary sources, and that the concerns that are expressed focus either on effects of alcohol on the father or on general religious tendencies toward austerity.

In the seventeenth century, both Robert Burton and Francis Bacon suggested that maternal drinking during pregnancy might have adverse consequences on offspring, although they apparently cite no specific data (Abel, 1984). During the "gin epidemic" in early eighteenth century England, several writers observed that children of drinking mothers were small, sickly, and mentally slow (Abel, 1984).

Several epidemiological studies in the mid and late nineteenth century by Howe, Bezzola, Sullivan et al. linked a variety of disorders, including stillbirth, infant mortality, and mental retardation, to maternal drinking during pregnancy. Of particular interest is Sullivan's observation that alcoholic women who had children with serious problems subsequently bore healthier children when imprisonment prevented them from drinking during pregnancy.

However, in an apparently highly scientific study published in 1910, Elderton and Pearson reported no relationship between drinking in parents and intelligence and appearance of children. Pearson was particularly active in the eugenics movement, and it should not be surprising that he and Elderton suggested that children of alcoholics might have problems either because parents and children shared "defective germ plasm," or because the parents provided a poor home environment. Some 30 years later, Haggard and Jellinik (1942) strongly denied that alcohol during pregnancy produced malformations.

Thus Montagu (1965) was presenting a generally accepted conclusion when he said:

> Unexpectedly, alcohol in the form of beverages, even in immoderate amounts, has no apparent effect on a child before birth. . . . (I)t now can be stated categorically . . . that no matter how great the amount of alcohol taken by the mother—or the father, for that matter—neither the germ cells nor the development of the child will be affected. (p. 114)

The statement was accepted but ironic, because at the time the statement appeared, Lemoine et al. were probably collecting their data on offspring of 127 alcoholic parents. They reported in 1968 that several of the children showed such a common set of abnormalities that maternal alcoholism could be inferred on the basis of their appearance. The abnormalities were in the three areas now associated with FAS: growth retardation, low intelligence, and facial anomalies. Published in French, although with an English abstract, the paper had little impact (Rosett & Weiner, 1984). Only with the reports of Jones and Smith, and Jones et al. in 1973, which described and named the fetal alcohol syndrome, did clinicians and researchers begin to focus on the dangers of prenatal exposure to alcohol.

A number of suggestions can be offered to the question, Why were the teratogenic effects of prenatal alcohol not described earlier? Most obvious is that earlier research produced highly inconsistent results with some apparently methodologically adequate studies finding no effects. Additionally, FAS children share many characteristics with children affected by other syndromes and show considerable variability in number and degree of dysmorphic features. Diagnosis cannot clearly be made in absence of knowledge of heavy maternal drinking (Rosett & Weiner, 1984). Finally, the belief in an effective placental barrier, generally accepted until the 1940s, may have impaired sensitivity to teratogenic influences of alcohol. Teratogenic action of a number of other drugs and maternal infections was clearly established only in the 1950s and 1960s (Moore, 1982).

The FAS cannot be diagnosed on the basis of a single set of criteria. Further, some symptoms, particularly of intellective and other neurological deficits, may not be recognized until the affected child is several years old; facial dysmorphology is also difficult to recognize in the newborn. Milder cases with fewer classic features may be particularly difficult to identify. Indeed, four of five cases at Boston City Hospital were identified only some time after birth (Rosett & Weiner, 1984).

The Fetal Alcohol Study Group of the Research Society on Alcoholism (Rosett, 1980) established minimal criteria for diagnosis of FAS, based largely on Clarren and Smith's (1978) summary of 245 cases. Diagnosis should be made only when three criteria are met:

Pre- and/or postnatal growth retardation (below the tenth percentile for body weight or length, or head circumference when corrected for gestational age).

Central nervous system dysfunction (neurological abnormality, mental impairment, or developmental delay).

Characteristic facial dysmorphology, involving at least two of three signs: (1) microcephaly (head circumference below third percentile); (2) micro-opthalmia and/or short palpebral fissures; (3) poorly developed philtrum, thin upper lip, and/or flattening of the maxillary area (See Figure for illustration and other physical characteristics).

In addition, numerous other features are commonly associated with FAS. Those reported by Clarren & Smith (1978) as occurring in more than 50% of cases are summarized in the Table. For clear diagnosis, a history of maternal drinking during pregnancy must be present. Pre- and postnatal growth retardation is the most common characteristic of FAS; affected infants are small even when gestational age is considered. Low birth weight is associated with a variety of other maternal factors, several of which, notably smoking, malnutrition, and drug abuse,

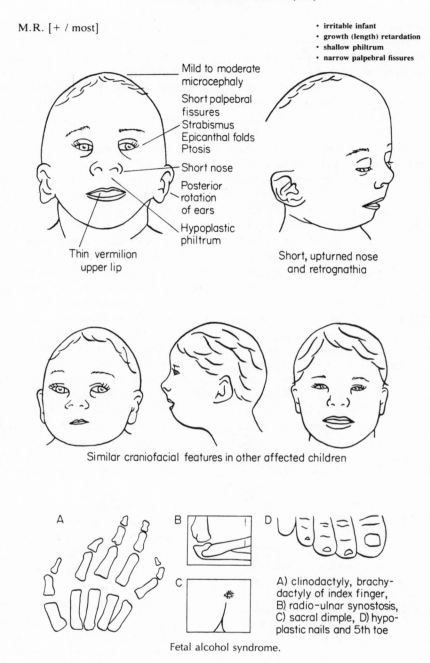

M.R. [+ / most]

- irritable infant
- growth (length) retardation
- shallow philtrum
- narrow palpebral fissures

Mild to moderate microcephaly

Short palpebral fissures
Strabismus
Epicanthal folds
Ptosis

Short nose

Posterior rotation of ears

Hypoplastic philtrum

Thin vermilion upper lip

Short, upturned nose and retrognathia

Similar craniofacial features in other affected children

A) clinodactyly, brachy-dactyly of index finger, B) radio-ulnar synostosis, C) sacral dimple, D) hypoplastic nails and 5th toe

Fetal alcohol syndrome.

also occur commonly among heavy drinkers; identification of the effects of drinking alone has been difficult. However, two lines of evidence strongly indicate that alcohol itself induces prenatal growth retardation. First, previously mentioned factors are rarely associated with the other features of FAS (Rosett & Weiner, 1984), and second, offspring of pregnant animals given alcohol show both growth retardation and FAS-characteristic facial anomalies when other factors have been eliminated or controlled (Abel, 1984).

A particularly striking aspect of alcohol-induced growth retardation is lack of catch-up growth. Typically,

infants who are either low weight at birth or who become low weight after birth through factors such as illness, malnutrition, or failure to thrive show accelerated growth after the condition has ended, which brings them back toward their expected weight (Tanner, 1978). Most FAS children show little if any catch-up growth; severely affected children may actually fall further behind. In milder cases, there may be partial or complete catch up. Again, animal research shows comparable results.

The major central nervous system dysfunction is mental retardation. Average IQ is about 70, although variability is high. Degree of retardation appears to vary di-

Principal Features of Fetal Alcohol Syndrome

Feature	Manifestation
Growth deficiency	
Prenatal	Height and weight at least two standard deviations below the mean[b]
Postnatal	Height and weight at least two standard deviations below the mean[b]; disproportionately diminished adipose tissue[a]
Central-nervous-system dysfunction	
Intellectual	Mild-moderate mental retardation[b]
Neurologic	Microcephaly[b]; poor coordination[a]; hypotonia[a]
Behavioral	Infancy: irritability[b]; Childhood: attention deficit disorder[a]
Facial anomalies	
Eyes	Short palpebral fissures[b]
Nose	Short, upturned[a]; hypoplastic philtrum[b]
Maxilla	Hypoplastic[a]
Mouth	Thinned upper vermilion[b]; Infancy: retrognathia[b]; Adolescence: micrognathia or relative prognathia[a]

Source: Modified after Clarren and Smith, 1978.

[a] Seen in >50% of cases.

[b] Seen in >80% of cases.

rectly with degree of facial dysmorphology. Attention deficit disorder, involving hyperactivity and impulsivity, frequently occurs. Again, animal research complements clinical findings: animals prenatally exposed to ethanol show learning deficits, high activity, and deficits in inhibition. Further, brains of animals prenatally exposed to alcohol show alterations in several structures, including the hippocampus, an area important for both memory and inhibition, but not in others, suggesting selective teratogenicity (Dewey & West, 1985). Other behavioral problems associated with FAS include sleep disturbances (sleeplessness and restlessness) and delayed development of motor coordination.

A variety of facial and cranial dysmorphologies are characteristic of FAS, as indicated in the Table. But some of Clarren and Smith's (1978) findings have been questioned by subsequent studies. Short palpebral fissures, for example, are not a clear delineator of FAS. Many other facial anomalies, including epicanthic folds, frequently occur.

Many other abnormalities may occur, including altered palmar crease, posterior rotation of ears, a variety of joint and limb anomalies, cardiac and urogenital anomalies, and neural tube defects. Heavy drinking during pregnancy also significantly increases the risk of spontaneous abortion, prematurity, stillbirth, and infant mortality.

Difficulty of diagnosing FAS on the basis of clinical signs alone should not be minimized. Many characteristics of FAS occur in other syndromes. In particular, symptoms of fetal hydantoin syndrome are very similar to those of FAS. Further, many people with epilepsy who are on anticonvulsant medication drink excessively. Some children will have been subjected to two teratogens, alcohol and phenytoin (dilantin), and may show even more severe characteristics of a fetal alcohol-hydantoin syndrome. Hodgkin's disease has been reported in one such case (Bostrom & Nesbit, 1985).

At-risk levels are difficult to specify for a number of reasons. Definitions of moderate and heavy drinkers vary from study to study and data on maternal drinking, being self-report, are of questionable reliability. In addition, only a small percentage of even alcoholic women have FAS children. In one study (Sokol, Miller, & Reed, 1980), e.g., 5 of 204 alcoholic women had an FAS child. As mentioned, many features of FAS are commonly associated with other agents and syndromes, and many occur in the absence of any obvious causative agent. Attribution problems abound, particularly in regard to FAE. Thus, although full FAS symptoms in conjunction with heavy maternal drinking lead to a diagnosis of FAS, attribution of some symptoms to light or moderate maternal drinking is more problematical. Additionally, a few episodes of binge drinking may have highly adverse effects.

"The full-blown fetal alcohol syndrome has been reported only in children whose mothers were 'heavy' drinkers during pregnancy" (Little, Graham, & Samson, 1982, p. 110). Little et al. report that the smallest amount of drinking associated with FAS was six bottles of beer daily throughout pregnancy. Abel (1984) has estimated that consumption by 72 mothers of FAS infants for whom individual drinking data were available was about 14 drinks per day. The factors that differentiate between alcohol abusers who do or do not have FAS or FAE children have not been identified. However, the fact that pregnant mice from two different strains who have been given comparable doses of alcohol have quite different blood-alcohol levels suggests that maternal differences in metabolism may be partly responsible (Chernoff, 1977, 1980).

The effect of lower levels of maternal drinking are much less clear. Abel (1984) suggests that linking effects with as few as two drinks daily would be difficult. Indeed, a prospective study conducted in Edinburgh (Plant, 1985) found that although the percentage of infants with two or more abnormalities increased with the mother's alcohol intake, a significant association occurred only among mothers who reported drinking 10 or more drinks in one day during the first trimester of pregnancy (abstainers = 11.0%; 1 to 9 units of alcohol = 15.3%; 10 or more units

= 35.6%). But Plant was unable to conclude that alcohol caused the problems, and suggested that some other factor, such as smoking, may have been responsible.

Prognosis for severe cases of FAS is poor. The damage has occurred before birth, and no specific treatment is possible. Central nervous system damage is irreversible, and, as stated, catch-up growth is unlikely. In addition, some neurological deficits and facial dysmorphologies may become apparent with age. Children with milder cases of FAS and FAE are, as would be expected, more likely to show catch-up growth and improved functioning.

Clearly FAS and FAE are totally preventable. All that is required is for alcohol-abusing pregnant women to stop or severely moderate their alcohol consumption. Unfortunately, that recommendation is more easily said than effected. Alcohol abuse is notoriously resistant to successful and long-lasting treatment, and many alcohol-abusing pregnant women continue to drink heavily even when aware of the risks to their offspring (Rosett & Weiner, 1984). Moreover, much damage to the embryo/fetus may already have occurred by the time the alcohol-abusing mother discovers she is pregnant. However, heavy-drinking pregnant women who moderate their drinking during the latter part of pregnancy after counseling are at less risk for having a damaged infant then are women who drink heavily throughout pregnancy (Rosett & Weiner, 1984).

However difficult, efforts should be made to help alcohol-abusing women to moderate or stop their drinking if they are at risk for becoming pregnant and certainly to reduce or stop their drinking if they are pregnant. More extensive counseling of this at-risk population is needed. Abel (1984) has reported cases indicating that mothers may be held legally responsible for their FAS children.

On the other hand, the risk of light alcohol consumption should not be exaggerated (Rosett & Weiner, 1984; Plant, 1985). In particular, women who have consumed light amounts of alcohol during pregnancy and have slightly deformed infants should not be made to feel guilty since any number of environmental or genetic factors may actually have caused the deformities. As Rosett and Weiner (1984) indicate, women should take precautions during pregnancy, but they do not have control over everything that may affect their baby.

Balancing the lack of strong evidence that light drinking causes defects are the facts that no safe level of maternal alcohol consumption during pregnancy is known (Little, Graham, & Samson, 1982) and that pregnant women and embryos/fetuses vary in their sensitivity to alcohol. Obviously, abstinence during pregnancy seems ideal, but realistic recommendations are far from clear. Rosett and Weiner (1984) provide a thoughtful discussion of issues involved in counseling women about risks of alcohol. Information about risks to offspring of prenatal alcohol, smoking, and other risk factors should be presented in required junior high school and high school health or science courses.

REFERENCES

Abel, E. L. (1984). *Fetal alcohol syndrome and fetal alcohol effects.* New York: Plenum.

Bostrom, B., & Nesbit, M. E. (1983). Hodgkin disease in a child with fetal alcohol-hydantoin syndrome. *Journal of Pediatrics, 103,* 760–762.

Çavdar, A. O. (1984). Fetal alcohol syndrome, malignancies, and zinc deficiency. *Journal of Pediatrics, 105,* 335.

Chernoff, G. F. (1977). The fetal alcohol syndrome in mice: An animal model. *Teratology, 15,* 223–230.

Chernoff, G. F. (1980). The fetal alcohol syndrome in mice: Maternal variables. *Teratology, 22,* 71–75.

Clarren, S. K., & Smith, D. W. (1978). The fetal alcohol syndrome. *New England Journal of Medicine, 298,* 1063–1067.

Dewey, S. L., & West, J. R. (1985). Organization of the commisural projection to the dentate gyrus is unaltered by heavy ethanol exposure during gestation. *Alcohol, 2,* 617–622.

Elderton, E. M., & Pearson, K. (1910). A first study of the influence of parental alcoholism on the physique and ability of the offspring. *Engenics Laboratory Memoir, 10,* 1–46.

Haggard, H. W., & Jellinik, E. M. (1942). *Alcohol explored.* Garden City, NY: Doubleday.

Jones, K. L., & Smith, D. W. (1973). Recognition of fetal alcohol syndrome in early infancy. *Lancet, 2,* 999–1001.

Jones, K. L., Smith, D. W., Ulleland, C. N., & Streissguth, A. P. (1973). Pattern of malformation in offspring of chronic alcoholic mothers. *Lancet, 1,* 1267–1271.

Lemoine, P., Harousseau, H., Borteryu, J. P., & Menuet, J. C. (1968). Les enfants de parents alchooliques: Anomalies observees a propos de 127 cas. *Ouest Medical, 21,* 476–482.

Little, R. E., Graham, J. M., Jr., & Samson, H. H. (1982). Fetal alcohol effects in humans and animals. In B. Stimmel (Ed.), *The effects of maternal alcohol and drug abuse on the newborn.* New York: Haworth.

Montagu, A. (1965). *Life before birth.* New York: Signet.

Moore, K. L. (1982). *The developing human* (3rd ed.). Philadelphia: Saunders.

Plant, M. (1985). *Women, drinking, and pregnancy.* London & New York: Tavistock.

Rosett, H. L. (1980). A clinical perspective of the fetal alcohol syndrome. *Alcoholism: Clinical and Experimental Research, 4,* 119–122.

Rosett, H. L., & Weiner, L. (1984). *Alcohol and the fetus.* New York: Oxford University Press.

Sokol, R. J., Miller, S. I., & Reed, G. (1980). Alcohol abuse during pregnancy: An epidemiological model. *Alcoholism: Clinical & Experimental Research, 4,* 135–145.

Tanner, J. M. (1978). *Fetus into man.* Cambridge, MA: Harvard University Press.

ROBERT T. BROWN
University of North Carolina,
Wilmington

ATTENTION DEFICIT DISORDER
FETAL HYDANTOIN SYNDROME
TERATOGEN

FETAL HYDANTOIN SYNDROME

The anticonvulsant agent phenytoin (Dilantin) appears to have teratogenic effects. Offspring of epileptic mothers who took phenytoin during pregnancy may show a complex of anomalies, the fetal hydantoin syndrome, that include growth deficiency, microcephaly (with associated mental deficiency), cleft lip and palate, low-set dysplastic ears, wide anterior fontanel, depressed nasal bridge, epicanthal fold, and hypoplasia of nails and terminal digits. This complex resembles that in fetal alcohol syndrome (Goodman & Gorlin, 1983; Kurczynski, 1983). Infants exposed prenatally to hydantoin are estimated to have about a 10% chance of developing the syndrome and an additional approximate 33% chance of showing some of the anomalies (Smith, 1982).

However, caution in inferring teratogenic action of hydantoin is necessary because the syndrome is based on observation of a relatively small number of case studies and because there is an absence of appropriate control groups. Incidence of malformations in offspring of epileptic mothers who took hydantoin is two or three time greater than that in offspring of mothers who have never had a seizure. Little information is available on offspring of epileptic women who did not take anticonvulsant medication during pregnancy. The effects of hydantoin on malformations cannot clearly be separated from those of seizures themselves (Goodman & Gorlin, 1983; Kurczynski, 1983), although the similarity of the symptoms to those of fetal alcohol syndrome supports the interpretation of teratogenicity of hydantoin. In any case, the risk of adverse effects of uncontrolled seizures on both the pregnant woman and the fetus may be greater than those of hydantoin (Kurczynski, 1983).

REFERENCES

Goodman, R. M., & Gorlin, R. J. (1983). *The malformed infant and child*. New York: Oxford University Press.

Kurczynski, T. W. (1983). Congenital malformations. In A. A. Fanaroff & R. J. Martin (Eds.), *Behrman's neonatal-perinatal medicine* (3rd ed., pp. 1035–1063). St. Louis: Mosby.

Smith, D. W. (1982). *Recognizable patterns of human malformation* (3rd ed.). Philadelphia: Saunders.

ROBERT T. BROWN
*University of North Carolina,
Wilmington*

DILANTIN
FETAL ALCOHOL SYNDROME

FEWELL, REBECCA R. (1936–)

Rebecca R. Fewell received her BA in sociology from Agnes Scott College, Georgia, in 1958. She then went on to receive her MA in 1969 and her doctorate in special education in 1972 from George Peabody College, Tennessee. On graduation she joined the Peabody faculty and remained there until 1979. While at Peabody, Fewell directed projects and a diagnostic training center for deaf-blind and handicapped children. Additionally, she was chairman of the special education department and was the elected faculty representative to the Peabody College Council on Student Policy.

Rebecca R. Fewell

Fewell's area of interest includes the continuation of the following programs: Program for Children with Down's Syndrome and Other Developmental Delays; the Supporting Extended Family Members program, a program for fathers, siblings, and grandparents of handicapped children; the Computer-Assisted Program Project for using resources at the University of Washington to serve children in rural areas throughout the United States; a research program comparing a direct instructional model to a cognitive mediated learning model for preschool intervention; and the Infant Health and Development Program for Premature Infants: Her other research involves the development of affective behavior and play skills in normal and handicapped children.

Fewell serves on the editorial board of five journals and is senior editor of *Topics in Early Childhood Special Education*. She has published over 75 articles, several books, and two tests, The Developmental Activities Screening Inventory and the Peabody Developmental Motor Scales and Activity Cards.

REFERENCES

Fewell, R. R. *Play assessment scale*. In preparation.

Fewell, R. R., & Langley, B. (1984). *Developmental activities screening inventory*. Austin, TX: Pro-Ed.

Fewell, R. R., & Vadasy, P. F. (Eds.). (1986). *Families of handicapped children: Needs and supports across the lifespan.* Austin, TX: Pro-Ed.

Folio, R., & Fewell, R. R. (1983). *Peabody developmental motor scales and activity cards.* MA: Teaching Resources.

Garwood, S. G., & Fewell, R. R. (1983). *Educating handicapped infants.* Rockville, MD: Aspen.

ROBERTA C. STOKES
Texas A&M University

FIELD DEPENDENCE–INDEPENDENCE

The concept field dependence (FD) and independence (FI) were introduced into psychology and education by H. A. Witkin (1954). He identified FD and FI as two distinct cognitive polarities that developed out of the theory of psychological differentiation. They were the terms used to accommodate broad patterns of psychological functioning associated with individual differences.

Witkin's research began with investigations of individual differences in the perception of the "upright" in the rod and frame, body adjustment, rotating room, and embedded figures tests. In each of these tests, subjects differed in the extent to which they used the external visual field or the body itself for locating the upright in space. The rod and frame test was used in early FD–FI research. Seated in darkness, the subject looks at a rod suspended in a frame. The rod and frame are independent of one another. The subject has the examiner adjust the rod to a perceived vertical position. How the subject rotates the rod in relation to the frame indicates field dependence or independence. At one extreme, when perception of the upright is dominated by the previous field (frame), this is designated field dependence. When the person sees the items as distinct from the surrounding field, this is designated field independence. The Embedded Figures Test (Witkin et al., 1977) is used more frequently and especially with younger children because of its simplicity. In this test, subjects are asked to locate a simple figure in a complex background. Witkin used this test to determine FD–FI in children between 3 and 9 years of age.

Many of the concepts derived from FD–FI styles are useful to special education. These are applicable to such issues as how children think, perceive, solve problems, and learn to relate to others. Field dependence-independence has been applied to the education of various groups, including the mentally retarded, gifted, physically disabled, and emotionally disturbed.

Tests used to determine FD–FI have aided in program planning both in school and at home. Moskowitz et al. (1981) used the embedded figures test with preschool children to determine FD–FI. He explored the early precursors of field dependence, which suggest that field-dependent children seek more emotional reassurances from their mothers thán field-independent children.

Keough (1982) discussed the importance of individual differences in educational and instructional planning and practical decisions for classroom management for exceptional children. This research stressed an increased need for the sensitivity to behavioral styles of children that is essential for teachers in diagnostic and remedial planning, as well as understanding children's interpersonal demands.

The embedded figures test and Piers-Harris Self-Concept Scale were used by Guyot et al. (1984) to access FD–FI in boys and girls in grades four to six. Results suggested that field independent girls had significantly higher self concept scores than field-dependent girls. Field dependent-independent boys showed no significant difference in self-concept scores.

Gargiula (1982) used the Children's Embedded Figures Test to measure FD–FI in retarded and nonretarded children of equal mental age. The educable mentally retarded were found to be significantly more field dependent, as were subjects characterized as impulsive.

The FD–FI may be helpful in planning and predicting concepts outcomes of cognitive restructuring programs for people with neurological impairment. Field independents will show greater lateral specialization of the hemispheres compared with field dependents (Witkin, 1979). Results showed that the left hemisphere would be for verbal and motor control processing and the right hemisphere for configuration-gestalt processing. People who are more field independent may have more developed cognitive restructuring skills, while people with more field dependence may lean toward interpersonal competencies, making this work very important for program planning.

Fitzgibbons (1965) found that field-dependent individuals are particularly attuned to social aspects of their surroundings. These persons are also better at learning materials with social content than field-independent people. This is a valuable finding for classroom learning. Fitzgibbons found that field-independent children often exhibit a function of lack of attention rather than ability. By bringing social material to attention, the performance of children who are field independent could be improved.

A final variable that has implications for education is how teachers and their related FD–FI styles affect students. Mahlios (1981) found that there were differences obtained regarding instructional behaviors among FD–FI teachers. The FD teachers seem to prefer greater interaction with pupils, while FI teachers preferred a more impersonal teaching situation. Consideration will be given to the combined effects of matched and mismatched teacher-student cognitive orientation in classroom interaction. Field dependent-independent students and teachers who were matched responded more positively to one another in both cognitive and personal characteristics

(Distefano, 1970). This may create an environment more conducive to learning.

REFERENCES

Distefano, J. J. (1970). Interpersonal perceptions of field independence and field dependence among teachers and students. *Dissertation Abstracts International, 31,* 463a–464a.

Fitzgibbons, D. (1965). Field dependence and memory for incidental material. *Perceptual & Motor Skills, 21,* 743–749.

Gargiulo, M. (1982). Reflection-impulsivity and field dependence-field independence in retarded and non-retarded of equal mental age. *Bulletin of the Psychonomic Society, 19,* 74–77.

Guyot, G. W., Fairchild, L. and Johnson, B. (1984). Embedded figures test performance and self concept of elementary school children. *Perceptual and Motor Skills, 58,* 61–62.

Keough, B. K. (1982). Temperament: An individual difference of importance in intervention programs. *Topics in Early Childhood Special Education, 2,* 25–31.

Mahlios, M. C. (1981). Instructional design and cognitive styles of teachers in elementary schools. *Perceptual & Motor Skills, 52,* 335–338.

Moskowitz, D. S., Dreyer, A. S. and Kronsberg, S. (1981). Preschool children's field independence prediction from antecedent and concurrent maternal and child behavior. *Perceptual & Motor Skills, 52,* 607–616.

Witkin, H. A. (1954). *Personality through perception.* Westport, CT: Greenwood.

Witkin, H. A., Moore, C. A., Goodenough, D. R., and Cox, P. W. (1977). Field dependent and independent cognitive styles. *Review of Educational Research, 47,* 1–64.

Witkin, H. A. (1979). Psychological differentiation: Current status. *Journal of Personality & Social Psychology, 37,* 1127–1145.

STEVEN GUMERMAN
Temple University

PERCEPTION
VISUAL-MOTOR AND VISUAL-PERCEPTUAL PROBLEMS
VISUAL PERCEPTION AND DISCRIMINATION

FILIAL THERAPY

Filial therapy is a therapeutic method developed by Guerney (1964) that teaches parents of emotionally disturbed children to conduct play sessions with their children. It can be used effectively with youngsters up to age 10 and can be practiced by one or both parents. Precursors to this work are reported by Freud (1959), Moustakas (1959), and Baruch (1949), all of whom employed parents as therapeutic agents. Filial therapy is promoted as using professional services much more effectively than the traditional 50-minute psychotherapy hour.

Filial therapy follows prespecified guidelines. Initially, parents of young children are brought together in groups of six to eight for didactic sessions with a trained psychotherapist. In these sessions, the goals and benefits of the therapy are explained, along with specific techniques to be employed. Play techniques are based on traditional Rogerian therapy, with empathy as a primary focus. Thus, structuring, restatement of content, and clarification of feelings are emphasized. Demonstrations of play therapy are conducted, with parents watching behind a one-way mirror. Next, parents practice their own play sessions, with other group members observing. After about eight weeks of group work, the parents begin conducting sessions at home with their own children. These sessions, initially once a week for 30 minutes, are gradually extended to 45 minutes once or twice weekly. Detailed notes or tape recordings are maintained, with supervision and discussion continued each week in the parents' group meetings.

Throughout the course of the parents' group sessions, a balance is maintained between didactic and dynamic processes (Andronico, Fidler, Guerney, & Guerney, 1967). Although parents continue to discuss content issues and refine their therapeutic techniques, emotional issues often arise. At such times, the therapist encourages discussion of internal feelings and motivations. In this way, conflicts that parents might have can be resolved within the group, thus preventing their expression at home with spouse or children.

The following goals for the play sessions are noted by Fidler, Guerney, Andronico, and Guerney, (1969): (1) to help the child change perceptions of the parents' feelings, attitudes, and behavior; (2) to allow the child—through the medium of play—to communicate needs and feelings to the parents and thus resolve anxiety-produced internalized conflicts; (3) to increase the child's sense of confidence and self-worth.

Guerney (1964) maintains that filial therapy has a number of benefits over more traditional treatment. It has long been acknowledged that it is difficult to remove a child from family and environment, treat that child, and expect changes to be maintained when the child is returned to the family. With filial therapy, the parent, being an agent of change, learns new attitudes and behaviors in conjunction with the child. Along the same lines, individual child therapy is often sabotaged by parents who are resentful or jealous of a therapist whom they feel has usurped their role as parents or whom they perceive as blaming them for the child's problem. Parents threatened by such situations may go so far as to remove the child from treatment just when real progress is beginning to be made.

Guerney also stresses that parents can have more of an impact on their child than can a surrogate. Rather than being involved with the secondary phenomena of transference and countertransference, children work out their conflicts directly with their parents. The increase in empathy and understanding evidenced by parents will likely extend their abilities to develop a productive and nurturing relationship with their child after the formal therapy has ended.

Guerney's (1964) observations of filial therapy groups conducted at the Rutgers University Psychological Clinic indicate positive results using this technique. However, the effectiveness of this method as compared with other therapeutic techniques has not been documented. Fidler et al. (1969) state that it does increase the leverage of professional time and physical resources and is clearly much less isolated from real life than traditional therapies.

REFERENCES

Andronico, M., Fidler, J., Guerney, B., & Guerney, L. (1967). The combination of didactic and dynamic elements in filial therapy. *International Journal of Group Psychotherapy, 17*, 10–17.

Baruch, W. (1949). *New ways in discipline.* New York: McGraw-Hill.

Fidler, J., Guerney, B., Andronico, M., & Guerney, L. (1969). Filial therapy as a logical extension of current trends in psychotherapy. In B. Guerney (Ed.), *Psychotherapeutic agents: New roles for nonprofessionals, parents, and teachers* (pp. 47–55). New York: Holt, Rinehart & Winston.

Freud, S. (1959). Analysis of a phobia in a five year old boy. In *Collected papers* (pp. 149–289). New York: Basic Books.

Guerney, B. (1964). Filial therapy: Description and rationale. *Journal of Consulting Psychology, 28*(4), 304–310.

Moustakas, C. W. (1959). *Psychotherapy with Children.* New York: Harper.

FRANCES F. WORCHEL
Texas A&M University

FAMILY COUNSELING
PARENT COUNSELING
PARENTS OF THE HANDICAPPED

FILIAL THERAPY, SPECIAL EDUCATION AND

Filial therapy was developed in the 1960s by Bernard Gurney and Michael Andronico (Andronico & Gurney, 1967). It is a "psychotherapeutic technique utilizing parents as therapeutic agents for their own children" (Hornsby & Applebaum, 1978). Primarily intended for emotionally disturbed children and their parents in outpatient school settings, filial therapy has been adapted to residential settings with borderline mentally retarded and autistic children (Hornsby & Applebaum, 1978; White, Hornsby, & Gordon, 1972). This approach is considered integrative; it empowers the parents as therapists and enlists them as agents of change. Instead of the child being taken away from the family to be helped, the message is clear that the parents are a necessary and integral part of the process.

Filial therapy is a method of treatment that can be used as a preventive or remedial approach to help parents become more effective in their parenting skills.

Although filial therapy has been used in the schools (Andronico & Gurney, 1967) to lighten the work loads of school psychologists, current usage is mainly in residential facilities where psychological therapy is the central treatment focus. A typical filial therapy session has a multiimpact format. After the family has undergone initial evaluation, designed to determine the internal dynamics of the family members, the filial sessions begin. The parent who is considered to be the most distant from the child is used as the "primary therapist." It is this parent who will work with the child in the therapy playroom. The psychologist supplies this patient with a "bug" (a hearing device placed in the ear) and retires with the other parent to an observation room. The psychologist gives suggestions and directions to the parent engaging in play with the child, and uses the other parent as a coobserver and resource. After the play session is over, the family and therapist process feelings, observations, and thoughts regarding the relationship and communication patterns between the primary therapist and the child. In addition, there is an emphasis on overall reactions to the filial therapy process. As sessions progress, the bug is removed and therapy focuses on generalizing what has been learned by the parent and child to the home setting. Ultimately, the goals of filial therapy are to enhance and improve family relations, communications, and behavior management and to increase motivation of the parents to succeed and be responsible for changes in the family system.

Filial therapy has not gained widespread recognition in the schools. However, parent training programs such as Parent Effectiveness Training (PET; Gordon, 1970), Systematic Training for Effective Parenting (STEP; Dinkmeyer & McKay, 1976), and Children: The Challenge (Dreikurs & Soltz, 1964), all use essentially the same principles of parents assuming cotherapeutic management of the child with the school. In other words, schools have recognized the importance of offering parental guidance. The resurrection of filial therapy in a residential setting perhaps reflects the reintegration of the emotionally disturbed child back into the public sector and the necessity for change to be supported by the family system.

Special education personnel may use the principles of filial therapy in one of three ways: (1) as a continuation of filial therapy with emotionally disturbed children reentering the public schools from residential or outpatient treatment; (2) where academic and behavioral deficits require support from the home environment; and (3) as a preventive measure in classes with behaviorally disturbed children. Modifications will certainly have to be made in the school setting. For example, the bug could be replaced by the teacher modeling appropriate academic or behavioral instruction in front of the parent or the parent and child engaging in academic or behavioral instruction with the educator observing and making suggestions. The benefits of filial therapy to the special educator include enhanced rapport with the child and parents, emphasizing a cooperative and holistic effort; reinforcement of appropriate learning from home, thereby assisting the child in generalization and transfer of training; and improved communication and interaction among family members.

In the last 20 years filial therapy has come full circle. The catalyst for its possible reentry into the public schools parallels deinstitutionalization. Residential care facilities have recognized the need to reintegrate the child back into the public sector. By parents acting as coagents of change, therapeutic gains are maintained in the family and the public schools.

REFERENCES

Andronico, M. P., & Gurney, B. (1967). The potential application of filial therapy to the school situation. *Journal of School Psychology, 6,* 7–12.

Dinkmeyer, D., & McKay, G. (1976). *Systematic training for effective parenting*; Circle Pines, MN: American Guidance Service.

Dreikurs, R., & Soltz, V. (1964). *Children: The challenge.* New York: Duell, Slone, & Pearce.

Gordon, T. (1970). *Parent effectiveness training.* New York: Wyden.

Hornsby, L. G., & Applebaum, A. S. (1978). Parents as primary therapists: Filial therapy. In N. L. E. Arnold (Ed.), *Helping parents help their children.* New York: Brunner/Mazel.

White, J. H., Hornsby, L. G., & Gordon, R. (1972). Treating infantile autism with parent therapists. *International Journal of Child Psychotherapy, 1,* 83–95.

DAVID FLETCHER-JANZEN
San Marcos Treatment Center
San Marcos, Texas

FINGERSPELLING

The American manual alphabet consists of 26 distinct hand configurations that represent the letters of the alphabet. Fingerspelling is the rapid execution of a series of these configurations to communicate words visually. As such, it is more a representation of written language than of spoken language because it excludes the phonological alterations and prosodic aspects of speech. Fingerspelling skills include the hand configurations, the characteristic positioning of the hand in a fixed central location, and the set of possible transition movements from one configuration to the next (Padden & LeMaster, 1985).

Dactylology (the study or use of the manual alphabet) has attributed the origin of fingerspelling to medieval monks who used it to communicate without breaking their vows of silence. A Spanish Benedictine monk, Pedro Ponce de Leon, is thought to have been the first person to use fingerspelling to instruct the deaf. His work was built on by another Spaniard, Juan Martin Pablo Bonet, who in 1620 published the first book on educating the deaf. This book included a diagram of a manual alphabet that is remarkably similar to the one used in the United States today. It is believed that this alphabet was later brought to France and used to improve the alphabet of Abbé Charles de l'Epée, founder of the first French public school for the deaf in the eighteenth century. It was de l'Epée's methods and alphabet that were later imported to the United States by Laurent Clerc and Thomas Hopkins Gallaudet. This alphabet, further modified and evolved, has become the American manual alphabet.

There are numerous manual alphabets in use in different countries around the world. The American manual alphabet, however, with only two exceptions (t and d), was adopted by the Fourth Congress of the World Federation of the Deaf in 1963 as the international hand alphabet. This was in part because English and French (which uses a very similar system) are the official languages of the federation, and in part because the American alphabet was already in use in many countries (Carmel, 1975; Schein, 1984).

Fingerspelling is generally used as an adjunct to sign language, especially to render proper nouns, technological terms for which no signs exist, and slang. To the uninitiated, fingerspelling seems an indistinguishable part of sign language. There are, however, several differences between signing and fingerspelling. Signs usually use one or two distinct hand configurations, while in fingerspelling there are as many configurations as there are letters in the word. Fingerspelling is done in a much smaller space than signing, with the hand remaining in a nearly fixed position as only the configuration changes. Palm orientation in fingerspelling is restricted almost exclusively to a palm out position, in contrast to signing, in which there is no such restriction. Another important difference is that while signing evolved as a means of communication in the deaf community, fingerspelling originated as an instructional tool (Padden & LeMaster, 1985).

Although fingerspelling is used primarily as a supplement to sign language, a method of manual communication exists that relies exclusively on the use of fingerspelling. This is known as the Rochester Method, after the Rochester School for the Deaf where the superintendent of the school, Zenas Westervelt, initiated its use in 1878. The method gradually fell into disuse after Westervelt's death in 1912, and though proponents of it still exist, it is seldom used today, not even in the school for which it was named (Schein, 1984).

American deaf people are noted for more frequent use, and more rapid execution, of fingerspelling than other sign communities throughout the world (Padden & LeMaster, 1985). This may in part be responsible for the phenomenon known as loan signs. These are signs that originated as fingerspelled words, but in which the number of hand configurations has been reduced to two. In addition, other features such as palm orientation and movement have been added so that a phonologically well-formed sign is produced (Battison, 1978).

REFERENCES

Battison, R. (1978). *Lexical borrowing in ASL.* Silver Springs, MD: Linstock.

Carmel, S. J. (1975). *International hand alphabet charts.* Rockville, MD: Studio Printing.

Padden, C. A., & LeMaster, B. (1985). An alphabet on hand: The acquisition of fingerspelling in deaf children. *Sign Language Studies, 47,* 161–172.

Schein, J. D. (1984). *Speaking the language of sign.* New York: Doubleday.

PEG EAGNEY
School for the Deaf, New York,
New York

AMERICAN SIGN LANGUAGE
DEAF EDUCATION

FITZGERALD KEY

The Fitzgerald key is used to teach deaf children to generate correct language structures. Developed by Elizabeth Fitzgerald, a deaf teacher, the key was originally described in 1926 in Fitzgerald's book, *Straight Language for the Deaf.* For the next 40 years it was widely used throughout the United States and Canada in schools and programs for the deaf (Moores, 1978; Myers & Hammill, 1976).

The key provides the deaf child with a visual guide for structuring sentences, thus helping to compensate for the lack of hearing. Fitzgerald (1976) recommended that it be used for all subjects and at all age levels. To facilitate its use she suggested that the key be painted in washable yellow paint across the top of the most prominent blackboard in the classroom.

The key consists of ordered (left-to-right) headings (key words) and six symbols that constitute a sentence pattern. Key words are used to classify new vocabulary. Nouns, for example, are classified under the key words what and who; adjectives under the key words how many, what kind, what color. Symbols are used to classify parts of speech for which there are no associated key words. For example, the symbol for verb is =; for pronoun ÷ Fitzgerald was careful to point out that each of the six written symbols should always be verbally paired with the name of the part of speech it represents. The teacher may also pair the symbol with its written name. Fitzgerald believed that the use of symbols helps children at beginning levels of instruction

to sense the difference between parts of speech more easily than terms such as verb, participle, etc.; however, she recommended that their use be dropped as soon as possible. The following example shows how words are combined into a sentence pattern using key words and symbols:

Who:		How many:	What color:	Whom:	Where:
What:			What		
=					
George brought	a	blue	car		to school

Initially, students are taught to combine words into simple phrases under appropriate key words (Moores, 1978). Instruction emphasizes the use of correct word order. Gradually, the complexity of the phrases is increased until students are able to work with the complete key to formulate sentences.

In 1947 Pugh (1955) published *Steps in Language Development for the Deaf,* a book of carefully sequenced language lessons using the key and based on the principles of instruction set forth by Fitzgerald. Although Pugh slightly modified Fitzgerald's approach, her book complemented Fitzgerald's so well that both books are traditionally used together (Myers & Hammill, 1976).

The Fitzgerald key also has been recommended as an instructional program for learning-disabled students with either severe auditory or visual modality problems (Myers & Hammill, 1976). The extent of its use with this population and the degree of success achieved in remediating learning disabilities has not been documented.

REFERENCES

Fitzgerald, E. (1976). *Straight language for the deaf.* Washington, DC: Alexander Graham Bell Association for the Deaf.

Moores, D. F. (1978). *Educating the deaf: Psychology, principles, and practices.* Boston: Houghton Mifflin.

Myers, P. I., & Hammill, D. D. (1976). *Methods for learning disorders* (2nd ed.). New York: Wiley.

Pugh, B. L. (1955). *Steps in language development for the deaf.* Washington, DC: Volta Bureau.

MARIANNE PRICE
Montgomery County
Intermediate Unit,
Norristown, Pennsylvania

DEAF EDUCATION
LANGUAGE DEFICIENCES AND DEFICITS
WRITTEN LANGUAGE OF HANDICAPPED

FOLLOW THROUGH

Follow Through was initiated through an amendment to the Economic Opportunity Act. Project Head Start had begun as an early intervention program for children from low-income families under this legislation (Rhine, 1981). Early reports on small groups of Head Start children had shown an average increase in IQ of about 10 points after a year of preschool, but the first major evaluation of Head Start showed initial gains dissipating soon after the children entered elementary school. Follow Through was intended to provide continued support when children were in the elementary grades to help preserve and enhance any gains made in preschool (Haywood, 1982).

Follow Through was plagued by insufficient funds and by conflicting interpretations of data gathered in evaluation studies of planned variations of different educational models. One of the largest studies, by Stebbins and colleagues in 1977 (Hodges & Cooper, 1981), used as primary measures of effectiveness the Metropolitan Achievement Test (MAT), the (Raven) Progressive Matrices, Coopersmith's Self-Esteem Inventory, and the Intellectual Achievement Responsibility Scale. Stebbins reported much variability in scores from site to site, but little significant difference among models. Models emphasizing basic skills facilitated learning of basic skills and yielded higher self-concept scores than other models. If models did not emphasize basic skills, they were not enhanced. No program model was superior to others in increasing cognitive conceptual skills. In general, where there were large effects, they were related to specific program goals (Hodges & Cooper, 1981). Careful consideration of the measures used by Stebbins suggests that high variability of test scores across settings should not have been surprising because of the tests used (only the MAT has unusually well-demonstrated reliability and validity). Other problems in determining the efficacy of Follow Through related to the difficulty of using a true experimental design, confounding variables, and sample loss.

Probably the safest statement to make about the Follow Through planned variation experiment is that with structured approaches such as applied behavior analysis or direct instruction models, scholastic achievement is facilitated, but clearly there is still much to be learned about compensatory programs and their effects.

REFERENCES

Haywood, H. C. (1982). Compensatory education. *Peabody Journal of Education, 59*, 272–300.

Hodges, W., & Cooper, M. (1981). Head Start and Follow Through: Influences on intellectual development. *Journal of Special Education, 15*, 221–238.

Rhine, W. R. (1981). Follow Through: Perspectives and possibilities. In W. R. Rhine (Ed.), *Making schools more effective.* New York: Academic.

SUE ALLEN WARREN
Boston University

HEAD START
HEAD START FOR THE HANDICAPPED

FOOD ADDITIVES

Over the past several years, one particularly fashionable explanation in the etiology of a number of learning disorders was proposed by Feingold et al. (Feingold, German, Brahm, & Slimmers, 1973). They contended that naturally occurring salicylates in fruits, vegetables, and other foods, artificial food colorings, and preservatives could produce a toxic reaction of cerebral irritability that could result in hyperactivity and other learning disorders in genetically predisposed children. This hypothesis has been subsequently revised by Feingold (1975a, 1976) to mitigate the importance of naturally occurring salicylates and to emphasize the role of two antioxidant preservatives, BHA (butylated hydroxyanisole) and BHT (butylated hydroxytoluene) (Feingold and Feingold, 1979). It is important to note that there has been a significant distinction made between food additives' allergic effect, which does occur for a small percentage of hyperactive children (Conners, 1980), and the toxic effect of these additives, which Feingold and Feingold (1979) have more recently hypothesized to explain the origins of learning disorders.

There has been some evidence posited (Brenner, 1979) to suggest that those children who appear to be affected by food additives differ biochemically from children who are not affected. Evidence that low concentrations of food dye (frequently referred to as Red Dye No. 3) used in a number of confections prevent brain cells from ingesting dopamine, a substance having significant effects on motor activity, providing this biochemical hypothesis with further impetus. In fact, in one seminal piece of research, Lafferman and Silbergeld (1979) concluded that the food dyes' blocking of dopamine is consistent with the notion that the dye could induce hyperactivity in some children.

Although some research has tentatively supported the mechanism of the toxic effect of certain food dyes for particular children, Feingold (1975a) has made a plethora of unsupported statements attesting to the efficacy of his additive-free therapeutic diet. In fact, Feingold (1975a) has even suggested that nearly half of his clinical practice evidenced complete remission of symptoms as a function of a diet that was additive-free. Despite the fact that these claims were not based on empirical data and were refuted later by other investigators (National Advisory Committee on Hyperkinesis and Food Additives, 1980), the claims from Feingold (1975b) still continued at high pitch; he contended that eliminating food additives would decrease motor incoordination and increase academic achievement for hyperactive children (Feingold, 1975b).

Feingold's claims resulted in a proliferation of reports by the popular press attesting to the potential link of food additives to hyperactivity (Ross & Ross, 1982). Further, there were also reports of behavioral improvements ascribed to additive-free diets (Ross & Ross, 1982). Understandably, the food industry perceived these claims as a direct threat and thus organized with the Food and Drug Administration committees to review the evidence pertaining to Feingold's claims. The committees concluded that there was no empirical evidence linking food additives to behavioral or learning dysfunctions in children. The committees further recommended (Ross & Ross, 1982) that carefully controlled empirical studies be conducted to test any validity of food additives in causing hyperactivity or other learning disorders in children.

Subsequently, a series of methodologically sophisticated studies were funded by the federal government. In them Feingold's hypotheses regarding food additives were put to careful tests. The results of these recent studies, which were reviewed by the National Advisory Committee on Hyperkinesis and Food Additives (1980), have generally "refuted the claim that artificial food colorings, artificial flavorings, and salicylates produce hyperactivity and/or learning disability." Based on their findings, the National Advisory Committee also recommended that further funding efforts in this area cease. While Conners' (1980) conclusions, in his lucid review of food additives, were similar to the National Advisory Committee report, he has recommended that future limited topics, including the effects of food dyes on brain chemistry, orthomolecular approaches, and other food substances, still receive careful investigation.

REFERENCES

Brenner, A. (1979). Trace mineral levels in hyperactive children responding to the Feingold diet. *Journal of Pediatrics, 94,* 944–945.

Conners, C. K. (1980). *Food additives and hyperactive children.* New York: Plenum.

Feingold, B. F. (1975a). *Why your child is hyperactive.* New York: Random House.

Feingold, B. F. (1975b). Hyperkinesis and learning disabilities linked to artificial food flavors and colors. *American Journal of Nursing, 75,* 797–803.

Feingold, B. F. (1976). Hyperkinesis and learning disabilities linked to the ingestion of artificial food colors and flavors. *Journal of Learning Disabilities, 9,* 551–559.

Feingold, H., & Feingold, B. F. (1979). *The Feingold cookbook for hyperactive children and others with problems associated with food additives and salicylates.* New York: Random House.

Feingold, B. F., German, D. F., Brahm, R. M., & Slimmers, E. (1973). Adverse reaction to food additives. Paper presented to the annual meeting of the American Medical Association, New York.

Lafferman, J. A., & Silbergeld, E. K. (1979). Erythrosin B inhibits dopamine transport in rat caudate synaptosomes. *Science, 205,* 410–412.

National Advisory Committee on Hyperkinesis and Food Additives. (1980). New York: Nutrition Foundation.

Ross, D. M., & Ross, S. A. (1982). *Hyperactivity: Current issues, research and theory* (2nd ed.). New York: Wiley-Interscience.

EMILY G. SUTTER
University of Houston, Clear Lake

RONALD T. BROWN
Emory University School of Medicine

DOPAMINE
FEINGOLD DIET
HYPERACTIVITY

FORNESS, STEVEN R. (1939–   )

Steven R. Forness attended the University of Northern Colorado, Greely, and received his BA in English and education in 1963 and an MA in educational psychology in 1964. After teaching high school for 2 years, Forness completed his EdD in 1968 in special education at the University of California, Los Angeles (UCLA). He remained at UCLA in various positions: special education coordinator in the mental retardation and child psychiatry department, associate professor, and full professor in 1977. In 1976 he became the inpatient school principal for the UCLA Neuropsychiatric Institute, a demonstration school for children with learning and behavior disorders. In 1985 he became the director of the Mental Retardation Training Program.

Forness's research has been in three main areas: (1) the direct classroom observation of children with mental retardation, the observation of first graders referred for special education (finding a significant difference from match nonreferred children in task attention), the observation of kindergarten children and the prediction of their placement at three-year follow-up, and the observation of TMR, EMR, and EH children and the differences in behavior

Steven R. Forness

related to achievement, teacher or peer rating, and other classroom variables; (2) studies focusing on how behaviorally disordered children's learning problems vary depending on how achievement is measured; and (3) psychiatric versus special education diagnosis.

Forness has published over 100 journal articles and four books, including a standard text in special education, *Education of Exceptional Learners* (1984) with Frank Hewett, and *The Science of Learning Disabilities* (1985) with Ken Kavale.

REFERENCES

Hewett, F., & Forness, S. (1984). *Education of exceptional learners* (3rd ed.). Newton, MA: Allyn & Bacon.

Kavale, K., & Forness, S. *The science of learning disabilities*. San Diego, CA: College-Hill.

STAFF

FORREST v. AMBACH

Muriel Forrest, a school psychologist with the Edgemont Union Free School District in Winchester, New York, was dismissed with only a five-day notice in May 1979. The district dismissed Forrest ostensibly because her work was unsatisfactory and she had refused to follow orders directing her to change. The dismissal was appealed to the Commissioner of Education for the State of New York (*In re Forrest*, 1980). Forrest based that appeal on three points. First was her contention that she had acquired tenure status. As a four-fifths-time employee, the district argued no, while Forrest argued yes on the basis of being included in the collective bargaining agreement (tenure status would mandate a formal hearing prior to dismissal). The second point (the crux of system procedure/professional standard interaction) involved the district's order that Forrest shorten reports, delete technical language, and refrain from making recommendations to parents prior to referrals being made to the Committee on the Handicapped. Forrest's position was that these requirements forced her to perform in a manner that violated her professional organization's ethical standards and state and federal law. The third issue was the district's refusal to permit her to present a paper at a professional conference, infringing, therefore, on a constitutionally protected right.

In April 1980, Commissioner Ambach dismissed the appeal on the basis that Forrest had failed to demonstrate that the speech in question is constitutionally protected and that her exercise of her rights was a substantial or motivating factor in the respondent board's decision to terminate her services. Ambach went on to say that

> the Education Law provides that an appeal to the Commissioner of Education may be brought by any party considering himself aggrieved, [and that] the person asserting the claims

must demonstrate that he or she is injured in some way by that action. Even if respondents were neglecting their statutory duties regarding handicapped children, an issue I do not here decide, petitioner failed to show how such neglect caused harm to her. Petitioner is not an aggrieved party within the meaning of Section 310 and her claim regarding respondents' performance of statutory duties which do not concern her are dismissed. (p. 5)

With that ruling in hand, Forrest sought judgment in the court to invalidate Ambach's decision (*Forrest* v. *Ambach*, 1981). Appearing as *amici curiae* were the National Association of School Psychologists, American Psychological Association, New York State Psychological Association, and the Westchester County Psychological Association. Justice Kahn rendered his decision late in 1980. In finding in part for Forrest, the court ordered that Commissioner Ambach review and reconsider the dismissal of Forrest from her position as a school psychologist. The court addressed two issues in the written opinion. First, whether Forrest was a tenured employee and therefore not subject to dismissal without a due process hearing, and second,

> whether the Commissioner was correct in declining to consider petitioner's specific allegations concerning the reason for her dismissal by holding that she lacked standing to challenge respondents' alleged neglect of their statutory duties regarding handicapped children. (p. 920)

With regard to the first question, the court upheld the commissioner's ruling that Forrest had not gained tenured status. However, the court went on to quickly add that the commissioner should have provided a forum for a review of the allegation made by Forrest. Forrest claimed that she was injured (loss of job) by the board's (district's) alleged misconduct. Justice Kahn identifies this as the "hub of her claim" and the commissioner's decision not to review whether the district was neglecting its statutory duties "resulted in a failure to have her grievance aired." Therefore, the opinion identifies the commissioner's determination as "a 'Catch 22' and is arbitrary and capricious in that there is not a rational basis therefore" (p. 920).

> While a school board is in the position of an employer, those professionals employed by a school board do have a level of professional competence and standards which must be recognized and respected, not only for the profession itself, but for the purpose of rendering the best service to the school board and ultimately to the students they service. *The ethical standards of any professional employed by a school board cannot be cavalierly dismissed as irrelevant to the employer-employee relationship, and may indeed become quite relevant in certain circumstances* (emphasis added). If, in fact, petitioner was dismissed solely due to her own professional standards as a psychologist, then her dismissal by said school board would be arbitrary, capricious and unconstitutional. (p. 920)

Justice Kahn affirms the special education legislation

and regulation and the explicit requirement of equal educational opportunity with a relevant reminder that "a school board should not be permitted to, in any way, impede the noble goals of such a law" (p. 920). Subsequent to the court's decision and directives, Ambach reheard Forrest's appeal and once again ruled in favor of the school district. Forrest appealed the decision to the state supreme court, and then the appellate division, losing each time. New York's highest court, the Court of Appeals, declined to review the case. The decision of Forrest accentuates the importance of professional standards and serves to underline the real and potential conflict that exists between such standards and system policy and procedure. In that sense, the decision provides an important foundation for establishing legal precedent in similar situations.

REFERENCES

Forrest v. *Ambach*, 436 N.Y.S. 2d 119, 107 Misc. 2d 920 (Sup. Ct. 1981).

In re Forrest. New York Education Department No. 10237 (April 2, 1980).

DAVID P. PRASSE
*University of Wisconsin,
Milwaukee*

ETHICAL ISSUES
NATIONAL ASSOCIATION OF SCHOOL PSYCHOLOGISTS

FOSTER HOMES FOR THE HANDICAPPED

Foster homes for handicapped children and adults have been used for many years (Sanderson & Crawley, 1982). With the advent of deinstitutionalization in the 1970s, alternatives to housing had to be considered. Although group homes were predicted to be the primary providers for this population, Roos (1978) affirmed that adoption or foster care would be the preferred residential placement. Willer and Intagliata (1982) compared group home and foster home placements on clients' achievement of self-care skills, adaptive behavior, community living skills, social skills, and community access. Interestingly, few differences were found across the two residential settings. Nevertheless, the authors concluded that family-care homes provided more opportunities to develop age-appropriate personal and interpersonal behaviors, while group homes provided more opportunities to develop community and independent living skills. Two major implications were made from these results. First, placement of handicapped persons into community residential facilities must be based on the individual needs of the client. Second, "group-home staff members could benefit from training in behavior-management techniques, whereas family-care providers could benefit from training in how to encourage residents to develop and utilize more independent community living skills" (Willer & Intagliata, 1982, p. 594). Although cost-effectiveness data were not examined, the authors concluded that the cost for foster care was significantly lower than for group-home placement.

Despite the issues of best placement, handicapped children and adults continue to be placed in foster homes. Many questions arise when considering these placements. What kinds of handicapped children are being placed in foster homes? What kinds of families take handicapped foster children? What are the needs of families with handicapped foster children?

It is estimated that over 500,000 children in the United States live in foster homes (Olsen, 1982). Foster homes have served a variety of children with developmental, emotional, physical, and medical problems. Traditionally, abused and neglected children have been in foster care. Many of these children are severely emotionally disturbed. Programs across the country have been developed to place severely mistreated children into safe and secure home environments. For example, the Intensive Treatment Homes (ITH) Project in Sacramento used a complete team approach for placing abused and neglected children into foster care (Harling & Harines, 1980). Less than half of the 43 children served in the first year of the project were able to return to their natural parents. One child was institutionalized, 2 were adopted, 11 were being considered for adoption, and the remaining 10 were referred for long-term foster care placement.

Foster homes for children with retardation and motor delays have been a constructive alternative to residential placement. For example, in a report by Taylor (1980), two case studies were presented from a foster parent's perspective. The achievements made by each of Taylor's foster children were remarkable. To meet the needs of foster parents such as these, Arizona developed a curriculum for foster parents of children with retardation (Drydyk, Mendeville, & Bender, 1980). The curriculum, Foster Parenting a Retarded Child, is available for purchase from the Child Welfare League of America, 67 Irving Place, New York, NY 10003.

Within the last few years, medically fragile children have been placed in foster homes. Often it is a nurse who will take a foster child with medical needs such as tracheotomy care, tube feeding, sterile dressing, and physical therapy. In many cases, these children would remain hospitalized indefinitely because of the biological parents' inability to provide care. Additionally, it was estimated that in 1983 the cost of foster care for these children was $1000 per month, while the average cost of a month's hospitalization was $10,500 (Whitworth, Foster, & Davis, 1983).

What kinds of families take handicapped foster children into their homes? Demographically, foster parents are often of low to middle socioeconomic status, have little or no education, are married, and have children of their own (Carbino, 1980; Enos, 1982; Hampson & Tavormina, 1980). The motives of foster parents vary from love of children, desire to help, and interest in children's well being to wanting a child to nurture or wanting a playmate for another child (Hampson & Tavormina, 1980). Many experience disruptive family patterns when a handicapped child is placed within their home; often handicapped children will be moved from one foster home to another.

The specific needs of foster parents vary depending on the child's handicap, tte family support system, and the coping abilities of the foster parents. Because of the reported emotional strain on families, it is critical that foster parents be provided with intensive orientation, training, and counseling sessions. Enos (1982) reports that foster parents leave foster care programs because of the unexpected demands of foster children, low payments, and interference with their own family's well being. Barsh, Moore, and Hamerlynck (1983) point out that foster parents of handicapped children have similar problems to those of the biological parents such as finding babysitters, transporting the child to clinics, and managing disruptive behavior. Furthermore, Edelstein (1981) reports that many foster parents go through a period of grieving when children are returned to their biological parents. It is clear that foster parents need to be aware of the problems inherent in foster parenting and to feel safe in discussing their feelings with professionals or other foster families (Foster, 1984). Training families in first aid, behavior management, therapeutic techniques, and crisis intervention may better prepare families for the care of a handicapped child. Foster homes provide an invaluable service to children with handicaps. Professionals serving handicapped children need to recognize the needs of foster parents in order to enhance the services provided to them and their foster children.

REFERENCES

Barsh, E. T., Moore, J. A., & Hamerlynck, L. A. (1983). The foster extended family: A support network for handicapped foster children. *Child Welfare, 62,* 349–359.

Carbino, R. (1980). *Foster parenting, an updated review of the literature.* New York: Child Welfare League of America.

Drydyk, J., Mendeville, B., & Bender, L. (1980). Foster parenting a retarded child. *Children Today, 9,* 10, 24–26.

Edelstein, S. (1981). When foster children leave: Helping foster parents grieve. *Child Welfare, 60,* 467–473.

Enos, S. L. (1982). More people to love you: Foster parents look at foster care. *Journal of Human Services Abstracts, 49,* 19.

Foster, P. H. (1984). Medical foster care: An ethnography. (Doctoral dissertation, University of Florida). Dissertation.

Hampson, R. B., & Tavormina, J. B. (1980). Feedback from the experts: A study of foster mothers. *Social Work, 25,* 108–112.

Harling, P. R., & Harines, J. K. (1980). Specialized foster homes for severely mistreated children. *Children Today, 9,* 16–18.

Olsen, J. (1982). Predicting the permanency status of children in foster care. *Social Work Research & Abstracts, 18,* 9–19.

Roos, S. (1978). The future residential services for the mentally retarded in the United States: A Delphi study. *Mental Retardation, 16,* 355–356.

Sanderson, H. W., & Crawley, M. (1982). Characteristics of successful family-care parents. *American Journal of Mental Deficiency, 86,* 519–525.

Taylor, S. W. (1980). Foster care: A foster mother's perspective. *Exceptional Parent, 10,* L4–L8.

Whitworth, J. M., Foster, P. H., & Davis, A. B. (1983). *Medical foster care for abused and neglected children of dysfunctional families.* Washington, DC: U.S. Department of Health and Human Services. Federal Grant #90-CA-0932.

Willer, B., & Intagliata, J. (1982). Comparison of family-care and group homes as alternative to institutions. *American Journal of Mental Deficiency, 86,* 588–595.

VIVIAN I. CORREA
University of Florida

ADOPTEES
CHILD CARETAKER EFFECTS
FAMILY COUNSELING

FOUNDATION FOR CHILDREN WITH LEARNING DISABILITIES (FCLD)

The Foundation for Children with Learning Disabilities (FCLD) is a charitable foundation incorporated in the state of New York and holding tax exempt status with the Internal Revenue Service. The FCLD is located at 99 Park Avenue, New York, NY 10016. It was founded in 1977 by Carrie Rozelle, who remains the president of the organization. The FCLD publishes *Their World*, an annual devoted to developing public awareness of learning disabilities. An annual benefit and other activities are carried out each year to raise funds to support the goals of FCLD.

In 1985 FCLD launched two major efforts aimed at service as well as public relations for the learning disabled. The FCLD has a grant program for public libraries to develop live programs for parents, teachers, learning-disabled children, and the public about learning differences. A second grant program has been designed and implemented to educate both the public and the judiciary about the potential link between learning disabilities and delinquency. The organization is devoted to developing public awareness of the problems associated with learning disabilities and to providing general educational services to the public on the topic. The FCLD does not provide direct services to learning-disabled children.

CECIL R. REYNOLDS
Texas A&M University

THEIR WORLD

FOUNTAIN VALLEY TEACHER SUPPORT SYSTEM IN MATHEMATICS

The 1967–1968 mathematics program teacher's guide for the Fountain Valley School District, California, includes the following mathematics content: numbers and numerals, geometry, measurement, applications, statistics and probability, sets, functions and graphs, logic, and problem solving. The teacher's guide also lists manipulative aids, audio-visual materials, and demonstration materials for use with elementary school-age students.

The outstanding feature of the Fountain Valley program is the mainstreaming of 60 educable mentally handicapped (EMH) and 30 educationally handicapped (EH) students into regular classes. The goal of the project was to determine whether they could be effectively educated in those settings. Effective education was defined as improvement in mathematics, reading, peer and teacher acceptance, and self-concept. The students were provided with individually prescribed programs of instruction that were based on daily assessment and prescription by a resource teacher. The resource teacher worked with regular classroom teachers to coordinate pupils' programs of instruction with regular classroom activities. Regular classroom teachers attempted to help handicapped students feel that they were valuable class members. Information available includes descriptions of scope, personnel, organization, services, instructional equipment and materials, budget, parent-community involvement, and evaluation.

Pre- and posttest assessments were administered to evaluate project objectives that were concerned with pupils' growth in academic achievement, acceptance by regular classroom teachers and students, and self-concept. Data indicate that EMR and EH students progressed an average of 12 months in mathematics and 9 to 11 months in reading. No difference was apparent in teachers' overall perception of handicapped versus nonhandicapped students as measured by Osgood's Semantic Differential. Also reported was the fact that the majority of students reached criterion levels of self-concept measures.

REFERENCES

Flint, D. (1971). *Supplement to district mathematics guide*. Fountain, Valley, CA: Fountain Valley School District.

Zweig, R. L. (1972) *Fountain Valley teacher support system in mathematics*. Huntington Beach, CA: Richard L. Zweig.

FREDERICKA K. REISMAN
Drexel University

ARITHMETIC INSTRUCTION
ARITHMETIC REMEDIATION

FOURTEENTH AMENDMENT RIGHTS

See EQUAL PROTECTION.

FOXX, RICHARD M. (1944–   )

Richard M. Foxx received his BA from the University of California, Riverside in 1967, his MA from California State University, Fullerton in 1970, and his PhD from Southern Illinois University in 1971. His major fields of interest include mental retardation, autism, and emotionally disturbed adolescents. He is considered a leading authority on the treatment of severe forms of maladaptive behavior.

Richard M. Foxx

His current interests include the development of nonintrusive methods of behavioral reduction and the study of the generalization of social skills, staff training, and the interface between environmental design and behavior analysis.

He is the author of several books. Among his most significant publications are *Increasing the Behavior of Retarded and Autistic Persons, Decreasing the Behaviors of Retarded and Autistic Persons*, and *Toilet Training the Retarded*. Foxx has also written many scientific articles and made 12 training films on the use of behavioral principles to treat mentally retarded and autistic individuals. He is a fellow in the American Psychological Association and American Association on Mental Deficiency and has won numerous awards and honors. Foxx is currently at the Anna Mental Health Center in Anna, Illinois.

REFERENCE

Foxx, R. M. (1982a). *Increasing the behavior of retarded and autistic persons*. Champaign, IL: Research.

STAFF

FRAGILE-X SYNDROME

As an X-linked form of mental retardation expressed more frequently in males than females, fragile-X (marker-X) is karotypically indicated by a structurally weak constriction on the X chromosome. Although fragile-X was reported in 1969 by Lubs, standard testing techniques frequently failed to identify affected individuals, resulting in false negative diagnoses. Insensitive tests masked the actual prevalence of fragile-X for several years. According to recent prevalence information, fragile-X is present in between 0.5 and 1.83/1000 males in the general population. Among female carriers of this sex-linked recessive trait, up to one-third may be significantly intellectually impaired. Proposals suggest that as much as 10% of mild mental retardation in females may be related to X-linked mental retardation (Moser, 1985). Confirmation of current estimates would place fragile-X second only to Down's syndrome as a chromosomally based cause of mental retardation (Hagerman, McBogg, & Hagerman, 1983).

Although mild to severe mental retardation is the most common correlate of fragile-X, other behavioral dysfunctions may also be present, including autism, self-mutilation, hyperactivity, psychosis, and impaired language (Hagerman et al., 1983; Nielsen, 1983). Affected individuals may appear phenotypically normal at birth, but later develop dysmorphic features. The most common features are large or prominent ears, large head circumference, elongated facial features, high arched palate, abnormally large testes (particularly postpubertally), and generalized hypotonia. Detection is through culture of tissues from individuals or from fetal fluid taken prenatally via amniocentesis. Accurate diagnosis occurs when the tissue is cultured in media deficient in folic acid and thymidine. Addition of 5-fluorodeoxyuridine (FUdR) further facilitates identification (Hagerman et al., 1983). Although the exact biochemical basis of the syndrome is not known and controlled treatment procedures have not been completed, high doses of folic acid reportedly result in improved behavior and learning ability in some cases (Hagerman et al., 1983). Currently a topic of intense research, subsequent data may modify or change existing knowledge regarding fragile-X.

REFERENCES

Hagerman, R. J., McBogg, P., & Hagerman, P. J. (1983). The fragile X syndrome: History, diagnosis, and treatment. *Developmental & Behavioral Pediatrics*, *4*, 122–130.

Lubs, H. A. (1969). A marker X chromosome. *American Journal of Human Genetics*, *21*, 231–244.

Moser, H. W. (1985). Biologic factors of development. In J. M. Freeman (Ed.), *Prenatal and perinatal factors associated with brain disorders* (NIH Publication No. 85-1149, pp. 121–161). Bethesda, MD: National Institute of Child Health ad Human Development.

Nielsen, K. B. (1983). Diagnosis of the fragile X syndrome (Martin-Bell syndrome). Clinical findings in 27 males with the fragile site at Xq28. *Journal of Mental Deficiency Research*, *27*, 211–226.

SHIRLEY PARKER WELLS
ROBERT T. BROWN
*University of North Carolina,
Wilmington*

AUTISM
CHROMOSOMAL ABNORMALITIES
CONGENITAL DISORDERS
DOWN'S SYNDROME
MENTAL RETARDATION

FRAIBERG, SELMA HOROWITZ (1918–   )

A native of Detroit, Michigan, Selma Horowitz Fraiberg received her BA (1940) and MSW (1945) from Wayne State University. She is currently professor of child psychoanalysis, University of Michigan, Ann Arbor.

As a social worker, Fraiberg advocated using appropriately trained social workers to work with children. Realizing that most caseworkers are trained to help adults, Fraiberg noted that resources are usually not available for a child with problems to be seen by any professional other than a caseworker. She feels that it is difficult, if not impossible, to draw hard and fast boundaries about where casework ends and other professions begin. A child with problems affects the lifestyle of an entire family, and that, she believes, is a casework problem. The family's problem is difficult to solve if the caseworker does not become involved in the child's problem. Fraiberg stresses that, to be effective, the caseworker must have appropriate training to work with children.

Selma Horowitz Fraiberg

Fraiberg's 1977 book, *Every Child's Birthright: In Defense of Mothering*, was written to publicize the practical aspects of research on the rearing of children. Much of the research studied the development of children from the Depression and the two world wars who grew up without their parents and frequently without other family as well. Her belief is that the survival of humankind depends at least as much on the nurturing care and love given to a child in infancy and childhood as it does on preventing war and surviving natural disasters. Another of Fraiberg's interests, how blind children develop and form bonding attachments when they cannot see their parents, was the basis of *Insights from the Blind: Comparative Studies of Blind and Sighted Infants* (1977).

REFERENCES

Fraiberg, S. H. (1977). *Every child's birthright: In defense of mothering*. New York: Basic Books.

Fraiberg, S. H., & Fraiberg, L. (1977). *Insights from the blind: Comparisons of blind and sighted infants*. New York: Basic Books.

E. VALERIE HEWITT
Texas A&M University

FRANCE, SPECIAL EDUCATION IN

Special education in France can be defined as "education combining pedagogical, psychological, social, medical, and paramedical actions. It is provided either by conventional establishments or by specialized establishments or departments" (Article 4, Law of Orientation, 1975). Recipients are "young subjects who, at a certain period of their life, in view of their active participation and integration in the community, are temporarily or lastingly in need of particular medical, social, pedagogical, or education procedures other than those provided for the general population" (Article 4, Law of Orientation, 1975). These definitions evolved over the past hundred years and are important in understanding how special education is provided in France at the present time.

Until the nineteenth century, assistance to handicapped children was dispensed by charitable institutions, mainly religious communities or philanthropic organizations, and was principally custodial. Saint Vincent de Paul (1581–1660) was one of the first to take an interest in the plight of abandoned children. The Abbe of l'Epee (1712–1789) founded the deaf and dumb institution of Paris, teaching language through dactylic signs. Valentin Hauy (1745–1752), founder of the Institute for Blind Youths, invented printing in relief for their instruction.

The mentally deficient, children then termed idiots or degenerates, were confined with adults to asylums, the precursors of modern psychiatric hospitals. There they received neither care nor education. However, the works of Esquirol, Itard, Seguin, and Bourneville foreshadowed a change in how handicapped children were to be treated. Bourneville considered the possibility of creating special classes providing the "necessary assistance and treatment to satisfy all the needs of the insane" (CRESAS, 1984).

The law of March 28, 1882, decreed compulsory education for all children. It highlighted the incapacity of some to follow the school curriculum and the fact that many children simply did not attend school. As a result of this law, some believed that a mentally defective child was a product of public, compulsory education. During this period, when mental specialists were turning their attention toward schooling, a number of educators were in favor of weeding out these "disturbing" elements. In 1905 Alfred Binet developed a system of identifying children maladjusted to conventional school: the metric intelligence scale. This instrument enabled qualifying all children less than

9 years old who were 3 years behind in their studies as feebleminded. The notion of an IQ is a logical outcome of this scale. The work of a committee led by Alfred Binet resulted in the promulgation of the law of April 15, 1909, relating to the creation of "refresher courses" for "backward" children of both sexes to be handled by teachers having undergone appropriate complementary training.

An educational system of segregated classes for the handicapped subsequently developed. From 25 special education classes in 1914, the number grew to 240 in 1939, 1145 in 1951, over 4000 in 1963, and over 16,000 in 1973. Recent statistics indicate a sharp decline in this number. Whereas in 1975–1976 a total of 141,007 pupils were in special public and private education courses, the figure dropped to 86,011 in 1983–1984. This is due to a general reduction of staff as well as to the creation of new institutions (notably psychopedagogical assistance groups and adaptation classes) and the development of a school integration policy.

During the 1970s, a vast movement in favor of integration, or the right to be different, developed in France, as elsewhere. It was ratified by the law of July 31, 1975. This law, decreeing compulsory education for all handicapped children and adolescents, accredits the principle of integration. It gives priority to upkeep in a normal working and living milieu, and, while assisting children and adolescents in finding the right solutions for their problems, maintains them in normal classes pending their admission to special establishments (using the cascade system). The primary aim of the integration principle is maintaining the largest possible number of handicapped children—taken in the most general sense of the term, from intellectual deficiency to physical disability—in ordinary schools. The main means to this end is through a transformation of the conventional school system.

Integration presents a number of advantages: pedagogical (the importance for the different branches of instruction of mediatory action by the other pupils and of a healthy relationship with the environment); social (development of the handicapped person's ability to adapt to living with a group of nonhandicapped pupils and better acceptance of this person by the group); and economic (the cost of integration being considerably lower than that of specialized establishments). However, integration must always be considered as a means to an end, and not as an end in itself. It cannot be a tenet, but only a guiding principle, the application of which must be adapted to particular circumstances. The present situation in France could be summed up in the phrase, "As much integration as possible, as much segregation as necessary."

According to statistics, pupils requiring special education are divided into 15 categories, depending on type of handicap. The Table shows the various types of handicaps being served and the relative and absolute numbers in each category.

Considering all age groups, pupils requiring special

Percentage of Children in Special Education Programs
in France: (1983–1984)

Type of Handicap	Number of Pupils	Percentage of Population Handicapped
Blind	1,421	0.4
Amblyopes	2,897	0.9
Deaf	6,775	2.0
Hard of hearing	2,165	0.6
Motor invalids	4,399	1.3
Motor handicapped (noncerebral)	7,174	2.1
Somatic-deficient (other physically deficient cases)	7,102	2.1
Nonseriously handicapped mentally deficient	243,625	72.6
Totally backward (not totally handicapped)	2,431	0.7
Totally deficient (not totally handicapped)	13,787	4.2
Slightly deficient	185,642	55.3
Child welfare cases	20,558	6.2
Serious psychiatric cases	11,059	3.3
Misfits	23,654	7.1

education represent approximately 3.5% of the total school population (beginning, elementary, and secondary) in France, the latter numbering some 12 million. Of 298,069 pupils in special education, 181,005 are boys and 117,064 girls, or 60.7% boys against 39.3% girls. Two additional facts should be considered concerning the slightly deficient: alone, they account for more than half of the child and adolescent population in special education; theirs is the only category showing a marked increase in numbers, progressing from 0.23% of handicapped children at age 6, to 4.9% at age 11 and 9.24% at age 14. As of age 15, the tendency is reversed.

For the most part, special education is the responsibility of the education ministry (on which public education is directly dependent), the health, social affairs, and solidarity ministries (under trusteeship), and the law ministry. The institutions and structures under the trusteeship of the health, social affairs, and solidarity ministries include the private medical and educational establishments in which education and medical care go hand in hand, the cost being reimbursed by health insurance and social assistance. These are the medico-pedagogical, medico-professional, and medico-educational institutions. Medical organizations include children's homes dispensing medical care (chronic afflictions), functional readaptation homes, treatment and postcure centers, etc. Organizations having a social and educational calling include children's villages, social assistance centers for children, etc. Reeducation of individual cases is handled in the medico-psycho-pedagogical centers (CMPM) and in daytime hospitals.

Altogether, these organizations handle approximately 40% of the children and adolescents in special education, primarily those who are physically handicapped, totally deficient, moronic, feebleminded, or afflicted with serious psychiatric or behavioral disorders; they also handle social classes. Few slightly deficient children are under their auspices. National education facilities coming under the heading of special education include the following:

1. For beginning or elementary schooling, there are special "refresher" courses," mainly in nursery schools or various specialized schools. Slightly more than 90% of handicapped children provided with schooling by the ministry of education attend these classes.
2. At the secondary level, specialized education sections (SES) in the secondary schools provide slightly intellectually deficient children with general education, preprofessional training, and workshop courses; there are also 81 state refresher schools for backward and slightly backward children who are also social cases. In addition, psychopedagogical assistance groups were set up as of 1970 to anticipate unadapted cases. Adaptation classes are attended on a temporary basis to enable especially difficult cases to follow the regular school courses.

This organizational structure forms a dense, complex network. It underwent considerable development up to the 1970s; at present, it is experiencing profound modifications. Special education will likely undergo major structural changes in the coming years.

Special education personnel, for the public and private sectors alike, is made up of specialized teachers having already taught ordinary classes. Public education instructors follow training courses, after which they pass an exam granting them the Aptness Certificate for Education of Retarded or Unadapted Children or Adolescents (CARI). The CARI comprises a general study program grouping the necessary information and problems for the specialized approach called for by the different options. These options are:

Specialized educators for children or adolescents who are deaf or hard of hearing.
Educators for amblyopic or blind children or adolescents.
Educators for somatic, physically or mentally handicapped children and adolescents.
Educators for children or adolescents suffering from troubles that are mainly of a psychological nature.
Specialized educators in charge of teaching and providing pedagogical assistance to unadapted children in beginning or elementary school.
Educators for unadapted adolescents and youths.

This division of options relates to specialized fields rather than to categories of pupils and should continue to sanction the development integration.

Moreover, the notion of a team is the very hub of all special education procedures. In addition to specialized educators, the teams include school psychologists, social workers, school medical service doctors, and various medical and therapeutic personnel, depending on objectives and need.

Several questions arise regarding special education in France. They may well provide a summary. What are special education methods in France? Personalized teaching takes into account the difficulties of each subject and the rate of acquisition and apprenticeship; progressive apprenticeship is based on analytical programming of subject matter; there is recourse to things concrete, to experimentation, to action on matter; there is an accent on motivation of the pupil, on teacher/pupil relations, on the lifestyle of the institution and its emotional climate; permanent attention to continuous observation and elaboration of an educational program based on teamwork are considered important. There is also prompt initiation of the necessary compensatory measures and therapy, flexible institutional or therapeutic solutions, and the taking into account of the evolutive and relative character of all maladjustments.

Where does school integration stand? In 1983–1984, 27,000 handicapped primary and secondary school pupils, or about 12% of all handicapped pupils, were enrolled in regular school courses. This means that integration in France is in its very first stages despite the measures taken in 1982 and 1983 in ministerial memorandums to encourage it. The special training programs for all teachers and the special information campaigns intended for all parents are expected to contribute to its development.

What evolution can we anticipate? First, strengthening of relations between the public education, assistance, and support networks and private institutions; then, better interministerial cooperation in the service of the public interest; continued support by the public for the principle of integration; the respect of individuality and personal distinctions; and the concrete affirmation of human solidarity.

REFERENCES

Bourneville, L. (1895). *Assistance to, treatment and education of, idiotic and degenerate children.* Paris: Alcan.

CRESAS Researchers. (1984). *Integration or marginalization? Aspects of special education* (Collection No. 2). Paris: l'Harmattan & INRP.

Labregere, A. (1976, June). *Handicapped persons, notes and documentary study.*

Petit, J. (1972). *Unadapted Children and Public Education.* Paris: Armand Colin.

DON BRASWELL
*Research Foundation, City
University of New York*

**BINET, ALFRED
CASCADE MODEL OF SPECIAL EDUCATION SERVICES**

FREE APPROPRIATE PUBLIC EDUCATION

One of the major provisions incorporated in the Education for All Handicapped Children Act (PL 94-142) is the requirement that all handicapped children and youths, ages 3 through 21, be afforded a free and appropriate public education (FAPE). Federal statutory requirements that mandate that services be provided to all children ages 3 through 5 and youths ages 18 through 21 apply to all states and U.S. territories except where state law or court order expressly prohibits the provision of FAPE to children or youths within these age ranges. Recently, the U.S. Congress passed legislation (P.L. 99-457) to extend federally-supported services to handicapped infants and toddlers, aged birth through two years of age.

The definition of a free and appropriate public education is comprised of three discrete, yet interrelated, provisions:

1. *Free.* Essentially this component of the FAPE mandate requires that special education and related services be provided at no cost to the parent or guardian.

2. *Appropriate.* This component of the FAPE principle requires that all special education and related services (1) be specifically tailored to the student's unique needs and capabilities (as established during the evaluation process); (2) conform to the content of the student's individualized education program (IEP); and (3) be provided in the least restrictive environment (LRE).

3. *Public Education.* The public education requirement mandates that all local, intermediate, or state agencies that directly or indirectly provide special education or related services must provide for FAPE. In meeting the FAPE requirements, public agencies (e.g., local school districts) may contract with private day or residential facilities to appropriately address the unique educational needs of a handicapped child or youth. Although the provision of FAPE does not fully apply to those handicapped children who, by parental discretion, are enrolled in private or parochial schools, these students must (by federal statute and regulation) be afforded genuine opportunities to participate in special education activities

supported under Education for All Handicapped Children Act funding.

Turnbull, Leonard, and Turnbull (1982) indicate that the provisions contained in the federal free and appropriate public education requirements have their foundations in several prominent civil rights court cases. These judicial decisions include *PARC* v. *Commonwealth of Pennsylvania, Mills* v. *D.C. Board of Education, Wyatt* v. *Stickney, New York State Association for Retarded Citizens* v. *Rockefeller, Diana* v. *State Board of Education,* and *Larry P.* v. *Riles.*

In establishing the concept of free and appropriate public education, the U.S. Congress (1983) statutorily defined FAPE as:

> Special education and related services which (A) have been provided at public expense, under public supervision and direction, and without charge, (B) meet the standards of the State educational agency, (C) include an appropriate preschool, elementary, or secondary school education in the state involved, and (D) are provided in conformity with the individualized education program required under section 614(a)(5).

In expanding on the legislative and judicial foundations supporting the provision of FAPE, Turnbull, Leonard, and Turnbull (1982) specify six major principles for the administration of special education: implementation of the zero reject concept, development of nondiscriminatory evaluation models, preparation of IEPs, maintenance of the full continuum of least restrictive placement options, administration of compliant due process systems, and the assurance of full parent participation in all programming decisions.

REFERENCE

Turnbull, A., Leonard, J. L., & Turnbull, H. R. (1982). *Educating handicapped children: Judicial and legislative influences.* Washington, DC: American Association of Colleges for Teacher Education.

U.S. Congress (1983). The Education of the Handicapped Amendments of 1983 (Public law 98-199). Washington D.C.: Government Printing Office.

GEORGE JAMES HAGERTY
Stonehill College

EDUCATION FOR ALL HANDICAPPED CHILDREN ACT OF 1975
INDIVIDUAL EDUCATION PLAN
LEAST RESTRICTIVE ENVIRONMENT
ZERO REJECT

FREEDOM FROM DISTRACTIBILITY

Numerous factor-analytic studies of the Wechsler intelligence scales have revealed *freedom from distractibility* as the third factor that underlies test performance. The first two factors are typically verbal comprehension and perceptual organization, each robust in its makeup and generally invariant in its subtest composition. The third, or distractibility factor, usually consists of the arithmetic, digit span, and coding/digit symbol subtests. Although the exact meaning of the factor remains to be discovered, it has been identified as the capacity to resist distraction (Wechsler, 1958); it is sometimes referred to as the anxiety triad (Lutey, 1977). Lutey stresses that the factor may be primarily a measure of number ability. Kaufman (1979) suggests that the factor may reflect a variety of cognitive faculties such as sequential processing, memory, or automatic functioning, rather than just the behavioral attributes of distractibility or anxiety.

The distractibility factor can play a key role in some individual test interpretations, but caution is advised against using it indiscriminately. The composition of the freedom from distractibility factor has been found to vary somewhat from one age group to another (e.g., coding A does not load meaningfully on the factor at ages 6½ and 7½); the factor is occasionally not isolated in factor-analytic studies (e.g., Reschly, 1978); and, when compared with the larger factors of verbal comprehension (information, similarities, vocabulary, and comprehension) and perceptual organization (picture completion, picture arrangement, block design, object assembly, and mazes), the third factor clearly accounts for a smaller percentage of variance.

The distractibility factor was first reported by Cohen (1952), who used a comparative factor analysis (considered a powerful exploratory technique at that time) to examine the performance of a group of psychiatric patients on the Wechsler-Bellevue. Expressing concern that the rationales for intelligence tests were intuitively developed and lacked needed experimental testing, Cohen found and labeled factor A (verbal), factor B (nonverbal organization), and factor C (freedom from distractibility). The last factor was found to include substantial loadings by the subtests that require alert, undistracted attention for good performance. He followed up this original work with a similar factor analysis of the standardization samples of the Wechsler Adult Intelligence Scale (WAIS) (Cohen, 1957). In this factor analysis he labeled factor C as memory. In the Wechsler Intelligence Scale for Children (WISC) (Cohen, 1959), he reverted to his original interpretation of factor C as freedom from distractibility.

Kaufman (1975) used three different methods of factor analysis in a comprehensive study of data from the standardization sample of the Wechsler Intelligence Scale for Children-Revised (WISC-R). He examined 11 age levels between 6½ and 16½ years. The principal-components technique produced two significant factors (similar to Wechsler's verbal and performance scales) at six age levels and three significant factors at five age levels, suggesting that a two-factor solution is insufficient. A principal-factor analysis was followed by varimax rotation of two-, three-, four-, and five-factor solutions. The two-factor rotation resulted in a clear verbal-performance division. The three-factor solution revealed the verbal comprehension, perceptual organization, and freedom from distractibility factors for 9 of the 11 age groups. In the four-factor solution, the three factors emerged at all 11 age levels. A quasi-specific factor and other individual subtest loadings were noted in the three-, four-, and five-factor rotations, but these were not meaningful in the sense that they varied appreciably from age to age and did not seem to represent any clearly defined dimension of intelligence.

A factor analysis of the Wechsler Adult Intelligence Scale-Revised (WAIS-R) was conducted by Parker (1983). The standardization sample was separated into nine age groups, the youngest being 16 to 17 and the oldest 70 to 74. The familiar three-factor solution was found across all nine age groups. However, the composition of the factors differed somewhat from WISC-R findings. Picture arrangement and, to a lesser extent, digit symbol each appeared to measure unique constructs more than the respective factors of perceptual organization and freedom from distractibility, with which they have been connected.

In an investigation of the factor structure of the Wechsler Preschool and Primary Scale of Intelligence (WPPSI), Hollenbeck and Kaufman (1973) divided the standardization sample into three age groups (4–4½, 5–5½, and 6–6½) and analyzed the test results. Several different factor-analytic procedures were used, yet, in each case, the WPPSI subtests separated clearly into distinct verbal and performance factors. This finding contrasts markedly with the results of similar analyses of the other Wechsler scales. The failure of a third factor to emerge on the WPPSI for young children—an age group that is characterized by distractible behavior—offers one good argument for not interpreting the third factor that emerges for older children and adults as freedom from distractibility.

A significant freedom from distractibility factor has been found in studies of various racial (Gutkin & Reynolds, 1981) and socioeconomic groups (Carlson, Reynolds, & Gutkin, 1983). However, these findings are not universal. Sandoval (1982), among others, reported that a three-factor solution emerged for whites but not for groups of black and Mexican-American children.

The three factors identified for normal youngsters and adults have also been found among special education populations. Van Hagen and Kaufman (1975) found the WISC-R factors for a sample of retarded children to be similar to the factors identified for normal children. The factors also bore a close resemblance to the WISC factors found for groups of institutionalized and noninstitutionalized retarded individuals (Baumeister & Bartlett, 1962a, 1962b). In the last studies, the third factor is labeled the trace or stimulus trace factor, referring to a hypothetical physiological basis for the construct involving disruption in the amplitude and duration of the stimulus trace. Nevertheless, the description of the trace factor corresponds to the description of freedom from distractibility and is conceivably another name for the same entity. Blaha and Vance (1979), using a hierarchical factor analysis for a sample of learning-disabled children, found a general (g) factor and three subgeneral factors, including an intact spatial-perceptual-mechanical factor, a verbal comprehension factor, and a freedom from distractibility factor. In addition, the third factor has been identified for numerous other exceptional groups using various factor-analytic procedures. More important, low scores on the third WISC-R factor seem to characterize the test performance of reading and learning-disabled children (Kaufman, 1979).

When should the freedom from distractibility factor be interpreted? Kaufman (1979) advises adhering to the Wechsler V-P dichotomy under ordinary circumstances. However, use of the factor-analytic trichotomy is indicated when the third factor is seen as reflecting a clear and unitary ability. In the event that there is a significant difference between any of the distractibility subtests and the individual examinee's mean scaled score (on either the verbal or the performance scales), Kaufman recommends that the other distractibility subtests be examined carefully. If these other scaled scores are in the same directional ball park as the significantly low- or high-distractibility score, it is wise to interpret this triad of subtest scores as a significant third factor that should then be compared with the other two factors.

If an examiner determines that an interpretation of the third factor is warranted, the matter of how to interpret the factor still remains. To automatically ascribe an explanation of distractibility to a child who scored low on arithmetic, digit span, and coding would be absurd if the child had concentrated on each task and attended closely to each item presented. A hypothesis of distractibility or anxiety should be substantiated by test behavior indicating an attention deficit or failure to concentrate. In addition to behavioral observations, other subtest scores, the nature of wrong responses, and conditions outside the testing situation must also be considered in a comprehensive and individualized interpretation. When sequencing ability is believed to be the difficulty (or the strength), the scaled score on the picture arrangement subtest should be examined for corroboration. Also, the examiner should look closely at background and referral information, noting any sequencing deficiency such as failure to follow directions. On the other hand, finger counting or writing and an inability to solve arithmetic problems during the time allowed, along with a low achievement level in math, all point to a difficulty with numerical symbols as a probable explanation for the third factor. By contrast, high scores on the three subtests coupled with evidence of very good achievement in mathematics suggest an interpretation of strength in number ability.

Lutey (1977) and Kaufman (1979) both warn against a simplistic interpretation of the third factor, stressing that the factor can yield valuable information if it is considered in a larger context that features the more global perspective of the entire test performance, the test behavior, and the personal history of the individual.

REFERENCES

Baumeister, A. A., & Bartlett, C. J. (1962a). A comparison of the factor structure of normals and retardates on the WISC. *American Journal of Mental Deficiency, 66,* 641–646.

Baumeister, A. A., & Bartlett, C. J. (1962b). Further factorial investigations of WISC performance of mental defectives. *American Journal of Mental Deficiency, 67,* 257–261.

Blaha, J., & Vance, H. (1979). The hierarchical factor structure of the WISC-R for learning disabled children. *Learning Disabilities Quarterly, 2*(4), 71–75.

Carlson, L., Reynolds, C. R., & Gutkin, T. B. (1983). Consistency of the factorial validity of the WISC-R for upper and lower SES groups. *Journal of School Psychology, 21,* 319–326.

Cohen, J. (1952). Factors underlying Wechsler-Bellevue performance of three neuropsychiatric groups. *Journal of Abnormal & Social Psychology, 47,* 359–365.

Cohen, J. (1957). The factorial structure of the WAIS between early adulthood and old age. *Journal of Consulting Psychology, 21*(4), 283–290.

Cohen, J. (1959). The factorial structure of the WISC at ages 7-6, 10-6, and 13-6. *Journal of Consulting Psychology, 23*(4), 285–299.

Gutkin, T. B., & Reynolds, C. R. (1981). Factorial similarity of the WISC-R for white and black children from the standardization sample. *Journal of Educational Psychology, 73,* 227–231.

Hollenbeck, G. P., & Kaufman, A. S. (1973). Factor analysis of the Wechsler Preschool and Primary Scale of Intelligence (WPPSI). *Journal of Clinical Psychology, 29*(1), 41–45.

Kaufman, A. S. (1975). Factor analysis of the WISC-R at 11 age levels between 6½ and 16½ years. *Journal of Consulting & Clinical Psychology, 43*(2), 135–147.

Kaufman, A. S. (1979). *Intelligent testing with the WISC-R.* New York: Wiley.

Lutey, C. (1977). *Individual intelligence testing: A manual and sourcebook* (2nd ed.). Greeley, CO: Lutey.

Parker, K. (1983). Factor analysis of the WAIS-R at nine age levels between 16 and 74 years. *Journal of Consulting & Clinical Psychology, 51*(2), 302–308.

Reschly, D. J. (1978). WISC-R factor structures among Anglos, Blacks, Chicanos, and Native-American Papagos. *Journal of Consulting & Clinical Psychology, 46,* 417–422.

Sandoval, J. (1982). The WISC-R factoral validity for minority groups and Spearman's hypothesis. *Journal of School Psychology, 20*(3), 198–204.

Van Hagen, J., & Kaufman, A. S. (1975). Factor analysis of the WISC-R for a group of mentally retarded children and adolescents. *Journal of Consulting & Clinical Psychology, 43,* 661–667.

Wechsler, D. (1958). *The measurement and appraisal of adult intelligence.* Baltimore, MD: Williams & Wilkins.

ALAN S. KAUFMAN
MARY E. STINSON
University of Alabama

FACTOR ANALYSIS
PROFILE ANALYSIS
PROFILE VARIABILITY
WECHSLER INTELLIGENCE SCALE FOR CHILDREN—
  REVISED

FRENCH, EDWARD LIVINGSTON (1916–1969)

Edward Livingston French began his professional career as a teacher at Chestnut Hill Academy in Philadelphia. Following three years of military service in World War II, he served as chief psychologist at the Training School at Vineland, New Jersey, where he was associated with Edgar A. Doll. In 1949 both French and Doll joined the Devereux Schools in Pennsylvania, French as director of psychology and education. French became a member of the board of trustees of the Devereux Foundation in 1954. Three years later he was made director of the foundation; in 1960 he became president and director.

Edward Livingston French

French received his PhD in clinical psychology from the University of Pennsylvania in 1950. He co-authored *How You Can Help Your Retarded Child.* His chapter on the Devereux Schools in *Special Education Programs within the United States* describes the principles of residential therapy on which the Devereux program is based. He served as president of both the Clinical Biochemistry and Behavioral Institute and the Division of School Psychologists of the American Psychological Association, and he was a trustee of the National Association of Private Psychiatric Hospitals.

REFERENCES

French, E. L. (1968). The Devereux Schools. In M. V. Jones (Ed.), *Special education programs within the United States*. Springfield, IL: Thomas.

French, E. L., & Scott, J. C. (1967). *How you can help your retarded child: A manual for parents*. New York: Lippincott.

PAUL IRVINE
Katonah, New York

FRENCH, JOSEPH L. (1928–   )

Joseph L. French earned his BS (1949) and MS (1950) from Illinois State University at Normal and his EdD (1957) in educational psychology and measurements from the University of Nebraska. He joined the special education and educational psychology faculty of Pennsylvania State University in 1964 and has remained there since. In that same year, he authored *The Pictorial Test of Intelligence*, used to assess the general intellectual level of normal and handicapped learners.

French has shown an interest in gifted adolescents since the 1950s and has been one of the pioneers in that area of research. He edited *Educating the Gifted* in 1959, a collection of articles on identifying and providing education and services for the gifted and creative. It was extensively revised in 1964. French has studied high school dropouts of high ability and the preparation of teachers of the gifted. He is also interested in test development and evaluation of educational programs. In addition, he has written various articles on intelligence and its assessment (French & Murphy, 1985) and on issues in school psychology (French, 1984).

French has been president of the School Psychology Division of the American Psychological Association (1975–1978) and president of The Association for the Gifted (1968–1971). He has also served as associate editor for *Exceptional Children, Diagnostique*, and the *Journal for the Education of the Gifted*.

REFERENCES

French, J. L. (1964a). *The Pictorial Test of Intelligence*. Boston: Houghton Mifflin.

French, J. L. (Ed.). (1964b). *Educating the gifted* (rev. ed.) New York: Holt, Rinehart, & Winston.

French, J. L. (1984). On the conception, birth, and early development of school psychology; with special reference to Pennsylvania. *American Psychologist, 39*, 976–987.

French, J. L., & Murphy, J. (1985). Intelligence, its assessment and its role in the comprehensive evaluation. In J. R. Bergan (Ed.), *School psychology in contemporary society*. Columbus, OH: Merrill.

ANN E. LUPKOWSKI
Texas A&M University

FREUD, ANNA (1895–1982)

Anna Freud was the youngest of Sigmund Freud's six children. She was educated at the Cottage Lyceum, and although an excellent student, left without a degree in 1912. Her father was her mentor in psychoanalytic theory and practice. Following the Nazi takeover of Austria, the family moved to London in 1938. Anna and her father remained professionally active and influential after their emigration. She was her father's devoted companion and associate until his death in 1939.

Anna Freud's many professional contributions resulted from her interest in applying psychoanalytic theory to the study of child development and in formulating and conducting psychotherapy appropriate to the special needs of young patients. Her work stimulated others, including Erik Erikson, whose study of psychoanalysis she encouraged. Her theoretical contributions included elaborating and extending her father's concept of ego defense mechanisms, particularly displacement and identification. She wrote prolifically, producing more than 100 articles and many important books, including *Introduction to the Technique of Child Analysis* (1927), *Psychoanalysis for Teachers and Parents* (1931), *The Ego and the Mechanisms of Defense* (1936), and *Psychoanalytic Treatment of Children* (1946). She also edited the 24-volume edition of her father's works (1953–1956).

Her interest in promoting child psychoanalysis led her to found in 1947 a clinic and a serial publication, both of which are still active. The Hampstead Child-Therapy Course and Clinic in London treats children and trains psychoanalytic child therapists; *The Psychoanalytic Study of the Child*, is a scholarly forum for theoreticians and practitioners.

Anna Freud received the highest professional recog-

Joseph L. French

nition of her contemporaries in 1970 when she was named the most outstanding living child psychoanalyst. Other distinctions include awards, medals, and honorary degrees from Clark, Yale, Columbia, and Harvard universities, and an honorary MD in 1972 from the University of Vienna.

Because of Anna Freud's modest and private nature, frustratingly little is known about her personal and professional development (Jackson, 1982). However, a memorial section of Volume 39 of *The Psychoanalytic Study of the Child* (1984) includes five papers discussing her contributions to the fields of law, developmental psychology, politics, and training in child analysis.

REFERENCE

Jackson, D. J. (1982). Psychology of the scientist: XLVI. Anna Freud. *Psychological Reports, 50*, 1191–1198.

PAULINE APPLEFIELD
*University of North Carolina,
Wilmington*

FREUD, SIGMUND (1856–1939)

Sigmund Freud, the founder of psychoanalysis, entered medical practice as a neurologist in Vienna in 1886. Psychoanalysis, developed out of Freud's clinical practice, revolutionized not only psychiatric treatment but man's view of himself. Freud introduced the concept of the unconscious mind and its influence on behavior. Free association and dream interpretation were developed as techniques for reaching the unconscious. Freud demonstrated the role of mental conflict in human development and identified the motivating forces of sexuality and aggression. He also identified the existence and importance of infantile sexuality, and the influence of childhood development on adult behavior. After the annexation of Austria by Nazi Germany in 1938, Freud moved to London, where he resided until his death the following year.

REFERENCES

Freud, S. (1933). *New introductory lectures on psycho-analysis.* New York: Norton.

Freud, S. (1970). *An outline of psychoanalysis.* New York: Norton.

Jones, E. (1953–1957). *The life and work of Sigmund Freud* (3 vols.). New York: Basic Books.

PAUL IRVINE
Katonah, New York

FRIEDREICH'S ATAXIA (FA)

Friedreich's ataxia (FA) applies to a varied group of problems whose major symptoms usually appear in the late childhood or early adolescent years. The condition is generally transmitted along family lines through Mendelian inheritance as an autosomal recessive trait, though some cases of dominant mode transmission have been recognized. At the core of the disorder is progressive dysfunction of the spinal cord and cerebellum. Cardiac muscle fiber degeneration may also be present.

The early signs of FA are an increasing disturbance of normal gait followed by progressive loss of muscular coordination in the upper extremities and trunk. Skeletal anomalies such as club foot, hammer toes, and highly arched feet, along with scoliosis, may be present. Cardiac failure, enlargement of the heart (or arrhythmias), nystagmus of the eyes, optical nerve atrophy, tremors, dysarthria, and feeding disorders may be noted. Loss of sensation, especially in the feet, is common in this disorder, and the risk of development of seizure disorders is high. The diagnosis of FA is completely reliant on these clinical manifestations. Lab findings are generally of little assistance in diagnosis, except for cases where electrocardiogram changes indicating myocarditis are observed. Most individuals with FA become wheelchair-bound and eventually bedridden. There is no known cure for this disorder, with death from myocardial failure in childhood, adolescence, or early adulthood the usual result.

Friedreich's ataxia has been separated diagnostically from other similar disorders such as ataxia-telangiectasia, Roussy-Levy syndrome, and Bassen-Kornzweig syndrome.

REFERENCES

Batshaw, M. L., & Perret, Y. M. (1981). *Children with handicaps: A medical primer.* Baltimore, MD: Brookes.

Bleck, E. E., & Nagel, D. A. (1982). *Physically handicapped children: A medical atlas for teachers.* New York: Grune & Stratton.

Vaughan, V. C., McKay, R. J., & Behrman, R. E. (1979). *Nelson textbook of pediatrics.* Philadelphia: Saunders.

JOHN D. WILSON
*Elwyn Institutes,
Elwyn, Pennsylvania*

GAIT DISTURBANCES
GENETIC COUNSELING

FROSTIG, MARIANNE (1906–1985)

Born in Vienna, Austria, Marianne Frostig received a degree as a children's social worker from the College of Social Welfare, Vienna, Austria, in 1926. Several years later, she and her neuropsychiatrist husband worked in a psychiatric hospital in Poland before he accepted a position in the United States. When the Nazis invaded Poland, they killed everyone in the hospital. In the United States, Fros-

Marianne Frostig (right)

tig earned the first BA ever issued by the New School for Social Research (1948). She received her MA (1940) from Claremont Graduate School and her PhD (1955) from the University of Southern California. She became ill and died while on a lecture tour in Germany.

Believing that every person is a unique individual who needs to be assessed and treated as such, Frostig was interested in finding the most appropriate education/treatment for each child. She thought that education should be adjusted to meet the needs of all children, especially those who, for various reasons, find learning difficult. To Frostig, a problem child is a child whose needs are not being met. *Education for Dignity* was intended to be a practical guide for the regular classroom teacher to meet those needs.

The Marianne Frostig Development Test of Visual Perception was the first test to segregate different visual abilities. Prior to this, all visual problems were grouped together. Frostig retired as director of the Marianne Frostig Center for Educational Therapy in 1972.

Frostig received the *Los Angeles Times* Woman of the Year Award and the Golden Key Award of the International Association for Children with Learning Disabilities. She has been included in *Who's Who of American Women, American Men and Women of Science*, and the *Dictionary of International Biography*.

REFERENCES

Frostig, M. (1976). *Education for dignity*. New York: Grune & Stratton.

Frostig, M., Lefever, D. W., & Whittlesey, J. R. B. (1964). *The Marianne Frostig Developmental Test of Visual Perception* (3rd. ed.). Palo Alto, CA: Consulting Psychologists.

E. VALERIE HEWITT
Texas A&M University

FROSTIG REMEDIAL PROGRAM

The Frostig Program of Visual Perception, developed in 1964, is designed to train children who have visual problems in perceptual and motor skills. Using a series of workbooks and worksheets, the program focuses on five areas. First, eye motor coordination, which involves drawing lines in carefully prescribed boundaries. Second, figure-ground, in which the child finds hidden figures in distracting and overlapping backgrounds. Third, perceptual constancy; here the child learns to recognize that an object remains the same even if its shape or color changes. Fourth, position in space; in this part of the program the child discovers that figures and objects remain the same although they may occupy different positions. Often, the child is provided with a model, then given several other models and is asked to select the shape or design that is exactly like the original. The fifth area is spatial relationships; at this point the child develops skills in perceiving positional relationships between objects or points of reference such as the arrangement of material or figures on a printed page (Bannatyne, 1971; Hallahan, & Kaufman, 1976).

The assumption underlying the Frostig program is that brain damage in children results in neurological disabilities giving rise to visual perceptual problems. This assumption, based on the seminal works of Goldstein, Strauss, Werner, and Cruickshank, concludes that manifestations of brain dysfunctions, usually perceptual problems, can occur even if no specific damage to the brain can be found (Hallahan & Kaufman, 1976). The Frostig program is one of several commercially developed training programs to aid learning-disabled children who exhibit perceptual deficiencies (Frostig & Maslow, 1973).

In conjunction with this program, the Frostig Developmental Test of Visual Perception was designed. This test purports to measure the five functions of visual perception and provides a means to compare children's performance with norms for their ages. The assumption on which the test is based, that visual perception is a critical element in school learning, has been questioned. Moreover, the effectiveness of the test and the Frostig training has not been documented. While the test itself provides an adequate measure of global perception of young children, its ability to assess specific areas of perceptual difficulty has not been shown. Mann (1978) cautions that a low score on the test should not be construed as a signal to begin a perceptual training program. In addition, he states that the test and its related training program has "stimulated wide and often injudicious programming for learning-disabled children" (p. 1276). More recently, critics have claimed that Frostig's names for traits are simply conjecture and the test and program both represent a psychometric era that has passed (Mitchell, 1985).

REFERENCES

Bannatyne, A. (1971). *Language, reading and learning disabilities*. Springfield, IL: Thomas.

Frostig, M., & Maslow, P. (1973). *Learning problems in the classroom*. New York: Grune & Stratton.

Hallahan, D., & Kaufman, J. (1976). *Introduction to learning disabilities*. Englewood Cliffs, NJ: Prentice-Hall.

Mann, L. (1978). Review of the Marianne Frostig developmental test of visual perception. In O. K. Buros (Ed.), *Mental measurements yearbook*. Highland Park, NJ: Gryphon.

Mitchell, J. V. (1985). *Ninth mental measurements yearbook*. Highland Park, NJ: Gryphon.

FORREST E. KEESBURY
Lycoming College

MOVIEGENICS
VISUAL-MOTOR AND VISUAL-PERCEPTUAL PROBLEMS
VISUAL PERCEPTION AND DISCRIMINATION

FUNCTIONAL CENTERS HYPOTHESIS

The functional centers hypothesis, the Soviet view of learning disorders expounded by and associated primarily with Vygotsky and Luria, was further investigated and supported by other researchers in the Soviet Union (Holowinsky, 1976). It is based on Pavlovian psychology and on the dialectical-materialistic interpretaton of human behavior: behavior, that is, on the elementary and higher levels, the product of phylogenetic, ontogenetic, and sociohistorical influences.

Central to the understanding of the hypothesis is the notion that an individual's mental functions (i.e., attention, memory, perception, thinking) are not only adaptive and acquired, but also are localized in and mediated by areas of cerebral cortex centers. Speech problems, language disorders, learning dysfunctions, and other handicaps are related to such centers but have psychoneurological etiologies. However, the functions "as complex functional systems with dynamic levels of localization in the brain" (Luria, 1980) are differentially related to various areas of the brain that are themselves highly differentiated in their structure. Mental functions are not, therefore, totally localized in particular/isolated areas of the brain (e.g., neuron, cortex), but operate as systems of functional combination centers. Localization in the Lurian brain for higher cortical function is dynamic, not static (Reynolds, 1981).

Mental functions appear in the developmental process first in elementary form as a result of natural development (determined by environmental stimulation). They then are changed primarily because of cultural development and self-regulated stimulation by the individual into a higher form (Vygotsky, 1978). Vygotsky considered voluntary control, conscious realization, social origins and nature, and mediation by psychological tools as characteristics of higher mental functioning (Wertsch, 1985). The development of speech is crucial because it provides new tools and signs that on mastery will clarify the operations of mental functioning to the individual.

Society plays a preeminent role in human development and functioning. In fact, higher mental functions (e.g., abstract thought, voluntary action) are formed during everyday activities. In a social context, they enable individuals to use a high level of organization, find new ways of regulating behavior, and establish new functional systems (Luria, 1978). Thus human beings can develop extracerebral connections and have the capacity to form numerous new functional systems and new functional centers in the cerebral cortex.

As a function is "a complex and plastic system performing a particular adaptive task and composed of a highly differentiated group of interchangeable elements" (Luria, 1980, p. 24), damage to any part of the cortical area can lead to a disintegration of the functional system. However, such a disturbance is likely to differ depending on the factors and on the role each part of the brain plays in the organization of the system during different stages of functional development (early or late).

In treating the learning disabled and mentally handicapped, the practitioner operates on the premise that a mental function may be performed by one of several intercenter connections in the functional centers. If one such connection is damaged—the damage or loss is not permanent—another system or cortical function can be trained to compensate for the deficit and take over the lost function. Thus restoring the disturbed or disorganized function is merely reorganizing that function and forming a new functional system.

REFERENCES

Holowinsky, I. Z. (1976). Functional centers hypothesis: The Soviet view of learning dysfunctions. In L. Mann & D. A. Sabatino (Eds.), *The third review of special education* (pp. 53–69). New York: Grune & Stratton.

Luria, A. R. (1978). L. S. Vygotsky and the problem of functional localization. In M. Cole (Ed.), *The selected writings of A. R. Luria* (pp. 273–281). White Plains, NY: Sharpe.

Luria, A. R. (1980). *Higher cortical functions in man* (2nd ed.). (B. Haigh, Trans.). New York: Basic Books. (Original work published 1962).

Reynolds, C. R. (1981). The neuropsychological basis of intelligence. In G. W. Hynd & J. E. Obrzut (Eds.), *Neuropsychological assessment and the school-aged child: Issues and procedures*. New York: Grune & Stratton.

Vygotsky, L. S. (1978). *Mind in society: The development of higher mental processes*. Cambridge, MA: Harvard University Press.

Wertsch, J. V. (1985). *Vygotsky and the social formation of mind*. Cambridge, MA: Harvard University Press.

HAGOP S. PAMBOOKIAN
Elizabeth City, North Carolina

ACTIVITY, THEORY OF
LURIA, A. R.
ZONE OF PROXIMAL DEVELOPMENT

FUNCTIONAL DOMAINS

Educators, psychologists, and other health professionals will often assess and describe a child's performance in a number of areas, called functional domains, in addition to describing the child's overall performance and development in a global fashion. Theoretically, an assessment of the child's strengths and weaknesses in the various domains gives a snapshot of the child's functional status or the child's performance and ability to do things most other children do. Functional status is closely related to the concept of health status in the health field (Starfield, 1974; Stein & Jessop, 1984) and to the concept of social competence in the early childhood field (Zigler & Trickett, 1978).

Although typologies for the number and name of the functional domains vary, they generally are divided into four major areas: physical, cognitive, social, and emotional. Sometimes, the social and emotional areas are considered together and called psychological or mental health. The key to assessments in all funtional domains is that behavior should be seen in a developmental context or framework so that the dynamic qualities of a child's development are considered (Walker, Richmond, & Buka, 1984).

Examples of behaviors or constructs that might be assessed under each functional domain are the physical (height and weight, activities of daily living); cognitive (intelligence, learning style); social (peer relationships, leadership skills); and emotional (self-concept, depression).

Because the measurements of these domains have been shown to be distinct, it is strongly recommended that researchers and practitioners do not try to combine the individual functional domain measures into an overall index or measure score (Eisen, Donald, Ware & Brook, 1980). Instead, a profile approach to the child's performance and functioning in terms of his or her strengths and liabilities in the various functional areas is preferred (Starfield, 1974). Assessments of a child's performance in various functional domain areas are much easier to translate directly into educational and other service programs for the individual child than more generic global index scores. This profile or multidimensional approach is recommended for both individual and group or population descriptions.

REFERENCES

Eisen, M., Donald, C. A., Ware, J. E., & Brook, R. H. (1980). *Conceptualization and measurement of health for children in the health insurance study*. Santa Monica, C.A. Rand.

Starfield, B. (1974). Measurement of outcome: A proposed scheme. *Millbank Memorial Fund Quarterly, 52*, 39–50.

Stein, R. E. K., & Jessop, D. J. (1984). Assessing the functional status of children. In D. K. Walker & J. B. Richmond (Eds.), *Monitoring child health in the United States*. Cambridge, MA: Harvard University Press.

Walker, D. K., Richmond, J. B., & Buka, S. L. (1984). Summary and recommendations for next steps. In D. K. Walker & J. B. Richmond (Eds.), *Monitoring child health in the United States*. Cambridge, MA: Harvard University Press.

Zigler, E. F., & Trickett, D. K. (1978). IQ, social competence and evaluation of early childhood intervention programs. *American Psychologist, 33*, 789–798.

DEBORAH KLEIN WALKER
Harvard University

ADAPTIVE BEHAVIOR
ASSESSMENT
INTELLIGENCE
MENTAL STATUS EXAMS

FUNCTIONAL INSTRUCTION

Functional instruction refers to the use of activities that involve skills of immediate usefulness to students as well as the employment of teaching materials that use real rather than simulated materials (Wehman, Renzaglia, & Bates, 1985). For example, a student could be taught to increase fine motor skills by assembling vocational products from local industry rather than by placing pegs in a board or stringing beads. Or a student could be required to place one cup at each place setting as opposed to placing one chip on each colored circle in an effort to teach one-to-one correspondence.

There are several reasons to support the use of functional instruction techniques, especially when considering the needs of severely handicapped students (Brown, Nietupski, & Hamre-Nietupski, 1976). First, the use of artificial materials and settings may fail to prepare students for the skills they will need to perform practical tasks in natural settings. One cannot make any inferences about the ability of severely handicapped students to generalize skills taught in simulated settings or with artificial materials to natural environments where these skills will be needed. Second, the actions required to do artificial tasks or materials may have little or no relation to the actions required in natural settings. For instance, labeling of plastic fruit and placing it in a small plastic shopping cart to be wheeled around the classroom may not prepare students for locating, selecting, bagging, and purchasing fruit in a local supermarket. Third, since the focus of education for severely handicapped students is on preparing them to function in heterogeneous adult environments, instruction should occur in community-based (natural) settings. It is only through instruction in such nonartificial settings that students will learn to attend to and respond to the myriad of activities of nonhandicapped individuals in such settings. In addition, instruction in community sites will enable students to discriminate among a variety of novel stimuli found in natural environments (e.g., different types of soap dispensers in public restrooms).

The proliferation of nonfunctional activities in classrooms can be traced to several possible origins (Wehman, Renzaglia, & Bates, 1985). First, the large amount of commercial material that has appeared on the market recently has significantly influenced the teachings of severely handicapped pupils. These commercially made materials are not always directly related to materials and activities that will be required by students in natural environments. Second, some educators believe that traditional nonfunctional activities (e.g., pegs in boards, stacking rings on post) are necessary for the student's readiness for more complex activities. Such a philosophy perpetuates the acquisition of isolated skills that have little correlation with skills needed in natural settings in adulthood. Unlike their nonhandicapped peers, severely handicapped individuals may not generalize skills taught in nonfunctional readiness activities to those needed in natural environments. Only with direct instruction of functional skills using nonartificial materials will severely handicapped students be able to exhibit competence in nonschool or postschool settings.

The use of functional materials and instruction involves the examination of individual needs in current and future environments. An ecological inventory (Brown et al., 1979) or ecological analysis (Wehman, Renzaglia, & Bates, 1985) can be conducted to determine individual student needs. By looking at aspects of the student's current environments (e.g., home, school, vocational site) and his or her future environments (e.g., group home, community recreation facility, vocational site), one can determine which skills will enable that student to function independently. By further breaking down current and future environments into subenvironments (e.g., group home: bathroom, living room, bedroom) and determining what activities are necessary in those subenvironments, one can determine the types of functional materials to be used during instruction. Careful consultation with parents or guardians as well as staff at future residential sites is also needed to ensure the functionality of skills targeted for instruction during the school years.

REFERENCES

Brown, L., Branston-McClean, M. B., Baumgart, D., Vincent, L., Falvey, M., & Schroeder, J. (1979). Using the characteristics of current and subsequent least restrictive environments in the development of curricular content for severely handicapped students. *AAESPH Review, 4,* 407–424.

Brown, L., Nietupski, J., & Hamre-Nietupski, S. (1976). Criterion of ultimate functioning. In M. A. Thomas (Ed.), *Hey, don't forget about me!* Reston, VA: Council for Exceptional Children.

Wehman, P., Renzaglia, A., & Bates, P. (1985). *Functional living skills for moderately and severely handicapped individuals.* Austin, TX: Pro-Ed.

CORNELIA LIVELY
University of Illinois,
Urbana-Champaign

ECOLOGICAL EDUCATION OF THE HANDICAPPED
EDUCABLE MENTALLY RETARDED
TRAINABLE MENTALLY RETARDED
TRANSFER OF LEARNING
TRANSFER OF TRAINING

FUNCTIONAL SKILLS TRAINING

Functional skills are generally considered to be those skills and competencies that are necessary for everyday living. These competencies are also referred to by many as "survival skills." The skills could be relatively simple for many people such as counting change from a basic purchase, reading the sign for a restroom in an unfamiliar location, or realizing when to walk across an unfamiliar intersection. They could also be more complicated and involve the balancing of a checkbook, the completion of an application for employment, or comparative shopping. Many students are able to acquire these types of skills either within their normal environment, through incidental learning, or through general instruction within a formal classroom setting. The exceptional child, however, may not be able to acquire these competencies through incidental learning in his or her environment, and may not be able to generalize and transfer classroom learning to everday situations out of the formal learning situation. Thus, the exceptional child may lose the opportunity to learn the very skills necessary for existence within our society.

Techniques for instruction of functional skills within the special education classroom will vary with the degree of impairment of the students involved. The techniques would include teaching of the "3 R's," generally referred to as the basics of academic instruction. Additionally, the social skills that are usually acquired by nonhandicapped students through environmental influences may require specific instruction by the special education teacher. Essentially, the teacher must decide whether to remediate deficits in academic subject areas or to concentrate on instruction in areas that could enable the student to function in as independent a manner as possible considering the limits of his or her abilities.

In functional reading, the sight-word approach is generally used to give a reading vocabulary. Teachers should consider the purpose of the instruction before selecting a method of instruction. In many cases, the level of literacy should be the level necessary for personal protection and information. Reading for protection requires minimal competence in reading itself, and must be practical for the survival of the individual (Palloway, Payne, Paton, & Payne, 1985). The sight vocabulary must include words such as restroom, men, women, danger, exit, walk, do not enter, and poison. For most special education students, vocational application of sight word skills would be a reasonable expectation. These skills would include those required to obtain and hold employment, to pass a driver's test, to complete a job application, and to order from a menu.

Functional skills training in mathematics should include those skills needed to provide a foundation for competence in vocational areas and daily living. Instruction should provide an understanding of measurement (both in carpentry and cooking), ordering, checking, paying bills, time, budgeting, purchasing, and making change. Mathematics is used much more in daily life than is realized by individuals who are able to assimilate knowledge without formal instruction. Consider the complexities involved in calculating a grocery bill, including taxes, without the ability to perform multiplication procedures, much less percent calculations. It is highly recommended that the use of a hand-held calculator be included in all programs of mathematics for special education students. Estimation should be included also so that the individual will be able to recognize correct and incorrect calculations. Counting of change is an extremely important aspect of functional mathematics skills for the handicapped. Remediation of deficits is not appropriate for the handicapped as a rule. Functional skills should be considered in mathematics prior to instruction in the more traditional mathematics operations. A project for developing survival skills for "regular" students is discussed by Frey-Mason (1985). This technique could easily be adapted for the special education population.

Training in functional skills in written language should emphasize legibility. A student should be instructed in signing his or her name, completing an employment application, taking an order, writing a personal check, and executing basic personal correspondence. The signature should be accomplished in cursive style; however, all other writing can be in either cursive or manuscript, whichever is more legible. A student will be able to write only what he or she is able to read in most cases; therefore, the amount of written language will depend to a great extent on reading skills. The use of microcomputers is encouraged for the handicapped in writing tasks. Lerner (1985) provides an overview of methods and theories of written language for the special child.

Frequently, the handicapped individual will require specific training in social skills. These should include specific instruction in developing appropriate peer relationships, classroom behaviors, and relationships with adults.

While many children are able to learn these skills from their environment, specific techniques should be considered for the special education child to enable him or her to function in a socially acceptable manner.

REFERENCES

Frey-Mason, P. (1985). Teaching basic mathematics and survival skills. *Mathematics Teacher, 78*, 669–671.

Lerner, J. (1985). *Learning disabilities: Theories, diagnosis, and teaching strategies* (4th ed.). Boston: Houghton Mifflin.

Palloway, E. A., Payne, J. S., Patton, J. R., & Payne, R. A. (1985). *Strategies for teaching retarded and special needs learners* (3rd. ed.). Columbus, OH: Merrill.

JAMES H. MILLER
JOHN F. CAWLEY
University of New Orleans

FUNCTIONAL DOMAINS
FUNCTIONAL VOCABULARY

FUNCTIONAL VISION

The term functional vision is associated with the name of Natalie Barraga, a pioneer figure in emphasizing the importance of helping children with severe visual limitations to use their residual visual abilities as effectively as possible (Barraga, 1964, 1970, 1976, 1980). The term functional vision, as defined by Barraga (1976, p. 15) denotes "how a person uses whatever vision he may have."

As Cartwright, Cartwright, and Ward (1984) have observed, the federal regulations for PL 94-142 have defined visual handicaps for school purposes so that the consideration of functional vision is primary. As defined in that law, "Visually handicapped means a visual impairment which, even with correction, adversely affects a child's educational performance." Thus the concept of functional vision is one that emphasizes what the visually handicapped child can do, rather than a particular type of physical visual limitation.

A functional vision assessment of children with visual problems attempts to determine how well a visually handicapped student is able to use the visual abilities and skills he or she possesses (Livingston, 1986). It usually involves the use of informal checklists that professionals working with the visually handicapped (e.g., teachers of visually impaired students, low-vision specialists, optometrists, orientation and mobility specialists) are asked to complete as per their particular observations.

The California Ad Hoc Committee on Assessment (Roessing, 1982) has developed a comprehensive criterion-referenced checklist for functional vision assessment. This covers the skills required for activities of daily living within a school setting, mobility, and academics. Barraga (1983) has developed the Program to Develop Efficiency in Visual Functioning, which provides an observational checklist and a diagnostic assessment procedure (DAP) for the developmental assessment of a wide range of visual skills. She also provides lesson plans to develop visual efficiencies.

Since children with multiple handicaps require specialized assessment, a number of functional vision assessment devices have been created to meet their needs. Among them is Langley's (1980) Functional Vision Inventory for the Multiply and Severely Handicapped.

REFERENCES

Barraga, N. C. (1964). *Increased visual behavior in low vision children*. New York: American Foundation for the Blind.

Barraga, N. C. (1970). *Teacher's guide for development of visual learning abilities and utilization of low vision*. Louisville, KY: American Printing House for the Blind.

Barraga, N. C. (1976). *Visual handicaps and learning: A developmental approach*, Belmont CA: Wadsworth.

Barraga, N. C. (1980). *Source book on low vision*. Louisville, KY: American Printing House for the Blind.

Barraga, N. C. (1983). *Visual handicaps and learning*. Austin, TX: Exceptional Resources.

Cartwright, G. P., Cartwright, C. A., & Ward, M. E. (1984). *Educating special learners* (2nd ed.). Belmont, CA: Wadsworth.

Langley, M. B. (1980). *Functional vision inventory for the multiple and severely handicapped*. Chicago: Stoelting.

Livingston, R. (1986). Visual impairments. In N. G. Haring & L. McCormick (Eds.), *Exceptional children and youth* (4th ed., pp. 398–429). Columbus, OH: Merrill.

Roessing, L. J. (1982). Functional vision: Criterion-referenced checklists. In S. S. Mangold (Ed.), *A teacher's guide to the special educational needs of blind and visually handicapped children*. New York: American Foundation for the Blind.

JANET S. BRAND
Hunter College, City University of New York

VISUAL IMPAIRMENT

FUNCTIONAL VOCABULARY

The development of functional reading vocabularies acquired significance as a result of the realization that the acquisition of functional academic skills was the upper limit of academic achievement for moderately/severely retarded persons (Gearheart & Litton, 1975). Prior to the time of that realization (late 1950s and 1960s) many curricula for the trainable retarded, although watered down, were not designed for functionality.

The content of an appropriate functional vocabulary (whether reading or speaking) is determined by analyzing the current and expected environmental demands for the student. Factors that influence the content include the age of the student, the degree of mobility independence the student has, the expected adult environment (e.g., shel-

tered workshop, competitive employment, custodial care), and the student's likes and dislikes. According to Musselwhite and St. Louis (1982), functional vocabulary content for severely handicapped persons should be based on client preferences and should be in the here and now rather than the future or past directed. They should also be words that occur with frequency. Many writers (Baroff, 1974; Holland, 1975; Lichtman, 1974; Schilit & Caldwell, 1980; Snell, 1983) have attempted to develop core functional lexicons or lists of sources for such lexicons. However, most researchers (including the mentioned writers) would agree that for a vocabulary to be truly functional, it must be based on an individual's experience and not on assumed common experience.

Bricker (1983) states that vocabulary instruction for moderately/severely retarded children must involve the primary caregiver (usually a parent). Instruction must involve association with an object, the client's use of the object, and word recognition in context. Guess, Sailor, and Baer (1978) provide support and extension for Bricker's statement. Functional words must be used consistently and frequently by all persons in the child's environment if they are to be learned (Musselwhite & St. Louis, 1982). According to Guess et al. (1978) and Bricker (1983), it is important to teach a child words that allow him or her to gain a degree of control over the environment, as these words are likely to lead to reinforcing consequences.

The content of a functional reading vocabulary for an individual is likely to change considerably over time. For elementary school-aged children, the content is usually aimed at warning signs and survival (e.g., danger, stop, men, women), whereas at the secondary and adult level, the content will include words associated with work, travel, and money management (Baroff, 1974; Drew et al., 1984). Sources for functional reading vocabularies include newspapers, street signs, price tags, job applications, recipes, telephone directories, and bank forms. Schilit and Caldwell (1980) produced a list of the 100 most essential career/vocational words, but Brown and Perlmutter (1971) contend that such lists are ineffective since they often do not match the experiences of individual clients.

Although most moderately retarded persons are severely limited with regard to reading, a number of researchers have been able to demonstrate that instruction based on a whole word/task analysis approach is effective (Brown et al., 1974; Sidman & Cresson, 1973). Any functional reading vocabulary should be taught in context. Snell (1983) offers an example of a pedestrian skills program during which students would take walks and read walk, don't walk, and stop signs. Brown et al. (1974) suggest a similar approach.

REFERENCES

Baroff, G. A. (1974). *Mental retardation: Nature, cause and management*. New York: Holsted.

Bricker, D. (1983). Early communication: Development and training. In M. E. Snell (Ed.), *Systematic instruction of the moderately and severely handicapped* (pp. 269–288). Columbus, OH: Merrill.

Brown, L., Huppler, B., Pierce, F., York, R., & Sontag, E. (1974). Teaching trainable level students to read unconjugated action verbs. *Journal of Special Education, 8,* 51–56.

Brown, L., & Perlmutter, L. (1971). Teaching functional reading to trainable level retarded students. *Education & Training of the Mentally Retarded, 6,* 74–84.

Drew, C. J., Logan, D. R., & Hardman, M. L. (1984). *Mental retardation. A life cycle approach.* St. Louis: Times Mirror/Mosby.

Guess, D., Sailor, W., & Baer, D. (1978). Children with limited language. In R. L. Schiefelbusch (Ed.), *Language intervention strategies* (pp. 101–143). Baltimore, MD: University Park Press.

Holland, A. (1975). Language therapy for children: Some thoughts on context and content. *Journal of Hearing Disorders, 40,* 514–523.

Lichtman, M. (1974). The development and validation of R/EAL: An instrument to assess functional literacy. *Journal of Reading Behavior, 6,* 167–182.

Musselwhite, C. R., & St. Louis, K. W. (1982). *Communication programming for the severely handicapped: Vocal and nonvocal strategies.* San Diego, CA: College-Hill.

Schilit, J., & Caldwell, M. L. (1980). A word list of essential career/vocational words for mentally retarded students. *Education & Training of the Mentally Retarded, 15*(2), 113–117.

Sidman, M. (1971). Reading and audio visual equivalencies. *Journal of Speech & Hearing Research, 14,* 5–13.

Sidman, M., & Cresson, O. (1973). Reading and cross modal transfer of stimulus equivalencies in severe retardation. *American Journal of Mental Deficiency, 77,* 515–523.

Snell, M. E. (1983). Functional reading. In M. E. Snell (Ed.), *Systematic instruction of the moderately and severely handicapped* (pp. 445–487). Columbus, OH: Merrill.

JAMES K. MCAFEE
Pennsylvania State University

FUNCTIONAL DOMAINS
FUNCTIONAL INSTRUCTION
FUNCTIONAL SKILLS
FUNCTIONAL VISION

FUTURE PROBLEM SOLVING PROGRAM (FPSP)

The Future Problem Solving Program (FPSP) is a year-long program for gifted children. Begun by E. Paul Torrance in 1974 as a high-school classroom project, the program has spread to all grade levels in all areas of the United States and more than 14 other countries. In 1985, it was estimated that approximately 120,000 students were participating in the program.

Based on the creative problem-solving process developed by Osborn (1967), the program challenges youngsters to follow a six-step process to solve futuristic problems. The regular program is divided into three age divisions: Juniors (grades 4–6), Intermediates (grades 7–9), and Seniors (grades 10–12). Each team receives three practice problems that are to be completed and sent to evaluators by designated due dates. After evaluation, the work is returned with scores and suggestions for improvement.

The most proficient teams are invited to participate in state FPSP Bowls held each spring. The three winning teams, one from each level, receive invitations to attend the International FPSP Conference, usually held in June.

The selection of topics to be studied each year is determined by a vote of students, coaches, and state FPSP directors. Topics have included such concerns as genetic engineering, artificial intelligence, feeding the world, and organ transplants.

The program also offers a purely instructional and non-competitive component for younger children, the Primary Division. Designed for children in grades K–3, the Primary Division also serves older children who are not yet ready for the complexity of the regular program. Like the regular program, the Primary Division provides three practice problems, which, when completed, are sent to evaluators who score them and return them with constructive comments. The topics for this division are of current concern and geared to the children's interests.

Crabbe (1985) provides a more detailed description of the program. Information regarding participation may be obtained from FPSP, St. Andrews College, Laurinburg, NC 28352.

REFERENCES

Crabbe, A. (1985). *The coach's guide to the Future Problem Solving Program.* Laurinburg, NC: Future Problem Solving Program.

Osborn, A. F. (1967). *Applied imagination* (3rd ed.). New York: Scribner's.

ANNE B. CRABBE
St. Andrews College

CREATIVE PROBLEM SOLVING
CREATIVITY
TORRANCE, E. PAUL

G

GAIT DISTURBANCES

Walking depends on the integration of sensory-motor-vestibular brain systems, as well as the functional strength and range of motion of the component body parts (Stolov & Clowers, 1981). Normal walking is developmentally linked to the orderly sequential integration of postural reflexes into automated smooth, adaptive responses that permit movement forward, backward, and up and down stairs by approximately 3 years of age. Clinical experience with children with impaired gaits suggests there may be as many gait disturbances as there are muscles and joints within the body.

Any skeletal or joint injury defect or disease that limits the normal range of joint motion produces a lack of fluidity in walking, or limping gait, because of necessary compensatory movements to maintain balance. Examples may be seen in children with arthritis, arthrogryposis, achondroplastic drawfism, and fractures. The shortening of one leg produces a characteristic pelvic tilt that can contribute to scoliosis or spinal curvature in a growing child. Pain or foot deformities can also produce a limping gait.

Cerebellar gait or ataxia is a wide-based gait with irregular steps and unsteadiness, with staggering on turning; it is characteristic of children who lack balance. Young children or those with developmental delay often walk with an ataxiclike gait, with arms elevated to assist with balance.

In hemiplegic gait, the child with spastic hemiplegia leans to the afflicted side and swings the affected leg out to the side and in a semicircle (circumduction). The antigravity muscles of upper extremities are often held fixed in flexor patterns.

In scissors gait, the legs are adducted and internally rotated so that with each step the child tends to trip over the opposite foot. Toe walking increases the balance difficulty. Steps are short, jerky, and slow, with many extraneous movements of the upper extremities to facilitate balance. This is the typical pattern for the child with spastic paraplegia or mild quadriplegic cerebral palsy.

Staggering or drunken giat is seen in persons with alcohol intoxication. It may also be observed in children with brain tumor, drug poisoning, or other central nervous system impairment.

Steppage gait is characterized by lifting the knees high to flop the foot down; foot drop is evident. Some children with initial stage muscular atrophy walk in this manner. Children with Duchenne muscular dystrophy show a gait somewhat similar to the steppage gait in initial stages. As their heel cords tighten these children walk more on their toes and often fall. To maintain their tenuous balance they lean back in lordosis. As weakness progresses, these children find it increasingly difficult to come to an erect position after a fall. They use their hands to "walk up their legs" to push themselves into an erect position and achieve balance. This process is the Gower's sign. These children are vulnerable in a regular school setting because a slight touch may disturb their precarious balance and weakness prevents their using their arms to catch themselves when falling; hence, serious head injuries and fractures can result.

The gait patterns of children with involuntary movement disorders are highly variable. Some individuals with athetoid and choreiform movements, which are severe and extensive, walk with a fair degree of speed and safety while their windmill involuntary movements occur. Others with less involuntary movement may have severe concomitant balance problems that require supportive safety devices.

Specific description, diagnosis, and medical intervention relative to gait disturbances usually occurs as a result of consultation among the pediatrician, orthopedist, and neurologist. Assistive devices such as braces, corsets, splints, canes, crutches, and wheelchairs require individualized fitting and training to provide the most effective locomotion compatible with health and safety. Readjustments in the nature and use of these devices must be adapted to changes owed to growth and disease status. Clinical experience suggests that many severely crippled children who learn crutch walking for short distances find the energy required for long distances dictates wheelchair mobility to conserve energy. Mobility evaluation, including transfer and self-care status, has been found to be essential in vocational planning for young adults with gait disturbances to help them achieve more realistic vocational goals. The orthotist (brace maker) and physical and occupational therapists may implement specific exercise and training for cane and crutch walking and assist in the selection and use of wheelchairs.

REFERENCES

Banus, B. S., Kent, C., Norton, Y., Sudiennick, D., & Becker, M. (1979). *The developmental therapist.* (2nd ed.). Thorofare, NJ: Slack.

Barr, M. L. (1979). *The human nervous system: An anatomic viewpoint* (3rd ed.). New York: Harper & Row.

Chusid, J. G. (1978). *Correlative neuroanatomy and functional neurology.* (16th ed.). Los Angeles: Lang Medical.

Stolov, W. C., & Clowers, M. R. (Eds.). (1981). *Handbook of severe disability* (stock #017-090-00054-2). Washington, DC: U.S. Government Printing Office.

RACHAEL J. STEVENSON
Bedford, Ohio

ATAXIA
ADAPTIVE PHYSICAL EDUCATION
MUSCULAR DYSTROPHY
PHYSICAL ANOMALIES

GALACTOSEMIA

Galactosemia, first described in 1908, is an inborn error of galactose metabolism resulting in an accumulation of galactose in the blood, tissues, and urine. Three types of galactosemia are known; each is due to a specific enzyme deficit. Classic galactosemia (the primary emphasis of this review) is the most prevalent and most severe form. It occurs in approximately 1/60,000 births and is attributed to a marked deficiency of galactose-1-phosphate uridyl transferase. Galactokinase deficiency, less severe, occurs in 1/500,000 births and leads to the development of cataracts. A rare form, with no clear clinical abnormalities, is attributed to a deficit of EDP-glucose-4-epimerase (Hug, 1979).

Symptoms of classic galactosemia begin shortly after birth with the infant taking food poorly, vomiting frequently, and often having diarrhea. Many affected infants die during the first few weeks of life. Biochemical changes of galactosemia have even been reported in the liver of a second trimester fetus, suggesting the development of the disorder in utero (Allen et al., 1980). Other clinical manifestations include cataracts, liver damage, proteinuria, and aminoaciduria. Continued ingestion of galactose may lead to mental retardation, malnourishment, progressive failure, and death (Hug, 1979).

Diagnosis is determined by severity of the symptoms, previous diagnosis of galactosemia in siblings or parents, and certain screening methods. Tests include urinalysis to detect the presence of protein, amino acids, or galactose, and a blood enzyme analysis (Gershen, 1975). Unfortunately, tests may require several weeks for analysis, by which time much damage may have occurred. Galacto-semia may also be diagnosed prenatally through amniocentesis.

Treatment consists of elimination of galactose and lactose from the diet immediately after birth. Since galactose is mainly formed by digestion of disaccharide lactose found in milk (milk sugar), a formula made from cow's milk is replaced with a meat-based or soybean formula. On dietary intervention, most effects subside. The infant gains weight; vomiting, diarrhea, liver anomalies disappear; and cataracts regress. Since the monosaccharide galactose does not occur in free form in foods, certain carbohydrates, lipids, and proteins that eventually metabolize to galactose must also be eliminated (Gershen, 1975). A balanced galactose-free diet should be maintained at least through age five or six; some physicians recommend rigid dietary control throughout life (Staff, 1982). The diet does not in any way cure the disorder, but reduces its effects on the developing person. Galactosemic women should adhere to the diet when they become pregnant to reduce levels of circulating toxins and resulting damage to the unborn fetus. Although affected women bear children, the frequency of ovarian failure is high (Kaufman et al., 1979).

With prompt initiation of dietary treatment, galactosemic children appear normal, or nearly so. However, even early dietary intervention may only partially reduce the degree and severity of cognitive damage; IQ scores cluster in the low-normal and mildly retarded range (Staff, 1982). On the other hand, others (e.g., Fishler, Koch, Donnell, & Wenz, 1980) report a more favorable outcome. Other specific difficulties may interfere with the education of treated galactosemic children. Perceptual-motor problems may be the most serious handicap and may account for low levels of academic achievement (Waisbren, Norman, Schnell, & Levy, 1983). Additionally, galactosemic children may have speech and language difficulties, short attention spans, and difficulty with spatial and mathematical relationships. They present no significant behavior problems except for occasional apathy and withdrawal. Galactosemic children have benefited from early diagnosis and diet therapy. However, relatively little is known about long-term outcomes as few follow-ups are available. More information on optimal management is needed.

REFERENCES

Allen, J. T., Gillett, M., Holton, J. B., King, G. S., & Pettit, B. R. (1980). Evidence of galactosemia in utero. *Lancet, 2,* 603.

Fishler, K., Koch, R., Donnell, G. N., & Wenz, E. (1980). Developmental aspects of galactosemia from infancy to childhood. *Metabolism, 19,* 38–44.

Gershen, J. A. (1975). Galactosemia: A psycho-social perspective. *Mental Retardation, 13*(4), 20–23.

Hug, G. (1979). Defects in metabolism of carbohydrates. In V. C. Vaughn, R. J. McKay, Jr., & R. E. Behrman (Eds.), *Nelson textbook of pediatrics* (11th ed., pp. 520–547). Philadelphia: Saunders.

Kaufman, F., Kogut, M. D., Donnell, G. N., Koch, R., & Goebels-
    mann, U. (1979). Ovarian failure in galactosemia. *Lancet, 2*,
    737–738.

Staff. (1982). Clouds over galactosaemia. *Lancet, 2*, 1379–1380.

Waisbren, S. E., Norman, T. R., Schnell, R. R., & Levy, H. L.
    (1983). Speech and language deficits in early-treated children
    with galactosemia. *Journal of Pediatrics, 102*, 75–77.

LINDA R. LONGLEY
ROBERT T. BROWN
*University of North Carolina,
Wilmington*

BIOCHEMICAL IRREGULARITIES
CONGENITAL DISORDERS
INBORN ERRORS OF METABOLISM

GALLAGHER, JAMES J. (1926–   )

James J. Gallagher earned his BS in psychology from the
University of Pittsburgh and his MS and PhD in child and
clinical psychology at Pennsylvania State University.
Currently, Gallagher is the director of the Frank Porter
Graham Child Development Center and Kenan professor
of education at the University of North Carolina at Chapel
Hill. During his professional career, Gallagher has worked
with and studied handicapped and gifted children, and has
been active in formulating public policies for these children (Gallagher, 1984).

Gallagher has worked a great deal in the areas of public
policy, serving as associate commissioner of education
(1967–1970) and the first chief of the Bureau of Education
for the Handicapped in the U.S. Office of Education; he
was also chairman of the Social Policy Committee for Research in Child Development (1977–1978). In his work as
chairman of the North Carolina Competency Test Commission (1977–1980), he emphasized the importance of
competency testing's role in remediation (Gallagher,

James J. Gallagher

1979). His Special Education Contract (Gallagher, 1972)
may have been instrumental in the development of the
individual education plan (IEP). He called for an agreement between the school and the exceptional child's family
that details the educational plan for the child and how the
objectives would be accomplished.

In addition to his work with handicapped children, Gallagher has been a leader in the field of gifted and talented
education. He served as president of the Council for Exceptional Children (1966), The Association for the Gifted
(1970), and the World Council for Gifted and Talented
Children (1981–1985).

REFERENCES

Gallagher, J. (1972). The special education contract for mildly
    handicapped children. *Exceptional Children, 38*, 527–535.

Gallagher, J. (1979). Minimum competency: The setting of edu-
    cational standards. *Educational Evaluation & Policy Analysis,
    1*, 62–67.

Gallagher, J. (1984). The evolution of special education concepts.
    In B. Blatt & R. J. Morris (Eds.), *Perspectives in special edu-
    cation.* Glenview, IL: Scott, Foresman.

Gallagher, J. (1985). *Teaching the gifted child* (3rd ed.). Boston:
    Allyn & Bacon.

Kirk, S., & Gallagher, J. (1986). *Educating exceptional children*
    (5th ed.). Boston: Houghton Mifflin.

ANN E. LUPKOWSKI
Texas A&M University

GALLAUDET, EDWARD M. (1837–1917)

Edward Miner Gallaudet, the originator of higher education for the deaf, was the youngest son of Thomas Hopkins Gallaudet, founder of the first school for the deaf in
the United States. While teaching in his father's school,
Gallaudet was chosen to organize a new school for the deaf
in Washington, DC, the Columbia Institution, which came
into existence in 1857 with Gallaudet as superintendent.
Believing that deaf students should have the same opportunity as hearing students to receive a higher education,
Gallaudet obtained legislation, approved by President
Lincoln, giving the Columbia Institution the power to
grant college degrees. A higher education department was
created, and in 1894 it was named Gallaudet College, in
honor of Edward Gallaudet's father.

An early eclectic in the education of the deaf, Gallaudet
advocated a system of instruction that combined the language of signs with speech and speech reading. He was
primarily responsible for the adoption of oral teaching
methods by the state residential schools for the deaf in the
United States.

REFERENCE

Boatner, M. T. (1959). *Voice of the deaf: A biography of Edward Miner Gallaudet*. Washington, DC: Public Affairs Press.

PAUL IRVINE
Katonah, New York

GALLAUDET, THOMAS HOPKINS (1787–1851)

Thomas Hopkins Gallaudet established the first school for the deaf in the United States in Hartford, Connecticut, in 1817, using methods that he had learned when visiting the *Institution Nationale des Sourds Muets* in Paris, and assisted by a teacher from that school, Laurent Clerc. Gallaudet served as principal of the Hartford school, later named the American School for the Deaf, until 1830, and continued on its board of directors for the rest of his life.

Gallaudet married one of his first students at the school. His oldest son, Thomas, became a minister to the deaf. His youngest son, Edward, established a school for the deaf in Washington, DC, the advanced department of which became Gallaudet College, named in honor of Thomas Hopkins Gallaudet.

REFERENCES

DeGerring, E. B. (1964). *Gallaudet, friend of the deaf*. New York: McKay.

Lane, H. (1984). *When the mind hears*. New York: Random House.

PAUL IRVINE
Katonah, New York

GALLAUDET COLLEGE

Gallaudet College, in Washington, DC, is the only liberal arts college for the deaf in the world. The college was formed in 1864 as a department of the Columbia Institution for the Deaf, now the Kendall School for the Deaf, by Amos Kendall, who had been postmaster general under President Andrew Jackson, and Edward Miner Gallaudet, superintendent of the Columbia Institution. The two men obtained the necessary federal legislation, which was signed by President Lincoln, to establish this national college for the deaf. In 1894 the college department became Gallaudet College, named in honor of Edward Miner Gallaudet's father, Thomas Hopkins Gallaudet, who established the first school for the deaf in the United States.

In addition to a distinguished record of success in the education of its students, Gallaudet College has provided much of the leadership in the education of the deaf in the United States. Its teacher-training program has provided both deaf and hearing teachers of the deaf. Many of the leaders in the field during the past century have been products of the Gallaudet College program.

REFERENCES

Boatner, M. T. (1959). *Voice of the deaf: A biography of Edward Miner Gallaudet*. Washington, DC: Public Affairs.

Gallaudet, E. M. (1983). *History of the College for the Deaf, 1857–1907*. Washington, DC: Gallaudet College Press.

PAUL IRVINE
Katonah, New York

GALTON, FRANCIS (1822–1911)

Sir Francis Galton, born in England in 1822, came from an intellectual family; his mother, Violetta Darwin, was the aunt of Charles Darwin, and his grandfather, Samuel Galton, was a fellow of the Royal Society. The youngest of a family of nine, he was brought up in a large house near Birmingham, where his father ran a bank. Galton was a precocious child. From material in Pearson's biography, Terman (1917) estimated Galton's childhood IQ at 200. He was the author of over 300 publications, including 17 books covering a broad range of topics.

Galton pioneered in the development of psychological testing and the formulation of the major genetic principle of segregation of inherited characteristics. He is perhaps best known for his work on the genetic basis of individual differences in intelligence as discussed in his book, *Hereditary Genius* (1869). He was an early proponent of eugenics, a term coined by him.

In his research on the relationship of the characteristics of parents and offspring, Galton discovered the phenomenon of regression toward the mean and developed the concept of correlation, a term first used by him. Galton's measure of correlation was later given mathematical refinement by Karl Pearson, who later wrote a biography of Galton (Pearson, 1914). A more recent biography was prepared by Forrest (1974).

REFERENCES

Forest, D. W. (1974). *Francis Galton: The life and work of a Victorian genius*. New York: Toplinger.

Galton, F. (1869). Heredity genius: An inquiry into its laws and consequences. London: Macmillan.

Galton, F. (1908). *Memories of my life*. London: Methuen.

Pearson, K. (1914). *The life, letters and labours of Francis Galton*. Cambridge, England: Cambridge University Press.

Terman, L. M. (1917). The intelligence quotient of Francis Galton in childhood. *American Journal of Psychology, 28*, 209.

ROBERT C. NICHOLS
DIANE JARVIS
*State University of New York,
Buffalo*

GAMES FOR THE HANDICAPPED

Games for the handicapped can serve both recreational and educational purposes. Games are the purest form of recreation in that they require cooperation among participants. However, games also require certain degrees of mental and physical skill. Even simple table games such as Parchesii necessitate decisions that involve unpredictable circumstances. Active games such as tug of war and football require strength and endurance as well as physical skill.

Recreational games for the handicapped can be categorized in a number of ways. First, there are interactive card games such as Uno and Old Maid, in which the players have to cooperate and compete with each other. Such games for the handicapped may have to be adjusted to the players' limitations by changing the rules or the nature of the cards, e.g., size of the print on the cards.

Second, there are table games such as Monopoly, checkers, and Trivial Pursuit, that stimulate critical thinking skills by the participants. They can be used to foster educational goals such as how to think logically and how to handle money. A third type of game involves varying degrees of movement and physical exercise, e.g., tossing a frisbee or a bean bag, or playing marbles.

Since 1975 a fourth type game for the handicapped, one played with a computer has become popular. Computer games can be modified or even designed to fit the motor and intellectual capabilities of handicapped students. For instance, in Star War-type games, the speed of the airships can be scaled up or down to adjust to the response characteristics of the players. Computer-assisted devices with programmable games have been found helpful in developing eye-hand coordination anticipatory skills, and intellectual curiosity (Polloway et al., 1985).

Special education teachers often use games to achieve their educational goals. Since games are usually conducted in informal atmospheres, the pressures to learn are not overbearing or evident to the student. In games the special education teacher is able to use guessing, searching, competition, and social interaction as means of instruction. Special education teachers use the informality and the basic elements of games to develop academic, visual, motor, and language skills, tactile sense, and body image (Schlein et al., 1985). In addition, games can be used to foster mimicry in language-disordered children.

In selecting or developing games for the handicapped, Carlson and Gingland (1979) suggest the following guidelines:

1. Games should be selected to help participants gain confidence in themselves.
2. Excessive physical or mental competition should be avoided.
3. Frustrating physical or mental work in games should be avoided.
4. Games in which the concentration time is appropriate to the participants' capabilities should be selected.
5. Quiet and active games should be alternated to avoid overstimulation.
6. Only one game should be introduced during a lesson.
7. Well-liked games should be repeated.
8. Rules and conduct of play should be flexible.
9. Games that require participants to use perceptual and motor skills should be included.

REFERENCES

Carlson, B., & Gingland, D. (1979). *Recreation for retarded teenagers and young adults*. New York: Abingdon.

Polloway, E., Payne, J., Patton, J., & Payne, R. (1985). *Strategies for teaching retarded and special needs learners*. Columbus, OH: Merrill.

Schlien, S., Tuckner, B., & Heyne, L. (1985). Leisure education programs for the severely disabled student. *Parks & Recreation, 17*(1), 74–78.

Wehman, P., & Schlein, S. (1981). *Leisure programs for handicapped persons: Adaptations, techniques and curriculum*. Baltimore, MD: University Park.

THOMAS BURKE
*Hunter College, City University
of New York*

CAMPING FOR THE HANDICAPPED
EQUINE THERAPY
RECREATION THERAPY

GAMMA-AMINOBUTYRIC ACID (GABA)

Gamma-aminobutyric acid (GABA) is a major inhibitory neurotransmitter in the central nervous system. Specific functions of the brain depend on adequate levels of neurotransmitters in the areas that control such functions. This knowledge has stimulated a search for drugs that can augment or reduce the supply of particular neurotransmitters. A deficiency of GABA has been associated with several diseases, including schizophrenia and epilepsy

(Hammond & Wilder, 1985). A new GABA-elevating drug, gamma-vinyl GABA, has had impressive therapeutic benefits for epilepsy patients. This drug crosses the blood brain barrier and causes a dose-dependent, long-lasting increase in brain concentrations of GABA.

Recent studies show the drug Piracetam, a GABA analogue, may be useful as an adjunct for the clinical remediation of dyslexia (Chase, Russell, Schmitt, & Tallal 1984; Wilsher, Atkins, & Manfield, 1985). Dyslexia is believed to result from a left cerebral hemisphere dysfunction. Piracetam has been found to increase verbal learning and improve performance on left hemisphere-related tasks. It is well tolerated and appears to have no negative effects. Further investigation is warranted on issues of dosage, duration, interaction with other remedial procedures, and the differential effects of Piracetam on the various subgroups of learning-disabled populations.

REFERENCES

Chase, C., Russell, G., Schmitt, R. L., & Tallal, P. (1984). A new chemotherapeutic investigation: Piracetam effects on dyslexia. *Annals of Dyslexia, 34,* 29–48.

Hammond, E. J., & Wilder, B. J. (1985). Gamma-vinyl GABA: A new antiepileptic drug. *Clinical Neuropharmacology, 8*(1), 1–12.

Wilsher, C., Atkins, G., & Manfield, P. (1985). Effect of Piracetam on dyslexics' reading ability. *Journal of Learning Disabilities, 18,* 19–25.

BARBARA S. SPEER
*Shaker Heights City School
District, Shaker Heights,
Ohio*

NEUROLOGICAL ORGANIZATION

GARGOYLISM

See HURLER'S SYNDROME.

GARRETT, EMMA (1846–1893)

Emma Garrett, seeking a way to demonstrate the effectiveness of the oral method of teaching the deaf, obtained a grant that enabled her, with her sister Mary, to establish the Pennsylvania Home for the Training in Speech of Deaf Children Before They Are of School Age, also known as the Bala Home. Located in Philadelphia, the home began operation in 1891. Emma Garrett was superintendent, and both sisters served as teachers. The Bala Home was widely influential as an example of the effectiveness of the oral method of teaching the deaf and of the efficacy of early intervention. Following Emma Garrett's death in 1893, her sister became superintendent of the Bala Home and carried on the work that the two of them had begun.

REFERENCE

Fay, E. A. (1893). *Histories of American schools for the deaf, 1817–1893* (Vol. 3). Washington, DC: Volta Bureau.

PAUL IRVINE
Katonah, New York

GARRETT, MARY SMITH (1839–1925)

Mary Smith Garrett, with her sister Emma, in 1891 founded in Philadelphia the Pennsylvania Home for the Training in Speech of Deaf Children Before They Are of School Age, also known as the Bala Home. Mary Garrett succeeded her sister as superintendent after Emma died in 1893. She continued in this position for the remainder of her life.

Mary Garrett was a leading advocate of the oral method of teaching the deaf and helped to develop a curriculum based on this approach. Her system of teaching oral communication was based on early intervention, with speech training beginning as early as 2 years of age. Through the efforts of Mary and her sister, Pennsylvania became the first state to appropriate funds for preschool speech and language training for deaf children.

Mary Garrett was instrumental in the enactment of legislation establishing a juvenile court and probation system for Pennsylvania. She was also a leader in the National Congress of Mothers, the forerunner of the National Congress of Parents and Teachers, where she promoted such social reforms as child labor laws and juvenile court legislation.

REFERENCE

Fay, E. A. (1893). *Histories of American schools for the deaf, 1817–1893* (Vol. 3). Washington, DC: Volta Bureau.

PAUL IRVINE
Katonah, New York

GARRISON, S. OLIN (1853–1900)

S. Olin Garrison, minister and educator, founded in New Jersey in 1887 the school for retarded children that later became the Training School at Vineland. The school featured a cottage system of small, homelike facilities, a strong educational program, and a research department that published some of the nation's most influential works on mental retardation. Garrison served as superintendent of the Training School until his death in 1900. He was also responsible for the establishment by New Jersey of the State Home for Girls and of a school for epileptic children.

REFERENCE

McCaffrey, K. R. (1965). *Founders of the Training School at Vineland, New Jersey: S. Olin Garrison, Alexander Johnson, Edward R. Johnstone*. Unpublished doctoral dissertation. Teachers College, Columbia University, New York.

PAUL IRVINE
Katonah, New York

GATES-MACGINITIE READING TESTS, SECOND EDITION

The purpose of the Gates-MacGinitie Reading Tests, Levels A through F, is to provide the teacher with an idea of the overall level of reading achievement of individuals and groups of students. These survey tests may be used to identify students who might profit from remediation or more advanced work. The tests can also be used to evaluate the general effects of instructional programs.

The tests have six levels ranging from primary through senior high school. All items on the tests are multiple choice. Each test level is color coded. All tests measure vocabulary and comprehension except the Basic R form, which also tests for letter recognition and letter sounds. Directions for administering the test are clear and easy to follow.

No specific diagnosis can be done, but the test norms are useful for deciding who would benefit from further diagnosis. Percentile ranks, normal curve equivalents, stanines, and grade equivalents are provided. Scoring can either be done by hand or through the Houghton Mifflin Scoring Service. This series of tests can provide the teacher with the information necessary to determine the general level of reading achievement of both individuals and groups. The tests have good validity. Reliabilities, while varying, are high.

REFERENCES

Gates-MacGinitie reading tests. (1978). In O. K. Buros (Ed.), *The eighth mental measurements yearbook* (Vol. II, pp. 1190–1193). Highland Park, NJ: Gryphon Press.

Teacher's manual: Gates-MacGinitie reading tests. (1978). Boston: Houghton Mifflin.

RONALD V. SCHMELZER
Eastern Kentucky University

GATES, MCKILLOP, HOROWITZ READING DIAGNOSTIC TESTS, SECOND EDITION

The Gates, McKillop, Horowitz Reading Diagnostic Test is a revised edition of the Gates-McKillop Reading Diagnostic Tests. Its purpose is to assess strengths and weaknesses in reading and, to a lesser degree, related areas, of children in grades 1 through 6. It may also be used to assess reading difficulties of older students.

The test battery consists of 15 individually administered tests divided into eight areas: (1) oral reading; (2) sentence reading; (3) flash words (sight words); (4) untimed words (word-attack skills); (5) word parts; (6) visual form of sounds (measures the child's ability to aurally recognize and associate a normal letter with its sound); (7) auditory tests, including auditory blending and auditory discrimination; and (8) written expression (spelling and an informal writing sample). Grade scores are given for each of the tests except the informal writing sample. The manual provides detailed instructions on how to administer and, to a lesser degree, interpret the results.

Although there is little technical data regarding the development of the test included in the manual, this limitation may not be serious, depending on how the test is used. The test appears to have good content validity and has value as a means of assessing particular reading problems. This test will yield more useful information if the administrator/evaluator is an experienced and skilled reading teacher and diagnostician.

REFERENCES

Gates-McKillop reading diagnostic tests. (1978). In O. K. Buros (Ed.), *The eighth mental measurement yearbook* (Vol. II, pp. 1252–1255). Highland Park, NJ: Gryphon Press.

Manual of directions: Gates, McKillop, Horowitz reading diagnostic tests. (1981). (2nd Ed.). New York: Teachers College Press.

RONALD V. SCHMELZER
Eastern Kentucky University

GAZE AVERSION

Eye contact, the study of facial characteristics during human intercourse, has been a topic that has always captivated inquiry. Why do we maintain eye contact during social interaction? What is there in facial cues that provide others social clues and to what do these clues address? Are there normal patterns of gaze aversion?

The answer to the last question is a definite yes. It is neither socially correct nor communicatively enriching to look continuously at another person's face. Researchers (Beattie, 1979) have advanced a hypothesis that gaze aversion is a technique that reduces distractibility and permits thinking and speech planning. Ehrlichman (1981) advanced this hypothesis, which his data supported, as a statement of cognitive interference. Simply, the hypothesis postulates that people look away more often during periods of speech hesitancy than during periods of fluency. Gaze aversion is used while thinking and planning the next speech pattern.

Coss (1979) believed that the dimensions of gaze in psychotic children were different in several respects. He ran three studies. The first examined 10 normal and 10 psychotic children during presentations of five models comprising a blank model and models with one through four concentric discoid elements separated by the same interpupillary distance as human eyes. The second experiment examined 15 psychotic children using models presenting two concentric discoid elements in vertical, diagonal, and horizontal orientations. The third experiment examined 10 normal and 10 psychotic children using five models comprising two schematic facing eyes as represented by concentric discoid elements. The psychotics looked longer at the models than did the normals. However, these groups did not differ for the model with two concentric discoid elements. Both groups, particulary the psychotics, looked less at the model presenting two concentric discoid elements than at the models presenting other arrangements of concentric discoid elements in the first experiment. Similarly, in the third experiment, both groups looked less at the model with two concentric discoid elements than at models with staring and averted irises. In sum, normals and psychotics did not differ appreciably in their gaze under varying conditions.

Currently, there is no data to support the long-standing belief that gaze aversion occurs with greater duration or more frequency among emotionally disturbed than among normal children. Scheman and Lockhard (1979) generated data from 573 children suggesting that gaze or stare is developmentally determined. Children under 18 months of age rarely establish eye contact. Children 18 months to 5 years do not avert their gaze. From 5 to 9 years, behavioral patterns specific to the youth are well established. This study took place in a suburban shopping center where the children were unprotected by parents' wishes when confronted by gaze from strange adults. This work lends strong support to the communication theory of gaze aversion. That, in turn suggests that gaze aversion is not solely a function of development, conditions, or emotional problems, but is a device that provides and protects concentration and is instrumental in speech production. Therefore, children with fluency difficulties, e.g., stutters, may have increased gaze aversion, a contention that is also supported in the research literature.

REFERENCES

Beattie, G. W. (1979). Planning units in spontaneous speech: Some evidence from hesitation in speech and speaker gaze direction in conversation. *Linguistics, 17,* 61–78.

Coss, R. G. (1979). Perceptual determinants of gaze aversion by normal and psychotic children: The role of two facing eyes. *Behavior, 3–4.* 228–253.

Ehrlichman, H. (1981). From gaze aversion to eye movement suppression: An investigation of the cognitive interference explanation of gaze patterns during conversation. *British Journal of Social Psychology, 20,* 233–241.

Scheman, J. D., & Lockhard, J. S. (1979). Development of gaze aversion in children. *Child Development, 50,* 594–596.

DAVID A. SABATINO
*West Virginia College
of Graduate Studies*

GEARHEART, BILL R. (1918–   )

Bill R. Gearheart earned his BA in math and physics from Friends University in Wichita, Kansas, in 1949. He received his MEd in school administration from Wichita State University in 1955 and his PhD in educational psychology and special education from the University of Northern Colorado in 1963. In the early part of his career in public education, Gearheart filled the roles of teacher, elementary principal, director of special services, and assistant superintendent. In 1966 he moved on to the university level and eventually became full professor. During his tenure at the University of Northern Colorado, Gearheart spent 6 years as director of the Navajo Education Project. Gearheart has taken early retirement and is currently serving as professor emeritus of special education at the University of Northern Colorado.

Gearheart's academic interests include preparation of regular classroom teachers to work with mildly handi-

Bill R. Gearheart

capped students, administration of special education, and professional writing in special education. He has been most profilic in this last area, writing numerous college texts in special education. Several revisions have been made of two of his major texts (Gearheart, 1973, 1977, 1981, 1985; Gearheart & Weishahn, 1976, 1980, 1984). Gearheart is a specialist in organizing educational programs for handicapped children and has been involved in legislation relating to handicapped children. He has been an active special education advocate at the national level. From 1967 to 1970, he served on the U.S. Office of Education panel involved in awarding federal grants in special education; for two of those years he served as chairperson. He spent 5 years as a field adviser to the Bureau of Education for the Handicapped, evaluating applications for research funds. Gearheart also has been a member of different federal site visit teams, visiting numerous major universities that offer the doctorate in special education. At the state level, Gearheart has been involved with special education projects for various state departments of education. In addition, he has assisted numerous local education agencies in planning and programming various special education services.

Involved in special education for over 25 years, Gearheart's major contributions to the field are twofold. First, he has written a dozen texts in special education (three in foreign translations). His development of practitioner-oriented texts has made his work familiar to many special educators and regular classroom educators. Second, he has been involved in the preparation of special educators at the doctoral level. His training contributions are seen in former students who now reside in more than half of the states and several foreign countries. A unique contribution to the field is Gearheart's directorship of the Navajo Education Project, initiating special education programming in Board of Indian Affairs schools of the Navajo reservation. Currently, Gearheart teaches courses at the University of Northern Colorado and conducts workshops on professional writing.

REFERENCES

Gearheart, B. R. (1973). *Learning disabilities: Educational strategies*. St. Louis: Mosby.

Gearheart, B. R. (1977). *Learning disabilities: Educational strategies*. (2nd ed.). St. Louis: Mosby.

Gearheart, B. R. (1981). *Learning disabilities: Educational strategies*. (3rd ed.). St. Louis: Mosby.

Gearheart, B. R. (1985). *Learning disabilities: Educational strategies*. (4th ed.). St. Louis: Mosby.

Gearheart, B. R., Weishahn, M. (1976). *The handicapped child in the regular classroom*. St. Louis: Mosby.

Gearheart, B. R., & Weishahn, M. (1980). *The handicapped child in the regular classroom*. (2nd ed.). St. Louis: Mosby.

Gearheart, B. R., & Weishahn, M. (1984). *The exceptional student in the regular classroom*. (3rd ed.). St. Louis: Mosby.

KATHRYN A. SULLIVAN
Texas A&M University

GENERAL APTITUDE TEST BATTERY (GATB)

The General Aptitude Test Battery (GATB) was developed by the U.S. Employment Service as a means of assisting clients (and those at state employment offices) in identifying possible successful occupational areas. The battery is composed of 12 separately timed and scored tests that measure nine aptitudes. Scores are then used to point out areas of client strengths and weaknesses. There are two forms, A & B. The nine tests measure (1) intelligence, the general learning ability of the client; (2) verbal aptitude, the ability to understand words and their relationships; (3) numerical aptitude, the ability to perform arithmetic quickly and accurately; (4) spatial aptitude, the ability to think visually of geometric forms and to recognize relationships resulting from the movement of objects in space; (5) form perception, the ability to perceive pertinent details and make visual discriminations; (6) clerical perception, the ability to discriminate similarities and differences in verbal material; (7) motor coordination, the ability to coordinate eyes and hands rapidly and accurately; (8) finger dexterity, the ability to move and manipulate small objects with the fingers rapidly and accurately; and (9) manual dexterity, the ability to move the hands skillfully in placing and turning motions.

Scores on the various subtests are correlated with occupations; tentative cutoff scores are provided for each occupational area. The GATB is one of the more researched aptitude test batteries presently available. The battery takes approximately 2 hours. The test administrator is certified to give the test by attending a workshop covering the test's administration and interpretation. Workshops are presented by state employment offices.

REFERENCES

Manual for the USES general aptitude test battery. Minneapolis, MN: Intran.

USES general aptitude test battery (1978). In O. K. Buros (Ed.), *The eighth mental measurement yearbook* (Vol. II, pp. 675–680). Highland Park, NJ: Gryphon Press.

RONALD V. SCHMELZER
Eastern Kentucky University

GENERAL CASE PROGRAMMING

The essence of general case programming is generalization. A teacher or trainer engaging in general case programming is systematically increasing the probability of skills learned in one setting being successfully performed in different settings with different target stimuli (Horner, Sprague, & Wilcox, 1982).

There are several trends in special education that coalesce to underscore the importance of general case programming. There has been a growing interest in training relevant age-appropriate skills that can be immediately used by a student in his or her real-life environment (Brown et al., 1979; Brown et al., 1983). For many students, particularly at the secondary level and above, this call for relevancy translates into community-based skills. Even though the community is the desired environment for performance, it presents a demanding set of circumstances for instruction. There are just too many different forms of transportation, restaurants, stores, people, jobs, etc., to train in all situations. Therefore, any training strategy must be efficient and promote generalization. The training examples a teacher selects must increase the likelihood of students performing correctly on similar but untrained examples and must be the fewest number of examples necessary to create this generalization. It is these two criteria that general case instruction is designed to meet.

Stimulus control is an important concept for general case programming. This control is achieved when environmental events, or discriminative stimuli, are able to cue correct performance. All stimuli have certain characteristics that are either relevant or irrelevant for correct performance. General case instruction teaches students to respond to the relevant stimulus characteristics and ignore the irrelevant by systematically varying the dimensions and levels of stimuli presented during instruction. By varying the dimensions and levels of stimuli, students come to identify a group or class of stimuli that share certain relevant characteristics and set the occasion for correct responding. The stimulus class comes to control the selection of correct responses because response characteristics have been automatically varied along with the variation in stimulus characteristics, creating a class of relevant or effective responses from the pool of all possible responses.

There are several guidelines that have been identified by Horner et al. (1982) for creating a general case curriculum:

1. Define the instructional universe by identifying all the situations in which a student is expected to produce a particular behavioral outcome.

2. Identify the range of relevant stimulus and response variation in the instructional universe by systematically analyzing the situations within which a student is expected to perform.

3. Select the minimum number of logistically feasible examples for training and testing that will sample the full range of stimulus and response variation.

4. Sequence teaching examples to produce the most efficient training possible.

5. Teach the examples using the most current instructional technology.

6. Test on nontrained probe examples to identify and eliminate error patterns.

It is obvious from the guidelines that a considerable amount of effort is applied during the preparation phase when creating a general case curriculum.

Research has shown that general case programming is more effective in obtaining generalized responding than single instance training or training on several similar instances of a particular skill. Generalized responding has been obtained via general case instruction for vending machine use (Sprague & Horner, 1984), preparing electronic capacitors for insulation (Horner & McDonald, 1982), and grocery shopping (McDonnell, Horner, & Williams, 1984).

REFERENCES

Brown, L., Branston, M. B., Hamre-Nietupski, H., Pumpian, I., Certo, N., & Gruenwald, L. A. (1979). A strategy for developing chronological age-appropriate and functional curricular content for severely handicapped adolescents and young adults. *Journal of Special Education, 13*, 81–90.

Brown, L., Nisbet, J., Ford, A., Sweet, M., Shiraga, B., York, J., & Loomis, R. (1983). The critical need for non school instruction in educational programs for severely handicapped students. *Journal of the Association for the Severely Handicapped, 8*, 71–77.

Horner, R. H., & McDonald, R. S. (1982). Comparison of single instance and general case instruction in teaching a generalized vocational skill. *Journal of the Association for the Severely Handicapped, 8*, 7–20.

Horner, R. H., Sprague, J., & Wilcox, B. (1982). General case programming for community activities. In B. Wilcox & G. T. Bellamy (Eds.), *Design of high school programs for severely handicapped students*. Baltimore, MD: Paul H. Brookes.

McDonnell, J. J., Horner, R. H., & Williams, J. A. (1984). Comparison of three strategies for teaching generalized grocery purchasing to high school students with severe handicaps. *Journal of the Association for the Severely Handicapped, 9*, 123–133.

Sprague, J. R., & Horner, R. H. (1984). The effects of single instance, multiple instance, and general case training on generalized vending machine use by moderately and severely handicapped students. *Journal of Applied Behavior Analysis, 17*, 273–278.

JOHN O'NEILL
Hunter College, City University of New York

GENERALIZATION
PROGRAMMED INSTRUCTION

GENERALIZABILITY THEORY

Generalizability theory was developed by Cronbach and his associates (Cronbach, Gleser, Nanda, & Rajaratnam,

1972) to evaluate the generalizability of results obtained when measurement is carried out for assessing, for example, differences among students. The theory is primarily concerned with identifying and estimating the variances associated with the effects present in the design used to collect the evaluation data. Variances are estimated within an analysis of variance (ANOVA) framework. These estimated variances are then used to describe the relative contribution of each effect to the observed variance and to compute measurement error variance and, if desired, generalizability coefficients for each factor of interest.

Two types of studies are conducted using generalizability theory: G (generalizability)-studies and D(decision)-studies. A G-study is carried out when developing a measurement procedure for use in a D-study later on. Thus, a G-study is designed to encompass the "universe of admissible observations" (Cronbach et al., 1972, p. 20); for instance, a universe including all the variables (factors) under which observations could be collected in subsequent D-studies. A D-study draws observations from the "universe of generalization," i.e., the universe to which we wish to generalize the results in a specific situation. The universe of generalization is then a subset of, or the same as, the universe of admissible operations. The results of a G-study are used to design D-studies. In many instances, however, a G- and D-study may be conducted using the same data set; for instance, the data are used both for making decisions and for improving the design of future D-studies so that the universe of admissible observations is the same as the universe of generalization.

Suppose a 20-item test is administered for diagnostic purposes to a sample of 30 referred students. To investigate the generalizability of the test for differentiating among the students, a G-study is conducted by first identifying the effects present in the linear ANOVA model associated with the design of the study. These effects are student, item, and student x item interaction, including random error. Next, using the ANOVA technique, the mean squares associated with each effect are obtained, and variances are estimated for each using a procedure such as that proposed by Cornfield and Tukey (1956). For the example above, the variances are estimated as follows: students-.0610 (22.13%), items-.0700 (25.82%), interaction-.1401 (51.68%).

Next, a D-study is carried out using the results of the G-study. First the estimated variances are examined. They show that approximately the same proportion of variation in the design is shown by the students and the items, while twice as much is attributable to the differences between students' responses to items and random error. The measurement error associated with differences among students is .0701/20 = .0025, since differences among students are shown in their differing responses to the same items. Divide by 20, since it is assumed that students are differentiated on the basis of their perform-

ance over all 20 items. A generalizability coefficient, ρ^2, analogous to a reliability coefficient, is estimated as

$$\hat{\rho}^2 = \frac{\text{student variance}}{\text{student variance and error variance}}$$

$$= \frac{.0610}{.0610 + .0035}$$

$$= .8971$$

In summary, from a generalizability analysis we estimate variance associated with each factor in the design, measurement error, and a generalizability coefficient associated with the factor of interest. The practitioner or researcher wishing to conduct generalizability analysis should read Brennan (1983), Fyans (1983), and Shavelson and Webb (1981).

REFERENCES

Brennan, R. L. (1983). *Elements of generalizability theory*. Iowa City, Iowa: American College Testing Program.

Cornfield, J., & Tukey, J. W. (1956). Average values of mean squares in factorials. *Annals of Mathematical Statistics, 27,* 907–949.

Cronbach, L. J., Gleser, G. C., Nanda, H., & Rajaratnam, N. (1972). *The dependability of behavioral measurements: Theory of generalizability for scores and profiles*. New York: Wiley.

Fyans, L. J. (Ed.). (1983). *Generalizability theory: Inferences and practical applications*. San Francisco: Jossey-Bass.

Shavelson, R. J., & Webb, N. M. (1981). Generalizability theory: 1973–1980. *British Journal of Mathematical & Statistical Psychology, 34,* 133–166.

GWYNETH M. BOODOO
Texas A&M University

RESEARCH IN SPECIAL EDUCATION

GENERALIZATION

Generalization is the demonstration of a behavior in circumstances other than those in which it was trained. The term is also used to refer to the occurrence of a behavior similar to, but different than, the learned behavior under the same circumstances as during training (Scruggs & Mastropieri, 1984). These two types of generalization are referred to as stimulus generalization and response generalization. Stimulus generalization, the type most commonly studied by special education researchers, may be said to have occurred when a learner demonstrates a skill or behavior in different surroundings, at different times, or with different people. For example, a student who is trained to insert the correct amount of change into a soda machine at school and subsequently performs the same skill at a recreation center is said to have generalized the response. Response generalization refers to the spread of effects to other related behaviors and is exemplified by a student opening a large can after having successfully learned to open a small can.

Generalization is necessary to the development of a wide repertoire of behavior. It was once assumed that generalization occurred automatically with the learning of a behavior, but this principle has not proven true, especially for handicapped learners (Stokes & Baer, 1977). If generalization is to occur, it must be a component of the actual training process (Baer, Wolf, & Risley, 1968).

There is a greater probability of success in training for generalization if several factors are addressed.

1. *Initial Training.* The behavior to be generalized should be firmly established in the learner's repertoire. Time between initial acquisition and training for generalization should be short. If conditions during training are tightly controlled, generalization may take more time than if initial training is "loose" (i.e., stimuli and responses are not narrowly defined).

2. *Stimulus Variables.* The stimulus variables to be changed (time, number, setting) should be manipulated systematically during training. There is little agreement whether this should be accomplished one variable at a time or all at one time. However, the more similarities between stimuli in the initial learning environment and those in the generalization environment, the easier the process for the learner (Stokes & Baer, 1977).

3. *Other Persons.* To the extent possible, significant others in the learner's environment should be included in the training. If they understand the purpose and method, they will be able to reinforce the learner whenever and wherever the behavior occurs.

4. *Reinforcers.* Artificial reinforcers should be faded as soon as possible and replaced by those reinforcers found in the environment in which behavior is most likely to occur. Likewise, regardless of the schedule of reinforcement used for training, an intermittent schedule should be in place before generalization is attempted. Intermittent reforcement will more closely resemble schedules found in the natural environment.

5. *Criteria for completion.* Criteria for successful generalization should be established. The number of exemplars required to assure generalization will vary, but training should continue until some spontaneous generalization is observed in nontraining environments (Stokes & Baer, 1977).

Success in training for generalization has varied and researchers differ in their opinions regarding its efficacy (Scruggs & Mastropieri, 1984). Some propose that failure to train for generalization is due to a lack of educational technology; others contend that inherent deficiencies in the intellectual functioning of handicapped persons make generalization difficult. The former analysis implies that new and better training techniques are needed and that the problem is a teaching one. The latter implies a learning problem and that attempts to train for generalization should be replaced by more effort spent training desired behaviors in the environments in which they are required (Scruggs & Mastropieri, 1984).

REFERENCES

Baer, D. M., Wolf, M. M., & Risley, T. R. (1968). Some current dimensions of applied behavior analysis. *Journal of Applied Behavior Analysis, 1,* 91–97.

Scruggs, T. E., & Mastropieri, M. A. (1984). Issues in generalization: Implications for special education. *Psychology in the Schools, 21,* 397–403.

Stokes, T. F., & Baer, D. M. (1977). An implicit technology of generalization. *Journal of Applied Behavior Analysis, 10,* 349–367.

SARA PANKASKIE
PAUL T. SINDELAR
Florida State University

TRANSFER OF TRAINING
TRANSFER OF LEARNING

GENERIC SPECIAL EDUCATION

Generic special education is a cross-categorical orientation to training teachers and delivering special education services to mild/moderately handicapped youngsters. This approach came about as a result of a variety of educational movements in special education. In the 1960s, there was growing dissatisfaction among educators with the use of traditional medical-model categories to identify handicapped pupils. This concern was due, in part, to increased recognition of the heterogeneity of learner characteristics within a specific handicap classification and to reports that many pupils have similar educational needs despite differences in their handicapping conditions (Hewett & Forness, 1984).

Legal requirements to educate handicapped children in the least restrictive educational environment according to an individualized educational plan (IEP) further eroded the historical categorical boundaries to instruction. According to PL 94-142, selection of instructional services for the handicapped is based on pupils' educational needs as determined by a committee of educators and parents who develop the IEP. After analyzing pupils' levels of performance, the appropriate educational placement is prescribed. A variety of instructional options have been developed to meet pupils' individual needs, including placement in regular classes, the use of consulting and itinerant special education teachers, resource and self-contained special education classes, special day schools, residential centers, hospital schools, and homebound instruction (Deno, 1973; Reynolds & Birch, 1982). The specific nature of instructional services, including decisions concerning curricula and teaching strategies, should be determined by the individual needs and instructional characteristics of the pupil rather; they should not be arbitrarily prescribed on the basis of the child's handicapping condition.

Concern for individualization is evident throughout the entire continuum of services provided by schools and agencies. From infant stimulation to vocational preparation programs that emphasize the transition from school to work, pupils who require special education services receive them based on their individual needs rather than on their categorical label. Within this context of individualization of instruction, generic special education focuses on identifying and meeting the learning needs and characteristics of specific pupils regardless of disability category. For example, owing to similarities in performance characteristics, many learning-disabled, mildly retarded, and emotionally disturbed youngsters may be effectively served in the same classroom with the same curricula.

As special education instructional services evolved from a rigid categorical approach to a functional orientation, so did teacher training programs change. With the support of federal funds in the early 1970s, several institutions of higher education initiated cross-categorical special education teacher training programs (Brady, Conroy, & Langford, 1984). These programs exhibited a variety of characteristics differentiating them from the traditional categorical orientation to teacher education. For example, each program's name described the role or function of the teacher rather than a particular handicapping condition (e.g., diagnostic-prescriptive teacher, consulting teacher). The programs were primarily developed at the master's degree level for already certified teachers, and although students were trained noncategorically, their certification remained categorical. Later, teacher training programs emphasized greater interaction with regular education, offered programs at both bachelor's and master's levels, and were located in states that began initiating noncategorical certification, primarily by collapsing certain categories into a general one. These training programs tended to collapse categorical course offerings to meet the challenge of noncategorical certification.

Associated with these movements in service delivery and teacher training has been a trend for state education agencies to develop noncategorical teacher certification in special education, growing from only 12 states in 1979 to 34 states and the District of Columbia in 1983 (Idol-Maestas, Lloyd, & Lilly, 1981). Names of these new certificates range from descriptions of pupils (e.g., learning handicapped, mildly handicapped) to descriptions of programs

(e.g., resource room specialist, diagnostic prescriptive teacher) to nonspecific terms such as generic special educator.

REFERENCES

Brady, M. P., Conroy, M., & Langford, C. A. (1984). Current issues and practices affecting the development of noncategorical programs for students and teachers. *Teacher Education & Special Education*, 7(1), 20–26.

Deno, E. N. (Ed.). (1973). *Instructional alternatives for exceptional children*. Arlington, VA: Council for Exceptional Children.

Hewett, F. M., & Forness, S. R. (1984). *Education of exceptional learners* (3rd ed.). Boston: Allyn & Bacon.

Idol-Maestas, L., Lloyd, S., & Lilly, M. (1981). A noncategorical approach to direct service and teacher education. *Exceptional Children*, 48(3), 213–220.

Reynolds, M., & Birch, J. W. (1982). Teaching exceptional children in all America's schools (2nd ed.). Reston, VA: Council for Exceptional Children.

CAROL ANDERSON
DOUGLAS J. PALMER
LINDA H. PARRISH
Texas A&M University

HOLISTIC APPROACH AND LEARNING DISABILITIES HUMANISM AND SPECIAL EDUCATION

GENETIC COUNSELING

In recent years, patients with a great variety of hereditary diseases have been referred for genetic evaluation and counseling (Nora & Fraser, 1981). There have been many advances in the management of hereditary disorders (e.g., plastic surgery, dietary manipulation, prenatal diagnosis, and most recently, gene therapy). Genetic counseling provides the vehicle for the transmission of relevant information needed by the client to make an informed decision about the treatment and prevention of hereditary disorders.

The first American genetic counseling center on record was the Eugenic Records Office in Cold Spring Harbor, New York, founded by Dr. Charles B. Davenport in 1915. Genetic counseling fell out of favor in the 1930s as the role of environment in human behavior became better understood. During the next 20 years, the study of genetics was predominantly an academic pursuit. Informal counseling was done by academicians who were primarily involved in basic genetic research rather than clinical medicine.

By the 1960s, great strides had been made in understanding human genetics. The new information gave counselors a broader and more scientific basis for telling families about the recurrence, risks, and inheritance patterns of an increasing number of diseases. The development of genetic tests based on blood and cell samples introduced the field of prospective counseling and helped shift counseling from primarily nonmedical settings to medical screening programs in hospitals and universities. Today, there are approximately 500 centers and satellite facilities specializing in genetics in the United States. Both the National Foundation–March of Dimes, 1275 Mamaroneck Avenue, White Plains, New York 10605, and the National Genetics Foundation, 250 West 57th Street, New York, NY, can direct those in need of counseling to an appropriate source.

Until recently, a professional providing genetic counseling was typically a physician with an interest in genetics, or a PhD geneticist with an interest in medicine. In the past 10 years, postdoctoral fellowship positions have prepared physicians and PhD geneticists in the full range of clinical genetics. In addition, genetic counselors with MS degrees emerged in response to a substantial increase in the number of individuals seeking genetic counseling and screening. The varied training and backgrounds of genetic counselors, and recognition by the American Society of Human Genetics for the need to certify counselors, led to the creation of a board certification process. Since 1981, hundreds of professionals have been certified by the American Board of Medical Genetics.

A good counselor needs a sound grasp of genetic principles, a wide knowledge of the scientific literature on diseases of possible genetic origin, and much empathy, tact, and good sense. The counselor may be in the role of information giver, facilitator of the counselee's decision process, psychotherapist, or moral advisor.

Genetic counseling usually begins with an individual wanting to know whether a disease suspected of being genetic will recur in close relatives. The traditional role of the counselor is to estimate P, the probability of recurrence, and when asked, to assist the client in deciding what is the appropriate action. In all cases, the decision must be left to the family. Clients may want to know whether they should have another baby. Others may want to know about the risk for affected children's children, or for the children of unaffected brothers and sisters. Prenatal diagnosis using cytogenetic or biochemical analyses of fetal cells, amniotic fluid, or mother's blood can now provide clear answers to questions concerning genetic disorders. In certain populations in which a severe genetic disorder is unusually high, such as Tay-Sachs disease, screening programs have been organized to detect and counsel heterozygotes (President's Commission for the Study of Ethical Problems in Medicine and Biomedical and Behavioral Research, 1983).

REFERENCES

President's Commission for the Study of Ethical Problems in Medicine and Biomedical and Behavioral Research. (1983).
Screening and counseling for genetic conditions. Washington, DC: U.S. Government Printing Office.

Nora, J. J., & Fraser, F. C. (1981). *Medical genetics: Principles and practice* (2nd ed.). Philadelphia: Lea & Febiger.

KENNETH A. ZYCH
*Walter Reed Army Medical
Center, Washington, D.C.*

**GENETIC FACTORS IN BEHAVIOR
HEREDITY
TAY-SACHS SYNDROME**

GENETIC FACTORS IN BEHAVIOR

Little is known about the genetics of human behavior, either normal or abnormal, and it is unlikely that there are specific genes for behavior or any other phenotypic trait. Behavior genetics is more complex than the study of genetic influences on physical traits because it is hard to define behavioral traits reliably, to assess them validly, and to control situational influences. Nonhuman species offer advantages of convenience and control for genetic research, but the lack of precise analogs between human and animal behavior, especially pathological behavior, limits the value of animal research for human behavior genetics.

However, a number of human pathological genes have more or less specific effects on behavior. The child with Phenylketonuria (PKU) is likely to be hyperactive and irritable, have outbursts of temper, abnormal postural attitudes, and agitated behavior; about 10% of those affected show psychotic behavior. Characteristic behavioral changes often precede the choreic movements in Huntington's chorea. Congenital cretinism, which may be recessively inherited, produces effects on personality. Perhaps the most striking example of a gene-induced behavioral defect is the bizarre tendency for self-mutilation in Lesch-Nyhan syndrome.

Chromosomal aberrations also have effects on behavior. Children with Down's syndrome are thought to be happier and more responsive to their environment than other children of comparable IQ; they often display musical ability. Girls with Turner's syndrome rate high on verbal IQ tests but below average on performance measures; they seem to have a deficit in perceptual organization. The XYY karyotype is alleged to show a predisposition to criminality and aggressive behavior; however, a causal link between an excess or deficiency of chromosomal material and a behavior phenotype is obscure.

There is more information about the genetics of abnormal behavior than about how normal behavior is encoded in the gene loci. Schizophrenia, with incidence in the 1% range, has been studied in families, and 2 to 5% of the parents and 6 to 10% of the siblings are affected. If a propositus and parent are both affected, the risk for the siblings is higher. Concordance is much greater for monozygotic than for dizygotic twin pairs. Children of schizophrenic parents raised by their natural parents and those raised by adoptive parents show the same incidence of schizophrenia. This finding seems to establish a role for heredity in schizophrenia. However, questions of genetic heterogeneity, the role of environmental stress, and the nature of the biochemical abnormalities associated with schizophrenia remain to be answered. At present, it does not seem reasonable to suspect a single gene-determined basic defect.

The affective disorders are somewhat similar to schizophrenia in terms of population incidence and frequency within families. It has been suggested that bipolar disease is an x-linked dominant disease, but so simple a hypothesis seems implausible on the basis of current evidence. Biochemical evidence of a single-gene basis for either the bipolar or the unipolar type is still lacking.

Developmental aphasia appears to be caused by the inability of the aphasic child to process auditory stimuli presented at a normal rate. This ability does develop eventually, but at a later age than average, and it is suspected to be an autosomal dominant trait (Thompson & Thompson, 1980). The evidence favoring the familial nature of dyslexia is compelling, but the factors that account for the aggregation of cases remain unclear. Some types of dyslexia seem to be influenced by the genes and it is speculated that dyslexia is an autosomal dominant condition with some degree of sex limitation (males are affected far more frequently).

By the application of biometrical genetics and twin studies, evidence for heritability has been found for infant behavior and temperament, introversion-extroversion, and neuroticism. Empirical evidence on sibling resemblance in intelligence published since 1915 in the United States and Europe, including more than 27,000 sibling pairs, showed that genetic factors are the major source of individual differences in intelligence. The most likely estimate of the sibling correlation for IQ in the population is +0.49 (Paul, 1980).

REFERENCES

Paul, S. M. (1980). Sibling resemblance in mental ability: A review. *Behavior Genetics*, *10*(3), 277–290.

Thompson, J. S., & Thompson, M. W. (1980). *Genetics in medicine* (3rd ed.). Philadelphia: Saunders.

KENNETH A. ZYCH
*Walter Reed Army Medical
Center, Washington, D.C.*

GENETIC TRANSMISSIONS

Genetics, the scientific study of heredity, is the phenomenon wherein biological traits appear to be transmitted from one familial generation to the next. Gregor Mendel, the nineteenth-century Austrian monk, did the seminal studies leading to the founding of the field of genetics. The history of human genetics since that time has included the development of cytogenetics, biochemical genetics, molecular genetics, immunogenetics, population genetics, applied genetics, and clinical genetics. The science of genetics has shown that inherited traits result from the transmission of the parents' genes to their offspring. Genes interact with one another and with their environment to produce distinctive characteristics or phenotypes. Therefore, offspring tend to exhibit phenotypes similar to those of their parents.

There are two types of cell division that occur within the human body. Mitosis is the process of cell division that occurs in all cells, except for the sex cells or gametes. Gametes are divided during the process of meiosis.

Critical to genetic transmission are chromosomes, which are the small, rod-shaped bodies located in the nuclei of each cell. Each normal human body cell has 23 pairs or 46 chromosomes. During mitosis, cells divide by duplicating themselves, and each daughter cell contains 46 chromosomes that are identical to the 46 chromosomes contained in the original cell. During meiosis, the gametes divide by splitting into two separate distinct cells that each contain 23 chromosomes of the original cell. During reproduction, the male and female gametes join and produce a zygote that contains 46 chromosomes. One pair of the 23 chromosomes is different in size and shape and this atypical pair is related to sex determination. In all mammals, the female has two similarly sized chromosomes, called X, while the male has one X and a smaller Y chromosome. If an ovum is fertilized by a Y-bearing sperm, the zygote will be a male, but if the ovum is fertilized by an X-bearing sperm, the zygote will be female.

The actual units of hereditary transmission are the deoxyribonucleic acid (DNA) molecules or genes residing at specific loci on the chromosome. A recent estimate has indicated there are over 30,000 structural genes per haploid set of 23 chromosomes. The different variants of genes that control a particular trait and occupy corresponding loci on the paired chromosomes are called alleles. For example, one allele, or variant, of the gene for eye color produces blue eyes, while a different allele produces brown eyes. The paternal and maternal alleles for eye color are aligned beside each other in two adjoining chromosomes of the offspring.

According to Mendel's laws, one allele dominates the other in the phenotypic expression of a heterozygous genotype (genetic constitution). Dominant alleles are represented by capital letters and recessive alleles with small letters. Whenever one or both parents are heterozygous for a trait, as often occurs, their children are not all likely to inherit the same genotype as distinguished from its physical appearance (phenotype). For example, a male inherits blue-eyed (b) alleles from both his mother and father. He is therefore homozygous for eye color (bb); both alleles are the same, the zygote is homogeneous for eye color. The boy will have blue eyes and can pass only an allele for blue eyes to his offspring. If the boy mates with a girl who has alleles only for brown eyes, she can pass only a brown-eyed (B) allele to their child. Since this child receives the blue allele (b) from one parent and the brown allele (B) from the other, the child is heterozygous for eye color (Bb). The child will have brown eyes because brown eye color is a dominant trait. Because so many different gene combinations can arise from two parents, two siblings seldom have the same genes, unless they come from the same zygote; these offspring are identical or monozygotic twins.

REFERENCES

King, R. C., & Stansfield, W. D. (1985). *A dictionary of genetics* (3rd ed.). New York: Oxford University Press.

Nora, J. J., & Fraser, F. C. (1981). *Medical genetics: Principles and practice* (2nd ed.). Philadelphia: Lea & Febiger.

Thaddeus, K. E. (1980). *Clinical genetics and genetic counseling.* Chicago: Year Book Medical.

Thompson, J. S., & Thompson, M. W. (1980). *Genetics in medicine* (3rd ed.). Philadelphia: Saunders.

KENNETH A. ZYCH
*Walter Reed Army Medical
Center, Washington, D.C.*

**CHROMOSOMAL ABNORMALITIES
GENETIC COUNSELING
KAROTYPE**

GENETIC VARIATIONS

The independent assortment of chromosomes during meiosis is a major reason for the variation of the genetic constitution in different individuals. Each gamete has 8 million possible combinations of chromosomes from the 23 pairs, and each set of parents has 7×1013 possible chromosome combinations to offer their children. Thus, with the incomplete exception of monovular twins, every person is and will be genetically unique.

While genetics is the study of biological variations, medical genetics is the study of those variations that result in, or predispose one to, disease. Genetic diseases make a considerable contribution to the burden of mortality and morbidity in childhood. Mendelian and chromosomal diseases account for about 12% to 15% of childhood mortality, with congenital malformations contributing an additional 25% to 30%. Of all individuals with IQs below 50, at least 40% have a chromosomal disorder (of which Down's syndrome accounts for about three-quarters); 15% have a single-gene disease (e.g., Huntington's disease, x-linked mental retardation, Tay-Sachs disease); and 45% have severe developmental malformation (Porter, 1982).

Generally, three major varieties of genetic disease afflict humans: Mendelian disorders caused by a single gene, cytogenetic disorders caused by chromosomal abnormalities, and multifactorial genetic diseases. In Mendelizing or single-gene diseases, the genetic factor is relatively simple. Three distinct patterns are recognized: dominant, recessive, and x-linked, of which there are 800, 550, and 100 known conditions, respectively. The most important of the genetic disorders of early development affect metabolism (e.g., phenylketonuria [PKU], a disorder of amino acid metabolism). Untreated, PKU results in severe mental retardation, decreased attention, and lack of responsiveness to the environment. Well-known autosomal dominant diseases are Huntington's disease, deafness (dominant forms), and neurofibromatosis (Von Recklinghausen disease). Cystic fibrosis is the most prevalent autosomal recessive disorder in white children. Tay-Sachs disease, also an autosomal recessive disorder, has a high prevalence rate among Ashkenazi Jews. Hemophilia is an x-linked recessive disease in which the blood fails to clot normally. Another genetic blood disease characterized by a tendency of the red cells to become grossly abnormal in shape is sickle cell disease, which affects about 0.25% of American blacks.

The second category of diseases results from failure of chromosomes to develop properly (chromosomal dysgenesis) during the formation of the oocyte or spermatocyte, or during conception and germination, resulting in an irreversibly abnormal chromosome makeup in the embryo. Extra and mismatched chromosomes, as well as structural anomalies, are major forms of dysgenesis. Examples of dysgenesis are trisomy 21, 18, and 13, as well as partial trisomies, mosaicisms, monosomies, deletions, and inversions. Sex chromosomal anomalies include Turner's syndrome and Klinefelter's syndrome (XXY). For the most part, the disorders in this category are not inherited, but they involve the genetic material, the chromosomes. Mental retardation and physical abnormalities are the most common consequences of chromosomal disorders.

The more common abnormal genetic conditions are multifactorial in their causation and are characterized by a complex interaction of genetic and environmental factors. The genetic effects are complex and determined by the interaction of many genes, each contributing a small effect. Cleft lip and palate, congenital dislocation of the hip, pyloric stenosis, talipes, and equinovarus are well-known examples; perhaps the best known examples are anencephaly and meningomyelocele, known collectively as neurological tube defects. Carcinogens have been found to induce some kind of chromosomal rearrangements that are associated with a variety of human cancers (Radman, Jeggo, & Wagner, 1982).

REFERENCES

Porter, I. H. (1982). Control of hereditary disorders. *Annual Review of Public Health, 3*, 277–319.

Radman, M., Jeggo, P., & Wagner, R. (1982). Chromosomal rearrangement and carcinogenesis. *Mutation Research, 98*, 249–264.

KENNETH A. ZYCH
*Walter Reed Army Medical
Center, Washington, D.C.*

GENETIC COUNSELING
GENETIC FACTORS IN BEHAVIOR

GENIE

The case of Genie involves an adolescent who experienced a degree of social isolation and experiential deprivation so far unparalleled in medical literature. The case came to light in 1970, when Genie was 13½ years of age.

From the age of 20 months to 13 years, 7 months, Genie was confined to a small bedroom at the rear of the family home. There, she was physically harnessed to an infant potty seat. At night, when she was not forgotten, she was removed from the harness and put into a sleeping bag which had been modified to hold Genie's arms stationary. She was then put into a crib with wire mesh sides and a wire mesh cover.

Genie received a minimum of care and stimulation. She was fed only infant food and wore no clothing. There was no TV or radio in the home, and as there were two doors separating her bedroom from the front of the house, where the remainder of the family lived, she could hear little of any family conversations. As her bedroom was set in the back of the house, away from the street, she heard few environmental noises. Her room contained only the potty and crib—no carpet, no pictures on the walls. The room's two windows were covered up except for a few inches at the top. Genie's mother, having become blind shortly after Genie's birth, was unable to care for Genie, and so it was Genie's father and brother who were her primary caretakers. Together, they committed many acts of cruelty and abuse, among which was their consistent unwillingness to talk to her and beatings inflicted on Genie for making noise.

When Genie was found, she was extremely malnourished. She weighed only 59 pounds and was only 54 inches tall. Never having been fed solid food, she was unable to chew or bite. She could not stand erect, and could barely walk. She was incontinent for feces and urine. Having been beaten for making noise, she was silent. She knew only a few words. She was essentially unsocialized and untrained.

Genie's case caught the attention of the scientific community because of the unique opportunity it offered for studying the human potential to "catch up" as it were—to develop social, cognitive, and linguistic knowledge after the typical points in development. Particular interest in Genie's potential for linguistic development was fostered by Lenneberg's (1967) critical age hypothesis for language acquisition. Lenneberg proposed that, as is the case with many maturationally timed species-specific behaviors, there is a critical period for first language acquisition—between the ages of two and puberty, beyond which a first language could not be learned. Genie faced the task of first language acquisition at 13½. Thus, her ability to learn language directly tested Lenneberg's hypothesis.

In the 9 years she was studied, Genie showed very uneven language learning ability. Most important in this regard is the striking contrast between her acquisition of morphology and syntax on the one hand and her acquisition of semantic knowledge on the other. Genie's acquisition of vocabulary and of how to express meaningful relations through words steadily progressed and increased, whereas her utterances remained largely ungrammatical and hierarchically flat (Curtiss, 1977, 1981, 1982). Genie's case, then, supports a weak form of Lenneberg's hypothesis in that while she developed some language, she did not acquire language fully or normally. Her case also suggests that different components of language are differentially vulnerable to the age at which language acquisition is carried out. In particular, her case points to the separability of a conceptual or referential linguistic component (which involves lexical knowledge and knowledge of semantic roles, and which is resilient in its developmental potential) from a grammatical component, which involves the constraints and rules of grammar, for which the acquisition potential appears to be far more maturationally constrained.

Although most of the scientific investigation carried out with Genie concentrated on her language development, a considerable number of standarized intelligence tests and tests of Piagetian operations were also administered. Remarkably, Genie evidenced 1 year's mental growth every year past her discovery and demonstrated full operational intelligence in spatial knowledge, with less developed ability in some other areas, specifically, those relying on verbal mediation.

The cognitive profile that Genie displayed lends support to a modular view of the mind in which grammar represents a distinct faculty of mind, separate from other components of language and separate from other mental abilities. For details regarding Genie's case history and language acquisition (see Curtiss, 1977). For details regarding her nonlinguistic cognitive abilities (see Curtiss, 1979). For a discussion of Genie's case and the critical age hypothesis, see Fromkin et al., 1974. For a discussion of Genie's case in connection with theories of language learning and cognitive development (see Curtiss, 1981 and 1982).

REFERENCES

Curtiss, S. (1977). *Genie: A psycholinguistic study of a modern-day "wild child."* New York: Academic.

Curtiss, S. (1979). Genie: Language and Cognition. *UCLA Working Papers in Cognitive Linguistics, 1,* 16–62.

Curtiss, S. (1981). Dissociation between language and cognition. *Journal of Autism & Developmental Disorders, 11,* 15–30.

Curtiss, S. (1982). Developmental dissociations of language and cognition. In L. Obler & L. Menn (Eds.), *Exceptional Language and Linguistics.* New York: Academic.

Fromkin, et al. (1974). The development of language in Genie: A case of language acquisition beyond the critical period. *Brain & Language, 1,* 81–107.

Lenneberg, E. H. (1967). *Biological foundations of language.* New York: Wiley.

SUSAN CURTISS
University of California,
Los Angeles

EXPRESSIVE LANGUAGE DISORDERS
LANGUAGE DEFICIENCIES AND DEFICITS
LINGUISTIC DEVIANCE

GENIUS

The original conception of genius was of a deity that would reside within an individual and have a profound influence on the development of his or her mental powers and spiritual growth. Recently the concept of genius has been subsumed within psychology and philosophy. Galton (1869) developed a quantitative concept of genius as an innate or inherited ability, and Lombroso (1891) conceived of genius as a manifestation of abnormal psychology—as akin to madness. Hirsch (1931) even proposed that the genius should be viewed as a separate psychobiological species.

The term genius is now used chiefly to denote exceptionally high talent, ability, or achievement. However, it has been largely supplanted by the terms gifted or gift-edness. As originally used in his research on heritability, Galton (1892) intended that genius should denote an "ability that was exceptionally high, and at the same time inborn" (p. VIII). However, he also suggested that it should not be considered a technical term. Galton attempted to demonstrate that genius or exceptional ability is inherited.

In approaching his monumental longitudinal study of gifted children, Terman (1925) used the term gifted, but he nevertheless titled the entire series of books that resulted *Genetic Studies of Genius.* It should be noted, however, that Terman had extended the concept of the origins of genius, "The origins of genius, the natural laws of its development, and the environmental influences by which it may be affected for good or ill, are scientific problems of almost unequalled importance for human welfare" (1925, p. V). Terman went on to suggest that there were three problems related to genius: its nature, its origins, and its cultivation. Clearly then, the stage was set for nature-nurture research.

Research on the origins and nurturance of genius has often taken the form of studies of eminent people or very high achievers. In Volume II of *Genetic Studies of Genius* (1926), Catherine Cox and others (including Lewis Terman) studied the early mental traits of 300 geniuses. Galton had also pioneered in this approach to the study of genius (1869). More recently the biographical research of the Goertzels (1962) continues this tradition, as reported in *Cradles of Eminence.*

Recent research by Bloom (1985), however, focused on living subjects who have achieved world recognition. The research by Bloom and his predecessors agrees in the finding that genius, giftedness, special talent, and high ability often appear as precocious behavior; for instance, accomplishments in youth that far exceed normal achievements. There is also increased recognition of the influence of family, schooling, and other variables in determining giftedness. The term genius is now used less frequently than it was, although it is sometimes evoked to denote truly exceptional giftedness.

REFERENCES

Bloom, B. S. (Ed.). (1985). *Developing talent in young people.* New York: Ballantine.

Cox, C. M. (1926). *Genetic studies of genius: Vol. II. The early mental traits of three hundred geniuses.* Stanford, CA: Stanford University Press.

Galton, F. (1869). *Hereditary genius* London: Macmillan.

Galton, F. (1892). *Hereditary genius* (2nd ed.). London: Macmillan.

Goertzel, V., & Goertzel, M. G. (1962). *Cradles of eminence.* Boston: Little, Brown.

Hirsch, N. D. M. (1931). *Genius and creative intelligence.* Cambridge, MA: Sci-Art Publisher.

Lombroso, C. (1891). *The man of genius.* London: Scott.

Terman, L. M. (1925). *Genetic studies of genius: Vol. 1. Mental and physical traits of a thousand gifted children.* Stanford, CA: Stanford University Press.

JOHN F. FELDHUSEN
Purdue University

GIFTED AND TALENTED CHILDREN
GIFTED CHILDREN

GEORGE, WILLIAM REUBEN (1866–1936)

William Reuben "Daddy" George was born on June 4, 1866, in the hamlet of West Dryden in central New York. As a young man, he moved to New York City, where he established a small manufacturing business. Through his church, George began working with children in one of the city's most oppressive slums. He had notable success with city gangs, forming his own "law and order" gangs, which transformed young people from lawbreakers to law enforcers. Because children from the slums were often not accepted into the summer fresh air programs for city children, George started a program that provided a camping experience in a rural setting for these needy young people. George's summer program began in 1890 on a farm at Freeville, near West Dryden, and continued until he conceived the idea of a permanent community for young people based on the structure of the U.S. government: "our glorious republic in miniature—a junior republic."

In 1895 George gave up his business to remain at Freeville at the end of the summer with a number of students to begin a year-round program. The community that they developed was based on the principles of self-support—the students worked for their food and lodging—and self-gov-

ernment—the students made and enforced the laws governing the community.

George's ideas attracted the attention of educators and social reformers, and of prominent men and women who provided much of the financial support for the "junior republic." There was great interest in other parts of the country as well, and George supervised the establishment of nine similar communities in other states. None of these institutions consistently followed George's principles, however, and he considered the expansion effort a failure.

At the Freeville junior republic, George developed an elaborate educational and social system based on the principles of self-government and self-support. "Nothing without labor" became the junior republic's motto. The students, or citizens, as they came to be called, attended school, worked in the various jobs that made the junior republic almost entirely self-sufficient, and ran their own government.

George's junior republic, an early demonstration of the progressive education principle of learning by doing, was a major force in the development of programs for deprived, delinquent, and troubled youths in schools and institutions in the first part of the century. George headed the junior republic until his death on April 25, 1936. It is a tribute to the power of his ideas that George's junior republic, which today enrolls 170 adolescents referred by public schools, courts, and parents, still carefully adheres to its founder's precepts of self-support and self-government.

REFERENCES

Holl, J. M. (1971). *Juvenile reform in the progressive era: William R. George and the junior republic movement.* Ithaca, NY: Cornell University Press.

Van Dyck, H. D., & Van Dyck, R. (1983). George junior republic: Fresh start for troubled teens. *Journal of the New York State School Boards Association*, pp. 15–20.

PAUL IRVINE
Katonah, New York

William Reuben George

GEORGIA STUDIES OF CREATIVE BEHAVIOR

The Georgia Studies of Creative Behavior is a research program devoted to the study of creativity. Established at the University of Georgia in 1966 by Torrance (1970), it continued and expanded a similar program of research and development at the University of Minnesota—the Minnesota Studies of Creative Behavior (1958–1966). The Minnesota and Georgia research program has been concerned with the identification of creative potential, developmental patterns in creative thinking abilities, predictions of adult creative achievement, future imaging, instructional models and strategies to enhance creative thinking, the presence of creativity in various population groups, teacher training, creative problem solving, and cross-cultural studies of creative behavior.

The contributions to theory and practice regarding creative behavior from the Minnesota and Georgia studies have been numerous. Significant achievements and events have included the development and refinement of a battery of creative thinking tests, the Torrance Tests of Creative Thinking (TTCT) (1966), for use from kindergarten through adulthood; a 22-year longitudinal study to assess the creative achievement of adults whose IQs and creativity had been tested in elementary school; the Incubation Model, an instructional model to enhance creative thinking and incubation; the wide-scale application of this model into the Ginn Reading 360 and 720 series; the Ideal-Pupil Checklist and the Torrance Checklist of Creative Positives; and the founding of the Future Problem Solving Program and the International Network of Gifted Children and their Teachers.

The program of the Georgia studies has been supported and directed by Torrance with the assistance of J. Pansy Torrance, numerous graduate research assistants from different countries, postdoctoral students, and visiting scholars. Torrance (1984) observed that graduate students throughout the world have participated in the studies through their questions, suggestions and research findings.

Headquarters for the Georgia Studies of Creative Behavior are at 185 Riverhill Drive, Athens, GA 30601. Current activities are concerned with investigating the nature of mentoring relationships; sociodrama as an instructional strategy; developing and revising the streamlined scoring procedures for the TTCT; and verbal and figural and work with the Torrance Center for Creative Studies at the University of Georgia in developing the Torrance Creative Scholars Program and the Torrance Creative Scholar-Mentor Network.

The work of the Minnesota and Georgia studies has resulted in the publication of over 1500 articles, over 35 books, monographs, instructional materials, films, filmstrips, and other creative learning materials. The collection of these materials and other references on creativity, giftedness, and future studies are contained in the library and archives of Torrance, which are housed at the University of Georgia Library and coordinated through the Torrance Center for Creative Studies.

REFERENCES

Torrance, E. P. (1974). *Georgia studies of creative behavior: A brief summary of activities and results (1966–1974)*. Unpublished paper, Department of Educational Psychology, University of Georgia, Athens.

Torrance, E. P. (1979). *Highlights: Georgia studies of creative be-*

havior (1970–1979). Unpublished paper, Department of Educational Psychology, University of Georgia, Athens.

Torrance, J. P. (1984a). *Over the years: Research insights of E. Paul Torrance*. Unpublished paper. Athens, GA: Georgia Studies of Creative Behavior.

Torrance, J. P. (1984). A retrospective view of the Minnesota and Georgia Studies of Creative Behavior. In *New Directions in Creativity Research* (pp. 65–73). Ventura, CA: National/State Leadership Training Institute on the Gifted and Talented.

MARY M. FRASIER
University of Georgia

CREATIVITY
TORRANCE CENTER FOR STUDY OF CREATIVE BEHAVIOR

GERSTMANN SYNDROME

The Gerstmann syndrome consists of a constellation of problems including finger agnosia, right-left orientation problems, inability to calculate or do math (acalculia), and inability to write (agraphia). When first described by Gerstmann (1940), Gerstmann syndrome was believed to be a discrete, localized neurological problem denoting damage specific to the left parietal lobe of the brain. Considerable disagreement currently exists regarding the specific nature and causes of Gerstmann syndrome. Benton (1961) argued that the syndrome was prematurely described and was based on a serendipitous combination of learning and behavior problems with a variety of causes. Others have argued over its precise nature, some holding that the underlying deficit is aphasic in nature and others arguing that Gerstmann syndrome is related to left-hemisphere neglect. The constellation of behaviors occurring in concert is rare and whether or not they represent a true syndrome is difficult to discern. At present, the syndrome is principally of historical and theoretical interest; there are few treatment implications beyond remediation of the specific symptomatology. Children with this constellation of problems would likely be seen as severely learning disabled and require extensive special education services.

REFERENCES

Benton, A. L. (1961). The fiction of the Gerstmann syndrome. *Journal of Neurology, Neurosurgery, & Psychiatry, 28*, 339–346.

Gerstmann, J. (1940). Syndrome of finger agnosia: Disorientation for right and left, agraphia, and acaculia. *Archives of Neurology & Psychiatry, 44*, 398–408.

CECIL R. REYNOLDS
Texas A&M University

ACALCULIA
AGRAPHIA

GESELL, ARNOLD LUCIUS (1880–1961)

Arnold Lucius Gesell was a high-school teacher and principal before entering graduate school at Clark University, where he received his doctorate in psychology in 1906. In 1911 he became assistant professor of education at Yale University, where he founded the Yale Clinic of Child Development and began the studies of child development that were to occupy him for the rest of his life. To improve his qualifications for this work, Gesell studied medicine at Yale, reveiving his MD degree in 1915. Gesell made a detailed, step-by-step analysis of infant behavior, establishing that infant behavior develops in an orderly manner through stages that are alike from child to child.

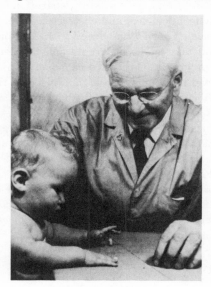

Arnold Lucius Gesell

Gesell became a household name in the United States, primarily because of three books that he coauthored: *Infant and Child in the Culture of Today* (1943), *The Child from Five to Ten* (1946), and *Youth: The Years from Ten to Sixteen* (1956).

In addition to his studies of normal development, Gesell made numerous investigations of deviations in development, including mental retardation, Down's syndrome, cretinism, and cerebral palsy. Following his retirement from Yale in 1948, Gesell continued his work at the Gesell Institute of Child Development, which was founded in his honor in 1950.

REFERENCES

Ames, L. B. (1961). Arnold L. Gesell: Behavior has shapes. *Science, 134,* 266–267.

Langfield, H. S., Boring, E. G., Werner, H., & Yerkes, R. M. (1952). *A history of psychology in autobiography* (Vol. 4). Worcester, MA: Clark University Press.

PAUL IRVINE
Katonah, New York

GESELL DEVELOPMENTAL SCHEDULES

GESELL DEVELOPMENTAL SCHEDULES

The Gesell Developmental Schedules were first published by Gesell and his colleagues in 1940, although updated administration and norms are reported by Gesell, Ilg, and Ames (1974) and Ames, Gillespie, Haines, and Ilg (1979). The schedules provide an empirical method of measuring the development of infants and young children from 4 weeks through 5 years of age. Items on the schedules are ordinally arranged, with behaviors typical of successive ages (e.g., 42 months, 48 months, 54 months) listed. The administration of the schedules requires direct observations of children's responses to stimulus objects such as toys and parent interviews.

Four areas of development are included in the schedules: motor, adaptive, language, and personal/social. Items include walking up and down stairs, saying words and sentences, and imitating drawing circles and crosses. Behavioral norms for ages 2½ through 5 years of age are reported in Ames et al. (1979). Interrater reliability coefficients over .95 have been found (Knobloch & Pasamanick, 1974).

REFERENCES

Ames, L. B., Gillespie, B. S., Haines, J., & Ilg, F. L. (1979). *The Gesell Institute's child from one to six: Evaluating the behavior of the preschool child.* New York: Harper & Row.

Gesell, A., Ilg, F., & Ames, L. B. (1974). *Infant and child in the culture of today* (rev. ed.). New York: Harper & Row.

Knobloch, H., & Pasamanick, B. (Eds.). (1974). *Gesell and Amatruda's developmental diagnosis* (3rd ed.). Hagerstown, MD: Harper & Row.

PATTI L. HARRISON
University of Alabama

BAYLEY SCALES OF INFANT DEVELOPMENT

GESELL SCHOOL READINESS TESTS

The Gesell School Readiness Tests (Ilg, Ames, Haines, & Gillespie, 1978), a behavior test for children ages 5 through 10 years, determines children's readiness for school and promotions to succeeding grade levels according to developmental level. The administration of the test requires about half an hour. The test consists of an interview with the child (questions about the child's age, birthday, number of siblings, and father's occupation); paper and pencil tests (writing name, address, date, and numbers); copying of forms (e.g., circle, triangle, square); finishing of a drawing of an incomplete man; right and left orientation; the Monroe Visual Tests; and questions about what the child likes to do best at home and at school.

Behavioral norms (i.e., the typical scores for children at each year from 5 through 10 years of age) are provided for each section of the instrument. Ilg et al. (1978) provide detailed descriptions of average children at each year from 5 through 10 years of age. Ilg et al. (1978) also report several psychometric characteristics of the tests. These include a description of the standardization sample and sex and group differences.

REFERENCES

Ilg, F. L., Ames, L. B., Haines, T., & Gillespie, C. (1978). *School readiness: Behavior tests used at the Gesell Institute* (rev. ed.). New York: Harper & Row.

PATTI L. HARRISON
University of Alabama

GESELL DEVELOPMENTAL SCHEDULES

GETMAN, GERALD N. (1913–   )

A native of Larchwood, Iowa, Gerald N. Getman received his doctor of optometry degree from Northern Illinois College of Optometry (NICO) in 1937. He also received an honorary doctor of ocular sciences degree from NICO in 1957, and an honorary doctor of sciences degree from the State University of New York College of Optometry in 1986. Though he spent much of his career in Luverne, Minnesota, Getman spent 8 years as director of research in child development at the Pathway School in Pennsylvania, and 11 years in education and research in California. He is now retired from optometric practice and serves numerous public and private schools as a special consultant on visually related learning problems.

Getman's principal contributions to special education have been equally divided between developmental/behavioral optometry and education. Having worked in research with Arnold Gesell from 1944 to 1950, Getman changed his concepts of vision development. With his help, the vision care of children is now widely available clinically from informed optometrists (Getman et al., 1949). Getman is widely considered the father of developmental optometry, and has broadly influenced the educational procedures for the guidance of the child with learning problems.

Gerald N. Getman

Getman has become a firm believer that parents must be involved in the preparation of children's learning programs if a child is to have the best preparation for today's increasingly technological and abstract culture. His book *How to Develop Your Child's Intelligence* has become an international text for both parents and teachers. In establishing programs, Getman sees no use for what he terms misleading clinical labels, holding that these ambiguous labels only create confusion instead of understanding (Getman, 1976).

Getman is the recipient of the Pioneer Award of the National Association for Children with Learning Disabilities and the Special Award of Distinction from the International Federation of Learning Disabilities. He is also the recipient of the Apollo Award, the highest commendation given by the American Optometric Association. He has been included in *Who's Who in the Midwest* and in numerous other such listings.

REFERENCES

Getman, G. N. (1976). *Teaching children with learning disabilities: Personal perspectives.* Columbus, OH: Merrill.

Getman, G. N., Gesell, A., Ilg, F., Bullis, G., & Ilg, V. (1949). *Vision, its development in infant and child.* New York: Hoeber.

E. VALERIE HEWITT
Texas A&M University

g FACTOR THEORY

Charles Spearman (1863–1945) proposed a general intellectual ability, *g*, to account for the fact that all mental abilities are to some degree positively intercorrelated (Spearman, 1904, 1927). Spearman considered *g* to be a hereditary general mental energy that is manifest most strongly in tasks involving "the education of relations and correlates" (i.e., inductive and deductive reasoning) and "abstractness."

Spearman developed the statistical method of factor analysis by which it is possible to determine the g loading of a test, or the proportion of variation in the test score that is shared with all other tests in the analysis. This led to Spearman's two-factor theory of mental ability, in which the variation of each measured ability is divided into two parts: a part owed to g and a part specific to the particular test. The two-factor theory was later expanded to admit the possibility of group factors, representing groups of tests that share variation in addition to their general and specific variation.

More recent studies have confirmed Spearman's observation that nearly all mental abilities are positively correlated. It has proved to be virtually impossible to devise a test that appears to involve mental ability that is not positively correlated with all other such tests when administered to a representative sample of people. Factor analysis of such positively correlating tests can always be made to yield a large general factor representing the variation that the tests share in common as indicated by their positive correlations. In such analyses, the tests with the highest g loadings tend to involve comprehension and abstract reasoning across a broad range of content. The greater the degree of mental manipulation of the input elements of the test items, the higher the general factor loading tends to be.

The observations that led Spearman to develop the theory of g are now well established; however, rival conceptualizations of the same observations have gained wide acceptance among psychologists. Thurstone (1938) extended Spearman's method of factor analysis to accommodate correlated factors and adopted the criterion of simple structure to determine the best set of multiple factors to represent the abilities contained in the tests being analyzed. The name primary mental abilities, which Thurstone attached to these factors, focused attention on the multiple differential abilities. The general factor, although still present, was hidden in the correlations among the primary factors. Following Thurstone, the number of known ability factors steadily increased. They have been organized into a model of the structure of intellect by Guilford (1967).

There is now general agreement that there are a number of distinct factors of mental ability that are substantially correlated with each other and that the correlation among the distinct factors represents a large general factor. The disagreement centers on which is most important, the multiple distinct factors or the single underlying general factor, g.

Jensen (1979, 1985) interpreted g as the basic biological factor of intelligence and attempted to relate it to general speed of mental processing. He pointed out that g, more than any other factor of ability, corresponds to the commonsense notion of intelligence, that it is most predictive of success in academic and occupational situations demanding mental ability. He also presented evidence concerning inbreeding depression that suggests that g is the ability that has been most subject to natural selection during the course of human evolution.

On the other hand, Dettermann (1982) suggested that g may simply be an artifact of the difficulty of obtaining independent measures of the specific components of human ability. He pointed out that any complex system will have interrelated parts, which will tend to produce a general factor of functioning. Attending to the general factor, however, will not help in understanding the components of the system, which must be studied if one is to gain insight into the nature of intelligence.

REFERENCES

Dettermann, D. K. (1982). Does 'g' exist? *Intelligence, 6,* 99–108.

Guilford, J. P. (1967). *The nature of human intelligence.* New York: McGraw-Hill.

Jensen, A. R. (1979). g: Outmoded theory of unconquered frontier? *Creative Science & Technology, 2,* 16–29.

Jensen, A. R. (1985). The nature of the black-white difference on various psychometric tests: Spearman's hypothesis. *Behavioral & Brain Sciences, 8,* 193–219.

Spearman, C. (1904). General intelligence, objectively determined and measured. *American Journal of Psychology, 27,* 229–239.

Spearman, C. (1927). *The abilities of man.* New York: Macmillan.

Thurstone, L. L. (1938). Primary mental abilities. *Psychometric Monographs, 1.*

ROBERT C. NICHOLS
DIANE JARVIS
*State University of New York,
Buffalo*

**CULTURE FAIR TESTS
INTELLIGENCE TESTING
SPEARMAN'S HYPOTHESIS OF BLACK WHITE
    DIFFERENCES**

GIFTED, COUNSELING THE

Gifted children do not necessarily become productive, high-achieving, gifted adults. During their schooling years, gifted students are faced with traditional choices and adjustments, as well as unique complications connected with their giftedness; therefore, counseling programs for the gifted need to be unique and multifaceted.

Counselors should be prepared to foster emotional development, socialization skills, academic preparation, career selection, and leadership training (Rice, 1985). Counselors should not assume that because students are gifted, they will be adept at making choices or being in control of their lives.

The dynamics of a counseling program for the gifted will usually consist of group and/or individual counseling sessions. Counseling goals should be predetermined with the unique attributes and needs of the gifted as a focus. Emotional and socialization issues may be addressed in group counseling through value clarification activities, philosophical debates, and moral dilemmas (Colangelo & Zaffran, 1979). However, with students who have personal social/emotional adjustment problems, individual counseling would be preferred (Rice, 1985).

Academic preparation and career selection counseling, although occasionally administered in group settings, should become an individualized process. Students should identify their own academic needs to prepare them for a variety of professions. Counselors may find themselves guiding gifted students in topics such as developing study skills, reading improvement, and test taking strategies, as well as course selection and sequencing (Barbe & Renzulli, 1981).

Individual counseling should be provided to gifted students to help them cope with the intricacies of giftedness. Self-management, self-discipline, self-perception, self-direction, and stress management are issues that need to be addressed by all gifted students.

Leadership training may be directed with individual or group counseling techniques. Giftedness does lend itself to the making of a leader; however, it does not ensure it. The development of leadership qualities should be an integral component of all gifted programs.

Counseling gifted students may occur in the counselor's office, the classroom, the hallway, on a field trip, or in any variety of settings. Several techniques that are applicable to counseling programs have been documented by Swassing (1985) as being effective with gifted students.

Mentorships are useful in aiding gifted students in developing necessary skills. The modeling that mentors often do teaches students methods for resolving conflicts.

Bibliotherapy is an excellent counseling technique. Many gifted students are avid readers and have reading abilities that enable them to comprehend a variety of materials. Biographies and autobiographies are excellent resources, for they provide models of successful individuals who demonstrated leadership qualities.

Swassing (1985) also advocates the use of humor in group and individual counseling activities. Using the wit of gifted students may relieve tension and provide an alternative means for attacking personal dilemmas. Humor may be used in problem solving, creative thinking, and self-perception activities.

REFERENCES

Barbe, W. B., & Renzulli, J. S. (Eds.). (1981). *Psychology and education for the gifted*. New York: Irvington.

Colango, N., & Zaffran, R. T. (1979). *New voices in counseling the gifted*. Dubuque, IA: Kendall/Hunt.

Rice, J. P. (1985). *The gifted: Developing the total talent*. Springfield, IL: Thomas.

Swassing, R. H. (1985). *Teaching gifted children and adolescents*. Columbus, OH: Merrill.

JONI J. GLEASON
University of West Florida

GIFTED CHILDREN
GIFTED CHILDREN AND TALENTED,
 UNDERACHIEVEMENT IN THE
GIFTED CHILDREN AND READING

GIFTED AND TALENTED, UNDERACHIEVEMENT IN THE

Student underachievement is failure to perform at expected levels in a given area, when these expectations are based on the student's past performance or area related aptitude measures. This failure to perform is not the result of sensory acuity limitations, health status, or a specific cognitive disability.

"Underachievement," or failure to perform (FTP), is a sociologically based concept in which a status is assigned to an individual based on the perception of him or her by others. "Failure to perform" is a label that is based on a performance predictor. It is possible that the predictor may be neither accurately measured nor relevant to performance in given task areas under specific conditions of instruction. For the purposes of this entry, it will be assumed that FTP has been appropriately identified.

In a population free of cognitive disabilities, FTP may reflect a number of factors. These factors include motivational, personality, interpersonal, and curricular instructional considerations. Failure to achieve appears to be a relatively complex phenomenon with multiple dimensions.

Motivation has two basic aspects: "direction or location" and "degree of need for success." Motivation may be of an extrinsic or external nature, or it can be characterized as intrinsic or internal (Newland, 1966). External motivation refers to a student responding to forces and demands outside of himself or herself. Extrinsic motivation is typified by students studying simply to pass an examination. In contrast, an example of intrinsic motivation would be a student's efforts to master an area to satisfy his or her personal achievement needs.

The observable aspects of personality may be viewed as an individual's consistent approach to life situations. While motivation may be thought of as efforts directed toward specific situations, personality reflects a consistent style of approaching a broad range of life situations including task achievement (Barron, 1975; Taylor & Ellison,

1975). This consistent life situation approach has, at least, an "inner" or "self" dimension and an "orientation-to-surrounding-situations" dimension. The inner dimension involves the self concept and is how persons perceive themselves across life settings (Dean, 1977). For example, students may think of themselves as not performing well under pressure. They may feel that their test grades frequently do not represent their actual knowledge in the tested area.

The second dimension of personality is based on the student's willingness to take risks (Doyle & Moen, 1978). This includes the entering of new situations and the making of efforts in areas where success is not always certain (Beery, 1975; Covington & Beery, 1976).

Affective and social issues are also important in school achievement. Personal adjustment is critical to a student's goals and on the student's energies available to pursue these goals. For example, some able students fail to achieve because of their oppositional behaviors towards teachers and parents (Hoeffel, 1980). Hoeffel (1980) has suggested that this is aggression, which results from the students' reduced ability to empathize with teachers and parents. The empathy training of students, based on role playing and other simulation based techniques, has been suggested as an intervention (Hoeffel, 1980).

Ruhland, Gold, and Feld (1978) and Veroff (1969) examined aspects of the school social forces that influence motivation. These influences appear to be developmental; early elementary school achievement appears to be relatively free of peer influences, while achievement in middle elementary and later grades seems very much shaped by peer influences.

Radin (1982) and Martin (1975) have found that parental-child interaction and parental models influence child achievement through support, warmth, and modeling. Combined with the findings of Veroff (1969) and Ruhland, Gold, and Feld (1978), it appears that social experiences and social stimuli at home and in school shape pupil motivation in school tasks. It is conceivable specific social skill deficits or unfavorable pupil parent interactions would have negative effects on school related motivation, unless special supportive intervention occurred.

Achievement has interpersonal, motivational, and personality influences, as well as curriculum influences. It is arguable that the needs of the gifted and talented might be best met through an individual educational plan approach (Swassing, 1985). This plan is based on a curriculum with the characteristics of content acceleration, content enrichment, content novelty, and content sophistication (Gallagher, 1984). Flexibility in programming, such as community-based program or other alternative educational approaches permit wider curriculum/program options to more fully motivate larger numbers of gifted and talented pupils (Swassing, 1985). Social and affective curriculum goals are also desirable to facilitate the more effective adult functioning of the gifted and talented, as well as their more integrated and more effective function in school (Lacy, 1979).

REFERENCES

Barron, F. (1969). *Creative person and creative process*. New York: Holt, Rinehart & Winston.

Beery, R. (1975). Fear of failure in the student experience. *Personnel & Guidance Journal, 54*, 190–203.

Covington, M. V., & Beery, R. (1976). *Self worth and school learning*. New York: Holt, Rinehart & Winston.

Hoeffel, E. (1978). *The antiachieving adolescent*. Unpublished doctoral dissertation, Boston University, Boston, MA.

Dean, R. S. (1977). Effects of self concept of learning with gifted children. *Journal of Educational Research, 70*, 315–318.

Doyle, K. E., & Moen, R. E. (1978). Toward the definition of a domain of academic motivation. *Journal of Educational Psychology, 70*, 231–236.

Gallagher, J. J. (1985). *Teaching the gifted child*. Boston: Allyn & Bacon.

Lacy, G. (1979). *The social and emotional development of the gifted and talented*. Albany, NY: University of the State of New York, State Education Department.

Newland, T. E. (1966). *The gifted in socioeconomic and educational perspective*. Englewood Cliffs, NJ.: Prentice Hall.

Radin, N. (1982). The unique contribution of parents to child-rearing. In S. G. Moore & C. R. Cooper (Eds.). *The Young Child: Reviews of Research* (Vol. 3, pp. 55–76). Washington, DC: National Association for the Education of Young Children.

Ruhland, D., Gold, M., & Feld, S. (1978). Role problems and the relationship of achievement motivation to scholastic performance. *Journal of Educational Psychology, 70*, 950.

Swassing, R. H. (1985). *Teaching gifted children and adolescents*. Columbus, OH: Merrill.

Taylor, C. W., & Ellison, R. L. (1975). Moving toward working models in creativity: Utah creativity experiences and insights. In I. A. Taylor & J. W. Getzels (Eds.), *Perspectives in creativity*. Chicago: Adline.

Veroff, J. (1969). Social comparison and the development of achievement motivation. In C. F. Smith (Ed.), *Achievement related motives in children*, 46–101. New York: Sage.

LeRoy Clinton
Boston University

GIFTED AND TALENTED CHILDREN

Gifted and talented children are now recognized in thousands of American schools as having learning and personal characteristics that are different from those of children of average and low ability. As a result of these differential characteristics, they have special educational needs and therefore a need for differentiated educational programs. Among the special characteristics of the gifted and talented are the following:

1. They learn new material rapidly and easily.
2. They are precocious. Talents appear early and advanced skills and achievement levels are much higher than grade placement.
3. They have large vocabularies, read early, are verbally fluent, and write well.
4. They reason well, understand easily, have intellectual depth, and are logical.
5. They have extended awareness of the world, respond to more elements of a situation, and are socially aware.

These characteristics lead to a set of special educational needs. Van-Tassel (1979) proposed the following list of special educational needs of gifted and talented children:

1. To be challenged to operate cognitively and affectively at complex levels of thought and feeling
2. To be challenged through opportunities for divergent production
3. To be challenged through work that demonstrates process/product outcomes
4. To be challenged by discussions among intellectual peers
5. To be challenged by experiences that promote understanding of human value systems
6. To be challenged by the opportunity to see interrelationships in all bodies of knowledge
7. To be challenged by special courses that accelerate pace and depth
8. To be challenged by exposure to new areas of learning
9. To be challenged by applying abilities to real problems
10. To be taught critical thinking, creative thinking, research, problem solving, coping with exceptionality, decision making, and leadership

Gifted children are those who have superior general intellectual ability. Talented children are those who show signs of special aptitude or ability in a specific area of the arts, sciences, business, etc. (Gagne, 1985). Renzulli (1979) suggests that giftedness also includes high levels of task commitment (motivation) and creativity. Feldhusen (1986) extended the conception of giftedness to include a self-concept that recognizes and accepts special talents or abilities. Gagne (1985), however, proposed that personal factors such as motivation, task commitment, and self-concept are not elements or factors of giftedness but rather are catalysts that facilitate the emergence and growth of general ability toward specialized talent or aptitude in a special area of human endeavor.

Schools sometimes identify the gifted and talented as early as kindergarten or first grade and provide special educational programs of service to them. Richert, Alvino, and McDonnel (1982) conducted a survey of the methods used to identify gifted and talented youths in the United States. They found a wide diversity of tests and rating scales being used (and misused) to identify gifted and talented children. They particularly noted that tests are often used in ways for which they were not intended and that the most significant deficiency in identification occurs in the area of leadership talent. However, they acknowledge that this is the most difficult area of giftedness to define.

Gallagher, Weiss, Oglesby, and Thomas (1983) conducted a survey of schools in the United States to determine which practices characterized special programs for the gifted. They found that the resource room/pullout model was most popular, followed by special advanced classes for the gifted at the elementary level. At the secondary level the most widely used provision was advanced or honors classes, while opportunities for independent study and research came in second.

Some states now mandate that all schools must provide special program services for gifted and talented youths. Many provide formula funding to the schools for the special education of these youths. There is increasing recognition that these youths need to be identified early and given differentiated educational opportunities if they are to realize their full potential. Recent research by Bloom (1985) indicates that gifted and talented youths should be identified early and given specialized instruction in their areas of special talent or ability. Through such special programming at school, and with support at home, gifted and talented children can reach high achievement as adults.

REFERENCES

Bloom, B. S. (Ed.). (1985). *Developing talent in young people.* New York: Ballantine.

Feldhusen, J. F. (1986). A conception of giftedness. In R. S. Sternberg & J. S. Davidson (Eds.), *Conceptions of giftedness.* New York: Cambridge University Press.

Gagne, G. (1985). Giftedness and talent: Reexamining a reexamination of the definitions. *Gifted Child Quarterly, 29,* 103–112.

Gallagher, J. J., Weiss, P., Oglesby, K., & Thomas, T. (1983). *The status of gifted/talented education.* Los Angeles: National/State Leadership Training Institute for the Gifted/Talented.

Renzulli, J. S. (1979). *What makes giftedness.* Los Angeles: National/State Leadership Training Institute for the Gifted/Talented.

Richert, E. S., Alvino, J. J., & McDonnel, R. C. (1982). *National report on identification.* Sewell, NJ: Educational Improvement Center-South.

Van-Tassel, J. L. (1979). A needs assessment model for gifted education. *Journal for the Education of the Gifted, 29,* 103–112.

JOHN F. FELDHUSEN
Purdue University

GENIUS
GIFTED CHILDREN
INTELLIGENCE

GIFTED CHILD QUARTERLY

The *Gifted Child Quarterly* is a major publication in the field of gifted education. It is published by the National Association for Gifted Children, 4175 Lovell Road, Box 30, Circle Pinese, Minnesota 55014. The quarterly was first published in 1954, two years after the founding of the National Association for Gifted Children. It carries articles on research and theory, book reviews, and descriptions of practice in gifted education. It is a refereed publication with a panel of 30 reviewers and an editor elected by the board of the association. All members of the association receive the quarterly as part of their membership privileges.

JOHN F. FELDHUSEN
Purdue University

GIFTED CHILDREN

The major pioneer of the scientific study of gifted children in the United States was Lewis Terman, whose research on intellectually gifted students refuted popular myths regarding the physical and social inferiority of highly able children and showed that gifted youths were largely neglected in school (Terman, 1925).

The research of Terman (1925), Hollingworth (1942), Cox (1926), Witty (1930), and others promoted the establishment of prototype programs for the gifted such as Cleveland's Major Work Program (Barbe, 1957), and special schools for talented students such as the Bronx High School of Science (Galasso & Simon, 1981). Federal support, however, was limited and gifted programming was limited to centers of interest within the major cities.

In 1957 the advent of Sputnik generated national concern regarding the quality of science education in the United States and a concomitant focus on gifted youth. This spurred a second wave of programs for the gifted, this time concentrating on students with specific academic ability, particularly in the sciences and mathematics. The National Education Association commenced its Project on the Academically Talented and issued a series of publications on educating children talented in a range of specific curriculum areas (Bish, 1975).

In 1972 the Marland Report (Marland, 1972) broadened concepts of giftedness still further by defining the gifted as those who possessed outstanding abilities or potential in the areas of general intellectual capacity, specific academic aptitude, creative or productive thinking, leadership ability, visual or performing arts, and psychomotor ability.

The Marland Report also established criteria for differentiated programming for the gifted arising out of the broader definition. Appropriate curriculum for the gifted was defined as (1) based on higher level cognitive concepts and processes; (2) involving instructional strategies that accommodate differentiated learning styles; and (3) accommodating a variety of special grouping arrangements.

The establishment of the Federal Office for the Gifted in 1974 and the appropriation of funding for the establishment of gifted programs led to the strengthening of state support agencies, the establishment of national networks, and increased cross-fertilization of ideas among states and centers of interest in gifted education. The passage of PL 95-561 in 1978 provided for the escalation of funding for gifted education at the federal level. In 1981, however, the Office of Gifted and Talented was eliminated along with many other federal programs.

The early 1980s saw a proliferation of research studies on the effectiveness of gifted programming in the United States. Richert (1982) surveyed methods used to identify gifted and talented youths and found great diversity in procedures. Gallagher, Weiss, Oglesby, and Thomas (1983) surveyed teachers and parents of the gifted to determine which program models are most frequently used and preferred; resource rooms were most common at the elementary level and special classes at the secondary level.

Definitions of giftedness determine program design and curriculum development. Tannenbaum (1983) offers one of the most promising of new definitions of giftedness in children. He states "giftedness . . . denotes their potential for becoming critically acclaimed performers or exemplary producers of ideas in spheres of activity that enhance the moral, physical, emotional, social, intellectual, or aesthetic life of humanity" (p. 86). He goes on to suggest five basic factors related to giftedness. They are (1) general intelligence, (2) special talents, aptitudes or ability, (3) nonintellective factors such as dedication and ego strength, (4) environmental conditions that are stimulating or supportive, and (5) chance factors. Feldhusen (1986) has added to that definition by suggesting that the gifted need a self concept that recognizes and accepts their unusual potential for high-level achievement. Feldhusen suggests that giftedness in a child or adolescent consists of psychological and physical predispositions for superior learning and performance in the formative years and high-level achievement or performance in adulthood.

REFERENCES

Barbe, W. B. (1957). What happens to graduates of special classes for the gifted? *Ohio State University Educational Research Bulletin, 36,* 13–16.

Bish, C. E. (1975). The academically talented project, gateway to the present. *Gifted Child Quarterly 19*(4), 271, 282–89.

Cox, C. M. (1926). *Genetic studies of genius: Vol. 2. The early mental traits of 300 geniuses*. Stanford, CA: Stanford University Press.

Feldhusen, J. F. (1986). A conception of giftedness. In R. J. Sternberg & J. E. Davidson (Eds.), *Conceptions of giftedness*. New York: Cambridge University Press.

Galasso, V. G., & Simon, M. (1981). Model program for developing creativity in science at the Bronx High School of Science. In I. S. Sato (Ed.), *Secondary programs for the gifted/talented* (pp. 55–57). Los Angeles: National/State Leadership Training Institute on the Gifted and Talented.

Gallagher, J. J., Weiss, P., Oglesby, K., & Thomas T. (1983). *The status of gifted, talented education: United States surveys of needs, practices and policies*. Los Angeles: National/State Leadership Training Institute on the Gifted and Talented.

Hollingworth, L. S. (1942). *Children Above 180 IQ*. New York: World Book.

Marland S. (1972). *Education of the gifted and talented*. Report to the Subcommittee on Education, Committee on Labor and Public Welfare. Washington, DC: U.S. Senate.

Richert, E. S. (1982). *National Report on Identification*. Sewell, NJ: Educational Improvement Centre-South.

Tannenbaum, A. J. (1983). *Gifted children, psychological and educational perspectives*. New York: Macmillan.

Terman, L. M. (1925). *Genetic studies of genius: Vol. 1. Mental and physical traits of a thousand gifted children*. Stanford, CA: Stanford University Press.

Witty, P. A. (1930). *A Study of 100 Gifted Children*. Lawrence, KA: Bureau of School Service and Research.

JOHN F. FELDHUSEN
Purdue University

GENIUS
GIFTED AND TALENTED CHILDREN

GIFTED CHILDREN, MINORITIES

Educators and the interested public encounter difficult issues in the area of minority students who are gifted and talented. Some areas of difficulty are definition, social-cultural or social-cultural-linguistic perspective, unbiased assessment, and special curricular and guidance-support.

Issues of definition, social-cultural perspective, and unbiased assessment will be considered from the vantage point of the Marland (1972) definition of "gifted and talented" persons. Essentially, Marland defined the gifted and talented as those with both a "potential for high performance" and a need for special intervention to realize this potential. In Marland's view, the gited and talented individual would demonstrate high achievement or high potential in at least one of the following areas: intellectual aptitude, academic achievement, creative or productive thinking, leadership, or visual and performing arts. Gallagher, Weiss, Oglesby, and Thomas (1983) found that 28 American states have definitions of gifted and talented that reflect the influence of Marland's (1972) definition.

The Marland and related gifted-talented definitions such as the one in the federal Gifted and Talented Act of 1978 imply that the value of a particular person's potential or performance is determined by his or her social-cultural context. Further, there is recognition of whether potential or achievement is "high." The use of local norms, e.g., might result in one decision, while the use of national norms would result in a different one.

Who are gifted and talented minority students? The answer to this question demands the consideration of several more fundamental issues: social-cultural context, unbiased assessment, and definition. Identification and screening procedures rest on social-cultural perspective view, assessment process, and selection criteria.

Sand painting is a traditional art form within segments of the southwestern Native American cultures. Might talent in this area be overlooked in typical American schools? If the answer is yes, the issue being raised involves social-cultural perspective and the valuing of efforts within a given context. One might argue that soapstone carving or storytelling are as much art forms as is portraiture. Some art forms have a greater tradition and are more valued than others in a given social-cultural setting. The risk is the ignoring of talent that may not be highly valued in the mainstream American social-cultural context.

The measurement of intellectual aptitude and academic achievement raises the concern of fair and accurate assessment. This concern includes the issues of unbiased assessment and status based on relative position. Unbiased assessment is the valid and reliable appraisal of student performance that is appropriate to a given student's cultural and linguistic background, as well as to that student's sensorial and physical status. Relative status refers to whether the identification of gifted and talented persons should be based on their status relative to other minority students or to students in general. Unbiasedness may be conceived to be a desirable characteristic of assessment, while relative status is a judgment criteria that may be used in screening and identification decisions.

LeRose (1978) and Mercer and Lewis (1978) offer approaches based on a relative-status approach to the identification of minority students who are gifted and talented. LeRose suggests a procedure whereby the percentage of the school population represented by a given minority group and a pupil's relative status within that group would be used to determine a minority student's status as gifted and talented. Mercer and Lewis suggest a different relative-status approach. Essentially, a yardstick measure is established within minority students. This comparative basis may then be used to interpret the relative performance of minority students and nonminority students.

The unbiasedness of standardized tests in minority populations has sometimes been sharply criticized. Kaufman and Kaufman (1983) have criticized the use of tests such as the WISC with minority students. The Kaufmans maintain that typical standardized aptitude tests result in biased assessments of minorities' abilities. Jensen (1983), in turn, has criticized the K-ABC battery that the Kaufmans offer as an alternative to the WISC. Jensen (1983) maintains the K-ABC battery yields higher but less valid scores for black students than does the WISC. Parker and Parker (1981) extend the criticism of tests to all written tests. The Parkers argue for a moratorium on written tests in the screening and the identification of gifted talented minority pupils; furthermore, they call for the use and the development of direct observation-based assessment procedures. Based on the authors cited, it might be concluded that standardized tests should be interpreted with utmost caution, if used at all, in the identification of gifted and talented minorities. Further data probably should be gathered, through direct observation, on a range of student behaviors across different situations.

Once identified and placed in programs, gifted and talented minority students may have special curriculum and support needs. These include curricular relevance to student goals and life experiences, the availability of appropriate role models, provision for a variety of learning styles, and support for the student's bridging of home, school, and societal values and expections.

Among others, Frasier (1979) and Colangelo and Lafrenz (1981) have spoken of the critical need for cultural awareness and sensitivity in the counseling/guidance of minority students. This awareness and sensitivity is of particular importance in career education for the gifted and talented minority student.

REFERENCES

Colangelo, N., & LaFrenz, N. (1981). Counseling the culturally diverse gifted. *Gifted Child Quarterly 25,* 27–30.

Frasier, M. M. (1979). Rethinking the issues regarding the culturally disadvantaged gifted. *Exceptional Children, 45,* 538–542.

Gallagher, J. P., Weiss, K., Oglesby, K., & Thomas, T. (1983). *Report on education of the gifted: Surveys and evidence of program effectiveness.* Los Angeles, CA: Natural Student Leadership Training Institution on the Talented and Gifted.

Jensen, A. R. (1983). The black-white difference on the K-ABC: Implications for future tests. *Journal of Special Education, 18,* 377–408.

Kaufman, A. S., & Kaufman, N. L. (1983). *K-ABC interpretive manual.* Circle Pines, MN: American Guidance Service.

LeRose, B. (1978). A quota system for gifted children: A viable solution. *Gifted Child Quarterly, 22,* 294–403.

Marland, S. P., Jr. (1972). *Education of the gifted and talented.* Washington, DC: U.S. Government Printing Office.

Mercer, J. R., & Lewis, J. F. (1978). Using the system of multicultural pluralistic assessment (SOMPA) to identify the gifted minority child. In A. Y. Baldwin, G. H. Gear, & L. J. Lucito (Eds.), *Educational planning for the gifted.* Reston, VA: Council for Exceptional Children.

Parker, R. H., & Parker, W. C. (1981). I ain't no group, I'm me. In W. L. Marks & R. Nystrand (Eds.), *Strategies for educational change: Recognizing the gifts and talents of all children.* Montclair, NY: Macmillan.

LeRoy Clinton
Boston University

GIFTED CHILDREN
GIFTED CHILDREN AND READING

GIFTED CHILDREN AND READING

Four basic reading goals have been offered, in one form or another, for gifted and talented pupils: (1) mechanical skills, (2) appreciation, (3) knowledge of the devices of composition and literature, and (4) evaluation and the application of written material (Barbe, 1961; Endres, Lamb, & Lazarus, 1969; Cushenbery & Howell, 1974). Dole and Adams (1983) have suggested that reading programs for the gifted are similar to programs for other students, but in gifted programs there is more stress on evaluation, analysis, research skills, rhetorical techniques, and independence.

Textual analysis, the use of genre examples, and the teaching of social-cultural-historical context are central in teaching rhetoric to students who are gifted and talented (Rindfleisch, 1981). Vida (1979) and Brown (1982) have stressed the instructional importance of well-selected examples of literary genres and nonfiction sources. The appreciation of good writing appears to be based on exposure to good writing and opportunities to react to this writing. McCormick and Swassing (1982) have highlighted the access to libraries and resource materials in their consideration of reading programs for the gifted and talented pupil. Further, the modeling of appreciation by significant others, teachers and parents, would seem also to facilitate students' appreciation of good writing.

Critical reading is the evaluation of writing content. Critical reading involves the evaluation of sources: what is known versus what is assumed or stated without support. Critical reading involves the analysis of the cogency of texts. Boothby (1980) has emphasized the differentiation of connotation and denotation. Miller (1982) has recommended that critical reading for the gifted stress propaganda devices, analogy, and the use of euphemism. Critical reading includes the evaluation and weighing of evidence, as well as the examination of the structure of written argument or presentation.

Creative reading involves interaction with text, problem solving, and the application of the content of text. In creative reading, a gifted and talented pupil ought to blend what is learned with previous knowledge. A basic goal of creative reading is a pupil's innovative application of knowledge. Torrance and Meyers (1970) have suggested that one instructional step toward creative reading is the setting of reading goals for gifted and talented pupils: (1) the resolution of an ambiguous statement or situation, (2) the presentation of a problem to be solved, or (3) the finding of missing information or a concept that is critical in an argument or explanation.

REFERENCES

Barbe, W. (1961). Reading aspects. In L. Fliegler (Ed.), *Curriculum planning for the gifted*. Englewood Cliffs, NJ: Prentice-Hall.

Boothby, P. (1980). Creative and critical reading for the gifted. *Reading Teacher, 33*, 674–676.

Brown, J. E. (1982). Supplementary materials for academically gifted English students. *Journal for the Education of the Gifted, 5*, 67–73.

Cushenbery, D., & Howell, H. (1974). *Reading and the gifted: A guide for teachers*. Springfield, IL: Thomas.

Dole, J. A., & Adams, P. J. (1983). Reading cirriculum for gifted readers: A survey. *Gifted Child Quarterly, 27*, 64–72.

Endres, M., Lamb, P., & Lazarus, A. (1969). Selected objectives in the English language arts. *Elementary English, 46*, 418–430.

McCormick, S., & Swassing, R. H. (1982). Reading instruction for the gifted: A survey of programs. *Journal for the Education of the Gifted, 5*, 34–43.

Miller, M. S. (1982). Using the newspaper with the gifted. *Gifted Child Quarterly, 23*, 47–49.

Rindfleisch, N. (1981). In support of writing. D. B. Cole & Ritt, Cornell (Eds.), *Respecting the pupil: Essays on teaching able students*. Exeter, NH: Phillips Exeter Press.

Torrance, E. P. & Meyers. R. E. (1970). *Creative learning and teaching*. NY: Harper & Row.

Vida, L. (1979). Children's literature for the gifted elementary school child. *Roeper Review, 1*, 22–24.

LeRoy Clinton
Boston University

GIFTED EDUCATION RESOURCE INSTITUTE

The Gifted Education Resource Institute was founded at Purdue University, West Lafayette, Indiana, in 1978 to (1) conduct research on gifted children; (2) provide graduate programs in gifted education at the MS and PhD levels; (3) offer services to schools in developing programs for the gifted; (4) conduct special programs for gifted youths on Saturdays and in summers; (5) make psychological services available for gifted youths in the areas of testing and counseling; and (6) disseminate information to schools and parents concerning the identification and education of gifted children. The institute is directed by Dr. John F. Feldhusen. Eight other professors in related disciplines serve as associated faculty at the institute. Approximately 15 graduate students are in residence each year working on grants and projects conducted by the institute. The institute also works closely with the Indiana Department of Education and Indiana schools in training teachers for work with the gifted and in developing educational programs for gifted and talented youth.

John F. Feldhusen
Purdue University

GIFTED HANDICAPPED

The gifted handicapped have been defined as "those who exhibit unusual gifts/talents in spite of physical, mental, emotional, or experiential handicaps" (Blacher-Dixon, 1977). This definition, however, is far too simplistic for one to understand the complexity of this seemingly contradictory category. To understand the category of gifted handicapped, one must understand each of the categories separately.

The experts in the field of gifted education disagree among themselves as to the appropriate definition of a gifted child. Burroughs (1979) writes of over 113 definitions of gifted children. Terman identified gifted as the 2% who score the highest on tests of intelligence (Clark, 1983). The federal government, through the Educational Consolidation and Improvement Act of 1983 (PL 97-35) defines the gifted as "children who give evidence of high performance capability in areas such as intellectual, creative, artistic, leadership capacity, or specific academic fields, and who require services or activities not normally provided by the school in order to fully develop such capabilities" (Section 582). Some define a gifted child as one possessing a cluster of characteristics (Renzulli, 1978), while others point to the latest research in biological differences in defining giftedness (Clark, 1983). All seem to agree, however, that giftedness implies superior ability and/or functioning in at least one specific area. Children are considered handicapped when their normal learning and development are impaired by one or more specific conditions so that special educational programming and related services are required to develop their abilities (Whitmore & Maker, 1985). "Gifted learners appear in every population of handicapped students with the obvious exceptions of the mentally retarded and severely developmentally disabled" (Clark, 1983). Different handicapping conditions affect the gifted child in varying ways. For example, the blind and visually impaired may possess the same levels of cognitive ability as the sighted, but they attain their maximum levels later. Among the deaf, there is a slower rate of development and difficulty in dealing with abstractions. Among the learning disabled and emotionally disturbed, problems are found in attention, perception, and ability to evaluate. For the physically handicapped, the rate and type of cognitive processes is comparable to that of the normal population (Maker, 1977).

Concern for the gifted handicapped surfaced in 1974 when Ed Martin, of the Bureau of Education for the Handicapped, spoke on historic patterns of discrimination affecting such youngsters. In 1975 a TAG (The Association of Gifted) committee on the gifted handicapped was formed. A TAG-sponsored topical conference was held in New Orleans in 1976. By 1977 the term gifted handicapped appeared in ERIC and Exceptional Children Educational Research indices (Porter, 1982).

Although no accurate statistics exist, a reasonable and perhaps conservative estimate is that 2% of all handicapped children can be classified as mentally gifted (Whitmore & Maker, 1985).

Children classified as gifted and handicapped require special educational programming both to accommodate one or more disabling conditions and to develop fully their potential for exceptional achievement in one or more areas (Whitmore & Maker, 1985). The deficit needs of these children are often so immediate that remediation becomes the primary concern. In this climate, evidence of giftedness is often overlooked (Clark, 1983) and those needs are not addressed.

Identification of the gifted handicapped learner will follow many of the same procedures of screening and multiple data collection that are typically used in identifying the gifted population. There are, however, some special factors that need to be considered in order to unmask the ability obscured by the disability. Pendarvis & Grossi (1980) present detailed identification procedures specific to each disability area. The federal government has supported some programs for identifying, diagnosing, and programming for gifted handicapped children. Three of the best known are the Chapel Hill, North Carolina, Training and Outreach Program; the RAPYHT (Retrieval and Acceleration of Promising Young Handicapped and Talented) Project; and the Rural School Gifted and Talented Project for Handicapped Children. All three programs were developed to identify and serve gifted, handicapped preschool-age children (Porter, 1982).

The barriers for the gifted handicapped are double those of the gifted nonhandicapped. First, the child must overcome or cope with difficulties presented by a handicapping condition. Second, the child must combat the prejudices of those who feel that handicapping conditions and giftedness are a contradiction in terms.

More and more attention is being given to this particular field; however, it is evident from the studies of people such as Whitmore and Maker (1985) that those disabled gifted who have become high achievers have done so despite discouragement, resistance, and rejection by many of those around them. Much work is yet to be done in the fields of identification, acceptance, and programming for the gifted handicapped if they are to fulfill the promise of their potential.

REFERENCES

Blacher-Dixon, J. (1977). *Preschool for the gifted handicapped: Is it untimely or about time?* Paper presented at the 55th Annual International Convention of the Council for Exceptional Children. (ERIC Document Reproduction Service No. ED 139 170).

Burroughs, M. (1979). *Restraints on excellence.* Hingham, MA: Teaching Resource.

Clark, B. (1983). *Growing up gifted.* Columbus, OH: Merrill.

Maker, J. (1977). *Providing programs for the gifted handicapped.* Reston, VA: Council for Exceptional Children.

Pendarvis, E., & Grossi, J. (1980). Designing and operating programs for the gifted and talented handicapped. In J. Jordan & J. Grossi (Eds.), *An administrative handbook on designing programs for the gifted and talented* (pp. 66–88). Reston, VA: Council for Exceptional Children.

Porter, R. (1982). The gifted handicapped: A status report. *Roper Review, 4*(3), 24–25.

Renzulli, J. (1978). What makes giftedness? Reexamining a definition. *Phi Delta Kappan, 60,* 180–184.

Whitmore, J., & Maker, J. (1985). *Intellectual giftedness in disabled persons.* Rockville, MD: Aspen.

MARJORIE WEINTRAUB
*Montgomery County
Intermediate Unit,
Norristown, Pennsylvania*

GIFTED CHILDREN
GIFTED CHILDREN, MINORITIES

GIFTED INTERNATIONAL

Gifted International is a journal published by the World Council for Gifted and Talented Children. The founding and current editor is Dr. Dorothy Sisk of the University of South Florida. The journal publishes theory, research on, and discussions of problems and practices in gifted education from around the world. In the first issue Sisk stated the following specific aims of the Journal:

1. Provide a forum for the exchange of research, identification procedures, curriculum, and good educational practices for the gifted and talented.

2. Generate cooperative sharing of gifted and talented practices and resources.

3. Stimulate cross-cultural research and provide opportunities for dissemination of findings.

The secretary of the World Council Sisk; subscription orders for *Gifted International* should be addressed to her at the College of Education, University of South Florida, Tampa, Florida.

JOHN F. FELDHUSEN
Purdue University

GILLINGHAM-STILLMAN: ALPHABETIC APPROACH

Anna Gillingham and Bessie Stillman derived their remedial training for children with specific disabilities in reading, spelling, and penmanship from the work of Dr. Samuel T. Orton. Orton was a neurologist who spent his career studying and treating children and adults with specific difficulties in reading, writing, and spelling. Both Gillingham and Stillman were teachers at the Ethical Culture Schools in New York City. Gillingham left the schools to become a research fellow under Orton at the Neurological Institute at Columbia-Presbyterian Medical Center, New York. She worked closely with Orton and then Stillman to devise and refine their teaching approach for children with specific language disabilities.

The Gillingham-Stillman approach is remedial, designed for children from third through sixth grades who have normal intelligence, normal sensory acuity, a tendency for letter or word reversals, and an inability to acquire reading and spelling skills by ordinary methods, for instance, "sight word methods even when these are reinforced by functional, incidental, intrinsic, or analytic phonics, or by tracing procedures" (Gillingham & Stillman, 1960, p. 17).

The technique is based on the close association of visual, auditory, and kinesthetic elements forming what has been called the language triangle. The following is the description of phonogram presentation from the manual by Gillingham and Stillman (1960):

Each new phonogram is taught by the following processes, which are referred to as associations and involve the associations between visual (V), auditory (A), and kinesthetic (K) records on the brain. Association I. This association consists of two parts—association of the visual symbol with the name of the letter, and association of the visual symbol with the sound of the letter: also the association of the feel of the child's speech organs in producing the name or sound of the letter as he hears himself say it. Association I is V-A and A-K. Part b. is the basis for oral reading.
Part a. The cord is exposed and the name of the letter is spoken by the teacher and repeated by the pupil.
Part b. As soon as the name has been really mastered, the sound is made by the teacher and repeated by the pupil.
Association II. The teacher makes the sound represented by the letter (or phonogram), the face of the card not being seen

by the pupil, and says "Tell me the name of the letter that has this sound." Sound to name is A-A, and is essentially oral spelling. Association III. The letter is carefully made by the teacher and its form, orientation, etc., explained. It is then traced by the pupil, then copied, written from memory, and finally written again with eyes averted while the teacher watches closely. This association is V-K and K-V. . . . Now, the teacher makes the sound, saying "Write the letter that has this sound." This association is A-K, and is the basis of written spelling. (p. 40)

Although the initial, primary focus is a direct approach to phonetic decoding via multiple sensory pathways, this is an integrated, total language approach. Each unit is established through hearing, speaking, seeing, and writing it. The visual, auditory, and kinesthetic patterns reinforce each other. It is a systematic, sequential approach, proceeding from the simple to the more complex in the orderly progression of language development. Such a concept originated in the works of Maria Montessori, Grace Fernald, and Samuel Orton. Currently, popular offshoots of the Gillingham-Stillman approach are Enfield and Greene's Project READ, the Slinglerland method, Spalding's Writing Road to Reading, the Herman method, and Traub's Recipe for Reading.

REFERENCES

Gillingham, A., & Stillman, B. (1960, 1970). *Remedial training for children with specific disability in reading, spelling and penmanship* (7th ed.). Cambridge, MA: Educators Publishing Service.

Orton, S. T. (1937). *Reading, writing and speech problems in children.* New York: Norton.

SYLVIA O. RICHARDSON
University of South Florida

READING DISORDERS
READING REMEDIATION

GLAUCOMA

See VISUALLY IMPAIRED.

GLIAL CELLS

In addition to the neuron, there are a variety of brain cells that function in a supportive role. These are the glial or neuroglial cells (Brodal, 1981). The glial cells are 5 to 10 times more numerous than neurons. The name is derived from the Greek derivative *glia*, which means glue. Originally, the glial cells were thought to function only as supportive tissue for the intricate neuronal matrix of the brain. While glial cells do play an important supportive role, it is now known that gial cells may play an even more dynamic, interactive, and regulatory role in brain function. For example, it is now known that many glial cells surround synaptic areas in an apparent network to restrict the escape of and specify the direction of neurotransmitter release between neurons. Glial cells may also play a nutritive role, providing a pathway from the vascular system to individual nerve cells (Rosenzweig & Leiman, 1982). Similarly, glial cells may assist in directing or redirecting blood flow, especially to active cerebral regions (Bloom, Lazerson, & Hofstadter, 1985). Glial cells also participate in regulating neuronal growth and direction of neuronal interaction (Cotman & McGaugh, 1980).

There are several types of glial cells, the most common being the astrocyte (Latin *astra* meaning star). Another common gial cell is the oligodendrocyte (Greek *oligo*, meaning few), which is considerably smaller than the astrocyte, with fewer processes and appendages. The third major glial cell type is the microglial, which, as its name implies, is very small. The microglial cells function in phagocytosis of neuronal debris.

Abnormal proliferation of glial cells is the basis of many types of cerebral tumors (astrocytomas). Also, the breakdown of glial cells (e.g., the axonal myelin sheath produced by the oligodendroglia) is the basis of certain degenerative brain disorders (e.g., multiple sclerosis).

Some recent anatomic findings in the brain of dyslexic individuals have demonstrated significant abnormalities in not only neuronal microstructure, but also glial cell development (Duffy & Geschwind, 1985; Galaburda & Kemper, 1979). These and similar findings suggest that glial cell abnormalities may play an important role in the expression of certain neurobehavioral disorders.

REFERENCES

Bloom, F. E., Lazerson, A., & Hofstadter, L. (1985). *Brain, mind, and behavior*. New York: Freeman.

Brodal, A. (1981). *Neurological anatomy* (3rd ed.). New York: Oxford University Press.

Cotman, C. W., & McGaugh, J. L. (1980). *Behavioral neuroscience*. New York: Academic.

Duffy, F. H., & Geschwind, N. (1985). *Dyslexia: A neuroscientific approach to clinical evaluation*. Boston: Little, Brown.

Galaburda, A. M., & Kemper, T. L. (1979). Cytoarchitectonic abnormalities in developmental dyslexia: A case study. *Annals of Neurology 6*, 94–100.

Rosenzweig, M. R., & Leiman, A. L. (1982). *Physiological Psychology*. Lexington MA: Heath.

ERIN D. BIGLER
Austin Neurological Clinic
University of Texas, Austin

CENTRAL NERVOUS SYSTEM
DENDRITES
MULTIPLE SCLEROSIS

GOALS, ANNUAL

See ANNUAL GOALS.

GOALS, USE OF

Educational goals serve three important functions: (1) to structure teaching and curriculum development, (2) to guide learners by helping them recognize errors and discriminate among responses, and (3) to structure the evaluation process (Bloom, Hastings, & Madaus, 1971).

The use of goals in special education was mandated in 1975 by the Education for All Handicapped Children Act (PL 94-142). Incorporation of educational goals into PL 94-142 was prompted by congressional concern for accountability, not by a desire to facilitate the educational purposes cited previously (Fuchs & Deno, 1982). In its fact finding for PL 94-142, Congress found that the special education needs of handicapped children were not being met fully and that the goal specification component of the law would ensure that schools would be accountable for the quality of the programs they provide to handicapped pupils (Turnbull & Turnbull, 1978).

Given this legal mandate, within the past 10 years, the writing of goals has become standard special education practice; i.e., teachers routinely write goals on students' individual educational programs (IEPs). Additionally, as mandated by PL 94-142, teachers are required to monitor their students' progress toward those goals. This typically translates into informal evaluations of student goal mastery approximately two to three times each year (Fuchs & Fuchs, 1984).

Despite the widespread use of goals and periodic evaluation of goal mastery in special education, research is scant on the effects of goal use among handicapped learners. Moreover, even within the regular education literature where empirical support for the general effectiveness of goals is provided, only limited information is available concerning specific dimensions of effective goal-writing procedures, and most studies have been conducted with adults (Fuchs, 1986).

Therefore, there is no meaningful data base concerning the general effectiveness of goals for handicapped pupils or the nature of specific dimensions of effective goals. Not surprisingly, it remains unclear whether special education teachers employ goals for instructional planning (Tymitz,

1981) or systematic progress monitoring (Fuchs & Fuchs, 1984) once they have fulfilled the legal requirement of completing goals on IEPs.

REFERENCES

Bloom, B. S., Hastins, J. T., & Madaus, G. F. (1971). *Handbook on formative and summative evaluation of student learning.* New York: McGraw-Hill.

Fuchs, L. S. (1986). *Use of goals with handicapped learners.* Unpublished paper, Vanderbilt University, Nashville, TN.

Fuchs, L. S., & Deno, S. L. (1982). *Developing goals and objectives for educational programs.* Washington, DC: American Association of Colleges for Teacher Education.

Fuchs, L. S., & Fuchs, D. (1984). Criterion-referenced assessment without measurement: How accurate for special education? *Remedial & Special Education, 5*(4), 29–32.

Turnbull, H. R., & Turnbull, A. P. (1978). *Free appropriate public education: Law and implementation.* Denver: Love.

Tymitz, B. L. (1981). Teacher performance on IEP instructional planning tasks. *Exceptional Children, 48,* 258–260.

LYNN S. FUCHS
DOUGLAS FUCHS
*Peabody College, Vanderbilt
University*

INDIVIDUAL EDUCATION PLAN
TEACHER EFFECTIVENESS

GODDARD, HENRY H. (1866–1957)

Henry Herbert Goddard received his PhD in psychology at Clark University. He taught at the Pennsylvania State Teachers College at West Chester before becoming director of research at The Training School at Vineland, New Jersey, in 1906. Specializing in the study of atypical children, his work at the Training School was a major influence on the education of mentally retarded children and adults in the United States. He established the first psy-

Henry H. Goddard

chological laboratory devoted to the study of the mentally retarded, and developed and tested educational methods for their instruction. He translated and adapted the Binet-Simon Intelligence Scale and inaugurated its use in the United States. He also participated in the development of the group tests used to classify the men in the U.S. armed forces in World War I. Goddard conducted a classic study of mental retardation as an inherited trait, reported in 1912 in *The Kallikak Family: A Study in the Heredity of Feeblemindedness.*

In 1918 Goddard was appointed director of the State Bureau of Juvenile Research in Ohio. From 1922 until his retirement in 1938, he was professor of abnormal and clinical psychology at Ohio State University.

REFERENCE

Goddard, H. H. (1912). *The Kallikak Family: A Study in the heredity of feeblemindedness.* New York: Macmillan.

PAUL IRVINE
Katonah, New York

GOLD, MARC (1931–1982)

Vocational training, job placement, and respect for the moderately, severely, and profoundly mentally handicapped was a vision Marc Gold forged into a reality. His interests during his teaching of the mentally retarded in Los Angeles led him to pursue a doctoral degree in experimental child psychology and special education. In 1969 he joined the University of Illinois faculty as a research professor and began working at the Institute for Child Behavior and Development.

Gold's strong philosophy of respect for persons with mental retardation acted as the foundation for all of his efforts. Gold (1980) believed that (1) the mentally handicapped are served best by training them in marketable skills; (2) individuals identified as mentally handicapped respond to learning best in a situation based on respect of their worth and capabilities; (3) given the appropriate training, the mentally retarded have the capability to demonstrate competence; (4) when a lack of learning occurs, it should first be interpreted as a result of inappropriate or insufficient teaching strategies rather than the individual's inability to learn; (5) intellectual testing is limiting to the mentally retarded; (6)) the labeling of people as mentally retarded is unfair and counterproductive; and (7) trainers should never assume that they are approaching the maximum potential of their learner.

Extolling this philosophy, Gold developed Try Another Way, a systematic training program for individuals who find it difficult to learn (1980). The strategies employed were physical prompts, modeling, manipulation of the learner's hands, and short specific phrases like, "Try another way." Task completion was met with silence as Gold believed no news is good news. The Try Another Way system is based on task analysis. Components of task analysis include method (the way the task is performed), content (the amount of steps the method is divided into), and process (the way the task is taught). Process is subdivided into format (the presentation of the material), feedback (cues so the learner knows what is wanted), procedure (description of the proposed training plan), criterion (the predetermined point when learning takes place), and data collection (the charting of steps accomplished and still to be mastered).

Gold's research (1972, 1973, 1974, 1976, 1981), consistently supports task analysis as a learning strategy with the autistic, deaf/blind, and multihandicapped for tasks such as self-help, mobility, and vocational and social skills.

In addition to the development of the Try Another Way system, Gold created an organization that disseminated information regarding the program, was the president of the Workshop Division of the Illinois Rehabilitation Association, was a member of the Executive Board of the American Association for the Education of the Severely/Profoundly Handicapped, was vice president of the Vocational Rehabilitation Division of the American Association on Mental Deficiency, and was consulting editor or member of the editorial board of *The American Journal of Mental Deficiency, Mental Retardation,* and *Education and Treatment of Children.*

REFERENCES

Gold, M. W. (1972). Stimulus factors in skill training of retarded adolescents on a complex assembly task: Acquisition, transfer, and retention. *American Journal of Mental Deficiency, 76,* 517–526.

Gold, M. W. (1973). Factors affecting production by the retarded: Base rate. *Mental Retardation, 11*(6), 41–45.

Gold, M. W. (1974). Redundant cue removal in skill training for the mildly and moderately retarded. *Education & Training of the Mentally Retarded, 9,* 5–8.

Gold, M. W. (1976). Task analysis of a complex assembly task by the retarded blind. *Exceptional Children, 4,* 78–84.

Gold, M. W. (1980). *Did I say that?* Champaign, IL: Research.

Gold, M. W., & Barclay, C. R. (1973a). The learning of difficult visual discriminations by the moderately and severely retarded. *Mental Retardation, 11*(2), 9–11.

Gold, M. W., & Barclay, C. R. (1973b). The effects of verbal labels on the acquisition and retention of a complex assembly task. *Training School Bulletin, 70*(1), 38–42.

SHARI A. BEVINS
Texas A&M University

GOLDEN, CHARLES J. (1949–   )

Charles J. Golden received his BA from Ponoma College in 1971 and his PhD in clinical psychology from the University of Hawaii in 1975. He completed in internship in clinical psychology at Hawaii State Hospital and established a neuropsychology laboratory at the University of South Dakota (1975–1978) and later at the University of Nebraska Medical Center (1978 to the present). His strongest interests are in the areas of psychological assessment, with a major emphasis on clinical neuropsychology.

He is best known for his work in the development of a standardized, American version of Luria's *methode clinique,* a neuropsychological investigation of individual cases known as the Luria-Nebraska Neuropsychological Battery. This battery attempts to integrate the qualitative approach to psychological assessment advocated by Luria with the quantitative, standardized approaches to assessment that have long characterized western psychology. It also tries to provide a broad evaluation of neuropsychological skills in a general battery applicable to a wide range of patients, administered in diverse settings with a minimum of equipment. The children's version of the battery addresses special education with the assessment of learning deficits suspected of having a neurological base.

Golden is also known for his study of the neurological basis of psychiatric disorders. His work includes an integration of test results from neurological procedures such as computerized tomography and regional cerebral blood flow with psychological and behavioral test results. As a result of this work, a subgroup of psychiatric patients with organic dysfunction that can be hypothesized to be the cause of their disorders has been found.

Golden's major publications include *Clinical Interpretation of Objective Psychological Test, Interpretation of the Halstead-Reitan Neuropsychological Battery: A Casebook Approach, Diagnosis and Rehabilitation in Clinical Neuropsychology, Item Interpretation of the Luria-Nebraska Neuropsychological Battery,* and *Interpretation of the Luria-Nebraska Neuropsychological Battery.*

REFERENCES

Golden, C. J. (1979). *Clinical interpretation of objective psychological test.* New York: Grune & Stratton.

Golden, C. J. (1981). *Diagnosis and rehabilitation in clinical neuropsychology.* Springfield, IL: Thomas.

Golden, C. J., Hammeke, T. A., Purisch, A. D., Berg, R. A., Moses, J. A., Jr., Newlin, D. B., Wilkening, G. N., & Puente, A. E. (1982). *Item interpretation of the Luria-Nebraska Neuropsychological Battery.* Lincoln: University of Nebraska Press.

Golden, C. J., Osmon, D., Moses, J. A., Jr., & Berg, R. A. (1980). *Interpretation of the Halstead-Reitan Neuropsychological Battery: A casebook approach.* New York: Grune & Stratton.

Moses, J. A., Jr., Golden, C. J., Ariel, R., & Gustavson, J. L. (1983, 1984). *Interpretation of the Luria-Nebraska Neuropsychological Battery* (Vols. 1 & 2). New York: Grune & Stratton.

STAFF

GOLDMAN-FRISTOE TEST OF ARTICULATION (GFTA)

The Goldman-Fristoe Test of Articulation (GFTA) (1986 edition) was designed to provide a systematic method for identifying and recording an individual's articulatory proficiency as a basis for establishing remedial strategies (Goldman & Fristoe, 1986). Normative data for GFTA are provided for individuals ranging in age from 2 to 16 years and above. Administration and scoring can be completed in approximately 45 minutes. The GFTA is comprised of three subtests that elicit spontaneous productions of 23 consonants and 12 consonant blends in various positions of words and sentences. Although this tool was not specifically designed to assess vowel and diphthong productions most can be observed and evaluated.

The sounds-in-words subtest consists of 35 large colored line drawings depicting objects and activities that are familiar to young children. Subjects are required to name the pictures as the examiner records misarticulations of target sounds. Evaluation of an individual's articulation skills in connected speech is obtained using the sounds-in-sentences subtest. Two narrative stories complemented by visual illustrations are read aloud by the examiner. As the client retells each story, the examiner evaluates accuracy of productions and records errors. The stimulability subtest yields information about the relative ease with which the client is able to produce a previously misarticulated sound at the syllable, word, and sentence level when provided with auditory and visual stimulation.

According to the authors, interpretation of test results is made by comparisons of responses across subtests. This assists the examiner in determining overall patterns of misarticulations and consistency of individual articulatory errors. Normative data and statistical analysis are provided in the examiner's manual.

REFERENCES

Goldman, R., & Fristoe, M. (1986). *Goldman-Fristoe Test of Articulation examiners manual*. Circle Pines, MN: American Guidance Service.

SUSAN MAHANNA-BODEN
TRACY CALPIN CASTLE
Eastern Kentucky University

ARTICULATION DISORDERS
GOLDMAN-FRISTOE-WOODCOCK
  AUDITORY SKILLS TEST BATTERY

GOLDMAN-FRISTOE-WOODCOCK AUDITORY SKILLS TEST BATTERY (G-F-W BATTERY)

The Goldman-Fristoe-Woodcock Auditory Skills Test Battery (G-F-W Battery) is designed to measure a broad spectrum of auditory abilities while providing detailed diagnostic information useful for instructional programming (Goldman, Fristoe, & Woodcock, 1974a). Normative data are provided for ages 3 through 80. The G-F-W Battery is comprised of 12 tests that are self-contained in five easel kits. Administration time is approximately 15 minutes per test.

The G-F-W Auditory Selective Attention Test measures an individual's ability to attend to and understand a message in the presence of systematically varied competing noise. The G-F-W Auditory Discrimination Test consists of three parts; part one provides a simple assessment of an individual's ability to discriminate among frequently confused speech sounds; parts two and three, used only with subjects exhibiting difficulty on part one, analyze the pattern of specific speech-sound discrimination errors. The G-F-W Auditory Memory Tests, designed to identify children and adults with short-term memory deficits, assess recognition memory, memory for content, and memory for sequence.

The seven tests comprising the G-F-W Sound-Symbol assessment are designed to measure prerequisite abilities for advanced language processes, including reading and spelling. These tests are described by the authors (1974b) as follows:

Test 1—Sound Mimicry measures the ability to imitate nonsense syllables immediately after auditory presentation

Test 2—Sound Recognition measures the ability to recognize isolated sounds comprising a word

Test 3—Sound analysis measures the ability to identify component sounds of nonsense syllables

Test 4—Sound blending measures the ability to synthesize isolated sounds into meaningful words

Test 5—Sound-Symbol Association measures the ability to learn associations between unfamiliar auditory and visual symbols

Test 6—Reading of Symbols measures the ability to make grapheme to phoneme translations

Test 7—Spelling of Sounds measures the ability to make phoneme to grapheme translations

The examiner's manual includes information for all subtests regarding derived scores, age equivalent scores, percentile ranks, standard scores, and stanines.

The G-F-W Battery is a test designed to evaluate various auditory abilities. It is useful to speech-language pathologists, audiologists, educational diagnosticians, reading specialists, learning-disability teachers, school psychologists, and counselors.

REFERENCES

Goldman, R., Fristoe, M., & Woodcock, R. W. (1974a). *Technical manual for Goldman-Fristoe-Woodcock Auditory Skills Test Battery*. Circle Pines, MN: American Guidance Service.

Goldman, R., Fristoe, M., & Woodcock, R. W. (1974b). *Goldman-Fristoe-Woodcock Auditory Skills Test Battery: Sound-symbol tests*. Circle Pines, MN: American Guidance Service.

TRACY CALPIN CASTLE
SUSAN MAHANNA-BODEN
Eastern Kentucky University

GOLDMAN-FRISTOE-WOODCOCK TEST OF AUDITORY DISCRIMINATION
GOLDMAN-FRISTOE TEST OF ARTICULATION

GOLDMAN-FRISTOE-WOODCOCK TEST OF AUDITORY DISCRIMINATION (G-F-W)

The Goldman-Fristoe-Woodcock Test of Auditory Discrimination (G-F-W) was designed to measure the auditory discrimination of speech sounds using both an ideal listening condition and a controlled background noise condition (Goldman, Fristoe, & Woodcock, 1970). This tool, comprised of a training procedure, a quiet subtest, and a noise subtest is contained in a compact easel kit. Normative data for G-F-W is available for individuals from ages 3 years 8 months to 70 years and older. Administration can be completed in approximately 13 minutes. A tape recorder is required for presentation of test stimuli.

The training procedure was designed to familarize the subject with the 61 line-drawn pictures of common objects used during the subtests and to teach the names associated with each picture. Completion of training occurs when the subject identifies each word picture association or is unable to match words with pictures after three trials.

When the training procedure is completed, the test tape containing two subtests (the quiet subtest, designed to measure auditory discrimination of speech sounds in the absence of background noise and the noise subtest, designed to assess discrimination abilities in the presence of competing background noise) is presented. The subject is instructed to point to one of four pictures on each plate while the examiner records the responses.

The authors report two levels of scoring. The first procedure is to count the frequency of errors during each subtest and translate these into either standard or percentile scores. The second procedure is designed for research purposes and involves the classification of errors into a speech sound matrix. Normative data are provided in the examiner's manual.

The G-F-W is an instrument used by speech language pathologists, audiologists, and educational specialists to assess an individual's ability to discriminate speech sounds under quiet and noisy conditions.

REFERENCES

Goldman, R., Fristoe, M., & Woodcock, R. (1970). *Goldman-Fristoe-Woodcock Test of Auditory Discrimination examiner's manual*. Circle Pines, MN: American Guidance Service.

TRACY CALPIN CASTLE
SUSAN MAHANNA-BODEN
Eastern Kentucky University

AUDIOGRAM
AUDITORY DISCRIMINATION

GOLDSTEIN, MAX A. (1870–1941)

Max A. Goldstein, an otolaryngologist, originated the acoustic method of teaching the deaf. The major significance of this method was that it used the student's residual hearing, an avenue largely neglected by educators of the deaf at the time. Goldstein employed amplification to train the student to use any remaining sound perception to understand spoken language and to guide his or her own voice in the production of speech. In 1914 Goldstein founded the Central Institute for the Deaf in St. Louis, where he demonstrated his methods and where he established the first two-year training program for teachers of the deaf and began the first nursery school for deaf children.

Goldstein was founder and editor of *The Laryngoscope*, a journal devoted to disorders of the ear, nose, and throat. To promote closer cooperation between teachers of the deaf and physicians, and to standardize teaching methods used in schools for the deaf, Goldstein established the professional society that later became the National Forum on Deafness and Speech Pathology. Goldstein served as president of the American Otological Society, the American

Max A. Goldstein

Laryngological, Rhinological, and Otological Society, and the organization that was the forerunner of the American Speech and Hearing Association.

REFERENCES

Goldstein, M. A. (1939). *The acoustic method*. St. Louis: Laryngoscope Press.

In memoriam: Dr. Max A. Goldstein, 1870–1941. (1941). *Laryngoscope. 51*, 726–731.

PAUL IRVINE
Katonah, New York

GOODENOUGH, FLORENCE LAURA (1886–1959)

Florence Laura Goodenough obtained the PhD degree in psychology under Lewis M. Terman at Stanford University after a number of years of experience as a teacher in the public schools and at the Training School at Vineland, New Jersey. Goodenough is well known for her Draw-A-Man Test, published in 1926, and the Minnesota Preschool Scale. As a researcher and an authority on research methodology, she was an innovator, applying a variety of research techniques to diverse research questions. Her *Experimental Child Psychology*, written with John E. Anderson, evaluated the pros and cons of numerous research methodologies. Goodenough served as president of the school psychology division of the American Psychological Association.

REFERENCES

Goodenough, F. L. (1926). *Measurement of intelligence by drawings*. Yonkers, NY: World Book.

Goodenough, F. L., & Anderson, J. E. (1982). *Experimental child study*. Darby, PA: Arden Library.

PAUL IRVINE
Katonah, New York

GOTTLIEB, JAY (1942–   )

Jay Gottlieb, now an associate professor in the department of educational psychology at New York University, received his PhD (1972) from Yeshiva University. Gottlieb (1981) is interested in mainstreaming and believes that more research is necessary to determine whether placing an exceptional child in a regular classroom is helpful or harmful to the child. Goodman, Gottlieb, and Harrison (1972) found that mentally retarded youngsters tend to be easily swayed by their more intellectually bright peers. These youngsters do not develop close relationships with other children; thus they do not always learn what is valued by others. Kaufman, Gottlieb, Agard, and Kukic

(1975) found that handicapped children did not progress in their school work more quickly when they were in segregated classrooms.

Gottlieb has used sociometric measures to study the social integration of learning-disabled children. Levy and Gottlieb (1984) found that there were few differences between the play habits of learning-disabled youngsters and their more normal peers, although the learning-disabled students tended to play alone more often. They did find that learning-disabled children had lower status than the nonlearning disabled. Nonlearning-disabled pupils played with about half of the learning-disabled pupils for whom they expressed liking. Gottlieb believes that issues like these, which are indirectly connected to the formal education of a child must be reviewed and evaluated if the child is to get the most out of the learning experience.

REFERENCES

Goodman, H., Gottlieb, J., & Harrison, R. H. (1972). Social acceptance of EMRs integrated into a nongraded elementary school. *American Journal of Mental Deficiency, 76*, 412–417.

Gottlieb, J. (1981). Mainstreaming: Fulfilling the promise? *American Journal of Mental Deficiency, 86*, 115–124.

Kaufman, M. J., Gottlieb, J., Agard, J. A., & Kukic, M. B. (1975). Mainstreaming: Toward an explication of the construct. *Focus on Exceptional Children, 7*, 6–17.

Levy, L., & Gottlieb, J. (1984). Learning disabled and non-learning disabled children at play. *Remedial & Special Education, 5*, 43–50.

E. VALERIE HEWITT
Texas A&M University

GOWAN, JOHN C. (1912–   )

John C. Gowan, who earned his BA at Harvard and his EdM and EdD at the University of California, Los Angeles, has spent his entire professional life in education. During his career, he has shown an interest in guidance, exceptional learners, creativity, and psychic science (Gowan, 1980). He was a faculty member at California State University, Northridge for over 25 years and is now a retired university professor and writer.

Gowan is known for his writing on guidance for gifted children (Gowan, Demos, & Kokaska, 1980); he has emphasized the special problems that these children may have such as a disparity between their social and intellectual development. He also has shown a great interest in the study of creativity and the influence of right-hemisphere imagery on creativity (Gowan, Khatena, & Torrance, 1981).

A leader in his field, Gowan has been president of the Association for Gifted (1971–1972), president of the National Association for Gifted Children (1974–1975), and editor of *Gifted Child Quarterly* (1974–1979). In addition, he was a Fulbright lecturer at the University of Singapore (1962–1963) and has been a visiting lecturer at the University of Hawaii (1965 and 1967), Southern Connecticut State College (1969), the University of Canterbury, New Zealand (1970) and Massey University, New Zealand (1975).

REFERENCES

Gowan, J. C. (1980). *Operations of increasing order*. Privately published.

Gowan, J. C., Demos, G. D., & Kokaska, C. J. (1980). *The guidance of exceptional children: A book of readings* (2nd ed.). New York: Longman.

Gowan, J. C., Khatena, J., & Torrance, E. P. (Eds.). (1981). *Creativity: Its educational implications* (rev. ed.). Dubuque, IA: Kendall-Hunt.

ANN E. LUPKOWSKI
Texas A&M University

GRADE EQUIVALENTS (GEs)

Grade equivalents (GEs) represent a popular, though much abused and often misinterpreted, score system for achievement tests. A GE is a representation of an average level of performance of all children at a specific grade level. For example, if, on a test of reading, the average number of questions correct (the mean raw score) for children in the third month of fourth grade (typically written as 4.3) is 40, then a raw score of 40 is assigned a GE of 4.3. If the average number correct for children in the second month of fifth grade is 43, then all scores of 43 are henceforth assigned a GE of 5.2, and so forth.

Grade Equivalents have numerous problems of interpretation and use, so much so that the 1985 *Standards for Educational and Psychological Testing* asks test publishers to take special care in explaining the calculation, interpretation, and appropriate uses of GEs for any particular test. Many users assume that GEs have the characteristics of standardized or scaled scores when, in fact, they do not. Often GEs are treated as being on an interval scale of measurement when they are only on an ordinal scale; i.e., GEs allow the ranking of individuals according to their performance but do not tell us anything about the distance between each pair of individuals. This problem can be illustrated as follows. If the mean score for beginning fourth graders (grade 4.0) on a reading test is 37, then any person earning a score of 37 on the test is assigned a GE score of 4.0. If the mean raw score of a fifth grader (grade 5.0) is 38, then a score of 38 would receive a GE of 5.0. A raw score of 37 could represent a GE of 4.0, 38 could be 5.0, 39 could be 5.1, 40 be 5.3, and 41, 6.0. Thus, differences of one raw score point can cause dramatic differences in the GE received. The differences will be highly inconsistent across grades with regard to magnitude of the difference in grade equivalents produced by constant changes in raw scores.

The Table illustrates the problems of using GEs to evaluate a child's academic standing relative to his or her peers. Frequently, in both research and clinical practice, children of normal intellectual capacity are diagnosed as learning disabled through the use of grade equivalents such as "two years below grade level for age" on a test of academic attainment. The use of this criterion for diagnosing learning disabilities or other academic disorders is clearly inappropriate (Reynolds, 1981, 1984). As seen in Table 1, a child with a GE score in reading 2 years below the appropriate grade placement for age may or may not have a reading problem. At some ages this is within the average range, whereas at others a severe reading problem may be indicated.

Grade equivalents tend to become standards of performance as well, which they clearly are not. Contrary to popular belief, GE scores on a test do not indicate what level of reading text a child should be using. Grade equivalent scores on tests do not have a one-to-one correspondence with reading series placement or the various formulas for determining readability levels.

Grade equivalents are also inappropriate for use in any sort of discrepancy analysis of an individual's test performance and for use in many statistical procedures for the following reasons (Reynolds, 1981):

1. The growth curve between age and achievement in basic academic subjects flattens out at upper grade levels. This can be seen in Table 1, where there is very little change in standard score values corresponding to 2 years below grade level for age after about grade 7 or 8. In fact, GEs have almost no meaning at this level since reading instruction typically stops by high school. This difficulty in interpreting GEs beyond about grade 10 or 11 is apparent in an analogy with age equivalents (Thorndike & Hagen, 1977). Height can be expressed in age equivalents just as reading can be expressed as GEs. It might be helpful to describe a tall first grader as having the height of an $8\frac{1}{2}$-year-old, but what happens to the 5 ft, 10 in. 14-year-old female? At no age does the mean height of females equal 5 ft, 10 in. Since the average reading level in the population changes very little after junior high school, GEs at these ages become virtually nonsensical, with large fluctuations resulting from a raw score difference of two or three points on a 100-item test.

2. Grade equivalents assume the rate of learning is constant throughout the school year and that there is no gain or loss during summer vacation.

3. Grade equivalents involve an excess of extrapolation, especially at the upper and lower ends of the scale. However, since tests are not administered dur-

Standard Scores and Percentile Ranks Corresponding to Performance "Two Years Below Grade Level for Age" on Three Major Reading Tests

Grade Placement	Two Years Below Placement	Wide Range Achievement Test		Woodcock Reading Mastery Test[a]		Stanford Diagnostic Reading Test[a]	
		SS[b]	%R[c]	SS	%R	SS	%R
2.5	K.5	72	1	—		—	
3.5	1.5	69	2	64	1	64	1
4.5	2.5	73	4	77	6	64	1
5.5	3.5	84	14	85	16	77	6
6.5	4.5	88	21	91	27	91	27
7.5	5.5	86	18	94	34	92	30
8.5	6.5	87	19	94	34	93	32
9.5	7.5	90	25	96	39	95	37
10.5	8.5	85	16	95	37	95	37
11.5	9.5	85	16	95	37	92	30

Source: Adapted from Reynolds (1981).

[a] Total test.

[b] All standard scores in this table have been converted for ease of comparison to a common scale having a mean of 100 and an SD of 15.

[c] Percentile rank.

ing every month of the school year, scores between the testing intervals (often a full year) must be interpolated on the assumption of constant growth rates. Interpolation between sometimes extrapolated values on an assumption of constant growth rates is a somewhat ludicrous activity.

4. Different academic subjects are acquired at different rates and the variation in performance varies across content areas so that "two years below grade level for age" may be a much more serious deficiency in math than in reading comprehension.

5. Grade equivalents exaggerate small differences in performance among individuals and for a single individual across tests. Some test authors even provide a caution on record forms that standard scores only, and not grade equivalents, should be used for comparisons.

Standard scores are a superior alternative to the use of GEs. The principal advantage of standardized or scaled scores with children lies in the comparability of score interpretation across age. By standard scores is meant scores scaled to a constant mean and standard deviation (SD), such as the Wechsler Deviation IQ, and not to ratio IQ types of scales employed by the early Binet and the Slosson Intelligence Test, which give the false appearance of being scaled scores. Ratio IQs or other types of quotients have many of the same problems as grade equivalents and should be avoided for many of the same reasons. Standard scores of the deviation IQ type have the same percentile rank across age since they are based not only on the mean but the variability in scores about the mean at each age level. For example, a score that falls two-thirds of a standard deviation below the mean has a percentile rank of 25 at every age. A score falling two-thirds of a grade level below the average grade level has a different percentile rank at every age.

Standard scores are more accurate and precise. When constructing tables for the conversion of raw scores into standard scores, interpolation of scores to arrive at an exact score point is usually not necessary. The opposite is true of GEs. Typically, extrapolation is not necessary for scores within three SDs of the mean, which accounts for more than 99% of all scores encountered. Scaled scores can be set to any desired mean and standard deviation, with the fancy of the test author frequently the sole determining factor. Fortunately, a few scales can account for the vast majority of standardized tests in psychology and education.

Nevertheless GEs remain popular as a score reporting system in special education. This popularity seems owed to the many misconceptions surrounding their use rather than any true understanding of children's academic attainment or how better to instruct them.

REFERENCES

Reynolds, C. R. (1981). The fallacy of "two years below grade level for age" as a diagnostic criterion for reading disorders. *Journal of School Psychology, 19*, 350–358.

Reynolds, C. R. (1984). Critical measurement issues in learning disabilities. *Journal of Special Education, 18*, 451–476.

Thorndike, R. L., & Hagen, E. P. (1977). *Measurement and evaluation in psychology and education.* New York: Wiley.

CECIL R. REYNOLDS
Texas A&M University

DIAGNOSIS IN SPECIAL EDUCATION SEVERE DISCREPANCY ANALYSIS

GRADE RETENTION

Grade retention involves the repetition of a particular grade level in school by a student. The practice is also known as grade repetition and nonpromotion, and by the commonly used terms of flunking, failing, or holding back a student. Typically, the term grade retention is used when the student is of elementary school age and is required to spend another academic year going over the same material. Such students may receive some individualized attention or curriculum the second year in the grade, but this is the exception rather than the rule. In a few school districts, retained students are promoted at midyear or on skill mastery to the next grade. The term subject repetition is used when a secondary school student fails one or more subjects, but not the grade, and has to repeat them.

Historically, the practice of grade retention can be traced back to the late sixteenth century, when schools in England first began grouping students according to age or lessons mastered. Students were placed in different rooms rather than taught all together, as had been the earlier European practice. With the assignment of students to graded classes in England during this period and in America during the nineteenth century, grade retention became a convenient and popular way of attempting to correct academic failure. From 1840 to 1930, approximately one out of two children was retained at least once during the first eight years of school, and little attention was paid to learning difficulties associated with immigrant status, native language differences, cultural factors, or intellectual handicaps. Over the next 30 years, the retention rate began to drop as its effect on children's social and emotional welfare was questioned. Many students, regardless of classroom performance, were "socially promoted" if they were overaged, oversized, or overly sensitive to failure. However, as the numbers of socially promoted students increased, standardized achievement test scores decreased and social promotion was singled out as one reason why some students who were awarded high-school diplomas were unable to adequately read, write, and compute.

In the late 1970s, federal, state, and local government agencies called for upgraded teaching standards, educational accountability, and a renewed emphasis on basic academic skills. Many states now require students to pass minimum competency tests to graduate from high school or be promoted from one grade to the next. Such legislation coupled with public support for raising academic standards impacted on the retention-promotion controversy in two important ways. First, schools began to place great emphasis on test scores to determine who should be promoted despite the fact that these tests overidentify minority students as failing, are usually not appropriate for special education students, and are not designed to predict who should be retained. Second, the implementation of strict promotion policies have directly affected retention rates. Where once state retention rates averaged about 4% over all grades, this figure has now about doubled. Some school districts currently are failing from 10 to 20% of their students, a phenomenon that is likely to increase the dropout rate among secondary students (Medway & Rose, 1986). Most children are retained either in the early elementary school grades to make sure that they have a good academic foundation, or prior to entrance into secondary school if there is a question about their ability to change classes and deal with older schoolmates.

Grade retention has been and continues to be a controversial educational practice. The arguments in favor of grade retention involve the following: (1) it allows the immature or developmentally delayed child time to catch up; (2) it prevents the child who is having difficulty from experiencing undue failure and frustration; (3) it makes classes homogeneous and easier to teach; (4) it preserves the meaning of school diplomas; and (5) children who repeat learn more than those who are promoted. The arguments against retention are (1) it can stigmatize and lower the self-image of the student; (2) it is an ineffective remediation strategy; (3) it discriminates against males, minorities, and the disadvantaged; (4) it is associated with students dropping out of school and committing crime; and (5) it delays a needed thorough psychological assessment of the child (Carstens, 1985; Medway & Rose, in press).

The existing research literature, despite methodological problems (Jackson, 1975), generally supports the antiretention position. Promoted students obtain scores on achievement tests that are, on the average, 34% greater than those of retained students (Holmes & Matthews, 1984). Research indicates academic benefits of retention for students in kindergarten, first, and second grades, but few benefits after sixth grade. Students who have been retained obtain lower scores on measures of personal adjustment than those who have been promoted (Holmes & Matthews, 1984), although the young child does not appear to suffer emotionally. Students placed in special educational programs, rather than just retained or promoted, usually fare the best, both academically and emotionally.

Research is just beginning to address the issue of what types of children are helped the most by grade retention. The best candidates for retention are children who are young, who have made some progress the first year in school, whose intelligence is at least low-average, who are not behavior problems, and who have parents who agree with the decision and help the child at home (Medway & Rose, 1986). There is no support for the position of retaining children who are small in stature, siblings of other retainees, or labeled "immature." No child should be retained before his or her teacher has tried alternative teaching approaches.

Handicapped students may be given minimum competency tests and may be subject to the same promotion and graduation standards as nonhandicapped students

(McCarthy, 1983). However, students should be given at least a year's notice prior to the enforcement of the promotion standard and grade requirements should be taught as part of the individualized educational program.

Numerous alternatives to grade retention and social promotion have been proposed; they attempt to directly remediate learning and adjustment problems. These include preventive programs such as preschool, readiness, and early childhood enrichment classes, and early identification of children in need of special education; remedial programs, transition classes, and tutoring; and intensive summer programs (Medway & Rose, 1986). For additional information on this topic see Germain and Merlo (1985) and Thompson (1980).

REFERENCES

Carstens, A. A. (1985). Retention and social promotion for the exceptional child. *School Psychology Review, 14,* 48–63.

Germain, R., & Merlo, M. (1985). Best practices in assisting in retention and promotion decisions. In A. Thomas & J. Grimes (Eds.), *Best practices in school psychology.* Stratford, CT: NASP Publications.

Holmes, C. T., & Matthews, K. M. (1984). The effects of nonpromotion on elementary and junior high school pupils: A meta-analysis. *Review of Educational Research, 54,* 225–236.

Jackson, G. B. (1975). The research evidence on the effects of grade retention. *Review of Educational Research, 45,* 613–635.

McCarthy, M. M. (1983). The application of competency testing mandates to handicapped children. *Harvard Educational Review, 53,* 146–164.

Medway, F. J., & Rose, J. S. (1986). Grade retention. In T. R. Kratochwill (Ed.), *Advances in school psychology* (Vol. 5). Hillsdale, NJ: Erlbaum.

Thompson, S. (1980). Grade retention and social promotion. *ACSA School Management Digest, Series 1, 20,* 1–36.

FREDERIC J. MEDWAY
University of South Carolina

RETENTION IN GRADE

GRAND MAL SEIZURES

Grand mal seizures, also known as tonic-clonic seizures, are perhaps the most familiar type of generalized seizures. They often serve as a model in describing the components of other types of seizures. Although not every element is found in every seizure, a grand mal seizure may contain the following: prodrome, aura, ictus, and postictal state. For several hours, or in some instances several days, the individual with epilepsy may feel vague anxiety or discomfort; this is usually sufficiently similar to past episodes to indicate an impending seizure. This period is known as the prodrome period. Although its precise cause is not yet known, the prodrome is not thought to result from abnormally increased activity in the brain. The aura period is

the period at the beginning of the paroxysmal discharge before consciousness is lost. In this state, the individual may describe unusual sensations such as numbness rising from the upper abdomen, faintness, or turning of the head and eyes. The aura is thought to be the consciously remembered portion of the seizure, and, therefore, is considered by many to be a part of the seizure (Golden, Moses, Coffman, Miller, & Strider, 1983). Specific characteristics of the aura are likely related to the anatomic site of origin of the seizure. Only about half of the patients with grand mal seizures, however, report such an aura.

The seizure itself, or ictus begins with tonic extension of all four extremities, and frequently with arching of the back and neck. This muscular activity coincides with a paroxysm of spikes on the EEG. The onset of the seizure is sometimes accompanied by a high-pitched cry caused by forcible expiration of air against the vocal cords resulting from sudden involuntary contraction of the respiratory and laryngeal muscles. As the patient falls, the body stiffens because of generalized tonic contraction of limb and trunk muscles. The legs usually extend and the arms flex partially. During the tonic phase, which lasts less than a minute, respiration stops as the result of sustained contraction of the respiratory muscles, and pallor or cyanosis (a bluish cast to the skin) may be seen. After the tonic stage, jerking or clonic movements occur in all four limbs for less than a minute. The tongue is sometimes bitten because of involuntary contractions of the masticatory muscles. Increased salivation and deep breathing may cause frothing at the mouth. A period of more relaxed unconsciousness follows, and lasts for about a minute. Relaxation of the anal and urethral sphincters usually occurs, with resultant incontinence. Tonic-clonic convulsions typically last a total of 3 to 5 minutes.

Following the seizure, the postictal period begins. Some individuals return to consciousness almost at once, with only minimal symptoms of headache or fatigue. Others pass through a period of unconsciousness or stupor, which can last for minutes or hours, often followed by confusion, headache, and fatigue. After regaining consciousness, the patient may remember the aura but not the ictal period. During the period of postictal confusion, the patient sometimes performs actions automatically such as undressing for bed or resisting restraint (Goldensohn, Glaser, & Goldberg, 1984). Often, if the patient was asleep or alone during the entire period of the seizure, the only evidence of its occurrence may be soiled clothing or a bitten tongue.

The fundamental mechanism(s) that triggers seizure activity remains unknown. Overall, seizures are considered to be the result of a primary disorder of the brain or to be symptomatic of and secondary to some other illness. In some cases, there is no identifiable cause for the seizures. Grand mal seizures also may be inherited. Goldensohn et al. (1984) note a child of the average patient with grand mal seizures has about 1 chance in 30 of developing seizures. Chusid (1973) lists the main causes of seizure activity to be genetic predisposition; birth factors, including infection and prematurity; infectious disorders including meningitis, brain abscess, encephalitis, fever, and parasites; toxic factors such as carbon monoxide poisoning, lead, mercury, and other metals, alcohol and various drugs, allergies, toxemia of pregnancy, and many other toxic medical conditions; trauma; various cerebrovascular disorders; metabolic and nutritional disturbances, including electrolyte imbalance, disorders of carbohydrate, protein, or fat metabolism, vitamin deficiency, and various endocrine disorders (e.g., disorders of menstruation); various tumors; and degenerative and inherited diseases, including multiple sclerosis.

REFERENCES

Chusid, J. G. (1973). *Correlative neuroanatomy and functional neurology* (15th ed.). Los Altos, CA: Lange.

Golden, C. J., Moses, J. A., Jr., Coffman, J. A., Miller, W. R., & Strider, F. D. (1983). *Clinical neuropsychology: Interface with neurologic and psychiatric disorders*, New York: Grune & Stratton.

Goldensohn, E. S., Glaser, G. H., & Goldberg, M. A. (1984). Epilepsy. In L. P. Rowland (Ed.), *Merritt's textbook of neurology* (pp. 629–650). Philadelphia: Lea & Febiger.

RICHARD A. BERG
West Virginia University
Medical Center, Charleston
Division

ABSENCE SEIZURES
ELECTROENCEPHLOGRAPH
EPILEPSY

GRAPHESTHESIA

Graphesthesia is a medical term used to define an individual's ability to identify numbers or figures written on the skin (Hensyl, 1982). For many years, tests of graphesthesia have been a part of the clinical neurological examination to determine the intactness and integration of sensory neural systems related to sensations from within the body, at a distance from the body, and outside the body.

Chusid (1986) reports that sensation may be divided into three types: superficial, concerned with touch, pain, temperature, and two-point discrimination; deep, concerned with muscle and joint position (proprioception), deep muscle pain, and vibration sense (pallesthesia); and combined, concerned with both superficial and deep sensory mechanisms involved in stereognosis (recognition and naming of familiar unseen objects placed in the hand) and topognosis (the ability to localize cutaneous (skin) stimuli). Stereognosis and topognosis probably depend on

the integrity of neural mechanisms within the cortex and are discriminatory in nature. The lower level mechanisms, such as touch, pain and temperature, seem more protective in nature.

Whether the form identification in graphesthesia is accomplished by identifying numbers traced on the fingertips (Reitan, 1979) or motor form replication (Ayres, 1980), there appears to be a developmental factor in responses favoring greater reliability in 8 to 11 year olds than in 5 to 6 years olds. Evaluations of graphesthesia are most useful and reliable when given as part of a battery of sensory, motor vestibular tests of sensory integrative function. These tests usually are given by therapists, psychologists, or neurologists with special training. It has been suggested (Ayres, 1980) that clusters of low scores on somatosensory tests (including graphesthesia) may be associated with a child's having difficulty with motor planning nonhabitual movement (apraxia). Children who have apraxia have severe problems learning fine motor skill tasks such as dressing and writing. A clear definition of the individual child's difficulty can lead to developmentally appropriate classroom responses and therapeutic intervention provided by related services such as occupational and speech therapy.

REFERENCES

Ayres, A. J. (1980). *Southern California Sensory Integration Tests examiner's manual* (revised ed.). Los Angeles: Western Psychological Services.

Ayres, A. J. (1981). *Sensory integration and the child.* Los Angeles: Western Psychological Services.

Chusid, J. G. (1986). *Correlative neuroanatomy and functional neurology.* (16th ed.). Los Angeles: Lange.

Hensyl, W. R. (Ed.) (1982). *Stedman's Medical dictionary*: Baltimore: Williams & Wilkins.

Reitan, R. M. (1979). *Manual for administration of neuropsychological test batteries for adults and children.* Tucson, AZ: Reitan Neuropsychology Laboratories.

RACHAEL J. STEVENSON
Bedford, Ohio

HALSTEAD-REITAN NEUROPSYCHOLOGICAL BATTERY
LURIA-NEBRASKA NEUROPSYCHOLOGICAL BATTERY
NEUROPSYCHOLOGY

GRAY ORAL READING TESTS

The Gray Oral Reading Tests are designed to measure growth in oral reading from early first grade to college and to help in the diagnosis of oral reading difficulties. Four forms (A, B, C, D) are available. Each form is made up of 13 oral reading passages that are graded according to difficulty. The first passage can be read by students who have completed the preprimer level; the last two are difficult enough to challenge good college students. Passage difficulty is based on vocabulary, concept difficulty, syllabic length of words, and length and complexity of sentence structure.

Students read approximately five of the passages; two easy, one at level, and two hard. To determine the students' grade equivalent, three measures are recorded for each passage: number of errors, reading time, and comprehension. The test can usually be given in about 10 minutes. When interpreting the test, the diagnostician looks for error patterns. The manual of directions gives examples of some of the patterns that may be encountered. The teacher determines how to remediate.

The oral reading passages, while somewhat out of date, were chosen with care and arranged in order of difficulty. Norms are given separately for boys and girls. This test is relatively old, but it has good content validity and can be used to classify patterns of errors and identify quality of oral reading.

REFERENCES

Gray Oral Reading Test (1974). In O. K. Buros (Ed.), *Tests in print II: An index to tests, test reviews, and the literature on specific tests* (p. 608). Highland Park, NJ: Gryphon Press.

Manual: Gray Oral Reading Tests. (1963). Indianapolis: Bobbs Merrill.

RONALD V. SCHMELZER
Eastern Kentucky University

GREAT BRITAIN, SPECIAL EDUCATION IN

See UNITED KINGDOM, SPECIAL EDUCATION IN THE.

GRIEVING PROCESS

It has been recognized for some time that parents of handicapped children often experience intense traumatic reactions to the diagnosis of their children. Further, these initial feelings are not the only ones that parents experience. It appears that parents go through a continual process of emotional fluctuation in the process of coming to terms with having a handicapped child (Searl, 1978). The intensity or degree of handicap does not seem to effect directly the appearance of these feelings. These reactions seem to occur regardless of when the parents become aware of the handicapping condition or how intense the condition is. For example, parents who have been informed that their

expected child will be handicapped early enough into a pregnancy to make numerous physical and financial preparations still have intense emotional reactions to the child's condition at the time of the child's birth. These reactions continue during the child's maturation (Roos, 1977). These feelings have often been likened to the mourning process experienced at the death of a loved one. Hence the reactions and the subsequent process of coming to terms with a handicapped person within the family has been labled the grieving process. Several authors have taken Kubler-Ross's developmental stage of reaction to dying and have applied it to the loss associated with parenting a handicapped child.

It has been suggested that parents go through a series of stages. Early work focused on stages of awareness, recognition, search for a cause, and acceptance (Rosen, 1955). Since that time, the literature has focused on psychological concerns, including guilt, denial, ambivalence, depression, anger, and acceptance. Studies of parental reaction often use vastly different terminology. Further, in these studies parents often report differing information concerning the onset, duration, and intensity of a specific feeling. Although the terminology is contradictory, there appear to be common experiences that parents of handicapped children report (Blacher, 1984). These stages are of varied intensity and duration, but seem to appear with predicted regularity. Further, these feelings are experienced throughout the parents' lives. Olshansky (1962) termed this experience "chronic sorrow," referring to the permanent and ongoing grieving that parents of handicapped children experience. Olshansky holds this is a natural and understandable process. Further, it is in the best interests of parents to work through these feelings at their own pace. Services should be provided to assist parents in managing and living with the handicapped child.

Professionals can play a role in helping parents adjust to the added pressures a handicapped person places on a family (Schleifer, 1971). The thrust of these professional efforts has been to secure appropriate services from the public sector, thus generally ignoring the emotional state of the parents. However, a more complete approach to meeting the needs of parents with handicapped children has received considerable attention during the 1980s. Many professionals have proposed that the grieving process can be an effective tool for understanding parental behavior and a powerful tool for counseling parents to understand and deal with their feelings (Blacher, 1985).

Some have found fault with this approach because of its inability to match all case studies and the misconception that parents resolve the grieving process. Allen and Afflect (1985) have proposed that because of such weaknesses, the grieving process should be disregarded. In place of the grieving process, they have proposed providing coping strategies to parents to help them better deal with the challenges of raising a handicapped individual. The emphasis is placed on problem resolution and emotional regulation. Coping strategies focus the parent on adjustment, which the stage approach to grieving processes often does not do.

Professionals need to be aware that the grieving process may adversely affect their relationship and interactions with parents of handicapped children. At least three considerations must be understood. First, parents may be experiencing a variety of emotional states at a given time. Single interactions may not be representative of the parents' levels of cooperation or enthusiam, but rather a stage in grieving (e.g., anger or guilt). Second, interaction with specific agency representives may cause emotional responses that are not expected by the professionals involved. This may not mean that a parent's total life is focused in that direction, but that current interactions are bringing out certain feelings. Third, parents may spend a prolonged amount of time in one stage or another. A parent may appear to be angry or sad during dealings with a professional. This does not mean that the parent will always remain in this emotional stage; the parent eventually may move on to other feelings in the process. Those who deal with parents must realize that not only do emotions affect interactions, but varied behaviors are normal and to be expected (Searl, 1978).

The implications of the grieving process to those who deal with the parents of the handicapped may be summarized as follows. First, parents often experience deep and intense feelings that may require counseling. Second, these feelings may continue for long periods of time. Third, feelings change at differing rates and/or varied sequences, necessitating flexibility in interpersonal dealings. Fourth, the grieving process is experienced by parents in an individual manner, necessitating interactions with parents to reflect an individual approach.

REFERENCES

Allen, D. A., & Affleck, G. (1985). Are we stereotyping parents? A postscript to Blacher. *Mental Retardation, 23,* 200–202.

Blacher, J. (1984). Sequential stages of parental adjustment to the birth of a child with handicaps: Fact or artifact? *Mental Retardation, 22,* 55–58.

Olshansky, S. (1962). Chronic sorrow: A response to having a mentally defective child. *Social Casework, 43,* 190–194.

Roos, P. (1977). Parents of mentally retarded people. *International Journal of Mental Health, 6,* 96–119.

Rosen, L. (1955). Selected aspects in the development of the mother's understanding of her mentally retarded child. *American Journal of Mental Deficiency, 59,* 522.

Schleifer, M. (1971). Let us all stop blaming the parents. *Exceptional Parent, 1,* 3–5.

Searl, S. (1978). Stages of parent reaction. *Exceptional Parent, 8,* 27–29.

ALAN HILTON
Seattle University

FAMILY COUNSELING
FAMILY RESPONSE TO HANDICAP

GROHT, MILDRED A. (1890–1971)

Mildred A. Groht, a prominent educator of the deaf and developer of one of the major methods of teaching language to deaf children, was a graduate of Swarthmore College, with an honorary doctorate from Gallaudet College. She began her career as a teacher at the New York School for the Deaf and later taught at the Maryland School for the Deaf. In 1926 she joined the faculty of the Lexington School for the Deaf in New York City, where she served as principal until her retirement in 1958.

A talented teacher, she proposed and developed the influential natural language method of teaching language to the deaf. Based on the premise that deaf children can best acquire language through activities that are a natural part of a child's life, Groht's method uses a variety of activities. The teacher consistently creates situations that provide the students with language experiences and continually talks to the children and encourages them to respond with speech. Such practice in real-life situations was seen as more effective than the traditional grammatical or analytical approach, with its emphasis on language analysis and drill. The use of natural methods has increased markedly, and most programs today use a mixture of natural and analytical approaches.

Groht described the natural method in her book *Natural Language for Deaf Children*. In its foreword, Clarence D. O'Connor, then superintendent of the Lexington School for the Deaf, called Groht, "one of America's most distin-

Mildred A. Groht

guished teachers of the deaf, particularly in the field of communication arts." He went on to say:

> She has increasingly expounded the philosophy that deaf children can acquire fluent use of English comparable to that of the hearing through what has come to be known as the 'natural' method, and through her own skillful teaching of deaf children and guiding of teachers she has demonstrated that this can be done without question. Through her writings, her demonstrations, and her lecture courses, and now through the chapters of this excellent book, she has very generously passed on to her coworkers the benefits of her rich experience in this specialized field.

Active in the Alexander Graham Bell Association for the Deaf, Groht served on the association's auxiliary board for a number of years and was named to its honorary board in 1965. She died in Ossining, New York, on December 11, 1971.

REFERENCE

Groht, M. A. (1958). *Natural language for deaf children*. Washington, DC: Alexander Graham Bell Association for the Deaf.

PAUL IRVINE
Katonah, New York

GROSENICK, JUDITH K. (1942–   )

Judith K. Grosenick received her BS (1964) in elementary education from the University of Wisconsin, Oshkosh (formerly Wisconsin State College, Oshkosh), and both her MS (1966) and PhD (1968) degrees in special education and emotional disturbance (respectively) from the University of Kansas, Lawrence. She is currently professor of education, University of Oregon, Eugene, as well as associate dean of teacher education, College of Education, University of Oregon, Eugene.

Originally an elementary school teacher, Grosenick en-

Judith K. Grosenick

countered more variation and more problems in children than she had expected or been trained to handle. With the realization that there existed more problems than solutions, she became more involved in the area of behavior disorders within the field of special education (Grosenick, 1981). She is perhaps best known for her development of in-service training programs for teachers who must deal with behaviorally disordered children in the classroom. She also has been involved in the areas of preparation of teachers and leadership personnel and knowledge building and dissemination. She has conducted data-gathering and analysis activities in the area of district-level programming for behavior-disordered children and youths. She has had information regarding issues and practices in the area of behavior disorders nationally disseminated (Grosenick & Huntze, 1983). Although actively involved in special education, Grosenick has a major interest in integrating special and regular education, not only in the public schools, but also in the teacher preparation programs (Grosenick & McCarney, 1984).

REFERENCES

Grosenick, J. K. (1981). Public school and mental health services to severely behavior disordered students. *Behavioral Disorders, 6*, 183–190.

Grosenick, J. K., & Huntze, S. L. (1983). *National needs analysis in behavior disorders: More questions than answers: Review and analysis of programs for behaviorally disordered children and youth*. Columbia, MO: Department of Special Education, University of Missouri, Columbia.

Grosenick, J. K., & McCarney, S. L. (1984). Preparation of teacher education in behavior disorders. *Teacher Education & Special Education, 7*, 100–106.

E. VALERIE HEWITT
Texas A&M University

GROSSMAN, HERBERT (1934–   )

Herbert Grossman attended Columbia University, where he obtained his doctorate (1967) in the field of clinical psychology. Grossman is currently with the special education department of California State University. He specializes in clinical child psychology and therapy.

Grossman was the coordinator of the Bilingual/Cross Cultural Special Education Program at California State University. From 1978 to 1980 he was the director of Project Hope, Peru.

ROBERTA C. STOKES
Texas A&M University

GROUP HOMES

The group home design is one model of alternate living environments designed to promote independent living for handicapped individuals in our society. As an alternative to large institutions, group homes provide a residential environment within a community that allows handicapped individuals to function as independently as possible while protecting their civil rights (Youngblood & Bensberg, 1983).

Historically, the developmentally disadvantaged in our society were placed in large institutions housing vast numbers of handicapped individuals. In 1969 Kugel and Wolfensberger reported that in the United States, 200,000 persons lived in over 150 public institutions for the retarded. An additional 20,000 resided in private institutions, with tens of thousands awaiting admittance to institutions for the mentally ill. For the most part, these institutions have been shown to be understaffed, overcrowded, and poorly managed. Violation of the rights of handicapped individuals came into serious question (e.g., *Wyatt* v. *Stickney*, 1972). As a direct result of this, and in keeping with the civil rights movement that was raging in the late 1960s, a large deinstitutionalization movement began.

The current philosophy is one of normalization, which maintains that developmentally disabled persons have the same legal and civil rights as any other citizen as guaranteed under the Fourteenth Amendment of the U.S. Constitution. Because most alternative living arrangements involve some departure from culturally normative practices, special attention to implementation of normalization and use of the "least restrictive environment" concept must underlie all such arrangements (Accreditation Council for Services for Mentally Retarded and Other Developmentally Disabled Persons, 1984).

To qualify for federal assistance, group homes must be established according to specific guidelines set forth by the Federal Agency of the Administration of Developmental Disabilities (WAC 275.36.010). According to these guidelines, a group home is defined as a residential facility in the form of a single dwelling, series of apartments, or other sound structures that allow for a pleasant and healthful environment for human life and welfare. This structure may be owned, leased, or be part of a larger facility serving other disabled individuals.

A group home is designed to serve a maximum of 20 mentally or physically disabled individuals who participate in various jobs, sheltered workshops, daycare centers, activity centers, educational facilities, or other community-based programs that are designed for their training, rehabilitation, and/or general well-being. These facilities must be located within reasonable proximity to those community resources that are necessary adjuncts to a training, education, or rehabilitation program. The living quarters should provide a homelike atmosphere and the residents should participate in the care of the facility and of themselves.

There are two major types of group home facilities. Both are designed to house 8 to 10 individuals. The first is a transitional group home. As the name implies, this home is designed to house adults (18 or older) with the goal that the handicapped person will move on to more independent living quarters (e.g., an apartment) once he or she has mastered important independent living skills. For individuals who exhibit less potential for being capable of independent living, long-term group homes are provided. These more permanent residences offer less restrictive environments than institutions, but not as independent an environment as transitional group homes. There are provisions even with long-term group homes that individuals be allowed to develop to their maximum potential. Thus, there are instances when individuals in long-term group homes have developed independent living skills to the extent that they can enter a transitional group home or can move directly into an independent living setting. Certain other groups of disabled individuals (e.g., deaf-blind) are also afforded chances for group home living. These facilities differ only in that they generally provide additional services to the transitional or long-term group home.

Group home facilities provide a wide range of services from legal assistance to sex education/family planning. The facilities, depending on states' funding patterns, are staffed by individuals ranging from house parents to supervisory professional staff members (Baker, 1977). Pros and cons of various staffing patterns are discussed by Youngblood and Bensberg (1983).

Establishing alternative living facilities (i.e., group homes) has not been always met with wholesale support, particularly by residents of communities where these residences are to be located. In keeping with the normalization principles and in accordance with state and federal guidelines for their establishment, group homes are to allow disabled individuals to experience community living to the maximum extent possible. Often residents of the community are concerned that their property values will fall because of group homes (Conroy & Bradley, 1985), or that a disabled resident might be dangerous. Researchers in the Pennhurst study found that resident attitudes following actual establishment of a group home were more positive than were attitudes toward the proposal of the same facility. The more negative attitudes were also directed toward group homes for the more severely disabled or mentally ill.

Research regarding the effects of group home living versus institutional living has been overwhelmingly positive. For example, the Pennhurst study (Conroy & Bradley, 1985) investigated whether disabled individuals ordered released from an institution following a court ruling and placed in alternative living environments, including group homes, were better off than a matched group of their peers who remained in the institution. Factors such as adaptive behavior, satisfaction with living arrangements, costs, and family and neighbor attitudes were examined. The study concluded: "the people deinstitutionalized under the Pennhurst court order *are* better off in *every* way measured . . . the results are not mixed" (pp. 322–323).

Just as residential services for the developmentally disabled today have met Wolfensberger's 1969 predictions, Willer (1981) has proposed that the concept of normalization and alternative living arrangements will again change in the future, out of necessity. He predicts "quality of life" concepts with emphasis on the individual will replace the group homes of today. Group homes as we know them, according to Willer, will be reserved for only the more severely disabled.

REFERENCES

Conroy, J. W., & Bradley, V. J. (1985). *The Pennhurst longitudinal study: A report of five years of research and analysis.* Philadelphia: Temple University, Developmental Disabilities Center. Boston: Human Services Research Institute.

Kugel, R. B., & Wolfensberger, W. (1969). *Changing patterns in residential services for the mentally retarded.* Washington, DC: President's Committee on Mental Retardation.

Standards for services for developmentally disabled individuals. (1984). Washington, DC: Accreditation Council for Services for Mentally Retarded and Other Developmentally Disabled Persons.

Willer, B. (1981). The future of residential services for mentally retarded persons. *Forum, 1*(4), 8–10.

Wyatt v. Stickney. 325F. Supp 781 (1972).

Youngblood, G. S., & Bensberg, G. J. (1983). *Planning and operating group homes for the handicapped.* Lubbock, TX: Research and Training Center in Mental Retardation.

JULIA A. HICKMAN
University of Texas, Austin

ADAPTIVE BEHAVIOR
DEINSTITUTIONALIZATION
EDGERTON, ROBERT B.
LEAST RESTRICTIVE ENVIRONMENT

GROUPING OF CHILDREN—IMPLICATIONS FOR SPECIAL EDUCATION

The grouping of children for organizational or instructional purposes is common practice in schools. For special education, the grouping process begins with the initial identification of the child as exceptional. As a consequence the child is, to some degree, set apart from the greater population of nonhandicapped children. Following initial classification, exceptional children are further grouped within a classroom structure, which, in most instances, still parallels the traditional categorical designations (e.g., a class for the educable mentally retarded, the learning disabled, the blind, etc.). Children within a given classroom share the same disability label.

The classification and labeling process is not neutral and both negative and positive consequences can result. The impact on a child's life can be profound and far-reaching (Hobbs, 1975). The benefits of labels tend to be organizational and group-oriented (e.g., a focal point for fiscal support and facilitation of communication among professionals). The negative consequences tend to be child-centered. Critics of categorically constituted groups point to numerous problems that can result from categorical labels: the tendency to blame the labeled child for the learning or behavior problem; the negative effects on teacher-student interaction and self-concept; the use of labels to excuse the child's lack of performance and the failure of the teaching effort; lowered expectations for student performance; teaching to the label rather than the child; lack of educational use of the labels; and inflexibility of categorical assignments. Comprehensive reviews of the labeling phenomenon are readily available in introductory textbooks on exceptional children.

Because of the many perceived shortcomings of categorical groups, an alternative approach to classroom grouping, termed noncategorical, is evolving in special education. Within the noncategorical approach, children's categorical disability labels are not the basis for classroom assignments. Rather, children are "grouped for instruction according to their performance on remedial tasks" (Hallahan & Kauffman, 1977). Groups constituted on children's instructional needs necessitate ongoing assessment of children's performance and flexibility. This will allow for frequent regrouping in keeping with student progress and changing instructional needs. A noncategorical group may actually be a mixed categorical group, as the children in almost all cases will have a categorical assignment even if it is not used as the basis for the classroom assignment. Even though there is strong support for noncategorical grouping and instruction (Hallahan & Kauffman, 1977), noncategorical classes are not enthusiastically embraced by all special educators (Gaar & Plue, 1983).

Each exceptional child must be assigned to a specific classroom setting. Since 1975, the least restrictive environment (LRE) provision of PL 94-142 has become the guiding principle in the placement of all handicapped children. For the severely or multiply handicapped, the LRE requirement has paved the way for special classes in regular school buildings and/or community settings (as opposed to segregated schools and institutions). For the mildly handicapped, the choice of class placement frequently involves a selection between a self-contained class, resource room, or regular education classroom. The decision has implications for student outcomes. Cegelka and Tyler (1970) reviewed studies comparing special class to regular class placement for educable mentally retarded (EMR) students. The data relative to academic performance either favored regular class placement or showed no differences between the two alternatives. Rejection and isolation of EMR students in regular class settings were reported in many of the studies reviewed. Another extensive review of special class versus regular class placement for exceptional children was conducted by Carlberg and Kavale (1980). They found that special class placement was inferior to regular class placement for below average IQ students, but that the special class was significantly superior to regular class placement for learning-disabled (LD) emotionally disturbed (ED), and behaviorally disordered (BD) students. In a review of resource room programs, Sindelar and Deno (1978) reported benefits for LD and ED, but not EMR, students.

Overall, the authors maintain that the results are inconclusive. However, the tentative finding of a differential effect for students of different exceptionalities under alternative class groupings is noteworthy. Further, research to clarify the interactive effect between exceptionality and type of group placement is essential if exceptional children are to be placed in group settings most beneficial to their growth and development.

REFERENCES

Carlberg, C., & Kavale, K. (1980). The efficacy of special versus regular class placement for exceptional children: A meta-analysis. *Journal of Special Education, 14*(3), 295–309.

Cegelka, W. G., & Tyler, J. L. (1970). The efficacy of special class placement for the mentally retarded in proper perspective. *Training School Bulletin, 67,* 33–68.

Gaar, B. L., & Plue, W. V. (1983). Separate versus combined categories for mental retardation and specific learning disabilities. *Learning Disabilities Quarterly, 6*(1), 77–79.

Hallahan, D. P., & Kauffman, J. M. (1977). Labels, categories, behaviors: ED, LD, and EMR reconsidered. *Journal of Special Education, 11*(2), 139–149.

Hobbs, N. (1975). *The futures of children.* San Francisco: Jossey-Bass.

Sindelar, P. T., & Deno, S. L. (1978). The effectiveness of resource programming. *Journal of Special Education, 12*(1), 17–28.

LIBBY GOODMAN
Pennsylvania State University

CASCADE MODEL OF SPECIAL EDUCATION
SYSTEMS OF CLASSIFICATION
LABELING

GROUP THERAPY

Group therapy is a general term that refers to any of the various types of therapeutic groups that share the broad purpose of increasing people's knowledge of themselves and others and giving people the skills necessary to enhance their personal competence. According to this general definition, group counseling, encounter groups, human relation groups, and skill-oriented groups are all types of group therapy. There are as many theoretical orientations to group therapy as there are to individual therapy. These include existentialism-humanism, gestalt, psychoanalytic, behavioral, rational-emotive therapy, reality therapy, transactional analysis, and others (Corey & Corey, 1977). The several types of group therapies plus the various theoretical orientations that may characterize group therapy make it difficult to make meaningful statements that generalize to the various types and models.

However, some generalizations do apply to most models of group therapy. First, participants can obtain honest feedback from others about how they appear to others. Thus, participants are provided with an opportunity to explore their style of relating to others and to learn more effective interpersonal skills. This feedback occurs in a group climate characterized by mutual caring and trust. Feedback from several persons, especially persons similar to a group participant, is often more powerful than a therapist's feedback in individual therapy.

Second, the group setting offers support for new behaviors and encourages experimentation. This norm of experimentation combined with the norms of feedback and support create a low-risk setting for participants to practice new behaviors such as showing compassion, intimacy, assertion, or disclosure of weaknesses.

Third, the sharing of experiences allows members to learn about themselves through the experiences of others, to experience emotional closeness, and to empathize with the problems of others. Participants learn that their problems and perceived inadequacies are not unique; they also learn new ways to cope with those problems. Some group therapists select group participants in a way that maximizes the opportunity for learning better ways of dealing with problems. For example, a group designed to help lonely children make friends would include some children who are at least moderately competent in friendship-making skills.

Fourth, group cohesiveness is necessary for a successful group. A cohesive group is characterized by mutual trust and respect and high levels of cooperation, support, encouragement, caring, productive problem solving, and the open expression of conflict. The group therapist directs much of his or her energies and skills to creating cohesive groups in which individuals experience the acceptance that is a necessary precondition for lowering defenses and risking new behaviors.

There are three major types of group therapy used in school settings: skill-oriented groups, personal growth groups, and specific focus therapy groups. The use of all three in schools is justified by the recognition that emotional and behavioral adjustment is important to a child's educational performance. Social-emotional problems like depression, loneliness, or anxiety affect school learning and adjustment.

Skill-oriented group therapy is the most widely accepted type of group therapy in school settings as it focuses on teaching specific adaptive skills such as communication, problem-solving, or social skills. An example of a skill-oriented therapy program is the structured learning therapy model developed and popularized by Goldstein (1981). In this model children with deficient social skills are taught skills through a procedure that employs instruction, modeling, behavior rehearsal, and feedback. Children in the group discuss each skill (e.g., expressing anger, offering help, disagreeing with another), citing their own examples of each skill. The skills are broken into component steps, and members practice the skills in role playing. They receive feedback from the group on their performance. Another example of a skill-oriented group is a communication skill group for adolescents. Members practice such skills as listening and perception-checking in the group setting and discuss how these skills apply outside the group.

In the personal growth group, the group setting provides the emotional support and encouragement necessary for the type of self-exploration that leads to a change in attitudes and behaviors. In schools, members of the group might share a common problem or situation such as having parents who are recently divorced. The group provides members with a place where they can express their feelings regarding their situations and discover that other people experience similar problems and feelings. These groups attempt to help members integrate their thinking and feelings and to experience greater self-acceptance. They are often directed to the normal person who is experiencing unusual stress or who wishes to become more self-actualized.

The specific focus therapy group attempts to correct an emotional or behavioral problem. An example is a group for highly anxious children. Children might share anxiety-producing situations and their reactions to those situations. They learn that different children are afraid of different situations, test the reality of their fears, and learn from other children how to cope with their anxieties. The group therapist might teach children how to use specific anxiety-management techniques such as relaxation, self-talk, or problem solving.

REFERENCES

Corey, G., & Corey, M. S. (1977). *Groups: Process and practice.* Belmont, CA: Wadsworth.

Goldstein, A. P. (1981). *Psychological skill training: The structured learning technique.* New York: Pergamon.

JAN N. HUGHES
Texas A&M University

FAMILY COUNSELING PSYCHOTHERAPY

GUADALUPE *v.* TEMPE ELEMENTARY SCHOOL DISTRICT

See DIANA *V.* STATE BOARD OF EDUCATION.

GUGGENBÜHL, JOHANN J. (1816–1863)

Johann Guggenbühl, a Swiss physician, was the originator of institutional care for the mentally retarded. Following an extensive study of cretinism, Guggenbühl established a hospital and school for mentally retarded children, the Abendberg, in the mountains of Switzerland. There he instituted for his students a program that combined healthful living, good diet, and medicine with an educational program that emphasized cognitive, sensory, and physical training. Guggenbühl found that his students, especially those who entered his school at an early age, showed improvement in both physical and mental development. Guggenbühl publicized his results widely, and institutions similar to his were established in many of the countries of Europe and in the United States.

Guggenbühl was much in demand and was often away from the Abendberg for extended periods, during which time the institution was poorly administered. This situation caused problems that, in conjunction with the high expectations that Guggenbühl had fostered, led to the closing of the Abendberg and the departure in disgrace of its founder. Nevertheless, Guggenbühl's contribution was monumental. He originated institutional care for the mentally retarded, demonstrated that young mentally retarded people could be helped to develop both physically and mentally, and developed a system of care and education that served as a model throughout the western world.

REFERENCE

Kanner, L. (1964). *A history of the care and study of the mentally retarded.* Springfield, IL: Thomas.

PAUL IRVINE
Katonah, New York

GUILFORD, J. P. (1897–   )

A native Nebraskan, J. P. Guilford was educated in psychology at the University of Nebraska, where Winifred Hyde interested him in psychological testing. During his graduate work at Cornell, Guilford was strongly influenced by Karl Dallenbach and Kurt Koffka.

Guilford spent most of his academic career at the University of Southern California. Aside from writing what some consider to be classic texts in psychological measurement (e.g., Guilford, 1942), Guilford is best known for his extensive work in factor analysis, through which he derived his structure of intelligence (SOI) model of intelligence (Guilford, 1967). Guilford's SOI model postulates some 120 distinct human abilities that contribute to overall intelligence. In special education, Guilford is best known for the application of his SOI model, particularly its concepts of convergent and divergent thought, to the development of programs to foster creativity and to improve the learning of gifted and creative children.

REFERENCES

Guilford, J. P. (1942). *Fundamental statistics in psychology and education*. New York: McGraw-Hill.

Guilford, J. P. (1967). *The nature of human intelligence*. New York: McGraw-Hill.

STAFF

**CONVERGENT AND DIVERGENT THINKING
STRUCTURE OF INTELLECT**

GUILLAIN-BARRÉ SYNDROME

Guillain-Barré syndrome is described as a peripheral polyneuritis resulting in symmetrical pain and weakness of the extremities (*Mosby's*, 1983). The condition was originally described by Guillain, Barré, and Strohl in 1916. It sometimes bears the names of all three physicians; other synonyms include acute febrile polyneuritis and Landry's paralysis (Durham, 1969; Magalini, 1971). Onset of Guillain-Barré syndrome may occur one to three weeks following a mild fever associated with immunization or viral infection (*Mosby's*, 1983). The presence of an upper respiratory infection prior to onset of symptoms has been reported in approximately half the cases (Dyck, 1979). Early signs are mild, and include weakness of the lower extremities, characterized by difficulty in walking, climbing stairs, or rising from a seated position. Weakness and paralysis develop in an ascending fashion either rapidly

(within hours) or more gradually, over a period of 7 to 10 days (Magalini, 1971). Bladder incontinence may occur, tendon reflexes are absent, and ocular nerves may be involved (Durham, 1969).

The course of Guillain-Barré syndrome varies widely; some individuals have extreme impairment (e.g., near total paralysis) and require nursing care, while others exhibit less severe symptoms. In nearly all cases, total remission occurs within a few weeks or months. The small number of patients for whom Guillain-Barré syndrome is fatal succumb to respiratory paralysis (Durham, 1969; Lechtenberg, 1982). The cause of Guillain-Barré syndrome is unknown, although exposure to a virus or bacterial infection is suspected (Dyck, 1979). Males and females, children and adults are affected equally. Treatment typically is limited to maintaining respiration and maximizing comfort. The administration of corticosteroid hormones has been associated with enhanced rate of recovery (Dyck, 1979). Physical therapy is advisable during the recovery period. During the acute and recuperative stages of Guillain-Barré syndrome, affected children may require special education, including homebound instruction for limited periods and related services (e.g., physical therapy). Educational programming should follow a multifactored evaluation and consultation with appropriate medical personnel.

REFERENCES

Durham, R. H. (1969). *Encyclopedia of medical syndromes*. New York: Harper & Row.

Dyck, P. J. (1979). Diseases of the peripheral nervous system. In P. B. Beeson, W. McDermott, & J. B. Wyngaarden (Eds.), *Cecil textbook of medicine* (pp. 899–913). Philadelphia: Saunders.

Lechtenberg, R. (1982). *The psychiatrist's guide to diseases of the nervous system*. New York: Wiley.

Magalini, S. (1971). *Dictionary of medical syndromes*. Philadelphia: Lippincott.

Mosby's medical and nursing dictionary. (1983). St. Louis: Mosby.

CATHY F. TELZROW
*Cuyahoga Special Education
Service Center, Maple
Heights, Ohio*

**CENTRAL NERVOUS SYSTEM
PHYSICAL DISABILITY**

H

HABILITATION OF THE HANDICAPPED

Habilitation is the process of using various professional services to help disabled persons maximize their vocational, mental, physical, and social abilities (Rosen, Clark, & Kivitz, 1977). Whereas the term rehabilitation connotes restoration of abilities, habilitation refers to the development of abilities that never existed. The term usually refers to programming for those with developmental disabilities such as cerebral palsy, mental retardation, epilepsy, autism, or sensory impairment.

Present-day habilitation programs have evolved from a decade of legislation and litigation addressing the rights and needs of the developmentally disabled. Three major pieces of legislation have promoted habilitation efforts: the Rehabilitation Act Amendments of 1973 (PL 93-112), the Education for all Handicapped Children Act of 1975 (PL 94-142), and the Education Amendments of 1976 (PL 94-482).

Sections 503 and 504 of the Rehabilitation Act mandate affirmative action for all employment openings, prohibit discrimination of the handicapped in hiring, training, advancement, and retention practices, and require that all programs be accessible to the handicapped. Compliance is necessary to retain federal funding.

The Education for all Handicapped Children Act and the Education Amendments of 1976 address the vocational educational needs of disabled individuals. Public Law 94-142 guarantees a free, appropriate, public education for handicapped children, the right to due process, an individualized educational program, and education in the least restrictive environment. Public Law 94-482 guarantees funding of vocational training programs for handicapped students.

Habilitation programs for handicapped students vary, but are similar in format to those described by Miller and Schloss (1982). Current programs focus not only on vocation, but also on academic, social, leisure, and interpersonal skills. Teaching procedures include identification of the handicap, assessment of skills, program design based on needs, interests, and skills of the individual, instruction, and behavior management and evaluation. Career education includes career awareness and exploration, development of vocational prerequisites, and preparation training. Goals of these training programs vary with the individual's skills and abilities.

REFERENCES

Goldberg, R. T. (1984). The human sciences and clinical methods: An historical perspective (Special issue). *Rehabilitation Literature, 45,* 340–344.

Kokaska, C. J., & Brolin, D. E. (1985). *Career education for handicapped individuals* (2nd ed.). Columbus, OH: Merrill.

Miller, S. R., & Schloss, P. J. (1982). *Career-vocational education for handicapped youth.* Rockville, MD: Aspen.

Rosen, M., Clark, G. R., & Kivitz, M. S. (1977). *Habilitation of the handicapped: New dimensions in programs for the developmentally disabled.* Baltimore, MD: University Park.

Trieschmann, R. B. (1984). Vocational rehabilitation: A psychological perspective (Special issue). *Rehabilitation Literature, 45,* 345–348.

CHRISTINE A. ESPIN
University of Minnesota

REHABILITATION
VOCATIONAL TRAINING

HABITUATION

Habituation is a decline in response to a stimulus that is presented repeatedly but that signals the onset of no other stimulus. For example, a loud noise may evoke a startle response at first but little response after its twentieth repetition. A new cuckoo clock may awaken people on the hour for the first few nights but not on later nights.

Because habituation is generally perceived as a relatively simple example of learning, it has been a popular focus for study by investigators interested in the physiology of learning. For example, the gill-withdrawal response of the sea slug *Aplysia* habituates after a tactile stimulus is repeated many times. The habituation can be traced to a single, identifiable synapse at which the presynaptic end bulb shrinks and releases less than normal amounts of its synaptic transmitter (Castellucci & Kandel, 1974).

Habituation may be taken as the opposite of distractibility. Someone who fails to habituate to a repeated stimulus will continue to be distracted by it. Biological factors that impair habituation also increase distractibility. Examples include damage to the frontal lobes of the cerebral cortex and a deficit of the synaptic transmitter acetylcholine (Carlton & Markiewicz, 1971). Infant rats fail to habituate before age 25 days (Feigley, Parsons, Hamilton, & Spear, 1972). This failure is attributed to the immaturity of certain areas of the brain, including the frontal cortex, prior to that age. High distractibility and slow habituation also characterize many children with an immature nervous system, including most of those who suffer from attention deficit disorder. Slow habituation also is associated with other behaviors that indicate a lack of inhibition such as impulsiveness, unresponsiveness to the threat of punishment, and failure to extinguish an unreinforced response.

Some investigators have used rate of habituation as a diagnostic technique to identify infants or young children who may have been exposed to factors that impair brain maturation. One study examined the rate of habituation by newborns as a function of alcohol use by their mothers during pregnancy (Streissguth, Barr, & Martin, 1983). Habituation was slightly but significantly slower among infants whose mothers drank alcohol during pregnancy, even if they drank a mean of less than one ounce of alcohol per day.

REFERENCES

Carlton, P. L., & Markiewicz, B. (1971). Behavioral effects of atropine and scopolamine. In E. Furchtgott (Ed.), *Pharmacological and biophysical agents and behavior* (pp. 345–373). New York: Academic.

Castellucci, V. F., & Kandel, E. R. (1974). A quantal analysis of the synaptic depression underlying habituation of the gill-withdrawal reflex in *Aplysia. Proceedings of the National Academy of Sciences, U.S.A., 71,* 5004–5008.

Feigley, D. A., Parsons, P. J., Hamilton, L. W., & Spear, N. E. (1972). Development of habituation to novel environments in the rat. *Journal of Comparative & Physiological Psychology, 79,* 443–452.

Streissguth, A. P., Barr, H. M., & Martin, D. C. (1983). Maternal alcohol use and neonatal habituation assessed with the Brazelton scale. *Child Development, 54,* 1109–1118.

JAMES W. KALAT
North Carolina State University

ATTENTION DEFICIT DISORDER-HYPERACTIVITY
BEHAVIOR MODIFICATION
DISTRACTIBILITY

HALDERMAN v. PENNHURST STATE SCHOOL AND HOSPITAL (1977)

The *Halderman* case was filed as a class-action suit by a resident (T. L. Halderman of the Pennhurst State School and Hospital (operated by the Commonwealth of Penn-

sylvania), the Pennsylvania Association of Retarded Citizens, and the United States of America against the Pennhurst State School and Hospital. The residents made a variety of claims that centered around the lack of rehabilitative and educational efforts at Pennhurst. The plaintiffs argued that custodial care was insufficient for involuntary placement in the Pennhurst institution since the plaintiffs were retarded and not considered dangerous.

In deciding the case, the federal judge for the eastern district of Pennsylvania, R. J. Broderick, made three rulings that have been of major importance in modifying special education services to the institutionalized retarded. Broderick ruled that retarded residents of state institutions have constitutional rights to minimally adequate habilitation services, to freedom from harm, and to the receipt of habilitation services in a nondiscriminatory manner. Broderick went on to rule in the *Halderman* case specifically that the resident's rights at Pennhurst had been violated because of failure to provide even minimally adequate habilitative services. In making his rulings, Broderick rejected the argument that improvements at Pennhurst were being made gradually and should be allowed to proceed at an incremental pace, that state law restricted the programs that could be offered, and that funding levels prevented minimally adequate habilitation programs.

Broderick wrote a lengthy decision that reviews assessment practices, programming, and management in institutional settings. All were directed at the provision of habilitative services and special education. For example, Broderick noted that although speech, hearing, and psychological evaluations had been completed on nearly all residents at approximately 3-year intervals, vocational assessments or evaluations of self-care skills were rarely conducted. Broderick saw a need for more extensive evaluations, stating that "Proper habilitation cannot be provided to retarded persons unless those responsible for providing such programs are aware of the individual's needs" (*Halderman* v. *Pennhurst*, 1977, p. 1305). Broderick required the development of individual educational plans for institutionalized retarded that would include (1) long- and short-term goals, (2) specification of the conditions under which the individual might achieve these goals, and (3) specification of the criteria to evaluate the individual's mastery of these goals.

Broderick placed many restrictions on the use of punishment, drugs, and physical restraints. He particularly ruled that lack of sufficient staff did not allow the use of otherwise inappropriate methods of control. Physical constraints, for example, could not be used just because insufficient staff were available to supervise self-injurious residents.

Broderick made strong statements indicating favorable sentiments toward the principles of normalization as applied to the severely and profoundly retarded as well. Since the court found that the environment at Pennhurst was not conducive to normalization, Broderick ruled that the residents were to be moved to community-based living facilities as part of the injunctive relief. He noted that each community facility would be required to provide minimally adequate habilitative services. Broderick's extensive rulings regarding the provisions of habilitative services, including detailed multidisciplinary assessment and movement toward normalization, have had significant impact on the deinstitutionalization of all but the most severely and profoundly mentally retarded. The rulings have impacted greatly the lives of those remaining in institutions such as Pennhurst.

CECIL R. REYNOLDS
Texas A&M University

NORMALIZATION
WOLFENSBERGER, WOLF

HALDOL

Haldol (haloperidol) is considered a major tranquilizer. Unlike thorazine, which is a phenothiazine, haldol is of the drug class butyrophenone, which tends to have a greater neuroleptic effect than phenothiazine (Bassuk & Schoonover, 1977). Haldol is similar in effect to the piperazine subgroup (e.g., Stelazine) of phenothiazines. Like similar antipsychotic drugs, haldol appears to block Dopamine receptors in the brain. In contrast to Chlorpromazine, haldol tends to produce less sedation, less decrease in blood pressure, and less change in temperature perception (McEvoy, 1984). Haldol is used primarily for symptomatic management of psychotic conditions. Haldol also appears to have more specific effects on agitated behavior. Thus, it tends to be used with psychotic individuals who also show assaultive behavior, with combative adolescents, and with hyperactive brain-impaired children (Bassuk & Schoonover, 1977). Haldol also has been used as an adjunct with manic-depressive patients in the manic phase during the initiation of lithium treatment (Jefferson, Greist, & Ackerman, 1983).

As may be expected from its actions, haldol produces anticholinergic side effects (i.e., dry mouth, blurred vision, urinary retention). Side effects (McEvoy, 1984) to haloperidol treatment usually develop during the initial days of treatment; they are similar to the side effects encountered during treatment with phenothiazines (parkinsonian symptoms: drowsiness or lethargy, drooling; neuromuscular reactions: motor restlessness, dystonic reactions, tardive dyskinesia; mental confusion, headache, dizziness, depression, and anxiety may also be seen). Haldol also lowers the seizure threshold, thus otherwise controlled seizures may recur. Abrupt withdrawal in a pediatric patient, especially after relatively high doses have been used, may

produce a syndrome of involuntary movements reminiscent of tardive dyskinesia in adults (Bassuk & Schoonover, 1977).

REFERENCES

Bassuk, E. L., & Schoonover, S. C. (1977). *The practitioner's guide to psychoactive drugs*. New York: Plenum.

Jefferson, J. W., Greist, J. H., & Ackerman, D. L. (1983). *Lithium encyclopedia for clinical practice*. Washington, D.C.: American Psychiatric Press.

McEvoy, G. K. (1984). *American hospital formulary service: Drug information 84*. Bethesda, MD: American Society of Hospital Pharmacists.

ROBERT F. SAWICKI
Lake Erie Institute of
Rehabilitation, Lake Erie,
Pennsylvania

DOPAMINE
STELAZINE

HALL, FRANK H. (1843–1911)

Frank Haven Hall, inventor of the braille typewriter, was a school superintendent prior to becoming superintendent of the Illinois Institution for the Education of the Blind in 1890. In 1892 Hall introduced the braillewriter, a braille typewriter that quickly replaced the laborious writing device then in use—a slate and hand-held stylus—and greatly speeded up the writing of braille. Hall then adapted his machine to print multiple copies. With its speed and efficiency, Hall's machine revolutionized bookmaking for the blind and made feasible the mass production of braille materials.

Frank H. Hall

Hall's experience at the Illinois institution convinced him that blind students should have the opportunity of participating fully in the activities of sighted individuals. He persuaded the school authorities of Chicago, who were considering the establishment of a boarding school for blind students, to establish day classes instead. As a result, the first public school day class for blind students was initiated in Chicago in 1900, with one of Hall's teachers as supervisor. The last decade of Hall's life was spent as superintendent of the Farmers' Institute of Illinois, where he effectively promoted the cause of agricultural education.

REFERENCE

Hendrickson, W. B. (1956). The three lives of Frank H. Hall. *Journal of the Illinois State Historical Society, 44,* 271–293.

PAUL IRVINE
Katonah, New York

HALL, G. STANLEY (1844–1924)

G. Stanley Hall established one of the first psychology laboratories in the United States, at Johns Hopkins University. Later, as the first president of Clark University, he instituted the first child psychology laboratory in the nation. A former student of Wilhelm Wundt in Leipzig, Hall was influential in introducing European theories and methods of psychology into the United States. He carried out pioneering studies of childhood, adolescence, senescence, human genetics, and the psychology of religion. Among Hall's students were many of the next generation of leaders in psychology and education, including John Dewey, James McKeen Cattell, Henry H. Goddard, and Lewis Terman. Hall published nearly 500 articles and books and founded four psychological journals. He was a leading figure in the formation of the American Psychological Association and was its first president.

REFERENCES

Hall, G. S. (1923). *Life and confessions of a psychologist.* New York: Appleton.

Watson, R. I. (1968). *The great psychologists.* New York: Lippincott.

PAUL IRVINE
Katonah, New York

HALLAHAN, DANIEL P. (1944–   )

Daniel P. Hallahan received his BA in psychology from the University of Michigan in 1967 and his PhD in edu-

Daniel P. Hallahan

cation and psychology from the University of Michigan in 1971. His major fields of interest include learning disabilities, attentional problems, cognitive behavior modification, and applied behavior analysis. His earliest work was in information processing. He suggested that many learning-disabled children exhibit strategy deficits when they attempt academic tasks (Hallahan, 1975). His recent research has focused on an educational intervention that will counteract such strategy deficiencies.

Hallahan is known for having popularized the notion of noncategorical education for the mildly handicapped and also for his research into the use of self-monitoring for children with attentional problems. His research is in the area of cognitive interventions, methods of making learning-disabled students independent learners, and policy analysis in special education.

Hallahan's principal publications include the *Handbook of Special Education, Introduction to Learning Disabilities,* and *Exceptional Children: Introduction to Special Education.* He has written other books as well as numerous articles concerning special education. Hallahan is currently teaching at the University of Virginia in Charlottesville.

REFERENCES

Hallahan, D. P. (1975). Comparative research studies on the psychological characteristics of learning disabled children. In W. M. Cruickshank and D. P. Hallahan (Eds.), *Perceptual and learning disabilities in children, Vol. 1: Psychoeducational practices* (pp. 29–60). Syracuse, NY: Syracuse University Press.

Hallahan, D. P., & Kauffman, J. M. (Eds.). (1981). *Handbook of special education.* Englewood Cliffs, NJ: Prentice-Hall.

Hallahan, D. P., Kauffman, J. M., & Lloyd, J. W. (1985). *Introduction to learning disabilities* (2nd ed.). Englewood Cliffs, NJ: Prentice-Hall.

Hallahan, D. P., & Kauffman, J. M. (1986). *Exceptional children:*

Introduction to special education (3rd ed.). Englewood Cliffs, NJ: Prentice-Hall.

REBECCA BAILEY
Texas A&M University

HALLERMANN-STREIFF SYNDROME (OCULO-MANDIBULO-FACIAL SYNDROME) (HSS)

Hallermann-Streiff syndrome (HSS) is a syndrome whose etiology is presently unknown. Children with HSS have multiple craniofacial malformations that often include a short head, thin skin, small face, eyes, and mouth, a reduction of hair, and a thin "beaked" nose that produces a birdlike appearance (Carter, 1978). Teeth may be present at birth; the small mouth, high palate, and absence of some teeth often result in dental problems. Congenital cataracts are frequently present, causing severe visual problems. In addition, hearing problems often occur.

Children with HSS are generally short in stature (usually less than the third percentile for height) with proportional dwarfism of extremities and hyperextensibility of joints. Small sexual organs are noted and spina bifida has been reported in some cases. Mental range extends from normal to moderate and, in some cases, severe retardation.

Special services will be required for hearing, vision, and speech problems. Because varying degrees of mental retardation may be present in HSS children, good diagnostic evaluations are important. In addition, there is a relatively substantial difference in the physical appearance of HSS children, therefore, psychological and guidance counseling may be necessary as the children mature because joint, motor, and spinal problems may develop. Mainstreamed settings with proper support services are usually the preferred educational settings.

REFERENCES

Carter, C. (Ed.). (1978). Medical aspects of mental retardation. (2nd ed.). Springfield: IL: Thomas.

Garlin, R., Cervenka, F., & Pruzansky, S. (1971). Facial clefting and its syndromes. The clinical delineation of birth defects. XI. Orafacial structures. Birth Defects, 8(7), 3–49.

SALLY L. FLAGLER
University of Oklahoma

PHYSICAL ANOMALIES
SPINA BIFIDA

HALLUCINOGENS

Blum (1984) describes three classes of hallucinogenic drugs: adrenergic compounds (e.g., mescaline, adrenaline); indole types (e.g., lysergic acid diethylamide [LSD]); and anticholinergic hallucinogens (e.g., scopolamine, atropine). An additional hallucinogen, which has been sold as everything from cocaine to LSD, is phencyclidine (PCP), which was originally marketed as an animal anesthetic. For a complete review of hallucinogenic agents, see Blum (1984).

In reviewing the personality characteristics of the users of hallucinogenic drugs, several trends have been noted. LSD users tend to be more introverted and artistic (McGothlin, Cohen, & McGothlin, 1966). Comparisons of personality test findings suggest that persons using hallucinogens are more socially distant, interpersonally suspicious, dominant, anxious, creative, and accident-prone (Kleckner, 1968). These trends have been replicated in additional studies (Pittel et al., 1970, cited in Leavitt, 1982), suggesting a contributory role for childhood chaos and above average stress in substance abuse.

The following are examples of characteristic hallucinogenic actions (Blum, 1984).

1. *Adrenergic types.* Examples of this class are peyote, mescaline analogs (e.g., DOM/STP 2,5-dimethoxy-4-methylamphetamine), epinephrine, and amphetamines. Characteristically, these drugs increase pulse rate, raise blood pressure, and act as a stimulant. Peyote tends to produce colored visual hallucinations as well as hallucinatory experiences. Sensations of depersonalization, ego distortion, and loss of time perception also have been described. The period of intoxication lasts from 4 to 16 hours, with aftereffects (e.g., delusions) occurring, in some cases for several months after intoxication.

2. *Indole types.* LSD-25 is the major example of drugs of this class; however, mushrooms containing psilocybin and the substance DMT (N-dimethyltryptamine) also are included. The major effects of LSD are related to its action on the central nervous system. Responses may be grouped into autonomic symptoms and perceptual symptoms. Autonomic effects include pupillary dilation, rise in blood pressure, and increase in pulse. Perceptual changes include distortions in which objects appear to lose their boundaries, colors are amplified, and new hues are formed. Sensory experiences also seem to merge (synesthesia: e.g., sounds may be perceived as having associated hues). Emotional responsiveness to such experiences and the range of sensory experience appear to be enhanced. LSD intoxication can become frightening since many of the distortions appear related to intrapersonal issues and situational ambience. The degree of perceptual discontinuity itself can produce panic, which in turn is amplified. The immediate effects of intoxication may last up to 48 hours, with usual periods being between 6 and 18 hours.

Of particular concern is the fact that an LSD experience may recur spontaneously (flashback) even 2 years after the last ingestion. Competing theories for the cause of such flashbacks include intense psychologic reliving and fatty storage of LSD, which creates a flashback on subsequent release of residual LSD. Attempting to calm and reassure an individual who is LSD intoxicated and experiencing a panic reaction is reported to be the most effective intervention. The focus of the technique is to reassure the individual that what is being experienced is a distortion that will stop and that he or she is not alone.

3. *Anticholinergic Types.* Examples include plants from which either atropine, or atropine-type alkaloids, or scopolamine may be derived (e.g., belladonna, henbane, mandrake, and datura species). Of particular concern is that the dosage necessary to produce intoxication with these substances is close to dosage that produces toxicity and sometimes poisoning. Along with expected anticholinergic effects, these drugs also may produce a toxic psychosis, lethargy, loss of attention, memory inefficiency for recent events, and delirium. Occasionally these drugs are added to other hallucinogens to increase their effect.

4. *Phencyclidine (PCP).* This substance has become increasingly available and abused owing to the ease of its creation. Besides PCP itself, there are many variations of the PCP formula that also produce hallucinogenic drugs. Effects generated by PCP appear to be related to dose and the chronicity of use. Initially, small doses produce a state similar to alcohol inebriation; larger doses produce analgesia (pain insensitivity) and disorientation; extremely large doses may produce unconsciousness and convulsions. Chronic usage of PCP has been followed by recurrent psychotic episodes, depression, and confusional syndromes. Chronic users, even during periods when the drug is not ingested, are reported to experience memory inefficiency, visual disturbance, disorientation, and communication difficulties. Of particular concern are outbursts of violence and general belligerent, assaultive, and antisocial behavior demonstrated by some intoxicated users. Unlike the visionary experience produced by other hallucinogenic drugs, PCP users experience body image distortions, frank thought disorganization, interpersonal negativism, and aggressiveness. Treatment during the intoxicated episode is symptomatic with a focus on hyperactivity and safety maintenance. Many abusers do not recall much of the intoxicated period, therefore PCP offers nothing in the way of existential experience. For the most part the cost of the inebriation far outweighs its benefit.

REFERENCES

Blum, K. (1984). *The handbook of abusable drugs.* New York: Gardner.

Kleckner, J. (1968). Personality differences between psychedelic drug users and non-users. *Psychology, 5,* 66–71.

Leavitt, F. (1982). *Drugs and behavior.* New York: Wiley.

McGothlin, W., Cohen, S., & McGothlin, M. (1966). Personality and attitude changes in volunteer subjects following repeated administration of LSD. *Excerpta Medica International Continuing Reports, 129,* 425–434.

ROBERT F. SAWICKI
Lake Erie Institute of
Rehabilitation, Lake Erie,
Pennsylvania

DRUG ABUSE

HALSTEAD APHASIA TEST

The Halstead Aphasia Test, Form M, was developed by Ward C. Halstead in cooperation with J. M. Wepman, R. M. Reitan, and R. F. Heimburger. It was published by the Industrial Relations Center, University of Chicago, in 1955. It is the pocket-size version of the Halstead-Wepman Screening Test for Aphasia (1949), which itself was a version of a 1935 test.

This test uses basically the same 51 test items and order of presentation as its predecessor. Test materials consist of plastic stimuli cards, which the patient views through a 2-inch by 1½-inch window, a manual, and scoring sheets. Criteria for evaluating subjects' responses and a diagnostic code and profile by which patients are classified into four aphasic categories (global, expressive-receptive, expressive, and receptive) are included in the manual. Administration time is 30 to 60 minutes.

Boone (1978) suggests that the Halstead Aphasia Test probes language comprehension in a limited way and does not discriminate between those who do and do not easily understand spoken language. Boone also points out that patients with hemianopsia have difficulty in viewing the stimuli through the small window.

Meier (1978) and Boone indicate that this test has some value as a screening tool, but both recommend more extensive testing measures to fully assess aphasics' linguistic abilities.

REFERENCES

Boone, D. R. (1978). Halstead Aphasia Test [review]. In O. K. Buros (Ed.), *The eighth mental measurements yearbook* (Vol. 2, pp. 1500–1501). Highland Park, NJ: Gryphon.

Halstead, W. C., Wepman, J. J., Reitan, R. M., & Heimburger, R. F. (1955). *The Halstead Aphasia Test.* Chicago: University of Chicago Press.

Meier, M. J. (1978). Halstead Aphasia Test [review]. In O. K. Buros (Ed.), *The Eighth Mental Measurements Yearbook* (Vol. 2., pp. 1501–1502). Highland Park, NJ: Gryphon.

K. SANDRA VANTA
Cleveland Public Schools,
Cleveland, Ohio

HALSTEAD-REITAN NEUROPSYCHOLOGICAL TEST BATTERY

Collectively, three separate test batteries are commonly referred to as the Halstead-Reitan Neuropsychological Test Battery. The adult battery (ages 15 and older) is entitled the Halstead Neuropsychological Test Battery for Adults; the older children's battery (ages 9 through 14) is called the Halstead Neuropsychological Test Battery for Children. A third battery for younger children (ages 5 through 8) is the Reitan-Indiana Neuropsychological Test Battery for Children. This differential terminology, which has resulted in confusion and inconsistent use of the proper battery name, is the result of an agreement between W. C. Halstead and his protégé, R. M. Reitan (Reitan, 1979), the two individuals credited with various aspects of the development and refinement of these batteries.

Despite terminology differences, the three batteries reflect conceptual similarities in their approaches to the assessment of brain-behavior relationships. The nuclear tests of the three batteries were originally developed by Halstead (1947) and later standardized and modified by Reitan. The adult battery is composed of the following tests: Category Test, Tactual Performance Test, Seashore Rhythm Test, Speech-Sounds Perception Test, Finger Oscillation Test, Trail-Making Test, Aphasia Screening Test, Sensory-Perceptual Disturbances Test, Lateral Dominance Test, and Strength of Grip Test. Reitan simplified several of these tests to create the battery for older children. The younger children's battery involved many more modifications of the original tests and the development of some entirely new tests (Reitan, 1979). It is common to use any of the three batteries in conjunction with the appropriate Wechsler Intelligence Scale, an achievement measure for children, or the Minnesota Multiphasic Personality Inventory (MMPI) for Adults (Boll, 1981).

All three batteries have proven to be effective in differentiating brain-damaged from normal functioning individuals, provided they are administered and interpreted properly by trained professionals. Reitan and Davison (1974) provide a detailed examination of the limitations and validity of these batteries.

REFERENCES

Boll, T. J. (1981). The Halstead-Reitan Neuropsychology Battery. In S. B. Filskov & T. J. Boll (Eds.), *Handbook of clinical neuropsychology* (pp. 577–607). New York: Wiley.

Halstead, W. C. (1947). *Brain and intelligence*. Chicago: University of Chicago Press.

Reitan, R. M. (1979). *Manual for administration of neuropsychological test batteries for adults and children*. Tucson, AZ: Reitan Neuropsychology Laboratories.

Reitan, R. M., & Davison, L. A. (1974). *Clinical neuropsychology*. New York: Hemisphere.

GALE A. HARR
*Maple Heights City Schools,
Maple Heights, Ohio*

LURIA-NEBRASKA NEUROPSYCHOLOGICAL BATTERY

NEUROPSYCHOLOGY

HAMMILL, DONALD (1934–   )

Donald Hammill received his BS degree in speech education in 1956, his MA in speech pathology in 1969, and an EdD in psychology/special education. From 1963 to 1965 he researched logopedics at Wichita State University.

He has served on the Council for Exceptional Children and the International Reading Association, the Society for Learning Disabilities and Remedial Education.

Hammill's interests include language development, learning disabilities, remedial education, and assessment methods. He has authored numerous tests, including the Test of Language Development and the Detroit Tests of Learning Aptitude.

In the 1970s Hammill demonstrated that disorder or ability models for learning disabilities were of questionable value to educators. This evidence was partly responsible for the 1977 guidelines for the implementation of PL 94-142, which minimized the use of ability tests. In addition, it opened the door for the increased use of behavioral or skill models for evaluation and classification (Hammill, 1974).

Hammill currently is president of PRO-ED Publishing Company in Austin, Texas.

REFERENCES

Hammill, D. D. (1974). Learning disabilities: A problem in definition. *Division for Children with Learning Disabilities Newsletter, 4*, 28–31.

Hammill, D. D., Bartel, N. R., & Bunch, G. O. (1982). *Teaching children with learning and behavior disorders* (3rd ed.). Boston: Allyn & Bacon.

Hammill, D. D., Leigh, J. E., McNutt, G., & Larsen, S. C. (1981). A new definition of learning disabilities. *Learning Disability Quarterly, 4*, 336–342.

RICK GONZALES
Texas A&M University

HANDEDNESS AND EXCEPTIONALITY

Handedness, though seemingly a phenomenon in its own right, is actually one component of a more general pattern of lateralization. Lateralization refers to the fact that most people tend to favor one side of their body over the other. A minority of individuals demonstrate inconsistent or weak lateralization, meaning they have a mixed pattern of hand dominance, foot dominance, eye dominance, or cerebral hemisphere dominance.

Research has documented that the left side of the brain controls the right side of the body, and vice versa, for basic sensory and motor activity, and that the left side of the brain is generally more efficient than the right side at processing language. These two facts, considered along with estimates that right-handers constitute approximately 90% of all humans, indicate that the most common pattern of lateralization includes both right-handedness and left hemisphere cerebral dominance for language. Left-handers, who are more apt to use both hemispheres of the brain for language than right-handers, might then be thought of as having weak or "deviant" lateralization. It is this deviant lateralization, of which handedness is but one component, rather than handedness per se, that has been linked to exceptionalities throughout the literature.

Deviant or weak lateralization may be inherited (Annett, 1964) or it may be caused by injury to the brain (Corballis & Beale, 1983). Whatever the etiology, deviation from the usual pattern of right-handedness and left hemisphere language representation can be manifested in a number of ways. On the positive side, weakly lateralized left-handers tend to be overrepresented among highly gifted and creative individuals. Leonardo da Vinci, Harpo Marx, and Charlie Chaplin are examples. On the negative side, left-handers may be particularly susceptible to a myriad of pathological conditions. Throughout the ages, left-handers have been overrepresented among schizophrenics, epileptics, and various types of criminals (Corballis & Beale, 1983).

Recent investigations have revealed a higher incidence of left-handedness in special education populations. Fein, Waterhouse, Lucci, Snyder, and Humes (1984) found 18% of a sample of school-age autistic children were left-handed. This figure is consistent with previous studies of autistic children, and is comparable to Satz's (1973) estimate of 83% right-handedness in retarded and epileptic populations. Those findings represent an approximate doubling of the left-handedness consistently found in normal populations. Other studies have found markedly greater frequencies of immune disease, migraine, and learning disabilities among left-handers (Geschwind & Behan, 1982).

Two other pathological conditions that have been linked to the deviant lateralization associated with left-handedness are dyslexia, a form of reading disability, and stuttering. The concept of dyslexia, first formulated about 100 years ago, has been surrounded by a great deal of controversy. Disagreement as to whether the disorder actually exists, its nature, and how it should be diagnosed

and treated abound. A distinction can be drawn between developmental dyslexia, which implies a developmental or maturational anomaly, and acquired dyslexia, which implies brain damage.

Orton (1928) proposed a unique theory for developmental dyslexia based on his own clinical experience with children suffering from reading and writing problems. Orton believed that reversals of letters and words occurred because the brains of dyslexic children lack cerebral dominance. He argued that the dominant hemisphere recorded events in the correct orientation (e.g., CAT), while the nondominant hemisphere recorded them in the reverse orientation (e.g., TAO). If a child failed to learn to suppress the activity of the nondominant hemisphere, the reversed word would intrude, creating left-right confusion. While Orton's theory generated much research, it soon became apparent that there was no evidence that mirror images of stimuli are projected to the nondominant hemisphere. As such, Orton's theory gradually lost favor.

Within the last 25 years, much progress has been made in understanding the neuropsychological processes involved in developmental dyslexia. Research has shown that dyslexics as a group are deficient in a wide variety of skills necessary for the development of adequate reading ability. Dyslexic children comprise a heterogeneous population that can be subdivided into groups, each with a distinct neurological deficit or cluster of deficits, which are related to dysfunction of left, right, or both cerebral hemispheres; and they may also be related to handedness. One subgroup of developmental dyslexia involves difficulty in integrating written symbols with their sounds, with resulting disability in developing phonic word analysis or decoding, skills often associated with a disordered function of the left cerebral hemisphere. Another subgroup manifests weaknesses in visual perception and memory for letters and whole-word configurations, resulting in problems with developing a sight vocabulary. The difficulties of this latter group have been associated with the impaired visuo-spatial functioning of the right side of the brain. A third subgroup demonstrates the difficulties of both of the other subgroups, suggesting dysfunction in both hemispheres (Hynd & Cohen, 1983).

It was also Orton (1937) who originated the dominance theory of stuttering. Stuttering was thought to be caused by a disruption of fine control of articulation resulting from lack of cerebral dominance. The more skilled and meticulous investigators became, however, the more frequently they failed to discover any neurological differences between stutterers and nonstutterers.

Recent investigators, however, suggest a return to the dominance theory, as convincing evidence continues to surface suggesting stutterers often exhibit deviant lateralization association with left-handedness. For example, Jones (1966) reported that four left-handers with a family history of left-handedness and bilateral speech representation experienced cessation of stuttering following surgical ablation of a portion of one hemisphere. Other neurosurgical reports have described epileptic stutterers as regaining fluent speech following surgery to either the right or left hemisphere to relieve epilepsy. Studies of stutterers and nonstutterers on dichotic listening tasks have reported a significantly greater number of stutterers than nonstutterers show a left ear advantage, implying right hemisphere language involvement (Corballis & Beale, 1983).

Despite the fact that it is still widely believed that stuttering is related to left-handedness, and in particular that it is caused by forcing a natural left-hander to write with the right hand, there is no evidence to show that changed handedness has any influence on cerebral representation of speech control. Moreover, it is difficult to separate left- or changed-handedness from the more general condition of weak or deviant lateralization.

Both dyslexia and stuttering occur more frequently among males than females. Since both of these conditions have been linked to weak or deviant lateralization, it seems contradictory that evidence suggests that generally females have weaker lateralization than males, both with respect to left hemispheric representation of language and right hemispheric representation of spatial functions (Corballis & Beale, 1983). This contradiction may be attributed to several different factors. First, males tend to be more susceptible to pathological influences at birth resulting in injury-induced deviant lateralization (Annett, 1964). Second, weaker female lateralization is specific to adults, as boys tend to lag behind girls in the development of lateralization (Bakker, Teunissen, & Bosch, 1976). The development of lateralization may be complete earlier in girls than in boys since girls generally reach puberty before boys. Dyslexia and stuttering typically develop well before puberty, when lateralization may be more highly developed in girls than in boys. Third, a factor more closely associated with males than females may actually trigger these two conditions. Geschwind and Behan (1982) believe that the male hormone, testosterone, slows development of the brain's left side, allowing the right hemisphere to assume some typically left-brain functions. The end result can be left-handedness or simply weaker or deviant cerebral lateralization.

Overall, there is convincing evidence that weak or deviant lateralization, of which handedness is one important component, is linked to various exceptionalities. While deviant lateralization should not be taken as a sufficient cause of learning disabilities, dyslexia, stuttering, or any of the other pathological conditions herein mentioned, it cannot be overlooked that those who manifest weak cerebral dominance are more apt to develop one of these afflictions than those who manifest strong lateralization.

REFERENCES

Annett, M. (1964). A model of the inheritance of handedness and cerebral dominance. *Nature, 204,* 59–60.

Bakker, D. J., Teunissen, J., & Bosch, J. (1976). Development of laterality-reading patterns. In R. M. Knights & D. J. Bakker (Eds.), *The neuropsychology of learning disorders* (pp. 207–220). Baltimore, MD: University Park Press.

Corballis, M. C., & Beale, I. L. (1983). *The ambivalent mind.* Chicago: Nelson-Hall.

Fein, D., Waterhouse, D., Lucci, D., Snyder, D., & Humes, M. (1984, Feb.). *Cognitive functions in left and right-handed autistic children.* Presentation at the annual meeting of the International Neuropsychological Society, Houston, TX.

Geschwind, N., & Behan, P. (1982). Left-handedness: Association with immune disease, migraine, and developmental learning disorder. *Proceedings of the National Academy of Science, U.S.A., 79,* 5097–5100.

Hynd, G. W., & Cohen, M. (1983). *Dyslexia: Neuropsychological theory, research, and clinical differentiation.* New York: Grune & Stratton.

Jones, R. K. (1966). Observations on stammering after localized cerebral injury. *Journal of Neurology, Neurosurgery, & Psychiatry, 29,* 192–195.

Orton, S. T. (1928). Specific reading disability-strephosymbolia. *Journal of the American Medical Association, 90,* 105–109.

Orton, S. T. (1937). *Reading, writing, and speech problems in children.* New York: Norton.

Satz, P. (1973). Left-handedness and early brain insult: An explanation. *Neuropsychologia, 11,* 115–117.

GALE A. HARR
*Maple Heights City Schools,
Maple Heights, Ohio*

DYSLEXIA
LEFT BRAIN-RIGHT BRAIN
STUTTERING

HANDICAPISM

Handicapism is a term created by Biklen and Bogdan (1976) to identify both an evolving social movement and a set of behaviors toward those with disabilities. It has been defined by its authors as "a theory and set of practices that promote unequal and unjust treatment of people because of apparent or assumed physical or mental disability" (p. 9). Handicapism is evident in our personal lives, social policy, cultural norms, and institutional practices (Biklen & Bogdan, 1976). Like racism and sexism, handicapism is evident in the language often used to describe disabled individuals. Such language tends to be discriminatory and serves to devalue the capabilities of the person (Heward & Orlansky, 1984; Mullins, 1979).

Common words and phrases that devalue rather than enhance a disabled person's characteristics include, "had a fit," "a basket case," and "ree tard." Handicapist phrases such as "he's a moron," handicapist humor such as "what did the twit say," and handicapist behavior, for instance, avoiding contact with a disabled person, are examples of handicapism in our personal lives. People with physical disabilities are often confronted with inaccessible entrances to buildings, bathrooms that do not accommodate wheelchairs, and public transporation systems that are difficult to use. Handicapism is also evident in the limited employment opportunities that prevail for the disabled, in media reporting that often transforms the severely disabled into objects rather than people, and in the attitudes of helping professions that often overlook the disabled person's need for privacy and human dignity.

Handicapism can be corrected. Major steps in eliminating it are (1) learning to identify and correct handicapist statements (Biklen & Bogdan, 1976); (2) providing persons with disabilities opportunities to participate in activities that make them part of the mainstream of society (Mullins, 1979); (3) demanding equal access to all facilities for all people (Biklen & Bogdan, 1976); and (4) recognizing that persons with disabilities deserve the same rights and services as those who are nondisabled.

REFERENCES

Biklen, D., & Bogdan, R. (1976, Oct.). Handicapism in America, *WIN*, 9–13.

Heward, W., & Orlansky, M. D. (1984). *Exceptional children* (2nd ed.) (p. 7). Columbus, OH: Merrill.

Mullins, J. B. (1979). Making language work to eliminate handicapism. *Education Unlimited*, June 1979, 20–24.

MARSHA H. LUPI
*Hunter College, City University
of New York*

CIVIL RIGHTS OF THE HANDICAPPED

HANDICAPPED, DEFINITION OF

The Education for All Handicapped Children Act of 1975 defines the handicapping conditions that are eligible for services that are reimbursable by the federal government. This law defines a handicapped individual:

as being mentally retarded, hard of hearing, deaf, speech impaired, visually handicapped, seriously emotionally disturbed, orthopedically impaired, other health impaired, deaf-blind, multi-handicapped, or as having specific learning disabilities, who because of those impairments need special education and related services.

(b) The terms used in this definition are defined as follows:

(1) "Deaf" means a hearing impairment which is so severe that the child is impaired in processing linguistic information through hearing, with or without amplification, which adversely affects educational performance.

(2) "Deaf-blind" means concomitant hearing and visual impairments, the combination of which causes such severe communication and other developmental and educational prob-

lems that they cannot be accommodated in special education programs solely for deaf or blind children.

(3) "Hard of hearing" means a hearing impairment, whether permanent or fluctuating, which adversely affects a child's educational performance but which is not included under the definition of "deaf" in this section.

(4) "Mentally retarded" means significantly subaverage general intellectual functioning existing concurrently with deficits in adaptive behavior and manifested during the developmental period, which adversely affects a child's educational performance.

(5)"Multihandicapped" means concomitant impairments (such as mentally retarded–blind, mentally retarded–orthopedically impaired, etc.), the combination of which causes such severe educational problems that they cannot be accommodated in special education programs solely for one of the impairments. The term does not include deaf-blind children.

(6) "Orthopedically impaired" means a severe orthopedic impairment which adversely affects a child's educational performance. The term includes impairments caused by congenital anomaly (e.g., clubfoot, absence of some member, etc.), impairments caused by disease (e.g., poliomyelitis, bone tuberculosis, etc.), and impairments from other causes (e.g., cerebral palsy, amputations, and fractures or burns which cause contractures).

(7) "Other health impaired" means (i) having an autistic condition which is manifested by severe communication and other developmental and educational problems; or (ii) having limited strength, vitality or alertness, due to chronic or acute health problems such as a heart condition, tuberculosis, rhematic fever, nephritis, asthma, sickle cell anemia, hemophilia, epilepsy, lead poisoning, leukemia, or diabetes, which adversely affect a child's educational performance.

(8) "Seriously emotionally disturbed" is defined as follows:

(i) The term means a condition exhibiting one or more of the following chracteristics over a long period of time and to a marked degree, which adversely affects educational performance:

(A) An inability to learn which cannot be explained by intellectual, sensory, or health factors;

(B) An inability to build or maintain satisfactory interpersonal relationships with peers and teachers;

(C) Inappropriate types of behavior or feelings under normal circumstances;

(D) A general pervasive mood of unhappiness or depression; or

(E) A tendency to develop physical symptoms or fears associated with personal or school problems.

(ii) The term includes children who are schizophrenic. The term does not include children who are socially maladjusted, unless it is determined that they are seriously emotionally disturbed.

(9) "Specific learning disability" means a disorder in one or more of the basic psychological processes involved in understanding or in using language, spoken or written, which may manifest itself in an imperfect ability to listen, think, speak, read, write, spell, or to do mathematical calculations. The term includes such conditions as perceptual handicaps, brain injury, minimal brain dysfunction, dyslexia, and developmental aphasia. The term does not include children who have learning problems which are primarily the result of vis-

ual, hearing, or motor handicaps, of mental retardation of emotional disturbance or of environmental, cultural, or economic disadvantage.

(10) "Speech impaired" means a communication disorder such as stuttering, impaired articulation, a language impairment, or a voice impairment, which adversely affects a child's educational performance.

(11) "Visually handicapped" means a visual impairment which, even with correction, adversely affects a child's educational performance. The term includes both partially seeing and blind children. (20 U.S.C. 1401(1), (15))

STAFF

EDUCATION FOR ALL HANDICAPPED CHILDREN ACT OF 1975

HANDICAPPED CHILDREN, SOCIAL MAINSTREAMING OF

Mainstreaming is a special education procedure designed to ensure that special students are serviced in the least restrictive environment in accordance with PL 94-142. Traditionally, a student who demonstrates academic proficiency in the special education class may qualify for regular classroom placement. Throughout this transition, academic performance is closely monitored but the affective domain may be ignored. Commonly, disregard for the affective development of the special education student socially segregates the student entering the regular classroom (Gresham, 1982; Ray, 1985; Sabortine, 1985).

There is an accumulated body of evidence that mainstreamed special education students are lacking social skills that would enable positive interactions with their peers (Gresham, 1982). In addition, the special education students are less accurate in appraising their own social standing as compared with their nonspecial education peers (Bruininks, 1978).

However, efforts to study empirically the social skill level of special education students have been fraught with methodological difficulties. The three most common methods for evaluating social ability have been teacher ratings, sociometric ratings, and direct observation (Gresham, 1982). These measures rest on the perceptions of peers and may not mirror actual social interactions among students (Gresham, 1982; Ray, 1985). Other measurement concerns include situation-specificity (e.g., playground to reading group), poor standardization, and vulnerability to events that precede the observation (Gresham, 1982).

In any case, a plethora of social skills training strategies have emerged to train social skills in the handicapped. Traditionally, social skills training has involved instrumental and classical learning techniques as well as modeling (Gresham, 1982). More recently, the concern over social mainstreaming has contributed to interest in cooperative learning strategies (Johnson & Johnson, 1986) and reverse mainstreaming (nonhandicapped students in special education classrooms, espoused by Jenkins, Speltz, and Odom (1985).

REFERENCES

Bruininks, V. L. (1978). Actual and perceived peer status of learning disabled students in mainstreamed programs. *Remedial & Special Education, 12,* 51–58.

Gresham, G. M. (1982). Misguided mainstreaming: The case for social skills training with handicapped children. *Exceptional Children, 48*(5), 422–431.

Jenkins, J. R., Speltz, M. L., & Odom, S. L. (1985). Integrating normal and handicapped preschoolers: Effects on child development and social interaction. *Exceptional Children, 52,* 7–17.

Johnson, D. W., & Johnson, R. T. (1986). Mainstreaming and cooperative learning strategies. *Exceptional Children, 52,* 553–561.

Ray, B. M. (1985). Measuring the social position of the mainstreamed handicapped child. *Exceptional Children, 52,* 57–62.

Sabortine, S. J. (1985). Social mainstreaming of handicapped students: Facing an unpleasant reality. *Remedial & Special Education, 6*(2), 12–16.

HARRISON C. STANTON
Texas A&M University

EDUCATION FOR ALL HANDICAPPED CHILDREN ACT OF 1975
MAINSTREAMING
SOCIAL SKILLS TRAINING

HANDICAPPED CHILDREN'S EARLY EDUCATION ASSISTANCE ACT (PUBLIC LAW 90-538)

The Handicapped Children's Early Education Program (HCEEP) began in 1968 with the passage of the *Handicapped Children's Early Education Assistance Act* (PL 90-538). The major goals of the program were to design experimental approaches to meet the special needs of young children with handicaps; to develop programs to facilitate the intellectual, mental, social, physical, and language development of the children; to acquaint the community with the problems and potential of young handicapped children; to coordinate with the local school system in the community being served; and to encourage parental participation in the development of programs. The program originally was comprised of one of its five current components—demonstration projects.

Demonstration Projects

To accomplish HCEEP's goals, the Act authorized grants and contracts to public and private agencies and organizations for the establishment of experimental preschool and early education demonstration projects. The chosen projects showed promise of developing comprehensive and innovative approaches for meeting the special needs of handicapped children from birth to eight years of age. These projects were expected to serve as models providing highly visible examples of successful practices, and encouraging others to initiate and/or improve services to young handicapped children. In this respect, HCEEP was viewed not as a direct service mechanism, but as an indirect mechanism for expanding and improving the quality of services.

Geographical dispersion of demonstration projects was extremely important for a program that relied on increasing services by example. Therefore, major efforts were made to establish demonstration projects in as many states as possible. An evaluation of the demonstrations, conducted when the first cohort had reached its third year of funding, indicated that the demonstrations were only beginning to pay off. To avoid losing the ground gained, and to assist the demonstrations in communicating the results of their efforts, it was decided to make outreach funds available. An additional component was added to HCEEP—the Outreach Component.

Outreach Projects

The Outreach Component, developed in 1972, had two goals: to stimulate and increase high quality services to preschool handicapped children, birth through eight years, and to stimulate replication of innovative models developed in the demonstration projects. Successful demonstration projects were expected to apply for outreach funds at the end of three years. To be even eligible for consideration, a demonstration project had to obtain funds from other sources to continue providing direct services to children and their families. Recently, projects not funded previously as early childhood demonstration projects have been allowed to compete for outreach funds.

State Plan Grants

The third component of HCEEP had its roots prior to 1976. Aware of the need for state planning to consider the needs of young handicapped children, HCEEP had made technical assistance available to states which desired to improve or expand services to the early childhood age range. The expectation was that federal funds would be available in the immediate future to help implement these states' plans. When such funds did become available in 1976 through the State Implementation Grant (SIG) initiative, states applying were awarded grants on a competitive basis. The goal of SIG was to assist state education agencies in building a capacity to plan for the initiation and expansion of early intervention services. To some degree, this planning process was expected to be enhanced simply by creating financial resources for an early childhood planning position within each state.

Public law 98-199 carried this initiative further with the creation of the current State Plan Grant Component. The state plan grant is intended to enable each state and territory to plan, develop, or implement a comprehensive service delivery system for special education and related services to handicapped children from birth to five years of age. States may apply for a grant to support planning, to support development, or to support implementation activities depending on their assessment of appropriateness and readiness. At least 30 percent of the HCEEP appropriation must be used for this component in recognition of the need for state commitments to serving these children.

Research Institutes

In 1977, the fourth component of HCEEP was initiated. In cooperation with the Research Projects Branch of the Office of Special Education Programs, HCEEP funded four research institutes to carry out longitudinal research. Topics of research included social, emotional, physical, cognitive, and behavioral aspects of the child; theories and methods of intervention; parent–child interaction; and assessment techniques.

The institutes were seen as investments in the future, paying off not only in terms of the immediate research results, but in terms of the training of future special education researchers and service providers. A second generation of institutes was funded in 1982 to investigate problems concerning services for autisticlike children, cost and efficacy data for early childhood interventions, and programming for parental involvement. In addition, another institute was funded in 1985 to focus on evaluating the impact of various methods of early intervention for handicapped children as a whole and in various subgroups.

Technical Assistance

In 1971, the Technical Assistance Development System (TADS) was funded to assist demonstration projects. From 1977 to 1982, two technical assistance systems, TADS and WESTAR, were operating in order to provide geographical coverage for the large number of demonstration projects and SIGs. When the number of demonstrations decreased in 1982, the need for technical assistance also was reduced and TADS again became the sole designated external provider of technical assistance to demonstration projects. A new technical assistance effort, the State Technical Assistance Resource Team (START), was funded in 1985 to provide assistance to the state plan grant projects.

JAMES BUTTON
United States Department of Education

HANDICAPPED CHILDREN'S EARLY EDUCATION PROGRAM (HCEEP)

The federal initiatives for research and service to young children with handicaps began in 1968 with the establishment of the Handicapped Children's Early Assistance Act. This act created the Handicapped Children's Early Education Programs (HCEEP) that were to develop, implement, and evaluate model preschool services. These services took direction from previious research and documentation of the positive results possible when children with handicaps received intervention early (Tjossem, 1974).

The stated purposes for HCEEP were to focus on all of the developmental aspects of the child, to provide parents with support and strategies to meet the needs of their child, to provide the parents with opportunities to participate in providing their child with an education, and to provide the community with information regarding the difficulties and potentials of young children with handicaps (Jordan, Hayden, Karnes & Wood, 1977). Individuals who have applied for funds to implement one of the programs provided statements of how they planned to meet the HCEEP purposes. These purposes were implemented with young children experiencing a variety of educational and developmental needs.

Information collected on these programs has expanded the knowledge and data base on successful intervention strategies with young handicapped children. These programs developed assessment tools, curricula, programming, and data collection strategies that serve as a foundation for today's early intervention services. This occurred as a result of the model services developed by the first group of funded projects. These projects demonstrated how to develop and operate model programs and provided technical assistance for the replication of their model. Some examples of projects are the Chapel Hill-Carrboro Outreach Project of North Carolina, the Rutland Center For Severely Emotionally Disturbed Children, the Curative Workshop, the Ski-Hi Project, the Portage Project, and the University of Washington (DeWeerd, 1981).

REFERENCES

DeWeerd, J. (1981). Early education services for children with handicaps: Where have we been, where are we now, and where are we going? *Journal of the Division for Early Childhood, 2,* 15–24.

Jordan, J. B., Hayden, A. H., Karnes, M. B., & Wood, M. M. (Eds.). (1977). *Early education for exceptional children: A handbook of exemplary ideas and practices.* Reston, VA: Council for Exceptional Children.

Tjossem, T. D. (1976). *Intervention strategies for high risk infants and young children.* Baltimore: University Park Press.

JACQUELINE E. DAVIS
SUE ALLEN WARREN
Boston University

EARLY CHILDHOOD, SPECIAL EDUCATION TOPICS IN EARLY EXPERIENCE AND CRITICAL PERIODS

HANDICAPPED GIFTED

See GIFTED HANDICAPPED.

HANDICAPPING CONDITIONS, HIGH INCIDENCE

See HIGH INCIDENCE HANDICAPS.

HANDICAPS, LOW INCIDENCE

See LOW INCIDENCE HANDICAPS.

HAND TEST

The Hand Test (Wagner, 1962) is unique among projective techniques that require storytelling. The stimuli provided to the individual are not whole scenes or figures but nine cards with line drawings of single hands. Each card shows a hand in a different position. A tenth blank card is included. Reaction time and responses are recorded during the administration, which averages about 10 minutes per case. Responses are scored into four categories for normative comparisons: impersonal, environmental, maladjusted, and withdrawal.

Another score that has received some support is the Acting-Out Score (AOS). The AOS seems to do well in differentiating between aggressive and nonaggressive children and between assaultive and nonassaultive delinquents. The AOS is also positively related to recidivism among juvenile offenders. Other validity data on the Hand Test are relatively scarce.

The Hand Test is quick and easy to administer and is useful in the evaluation of children and adolescents with emotional and behavioral problems. However, it should not be used with extensive training in projective assessment and then principally as a cue to further exploration of problem areas of personality (Koppitz, 1982).

REFERENCES

Koppitz, E. M. (1982). Personality assessment in the schools. In C. R. Reynolds & T. B. Gutkin (Eds.), *The handbook of school psychology*. New York: Wiley.

Wagner, E. E. (1962). *The Hand Test: Manual for administration, scoring, and interpretation*. Akron, OH: Mark Jones.

CECIL R. REYNOLDS
Texas A&M University

HANDWRITING

Handwriting is an essential tool for recording, expressing, and communicating human thought. It is a traditional element of the elementary school curriculum, and considerable time and energy are devoted to its mastery. Handwriting is not a discrete and separate skill, however, but an integral part of the writing process. A general goal of writing instruction is to make the act of handwriting so automatic that it can be produced with maximum efficiency and minimum effort, enabling students to deploy more of their attention to higher order writing processes such as purpose, content, or organization (Graham, 1982a).

Although it is generally assumed that a large percentage of handicapped children and youths have handwriting difficulties, it is difficult to substantiate or refute this assumption. Very little empirical evidence on the handwriting characteristics of handicapped students is available, and an examination of the information that has been gathered suggests that students with different disabilities may have different characteristics and ultimately different instructional needs. For example, Love (1965) found that the quality of mentally retarded students' handwriting was superior to that of normally achieving peers, but their speed of writing was significantly slower. In contrast, Graham, MacArthur, Malouf, and Skarovold (1985) reported that learning-disabled students' speed of writing was within the normal range, but the quality of their penmanship was not.

With the exception of specific technological adaptations for the physically disabled and the use of braille with the blind, handwriting instruction for the handicapped has, in large part, been based on traditional procedures and techniques used to teach normally achieving students. Instruction has been aimed at assisting students to develop a handwriting style that is, first and foremost, legible and that can be produced quickly and fluently. Furthermore, most handicapped students are taught two styles of writing: manuscript in the lower primary grades and cursive in middle and upper elementary grades. There is considerable controversy, however, surrounding this practice. Some experts have indicated that it is more difficult to master two styles than it is to perfect one. Nevertheless,

it is not clear which style should be taught. According to Graham and Miller (1980), the evidence collected to date is not conclusive and the relative effectiveness of the two styles has not been adequately established.

Although it is not clear when handwriting instruction for handicapped students should begin, it is generally agreed that correct habits of posture, grip, and paper position should be established as soon as possible and sustained throughout the student's educational career. Desirable procedures for teaching the formation of individual letters include consistent demonstrations on how to form letters; the use of physical prompts and cues; considerable practice tracing, copying, and writing individual letters from memory; and corrective feedback and reinforcement followed by self-correction of malformed letters (Graham & Madan, 1981). Once the formation of letter forms is mastered, speed of production is gradually increased by having students practice their skills in meaningful written assignments. For some handicapped students, it may be necessary to use reinforcement, self-regulation procedures, and self-competition to increase fluency (Graham & Miller, 1980).

Despite the important role that evaluation plays in the development and modification of instructional programs for the handicapped, the assessment of students' handwriting performance has generally been nonexistent or informal. Informal procedures typically consist of examining a handwriting sample for particular trends or characteristics. The reliability and validity of such procedures is questionable (Graham, 1982b). Although there are several standardized handwriting assessment instruments presently available, it does not appear that they are used by many teachers (Graham, 1986). The Zaner-Bloser scale (Barbe, 1979) is the most popular standardized instrument; it was designed to be used in conjunction with the Zaner-Bloser Handwriting Program.

Even though there do not appear to be any significant differences in the handwriting quality and speed of left- and right-handed writers, special instructional provisions should be made for handicapped students who are left-handed (Graham & Miller, 1980). Finally, some experts have suggested that letter reversals are indicative of brain injury or central nervous system dysfunction. The validity of this assertion for the vast majority of handicapped students has not been adequately demonstrated.

REFERENCES

Barbe, W. (1979). *The Zaner-Bloser Evaluation Scales*. Columbus, OH: Zaner-Bloser.

Graham, S. (1982a). Composition research and practice: A unified approach. *Focus on Exceptional Children, 14,* 1–16.

Graham, S. (1982b). Measurement of handwriting skills: A critical review. *Diagnostigue, 8,* 32–42.

Graham, S. (1986). A review of handwriting scales and factors that contribute to variability in handwriting scores. *Journal of School Psychology, 24,* 63–71.

Graham, S., MacArthur, C., Malouf, D., & Skarvold, J. (1985). An examination of LD students' writing under three conditions. Presentation at 7th International Conference on Learning Disabilities, New Orleans, LA.

Graham, S., & Madan, A. (1981). Teaching letter formation. *Academic Therapy, 16,* 389–396.

Graham, S., & Miller, L. (1980). Handwriting research and practice: A unified approach. *Focus on Exceptional Children, 13,* 1–16.

Love, H. (1965). Comparison of quality, speed and use of handwriting among special and regular classroom children. *Journal of Educational Research, 58,* 475–477.

STEVE GRAHAM
University of Maryland

DYSGRAPHIA
REVERSALS IN READING AND WRITING

HARD OF HEARING

See DEAF.

HARING, NORRIS G. (1923–   )

Norris G. Haring obtained a BA from Kearney State Teachers College (Nebraska) in 1948. He went on to the University of Nebraska, receiving an MA in 1950 and an EdD from Syracuse University in 1956. He is presently professor of education (special education) and director of the Washington Research Organization in the College of Education at the University of Washington.

Haring's major field of interest lies in dealing with exceptional children in the classroom environment. Haring's philosophy about exceptional children is that they should have the benefit of experiences with their nonexceptional peers whenever possible because they will eventually be required to achieve a satisfactory adjustment within a predominantly normal society (Haring, Stern, & Cruickshank, 1958).

Haring's major research has dealt with the behavior management of children with learning disabilities and behavioral disorders in the classroom. His textbook on this subject, *Educating Emotionally Disturbed Children* (1962), is now considered a classic.

Subsequent research concentrated on the development and refinement of the learning environment and the ecology that promotes adaptive social behavior. This research resulted from work with the emotionally disturbed and behaviorally disordered and investigations of classroom performance measurement and data-based decisions in terms of instructional procedures, methodology, and curriculum. The application of behavioral principles in special education guided his research for nearly 10 years. His book *Exceptional Teaching* (1980) concentrates on the application of precision teaching strategies in regular and self-contained classrooms. Haring is known for the research and development of behaviorally validated stages of learning in a learning hierarchy.

Haring was the director of the Experimental Education Unit at the University of Washington for 12 years. During that period he became interested in the application of modern behavior technology to the education of the severely handicapped. Haring worked with national leaders in the field to develop the Association for Persons with Severe Handicaps (TASH), and served as founding president of that organization. Most recently, he directed the Washington Research Organization in a series of studies designed to investigate ways to promote generalization with severely handicapped students and the application of research information to facilitate their transition to vocational success and adult life.

REFERENCES

Haring, N. G., & Phillips, E. L. (1962). *Educating emotionally disturbed children.* New York: McGraw-Hill.

Haring, N. G., & Schiefelbusch, R. L. (Eds.). (1967). *Methods in special education.* New York: McGraw-Hill.

Haring, N. G., Stern, G., & Cruickshank, W. M. (1958). *Attitudes of educators toward exceptional children.* Syracuse, NY: Syracuse University Press.

Haring, N. G., & Whelan, R. J. (1965). Experimental methods in education and management of emotionally disturbed children. In N. J. Long, W. C. Morse, & R. G. Newman (Eds.), *Conflict in the classroom: The education of emotionally disturbed children.* Belmont, CA: Wadsworth.

White, O. R., & Haring, N. G. (1980). *Exceptional teaching* (2nd ed.). Columbus, OH: Merrill.

ELIZABETH JONES
Texas A&M University

HARVARD EDUCATIONAL REVIEW

The *Harvard Educational Review* was first published in 1931 under the name of *Harvard Teachers Record* by the offices of the Harvard Graduate Schools of Education. The present name was taken in 1937. This journal consists of opinions and research related to the field of education. Articles are read blind, then selected, edited, and published by an editorial board of graduate students from various Harvard schools. The selection process of the editorial board involves the distribution of letters to the faculty requesting nominations from the student body and the posting of information on bulletin boards at Harvard schools asking the students to apply for consideration. Students are then selected according to their ability and by their diversity of interests. The board of 20 students is balanced among men and women and minorities, each of whom receive a small stipend. There is one chairperson who receives a slightly larger stipend. This position changes yearly.

Fifty-four volumes have now been published and there are an estimated 10,000 in circulation annualy. Each journal, published quarterly, contains on the average three manuscripts equaling 500 to 550 pages a year.

TERESA K. RICE
Texas A&M University

HAÜY, VALENTIN (1745–1822)

Valentin Haüy, a French pioneer in the education of the blind, developed a system of raised letters with which he taught blind students to read and write, providing one of the earliest demonstrations that it is possible for a blind person to be educated. It was one of Haüy's students, Louis Braille, who later developed the system in use today, replacing Haüy's raised letters with a system of dots.

In 1784, with support from a philanthropic society, Haüy established in Paris the first school for the blind that admitted both blind and sighted children and educated them together. The great success of Haüy's school led to the rapid development of similar schools throughout Europe.

REFERENCE

Ross, I. (1951). *Journey into light*. New York: Appleton-Century-Crofts.

PAUL IRVINE
Katonah, New York

HAVIGHURST, ROBERT J. (1900–   )

A native of DePere, Wisconsin, Robert J. Havighurst received his BA (1921) from Ohio Wesleyan and his PhD (1924) from Ohio State University. He has been a professor of education at the University of Chicago since 1941.

Originally a chemistry educator, Havighurst has been an assistant professor of chemistry and an assistant professor of physics. He became an associate professor of science education (1932) at Ohio State University.

In 1943 Havighurst introduced his theory of developmental tasks (Havighurst, 1979). These "tasks" are skills, knowledge, functions, or attitudes that an individual normally acquires during a specific period of life. To develop properly, three conditions must be met: (1) physical mat-

Robert J. Havighurst

uration; (2) cultural expectation; and (3) personal values. Havighurst believes that there are sensitive periods (teachable moments) when a person is most ready to learn a new skill. If a task is not learned at its appropriate time, it is much more difficult to learn later. In conjunction with these tasks are developmental stages: (1) infancy and early childhood; (2) middle childhood; (3) adolescence; (4) early adulthood; (5) middle age; and (6) late maturity.

Havighurst has found that adolescents prefer the approval of the larger community to that of the peer group (Havighurst, 1970). Most rewards from this group are not important to the larger society. The larger society usually does not reward the adolescent meaningfully, therefore the child refuses to be socialized. Havighurst believes that the larger society, especially the school system, must learn to provide important reinforcement to adolescents, especially minority, disadvantaged youths.

REFERENCES

Havighurst, R. J. (1970). Minority subcultures and the law of effect. *American Psychologist, 25*(4), 313–322.

Havighurst, R. J. (1979). *Developmental tasks and education* (4th ed.). New York: Longman.

E. VALERIE HEWITT
Texas A&M University

HAWTHORNE EFFECT

The experimental findings that led to the use of the term Hawthorne effect resulted from research done primarily between 1927 and 1932 at the Hawthorne plant of Western Electric. Investigators isolated a group of workers and then systematically varied such working conditions as rest periods and length of the work day. Over time, productivity steadily increased even in instances where more favorable working conditions were replaced with those originally in effect. The researchers in the Hawthorne study explained these results in terms of the workers' response to the special attention that they received in a novel situation (Roethlisberger & Dickson, 1939).

The Hawthorne effect is demonstrated when people are highly compliant in settings that they perceive to be innovative or experimental. As originally studied in industry, it resulted in greater worker productivity regardless of specific experimental manipulations. Writers now use the term Hawthorne effect in nonindustrial research contexts to indicate increased subject compliance with the perceived wishes of the experimenter (Sears, Freedman, & Peplau, 1985). In some cases, these subject responses might represent a rival account for results attributed to manipulations of the independent variable(s).

A number of critics have questioned the meaning of the Hawthorne study results and, by implication, the validity of the concept of the Hawthorne effect. For example, Parsons (1974) offered an operant conditioning interpretation emphasizing the special setting where there was a high level of feedback and contingency between individual productivity and reward. Luthans (1981) asserted that the subjects' performance was strongly influenced by the impact of working together in a small group where the members received atypical rewards and supervision. Despite the fact that adults have supposedly shown the Hawthorne effect in several field studies, at least one study with elementary school students did not find evidence for the effect (Cook, 1967).

Although it has been difficult in specific instances to demonstrate the Hawthorne effect, the concept has important implications for the evaluation of educational and treatment innovations. To be certain that experimental interventions are responsible for observed changes, researchers must employ control groups where subjects receive attention, but not intervention, in a novel situation. A Hawthorne effect in special education classroom innovations would initially accelerate the benefits of a given program, but as the program became routine, the positive effects of its novelty would be expected to dissipate.

REFERENCES

Cook, D. (1967, June). *The impact of the Hawthorne effect on experimental designs in educational research.* U.S. Office of Education, No. 0726. Washington, DC: U.S. Government Printing Office. (ERIC Document Reproduction Service No. ED 0021 308).

Luthans, F. (1981). *Organizational behavior.* New York: McGraw-Hill.

Parsons, H. (1974). What happened at Hawthorne? *Science, 183,* 922–932.

Roethlisberger, F., & Dickson, W. (1939). *Management and the worker.* Cambridge, MA: Harvard.

Sears, D., Freedman, J., & Peplau, L. (1985). *Social psychology* (5th ed.). Englewood Cliffs, NJ: Prentice-Hall.

LEE ANDERSON JACKSON, JR.
*University of North Carolina,
Wilmington*

MOTIVATION
PROGRAM EVALUATION
RESEARCH IN SPECIAL EDUCATION

HAYDEN, ALICE HAZEL (1909–   )

Alice Hazel Hayden holds her BS and MS degrees from Oregon State University and a PhD from Purdue University. She administers several projects that are designed to develop replicable models for the individualization of instruction and for the integration of handicapped with nonhandicapped children.

One of her principal publications is *The Improvement of Instruction,* coedited with Norris G. Haring, a book of readings from a workshop designed to provide the classroom teacher with information about various ways of choosing instructional programs to accomplish teaching objectives and to assist teachers in arranging better classroom conditions to improve instruction. Her book *Systematic Thinking of Education,* coedited with Gerald M. Torkelson, discusses the technology of education and technology in teaching. It suggests that teachers and the school as an institution must be responsive to the world community and the advancing instruments and processes that people continue to create for a better life in order to convey the most current techniques and advancements in education to students.

Hayden is the author of numerous articles and was the guest editor of the Winter 1971–1972 issue of *Educational Horizons,* an issue that focused on education for the very young. Hayden is a professor of education and associate director of the experimental unit of the Child Development and Mental Retardation Center at the University of Washington, Seattle.

REFERENCES

Hayden, A. H., & Haring, N. G. (1972). *The improvement of instruction.* Special Child.

Hayden, A. H., & Torkelson, G. M. (1973). *Systematic thinking about education.* Phi Delta Kappa Educational Foundation.

REBECCA BAILEY
Texas A&M University

HAYWOOD, H. CARL (1931–   )

Carl Haywood attended West Georgia College from 1948 to 1950. He was in the U.S. Navy until 1954, at which time he returned to San Diego College. There he obtained his BA in 1956 and his MA in 1957 in the field of psychology. He then went on to receive his doctorate in clinical psychology in 1961 from the University of Illinois, with minors in experimental psychology and education.

H. Carl Haywood

Haywood was director of the John F. Kennedy Center for Research on Education and Human Development from 1971 to 1983; since 1980 he has been associated with Vanderbilt University as professor of psychology, George Peabody College; professor of neurology, School of Medicine; and senior fellow, Institute for Public Policy Studies. His current position includes continued responsibility for the cognitive development research program of the Kennedy Center.

Haywood's areas of scholarly interest and research emphases include intellectual development, cognitive development and education, learning efficiency, psychopathology, and public policy relating to the welfare of children.

He is currently a member of the Governor's Task Force on Healthy Children, State of Tennessee, and a member of the National Advisory Child Health and Human Development Council, National Institutes of Health.

Haywood has served as editor of the *American Journal of Mental Deficiency* and has been an advisory editor and reviewer for numerous other journals. He has published over 100 articles, books, and reviews in the field of mental retardation. His major works include *Educacion y desarrollo de la inteligencia; Intrinsic Motivation: A New Direction in Education; Social-Cultural Aspects of Mental Retardation; Brain Damage in School Age Children.*

REFERENCES

Haywood, H. C. (1968). *Brain damage in school children.* Washington, DC: Council for Exceptional Children.

Haywood, H. C. (1970). *Socio-cultural aspects of mental retardation.* New York: Appleton-Century-Crafts.

Haywood, H. C. (1971). *Intrinsic motivation: A new direction in education.* Toronto, Ontario: Holt, Rinehart, & Winston.

Haywood, H. C. (1982). *Educacion y desarrollo de la inteligencia.* Caracas, Venezuela: CINTERPLAN.

ROBERTA C. STOKES
Texas A&M University

HEAD INJURY

Head injury produces many observable changes and many more less obvious changes in a child's cognitive functions. There often remain subtle deficits that influence behavior in diffuse ways or that remain unnoticed until later stages of development are reached. Assessment of the nature and extent of the consequences of brain damage in children is more difficult and challenging than with adults, yet, effective treatment and remediation require an objective appraisal of cognitive strengths and weaknesses. Underestimating the capacity of recovery may lead to delayed rehabilitation, with efforts aimed at the consequences of the injury rather than at preventive therapy (Stover & Zeiger, 1976). On the other hand, underestimating the extent of the impairment may lead to excessive stress or problems in emotional adjustment. Clearly, even mild head injury can represent a significant disruptive event to children and their families unless the consequences are evaluated properly and effective rehabilitation is instituted.

For a time it was generally believed that brain damage sustained early in life was associated with less deleterious effects than that sustained later in life (Kennard principle). Children were thought to have a more resilient nervous system since they appear to recover more rapidly than adults, experience less persistent symptoms (Black et al., 1969), and report postconcussion symptoms less often (Rutter, Chadwick, & Shaffer, 1983). However, this notion is only partially accurate at best (Bolter & Long, 1985).

Children do grow out of some early deficits, but not others. Klonoff, Low, and Clark (1977) found that after mild head injury, some children demonstrated persistent weakness in cognitive functions 4 to 5 years after trauma. In some cases, dysfunction may appear only later in the course of development (Goldman, 1971, 1972, 1974; Teuber & Rudel, 1962). For example, damage to the immature frontal lobes of a young child may not produce behavioral manifestations until much later in development when those cortical areas would normally assume functional prominence (Russell, 1959). It is likely that the effects of head injury in children combine with other functions in their development and have widespread effects (Korkman, 1980). Age is only one variable in determining the extent of recovery. In addition to age, one must consider location, nature, and extent of the injury to determine the effects on subsequent behavior.

The pathophysiology of brain injury is similar in children and adults. Severity of injury is usually measured by duration of coma or posttraumatic amnesia (PTA), although both are difficult to assess in younger children (Leigh, 1979). As a general guide, children experiencing coma of over 7 days seldom recover to their premorbid level. Even coma of less than 7 days or PTA of over 3 weeks usually is associated with some permanent cognitive impairment (Stover & Zeiger, 1976).

After severe head injury, impaired physical functions rapidly improve, whereas cognitive dysfunctions may resolve less quickly. Head injury frequently affects intelligence, memory, speech and language, and other functions. The effects on cognitive functions are pervasive during the first 6 months following injury (Levin & Eisenberg, 1979). Later in recovery, the effects often are characterized by slowed information processing, poor problem-solving ability, impulsivity, distractibility, and poor stress tolerance with irritability and emotional lability. Common behavioral symptoms include hyperkinesis (32%), discipline problems (10%), and lethargy (87%) (Black et al., 1969). These effects are observed in school performance and in neuropsychological testing. More important is the finding that children suffering even mild head trauma, with little or no coma or PTA, demonstrate attenuated cognitive abilities. Children are undergoing significant developmental changes and even mild brain damage can cause developmental setbacks resulting in immature behaviors. Such damage may cause a loss of previously mastered skills as well as compromise future acquisition of skills.

In addition to physical impairment and cognitive dysfunction, the brain-injured child is at risk for the development of *emotional problems*. The risks are greater in those with low IQ and low socioeconomic class, or those from parents who have divorced (Rutter et al., 1980). However, emotional problems are most likely to occur when there is also abnormal neurophysiological activity (Rutter, 1981). To aid in recovery from head injury, children should be afforded less distractible areas of study, more external cuing and assistance in planning, and more time to complete their tasks. Care should be taken to ensure that they are working at a level that will produce some successes. With proper structuring of their environment and effective social support, more rapid recovery and possibly greater recovery are possible.

REFERENCES

Black, P., Jeffries, J. J., Blumer, D., Wellner, A., & Walker, A. E. (1969). The postraumatic syndrome in children. In A. E. Walker, W. F. Caveness, & M. Critchley (Eds.), *Late effects of head injury* (pp. 142–149). Springfield: IL: Thomas.

Bolter, J. F., & Long, C. J. (1985). Methodological issues in research in developmental neuropsychology. In L. C. Hartlage & C. F. Telzrow (Eds.), *The neuropsychology of individual differences* (pp. 41–59). New York: Plenum.

Goldman, P. S. (1971). Functional development of the prefrontal cortex in early life and the problem of neuronal plasticity. *Experimental Neurology, 3,* 366–387.

Goldman, P. S. (1972). Developmental determinants of cortical plasticity. *Acta Neurobiologica Experimentalis, 32,* 495–511.

Goldman, P. S. (1974). An alternative to developmental plasticity: Heterology of CNS structures in infants and adults. In D.

Stein, J. Rosen, & N. Butters (Eds.), *Plasticity and recovery of function in the central nervous system* (p. 109). New York: Academic.

Klonoff, H., Low, M. D., & Clark, C. (1977). Head injuries in children: A prospective five year follow-up. *Journal of Neurology, Neurosurgery, & Psychiatry, 40,* 1211–1219.

Korkman, M. (1980, March). *An attempt to adapt methods of Luria for diagnosis of cognitive deficits in children.* Paper presented at the INS Third European Conference, Chianciano, Italy.

Leigh, D. (1979). Psychiatric aspects of head injury. *Psychiatric Digest, 40,* 21–33.

Levin, H. S., & Eisenberg, H. M. (1979). Neuropsychological impairment after closed head injury in children and adolescents. *Journal of Pediatric Psychology, 4,* 389–402.

Russell, W. R. (1959). Brain memory learning; A neurologist's view. Oxford: Clarendon Press.

Rutter, M. D. (1980). Psychological sequelae of brain damage in children. *American Journal of Psychiatry, 138,* 1533–1544.

Rutter, M., Chadwick, O., & Shaffer, D. (1983). Head injury. In M. Rutter (Ed.), *Developmental Neuropsychiatry* (pp. 83–111). New York: Guilford.

Rutter, M., Chadwick, O., Shaffer, D., & Brown, G. (1980). A prospective study of children with head injuries: I. Design and methods. *Psychological Medicine, 10,* 633–645.

Stover, S. L., & Zeiger, H. E., (1976). Head injury in children and teenagers: Function/recovery correlated with the duration of coma. *Archives of Physical Medicine and Rehabilitation, 57,* 201–205.

Teuber, H. L., & Rudel, R. G. (1962). Behavior after cerebral lesions in children and adults. *Developmental medicine and Child Neurology, 4,* 3–20.

CHARLES J. LONG
*University of Tennessee,
Memphis
Memphis State University*

**BIRTH INJURIES
BRAIN DAMAGE
BRAIN DISORDERS
NEUROPSYCHOLOGY**

HEAD START

Head Start began in 1965 as a federally funded 8-week summer program for over 550,000 children from low-income families. Its initiation reflected the era's optimism for the role of preschool education in fighting the effects of poverty. It also reflected the environmentalist view of intellectual development, a belief in a critical period for human learning, the recommendations in the 1962 report of the President's Panel on Mental Retardation, and the need for a highly visible symbol of President Lyndon Johnson's war on poverty. By 1972 most programs ran the full year.

Head Start was intended to counteract negative environmental effects because of the well-known relationships between low school achievement and such factors as poverty, racial/ethnic membership, and socioeconomic status. Those factors were believed to be related to developmental and ecological variables that should be subject to modification. Early intervention was expected to eliminate the progressive decline in intellectual functioning and academic achievement that was typical of many children from poor families. Head Start emphasized local community involvement and autonomy; therefore, programs varied greatly across sites. The government encouraged parent volunteers and parent training, and published numerous training materials.

Research support for the expectation that preschool education would counteract effects of environmental disadvantages came from early reports of experimental preschool programs for poor, black children begun in 1958 by Susan Gray in Tennessee, Martin Deutsch in New York City, and David Weikart in Michigan (Lazar & Darlington, 1982). Their experimental work was theoretically anchored, carefully monitored, designed, and implemented by skilled professional educators and psychologists. However, for early Head Start programs there was not enough time for advance planning of curriculum and evaluation and limited direct supervision and monitoring of actual experiences of children. There were also too few teachers trained in early childhood education and a limited amount of in-service training for teachers and volunteers. Ironically, a program for disadvantaged children began at a disadvantage.

Head Start placed strong emphasis on medical, dental, and social services; initially, these were the most readily documented benefits. Millions of children were vaccinated, had vision and hearing tests, and received medical and dental examinations. A substantial percentage also received medical and dental treatment.

Early evaluation of sustained effects on cognitive and academic skills raised serious doubts about the program's effect on academic skills (Cicirelli, 1969). Media coverage was extremely negative. The program was modified. A Planned Variations project was devised to seek factors related to successful intervention. Training programs for Head Start personnel were greatly expanded.

Data from dozens of Head Start studies comparing group averages of Head Start graduates with averages of children without preschool programs lead to these conclusions: Head Start has positive effects on intellectual development (although in most studies average test scores are somewhat below the national average); Head Start children have fewer retentions in grade and fewer special education placements (although they still contribute disproportionately to special education and retention); some Head Start programs produce advantages in reading or arithmetic as measured by standardized tests; different curricula do not appear to produce differential effects (al-

though such differences are found in experimental preschool programs for high-risk children); most parents of Head Start children are highly supportive; and full-year Head Start programs are superior to short summer ones. Positive effects reported in some studies include improvement in social behavior, parent-child interactions, skills of parents, and nutrition (Haywood, 1982; Hubbell, 1983).

As evidence of program efficacy increased, criticisms from professionals decreased and public approval increased. A highly laudatory article in the national newspaper *USA Today* (Kanengiser, 1985) described Martin Deutsch's recent report that his group of Head Start graduates were more likely to finish high school, go to college, and hold full-time jobs than similar children who had no preschool experience. Such findings suggest that Head Start may affect motivation for education.

Edward Zigler, who was Head Start's first federal administrator, viewed Head Start's goal as the development of social competence. He commented that when one realistically examines its true effectiveness, it cannot be dismissed as a failure, but neither should so fragile an effort over one year of a child's life be viewed as the ultimate solution to poverty, illiteracy, and failures in life (Zigler, 1979).

REFERENCES

Cicirelli, V. G. (1969). Project Head Start, a national evaluation: Summary of the study. In D. G. Hayes (Ed.), *Britannica Review of American Education* (*Vol. 1*). Chicago: Encyclopedia Britannica.

Haywood, H. C. (1982). Compensatory education. *Peabody Journal of Education, 59*, 272–300.

Hubbell, R. (1983). *A review of Head Start research since 1970.* Washington, DC: Administration for Children. Youth, and Families (Superintendent of Documents, U.S. Government Printing Office.

Kanengiser, A. (1985, Oct. 3). Head Start really gives a head start. *USA Today,* 4D.

Lazar, I., & Darlington, R. (1982). Lasting effects of early education: A report from the consortium for longitudinal studies. *Monographs of the Society for Research in Child Development. 47* (serial nos. 2–3).

Zigler, E. (1979). Project Head Start: Success or failure? In E. Zigler & J. Valentine (Eds.), *Project Head Start: A legacy of the war on poverty.* New York: Free Press.

SUE ALLEN WARREN
JACQUELINE E. DAVIS
Boston University

EARLY EXPERIENCE AND CRITICAL PERIODS
EARLY IDENTIFICATION OF HANDICAPPED CHILDREN
EDUCATION FOR ALL HANDICAPPED CHILDREN ACT OF 1975
HEAD START FOR THE HANDICAPPED
PRESCHOOL ASSESSMENT
ZIGLER, EDWARD

HEAD START FOR THE HANDICAPPED

Head Start services began in 1965 with the Economic Opportunity Act. The goal was to provide "comprehensive developmental services for preschool children from low-income families" (Lasher, et al., 1978). In 1972 Congress amended the Economic Opportunity Act with PL 92-424, which required Head Start programs to include children with handicaps. It was mandated that at least 10% of the national enrollment in Head Start programs must include children with handicaps. In 1974 the Head Start Economic Opportunity and Community Partnership Act changed that quota to 10% of the total enrollment in each state (Zigler & Valentine, 1979).

Comprehensive and individualized services had always been a purpose of Head Start programs. There was a focus on the child's overall growth and development, which meant that the program included identification and treatment of health and medical problems. It is possible that this focus helped to prevent and/or ameliorate many handicaps through the early identification and treatment of hearing, vision, and physical impairments (Zigler & Valentine, 1979).

The spirit of the legislated mandates sought to include children with handicaps to expand the population within the low-income communities for whom the services would be available. Those responsible for implementing the changes felt that the mandate would help to acknowledge that many children in Head Start were at risk for handicaps for additional reasons; they hoped to expand on the nature and types of needs for which services would be provided. The legislative mandates to include children with handicaps was an opportunity and challenge to Head Start to further the individualized and comprehensive services.

Earlier, Skeels and Dye (1939) documented that infants who were orphans and who were identified as retarded showed dramatic improvements in their IQs when they were provided with special attention and stimulation. Those gains were maintained into adult life. This and other research provided direction for the federal initiatives for young children with handicaps. These began in 1968 with the establishment of the Handicapped Children's Early Education Assistance Act, which created the Handicapped Children's Early Education Programs (HCEEP).

Evaluating the overall impact of Head Start for children with handicaps has been as difficult as evaluating the impact of early intervention for children with handicaps in any program. The Administration for Children, Youth, and Families (ACYF) sponsored annual surveys to report the percentages of handicapping conditions being served. By 1977 data indicated that approximately 11% of those enrolled were handicapped. However, these data varied greatly from 1978 to 1982. The reasons for this variation were in part owed to the identification process. More than half of the children identified as handicapped had been identified through the normal enrollment procedures that did not include a specific assessment. Therefore, the data on the nature of handicapping conditions must be interpreted with caution.

The areas of change measured to determine impact of services were academic achievement, increased intellectual functioning, and social competence. Initially there were concerns regarding the lack of individualized service plans for some children and the lack of early childhood special education training for some teachers (Hubbell, 1983). But Head Start provided additional training for their staff and created the position of coordinator for services for children with handicaps (Lasher et al., 1978).

Positive changes were shown for young children with handicaps (Hubbell, 1983; Zigler & Valentine, 1979), but the degree of change or the length of time the change was maintained was not as clear. Failure to find efficacy may have been related to the difficulty of planning for evaluation of a program that was to be implemented on a short timeline, variability in Head Start programs across the country, differences in training skills of teachers, and the choice of variables to be measured.

REFERENCES

Hubbell, R. (1983). *A review of Head Start research since 1970.* Washington, DC: U.S. Government Printing Office.

Lasher, M., Mattick, I., Perkins, F., von Hippel, C., & Hailey, L. (1978). *Project Head Start: Mainstreaming preschoolers series.* Washington, DC: U.S. Government Printing Office.

Skeels, H., & Dye, H. (1939). A study of the effects of differential stimulation on mentally retarded children. *Proceedings of the American Association of Mental Deficiency, 44,* 144–136.

Zigler, E., & Valentine, J. (Eds.). (1979). *Project Head Start: A legacy of the war on poverty.* New York: Free Press.

JACQUELINE E. DAVIS
SUE ALLEN WARREN
Boston University

EARLY IDENTIFICATION OF THE HANDICAPPED
FOLLOW THROUGH
HEAD START
PRESCHOOL ASSESSMENT

HEALTH IMPAIRMENTS

Public Law 94-142 divided the classification of physical handicaps into two categories for purposes of special education: orthopedic impairments and health impairments (Bigge & Sirvis, 1986). The second category of health impairments consists of physical conditions that affect a child or youth's educational performance such as "limited strength, vitality or alertness due to chronic or acute health problems such as a heart condition, tuberculosis, rheumatic fever, nephritis, asthma, sickle cell anemia, hemophilia, epilepsy, lead poisoning, leukemia, or diabetes (*Federal Register*, 1977, p. 42478). Such children are often diagnosed and managed medically and socially as chronically ill children. Data collected by the federal government regarding children and youths receiving special education and related services under PLs 94-142 and 89-313 found that 54,621 children had been identified as health impaired, and as such should receive some form of special education and related services.

REFERENCES

Bigge, J., & Sirvis, B. (1986). Physical and health impairments. In N. G. Haring & L. McCormick (Eds.), *Exceptional children and youth*. (4th ed., pp. 313–354). Columbus, OH: Merrill.

U.S. Office of Education. (1985). *Seventh annual report to Congress on the implementation of Public Law 94-142: The Education of All Handicapped Children Act*. Washington, DC: U.S. Government Printing Office.

LESTER MANN
*Hunter College, City University
of New York*

**CHRONIC ILLNESS IN CHILDREN
ORTHOPEDIC IMPAIRMENTS**

HEALTH MAINTENANCE, INVASIVE PROCEDURES FOR

In accordance with PL 94-142, some invasive procedures for health maintenance are required to be performed by the teacher or other school personnel during the school day if required for the child to attend school and if no health care professional is available. Procedures that do not require a sterile field and that may be routinely performed by parents may be required to be performed by school-based personnel. Procedures such as ostomy maintenance, injection, catheterization, suctioning, or tube feeding may need to be conducted by the teacher, an aide, or a trained volunteer for the child to be in school all day.

Specific health maintenance activities have been deemed a part of the teacher's responsibility if no health care specialist is available. Whenever possible, the child should perform the maintenance activities independently. When this is not possible because of the child's age, physical, sensory, or cognitive functioning, the teacher should (1) provide only the level of supervision, support, or intervention required by the student; (2) develop a program or procedure wherein the child learns to take care of as much of the maintenance activity as possible; (3) carry out the procedure when required under the direction of the parents, school system health officer, and child's physician and therapist; (4) obtain training in basic first aid and cardiopulmonary resuscitation as a general protection prior to conducting any health maintenance activity; and (5) have a school board and school-based policy in writing defining procedures to be followed. Depending on school or district policy, aides, volunteers, or secretaries may be trained to carry out a specific procedure so that the teacher may continue to teach and supervise academic activities during the time of the procedure.

Depending on local, state, and federal policy, the teacher may be required to (1) have a witness when carrying out any invasive procedure, and (2) record all procedures, including time, observations of health, and general impressions of the adequacy of the intervention. Record keeping systems must be employed each time a procedure is conducted (Dykes & Venn, 1983).

REFERENCE

Dykes, M. K., & Venn, J. (1983). Using health, physical and medical data in the classroom. In J. Unbreit (Ed.), *Physical disabilities and health impairments: An introduction*. Columbus, OH: Merrill.

MARY K. DYKES
University of Florida

**HEALTH MAINTENANCE PROCEDURES
HOSPITAL SCHOOLS
MEDICALLY FRAGILE STUDENT**

HEALTH MAINTENANCE PROCEDURES

Under PL 94-142, educators may be held responsible for monitoring specific health maintenance activities required in order for the child to attend school. Teachers may oversee students taking medication, conducting bowel and bladder maintenance procedures, and adjusting braces. In addition, monitoring of such health maintenance equipment as ventilators, cardiac monitors, reciprocal braces, and shunts may be a part of required teacher activity. Before monitoring or helping with any health maintenance activity, the teacher should have a written school district and school policy to follow, have completed first aid and cardiopulmonary resuscitation courses, have been trained by parents and a school health official, and have written, dated, and signed specific directions requesting that a procedure be carried out while the child is at school.

Whenever possible, the student should be responsible for carrying out all health maintenance activities. Medications should be taken by the student in the presence of an adult who checks the prescription bottle for name, directions for administration, and the log for last time taken. If students are incapable of carrying out the required procedure (e.g., catheterization), they should be taught the procedure as soon as possible if there is enough potential motor and intellectual skill to carry out the task.

Issues of liability should be taken into account (1) accountability for which or how much medication was taken; (2) record keeping when monitoring equipment (e.g., a log should be kept of date, time, signature, and any signs of abnormal functioning of the child or the equipment; (3) written procedures for administration of medication; and (4) written school board policy for protocols to follow in meeting routine and emergency health maintenance needs of the child (Dykes & Venn, 1983).

REFERENCE

Dykes, M. K., & Venn, J. (1983). Using health, physical and medical data in the classroom. In J. Unbreit (Ed.), *Physical disabilities and health impairments: An introduction.* Columbus, OH: Merrill.

MARY K. DYKES
University of Florida

HOSPITAL SCHOOLS
MEDICALLY FRAGILE STUDENT

HEARING IMPAIRED

See DEAF.

HEBER, RICK F. (1932–   )

Rick Heber was born January 12, 1932. He received his BA degree from the University of Arkansas in 1953. After a year as principal of the Manitoba School for Mental Deficiency, Heber attended Michigan State University, obtaining his MA degree there in 1955. He then went to George Peabody College, taking his PhD in 1957. Heber joined the faculty of the University of Wisconsin, Madison in 1959 as coordinator of the special education program.

Heber is best known for his work as principal investigator in the Milwaukee Project and the subsequent controversies surrounding the project. Heber was a member of the faculty of the University of Wisconsin, Madison when he was indicted on charges stemming from the misuse of federal funds allocated to the project. He was subsequently convicted and served time in the federal prison in Bastrop, Texas. Previously a respected scholar in the field of mental retardation, his academic work on the Milwaukee Project has been called into serious question. It is now questionable whether the project ever actually existed as it had been described by Heber.

REFERENCES

Heber, R. F. (1970). *Epidemiology of mental retardation.* Springfield, IL: Thomas.

Heber, R. F., & Garber H. (1975). The Milwaukee Project: A study of the use of family intervention to prevent cultural-familial mental retardation. In B. Z. Friedlander, G. Kirk, & G. Sterritt (Eds.), *The exceptional infant* (Vol. 3). New York: Brunner/Mazel.

CECIL R. REYNOLDS
Texas A&M University

MILWAUKEE PROJECT, THE

HEELCORD OPERATION

The heelcord operation is an orthopedic surgical treatment for children with spastic cerebral palsy. It is performed to compensate for equinus, a condition in which the foot is involuntarily extended owing to contracted tendons in the heel. Palsied children with equinus often have severe gait problems (Batshaw & Perret, 1981). The operation itself involves cutting and lengthening the Achilles tendon and rotating the heel to a normal position. The operation is typically followed by 6 weeks in a cast and roughly 6 months of physical therapy.

Without surgery, treatment of this condition is often painful and unsuccessful. It involves the use of braces, splints worn at night, and regular heelcord stretching exercises. The success rate of the operation is very high. Research has shown an overall recurrence rate for patients receiving surgery of only 9%, although recurrence is related to age; 2 year olds, for example, have a recurrence rate of 75% (Lee & Bleck, 1980).

REFERENCES

Batshaw, M. L., & Perret, Y. M. (1981). *Children with handicaps: A medical primer.* Baltimore, MD: Brookes.

Lee, C. L., & Bleck, E. E. (1980). Surgical correction of equinus deformity in cerebral palsy. *Developmental Medicine and Child Neurology, 22,* 287–294.

THOMAS E. ALLEN
Gallaudet College

CEREBRAL PALSY

HEGGE, KIRK, KIRK APPROACH

Hegge, Kirk, and Kirk (1936) formulated the phono-grapho-vocal method of remedial reading while teaching educable mentally retarded children. Emphasizing programmed learning techniques, this method incorporates sound blending and kinesthetic experiences (Kirk, 1983). Basic to this method is a set of remedial reading drills presented in four parts. Part I provides drills in sounding out consonants, short vowels, and vowel combinations such as *ee, ay, ow, ing, all, ight, ur,* and the final *e* marker. Drills in Part I are printed on one line from left to right reinforcing directional patterns in reading. Early drills are simple, showing that only the initial consonant changes in words such as sat-mat-rat. More complex drills are successively introduced by changing the first and last consonant of words. After repeated drills on the consonants, the short vowels, a, e, i, o, and u, are emphasized.

In Part II words are presented using the sounds already learned in Part I. Children are taught to read hand as h-an-d instead of h-a-n-d. Through frequent review and drills (the hallmark of this method) children move from vocalizing and recognizing simple sounds to incorporating these sounds into words.

Parts III and IV are for those children who, after having been repeatedly drilled on the sound blends in Parts I and II, are beginning to read by rapidly sounding out words. Part III requires children to read new words in syllables or wholes.

In Part IV of this approach children are drilled on sounds that could not be systematically presented in earlier drills. Reinforcement drills are used with children who exhibit problems in specific areas such as confusing b, d, and p or m and n (Kirk, 1940).

Kirk (1940) warns that the Hegge, Kirk, Kirk method, developed in 1936, should not be used as a general teaching method or for children in higher grade levels. Rather it is applicable to first-, second-, and third-grade students whose reading level is at least 2 years below the norm, who are trainable in sound blending, and who demonstrate the desire to learn to read. This program will be of little value to those children who are accurate but slow readers because they already possess the skills inherent in the practice drills.

REFERENCES

Hegge, T., Kirk, S., & Kirk, W. (1936). *Remedial reading drills.* Ann Arbor, MI: Wahr.

Kirk, S. (1940). *Teaching reading to slow-learning children.* Cambridge, MA: Riverside.

Kirk, S., & Gallagher, J. (1983). *Educating exceptional children.* (4th ed.). Boston: Houghton Mifflin.

FORREST KEESBURY
Lycoming College

ORTON-GILLINGHAM METHOD
READING DISORDERS
READING REMEDIATION

HEINICKE, SAMUEL (1727–1790)

Samuel Heinicke, a German educator, founded the first oral school for the deaf about 1755. He established Germany's first public school for the deaf in 1778 at Leipzig. Using published accounts of the teaching of deaf children by Jacob Pereire and others, Heinicke devised a highly successful method for teaching reading, writing, speech, and speech reading to deaf students, a method that formed the basis for the later development of the oral method in Germany by Moritz Hill.

Some of Heinicke's ideas anticipated later educational practice. He taught the reading of whole words before teaching the letters. He advocated classes at the University of Leipzig for preparing teachers of the deaf, and attempted, apparently unsuccessfully, to establish with the university provision for his deaf students to participate in university activities. Heinicke's work was continued after his death by his widow, who took charge of his school, and his son-in-law, who established a school for the deaf near Berlin.

REFERENCE

Bender, R. E. (1970). *The conquest of deafness.* Cleveland, OH: Case Western Reserve University Press.

PAUL IRVINE
Katonah, New York

HELEN KELLER INTERNATIONAL

Founded in 1915, Helen Keller International assists governments and agencies in developing countries in providing services to prevent or cure eye diseases and blindness and to educate or rehabilitate the blind and visually impaired. Subsumed under Helen Keller International are the Association for Chinese; Permanent Blind Relief War Fund; American Braille Press for War and Civilian Blind; and the American Foundation for Overseas Blind (Gruber & Cloyd, 1985).

The organization offers courses for teachers of blind children and adults as well as for field workers dealing with the rural blind. A training focus is prevention and treatment of blindness caused by malnutrition, trachoma, cataracts, and other eye diseases. Additionally, there are programs to prepare volunteers to counsel families of blind babies.

An important function of this international agency is the collection and compilation of statistics on blindness throughout the world. Publications include an annual report, a newsletter, fact sheets, technical reports, educational materials, and training information. There is one annual conference and an annual board meeting. Headquarters are at 15 West 16th Street, New York, NY 10011.

REFERENCE

Gruber, K., & Cloyd, I. (1985). *Encyclopedia of associations* (Vol. 1, 20th ed.). Detroit, MI: Gale Research.

C. MILDRED TASHMAN
College of St. Rose

HEMIBALLISMUS

Hemiballismus is a rare condition that is characterized by violent, flinging, involuntary movements in the extremities on one side of the body. The movements are typically more pronounced in the arm than in the leg and may be severe enough to cause bruising of the soft tissues or exhaustion. Involvement also has been reported in the muscles of the neck. Hemiballistic movements disappear during sleep.

Onset of the condition usually occurs in adulthood and often is associated with a prior cerebral vascular accident (stroke) involving the subthalamic nucleus. Tumors rarely are involved but hemiballism occasionally occurs in multiple sclerosis. In a few instances, the severity of hemiballism spontaneously subsides after several weeks. Death from exhaustion, pneumonia, or congestive heart failure within 4 to 6 weeks of onset also has been reported. Severe movement abnormalities may persist for several months or years without noticeable diminution in many of those who survive these initial weeks. Hemiballistic movements also may subside and be replaced by milder hemichoreatic movements in some instances.

Chlorpromazine and Haloperidol have been reported to substantially reduce or eliminate hemiballistic movements over a period of 3 months to more than 1 year. In some individuals, medications have been reduced gradually and ultimately eliminated with no reoccurrence of the condition. The prognosis has become more optimistic in recent years owing to increased use of these medications. Fatalities are rare.

REFERENCES

Berkow, R. (Ed.). (1982). *The Merck manual of diagnosis and therapy* (14th ed., 1359). Rahway, NJ: Merck, Sharp & Dohme.

Fahn, S. (1985). Neurologic and behavioral diseases. In J. Wyngaarden & L. Smith, Jr. (Eds.), *Cecil textbooks of medicine* (17th ed., 2075). Philadelphia: Saunders.

Kalawanis, H. L., Moses, H., Nausieda, P. A., Berger, D., & Weiner, W. J. (1976). Treatment and prognosis of hemiballismus. *New England Journal of Medicine, 295,* 1348–1350.

Magalini, S., & Scarascia, E. (1981). *Dictionary of medical syndromes* (2nd ed., pp. 110–111). Philadelphia: Lippincott.

DANIEL D. LIPKA
*Lincoln Way Special Education
Regional Resource Center,
Louisville, Ohio*

CHOREA
MULTIPLE SCLEROSIS

HEMIPARESIS

Hemiparesis is a topographic term used to describe a person who has a slight paralysis affecting one side of the body (with muscular weakness on that side). Hemiparesis may be facial in nature and vision and hearing deficits may be contributory deficits. The cause (etiology) of the hemiparesis may be a disease, injury, or congenital defect that occurred before, at, or after birth. The nature of the etiology is important to educational and vocational plans, and is best determined during evaluation by a skilled neurologist. Two questions are relevant: Is the causal agent progressive? In addition to the evident weakness, what sensory/motor/vestibular damage, if any, is also present?

Weakness on one side of the body may be accompanied by a loss of pain sensitivity (hemianalgesia). Hemianesthesia, one-sided anesthesia, or loss of tactile sensibility on one side of the body, also may be a component feature. The pattern of sensory loss may not be on the same side as the motor loss. The importance of knowing about pain, heat, and cold sensibility loss relates to protection of the individual from burns, freezing, and injuries that could be more serious impairments than the obvious weakness. Both sensory deprivation and balance deficits (cerebellar/vestibular) have profound implications for safety in transportation to and from school, school activities, self-care, and realistic vocational plans for the individual child.

REFERENCES

Berkow, R. (Ed.). (1982). *The Merck manual of diagnosis and therapy* (14th ed.). Rahway, NJ: Merck, Sharp & Dohme.

Evarts, E. V. (1979). Brain mechanisms of movements. *Scientific American, 241,* 164–173.

Hensyl, W. R. (Ed.). (1982). *Stedman's medical dictionary* (24th ed.). Baltimore, MD: Williams & Wilkins.

RACHAEL J. STEVENSON
Bedford, Ohio

ADAPTED PHYSICAL EDUCATION
HEMIPELGIA
PHYSICAL ANOMALIES

HEMIPLEGIA

Hemiplegia is a topographic term used to describe a person who has a movement disorder or paralysis of both limbs on the same side of the body owing to congenital defect, disease, or injury to the brain or central nervous system (CNS). The extent and nature of the disturbance of functional performance experienced by the individual is determined by the age at which the impairment occurs, the severity and location of the damage of the CNS, and the etiology of the injury.

Clinical experience suggests that the terms hereditary hemiplegia, infantile hemiplegia, and spastic hemiplegia often are used to describe an individual who has suffered damage during the developmental period—generally to age 8 to 12 years. In this category, the neurological condition may not be progressive, but the clinical symptoms observed may change with maturation. Hemiplegia may be used to describe the completed stroke, in which a person has a sudden onset of weakness or other neurological symptoms of both limbs on the same body side as a result of injury to a blood vessel in the brain (cerebrum, cerebellum, or brain stem). A stroke usually suggests a cerebrovascular accident (CVA). Precipitating causes of CVA in children include sickle cell disease crisis and trauma (especially to children with hemophilia).

The increased muscle tone in the antigravity muscles on the affected side is the most obvious symptom of the child with spastic hemiplegia; however, the associated damage and sensory deficits may have more profound impact on plans for educational and vocational intervention. Vision, hearing, and touch, hot/cold and position sense and balance may be impaired and seriously affect a child's ability to learn complex motor skills. Specific aphasias, language processing problems, and seizures are common concomitants of this condition. It would be expected that close medical, school, and parent cooperation would need to be established, with appropriate evaluation and intervention of related service therapists to prevent deformity and maximize opportunity for a schoolchild with hemiplegia and associated deficits.

REFERENCES

Berkow, R. (Ed.). (1982). *The Merck manual of diagnosis and therapy* (14th ed.). Rahway, NJ: Merck, Sharp & Dohme.

Hensyl, W. R. (Ed.). (1982). *Stedman's medical dictionary* (24th ed.). Baltimore, MD: Williams & Wilkins.

Stolov, W. C., & Clowers, M. R. (Eds.). (1981). *Handbook of severe disability* Washington, DC: U.S. Government Printing Office. (stock #017-090-00054-2).

RACHAEL J. STEVENSON
Bedford, Ohio

ADAPTED PHYSICAL EDUCATION
HEMIPARESIS

HEMISPHERECTOMY

Hemispherectomy (surgical removal of one cerebral hemisphere) is an uncommon procedure, usually reserved for children with widespread damage affecting one cerebral hemisphere, such as intracerebral tumor(s) (Gott, 1973), intractable seizures, or congenital/infantile hemiplegia (Ameli, 1980; Campbell, Bogen, & Smith, 1981; Dennis & Kohn, 1975; Dennis & Whitaker, 1976; Kohn & Dennis, 1974; Smith, 1974; Verity, et al., 1982). Adult hemispherectomy patients generally demonstrate severe, nonrecoverable deficits (e.g., hemiparalysis and cognitive impairment) after surgery. In contrast, some hemispherectomized children show good recovery of sensorimotor function with fairly normal development of many cognitive abilities. For example, Smith (1974) described a case of juvenile hemispherectomy in which the patient developed above average verbal and normal nonverbal capabilities and went on to graduate from college.

While there is considerable variability in the findings, the extent of recovery after hemispherectomy appears to be, at least in part, age related. The fact that young children clearly show better recovery than adults (Campbell et al., 1981; Chadwick, Rutter, Thompson, & Shaffer, 1981; Smith, 1974; Smith & Sugar, 1975) suggests that young brains have biological equivalence or bilateral representation of many functions (Ameli, 1980; Smith, 1974). This equivalence declines during the first decade of life (Dennis & Kohn, 1975; Dennis & Whitaker, 1976; Smith, 1974), and once functions are lateralized they cannot be easily transferred (Smith, 1974).

In the intact, mature brain, one hemisphere (generally the left) mediates language function and processes information sequentially and analytically. The other hemisphere usually has limited language capability, processes information in a simultaneous/integrative manner, and is involved primarily in nonverbal, spatial, constructional, and visuo-spinal memory functions (Smith, 1974; Zaidel, 1981). This pattern of functional lateralization develops during childhood but it can be altered. Up to the age of about 5 years, either hemisphere seems to be capable of developing language (Zaidel, 1978); compensation appears to be most successful with hemispherectomy before 1 year of age (Dennis & Kohn, 1975; Smith, 1974).

While compensation for language deficits is given precedence following early left or right hemispherectomy (Campbell et al., 1981; Dennis & Kohn, 1975; Kohn & Dennis, 1974; Smith & Sugar, 1975), careful study reveals that recovery is not equivalent for all language functions. Comprehension appears to be more bilaterally represented, whereas speech is more lateralized (Campbell et al., 1981; Zaidel, 1978); semantic deficits remain following right hemispherectomy (Zaidel, 1977).

The considerably lesser recovery of right hemisphere functions as compared with recovery from language deficits (Dennis & Kohn, 1975; Kohn & Dennis, 1974; Smith

& Sugar, 1975) is to some extent reflected in IQ scores, which in all cases are greater for verbal IQ than performance IQ regardless of the hemisphere removed (Kohn & Dennis, 1974; Smith & Sugar, 1975). However, this may also reflect greater emphasis on language capabilities in education, or limitations of testing procedures (Smith & Sugar, 1975).

Additionally, such recovery patterns may reflect existing impairments of the remaining hemisphere (Smith & Sugar, 1975), or removal of the restraining influence of neural systems already having acquired functional dominance (St. James-Roberts, 1975). Thus any conclusion from the study of hemispherectomized individuals must be reached with appropriate caution.

REFERENCES

Ameli, N. O. (1980). Hemispherectomy for the treatment of epilepsy and behavior disturbance. *Canadian Journal of Neurological Sciences, 7,* 35–38.

Campbell, A. L., Bogen, T. E., & Smith, A. (1981). Disorganization and reorganization of cognitive and sensorimotor functions in cerebral commissurectomy. *Brain, 104,* 493–511.

Chadwick, O., Rutter, M., Thompson, J., & Shaffer,D. (1981). Intellectual performance and reading skills after localized head injury in children. *Journal of Child Psychology and Psychiatry, 22,* 117–139.

Dennis, M., & Kohn, B. (1975). Comprehension of syntax in infantile hemiplegics after cerebral hemidecortication: Left-hemisphere superiority. *Brain & Language, 2,* 472–482.

Dennis, M., & Whitaker, H. A. (1976). Language acquisition following hemidecortication: Linguistic superiority of the left over the right hemisphere. *Brain & Language, 3,* 404–433.

Gott, P. S. (1973). Cognitive abilities following right and left hemispherectomy. *Cortex, 9,* 266–274.

Kohn, B., & Dennis, M. (1974). Patterns of hemispheric specialization after hemidecortication for infantile hemiplegia. In M. Kinsbourne & W. L. Smith (Eds.), *Hemispheric disconnection and cerebral function* (pp. 34–47). Springfield, IL: Thomas.

St. James-Roberts, I. (1979). Neurological plasticity, recovery from brain insult, and child development. *Advances in Child Development and Behavior, 4,* 253–319.

Smith, A. (1974). Dominant and nondominant hemispherectomy. In M. Kinsbourne & W. L. Smith (Eds.), *Hemispheric disconnection and cerebral function* (pp. 5–33). Springfield, IL: Thomas.

Smith, A., & Sugar, O. (1975). Development of above normal language and intelligence 21 years after left hemispherectomy. *Neurology, 25,* 813–818.

Verity, C. M., Strauss, E. H., Moyes, P. D., Wada, J. A., Dunn, H. G., & Lepointe, J. S. (1982). Long-term follow-up after cerebral hemispherectomy: Neurological, radiologic, and psychological findings. *Neurology, 32,* 629–639.

Zaidel, E. (1977). Unilateral auditory language comprehension on the Token Test following cerebral commissurectomy and hemispherectomy. *Neuropsychologia, 15,* 1–18.

Zaidel, E. (1978). Auditory language comprehension in the right hemisphere following cerebral commissurectomy and hemispherectomy: A comparison with child language and aphasia. In A. Caramazzo & E. G. Zurif (Eds.), *Language acquisition and breakdown: Parallels and divergencies* (pp. 229–275). Baltimore, MD: Johns Hopkins.

Zaidel, E. (1981). Performance on the ITPA following cerebral commissurectomy and hemispherectomy. *Neuropsychologia, 17,* 259–280.

CHARLES J. LONG
GERI R. ALVIS
University of Tennessee,
Memphis
Memphis State University

CEREBRAL DOMINANCE
LEFT BRAIN-RIGHT BRAIN

HEMISPHERIC ASYMMETRY, SEX DIFFERENCES IN

Hemispheric asymmetry refers to the fact that the left and right hemispheres of the brain specialize in different forms of information processing. For most individuals, the left hemisphere is more efficient at processing information logically and sequentially (e.g., spoken and written language), while the right hemisphere is better suited to processing spatially and holistically (e.g., visual spatial tasks). However, because most tasks include both linguistic and spatial aspects, cognitive processing generally involves both hemispheric functions, though they may vary in emphasis from moment to moment (Gaddes, 1985).

Considerable research exists to support a sex difference in hemispheric asymmetry at all age levels. The evidence indicates that males characteristically are more proficient with their right hemispheres and females with their left, suggesting a male spatial superiority and a female verbal superiority. Thus, when a task can be performed either by left or right hemisphere mechanisms, males are more likely to use a nonverbal, spatial strategy for problem solving, while females are more apt to use a verbal strategy (McGlone & Davison, 1973).

In a study of children who were followed from ages 5 to 9 (Buffery, 1976), it was discovered that both sexes preferred to process material that was easy to verbalize with the left hemisphere, although the asymmetry was more pronounced in girls, especially as they grew older. Both sexes also used predominantly right hemispheric processing for material that was difficult to verbalize. Hemispheric asymmetry for cross-modal analysis was found to emerge around age 8 in boys and age 7 in girls. These findings suggest that girls up to the age of 8 might be expected to be more competent than boys in following purely verbal instructions, while boys might be better at understanding spatial diagrams or pictorial material.

In another study with children ages 6 through 13, no

sex differences were found on 11 of the 20 subtests of the Spreen-Benton Aphasia Battery (Gaddes & Crockett, 1975). In light of other studies that have shown sex differences in verbal skills, the investigators concluded that since all tasks could be solved by either a verbal or nonverbal strategy, boys and girls most likely achieved the same levels of success by using different tactics. Sex differences in relative maturation rates of the two hemispheres, relative degree of specialization of the two hemispheres, and other factors have been noted. Though much research remains to be done before we fully understand the nature of sex differences in hemispheric functioning, they do exist and they are developmental to at least some degree.

It is likely that such findings have significant implications for the education of children. Additional research is needed to apply this knowledge to the development of appropriate teaching strategies.

REFERENCES

Buffery, A. W. H. (1976). Sex differences in the neuropsychological development of verbal and spatial skills. In R. M. Knights & D. J. Bakker (Eds.), *The neuropsychology of learning disorders: Theoretical approaches* (pp. 187–205). Baltimore, MD: University Park Press.

Gaddes, W. H. (1985). *Learning disabilities and brain function: A neuropsychological approach* (2nd ed.). New York: Springer-Verlag.

Gaddes, W. H., & Crockett, D. J. (1975). The Spreen-Benton Aphasia Tests: Normative data as a measure of normal language development. *Brain & Language, 2,* 257–280.

McGlone, J., & Davison, W. (1973). The relation between cerebral speech laterality and spatial ability with special reference to sex and hand preference. *Neuropsychologia, 11,* 105–113.

GALE A. HARR
Maple Heights City Schools,
Maple Heights, Ohio

CEREBRAL DOMINANCE
LEFT BRAIN-RIGHT BRAIN

HEMISPHERIC FUNCTIONS

Hemispheric functions refers to the specialization of each cerebral hemisphere of the brain for various processes. The right hemisphere usually has been associated with processing information in a simultaneous, spatial, and holistic fashion (Speery, 1974). In contrast, the left hemisphere of the brain has been shown to best process information in a sequential, temporal, and analytic mode (Speery, Gazzaniga, & Bogen, 1969).

Although hemispheric lateralization usually refers to the processing of specific information by predominantly one hemisphere, undifferentiated hemispheric preference for the processing of certain information also exists. Gordon (1974), for example, found that when melodies recorded from an electric organ were simultaneously presented, one to each ear, no hemispheric superiority was noted. Few reliable hemispheric differences were noted for lower level sensory elements such as brightness, color, pressure, sharpness, pitch, and contour (Gordon, 1970). Symmetrical processing of information does not occur on tasks that require complex cognitive processes such as categorization, integration, and abstraction. As the level of cognitive complexity increases, so does the lateralization for the task in question.

The notion of lateralization of functions within cerebral hemispheres can be dated back to the late 1800s, when Broca and Wernicke demonstrated that aphasia (or the inability to express or comprehend language) resulted from lesions to the left hemisphere. Moreover, the left hemisphere was portrayed as the dominant hemisphere by virtue of its leading role in such activities as speech and calculation, whereas the right hemisphere was seen as the minor hemisphere, serving activities associated with perception and sensation (Geschwind, 1974).

Invasive techniques that have been used to investigate brain functioning consist of electrical stimulation of the brain, hemispheric anesthetization, and split-brain research. Direct electrical stimulation of the brain was pioneered by Penfield (Penfield & Roberts, 1959) as a means of map areas of the brain that controlled specific functions prior to other surgical procedures. Given that the brain does not contain pain receptors, electrical stimulation was applied to various parts of the brain while the patient was fully conscious. This technique has been successful in examining areas of the brain associated with vision, hearing, olfaction, and haptic sensations.

Another invasive technique to investigate speech lateralization involved the injection of sodium amytal to the carotid artery, which is located on either the right or left side of the patient's neck. This procedure, which is commonly referred to as the Wada test (Wada & Rasmussen, 1960), quickly anesthetizes or temporarily paralyzes the hemisphere that receives the injection. The hemisphere is anesthetized for approximately 3 to 5 minutes, thereby enabling the examiner to assess which hemisphere is responsible for processing linguistic information. The last invasive technique, split-brain surgery, involves the severing of the corpus callosum, a large band of nerve fibers that permit the left and right hemispheres to communicate with one another. This procedure is primarily performed to prevent the spreading of a seizure from a focal point in one hemisphere to the other hemisphere by way of the corpus callosum. By severing the corpus callosum, communication between the hemispheres is blocked, thereby allowing the examiner to determine the hemispheric lateralization for such functions as language, visual discrimination, touch, olfaction, and motoric control (Hacaen, 1981).

Research that has resulted from the use of the preceding techniques has found that the right hemisphere plays a dominant role in processing certain information. Specifically, the right hemisphere is dominant for processing nonlinguistic information involving nonverbal reasoning, visual-spatial integration, visual-constructive abilities, haptic perception, pattern recognition, and other related tasks (Dean, 1984). Conversely, the left hemisphere has been shown to be responsible for tasks that require speech, general language, calculation, abstract verbal reasoning, etc. (Dean, 1984).

Noninvasive techniques for investigating hemispheric specializations have also been employed. The dichotic listening technique attempts to determine if auditory information for verbal and nonverbal information is lateralized to one hemisphere. Here, the subject is simultaneously presented with different information in each ear and is required to recall or recognize the information presented. Given that greater numbers of nerve connections cross over from ear to hemisphere, the hemisphere opposite the ear that obtains the greatest number of correct responses (ear advantage) is inferred to be the functional hemisphere for the specific information presented. For example, most normal children and adults have a right-ear advantage (left hemisphere) for linguistic information (Dean & Hua, 1982). When nonverbal auditory information such as tones are presented, a left-ear advantage (right hemisphere) is found for most normal right-handed individuals (Kimura, 1967). The dichotic listening paradigm has been successful in suggesting specific functions of each hemisphere.

Similar to the dichotic listening methodology, the split visual-field technique presents visual information to either the left or right visual half fields. It should be noted that each retina is separated into a left and right half visual field. Therefore, information presented to the two left halves of each retina is processed by the right hemisphere and, conversely, information presented to the two right halves is processed by the left hemisphere. To study the lateralization of visual stimuli, different information is simultaneously presented on a tachistoscope. As would be expected, a right visual half advantage (left hemisphere) is found for linguistic information (Marcel & Rajan, 1975) while a left visual half advantage (right hemisphere) has been noted for nonverbal spatial information (Kimura & Durnsford, 1974). One noted difficulty with this technique, however, is the attentional scanning of the stimuli that occurs once the information has been presented (Dean, 1981).

Differences in hemispheric specializations may be due, in part, to anatomical differences of the cortical hemispheres. In examining anatomical differences, it was found that the left temporal planum structure that serves language functions is larger than the right temporal planum (Geschwind & Levitsky, 1968). Similarly, the Sylvian fissure, a large lateral depression in the brain that contains the major speech area, is found to be larger for the left side of the Sylvian fissure than the right (Geschwind, 1974). In addition, the left hemisphere is noted to be approximately 5 gr heavier than the right hemisphere. Another anatomical difference is the projection of nerve fibers from the left hemisphere that cross over earlier at the base of the brain than do nerve fibers from the right hemisphere. Such structural differences between the hemispheres may partially account for cerebral lateralization of specific functions.

When gender differences are examined, subtle anatomical dissimilarties between males and females are found to exist shortly after birth. Perhaps more striking than anatomical are functional changes that exist between adult male and female brains (Kolata, 1979). As a group, males have been shown to perform better on tasks of spatial ability than females, who present superior verbal facility (Witelson, 1976). The spatial ability of males may be partially due to an earlier right hemisphere lateralization of spatial functions. Males also have been shown to have an earlier hemispheric specialization for language, while females are noted to be less consistent in lateralization for language activities (Levy, 1973). This less established hemispheric specialization for females, however, can be contrasted to their firmer lateralization for peripheral activities such as handedness (Annett, 1976) and visually guided motor activities (Dean, Rattan, & Hua, in press). That is, while females are more bilateral for cognitive activities such as language, they have more established preference than do males for consistently using the same hand, ear, eye, etc., for related activities.

This paradoxical finding for females seems to be a function of the tenuous relationship between lateral preference patterns for peripheral activities and hemispheric specialization for language. Inferring hemispheric lateralization from lateral preference patterns from simple measures of handedness should be cautioned against. Dean (1982) has shown that lateral preference is a factorially complex variable and a function of the system (e.g., eyes, ears, hands, etc.) under study. Lateral preference patterns, then, may be more heuristically represented on a continuum from entirely left to entirely right instead of categorically as either left or right.

REFERENCES

Annett, M. (1976). Hand preference and the laterality of cerebral speech. *Cortex, 11*, 305–329.

Dean, R. S. (1981). Cerebral dominance and childhood learning disorders: Theoretical perspectives. *School Psychology Review, 10*, 373–380.

Dean, R. S. (1982). Assessing patterns of lateral preference. *Clinical Neuropsychology, 4*, 124–128.

Dean, R. S. (1984). Functional lateralization of the brain. *Journal of Special Education, 18*, 239–256.

Dean, R. S., & Hua, M. S. (1982). Laterality effects in cued auditory asymmetries. *Neuropsychologia, 20*, 685–690.

Dean, R. S., Rattan, G., & Hua, M. S. (in press). Patterns of lateral preference: An American-Chinese comparison. *Neuropsychologia*.

Geschwind, N. (1974). The anatomical basis of hemispheric differentiation. In S. J. Dimond & J. G. Beaumont (Eds.), *Hemisphere function in the human brain*. New York: Wiley.

Geschwind, N., & Levitsky, W. (1968). Human brain: Left-right asymmetries in temporal speech region. *Science, 161*, 186–187.

Gordon, H. W. (1970). Hemispheric asymmetries in the perception of musical cords. *Cortex, 6*, 387–398.

Gordon, H. W. (1974). Auditory specialization of the right and left hemispheres. In M. Kinsbourne & W. L. Smith (Eds.), *Hemispheric disconnection and cerebral function*. Springfield, IL: Thomas.

Hecaen, H. (1981). Apraxias. In S. B. Filskov & T. J. Boll (Eds.), *Handbook of clinical neuropsychology*. New York: Wiley.

Kimura, D. (1967). Functional asymmetry of the brain in dichotic listening. *Cortex, 3*, 163–178.

Kimura, D., & Durnsford, M. (1974). Normal studies on the function of the right hemisphere in vision. In S. J. Dimond & J. G. Beaumont (Eds.), *Hemisphere function in the human brain*. London: Elek Scientific.

Kolata, G. B. (1979). Sex hormones and brain development. *Science, 205*, 985–987.

Levy, J. (1973). Lateral specialization of the human brain: Behavioral manifestations and possible evolutionary basis. In J. A. Kriger (Ed.), *The biology of behavior*. Corvallis, OR: Oregon State University Press.

Marcel, T., & Rajan, P. (1975). Lateral specialization of recognition of words and faces in good and poor readers. *Neuropsychologia, 13*, 489–497.

Penfield, W., & Roberts, L. (1959). *Speech and brain mechanisms*. Princeton, NJ: Princeton University Press.

Rattan, G., & Dean, R. S. (in press). Cerebral dominance. In C. R. Reynolds & L. Mann (Eds.), *Encyclopedia of special education: A reference for the education of the handicapped and other exceptional children and youth*. New York: Wiley.

Speery, R. W. (1974). Lateral specialization in the surgically separated hemispheres. In F. O. Schmitt & F. G. Worden (Eds.), *The neurosciences: Third study program*. New York: Wiley.

Speery, R. W., Gazzaniga, M. S., & Bogen, J. H. (1969). Interhemispheric relationships: The neocortical commissures: Syndromes of hemisphere disconnection. In P. Vinken & G. W. Bruyn (Eds.), *Handbook of clinical neurology (Vol. 4)*. New York: Wiley.

Wada, J. A., & Rasmussen, T. (1960). Intracarotid injection of sodium amytal for lateralization of cerebral speech dominance: Experimental and clinical observation. *Journal of Neurosurgery, 17*, 266–282.

Witelson, S. F. (1976). Abnormal right hemisphere specialization in developmental dyslexia. In R. M. Knights & D. F. Bakker (Eds.), *Neuropsychology of learning disorders: Theoretical approaches*. Baltimore, MD: University Park Press.

GURMAL RATTAN
*Indiana University of
Pennsylvania*

RAYMOND S. DEAN
*Ball State University
Indiana University School
of Medicine*

CEREBRAL DOMINANCE
LEFT BRAIN-RIGHT BRAIN

HEMOPHILIA AND SPECIAL EDUCATION

Hemophilia ("bleeder's disease") is an hereditary disorder of the blood clotting process caused by an inadequacy of certain coagulation factors within the blood. The deficiency may be in one or more of the 10 blood plasma proteins required for normal clotting. Hemophilia may be classified as severe, moderate, or mild based on the degree of factor deficiency, but actual bleeding episodes will vary in affected persons. The disorder is genetically transmitted in a sex-linked recessive pattern from mothers to male offspring, accounting for 85 to 90% of all cases. In rare instances, girls may have other forms of the condition. (Cartwright, Cartwright, & Ward, 1984; Lindemann, 1981).

While once almost always a life-threatening condition, medical advances in the last 25 years have significantly reduced morbidity. Technological and philosophical changes in medical treatment now allow many hemophiliacs to prevent or recover rapidly from bleeding episodes and enjoy increased freedom of activity, including regular attendance at school (Baum, 1982).

Evidence indicates that children with hemophilia require mainstreamed educational opportunity. School achievement is at risk only as the result of possible school absences and the debilitating effects of pain associated with the swelling of tissues and joints. Major school modifications may be required in transportation, mobility, and physical education activities. Maintenance of normalized school involvement to the greatest extent possible is essential for educational and psychosocial development (Walker & Jacobs, 1984).

The emotional adjustment of the child with hemophilia is of central concern to special education. Low self-esteem, delays in masculine identification, denial, prolonged immaturity, and depression characterize the emotional development of many hemophiliacs. The psychological implications of the disorder are particularly important for the preschool, early childhood, and adolescent patient, and for the family. In the early childhood period (ages 4 to 8), the hemophiliac experiences the limitations imposed by the condition; these include the inability to engage in many physical and exploratory activities important for both learning and social adjustment (Cerreto, 1986). Possible special educational opportunities for limited physical participation or the presentation of equivalent educational activities may be desirable.

The adolescent with hemophilia must face the usual emotional stress of that period with the complications of a chronic disorder, including its implication of lifelong restrictions. Its limitations on physical activity, and the potential danger of using alcohol or drugs that may interact with medication. Concentrated emotional guidance and support is fundamental to the adolescent hemophiliac (Eisenberg, Sutkin, & Jansen, 1984; Lindemann, 1981).

The role of the special educator is seen primarily as maintaining the child in the regular program with support and resource assistance if necessary, as helping the classroom teacher bridge periods of absence, and as promoting home-school contact to offer support and relief to the parents of children with hemophilia.

REFERENCES

Baum, D. D. (Ed.). (1982). *The human side of exceptionality*. Baltimore, MD: University Park.

Cartwright, G. P., Cartwright, C. A., & Ward, M. J. (1984). *Educating special learners* (2nd ed.). Belmont, CA: Wadsworth.

Cerreto, M. C. (1986). Developmental issues in chronic illness: Implications and applications. *Topics in Early Childhood Special Education, 5*, 4.

Eisenberg, M. G., Sutkin, L. C., & Jansen, M. A. (Eds.). (1984). *Chronic illness and disability through the life span: Effects on self and family*. New York: Springer.

Lindemann, J. E. (1981). *Psychological and behavioral aspects of physical disability*. New York: Plenum.

Walker, D. K., & Jacobs, F. H. (1984). Chronically ill children in school. *Peabody Journal of Education, 61*, 28–74.

RONALD S. LENKOWSKY
*Hunter College, City University
of New York*

**ATTITUDES TOWARD HANDICAPPED
FAMILY RESPONSE TO A HANDICAPPED CHILD**

HEREDITY

Heredity refers to the phenomenon of progeny being biologically similar to their parents. Genetics is the science or study of heredity; it includes the study of the variation of inherited characteristics. Genetics has shown that units called genes, which store information and control heredity, are transmitted from parent to progeny during the reproductive process. These genes interact with each other and with the environment to produce distinctive characteristics.

Genetics is a relatively recent science with most discoveries occurring in the twentieth century. Advances in genetics since 1950 have dramatically increased our understanding of phenomena such as the origin of life, the structure of living material, and evolution. The application of genetic theory has yielded a better understanding of certain human diseases, a clearer picture of the nature versus nurture controversy, and improvements in plant and animal breeding (Cavalli-Sforza, 1977).

Gregor Mendel, who is credited with founding the science of genetics, discovered that hereditary traits are controlled by units (genes) that are independent of each other and transmitted separately from parents to offspring. Each progeny contains one set of genes from each parent, and thus possesses two genes for each of the thousands of characteristics present (except for sex-linked characteristics). For example, the ABO blood groups in humans are determined by three forms of a gene, A, B, and O. A and B are codominant and both are dominant to O. Possible combinations of these three forms produce the four different blood groups in the following manner: combinations AA and AO produce type A; combinations BB and BO produce type B; combination AB produces type AB; and combination OO produces type O. The recombinations of the different forms (alleles) of a gene increase substantially the variations present in sexually reproducing organisms.

The study of human genetics has advanced our understanding of inherited defects and diseases in humans. Many inherited defects and diseases result from the presence of an abnormal form of a gene. The defective genes produce abnormal substances that do not function properly. In some cases, a single abnormal gene is sufficient to produce an abnormal characteristic (a dominant disorder). In other cases, the gene from both parents must be abnormal for the defect to be expressed (a recessive disorder). The determination of the genetic cause of a defect has, in some situations, led to corrective treatment. Phenylketonuria (PKU) is the best known example.

Medical advances have led to the control of many infectious and other types of human diseases. As genetic knowledge increases, diseases previously not recognized as such have been found to have a substantial genetic basis. McKusick's (1983) catalog of human inheritance lists thousands of human traits, many of which are genetic diseases of medical importance. Behavioral traits such as schizophrenia intelligence, and special talents, are but a few of the traits shown to have a definite genetic component. These and many other traits are affected by environmental factors. The environmental-gene interactions that occur are complex and poorly understood. Further elucidation of these factors will provide a basis for a better and more complete treatment of some human diseases (Hartl, 1985).

Genetic studies of populations, organisms, and the molecular structure and function of DNA have determined that mutations (changes in DNA) are the ultimate source of the variability in organisms. Generally speaking, genes are transmitted unchanged from one generation to the next. However, spontaneous mutations of genes occur at a very low frequency, and it has been shown that different genes have different spontaneous mutation rates. Certain agents, called mutagens, cause a gene to change structure (mutate) and dramatically increase the mutation rate. Examples of mutagens are ionizing radiation from radioactive materials and X-rays, nitrous acid, acridine dyes (such as acridine orange), and ultraviolet light (Strickberger, 1985). Most mutations are deleterious and, when expressed in an organism, render it less fit to survive. A small percentage, however, are neutral or positive in effect, and are passed from generation to generation thus increasing variability. The determination that populations of organisms change over time because of environmental forces acting on the inherent variation provided by mutations (and shuffled by hereditary processes) has filled one of the major gaps in the theory of evolution proposed by Darwin (Parkin, 1979).

REFERENCES

Cavalli-Sforza, L. L. (1977). *Elements of human genetics* (2nd ed.). California: Benjamin.

Hartl, D. L. (1985). *Our uncertain heritage: Genetics and human diversity* (2nd ed.). New York: Harper & Row.

McKusick, V. A. (1983). *Mendelian inheritance in man* (6th ed.). Baltimore, MD: Johns Hopkins University Press.

Parkin, D. T. (1979). *An introduction to evolutionary genetics*. Baltimore, MD: University Park Press.

Strickberger, M. W. (1985). *Genetics* (3rd ed.). New York: Macmillan.

JAMES F. MERRITT
*University of North Carolina,
Wilmington*

CONGENITAL DISORDERS PHENYLKETONURIA

HERPES SIMPLEX I AND II

Although clinically and pathologically described since 100 AD, herpesvirus hominus (HVH) was not located until the 1920s; the existence of two antigenic types was not known until the 1960s; and genital herpes was not recognized as a venereal disease until the late 1960s. In the past, infection above and below the waist have generally been attributed to oral herpes (HVH-1) and genital herpes (HVH-2), respectively. However, the site of the infection does not always point to the particular type of herpes; both types now appear in both the genital and oral areas. Increased frequency of oral genital sex play may be responsible for the spread of location (Bahr, 1978).

Genital herpes is a highly contagious and prevalent venereal disease characterized by the appearance of pus-containing sores in the genital region. Twenty million Americans (Eastman, 1983) and as much as 30% of the young, sexually active population (Hastings, 1983) may have genital herpes. With society's changing mores regarding sexual activity outside of marriage, increasing numbers of sexual partners, and increasing acceptance of oral sex, the number of people, including adolescents, with genital manifestations of both genital and oral herpes will probably remain high. Genital herpes has serious effects on both affected individuals and their offspring.

The transfer of genital herpes usually occurs through genital or oral-genital contact. Autoinoculation from infected to uninfected areas of the body commonly occurs through touching the infected area during masturbation, washing, or inspection (Himell, 1981). Inanimate objects such as toilet seats, towels, and medical equipment are generally believed not to contribute to the spread (Lukas & Corey, 1977). However, the herpes virus may survive for up to 72 hours on inanimate items such as clothing, towels, toilet seats, and medical equipment (Eastman, 1983).

Active infection begins on average 6 days after exposure (range 2 to 20 days) and lasts approximately 3 weeks, with symptoms most severe between days 10 and 14. Once in the person, the virus can be reactivated with symptoms lasting 10 to 21 days. The duration of subsequent infections is generally shorter and less painful. Patients experience an average of four recurrences a year (Himell, 1981).

Genital and oral herpes have been linked with carcinoma of the cervix and lip, respectively. In addition, the occurrence of spontaneous abortion during the first trimester of pregnancy is three times greater in women who have genital herpes (Naib, Nahmias, Josey, & Wheeler, 1970).

Friendship and Family Living Concerns

Adolescents with genital herpes are frequently concerned about transmitting the disease to close friends or family members. This may be a genuine concern. However, careful and precise hygienic methods usually prevent spreading the infection. The herpes victim should thoroughly clean bathroom facilities after using them. During periods when the disease is active or their genital sores are at the weeping stage, victims should not bathe with others in hot tubs or sit on edges of hot tubs and swimming pools.

Because of possible recurrences of infection, genital herpes victims sometimes fear that family members and friends will learn about their plight. If victims understand that direct and intimate sexual contact is the primary mode of transmission, these fears may be reduced.

Oral Acyclovir Treatment

Recently the U.S. Food and Drug Administration has approved treatment of herpes through the oral use of the antiviral drug acyclovir. One study (Reichman et al., 1984) has shown that patients who received acyclovir after the onset of a recurrent episode showed decreased duration of virus shedding, time to crust, and time to lesion healing relative to those receiving a placebo. However, acyclovir and placebo groups did not differ in duration of itching and pain or in duration of subsequent recurrence. Further, the two groups did not differ in time to next recurrence, suggesting that acyclovir therapy does not affect the latent state. Although oral acyclovir suppresses genital herpes in patients with frequent recurrences, drug resistance is a potential problem. The long-term safety of oral acyclovir is not known. Unfortunately, acyclovir is expensive, costing $15 to $55 to treat each recurrence.

Sexual Concerns

Having genital herpes does not mean that victims are always infectious; appropriate care can minimize the possibility of transmitting the disease to sexual partners. Prevention should begin with the prodrome, the tingling or itching sensation that many victims have several hours or days before sores are seen. The prodrome state may be infectious itself, and should be thought of as the beginning of the contagious period. Therefore, no oral-genital or genital sexual intercourse should occur from the start of the prodrome to the completion of the healing process as indicated by the disappearance of lesions. Condoms do not prevent the transmission of the disease during an outbreak because the virus can pass through pores in the condom.

Incidence of cervical herpes has dramatically increased. Females are generally not aware that they have the disease until a gynecological examination has been performed. Since the cervix contains few nerve endings, the victim does not experience the discomfort usually associated with genital herpes. A vaginal discharge may occur; this usually motivates the woman to seek medical attention. Since these victims do not experience the prodrome or discomfort, they may be unaware that they are having a recurrence. At the first signs of sores on the cervix, restriction of sexual behavior becomes necessary. Women can be taught self-pelvic exam by a health care provider to enable them to recognize cervical lesions. Also, female victims should be aware that they can spread the virus to the cervix during outbreaks if they use tampons.

Herpes victims also should be aware that having the disease does not immunize against reinfection, as is frequently the case with other diseases. Thus a herpes victim can be reinfected by having sexual relations with a partner who is experiencing a genital herpes attack.

Psychological Consequences

Herpes can have serious psychological consequences, especially for adolescents. Luby (1981) has noted a sequence of responses to genital herpes: (1) shock and emotional numbing; (2) search for an immediate cure; (3) development of feelings of isolation and loneliness and fear that companionship, sexual relations, and children are not in one's future; (4) anger, which can reach homicidal proportions, directed toward the person who is believed to be the transmitter of the disease (at this point fear generalizes and anxiety may result); (5) a "leper" effect, accompanied by depression, which may deepen with time and recurrences. Common feelings at this point include hopelessness, guilt, unworthiness, and self-hatred. Some people become suicidal. Finally, developing herpes can make manifest any latent psychopathology.

Not all victims are emotionally affected, but for many adolescents, it can become a psychologically crippling experience. Individual counseling or membership in a herpes self-help group may be helpful. Herpes self-help groups generally work to achieve several goals, including relief from isolation and loneliness, establishment of a new social network, provision of mentors, and ventilation of rage. If depression with sleep disorder, loss of appetite, psychotic symptoms, or suicidal ideation occur, a psychiatric referral may be required (Luby, 1981).

Effects on Offspring

Genital herpes may have devastating effects on affected newborns. Although frequently classified with other maternal infections such as rubella, as in the TORCH complex, herpes generally affects newborns during birth rather than prenatally, Neonates may contract the infection during birth as they pass through an infected maternal genital tract or contact the virus through ruptured fetal-maternal membranes. Risk of infection of newborns during birth is higher among women who had primary infection during pregnancy or lesions present at delivery than among mothers with recurrent herpes during pregnancy and no lesions at delivery.

Symptoms of infection, which may or may not include the presence of vesicles, appear a few days after birth. The severity ranges from mild skin infection to death. Common symptoms include irritability, jaundice, and respiratory distress. About 50% of affected infants will show signs of neurologic damage, including seizures, palsy, and coma. Encephalitis and other potentially lethal disorders may develop. A large percentage of affected newborns die; most survivors show sequelae such as mental retardation, epilepsy, and sensory impairments (Douglas, 1985). In order to avoid infecting newborns, known affected mothers with an active infection generally deliver via cesarean section.

Rarely, herpes infection can be spread prenatally to the embryo or fetus. The newborn will show signs common to the TORCH complex, including microcephaly, microphthalmia, chorioretinitis, and seizures (Douglas, 1985).

Teachers, coaches, and others who work with students who have herpes can help by being empathic listeners and having an understanding of the disease that enables them to dispel myths and untruths regarding herpes. Also, they can help students develop a realistic view of their situation by stressing that the disease can be medically managed and is not fatal.

Adolescents' self-esteem can be deeply affected. If this occurs, referral to the school's guidance counselor or family physician should be arranged. Suicide cannot be ruled out. The teacher or coach should not hesitate in making a referral to the guidance counselor or to a mental health professional if emotional disturbances are noted. Remind the victims that they need to isolate active lesions, not themselves.

Assistance can be found at a local chapter of HELP. If there is no local phone number, contact the National Herpes Resource Center, PO Box 100, Palo Alto, CA 94302.

REFERENCES

Bahr, J. (1978, January/February). Herpesvirus hominis type 2 in women and newborns. *American Journal of Maternal Child Nursing*, pp. 16–18.

Douglas, R. G., Jr. (1985). Herpes simplex virus infections. In J. G. Wyngaarden & L. H. Smith, Jr. (Eds.), *Cecil Textbook of medicine* (17th ed., pp. 1714–1717). Philadelphia: Saunders.

Eastman, P. (1983). Genital herpes also spread by non-sexual contacts. *Nutrition Health Review, 27*, 10.

Hastings, W. (1983). Providing hope for herpes patients. *Psychology Today, 14*, 28.

Himell, K. (1981, November/December). Genital herpes: The need for counseling. *Journal of General Nursing*, pp. 446–447.

Luby, E. (1981, December). *Presentation at the National Genital Herpes Symposium*, Philadelphia. *The Helper, 3*(4), 2–3.

Lukas, J., & Corey, L. (1977). Genital herpes simplex virus infection: An overview. *Nurse Practitioner, 7*, 7–10.

Naib, Z., Nahmias, A., Josey, W., & Wheeler, J. (1970). Association of maternal genital herpetic—infection with spontaneous abortion. *Obstetrics & Gynecology, 35*, 260–263.

Reichman, R. C., Badger, G. J., Mertz, G. J., Corey, L., Richman, D. D., Connor, J. D., Redfield, D., Savoia, M. C., Oxman, M. N., Bryson, Y., Tyrrell, D. L., Portnoy, J., Creigh-Kirk, T., Keney, R. E., Ashikaga, T., & Dolin, R. (1984). Treatment of recurrent genital herpes simplex infections with oral acyclovir. *Journal of the American Medical Association, 251*(16), 2103–2107.

C. SUE LAMB
GINGA COLCOUGH
ROBERT T. BROWN
JANE SPARKS
University of North Carolina, Wilmington

DEPRESSION
TORCH COMPLEX

HESS, ROBERT D. (1920–   )

Robert D. Hess received his BA at the University of California, Berkeley in 1947. He obtained his PhD in devel-

opmental psychology at the University of Chicago in 1950. He is presently with the School of Education at Stanford University.

Hess's major interests have focused on the relationships of teachers who interact with young children's home life, external reality, and inner life within the atmosphere of the classroom. Hess feels the future of any society lies in its ability to train or socialize the young, and that the cultural distance and status differential between home and classroom are considerable (Hess & Croft, 1972). To be effective, the school must find ways to deal with those subcultural influences on the learning and teaching climate of the classroom. The current growth of programs in early education and the large-scale involvement of the schools and federal government is not a transitory concern; it represents a fundamental shift in the relative roles and potential influence of the two major socializing institutions of the society, the family and the school (Hess & Bear, 1968). Experimentation and social experimentation are badly needed.

Some of Hess's major works include *Teachers of Young Children*; *Early Education: Current Theory, Research, and Action*; and *Family Worlds: A Psychosocial Approach to Family Life*.

REFERENCES

Hess, R. D., & Bear, R. M. (1968). *Early education: Current theory, research, and action*. Chicago: Adline.

Hess, R. D., & Croft, D. J. (1972). *Teachers of young children*. Boston: Houghton Mifflin.

ELIZABETH JONES
Texas A&M University

HETEROPHORIA

See STRABISMUS, EFFECT ON LEARNING.

HEWETT, FRANK M. (1927–   )

Frank M. Hewett received his MA in 1958, and PhD in 1961, in clinical psychology from the University of California, Los Angeles (UCLA). He remained at UCLA as principal of the Neuropsychiatric Institute School until 1964. He then joined the faculty in the Graduate School of Education, gaining his present status of professor of education and psychiatry in 1971.

Hewett's work has mainly dealt with the emotionally disturbed population, yet his contribution to the area of learning disabilities has been described as vital (Haring & Bateman, 1977, p. 47). Instead of entering the debate on the definition or etiology of learning disabilities, Hewett has sought educational strategies that allow a wider portion of public school children to learn effectively and efficiently. From a generalist orientation, he developed a sequence of educational tasks that delineate six levels of learning competence (Hewett & Taylor, 1980). These levels of learning competence are a synthesis of work on developmental stages done by Kephart, Piaget, Maslow, Freud, and others. Hewett's competence levels were operations directly related to classroom learning (Haring & Bateman, 1977). Hewett's principal publications include *Education of Exceptional Learners* and *The Emotionally Disturbed Child in the Classroom: The Orchestration of Success.*

REFERENCES

Haring, N. G., & Bateman, B. (1977). *Teaching the learning disabled child.* Englewood Cliffs, NJ: Prentice-Hall.

Hewett, F. M., & Forness, S. (1984). *Education of exceptional learners* (3rd ed.). Boston: Allyn & Bacon.

Hewett, F. M., & Taylor, F. (1980). *The emotionally disturbed child in the classroom: The orchestration of success* (2nd ed.). Boston: Allyn & Bacon.

ELAINE FLETCHER-JANZEN
Texas A&M University

HIGHER EDUCATION CONSORTIUM FOR SPECIAL EDUCATION (HECSE)

The Higher Education Consortium for Special Education (HECSE) is an independent, nonprofit membership organization of institutions of higher education that maintain doctoral programs in special education. Founded in 1968, HECSE provides its approximately 30 member institutions with a national vehicle for program advocacy, information dissemination, and collaborative personnel training.

Membership in the HECSE is open to those universities that prepare doctoral-level special education professionals and maintain programs in at least two areas of graduate-level specialization. The HECSE members annually elect a consortium president who oversees meetings and the development of professional activities related to the improvement of doctoral training programs. The national office of HECSE transfers to the employing institution of each successive consortium president.

The HECSE (1984) has articulated a mission of advocacy and service on behalf of member institutions through the following activities:

Representing the interests and positions of member institutions through the preparation of policy papers;

testifying before federal and state deliberative bodies.

Upgrading the administrative and decision-making skills of special education leadership personnel.

Coordinating with other national organizations and professional groups to effect improvements in the special education service delivery system, particularly emphasizing advances in special education leadership training.

REFERENCE

Higher Education Consortium for Special Education. (1984). *Indicators of quality in special education doctoral programs.* Columbia, MO: Author.

GEORGE JAMES HAGERTY
Stonehill College

HIGH-INCIDENCE HANDICAPS

Although often used synonomously, the terms incidence and prevalence are not equivalent and therefore interchangeable use is erroneous. Marozas, May, and Lehman (1980) note that incidence represents new cases during some specified period of time (frequently one year), while prevalence denotes the total number of individuals affected at any particular point in time. Hypothetically, a school system might find 75 previously unidentified cases of learning disabilities during a specific academic year. If 150 previously identified cases are then added, prevalence is 225. This total may then be used to specify a prevalence rate; if the school system contains 10,000 students the prevalence rate is 225/10,000, or about 2%.

Prevalence and incidence need not reflect the same proportions of the population. For example, if an effective preventive technique could be found to prevent the occurrence of a disabling condition (but not remediate it), the incidence rate (new cases) aproaches zero. However, the prevalence rate would fall off more gradually since existing cases would continue. The terms are related but distinct. Blurring the distinction can result in the development of inaccurate statistics or the erroneous interpretation of statistics.

The expression high-incidence handicapped refers to an exceptionally large proportion of a particular type of exceptionality during some particular period of time relative to the incidence of other conditions. The expression high incidence is arbitrarily defined, however, as no specific numerical proportion is required. Unfortunately, the special education literature provides mention of both high-incidence and high-prevalence handicap; therefore, the reader must keep this distinction in mind.

High-incidence handicapped can only be meaningful

when thought of in connection with other handicapping conditions. These conditions are often referred to as categories of exceptionality. Currently, the U.S. Department of Education accepts 10 categories of handicapping conditions, although individual states often alter these basic categories. Garrett and Brazil (1979), for example, identified 13 categories used across the 50 states. Most states did not recognize all 13 categories, and two states recognized no multiple categories of exceptionality, preferring instead to offer special education to children in need of special assistance.

The recognized incidence (and for that matter prevalence) of exceptional students and of specific categories of exceptionality is a much debated topic. Several factors are responsible for the often divergent estimates. Principal among these factors are the relative vagueness of some definitions, the use of varied definitions across states, the level of emphasis placed on identification, imprecision in identification practices, and the movement of individuals from one category to another. Further, the incidence of some handicaps appears to vary over time (Algozzine & Korinek, 1985), possibly as a result of the particular handicap's social acceptability.

Despite difficulties in establishing precise incidence rates, several categories possess generally accepted levels that represent a significant proportion of the school-aged handicapped population. Approximately 11% (Algozzine & Korinek, 1985) of the total school-aged population now receives special education services in the public schools. Some handicapping conditions (e.g., visual and hearing impairments) represent a long-standing pattern of low incidence rates. Others, notably language disorders, learning disabilities, mental retardation, and behavioral (emotional) *disorders* occur in sufficient numbers to be considered high incidence.

Strictly, the concepts of low incidence or high incidence might have little more than a descriptive capacity for denoting the likelihood (probability) of occurrence. There are, however, at least two fundamental considerations that will help the value of the term. The first is the rapid expansion of the number of high-incidence handicaps. Ysseldyke and Algozzine (1984) suggest that a high-incidence group might include the learning disabled, the mentally retarded, the behaviorally (emotionally) handicapped, and the language disordered. A high-incidence group constituted in this way would represent in excess of 90% of the handicapped students served in the public schools. Algozzine and Korinek (1985) reached a similar conclusion. However, the authors also noted that of the categories included in high-incidence exceptionalities, learning disabilities was by far the most rapidly expanding and largest category, and emotional disturbance the smallest. Within the high-incidence handicapped group, both learning disabilities and emotional disorders are rapidly expanding, learning disabilities phenomenally. Two are decreasing (mental retardation and speech-language disordered). Yet overall incidence of high-incidence handicaps is increasing at a rate in sharp contrast to the near stable levels of the low-incidence handicapped. Current statistics and projections of future trends demonstrate the group's influence on the special education service delivery system.

Beyond the sheer size of the high-incidence group, a second important matter, that of programming through combining several traditional high-incidence categories, has emerged. Sometimes this is viewed as noncategorical special education, though that seems to be a misnomer (Hallahan & Kauffman, 1982) as most special educators do not mean to imply the deletion of all categories of exceptionality. Lilly (1979), for example, presented a limited noncategorical or high-incidence approach that included the educable mentally retarded, the behaviorally (emotionally) disordered, and the learning disabled. In Lilly's view, the prevalence of the groups, the identification techniques that are used, the behavioral characteristics, and the instructional strategies are sufficiently similar to make further nosological classification unnecessary. In stressing the use of a data-based instructional model, Lilly observed little to encourage the continuation of traditional categorical classification and programming for these groups. It should be noted that speech- and language-impaired individuals were not included in Lilly's (1979) proposal, presumably because the similarity of this category to the high-incidence group lies only in the matter of incidence/prevalence.

Miller and Davis (1982) generally found points of agreement with Lilly's (1979) position. Among the more convincing evidence was the observation of Connor (1976) that cross-categorical teacher education had gained momentum and the results of a survey by Belch (1979) that identified an increasing number of states offering cross-categorical (comprehensive) certification. Both trends may be interpreted as heightened interest in the viability of the high-incidence handicapped concept, although the majority of states continue to organize services in line with the traditional handicapping conditions.

REFERENCES

Algozzine, B., & Korinek, L. (1985). Where is special education for students with high prevalence handicaps going? *Exceptional Children, 51*, 388–394.

Belch, P. J. (1979). Toward noncategorical teacher certification in special education—Myth or reality? *Exceptional Children, 46*, 129–131.

Connor, F. P. (1976). The past is prologue: Teacher preparation in special education. *Exceptional Children, 42*, 366–378.

Garret, J. E., & Brazil, N. (1979). Categories used for identification and education of exceptional children. *Exceptional Children, 45*, 291–292.

Hallahan, D. P., & Kauffman, J. M. (1982). *Exceptional children: Introduction to special education* (2nd ed.). Englewood Cliffs, NJ: Prentice-Hall.

Lilly, M. S. (1979). *Children with exceptional needs*. New York: Holt.

Marozas, P. S., May, D. C., & Lehman, L. C. (1980). Incidence and prevalence: Confusion in need of clarification. *Mental Retardation, 18,* 229–230.

Miller, T. L., & Davis, E. E. (1982). The mildly handicapped: A rationale. In T. L. Miller & E. E. Davis (Eds.), *The mildly handicapped student* (pp. 3–16). New York: Grune & Stratton.

Ysseldyke, J. E., & Algozzine, B. (1984). *Introduction to special education*. Boston: Houghton Mifflin.

TED L. MILLER
*University of Tennessee,
Chattanooga*

**CATEGORICAL EDUCATION
LOW INCIDENCE HANDICAPS**

HIGH INTEREST–LOW VOCABULARY

High interest–low vocabulary refers to reading materials that have been designed to interest older students who have low vocabularies and low reading levels. Often, adolescents who have reading levels in the lower elementary grade levels become even more frustrated if given the reading books that have been designed for their reading levels. Such reading books can insult the adolescents since they are geared for the interest level of a third grader, not a ninth grader.

Many publishers have designed materials to deal with this problem. For example, the *Corrective Reading* series (Engelmann, et al., 1978) is designed for students from fourth to twelfth grade who have not developed adequate reading, decoding, and comprehension skills. The vocabulary introduced in these stories is very controlled. Only word patterns that have been taught and practiced are included in the lessons (low vocabulary). More important, however, the interest level of the stories is geared to the older reader; the topics covered do not insult the older reader by assuming his or her interests are similar to those of a third grader.

Other published materials are also designed to be used as supplements for the older, lower reader's instructional program. Mercer and Mercer (1985) present a listing of 35 such materials, with corresponding reading grade levels and approximate interest grade levels. The *Pal Paperback Kits* (Xerox Education Publications) and the *Mystery Adventure Series* (Benefic Press) are two examples. These series, however, do not present as carefully sequenced phonetic skills as a linguistic basal reader series or *Corrective Reading* series previously mentioned.

REFERENCES

Engelmann, S., Johnson, G., Hanner, S., Carnine, L., Meyers, L., Osborn, S., Haddox, P., Becker, W., Osborn, W., & Becker, J.

(1978). *Corrective reading program*. Chicago, IL: Science Research.

Mercer, C. D., & Mercer, A. R. (1985). *Teaching students with learning problems* (2nd ed.). Columbus, OH: Merrill.

THOMAS E. SCRUGGS
MARGO A. MASTROPIERI
Purdue University

**READING DISORDERS
READING IN THE CONTENT AREAS
READING REMEDIATION**

HIGH RISK

The phrase high risk refers to a baby at risk for the development of a handicapping condition owing to factors present prior to conception, during pregnancy, delivery, or the first three years of life. Presently, couples contemplating having a baby take a 3 to 5% chance of producing a high-risk child (Deppe, Sherman, & Engel, 1981). This percentage can be reduced by developing awareness of factors that can place a child at risk and taking steps to minimize their impact.

The first set of factors that place a child at risk occurs prior to conception and is hereditary in nature. Hereditary factors include the genetic history of both parents. Specifically, parents may produce a high-risk child if either has a mentally or physically handicapped child in the extended family; is a known or suspected carrier of a chromosome abnormality; is black or of Jewish or Mediterranean descent. In addition, hereditary factors include previous miscarriages during the first trimester of pregnancy and a maternal age greater than 35 at the time of anticipated birth. Couples falling into any of these categories may seek genetic counseling to estimate the risk of occurrence of a genetic disorder, understand options available for dealing with the risk, decide on a course of action, and increase their knowledge of diagnosis, prognosis, and management techniques available.

The second set of factors increasing the probability of producing a high-risk child occurs during pregnancy. Specific factors include maternal malnutrition, use of alcohol or drugs, smoking, and exposure to diseases. Maternal malnutrition has been related to mental retardation, cerebral palsy, and learning disabilities. Use of alcohol during pregnancy has been linked to mental retardation, joint distortions, facial abnormalities, and congenital heart disease (Furey, 1982). Medicine purchased over the counter or by prescription may adversely influence the health of a baby. For example, handicapped babies were born to women using thalidomide. Similarly, there is an increased incidence of vaginal cancer in young women whose mothers used diethylstilbestrol to prevent miscarriages. Other drugs, such as heroin, have been linked to an increased incidence of low birth weight, intrauterine growth, retardation, and prematurity (Crain,1984). Smoking has been associated with smaller birth weight and may be a factor in sudden infant death syndrome. Exposure to diseases such as German measles is associated with visual impairments, hearing impairments, and heart disease. Couples anticipating the birth of a child can take precautionary steps to reduce the chance of producing a high-risk baby. These steps include proper diet, use of medicines only under the supervision of a physician, limited consumption of alcohol, and no cigarette or drug use.

The third set of factors associated with the birth of high-risk babies occurs during the perinatal period. These factors include the use of an anesthesia, hemorrhage, knotting of the umbilical cord, and shock owing to loss of blood in the mother (Cartwright, Cartwright, & Ward, 1984). All of these factors may cause fetal anoxia (lack of oxygen), resulting in mental retardation, cerebral palsy, or convulsive disorders.

Finally, factors placing a child at high risk may occur from birth to 3 years of age and include physical trauma, deprivation, and severe infection. Physical traumas such as accidents may result in brain damage or a physical handicap. Similarly, children who suffer nonaccidental injuries such as child abuse may be brain damaged, physically handicapped, or emotionally disturbed. Deprivation includes physical neglect (e.g., inadequate levels of medical attention, food, clothing, supervision, and housing) and emotional neglect (an environment nonconducive to a child's learning and development). Severe infections such as meningitis, rheumatic fever, or encephalitis frequently result in hearing impairments, heart damage, or convulsive disorders. Many of the factors placing a child at risk from birth to three years of age can be controlled by parents or professionals. Careful supervision of young children, adequate physical and emotional care, and prompt medical attention can minimize the impact of high-risk factors during the first three years of life.

REFERENCES

Cartwright, G. P., Cartwright, C. A., & Ward, M. E. (1984). *Educating special learners*. Belmont, CA: Wadsworth.

Crain, L. S. (1984). Prenatal causes of atypical development. In M. J. Hanson (Ed.), *Atypical infant development* (pp. 27–55). Baltimore, MD: University Park Press.

Deppe, P. R., Sherman, J. L., & Engel, S. (1981). *The high risk child: A guide for concerned parents*. New York: Macmillan.

Furey, E. M. (1982). The effects of alcohol on the fetus. *Exceptional Children, 49*, 30–34.

MAUREEN A. SMITH
Pennsylvania State University

HIGH-RISK REGISTRY

A high-risk registry is based on the premise that early identification of infants and young children with handicaps is critical to the success of an early intervention treatment program. The registry contains factors associated with an increased risk for the development of a handicapping condition (Feinmesser & Tell, 1974). These factors typically include birth weight of less than 1500 gr; billirubin level of less than 20 mg/100 ml of serums; exposure to or the presence of bacterial infections such as meningitis; exposure to or the presence of nonbacterial infections such as rubella or herpes; multiple apneic spells; and 5-minute Apgar scores less than 5.

The Apgar score (Apgar, 1953) is a simple measure of neonatal risk routinely obtained during the medical assessment of a newborn infant 1 and 5 minutes after delivery. The infant's heart rate, respiration, reflex irritability, muscle tone, and skin color are rated on the basis of 0, 1, or 2. For example, a heart rate between 100 and 140 beats per minute is rated a 2, while a heart rate less than 100 beats per minute is rated 1; no heartbeat is rated 0. A composite score reflects the infant's ability to adapt to the postnatal environment (Gorski, 1984).

The staff at a hospital participating in a high-risk registry typically completes a card after each live birth. Information regarding birth weight, billirubin levels, the presence of bacterial or nonbacterial infections, apneic spells, and Apgar scores is provided by the obstetric staff or the attending physician. Maternal interviews provide additional information regarding exposure to bacterial or nonbacterial infections and any parental concern for the health of the baby. The presence of any one of these factors tentatively identifies an infant as at risk and warrants referral for additional evaluation at 6, 9, and 12 months of age. If during subsequent evaluation, the baby no longer displays any abnormal characteristics, and if parents express no concern, the baby's name is removed from the files. If subsequent evaluation does indicate the presence of a handicap, the parents are encouraged to pursue additional assessment, a medical evaluation, and a treatment program.

REFERENCES

Apgar, V. (1953). A proposal for a new method of resolution of the newborn infant. *Current Researchers in Anesthesia & Analgesia, 32*, 260–267.

Feinmesser, M., & Tell, L. (1974). Evaluation of methods for detecting hearing impairment in infancy and early childhood. In G. T. Mencher (Ed.), *Early identification of hearing loss* (pp. 102–113). Pratteln, Switzerland: Thur AG Offsetdruck.

Gorski, P. A. (1984). Infants at risk. In M. J. Hanson (Ed.), *Atypical infant development* (pp. 59–75). Baltimore, MD: University Park Press.

MAUREEN A. SMITH
Pennsylvania State University

EARLY EXPERIENCE AND CRITICAL PERIODS
EARLY IDENTIFICATION OF HANDICAPPED CHILDREN
HIGH RISK
INFANT STIMULATION
PREMATURITY/PRETERM

HISKEY-NEBRASKA TEST OF LEARNING

The Hiskey-Nebraska Test of Learning Aptitude (HNTLA) is individually administered to assess the learning aptitude of persons age 3 through 17. The test is appropriate for use with deaf and hard-of-hearing persons as well as those without sensory defects. The HNTLA is composed of 12 subtests; 3 of the 12 are administered to subjects of all ages; 5 are administered only to children under age 12; and 4 are administered only to students over age 11. Items are uniformly administered either in pantomime fashion or by verbal directions. Examinees respond to items motorically, by pointing to one of several response alternatives, drawing picture parts, or manipulating objects such as beads, colored sticks, picture cards, or wooden blocks. The type of tasks on the HNTLA range from memory for color sequences to puzzle completion, picture analogy, and spatial reasoning. The tasks administered to children ages 3 to 11 primarily involve short-term visual memory, perceptual organization, visual discrimination abilities, and freedom from distractibility. The tasks administered to older examinees primarily involve perceptual organization, visual discrimination abilities, and analogical reasoning.

An examinee's raw score is based on the median subtest performance and converted to a learning age (LA) if pantomimed directions were used or a mental age (MA) if verbal directions were used. Learning ages are based on norms for deaf children; MAs are based on norms for hearing children. By using norms tables, LAs and MAs can be converted to learning quotients and IQs respectively. The current edition of the HNTLA was normed in 1966 for hearing and deaf children. Reviewers have consistently noted the lack of more current reliability or validity for the test, but frequently acknowledge it as the best, and only appropriate, device available for the assessment of deaf children. It is a useful instrument for evaluating the intellectual functioning of children with language disorders.

REFERENCES

Bolton, B. F. (1978). Review of the Hiskey-Nebraska Test of Learning Aptitude. In O. K. Buros (Ed.), *The eighth mental measurements yearbook* (pp. 307–308). Highland Park, NJ: Gryphon.

Mira, M., & Larson, A. D. (1986). Review of the Hiskey-Nebraska Test of Learning Aptitude. In D. J. Keyser & R. C. Sweetland (Eds.), *Test critiques* (Vol. 3, pp. 331–339). Kansas City, MO: Test Corporation of America.

Newland, T. E. (1972). Review of the Hiskey-Nebraska Test of Learning Aptitude. In O. K. Buros (Ed.), *The seventh mental measurements yearbook* (pp. 738–740). Highland Park, NJ: Gryphon.

Salvia, J., & Ysseldyke, J. E. (1985). *Assessment in special and remedial education* (3rd. ed.). Boston: Houghton Mifflin.

GEORGE MCCLOSKEY
*American Guidance Service,
Circle Pines, Minnesota*

ASSESSMENT
INTELLIGENCE TESTING

HISPANIC HANDICAPPED

Hispanic students make up a large and growing segment of the school population. While they do not share a singular cultural tradition nor an identical linguistic code, these students who have ties to Mexico, South and Central America, and the Caribbean share a variety of common characteristics. Unfortunately, many of these characteristics place them at risk in America's schools. Many are poor, have limited proficiency in English, and are acculturated into a system of values and cognitive styles that may conflict with the dominant culture in schools. Owing, in part, to these characteristics, controversy has surrounded the delivery of special education services to these children. Specifically, the adequacy of assessment and intervention practices for handicapped Hispanic children are two issues that have received a great deal of attention.

Under PL 94-142, children are not to be identified as handicapped on the basis of socioeconomic, cultural, or linguistic differences. However, owing to these factors, many Hispanic pupils are referred, assessed, and ultimately placed in special education programs. Recent surveys by the Office of Civil Rights report that the percentage of students identified as learning disabled differs for Hispanic and white students (GAO Report, 1981). Although there are a variety of possible reasons for the differences in representation, one of the critical factors concerns the adequacy of assessment instruments and procedures to identify handicapped Hispanic children.

Tests are administered in schools for a number of purposes. In an effort to promote equality of categorization and placement, and to prevent bias or subjectivity, educational and psychological tests are used. However, uninformed and/or indiscriminate use and interpretation of these tests with many minority pupils can result in the incorrect identification of these youngsters as handicapped. For example, prior to any formal assessment to determine a handicapping condition, assessment staff are required to ascertain pupils' dominant language proficiency. Frequently, the language assessment scales (LAS) are administered by paraprofessionals with limited training in bilingual education, special education, or assessment. Despite the questionable nature of this assessment activity, these tests results are then used to determine the appropriateness of intervention and assessment procedures. Assuming language dominance is accurately identified, there remain a number of issues that influence the use of intellectual and achievement assessment data: specifically, tests as measures of competence versus performance and test content.

The first issue concerns the perception of intelligence test performance as an indicator of cognitive capacity (Bortner & Birch, 1970). Cognitive test results may be heavily influenced by the nature and content of previous formal and informal educational experiences (Sternberg, 1984). Unless previous educational experiences have been appropriate to the child, it is highly unlikely that assessment will provide an accurate indication of academic potential, although it may well be indicative of future academic performance. An example of the influence of educational context and learner characteristics may be found in the literature concerning cooperative versus competitive education. Students from minority groups tend to perform comparably to their nonminority peers in cooperative settings while demonstrating typical achievement discrepencies in competitive settings (Kagan, 1983).

The second assessment issue involves test content. A variety of nonverbal cognitive measures have been recommended for use with pupils with limited English proficiency. However, minority pupils' performance on these tests shows greater differences than in the verbal tests they were designed to replace (Jensen, 1982). While these tests do not require verbal output on the part of the examiner, investigators involved in the cross-cultural study of cognition have found that many of these performance-type tests have underlying verbal/language components that are not readily apparent but that have definite implications for test performance (Gallimore & Price-Williams, 1980). Different cultural groups may have different experiences, values, and perceptions of the tasks; these may influence an individual's motivation and orientation to the task. This would suggest that while within group comparisons of test performance might be possible, between group comparisons are likely to be faulty and deceptive.

Due to their unique ethnic, linguistic, and socioeconomic status, Hispanic handicapped children may also have instructional needs that differ from those of their peers. However, the capability of school districts to meet those needs is limited by such factors as lack of trained personnel in special and bilingual education, appropriate materials, and policies within state education agencies. Proponents of bilingual education claim that children who are not proficient in English need to receive instruction in their primary mode of communication to be able to maximize their learning. While this position is a basis for the bilingual instruction of many children, handicapped His-

panic youngsters have not been systematically included in specially designed programs for bilingual handicapped youngsters (Bergin, 1980).

A recent review by Chinn (1982) identified unique instructional programs used with culturally different handicapped children. One instructional approach for Hispanic handicapped pupils with limited English proficiency involves interfacing bilingual and special education programs to apply the intervention techniques inherent in those programs. The goal is to provide the needed cultural and linguistic emphasis as well as special instructional methods. Examples of exemplary bilingual-special education efforts include the Responsive Environment Program for Spanish American Children (REPSAC) in Clovis, New Mexico; the Psycholinguistic Learning Disabilities in Mexican American Students program in Coachella, California; Early On (for severely and multiply handicapped) in San Diego, California; and the Coordinated Services for Handicapped LESA Students in Houston, Texas.

Excellent guides to resources for intervention efforts, research, and training concerning Hispanic handicapped pupils include publications from the National Clearing House for Bilingual Education and The Council for Exceptional Children, Reston, Virginia.

Meeting the educational needs of handicapped Hispanic youngsters will require extensive study of the impact of cultural and linguistic factors on the cognitive functioning and socialization of these pupils in America's schools. Unfortunately, there is limited research information in these areas. As such, one of the critical problems is the lack of educational leadership personnel to engage in research and development efforts.

REFERENCES

Bergin, V. (1980). *Special education needs in bilingual programs.* National Clearinghouse for Billingual Education. Lanham, MD: Eagle One Graphics.

Bortner, M., & Birch, H. (1970). Cognitive capacity and cognitive competence. *American Journal of Mental Deficiency, 74,* 735–744.

Chinn, P. C. (1982). Curriculum development for culturally different exceptional children. In C. H. Thomas & J. L. Thomas (Eds.), *Billingual special education resource guide.* Phoenix, AZ: Oryx.

Gallimore, R., & Price-Williams, D. (1980). The cultural perspective. In B. K. Keogh (Ed.), *Advances in special education* (Vol. 2, pp. 165–192). Greenwich, CT: JAI.

Jensen, A. (1982). Reaction time and psychometric g. In H. J. Eysenck (Ed.), *A model for intelligence.* Berlin: Springer-Verlag.

Kagan, S. (1983). Cooperative learning and the handicapped Hispanic child. Paper presented at the 1983 Conference on Handicapped Hispanic Children, Texas A&M University, College Station.

Sternberg, R. J. (1984). What should intelligence tests test? Implications of a triarchic theory of intelligence for intelligence testing. *Educational Researcher*, 5–15.

DOUGLAS J. PALMER
ARTHUR HERNANDEZ
Texas A&M University

DIEGO GALLEGOS
Texas A&M University
San Antonio Independent
School District

ASSESSMENT
BILINGUAL EDUCATION
CULTURAL BIAS IN TESTS

HISTORY OF SPECIAL EDUCATION

Prehistoric societies, whose survival could depend on the fitness of each member, did not protect children who were born with defects, generally allowing them to die at birth or in infancy. Some ancient peoples, believing that physical deformities and mental disorders were the result of possession by demons, rejected, punished, or killed those who were afflicted. However, there is some evidence of handicapped persons being treated with kindness, or even revered as possessed of supernatural powers.

The ancient Greek and Roman societies gave us the first recorded attempts at the scientific understanding and treatment of disability in children. Some physicians and scholars in these cultures began to look on such conditions as treatable, and although infanticide was common, some efforts were made to preserve the lives of handicapped children.

In the Middle Ages, handicapped persons were often objects of amusement, and sometimes were used for entertainment. More often, however, they were derided, imprisoned, or even executed. During this period, the church began to foster humane care for handicapped people and to provide asylums for them. The Renaissance brought a greater belief in the value of human life, and laid the groundwork for the popular revolutions that later overthrew the domination of royalty in much of Europe and in America. Interest in educating handicapped children, then, grew out of the new humanism of the Renaissance, the belief in the worth of every individual, and the associated struggles for freedom for the common man.

Education of the Hearing Impaired

Special education, as the scientific study and education of exceptional children, can be said to have started about 1555 when a Spanish monk, Pedro Ponce de Leon (1520–1584), taught a small number of deaf children to read, write, and speak, and to master the academic subjects. Another Spaniard, Juan Pablo Bonet (1579–1629?), in 1620 wrote the first book on the education of the deaf, describing his methods, probably derived from those of Ponce de Leon, and setting forth a one-handed manual alphabet that provided the basis for the alphabet in use today.

In England in 1644, John Bulwer (1614–1684) published the first book in English on the education of the deaf. This was followed in 1680 by the most significant of the early books in English, *Didasopholus; or, the Deaf and Dumb Man's Tutor*, by George Dalgarno (1628?–1687). The author made the startling assertion that deaf people have as much capacity for learning as those who can hear, and outlined instructional methods that came to be widely used by subsequent educators.

The first permanent school for the deaf in Great Britain was established in 1767 in Edinburgh by Thomas Braidwood (1715–1806). Braidwood's school was successful from the beginning, and in 1783 he moved it to Hackney, near London, to draw students from the larger population of the London area. Braidwood's nephew and assistant, Joseph Watson (1765–1829), later established the first school in Great Britain for poor deaf children, in the London area. Braidwood's method combined manual and oral elements, teaching his students a manual alphabet and signs as well as articulation.

In Germany, at about the same time, Samuel Heinicke (1729–1784) was developing a purely oral method of instruction, emphasizing the development of lip reading and speaking skills. Heinicke's method, as further developed by Friedrich Moritz Hill (1805–1874), was the basis for the oral method that became accepted practice throughout the world.

In France, Abbé Charles Michel de l'Epée (1712–1789) and Abbé Roch Ambroise Sicard (1742–1822) were developing the modern language of signs. Based on earlier work by Jacob Pereire (1715–1790), the instructional system was characterized by use of signs and a manual alphabet for communication. The French system also emphasized training of the senses of sight and touch, a forerunner of the sensory training that became an integral part of special education in the next century.

Organized education for deaf children in the United States began with the training of Thomas Hopkins Gallaudet (1787–1851) by Sicard in the French method of teaching the deaf. Gallaudet, who had been chosen to start America's first school for the deaf, returned to Hartford, Connecticut, well trained in Sicard's methods and accompanied by Laurent Clerc (1785–1869), a deaf teacher of the deaf recruited in France. In 1817 they established the first school for the deaf in the United States, now the American School for the Deaf. This was the first educational program for exceptional children established in the United States. The New York Institution for the Deaf opened the next year, and by 1863 there were 22 schools for the deaf in the nation. In 1867 the first oral schools for the deaf were established in the United States, the Clarke School for the Deaf in Massachusetts and the Lexington School for the Deaf in New York. Gallaudet College, the only liberal arts college for the deaf in the world, was established in 1864. The first day school classes for any exceptionality in the United States were established for deaf children in Boston in 1869. Adult education for the deaf began in New York City in 1874.

The subsequent development of services for the deaf in the United States was aided immeasurably by a number of prominent advocates, most notably Alexander Graham Bell (1847–1922), inventor of the telephone and tireless worker for education for the deaf, and Helen Keller (1880–1957), who, deaf and blind from early childhood, was a living example of the effectiveness of special educational methods in overcoming even the most severe handicaps.

The development of services for the deaf were, in the United States and elsewhere, hindered by bitter disagreements between advocates of the oral and the manual methods of instruction, with a resulting absence of cohesive effort toward common goals. In recent years these differences have been to a great extent reconciled, with a majority of programs using a combined oral-manual system of communication usually referred to as total communication or the simultaneous method.

Education of the Visually Impaired

Education for the blind began in France with the work of Valentin Haüy (1745–1822), a French philanthropist who, in 1784, founded the National Institution for the Young Blind in Paris. The school admitted both blind and sighted students so as not to isolate blind students from their sighted peers. Its success led to the formation of seven similar schools in Europe during the next 15 years. The first school for the blind in the United States, now the Perkins School for the Blind in Watertown, Massachusetts, was incorporated in 1829 with Samuel Gridley Howe (1801–1876) as its first director. There followed a rapid development of residential schools for the blind, which soon began also to enroll partially seeing students. These residential schools provided the nation's only education services to visually impaired children until the development of special classes in the public schools, a movement that began with the formation of a special class for the blind in Chicago in 1900. The first special class for partially seeing children was opened 13 years later in Boston.

Crucial to the education of blind students was the development of a system of reading and writing. Haüy developed a system of embossed letters to be read with the fingers and, using this system, he printed the first books for the blind. Raised letters proved to be extremely difficult to read, however, and it was Louis Braille (1809–1852), blind from childhood and one of Haüy's students, who developed the system of reading that has become universal. Known as braille, the system uses raised dots to represent the letters of the alphabet. For many years all braille materials had to be prepared individually by hand. The availability of materials in braille was greatly ex-

panded by two inventions by Frank H. Hall (1843–1911), a braille typewriter (1892) and a braille printing system (1893). English-language braille, which developed in many variations, was standardized in 1932 with an international agreement on the code that is now called Standard English Grade Two.

Education of the Mentally Retarded

Education for children with mental retardation began with the attempt by a French physician, Jean Marc Gaspard Itard (1775–1838), to educate an 11-year-old boy who had been found living as a savage in the woods. Itard's efforts to educate and civilize the boy were only partially successful, apparently because the boy was mentally retarded. Itard documented his methods in a book, *The Wild Boy of Aveyron* (1801). The instructional procedures that he described formed the basis for more than a century of development in the education of those with mental retardation, most notably by Edouard Seguin (1812–1880) in France and the United States and Maria Montessori (1870–1952) in Italy. Seguin, in his influential book *Idiocy and Its Treatment by the Physiological Method*, published in 1866, enunciated many ideas that have persisted to the present time: education of the whole child, individualization of instruction, beginning instruction at the child's current level of functioning, and the importance of rapport between teacher and pupil. These concepts and Seguin's emphasis on sensory training were incorporated in the twentieth century into the famous Montessori method, used worldwide in the education of both handicapped and nonhandicapped children. Ovide Decroly (1871–1932) in Belgium developed an effective curriculum for mentally retarded children early in the twentieth century and established schools that served as models throughout Europe. Alfred Binet (1857–1911), working in the public schools of Paris, made an immense contribution with the invention of intelligence testing, providing in 1905 the first objective instrument for selecting children for placement in special education services.

The first instance of schooling for children with mental retardation in the United States took place in 1839, when a blind, mentally retarded student was admitted to the Perkins Institute for the Blind in Massachusetts. The first school designed specifically for children with mental retardation, a residential facility, was opened in 1848 in Barre, Massachusetts, by Hervey Backus Wilbur (1820–1883). Public residential facilities for mentally retarded children and adults were opened in all parts of the country during the next half century and by 1917 all but four states were providing institutional care for the mentally retarded.

The first public school special class for children with mental retardation was formed in Germany in 1859, and a small number of such classes were formed in other European nations during the next several decades. In the

United States the first public school special class for mentally retarded children was opened in 1896 in Providence, Rhode Island.

Education of Children with Orthopedic Handicaps and Other Health Problems

There were few special educational provisions for children with orthopedic handicaps and health impairments prior to the twentieth century. In the United States the first special class for orthopedically handicapped children was established in the Chicago public schools in 1899 or 1900. A class for students with lowered vitality was initiated in Providence, Rhode Island, in 1908, and a class for children with epilepsy was formed in Baltimore, Maryland, in 1909.

Education of Emotionally Handicapped/Behaviorially Disordered Children

References to children emotionally disturbed do not appear in the scientific literature until the nineteenth century; there is a puzzling absence of references to the subject in any literature prior to that time. The first description of childhood psychosis was published in 1838 by Jean Etienne Esquirol (1772–1840) in *Des Maladies Mentales*, a work that constituted the first scientific treatment of mental illness.

The development of school services for children with emotional handicaps is not easy to trace because of imprecision in the classification of handicaps, difficulty in diagnosis, and a tendency to place children with these types of problems in classes designed for children with other handicaps. Late in the nineteenth century, a few schools in the United States began to make formal provision for emotionally handicapped students. The New Haven, Connecticut, public schools in 1871 established a class to provide for children exhibiting unmanageable behavior; classes for unruly boys were formed in the public schools of New York City in 1874. It is noteworthy that these were the first public school special classes for exceptional students to be established in the United States.

It was not until the 1930s that children with severe emotional problems began to be studied in a systematic way, and even then public schools were slow to accept responsibility for educating these students. But with psychiatry developing as a discipline, with individual differences a central topic in psychology, and with psychological testing increasingly useful as a diagnostic tool, schools began to assume responsibility for educating these students and for developing programs based on psychiatric diagnosis and treatment recommendations.

The years since World War II have been characterized by the rapid development of services for handicapped children in the United States, with greatly increased involvement of parents and governmental entities.

Parent Involvement

Parents of handicapped children, who had long been in the background of special education, began in the 1940s and 1950s to organize themselves to represent the needs of handicapped children and, where necessary, to provide educational services for those handicapped children not being served by the public schools. Organizations such as the National Association of Retarded Citizens, the United Cerebral Palsy Association, and the Association for Children with Learning Disabilities have been major forces in the development of public school services for all handicapped children. They have had great influence in establishing the educational rights of handicapped children and their families, obtaining legislation relating to the rights of handicapped persons, changing attitudes toward the handicapped, and establishing the right of parents to participate in public school decisions about their child.

Legislative and Governmental Action

The federal government conducted a variety of programs designed to improve educational services for handicapped children in the years following World War II. These governmental activities included grants to the states to assist in the development of new programs for handicapped children, funding of research and demonstration projects, funding of training of special education personnel, establishment of regional resource centers for teachers, and establishment of a network of centers for deaf-blind children. In 1967 the Bureau of Education for the Handicapped was established in the U.S. Office of Education to administer the training, research, and educational programs supported by the federal government throughout the nation.

The landmark legislation for the handicapped in the United States is PL 94-142, the Education for All Handicapped Children Act, enacted by Congress in 1975. Its stated purpose is ensuring that all handicapped children have available a free appropriate public education that provides special education and related services as needed to meet the student's unique needs. Public Law 94-142 required that state and local education agencies ensure that all children who are handicapped be identified and evaluated; that a comprehensive, nondiscriminatory, multidisciplinary educational assessment be made; that a reassessment be made at least every 3 years; that a written individualized educational plan (IEP) be developed and maintained for each child who has been determined to be handicapped; and that each child be educated in the least restrictive environment that is consistent with his or her handicap. The law also granted certain rights to parents to review their child's school record; to obtain an independent evaluation of the child; to receive written notice prior to placement in special education services; and to have an impartial hearing if they wish to challenge the proposed classification or placement of their child. Compliance with the requirements of PL 94-142 has brought modest amounts of federal financial aid to the states, to be used with state and local funds to support the cost of educating handicapped children.

A far-reaching effect of PL 94-142 has been the virtual elimination of the exclusion of handicapped children from school. As the title of the act states, the legislation provides for the education for all handicapped children.

A number of court decisions laid the groundwork for the enactment of PL 94-142. The decision in *Pennsylvania Association for Retarded Children* v. *Commonwealth of Pennsylvania* in 1972 established that it is the responsibility of the public schools to provide appropriate programs for handicapped children, and ruled that a child may not be excluded from school without due process. *Mills* v. *Board of Education* in the same year established that a handicapped child may not be denied an appropriate, publicly supported education, and that a lack of funds may not be used by the school system as a reason for failing to provide the services to which a handicapped child is entitled.

Section 504 of the Vocational Rehabilitation Act of 1973 (PL 93-112) serves as a statement of civil rights for the handicapped, providing that no otherwise qualified handicapped individual will, because of his or her handicap, be denied participation in any activity or program that receives federal financial assistance. This provision established public education as a right for all handicapped children, regardless of how serious the handicap might be, and is also the basis for a nationwide effort to make school buildings accessible to the handicapped.

Growth in Services

Special education services expanded rapidly after World War II, both in numbers and types of children served. There was an explosion of new special classes and special schools, and of college and university preparation programs for special education personnel. New populations of handicapped children were included in the population served, including trainable mentally retarded children, previously served primarily in institutions or in special schools operated by parent groups, and, beginning in the 1960s, learning-disabled children, a group that had mostly been achieving poorly in regular classes or misplaced in special classes for students with other kinds of handicaps. In addition, there developed an increased interest in special programs for a group of students who are not handicapped but who are generally included in the definition of exceptional children: gifted and talented children. Programs for these students appeared only slowly, as they lacked strong support from most educators. Consequently, programs for the gifted and talented have not shown the rapid growth that took place in programs for handicapped students.

Early education, or preschool education, for handi-

capped children, long provided for deaf children and for those with cerebral palsy and other physical handicaps, became generally available for other categories of handicapped children in the 1970s. This development was based on research findings corroborating commonly held beliefs that that development of young children can be changed through early educational intervention. Often initiated with federal funding, these programs provided several new emphases in special education, including organized "child-find" procedures to locate young children in need of special programming, improved multidisciplinary approaches, and parent education.

Under the provisions of PL 94-142 and Section 504 of the Vocational Rehabilitation Act, public schools are required to make appropriate educational services available to students with severe, profound, and multiple handicaps, a category that includes various degrees and combinations of mental retardation, behavior disorders, physical handicaps, and sensory handicaps. Programs for such severely handicapped children, many of whom were previously unserved by the public schools, have become a major element of special education and have brought with them services such as physical therapy and occupational therapy that had not previously been considered the province of the schools. These programs also have necessitated the downward extension of the curriculum to include instruction in infant-level self-help skills.

Increased enrollment of handicapped students in vocational education programs was fostered by the Vocational Education Amendments of 1976 (PL 94-482), which require each state to allocate 10% of its vocational funds for the education of handicapped students. Increasingly, since enactment of these amendments, high-school students with handicaps have had available to them a variety of occupational preparation options, both in regular and special vocational education programs.

The explosion of technology that characterizes our time has directly benefited handicapped students in some significant ways. The use of computers by handicapped children is becoming commonplace, as it is for all students. Improved prostheses, motorized wheelchairs, and other transportation devices have greatly increased the mobility of physically handicapped children. The deaf have benefited from vastly improved hearing aid technology and increased captioning of films and television programs.

Of special significance are telecommunication devices for the deaf, the best known being the teletypewriter and teleprinter (TTY), a device that enables the deaf to communicate by telephone, typing into the system messages that are then printed at the receiving end. Reading for the blind is being transformed by a number of devices. The recorded "talking book" can now be enhanced by a technique known as compressed speech, which can double the speed at which the recording is played without producing distortion in pitch or quality. The Optacon converts print into a vibrating image that can be read with the fingers.

The Kurzweil Reading Machine converts print into spoken English. In the important area of mobility, the Sonicguide aids the blind person by producing a sound that indicates the presence of an object that lies in his or her path, and its distance. Unfortunately, because of the cost of such devices, their general use lies in the future.

The 1970s saw the emergence of mainstreaming and least restrictive environment as dominant concepts in special education. The requirement in PL 94-142 that handicapped students be educated in the least restrictive environment was a reaction to doubts about the educational and social efficacy of the existing special class model, and about the willingness of the schools to give handicapped students access to the regular school program. As a result of this requirement of PL 94-142, there have been significant shifts in special education placements in the last decade, with a trend toward a reduction in placements in residential schools and special day schools and increased enrollment of handicapped students in special classes in regular school buildings and in regular classes, usually with assistance in the form of some type of supplementary special instruction. Placement in less restrictive environments, and the provision of appropriate educational services in this context, while not without its difficulties, is serving to eliminate needless segregation of handicapped students.

REFERENCES

Bender, R. (1970). *The conquest of deafness.* Cleveland, OH: Case Western Reserve.

Blatt, B., & Morris, R. J. (1984). *Perspectives in special education: Personal orientations.* Glenview, IL: Scott, Foresman.

Despert, J. L. (1965). *The emotionally disturbed child—Then and now.* New York: Brunner.

Fancher, R. E. (1979). *Pioneers of psychology.* New York: Norton.

Fancher, R. E. (1985). *The intelligence men: Makers of the I. Q. controversy.* New York: Norton.

Gannon, J. R. (1981). *Deaf heritage: A narrative history of deaf America.* Silver Spring, MD: National Association of the Deaf.

Hatlen, P. H., Hall, A. P., & Tuttle, D. (1980). Education of the visually handicapped: An overview and update. In L. Mann & D. A. Sabatino (Eds.), *The fourth review of special education* (pp. 1–33). New York: Grune & Stratton.

Irwin, R. B. (1955). *As I saw it.* New York: American Foundation for the Blind.

Jan, J. E., Freeman, R. D., & Scott, E. P. (1977). *Visual impairment in children and adults.* New York: Grune & Stratton.

Kanner, L. (1964). *A history of the care and study of the mentally retarded.* Springfield, IL: Thomas.

Kanner, L. (1970). Emotionally disturbed children: A historical review. In L. A. Faas (Ed.), *The emotionally disturbed child: A book of readings.* Springfield, IL: Thomas.

Kirk, S. A., & Gallagher, J. J. (1983). *Educating exceptional children* (4th ed.). Boston: Houghton Mifflin.

Koestler, F. A. (1976). *The unseen minority: A social history of blindness in the United States.* New York: McKay.

Lane, H. (1984). *When the mind hears.* New York: Random House.

Lerner, J. (1985). *Learning disabilities: Theories, diagnosis, and teaching strategies* (4th ed.). Boston: Houghton Mifflin.

Lowenfeld, B. (1975). *The changing status of the blind: From separation to integration.* Springfield, IL: Thomas.

Moores, D. F. (1982). *Educating the deaf: Psychology, principles, and practices* (2nd ed.). Boston: Houghton Mifflin.

Reynolds, M. C., & Birch, J. W. (1977). *Teaching exceptional children in all America's schools.* Reston, VA: Council for Exceptional Children.

Rosen, M., Clark, G. R., & Kivitz, M. S. (Eds.). (1976). *The history of mental retardation: Collected papers.* Baltimore, MD: University Park Press.

Ross, I. (1951). *Journey into light: The story of the education of the blind.* New York: Appleton-Century-Crofts.

Scheerenberger, R. C. (1983). *A history of mental retardation.* Baltimore, MD: Brookes.

Smith, S. (1983). *Ideas of the great psychologists.* New York: Harper & Row.

Swanson, B. M., & Willis, D. J. (1979). *Understanding exceptional children and youth.* Chicago: Rand McNally.

Wallin, J. E. W. (1955). *Education of mentally handicapped children.* New York: Harper & Row.

Watson, R. I. (1968). *The great psychologists: From Aristotle to Freud* (2nd ed.). Philadelphia: Lippincott.

Wiederholt, J. L. (1974). Historical perspectives on the education of the learning disabled. In L. Mann & D. A. Sabatino (Eds.), *The second review of special education* (pp. 103–152). Philadelphia: JSE.

PAUL IRVINE
Katonah, New York

HUMANISTIC SPECIAL EDUCATION
LEGAL REGULATIONS OF SPECIAL EDUCATION
MAINSTREAMING
SCHOOL ATTENDANCE OF THE HANDICAPPED

HOBBS, NICHOLAS (1915–1983)

Nicholas Hobbs began his professional career as a high school teacher, earned his PhD degree in clinical psychology from Ohio State University in 1946, and served on the faculties of Teachers College, Columbia University, Louisiana State University, and George Peabody College of Vanderbilt University. From the time of his arrival at George Peabody College in 1951 until his retirement in 1980, he held a number of positions, including chairman of the division of human development, director of the Center for the Study of Families and Children, which he created, and provost of Vanderbilt University.

Hobbs was widely known for his pioneering Project Re-ED, dedicated to "the reeducation of emotionally disturbed children." An educational approach to the treatment of emotionally disturbed children, Project Re-ED, which grew into a nationwide program, is described in Hobbs's *The Troubled and Troubling Child.*

Hobbs was appointed to a number of presidential panels and commissions and participated in the creation of the Peace Corps. He served as president of the American Psychological Association.

REFERENCES

Hobbs, N. (1982). *The troubled and troubling child.* San Francisco: Jossey-Bass.

The legacy of Nicholas Hobbs: Research on education and human development in the public interest, Part I. (1983). *Peabody Journal of Education, 60*(3).

The legacy of Nicholas Hobbs: Research on education and human development in the public interest, Part II. (1984). *Peabody Journal of Education, 61*(3).

PAUL IRVINE
Katonah, New York

HOBSON v. HANSEN

Hobson v. *Hansen* (1967) was the first case in which the federal courts chose to become involved in the racial issues of testing for placement in educational programs. *Hobson* centered around the controversial practice in the District of Columbia of using educational tracking. *Hobson* subsequently challenged the legality of within school district disparities in the allocation of financial and educational resources. These disparities resulted in greater resources being given to white children placed in higher level programs than black children, who were disproportionately placed in lower level educational tracks. All placements had been made on the basis of group-administered standardized tests of intelligence and achievement. In considering this case, the court expressed much concern that the placement had occurred primarily, or in some cases exclusively, on the basis of standardized tests.

As Bersoff (1982) has reported, despite the genuine intent of the Washington, DC school district in remediating severe academic deficiencies of black children, the court, in *Hobson*, eventually ruled against the district because of the resultant disproportionality in the different educational tracks. The court wrote that "in those schools with a significant number of white and Negro students a higher proportion of Negroes will go into the Special Academic (EMR) Tract than will white students" (p. 456). The court determined that the placement system as actually practiced violated the equal protection clause of the Fourteenth Amendment to the Constitution. The court ruled that ability grouping was justified when it resulted in racial disproportionality only when the assessment measures and judgments of ability were based on children's innate ability or genetic endowment and not current skill

or ability levels. Though many special educators and psychologists would continue to take issue with this position, the court ventured into even more controversial ground when it asserted that only when ability grouping is based on innate ability, would special education be "reasonably related to the purposes of education" (p. 512).

Bersoff (1982) has asserted that when viewed in its entirety, *Hobson* was not nearly so much a rejection of testing practices as it seems, but was more "the condemnation of rigid, poorly conceived classification practices that negatively affect the educational opportunities of minority children. The court's major concern was not the tests but the inflexibility of ability grouping as practiced by the school system, the stigmatizing effect on blacks, and its failure to provide sufficient resources to those in the lower tracks, resulting in generally poor teaching" (pp. 1047–1048). The court held that the end result was to relegate EMR students to a permanent class of inequality.

The court in *Hobson* was more impressed with the results of individual assessment, however, and did favor the use of individually administered tests by psychologists for placement in special educational programs. When re-evaluated by psychologists under the conditions of individual assessment, the court found that nearly two-thirds of the children placed into EMR programs on the basis of group test results had been misclassified.

REFERENCE

Bersoff, D. N. (1982). The legal regulation of school psychology. In C. R. Reynolds & T. B. Gutkin (Eds.), *The handbook of school psychology.* New York: Wiley.

CECIL R. REYNOLDS
Texas A&M University

INTELLIGENCE TESTING
LARRY P.
MARSHALL v. GEORGIA
MENTAL RETARDATION
SIX-HOUR RETARDED CHILD

HOLISTIC APPROACH AND LEARNING DISABILITIES

Holism is defined as "a theory that the universe and especially living nature is correctly seen in terms of interacting wholes . . . that are more than the mere sum of elementary particles" (*Webster's New Collegiate Dictionary,* 1979). Holism, as applied to teaching and learning, suggests an approach whereby variables are not broken down into their component parts, but are examined within the context in which they occur. This type of learning is ongoing and is not fragmented into discrete segments or skills (McNutt, 1984). In contrast, behaviorists contend that each learning task can be analyzed, segmented, and sequenced in a hierarchical order; the individual parts must be learned before the whole (the sum of the parts) can be understood. Holists believe this to be a piecemeal approach that results in learning that is irrelevant and boring (Heshusius, 1984).

Until recently the major approaches used with children who are learning disabled have been reductionist in their orientation. According to Poplin (1984a), the psychological process approach, the behaviorist approach, and the cognitive-strategies approach, all of which have been used in treating learning disabilities, share several assumptions: the learning process is divided into segments; the focus is on deficits of the individual instead of strengths; and there are right and wrong ways to process information. Holists do not agree with these assumptions and, in fact, would argue that operating in this manner hinders learning in the learning-disabled student.

> Applied to learning disabilities, holistic inquiry lends credence to the argument that processes such as memory can neither be viewed experimentally nor taught separately, and that a child's memory for academic tasks may depend more on what the child already knows and feels and her/his interests than on the function or dysfunction of any hypothetical construct. (Poplin, 1984a, p. 290)

Those advocating a holistic approach for teaching children with learning disabilities (Heshusius, 1984; Leigh, 1980; Poplin, 1984a, 1984b; Rhodes & Dudley-Marling [in press]) argue that these students need a curriculum that is rich in language and that provides frequent opportunities to engage in reading and writing. Learning-disabled students, however, often read in a slow, laborious, and disfluent manner. Rhodes and Dudley-Marling (in press) posit that disfluent readers are afraid to take risks in the process of reading and writing. These readers believe that reading and writing are done in order to practice the form of language, word recognition, spelling, and mechanics. They do not understand that the goal is to derive and communicate meaning from their reading. According to Pflaum and Bryan (1982), fluent readers use the three language systems, graphophonics, syntax, and semantics, in an interrelated way to determine meaning, while disabled readers rely mainly on graphophonics. Holists feel that learning-disabled students need to learn to treat reading and writing as language rather than as discrete sets of skills that have little meaning or relevance to the reader.

Leigh (1980) puts forth seven major principles of the whole language philosophy that provide a comprehensive description of a holistic approach to teaching:

1. Reading, writing, speaking, and listening are closely interrelated language processes rather than separate, autonomous academic skills.
2. The fundamental purpose of any language activity is to acquire, mediate, or express meaning.
3. Language, in all forms, involves an interactive process that occurs in social contexts.
4. Oral and written language are learned rather than taught.
5. Children need competence in using language for several different functions.
6. Whole-language evaluation should be based on naturalistic, observational procedures that focus on comprehension.
7. The teacher's attitudes and competencies are essential determinants of the effectiveness of a whole-language program (pp. 63–68).

A classroom for the learning disabled facilitates learning in accordance with these principles by providing a language-rich environment. The holistic classroom is a place where children have frequent opportunities to engage in reading and writing and to be exposed to demonstrations of the natural purposes and joy of written language (Dudley-Marling, in press). School goals become the same as life goals, and children learn because the material is relevant, purposeful, and meaningful.

In holistic classrooms, teachers demonstrate a purpose for reading and writing. They write notes to students and encourage them to write notes and letters to each other. Daily schedules and lunch menus are posted in the room. Teachers write directions for assignments or class activities. Pictures of students are posted along with their biographies. Teachers and students label items in the classroom, display their writing, and read aloud to each other. Teachers and students also talk about reading, writing, and thinking. Communication is at the heart of the process by which intelligence develops (Sadler & Whimbey, 1985). When students have the opportunity to articulate their thinking and receive feedback they develop their cognitive skills. In holistic learning-disabled classrooms, students and teachers discuss books they have read or pieces they have written. Teachers share problems they have had in comprehending stories or writing papers or poems. This encourages students to think of similar situations in which they have been involved. The awareness helps them to monitor their thought processes and feel more comfortable with reading and writing processes.

A holistic classroom also provides opportunities for students to engage in reading and writing. There are reading centers that contain a variety of reading materials, e.g., books, newspapers, magazines, comics, and cookbooks. Writing centers are complete with pencils, papers, and reasons for writing. Students write journals, stories, notes, poems, plays, or recipes. Students read and write together in groups to help one another be creative or to overcome obstacles. Holistic teachers plan activities that show reading and writing is useful. For example, a cooking project includes finding recipes in books, writing grocery lists, writing and reading recipes, and talking about the experience.

The holistic classroom is a place where teaching and learning is an interactive process with the emphasis on the meaning, not the form, of language. Learning-disabled students benefit in this meaningful environment. Segmenting learning into discrete parts can discourage reluctant learners with its repetition and boredom. Holistic learning, on the other hand, motivates students because it is meaningful, purposeful, and relevant.

REFERENCES

Dudley-Marling, C. C. (in press). Creating a rich language environment for written language learning. *Teaching Exceptional Children*.

Heshusius, L. (1984). Why would they and I want to do it? A phenomenological-theoretical view of special education. *Learning Disability Quarterly* 7(4), 363–368.

Leigh, J. E. (1980). Whole-language approaches: Premises and possibilities. *Learning Disability Quarterly*, 3(4), 62–69.

McNutt, G. (1984). A holistic approach to language arts instruction in the resource room. *Learning Disability Quarterly*, 7(4), 315–320.

Pflaum, S. W., & Bryan, T. H. (1982). Oral reading research and learning disabled children. *Topics in Learning and Learning Disabilities, 1*, 33–42.

Poplin, M. S. (1984a). Summary rationalizations, apologies and farewell: What we don't know about the learning disabled. *Learning Disability Quarterly, 7*(2), 130–135.

Poplin, M. S. (1984b). Toward an holistic view of persons with learning disabilities. *Learning Disability Quarterly*, 7(4), 290–294.

Rhodes, L. K., Dudley-Marling, C. C. (in press). *Teaching literacy to learning disabled and remedial students*. Portsmouth, NH: Heinemann Educational Books.

Sadler, W. A., Jr., & Whimbey, A. (1985, Nov.). A holistic approach to improving thinking skills. *Phi Delta Kappan*, 199–203.

Webster's New Collegiate Dictionary (1979). Springfield, MA: Merriam.

NANCY J. KAUFMAN
University of Wisconsin, Stevens Point

ECOLOGICAL ASSESSMENT
ECOLOGICAL EDUCATION FOR THE HANDICAPPED

HOLLAND, SPECIAL EDUCATION IN

See NETHERLANDS, SPECIAL EDUCATION IN.

HOLLINGWORTH, LETA A. S. (1886–1939)

Leta A. S. Hollingworth, psychologist, received her PhD from Teachers College, Columbia University, in 1916, after serving as a high-school teacher in Nebraska and as a clinical psychologist in New York City. She was a member of the faculty of Teachers College from 1916 until her death in 1939.

Hollingworth made pioneering studies of the psychology of women, correcting prior misconceptions regarding differences in abilities between the sexes and providing the basis for her strong advocacy of professional equality between men and women. She was a leader in the establishment of standards for clinical psychologists and carried out significant investigations of both mentally retarded and gifted children.

REFERENCES

Gates, A. I. (Ed.). (1940). Education and the individual. *Teachers College Record, 42*, 183–264.

Hollingworth, H. L. (1943). *Leta Stetter Hollingworth*. Lincoln: University of Nebraska Press.

Hollingworth, L. (1926). *Gifted children: Their nature and nurture*. New York: Macmillan.

PAUL IRVINE
Katonah, New York

HOLT, WINIFRED (1870–1945)

Winifred Holt founded the New York Association for the Blind in 1905. She was responsible for the creation of the committee that eventually became the National Society for the Prevention of Blindness. With a special interest in training and employment for the blind, she developed the New York Lighthouse, a workshop devoted to education, employment, and recreation for the blind. Dedicated by President William Howard Taft in 1913, the Lighthouse

Winifred Holt

was so successful that Lighthouses were established in many cities in the United States, and eventually in 34 other countries.

A leader in the campaign to get blind children into the public schools, Holt helped the New York City Board of Education to establish its program for the education of blind students in classes with sighted children. She wrote two influential books, a biography of Henry Fawcett, the blind English postmaster-general, and *The Light Which Cannot Fail*, which contained stories about blind men and women and a useful "handbook for the blind and their friends." In 1922 Holt married Rufus Graves Mather, a research and lecturer on art who joined her in her work for the blind.

REFERENCES

Bloodgood, E. H. (1952). *First lady of the Lighthouse.* New York: The Lighthouse, New York Association for the Blind.

Holt, W. (1914). *A beacon for the blind: Being a life of Henry Fawcett, the blind postmaster-general.* Boston: Houghton Mifflin.

Holt, W. (1922). *The light which cannot fail.* New York: Dutton.

PAUL IRVINE
Katonah, New York

HOLTZMAN, WAYNE H., JR. (1948–   )

Wayne Holtzman received his BA from the University of Texas, Austin (1971) in liberal arts, with emphasis in foreign languages and psychology. He received his MA in bilingual education (1973) from Antioch College, and his PhD in school psychology (1980) from the University of Texas, Austin.

Holtzman's first experiences in the field of special education were as a bilingual school psychologist in Austin, Texas. It was there that he formed the opinion that the needs of Hispanic children were great, and that few school

Wayne H. Holtzman, Jr.

personnel have sufficient training to deal with them effectively. His interest in special education was paralleled by a focus in bilingual education that culminated in his serving as a coordinator and director of federally funded educational research projects in bilingual education.

In 1982 Holtzman taught in the department of psychology at the National University in Mexico City. He returned to the University of Texas, Austin in 1984 to coordinate the master's program in bilingual special education. That year, he also served as co-director of the Young Psychologists Program at the International Congress of Psychology.

Holtzman is currently interested in the creation of an infant and preschool developmental scale in Spanish to be used in Latin America. He is also interested in international education in general, and the improvement of special education services throughout Latin America.

ELAINE FLETCHER-JANZEN
Texas A&M University

HOLTZMAN, WAYNE H., SR. (1923–   )

Wayne H. Holtzman, Sr. received his BS in chemistry (1944) and his MS (1947) from Northwestern University. He received his PhD (1950) in psychology and statistics from Stanford University. Holtzman's major field of study is personality psychology specializing in educational psychology.

He has written numerous books and articles; among his most significant are *Tomorrow's Parents, Survey of Study Habits and Attitudes, Forms C and S,* and *Holtzman Inkblot Technique.* The inkblot technique focuses on the analysis of inkblots to determine a person's mode of perception. It is a method designed to stir one's imagination in order to study their personality. Holtzman revised the original inkblot method by using more inkblots with simplified procedures for administration.

During 1953–1954, he received a faculty research fellowship from the Social Science Research Council. In 1962, his research in the field of inkblot perception and personality was recognized by the Helen D. Sargent Memorial Award from the Menninger Foundation and in 1962–1963, he was awarded a fellowship at the Center for Advanced Study in the Behavioral Sciences, Stanford, California. In 1979 he was appointed "Profesor Honorario" at the Universidad San Martin de Porres in Lima, Peru, and received the Doctor of Humanities degree from Southwestern University in Georgetown, Texas in 1980.

Currently, Holtzman is President of the Hogg Foundation for Mental Health at the University of Texas where he serves as Hogg Professor of Psychology and Education.

REFERENCES

Holtzman, W. H. (1961). *Holtzman Inkblot Technique.* New York: Psychological Corp.

Holtzman, W. H. (1965). *Tomorrow's Parents.* Austin: University of Texas Press, p. 371.

Holtzman, W. H., & Brown, W. F. (1967). *Survey of Study Habits and Attitudes, Forms C and S.* New York: Psychological Corp.

REBECCA BAILEY
Texas A&M University

HOMEBOUND INSTRUCTION

Homebound instruction is defined as education for the child confined to home owing to illness, physical injury, or emotional condition provided by an itinerant or visiting teacher. A child is eligible for a home instruction program if school attendance is made impossible by such physical or emotional conditions. Public Law 94-142 has categorized home instruction as one of the most restrictive in the available cascade of services; as a result, such placement is to be considered temporary whenever possible (Berdine & Blackhurst, 1985).

The homebound teacher is used as the provider of this instruction in those areas or school districts where such services are available. The homebound instructional component must consist of direct service to the child and regular consultation with in-school personnel, as the nature of the service will vary from helping students at home for short periods of time to maintain the pace and assignments of their classes, to providing a complete instructional program for those confined for longer periods. Authorities agree that regular liaison with school and peers to maintain contacts and social skills is vital to the student on homebound instruction, who must be brought back to school as quickly as the handicapping condition allows (Polloway, Payne, Patton, & Payne, 1985).

Some instances of the abuse of homebound instruction have been noted in urban areas with relatively high frequency use of such services, primarily with disruptive, delinquent, or emotionally disturbed students prohibited from school for behavioral reasons. Homebound services for the emotionally handicapped also have been overemployed with disadvantaged, black, and male students (Safer, 1982). Additional criticisms of home instruction include the danger of segregating children for prolonged periods of time, the expense to school systems, and the use of inadequately trained teachers as service providers (Haring, 1982).

New directions in special education are extending traditional homebound instruction to include home-based services for severely handicapped children, deaf and blind infants and preschool children, the mentally retarded, and other high-risk infants (Cartwright, Cartwright, & Ward,

1984). These services include the use of teacher-trainers to teach parents and children, with emphasis on self-help skills, communications, and language arts using the natural surroundings of the home environment to promote development (Kiernan, Jordan, & Saunders, 1984).

Technological advances in telecommunications and computer-linked instruction increasingly assist the homebound child and teacher until a return to a less restrictive environment is accomplished (Kirk & Gallagher, 1986).

REFERENCES

Berdine, W. H., & Blackhurst, A. E. (1985). *An introduction to special education* (2nd ed.). Boston: Little, Brown.

Cartwright, G. P., Cartwright, C. A., & Ward, M. J. (1984). *Educating special learners* (2nd ed.). Belmont, CA: Wadsworth.

Haring, N. R. (Ed.). (1982). *Exceptional children and youth.* Columbus, OH: Merrill.

Kiernan, C., Jordan, R., & Saunders, C. (1984). *Stimulating the exceptional child: Strategies for teaching communication and behavior change to the mentally disabled.* Englewood Cliffs, NJ: Prentice-Hall.

Kirk, S. A., & Gallagher, J. J. (1986). *Educating exceptional children* (5th ed.). Boston: Houghton Mifflin.

Polloway, E. A., Payne, J. S., Patton, J. R., & Payne, R. A. (1985). *Strategies for teaching retarded and special needs learners.* Columbus, OH: Merrill.

Safer, D. J. (1982). *School programs for disruptive adolescents.* Baltimore, MD: University Park.

RONALD S. LENKOWSKY
Hunter College, City University of New York

CASCADE MODEL OF SPECIAL EDUCATION
LEAST RESTRICTIVE ENVIRONMENT

HOMEWORK

Time spent on homework is generally related to academic achievement. This conclusion has been supported in studies conducted since the early 1900s. Keith (1982) found that homework has a higher correlation with better grades in school than any other factor except intellectual ability. Walberg (1984) found, after a review of 15 studies on graded homework, that such assignments have three times more influence on student achievement than the education, income level, or occupational status of the parents. The relative effectiveness of assigning homework versus not assigning homework results in an achievement gain of approximately .30 of a standard deviation. By grading homework, a teacher can almost triple the effectiveness of this strategy over merely assigning it for practice.

Austin (1979), after reviewing 23 experimental studies focusing on mathematical homework, concluded that the effects of homework are cumulative, more effective in enhancing computational skills than problem-solving skills, and not related to students' attitudes toward mathematics. Keith (1982) reported that if students are required to do more homework and actually do it, the potential benefits are large. Low-ability high-school students doing only one to three hours of homework per week achieve the same grades as do middle-ability students doing no homework. In high-performance private schools, students are assigned at least twice as much homework as in the average public school (Coleman, Hoffer, & Kilgore, 1981).

It is not simply a question of requiring more homework to achieve higher performance. The benefits depend on how well designed, supervised, and monitored such assignments are. Keith (1982) has concluded that at some point, increased homework will probably bring smaller and smaller returns. It is probably safe to assume, however, that most students are a long way from the point of diminishing returns regarding homework. Some general rules for homework assignments are (1) require it on a regular schedule; (2) evaluate it by grades or feedback as soon as possible after the assignment; (3) make it an integral part of the in-class activities; and (4) base it on content that will be evaluated on tests.

REFERENCES

Austin, J. D. (1979). Homework research in mathematics. *School Science & Mathematics, 79,* 115–121.

Coleman, J. S., Hoffer, T., & Kilgore, S. (1981). Cognitive outcomes in public and private schools. *Sociology of Education, 55*(23), 65–76.

Keith, T. Z. (1982). Time spent on homework and high school grades: A large sample path analysis. *Journal of Educational Psychology, 74*(2), 246–253.

Walberg, H. J. (1984). Improving the productivity of America's schools. *Educational Leadership, 41*(8), 19–27.

ROBERT A. SEDLAK
University of Wisconsin, Stout

ACHIEVEMENT NEED
TEACHER EFFECTIVENESS

HORSEBACK RIDING FOR THE HANDICAPPED

See EQUINE THERAPY.

HORTICULTURAL THERAPY

Horticultural therapy is also known as hortitherapy, agritherapy, therapeutic horticulture, plant therapy, and hort-therapy. Horticultural therapy for handicapped per-

sons has its roots in the nineteenth century, during the rise of the large state institutions. Many of these institutions were located in rural areas and included areas for propagation of crops. Residents were trained to plant, care for plants, and harvest. The purpose of this farming was primarily economic rather than therapeutic. However, as a secondary benefit many residents were able to obtain work in agriculture and, in factor, before World War II, agriculture was one of the strongest occupational areas for the handicapped.

Contemporary hortitherapy has several underpinnings. It may be a branch of occupational therapy (Burton & Watkins, 1978) used to enhance motor development. It has also been employed as a form of psychotherapy (Watson & Burlingame, 1960) to develop motivation and provide clients with a sense of responsibility for living things (Saever, 1985). Horticultural therapy has also been used as a vocational activity (Downey, 1985; Good-Hamilton, 1985; Schrader, 1979). Such training may be in a sheltered work setting or in a vocational school program for competitive employment.

There are a number of unique hortitherapy programs. Burton and Watkins (1978) described a public school program for physically handicapped students in which academic concepts were taught while students were involved in plant care. The program was designed from a Piagetian point of view and was transdisciplinary, incorporating physical, occupational, and speech therapy, and classroom instruction. Saever (1985) employed agritherapy with learning-disabled students (8 to 12 years old) as a means of promoting responsibility, order, and structure, following through on plans, respect for nature, cooperative effort, and positive relationships with adults. Good-Hamilton (1985) described another public school program in which trainable mentally retarded students and learning-disabled students worked in greenhouse production to develop vocational skills (primarily work habits). More than 50% of the students were able to obtain employment at the conclusion of training. There is a professional hortitherapy organization, the National Council for Therapy and Rehabilitation Through Horticulture (NCTRH), which was started in 1973.

REFERENCES

Burton, S. B., & Watkins, M. (1978). *The green scene: Horticultural experiences for the physically impaired student.* Paper presented at the 56th annual International Conference, Council for Exceptional Children, Kansas City, MO.

Downey, R. S. (1985). Teaching the disadvantaged and handicapped. *Agricultural Education Magazine, 57*(8), 5–7.

Good-Hamilton, R. (1985). Plants breed success. *Agricultural Education Magazine, 57*(8), 8–10.

Saever, M. D. (1985). Agritherapy, plants as learning partners. *Academic Therapy, 20*(4), 389–397.

Schrader, B. (1979). *Working hands and 3,000 chrysanthemums. Special report: Fresh views on employment of mentally handi-*

capped people. Washington, DC: President's Committee on Employment of the Handicapped.

Watson, D. P., & Burlingame, A. W. (1960). *Therapy through horticulture.* New York: Macmillan.

JAMES K. MCAFEE
Pennsylvania State University

OCCUPATIONAL THERAPY
VOCATIONAL TRAINING

HOSPITALIZATION AND SPECIAL EDUCATION

Hospital instruction involves teaching the special education pupil who is recovering from illness or accident in the hospital setting. Typically, such instruction is viewed as part of a temporary delivery system (Cartwright, Cartwright, & Ward, 1984). As long-term hospital placements are by far the most restrictive environments available to the handicapped child, the provisions of PL 94-142 require increasingly more sophisticated in-district school special education programs and shorter durations for hospital or homebound physically or emotionally handicapped children (Kirk & Gallagher, 1986).

Educational strategies for hospitalized children should reflect appropriate pupil needs. Itinerant teachers or full-time personnel based in hospital schools are required to meet those instructional objectives indicated by the child's individual education plan (IEP). These objectives will differ according to student age and level of function and will show up in the special education curriculum employed. Suggested strategies include emphasis on activities of daily living and game participation at the early childhood level, reading and math concentration for the primary grade child, language arts and math for the pupil of intermediate age, language arts, math, and science for junior high school students, and science, math, social studies, and English for the high school hospital curriculum. Teacher preparation will be required so that special educators providing hospital instruction will be capable of meeting these aspects of curriculum (Kneedler et al., 1984; Larsen & Poplin, 1980).

Special educators must be aware of the predisposition of hospitalized children to develop emotional problems. Such emotional concomitants have been termed "hospitalisms." One additional role for the special educator is to serve as part of the counseling, medical, and support service team offering relief for the psychosocial factors accompanying hospital placements (Suran & Rizzo, 1983).

Future considerations for students requiring hospital instruction for both acute and chronic conditions will involve liaison between providers of the special services and in-school instructors.

REFERENCES

Cartwright, G. P., Cartwright, C. A., & Ward, M. J. (1984). *Educating special learners* (2nd ed.). Belmont, CA: Wadsworth.

Gearheart, B. R., & Weishahn, M. W. (1984). *The handicapped student in the regular classroom* (3rd ed.). St. Louis: Mosby.

Kirk, S. A., & Gallagher, J. J. (1986). *Educating exceptional children* (5th ed.). Boston: Houghton Mifflin.

Kneedler, R. D., Hallahan, D. P., & Kauffman, J. M. (1984). *Special education for today.* Englewood Cliffs, NJ: Prentice-Hall.

Larsen, S. C., & Poplin, M. S. (1980). *Methods for educating the handicapped: An individualized education program approach.* Boston: Allyn & Bacon.

Suran, B. G., & Rizzo, J. V. (1983). *Special children: An integrative approach.* Glenview, IL: Scott, Foresman.

RONALD S. LENKOWSKY
*Hunter College, City University
of New York*

HOMEBOUND INSTRUCTION
HOMEWORK
HOSPITAL SCHOOLS

HOSPITAL SCHOOLS

If a child is confined to home or to a hospital for a long period of time and is unable to attend class elsewhere because of a physical impairment or injury, instruction can continue through a "hospital school." Hospital school has been defined by Page (1977) as "school provided in a hospital for the education of children who are hospital patients." The tenth edition of ERIC descriptors (1984) lists "schools in hospitals for formal instruction of hospitalized children." Teaching at hospital schools is usually done by itinerant teachers assigned by school systems to help tutor homebound children for an hour or more per day or as their condition permits. The caseload of the teacher may vary according to the type of children served and the type of academic help needed.

According to Kirk and Gallagher (1986), some larger children's hospitals run their own schools to meet the needs of children who are recovering from acute illness, serious accident, or surgery. These larger hospitals may hire a full-time teacher instead of using the itinerant teacher. Often, in the case of psychiatric hospitals, children may be so seriously disordered that they must remain in their wards and not leave to attend a residential school on the grounds (Kirk & Gallagher, 1986). In either case, the teacher maintains contact between homebound or hospitalized students and their regular teachers and schools.

Placement in a hospital school setting is intended to be of short duration during diagnosis, treatment, and convalescence. Handicapped children admitted to such programs are normally those with severe physical handicaps, but demonstrating normal or near normal intelligence (Kirk & Gallagher, 1986).

REFERENCES

ERIC. (1984). *Thesaurus of ERIC descriptors* (10th ed.). Phoenix, AZ: Oryx Press.

Kirk, S., & Gallagher, J. (1986). *Educating exceptional children* (5th ed.). Boston: Houghton Mifflin.

Page, G. T. (1977). Hospital school. In G. T. Page & J. B. Thomas (1977). *International dictionary of education*. New York: Nichols.

MARIBETH MONTGOMERY KASIK
Governors State University

HOMEBOUND INSTRUCTION
HOMEWORK

HOUSE, BETTY J. (1923–)

Betty J. House earned her BA from Oklahoma University in 1948 and her MA from Brown University in 1949. She received her PhD in 1952 from the University of Connecticut. Beginning as a research assistant at the University of Connecticut in 1954, she has remained there throughout her career and has been a professor in residence in the department of psychology since 1972. Her research interests include learning, memory, cognitive processes, intelligence, and mental retardation.

In collaboration with her husband, Dr. David Zeaman, House has conducted research in mental retardation for over 30 years. A permanent laboratory was established for their research at the Mansfield State Training School in Connecticut; the National Institute of Mental Health provided funding for their projects for over 20 years. The major accomplishment of their research has been the development and elaboration of an attention theory of retardation discrimination learning. Their model was first published in 1963. A history of their research and theory development from 1963 to 1979 can be found in Ellis' *Handbook of Mental Deficiency, Psychological Theory and Research* (1979).

House has been associate editor of the *American Journal of Mental Deficiency* from 1975 to the present. She was a consulting editor for *Child Development* from 1968 to 1981 and has been a consulting editor for the *Journal of Experimental Child Psychology* from 1969 to the present. She served as associate editor for *Psychology Bulletin* from 1982 to 1984 and became editor in 1985.

REFERENCE

Zeaman, D., & House, B. J. (1970). A review of attention theory. In N. R. Ellis (Ed.), *Handbook of mental deficiency, psychological theory and research* (2nd ed.). Hillsdale, NJ: Erlbaum.

KATHRYN A. SULLIVAN
Texas A&M University

ZEAMAN, DAVID
ZEAMAN-HOUSE RESEARCH

HOUSE-TREE-PERSON (HTP)

The House-Tree-Person (HTP), devised by J. N. Buck (1948, 1966), is a projective drawing technique widely used as a measure of personality adjustment in children and adults. Although a variety of administration procedures exist, the individual is typically asked to draw (in pencil) a picture of a house, a tree, and a person, either on a single $8\frac{1}{2} \times 11$ in. sheet of paper or, as originally proposed by Buck, on three separate sheets. An inquiry phase may follow during which the individual is asked to describe and interpret the drawings. A quantitative scoring system was devised by Buck and a set of qualitative interpretations has been provided by Jolle (1971). Bieliauskas (1980) has compiled a bibliography and review of research on the HTP.

REFERENCES

Bieliauskas, V. J. (1980). *The House-Tree-Person research review*. Los Angeles: Western Psychological Services.

Buck, J. N. (1948). The H-T-P technique: A qualitative and quantitive scoring manual. *Journal of Clinical Psychology, 4*, 317–396.

Buck, N. N. (1966). *The House-Tree-Person technique: Revised manual*. Los Angeles: Western Psychological Services.

Jolle, I. (1971). *A catalogue for the qualitative interpretation of the House-Tree-person (H-T-P)*. Los Angeles: Western Psychological Services.

ROBERT G. BRUBAKER
Eastern Kentucky University

PERSONALITY ASSESSMENT

HOWE, SAMUEL GRIDLEY (1801–1876)

Samuel Gridley Howe, pioneer educator of the blind and the mentally retarded, was a Massachusetts physician who became superintendent of that state's first school for the blind, which opened in Howe's home in 1832. Later named the Perkins Institution and Massachusetts School for the Blind, Howe's school led in the development of programs to enable blind students to become academically competent, self-reliant, and competitively employable. Howe's most famous student was a deaf-blind child, Laura Bridgeman, and the school's success in educating her led Helen Keller's father (50 years later) to appeal to the Perkins Institution for help, with the result that Anne Sullivan became young Helen's teacher.

Howe published books for the blind, and through appeals to Congress was instrumental in the establishment of the American Printing House for the Blind in 1879. Howe accepted a blind, mentally retarded student in 1839, demonstrated that such a child could be successfully educated, and, in 1848, established an experimental program at Perkins for blind, mentally retarded students. With encouraging results in this program, Howe convinced the legislature that education of the mentally retarded should be a public responsibility, and a state school for the mentally retarded was authorized. That school, established in 1855, became the Walter E. Fernald State School.

REFERENCES

Kanner, L. (1964). *A history of the care and study of the mentally retarded.* Springfield, IL: Thomas.

Scheerenberger, R. C. (1983). *A history of mental retardation.* Baltimore, MD: Brookes.

Schwartz, H. (1956). *Samuel Gridley Howe, social reformer.* Cambridge, MA: Harvard University Press.

PAUL IRVINE
Katonah, New York

HUMANISM AND SPECIAL EDUCATION

Humanistic approaches to education draw heavily from humanistic philosophy and humanistic psychology. Examples may be found in the alternative or free schools, the most prominent of these being Summerhill founded by A. S. Neill (1960). It was Neill's belief that children do not need teaching as much as they need love, understanding, approval, and responsible freedom. Self-direction, self-evaluation, and self-fulfillment were emphasized at his school. Another humanistic approach to education is Brown's (1971) confluent education. Believing that education of the whole person is important, he described confluent education as a philosophy and a process of teaching and learning that focuses on both the affective and the cognitive domains. Other humanistic strategies include Simon's values clarification exercises, Kohlberg's moral development activities, Ojemann's causal orientation,

Glasser's classroom meetings, Palomares' magic circle, Dinkmeyer's Developing Understanding of Self and Others, Alschuler's organizational approach, Redl's life space interviewing, and Weinstein's trumpet technique. Whatever the approach or strategy, all seem to be directed toward the goal of the fullest use of capacities by all human beings (Simpson & Gray, 1976).

Prior to 1800 little or no attention was given to the development of the capacities of the handicapped. Among the earliest to provide humane treatment was Pinel. His methods, which became known as moral treatment, were elaborated on and extended by his students and admirers, the best known of whom was perhaps Itard. Not only did Itard attempt to socialize a boy found in the forests of Aveyron, France, but he also attempted to understand the mind and emotions of the child and to feel with and care for him.

The first handicapped children to receive the attention of organized groups were probably the blind and deaf. Noteworthy here is the work of Howe, who was able to make a significant breakthrough in the education of these special children owing, in part, to his unique ability to understand their inner world. Also influential was Rush, whose emphasis on love-oriented methods of control foreshadowed current appeals for more caring relationships with children (Kauffman, 1981; Suran & Rizzo, 1979).

The positivism and humane care associated with moral treatment in the first half of the 1800s gave way to pessimism and dehumanizing institutionalization that continued into the 1900s. In works such as *Christmas in Purgatory, Exodus from Pandemonium,* and *Souls in Extremis,* Blatt (1981) revealed how society treated the mentally retarded. *In and Out of Mental Retardation* is his plea for more humane treatment. "This book took 30 years to write," he said, "and I hope it will teach someone that what we can learn from the life of Helen Keller isn't only that she was educable but that all people are educable" (p. xv). Echoing Blatt were persons such as Baum (1982), Hobbs (1974), and Long, Morse, and Newman (1980). Others calling for freedom, openness, and humanism in special education included Dennison, Grossman, Knoblock, Schultz, Heuchert, and Stampf (Kauffman, 1981).

As attitudes began to change, the rights of children were reinforced at three distinct levels: policy statements of national and international organizations such as the Bill of Rights for Children; court decisions such as *Brown v. Board of Education,* providing equal access to educational opportunities; and legislation enacted by Congress, the most important being the Education for All Handicapped Children Act (PL 94-142) passed in 1975 to ensure a free and appropriate public education for all special children (Suran & Rizzo, 1979). However, with regard to the legislation, Morse (1979) noted that the child too often got lost. He called for the humanization of special education with the individual student as the focus. Fischer and Rizzo (1974), Newberger (1978), Shelton (1977), and Zeff (1977) were among those suggesting ways to humanize special education. Fischer and Rizzo offered the following suggestions in their paradigm for humanizing special education. Recognize that special children are experiencing, purposive beings; deemphasize testing and give priority to assessing how the child does what in specific circumstances; replace diagnosis with concrete recommendations; allow the child to be a co-assessor/planner (Rayder, 1978); provide students with access to their files, allowing them to have input; and shift focus from limitation to possibility, with the child participating in the direction of his or her life as much as possible.

Newsberger presented a mainstreaming reintegration process, situational socialization, through which the handicapped could be helped to acquire the knowledge, behaviors, and attitudes needed to interact successfully with others. Shelton focused on considerations necessary when planning a successful affective program for the learning disabled. Zeff described the implementation and outcome of a group tutorial program designed to help underachieving students.

An illustrative humanistic approach to special education is in operation at the P. K. Yonge School in Florida. There all pupils are in regular heterogeneous classroom groups. Goals are that each student develop increasingly positive perceptions of himself or herself; accept increasing responsibility for his or her behavior and learning; develop those skills and attitudes necessary for effective group living and interaction; learn to adapt to change and affect change constructively; become an effective lifelong learner; and find real meaning in life. Underlying values include sensitivity, authenticity, self-realization, involvement, creativity, pursuit of excellence, and responsibility (Brown, 1973).

Humanistic approaches to teacher education have been proposed in order to prepare humanistic teachers of special children (Bruininks, 1977; Simpson & Gray, 1976). In these programs teacher education is not centered on learning how to teach but rather on learning how to use one's self and surroundings to help students learn (Wass, Blume, Combs, & Hedges, 1974).

A teacher who devises an education for special children based on a humanistic model will be more of a resource and catalyst for children's learning than a director of activities. The classroom atmosphere will be nontraditional, affectively charged, and personal (Kauffman, 1981). Interactions between the teacher and students will be characterized by respect and acceptance, and students' needs for identity, achievement, and individual treatment will be recognized. Demeaning, authoritarian practices have no place in a humanistic classroom (Bernard & Huckins, 1974).

REFERENCES

Baum, D. D. (Ed.). (1982). *The human side of exceptionality.* Baltimore, MD: University Park Press.

Bernard, H. W., & Huckins, W. C. (1974). *Humanism in the classroom.* Boston: Allyn & Bacon.

Blatt, B. (1981). *In and out of mental retardation.* Baltimore, MD: University Park Press.

Brown, G. I. (1971). *Human teaching for human learning.* New York: Viking.

Brown, J. W. (1973). *A humanistic approach to special education.* (Resource Monograph No. 8). Gainesville, FL: P. K. Yonge Laboratory School.

Bruininks, V. L. (1977). A humanistic competency-based training for teachers of learning disabled students. *Journal of Learning Disabilities, 10,* 518–526.

Fischer, C. T., & Rizzo, A. A. (1974). A paradigm for humanizing special education. *Journal of Special Education, 8,* 321–329.

Hobbs, N. (1974). *The future of children.* San Francisco: Jossey-Bass.

Kauffman, J. M. (1981). *Characteristics of children's behavior disorders* (2nd ed.). Columbus, OH: Merrill.

Long, N. J., Morse, W. C., & Newman, R. G. (1980). *Conflict in the classroom* (4th ed.). Belmont, CA: Wadsworth.

Morse, W. C. (Ed.). (1979). *Humanistic teaching for exceptional children.* Syracuse, NY: Syracuse University Press.

Neill, A. S. (1960). *Summerhill.* New York: Hart.

Newberger, D. A. (1978). Situational socialization: An affective interaction component of the mainstreaming reintegration construct. *Journal of Special Education, 12,* 113–121.

Rayder, N. F. (1978, Mar.). *Public outcry for humane evaluation and isomorphic validity.* Paper presented at the meeting of the American Educational Research Association, Toronto, Canada.

Shelton, M. N. (1977). Affective education and the learning disabled student. *Journal of Learning Disabilities, 10,* 618–624.

Simpson, E. L., & Gray, M. A. (1976). *Humanistic education: An interpretation.* Cambridge, MA: Ballinger.

Suran, B. G., & Rizzo, J. V. (1979). *Special children: An integrative approach.* Glenview, IL: Scott, Foresman.

Wass, H., Blume, R. A., Combs, A. W., & Hedges, W. D. (1974). *Humanistic teacher education: An experiment in systematic curriculum innovation.* Fort Collins, CO: Shields.

Zeff, S. B. (1977). A humanistic approach to helping underachieving students. *Social Casework, 58,* 359–365.

GLENNELLE HALPIN
Auburn University

ECOLOGICAL EDUCATION OF THE HANDICAPPED
HISTORY OF SPECIAL EDUCATION

HUMAN RESOURCE DEVELOPMENT (HRD)

Human resource development (HRD) in special education involves the implementation of approaches and interventions designed to improve the functioning of professionals and paraprofessionals in their delivery of special education services. The need for HRD in special education has been exacerbated by four historical trends and events: (1) the changing nature of special education, (2) burnout of special services providers, (3) new professional and legal requirements, and (4) the increasing demand for special education services. The changing nature of special education is evident in many ways, including the introduction of new technologies such as microcomputers. For special services providers to keep abreast of advances, it is important that they participate in skill and knowledge development activities. Burnout and stress has been recognized as an important problem for many types of employees, and a recent review of the literature suggests that special services providers are not exempt from burnout and high levels of job-related stress (Cherniss, 1985).

The HRD approaches and interventions may have the potential for reducing burnout and stress in special education by enriching the work experience of special services providers. The significance of HRD for special education is further underscored by changing professional and legal requirements. The advent of PL 94-142, for example, placed new demands on many special service providers such as multidisciplinary team decision making. It has been argued (Yoshida, 1980) that special services providers and others may have been ill prepared to participate in team decision making. The need for HRD in special education is evident from the increasing demand for special education services. As Sarason (1982) has noted, it is unlikely that traditional approaches to training will be able to generate the number of individuals needed to provide the requested services. Therefore, it is also important to engage various nonprofessional groups (e.g., classroom instructional aides, parents, and even students) in special education HRD.

In contrast to traditional staff development efforts, which have almost exclusively focused on technical competencies, HRD interventions can focus on a broad spectrum of areas that might be functionally related to job performance. These areas include: (1) technical competencies, (2) interpersonal competencies, (3) professional responsibilities, and (4) job satisfaction. Technical competencies refer to job-related knowledge and skills. Interpersonal competencies concern conflict resolution and assertiveness skills that are important to maintaining productive work relationships. Professional responsibilities encompass fulfilling job-related duties in a reliable and timely manner. Job satisfaction is a multidimensional concept referring to both task satisfaction and satisfaction with the organizational climate of the work setting.

Interventions intended to develop these HRD areas can be implemented within the context of several general approaches to HRD, such as in-service training, supervision, consultation, team building, job design, and professional self-management. In-service training has typically involved performance evaluations, participation in conventions and workshops, reading of professional literature, and courses at local colleges (Maher, Cook, & Kruger, in

press). Supervision that is intended to facilitate HRD might involve participatory decision making, goal setting, performance review, and feedback activities. Consultation for the purpose of HRD is voluntarily engaged in by the consultee and might involve the consultee in activities similar to those described with respect to supervision. Team-building approaches to HRD can focus on either improving the functioning of existing work teams or the development of new work teams (Woodman & Sherwood, 1980). Job design as an HRD approach focuses on changing elements of work tasks and setting work conditions so that tasks can be performed in an exemplary manner (Gilbert, 1978). A sixth and newly emerging approach to HRD is professional self-management (Maher, 1985). Professional self-management is characterized by self-initiated and self-sustained efforts to improve one's management of time, stress, intervention cases, interpersonal conflicts, and continuing education.

REFERENCES

Cherniss, C. (1985). Stress, burnout, and the special services providers. *Special Services in the Schools, 2*, 45–61.

Gilbert, T. (1978). *Human competence: Engineering worthy performance.* New York: McGraw-Hill.

Maher, C. A. (1985). *Professional self-management: Techniques for special services providers.* Baltimore, MD: Brookes.

Maher, C. A., Cook, S. A., & Kruger, L. J. (in press). A behavioral approach to human resources development in schools. In C. A. Maher and S. G. Forman (Eds.), *Providing effective educational services: Behavioral approaches.* Hillside, NJ: Erlbaum.

Sarason, S. B. (1982). *The culture of the school and the problem of change* (2nd ed.). Boston: Allyn & Bacon.

Woodman, R. W., & Sherwood, J. J. (1980). The role of team development in organizational effectiveness. *Psychological Bulletin, 88*, 166–186.

Yoshida, R. K. (1980). Multidisciplinary decision making in special education: Review of the issues. *School Psychology Review, 9*, 221–227.

CHARLES A. MAHER
Rutgers University

LOUIS J. KRUGER
Tufts University

MULTIDISCIPLINARY TEAMS
PERSONNEL TRAINING IN SPECIAL EDUCATION

HUMPHREY, ELLIOTT S. (1888–1981)

Elliott S. (Jack) Humphrey, after early experiences as a jockey and a cowboy, made a career of the breeding and training of animals. He trained lions and tigers for circuses, and bred some of the dogs used by Admiral Richard

Elliott S. Humphrey

E. Byrd in his Antarctic expedition. Dorothy Eustis, who later founded The Seeing Eye, the first American organization to train dogs as guides for the blind, hired Humphrey to breed and train guide dogs for the blind. His teaching methods are credited with the immediate success of The Seeing Eye when it was established in 1928. His methods are used today by more than half a dozen other programs that train guide dogs. Faced with difficulty in finding competent instructors for The Seeing Eye, Humphrey designed and operated a school for instructors that provided not only teachers needed at The Seeing Eye but staff for other guide-dog programs as well. Humphrey published a book on the breeding of working dogs, and lectured on his specialty at Columbia University. During World War II he served as a commander in the Coast Guard, with responsibility for organizing and directing a school for dog trainers for the armed forces.

REFERENCES

Humphrey, E. S., & Warner, L. H. (1934). *Working dogs*. Baltimore, MD: Johns Hopkins University Press.

Putnam, P. B. (1979). *Love in the lead*. New York: Dutton.

PAUL IRVINE
Katonah, New York

HUNGERFORD, RICHARD H. (1903–1974)

Richard H. Hungerford, a leader in the field of mental retardation, served from 1942 to 1953 as director of the Bureau for Children with Retarded Mental Development in the New York City public schools. Subsequently he was superintendent of the Laconia, New Hampshire, State School; executive director of the Gulf Bend Center for Children and Youth in Victoria, Texas; executive director of Mental Health and Mental Retardation Services for the diocese of Galveston-Houston; and professor of special education at Boston University.

During the 1940s, Hungerford developed for New York City's schools a comprehensive curriculum for mentally retarded students that emphasized specific occupational preparation, training in home living skills, and activities aimed at the development of social competence. In 1943 he co-founded, with Chris J. DeProspo, *Occupational Education*, a journal for teachers of mentally retarded pupils. Hungerford's thoughtful writings, especially his beautifully written essays, such as "On Locusts," inspired both laymen and colleagues in the field of mental retardation. Hungerford served as president of the American Association on Mental Deficiency and was editor of its *American Journal of Mental Deficiency* from 1948 to 1959.

REFERENCES

Blatt, B. (1975). Toward an understanding of people with special needs: Three teachers. In J. M. Kauffman & J. S. Payne (Eds.), *Mental retardation: Introduction and personal perspectives*. Columbus, OH: Merrill.

Hungerford, R. H. (1950). On locusts. *American Journal of Mental Deficiency, 54*, 415–418.

PAUL IRVINE
Katonah, New York

HUNT, JOSEPH McVICKER (1906–   )

Joseph McVicker Hunt was born in Scottsbluff, Nebraska, on March 19, 1906. He attended the University of Nebraska, receiving his BA degree there in 1929 and his MA

Joseph McVicker Hunt

in 1930. He then went to Cornell University, receiving his PhD degree in 1933. On graduating, he became a National Research Council fellow in psychology, spending the year 1933–1934 at New York Psychiatric Institute and Columbia University and 1934–1935 at Worcester State Hospital and Clark University. After a year as visiting assistant professor of psychology at the University of Nebraska in 1935, Hunt went to Brown University as instructor in psychology in 1936, advancing to assistant professor in 1938 and associate professor in 1944. While at Brown, Hunt became associated with Butler Hospital in Providence, Rhode Island, acting as research associate (1944–1946) and as director (1946–1951). In 1951 Hunt joined the department of psychology at the University of Illinois as professor of psychology, a position he held until gaining professor emeritus status in 1974.

Hunt is well known for his many studies in child psychology. Aside from being professor of psychology, he was also professor of early education at the University of Illinois (1967–1974). He was chair of the White House Task Force on Early Childhood Education and was instrumental in the preparation of the report "A Bill of Rights for Children." That report recommended extending Head Start programs to very young children and promoted a follow-through program that would extend the age limits of head start children.

Hunt's long list of publications have dealt with problems of clinical psychology, child psychology, social casework, personality and behavior disorders, and intelligence.

REFERENCES

Hunt, J. McV. (1965). Intrinsic motivation and its role in psychological development. *Proceedings of the Nebraska Symposium on Motivation* (pp. 189–282). Lincoln: University of Nebraska Press.

Hunt, J. McV. (1950). *Measuring results in social casework: A comparison of diagnostic and functional casework concepts.* New York: Family Service Association of America.

RAND B. EVANS
Texas A&M University

HUNTER'S SYNDROME (MUCOPOLY SACCHARIDOSIS II)

Hunter's syndrome (mucopoly saccharidosis II), which resembles Hurler's syndrome (MRS-I), is transmitted as an X-linked recessive trait that occurs primarily in males. Growth during the first 2 years is normal, with malformations occurring during years 2 to 4. There are two types of Hunter's syndrome, A (severe) and B (mild). In type A,

there is no clouding of corneas and death usually occurs before year 15. Concomitant mental retardation and learning levels are higher than for children with Hurler's syndrome (Carter, 1978). However, behavior disorders and hyperactive and destructive behavior is often seen as a result, and the children tend to become difficult to manage as they mature. With type B, survival rates may extend to age 50, with fair intelligence possible. (Wortis, 1981).

Children having Hunter's syndrome will appear short in stature with stiff joints and a large abdomen (associated with enlarged organs like the spleen and liver). Children have a large head, prominent forehead, long skull, and coarse eyebrows. Thick lips, broad flat nose, and misaligned teeth are seen as the child develops. Hairiness, especially in brows and lashes, is characteristic and usually apparent by 2 to 4 years of age. Hands are clawlike, with short and stubby fingers; stiff hands and feet may present mobility and coordination problems (Lemeshaw, 1982).

Mental retardation occurs in varying degrees but because development is normal to age 2 or beyond, cognitive and verbal capabilities may be higher than in other syndromes having similar physical characteristics. Motor retardation may be more likely as the child matures. Seizures also have been noted in older children. Progressive nerve deafness and occasional vision problems are present in some Hunter's syndrome children (Illingworth, 1983). Many learning-disabledlike symptoms (low attention span, hyperkinesis, negative behavior) may also be displayed.

Health and behavior problems, coupled with the motoric and mental disabilities that occur later in development, may require placement in a more restricted setting than the regular classroom. Visual, speech, and hearing impairments that may occur will need to be assessed and remediated by a special education specialist. Physical and occupational therapy may also be necessary.

REFERENCES

Carter, C. (Ed.). (1978). *Medical aspects of mental retardation* (2nd ed.). Springfield, IL: Thomas.

Illingworth, R. (1983). *Development of the infant and young child: Abnormal and normal* (7th ed.). New York: Churchill, Livingstone.

Lemeshaw, S. (1982). *The handbook of clinical types in mental retardation.* Boston: Houghton Mifflin.

Wortis, J. (Ed.). (1981). *Mental retardation and developmental disabilities: An annual review.* New York: Brunner/Mazel.

SALLY L. FLAGLER
University of Oklahoma

HURLER'S SYNDROME
MENTAL RETARDATION
PHYSICAL ANOMALIES

HUNTINGTON'S CHOREA

Huntington's chorea, or Huntington's disease, is a degenerative condition, the progression of which is insidious. Its onset generally occurs between 25 and 50 years of age and is characterized by involuntary, irregular, jerking movements (i.e., chorea). Although the condition is often not correctly diagnosed until the onset of the chorea, Bellamy (1961) found that 29% of his patients manifested emotional disturbance prior to the abnormal motor movements. As the disease progresses, mental deterioration occurs and, after 10 to 20 years, ends with the death of the afflicted individual.

Huntington's chorea is rare; most prevalence studies agree that it occurs in from 4 to 7 individuals per 100,000 in the population. Although it was long thought not to occur among certain ethnic groups (e.g., Jewish families), such is not the case. However, it is apparently true that, among Japanese, the disease occurs at a much lower rate (about .4 per 100,000).

The major symptoms of the disease had been reported in earlier literature by several individuals: Charles O. Waters in 1841, Charles L. Gorman in 1848, George B. Wood in 1855, and Irving W. Lyon in 1863. Nevertheless, George S. Huntington is widely considered to deserve the use of his name in the medical nomenclature because his 1872 description of the symptoms of the disease was so accurate (DeJong, 1973).

Huntington's chorea is transmitted by a dominant autosome. It is the only psychiatric disorder that follows a simple Mendelian ratio. That is, half of the children of a parent who carries the gene will become afflicted (Coleman, 1964). The prevalence could be reduced to zero in one generation if affected individuals would forego bearing children. Nevertheless, this solution is difficult to implement because the carrier is often unaware of the problem until after the prime reproductive years. In addition, since the disease is believed to originate as a defective gene mutation, abstinence on the part of the gene carrier from parenthood remains only a partial solution.

Unfortunately, there is no cure for Huntington's chorea. Though both drug therapy and neurosurgery have been applied successfully to alleviate the symptoms of the disease, the ultimate problem is most likely to be resolved through prevention. By discovering precisely the affected genetic structure, an early detection system will be found, thus overcoming the basic difficulty in genetic counseling.

REFERENCES

Bellamy, W. E., Jr. (1961). Huntington's chorea. *North Carolina Medical Journal, 22,* 409–412.

Coleman, J. C. (1964). *Abnormal psychology and modern life* (3rd ed.). Chicago: Scott, Foresman.

DeJong, R. N. (1973). The history of Huntington's chorea in the United States of America. In A. Barbeau, T. Chase, & G. W. Paulson (Eds.), *Advances in neurology—Huntington's chorea* (Vol. 1). New York: Raven.

RONALD C. EAVES
Auburn University

CHOREA
GENETIC COUNSELING

HURLER'S SYNDROME

Hurler's syndrome (gargoylism; lipochondrodstrophy) is an inherited metabolic disorder that can affect an individual's physical or mental development. There are two distinct forms of this disease (Stanbury, Wyngaarden, & Fredrickson, 1966). The milder form of this disorder results from an inherited sex-linked recessive gene commonly carried by the X chromosome of the twenty-third pair of chromosomes. It is more likely to be expressed in the male population. The more severe form is inherited by way of an autosomal recessive gene that may affect any one of the 22 genes inherited from either parent (Robinson & Robinson, 1965).

In its milder form, clinical indicators of Hurler's may not be evident at birth, although symptoms generally begin to appear by 6 months of age. By 2 years of age, affected children may reflect retarded physical or mental growth. In its more severe form, individuals may manifest a variety of physical characteristics. Owing to a build up of mucopolysaccharides throughout the body, abnormal growths will result. Tissues in the liver, heart, lungs, and spleen are most often the areas affected. Abnormal lipid deposits may result in lesions in the gray matter of the brain. Even in its severe form, this genetic defect accounts for less than 1% of the severe mental retardation in children.

Physical characteristics of this disorder typically include an underdeveloped body with significant disproportion between the head and body. Limbs are short and mobility may be limited as fingers and toes are often fixed in a partial flexed position. Bone abnormalities may affect the vertebrae and result in a shortened neck and protruding belly, with possible umbilical hernia.

Individuals severely affected by Hurler's disease often have an enlarged head and protruding forehead. Facial characteristics may include bushy eyebrows, a saddle-shaped nose, double chin, and enlarged tongue. The more common form of this disorder is characterized by dwarfism and corneal clouding. In this more severe form of the disorder, individuals may live only into their teens, with death resulting from heart failure or respiratory disease. In milder cases, there is an absence of corneal clouding and dwarfism, but there is a high frequency of deafness from nerve damage.

Recent diagnostic advances in detecting fetal abnormalities have accurately confirmed the presence of Hurler's as early as 14 to 16 weeks into gestation. This diagnosis is made on the bases of finding elevated levels of the compound mucopolysaccharide in amniotic fluid (Henderson & Whiteman, 1976). A positive in vitro diagnosis of Hurler's syndrome is questionable owing to the variety of related diseases. As advances are made in microtechnology, the efficacy of in vitro diagnosis will increase.

REFERENCES

Henderson, H., & Whiteman, P. (1976). Antenatal diagnoses of Hurler's disease. *Lancet, 2*, 1024–1025.

Robinson, H. B., & Robinson, N. M. (1965). *The mentally retarded child*. New York: McGraw-Hill.

Stanbury, J. B., Wyngaarden, J. B., & Fredrickson, D. S. (Eds.). (1966). *The metabolic bases of inherited diseases* (2nd ed.). New York: McGraw-Hill.

FRANCINE TOMPKINS
University of Cincinnati

AMNIOCENTESIS
CHROMOSOMAL ABNORMALITIES

HYDROCEPHALUS

Hydrocephalus is a condition in which there is an abnormal accumulation of cerebrospinal fluid within the skull. As the fluid accumulates, the upper portion of the skull gradually increases in size out of proportion to the rest of the body. Left untreated, the condition usually produces several sequelae that end in the death of the patient. The three primary causes of the accumulation of fluid are overproduction of cerebrospinal fluid, defective absorption of the fluid, and interference with the circulation of the fluid. Underlying causes of the accumulation are often associated with meningitis, spina bifida, or tumors.

Thomson (1974) offered two criteria that should arouse suspicion of hydrocephalus in infants: (1) an increase in the circumference of the head of more than 1 inch during each of the first 2 months of life (and much less subsequently) and (2) the circumference of the head exceeds that of the infant's chest. Other visible characteristics include prominent veins in the scalp, separation of the sutures of the skull, widely spaced eyes, and a somewhat flattened nose. Internally, the brain becomes compressed downward, particularly when the condition occurs after the cranial sutures have closed. The pressure, which results from the abundance of cerebrospinal fluid, interferes with proper mental functioning. This often leads to behavioral symptoms, including listlessness, irritability, and retardation. As the disease progresses, the senses, particularly vision, become affected. Toward the end of its course, the patient may become paralyzed and experience convulsive seizures.

Although the pathology was not fully understood, the basic approach to the treatment of hydrocephalus has been known for at least 150 years. For example, Meindl, cited by Jordan (1972), recounted two successful surgical treatments of hydrocephalus by tapping the ventricles of the brain as early as 1829. However, the procedure, which was introduced by a Dr. Conquest, was criticized and eventually abandoned. Unfortunately, the technology that would make successful treatment commonplace was not to become available until the 1950s.

Many ingenious procedures have been devised to diagnose and treat hydrocephalus. A recent development that has led to great optimism in the assessment of the degree and cause of hydrocephalus is the use of computerized axial tomography (CAT scan). This technology involves the radiological scanning of the skull cavity in thin "slices," thus allowing the diagnostician to localize the site of a tumor or other blockage. Nevertheless, the CAT scan currently exhibits several problems (McAllister, Hankinson, & Sengupta, 1978) that may or may not be overcome with improved technology.

An early treatment approach reported by Ingraham and Matson (1954) is the ventriculo-ureterostomy procedure, in which, following the removal of one kidney, the ventricular cavity of the skull is connected to the ureter via a plastic tube. Thus, the excess cerebrospinal fluid is drained into the bladder and evacuated along with the urine produced by the remaining kidney. This procedure and the others to follow are referred to as shunt procedures because the excess fluid is diverted from the cranium to a part of the body that can absorb or excrete it. The two procedures most common today both employ an unidirectional valve (usually the Hakim or the Prudenz, sometimes in combination with the antisiphon valve). In ventriculo-atrial shunting, the cerebrospinal fluid is diverted to the right atrium of the heart. When the ventriculo-peritoneal shunt is used, the fluid is passed into the peritoneal cavity (stomach).

Although successful shunts often result in the arrest of the normal course of the condition, three problems may complicate the treatment: 1) extreme care is necessary to avoid infection; 2) revision or replacement of a valve is necessary when it becomes blocked or malfunctions in some way, and the tube used to drain the fluid may become dislodged and require adjustments; and, 3) epilepsy is a frequent sequela to operative treatment and shunt-related infection (Blaauw, 1978).

REFERENCES

Blaauw, G. (1978). Hydrocephalus and epilepsy. In R. Wullenweber, H. Wenker, M. Brock, & M. Klinger (Eds.), *Treatment of hydrocephalus—Computer tomography* (pp. 37–41). Berlin: Springer-Verlag.

Ingraham, F. D., & Matson, D. M. (1954). *Neurosurgery of infancy and childhood.* Springfield, IL: Thomas.

Jordan, T. E. (1972). *The mentally retarded* (3rd ed.). Columbus, OH: Merrill.

McAllister, V. L., Hankinson, J., & Sengupta, R. P. (1978). Problems in diagnosis with computerized tomography (CT). In R. Wullenweber, H. Wenker, M. Brock, & M. Klinger (Eds.), *Treatment of hydrocephalus—Computer tomography* (pp. 61–74). Berlin: Springer-Verlag.

Thomson, W. A. R. (1974). *Black's medical dictionary* (30th ed.). New York: Harper & Row.

RONALD C. EAVES
Auburn University

**MENINGITIS
SPINA BIFIDA**

HYPERACTIVITY

Hyperactivity, with its constellation of symptoms, is the problem most frequently referred to child guidance clinics in the United States (Barkley, 1981). The term is used interchangeably with attention deficit disorder (ADD). Over the past several years, there has been a consensus among researchers on the importance of attentional deficits in children previously receiving the label of hyperactivity (Douglas & Peters, 1979). In recognition of recent research demonstrating that hyperactivity is more of a cognitive than a motoric problem (Douglas, 1983), the American Psychiatric Association (1980) relabeled this syndrome as attention deficit disorder (ADD). As currently classified in the American Psychiatric Association *Diagnostic and Statistical Manual-III* (DSM-III), ADD refers to those related behavioral syndromes that are characterized by (1) developmentally inappropriate inattention (failure to complete activities, distractibility, difficulty in concentrating on tasks and sticking to play, and the appearance of not listening); (2) impulsivity (difficulty with organizing and with waiting for turns, shifting from activity to activity, acting before thinking, calling out in class, and needing much supervision); (3) and hyperactivity (excessive running, climbing, and moving, awake and asleep, difficulty in staying still and staying seated, fidgeting). DSM-III indicates that there are two types of ADD: with hyperactivity and without.

Onset of the disorder must be prior to the age of 7 with a duration of at least 6 months, and without evidence of severe or profound mental retardation, affective disorder, or psychosis. Academic difficulties, conduct problems, low self-esteem, immaturity, poor peer relationships, and spe-

cific developmental disorders are frequently associated with the ADD syndrome (Donnelly & Rapoport, 1985).

Douglas (1980) has proposed that there may even be another type of attentional deficit characteristic of hyperactive children, one involving selective attention. According to Douglas (1980), this deficit involves the tendency of a hyperactive child to have the attention captured by the salient aspects of situations to such an extent that the child fails to process more subtle aspects. Furthermore, hyperactive children may have a greater need for stimulation and may actually be stimulus seeking. Douglas (1980) has also postulated that most of the behavioral and cognitive aberrations in these children have their origins in deficits of sustained attention, poor inhibitory control, and faulty modulation of the arousal levels necessary for meeting task demands. This constellation of deficits has been described as an inability to stop, look, listen, and think (Douglas, 1980). A model of the deficits, problems, and difficulties as experienced in hyperactive children is presented in the Figure.

In examining the Figure, the term metaprocesses refers to the notion that these children may be impaired in their capacity to apply deliberate effort to tasks requiring a breakdown and analysis of a problem. Thus, their ability

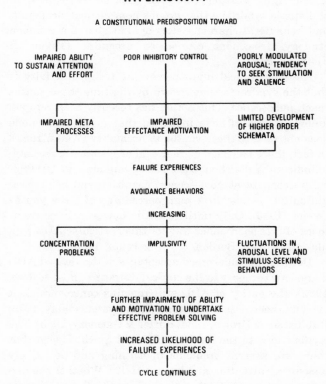

A model of deficits, problems, and difficulties seen in children with hyperactivity. (Reprinted by permission from V. I. Douglas (1980). Higher mental processes in hyperactive children. In R. M. Knights & D. J. Bakker (Eds.), *Treatment of hyperactive and learning disordered children.* Baltimore, MD: University Park Press).

to reflect on what they already know in order to approach and solve a novel problem is typically impaired. An impairment in effectance motivation suggests that ADD children do not remain sufficiently involved long enough, intensively enough, or effectively enough to develop intrinsic motivation. Finally, limited development of higher order schemata suggests that ADD youngsters perceive their world less carefully than do their normally developing peers, thereby placing limits on future learning. In the development of this model, Douglas (1980) has concluded that much of the available research points to a serious deficit in the higher order mental functioning of hyperactive children.

Prior to the current diagnostic label of attention deficit disorder (American Psychiatric Association, 1980), this syndrome was frequently referred to as minimal brain dysfunction (Cantwell, 1977). Recently it has been called hyperkinetic reaction of childhood. The various labels reflect a number of changes in the conceptualization of the disorder throughout the clinical and research literature. Unfortunately, until recently, our knowledge of hyperactivity was largely based on clinical myth (Ross & Ross, 1982) rather than on empirical reality. For example, numerous investigations have pointed out that the majority of children having received such labels do not have demonstrable brain damage and in fact fail to evidence subtle neurological signs. Further, there has been no real validation of a single syndrome that groups neurological, academic, and behavioral characteristics or that shares a common etiology, treatment course, or prognosis (Taylor & Fletcher, 1980).

Another clinical myth pertaining to hyperactivity is that the syndrome is outgrown by the time these youths reach pubescence. This notion has recently been refuted; follow-up studies have indicated that maturation alone does not restore these youths to normality (Weiss, 1983). In fact, there has been a great deal of systematic research to indicate that although the basic symptoms of ADD typically dissipate at adolescence, cognitive and behavioral difficulties persist in a high percentage of these youths (Weiss, 1983). Only until recently, however, have treatment efforts been under way for this particular ADD population (Brown, Borden, & Clingerman, 1985).

Despite the widespread acceptance of the revised ADD diagnostic category in the clinical literature (Ross & Ross, 1982), the entity of ADD still remains controversial; it even has been assailed by some investigators (Quay, 1979; Rubinstein & Brown, 1984; Rutter & Garmezy, 1983). The student new to the field of ADD will quickly learn that there are several problems in defining and objectively measuring attention and hyperactivity. Whether the disorder must be demonstrated across multiple situations is still largely unclear (Donnelly & Rapoport, 1985). Some investigators have gone so far as to insist that there is no real empirical support for the entity of an ADD disorder

(Quay, 1979); in fact, psychiatrists in the United Kingdom rarely differentiate ADD from conduct disorders.

Many treatment approaches have been systematically investigated for use with hyperactive children, but stimulant medication remains the best documented therapy in child psychiatry (Gittelman, 1983). Specifying target behaviors for successful drug therapy in these children is critical (Sprague, 1979), and the special education teacher may prove helpful to the practicing physician in documenting behavioral changes in the classroom so as to determine response to pharmacotherapy (Ullmann & Sleator, 1985). Parent ratings of children's behavior in determining efficacy to stimulant medication may also prove useful.

Careful attention must also be paid to any untoward side effects resulting from stimulant medication. Moreover, it should be recognized that stimulant drugs are not a panacea; improved functioning only sustains for the period of time that the hyperactive child is receiving the medication (Brown et al., in press). Unfortunately, the effects of long-term stimulant drug use in hyperactive children still remains unknown. Further, there is mounting research to suggest that long-term drug use may result in psychological side effects, including diminished self-esteem and learned helplessness (Borden, 1986). Although there has been a recent trend to supplement drug therapy with other psychological therapies, these approaches have proven to be largely unsuccessful (Abikoff & Gittelman, 1985; Brown, Wynne, & Medenis, 1985; Brown et al., in press). Thus, the search for optimal treatment approaches for this troublesome population still remains an area for investigation.

REFERENCES

Abikoff, H., & Gittelman, R. (1985). Hyperactive children treated with stimulants: Is cognitive training a useful adjunct? *Archives of General Psychiatry, 42,* 953–961.

American Psychiatric Association. (1980). *Diagnostic and statistical manual of mental disorders* (3rd ed.). Washington, DC: American Psychiatric Association.

Barkley, R. (1981). Hyperactivity. In E. Mash & L. Terdal (Eds.), *Behavioral assessment of childhood disorders* (pp. 127–184). New York: Guilford.

Borden, K. A. (1986). *Attributional outcomes: The subtle messages of treatments for attention deficit disorder.* Unpublished doctoral dissertation, University of Illinois at Urbana-Champaign.

Brown, R. T., Borden, K. A., & Clingerman, S. R. (1985). Pharmacotherapy in ADD adolescents with special attention to multimodality treatments. *Psychopharmacology Bulletin, 21,* 192–211.

Brown, R. T., Borden, K. A., Wynne, M. E., Schleser, R., & Clingerman, S. R. (in press). Methylphenidate and cognitive therapy with ADD children: A methodological reconsideration. *Journal of Abnormal Child Psychology.*

Brown, R. T., Wynne, M. E., & Medenis, R. (1985). Methylphenidate and cognitive therapy: A comparison of treatment approaches with hyperactive boys. *Journal of Abnormal Child Psychology, 13,* 69–87.

Cantwell, D. P. (1977). Psychopharmacologic treatment of the minimal brain dysfunction syndrome. In J. M. Weiner (Ed.), *Psychopharmacology in childhood and adolescence (pp. 119–148). New York: Basic Books.*

Donnelly, M., & Rapoport, J. L. (1985). Pharmacological treatment of attention deficit disorder. In J. M. Wiener (Ed.), Diagnosis and pharmacology of childhood and adolescent disorders (pp. 179–197). New York: Wiley.

Douglas, V. I. (1980). Higher mental processes in hyperactive children: Implications for training. In R. M. Knights & D. J. Bakker (Eds.), *Rehabilitation, treatment, and management of learning disorders* (pp. 65–91). Baltimore, MD: University Park Press.

Douglas, V. I. (1983). Attentional and cognitive problems. In M. Rutter (Ed.), *Developmental neuropsychiatry* (pp. 280–329). New York: Guilford.

Douglas, V. I., & Peters, K. G. (1979). Toward a clearer definition of the attentional deficit in hyperactive children. In G. A. Hale & M. Lewis (Eds.), *Attention and the development of cognitive skills* (pp. 173–247). New York: Plenum.

Gittelman, R. (1983). Hyperkinetic syndrome: Treatment issues and principles. In M. Rutter (Ed.), *Development neuropsychiatry* (pp. 437–449). New York: Guilford.

Quay, H. C. (1979). Classification. In H. Quay & J. S. Werry (Eds.), *Psychopathological disorders of childhood* (pp. 1–42). New York: Wiley.

Ross, D. M., & Ross, S. A. (1982). *Hyperactivity: Current issues, research, and theory* (2nd ed.). New York: Wiley.

Rubinstein, R., & Brown, R. T. (1984). An evaluation of the validity of the diagnostic category of attention deficit disorder. *American Journal of Orthopsychiatry, 54,* 398–414.

Rutter, M., & Garmezy, N. (1983). Developmental psychopathology. In P. Mussen (Ed.), *Handbook of child psychology Vol. 4,* (4th ed.) (pp. 775–912). New York: Wiley.

Sprague, R. L. (1979). Assessment of intervention. In R. L. Trites (Ed.), *Hyperactivity in children: Etiology, measurement, and treatment implications* (pp. 217–229). Baltimore, MD: University Park Press.

Taylor, G., & Fletcher, J. M. (1983). Biological foundations of "specific developmental disorders": Methods, findings, and future directions. *Journal of Clinical Child Psychology, 46,* 46–65.

Ullman, R. K., & Sleator, E. K. (1985). Attention deficit disorder children with or without hyperactivity: Which behaviors are helped by stimulants? *Clinical Pediatrics, 24,* 547–551.

Weiss, G. (1983). Long-term outcome: Findings, concepts, and practical implications. In M. Rutter (Ed.), *Developmental neuropsychiatry* (pp. 422–436). New York: Guilford.

RONALD T. BROWN
*Emory University School
of Medicine*

PHILLIP JENKINS
University of Kentucky

ATTENTION SPAN
ATTENTION DEFICIT DISORDER
HYPERKINESIS
HYPERTHYROIDISM

HYPERCALCEMIA

See INFANTILE HYPERCALCEMIA.

HYPERKINESIS

Hyperkinesis, previously believed to be a behavioral pattern associated with neurological dysfunction, is a widely used diagnostic classification for children with a high degree of activity combined with disordered or unmanageable behavior. It has been argued that a more appropriate label for these children might be attentional impulsivity disorder in view of the fact that attentional disturbances are so salient in the clinical descriptions of hyperkinetic children (Douglas & Peters, 1979). In fact, in the third edition of the *Diagnostic and Statistical Manual of Mental Disorders* (DSM III) hyperkinesis as a syndrome is described as attention deficit disorder (ADD). Specific diagnostic criteria include impulsivity, short attention span, overactivity, fidgetiness, and overdemanding, inattentive, and disruptive behavior (American Psychiatric Association, 1980).

Over the past two decades, hyperkinesis has been a significant focus of study not only because of its widespread prevalence in special education settings, but also because children so diagnosed often experience other significant problems. Loney (1980) has indicated that the "four As" of activity, attention, aggression, and achievement deserve careful consideration by clinicians and that there may be at least four overlapping but separable syndromes related to ADD; specifically, attention deficit disorder with hyperactivity, aggression, conduct disorder, and learning disability.

Contrary to popular clinical lore, which has suggested that hyperkinesis dissipates with age, it has recently been demonstrated that adolescents and young adults who had been diagnosed as hyperkinetic in childhood continue to experience difficulties in many areas of social functioning and personal well-being (Thorley, 1984). Thus, hyperkinesis remains a problem not only to be studied and treated in childhood but also in adolescence and adulthood as well.

REFERENCES

American Psychiatric Association. (1980). *Diagnostic and statistical manual of mental disorders* (3rd ed.). Washington, DC: Author.

Douglas, V. I., & Peters, K. G. (1979). Toward a clearer definition of the attentional deficit in hyperactive children. In G. A. Hale & M. Lewis (Eds.), *Attention and the development of cognitive skills* (pp. 173–247). New York: Plenum.

Loney, J. (1980). Hyperkinesis comes of age: What do we know and where should we go? *American Journal of Orthopsychiatry, 50,* 28–42.

Thorley, G. (1984). Review of follow-up and follow-back studies of childhood hyperactivity. *Psychological Bulletin, 96,* 116–132.

RONALD T. BROWN
*Emory University School
of Medicine*

ATTENTION-DEFICIT DISORDER-HYPERACTIVITY
HYPERTHYROIDISM

HYPERLEXIA

Hyperlexia is a condition characterized by precocious word calling skills that exceed levels of performance expected on the basis of intellectual ability. Although reading, or word calling, skills are high, there is usually poor reading comprehension. The condition has been reported since the 1940s (Bergman & Escalona, 1948), with more reports in the next decade (Eisenberg & Kanner, 1956; Mahler & Elkisch, 1953). The term hyperlexia was first used by Silberberg and Silberberg (1967), who suggested that the condition might be related to a neurological abnormality characterized by advanced development of specific brain functions. As recently as 1969, Cain reviewed the literature to date and concluded that there was no explanation for the phenomenon. Since that time there have been a number of studies of hyperlexic children (Hartlage & Hartlage, 1973; Huttenlocher & Huttenlocher, 1973; Mehegan & Dreifuss, 1972; Richman & Kitchell, 1981; Torrey, 1973), but there is still no consensus concerning the exact nature or etiology of the condition. One possible reason for the lack of agreement about the condition involves different characteristics supposedly associated with hyperlexia. Some researchers (e.g., Huttenlocher & Huttenlocher; Mehegan & Dreifuss; Silberberg & Silberberg) consider retarded language development to be a common correlate of the disorder, but other researchers (Durkin, 1966; Torrey, 1973) have found hyperlexia without these conditions.

The importance of a concurrent language disorder as a diagnostic feature of hyperlexia appears to be crucial for the development of a conceptual model of the disorder. Some researchers (e.g., Benton, 1978) contend that hyperlexia may be a unique form of language disorder found in many dyslexics; others (e.g., Hartlage & Hartlage, 1973) report that in hyperlexics there is a mirror image of the profile associated with dyslexia, in which hyperlexics score highest on such sequencing tasks as Wechsler coding and digit span, and poorest on such spatial tasks as Wechsler block design and object assembly subtests.

Hyperlexia has been reported in such subnormal populations as children with autism and severe mental retardation (Bender, 1955; Mehegan & Dreifus, 1972) as well as in more intellectually normal children (Healy, et al., 1982; Richman & Kitchell, 1981). Thus, intellectual level by itself does not seem to be a specific factor in the condition. One recent study (Graziani, 1985) found that some hyperlexic preschool children who tested in the mentally retarded range were subsequently found to have average intellectual ability, while other hyperlexic preschoolers with average intellectual ability showed subsequent regression in intellectual level. Thus, the relationship of hyperlexia to mental ability is difficult to predict owing to the variably interactive effects of reading-related activities on intellective functions at differing ages.

REFERENCES

Bender, L. (1955). Twenty years of clinical research on schizophrenic children. In G. Kaplan (Ed.). *Emotional problems of early childhood.* New York: Basic.

Benton, A. L. (1978). Some conclusions about dyslexia. In A. L. Benton & D. Pearl (Eds.), *Dyslexia.* New York: Oxford University Press.

Bergman, P. & Escalona, S. (1948). Unusual sensitivities in very young children. *Psychoanalytic Study of the Child.* New York: International Universities Press.

Cain, A. C. (1969). Special "isolated" abilities in severely psychotic children. *Psychiatry, 32,* 137–149.

Durkin, D. (1966). *Children who read early.* New York: Teacher's College Press.

Eisenberg, L., & Kanner, L. (1956). Early infantile autism, 1943–1955. *American Journal of Orthopsychiatry, 26,* 556–566.

Graziani, L. (1985, Feb.). *The neurological basis of language and reading disorders.* Paper presented at the meeting of the Association for Children and Adults with Learning Disabilities, San Francisco.

Hartlage, L. C., & Hartlage, P. L. (1973, May). *Hyperlexia in severely, moderately, and mildly retarded children.* Paper presented at American Association on Mental Deficiency, Minneapolis.

Healy, J. M., Straw, S. B., Schreiner, R., Reynolds, R. E., Taylor, M., & Steffensen, N. S. (1982). The enigma of hyperlexia. *Reading Research Quarterly, 17,* 319–338.

Huttenlocher, P. R., & Huttenlocher, J. (1973). A study of children with hyperlexia. *Neurology, 23,* 1107–1116.

Mahler, M. S., & Elkisch, P. (1953). Some observations on disturbances of the ego in a case of infantile psychosis. *Psychoanalytic Study of the Child.* New York: International Universities Press.

Mehegan, C. C., & Dreifuss, F. E. (1972). Hyperlexia: Exceptional reading ability in brain-damaged children. *Neurology, 22,* 1105–1111.

Richman, L. C., & Kitchell, M. M. (1981). Hyperlexia as a variant of developmental language disorder. *Brain & Language, 12,* 203–212.

Silberberg, N. E., & Silberberg, M. C. (1967). Hyperlexia: specific word recognition skills in young children. *Exceptional Children, 34,* 41–42.

Torrey, J. (1973). Learning to read without a teacher. In F. Smith (Ed.), *Psycholinguistics and reading.* New York: Holt, Rinehart & Winston.

LAWRENCE C. HARTLAGE
Evans, Georgia

READING DISORDERS
READING REMEDIATION

HYPEROPIA

Hyperopia is a visual disorder that results from an error of refraction. Refraction is a process by which light rays are gathered and focused onto certain portions of the retina. The hyperopic eye is too short and too weak to allow this process to take place normally (Heward & Orlansky, 1984). As a result, hyperopia develops. This impedes near vision and is commonly referred to as farsightedness.

The average, normal infant is born farsighted. As the child matures, the hyperopia decreases. This is especially true during puberty, when children who began life without the hyperopic trait will become nearsighted (Michelson, 1980). Children who are left with some farsightedness will become aware of it at different times depending on severity or occupational demands.

Hyperopia is easily treated through the prescription of glasses or contact lenses. However, if untreated, hyperopia can have significant impact on classroom performance. Since a hyperopic student will have difficulty in focusing on near objects, it may become difficult to perform certain academic functions.

REFERENCES

Heward, W. L., & Orlansky, M. D. (1984). *Exceptional children.* Columbus, OH: Merrill.

Michelson, P. E. (1980). *Insight into eyesight.* Chicago: Nelson-Hall.

JOHN R. BEATTIE
University of North Carolina,
Charlotte

VISUAL ACUITY
VISUAL EFFICIENCY

HYPERTELORISM

Hypertelorism is a descriptive term designating wide orbital separation characterized by separation of the eyes. This represents a retention of the wide, primitive interorbital angle. While early studies suggested a single cause, subsequent evaluations show great variety in the clinical and radiologic appearances of the skull. The condition is distinguished from telecanthus (lateral displacement of the medical canthal tissue), where the interocular (between the eyes) distance is normal (Duke-Elder, 1963).

The retention of a wide interorbital angle is attributed to early ossification of the lesser wings of the sphenoid bone, fixing the orbits in lateral positions. An alternative hypothesis suggests the anomaly results from failure of maxillary process development with compensatory overgrowth of the frontonasal process. Further, it is important to differentiate this anomaly from physiologic variance often associated with racial groups and patients with secondary hypertelorism. Secondary forms follow disturbances in development resulting from various disorders such as frontal encephalocele and trauma. The primary, dysgenetic type may accompany a variety of congenital disorders, including craniofacial abnormalities and many chromosomal aberrations (Jones & Jakobiec, 1979).

Divergent strabismus is the most common associated ocular disorder, although other abnormalities such as microphthalmos, microcornea, and optic atrophy may occur. Mentation is generally good and most patients are described as even-tempered and gentle.

The significance of this anomaly is minimal to the educator except as a clue to other developmental defects. In general, the eye, face and brain develop concurrently; defects in one area suggest the possibility of defects in another. Only if associated with ocular or central nervous system defects would this anomaly be of particular significance.

REFERENCES

Duke-Elder, S. (1963). *System of ophthalmology: Vol. III, Part 2, Congenital deformities.* St. Louis: Mosby.

Jones, I. S., & Jakobiec, F. A. (1979). *Diseases of the orbit.* Hagerstown, MD: Harper & Row.

GEORGE R. BEAUCHAMP
Cleveland Clinic Foundation,
Cleveland, Ohio

HYPERTHYROIDISM

Hyperthyroidism is an endocrinological disorder that is characterized by excessive functional activity in the production of thyroid hormones. The resulting condition is generally marked by increased metabolic rate, protrusion of the eyes, enlargement of the thyroid gland, high blood pressure, and rapid heart rate. This disease is genetically determined, runs in families, affects females more than males, and requires a physician's diagnosis and subsequent treatment. Parents, teachers, and the school psychologist should work closely with the child's physician in providing intervention (Gardner, 1969).

Throughout the early literature many terms were used to describe the disorder (Mornex & Orgiazzi, 1980). Unique aspects of individual cases generally were detailed, as in Grave's 1835 work with patients having heart and eye swelling and Von Basedow's 1840 reporting of eye and thyroid enlargement. Both describe the disorder of hyperthyroidism and its synonym thyrotoxicosis.

The American Thyroid Association has provided a system of classification from which various types of hyperthyroidism can be differentiated (Werner, 1969). All of these categories are similar with respect to the involvement of excess thyroid hormones without a normal regulating control in the body. The severity of the symptoms varies by the level and duration of the hypersecretion of thyroid hormones. The patient generally complains of fatigue and is perceived by others as being nervous, irritable, and overactive, and as having mild tremors.

Children with congenital hyperthyroidism have been observed to be restless, to overeat without weight gain, and to experience high temperatures. Hyperthyroidism is extremely rare before age 5; approximately 10% of patients are under 10. Although females have a disproportionate representation of 6:1 over males, the prevalency is equal between the sexes for children ages 10 to 15 years. The disorder progresses rapidly from early symptoms to the expression of behavioral problems and subsequent decline in school performance. Accelerated body growth without modification of final height has been reported (Mornex & Orgiazzi, 1980).

Confusion of hyperthyroidism with emotional disorders is common and necessitates a careful diagnosis by a physician. Research has shown that abnormally high levels of thyroid hormones in the body are associated with and may precipitate psychopathology in hyperthyroidism (Zeitlhofer, Saletu, Stary, & Ahmandi, 1984). Psychopathology sometimes masks the underlying disorder of hyperthyroidism, and the aberrant behavior diminishes following antihyperthyroid treatment. It is assumed that the chemical imbalance inhibits efficient processing of the central nervous system and that pathological behaviors result.

Treatment of hyperthyroidism is either ablative (surgery, radioactive iodine) or conservative (drug therapy), or a combination of both. When a tumor is thought to be the cause of hyperthyroidism, surgery is necessary. However, the removal of the thyroid gland then may reverse its symptomatology, resulting in hypothyroidism. Antihyperthyroid medication is generally the choice of treatment, in combination with supportive counseling.

Prognosis is poor owing to the lack of a completely satisfactory treatment. The disorder is probably lifelong and requires lengthy treatment. Special educators should work closely with the physician and school psychologist in adapting the educational environment to the unique needs of the child with hyperthyroidism.

REFERENCES

Gardner, L. (1969). *Endocrine and genetic disease in childhood.* Philadelphia: Saunders.

Mornex, R., & Orgiazzi, J. J. (1980). Hyperthyroidism. In M. De Visscher (Ed.), *The thyroid gland* (pp. 275–369), New York: Raven.

Werner, S. C. (1969). Classification of thyroid diseases. *Journal of Clinical Endocrinology & Metabolism, 29,* 860–862.

Zeitlhofer, J., Saletu, B., Stary, J., & Ahmandi, R. (1984). Cerebral function in hyperthyroid patients: Psychopathology, psychometric variables, central arousal and time perception before and after thyreostatic therapy. *Neuropsychobiology, 2,* 89–93.

Scott W. Sautter
Peabody College, Vanderbilt University

EMOTIONAL DISORDERS
HYPOTHYROIDISM

HYPERTONIA

Hypertonia, or hypertonicity, is a nonspecific state of increased skeletal muscle tone or partial contraction. The term often is used interchangeably with spasticity, but spasticity generally is viewed as a more pronounced degree of pathologic hypertonicity. Hypertonia occurs because of excessive motor unit activity within the muscle fibers; it is an indicator of neurologic dysfunction. Hypertonia is best represented by a continuum, from slightly above normal muscle tone to severely rigid. Muscle tone is often variable throughout different locations of the body. A person's level of arousal, body position in relation to gravity, and activity often will influence the degree of hypertonia that is present.

Some people may have a higher state of normal muscle tone (e.g., athletes or soldiers), but this generally is not considered to be pathologic hypertonicity or spasticity. Normal muscle tone is a state of tension or partial contraction that provides postural stability and allows people to maintain themselves in an upright position against the force of gravity. When damage occurs to the central nervous system (CNS) and especially the cortex of the brain, hypertonia often is seen in the extremities. This damage may occur in a wide variety of CNS disorders including cerebral vascular accident (CVA), traumatic closed head injury, cerebral palsy, and dystonia. The location and severity of damage to the CNS determines the location and severity of abnormal hypertonia in the body. The increased muscle tone associated with hypertonia reduces the amount of mobility and increases the stability in the joints of the affected extremity. This decreased mobility and increased stability restrict normal movement from occurring in the involved body parts.

Electromyographic (EMG) studies are the most precise method of detecting or delineating muscular hypertonia because the excessive motor unit activity within the muscles can be detected as electrical impulses. Clinical identification also can be made by eliciting exaggerated stretch reflexes or by observing the person engaging in different postures or positions. Abnormal hypertonia, if left untreated, may result in compensatory movement patterns or postures in parts of the body that are less impaired. Permanent muscle shortening, which in turn results in joint contracture and skeletal deformity, is often the end result of more severe forms of hypertonia.

Treatment for hypertonia includes a variety of medical, surgical, and therapeutic approaches. Numerous medications have been used with limited success, often because of unwanted side effects. Splinting and bracing also may be used to prevent muscle shortening and permanent deformity, but these approaches only address the symptoms rather than the condition itself. Physical management or manipulation techniques such as neurodevelopmental treatment (NDT) and proprioceptive neuromuscular facilitation (PNF) have become increasingly effective and popular because they are believed to have some impact on the complex mechanisms that sustain hypertonia. When permanent muscle shortening or joint contracture occur secondary to hypertonia, orthopedic surgery to lengthen tendons or connective tissue often is needed. In some cases of severe hypertonia, it may be necessary to insert a pin or surgically fuse a joint to prevent further deformity or dislocation.

REFERENCES

Bishop, B. (1977). Spasticity: Its physiology and management, Part 1. Neurophysiology of spasticity: Classical concepts. *Physical Therapy, 57,* 371–376.

Campbell, P. (1984). Basic considerations in programming for students with movement difficulties. In M. Snell (Ed.), *Systematic instruction of the moderately and severely handicapped* (2nd ed., pp. 168–202). Columbus, OH: Merrill.

Rasch, P. J., & Burke, R. K. (1979). Physiology of muscular contraction. In P. J. Rasch & R. K. Burke (Eds.), *Kinesiology and applied anatomy* (6th ed., pp. 203–221). Philadelphia: Lea & Febiger.

Wyke, B. (1976). Neurological mechanisms in spasticity: A brief review of some current concepts. *Physiotherapy, 62,* 316–319.

DANIEL D. LIPKA
*Lincoln Way Special Education
Regional Resource Center,
Louisville, Ohio*

HYPOTONIA
PHYSICAL DISABILITIES

HYPNOSIS

While no generally accepted definition exists, hypnosis is usually considered to be an altered state of consciousness characterized by a heightened susceptibility to suggestion. As an altered state of consciousness, hypnosis is seen as a condition distinct from sleep or wakefulness, perhaps similar to deep meditation, yoga, or some other trancelike state. The heightened susceptibility characteristic relates to the observation that the hypnotized person accepts ideas more uncritically and wholeheartedly than ordinarily (American Society of Clinical Hypnosis, 1973).

Research suggests that the practice of hypnosis extends far back into the history of man. Support for such claims is found in ancient writings from many cultures, including India, Persia, China, and Egypt (Gravitz & Gerton, 1984). The modern history of hypnosis began with Franz Anton Mesmer, a Viennese physician of the late eighteenth and early nineteenth centuries. Mesmer is most famous for his theory of hypnotism as animal magnetism, a force that he believed came from within living bodies and was passed to other living bodies and objects. Mesmer's animal magnetism supposedly could be used to cure serious illnesses. His work gave raise to the term mesmerism, a synonym for hypnosis.

Mesmer's work came to the attention of James Braid, a Scottish physician of the early nineteenth century. Braid, who coined the term hypnotism, rejected Mesmer's animal magnetism theory but emphasized the importance of suggestion and concentration in hypnosis. Braid's experience lead him and others to use hypnosis in the treatment of disease; during the 1800s this technique was used successfully as an anesthetic for many surgical procedures (Hilgard & Hilgard, 1975).

Since Braid's time, the use of hypnosis has gone through several periods of public and professional interest and disinterest, and has been studied by such famous scientists as Charles Darwin and Sigmund Freud. Presently, the interest in hypnosis as a medical and psychological aid is high and research into its effective use is expanding. Hypnosis is now viewed by the majority of the professional community as a respectable and useful technique for helping with medical and psychological problems.

Little agreement about the nature of hypnosis exists among the authorities in the field. Numerous competing theories have been proposed, but none seem to explain adequately the phenomenon and no theory has gained wide acceptance. Many theories fit into one of two categories, physiological and psychological. Physiological theories of hypnosis emphasize physical changes that are reported to occur during or as a result of hypnosis: alteration in metabolism, changes in the nervous system, and unusual electrical activity in the brain. Psychological theories stress the importance of psychological factors: learning, suggestion, role-playing, and modeling.

Ernest R. Hillard, a leader in the scientific study of

hypnosis, has proposed a neodissociation theory, which holds that hypnotic procedures rearrange control systems in the brain (Hilgard, 1977). Research by Hilgard and others supports this model. However, at the present time, the scientific understanding of hypnosis is at an early stage of development.

Regardless of the true nature of hypnosis, it can be used to produce some conditions in a subject that are helpful and therapeutic: relaxation, concentration, the ability to put oneself in imaginary situations, and the capacity to accept suggestions more fully. These conditions provide a basis for the application of hypnosis to the treatment of a number of medical and psychological problems.

Hypnosis has been used successfully alone or in combination with other treatment methods in dealing with the following: emotional problems, including anxiety; control of pain; surgery; psychosomatic problems; obesity and dietary problems; smoking; pediatric problems; neurological problems; rehabilitation; conditions related to obstetrics and gynecology; skin problems; sexual dysfunction; and dental procedures. Practical application of hypnosis is extensive.

REFERENCES

American Society of Clinical Hypnosis–Education and Research Foundation (1973). *A syllabus on hypnosis and a handbook of therapeutic suggestions*. Des Plains, IL: Author.

Gravitz, M. A., & Gerton, M. I. (1984). Hypnosis in the historical development of psychoanalytic psychotherapy. In W. C. Wester & A. H. Smith (Eds.), *Clinical hypnosis: A multidisciplinary approach*. Philadelphia: Lippincott.

Hilgard, E. R. (1977). *Divided Conscienceness*. New York: Wiley.

Hilgard, E. R., & Hilgard, J. R. (1975). *Hypnosis in the relief of pain*. Los Altos, CA: Kaufman.

ROBERT R. REILLEY
Texas A&M University

PSYCHOSOCIAL ADJUSTMENT
PSYCHOTHERAPY

HYPOACTIVITY

Hypoactivity is a condition characterized by insufficient or inadequate motor activity and the inability to focus and sustain attention on external stimuli. Myers and Hammill (1969) describe the hypoactive child as one who is lethargic and quiet, and who causes little disturbance in the classroom. These children are more difficult to recognize and identify than are their hyperactive counterparts, and their problems may escape detection.

Although hyperactive and hypoactive children are at opposite ends of an activity level continuum, both show attentional deficits that may interfere with learning. Dykman, Ackerman, Clements, and Peters (1971) discuss the child who is unable to focus attention on the written or spoken word, and who, therefore, cannot easily learn to read or spell. Most frequently, such attention deficits take the form of impulsivity and overreaction to stimuli. However, in the case of hypoactive children, inhibition, passivity, and underreaction to stimuli are symptomatic of the deficit.

The Russian psychologist A. R. Luria (1959, 1961) has written extensively on attention deficits, and has addressed the problem of hypoactivity specifically. He refers to the syndrome of cerebral asthenia, characterized by an inability to concentrate, distractibility, and short attention span. Luria points out that this syndrome often can be expressed in two externally different but essentially similar forms. He states that nervous processes are reducible to the two basic components of excitation and inhibition, present in all individuals. The strength, concentration, equilibrium, and mobility of excitation and inhibition may be affected by brain pathology. If the pathological state of the cortical cells primarily affects the inhibitory processes, the child displays excessive impulsivity and the loss of control associated with hyperactivity. However, if the pathology is expressed in a decline of the excitatory processes, the child experiences a sharp fall of the tone of the nervous processes and enters into a state of passivity. Luria refers to such children as inhibitory types and describes them as sluggish, torpid, and slow to form new positive reactions to stimuli, much like the hypoactive, learning-disabled child.

Although the literature reflects considerable research focused on hyperactivity, there have been relatively few studies dealing with the hypoactive child. Luria (1961) investigated the role of speech as an influence on the disequilibrium between the basic nervous processes. In experiments that required sustained, focused attention, he found inhibited children failed to make correct motoric responses to stimuli. However, when these children were asked to respond verbally as well as motorically, the accuracy and frequency of their responses increased significantly. Luria concluded that the combination of verbal and motoric responses tones up the activity level of the child, and that the compensatory influence of speech serves to heighten the level of the excitatory processes.

Research by Ozolins and Anderson (1980) showed that behavioral approaches could be used successfully to influence the performance of hypoactive children. In experiments requiring sustained attention, the authors found that such children performed better when given feedback reinforcing correct answers. Knowledge of errors served only to increase already excessive levels of inhibition and reduced correct answers. Positive reinforcement made this group feel more secure and less inhibited in their responses.

REFERENCES

Dykman, R. A., Ackerman, P. T., Clements, S. D., & Peters, J. E. (1971). Specific learning disabilities: An attentional deficit syndrome. In H. R. Myklebust (Ed.), *Progress in learning disabilities* (Vol. 2, pp. 56–94). New York: Grune & Stratton.

Luria, A. R. (1959). Experimental study of the higher nervous activity of the abnormal child. *Journal of Mental Deficiency Research, 3,* 1–22.

Luria, A. R. (1961). *The role of speech in the regulation of normal and abnormal behavior.* New York: Liveright.

Myers, P. I., & Hammill, D. D. (1969). *Methods for learning disorders.* New York: Wiley.

Ozolins, D. A., & Anderson, R. P. (1980). Effects of feedback on the vigilance task performance of hyperactive and hypoactive children. *Perceptual and Motor Skills, 50*(2), 415–424.

BARBARA S. SPEER
*Shaker Heights City School
District, Shaker Heights,
Ohio*

**ATTENTION DEFICIT DISORDER—HYPERACTIVITY
ATTENTION SPAN**

HYPOGLYCEMIA

Hypoglycemia is a physiological disorder in which a sudden rise and then rapid decrease in blood glucose level occurs within 1 to 3 hours. This abrupt drop in blood glucose sends the body into a condition of near shock that may be exacerbated by stress (Sorochan, 1981). Concomitant symptomatology may include lethargic behavior (unmotivated, fatigued, withdrawn, depressed); erratic behavior (mental confusion, unprovoked anxiety, hyperactivity, aggression); and a craving for sweets (Knapczyk, 1979). This condition of low blood glucose level marks the disorder of hypoglycemia. It is differentiated from hyperglycemia, in which the body has abnormally high blood glucose levels.

The diagnosis of hypoglycemia is made by a physician, who measures the blood glucose level at different times (e.g., before eating, immediately after eating, and a few hours after eating). Before eating, the level is low; it rises after eating and then falls after a few hours. If the rate of the drop in blood glucose level exceeds the normal range for the individual's age group, then the diagnosis of hypoglycemia is positive.

One out of 10 individuals is born with a hypersensitive pancreas (Sorochan, 1981) and is physically incapable of processing large quantities of sugar (or its various derivatives) in foods. The pancreas then produces excess insulin that results in the rapid drop of the blood glucose level. This in turn produces adverse behavior because the brain and other organs depend on an adequate supply of blood glucose for energy.

Some researchers have investigated the relationship between hypoglycemia and behavioral disorders (Knapczyk, 1979) and aggression and psychiatric symptoms (Virkkunen, 1982). Many researchers have concentrated on the area of diet, particularly the reduction of carbohydrates. One of the most effective treatments of hypoglycemia may be a well-controlled elimination diet that advocates six or more meals a day instead of three. The intention is to reduce sugar consumption as well as decrease the amount of time in which the individual is in the low blood glucose state.

Even though hypoglycemia should be diagnosed by a physician, school administrators, psychologists, and teachers also should be aware of the disorder. Consistent observation of a child's erratic behavior following eating may indicate hypoglycemia, and referral to a physician may be in order.

REFERENCES

Knapczyk, D. R. (1979). Diet control in the management of behavior disorders. *Behavioral Disorders, 1,* 2–9.

Sclafani, A. (1982)., On the role of hypoglycemia in carbohydrate appetite. *Appetite, 3,* 227–228.

Sorochan, W. D. (1981). *Promoting your health.* New York: Wiley.

Virkkunen, M. (1982). Reactive hypoglycemic tendency among habitually violent offenders: A further study by means of the glucose tolerance test. *Neuropsychobiology, 1,* 35–40.

SCOTT W. SAUTTER
*Peabody College, Vanderbilt
University*

**ACTING OUT
BEHAVIORAL DISORDERS
HYPERGLYCEMIA**

HYPOTHYROIDISM

Congenital hypothyroidism is an endocrinological disorder resulting from a deficient production of thyroid hormones. If left untreated for a period of 1 to 3 months postnatally, severe mental retardation occurs. Acquired hypothyroidism in childhood does not have as devastating an effect on intelligence as the congenital form. However, this condition is associated with fatigue, poor growth, cold intolerance, aggressive behavior, and depression. Research has shown that acquired hypothyroidism impairs psychological, neurological, and behavioral patterns (Gardner, 1969).

There appear to be sufficient data to support the hypothesis of critical periods of brain development that require adequate supplies of thyroid hormones (Hulse, 1983). The fetus is largely dependent on its own thyroid gland because little of the mother's thyroxine crosses the placenta. Thyroid hormones have been determined to be critical in the development of the central nervous system. It has been postulated that even before birth, hypothyroidism may cause cerebral and cerebellar impairment. Current research is examining the extent to which changes in brain-behavioral relationships are reversible through early treatment. Evidence suggests that early diagnosis through neonatal screening and subsequent treatment is of major importance for the prevention of lifelong complications of congenital hypothyroidism.

The effects of hypothyroidism on the developing brain are accumulated through complex interactions. The diversity and speed at which brain growth is delayed by the absence or lack of thyroid hormones adversely affects dendritic growth and synaptic connections (Birrell, Frost, & Parkin, 1983). The overall consequence is severe mental retardation.

Hulse (1983) reported that early researchers investigating hypothyroidism recognized that both age and severity of the retardation were important variables at the time of treatment, but were not always predictive in the assumed direction. Later, more detailed studies demonstrated the need for treatment prior to 1 to 3 months postnatally for good prognosis of congenital hypothyroidism (Rovet, Westbrook, & Ehrlich, 1984). The diagnosis and treatment are conducted by a physician. School personnel should work closely with the physician in designing and implementing intervention programs.

A good prognosis will stem from continued early diagnosis and treatment from routine neonatal screening. The successfully treated cases have had normal intelligence, some behavioral disorders, and minor motor incoordination. If remedial programs are required, careful delineation of the child's strengths and weaknesses may indicate specific interventions. Participation in the daily activities of school and its general milieu will promote mental and physical growth of the child with treated hypothyroidism.

REFERENCES

Birrell, J., Frost, G. J., & Parkin, J. M. (1983). The development of children with congenital hypothyroidism. *Developmental Medicine & Child Neurology, 4,* 512–519.

Gardner, L. (1969). *Endocrine and genetic disease in childhood.* Philadelphia: Saunders.

Hulse, A. (1983). Congenital hypothyroidism and neurological development. *Journal of Child Psychology & Psychiatry, 4,* 629–635.

Rovet, J. F., Westbrook, D. C., & Ehrlich, R. M. (1984). Neonatal thyroid deficiency: Early temperamental and cognitive characteristics. *Journal of the American Academy of Child Psychiatry, 1,* 10–22.

SCOTT W. SAUTTER
Peabody College, Vanderbilt University

HYPOACTIVITY
HYPOGLYCEMIA

HYPOTONIA

Hypotonia, or hypotonicity, is a nonspecific state of decreased skeletal muscle tone or partial contraction. The term may occasionally be used interchangeably with flaccidity, but flaccidity is generally viewed as an absence of muscle tone. Hypotonia occurs because of reduced motor unit activity within the muscle fibers. It is an indicator of neurologic dysfunction or muscle disease. Hypotonia is best represented by a continuum, from slightly below normal muscle tone to complete flaccidity; it is often variable throughout different locations of the body. Although hypotonia occurs in the absence of voluntary control, a person's level of arousal, body position in relation to gravity, and activity may influence the degree of hypotonia that is present.

Some people may have a lower state of normal muscle tone (resulting in poor posture), but this is generally not considered to be pathologic hypotonicity. Normal muscle tone is a state of tension or partial contraction that provides postural stability and allows a person to maintain himself or herself in an upright position against the force of gravity. When damage occurs to parts of the central nervous system (CNS), especially the cerebellum of the brain, hypotonia may be seen in the trunk or extremities. Peripheral nerve injuries typically result in flaccidity in the involved extremity. Some congenital impairments or syndromes such as muscular dystrophy or Down's syndrome have varying degrees of muscular hypotonia. The decreased muscle tone associated with hypotonia reduces the amount of stability and increases the mobility in the joints of the affected extremity. This decreased stability and increased mobility reduce the postural capacity of the individual and often makes movement of body parts more strenuous.

Electromyographic (EMG) studies are the most precise method of detecting or delineating muscular hypotonia because the reduced motor unit activity within the muscles can be detected as electrical impulses. Clinical identification is more commonly used to detect hypotonia by observing the person engaged in different postures or positions. Abnormal hypotonia, if left untreated, may result in compensatory movement patterns or postures; in some cases, a person with hypotonicity may be prone to obesity. Skeletal deformity, particularly in the spine (scoliosis, etc.), is often the end result of many forms of hypotonia, but the extremities are rarely involved.

Treatment for hypotonia includes a variety of surgical or therapeutic approaches. Splinting and bracing may be used to prevent spinal curvature and permanent deformity, but these approaches only address the symptoms and not the condition itself. Physical management or manipulation techniques such as neurodevelopmental treatment (NDT) and proprioceptive neuromuscular facilitation (PNF) also have been tried, but the effectiveness has been less than with hypertonia. When permanent orthopedic deformities occur secondary to hypotonia, orthopedic surgery may be necessary to insert a pin or surgically fuse the spine or other joints to prevent further deformity or dislocation. Educational performance may be influenced by hypotonia in regard to activities involving sensory motor functioning. Hypotonia may be mild enough to have no discernible effect on educational performance or may be so severe as to prevent a person from sitting or holding his or her head upright. Mental retardation or other disturbances in intellectual functioning may exist concurrently with hypotonia, requiring multidisciplinary educational intervention.

REFERENCES

Campbell, P. (1984). Basic considerations in programming for students with movement difficulties. In M. Snell (Ed.), *Systematic instruction of the moderately and severely handicapped*. Columbus, OH: Merrill.

Packer, R. J., Brown, M. J., & Berman, P. H. (1982, Dec.). The diagnostic value of electromyography in infantile hypotonia. *American Journal of the Disabled Child, 136,* 1057–1059.

Rasch, P. J., & Burke, R. K. (1979). Physiology of muscular contraction. In P. J. Rasch & R. K. Burke (Eds.), *Kinesiology and applied anatomy* (6th ed.). Philadelphia: Lea & Febiger.

DANIEL D. LIPKA
*Lincoln Way Special Education
Regional Resource Center,
Louisville, Ohio*

MUSCULAR DYSTROPHY

HYPOXIA

Hypoxia means lowered levels of oxygen intake. Lowered oxygen levels cause changes in pH balance, energy use, and tissue perfusion (Freeman, 1985a). The degree of change varies with the duration and severity of the episode. In extreme, it can lead to death. Hypoxia may occur in infants (1) requiring mechanical ventilation because their lungs are unable to absorb inspired oxygen; (2) with recurring apnea; (3) with heart disorders that prevent oxygenated blood from reaching vital tissues; and, more rarely (4) with severe anemia. In the last case, the underlying factor is the blood's inability to transport oxygen even though the heart and lungs are functioning normally (Parry & Adams, 1985).

Neonatal hypoxia may cause irreversible damage, especially to the brain. Developing brain tissue is particularly susceptible to lowered oxygen levels as well as other insults. The effects of hypoxia are highly variable; some infants who experience hypoxia do poorly, but most recover well. Recent research suggests a threshold effect: A range of degrees of hypoxia can be tolerated without obvious effect, but severity beyond the threshold produces damaging effects. Normal term infants of normal weight are presumed to have the highest threshold, and thus can best withstand minor degrees of hypoxia. Conditions that lower the threshold are those that "weaken" the infant and his or her ability to handle stress. Two such conditions are prematurity and low birth weight (Freeman, 1985b).

Maternal hypoxia, caused, for example, by severe pneumonia, may adversely affect the developing fetus, causing severe malformations in the brain itself (Goodlin, Heidrick, Papenfuss, & Kubitz, 1984).

Cerebral palsy is the most common defect associated with hypoxia; it is seen in 10 to 26% of survivors. Other possible sequelae are hydrocephalus, seizures, brain hemorrhage, and mental retardation. Hypoxia may also be one cause of learning disorders and deficits in fine and gross motor coordination (Parry, Baldy, & Gardner, 1985). Hypoxia is one component in a series of events that often progress to a condition termed asphyxia.

REFERENCES

Freeman, J. (1985a). Introduction. In J. F. Freeman (Ed.), *Prenatal and perinatal factors associated with brain damage* (NIH Publication No. 85–1149, pp. 1–11). Bethesda, MD: National Institutes of Health.

Freeman, J. (1985b). Summary. In J. Freeman (Ed.), *Prenatal and perinatal factors associated with brain damage* (NIH Publication No. 85–1149, pp. 13–32). Bethesda, MD: National Institutes of Health.

Goodlin, R. C., Heidrick, W. P., Papenfuss, H. L., & Kubitz, R. L. (1984). Fetal malformation associated with maternal hypoxia. *American Journal of Obstetrics and Gynecology, 149*(2), 228–229.

Parry, W., & Adams, N. (1985). Acid-base homeostasis and oxygenation. In G. Merenstein & S. Gardner (Eds.), *Handbook of neonatal intensive care* (pp. 239–252). St. Louis: Mosby.

Parry, W., Baldy, M., & Gardner, S. (1985). Respiratory diseases. In G. Merenstein & S. Gardner, (Eds.), *Handbook of neonatal intensive care* (pp. 301–344). St. Louis: Mosby.

BRENDA POPE
*New Hanover Memorial
Hospital, Wilmington,
North Carolina*

APNEA
ASPHYXIA
PREMATURITY

HYSTERICAL PERSONALITY

Hysterical personality (or histrionic disorder) is a type of personality disorder characterized by an inordinate need for attention, affection, and stimulation. Behavior resulting from this need often includes exaggerated expression of emotion, overreaction to minor events, frequent attempts to draw attention to oneself, tantrums, and intense seeking of activity and excitement (American Psychiatric Association, 1980). With the publication of the third edition of the *Diagnostic and Statistical Manual of Mental Disorders* (DSM-III) in 1980, the term histrionic personality disorder has replaced the older hysterical personality as the official designation of this condition.

Since it is classified as a personality disorder, this condition is considered to be deeply embedded in the individual's makeup, pervasive in its influence on the person's behavior, and likely to last over a long period of time. The histrionic personality is chronic rather than acute and represents the individual's usual or typical way of acting, as opposed to an isolated response to some life event. The behavior pattern persists in spite of being seriously maladaptive and resulting in considerable impairment to the individual's interpersonal functioning.

In terms of underlying causes, Theodore Millon (1981) views the histrionic personality disorder as resulting from a fear of independence or autonomy coupled with an exaggerated desire for social approval and attention, "an insatiable and indiscriminate search for stimulation and affection" (p. 60). While dependent on others for attention and affection, histrionics are not content to be passive. To the contrary, they take the initiative in attracting attention by a variety of methods: seductive ploys, hyperalertness to the needs of others, exhibitionism, and persistent attention-seeking behavior. Active-dependent and gregarious are terms considered appropriate for this group (Millon, 1981).

Histrionics tend to have a limited and shallow internal life. They focus primarily externally, attending to others who may provide the attention and novelty they crave. This external preoccupation, along with tendencies to repress or deny inner feelings, results in an individual with very little capacity for insight or self-understanding. Not surprisingly, histrionics show meager interest in intellectual achievement or analytic thinking.

Ironically, histrionics experience their greatest failure in the very arena in which they strive so hard for success: interpersonal relations. They are perceived by others as immature, egocentric, self-centered, vain, and demanding (American Psychiatric Association, 1980). This personality disorder is associated with shallow, superficial friendships that tend to be brief in duration owing to the histrionics' constant need to impress new individuals and thus assure the constant stream of attention they crave. Their social relationships have been described as seductive, dramatic, and capricious (Millon, 1981).

In addition to its pure form, histrionic personality disorder frequently appears in combination with other illnesses. Drug abuse, depression, anxiety, conversion disorders, and a variety of physical complaints are common. Combinations of histrionic personality with other personality disorders are also to be expected.

Treatment of this condition is hampered by the histrionic's strong tendency to be demanding, seductive, self-centered, and manipulative. Impulsive behavior, including suicide attempts and threats, is not unusual (Reid, 1983). At the same time, shallow emotions and limited personal commitment threaten the continuance of the therapeutic relationship. These individuals, however, do experience periods of intense anxiety and depression requiring psychotherapy and support. Tupin (1981) provides additional information on the diagnosis and treatment of this condition.

REFERENCES

American Psychiatric Association. (1980). *Diagnostic and statistical manual of mental disorders* (3rd ed.). Washington, DC: Author.

Millon, T. (1981). *Disorders of personality DSM-III: Axis II*. New York: Wiley.

Reid, W. H. (1983). *Treatment of the DSM-III psychiatric disorders*. New York: Brunner/Mazel.

Tupin, J. P. (1981). Histrionic personality. In J. R. Lion (Ed.), *Personality disorders: Diagnosis and management* (2nd ed.). Baltimore, MD: Williams & Wilkins.

ROBERT R. REILLEY
Texas A&M University

CHARACTER DISORDER
MENTAL ILLNESS

I

IDIOT

Idiot is an archaic term used from the turn of the century through the 1950s to denote a retarded individual whose measured IQ fell below 25 or 30. It represented the most severe level of mental retardation and was used comparatively with lesser degrees of retardation (i.e., imbecile and moron). The term acquired a pernicious quality among lay people over the years of its use and, during the 1950s, led to several revised systems of nomenclature. In America the classification system that was to become most widely adopted was published by the American Association on Mental Deficiency (Heber, 1959). This classification system replaced the term, idiot, with the current levels of severe and profound retardation.

Originally, the terms idiocy, imbecility, and moronity represented the three levels of mental deficiency (otherwise known as amentia or feeblemindedness). These terms were considered separate from dementia, which denoted those who had acquired mental illnesses. Amentia, on the other hand, denoted "persons whose minds (had) never developed very far" (Peterson, 1925, p. 20).

The exact level of functioning of individuals designated as idiots has never been clear. However, attempts to characterize the level often focused on the use of language. In general such individuals could learn only a few simple words, but were not capable of substituting words for objects in their behavior. In addition, they were not expected to learn to wash or dress themselves and were generally cared for in institutions. Finally, the mental age of those classified as idiots did not exceed three years.

REFERENCES

Heber, R. F. (1959). A manual on terminology and classification in mental retardation. *Monograph Supplement American Journal of Mental Deficiency, 64.*

Peterson, J. (1925). *Early conceptions and tests of intelligence.* Chicago: World Book.

RONALD C. EAVES
Auburn University

AAMD CLASSIFICATION SYSTEMS
HISTORY OF SPECIAL EDUCATION

IDIOT SAVANT

This apparent contradiction in terms refers to an individual who, though performing as a psychotic or retarded individual in most respects, displays one or more skills at a much more advanced level. The savant behavior may take the form of outstanding memory, quantitative ability, musical or other artistic talent, or mechanical facility. The term, idiot savant behavior, is not commonly found in the literature today. In order to avoid the stigma and other emotionality associated with the term, it has been replaced by the rubric, splinter skill.

A classic example of this type of skill was demonstrated by a 14-year-old inmate of a Virginia mental institution during the 1970s. Given a stranger's birth date, this youngster was instantly able to tell the stranger the exact number of years, months, and days he had been alive. Given the individual's birth date only once, the boy was able to repeat this phenomenon for any date in the future, even though he did not see or communicate with the stranger for lengthy intervals. Another patient in the same state hospital was able to quickly tell how long ago any major world event occurred. It was unnecessary to give this patient the date of the events; these he had memorized. The latter youngster had a twin brother, also an inmate of the institution, who displayed no such savant behavior.

Another classic case, this one described in the literature, was that of the genius of Earlwood Asylum, who built excellently detailed model ships (Tredgold & Soddy, 1956). In one of his constructions, the "genius" employed over 1 million miniature wooden pegs, producing a model ship that was 10 ft long. He wore a naval captain's attire and exhibited great pleasure when his work was admired by visitors, exclaiming how clever he was while patting his head (Kisker, 1964).

A final example describes savant behavior in the form of outstanding artistic ability. A psychotic adult inmate of a Georgia mental institution during the 1970s exhibited exceptional ability in producing line drawings of mechanical objects (e.g., helicopters, trailer trucks). He drew perfect curves and straight lines even though all of his work was completed freehand. The drawings were accurately detailed and of excellent quality. A peculiarity of his work was the lettering on the objects pictured. All letters and numerals were reversed and presented in backward order. Occasionally, the orthography included material evidently taken from the hospital ward environment (e.g., the words "EXIT" or "PULL").

As can be seen from the preceding descriptions, the skill displayed by such individuals is isolated. In most respects, the so-called idiot savant manifests behavior that is consistent with the labels of mental retardation or psychosis. Although severely mentally handicapped people may demonstrate savant behavior, generally, their levels of retardation are mild. There is no known cause for the phenomonon; it has received relatively little attention from scientists, probably because it is generally harmful to no one and beneficial to many.

REFERENCES

Kisker, G. W. (1964). *The disorganized personality*. New York: McGraw-Hill.

Tredgold, R. F., & Soddy, K. (Eds.). (1956). *A text-book of mental deficiency* (9th ed.). Baltimore, MD: Williams & Wilkins.

RONALD C. EAVES
Auburn University

MENTAL RETARDATION

IEP

See INDIVIDUALIZED EDUCATIONAL PLAN.

ILLINOIS TEST OF PSYCHOLINGUISTIC ABILITIES (ITPA)

The Illinois Test of Psycholinguistic Abilities (ITPA; Kirk, McCarthy, & Kirk, 1968) was designed to measure a child's verbal and nonverbal language comprehension and production abilities. The ITPA was the dominant representative of an approach to evaluation that gained popularity in the late 1960s with the growth of the learning-disabilities movement. That approach was based on three major assumptions regarding the psychological processes that underlie learning: (1) the specific processes necessary for language development and academic achievement can be identified; (2) these processes can be broken down into discrete abilities and assessed separately; and (3) these abilities can be remediated to produce improvement in language and academic skills.

The ITPA has been the subject of extensive research and debate since its publication. Critics have questioned its theoretical foundation, technical adequacy, and edu-

cational relevance. As to theory, the model of psycholinguistic functioning on which the ITPA was based is widely regarded as outmoded (see Reid & Hresko, 1981, for a detailed review of Osgood's model and an examination of the ITPA). Technical adequacy has been called into question with respect to the test's validity, reliability, and standardization (Sattler, 1982). Finally, studies of remediation programs based on the ITPA have not supported the value of this assessment approach for improving either psycholinguistic or academic skills (Newcomer & Hammill, 1976). While the ITPA represented an early and significant attempt to assess underlying cognitive processes and to forge a link between assessment and instruction, it has retained little support as a diagnostic instrument or intervention model.

REFERENCES

Kirk, S., McCarthy, J., & Kirk, W. (1968). *The Illinois Test of Psycholinguistic Abilities*. Urbana, IL: University of Illinois Press.

Newcomer, P. L., & Hammill, D. D. (1976). *Psycholinguistics in the schools*. Columbus, OH: Merrill.

Reid, D. K., & Hresko, W. P. (1981). *A cognitive approach to learning disabilities*. New York: McGraw-Hill.

Sattler, J. M. (1982). *Assessment of children's intelligence and special abilities* (2nd ed.). Boston: Allyn & Bacon.

MARY LOUISE LENNON
RANDY ELLIOT BENNETT
*Educational Testing Service,
Princeton, New Jersey*

KIRK, SAMUEL
MEASUREMENT
PSYCHOLINGUISTICS

IMAGERY

Imagery is the mental representation of objects, events, or concepts in some nonverbal form, a process thought to be basic to human functioning. While this representation is often assumed to be visual such as a picture according to Klinger (1981), mental imagery includes any of the almost unceasing sensationlike experiences that are a part of our stream of consciousness and that are representative of any of our sense modalities. Although the study of mental imagery was a central part of psychology until 1920, interest by psychologists in the United States in this phenomenon did not become active until the 1960s, with the work of psychologists such as Eleanor and James Gibson, Piaget, Neisser and others. These psychologists were concerned with determining how the brain constructs and stores models through which sense can be made of the sensations that occur as the individual interacts with the environment. This latter process, labeled perception, guides the individual's actions or response to the environment. Thus the imagery constructed by an individual is central to psychological functioning and whoever can shape that imagery holds a powerful tool for controlling and altering human functioning, whether the shaper be the individual or another person (Klinger, 1981).

The facilitative effect of imagery on comprehension and recall or memory was described by early Greek scholars and experienced by Roman orators as they delivered lengthy speeches using imagery as a mnemonic tool. Recent pioneering work of Canadian psychologist Allan Paivio has provided theoretical explanations and firm empirical support for this aspect of imagery. Paivio (1971) effectively developed the case for dual coding of information by individuals. In dual coding retrieval of information is enhanced by the fact that many concrete words or concepts can be represented in both verbal and imagery systems, thus providing dual cues for recalling the information. Present investigations on imagery as an important concept in cognitive psychology are focusing on individual differences in imagery, its usefulness in problem solving and other complex human behaviors including creativity, imagery through sensory modalities other than the visual, and the possibility of affective coding of experiences.

Mental imagery appears to play a critical role in the creative processes in diverse fields, from architecture to molecular science (Shepard, 1978). The ability to process information through imagery has been used to predict and enhance creative imagination in children and adults (Khatena, 1979). In addition, directed focusing of imagery has been found to be a powerful enhancer, eliciting from the individual a holistic and directly felt bodily sense of a situation or issue (Gendlin, 1980). Perfection of various athletic or performance skills, as well as a wide variety of classroom applications, have evolved, and scripts have been developed for using such guided imagery (Roberts, 1983). Rose (1980) describes his technique for using guided fantasies in the elementary classroom to acquire new concepts, build confidence for oral reports, or handle conflicts. In special education, imagery can be used to help individuals identify negative or positive attitudes regarding a physical disability (Morgan, 1980).

Imagery has been a particularly useful tool for the psychotherapist: the patient expresses in drawings or paintings, to be interpreted clinically, information unlikely to have been offered verbally. The advantage of this type of communication is that it is given in less threatening situations, avoiding times when the patient may be withdrawn, overly aroused, or frightened. In addition, imagery can be used to establish empathetic understanding, manage anxiety and stress, and even reduce pain, giving symptomatic relief to patients. Through imagery, then, humans can alter in positive ways both mental and physical functioning, their own as well as that of others.

REFERENCES

Gendlin, E. T. (1980). Imagery is more powerful with focusing: Theory and practice. In J. E. Schorr, G. E. Sobel, P. Robin, & J. A. Connella (Eds.), *Imagery. Its many dimensions and applications.* New York: Plenum.

Khatena, J. (1979). *Teaching gifted children to use creative imagination imagery.* Starkville, MI: Allan.

Klinger, E. (Ed.). (1981). *Imagery. Concepts, results and applications.* New York: Plenum.

Morgan, C. (1980). Imagery experiences of disabled persons. In J. E. Schorr, G. E. Sobel, P. Robin, & J. A. Connella (Eds.), *Imagery. Its many dimensions and applications.* New York: Plenum.

Paivio, A. (1971). *Imagery and verbal processes.* New York: Holt, Rinehart & Winston.

Roberts, N. M. (1983). Imagery: A second look: Expanding its use in the classroom. *Reading Improvement, 20*(1), 22–27.

Rose, R. (1980). Guided fantasies in elementary classrooms. In J. E. Schorr, G. E. Sobel, P. Robin, & J. A. Connella (Eds.), *Imagery. Its many dimensions and applications.* New York: Plenum.

Shepard, R. N. (1978). Externalization of mental images and the act of creation. In B. S. Randhawa & W. E. Coffman (Eds.), *Visual learning, thinking, and communication.* New York: Academic.

PATRICIA A. HAENSLY
Texas A&M University

CREATIVITY
HYPNOSIS

IMPERSISTENCE

See PERSEVERATION.

IMPULSE CONTROL

An impulse is a psychological term given to a feeling that results in an action. As used here, it refers to a trait normally measured by a test such as the Matching Familiar Figures Test. The resulting outcome of the test is an indication of whether the learner is reflective or impulsive. A reflective learner examines a stimulus slowly and takes more time to make a decision than an impulsive learner. Generally, there is some relationship between impulsive responders and high error rates. Thus, there is a need to control the response rate of the learner to cut down on errors (Kagan, Pearson, & Welch, 1966; Kendall & Wilcox, 1979).

The predominant method for the control of impulsive behavior is cognitive training (Kendall & Finch, 1978; Kendall & Wilcox, 1979, 1980). Recently, investigators have combined cognitive and behavioral methods. Two of the most successful strategies for the control of impulsive behavior are modeling and self-instructional training. Modeling is based on social learning theory. A learner observes a high-status adult or peer engaging in acts that are reflective and purposeful. If the tasks performed by the model are similar to the types of tasks to be performed by the learner, there is a likelihood that the reflective behavior will be modeled by the learner. As the tasks become dissimilar, the degree of transfer decreases.

Self-instructional training is based on a theory that states that voluntary control over motor behavior requires the internalization of verbal commands (Meichenbaum & Goodman, 1971). To improve impulsive behavior by self-instruction, the learner verbalizes either aloud, in a whisper or subvocally. The practice becomes a thinking-out-loud intervention that reminds a learner to slow down, to be careful, and to follow the steps in a process.

Cognitive modeling plus self-instructional training is generally superior to cognitive modeling alone. The following five-step procedure has been used successfully to control impulsive behavior: (1) the leader models a reflective problem-solving style using overt self-instructions; (2) the learner is guided by the teacher through the same problem with verbal instructions; (3) the learner solves the problem while providing overt self-instruction; (4) the learner solves the problem while whispering; and (5) the learner solves the problem with subvocal self-instruction. This procedure appears to work well for modifying impulsive behavior on specific tasks but general classroom behavior on unrelated tasks remains unchanged.

Adding a response cost procedure to the cognitive modeling and self-instructional training enhances the training program for the control of impulsive behavior (Meichenbaum & Anarnow, 1979). In response cost, a punishment procedure is imposed for errors. The procedure is designed to discourage the child from making quick responses. Positive reinforcement is not a highly effective strategy to add to cognitive modeling and self-instructional training. The problem with using positive reinforcement in this process is that lucky guesses may be reinforced and thus maladaptive problem-solving strategies may be maintained.

Another approach to cognitive training involves the following six-step problem-solving sequence (Meichenbaum & Goodman, 1971): (1) problem definition; (2) problem approach; (3) focusing attention; (4) problem solution; (5) self-reinforcement; and (6) coping with errors. In studies following this sequence, there is a greater generalization of reflective behavior if the training deals with self-statements that are global rather than problem specific. If training focuses only on a specific problem situation, the generalization of reflective behavior is restricted. If the

problem situations are broad and the strategies applicable to a wide range of behavior, generalization will be enhanced.

A final procedure for the control of impulsive behavior is the imposed delay. Students are prevented from responding for a specified number of seconds after a problem is presented. Used in isolation, learners will slow down in their responding time but errors will not change. To be effective, the strategy must be coupled with other strategies discussed previously.

REFERENCES

Kagan, J., Pearson, L., & Welch, L. (1966). Modifiability of an impulsive tempo. *Journal of Educational Psychology, 57,* 359–365.

Kendall, P. C., & Finch, A. J. (1978). A cognitive-behavioral treatment for impulsivity: A group comparison study. *Journal of Consulting & Clinical Psychology, 46,* 110–118.

Kendall, P. C., & Wilcox, L. E. (1979). Self-Control in children: Development of a rating scale. *Journal of Consulting & Clinical Psychology, 47,* 1020–1029.

Kendall, P. C., & Wilcox, L. E. (1980). Cognitive-behavioral treatment for impulsivity: Concrete versus conceptual training in non-self-controlled problem children. *Journal of Consulting & Clinical Psychology, 48,* 80–91.

Meichenbaum, D. H., & Anarnow, J. (1979). Cognitive-behavioral modification and metacognitive development: Implications for the classroom. In P. C. Kendall & S. D. Hollon (Eds.), *Cognitive-behavioral interventions: Theory, research, and procedures.* New York: Academic.

Meichenbaum, D. H., & Goodman, J. (1971). Training impulsive children to talk to themselves: A means of developing self-control. *Journal of Abnormal Psychology, 77,* 115–126.

ROBERT A. SEDLAK
University of Wisconsin, Stout

BEHAVIOR MODELING
BEHAVIOR MODIFICATION
SELF-MONITORING

IMPULSIVITY-REFLECTIVITY

Impulsivity-reflectivity is a cognitive dimension defined by Kagan (1965) that describes the way children resolve uncertainty. Impulsivity-reflectivity describes the tendency to reflect on the validity of problem solving when several choices are presented. The instrument most often used to measure reflectivity and impulsivity in children is the Matching Familiar Figures Test (MFFT). Based on test performance, reflective children will make fewer errors and have longer response latencies than impulsive children (Kagan, 1965). The test format involves presentation of a figure such as a boat, animal, or pair of scissors with as many as eight facsimiles differing in one or more details. The subject is asked to select from the alternatives, the one that exactly matches the figure. Time and response are computed. Children who score above the median on the MFFT response time and below the median on errors are called reflective. Children who score below the median on response time and above the median on errors are called impulsive (Messer, 1976). Impulsive children tend to respond quickly and make many mistakes; reflective children tend to respond more slowly and carefully and make fewer errors (Finch, 1982).

Educators and psychologists have used impulsivity and reflectivity as a way to implement programs for childhood education (Borkowski, 1983; Finch, 1982). This has been useful with emotionally disturbed children who display problem behavior (Finch, 1982). Finch also examined reflectivity and impulsivity in WISC-R performance in children with behavior problems. Reflective children scored significantly higher than impulsive children on verbal, performance, and full-scale IQ. Although there is no evidence that consistently links impulsivity and reflectivity to IQ scores, this does suggest that cognitive style may be related to performance on standard intelligence tests.

Sergeant (1979) expored hyperactivity, impulsivity, and reflectivity and their relationship to clinical child psychology. The MFFT was used to measure hyperactivity. Although impulsivity is thought to be related to hyperactivity, their research showed that measuring hyperactivity by determining the level of impulsivity could be misleading. Impulsivity-reflectivity has been found to be related to other clinical syndromes including brain damage, epilepsy, and mental retardation (Messer, 1976). This work also indicates that impulsivity and reflectivity may be related to school performance as shown by the greater impulsivity in children with learning disabilities, reading problems, and general school failure. Messer found that reflective children will gather information more carefully and systematically than impulsive children. This same study indicated that reflectivity and impulsivity cannot accurately be measured in preschool children, since they have not yet learned to examine alternatives.

Social reasoning has also been measured in reflective and impulsive children (Peters & Bernfeld, 1983) by using the Peabody Picture Vocabulary and the MFFT. Reflective children made decisions more slowly; impulsive children made decisions more rapidly. Reflective children favored a more direct approach; impulsive children favored a more passive approach.

Kagan (1983) studied children who were given visual matching problems. The subjects with fast response times and higher error scores made more errors in reading words than subjects with long decision-making times and lower error scores. This supported the notion that primary-grade children who reflected over alternative hypotheses would be more accurate in word recognition than children who reported hypotheses impulsively.

Reflectivity and impulsivity seem to develop with age as children typically become more reflective as they grow older (Messer, 1976). Messer reported that response times increased with age, while the amount of errors decreased. Siegelman (1969) examined the ways in which reflective and impulsive children of different ages actually deploy alternatives and scan the objects presented to them. The hypothesis was that impulsive children devote a greater amount of time to a chosen stimulus and ignore the alternatives, in contrast to the reflectives, who spent more time weighing alternatives. Results suggested that impulsive and reflective children may be using different search strategies. This indicates that the impulsive dimension may be modifiable. Kagan (1983) and Messer (1976) found that impulsivity may be modified by teaching impulsives to improve their scanning strategies. The researchers accomplished this by having children who were impulsive verbalize what they were doing.

Impulsivity and reflectivity have also been examined from a teaching perspective that has implications for classroom learning. Teachers need to be aware of individual differences among children to cope with each individual learner. Readance and Bean (1978) reported that the impulsive child has a tendency to act on his or her initial response with little reflection when solving problems. A reflective child usually delays, weighing all choices available. Reflective children are not necessarily brighter or better learners; however, the research did suggest that teachers may perceive impulsive children less favorably. Reflective students were seen as highly attentive. Impulsive boys were seen as less able to concentrate in class. This supported the notion that this particular individual difference of impulsivity and reflectivity is important for classroom learning. Evidence supports the contention that the cognitive dimension of impulsivity and reflectivity is an important individual difference. This dimension will play a role in helping assess a child's ability, ultimately improving the learning process within the field of special education.

REFERENCES

Borkowski, J. G., Peck, V. A., Reid, M. K. and Kurtz, B. E. (1983). Impulsivity and strategy transfer: Metamemory as mediator, *Child Development, 54*, 469–473.

Finch, A. J., Saylor, C. F. and Spirito, A. (1982a). Impulsive cognitive style and impulsive behavior in emotionally disturbed children. *Journal of Genetic Psychology, 141*, 293–294.

Finch, A. J., Spirito, A. and Brophy, C. J. (1982b). Reflection-impulsivity and WISC-R performance in behavior-problem children. *Journal of Genetic Psychology, 111*, 217–221.

Kagan, J. (1965). *Conceptual development in children.* New York: International University Press.

Kagan, J. (1983). Reflection-impulsivity and reading ability in primary grade children. *Child Development, 54*, 609–628.

Messer, S. B. (1976). Reflection-impulsivity: A review. *Psychological Bulletin, 83*, 1026–1052.

Peters, R. D., & Bernfeld, G. A. (1983). Reflection-impulsivity and social reasoning. *Developmental Psychology, 19,* 78–81.

Readance, J. E., & Bean, T. W. (1978). Impulsivity-reflectivity and learning: An individual difference that matters. *College Student Journal, 11,* 367–371.

Siegelman, E. (1969). Reflective and impulsive observing behavior. *Child Development, 40,* 1213–1222.

Sergeant, J. A., Van Velthoven, R. and Virginia, A. (1979). Hyperactivity, impulsivity and reflectivity. *Journal of Child Psychology & Psychiatry, 20,* 47–60.

STEVEN GUMERMAN
Temple University

CREATIVE PROBLEM SOLVING
IMPULSE CONTROL

INBORN ERRORS OF METABOLISM

Inborn errors of metabolism, recently classified as a group of genetic diseases, involve single-gene defects that interfere with the process of metabolism. Metabolism refers to the process in which the body breaks down food into fats, proteins, and carbohydrates. The conversion of the food into energy to maintain the life cycle of body cells is carried out by enzymes. The enzymes assist in the maintenance of homeostasis and the control of functions of blood pressure, blood sugar levels, and rate of growth. A single-gene defect may lead to a missing or malfunctioning enzyme, which if left untreated, may result in severe mental retardation or impaired bodily functions such as poor digestion. Such disorders occur in approximately 1 in 5000 births (Batshaw & Perret, 1981).

Robinson and Robinson (1965) divided metabolic disorders into three areas: (1) ongoing faulty digestive processes identified by biochemical substances in the urine or the bloodstream; (2) storage diseases in which materials are stored because of decreased rate of metabolism or overproduction; and (3) disorders in endocrine secretions that result in anomalies in the structure of the brain and cranium or other difficulties.

Koch and Koch (1974) reported that 40 to 50 such serious diseases often are passed on by consanguineous parents. The body is constantly producing, maintaining, and recycling cells. In the metabolic process of mitosis, the cell dies and is recycled and changed into chemicals and proteins. These components are then absorbed and reused by the body. Any genetic disease that interferes with the process is called an inborn error of metabolism. For many metabolic disorders, there is no effective therapy. For some, therapy is successful only if begun immediately. When untreated, profound mental retardation, seizures, aberrant behavior, and stunted growth may accompany the metabolic abnormality. Some inborn errors of metabolism (e.g., Gaucher's) are asymptomatic and may pose little threat to a reasonably normal existence (Stanbury, Wyngaarden, & Fredrickson, 1978). However, many of these disorders have serious consequences and may be fatal if untreated. Age of onset affects severity. In several of the lipid storage diseases such as Gaucher's and Niemann-Pick disease, if the disorder is manifested during the infantile period when the brain is being myelinated, the result is a much more serious disability. Conversely, many of the hereditary metabolic disorders such as gout, hemochromatosis, or familial periodic paralysis do not become fully manifest until adulthood.

In galactosemia, a carbohydrate disorder, the infant appears normal at birth. However, because of a missing enzyme, the sugar or galactose is not used properly. It accumulates in the blood, body tissue, and urine. The injurious waste products can cause brain damage if proper dietary controls are not exercised immediately. The affected individual is unable to metabolize the galactose in milk. If milk is withheld, the development will proceed normally.

Phenylketonuria (PKU) is the most well-known and most successfully treated metabolic disorder. Two similar recessive genes, one from each parent, combine and produce a deficiency of the liver enzyme that normally breaks down the amino acid phenylalanine (Telford & Sawrey, 1977). The parents are carriers of the defective genes but are not themselves affected. Brain damage results from an accumulation of phenylalanine, one of the nine amino acids essential for growth. Prenatal diagnosis does not detect PKU and a child has no symptoms in infancy, hence early screening is critical. More than 90% of all newborns in the United States are tested for PKU (Bearn, 1979). While it is not a general test for mental retardation, it does successfully detect PKU and a few other rare inborn errors. The currently used heel stick test was developed by Dr. Robert Guthrie in 1959 (Guthrie, 1972). Phenylketonuria occurs at a rate of 1/14,000 births. Parents who have one affected child have a 25% chance of having another (Batshaw & Perret, 1981). In the past, this disorder led to death or severe mental retardation. Diet therapy has greatly improved prognosis. However, early treatment is not perfect. Individuals with PKU are still found to score significantly lower on IQ tests than their parents. Longitudinal studies of PKU children have found a high incidence of perceptual difficulties that interfere with academic achievement (Koch & Koch, 1974). Diet therapy can lead to malnutrition because of reduced food intake. It also is problematic to gain the full cooperation of the affected individual.

Robinson and Robinson (1965) detailed several of the storage diseases. Hurler's disease, gargoylism, results in a deformed and stunted body as well as mental retardation. Affected individuals also may exhibit visual and hearing impairments. Gaucher's, when severe, is manifested by enlarged liver, spleen, and lymph nodes. Most do not live beyond adolescence.

Some of the inherited metabolic disorders are sex linked. Hemochromatosis is more common in males because the menstrual cycle in females decreases the iron stored in the system. Hemophilia, Fabray's disease, childhood muscular dystrophy, and hyper-uricemia all occur predominantly in males.

Some metabolic disorders appear to improve as the affected individual ages (Stanbury, Wyngaarden, & Fredrickson, 1978). Some galactosemics gradually develop the ability to metabolize galactose. Individuals with adrynamia epidocis hereditaria and periodic paralysis may also cease to have attacks as they grow older.

Inborn errors of metabolism are the subject of continued intensive research. Reports of newly discovered syndromes frequently are announced. Screening still offers the best hope. The most direct method detects qualitative changes in the structure of the protein (Bearn, 1979). Mass screening for all possible single gene defects is still prohibitive financially. Therefore, with the exception of PKU, the focus is on families and at-risk populations. Bearn (1979) suggests that amniocentesis and the use of cultured fibroblasts will increase in the years ahead as a means of making screening programs more comprehensive. Currently, scientists apply a sophisticated battery of laboratory procedures to identify and elucidate suspected metabolic disorders. A more detailed account can be found in the works of Stanbury, Wyngaarden, and Fredrickson (1978).

REFERENCES

Batshaw, M. L., & Perret, Y. M. (1981). *Children with handicaps: A medical primer.* Baltimore, MD: Brooks.

Bearn, A. G. (1979). Inborn errors of metabolism and molecular disease. In P. Beeson, W. McDermott, & J. Wyngaarden (Eds.), *Cecil textbook of medicine* (15th ed., pp. 40–48). Philadelphia: Saunders.

Guthrie, R. (1972). Mass screening for genetic disease. *Hospital Practice, 7,* 93.

Kelly, T. E. (1975). The role of genetic mechanisms in childhood handicaps. In R. Haslam & P. Valletutti (Eds.), *Medical problems in the classroom: The teacher's role in diagnosis and management* (pp. 113–215). Baltimore, MD: University Park.

Koch, R., & Koch, K. (1974). *Understanding the mentally retarded child: A new approach.* New York: Random House.

Robinson, H. B., & Robinson, N. M. (1965). *The mentally retarded child: A psychological approach.* New York: McGraw-Hill.

Stanbury, J. B., Wyngaarden, J. B., & Fredrickson, D. S. (Eds.). (1978). *The metabolic bases of inherited disease.* New York: McGraw-Hill.

Telford, C., & Sawrey, J. (1977). *The exceptional individual.* Englewood Cliffs, NJ: Prentice-Hall.

SALLY E. PISARCHICK
*Cuyahoga Special Education
Service Center, Maple
Heights, Ohio*

**GALACTOSEMIA
GENETIC COUNSELING**

**GENETIC TRANSMISSIONS
HURLER'S SYNDROME
PHENYLKETONURIA**

INCIDENCE

The term incidence refers to the estimated number of people in a given population who possess or exhibit a given characteristic at some point during their lives (Blackhurst & Berdine, 1981). Dunn (1973) believes that incidence gives the rate of occurrence of a condition while Schifani, Anderson, and Odle (1980) define incidence as the number of new cases of handicapped children identified in a given period of time—usually a year. Incidence most often relates to the occurrence of some characteristic.

Incidence is often confused with prevalence but the two terms have different meanings. Prevalence refers to currently existing handicapped children as opposed to those who might be considered exceptional at some point in their lives. Incidence results in a higher figure since it estimates future occurrence, where prevalence deals with a point in time figure.

Because incidence is an estimate, it is more difficult to validate or substantiate. Meyen (1978) states that state education agencies and school districts generally establish prevalence rates when conducting needs assessment surveys. He suggests that future surveys and studies would be better able to establish incidence rates given the data becoming available from referral requests for service under PL 94-142. For general education planning purposes prevalence estimates continue to be used.

Educational planning requires an estimate of the number of handicapped children requiring service. If program planners, for example, assume the incidence of mental retardation is 3% and project needed programs and services based on that figure, the result could be an overestimate of 100% if the actual prevalence was $1\frac{1}{2}\%$.

REFERENCES

Blackhurst, A. E., & Berdine, W. H. (Eds.). (1981). *An introduction to special education.* Boston: Little, Brown.

Dunn, L. M. (Ed.). (1973). *Exceptional children in the schools.* New York: Holt, Rinehart, & Winston.

Meyen, E. L. (1978). *Exceptional children and youth: An introduction.* Denver: Love.

Schifani, J. W., Anderson, R. M., & Odle, S. J. (Eds.). (1980). *Implementing learning in the least restrictive environment.* Baltimore, MD: University Press.

PHILIP R. JONES
*Virginia Polytechnic Institute
and State University*

DEMOGRAPHY OF SPECIAL EDUCATION

INCORRIGIBILITY

Incorrigibility is a term that appears in the legal code of most states as one of three descriptors used to define juvenile delinquency. The term is badly outdated but remains in use as part of the legal language of the juvenile justice system. Incorrigibility is used in legal codes in conjunction with dependence and delinquency to establish the parameters of juvenile justice systems. However, behaviors associated with this antiquated legal descriptor have changed significantly over time.

For example, running in halls, chewing gum, making noise, wearing improper clothes, and getting out of turn in line were listed frequently by many educators as major incorrigible behaviors prior to World War II. Today, however, the major offenses in 8000 schools are rape, robbery, assault, personal theft, burglary, disorderly conduct, drug abuse, arson, bombings, alcohol abuse, and weapons possession. Incorrigibility has been a major concern of parents and educators since recorded history. Obviously, the problems are becoming more serious as time progresses. Classroom conduct has deteriorated from the level of misconduct to felonies committed by youths under age 18 (Stoops, Rafferty, & Johnson, 1981).

Incorrigibility means that a student's behavior is unacceptable and that the student is out of control. Lack of discipline tops the Gallup Poll in 1980 as the major problem facing the nation's schools (Gallup Poll, 1980). One in four respondents listed incorrigibility as their primary concern in today's schools. Low-income and minority groups were particularly affected. Taxpayers, parents, and the public in general view incorrigibility as one of the worst examples of ineffectiveness in America's educational system (Aird, 1981).

Incorrigibility is associated with juvenile delinquency. Crime among children is increasing and the adult community's responses seem only to exacerbate the problem (Cohen, Intili, & Robbins, 1979). If the situation is to be corrected at all, then community attitudes must be changed. Parents, teachers, and the community at large need to be aware of the school. The community needs to become involved and work cooperatively to alleviate this deterioration of the educational system.

Statistics show that 73% of the nation's schools experience a major crime every 5 months, and 50% report more than one major crime in a semester. In any year, 3% of all children are referred to juvenile court (Achenbach, 1975). The national average of punishable offenses is a disturbing 6.8%/1000 enrollments (National Center for Educational Statistics, 1978).

Teachers become frustrated as their role as mentor becomes more that of disciplinarian, police officer, prosecutor, and judge. Teachers do not prepare professionally to be either police officers or prison wardens; they do so to educate the nation's youth in the hope that brighter minds and worthy skills will progress to a better tomorrow. Because of high rates of behavioral problems and the increasing frequency of crimes at school, the status of teaching as a career is declining. A third of the nation's teachers would opt for a different career. Only 48% of those responding in the 1980 Gallup Poll indicated that they would like a son or daughter to become a teacher, compared with 75% in 1969 and 60% in 1972.

Stress has become synonymous with teaching and a reason for teachers to leave education. One student death per week from violent assault was reported by the head of security in one large school district; 5% (52,000) of the nation's secondary school teachers are physically attacked each year, with 10,000 requiring medical attention. More than 5000 teachers are attacked on high-school campuses each month (Stoops, Rafferty, & Johnson, 1981). In addition, 60,000 teachers are robbed, and 12% (120,000) lose personal property from theft or damage. Boycotting or avoiding particular instructors is the excuse used by 30 to 50% of students reporting absenteeism; up to 40% of high-school students are absent each day without cause; and taxpayers spent some $1 billion to repair school vandalism in 1979.

The presence of juvenile incorrigibility in society has reached staggering proportions. The prison population in Illinois doubled from 1972 to 1982 and so did the annual cost per inmate. In most states, the prison system is the major competitor with public education for state general revenue funds. Are students graduating from crime in school to those of worse degree? A report in the *Illinois School Board Journal* (Gierach, 1981) revealed that more than half of all crime in the state was committed by persons under 21. Juvenile arrests nationally account for 51% of all property crimes, 23% of all violent crimes, and 43% of other serious crimes (Miller, Sabatino, Miller, & Stoneburner, 1979). More crimes are committed by youths under 15 than adults over 23. The description of the typical offender is a male school dropout with a history of misdemeanors, driving offenses, and sporadic employment.

The Carnegie Council Policy Studies (Kerr & Ragland, 1979) estimated that one-third of today's youths are ill educated, ill employed, and ill equipped to compete successfully in society. The education system must make amends. If incorrigibility is to be deterred before it develops into a lifelong pattern, the school must accept responsibility and do its utmost to change juvenile delinquents' course of destiny. The ill educated, ill employed, and ill equipped must be rerouted to provide them with the skills necessary to compete and survive in today's world. The need for society to understand what sets incorrigible behavior into motion, and the willingness to shape that behavior, is not simply important, it is critical.

REFERENCES

Achenbach, T. M. (1975). The historical context of treatment for delinquent and maladjusted children: Past, present, and future. *Behavioral Disorders, 1*, 3–14.

Aird, R. B. (1981, Sept.). Motivation: Key to educational problems. *Phi Delta Kappan, 63,* 56–58.

Cohen, E., Intili, J., & Robbins, S. (1979). Task and authority: A sociological view of classroom management. In D. Duke (Ed.), *Classroom management: The 78th yearbook of the National Society for the Study of Education.* Chicago: University of Chicago Press.

Gallup Poll. (1980). School ratings up slightly; discipline still top problem. *Phi Delta Kappan, 6,* 206.

Gierach, W. E. (1981, May–June). Working together, schools and courts can stem the flow of young criminals. *Illinois School Board Journal,* 14–16.

Kerr, M., & Ragland, E. (1979). Pow wow: A group procedure for reducing classroom behavior problems. *Pointer, 24,* 92–96.

Miller, T., Sabatino, D., Miller, S., & Stoneburner, R. (1979, Feb.). Adolescent violent behaviors directed at the schools: Problem and prevention. *Counseling and Human Development, 11,* 1–8.

National Center for Educational Statistics (NCES) (1978). *Digest of education statistics.* Washington, DC: U.S. Government Printing Office.

Stoops, E., Rafferty, M., & Johnson, R. E. (1981). *Handbook of education administration* (2nd ed.). Boston: Allyn & Bacon.

DAVID A. SABATINO
University of Wisconsin, Stout

CONDUCT DISORDER
DISCIPLINE
JUVENILE DELINQUENCY

INDEPENDENT LIVING

The concept of normalization is based on the principle of allowing handicapped individuals, to the maximum extent possible, the opportunity to interact with nonhandicapped individuals in the community and society. The emphasis is placed on allowing the handicapped to socially integrate into the community through independent living. There are basic skills needed by the handicapped in order to function independently. These skills include self-help, social skills, domestic maintenance, employment, and recreation. These skills are sometimes referred to in the literature as functional skills, self-help skills, practical skills, and daily living skills. Research by Aninger and Bolinsky (1977) and others indicate that handicapped individuals, including the mentally retarded, can, with proper training and preparation, live independently in the community. Other researchers who have evaluated community-based programs for the handicapped such as Crnic and Pym (1979) report that the most important factors for successful independent living include stimulating motivation, teaching behavioral skills, and providing environmental support. Many of the problems that occur have been found to be related to loneliness and lack of social support systems, including peer contact.

According to Cartwright, Cartwright, and Ward (1984), the majority of individuals with disabilities desire to live independently. However, to achieve independence, adaptations must be made in the home living environment. For example, adaptations for a severely handicapped person would include an intercom system, kitchen with adapted appliances and controls, accessible sinks and showers, and wheel-in showers. Outside the home environment, other areas of consideration are transportation and employment. In terms of transportation, personal mobility may be achieved with computer-controlled wheelchairs, Sonicguide electronic glasses, and other technological devices such as the Voice Data Entry Terminal System. This system allows the handicapped individual a way to control the immediate environment.

Section 503 and 504 of the Vocational Rehabilitation Act of 1973 guarantee that the handicapped cannot be denied access to housing, jobs, or transportation because of their disability. Employment is also an essential component of independent living. There is a wide range of possible jobs appropriate for the handicapped. However, this depends on the skill and knowledge level of the individual. The major goal of rehabilitation agencies is to assist the handicapped individual with obtaining and keeping a job. Some handicapped individuals will be able to compete in the regular job market. There are others with more serious disabilities who are unable to compete and are limited to sheltered workshops and work activity centers. The sheltered workshop employs disabled adults to perform various jobs that have been subcontracted from companies and firms. All employees of the workshop receive wage based on attendance, satisfactory job performance, and adequate social behavior. The work activity center, which is often operated by the workshop, is designed for those who are not able to perform satisfactorily in a sheltered workshop or who may be in need of additional training before entering a workshop.

REFERENCES

Aninger, M., & Bolinsky, K. (1977). Levels of independent functioning. *Mental Retardation, 15*(4), 12–13.

Cartwright, G. P., Cartwright, C. A., & Ward, M. E. (1984). *Educating special learners* (2nd ed.). Belmont, CA: Wadsworth.

Crnic, K. A., & Pym, H. A. (1979). Training mentally retarded adults in independent living skills. *Mental Retardation, 17,* 13–16.

JANICE HARPER
North Carolina Central University

DEINSTITUTIONALIZATION
NORMALIZATION

INDIVIDUALIZATION OF INSTRUCTION

Individualization of instruction is a method of teaching in which instruction is tailored to the unique needs of students, enabling them to advance at their own rates and to achieve their potential. Individualized instruction requires that students be placed individually within a curriculum or sequence of objectives, and that teaching methods be prescribed so as to maximize individual growth and accomplishment. Both elements—placement and prescription—are essential to the process. Schwartz and Oseroff (1975) traced the roots of individualized instruction to Harris, who in 1868 "vigerously [sic] challenged the validity of requiring all pupils to do the same amount of work and to advance at the same time" (p. 26). Nonetheless, formal recognition of its critical role in special education awaited the enactment of PL 94-142, the Education for All Handicapped Children Act, in 1975.

Public Law 94-142 assigned to state and local agencies the responsibility to provide free, appropriate education to meet the unique needs of exceptional children. The act delineated guidelines for individualized placement and prescription by requiring an individual educational program (IEP) for every student. The IEP includes statements of present levels of educational performance, annual goals, short-term objectives, and specific educational services to be provided. Ideally then, an IEP must embody the elements of individualized instruction and in so doing "represents a formalization of the diagnostic/prescriptive approach to education" (Safer, Morrissey, Kaufman, & Lewis, 1978, p. 1).

Individualized placement within a curriculum or sequence of objectives may be accomplished through a variety of means. Many curricula include placement tests that can be used to identify the material that students have and have not mastered. However, these instruments are apparently not developed with the same rigor as standardized tests because their technical properties (reliability and validity) often fall short of established standards. Criterion-referenced tests, those that sample performance within a specified instructional domain, have stronger technical properties but may not necessarily correspond to particular curricula. Recent efforts to link performance on criterion-referenced tests to placement levels within curricula bode well for their continued use in the future. Precision teaching (PT) and data-based program modification (DBPM) define instructional levels in terms of performance within the curriculum itself and represent another useful alternative for making individualized placements.

The prescription of individualized instructional methodologies represents a more difficult problem since efforts to predict how teaching methods interact with learner characteristics have not yet proved fruitful. At the present, post hoc validation represents the most well-established approach to determining the effectiveness of instructional programs (Salvia & Sindelar, 1982). Frequent and repeated assessments of performance are evaluated against predetermined criteria to establish the adequacy of an instructional program. Here again, PT and DBPM provide methodologies for conducting such post hoc analyses.

Individualization of instruction is not synonymous and should not be confused with one-to-one instruction. The latter may or may not be individualized; the former may be accomplished with groups. Similarly, individualized instruction does not necessarily require that students work independently on seat work tasks. Effective individualized instruction can occur in teacher-led groups (Stevens & Rosenshine, 1980).

REFERENCES

Safer, D., Morrissey, A., Kaufman, J., & Lewis, L. (1978). Implementation of IEPs: New teacher roles and requisite support systems. *Focus on Exceptional Children, 10,* 1–20.

Salvia, J., & Sindelar, P. T. (1982). Aptitude testing and alternative approaches to maximizing the effects of instruction. In T. L. Miller & E. E. Davis (Eds.), *The mildly handicapped student* (pp. 221–240). New York: Grune & Stratton.

Schwartz, L., & Oseroff, A. (1975). *The clinical teacher for special education: Vol. 1. Establishing the model.* Final Report, USOE, HEW/BEH Grant No. OEG-0-71-1688 (603). Tallahassee, FL: Florida State University.

Stevens, R., & Rosenshine, B. (1980). Advances in research on teaching. *Exceptional Education Quarterly, 2,* 1–9.

PAUL T. SINDELAR
RHONDA COLLINS
Florida State University

DATABASED INSTRUCTION
INDIVIDUALIZED EDUCATION PLAN
PRECISION TEACHING

INDIVIDUALIZED EDUCATION PLAN (IEP)

IEP is the acronym for the individualized educational program that must now be written for each identified handicapped child prior to his or her placement in a special education program. Public Law 94-142, the Education of All Handicapped Children Act (1975), required that states receiving federal funds for special education services develop and implement a written statement by October 1977, as to what unique educational services each handicapped child is to receive. At a minimum it is mandatory that each written program include the following:

1. A statement of the child's present levels of performance.

2. A statement of annual goals, including long- and short-term institutional objectives.

3. A statement of special education and related services to be provided to the child, and the extent to which the child will be able to participate in regular education programs.

4. The projected dates for initiation of services and anticipated duration of the services.

5. Appropriate objective criteria and evaluation procedures and schedule for determining, on an annual basis at least, whether the short-term instructional objectives are being achieved. (Federal Register, p. 42491)

Under these guidelines, a meeting must be held at least once a year to review and, if necessary, revise the educational program as originally outlined. It is obvious that the goals—long- or short-range—specified in the initial IEP would periodically be in need of revision for a number of reasons: the original goals may be inappropriate for the individual child, or the child may meet or make progress on many of the goals, thus requiring revision and development of new goals.

According to some authorities (e.g., Reynolds, Gutkin, Elliot, & Witt, 1984), once a year reviewing is not enough to ensure the best educational programming for a handicapped child. They do, however, acknowledge that this mandated requirement is far better than prior practices which seldom ensured the review of educational plans for handicapped students.

Although the intent of the law is commendable, the actual implementation is often less than satisfactory. One example involves the extent to which the IEP is in fact individualized for the child. It is not uncommon for educational programs to be designed specific to the child's classification (e.g., learning disabled) rather than the unique abilities of the child involved. Often individualized educational programs will simply be a reflection of the specific district or school the child attends. For example, states will frequently mandate that all children meet certain objectives within a given subject (e.g., reading). Therefore, it is not uncommon to find the short-range objectives specified for the learning-disabled child in reading to be simply a list of the reading objectives common to the district. This practice would seem in direct contradiction to the intent of the law and certainly not always in the best interests of the handicapped child involved.

The law also stipulates who should be present at each IEP meeting, whether it be for the purposes of developing, reviewing, or revising a child's IEP. The educational agency is charged with ensuring that those individuals are present. They include:

1. A representative of the public agency, other than the child's teacher, who is qualified to provide or supervise the provision of special education.

2. The child's teacher.

3. One or both of the child's parents.

4. The child, when appropriate.

5. Other individuals at the discretion of the parent or agency. If the child is being evaluated for the first time, a member of the evaluation team must participate in the meeting, or a representative of the public agency, the child's teacher, or some other person who is knowledgeable about the evaluation procedures used with the child and is familiar with the results of the evaluation must be present. (Federal Register, p. 42490)

In keeping with another major intent of PL 94-142, to protect the rights of parents of handicapped children to fully participate in their child's education, each public agency is charged with the responsibility of exerting maximum effort in ensuring that one or both parents are present at meetings where the IEP is developed, reviewed, and revised. To be in compliance with the law, the public agency serving the handicapped child must have proof that they not only gave parents notice of the meeting, including all details, but that the meeting was arranged at a time that is mutually convenient to all involved. If the parents cannot attend the meeting, the agency must show that parent participation was elicited via other means, e.g., telephone conversations. Whether or not the parents are able to attend, they are to be given a copy of the IEP.

Various studies have been conducted investigating parental participation in IEP development and planning (e.g., Lusthaus, Lusthaus, & Gibbs, 1981; Polifka, 1981; Roit & Pfohl, 1984; Scanlon, Arick, & Phelps, 1981; Yoshida, Fenton, Kaufman, & Maxwell, 1978). Yoshida et al. (1978) found that educational personnel involved in the planning meeting expected parents to simply provide information as opposed to actively participating in the decisions as to what would constitute the plan. Interestingly, results of a parental survey conducted by Lusthaus et al. (1981) found that parents agreed that their role should be that of information giver and receiver instead of equal decision maker. Roit and Pfohl (1984) indicated that printed information provided parents regarding PL 94-142 and their rights (including their right to participate in the IEP process) was often not comprehensible to a large number of parents. This is one variable that should be addressed in helping agencies meet not only the letter but also the intent of the law (Roit & Pfohl, 1984).

Polifka (1981) reported on the results of a survey conducted as part of the Iowa Department of Public Instruction evaluation of special education services by a specific area agency. He found that parent satisfaction with the services their child received was significantly related to, among other variables, whether they were asked to help develop the IEP and whether they were invited to a meeting to review the IEP. It is impossible to determine the actual involvement these parents were allowed or whether the involvement was responsible for their satisfaction, but it does seem that active involvement should be fostered not only to ensure compliance but to promote active decision-making roles for the parents of handicapped children.

REFERENCES

Federal Register. (1977). Regulations implementing Education for All Handicapped Children Act of 1975. Washington, DC: Department of Health, Education, and Welfare.

Lusthaus, C. S., Lusthaus, E. W., Gibbs, H. (1981). Parents' role in the decision process. *Exceptional Children, 48*(3), 256–257.

Polifka, J. C. (1981). Compliance with Public Law 94-142 and consumer satisfaction. *Exceptional Children, 48*(3), 250–253.

Reynolds, C. R., Gutkin, T. B., Elliot, S. N., & Witt, J. C. (1984). *School psychology: Essentials of theory and practice*. New York: Wiley.

Roit, M. L., & Pfohl, W. (1984). The readability of PL 94-142 parent materials: Are parents truly informed? *Exceptional Children, 50*(6), 496–506.

Scanlon, C. A., Arick, J. R., Phelps, N. (1981). Participation in development of the IEP: Parents' perspective. *Exceptional Children, 47*(5), 373–376.

Yoshida, R., Fenton, K., Kaufman, M. J., & Maxwell, J. P. (1978). Parental involvement in the special education pupil planning process: The school's perspective. *Exceptional Children, 44*, 531–533.

JULIA A. HICKMAN
University of Texas, Austin

PARENTS OF THE HANDICAPPED
PUBLIC LAW 94-142

INDIVIDUAL VARIABILITY

See TEST SCATTER.

INFANT ASSESSMENT

The term infant assessment has come to represent a variety of formal and informal screening and diagnostic procedures used for the systematic collection of data. The initial purpose of assessment is to determine whether development of the infant is progressing normally.

Recent advances in genetics and biochemistry have made it possible to begin this assessment process prior to the birth of the infant. Information about the health of the mother and her fetus, including the identification of genetic and chromosomal disorders, can be obtained through prenatal diagnostic techniques.

The common areas of focus for the assessment of infants from birth through 2 years of age include physical and sensory attributes, cognitive and general communication abilities, and social/emotional responses and interactions.

Infant assessment begins with procedures that can be carried out quickly and inexpensively. These screening measures constitute the initial stage of the assessment process and allow for the identification of at-risk infants (i.e., individuals with known or suspected disorders or developmental delays).

For those infants considered to be at risk, the focus of assessment is expanded to include more in-depth or diagnostic procedures. The purpose for using diagnostic measures is to collect information that will help to identify and understand the nature of an impairment as it affects the development of the infant.

Screening and diagnostic information can be gathered through the combined use of direct testing (using standardized norm, criterion, or curriculum reference measures), naturalistic observations, and parent interviews. The resulting information is analyzed and used to make strategic diagnostic, placement, and intervention decisions.

Historically, the assessment of infants can be traced back to the intelligence testing movement of the nineteenth and twentieth centuries (Brooks & Weintraub, 1976). Among the first tests designed specifically for the purpose of gathering normative data on infant behavior were Gesell's Developmental Schedules and Bayley's California First Year Mental Scale.

Although many advances have been made in the development of diagnostic instruments, a lack of predictive validity for these standardized measures has continued to be the major issue in infant assessment. Research has consistently shown that it is not possible to predict the future cognitive performance of a child on the bases of infant test results (McCall, 1979).

According to Lewis and Fox (1980), the major reason for this lack of predictive validity is the nature of the tests themselves, in that the resulting scores are inaccurate indicators of a child's functioning. Lewis and Fox point out that it is not possible to validly predict future infant performance without considering the nature of parent-infant interactions and the influence these interactions can have on the future development of the child. Kagan and Moss (1962) have concluded that the predictive validity of infant assessment tests could be improved if the socioeconomic status of the parents was combined with the child's test scores.

While there is little long-range predictive validity in the assessment of normal infants, research with handicapped infants (DuBose, 1977; Meir, 1975) has provided evidence that predictive validity is greater with severely handicapped individuals. This increase appears to be related to the overall rate of development in the infant. Unlike normally developing infants, who are in a constant state of change (Honzik, 1976), infants with severe delays or deficits often exhibit very low-functioning behaviors that remain relatively stable, and thus more predictable over time (Brooks-Gunn & Lewis, 1981).

The assessment of handicapped populations raises another issue related to validity. Fewell (1983) points out that tests may require infants to perform many fine motor manipulations. Under these testing conditions children with motor handicaps suffer an obvious disadvantage unless the examiner systematically modifies evaluation procedures.

It is clear that the most pervasive issue with respect to the validity of assessing infant behavior is that it may not be possible to accurately predict long-range performance based on early test results. As Sheehan and Gallagher (1984) suggest, it may be more productive for infant assessment to be used to address immediate needs of diagnoses, placement, and intervention rather than long-range predictions of a child's developmental outcome.

As a result of continuing dialogue and research on infant assessment, many guiding principles have been offered in an attempt to achieve greater assessment reliability and validity. Although it is not possible to detail all of the information presented in the literature, the following summary represents an overview of suggestions as discussed by Bailey and Wolery (1984) and Sheehan and Gallagher (1984).

The assessment process should begin with the identification of the specific behaviors to be measured. Following this identification, selection of appropriate screening and diagnostic measures can be made. In-depth, diagnostic procedures must include the use of reliable and valid standardized tests (with appropriate use of adaptive equipment), multiple, systematic observations of the infant in various settings and situations, and parent interviews.

The collection and subsequent analysis of assessment data should be conducted by a multidisciplinary team, which might include a pediatrician, a psychologist, a communications specialist, and a physical therapist as well as the parents of the infant. The resulting information is used for the purpose of establishing appropriate objectives for intervention. This process of assessment also must include an evaluation of the intervention program.

REFERENCES

Bailey, D. B., & Wolery, M. (1984). *Teaching infants and preschoolers with handicaps.* Columbus, OH: Merrill.

Brooks, J., & Weintraub, M. (1976). A history of infant intelligence testing. In M. Lewis (Ed.), *Origins of intelligence* (pp. 19–58). New York: Plenum.

Brooks-Gunn, J., & Lewis, M. (1981). Assessing young handicapped children: Issues and solutions. *Journal of the Division for Early Childhood, 2,* 84–95.

DuBose, R. F. (1977). Predictive value of infant intelligence scales with multiply handicapped children. *American Journal of Mental Deficiency, 81*(4), 388–390.

Fewell, R. (1983). Assessing handicapped infants. In S. G. Garwood & R. R. Fewell (Eds.), *Educating handicapped infants.* Rockville, MD: Aspen.

Honzik, M. (1976). Value and limitations of infant tests: An overview. In M. Lewis (Ed.), *Origins of intelligence.* New York: Plenum.

Kagan, J., & Moss, H. A. (1962). *Birth and maturity: A study in psychological development.* New York: Wiley.

Lewis, M., & Fox, N. (1980). Predicting cognitive development from assessment in infancy. *Advances in Behavioral Pediatrics, 1,* 53–67.

McCall, R. B. (1979). The development of intellectual functioning in infancy and the prediction of later I.Q. In J. Osofsky (Ed.), *Handbook of infant development.* New York: Wiley.

Meir, J. H. (1975). Screening, assessment and intervention for young children at developmental risk. In N. Hobbs (Ed.), *Issues in the classification of children* (Vol. 2). San Francisco: Jossey-Bass.

Sheehan, R., & Gallagher, R. J. (1984). Assessment of infants. In M. J. Hanson (Ed.), *Atypical infant development.* Baltimore, MD: University Park Press.

FRANCINE TOMPKINS
University of Cincinnati

ASSESSMENT
DEVELOPMENTAL MILESTONES
INFANT STIMULATION
MEASUREMENT

INFANTILE AUTISM

See AUTISM.

INFANTILE HYPERCALCEMIA

Infantile hypercalcemia (also called hypercalcemia, or William's syndrome) is a rare syndrome whose etiology is uncertain. It is characterized by abnormal calcium chemistry and is associated with circulatory and cardiac (particularly supravalvular aortic stenosis) defects. Many children with this syndrome have low birth weights. They may have heart murmurs, kidney problems, and gastrointestinal problems early in life. There may be reduced muscle tone and general motor difficulties (listlessness, lethargy), also noted in infants. Most children will have mild to moderate mental retardation, although some children may have normal intelligence. Some mild neurologic dysfunction has been noted (Bergsma, 1979).

Children are short in stature (and skeletal defects are often seen), with pointed chins and ears, and are often described as having elflike features (full cheeks, small, broad foreheads). Wide-spaced and squinted eyes with epicanthal folds are typical. Teeth tend to be underdeveloped but the mouth is wide with a "cupid-bow" upper lip. No significant characteristics in upper or lower extremities are usually noted (Lemeshaw, 1982).

Because of the varying degree of mental retardation and concomitant health and skeletal problems that may exist, a comprehensive assessment is necessary for proper placement of these children. Support medical services are usually required, and in some instances children will respond to medical treatment and surgery. Motoric problems may cause extensive immobility and may result in more restricted education placement than in a regular classroom. This decision can be made only by a complete evaluation of all the factors of this syndrome. Related services are often necessary as well.

REFERENCES

Bergsma, D. (1979). *Birth defects compendium* (2nd ed.). New York: National Foundation, March of Dimes.

Lemeshaw, S. (1982). *The handbook of clinical types in mental retardation*. Boston: Allyn & Bacon.

SALLY L. FLAGLER
University of Oklahoma

HUNTER'S SYNDROME
HURLER'S SYNDROME
MENTAL RETARDATION
PHYSICAL ANOMALIES

INFANT STIMULATION

The term infant stimulation is used to represent a variety of early intervention activities (i.e. perceptual, sensorimotor, cognitive, language, and/or social/emotional) that are designed to facilitate development. The value of early intervention is based on a body of research that has demonstrated that infants, including those with handicaps, are capable of learning as a result of sustained, meaningful interactions with people and events within their environment (Osofsky, 1979).

It is believed that early experiences of the infant serve as the foundation for future growth of the individual. According to developmental theory, an infant's early sensorimotor experiences such as visually tracking and reaching for objects are precursors for later cognitive attainments such as object permanence, means-ends, and spatial relationships (Gallagher & Reid, 1981).

Since many at-risk infants (i.e., infants with known or suspected handicapping conditions) manifest deficits in perceptual or sensorimotor areas, early intervention is particularly important. Deficits that limit an infant's interaction with his or her physical and social environment often will result in delayed or deficient development (Bobath & Bobath, 1972).

Currently, there is no clear agreement about how much or what type of stimulation is most effective for facilitating development. This issue is unresolved because it is not known how to validly evaluate the effects of stimulation activities. There is general agreement, however, that the stimulation of infants does have a positive effect on immediate and future development (Alberto, Briggs, & Goldstein, 1983; Hanson & Hanline, 1984; Sheehan & Gallagher, 1983).

Over the years many programs have been developed for the purpose of stimulating the development of handicapped and at-risk infants. Detailed reviews of these programs (Bailey, Jens, & Johnson, 1983; Sheehan & Gallagher, 1983) reveal that they vary greatly in their content and effectiveness.

Infant stimulation programs can be center-based (i.e., carried out by professionals in hospitals, clinics, or schools) or home-based (i.e., conducted by parents and professionals within the infant's home). There are also programs that combine center-based instruction with a home-based component.

Despite the recent increase in educational programs for infants with handicapping conditions, there is a lack of empirical evidence supporting the effectiveness of most of these programs. This may be due, in part, to the lack of unified standards for the development of curricula (Karnes & Teska, 1975).

Fortunately, there are general guidelines suggested for the purpose of guiding the development of programs, including the selection of intervention methods and materials, as well as program evaluation. According to these guidelines, there is a clear need for programs to use a sound theoretical framework to direct instructional content and intervention strategies. Professionals need to be clear about the purpose of instruction and to identify the population(s) most appropriate for their programs.

Activities must be meaningful and instruction should emphasize natural learning opportunities and interactions within a variety of domains (i.e., perceptual, cognitive, psycho-motor, and social/emotional). Staff must be properly trained and a program evaluation plan developed. Most important, any stimulation or early intervention program must involve the parents and family of the infant.

REFERENCES

Alberto, P. A., Briggs, T., & Goldstein, D. (1983). Managing learning in handicapped infants. In S. G. Garwood & R. R. Fewell

(Eds.), *Educating handicapped infants* (pp. 417–454). Rockville, MD: Aspen.

Bailey, D. B., Jr., Jens, K. G., & Johnson, N. (1983). Curricula for handicapped infants. In S. G. Garwood & R. R. Fewell (Eds.), *Educating handicapped infants* (pp. 387–416). Rockville, MD: Aspen.

Bobath, K., & Bobath, B. (1972). Cerebral palsy. In P. H. Pearson & C. Williams (Eds.), *Physical therapy services in the developmental disabilities.* Springfield, IL: Thomas.

Gallagher, J., & Reid, D. K. (1981). *The learning theory of Piaget and Inhelder.* Monterey, CA: Brooks/Cole.

Hanson, M. J., & Hanline, M. F. (1984). Behavioral competencies and outcomes: The effects of disorder. In M. J. Hanson (Ed.), *Atypical infant development* (pp. 109–178). Baltimore, MD: University Park Press.

Karnes, M. B., & Teska, J. A. (1975). Children's response to intervention programs. In J. J. Gallagher (Ed.), *The application of child development research to exceptional children.* Reston, VA: Council for Exceptional Children.

Osofsky, J. D. (Ed.). (1979). *Handbook of infant development.* New York: Wiley.

Sheehan, R., & Gallagher, R. J. (1983). Conducting evaluations of infant intervention programs. In S. Garwood & R. R. Fewell (Eds.), *Educating handicapped infants.* Rockville, MD: Aspen.

FRANCINE TOMPKINS
University of Cincinnati

ENRICHMENT
INFANT ASSESSMENT

INFORMAL READING INVENTORY (IRI)

Informal reading inventory (IRI) is a generic term that refers to some type of nonstandardized technique used to assess aspects of reading performance. According to Smith and Johnson (1980), the most informal application of the diagnostic method involves having the child read selections of material silently and orally, asking comprehension questions about what has been read, and making note of the quality of reading, particularly word identification errors. Typically, the reading selections cover a range of grade or difficulty levels, from the preprimer through the eighth or ninth reader levels, as found in basal reading series. The comprehension questions based on the reading passages are usually of three types: factual or literal recall; inferential thinking; and vocabulary knowledge.

Johnson and Kress (1965) identified four purposes for administering an informal reading inventory. The IRI can be used to determine the level at which a reader can function independently, the level at which he or she can profit from instruction, the level at which the reader is frustrated by the material, and the level of listening comprehension. Results of an IRI aid in determining specific strengths and weaknesses in reading, thus leading to a

program of instruction or remediation. Also, the results of an IRI enable the reader to become aware of his or her own abilities and can be used as a measure of reading progress.

Betts (1946) established the earliest criteria for determining the four pedagogical levels. He determined that a child should read words in context with 99% accuracy and answer 90% of the comprehension questions correctly to be able to handle material independently. In order to profit from instruction in certain materials, the reader should recognize 95% of the words in context and respond correctly to comprehension questions with 75% accuracy. When the reader can recognize words with only 90% accuracy, or respond correctly to only half of the comprehension questions, then the material is too difficult and is frustrating. Finally, listening comprehension is determined by reading selections to the child with the expectation that he or she will answer 75% of the related questions correctly.

REFERENCES

Betts, E. A. (1946). *Foundation of reading instruction.* New York: American Book.

Johnson, M. S., & Kress, R. A. (1965). *Informal reading inventories.* Newark, DE: International Reading Association.

Smith, R. J., & Johnson, D. D. (1980). *Teaching children to read* (2nd ed.). Reading, MA: Addison-Wesley.

JOHN M. EELLS
*Souderton Area School District,
Souderton, Pennsylvania*

BASAL READER
CLOZE TECHNIQUE
READING

INFORMATION PROCESSING

Webster's Third World International Dictionary defines a *process* as:

> The action of moving forward progressively from one point to another on the way to completion; the action of passing through continuing development from a beginning to a contemplated end; the action of continuously going along through each of a succession of acts, events, to developmental stages.

Succinctly, process may be considered a manipulation. Information processing, then, in the context of psychological study, is the manipulation of incoming stimuli, and existing or stored information, and the creation of new information by the human brain. This would include such common activities as perception, encoding, decoding, retrieval from memory, rehearsal, general reasoning ability, and a growing multitude of "new" cognitive processes. As new theories of cognitive processes occur, new names and new constructs are devised and added to the list. Implicit in theories of information processing is the assumption that each individual's behavior is determined by the information processing that occurs internally. In combination, the form, depth, and breadth of information processing is what controls behavior, overt and covert, though in all likelihood in a reciprocal relationship with the outside world.

Information processing is in the midst of a revival of study in psychology and related fields, generally under the rubric of cognitive science. During the age of behaviorism, when only clearly observable behaviors were appropriate for study, research on the internal processes of the mind continued but at a much slower pace. There were clear biases present in many journals against the publication of such work. During the 1960s a resurgence began that came to full force only in the 1980s. This resurgence was in some ways related to advances in computer technology, as analogies to computer terminology are common and provide a paradigm for how humans might analyze information. In special education, information processing has always been a major interest because of its relationship to learning and the remediation of learning disorders (Mann, 1979). Disturbances of normal information processing are believed to be at the core of the etiology of learning disabilities. The terminology of information processing has fluctuated over the years, with central processing being the most frequently used alternative term.

Since at least the early 1900s, special educators have been interested in training children in various information-processing methods as a technique for the remediation of learning disorders. Past efforts to improve academic skills through the training of processing have been notable in their failures (Glass, 1983; Mann, 1979; Myers & Hammill, 1969; Reynolds, 1981). With the revival of cognitivism has come a new wave of cognitive processes and higher order information-processing strategies to train. The effectiveness of training cognitive processes for the purpose of improving academic skills has yet to be demonstrated, and the potential of such efforts has been hotly debated (Gresham, 1986; Haywood & Switzky, 1986a, 1986b; Reynolds, 1986).

The information-processing skills of exceptional children will always be of interest to special educators. Most mentally handicapped children have some form of information processing disorder, whether it is a mild deviation from the average skill level of other same-age children or a massive disruption of higher order skills. Treating these children requires extensive knowledge of their information-processing skills.

Theories of information processing abound. The best theory on which to base generalizations about a child may vary from child to child. New theories are being formulated and old theories revised almost daily in this rapidly expanding area of research. However, we must be particularly careful in evaluating work in information pro-

cessing for its application to special education. As Mann (1979) reminds us, many fads in information processing have come and gone and too many of the "new" information processing approaches are simply yesterday's failures shrouded in new jargon and repackaged for today's thinking.

Contemporary information processing models attempt to duplicate or prepare a representation of the internal flow of information in the brain. The various information-processing theories create numerous variations in number and arrangement of subsystems of processing. Information-processing models of human thinking can be represented mathematically, though most often researchers prefer to display the theory as a series of boxes connected by various arrows, much as in a flowchart with feedback loops and various checks and balances.

There are basically only three kinds of models. The first treats information processing as a linear activity, a form of processing that is serial, wherein stages of processing are linked in a straight line and the output of one stage is the input for the next stage; processing proceeds very much in a sequential step-by-step manner. Each stage must await the outcome of the preceding stage. The second primary model of processing does not need to wait for each link in the chain to be completed, but rather carries on parallel processing, doing many tasks simultaneously without awaiting output from a prior step. In parallel processing, several stages can access output from any other stage at the same time. An information processing theory with both components interlinked (serial stages and parallel stages) is a hybrid model (Kantowitz, 1984). These models tend to be more complex but may not always be more useful.

Information processing has progressed to the point of now being a major force in experimental psychology. It is likely to continue to occupy a significant amount of space in the leading scientific journals of psychology for some years to come. Discussions, reviews, and research related to information processing and its related theories will grow in importance in journals related to the education of exceptional children.

REFERENCES

Glass, G. V. (1983). Effectiveness of special education. *Policy Studies Review, 2*, 65–78.

Gresham, F. (1986). On the malleability of intelligence: Unnecessary assumptions, reifications, and occlusion. *School Psychology Review, 15*, 261–263.

Haywood, H. C., & Switzky, H. N. (1986a). The malleability of intelligence: Cognitive processes as a function of polygenic-experiential interaction. *School Psychology Review, 15*, 245–255.

Haywood, H. C., & Switzky, H. N. (1986b). Transactionalism and cognitive processes: Reply to Reynolds and Gresham. *School Psychology Review, 15*, 264–267.

Kantowitz, B. H. (1984). Information processing. In R. Corsini

(Ed.), *Encyclopedia of psychology* (Vol. 2). New York: Wiley-Interscience.

Mann, L. (1979). *On the trail of process*. New York: Grune & Stratton.

Myers, P., & Hammill, D. (1969). *Methods for learning disorders*. New York: Wiley.

Reynolds, C. R. (1981). Neuropsychological assessment and the habilitation of learning: Considerations in the search for the aptitude × treatment interaction. *School Psychology Review, 10*, 343–349.

Reynolds, C. R. (1986). Transactional models of intellectual development, yes. Deficit models of process remediation, no. *School Psychology Review, 15*, 256–260.

CECIL R. REYNOLDS
Texas A&M University

PERCEPTUAL DEVELOPMENT (LAG IN)
PERCEPTUAL TRAINING
RECIPROCAL DETERMINISM
REMEDIATION, DEFICIT-CENTERED MODELS OF
SEQUENTIAL AND SIMULTANEOUS COGNITIVE
　PROCESSING

INFORMED CONSENT

See CONSENT, INFORMED.

INITIAL TEACHING ALPHABET (i/t/a)

The Initial Teaching Alphabet, popularly known as i/t/a, was devised by Sir James Pitman of England. His work was the amalgamation of earlier work done by British advocates of the simplification of English spelling. Pitman promoted the concept of a simplified spelling of the English language requiring the addition of new symbols that augmented the alphabet from 26 characters to 44 characters. These early efforts at changing the orthography of English were known as the Augmented Roman Alphabet (Aukerman, 1971).

The 44-character Augmented Roman Alphabet was developed and publicized by the Pitman organization in 1960 under the original title Initial Teaching Medium (Aukerman, 1971). The purpose behind the development of the new orthographic system was to permit a one-letter character to represent only one English sound or phoneme. Twenty characters were added for speech sounds not represented by a single letter of the English alphabet, and no characters were provided for q and x. No distinction was made between lower-case and capital letters; capital letters were a larger type size of the lower-case form. Use of the augmented alphabet was proposed for teaching beginning reading only.

The i/t/a was used in British and American schools in the 1960s and the early 1970s. The i/t/a provided beginning readers with a true sound-symbol approach to encoding and decoding the sounds of the English language. It made phoneme-grapheme correspondence more regular and simplified spelling for beginning readers. Downing (1964) stated that i/t/a was not a method of instruction; rather, it was a teaching tool that could be used with any type of reading instruction.

Research comparing i/t/a instruction and traditional orthographic (TO) instruction was conducted in England by John Downing (1964). Longitudinal studies showed that even though various instructional methods were used, i/t/a-trained students showed significant differences in the speed with which they learned to read, their levels of comprehension, their spelling levels, and their creative writing abilities.

The i/t/a program in the United States, Early to Read, was developed by Albert Mazurkiewicz and Harold Tanyzer (1966). This program, like the British i/t/a, was divided into three phases. In Phase I, students were introduced to the i/t/a characters through the use of the language-experience approach. Phase II reinforced and extended writing, spelling, and reading skills. Phase III, which usually began during the second year of instruction, emphasized the transfer to TO. Early to Read differed from the British program in that a new reading series was written. British publishers transliterated the *Janet and John* basal series into i/t/a.

Mazurkiewicz (1967) conducted the first i/t/a research in the United States in Bethlehem, Pennsylvania. This initial study and later studies showed that pupils instructed in i/t/a continuously showed better abilities in word discrimination, word knowledge, spelling, and creative writing.

The Initial Teaching Alphabet Foundation at Hofstra University was founded to collect and disseminate information on the i/t/a. In reviewing 70 control group studies that compared i/t/a programs to TO, Block (1971) found that two-thirds of the studies indicated that i/t/a was more successful in teaching beginning and writing skills, that one-third showed i/t/a equally as successful as TO, and that no studies showed adverse effects of using the i/t/a approach.

Block (1971) cites the following as frequent criticisms to i/t/a: (1) children who learn i/t/a have difficulty transferring to TO; (2) i/t/a materials and training are expensive; (3) the majority of the children's environment uses TO; and (4) children in i/t/a programs experience the Hawthorne effect.

Downing (1979) reviewed the use of i/t/a with exceptional children. He reported that even though i/t/a had been successful in teaching reading disabled, mentally retarded, culturally disadvantaged, bilingual, and emotionally disturbed and socially maladjusted children to read, further research is needed. Longitudinal studies in Britain showed that the gifted benefited most from the i/t/a method (Downing, 1979).

REFERENCES

Aukerman, R. C. (1971). *Approaches to beginning reading*. New York: Wiley.

Block, J. R. (1971). *i.t.a.—A status report—1971: The beginnings of a second decade*. Hempstead, NY: Initial Teaching Alphabet Foundation.

Downing, J. (1964). The i.t.a. (Initial Teaching Alphabet) reading experiment. *Reading Teacher, 18*, 105–109.

Downing, J. (1979). "i.t.a." in special education. *Special Education in Canada, 53*, 25–27.

Mazurkiewicz, A. J. (1967). *The Initial Teaching Alphabet in reading instruction, evaluation-demonstration project on the use of i.t.a.* Bethlehem, PA: Lehigh University.

Mazurkiewicz, A. J., & Tanyzer, H. J. (1966). *The i.t.a. handbook for writing and spelling: Early-to-read i.t.a. program*. New York: Initial Teaching Alphabet Publications.

JOYCE E. NESS
*Montgomery County
Intermediate Unit,
Norristown, Pennsylvania*

READING DISORDERS
READING REMEDIATION

INSATIABLE CHILD SYNDROME

Insatiable child syndrome has been described by Levine, Brooks, and Shonkoff (1980) as chronic insatiability that may accompany attention deficit disorder. As described by these authors, insatiable children have a persistent quest for satisfaction, never obtained, that may focus on food, specific activities, or material goods. They are often whiny and irritable and are described by parents as unpleasant, demanding, and difficult to live with. Insatiability may be biological (i.e., a constitutional trait) or it may be acquired. In the latter case, insatiability develops in late infancy or beyond and may result from insecurity or feelings of deprivation and hunger. The chronically insatiable child may, for example, ask unrelentingly for a new toy, yet when getting it, find that it has lost all attraction; demand an inordinate amount of adult attention, tolerating no diversion of attention for another child, another adult, or another activity; or demand that the teacher be available at all times, resenting interactions with other children (Levine et al., 1980).

"Chronic insatiability is a difficult management problem" (Levine et al., 1980, p. 239). Teachers and parents of such children are often weary and frustrated from contact with the child. Specific intervention strategies and gen-

eral goals have been provided by Levine et al. (1980), but their implementation depends on a correct diagnosis. The etiology will dictate in many cases the specific approach to treatment. In general, one must focus on building the child's capacity to delay gratification, build tolerance for not having adult attention, and encourage the sharing of possessions with others. At school, the use of attention and special one-on-one times may be used as reinforcement for more appropriate behavior. If the child's sense of competency, self-sufficiency, and self-esteem can be enhanced through school activities, insatiability may diminish. In all cases, consultation with special education support staff, particularly the school psychologist, will be needed, along with coordination with efforts at home. Well-rounded, comprehensive intervention programs are required for success in treating the insatiable child.

REFERENCE

Levine, M. D., Brooks, R., & Shonkoff, J. P. (1980). *A pediatric approach to learning disorders*. New York: Wiley.

CECIL R. REYNOLDS
Texas A&M University

ATTENTION DEFICIT DISORDER

IN-SERVICE TRAINING FOR SPECIAL EDUCATION TEACHERS

In-service training for special education teachers is not clearly defined. Definitions abound (Hite, 1977; Johnson, 1980; Langone, 1983). Significant differences exist on the subjects of purpose, need, responsibility, and format. In general, however, any training of special education teachers after they have begun functioning as full professionals may be labeled in-service training. Over the past decades, the focus of in-service training for special education teachers has ranged from remedying the deficiencies in preservice training programs (i.e., undergraduate and in some cases graduate degree programs) to implementing new instructional technology.

Some special education teachers view in-service training as a means of increasing communication and reducing the isolation that is prevalent in an occupation in which contact with nonhandicapped students and other adults is limited. In-service training is a way of achieving social mobility in the educational profession, not only by acquiring credentials that are necessary for more responsible positions and higher salaries, but also by gaining wider visibility in the professional world. In-service training continues to be one avenue by which an individual special education teacher's personal interest and needs can be served. In-service training can also aid the school in implementing new educational programs by helping teachers acquire understanding, skills, and attitudes essential to the roles they are to play in the new programs. In sum, the purpose of in-service training for special education teachers usually reflects one or more of the following: job or program improvement, professional growth, personal growth (Rubin, 1971).

In the 1970s and 1980s the need for in-service training of special education teachers has been intensified by social and educational forces. Foremost among the social forces affecting the schools has been the movement to secure equal educational opportunity for handicapped students. The movement is embodied in the Education for All Handicapped Children Act of 1975 (PL 94-142). Public Law 94-142 put heavy demands on special education (and regular education) teachers and administrators—demands that they were not necessarily trained to meet. For example, many special education teachers had to learn to function as resource teachers rather than as teachers of their own special education self-contained students. Teachers trained prior to the late 1970s were ill prepared to meet the challenge of PL 94-142. Recognizing the need previously described, PL 94-142 provided for a comprehensive system of personnel development (CSPD) in each state. The CSPD is based on annual needs assessment and encompasses in-service training as well as preservice training.

Two recent forces within the education community have also increased the need for in-service training of special education teachers: an awareness of the limits of preservice training programs and an infusion of instructional technology. For decades teacher educators focused their attention on raising the standards of preservice special education teacher training programs. During this time period, in-service training was primarily viewed as a means to remedy the deficiencies in the preservice programs. In the late 1970s teacher educators began to realize that preservice training programs only prepare beginning teachers, not accomplished teachers (Howey, 1978). In addition, teacher educators also began to realize that some teaching competencies are better learned on the job, with the benefit of experience, and that other competencies cannot be learned anywhere else. For example, it is difficult to see how special education teachers can internalize complex organizational strategies or transfer principles of growth and development to instructional decisions without more substantive teaching experience than is generally provided in preservice training programs.

A final reason why the need for in-service training has been intensified in the 1980s is the recent infusion of instructional technology into special education programs. Bennett and Maher (1984) have identified training special education teachers for effective use of instructional technology as a critical in-service need. For example, special education teachers must learn to capitalize on the potential of instructional technology. Technology such as computer-assisted instruction can bring about more productive use of the teacher's and the student's time. Of particular importance is its capacity to provide instruction that is truly individualized for each handicapped student.

In-service training of special education teachers does not have an established framework. The responsibility for it is not fixed. Institutions of higher education, state departments of education, and local school districts have not embraced in-service training as a basic commitment. The roles different groups play in in-service training of special education (and regular education) teachers are changing. The realignment of power in teacher education has altered or abolished traditional roles. New roles are becoming defined for some groups for example, the state departments of education and teachers, but not for others. Higher education is particularly affected. Its role in organizing and conducting in-service training is being taken over by teachers and collaborators (Edelfelt, 1979).

Frequently used formats for in-service training of special education teachers include on-site after school workshops, release-time activities, teacher centers, and on-site college or university courses (Swenson, 1981). Among these formats, the teacher center reflects the new role played by teachers. Teacher centers are places where teachers determine their own needs, seek assistance, and develop materials or strategies to solve problems. Teacher center instructors are themselves classroom teachers, sharing their own practical, classroom-developed materials; or they are advisors—formerly classroom teachers—who view their job as stimulating, supporting, and extending a teacher's own direction of growth. Attendance at teacher center classes is voluntary, not prescribed by the school district; if indirectly required (e.g., as a way to spend release time), programs offered are based on teachers' expressions of their own training needs (Devaney & Thorn, 1975).

Collaboration as a feature of in-service training is present in some teacher centers, but it is not a distinguishing feature of them as it is of another format, the consortium of two or more educational agencies. Probably the most common type of cooperative format is a college or university and a school system working together. A variety of other cooperative approaches exist, for example, the cooperation of several school districts or several colleges and universities within the same geographic region.

With the increased attention in the 1970s and 1980s has come a move to evaluate and reform in-service training. Teachers are widely known to be dissatisfied with inservice training (Johnson, 1980; Rubin, 1978). There exists little empirical evidence that in-service training has any significant effect on the behavior of special education teachers (Langone, 1983). Johnson (1980) lists the following problems with inservice training:

1. In-service education has not placed enough emphasis on improving school program or teacher performance.

2. In-service education has not addressed teachers' urgent, day-to-day needs.

3. In-service education has been required of teachers and imposed and delivered by others.

4. In-service education has violated many principles of good teaching.

5. In-service education has been fragmented, unsystematic, devoid of a conceptual framework. (pp. 29–30)

REFERENCES

Bennett, R., & Maher, C. (Eds.). (1984). *Microcomputers and exceptional children*. New York: Haworth.

Devaney, K., & Thorn, L. (1975). *Exploring teachers' centers*. San Francisco: Far West Laboratory for Educational Research and Development.

Edelfelt, R. (1979, April). Inservice teacher education: A concept, an overview. *National Council of States on Inservice Education Inservice Newsletter, 15*, 4–11.

Hite, H. (1977). Inservice education: Perceptions, purposes, and practices. In H. Hite & K. Howey (Eds.), *Planning inservice teacher education: Promising alternatives* (pp. 1–20). Washington, DC: American Association of Colleges for Teacher Education.

Howey, K. (1978, March). *Inservice teacher education: A study of the perceptions of teachers, professors and parents about current and projected practice*. Paper presented at the meeting of the American Educational Research Association, Toronto (ERIC Document Reproduction Service NO. ED 152 701).

Johnson, M. (1980). *Inservice education: Priority for the '80s*. Syracuse, NY: National Council of States on Inservice Education, Syracuse University.

Langone, J. (1983). Developing effective inservice for special educators. *Journal for Special Educators, 19*(3), 33–47.

Rubin, L. (1971). *Improving in-service education: Proposals and procedures for change*. Boston: Allyn & Bacon.

Rubin, L. (1978). *Perspectives on preservice and inservice education*. Syracuse, NY: National Council of States on Inservice Education, Syracuse University.

Swenson, R. (1981). The state of the art in inservice education and staff development in K-12 schools. *Journal of Research & Development in Education, 15*(1), 2–7.

PHILLIP J. MCLAUGHLIN
University of Georgia

**TEACHER CENTERS
TEACHER EFFECTIVENESS**

INSIGHT (IN THE GIFTED)

Advocates of the gestalt school typically believe that learning takes the form of an insight, a sudden occurrence of a reorganization of the field of experience, as when one has a new idea or discovers a solution to a problem. Two authors (Koffka, 1929; Kohler, 1929) used a variety of problem situations to study the role of insight in the learning of animals. For example, Kohler studied chimpanzee behaviors associated with retrieving a banana that had been placed out of reach by the investigator. As opposed to trial-and-error behavior, the chimpanzee successfully reached the banana as if by plan. Thus, Kohler interpreted the insight involved as a seeing of relations or a putting together of events that were internally represented.

Insight has also been described in human beings by researchers such as Wertheimer (1945) and Sternberg and Davidson (1983). Wertheimer studied children's insightful solutions to geometric problems. Some children used a rote fashion to solve problems; others, however, could see the essential structure of a problem situation, and consequently used insight as their approach to learning. Sternberg and Davidson, on the other hand, developed a subtheory of intellectual giftedness based on the centrality of insight skills.

In a later work, Davidson and Sternberg (1984) proposed that insight involves not one, but three separate but related psychological processes. They refered to the products of the three operations as insights, understood in terms of three types of insight skills: (1) selective encoding, by which relevant information in a given context is sifted from irrelevant information; (2) selective combination, by which relevant information is combined in a novel and productive way; and (3) selective comparison, by which new information is related in a novel way to old information.

The authors' three-process view of insight constitutes what they believe to be a subtheory of intellectual giftedness. Whereas selective encoding involves knowing which pieces of information are relevant, selective combination involves knowing how to blend together the pieces of relevant information. Selective comparison involves relating the newly acquired information to information acquired in the past (as when one solves a problem by using an analogy). In addition, the authors reason that the three processes are not executed in simple serial order, but rather, continually interact with each other in the formation of new ideas. Thus, it is the products of these operations that they refer to as insights.

To test their subtheory, Davidson and Sternberg (1984) completed three experiments with gifted and nongifted children in grades 4, 5, and 6. Results of all three experiments support the subtheory of intellectual giftedness. It was learned that insight plays a statistically significant role in the learning of the gifted as compared with that of the nongifted.

Davidson and Sternberg (1984) suggest several benefits of their approach to understanding and assessing intellectual giftedness over alternative psychometric and information-processing approaches. First, they propose that their theoretically based approach deals with what it is that makes the gifted special. For example, they believe that what primarily distinguishes the intellectually gifted in their performance is not that they are faster, but that they are better in their insightful problem-solving skills. Second, because their measurement of insight skills has no demands on prior knowledge, their approach is appropriate for individuals with nonstandard backgrounds.

REFERENCES

Davidson, J. E., & Sternberg, R. J. (1984). The role of insight in intellectual giftedness. *Gifted Child Quarterly. 28*(2), 58–64.

Koffka, K. (1929). *The growth of the mind* (2nd ed.). New York: Harcourt.

Kohler, W. (1929). *Gestalt psychology.* New York: Liveright.

Sternberg, R. J., & Davidson, J. E. (1983). Insight in the gifted. *Educational Psychologist. 18*(1), 51–57.

Wertheimer, M. (1945). *Productive thinking.* New York: Harper & Row.

JUNE SCOBEE
University of Houston, Clear Lake

INSTITUTE FOR RESEARCH ON LEARNING DISABILITIES, TEACHERS COLLEGE, COLUMBIA UNIVERSITY

The Institute for the Study of Learning Disabilities at Teachers College, Columbia University, was established in 1977 as one of five centers funded by the federal government to carry out research in learning disabilities. The institute's research work was guided by the proposition that learning-disabled (LD) children's learning problems may be caused by their difficulties in processing information. It was postulated that LD children's academic failures are the result of interactions between their ways of processing information and the information-processing demands made on them by the instructional methods used in their classrooms (Connor, 1983). Research evidence at the institute suggested that some LD learners may perform like younger and less mature children on tasks such as arithmetic computation as a consequence of information-processing difficulties.

Two options for intervention were investigated. The first was manipulating instructional variables to make instruction more effective. The second was teaching learning-disabled children how to use cognitive skills effectively, and to use metacognitive strategies to reduce the gaps in learning that are found between these children and non-LD children. Both types of intervention options were found to be effective.

Exploring the first option, Bryant et al. (1980) found that methods and materials that avoided information processing "overloading" during instruction were beneficial in assisting LD students to learn better. They assisted by (1) reducing the unit size in reading; (2) providing the teacher with a special focus during instruction; (3) reduc-

ing competition in students' possible responses to instruction; (4) teaching all skills to mastery; (5) providing distributive practice and review; and (6) training for transfer.

As to the second option, LD students were found to benefit considerably through the direct teaching of cognitive strategies. It was shown that these students could use such strategies effectively in memorizing information, that they could be taught to use linguistic cues more effectively, and that their use of metacognitive skills resulted in increased comprehension and use of information (Kimmel & MacGinitie, 1982).

The institute also carried out specific investigations into the implications for reading comprehension of the connection between the characteristics of the text being read and the reader (Williams & Taylor, 1982). Since LD and non-LD learners performed similarly in experiments dealing with this connection, it was concluded that the judicious use of a variety of reading techniques found to be successful with normal readers might also benefit learning-disabled readers.

Institute research also confirmed that although it is reading problems that are most often the reason for a child being classified as learning disabled, such a child is often deficient in arithmetic achievement as well. On the positive side, it was found that instruction based on a direct instructional model can be effective in teaching learning-disabled students to master both simple and relatively complex skills (Fleischner & Garnett, 1979).

REFERENCES

Bryant, N. D., Fayne, H., & Gettinger, M. (1980). *Applying the mastery model to sight word instruction for disabled readers* (Technical Report No. 2). New York: Teachers College, Columbia University, Research Institute for the Study of Learning Disabilities.

Connor, F. P. (1983). Improving school instruction for learning disabled children: The Teachers College Institute. *Exceptional Child Quarterly, 4*, 23–44.

Fleischner, J. E., & Garnett, K. (1979). *Mastery of basic number facts by learning disabled students: An intervention study* (Technical Report No. 17). New York: Teachers College, Columbia University, Research Institute for the Study of Learning Disabilities.

Kimmel S., & MacGinitie, W. (1982). *Children with a perseverative text interpretation strategy: The effects of text organization* (Technical Report No. 18). New York: Teachers College, Columbia University, Research Institute for the Study of Learning Disabilities.

Williams, J. P., & Taylor, M. B. (1982). *Factors in the comprehension of expository text in normally achieving and learning-disabled children* (Technical Report No. 18). New York: Teachers College, Columbia University, Research Institute for the Study of Learning Disabilities.

LESTER MANN
Hunter College, City University of New York

CHICAGO INSTITUTE
DIRECT INSTRUCTION
INSTITUTES FOR RESEARCH ON LEARNING DISABILITIES
METACOGNITION

INSTITUTE FOR RESEARCH ON LEARNING DISABILITIES, UNIVERSITY OF KANSAS

The University of Kansas Institute for Research on Learning Disabilities (KU-IRLD) was established in 1977 as one of five centers funded by the federal government to carry out research into learning disabilities. Its major mission was to develop a validated intervention model sufficiently powerful to affect the academic performance of learning-disabled adolescents (Schumaker, Deshler, Alley, & Warner, 1983).

Because members of the institute did not feel comfortable with the limited amount of empirical information available on the characteristics of learning-disabled adolescents, the institute's initial work was directed toward the establishment of a comprehensive epidemiological data base. This was created through epidemiological research and subsequent cross validation in Kansas school districts. Epidemiological findings were reported in a variety of KU-IRLD research reports (e.g., by Deshler, Schumaker, Alley, Warner, & Clark, 1982). Some of the findings were (1) learning-disabled (LD) students are when compared with low-achieving (LA) students, significantly different in respect to academic and cognitive factors but not in respect to social, medical, or environmental ones; (2) LD adolescents reach a plateau of basic skills during the secondary grades so that adolescence is usually a time of little growth for them; (3) LD adolescents demonstrate deficiencies in study skills and strategies, e.g., 85% of the Kansas students studied were deficient in such areas as test-taking skills and study skills (Alley, Deshler, & Warner, 1979); (4) many LD adolescents exhibit immature executive functioning, i.e., the ability to create and apply cognitive strategies to novel problems; (5) many adolescent LD students demonstrate social skills deficiencies; and (6) school demands increase with the age of the child, and the complexity of school settings appear to contribute as much to the LD adolescent's academic failures as his or her deficits.

During its second year, the institute developed an intervention model congruent with the institute's major epidemiological findings. This included a learning strategies approach as the core component of the intervention model, designed to teach students how to learn rather than how to master particular subject matter content. To assist in learning strategy training, the institute designed a series of learning strategy packets matched to the major curriculum demands of the secondary school. These were vali-

dated and refined for individual students (Deshler, Schumaker, Alley, Warner & Clark, 1982).

Other efforts of the KU-IRLD included the development of a social skills curriculum to teach generalizable social skills to LD and other mildly handicapped students. A number of studies also were carried out to train school-related social skills, job-related social skills, and general social skills. An effort also was made to teach the students how to generalize these skills (Schumaker & Ellis, 1982). A social skills curriculum was developed from these studies.

Another emphasis of the institute was to design procedures that modify the ways in which classroom instruction is provided to students. Thus textbook chapters were transferred onto audiotapes and students taught how to use comprehension and organizational strategies to manage the transferred content. An advanced organizer technique to be used by content teachers prior to presenting lectures was designed by Lentz (1982).

Other efforts on the part of KU-IRLD staff were directed toward the development of teaching methodologies based on learning principles, and the design of generalization procedures that would be powerful enough so that LD adolescents would be able to use them to transfer the skills they learned in the resource room to a variety of academic and nonacademic contexts. Still further research and curriculum development efforts focused on the teaching of motivation skills to adolescent LD students. These skills would help them to accept responsibility for their own educaation and independent functioning.

REFERENCES

Alley, G. R., Deshler, D. D., & Warner, M. M. (1979). Identification of learning disabled adolescents: A Bayesian approach. *Learning Disabilities Quarterly, 2,* 76–83.

Deshler, D. D., Schumaker, J. B., Alley, C. R., Warner, M. M., & Clark, F. L. (1982). Learning disabilities in adolescent and young adult populations. *Focus on Exceptional Children, 15,* 1–12.

Lentz, B. K. (1982). *The effect of advance organizers on the learning and retention of learning disabled adolescents within the context of a cooperative planning model.* Dissertation. University of Kansas, Lawrence.

Schumaker, J. B., Deshler, D. D., Alley, C. R., & Warner, M. M. (1982). *The evaluation of a learning strategies intervention model for LD adoelscents* (Research Report No. 67). Lawrence: University of Kansas Institute for Research in Learning Disabilities.

Schumaker, J. B., & Ellis, E. S. (1982). Social skills training with LD adolescents: A generalization study. *Learning Disability Quarterly, 5,* 295–304.

STAFF

INSTITUTE FOR RESEARCH ON LEARNING DISABILITIES, CHICAGO

INSTITUTE FOR RESEARCH ON LEARNING DISABILITIES,
UNIVERSITY OF MINNESOTA

INSTITUTE FOR RESEARCH ON LEARNING DISABILITIES, UNIVERSITY OF MINNESOTA

The University of Minnesota Learning Disabilities Institute was one of five institutes created by the federal government to carry out intensive and sustained research into learning disabilities. The original federal mandate indicated that the development of empirically demonstrated interventions was to be the major charge of the new institutes. Nevertheless, the Minnesota institute focused its efforts on the assessment of the characteristics of children referred for psychoeducational evaluation or identified as being eligible for special education services under the rubric of learning disabilities. Institute members investigated the methods employed by schools for planning instructional evaluations, the extent to which children referred for learning disabilities services benefited from the instruction they received through these services, and the effectiveness of specific instructional programs provided to learning-disabled (LD) students.

The institute's major findings raised serious concerns about learning disability assessment and decision-making practices. These were found to be too often vague or subjective. The Minnesota institute's work raised questions about "automatic testing of children thought to have learning disabilities . . . often with technically inadequate devices . . ." (Ysseldyke et al., 1983). The research also questioned the effectiveness of team decisions regarding the diagnosis and programming of LD students. School teams were found to make decisions "less on data than on subjective teacher or student variables and on inconsistent and indefensible criteria" (Ysseldyke et al., 1983, p. 87).

The institute concluded that classroom-based interventions should be instituted at the point of an academically troubled child's referral rather after the laborious sequence of referral, assessment, and decision making. In addition, the institute investigated the values of curriculum-based assessment devices and noted that special education teachers might prefer these to standardized achievement and other tests to guide their instructional efforts. Curriculum-based devices were generally found to be as reliable and valid as commercial devices, while being more useful for ongoing decision making about instruction (Mirkin, Deno, Tindal, & Kuehnle, 1982). The institute concluded that learning-handicapped students make better progress if teachers apply specific data-use strategies, based on curricular assessment, to teach them; teachers should not rely soley on their own judgments.

The work of the Minnesota institute called into question many of the diagnostic, placement, and educational decision-making processes at work in the field of learning disabilities. The institute also criticized the construct of learning disabilities. It did so on the basis of findings that students diagnosed as learning disabled did not differ significantly from other students with academic difficulties who were not so diagnosed. For support and criticism of the Minnesota institute's work, see Keogh (1983) and McKinney (1983).

REFERENCES

Keogh, B. K. (1983). A lesson from Gestalt psychology. *Exceptional Education Quarterly, 4*, 115–127.

McKinney, J. D. (1983). Contributions of the Institutes for Research on Learning Disabilities. *Exceptional Education Quarterly, 4*, 129–144.

Mirkin, P., Deno, S., Tindal, G., & Kuehnle, K. (1982). Frequency of measurement and data utilization strategies as factors in standardized behavioral assessment of academic skill. *Journal of Behavioral Assessment, 4*, 361–370.

Ysseldyke, J. E., Thurlow, M., Graden, J., Wesson, C., Algozzine, B., & Deno, S. (1983). Generalizations from five years of research on assessment and decision making: The University of Minnesota Institute. *Exceptional Education Quarterly, 4*, 75–93.

LESTER MANN
*Hunter College, City University
of New York*

INSTITUTE FOR RESEARCH ON LEARNING DISABILITIES,
CHICAGO
INSTITUTES FOR RESEARCH ON LEARNING DISABILITIES,
UNIVERSITY OF KANSAS

INSTITUTE FOR RESEARCH ON LEARNING DISABILITIES, UNIVERSITY OF VIRGINIA

The University of Virginia Learning Disabilities Research Institute (LDRI) was established in 1977 at the University of Illinois at Chicago as one of five centers funded by the federal government to carry out research into learning disabilities.

The major focus of the University of Virginia Learning Disabilities Research Institute was on the development and validation of educational interventions to assist learning-disabled (LD) children with attentional difficulties (Hallahan, et al., 1983). The LDRI was particularly interested in the usefulness of remedial efforts that proceeded on a cognitive basis as compared with those that directly approached learning problems through the remediation of academic skill deficits.

Researchers at LDRI found that many LD children who suffer from attentional problems, and who could be categorized as strategy deficient, are unable to use task-appropriate strategies. The investigators thus developed and evaluated the effects of cognitive strategy training, metacognitive training, and cognitive behavioral training on the attentional deficits of the learning-disabled children. Information-processing investigations also were carried out, often in tandem with cognitive training efforts.

Much of the LDRI's research interest focused on the direct application of cognitive-metacognitive and cognitive behavior modification CBM training on the acquisition of specific academic skills. Relative to broad academic skill training, the institute found that the strategic breakdowns of LD students could be helped by training the students to effectively use problem-solving strategies. In more specific areas, there was research into spelling and handwriting acquisition (Kosiewicz, Hallahan, Lloyd, & Graves, 1982) and into arithmetic (Lloyd, Cameron, Cullinan, Kauffman, & Kneedler, 1981). Adult-child interactions and the psychometric properties of the Woodcock-Johnson Psychoeducational Battery also were investigated by the Virginia institute.

REFERENCES

Hallahan, D. P., Hall, R. J., Ianna, S. O., Kneedler, R. D., Lloyd, J. W., Loper, A. P., & Reeve, R. E. (1983). Summary of research findings at the University of Virginia Learning Disabilities Research Institute. *Exceptional Education Quarterly, 4*, 95–114.

Kosiewicz, M. M., Hallahan, D. P., Lloyd, J. W., & Graves, A. W. (1982). Effects of self-instruction and self-correction procedures on handwriting performance. *Learning Disability Quarterly 5*, 71–78.

Lloyd, J. W., Cameron, N. A., Cullinan, D., Kauffman, J. M., & Kneedler, R. D. (1981). Addition strategy training with learning-disabled children (Technical Report No. 49). Charlottesville, VA: University of Virginia, Learning Disabilities Research Institute.

LESTER MANN
*Hunter College, City University
of New York*

INSTITUTES FOR RESEARCH ON LEARNING DISABILITIES
LEARNING DISABILITIES
RESEARCH IN SPECIAL EDUCATION

INSTITUTE FOR THE STUDY OF LEARNING DISABILITIES, CHICAGO

The Chicago Institute for the Study of Learning Disabilities was established in 1977 as one of five centers funded by the federal government to carry out research into learning disabilities. One of the institute's major roles was to conduct research on the terms used in the federal defini-

tion of learning disabilities: oral expression and listening, oral reading and reading comprehension, and learning and memory (Bryan, Pearl, Donahue, Bryan, & Pflaumm, 1983).

Oral expression and listening were examined within an interactionist framework. The use of language in social contexts was assessed. The institute also evaluated the ways in which personality factors and teacher strategies affected oral reading rates and comprehension. Laboratory studies were conducted on children's rates of learning and memory functioning. Still other studies sought to determine how varying models and classrooms influenced learning-disabled (LD) schoolchildren's achievement and behavior.

Some of the evidence accumulated through the Chicago institute's investigations indicated that the learning-disabled children studied, while scoring within the average range of intellectual functioning on intelligence tests, consistently averaged approximately half a standard deviation below their normally achieving classmates. In reading and mathematics, inner-city LD children were found to score 2 to 4 years below national norms on achievement tests, while suburban LD children scored only slightly below the national norms. Learning-disabled children low in reading were also low in mathematics.

An important finding at the Chicago institute was that there were great similarities among various samples of LD students. Thus LD groups that were divergent on demographic and achievement measures still responded, while in the institute's research programs, more similarly to each other than to groups of nonlearning-disabled students. Furthermore, there were persistent personality and behavioral differences between LD and non-LD students. Investigations at the Chicago institute also found that interventions successful with LD children were likely to improve the school performance of non-LD students.

Other research at the institute suggested that LD students who failed in one situation tended to anticipate failure in subsequent situations. This led the investigators to conclude that general pessimism ". . . leads the LD child to avoid new challenges and to engage in maladaptive behavior" (Bryan, et al., 1983, p. 17). Other important research at the institute suggested that LD students are highly motivated to seek peer approval and that their marginal social status and learning difficulties may lead them to seek attention from peers through socially unacceptable means (Pearl & Bryan, 1982).

REFERENCES

Bryan, T., Pearl, R., Donahue, M., Bryan, J., & Pflaumm, S. (1983). The Chicago Institute for the Study of Learning Disabilities. *Exceptional Child Quarterly, 4*, 1–22.

Pearl, R., & Bryan, T. L. (1982, February). *Learning disabled children's self esteem and desire for approval*. Paper presented to the International Conferences of the Association for Children with Learning Disabilities, Chicago.

LESTER MANN
*Hunter College, City University
of New York*

INSTITUTES FOR RESEARCH IN LEARNING DISABILITIES
INSTITUTE FOR RESEARCH ON LEARNING DISABILITIES, UNIVERSITY OF VIRGINIA

INSTITUTES FOR RESEARCH ON LEARNING DISABIILTIES

The Institutes for Research on Learning Disabilities were created to encourage basic and applied research in order to develop and validate successful practices with learning-disabled (LD) pupils. Originally sponsored by the Bureau of Education for the Handicapped and later funded through Special Education Programs within the Department of Education, the five 6-year institutes were awarded on a contractual basis to the University of Illinois—Chicago Circle, Teachers College at Columbia University, the University of Kansas, the University of Minnesota, and the University of Virginia.

The Chicago Institute for the Study of Learning Disabilities focused on the social competence of LD children. Studies addressed LD pupils' communicative competence and reading abilities, causal attributions of success and failure, and the immediate impression the pupils make on naive observers (Bryan, Pearl, Donahue, Bryan, & Pflaum, 1983).

The Teachers College Institute at Columbia University was organized as five task forces, each of which conducted research in a specific academic skill area (Connor, 1983). One task force studied memory and study skills of LD students (Gelzheiser, 1982; Shepherd, Frank, Solar, & Gelzheiser, 1982). Two task forces investigated learning problems in the basic skills of arithmetic, reading, and spelling (Fleischner & Garnett, 1979; Fleischner, Garnett, & Preddy, 1982). The final two task forces studied reading comprehension, one from the perspective of interaction of text and reader and one from the perspective of semantics and application of schemata (Williams, 1986).

At the University of Kansas institute, research concentrated on the problems of LD adolescents. Epidemiological studies revealed the unique characteristics of LD students of high school age, and a curriculum comprised of strategy training, social skills, modified materials, and instructional procedures was investigated and developed (Schumaker, Deshler, Alley, & Warner, 1983).

The major purpose of the University of Minnesota's Institute for Research on Learning Disabilities was to study the assessment of LD children. This research incorporated two major lines of investigation. The first explored the characteristics of students referred for psychoeducational evaluation and of those found eligible for placement in school-based LD programs (Ysseldyke, Thurlow, Graden, Algozinne, & Deno, 1983). The second line of research developed and validated repeated and direct assessment procedures for assessing students' academic progress and for formatively developing effective instructional programs (Deno, 1985).

The University of Virginia Learning Disabilities Research Institute focused its efforts on LD students with attention problems. It emphasized developing cognitive behavior modification techniques that improve children's on-task behavior and that provide children with strategies for approaching academic tasks. Studies included investigations of metacognition, information processing, self-recording of task-related behavior, and strategy training (Hallahan et al., 1983).

The work of the five Institues for Research on Learning Disabilities began amidst considerable controversy about the nature of learning disabilities (McKinney, 1983). Nevertheless, it is generally accepted that the institutes, through the collective resources of many investigators pursuing a complex set of problems in programmatic fashion, contributed significantly to what we now know about the nature and treatment of learning disabilities (Keogh, 1983; McKinney, 1983).

REFERENCES

Bryan, T., Pearl, R., Donahue, M., Bryan, J., & Pflaum, S. (1983). The Chicago Institute for Study of Learning Disabilities. *Exceptional Education Quarterly, 4*(1), 1–22.

Connor, F. P. (1983). Improving school instruction for learning disabled: The Teachers College Institute. *Exceptional Education Quarterly, 4*(1), 23–44.

Deno, S. L. (1985). Curriculum-based measurement: The emerging alternative. *Exceptional Children, 52*, 219–232.

Fleischner, J. E., & Garnett, K. (1979). *Arithmetic learning disabilities: A literature review* (Research Review Series 1979–1980, Vol. 4). New York: Teachers College, Columbia University, Research Institute for the Study of Learning Disabilities.

Fleischner, J. E., Garnett, K., & Preddy, D. (1982). *Mastery of basic number facts by learning disabled students: An intervention study* (Technical Report No. 17). New York: Teachers College, Columbia University, Research Institute for the Study of Learning Disabilities.

Gelzheiser, L. M. (1982). *The effects of direct instruction on learning disabled children's ability to generalize study behaviors for deliberate memory tasks.* Unpublished doctoral dissertation, Teachers College, Columbia University.

Hallahan, D. P., Hall, R. J., Ianna, S. O., Kneedler, R. D., Lloyd, J. W., Loper, A. B., & Reeve, R. E. (1983). Summary of research findings at the University of Virginia Learning Disabilities

Research Institute. *Exceptional Education Quarterly, 4*(1), 95–114.

Keogh, B. K. (1983). A lesson from Gestalt psychology. *Exceptional Education Quarterly, 4*(1), 115–128.

McKinney, J. D. (1983). Contributions of the Institutes for Research on Learning Disabilities. *Exceptional Education Quarterly, 4*(1), 129–144.

Schumaker, J. B., Deshler, D. D., Alley, G. R., & Warner, M. M. (1983). Toward the development of an intervention model for the learning disabled adolescents: The University of Kansas Institute. *Exceptional Education Quarterly, 4*(1), 45–74.

Shepherd, J. J., Frank, B., Solar, R. A., & Gelzheiser, L. M. (1982). *Progress report*. New York: Teachers College, Columbia University, Research Institute for the Study of Learning Disabilities.

Williams, J. P. (1986). The role of phonemic analysis in reading. In J. K. Torgeson, & B. Y. L. Wong (Eds.), *Psychological and educational perspectives on learning disabilities*. Orlando, FL: Academic.

Ysseldyke, J., Thurlow, M., Graden, J., Wesson, C., Algozzine, B., & Deno, S. (1983). Generalizations from five years of research on assessment and decision making: The University of Minnesota Institute. *Exceptional Education Quarterly, 4*(1), 75–94.

Douglas Fuchs
Lynn S. Fuchs
Peabody College, Vanderbilt University

INSTITUTE FOR RESEARCH ON LEARNING DISABILITIES, CHICAGO
INSTITUTE FOR RESEARCH ON LEARNING DISABILITIES, UNIVERSITY OF MINNESOTA
INSTITUTE FOR RESEARCH ON LEARNING DISABILITIES, TEACHERS COLLEGE, COLUMBIA UNIVERSITY
INSTITUTE FOR RESEARCH ON LEARNING DISABILITIES, UNIVERSITY OF KANSAS
INSTITUTE FOR RESEARCH ON LEARNING DISABILITIES, UNIVERSITY OF VIRGINIA

INSTITUTIONALIZATION

In the past, handicapped persons (notably persons with mental retardation or mental illness) were left to fend for themselves, were shut away in rooms or houses, or worse, were placed in prisons (Wolfensberger, 1972). This often resulted in illness or death: a situation that led to the establishment of institutional residences in the nineteenth century. These facilities, called hospitals, asylums, or colonies, were constructed in rural areas with residents having little contact with community members. The original intent of such facilities was to provide a higher level of care for handicapped persons needing such care. Anywhere from 500 to 5000 residents were maintained in each facility. The facilities often had large staffs and became communities unto themselves.

Handicapped residents of institutions typically were not prepared to live and work in the community. Emphasis was placed on physical care in contrast to vocational preparation. In addition, the standard of care often was poor. Residents lived in barracks-style arrangements that were dehumanizing. Crowding was commonplace, with waking hours spent in idle activity.

Placement in a residential facility was often for life. Through the 1950s, the number of handicapped persons residing in institutions increased. Then, with the advent of the deinstitutionalization movement, promoted by those who thought the physical and social environment of institutions to be detrimental, the resident institutional population declined. From 1955 to 1973, the resident population declined from 500,000 to 250,000 in spite of a 40% increase in the U.S. population (Telford & Sawrey, 1977). Currently, the emptying of residential institutions has slowed, with most states controlling new admissions instead of removing residents.

While many formerly institutionalized handicapped persons can be accommodated in the community, care and treatment facilities have not kept pace with the deinstitutionalization movement. Consequently, a number of those who returned to the community have been unable to obtain needed services and have become part of the homeless contingent found in many cities. Institutions will always be required for at least some small segment of the handicapped population. However, with early intervention, education, and community-based alternatives, few individuals will require intensive and lifelong care.

REFERENCES

Arnhoff, F. N. (1975). Social consequences of policy toward mental illness. *Science, 188,* 1277–1281.

Telford, C. W., & Sawrey, J. M. (1977). *The exceptional individual* (2nd ed.). Englewood Cliffs, NJ: Prentice-Hall.

Wolfensberger, W. (1972). *The principle of normalization in human services.* Downsview, CT: National Institute of Mental Retardation.

Patricia Ann Abramson
*Hudson Public Schools,
Hudson, Wisconsin*

COMMUNITY RESIDENTIAL PROGRAMS
DEINSTITUTIONALIZATION

INSTITUTION NATIONALE DES SOURDS-MUETS

The Institution Nationale des Sourds-Muets, the first public nonpaying school for the deaf in the world, was founded in Paris in 1755 by the Abbot Charles Michel de l'Epée (1712–1789). Its name was changed in 1960 to Institut National de Jeunes Sourds (INJS) (National Institute for Young Deaf). Despite its location in the heart of Paris, it has retained spacious grounds (19,300 square meters) comprising playgrounds, gardens, orchards, and vegetable gardens.

Institut National des Jeunes Sourds (Paris)

De l'Epée started to teach the deaf when he was asked to give religious instruction to two deaf twin sisters who communicated by signs. He understood that signs could express human thought as much as oral language and decided to use them for his teaching. However, probably unaware that a more elaborate sign system existed among the Paris deaf community (Moody, 1983), de l'Epée felt compelled to create additional signs. These, the methodical signs, were intended to expand the vocabulary and to adapt the existing signs so as to follow French syntax and morphology. The successor of de l'Epée was the abbot Sicard (1808), who continued to expand the methodical signs. However, their excessive development resulted in a cumbersome system unsuitable for communication. During his tenure, a trend towards greater use of natural signs gained momentum and was established as a principle by the following director, Bébian (Moores, 1978).

As early as 1805, the institute's physician, J. M. Itard (1821), introduced auditory and speech training for some pupils, and tried to teach speech to Victor, the wild child of the Aveyron (Lane, 1981). Bébian, who took charge in 1817, is probably the first protagonist of a bilingual education. He considered that the acquisition of French was facilitated when concepts were first established through signs. This official use of natural sign language allowed more and more former pupils to become teachers. Already under Sicard, however, some deaf teachers had been trained; in 1816 one of them, Laurent Clerc, accompanied Thomas Hopkins Gallaudet back to the United States to establish a school along the same model as the Paris institution.

During most of the nineteenth century, sign language for teaching flourished, although its use was criticized by Itard and his followers. The latter were unsuccessful in defending oralism until the 1880 Milano Congress of Educators of the Deaf, which decided that signs were inappropriate for teaching and had an adverse effect on the acquisition of spoken language. Signs were henceforth suppressed, and deaf teachers discharged.

For the rest of the nineteenth century and for more than two-thirds of the twentieth, oral education prevailed as the only official method. Signs were tolerated among pupils as a low-grade communication medium, although they were still covertly used by some teachers. Following the congresses of the World Federation of the Deaf in Paris (1971) and Washington (1975), a renewal of interest in sign language took place in France. This movement has shaken the strictly oralist position of the INJS and other European schools for the deaf and has led several of its teachers to adopt a total communication philosophy. Today the INJS is a place where energies are expended in several directions in an attempt to revitalize deaf education. The school, which formerly was entirely residential, presently has a larger population of day pupils. Efforts are being made towards mainstreaming and some teachers have become itinerant in order to support pupils integrated into ordinary schools. Sign language teaching is organized within the institution and several teachers use it in their classrooms. Training of interpreters for the deaf has been organized. Other teachers have adopted cued speech, while some have remained exclusively oral. The venerable library contains many publications by former deaf teachers and pupils, including detailed accounts of the life of the deaf community in eighteenth- and nineteenth-century France.

The INJS deserves the title of cradle of sign language for deaf education. In its front courtyard, visitors are greeted by the statue of the Abbot de l'Epée, to whose robe clings a grateful deaf child. Many deaf people throughout the world consider de l'Epée as their spiritual father, and the INJS as the living historical landmark of his action.

REFERENCES

Itard, J. M. (1821). *Traité des maladies de l'oreille et de l'audition.* Paris.

Lane, H. (1981). *L'enfant sauvage de l'Aveyron.* Paris: Payot.

Moody, B. (1983). *La langue des signes.* Vincennes, France: International Visual Theatre.

Moores, D. F. (1978). *Educating the deaf: Psychology, principles and practices.* Boston: Houghton Mifflin.

Sicard, A. (1808). *Théorie des signes.* Paris: Dentu, Delalain.

OLIVIER PÉRIER
Université Libre de Bruxelles,
Centre Comprendre et Parler,
Belgium

DEAF EDUCATION
TOTAL COMMUNICATION

INSTRUCTIONAL MEDIA/MATERIALS CENTER

Virtually every school district, intermediate unit, and co-operative supports an instructional media/materials center as part of its overall educational effort. Originally, local instructional media centers dealt mainly with audiovisuals (films, filmstrips, multimedia kits, slide-tapes, audiotapes, videotapes) and concentrated primarily on responding to teachers' requests for audiovisual materials and for loan and maintenance of audiovisual equipment.

The implementation of PL 94-142 has expanded the functions of many instructional media/materials centers that today house teacher centers, professional libraries, and collections of textbooks, print materials, and adaptive devices (in addition to audiovisuals). The range of services may include circulation of new products through on-site borrowing, by mail or mobile units; information searches; in-service training; development of print and nonprint products for local use; dissemination of information on promising practices and products; assistance with the selection and adoption of new practices; and participation in school improvement programs. Some instructional media/materials centers also provide microcomputer workshops, software development, software reviews and guides, and microcomputer libraries.

JUDY SMITH-DAVIS
*Counterpoint Communications
Company, Reno, Nevada*

IN-SERVICE TRAINING OF SPECIAL EDUCATION
INSTRUCTIONAL TECHNOLOGY FOR THE HANDICAPPED

INSTRUCTIONAL PACING

Since the early 1970s many educational researchers have directed their efforts toward identifying teaching activities and classroom conditions that foster student learning. As education has progressed from a service provided for the few to a service provided for all children, including the most severely handicapped of our society, the need for more effective and efficient instructional programs has become evident. A considerable portion of recent educational research has focused on validating the effectiveness of specific educational approaches. Instructional pacing, or the rate of stimulus presentation, has been proposed as a teaching behavior that may have a direct impact on student learning.

There are several temporal variables that determine the pacing of a teacher's lesson. Teacher wait-time is generally defined as the amount of time a teacher waits for a student's repsonse after presenting a question or stimulus. Researchers (Fagan, Hassler, & Szabo, 1981; Rowe, 1974) have suggested that extended teacher wait-time leads to more frequent and more accurate responses. These findings also have been substantiated in the field of special education with multiply handicapped children.

A second temporal variable, the intertrial interval, is the time that elapses between the end of one learning trial and the beginning of the next. In studies with autistic children, short intertrial intervals of 1 to 4 seconds have been shown to result in more rapid learning (Koegel, Dunlap, & Dyer, 1980) and lower levels of self-stimulatory behaviors (Dunlap, Dyer, & Koegel, 1983) than long intervals of 5 to 26 seconds.

Englert (1984) has examined presentation rates in the context of special education. She found that teacher interns who were judged to be more effective, based on their students' achievement, presented a significantly higher number of trials per minute than interns judged to be less effective. The effective interns were said to have maintained a brisker lesson pace.

Although extended teacher wait-times and shortened intertrial intervals may seem to be theoretically opposed, the proponents of the direct instruction model and commercial curricula based on it advocate a similar approach. They suggest allowing students ample time to respond to a task and shortening the time between tasks. Future research may help in establishing firm instructional pacing guidelines for special education professionals.

REFERENCES

Dunlap, G., Dyer, K., & Koegel, R. L. (1983). Autistic self-stimulation and intertrial interval duration. *American Journal of Mental Deficiency, 88*, 194–202.

Englert, C. S. (1984). Effective direct instruction practices in special education settings. *Remedial & Special Education, 5*(2), 38–47.

Fagan, E. R., Hassler, D. M., & Szabo, M. (1981). Evaluation of questioning strategies in language arts instruction. *Research in the Teaching of English, 15*, 267–273.

Koegel, R. L., Dunlap, G., & Dyer, K. (1980). Intertrial interval duration and learning in autistic children. *Journal of Applied Behavior Analysis, 13*, 91–99.

Rowe, M. B. (1974). Wait-time and rewards as instructional variables, their influence on language, logic, and fate control: Part one—wait-time. *Journal of Research in Science Teaching, 11*(2), 81–94.

GREG VALCANTE
University of Florida

AUTISM
DIRECT INSTRUCTION
TEACHER EFFECTIVENESS

INSTRUCTIONAL TECHNOLOGY FOR THE HANDICAPPED

Instructional technology, also known as educational technology, is a term that has been used to describe a wide range of tools or techniques developed to simplify or enhance educational efforts by either the learner or the teacher. Although commonly thought of as mechanical or electronic devices (e.g., computers and calculators) and instructional media (e.g., filmstrips and videotapes), certain assessment strategies (e.g., precision teaching and applied behavioral analysis procedures), and curriculum designs (e.g, specific competencies/technology design or objective-based instruction) also may be considered instructional technology. The key element in classifying something as instructional technology seems to be that the device or technique is the result of the application of a scientific principle to an educational concern.

Aside from assessment methodologies, curriculum design, and microcomputers, all of which have broad applications across exceptionalities, there has been continued development over the past several years of technology to meet specific needs of particular handicapping conditions. Examples of instructional technology developed for specific exceptionalities follows:

1. For the physically handicapped there is a wide range of adapted equipment such as specially designed writing instruments and customized wheelchairs, such as the Levo Stand-Up (American Stair-Glide Corporation, 1981).

2. For the communication disordered or multiply and severely handicapped, there are computerized word processing systems, augmentive communication boards (Yoder, 1980), and the Ability Phone (Lincoln Telephone Service and Supply, 1983).

3. Hearing-impaired people are offered hearing aids and a multitude of telecommunication devices for the deaf such as the teletypewriter and printer (Levitt, Pickett, & Houde, 1980).

4. Visually impaired people have available devices for obtaining written information such as an Imager 100EVA (Apollo, 1983), a video visual magnifier, or a Micro Brailler 2400 (Triformation Systems, 1983), devices for increasing mobility such as sonic detectors or laser canes (Nurion, 1983), and talking calculators and other instruments to aid computation.

Advances in instructional technology have had, and will continue to have, significant impact on the education of the handicapped by increasing efficiency of instruction, student access to information, and student ability to display knowledge. However, especially in the area of electronic and mechanical advances, with each new development there is usually a cost. Often there is disagreement among school systems, insurance companies, and public assistance agencies about who should bear the responsibility for the cost of expensive devices; this is a dilemma for which there is no simple solution but one that must be resolved if the handicapped are to continue to benefit from the full range of instructional technology.

The *Journal of Special Education Technology*, a quarterly publication of Utah State University, the Association for Special Education Technology, and the Technology and Media Division of the Council for Exceptional Children deals specifically with research and presentations of innovative practices in the application of instructional technology with the handicapped.

REFERENCES

American Stair-Glide. (1981). *Levo stand-up*. Grandview, MO: Author.

Apollo Electronic Visual Aids. (1983). *Imager model 100*. Chasworth, CA: Author.

Levitt, H., Pickett, J., & Houde, R. (1980). *Sensory aids for the hearing impaired*. New York: Institute for Electrical and Electronics Engineering Press.

Lincoln Telephone Service and Supply. (1983). *Ability phone*. Trafford, PA: General Concepts.

Nurion. (1983). *Laser cane*. Wayne, PA: Author.

Triformation Systems. (1983). *Micro brailler 2400*. Stuart, FL: Author.

Yoder, D. (1980). Communication systems for nonspeech children. In D. Bricker (Ed.), *Language intervention with children: Vol. 2. New directions for exceptional children*. San Francisco: Jossey-Bass.

KATHY RUHL
Pennsylvania State University

AUGMENTATIVE COMMUNICATION SYSTEMS
COMPUTER USE WITH THE HANDICAPPED
ELECTRONIC COMMUNICATION DEVICES

INTEGRATED THERAPY

The provision of specialized therapy services in the classroom and in other natural environments has been termed integrated therapy (Nietupski, Schutz, & Ockwood, 1980; Sternat, et al., 1977). Integrated therapy has a number of advantages over the isolated therapy model, in which students are removed from their classroom for therapy in a segregated environment, usually a clinic or therapy room. One advantage is the potential for continuous as opposed to episodic training sessions. Therapists and classroom teaching staff are able to coordinate both training goals and procedures. Moreover, in an integrated therapy model, there are more opportunities for sharing of professional skills and information concerning students' programs.

Another important advantage of integrated therapy conditions is the potential to enhance generalization. This is particularly critical for very young and severely handicapped students who often fail to perform new skills in other than the training environment.

There are many other theoretical and practical considerations (e.g., the importance of longitudinal intervention in natural environments, the reality of limited resources and personnel) that suggest the superiority of integrated therapy conditions in most school situations, but these considerations are less important than professional commitment. The effectiveness of integrated therapy depends on the willingness of teachers and therapists to alter traditional beliefs and practices and negotiate new role functions. They must discard the notion that only a therapist can provide therapy and agree to share intervention responsibilities in natural settings.

REFERENCES

Nietupski, J., Scheutz, G., & Ockwood, L. (1980). The delivery of communication therapy services to severely handicapped students: A plan for change. *Journal of the Association for the Severely Handicapped, 5*(1), 13–23.

Sternat, J., Messina, R., Nietupski, J., Lyon, S., & Brown, L. (1977). Occupational and physical therapy services for severely handicapped students: Toward a naturalized public school service delivery model. In E. Sontag, J. J. Smith, & N. Certo (Eds.), *Educational programming for the severely & profoundly handicapped.* Reston, VA: Council for Exceptional Children.

LINDA MCCORMICK
University of Hawaii

LEAST RESTRICTIVE ENVIRONMENT
MAINSTREAMING

INTELLECTUAL DEFICIENCY

See MENTAL RETARDATION; SEE INTELLIGENCE.

INTELLIGENCE

Intelligence is an ancient concept, but useful measures of intelligence are a relatively recent invention. The early mental tests developed in the late nineteenth century emphasized measures of sensory acuity, reaction time, memory, sensitivity to pain, and color preferences; they were clearly failures as indicators of a commonsense notion of intelligence.

The first successful intelligence test was developed in Paris by Alfred Binet and Theodore Simon in 1905. The Binet tests differed from their unsuccessful predecessors in two important respects. First, they sacrificed precision to measure more global mental abilities such as memorizing sentences, following instructions, distinguishing between abstract words (such as "liking" and "respecting"), and constructing sentences to include three given words (such as "Paris," "gutter," and "fortune"). Second, they used age norms for evaluating the performance of a given child and as the criterion for intelligence.

Binet and Simon, in their work with children, saw that mental capabilities increase steadily with age. This observation provided a criterion for identifying good intelligence test items, a good item being one on which older children perform better, on average, than younger children. Each task was assigned an age level, which was the age at which half the children could correctly perform the task. Mental performance was thus measured on an age scale, and a child's mental age could be determined by his or her performance on the age-graded series of tasks. The test worked. Children who were mentally advanced (i.e., their mental age was above their chronological age) generally were considered bright by their teachers, while children whose mental age was below their chronological age generally were considered dull. The concept of mental age proved to be the key to intelligence. It provided a scale that corresponded to the commonsense notion of intelligence, and it provided a method of identifying good measures of intelligence without solving the difficult problem of defining exactly what intelligence is.

Soon after the Binet scales were published, the German psychologist William Stern developed the concept of intelligence quotient or IQ. Stern saw that a child who is a year ahead at age 6 is more advanced than one who is a year ahead at age 9. The proper measure of intelligence is the ratio of mental age to chronological age, not the difference. To obtain the IQ, Stern divided the mental age by the chronological age and multiplied by 100 to get rid of the decimals. A 5-year-old child who has a mental age of 6 and a 10-year-old who has a mental age of 12 both obtain an IQ of 120. The IQ is thus a measure of rate of mental growth. A child whose mental abilities are developing 20% faster than those of the average child will obtain an IQ of 120.

The Binet test proved to be remarkably robust when transported to other countries. It was not only in Paris that the average 7-year-old was barely able to repeat five digits read to him or her and to indicate certain omissions in drawings, but in Germany, England, and America as well. This relative constancy of age scale was one of the first indications that something basic was being measured by the IQ. A number of translations and revisions of the

Binet tests were undertaken. The most successful of these was the Stanford Binet developed by Louis M. Terman and associates at Stanford University. The Stanford revisions of the Binet published in 1916 and 1937 greatly improved the technology of test construction and standardization while retaining the basic concepts of mental age and IQ as the operational definition of intelligence.

The Stanford Binet became the standard for the evaluation of other tests that were developed; the mental-age concept thus was at the root of modern conceptions of intelligence. The IQ derived from mental age is no longer used in intelligence measurement, however, because it presents several technical difficulties. One of the major difficulties with the mental-age scale is that growth of mental ability, like physical growth, slows during adolescence and then stops altogether by about age 16 or 18. For this reason, the ratio IQ is not a meaningful index of intelligence for adults. Most current tests of intelligence compare the subject's test performance with a representative sample of the population of the same age and express the relative performance in terms of an IQ scale that has a mean of 100, a standard deviation of 15, and a normal distribution in the standardization sample. This procedure produces an identical distribution of scores at all ages. Although this distribution of IQ scores is now forced in the standardization of most tests, it was originally adopted because it was similar to the distribution of ratio IQs actually observed in the 1937 standardization of the Stanford Binet.

While the development of intelligence tests was proceeding almost entirely on a pragmatic basis, psychologists were developing measures of more specific abilities for the investigation of the structure of intelligence. The statistical method of factor analysis was developed to aid in the attempt to infer the structure of intelligence from the intercorrelations of a number of ability tests. Although the statistical method is complex, the basic idea of factor analysis is simple. If several tests tend to correlate more highly with one another than they do with other tests, this is an indication that these tests measure something that is not shared by the other tests, at least not as strongly. Such a cluster of highly correlating tests can be considered to be evidence of the operation of some common factor that is causing the tests to vary together. Factor analysis provides a method of determining the number of such common factors in a given collection of tests and the relationship of the tests to the factors so that the underlying factors can be measured.

An early form of factor analysis was developed by Spearman (1927), who was impressed by the fact that almost all mental abilities are positively correlated. People who perform relatively well on one test such as memory also tend to perform well on other tests, such as completion of sentences. Spearman interpreted this as evidence of a general factor of intelligence, which he called g. His method of factor analysis was intended to reveal the degree to which each test was saturated with this general factor.

The statistical method of factor analysis was developed further by Thurstone (1938), who used the method to identify several ability factors, including verbal comprehension, word fluency, number ability, spatial visualization, rote memory, and reasoning. These factors were all positively correlated with each other. This would fit in with Spearman's concept of general intelligence, but Thurstone chose to emphasize the factors' separate identities by calling them primary mental abilities. The work of Thurstone has been extended by a number of investigators, who have identified ever larger numbers of factors.

A leading figure in this effort has been Guilford (1967), who organized the known ability factors according to the mental operation, the content, and the product involved in the tests. This three-way classification of factors was displayed graphically as a cube, which Guilford called the structure-of-intellect model. This model has the advantage of organizing a diverse collection of abilities into a meaningful structure. Such a model is also a useful guide for research, since it predicts the nature of new factors that have not yet been identified. Although the model is a useful organizing schema for a diverse collection of abilities, it does not pretend to be a model of the brain structures that produce these abilities. In addition, it has not yet provided much insight into the underlying causes of the differential abilities.

Most of the 120 abilities represented in the structure-of-intellect model have not yet been adequately identified and measured. The Educational Testing Service (ETS) has published a kit of reference tests for the ability factors that have been found in more than one laboratory and that are generally accepted as being identifiable. The factors to be represented in the kit were selected with the aid of an advisory committee consisting of leading researchers in the ability field. There was consensus on 23 factors. The following are examples of these factors: associational fluency (the ability to produce rapidly words that share a given area of meaning or some other common semantic property); associative memory (the ability to recall one part of a previously learned but otherwise unrelated pair of items when the other part of the pair is presented); logical reasoning (the ability to reason from premise to conclusion, or to evaluate the correctness of a conclusion); and spatial orientation (the ability to perceive spatial patterns or to maintain orientation with respect to objects in space).

There is indeed a diversity of mental abilities that can be separately identified and measured. A critical question that remains unanswered is why this particular set of differential abilities exists. Are there different biological structures in the nervous system that are used in performing the different mental tasks? Do certain critical experiences or learning opportunities promote the development of abilities represented by the different factors? We do not know.

As we have seen, there are two approaches to the measurement of intelligence. One focuses on a single factor of general ability with little concern for its different aspects. The other emphasizes the analysis of intelligence into component abilities with little concern for the fact that the components tend to be positively correlated. Both of these approaches are correct in the sense that they attend to real aspects of ability. There are, indeed, a number of factors of ability that can be separately measured. These factors are all positively correlated with each other. Studies typically find that about half the common variance in a diverse set of tests can be accounted for by a single general factor, with the remaining half attributable to differential factors. A hierarchical organization is clearly suggested, but this does not solve the problem of where the major research emphasis should be placed. One might consider the differential abilities to be of major interest with their intercorrelations attributed to relatively trivial factors, such as measurement bias, common environmental influences, and the like. On the other hand, one might consider the most important area to be that which the differential abilities share in common, with their specific variance attributed to relatively trivial factors. Two contrasting points of view on this topic are presented by Jensen (1979) and Carroll (1976).

The two approaches may be compared in terms of their contribution to two important goals: prediction and understanding. General intelligence and aptitude tests have grown up in the prediction arena and generally are considered to have achieved remarkable success, particularly in predicting performance in school and in academically related occupations. If measures of differential aptitudes or more specific abilities are to be useful predictors, they must surpass the high standard established by the general aptitude test; this they have not been able to do (McNemar, 1964).

The presence of a number of specific ability factors along with the preeminently important factor of general intelligence can be seen as analogous to the relationships among a variety of anatomical measurements of a group of people. People differ greatly in size, and large people tend to exceed small people on almost all anatomical measures; thus, there is a general size factor. In addition, people differ in corpulence and in stature, so that longitudinal measurements (such as length of arms, legs, and torso) tend to correlate more highly with each other than with measures of girth (such as circumference of neck, waist, and thigh), which tend to form another homogeneous cluster. Thus instead of describing people as relatively large or small, it is possible to describe the human physique in terms of correlated height and weight factors. Further analysis most likely would identify a long-waisted versus short-waisted factor, and factors specific to particular areas of the body, such as facial physiognomy, hand configuration, etc. The relative usefulness of the various anatomical factors for prediction would depend on the performance criteria of most interest. If all the criteria involved breaking through barriers of some sort, the general size factor would probably be most important, even though, for example, the hand factors might seem on the surface to be more relevant for barriers to be broken with the hand.

The analysis of intelligence into its components seems to be a promising route to understanding. For example, Carroll (1976) analyzed the detailed mental operations that are required by the tasks involved in each of the 23 factors in the ETS kit. This analysis suggests that each factor may involve operations that depend primarily on a specific aspect of mental functioning. For example, memory span depends primarily on storage and retrieval from short-term memory; fluency factors involve a scanning of long-term memory; and verbal comprehension depends on the contents of the "lexicosemantic store." It seems reasonable to expect that when the mechanism of storage and retrieval of information in memory and the mechanism of logical mental operations are finally understood, there will be a clear correspondence between the underlying process and the factor structure of overt performance.

The computer analogy has recently been very influential in the field of cognitive psychology. The development of methods to precisely measure the time required for various elementary components of mental operations seems to promise new understanding of the underlying process of human abilities (Sternberg, 1977). On the other hand, Jensen (1980) has reported a substantial correlation between general speed of mental processing and intelligence, which tends to focus attention back on the general factor. It is still too early to tell what may be the outcome of this promising new direction of research on intelligence.

Throughout most of its history intelligence has been a subject of public controversy. This is doubtlessly because of the high value placed on intelligence in our society and because of its association with academic and economic achievement. The controversy has centered around the relative importance of heredity and environment in producing individual differences in intelligence and on the extent and causes of differences in intelligence among various racial, ethnic, and socioeconomic groups.

REFERENCES

Carroll, J. B. (1976). Psychometric tests as cognitive tasks: A new "structure of intellect." In L. B. Resnick (Ed.), *The nature of intelligence*. Hillsdale, NJ: Erlbaum.

Dettermann, D. K. (1982). Does "*g*" exist? *Intelligence, 6*, 99–108.

Guilford, J. P. (1967). *The nature of human intelligence*. New York: McGraw-Hill.

Jensen, A. R. (1979). "*g*": Outmoded theory or unconquered frontier? *Creative Science & Technology, 2*, 16–29.

Jensen, A. R. (1980). Chronometric analysis of intelligence. *Journal of Social & Biological Structures, 3*, 103–122.

McNemar, Q. (1964). Lost: Our intelligence? Why? *American Psychologist, 19*, 871–882.

Spearman, C. (1927). *The abilities of man.* New York: MacMillan.

Sternberg, R. (1977). *Intelligence, information processing and analogical reasoning: The componential analysis of human abilities.* Hillsdale, NJ: Erlbaum.

Thurstone, L. L. (1938). Primary mental abilities. *Psychometric Monographs*, No. 1.

ROBERT C. NICHOLS
DIANE JARVIS
*State University of New York,
Buffalo*

CULTURAL BIAS IN TESTING
DEVIATION IQ
GRADE EQUIVALENTS
INTELLIGENCE TESTING
JENSEN, A. R.
KAUFMAN ASSESSMENT BATTERY FOR CHILDREN
NATURE VERSUS NURTURE
RATIO IQ
STANFORD BINET INTELLIGENCE SCALE
WECHSLER SCALES

INTELLIGENCE: A MULTIDISCIPLINARY JOURNAL

Intelligence is a relatively new journal, first appearing in January 1977 and published quarterly since that time. It has been edited since its inception by Douglas Detterman. David Zeaman and Robert Sternberg served as associate editors until 1984; no associate editors are currently listed. Joseph Hogan, III, served as book review editor until 1980, when James Pellegrino took the position. After 1981 book reviews were infrequent and the journal no longer lists a book review editor. *Intelligence* has a large editorial board comprised of notable scholars from different disciplines within the behavioral sciences.

When *Intelligence* was established in 1977, there were no other journals devoted exclusively to basic research in human intelligence, even though many prestigious journals were available in the field of learning. By establishing a new journal, the founder sought to "formalize the importance of the study of human intelligence and the major role it has played in the development of the behavioral sciences" (p. 2).

Intelligence is a scientifically oriented journal, publishing papers that make a substantial contribution to the understanding of the nature and function of intelligence. The journal is devoted to the publication of original research, but also accepts theoretical and review articles. Studies concerned with application are considered only if the work also contributes to basic knowledge. The journal is multidisciplinary in nature. Of interest to special educators are the many empirical studies published in the field of mental retardation. Other types of studies include early childhood development, measurement of individual differences, and issues in cultural test bias.

REFERENCE

Detterman, D. K. (1977). Is *Intelligence* necessary? *Intelligence: A Multidisciplinary Journal,* 1(1), 1–3.

KATHRYN A. SULLIVAN
Texas A&M University

INTELLIGENCE QUOTIENT

The intelligence quotient represents a measurement concept that was used extensively in the early days of intelligence testing but is less commonly used today. After Alfred Binet's death in 1911, Stern (1914) introduced the notion of a mental quotient, suggesting that the index of intellectual functioning derived from the Binet-Simon Scale could be expressed as the ratio of a test taker's mental age to his or her chronological age multiplied by 100 to eliminate decimals ($MQ = 100 \times MA/CA$). This *MQ* represented something about a person's rate of mental growth up to the time of the test. If examinees earned a mental age (MA) equivalent to chronological age (CA), their mental quotient (MQ) would be 100. An MQ of 100 represented average performance.

Working at Stanford University in California, Lewis M. Terman developed what was to become the most widely used American version of the Binet test, the Stanford-Binet. Terman (1916) incorporated Stern's notion of a mental quotient but renamed it, calling it a ratio intelligence quotient, or IQ.

The concept of the ratio intelligence quotient became increasingly popular, but it was used in a number of inappropriate ways. Its decline over the last quarter century can be attributed to a number of inherent characteristics that have been highly criticized by measurement specialists and practitioners.

Because the ratio intelligence quotient has minor differences in the magnitude of its standard deviation at various ages, a constant intelligence quotient from one age to another does not represent the same relative status. Similarly, even if the test taker's relative status remained the same from one year to another, the intelligence quotient would have to change. This suggests that intelligence quotients at different age levels are not comparable statistically (Tyler & Walsh, 1979). For example, a very bright child could obtain a higher IQ at age 12 than at age 6, even if the child's growth rate was unchanged. This difference would simply be due to the differences in the variability or standard deviations, with the variability of the IQ distribution being greater for 12 year olds than for 6 year olds.

Critics also point to the conceptual difficulty of the ratio intelligence quotient. For example, a 5 year old with a mental age of 6 and a 10 year old with a mental age of 12 would both have identical intelligence quotients of 120. However, the 6 year old is a year advanced in mental age while the 10 year old is 2 years advanced.

Another criticism of the intelligence quotient relates to its inability to describe adult intelligence (Tyler & Walsh, 1979). Critics suggest that like physical growth, adult mental growth lacks the predictable regularity characteristic of the mental development of children. Age standards lack meaning after the mid-teens, rendering mental age and therefore the intelligence quotient concept meaningless.

Owing to these criticisms of the ratio intelligence quotient, most major intelligence tests today yield IQs but not ratio intelligence quotients. For example, since the 1960 revision of the Stanford-Binet, the ratio intelligence quotient has been replaced by the deviation IQ. Major intelligence tests such as the Wechsler and McCarthy scales and the Kaufman Assessment Battery for Children (K-ABC) do not yield ratio intelligence quotients. However, several other intelligence tests in use today retain the concept of the ratio intelligence quotient, including the Leiter International Performance Scale, the Slosson Intelligence Test, and the Quick Test. Because of the inherent limitations of the ratio intelligence quotient, IQs yielded from these tests should be interpreted cautiously.

REFERENCES

Stern, W. (1914). *The psychological methods of testing intelligence*. Baltimore, MD: Warwick & York.

Terman, L. M. (1916). *The measurement of intelligence*. Boston: Houghton Mifflin.

Tyler, L. E., & Walsh, W. B. (1979). *Tests and measurements*. Englewood Cliffs, NJ: Prentice-Hall.

MARK E. SWERDLIK
Illinois State University

DEVIATION IQ
IQ
RATIO IQ

INTELLIGENCE TESTING

Intelligence testing, although called by many different names and used in many different forms, has been around for many centuries (Anastasi, 1982). The Chinese have been using mental tests for 3000 years, and in the seventh and eighth centuries the Imperial Court established tests of speaking and writing and verbal and nonverbal reasoning that are similar to tasks on today's tests. The ancient Greeks, followers of Socrates, and universities in the Middle Ages, all developed methods of assessing intellectual skills.

As summarized by Kaufman (1983), the 1800s saw the beginning of the development of ideas about mental abilities and methods of measuring intelligence; these ideas formed the foundation for contemporary assessment. Not surprisingly, the scholars involved in the roots of intelligence testing were concerned with the two extremes of ability. Jean Esquirol in the early 1800s and Edouard Seguin in the mid-1800s, two French physicians, studied intelligence of mentally retarded individuals. Francis Galton, in the mid-to-late 1800s, focused on the ability of men of genius. In the 1890s, James McKeen Cattell brought intelligence testing to the United States.

Esquirol's contributions included distinguishing between those people with very low intelligence, or the mentally retarded, and those people with emotional disturbances. He indicated that there is a hierarchy of retardation along a continuum, and coined terms like imbecile and idiot to describe different levels of mental deficiency. Although Esquirol studied several procedures, he concluded that a person's use of language is the most dependable criterion for determining intelligence, a philosophy that is apparent on many intelligence tests today.

Seguin rejected the notion that mental retardation is incurable and served as a pioneer in education for the mentally retarded. Unlike Esquirol, Seguin stressed the importance of sensory discrimination and motor control as aspects of intelligence. He developed procedures that were adopted by later developers of performance and nonverbal intelligence tests. An example is the Seguin Form board, which requires rapid placement of variously shaped blocks into their correct holes.

The English biologist Galton was primarily responsible for developing the first comprehensive individual intelligence test. As part of his research of men of genius and the heredity of intelligence, he administered tasks of sensory discrimination and sensory motor coordination in his Anthropometric Laboratory. His belief that intelligence comes to us through the senses led to the development of tasks such as weight discrimination, reaction time, strength of squeeze, and visual discrimination.

In the early 1890s, Cattell, an assistant in Galton's laboratory, established similar laboratories in the United States. During this time, Cattell used the term mental test for the first time in the psychological literature. Cattell shared Galton's view that intelligence is best measured through sensory tasks, but expanded his mentor's ideas by emphasizing that test administration must be standardized so that results are comparable from person to person and time to time.

In the early 1900s, significant advances were made in both individual and group intelligence testing (Sattler, 1982; Vane & Motta, 1984). In France, Alfred Binet, assisted by Theophile Simon and Victor Henri, rejected Galton's notions about the sensory and motor aspects of intelligence and claimed that tests of higher mental processes more effectively distinguish among the individual differences in people's intellectual abilities. This group developed numerous tests of complex intellectual functions such as memory, comprehension, imagination, and moral sentiments. The specific appointment by the French minister of public instruction to study the education of retarded children led to the development of the individually administered Binet-Simon Scale in 1905, constructed to separate mentally retarded and normal children in the Paris public schools. Two of the key aspects of Binet's approach to intelligence testing were that he "discarded the specific test for the specific ability and took a group of tests which seemed to cover in general the chief psychological characteristics that go to make up intelligence. And, further, as the norm or standard of intelligence he took what the average child at each age could do" (Pintner & Patterson, 1925, p. 7).

The Binet-Simon Scale, including the 1911 revision that extended through adulthood, was almost immediately adapted and translated in the United States. The most successful revision was Terman's Stanford-Binet Scale in 1916. Terman carefully standardized his scale and introduced the application of the term intelligence quotient (mental age divided by chronological age multiplied by 100). The Stanford-Binet was widely adopted by individual examiners in the United States, and it is still popular today. The Binet was revised and restandardized in 1937, revised in 1960, and again restandardized in 1972. A thoroughly new version of the Binet will soon be released. The ratio IQ, although retained in the 1937 Binet, was replaced by the deviation IQ (a standard score with a mean of 100 and standard deviation of 16) for the 1960 and 1972 Stanford-Binets.

David Wechsler, in 1939, was the first to challenge the Stanford-Binet monopoly on individual intelligence tests by publishing the Wechsler-Bellevue Scale. Wechsler, like Binet, included the concept of global intelligence in his scale, but instead of having one score, as did the Stanford-Binet, he included three scores: a verbal IQ, a performance IQ, and a full-scale IQ. Wechsler did not employ the methodology of the Stanford-Binet, which used a large number of brief and primarily verbal tasks. His scale was limited to a small number of longer tasks, half of them verbal and half nonverbal. Several versions of the Wechsler scales have been published since his Wechsler-Bellevue, and the types of tasks on later versions are virtually identical to the first scale. The main sources of Wechsler's verbal tasks were the Binet and the Army Group Examination Alpha; his performance tests came primarily from the Army Group Examination Beta and the Army Individual Performance Scale Examination.

The methods of the individual assessment of intelligence changed little until the 1980s. In 1983 Alan and Nadeen Kaufman published the Kaufman Assessment Battery for Children (K-ABC). The K-ABC attempted to respond to contemporary assessment needs not met by the Stanford-Binet and Wechsler scales and tried to be sensitive to the emphasis being placed on the psychoeducational assessment of children with learning disabilities, neuropsychological evaluation, and nonbiased assessment. The K-ABC includes a theoretical rationale for the scale based on research in cognitive psychology and neuropsychology; organization of tasks into scales that indicate the process required for their problem solution, rather than their verbal or nonverbal content; and the separation of tasks requiring the ability to solve new or unfamiliar problems (intelligence) from tasks requiring considerable verbal ability and factual knowledge (achievement). The Kaufmans are currently developing a new intelligence battery for adolescents and adults based on an application and extension of their conception of intelligence for individuals ages 11 and above.

The widespread use of group intelligence tests began, like the first Binet Scale, to meet a practical need (Anastasi, 1982). The entry of the United States into World War I in 1917 required a rapid means of classifying 1.5 million recruits for assignment into different types of training, discharge from service, and officer ability. A committee of the American Psychological Association, headed by Robert M. Yerkes, was directed to develop two group intelligence tests; these came to be known as the Army Alpha and Army Beta. The former, a verbal test modeled after the Binet, was designed for general use with literate recruits; the latter employed nonverbal items and was designed for illiterate recruits, or those recent immigrants who did not speak English well. (The Army Individual Performance Scale, mentioned previously, was given to those recruits who could not be tested validly on either the Army Alpha or Army Beta.).

The tests were released for civilian use soon after the war ended. Because of the belief that intelligence tests were better than teacher evaluations for identifying abilities, these tests became widely accepted in education (Vane & Motta, 1984). A short time after, revisions of the Army tests, as well as new group intelligence tests that used the Army tests as models, were being administered to thousands of preschool through graduate students all over the country, and to special adult groups such as employees or prisoners. The group format was attractive because it allowed the testing of many individuals simultaneously and it incorporated simple administration procedures that required little examiner training. The rapid growth of group intelligence testing resulted in the development of 37 group tests in only 5 years! (Pintner, 1923).

A new surge in group intelligence testing occurred in 1958, after the launching of Sputnik. The passage of the National Defense Education Act provided funds for states to test the abilities of schoolchildren and identify outstanding students. This testing was facilitated by the development of optical scanning for test scoring by Lindquist in 1955. Also in 1958, the National Merit Scholarship program was established to select exceptional high-school students. According to Vane and Motta (1984), another significant upturn in testing happened in the late 1970s, and this interest continues to this day.

Intelligence tests, both group and individual, are used in many different ways today. The largest users of intelligence tests are schools. Group intelligence tests are used at the preschool and kindergarten levels to distinguish children who are ready to participate in educational activities from those who need remedial preparation. At the elementary, middle, and high-school levels, group tests are used to identify exceptional and handicapped students, and to aid in forming homogeneous ability groups within classrooms. Group intelligence tests are commonly used as one criterion for admission into colleges and universities. Individual intelligence tests have been administered for over half a century by well-trained clinicians for psychological, psychoeducational, and neuropsychological diagnosis. The passage of the Education of All Handicapped Children Act of 1975 (PL 94-142) resulted in the common use of individual intelligence tests as part of larger assessment batteries for the placement of children in special education programs for the mentally retarded, learning disabled, emotionally disturbed, and so forth, and for the development of individual educational programs for these children. For adults, group and individual intelligence tests are used in a variety of settings, including business and industry, prisons, mental health centers, hospitals, and private clinical practice.

Group intelligence tests find their principal application in education, business, government, and military, in circumstances where it is feasible to obtain valid test data from many individuals at once; they are useful as well with individuals who are able to take a test by themselves without need of an examiner. In contrast, individual intelligence tests are used in clinics and special education centers, where an intensive study of individual clients is needs and a trained examiner is necessary to secure valid test results. The reasons for using group and individual tests are many and provide a basis for understanding the type of information provided by the two testing formats. A summary of these reasons, as reported by Anastasi (1982), follows.

Group tests can be administered to a large number of individuals at the same time by using booklets of printed items and forms for the examinee to indicate his or her answer. The training and experience required by the examiner is minimal, as most group tests only require the examiner to read simple instructions and accurately keep time. The minimal role of the examiner in group testing provides more uniform testing conditions than in individual testing.

Objective scoring is a key aspect of group tests. Test items are usually multiple choice, true-false, or some other type that produces responses that can be scored as correct or incorrect with no deliberation. Items on group tests can usually be scored by a clerk or a computer. In addition, group tests typically include answer sheets, separate from the test booklets that contain the items, allowing economical reuse of test booklets.

Because group tests can be administered to large groups of individuals at the same time, larger numbers of individuals can be used in the standardization programs for group tests than for individual tests. Group test norms are generally better established because they are based on standardization samples of 100,000 to 200,000 instead of the 1000 to 4000 used for individual tests.

On the other hand, individual intelligence tests have several characteristics that make them suitable for a variety of clinical purposes. In individual testing, the examiner has the opportunity to obtain cooperation, establish rapport, and enhance motivation of the examinee. The trained examiner in individual testing detects, reports, and uses in the interpretation of test scores the many characteristics of the examinee that may affect test performance such as anxiety, fatigue, and problem-solving style. In addition, some individuals such as emotionally disturbed and mentally retarded children and adults may perform better on individual tests than on group tests. Since most group tests require the examinee to read instructions and test items, individually administered tests, which demand little or no reading, are especially useful for learning-disabled and retarded individuals, and others who may have reading problems.

Individual intelligence tests, because they typically include short questions that require oral and open-ended responses, allow examinees to give creative and original responses to items. In individual testing, examinees are not limited to selecting one of four multiple choice answers or indicating if an item is true or false. The contents of an examinee's response on an individual intelligence test can therefore be analyzed in order to generate hypotheses about, for example, the examinee's creativity, style of thinking, cognitive development, or defense mechanisms.

Another aspect of individual intelligence testing concerns the flexibility of administration. On a group test, an examinee is required to respond to all items, or as many items as he or she can in a certain time limit. On an individual test, testing time is more effectively used because the examinee is administered only those items in the range appropriate to his or her ability level. This characteristic of individual tests helps avoid the boredom an examinee may have when working on items that are too easy or the frustration of working on items that are too difficult.

There are many group intelligence tests, but most have the characteristics noted previously: multiple choice items with four or five choices for each question and test booklets with separate answer sheets for recording responses. Also, most group tests provide deviation IQs or similar standard scores. Since there is no flexibility to present more or less difficult items based on the examinee's performance, most group intelligence tests consist of a series of multilevel tests, each designated for a particular age, grade, or level of difficulty.

Two widely used group intelligence tests are the Otis-Lennon School Ability Test (OLSAT) and the Cognitive Abilities Test (CAT). The OLSAT is a test of general intelligence, primarily verbal intelligence, with five separate levels of the test for grades 1 through 12. The spiral omnibus format is used from the fourth grade level up; for each block of 5 to 10 items of the same type, the easiest is presented first, followed by the next easiest, and so on; this results in a rising spiral of item difficulty. The items are categorized into three parts: I Classification, II Analogies, and III Omnibus (e.g., mathematical reasoning, verbal comprehension, following directions). At each level of the OLSAT, scores are expressed as a School Ability Index, or a normalized standard score with a mean of 100 and standard deviation of 16. Age- and grade-based percentile ranks and stanines also may be obtained. Norms for the OLSAT are based on a representative standardization sample of 130,000 students from 70 school districts.

The CAT contains 10 levels, two primary levels for kindergarten through third grade, and eight levels of a Multilevel Edition for grades 3 through 12. Unlike the OLSAT, the CAT measures verbal, nonverbal, and quantitative intelligence. The eight levels of the Multilevel Edition are divided into three batteries: verbal (vocabulary, sentence completion, verbal classification, verbal analogies); quantitative (quantitative relations, number series, equation building); and nonverbal (figure classification, figure analogies, figure analysis). Also, unlike the OLSAT, the CAT does not yield a single score of general intelligence, but yields separate scores from the three batteries. The manual advises against combining the three scores into a total score. Scores for the three batteries are expressed as standard scores (mean of 100 and standard deviation of 16); percentile ranks and stanines are also available. The CAT was standardized on a representative sample of 18,000 students for each of 10 groups.

The OLSAT and CAT are representative of the many available and commonly used group intelligence tests. They illustrate that although such tests have many similarities, there are also differences in format, abilities measured by the tests, and the test author's philosophies.

Unlike group intelligence tests, individual intelligence tests display more of a variety of items among the different tests, as well as within the same test. Items are seldom in a multiple choice format, and the use of paper and pencil is only occasionally required. Individual intelligence tests typically require the examinee to give a short verbal response; manipulate objects such as blocks, pictures, or puzzle pieces; or point to pictures, symbols, or designs. The examinee does not respond to all items on the test, as administration to each individual examinee is limited to only those items in his or her range of ability. All individual intelligence tests require highly trained examiners who are thoroughly knowledgeable in psychological research and theory, and who have received extensive practical clinical training under careful supervision.

The most commonly used individual intelligence tests are the Stanford-Binet, the Wechsler, and the Kaufman Assessment Battery for Children. These tests all contain items measuring verbal, nonverbal, and quantitative skills, but there are major differences in how the tests report scores in general, global intelligence, and in separate ability areas.

The 1973 version of the Stanford-Binet measures general intelligence of individuals 2 years through adult, although norms are not provided above age 18. A total of 142 subtests is arranged by half year or year-age levels; the subtests included at a given age level are those that are supposed to be passed by about half of the children tested at that age level. Testing begins at a level slightly below the estimated mental age of the examinee, and thus the first items should be fairly easy. The examiner first tries to establish a basal level for each examinee (an age level at which all tasks are passed); then, testing continues, level by level, until the examinee reaches a level where all subtests are failed, establishing a ceiling. Some of the Binet subtests cover vocabulary, copying a square, opposite analogies, number concepts, naming objects, picture memories, and similarities and differences. The Stanford-Binet yields only one score of general, global intelligence—a deviation IQ with a mean of 100 and standard deviation of 16. An age equivalent score, called a mental age, is also available. The Stanford-Binet was standardized with a presumably representative sample of 2351 children and adolescents, although specific percentages of individuals from different racial, socioeconomic, or regional backgrounds are not reported.

A revision of the Stanford-Binet is currently being developed. The new test promises to be different from earlier versions. According to Thorndike (1985), there will be 15 subtests instead of the large number on the previous versions. Subtests will be categorized into four areas: verbal reasoning, visualizing and visual reasoning, quantitative comprehension, and short-term memory. Scaled scores will be available for each of the 15 subtests, the 4 categories, and a total composite. As with the 1973 version, the revision is intended for use with individuals 2 years of age through adult.

There are three Wechsler intelligence scales: the Wechsler Preschool and Primary Scale of Intelligence (WPPSI), for children ages 4 through 6½ years; the Wechsler Intelligence Scale for Children–Revised (WISC-R), for children ages 6 through 16 years; and the Wechsler Adult Intelligence Scale–Revised (WAIS-R), for individuals ages 16 through 74 years. Each of the three Wechsler scales has 11 or 12 subtests divided into verbal and performance (nonverbal) scales. The WPPSI verbal subtests cover information, vocabulary, arithmetic, similarities, comprehension, and sentences; the performance subtests are animal house, picture completion, mazes, geometric design, and block design. The WISC-R and WAIS-R verbal subtests are information, similarities, arithmetic, vocabulary, comprehension, and digit span, while performance subtests include picture completion, picture arrangement, block design, object assembly, coding (called digit symbol on the WAIS-R), and mazes (not included on the WAIS-R). Unlike the Stanford-Binet, all individuals are administered all subtests, although the use of special starting and discontinue rules limit administration to only those items in each subtest that are appropriate for the functioning level of the individual. Also, unlike the 1973 version of the Stanford-Binet, the Wechsler scales yield a variety of scores. Performance on the subtests is expressed as a scaled score with a mean of 10 and standard deviation of 3. There are three IQs (normalized standard scores with a mean of 100 and standard deviation of 15): verbal IQ, performance IQ, and full-scale IQ. All three scales were standardized with representative standardization samples: 1200 standardization subjects for the WPPSI; 2200 for the WISC-R; and 1880 for the WAIS-R. The WISC-R is currently the most widely used individual intelligence test for children and adolescents. The WAIS-R is virtually the only commonly used individual test battery for adults. Both tests, and their predecessors, the WISC and WAIS, have been the subjects of thousands of research studies.

The Kaufman Assessment Battery for Children (K-ABC), for children ages 2½ through 12½ years, contains several contemporary features not found on the Stanford-Binet and WISC-R or any of the previously discussed group intelligence tests. First, the K-ABC was constructed from research and theories of information processing developed independently by neuropsychologists and cognitive psychologists. Second, the K-ABC defines intelligence as the ability to process information in two ways: sequentially (solving problems in serial or temporal order) and simultaneously (integration and synthesis into a gestalt to solve problems). The K-ABC defines intelligence as the ability to solve new and unfamiliar problems, rather than as knowledge of facts. However, subtests that measure factual knowledge (e.g., vocabulary, arithmetic, reading) are included on the K-ABC in a separate achievement scale. Some of the tests on this scale are considered to be measures of intelligence by adherents to the Binet-Wechsler model. Third, the K-ABC was developed to provide information about appropriate remedial interventions that teachers can use with children who have learning difficulties.

The K-ABC sequential processing subtests include hand movements, number recall, and word order; simultaneous processing subtests are magic window, face recognition, gestalt closure, triangles, matrix analogies, spatial memory, and photo series. The achievement subtests are expressive vocabulary, faces and places, arithmetic, riddles, reading/decoding, and reading/understanding.

Children are administered 7 to 13 of the 16 subtests depending on their age. Within each subtest, starting and discontinue rules are used to limit the administration of items to those within the child's level of performance.

Scores for the K-ABC include scaled scores (mean of 10, standard deviation of 3) for all mental processing (intelligence) subtests andd standard scores (mean of 100, standard deviation of 15) for the global scales and the achievement subtests. The five global scales are sequential processing, simultaneous processing, mental processing (a composite of the sequential and simultaneous scales and a measure of general intelligence), achievement, and nonverbal (consisting of the processing subtests that require no verbalization and can be administered in pantomime). For the subtests and global scales, national percentile ranks, stanines, age equivalents, and grade equivalents are also available. The inclusion of measures of intelligence and achievement in the same test battery is useful for the assessment of learning disabilities. Sociocultural norms allow an individual child to be compared with others of the same racial background and socioeconomic status. The K-ABC was normed with a representative national sample of 2000 children; an additional group of 496 blacks and 119 whites was tested to help develop the sociocultural norms.

The discussions of the Stanford-Binet, Wechsler scales, and K-ABC provide examples of traditional and more recent alternatives for measuring intelligence. Other individual intelligence tests include the McCarthy Scales of Children's Abilities, for children ages 2½ through 8½ years, which measures verbal, nonverbal, quantitative, memory, and motor skills; the Leiter International Performance Scale, a nonverbal scale for children ages 2 through 18; the Woodcock-Johnson Psycho-Educational Battery, a cognitive, achievement, and interest battery for ages 3 through adult; and the Slosson Intelligence Test, a quick screening test for individuals over 4 years of age.

Intelligence testing has been a controversial topic since the 1960s (Kaufman, 1979). The most pressing issues that are debated within both professional and public forums concern test bias, the influence of heredity versus environment on IQ, race differences in test scores, and disproportionate placement of minority children into special education classes such as those for the retarded or gifted. These issues have been the subject of research, debate, federal guidelines, laws, and lawsuits. Just as major law cases differ on whether intelligence tests are unfair to minority children (*Larry P.* v. *Riles*; PASE decision in Chicago), so do professionals in the field of intelligence testing continue to disagree on these issues. It is likely that the future will be filled with arguments on the appropriate use of intelligence tests and claims that they should be banned; at the same time, it is equally certain that there will continue to be a proliferation of new and revised instruments of both the individual and group variety.

REFERENCES

Anastasi, A. (1982). *Psychological testing* (5th ed.). New York: Macmillan.

Kaufman, A. S. (1979). *Intelligent testing with the WISC-R*. New York: Wiley.

Kaufman, A. S. (1983). Intelligence: Old concepts—new perspectives. In G. W. Hynd (Ed.), *The school psychologist: An introduction* (pp. 95–117). Syracuse, NY: Syracuse University Press.

Pintner, R. (1923). *Intelligence testing*. New York: Holt, Rinehart & Winston.

Pintner, R., & Patterson, D. G. (1925). *A scale of performance*. New York: Appleton.

Sattler, J. M. (1982). *Assessment of children's intelligence and special abilities* (2nd ed.). Boston: Allyn & Bacon.

Thorndike, R. L. (1985, April). *An introduction to the revised Stanford-Binet for school psychology educators*. Paper presented at the conference of the Trainers of School Psychologists, Las Vegas, NV.

Vane, T. R., & Motta, R. W. (1984). Group intelligence tests. In G. Goldstein & M. Hersen (Eds.), *Handbook of psychological assessment* (pp. 100–116). New York: Pergamon.

ALAN S. KAUFMAN
PATTI L. HARRISON
University of Alabama

INTELLIGENCE
INTELLIGENCE QUOTIENT
INTELLIGENT TESTING

INTELLIGENT TESTING

Intelligent testing is a philosophy or model of assessment widely espoused and best represented in the writings of Kaufman et al. (Kaufman, 1979; Kaufman & Kaufman, 1977; Reynolds & Clark, 1982; Reynolds & Kaufman, 1986). The intent of the intelligent testing model is to bring together empirical data, psychometrics, clinical acumen, psychological theory, and careful reasoning to build an assessment of an individual leading to the derivation of an intervention to improve the life circumstances of the subject. The promulgation of this philosophy was prompted by many factors, but particularly extremist approaches to the use of tests.

Conventional intelligence tests and even the entire concept of intelligence testing have been the focus of considerable controversy for several decades. Always the subject of scrutiny, the past two decades have witnessed intelligence tests placed on trial in the federal courts (Larry P., 1979; PASE, 1980), state legislatures (New York's "trust-in-testing" legislation), the lay press, and open scholarly forums (Reynolds & Brown, 1984). At one extreme are issues such as those brought up by Hilliard (1984), who con-tends that IQ tests are inherently unacceptable measurement devices with no real utility. At the other extreme are such well-known figures as Herrnstein (1973) and Jensen (1980), who believe the immense value of intelligence tests is by now self-evident. While critics of testing demand a moratorium on their use with children, psychologists often are forced to adhere to rigid administrative rules that require the use of precisely obtained IQs when making placements or diagnostic decisions. No consideration is given to measurement error, the influence of behavioral variables on performance, or appropriate sensitivity to the child's cultural or linguistic heritage.

A middle ground is sorely needed. Tests must be preserved, along with their rich clinical heritage and their prominent place in the neurological, psychological, and educational literature. At the same time, the proponents of tests need to be less defensive and more open to rational criticism of the current popular instruments. Knowledge of the weaknesses as well as the strengths of individually administered intelligence tests can serve the dual functions of improving examiners' ability to interpret profiles of any given instrument and enabling examiners to select pertinent supplementary tests and subtests to secure a thorough assessment of the intellectual abilities of any child, adolescent, or adult referred for evaluation. The quality of individual mental assessment is no longer simply a question answered in terms of an instrument's empirical or psychometric characteristics. High reliability and validity coefficients, a meaningful factor structure, and normative data obtained by stratified random-sampling techniques do not ensure that an intelligence test is valuable for all or even most assessment purposes. The skills and training of the psychologist engaged in using intelligence tests will certainly interact with the utility of intelligence testing beyond the level of simple actuarial prediction of academic performance. Intelligent testing provides an appropriate model.

With low-IQ children, the primary role of the intelligent tester is to use the test results to develop a means of intervention that will "beat" the prediction made by global IQs. A plethora of research during the twentieth century has amply demonstrated that very low-IQ children show concomitantly low levels of academic attainment. The purpose of administering an intelligence test to a low-IQ child, then, is at least twofold: (1) to determine that the child is indeed at high risk for academic failure, and (2) to articulate a set of learning circumstances that defeat the prediction. For individuals with average or high IQs, the specific tasks of the intelligence tester may change, but the philosophy remains the same. When evaluating a learning-disabled (LD) child, for example, the task is primarily one of fulfilling the prediction made by the global IQs. Most LD children exhibit average or better general intelligence, but have a history of academic performance significantly below what would be predicted from their intelligence test performance. The intelligent tester takes on the responsibility of preventing the child from becoming an "outlier" in the prediction; i.e., he or she must design a set of environmental conditions that will cause the child to achieve and learn at the level predicted by the intelligence test.

When psychologists engage in intelligent testing, the child or adult becomes the primary focus of the evaluation and the tests fade into the background as only vehicles to understanding. The test setting becomes completely examinee oriented. Interpretation and communication of test results in the context of the individual's particular background, referral behaviors, and approach to performance on diverse tasks constitute the crux of competent evaluation. Global test scores are deemphasized; flexibility, a broad base of knowledge in psychology, and insight on the part of the psychologist are demanded. The intelligence test becomes a dynamic helping agent, not an instrument for labeling, placement in dead-end programs, or disillusionment on the part of eager, caring teachers and parents.

Intelligent testing through individualization becomes the key to accomplishment; it is antithetical to the development of computerized or depersonalized form reporting for individually administered cognitive tests such as espoused by Alcorn and Nicholson (1975) and Vitelli and Goldblatt (1979) (Reynolds, 1980a, 1980b). For intelligent testers, it is imperative to be sensitive and socially aware, and to be aware that intelligence and cognition do not constitute the total human being. The intelligence testing model is inconsistent with "checklist" approaches to the development of individual education plans (IEPs). It is a mode of true individualization and does not lend itself to mimeographed IEPs that are checked off, or to special education programs where all children are taught with the same methodology. Computer-generated reports with "individualized" recommendations are anathema to the intelligent testing philosophy.

Intelligent testing urges the use of contemporary measures of intelligence as necessary to achieve a true understanding of the individual's intellectual functioning. The approach to test interpretation under this philosophy has been likened to the approach of a psychological detective (Kaufman, 1979). It requires melding of clinical skill, mastery of psychometrics and measurement, and extensive knowledge of cognitive development and intelligence. A far more extensive treatment of this approach to test interpretation appears in the book *Intelligent Testing with the WISC-R* (Kaufman, 1979). Discussion of applications of this philosophy to preschool children may be found in Kaufman and Kaufman (1977) and Reynolds and Clark (1982).

Clinical skills with children are obviously important to the intelligent tester in building rapport and maintaining the proper ambiance during the actual testing. Although adhering to standardized procedures and obtaining valid scores are important, the child must remain the lodestar

of the evaluation. Critical to the dynamic understanding of the child's performance is close, insightful observation and recordings of behavior during the testing period. Fully half the important information gathered during the administration of an intelligence test comes from observing behavior under a set of standard conditions. Behavior at various points in the course of the assessment often will dictate the proper interpretation of test scores. Many individuals earn IQs of 100, but each in a different manner, with infinite nuances of behavior interacting directly with a person's test performance.

Knowledge and skill in psychometrics and measurement are requisite to intelligent testing. The clinical evaluation of test performance must be directed by careful analyses of the statistical properties of the test scores, the internal psychometric characteristics of the test, and the data regarding their relationship to external factors. As one example, difference scores have long been of inherent interest for psychologists, especially between subparts of an intelligence scale. Difference scores are unreliable, and small discrepancies between levels of performance may be best attributed to measurement error. If large enough, however, difference scores can provide valuable information regarding the choice of an appropriate remedial or therapeutic program. The psychometric characteristics of the tests in question dictate the size of the differences needed for statistical confidence in their reflecting real rather than chance fluctuations. Interpretation of subscale differences often requires integrating clinical observations of the child's behavior with data on the relationship of the test scores to other factors, and with theories of intelligence, but only after first establishing that the differences are real and not based on error.

One major limitation of most contemporary intelligence tests is their lack of foundation in theories of intelligence, whether these theories are based on research in neuropsychology, cognitive information processing, factor analysis, learning theory, or other domains. Nevertheless, many profiles obtained by children and adults on intelligence tests are interpretable from diverse theoretical perspectives, and can frequently be shown to display a close fit to one or another theoretical approach to intelligence. Theories then become useful in developing a full understanding of the individual. Competing theories of intelligence abound (Reynolds, 1981; Vernon, 1979; White, 1979).

Well-grounded, empirically evaluated models of intellectual functioning enable one to reach a broader understanding of the examinee and to make specific predictions regarding behavior outside of the testing situation. Predictions will not always be correct; however, the intelligent tester has an excellent chance of making sense out of the predictable individual variations in behavior, cognitive skills, and academic performance by involving the nomothetic framework provided by theory. The alternative often is to be stymied or forced to rely on trial-and-error or anecdotal, illusionary relationships when each new set of profile fluctuations is encountered. Theories, even speculative ones, are more efficient guides to developing hypotheses for understanding and treating problems than are purely clinical impressions or armchair speculations.

Through the elements of clinical skill, psychometric sophistication, and a broad base of knowledge of theories of individual differences emerges intelligent testing. None is sufficient, yet, when properly implemented, these elements engage in a synergistic interaction to produce the greatest possible understanding. The intelligent testing model places a series of requirements on the test but also on the tester; not every test can be used intelligently nor can everyone be an intelligent tester. The examiner's breadth of knowledge of psychometrics, differential psychology, child development, and other areas is crucial. Equally, the test must have multiple scales that are reliable, with good validity evidence, and be standardized on a sufficiently large, nationally stratified random sample. The test must offer the opportunity for good clinical observations. Without all of these characteristics, intelligent testing is unlikely to take place; when it does, however, the child is certain to benefit.

REFERENCES

Herrnstein, R. (1973). *IQ in the meritocracy*. Boston: Little, Brown.

Hilliard, A. G. (1984). IQ testing as the emperor's new clothes: A critique of Jensen's bias in mental testing. In C. R. Reynolds & R. T. Brown (Eds.), *Perspectives on bias in mental testing.* New York: Plenum.

Jensen, A. R. (1980). *Bias in mental testing*. New York: The Free Press.

Kaufman, A. S. (1979). *Intelligent testing with the WISC-R*. New York: Wiley-Interscience.

Kaufman, A. S., & Kaufman, N. L. (1977). *Clinical evaluation of young children with the McCarthy scales*. New York: Grune & Stratton.

Reynolds, C. R., (1980a). Two commerical interpretive systems for the WISC-R. *School Psychology Review, 9*, 385–386.

Reynolds, C. R. (1980b). Review of the TARDOR interpretive scoring system for the WISC-R. *Measurement & Evaluation in Guidance, 14*, 46–48.

Reynolds, C. R. (1981). The neuropsychological basis of intelligence. In G. W. Hynd & J. E. Obrzut (Eds.), *Psychoeducational assessment of the school aged child: Issues and procedures*. New York: Grune & Stratton.

Reynolds, C. R., & Brown, R. T. (Eds.). (1984). *Perspectives on bias in mental testing.* New York: Plenum.

Reynolds, C. R., & Clark, J. H. (1982). Cognitive assessment of the preschool child. In K. Paget & B. Bracken (Eds.), *Psychoeducational assessment of preschool and primary aged children*. New York: Grune & Stratton.

Reynolds, C. R., & Kaufman, A. S. (1986). Assessment of children's intelligence with the Wechsler scales. In B. Wolman (Ed.), *Handbook of intelligence*. New York: Wiley-Interscience.

Vernon, P. A. (1979). *Intelligence: Heredity and environment*. San Francisco: Freeman.

Vitelli, R., & Goldblatt, R. (1979). *The TARDOR interpretive scoring system for the WISC-R*. Manchester, CT: TARDOR.

White, W. (Ed.). (1979). Intelligence [Special issue]. *Journal of Research & Development in Education, 12*(1).

CECIL R. REYNOLDS
Texas A&M University

ASSESSMENT
CULTURAL BIAS IN TESTING
INTELLIGENCE TESTING
KAUFMAN, ALAN S.
REMEDIATION, DEFICIT-CENTERED MODELS OF
SEQUENTIAL AND SIMULTANEOUS COGNITIVE-
  PROCESSING

INTERACTIVE LANGUAGE DEVELOPMENT

The notion of interactive language development has its roots in the philosophy of pragmatism and in child language pragmatics research. Pragmatics refers to the study of the social uses of language and research in the area of pragmatic language development in children. It is concerned primarily with three major focuses: (1) understanding how children learn to adapt their language to various linguistic and nonlinguistic contexts; (2) tracking development relative to the increasing repertoire of language functions; and (3) determining the role of social context in facilitating various aspects of language development (Bates, 1976; Prutting, 1982).

Interactive language development approaches rely heavily on social psychological research involving the study of adult-child interaction. Rees (1982) found a recurring theme in this literature: that pragmatic considerations have a prominent role in language acquisition "not only as a set of skills to be acquired but as motivating and explanatory factors for the acquisition of the language itself" (p. 8). Rees argues that pragmatic interactional factors assume an important role in the child's mastery of native language. Interactional factors may be seen as the source or origin of language in the child. Bruner (1975) cites the interaction between mother and infant during the first year of life, particularly in shared attention objects, people, and events of interest, as the basis of the child's capacity for reference and more broadly for meaning that eventually characterizes the human use of linguistic symbols.

Second, pragmatic interactional factors may be seen as the motivation for language learning as exemplified in the research of Halliday (1975) and Bates (1976). These researchers demonstrate how communicative functions emerge prior to the acquisition of linguistic skills. In addition to forming the basis for the development of particular linguistic structures, pragmatic interactional factors explain the development of linguistic style and code switching ability. As Rees (1982) notes, "language users typically control a range of style and code variants that are appropriate to particular listeners and particular settings, and they use these variants in establishing and maintaining social role relationships. . . ." (p. 10). Children as young as 3 or 4 years have been found to use different styles or "registers" for speaking to their parents, siblings, friends, strangers, younger and older children (Gleason, 1973; Snow & Ferguson, 1977).

As descriptions of the acquisition of pragmatic interactional abilities increased in the normal child language literature, language and communication practitioners began to develop pragmatically based assessment and intervention programs for disordered children (Prinz, 1982). Professionals involved in the treatment of language-disordered children stressed the importance of viewing communication as an interpersonal behavior that occurs in interaction with the environment. The interactional component, in which language is used to establish and maintain contact with other persons, is an integral part of many current intervention programs for language-disabled children. Specific procedures have been developed to facilitate the child's communication with the environment, including initiating and sustaining communicative interactions with others, consideration of a listener's perspective when encoding messages, and appropriate responses to listener feedback indicating a lack of understanding. Procedures for pragmatic interactional language treatment are discussed in Wilcox (1982).

REFERENCES

Bates, E. (1976). Pragmatics and sociolinguistics in child language. In D. Morehead & A. Morehead (Eds.), *Normal and deficient child language*. Baltimore, MD: University Park Press.

Bruner, J. (1975). The ontogenesis of speech acts. *Journal of Child Language, 2,* 1–20.

Gleason, J. (1973). Code-switching in children's language. In T. Moore (Ed.), *Cognitive development and the acquisition of language*. New York: Academic.

Halliday, M. (1975). *Learning how to mean*. London: Arnold.

Prinz, P. M. (1982). Development of pragmatics: Multi-Word level. In J. V. Irwin (Ed.), *Pragmatics: The role in language development*. La Verne, CA: Fox Point and University of La Verne Press.

Prutting, C. (1982). Pragmatics as social competence. *Journal of Speech & Hearing Disorders, 47,* 123–134.

Rees, N. (1982). An overview of pragmatics or what is in the box? In J. V. Irwin (Ed.), *Pragmatics: The role in language development*. La Verne, CA: Fox Point and University of La Verne Press.

Snow, C., & Ferguson, C. (1977). *Talking to children: Language input and acquisition*. Cambridge, England: Cambridge University Press.

Wilcox, M. (1982). The integration of pragmatics into language therapy. In J. V. Irwin (Ed.), *Pragmatics: The role in language development*. La Verne, CA: Fox Point and University of La Verne Press.

PHILIP M. PRINZ
Pennsylvania State University

LANGUAGE THERAPY
SOCIAL LEARNING THEORY
THEORY OF ACTIVITY

INTERDISCIPLINARY TEAMS

Before any child receives special education services, he or she must receive an individual assessment to identify areas of educational need, determine the child's aptitude for achievement, and identify other factors that might be interfering with school performance. This individual assessment is the basis for all instructional planning. With the advent of PL 94-142 came the requirement that an interdisciplinary team (IDT), also known as a multidisciplinary team (MDT), be used to determine pupil eligibility for special education services. Public agencies assessing children suspected of having a handicapping condition must include the following in their interdisciplinary team (Federal Register, 1977, 121a.540):

(A) (1) The child's regular teacher; or
    (2) If the child does not have a regular teacher, a regular classroom teacher qualified to teach a child of his or her age; or
    (3) For a child of less than school age, an individual qualified by the State Educational Agency to teach a child of his or her age; and
(B) At least one person qualified to conduct individual diagnostic examinations of children such as a school psychologist, speech language pathologist, or remedial reading teacher.

Since PL 94-142, IDTs have become incorporated into the organizational routine of most school systems in the United States. Nevertheless, school professionals, parents, and the general public have expressed differing views their value (Masters & Mori, 1986).

The IDT model is often cited as the organizational unit best suited to making evaluation and programming decisions because the different perspectives made possible by it prevent biased eligibility and placement decisions (Abelson & Woodman, 1983). However, there is no empirical evidence to support the use of teams. Ballard-

Campbell and Semmel (1981) suggest forces such as litigation, parental and educator opinions, and state-level administrative practices, rather than research evidence, have been responsible for the spread of interdisciplinary practices.

Indeed, recent research findings concerning the effectiveness of the IDT model are discouraging. According to Ysseldyke (1983), the IDT model uses conceptual definitions that have not been translated into scientific or practical assessment procedures.

While IDT functioning has been widely researched, the results have been mixed; some inquiries into whether IDTs make better decisions than individuals have revealed few differences between decisions made by IDTs and those made by individual decision makers (Pfeiffer, 1982). Some researchers (Pfeiffer & Naglieri, 1983) have demonstrated that teams make more consistent and less variable decisions than do individuals. Interpretive and methodological differences between positive and negative studies make it difficult to arrive at definitive answers.

REFERENCES

Abelson, M. A., & Woodman, R. W. (1983). Review of research on team effectiveness: Implications for teams in schools. *School Psychology Review, 12*(2), 125–138.

Ballard-Campbell, M., & Semmel, M. I. (1981). Policy research and special education issues affecting policy research and implementation. *Exceptional Education Quarterly, 2*, 59–68.

Masters, L. F., & Mori, A. A. (1986). *Teaching secondary students with mild learning and behavior problems.* Rockville, MD: Aspen.

Pfeiffer, S. I. (1982). Special education placement decisions made by teams and individuals. *Psychology in the Schools, 19*, 335–340.

Pfeiffer, S. I., & Naglieri, J. A. (1983). An investigation of multidisciplinary team decision-making. *Journal of Learning Disabilities, 15*(10), 586–590.

Ysseldyke, J. E. (1983). Current practices in making psychoeducational decisions about learning disabled students. *Journal of Learning Disabilities, 16*(4), 226–233.

JOSEPH M. RUSSO
*Hunter College, City University
of New York*

ASSESSMENT
MULTIDISCIPLINARY TEAMS
PUBLIC LAW 94-142

INTERNATIONAL CHILD NEUROLOGY ASSOCIATION

The International Child Neurology Association, composed of child neurologists and related professionals, is dedicated to improving the care and treatment of infants and children with neurological disorders. The association seeks to advance child neurology by encouraging scientific research and exchange of knowledge in the field. It coordinates international conferences and publications. The *International Review of Child Neurology Series* is the official publication of the International Child Neurology Association.

MARILYN P. DORNBUSH
Atlanta, Georgia

INTERNATIONAL CLASSIFICATION OF DISEASES (ICD)

The International Classification of Diseases (ICD) is used to classify morbidity and mortality data for statistical purposes and to index hospital records on diseases and operations for information storage and retrieval. Classifying operations for this purpose has traditionally involved structuring according to type of operative procedure, anatomic site, or a combination of these two methods. Surgical specialty serves as the primary axis for classification in the present ICD as well as in most hospitals. The way in which a classification system of diseases is applied depends on the particular data to be classified and on the final product desired. As of yet, there exists no internationally agreed on method for classifying multiple causes of death.

Although the statistical study of diseases began as early as the 1700s, the roots of the ICD are found in the work of William Farr (1807–1883), a medical statistician who produced the best classification of diseases for his time—the International List of Causes of Death. Although this classification was never universally accepted, it did lay the basis for classifying by anatomical site. In the early 1900s, Dr. Jacque Bertillon prepared the Bertillon Classification of Causes of Death. Several revisions were put forth and, in 1923, M. Michel Huber (Bertillon's successor) managed to involve other international organizations such as the Health Organization of the League of Nations, in drafting revisions, stating that the system should be reviewed every 10 years. The Sixth Decennial Revision Conference was marked by the adoption of a system calling for international cooperation in establishing national committees on vital and health statistics to coordinate statistical activity in the United States as well as through the World Health Organization. The present ICD is in its eighth revision, finalized in 1964.

The eighth revision of the ICD is an extension of the system of causes of morbidity and mortality. Furthermore, it provides a means for developing an efficient basis for indexing diagnostic information on hospital charts so that this data may later be reviewed and studied. The ICD is divided into 17 main sections, among them: diseases caused by well-defined infective agents; endocrine, neoplasmic, metabolic, and nutritional diseases; mental diseases; complications of pregnancy and childbirth; diseases of the perinatal period; ill-defined conditions; and a classification of injuries (puncture, burn, or open wound). The last category involves a dual classification system: external cause and nature of injury. This section is designed to bear the numbers 800–999; external cause is distinguished by the prefix "E," while nature of injury is distinguished by the prefix "N." Although the broad section headings aid organization, much significance should not be placed on their inherent value, since they have never represented a consistent collection of disease conditions to serve as statistically stable and usable areas. The detailed list is comprised of 671 categories, in addition to 187 categories characterizing injuries according to the nature of the wound, and 182 categories classifying external causes of injuries. A decimal numbering system is used; thus the categories are designated by three-digit numbers. The initial two digits pinpoint important or summary groups, while the third digit sections each group into categories representing classifications of diseases according to a specific axis of specific disease entities. The three-digit categories are not numbered consecutively. Four-digit subcategories provide additional specificity regarding etiology or manifestations of the condition. While the list of categories in the ICD provides a structure for classification, it is essential to be familiar with the diagnostic terms included within each category before the ICD can be of practical use.

MARY LEON PEERY
Texas A&M University

INTERNATIONAL JOURNAL OF CLINICAL NEUROPSYCHOLOGY (IJCN)

The *International Journal of Clinical Neuropsychology* (IJCN) is the official journal of the National Academy of Neuropsychologists. Initially published in 1979 under the name *Clinical Neuropsychology*, the journal was renamed in 1984 to reflect a growing readership and contributors from 23 countries. The IJCN is published by the MelNic Press, Madison, Wisconsin, on a quarterly basis. It is listed in Psychological Abstracts and Current Content/Clinical Practice.

Clinical neuropsychology is the application of our knowledge of brain-behavior relationships. As such, the journal is primarily devoted to the publication of research findings and related articles intended to enhance the readers' ability to understand, measure, and treat maladaptive human behaviors dependent on brain functioning. Generally, contributors to IJCN are researchers or practitioners from various fields concerned with human brain functioning and their behavioral correlates, including clinical neuropsychology, psychiatry, and neurology. All articles are peer reviewed by members of the IJCN Editorial Review Board, with selected articles published quarterly.

RICHARD G. PETERS
Ball State University

RAYMOND S. DEAN
Ball State University
Indiana University School
of Medicine

INTERNATIONAL READING ASSOCIATION (IRA)

The International Reading Association (IRA) is a nonprofit professional organization devoted to the improvement of reading instruction (IRA, 1985). Membership in IRA is open to individuals who are interested in the field of reading, including teachers, administrators, reading specialists, special educators, college-level instructors and researchers, psychologists, librarians, and parents. In addition, membership is also available to institutions and agencies that are involved with the teaching of reading or the preparation of reading teachers. The IRA endorses the study of reading as a process, promotes research into improvement of reading programs, and advocates better teacher education. The organization is also closely involved with the worldwide literacy movement and the role of reading in the general welfare of society and individuals, as promulgated in the IRA Code of Ethics (1985).

The IRA is comprised of over 1150 councils and national affiliates in various countries around the world. Local, national, and international meetings and conventions provide an opportunity for members to come together. The four major professional journals and numerous individual volumes on reading-related topics published annually by IRA provide other means through which members are kept informed of current practices in reading education.

REFERENCES

Committee on Professional Standards and Ethics. (1985). IRA Code of Ethics. *Reading Teacher, 39*(1), 56–57.

International Reading Association. (1985). Newark, DE: Author.

JOHN M. EELLS
Souderton Area School District,
Souderton, Pennsylvania

READING
READING REMEDIATION

INTERNATIONAL YEAR OF DISABLED PERSONS, 1981

The General Assembly of the United Nations proclaimed 1981 the International Year of Disabled Persons (Resolution 31/123, December 16, 1976). Previous initiatives had set the stage. These included the Declaration on the Rights of Mentally Retarded Persons (Resolution 2856 [xxvi], adopted on December 20, 1971) and the Declaration on the Rights of Disabled Persons (Resolution 3447 [xxx], adopted December 9, 1975).

The resolution on the International Year of Disabled Persons stressed the theme of full participation by persons with disabilities in the social, political, and economic life and development of the societies in which they live. It also promoted national and international efforts to provide disabled persons with proper assistance, training, care, and guidance, and encouraged study and research projects designed to facilitate the practical participation of disabled persons in daily life by improving such things as transport and access. One hundred and thirty-one countries took an active part in the International Year of Disabled Persons. They formed national commissions and carried out national programs, many of them focusing formally on the problem of disability for the first time.

Perhaps the greatest contribution of the International Year of Disabled Persons at the world level was the development by the United Nations of a World Plan of Action. The plan was adopted by the General Assembly at its 34th session, which concluded in December 1979. The plan set forth (on a global scale) the steps nations, nongovernment organizations, the United Nations, and individuals must take to continue the commitment and momentum of the International Year of Disabled Persons (Resolution A/RES/34/158, adopted January 30, 1980). Activities included measures at the national, regional, and international levels, including the organization of meetings and symposiums, the development of statistical data on disability, a review of existing legislation relating to disabled persons, the development of mass media campaigns relating to disability, and the identification of prophylaxis for disease and the prevention of disability.

On December 3, 1982, at the conclusion of its 37th session and the end of the International Year of Disabled Persons, the United Nations' General Assembly proclaimed the United Nations Decade of Disabled Persons, 1983–1992. It also formally adopted the World Program of Action, with its stress on the prevention of disability and its effort to identify major problems facing people with disabilities throughout the world, and made recommendations of actions to be taken to respond to these problems. The majority of recommendations address strategies for prevention, rehabilitation, and equalization of opportunity. The last category includes such issues as legislation, the physical environment, income maintenance, and social security, education and training, employment, recreation, culture, religion, and sports.

REFERENCES

National Organization on Disability. (1983). *International year of disabled persons, the story of the U.S. council for IYPD*. Washington, DC: Author.

Rehabilitation International. (1981). *International statements on disability policy*. New York: Author.

United Nations. (1983). *For the benefit of the disabled, activities undertaken during the international year of disabled persons*. New York: Author.

United Nations. (1983). *U.N. decade of disabled persons, 1983–1992: World programme of action concerning disabled persons*. New York: Author.

United Nations General Assembly adopts IYPD action plan. (1980). *International Rehabilitation Review, 1,* 1.

United Nations proclaims 1983–1992 decade of disabled persons (1982). *International Rehabilitation Review,* 4th quarter, 1.

CATHERINE HALL RIKHYE
*Hunter College, City University
of New York*

INTERPRETERS FOR THE DEAF

Interpreters for the deaf are hearing individuals who listen to a spoken message and communicate it in some way to hearing-impaired people. In interpreting it is permissible to depart from the exact words of the speaker to paraphrase, define, and explain what the speaker is saying. Interpreting is differentiated from translating, which is a verbatim presentation of another person's remarks (Quigley & Paul, 1984).

Until 1964 interpreters were mainly family friends or relatives who knew sign language (Levine, 1981). In 1964 the National Registry of Interpreters for the Deaf was established to promote the recruitment and training of interpreters, to clarify their functions, to specify the competencies required for interpreting, and to maintain a list of certified interpreters.

There are various types of interpreters for the deaf: sign language interpreters, who communicate what has been said in some form of sign language or finger spelling; oral interpreters, who inaudibly repeat the speaker's message, (clearly enunciated and somewhat more slowly) to facilitate its speech reading by deaf persons (Northcott, 1984); and reverse interpreters, who convert a deaf person's sign language or difficult to understand speech into normally spoken English (Bishop, 1979). Specialized interpreters, familiar with the pertinent technical language, serve in legal, medical, psychiatric, and rehabilitative settings. Educational interpreters facilitate the mainstreaming of deaf students in schools and universities. Theatrical interpreters sign operatic performances and Broadway shows (Kanter, 1985).

The first case involving PL 94-142, the Education for all Handicapped Children Act, decided by the U.S. Supreme Court, was a demand for a sign language interpreter by the parents of a mainstream deaf child, Amy Rowley. The Court decided that this particular deaf child did not need an interpreter. However, in other cases, sign language interpreters have been ordered, even for elementary school students when teachers state that interpreters are needed for pupils to benefit from their classes and actively participate in them (DuBow & Geer, 1983). In 1982 the U.S. Court of Appeals mandated state vocational rehabilitation agencies to provide interpreters for deaf clients attending college.

The Vocational Rehabilitation Act of 1965 provided that interpreter services must be included as part of vocational rehabilitation services. Since then, most states have mandated that deaf individuals must be offered sign language interpreters whenever their civil rights are involved. Interpreter training programs are available throughout the United States. Many colleges offer an AA, or BA degree in interpreting.

REFERENCES

Bishop, M. (1979). *Mainstreaming.* Washington, DC: Alexander Graham Bell Association for the Deaf.

DuBow, S., & Geer S. (1983, July). Education decisions after Rowley. *National Center for Law and the Deaf Newsletter,* pp. 1–3.

Kanter, A. (1985, Summer). *A night at the opera.* N.T.I.D. Focus, pp. 3–4.

Levine, E. (1981). *The ecology of early deafness.* New York: Columbia University Press.

Northcott, W. (1984). *Oral interpreting: Principles and practices.* Baltimore, MD: University Park Press.

Quigley, S., & Paul, P. (1984). *Language and deafness.* San Diego, CA: College Hill Press.

ROSEMARY GAFFNEY
Hunter College, City University
of New York

DEAF EDUCATION
LIPREADING—SPEECHREADING

INTERVENTION

Intervention consists of all planned attempts to promote the general welfare of exceptional individuals. There are three broad types of interventions: preventive, remedial, and compensatory.

Efforts to thwart the appearance of handicapping problems are considered preventive. For example, phenylketonuria is an inherited condition that ultimately results in brain damage and arrested mental development. Early diagnosis and intervention via a special diet effectively prevent the otherwise predictable neurological damage and mental retardation. Though it is not invariably so, preventive interventions are most often introduced by the medical profession.

Remedial intervention is the process of overcoming a deficit by correcting or otherwise improving it directly. When a handicapped reader is taught to read at a level that is comparable to that of his or her peer group, it is called remedial intervention. Remedial interventions are generally introduced by the education profession.

In compensatory intervention, the usual approach is to provide a child with the means to circumvent, substitute, or otherwise offset an irremediable deficit. The best known and most widely used compensatory interventions consist of teaching a child to use technological advances that at least partially obviate the need for remediation. For example, the recent development of close-captioned television programs effectively compensates for the inability of deaf people to hear the program.

Several theoretical models exist by which interventions may be classified. They include biophysical, psychological, behavioral, ecological, and sociological models. In the following sections, each model is discussed and at least one example is provided to illustrate an application of the model. The illustrations are often not pure applications but may borrow from other theoretical models.

Biophysical theorists believe that abnormalities result from physical anomalies within the organism. The causes of affective, cognitive, and motoric difficulties may be either endogenous (i.e., originating within the body) or exogenous (originating outside of the body), and generally are considered to be genetic, nutritional, neurological, or biochemical in nature.

Genetic counseling is an intervention intended to prevent hereditary disorders from occurring. Prime candidates for genetic counseling are adults who have known hereditary disorders or who find themselves in circumstances that increase the probability of bearing a child with a genetic disorder. Sickle cell anemia, hemophilia, and osteogenesis imperfecta (tarda) are just three conditions that are genetically caused and, therefore, can be prevented through genetic counseling. On the other hand, genetic counselors provide a service to older couples by informing them of the probabilities of bearing a child with a genetic abnormality such as Down's syndrome.

Nutritional deficiencies can result in severe, irreversible intellectual and physical disorders. Although nutritional problems are not particularly extensive in the United States, they do exist; in many third world nations (e.g., Ethiopia) the extent of such disorders is nothing short of catastrophic. The introduction of a balanced, nutritional diet is the obvious biophysical intervention of choice.

Neurological damage incurred following accidents, low levels of oxygen in the blood, etc., also result in behavioral abnormalities. When instruction in sign language is used with victims of electrical shock or stroke in order to circumvent the resulting neurological impairment, a compensatory intervention is implemented.

Remedial interventions are also employed to overcome assumed neurological dysfunctions. For instance, cognitive interventions are those that deal with teaching the individual how to think. Such interventions primarily intend to improve perception, memory, and problem solving. Included here are approaches often referred to as process or ability training (Mann & Sabatino, 1985; Ysseldyke & Algozzine, 1984). Often, the tasks involved are neuropsychologically specific. That is, they are characterized by modality specificity (e.g., auditory, visual, or haptic) or hemisphere specificity (i.e., they are analytical, sequential, and highly language-based or global, simultaneous, and nonlanguage-based). Cognitive intervention strategies cover a wide range of topics (Hallahan, 1980). They remain among the most controversial approaches to intervention.

The core belief in the psychological intervention model is that abnormality is the result of internalized conflicts that prevent the individual from fully participating in the social and academic environment. According to the earliest view, that of Freud's psychoanalysis, these conflicts interfere with the individual's normal progression through several stages of personality development presumed to take place during childhood and adolescence.

An outgrowth of Freudian psychology, the psychodynamic model seeks to reduce the individual's conflicts by helping him or her to better understand both behavior and the reasons for exhibiting it. Fritz Redl was one of the primary contributors to this approach, introducing such classroom techniques as the life space interview (LSI). The LSI is actually a set of interventions designed to take place immediately following crisis situations. The interventions have a temporal advantage over traditional therapy in that life events are not allowed to grow distant before the child and the teacher or therapist deal with them. Psychoeducational approaches are an outgrowth of the work of Fritz Redl and have been proposed by his students and coworkers. These interventions are deliberate attempts to adapt psychodynamic concepts to the classroom environment.

Although the behavioral intervention tradition in special education is often tied most closely to B. F. Skinner's work in instrumental (or operant) conditioning, its roots are much broader. It is true that most of the interventions known today as behavior modification do stem from Skinner's ground-breaking research in reinforcement, punishment, and extinction. However, many of the more powerful interventions being introduced to the field lately (e.g., in the writings of Kathryn Blake, Siegfried Engelman, and Douglas Carnine) come from the traditional psychological research on concept learning, verbal learning, discrimination learning, and problem solving.

Both approaches share the common characteristic that the specific techniques they employ have been well validated through a rich research history. However, they are somewhat particular in their effects. Generally, conditioning approaches powerfully affect the motivation of the individual. That is, they provide the individual with the need or desire (the motive) to act in a specific manner. They probably influence the acquisition of skills as well, but their primary effect is motivational. On the other hand, conditions that influence the various types of learning primarily affect the speed with which the individual acquires, retains, and transfers new skills. Both behavioral interventions are powerful, well-documented approaches that enjoy considerable support in the research literature.

In contrast to proponents of the biophysical and psychological models, ecological theorists consider disturbance to be the result of the dynamic interaction between the child and the environment (Rhodes & Tracy, 1974). According to the ecological intervention approach, such events as physical abuse by the parents, slothful behavior by the child, or the death of a sibling are not isolated phenomena, but are interactive in nature. That is, the individual's behavior and other environmental conditions both affect and are affected by the people and conditions within the ecosphere. Consequently, advocates of this model discuss disturbed environments, not disturbed people.

Given their views on disturbance, it follows that ecological practitioners attempt to intervene on entire ecologies or at least those aspects of the environment considered to be disturbed. In practice, this means that virtually any existing intervention may be used within the ecological model if it is considered to be of potential benefit. For instance, the biophysical intervention of drug therapy, the psychodynamic LSI, and such behavioral techniques as positive reinforcement and extinction would not be unusual within an ecological intervention system.

Without question, the best known implementation of an ecological intervention system is that of Project Re-Ed (Hobbs, 1966). In this project, children are temporarily removed from their homes to a residential setting that focuses on education. Two teacher-counselors are responsible for eight children during the day and at night. During their relatively brief stay in the residential facility, the teacher-counselors, aided by a host of supportive personnel, "reeducate" their charges regarding the virtues of trust, competence, cognitive control, the healthy expression of feelings, etc. Prior to the reintegration of the child into the community, additional staff members prepare the home and the community for his or her return. It is the liaison teacher's task to ensure that the faculty and staff of the child's school are sufficiently aware of the child's needs so as to provide effectively for them. The psychiatric social worker engages community services (e.g., family counseling) that are expected to be needed to enhance the probability that the child's return will be successful.

Three distinct views characterize the sociological intervention model: (1) labeling theory, (2) societal rule breaking and rule following, and (3) anomie. Specific interventions that are the result of these views are difficult to identify. Rather, in labeling theory and societal rule breaking and rule following, the opposite seems true; i.e., it may the interventions themselves that lead to deviance (as it is termed by sociologists).

Labeling theorists suggest that deviance itself is sometimes the result of the painfully focused attention that the individual's behavior may receive. They contend that labels such as troublemaker and dunce are pejorative and can actually be powerful stimuli for deviant behavior. Some individuals (e.g., Lemert, 1962) further contend that the most debilitating form of deviance is that which results from a falsely applied label (i.e., instances in which significant deviance did not exist until after the application of the label). Since the label was falsely applied, there is little hope that the child will work to overcome the "deviance"; instead, it is likely that the label itself will produce rebellion and other forms of deviance where none existed before.

Unlike other perspectives, sociological theorists generally view abnormality as behavior that is significantly contrary to the rules established by society. Since normal people break rules some of the time and abnormal individuals follow established rules much or even most of the time, it is important to note the agents who enforce societal rules (e.g., police, teachers) are in the unhappy position of deciding which rule breakers to label as abnormal. Clearly, only a few rule breakers are labeled by society. Since deviance is only a vaguely defined concept, it seems certain that many injustices in the form of false positives and false negatives are committed. In particular, many believe that individuals from poor or culturally different backgrounds are especially susceptible to the application of false labels. Such logic would seem to support the notion of labeling theory.

Anomie refers to deviance that results from social changes that occur at rates too fast for society to effectively establish norms for behavior. One example might be the United States' rapid shift from an agrarian society (in which large families were an advantage) to modern U.S. society, in which the role of children remains marked by ambiguity. The frustrations one feels in attempting to deal with an inoperable vending machine or a billing error committed by a computer are minor examples of anomie.

Interventions based on sociological models are difficult to implement. Nevertheless, society has implemented a number of them in an attempt to prevent or remediate deviance. Local, state, and federal police forces are intended to both prevent and enforce societal rules that have

been codified into laws. Our judicial system is intended to mete out justice to those accused of offenses. Public school programs clearly play a similar role, particularly with regard to values and mores that have not been codified as laws. Prison systems and youth detention centers assume both a punitive and a remedial intervention role where lawbreakers are concerned. Some recent attempts by society to intervene more effectively include an increase in mental health centers, better organized community services, crisis intervention centers, suicide help lines, normalization projects, and not least, public school mainstreaming of handicapped children.

REFERENCES

Hallahan, D. (Ed.). (1980). *Teaching exceptional children to use cognitive strategies*. Rockville, MD: Aspen.

Hobbs, N. (1966). Helping disturbed children: Psychological and ecological strategies. *American Psychologist, 21*, 1105–1115.

Lemert, E. (1962). Paranoia and the dynamics of exclusion. *Sociometry, 25*, 2–20.

Mann, L., & Sabatino, D. A. (1985). *Foundations of cognitive processes in special and remedial education*. Rockville, MD: Aspen.

Rhodes, W. C., & Tracy, M. I. (Eds.). (1974). *A study of child variance: Conceptual models* (Vol. 1). Ann Arbor: University of Michigan.

Ysseldyke, J. E., & Algozzine, B. (1984). *Introduction to special education*. Boston: Houghton Mifflin.

RONALD C. EAVES
Auburn University

JAMES A. POTEET
Ball State University

**BEHAVIOR MODIFICATION
CHILD PSYCHOLOGY
ECOLOGICAL ASSESSMENT**

IQ

In psychoeducational assessment, a difference exists between an IQ and an intelligence quotient or ratio IQ. Since the ratio IQ or intelligence quotient has decreased in use, the IQ has taken on more of a generic meaning as an index of a test taker's current level of intellectual functioning or general cognitive ability. The IQ has been found useful in understanding and predicting a number of important behaviors such as academic achievement (Sattler, 1982). In addition, diagnoses of a variety of learning disorders such as mental retardation and learning disabilities are dependent in part on determining the IQ of the student.

A test taker's composite performance on a test consisting of cognitive or intellectual tasks is represented by the IQ score. Intelligence tests can be very different from each other in item composition and consequently may yield divergent IQ estimates for the same individual. The magnitude of the IQ score and the interpretation of its meaning is dependent on the test author's theory or definition of intelligence. For example, the Wechsler Intelligence Scales yield verbal and performance IQs and a full-scale IQ. The meaning of these IQ estimates relate to Wechsler's theory of intelligence, which includes verbal and nonverbal reasoning and a heavy emphasis on language and acquired knowledge such as is tapped on the information, vocabulary, and arithmetic subtests. This theory is in contrast to Kaufman and Kaufman's (1983) definition of intelligence, which minimizes the role of language and acquired knowledge. Interpretations of IQ estimates based on Wechsler's and Kaufman and Kaufman's definitions of intelligence will certainly be different; the tests would likely yield different IQ estimates for the same individual.

Although most tests of intelligence currently in use yield IQs, they do not yield intelligence quotients representing the ratio of the test taker's mental age to his or her chronological age multiplied by 100. Rather, these intelligence tests provide tables for converting raw scores into age-corrected deviation standard scores or IQs.

David Wechsler, author of the Wechsler Intelligence Scales, proposed what he called a deviation IQ. The deviation IQ is a measure that describes how much a test taker's intellectual ability deviates from the average performance of others or the same chronological age within the standardization sample. Initially, developing a test to measure adult intelligence, Wechsler (1939) culled the standarization sample's data and constructed tables so that the person who scored at the average level for his or her age group would receive an IQ of 100. The standard deviation for all age groups was set at 15 by Wechsler. For the Wechsler Intelligence Scale for children, IQs were obtained by comparing a child's performance with the average performance of those in his or her age group. This deviation IQ is a standard score that represents how many standard deviations above or below the average the test taker's intellectual ability falls. To further aid in communicating the meaning of the IQ to nonprofessionals, IQ standard scores are often translated into a descriptive classification such as mentally deficient, a percentile rank, or an age equivalent.

The deviation IQ now represents the most common composite standard score yielded by intelligence tests, including the three Wechsler scales and the Stanford-Binet. This popularity can be attributed primarily to the deviation IQ's overcoming many of the criticisms leveled at the ratio intelligence quotient. The means and standard deviations are equal across all age levels for the deviation IQ, allowing comparability for similar IQs across different ages. However, it is important for the test user to remember that deviation IQs yielded by different intelligence tests can only be compared if they have the same or similar standard deviations.

Finally, the generic terms IQ and IQ tests have often been misinterpreted by nonprofessionals and they possess a number of unfortunate negative connotations. The IQ test and the IQ have also been the subject of litigation in state and federal courts (Jensen, 1980). As a result of these negative connotations and litigation, some contemporary test developers have avoided the term IQ in labeling their composite standard scores yielded from their intelligence tests. For example, McCarthy's (1972) General Cognitive Index (GCI) and Kaufman and Kaufman's (1983) Mental Processing Composite (MPC) can be used interchangeably with the IQ.

REFERENCES

Jensen, A. R. (1980). *Bias in mental testing.* New York: Free Press.

Kaufman, A. S., & Kaufman, N. S. (1983). *Kaufman Assessment Battery for Children.* Circle Pines, MN: American Guidance Service.

McCarthy, D. (1972). *Manual for the McCarthy scales of children's abilities.* New York: Psychological Corporation.

Sattler, J. M. (1982). *Assessment of children's intelligence and special abilities.* Boston: Allyn & Bacon.

Wechsler, D. (1939). *The measurement of adult intelligence.* Baltimore, MD: Williams & Wilkins.

MARK E. SWERDLIK
Illinois State University

DEVIATION IQ
INTELLIGENCE
INTELLIGENCE TESTING

IRWIN, ROBERT BENJAMIN (1883–1951)

Robert Benjamin Irwin, blind from the age of five, in 1909 became superintendent of classes for the blind in the Cleveland, Ohio, public schools, one of the first school systems in the United States to educate blind children. He organized braille reading classes and, most significantly, established the first "sight-saving" classes for partially seeing students rather than group them with blind children.

Irwin became director of research and education for the newly formed American Foundation for the Blind in 1923, and served as its executive director from 1929 until his retirement in 1950. He promoted federal legislation relating to the blind, including laws authorizing the Library of Congress to manufacture and distribute "talking books" and books in braille, providing Social Security for the blind, providing income tax exemptions for the blind, and giving priority to the blind in the operation of vending stands in federal buildings. Believing that the blind

Robert Benjamin Irwin

should not be segregated, he opposed a movement to establish a national college for the blind.

REFERENCES

Allen, A. (1952). Robert B. Irwin—A lifetime of service. *New outlook for the blind, 46,* 1–3.

Irwin, R. B. (1955). *As I saw it.* New York: American Foundation for the Blind.

PAUL IRVINE
Katonah, New York

ITA

See INITIAL TEACHING ALPHABET.

ITALY, SPECIAL EDUCATION IN

Many parallels exist between the development of special education in Italy and the United States. Historically, exceptional children were separated from their normal peers in both countries. In addition, national legislation (PL 94-142 in the United States and Law 517 in Italy) has had a significant impact on the provision of services to exceptional students. While similarities exist, differences also exist that reflect the unique sociocultural and political atmospheres of Italy and the United States.

Until the late 1960s in Italy (as in the United States), disabilities were dealt with in a traditional fashion. The less severely disabled children attended regular schools, although most of them were compelled to attend special ("differential" was the Italian name) classes.

Many large institutions cared for the most severely disabled (e.g., the visually and auditorially impaired, severely mentally retarded, autistic, and brain damaged). The children spent most of their time within the institution and had little contact with the community. Most institutions were run by people from religious orders and were financed by state and/or local government.

Services provided by institutions were mainly custodial, since the underlying philosophy regarding the possibility of educating this kind of child was pessimistic. In contrast, the philosophy behind the differential classes was more optimistic. Children were thought to be capable of learning basic academic skills and adjusting to the demands of society. The differential classes were made up of few children and their teachers often were more experienced (if not more skilled) than regular teachers. In addition, the curricula were not special but were similar to those adopted in regular schools, the major difference being that the pace of teaching and learning was much slower. Before long, however, this educational philosophy collapsed as a result of many unexpected social, political, psychological, and educational pressures.

Profound social, political, and cultural change occurred in 1968. No institution was spared from criticism. The school and health systems, in particular, were targets of bitter criticism, as they were thought to be the cultural strongholds of the political establishment. In 1977 a law was passed (Law 517) that required all handicapped children to be mainstreamed into regular classes regardless of the nature and severity of the handicap. This produced severe changes in educational and social policies. The medical model was no longer dominant, having been replaced by a blend of somewhat idealistic views that held that any developmentally disabled child has the right to be socialized—a vague term from which many meanings can be conveyed.

Law 517 allowed parents of disabled children to enroll them in the nearest school in the community in the grade appropriate to their chronological age regardless of the severity of the problem. In Italy the average regular class of about 15 students enables the school schedule to be relatively flexible. The school principal assigns one support teacher at the ratio of one to every four disabled children. The teachers are responsible for organizing their teaching time and deciding which curricula to use, the length of time to devote to individual or group education, the place to instruct children (e.g., regular classrooms vs. resource rooms), and other important educational decisions. With few exceptions, the trend is to give the disabled child as much within-classroom teaching as possible in an attempt to minimize the social stigma connected with being taken out of the room or attending a special facility.

In spite of some successes (e.g., more positive attitudes toward disabled children), mainstreaming policy and implementation have not gone uncriticized. All of the criticisms are a reflection of a lack of pragmatism that tends to run through Italian reforms and laws.

First, the dogmatic core of Law 517 has been the target of bitter attacks. Keeping disabled children in regular classes at any cost actually may be detrimental to their learning, since their special needs for individual treatment are unlikely to be met. Second, "socialization," the cornerstone of present educational policy, is not well defined and has acquired various meanings, ranging from a pure acceptance of disabled children on the part of the school system to supplying these children with refined academic and adaptive skill repertoires. Therefore, the need to operationalize this term is strongly felt by psychologists. Third, the amount of time special education teachers can spend with the children is too limited. Considering that most Italian schools have only part-time programs (from 8:30 A.M. to 12:30 P.M.), each child is likely to receive only one hour a day of individualized help.

To overcome the last criticism, most regional regulations (regions are an administrative subdivision of the Italian political system) decree that every child who is not self-sufficient is entitled to a personal assistant (most of the time a teacher serves in this capacity) whose basic function is to take care of the student's physical needs.

Last, Italian support teachers often are not well trained. The syllabus guiding their preparation is still heavily affected by the medical model and allows little time for them to acquire the necessary educational and instructional skills.

Following the passage of Law 517, most institutional settings were expected to close. However, many managed to survive by changing their goals and strategies. Most have been transformed into regular schools where mainstreaming has been carried out. Some accepted the few disabled children who could not possibly be accepted by any school because of the severity of their problems. Some turned into sheltered workshops.

REFERENCE

Meazzini, P., & Nisi, A. (1985). Behavior modification for developmentally disabled children: The state of the art in Italy. *Analysis & intervention in Developmental Disabilities, 5,* 211–221.

THOMAS OAKLAND
JEFF LAURENT
University of Texas, Austin

PAOLO MEAZZINI
University of Rome

ITARD, JEAN M. G. (1775–1838)

Jean Itard, a French physician who served on the medical staff of the famous National Institution for Deaf Mutes in Paris, is best known for his work with the wild boy of Aveyron. This child of 11 or 12 was found naked in the woods, where he had been living as a savage. He was brought to Itard for training, and Itard set out to civilize the boy, to teach him to speak and to learn. Five years of work with the boy, whom Itard named Victor, led to the conclusion that his pupil was mentally retarded. Victor learned to read and write many words and could even exchange simple written communications with others, but he never learned to speak. He became socialized to some degree; he could, for example, dine in a restaurant with his tutor. The experiment ended unhappily when, with the onset of puberty, Victor changed from a gentle boy into a rebellious youth. Itard abandoned his work with the boy, and Victor lived in custodial care until his death at the age of about 40.

Itard's work was not in vain, however. He demonstrated that mentally retarded individuals could be trained in both cognitive and social skills, and he provided essential groundwork for the development of the first educational programs for mentally retarded children by Edouard Seguin and others.

REFERENCES

Itard, J. M. G. (1932). *The wild boy of Aveyron.* New York: Appleton-Century-Crofts.

Kanner, L. (1960). Itard, Seguin, Howe—Three pioneers in the education of retarded children. *American Journal of Mental Deficiency, 65,* 2–10.

Lane, H. (1976). *The wild boy of Aveyron.* Cambridge, MA: Harvard University Press.

PAUL IRVINE
Katonah, New York

ITINERANT SERVICES

Itinerant services are resource programs on wheels. This program model is most practical in areas that have limited funds for full-time services in each school or that do not have enough eligible children to warrant a full-time teacher. In addition to serving schools, itinerant services can provide instruction in the hospital or home to recuperating and chronically ill children by establishing a curriculum and offering teaching services.

Visual impairment was one of the first areas to demonstrate that itinerant instruction on a resource basis could be used in conjunction with a regular school program. Only a decade or two ago, according to Reynolds and Birch (1977), it was common in many states to have blind and partially sighted students automatically referred and placed in residential schools. Recently it has become the prevailing practice in a great many school districts to start visually impaired children in regular school programs and to maintain them there by delivering the special instruction they need in that environment or nearby resource rooms. Currently, in many states, there are more legally blind children being educated in regular classes as a result of itinerant service programs than are being educated in special schools or classes for the blind (Deighton, 1971). Although itinerant services as a derivative of the resource room have been used primarily with visually handicapped children, this program model is being employed with hearing handicapped, emotionally disturbed, learning-disabled, and gifted children.

A comparative study, designed by Pepe (1973), concerned the effectiveness of itinerant services and resource room programs serving children with learning disabilities. Each group consisted of 20 students identified as learning disabled, of average ability, and 9 to 12 years of age. There was no significant difference in the treatment effect gains of students, indicating that the itinerant and resource room programs were equally effective in providing services for mildly learning-disabled children. Since there was no significant difference in gains made by students of comparable ability who were afforded less time by the special education teachers, the itinerant programs appeared to be more efficient. Similar results were obtained by Sabatino (1971).

Difficulties in operating itinerant services are described by Wiederholt, Hammill, and Brown (1978). First, teachers must carry their materials from school to school. Second, they frequently must work in the furnace room, in the lunchroom, or in the principal's or counselor's office, and may even share a room with other staff. Third, they are rarely able to provide instruction on a daily basis. Fourth, the fact that they may serve several schools makes it difficult for them to develop social and professional bonds.

An advantage of itinerant services is flexible scheduling, allowing the student's instructional program to be altered to meet changing needs. Because large numbers of young children with developing problems can be accommodated less expensively, later severe disorders may be prevented, making room for the handicapped students for whom self-contained classes were originally developed. Through itinerant services, most students can receive help in their neighborhood schools; thus, the necessity of busing handicapped children is reduced. Finally, in contrast to the self-contained special class program, children start the day in an integrated program with their age mates and become special for specific services. The itinerant service setting helps avoid the stigma of the special class.

REFERENCES

Deighton, L. C. (1971). *The encyclopedia of education* (Vol. 4). New York: Macmillan.

Pepe, H. J. (1973). A comparison of the effectiveness of itinerant and resource room model programs designed to serve children with learning disabilities (Doctoral dissertation, University of Kansas, 1973). *Dissertation Abstracts, 34*, 7612A.

Reynolds, M. C., & Birch, J. W. (1977). *Teaching exceptional children in all America's schools.* Reston, VA: Council for Exceptional Children.

Sabatino, D. A. (1971). An evaluation of resource rooms for children with learning disabilities. *Journal of Learning Disabilities, 4*, 341.

Weiderholt, J. L., Hammill, D. D., & Brown, V. (1978). *The resource teacher.* Boston: Allyn & Bacon.

WARNER H. BRITTON
Auburn University

HOMEBOUND INSTRUCTION
ITINERANT TEACHER
RESOURCE ROOM

ITINERANT TEACHER

An itinerant teacher has received specialized training in a particular category and provides services to homebound students, or students in hospital programs. The itinerant teacher may also travel between schools within a district, or between districts. The service rendered supplements the instruction provided by the student's classroom teacher. Although teaching is the major responsibility of itinerant teachers, they are involved in related activities such as procuring special materials, conferring with parents, assessing students, or participating in case conferences (Dejnozka & Kapel, 1982). According to Wiederholt, Hammill, and Brown (1978), itinerant teachers must also be able to manage daily details, such as scheduling and grading. In addition, they must possess considerable knowledge of many specific school-related abilities, including reading, spelling, writing, arithmetic, spoken language, and classroom behavior.

The use of itinerant teachers has developed particularly in the field of speech and hearing handicaps, where only small group or individual instruction will work. In the past few years, itinerant teachers have been employed to serve learning-disabled, emotionally disturbed, and gifted students.

Disadvantages, reported by Ellis and Mathews (1982), indicate that itinerant teachers have larger caseloads than special education teachers with a self-contained classroom, which usually has an established teacher-pupil ratio prescribed by state law. The larger caseload often prevents the itinerant teacher from becoming completely familiar with the child. According to Cohen (1982), the role of the itinerant teacher has several drawbacks. For example, itinerant teachers rarely become accepted as a part of a school faculty because they are divided between schools. They are available only on a limited basis, creating problems in scheduling. Because of their itinerant schedules, these teachers are sometimes perceived to be inaccessible both by classroom teachers and parents. Itinerant teachers confess that at times their instructional roles seem dictated by schedule rather than by choice. In addition, the physical burden of transporting materials between resource rooms, the sharing of locations with other staff, and the general feeling of isolation can make itinerant teachers question their contribution to a school's program.

Advantages to employing an itinerant teacher occur when the teacher serves as an in-school consultant based on broad experience with many children exhibiting different educational and behavioral problems. More children can be served by itinerant teachers working extensively with classroom teachers through indirect services to students with mild problems. Another important advantage, according to Deighton (1971), is the effect of changing the attitude of the classroom teacher in dealing with the special student. As the classroom teacher becomes more skillful in meeting the needs of the special child, the itinerant teacher can become involved in the more severe cases that require direct services.

REFERENCES

Cohen, J. H. (1982). *Handbook of resource room teaching*. New York: Aspen.

Deighton, L. C. (1971). *The encyclopedia of education* (Vol. 4). New York: Macmillan.

Dejnozka, E. L., & Kapel, D. E. (1982). *American educators' encyclopedia*. Westport, CT: Greenwood.

Ellis, J. R., & Mathews, G. J. (1982). *Professional role performance difficulties of first year itinerant specialists*. Northern Illinois University: Educational Resources Information Center.

Wiederholt, J. L., & Hammill, D. D., & Brown, V. (1978). *The resource teacher*. Boston: Allyn & Bacon.

WARNER H. BRITTON
Auburn University

HOMEBOUND INSTRUCTION
ITINERANT SERVICES
RESOURCE TEACHER

J

JAPAN, SPECIAL EDUCATION IN

On the basis of a 1980 national survey, it is estimated that the number of disabled persons in Japan is approximately 3.5 million. Among them, 2.1 million are physically disabled, 0.4 million are mentally retarded, and 1 million are mentally ill. This number indicates only those whose disabilities are sufficiently serious to entitle them to rehabilitation services, care programs, and other measures provided under three major laws that address the needs of the handicapped: the Law for the Welfare of Physically Disabled Persons (Law 283 of 1949), the Law for the Welfare of Mentally Retarded Persons (Law 37 of 1960), and the Mental Health Law (Law 123 of 1950). It is believed that if persons with milder disabilities were included, the number would be over 5 million, or approximately 5% of the total population of Japan (117 million in 1980).

Japan offers special education for handicapped children in two distinct forms: in special schools for the handicapped and in special classes within ordinary elementary and lower secondary schools. As of 1982, there were almost 95,000 pupils being taught in almost 800 special schools serving blind, deaf, mentally retarded, physically impaired, and health-impaired youngsters ranging from kindergarten to upper secondary school level. Over 205,000 pupils were being served in almost 22,000 special classes at the elementary and lower secondary school levels; these included the partially sighted, hard of hearing, mentally retarded, physically impaired, health impaired, speech impaired, and emotionally disturbed.

Special classes and special schools are operated under the school system of the Ministry of Education. For more severely involved students, there are public and private daycare centers operated through the Ministry of Health and Welfare. A special child-rearing allowance is given to guardians caring for moderately or severely mentally or physically handicapped persons under the age of 20 in their homes. An additional grant is given when severely handicapped persons, regardless of age, require special care at home on a daily basis.

There are 72 schools for the blind (1 national, 69 local, and 2 private), 110 schools for the deaf (1 national, 108 local, and 1 private), 431 schools for the mentally retarded (42 national, 378 local, 11 private), 174 schools for the physically impaired (1 national, 171 local, and 2 private), and 95 schools for the health impaired (94 local and 1 private).

Compulsory education has been in effect in schools for the blind and the deaf since 1948, and in schools for the mentally retarded, physically impaired, and health impaired since 1979. Special education in Japan began with the foundation of the School for the Blind and Deaf in Kyoto in 1878. Two years later, in 1880, the Rakuzenkai School for the Blind was established in Tokyo. In 1885 the Rakuzen-kai School was placed under the jurisdiction of the Ministry of Education and renamed the School for the Blind and Deaf. By placing the responsibility for schools for the deaf and the blind squarely with the Ministry of Education, impetus was given to focusing on educational services rather than charitable services for handicapped youngsters. In 1890 the Elementary School Ordinance was enacted; this set up criteria for the establishment of schools for the deaf and the blind. The number of schools in this category gradually increased. The Ordinance on Schools for the Blind and for the Deaf of 1923 legally incorporated this kind of special education into the public school system. An increasing number of private schools were converted into public schools and prefectural governments were obligated to establish such schools.

During the first phase of special education in Japan, from the late Meiji period (1868–1912) to the early Taisho (1912–1926), school education for mentally retarded, physically impaired, and health-impaired youngsters was, for the most part, left to private management and charity. The first provision was a special class for educable mentally retarded children in the Matsumoto Elementary School in Nagano Prefecture in 1890. This was followed by a smattering of special classes in a small number of schools in the late 1890s. Special classes were established under a Ministry of Education ordinance on an experimental basis in 1907. Then came a period, lsting until approximately 1940, when it was thought that mentally retarded children and youths should be exempted from compulsory education. An attempt was made to incorporate the mentally retarded as much as possible into the ordinary educational system. This prevailed until 1940, when the Shisei Elementary School, dealing exclusively with mentally retarded youngsters, was set up in Osaka. Education, rather than simple medical rehabilitation, became the focus for the health- and physically impaired during the 1920s. During the late 1950s it began to be recognized that a wide range of special educational services was necessary to meet the needs of other, divergent categories of handicapped children such as the speech disordered, the emotionally handicapped, and the multiply handicapped.

The special education teacher training system involves 4-year training courses in national universities offering teacher-training courses. There are training courses for teachers of the blind in two universities, for the deaf in six universities, for the physically impaired in three, for the health impaired in one, for the speech-disordered in four, and for the generally handicapped in 47. There are also courses allowing teachers with regular certificates to acquire the credits required for special education teachers. Additionally, the Ministry of Education and the prefectural boards of education offer training courses for credit certification. The teacher certificate for special education is classified into two types: the regular teacher certificate for teachers of the deaf, blind, or handicapped, for which one must first hold a teaching certificate for kindergarten, elementary, lower, or upper secondary school; and the certificate for teaching specialized courses in schools for the handicapped.

Organizations for the disabled in Japan were established primarily in the postwar period. There are 102 organizations registered in the Japanese Council for the International Year of Disabled Persons, and 135 organizations registered in the list of Unions for the Mentally and Physically Handicapped drawn up by the National Council of Social Welfare (November 1978). Groups working for the disabled have been divided into six broad categories by Kojima (1981). The first category is composed of professional study groups organized by type of disability (e.g., the Society for Rehabilitation Medicine, the Japanese Association for the Study of Mental Retardation, the Japanese Society for Crippled Children). The second category comprises the groups organized by the disabled themselves (e.g., the All-Japan League of the Deaf and Dumb, the Japan League of Societies for the Blind, the National Meeting of Wheelchair Users, the National Federation of Organizations for Physically Handicapped Persons). The third category is made up of those groups organized by parents of the disabled (e.g., the National Parents' Union for the Mentally Handicapped, the National Parents' Federation for Autistic Children, the Parents' Association for Mentally and Physically Handicapped Children). The fourth category includes groups created by people with specific or rare diseases and their parents (e.g., the National Association of Patients with Multiple Sclerosis, the Association of Patients with Bechet's Disease, the Association of Patients with Diabetes Mellitus). Groups related to institutions for the disabled constitute the fifth category (e.g., the National Council of Social Welfare Institutions for the Blind, the National Council of Homes for Physically Weak Children, the National Administrative Council of Hospital Homes for Crippled Children). Groups relating to schools for the disabled are the sixth category of organizations relating to the handicapped (e.g., the National PTA Union of Special Schools for Physically or Mentally Handicapped Children, the National League for Promotion of Education for Exceptional Children, the National Society of Special School Masters).

Legal provisions for the advancement and welfare of the disabled are derived from the constitution of Japan (1946) and from various laws established under the welfare, education, and labor divisions of government. Based on constitutional provisions, there are currently over 20 laws designed to maintain the rights of the disabled in education, welfare, and employment. All of this legislation has been enacted since World War II. First, the Child Welfare Law and School Education Law were established (1947). With the enactment of the Worker's Accident Compensation Law (1947), the need to rehabilitate workers was addressed. The Law for the Welfare of Physically Handicapped Persons was enacted in 1949, and the Law for the Welfare of Mentally Retarded Persons was enacted in 1960. By the 1960s numerous laws addressing the needs of the disabled had been enacted, however, new problems involving such issues as the needs of the multiply disabled had emerged. Political parties and organizations involved with the handicapped stressed the need for laws that would bridge the gaps between existing laws, strengthen coordination between legislation and administration, and extend services to all disabled persons. This led to the establishment in 1970 of the Fundamental Law for Countermeasures Concerning Mentally and Physically Handicapped Persons. The School Education Law of 1947, which provided a limited education policy for disabled children, was superseded in 1979 by a government ordinance that ensured compulsory education for all disabled children, including the severely and multiply handicapped, the mentally retarded, and the health impaired.

In Japan government operates at three levels, the national, the level of the 57 prefectures (which includes the 10 largest cities), and the level of approximately 3300 cities, towns, and villages. Welfare services authorized by the Law for the Welfare of the Physically Handicapped and the Law for the Welfare of the Mentally Retarded are provided through each of these governmental levels of organization. The national government bears final administrative responsiblity for the rehabilitation of the disabled, including responsibility for such central resources as the National Center for the Handicapped; it operates by discharging the provision of direct services to disabled people to the governors and mayors of local areas. Most of the local government costs of rehabilitation services are paid from national government subsidies. Half the cost of facility construction is paid by national government subsidies. Three ministries are principally responsible for rehabilitation services, the Ministry of Health and Welfare, the Ministry of Labor, and the Ministry of Education. Some services also are offered by the Ministry of Construction and the Ministry of Transport. The work of these five ministries is coordinated through the Central Council to Plan Countermeasures for Mentally and Physically Disabled Persons, which operates within the office of the prime minister. Further resources on special education in Japan include the Japanese Society for Rehabilitation of the Disabled (1983); Koike (1983); and Kojima, (1981).

REFERENCES

Japanese Society for Rehabilitation of the Disabled. (1983). *Rehabilitation services for disabled persons in Japan* (3rd ed.). Tokyo: Author.

Koike, F. (1983). Rehabilitation in Japan: Progress and problems. In *Seventh Asia/Pacific Conference of Rehabilitation International: Country reports from member countries in the Asia/Pacific region*. New York: Rehabilitation International.

Kojima, Y. (Ed.). (1981). *Disabled people in the Japanese community*. Tokyo: Japan Council for the International Year of Disabled Persons.

CATHERINE HALL RIKHYE
*Hunter College, City University
of New York*

CHINA, SPECIAL EDUCATION IN

JARGON APHASIA

Jargon aphasia refers to an expressive language deficit in which a dysphasic individual produces a profusion of unintelligible utterances. Language structure may be retained, but meaning is unclear. Intonation, rhythm, and stress patterns are normal. Speech is fluent with few if any of the hesitations or pauses characteristic of some other dysphasic speech patterns. Bizarre responses, often consisting of clichés, stock phrases, neologisms, and unusual word combination patterns are produced. Speakers seem unaware that their utterances are not meaningful, and receptive language is impaired.

Although meaningless to the listener, Eisenson (1973) feels that jargon may not be so to the speaker. Analysis of a patient's jargon speech revealed some regular sound and morpheme substitutions, confirming Eisenson's impression that some underlying meaning may exist. Eisenson considers jargon aphasia to be a transitory condition rather than a true aphasic condition.

REFERENCE

Eisenson, J. (1973). *Adult aphasia: Assessment and treatment*. New York: Appleton-Century-Crofts.

K. SANDRA VANTA
*Cleveland Public Schools,
Cleveland, Ohio*

APHASIA
DEVELOPMENTAL APHASIA
DYSPHASIA
EXPRESSIVE DYSPHASIA

JENSEN, ARTHUR R. (1923–   )

Arthur Jensen has been on the faculty of the University of California in Berkeley since 1958. He is currently a professor of educational psychology and a research psychologist at the Institute of Human Learning. A graduate of the University of California, Berkeley, and Columbia University, he was a clinical psychology intern at the University of Maryland Psychiatric Institute and a postdoctoral research fellow at the Institute of Psychiatry, University of London, where he studied with and was heavily influenced by Hans Eysenck.

Jensen turned to the study of differential psychology after a decade of research on classical problems in verbal learning. In 1969 he argued that genetic, as well as environmental and cultural, factors should be considered for understanding not only individual differences, but also social class and racial differences in intelligence and scholastic performance (Jensen, 1969). This hypothesis, that both individual and racial differences in abilities are in part a product of the evolutionary process and have a genetic basis, created a storm of protest from scientists and educators. The subject is still a sensitive one and has been explicated by Jensen in several books such as *Bias in Mental Testing* (1980) and *Straight Talk About Mental Tests* (1981). The controversy has also led him to two other areas of research: the study of culture bias in psychometric tests and the investigation of the nature of g (the general intelligence factor).

Jensen presently views the g factor as (1) reflecting some property or processes of the human brain manifest in many forms of adaptive behavior in which individuals (and probably populations) differ; (2) increasing from birth

Arthur R. Jensen

to maturity and declining in old age; (3) showing physiological as well as behavioral correlates; (4) having a hereditary component; (5) being subject to natural selection in the course of human evolution; and (6) having important educational, occupational, economic, and social correlates in all industrialized societies.

Author of over 300 publications, Jensen has been a Guggenheim fellow (1964–1965), a fellow of the Center for Advanced Study in the Behavioral Sciences (1966–1967), and a research fellow at the National Institute of Mental Health (1957–1958).

REFERENCES

Jensen, A. R. (1969). How much can we boost I.Q. and scholastic achievement? *Harvard Educational Review, 39,* 1–123.

Jensen, A. R. (1980). *Bias in mental testing.* New York: Free Press.

Jensen, A. R. (1981). *Straight talk about mental tests.* New York: Free Press.

ELAINE FLETCHER-JANZEN
Texas A&M University

CULTURAL BIAS IN TESTS
g FACTOR THEORY

J.E.V.S.

The J.E.V.S. evaluation was developed by the Jewish Employment Vocational Service in Philadelphia, Pennsylvania, during the 1960s. It takes approximately 2 weeks to evaluate the capabilities of a client in a wide range of employment skills. The initial stages of the procedures are with simple work samples that are gradually advanced to more complex skills.

The J.E.V.S. programs measure many employment variables, including information concerning a person's vocational potential. The work samples provided enable an evaluator to assess the client's potential for competitive employment and to assess functional abilities in spatial and perceptual skills and manual dexterity. The objective areas of the J.E.V.S. program provide information concerning the client's interests, behaviors, and aptitudes in work-related situations. The program is divided into two major review areas: VIEWS (Vocational Information and Evaluation Work Samples) and VITAS (Vocational Interests, Temperments and Aptitude Systems).

The J.E.V.S. programs evaluate two factors that are inherent in work-related situations: the specific and the global. Specific factors include discrimination skills, counting ability, eye-hand-foot coordination, finger dexterity, following diagrammatic instructions, following a model, motor coordination, manual dexterity, measuring ability, numerical ability, forms perception, clerical perception, spatial discrimination, size discrimination, and the use of hand tools. The four global factors are accuracy,

following oral instructions, neatness, and organizational ability.

REFERENCE

Vocational Research Institute. (1973). *Work sample evaluator's handbook.* Philadelphia: Jewish Employment and Vocational Services.

PAUL C. RICHARDSON
*Elwyn Institutes, Elwyn,
Pennsylvania*

VOCATIONAL EVALUATION

JOHNSON, DORIS (1932–   )

Doris Johnson was awarded a BA degree in speech pathology from Augustana College in 1953. She then went on to receive her MA in speech and language pathology in 1955 and her PhD in counselor education in 1971 from Northwestern University. She is currently professor and head of the Learning Disabilities Program at Northwestern University. She has trained learning disabilities specialists, and has long been involved in research at the Center for Learning Disabilities at the university. Johnson primarily has studied the relationships among oral language, reading, and writing.

Johnson and Myklebust (1967) were among those who called attention to the significance of language disorders in learning disabilities. Johnson described a specific disabilities model of learning disabilities; the model showed that there are certain abilities required for normal language development (Johnson & Myklebust, 1967). This position holds that such abilities can be measured and deficits remediated.

Johnson has received numerous honors such as the Outstanding Service Award from the Association of Children with Learning Disabilities. She became a fellow of the American Speech and Hearing Association in 1976. She is best known for two publications: *Learning Disabilities: Educational Principles and Practices* (1967) and *Dyslexia in Childhood* (1965). She is currently coediting *Adults with Learning Disabilities: Clinical Studies* (in press).

REFERENCES

Johnson, D. J. *Adults with learning disabilities* (in press) Orlando, FL: Grune & Stratton.

Johnson, D. J., & Myklebust, H. (1965). Dyslexia in childhood. In J. Hellmuth. (Ed.), *Learning disorders.* Seattle, WA: Special Child.

Johnson, D. J., & Myklebust, H. (1967). *Learning disabilities: Educational principles and practices.* New York: Grune & Stratton.

STAFF

JOHNSON, G. ORVILLE (1915–)

G. Orville Johnson was born June 23, 1915, in Cameron, Wisconsin. He attended the University of Wisconsin, Milwaukee (then Milwaukee State Teachers College), receiving his BS degree in 1938. He obtained his EdM from the University of Illinois in 1949 and his EdD in 1950 from the same institution. Between his undergraduate and graduate years, Johnson worked as a public school teacher in Sheboygan and Wawatosa, Wisconsin. He was principal of the South Wisconsin Colony and Training School in 1946–1947. He was an assistant professor at the University of Illinois from 1949 to 1951. In 1951 he went to the University of Denver, where he became associate professor of education and director of special education. On leaving Denver in 1954, Johnson served as professor at the University of Syracuse, Ohio State University, and the University of South Florida, Tampa.

Johnson is associate editor of *Exceptional Children*. His research work has focused on psychological characteristics of the mentally retarded and how classification or labeling affects them. In Johnson's view, the two basic classifications, behavioral and medical, are not mutually exclusive. For an individual with mental retardation to be described adequately and classified, he or she must be described in both medical and behavioral terms.

Some of Johnson's major works include *Educating the Retarded Child, Education of Exceptional Children and Youth,* and *Learning Performance of Retarded and Normal Children.*

REFERENCES

Johnson, G. O., & Kirk, S. A. (1951). *Educating the retarded child.* Boston: Houghton Mifflin.

Johnson, G. O., & Cruickshank, W. A. (1975). *Education of exceptional children and youth.* Englewood Cliffs, NJ: Prentice-Hall.

Johnson, G. O., & Blake, K. A. (1969). *Learning performance of retarded and normal children.* New York: Syracuse University Press.

Johnson, G. O. (1963). *Education for the slow learner.* Englewood Cliffs, NJ: Prentice-Hall.

ELIZABETH JONES
Texas A&M University

JOHNSTONE, EDWARD RANSOM (1870–1946)

Edward Ransom Johnstone began his career as a teacher and principal in the public schools of Cincinnati. He then served as a teacher in the Indiana School for Feeble Minded Youth, subsequently becoming principal there. In 1898 he moved to the Training School at Vineland, New Jersey, where he was employed as vice principal under the Reverend Stephen Olin Garrison, who had founded the school 10 years before. After Garrison's death in 1900, Johnstone was made superintendent. He became executive director in 1922, and director emeritus in 1944.

During Johnstone's years there, the Training School exerted tremendous influence on the education and training of mentally retarded children and adults, on the preparation of teachers of handicapped children, and on educational testing. Johnstone founded a research laboratory with Henry H. Goddard as director. There numerous studies were conducted using data from the school's mentally retarded population. A summer school was conducted for teachers.

Johnstone inaugurated *The Training School Bulletin,* an influential journal in special education from its inception in 1904. Johnstone served on numerous boards and commissions and was elected to two terms as president of the American Association on Mental Deficiency.

REFERENCES

McCaffrey, K. R. (1965). *Founders of the Training School at Vineland, New Jersey: S. Olin Garrison, Alexander Johnson, Edward R. Johnstone.* Unpublished doctoral dissertation. Teachers College, Columbia University, New York.

The Training School Bulletin. (1947, May), 44.

PAUL IRVINE
Katonah, New York

JOINT TECHNICAL STANDARDS FOR EDUCATIONAL AND PSYCHOLOGICAL TESTS

See STANDARDS FOR EDUCATIONAL AND PSYCHOLOGICAL TESTING.

JONES, REGINALD L. (1931–)

Reginald L. Jones graduated cum laude with a major in psychology from Morehouse College, Atlanta, Georgia, in 1952. He then received his MA in clinical psychology from Wayne State University. In 1959 he obtained his doctorate in psychology (with a minor in special education) from Ohio State University.

Jones currently is professor of Afro-American studies and education, University of California, Berkeley. He was chairman of Berkeley's department of Afro-American studies from 1975 to 1978 and 1983 to 1985. He was coordinator of the joint PhD program in special education in 1976–1977. Jones also has been professor and vice chairman, department of psychology, at Ohio State; pro-

Reginald L. Jones

fessor and chairman, department of education, University of California, Riverside; and professor and director, University Testing Center, Haile Sellassie I University (Ethiopia).

Jones has authored an extensive number of articles and reviews in special education, psychological and educational assessment, and other topics. He is especially noted for his work on special education labeling, attitudes toward handicapped persons, and the special education of minority children. He is a recipient of the J. E. Wallace Wallin Award, the Council for Exceptional Children's highest honor (1983), and of the Scholarship Award of the Association of Black Psychologists (1979).

Jones has served on the editorial board and as consultant for numerous journals on psychology and education and has been associate editor of the *American Journal of Mental Deficiency* (1975–1977) and editor of *Mental Retardation* (1979–1983). Jones's books include *Black Psychology* (1980) and *Mainstreaming and the Minority Child* (1976). Jones's current work and research are in the areas of black human development and psychological and educational assessment.

REFERENCES

Jones, R. L. (1976). *Mainstreaming and the minority child*. Reston, VA: Council for Exceptional Children.

Jones, R. L. (1980). Black psychology (2nd ed.). NY: Harper & Row.

STAFF

JORDAN LEFT-RIGHT REVERSAL TEST

The Jordan Left-Right Reversal Test (the Jordan) is a norm-referenced measure of visual reversal of letters, numbers, and words intended for use with individuals from age 5 years through adulthood. The current version, the second revision, was published by Academic Therapy Publications in 1980. The first edition was published in 1974 (Jordan, 1980). The test is untimed but typically requires about 20 minutes for administration and scoring. Two levels or forms are available, the first for ages 5 to 8 years and the second for ages 9 years and up.

The Jordan was standardized on children ages 5 through 12 years only; it should not be used outside this age range despite the author's claim for utility through adulthood. Very little data are given on the sample, far too little to allow for an adequate appraisal of its quality and representativeness, though the sample was large. Only test-retest reliability data are reported, but even this was miscalculated. Internal consistency evidence, as required by the Standards for Educational and Psychological Testing (Committee, 1984) is not reported, although ample data for such calculations were available to the author. Validity evidence is limited and the scaling of the norms is cumbersome. The Jordan is an interesting and innovative test that could have filled a gap in the assessment of children with a variety of learning disabilities. However, the psychometric ineptness apparent in the development, standardization, and investigation of the scale's validity and reliability render it useful only for an informal appraisal.

REFERENCES

Committee to Revise the Standards. (1984). *Standards for educational and psychological testing*. Washington, DC: American Psychological Association.

Jordan, B. T. (1980). *Jordan left-right reversal test*. Novato, CA: Academic Therapy.

CECIL R. REYNOLDS
Texas A&M University

JOURNAL FOR EDUCATION OF THE GIFTED (JED)

The *Journal for Education of the Gifted* (JED) is the official journal of the Association for the Gifted (TAG), a division of the Council for Exceptional Children. Members of TAG receive JEG as a benefit of membership. Founded in 1978, JEG is published quarterly.

The journal provides a forum for the analysis and communication of knowledge about the gifted and talented, and for the exchange of ideas and diverse points of view regarding the education of gifted and talented students. Articles in the journal include theoretical and position papers, descriptive research, evaluation, and experimental research. The JEG specifically solicits (1) original research with relevance to the education of the gifted and talented; (2) theoretical and position papers; (3) descriptions of innovative programming and instructional practices for the gifted and talented based on existing or on novel models of gifted education; (4) reviews of literature related to gifted education; and (5)historical reviews. All submissions are referred following a blind reviewing process. Manuscript preparation follows the American Psychological Association style manual. Beverly N. Parks of Wayne State University in Detroit is the current editor.

CECIL R. REYNOLDS
Texas A&M University

JOURNAL OF ABNORMAL CHILD PSYCHOLOGY

The *Journal of Abnormal Child Psychology* first appeared in 1973. The journal focuses on psychopathology research and theory in childhood and adolescence. It is published quarterly, with approximately 650 pages per issue. Published works include empirical investigations in assessment, etiology, treatment (within community and correctional institutions), prognosis and follow-up, pharmacological intervention, epidemiology, and research related to the ecology of pathological behavior. Studies usually focus on neuroses, organic dysfunctions, delinquency and behavioral disorders, psychosomatic conditions, and mental retardation. Experimental and correlational studies are of interest, as well as significant case studies and reports detailing ongoing projects.

MARY LEON PEERY
Texas A&M University

JOURNAL OF APPLIED BEHAVIOR ANALYSIS (JABA)

The *Journal of Applied Behavioral Analysis (JABA)* is published by the Society for the Experimental Analysis of Behavior (SEAB). Its purpose is to supply an outlet for the publication of original research on applications of the analysis of behavior.

The first issue of *JABA* appeared in 1968 under the editorship of Montrose M. Wolf of the University of Kansas. He remained editor until 1970. The most recent editor is Brian A. Iwata of Johns Hopkins University School of Medicine. The editor is appointed by the SEAB board of directors. The editorial board is then appointed by the editor. Editors typically serve 3-year terms.

JABA publishes articles on the general subject of applied behavior analysis. It has published articles on topics relating to behavior therapy and behavioral control paradigms and other subjects of interest to those dealing with special education populations.

RAND B. EVANS
Texas A&M University

JOURNAL OF AUTISM AND DEVELOPMENTAL DISORDERS

The *Journal of Autism and Developmental Disorders* was first published under the title of the *Journal of Autism and Childhood Schizophrenia*. It was born from the collaboration of Leo Kanner, regarded as the founding father of child psychiatry in the English-speaking world, and publisher V. H. Winston, the father of an autistic child. The journal was dedicated to stimulating and disseminating from diverse sources "ways to understand and alleviate the miseries of sick children." As founding editor and the discoverer of autism, Kanner convened a task force of outstanding researchers and clinicians to contribute from multidisciplinary sources. Fields such as ethology, genetics, psychotherapy, chemotherapy, behavior modification, special education, speech pathology, and neurobiology contributed. Research was conducted by investigators from the professions of medicine, psychology, neuroscience, biochemistry, physiology, and education. The unifying basis for the publication of such diverse material was the direct relevance to the understanding and remediation of autism, childhood psychoses, and related developmental disorders.

In 1974 Eric Schopler took over as editor of the journal, with Michael Rutter collaborating as European editor. Editorial policies remained the same, but there was increasing emphasis on studies demonstrating the connection between basic research and clinical application. Toward that end a "Parents Speak" column was added. It was intended to raise issues of practical concern not always accessible to current research methodologies and research issues not always clear as to their practical implications. The purpose of the column was to provide a forum for parents and researchers.

By 1979 the title of the journal was changed from the *Journal of Autism and Childhood Schizophrenia* to its current title. This change reflected primarily the growth of empirical knowledge. Initially, autism was regarded as the earliest form of childhood schizophrenia. However, increasing data suggested that autism and childhood schizophrenia were different both in onset and symptoms. Autism was usually related to early onset, before age 3, while childhood schizophrenia came with later onset and somewhat different symptoms. Moreover, the effects of development were recognized for a wide range of disorders, as was the coexistence of autism with other developmental disorders such as mental retardation. An unusual convergence of scientific knowledge and political action occurred when autism was included in the Developmental Disabilities Act of 1975. The journal's change of title and scope was intended to proclaim this infrequent marriage of science and policy.

ERIC SCHOPLER
*University of North Carolina,
Chapel Hill*

JOURNAL OF CLINICAL CHILD PSYCHOLOGY

The *Journal of Clinical Child Psychology* is published on behalf of Section 1 (Clinical Child Psychology) of Division 12 (Clinical Psychology) of the American Psychological Association. It provides a forum for reflective comment by those concerned with children and youths. The journal is problem- rather than discipline-oriented. It publishes the views of all child advocates including students, consumers of child mental health services, and individuals from nonpsychological disciplines.

Manuscripts are solicited in American Psychological Association format. Occasional issues deal with special topics related to common problems of children; they may be published as special issues devoted to a single topic. The journal is published quarterly in one volume by Lawrence Erlbaum Associates, 365 Broadway, Hillsdale, NJ 07642. It is edited by Dr. June Tuma. The editorial address is Department of Psychology, Louisiana State University, Baton Rouge LA 70803.

LAWRENCE C. HARTLAGE
Evans, Georgia

JOURNAL OF COMMUNICATION DISORDERS

The first volume of the *Journal of Communication Disorders* was published in 1967 by the North Holland Publishing Company. It is now published by the Elsevier Publishing Company. The editor is R. W. Rieber of John Jay College and Columbia University in New York. He founded the journal and has held the editorial position since the inception. There are two associate editors and approximately 39 consulting editors. The journal is a bimonthly publication and has a present circulation of 1200. It publishes approximately 600 pages a year and an average of six manuscripts an issue. Manuscripts are selected according to the referral method. The editor reads the articles, sends them to consulting editors, and then chooses the articles to be published.

The aim of the journal has remained the same from the beginning: to publish articles on "problems related to the various disorders of communication, broadly defined." Its interest include the biological foundations of communications as well as psychopathological, psychodynamic, diagnostic, and therapeutic aspects of communication disorders.

TERESA K. RICE
Texas A&M University

JOURNAL OF CONSULTING AND CLINICAL PSYCHOLOGY

The *Journal of Consulting and Clinical Psychology* was first published in 1937 by the American Psychological Association (APA) under the name *Journal of Consulting Psychology*. Its managing editor was J. P. Symonds.

Fifty-four volumes have been published as of April 1986 and the total circulation is 1200. The editor, appointed by the APA, is Alan E. Kazdin of the University of Pittsburgh School of Medicine and the Western Psychiatric Institute and Clinic. There are four associate editors and approximately 50 consulting editors appointed by the editor.

The journal publishes original contributions on such topics as the development and use of techniques of diagnosis and treatment in disordered behaviors; studies of populations of clinical interest; studies of personality and of its assessment and development related to consulting and clinical psychology; cross-cultural and demographic studies of interest for behavioral disorders; and case studies relevant to the preceding topics.

The journal considers manuscripts dealing with the diagnosis or treatment of abnormal behaviors. Manuscripts are submitted blind and reviewed by a board of consulting editors. The journal receives approximately 1000 manuscripts a year and about 18% of these are published.

TERESA K. RICE
Texas A&M University

JOURNAL OF FLUENCY DISORDERS

The *Journal of Fluency Disorders* was begun in 1972 by Anthony Zenner at the University of South Florida, Tampa. The need for such a journal had been noted for several years by leaders in the areas of fluency and fluency disorders.

The *Journal* publishes full length research and clinical papers, descriptions of new apparatus, novel applications of existing procedures, case studies, evaluations of traditional therapy and research programs, and film and book reviews. The *Journal* has 38 review editors from Europe, Asia, Australia, and North America. It is considered the international authoritative source of information in the areas of fluency and fluency disorders.

CECIL R. REYNOLDS
Texas A&M University

JOURNAL OF LEARNING DISABILITIES

The *Journal of Learning Disabilities* is a multidisciplinary publication containing articles on practice, research, and theory related to learning disabilities. It includes reports of research, opinion papers, and cases, and discussions of issues that are the concern of all disciplines engaged in the field. Book reviews and letters to the editor also are welcome. The journal is a refereed publication, with reviewers typically being editorial board members serving rotational terms. The journal has published consecutively since 1968. Ten issues are published yearly: publication is monthly (except June/July and August/September, which are combined). J. Lee Weiderholt is currently editor-in-chief. The journal is published by PRO-ED, Inc., 5341 Industrial Oaks Blvd., Austin, TX, 78735. Subscription information is available from the publisher.

ROBERTA C. STOKES
Texas A&M University

JOURNAL OF MENTAL DEFICIENCY RESEARCH

The *Journal of Mental Deficiency Research* was the result of team research into the genetic aspects of mental handicaps carried out under the leadership of Lionel Penrose at the Kennedy-Galton Centre in England during the 1950s. In 1956, Barry Richards was appointed editor and remained in the position for 25 years.

From the beginning, the *Journal* had a high number of submissions from non-Anglo-Saxon researchers and reflected a multidisciplinary theme with articles in psychology, social-psychology, and genetics. The *Journal* appears in over 40 countries and aims to increase knowledge of the causes, prevention, and treatment of mental handicaps.

STAFF
Texas A&M University

JOURNAL OF PSYCHOEDUCATIONAL ASSESSMENT

The *Journal of Psychoeducational Assessment* presents empirically based and methodologically sound research that provides implications for practicing psychologists, special educators, educational diagnosticians, academic trainers, and others with an interest in psychoeducational assessment. Published works include studies describing research or theoretical positions, assessment strategies, diagnostic procedures, the relationship between assessment and instruction, comparisons of existing instruments, and reviews of assessment strategies, techniques, and instrumentation. Unsolicited test and book reviews are also of interest. The journal focuses on issues relevant to the practitioner and his or her needs. It is published quarterly. Subscriptions may be obtained by writing to Grune & Stratton, Inc., Journal Subscription Fulfillment Department, 6277 Sea Harbor Drive, Orlando, FL 32821, (305) 345-2777.

MARY LEON PEERY
Texas A&M University

JOURNAL OF SCHOOL PSYCHOLOGY (JSP)

The *Journal of School Psychology* (JSP) is school psychology's oldest and most prestigious journal; it first appeared in 1963. Its 58 original founders and shareholders provided the capital necessary to launch JSP. In its first editorial, Smith (1963) states:

> The main purpose of the *Journal of School Psychology* is to provide an outlet for research studies and articles in professional school psychology. It is a scientifically oriented journal devoted to the publication of original research reports, reviews, and articles, with the aim of fostering the expansion of school psychology as an applied science. (p. 2)

This statement of purpose has remained largely unchanged during the last 20 years.

Various persons have been instrumental to JSP's growth and development. Three officers comprise a board of directors that represents the corporation. During the past decade, officers have included president James Eikeland, vice president Marcia Shaffer, and secretary-treasurer William Farling. Four editors helped guide JSP's growth: Donald Smith (1963–1968), Jack Bardon (1968–1971), Beeman Phillips (1972–1981), and Thomas Oakland (1981–1986). Raymond Dean took over as editor in January of 1987. An estimated 200 persons have served as editorial consultants to JSP.

Nine hundred and ten persons authored or coauthored one or more articles for JSP during its first 20 years (Oakland, 1984). Among these 910, 764 contributed one article, and 8 contributed 7 or more articles. The most prolific contributors to JSP are actively engaged in other scholarly and professional activities. Six thousand seven hundred twenty-two separate references are cited within the 709 articles. Thus, JSP has enabled numerous persons to make contributions to the science and profession of school psychology. The articles discuss a range of topics that reflect the breadth of school psychology literature and its practice.

REFERENCES

Oakland, T. (1984). The *Journal of School Psychology*'s first twenty years: Contributions and contributors. *Journal of School Psychology, 22,* 239–250.

Smith, D. (1963). Editor's comments: Genesis of a new *Journal of School Psychology. Journal of School Psychology, 1,* 1–4.

THOMAS OAKLAND
University of Texas, Austin

SCHOOL PSYCHOLOGY

JOURNAL OF SPECIAL EDUCATION

The *Journal of Special Education* is a quarterly published by PRO-ED, Inc., 5341 Industrial Oaks Blvd., Austin, TX,

78735. Lynn and Douglas Fuchs are the co-editors-in-chief.

The *Journal of Special Education* first began publishing in October 1966, at a time when modern-day special education was still in its infancy and there were few independent publications. It was early known for its willingness to serve as a forum for controversial issues, even during periods when consensus rather than discussion was preferred on many issues. A number of special issues have become classics.

The *Journal of Special Education* has chosen to be an elitist publication, holding to the highest standards of scholarship. As such, it has continued to be respected by the professional community. It assumes a broad perspective as to what constitutes special education and has encouraged the emergence of new points of view in the field.

Representing no particular professional organization or ideology of research or practice, the *Journal of Special Education* has sought to sustain a nondoctrinaire position relative to the field it serves. It is considered by many the flagship of special education publishing.

LESTER MANN
*Hunter College, City University
of New York*

JOURNAL OF SPEECH AND HEARING DISORDERS

The *Journal of Speech and Hearing Disorders* is a quarterly publication that accepts articles, reports, and letters pertaining to the nature and treatment of disordered speech, hearing, and language, and to the clinical and supervisory processes by which this treatment is provided. The journal was first published in 1936 with G. Oscar Russell serving as editor. It is now published by the American Speech, Language and Hearing Association. The editor is Laurance B. Leonard of Purdue University. Leonard, in turn, chose his editorial consultant and associate editors, which number approximately 150.

The journal receives about 200 submissions yearly; only about 60 are published, totaling an estimated 450 pages per year. The journal, now in Volume 56, has reached a total circulation of 57,000.

TERESA K. RICE
Texas A&M University

JOURNAL OF THE AMERICAN ASSOCIATION FOR THE SEVERELY HANDICAPPED

See AMERICAN ASSOCIATION FOR THE SEVERELY HANDICAPPED.

JOURNAL OF VISUAL IMPAIRMENT AND BLINDNESS

The *Journal of Visual Impairment and Blindness* is published monthly, except in July and August, by the Publications and Information Services Department of the American Foundation for the Blind. It is an interdisciplinary journal of record for practitioners and researchers professionally concerned with blind and visually impaired persons. It provides an impartial forum and seeks to draw on a wide variety of fields to further work for the visually impaired.

Each journal includes five types of signed papers: articles, short reports, comments, letters to the editor, and meeting reports. One feature, "Random Access," continually updates the impact of technology on visually impaired and blind persons. Most issues include a variety of topics addressing both practical and research issues. Occasional special issues focus on a single, relevant topic. Articles are on issues pertinent to all ages. A sampling of some of the topics covered follows: parental concerns and involvement, issues in the education of the visually impaired and blind, assessment, language development, residential schools, rehabilitation, employment, orientation and mobility, and physical fitness.

Persons from any field who are interested in and concerned about the visually impaired and blind will find this journal beneficial and informative.

ANNE CAMPBELL
Purdue University

JOURNALS IN EDUCATION OF HANDICAPPED AND SPECIAL EDUCATION

See SPECIFIC JOURNAL.

JUKES AND THE KALLIKAKS

In the late nineteenth and early twentieth centuries, Americans became increasingly concerned with overpopulation and unrestricted immigration. It was believed that the high birth rate of the mentally defective would have an adverse impact on the economy and social order. The eugenics movement promoted compulsory sterilization of people with undesirable traits as well as restricted immigration of unwanted races (Bajema, 1976). Research on human pedigrees provided scientific support for these efforts by showing that mental retardation and other undesirable traits tend to run in families over a number of generations. Many studies of family degeneracy were published, but the two most influential were based on the pedigrees of the Juke and the Kallikak families.

One of the most influential studies of family degeneration, *The Jukes*, written by Richard L. Dugdale as a report for the Prison Association of New York (Dugdale, 1895), was the first comprehensive study of the history of an entire family over a number of generations. By examining prison records, Dugdale discovered a family with a long history of arrest and dependence on charity. Dugdale traced 709 members of the Juke family, spanning seven generations, who were related by blood, marriage, and cohabitation.

Dugdale found that the Juke family had a high incidence of feeblemindedness, pauperism, prostitution, illegitimacy, and crime among its members. The family tended to marry its own members and produce large numbers of offspring. Dugdale calculated the cost of the Juke family in confinement and charity to be over $1 million (over $12 million in 1985).

The study concluded that crime and poverty are mainly the result of heredity, but that the environment does have some influence. Dugdale argued that crime and poverty are avoidable if the proper environmental conditions are met. He advocated a program of industrial education and personal hygiene, with imprisonment only as a last resort for the habitual criminal. Heredity was viewed as an innate force that impinged on individuals throughout their lives. In spite of Dugdale's emphasis on environmental interventions, his report of the Juke family was widely used in support of the argument that only heredity determines human behavior and consequently poverty and crime.

Although Dugdale claimed that his data-gathering methods were sound, the study has been severely criticized on methodological grounds (Gould, 1981). One problem is that feebleminded individuals were identified mainly on the basis of hearsay, rather than by testing or other standardized methods. In addition, it has been charged that the self-fulfilling prophecy may have biased the results, in that the researcher's strong expectations may have influenced his judgment of the cases.

A follow-up of the Juke family (Estrabrook, 1915) reported that the incidence of feeblemindedness, prostitution, pauperism, illegitimacy, and crime had continued at about the same rate as reported by Dugdale. This report argued against imprisoning people with criminally weak intellects, proposing instead that they receive permanent custodial care and sterilization. Sterilization was particularly advocated because the mentally impaired produced large numbers of offspring and put high demands on charity. It was claimed that the Juke family history demonstrated that criminal fathers would produce criminal offspring, making sterilization the only remedy.

The second most influential study of family degeneracy was Henry Goddard's 1912 book *The Kallikak Family: A Study of the Heredity of Feeble-Mindedness* (Goddard, 1912).

Goddard's work was based on the family background of a young girl with the pseudonym of Deborah Kallikak; she was a resident at the Vineland Training School for Feeble-Minded Girls and Boys in New Jersey. Deborah's family was traced back through six generations to Martin Kallikak. Martin first married a woman of good repute and founded a line of offspring that were upstanding citizens of normal intelligence. Martin Kallikak also had an illegitimate child with a barmaid, and this branch of the family produced large numbers of criminals, feebleminded, and charity cases. Goddard summarized the findings as follows:

> The Kallikak family presents a natural experiment in heredity. A young man of good family becomes through two different women the ancestor of two lines of descendants,—the one characterized by thoroughly good, respectable, normal citizenship, with almost no exceptions; the other being equally characterized by mental defect in every generation. . . . In later generations, more defect was brought in from other families through marriage. . . .
>
> We find on the good side of the family prominent people in all walks of life and nearly all of the 496 descendants owners of land or proprietors. On the bad side we find paupers, criminals, prostitutes, drunkards, and examples of all forms of social pest with which modern society is burdened (Goddard, 1912, p. 116).

It is interesting to note that Goddard interpreted the striking difference between the two lines of the Kallikak family as evidence for the strong influence of heredity, an interpretation uncritically accepted at the time. Later writers have pointed out, however, that this difference is actually stronger evidence for the importance of the environment, since the two lines of the family have a common ancestor, yet differed greatly in social standing (Smith, 1985).

Goddard's methodology has been subject to the same criticism as was Dugdale's study of the Jukes. He relied on untrained field workers to make diagnostic decisions about the mental abilities and personalities of family members, both living and dead. For example, the following report of a home visit was submitted by a research associate.

> The girl of twelve should have been at school, according to the law, but when one saw her face, one realized it made no difference. She was pretty, with olive complexion and dark languid eyes, but there was no mind there. . . . Benumbed by this display of human degeneracy, the field worker went out into the icy street (Goddard, 1912, p. 73).

There is also uncertainty over whether Goddard's original diagnosis of Deborah's feeblemindedness was correct (Smith, 1985). Smith reviewed Goddard's diagnostic evidence and concluded that using modern standards, Deborah would not be classified as mentally retarded.

Although the studies of the Jukes and the Kallikaks are seriously flawed by present-day standards, they provided all the evidence that was needed to convince the eugenicists of the time that something must be done to stem the proliferation of mental defects. Armed with these inflammatory studies, they successfully lobbied for compulsory sterilization laws in 30 states, and helped pass the Immigration Restriction Act of 1924.

REFERENCES

Bajema, C. J. (1976). *Eugenics then and now.* Stroudsburg, PA: Hutchinson & Ross.

Dugdale, R. L. (1895). *The Jukes: A study in crime, pauperism, disease, and heredity.* (5th ed.). New York: AMS.

Estrabrook, A. H. (1915). *The Jukes in 1915.* New York: Macmillan.

Goddard, H. H (1921). *The Kallikak family: A study in the heredity of feeble-mindedness.* New York: Macmillan.

Gould, S. J. (1981). *The mismeasure of man.* New York: Norton.

Smith, J. D. (1985). *Minds made feeble: The myth and legacy of the Kallikaks.* Rockville, MD: Aspen.

ROBERT C. NICHOLS
DIANE J. JARVIS
*State University of New York,
Buffalo*

EUGENICS
HEREDITY
SOCIOECONOMIC STATUS

JUVENILE ARTHRITIS

See ARTHRITIS, JUVENILE.

JUVENILE CEREBROMACULAR DEGENERATION

Juvenile cerebromacular degeneration is a progressive disorder transmitted on an autosomal recessive basis. If the onset occurs between the ages of 1 and 3 years, it may be known as infantile cerebromacular degeneration or Bielschowsky syndrome. The juvenile variety occurs at 5 to 7 years of age and may also be known as Spielmeyer-Vogt disease. Both types involve a degenerative process of the gray matter of the brain and are generally classified with the lipid storage diseases, the most common of which is Tay-Sachs or amaurotic familial idiocy (Behrman & Vaughan, 1983).

Onset usually begins with visual disturbances because of degenerative changes in the retina. These range from retinitis pigmentosa to generalized retinal atrophy resulting in blindness, despite the fact that the pupils may remain reactive to light. The visual disturbances are fol-

lowed by a progressive degeneration of cortical gray matter, which may be detected by EEG exam long before observable behavioral changes are seen. The child may develop seizures, become hyperactive, and show a severe pattern of cognitive and motor degeneration. Speech is lost as are most other motor functions. The later the onset of the disease, the slower it progresses. Some have survived into adolescence but there remains no cure for the disorder (Behrman & Vaughan, 1983). Treatment consists only of symptom alleviation and supportive care. Many eventually require feeding through gastrostomy tube (Kolodny, 1979).

A blood test can detect carriers of the disease: it is strongly recommended for all those of Ashkenazic Jewish background where heterogenous carriers have been identified at the rate of about 1:30 (Bennett, 1981).

REFERENCES

Behrman, R., & Vaughan, V. (1983). *Nelson textbook of pediatrics* (12th ed.). Philadelphia: Saunders.

Bennett, J. (1981). *Diseases, the nurse's reference library series* Horsham, Pennsylvania: Informed Communications Book Division.

Goodman, A., & Motulsky, R. (Eds.). (1979). *Genetic disorders of Ashkenazi Jews.* New York: Raven.

Kolodny, E. H. (1979). Tay-Sachs disease. In A. Goodman & R. Motulsky (Eds.), *Genetic disorders of Ashkenazi Jews.* New York: Raven.

JOHN E. PORCELLA
*Rhinebeck Country School,
Rhinebeck, New York*

TAY-SACHS SYNDROME

JUVENILE COURT SYSTEM AND THE HANDICAPPED

The number of delinquents with handicapping conditions being disposed of by the juvenile courts is not known since this datum currently is not recorded by any U.S. governmental office. In a recent study, Nelson, Rutherford, and Wolford (1985) reported that the prevalence of handicapping conditions among incarcerated youth is approximately two times that expected in a hypothetical average school. The implication of this study is that a higher number of juveniles with handicapping conditions are being disposed of by the courts.

The juvenile courts are organized in various manners within the different states. Whatever their organizational structure, they process juvenile cases under a separate system that is based on concepts of nonculpability and rehabilitation (U.S. Department of Justice, 1983). In 1899, Illinois established the first juvenile court based on the concept that a juvenile is worth saving and is in need of treatment rather than punishment, and that the juvenile court had a mission to protect the juvenile from the stigma of criminal proceedings.

Juvenile courts differ from criminal courts in that the language used in juvenile courts is less harsh. A juvenile court accepts "petitions of delinquency" rather than criminal complaints; conducts "hearings," not trials; adjudicates "juveniles to be delinquent" rather than guilty of a crime; and orders one of a number of available dispositions rather than sentences (U.S. Department of Justice, 1983).

The number of juveniles under the age of 21 who were processed through the juvenile courts during 1980 was 1,345,200. There were approximately three times more male than female cases being disposed of by the courts (U.S. Department of Justice, 1983). In 1977, 83% of the under-18-year-old population was held in detention facilities prior to court disposition (including 122,503 in jails and 507,951 in other juvenile detention facilities) as suspected delinquent or status offenders (U.S. Department of Justice, 1980).

Once referred to a juvenile court, a juvenile may be located at an intake facility or a detention facility that is either secured (similar to a jail facility) or nonsecured. During the judicial process, a juvenile may experience several of the following hearings: the detention hearing; the preliminary hearing; the fitness hearing (to certify as an adult or juvenile); the hearing of motions filed; the adjudication hearing (a hearing of fact); or the disposition hearing (placement, release, and probation) (U.S. Department of Justice, 1980).

A study by the U.S. Department of Justice (1980) to determine the relationship between juvenile delinquency and learning disabilities found that learning-disabled youths are disproportionately referred to the juvenile justice system and that the juvenile courts need to use procedures for identifying and referring learning-disabled youths for remediation. These findings suggest that the juvenile court could expand its available range of dispositional alternatives by incorporating the use of special education program options.

Few studies have attempted to determine the current relationship between the juvenile court and special education. Karcz (1984) found that youths in a juvenile court secure detention facility in Lake County, Illinois, who were suspected of having handicapping conditions, or who had handicaps, were provided with screening for handicapping conditions, referral for diagnosis, an interim special education program at the detention facility, guarantees of due process procedures, and transition services through a new special education-related service position known as the Youth Advocate Liaison (YAL). As a result of these efforts, the YAL program increased the likelihood that the average detainee with handicapping conditions would attend school in the home school district.

Other model special education programs that could support the juvenile courts' deliberations during the various hearings previously listed were not to be found. Intake officers, administrators of probation services, juvenile court judges, and probation officers have not been apprised of the relevance of PL 94-142 (the Education for All the Handicapped Children Act of 1975), nor is there any evidence that they are using the provisions of this act.

REFERENCES

Brown, E. J., Flanagan, T. J., & McLeod, M. (Eds.). (1983). *Sourcebook of criminal justice statistics, 1983* (pp. 478–479, U.S. Department of Justice, Bureau of Justice, Bureau of Justice Statistics). Washington, DC: U.S. Government Printing Office.

Karcz, S. A. (1984). *The impact of a special education related service on selected behaviors of detained handicapped youth* (pp. 7–8). Unpublished doctoral dissertation, University of Syracuse, New York.

Karcz, S. A., Paulson, D. R., & Mayes, W. T. (1985, Oct.). Abrupt transitions for youth leaving school: Models of interagency cooperation. *Techniques, 1*(6), 497–499.

Nelson, C. M., Rutherford, R. B., & Wolford, B. J. (1985). *Juvenile and adult correctional special education data* (Corrections 1/Special Education Training [C/SET] Project). Washington, DC: U.S. Department of Education.

U.S. Department of Justice. (1980). *Juvenile justice: Before and after the onset of delinquency* (pp. 19, 22, 18). Washington, DC: U.S. Government Printing Office.

U.S. Department of Justice. (1983). *Report to the nation on crime and justice: The data* (pp. 60, 64, 69, National Criminal Justice Reference Series, NCJ-87060). Rockville, MD: Bureau of Justice Statistics.

STAN A. KARCZ
University of Wisconsin, Stout

CONDUCT DISORDER
JUVENILE DELINQUENCY

JUVENILE DELINQUENCY

Prior to the enactment of the federal Juvenile Delinquency Act in 1938, juvenile offenders violating the laws of the United States were subject to prosecution in the same manner as adults. Since the act, juvenile delinquents have been treated procedurally as juveniles even though juvenile delinquency is defined as the violation of the law of the United States committed by a person prior to his eighteenth birthday that would have been a crime if committed by an adult (Karcz, 1984). Official delinquency refers to those encounters with the law where the juvenile custody (called an arrest for adults) is entered into the recordbooks. Any act that could place the juvenile who committed it in jeopardy of adjudication if it were to be detected is delinquent behavior (Hopkins, 1983).

Broadly speaking, there are two categories of youngsters committing a delinquent offense: status offenders and juvenile offenders. Status offenses are those subject to legal action only if committed by a juvenile. Examples of status offenses are truancy, incorrigibility, smoking, drinking, and being beyond the control of the parent or guardian (Hopkins, 1983). An adult committing the same offense would not be charged with violation of the law. The category status offender includes the following: minors in need of supervision (MINS), dependent minors, and neglected and abused minors. The Juvenile Justice and Delinquency Act of 1974 requires that status offenders be removed from juvenile detention experiences and from correctional institutions.

A major difference between juvenile offenders and adult offenders is the importance that the juvenile places on gang membership and the tendency of the juvenile to engage in group criminal activity. Violent juvenile offenders, however, have similar characteristics to those of adult felons. Juvenile offenders and adult felons are predominately male, disproportionately black and Hispanic as compared with their proportion in the population, typically disadvantaged, likely to exhibit interpersonal difficulties and behavioral problems both in school and on the job, and likely to come from one-parent families with a high degree of conflict, instability, and inadequate supervision (U.S. Department of Justice, 1983).

In 1981 juveniles under 18 years of age committed 18.5% (or 73,506) of all the violent offenses committed in the United States. Violent offenses include murder, negligent manslaughter, forcible rape, robbery, and aggravated assault. Juveniles under 18 committed 37% (or 567,923) of all property crimes. Property crimes include burglary, larceny-theft, motor vehicle theft, and arson (U.S. Department of Justice, 1983).

The U.S. Department of Justice and Delinquency Prevention Office (1977) found that juvenile delinquents are typically males who limited or lowered their educational goals to high school—or whose mothers did—and who showed much higher delinquency rates than those whose aspirations/expectations were college oriented; or blacks from a large family with poor father-son interaction and from a low-quality neighborhood. Ng (1980) supports the position that poor family relationships, undesirable peer associations, poor choice of free time activities, and inadequate moral development are the preconditions of juvenile delinquency. Undesirable peer associations is also an immediate factor contributing to juvenile delinquency. Glueck and Glueck (1968) found that juvenile delinquents come from families characterized by greater family disorganization, greater alcoholism, more criminality, more separations, more divorces, less supervision of children,

and fewer home rules such as those relating to meals and bedtime. The Gluecks also found that more delinquents are struck down by motor vehicles than nondelinquents, 14% compared with 5%. Perhaps most strikingly, however, they found that 98% of the juvenile delinquents reported having friends who are delinquents compared with only 7% of the nondelinquents.

Despite the number of reported offenses, Empey and Erickson (1966) state that 90% of delinquent acts go undetected and never enter into the official records. Age, however, plays an important role in facilitating a decrease in delinquent behavior. Hopkins (1983) states that boys who were official delinquents showed a decline in criminal behavior into adulthood. This decrease in delinquent behavior implies that some form of "learning" has taken place for the maturing delinquent. This suggests that society should ascertain the nature of this learning activity and use such knowledge with the predelinquent.

REFERENCES

Empey, L. T., & Erickson, M. L. (1966). Hidden delinquency and social status. *Social Forces, 44,* 546–554.

Glueck, S., & Glueck, E. (1968). *Delinquents and nondelinquents in perspective.* Cambridge, MA: Harvard University Press.

Hopkins, J. R. (1983). Adolescence: The transitional years (pp. 327, 329, 339). NY: Academic.

Karcz, S. A. (1984, Aug.). *The impact of a special education related service on selected behaviors of detained handicapped youth* (pp. 31, 32) (dissertation). Syracuse, NY: Syracuse University.

Ng, A. M. (1980). Family relationships and delinquent behavior. Doctoral Dissertation, Columbia University, New York.

U.S. Department of Justice. (1983, Oct.). *Report to the nation on crime and justice: The data* (p. 33). National Criminal Justice Reference Service, Box 6000, Rockville, MD 20850.

U.S. Department of Justice, Bureau of Justice Statistics (1984). In E. J. Brown, T. J. Flanagan, & M. McLeod (Eds.), *Sourcebook of criminal justice statistics—1983* (pp. 421, 424, 425, 428, 429). Washington, DC: U.S. Government Printing Office.

U.S. Juvenile Justice and Delinquency Prevention Office. (1977). *City life and delinquency: Victimization, fear of crime and gang membership* (p. 61). Washington, DC: U.S. Government Printing Office.

STAN A. KARCZ
University of Wisconsin, Stout

CONDUCT DISORDER
DISADVANTAGED CHILD
DISCIPLINE
JUVENILE COURT SYSTEM AND THE HANDICAPPED

K

KAISER-PERMANENTE DIET

The Kaiser-Permanente diet, frequently referred to as the Feingold diet, was proposed by Feingold (1975) for the management of learning and behavioral disorders in children. Feingold's diet essentially eliminates the chemical additives that are frequently added to foods to enhance their longevity. Rooted in the basic premise of the Kaiser-Permanente diet is the assumption that children with hyperactivity, or other learning and behavioral disorders, have a natural toxic reaction to these artificial additives. Specifically, the diet forbids artificial colors and flavorings and foods containing natural salicylates including a number of nutritious fruits and vegetables.

Despite the vogue of the Kaiser-Permanente diet in many households across the country, Feingold's (1976) claim that the diet would ameliorate behavioral and learning disturbances has received scant support in the research literature (Kavale & Forness, 1983). Although Conners (1980) has indicated that a small percentage of hyperactive children do respond to some type of dietary intervention, it still remains unclear whether the improvement is actually a function of the diet itself or the regimen associated with the diet. Nonetheless, despite the dubious validity of Feingold's (1975, 1976) claims, many parents are loyal followers of Feingold's diet and have formed a national association to laud its efficacy and warn the public about the harmful effects of food additives for children.

REFERENCES

Conners, C. K. (1980). *Food additives and hyperactive children.* New York: Plenum.

Feingold, B. F. (1975). *Why your child is hyperactive.* New York: Random House.

Feingold, B. F. (1976). Hyperkinesis and learning disabilities linked to the ingestion of artificial food colors and flavors. *Journal of Learning Disabilities, 9*(9), 551–559.

Kavale, K. A., & Forness, S. R. (1983). Hyperactivity and diet treatment: A meta-analysis of the Feingold hypothesis. *Journal of Learning Disabilities, 16*(6), 324–330.

author block
EMILY G. SUTTER
*University of Houston, Clear
    Lake*

RONALD T. BROWN
*Emory University School
    of Medicine*

ADDITIVE-FREE DIETS
FEINGOLD DIET
HYPERACTIVITY
IMPULSE CONTROL

KANNER, LEO (1894–1981)

Leo Kanner, "the father of child psychiatry," was the founder of the Johns Hopkins Children's Psychiatric Clinic and the author of the widely used textbook *Child Psychiatry.* Born in Austria, he came to the United States in 1924 and was naturalized in 1930.

Associated with Johns Hopkins University from 1928 until his death, Kanner was the first to describe infantile autism, which he characterized as the innate inability of certain children to relate to other people. A prolific author who once hoped to be a poet, Kanner published more than 250 articles and books on psychiatry, psychology, pediatrics, and the history of medicine.

REFERENCES

Kanner, L. (1964). *A history of the care and study of the mentally retarded.* Springfield, IL: Thomas.

Kanner, L. (1979). *Child psychiatry* (4th ed.). Springfield, IL: Thomas.

PAUL IRVINE
Katonah, New York

KARNES, MERLE B. (1916–   )

Merle Karnes received her BS (1937) at Southeast Missouri State Teachers College and her MS (1941) and EdD (1948) at the University of Missouri in elementary education. She also has pursued postdoctoral work in special education, handicapped and gifted, at the University of Illinois. Throughout her career, Karnes has been particularly interested in atypical children, both gifted and

Merle B. Karnes

REFERENCES

Karnes, M. B. (Ed.). (1983). *The underserved: Our young gifted children.* Reston, VA: Council for Exceptional Children.

Karnes, M. B., Shwedel, A. M., & Kemp, P. B. (1985, April). Maximizing the potential of the young gifted child. *Roeper Review, 7*(4), 204–209.

Karnes, M. B., Shwedel, A. M., & Lewis, G. F. (1983). Long-term effects of early childhood programming for the gifted/talented handicapped. *Journal for the Education of the Gifted, 6*(4), 266–278.

Karnes, M. B., Shwedel, A. M., & Linnemeyer, S. A. (1982). The young gifted/talented child: Programs at the University of Illinois. *Elementary School Journal, 82*(3), 195–213.

ANN E. LUPKOWSKI
Texas A&M University

handicapped. Currently, she is a professor of education at the University of Illinois, Urbana-Champaign, where she coordinates a graduate training program in gifted education and directs research projects with gifted and handicapped children.

Karnes is known especially for her work with gifted preschool children (Karnes, Shwedel, & Kemp, 1985; Karnes, Shwedel, & Linnemeyer, 1982): those from low-income homes, the gifted/talented handicapped, and those who are nonhandicapped from more affluent homes. She and her staff have developed an effective model for young gifted/talented children; it is known as RAPYHT (Retrieval and Acceleration of Promising Young Handicapped and Talented; Karnes, Shwedel, & Lewis, 1983). Its development and dissemination have been funded since 1975 by the Office of Special Programs, and it is being replicated in over 20 states. In addition, Karnes edited the book *The Underserved: Our Young Gifted Children* (1983), which is one of the few books available on gifted preschool children. She has devoted more than 20 years to developing and disseminating models for the education of young children from low-income homes and for handicapped children.

Karnes is active in many national organizations; she served as president of the National Council of Administrators of Special Education and of the Division of Early Childhood of the Council for Exceptional Children. She is currently the editor of the *Journal of the Division for Early Childhood.* In 1973 Karnes received the J.E. Wallin Award from the Council for Exceptional Children for her outstanding contributions to exceptional children. At the 1986 National Convention of the Council for Exceptional Children, held in New Orleans, she received an award from the Division of Early Childhood for her outstanding contributions to young exceptional children. Among the many other honors bestowed on her, she has received two honorary doctorates.

KARYOTYPE

Karyotype is the chromosome set or constitution of an individual. Each species has a characteristic karyotype, not only with respect to chromosome number and morphology, but also with respect to the genes on each chromosome. Chromosomes are typically visualized in peripheral lymphocytes that have been placed in tissue culture, stimulated to divide, arrested in metaphase, and osmotically swelled. When prepared for analysis, the chromosomes of a human metaphase cell appear under the microscope as a chromosome spread. To analyze such a spread, the chromosomes are cut out from a photomicrograph and arranged in pairs in a standard classification. This process is called karyotyping.

Standardization of Karyotype nomenclature has been accomplished through a series of conferences sponsored by the National Foundation-March of Dimes. The medical applications of chromosomal analysis include clinical diagnosis, linkage and mapping, polymorphism, study of malignancy, role in reproductive problems, and prenatal diagnosis. Since the advent of karyotyping and definition of the normal number of chromosomes in 1956, large numbers of chromosomal anomalies have been described. Down's syndrome or trisomy 21 is the most common chromosomal abnormality associated with karyotyping. Sources for more in depth reading are cited below.

REFERENCES

King, R. C., & Stansfield, W. D. (1985). *A dictionary of genetics* (3rd ed.). New York: Oxford University Press.

Nora, J. J., & Fraser, F. C. (1981). *Medical genetics: Principles and practice* (2nd ed.). Philadelphia: Lea & Febiger.

Thaddeus, K. E. (1980). *Clinical genetics and genetic counseling.* Chicago: Year Book Medical.

Thompson, J. S., & Thompson, M. W. (1980). *Genetics in medicine* (3rd ed.). Philadelphia: Saunders.

KENNETH A. ZYCH
*Walter Reed Army Medical
Center, Washington, D.C.*

CHROMOSOMAL ABNORMALITIES
DOWN'S SYNDROME
GENETIC COUNSELING

Alan S. Kaufman

KAUFMAN, ALAN S. (1944–   )

Alan S. Kaufman received his BA in natural science in 1965 from the University of Pennsylvania, his MA in educational psychology in 1967 from Columbia University, and his PhD, with a major in psychology and a minor in measurement, research, and evaluation in 1970, also from Columbia University. His major field of interest is in educational psychology, with emphasis on intelligence, its measurement, and psychometrics.

Kaufman has published over 40 articles on assessment in professional journals in the fields of school psychology, special education, clinical psychology, and educational psychology. Over 10 of these studies deal with the Wechsler Intelligence Scale for Children—Revised, an intelligence scale for children. These studies focus principally on the application of psychometric techniques to the clinical analysis of profiles. Kaufman's principal publications include *Intelligent Testing with the WISC-R* (Kaufman, 1979) and *Clinical Evaluation of Young Children with the McCarthy Scales* (Kaufman & Kaufman, 1977). His volume on the WISC-R is one of the most widely cited works in school psychology and is the standard text on this topic in the field. Kaufman was well equipped to author these volumes. From 1968 until 1974 he was employed in several positions at The Psychological Corporation, where he was project director for development of the WISC-R and for the McCarthy scales. Involved in other projects as well, Kaufman's influence on assessment in special education has been extensive over the last two decades.

Recently, Kaufman has become widely known in the field of special education as a test author himself. With his wife and scholarly colleague Nadeen Kaufman, he published, in 1983, the Kaufman Assessment Battery for Children (K-ABC), an intelligence battery for children aged $2\frac{1}{2}$ to $12\frac{1}{2}$ years. The K-ABC successfully challenged established views of intelligence and became a diagnostic tool based on underlying neuropsychological processes in cognition. The K-ABC was followed by the Kaufman Test of Educational Achievement (K-TEA; Kaufman & Kaufman, 1985), a battery for most achievement areas, such as reading comprehension and mathematics. An adult version of the K–ABC may prove revolutionary in the assessment of adult intelligence.

Kaufman's relatively short career has contributed to the field of special education in a pervasive and practical way. He has provided diagnostic and evaluative guidance to the practitioners who identify and teach exceptional children, and remains on the cutting edge of progress in assessment.

A student of Robert L. Thorndike, author of the Stanford-Binet Intelligence Scale, Fourth Revision, Kaufman has continued a tradition of psychometric excellence in his work while finding appropriate means of melding psychometrics with the clinical acumen of the trained examiner. His philosophy of "intelligent testing" has been widely adopted in test interpretation at all levels. Kaufman also is well known as a mentor in school psychology; his former students include Patti L. Harrison, Cecil R. Reynolds, Randy W. Kamphaus, Jack Naglieri, Bruce Bracken, Kathleen Paget, and Steve McCallum, among other notables. Kaufman is presently a professor of educational psychology at the University of Alabama.

REFERENCES

Kaufman, A. S. (1979). *Intelligent testing with the WISC-R*. New York: Wiley-Interscience.

Kaufman, A. S., & Kaufman, N. L. (1977). *Clinical evaluation of young children with the McCarthy scales*. New York: Grune & Stratton.

Kaufman, A. S., & Kaufman, N. L. (1983). *Kaufman Assessment Battery for Children*. Circle Pines, MN: American Guidance Service.

Kaufman, A. S., & Kaufman, N. L. (1985). *Kaufman Test of Edu-*

cational Achievement. Circle Pines, MN: American Guidance Service.

CECIL R. REYNOLDS
Texas A&M University

INTELLIGENT TESTING
KAUFMAN, NADEEN L.
KAUFMAN ASSESSMENT BATTERY FOR CHILDREN
KAUFMAN TEST OF EDUCATIONAL ACHIEVEMENT
WECHSLER INTELLIGENCE SCALE FOR CHILDREN-REVISED

Nadeen L. Kaufman

KAUFMAN, NADEEN L. (1945–   )

Born Nadeen Bengals in New York City, Nadeen Kaufman received her BA in education from Hofstra University in 1965. She then taught an elementary grade class of learning-disabled children prior to returning to higher education to pursue graduate training at Columbia University. Kaufman earned her MA in educational psychology from Columbia in 1972, followed by an EdM in learning and reading disabilities in 1975. She earned her EdD from Columbia in the field of special education (specializing in neuroscience applications) in 1978. During the period 1972 to 1978, Kaufman worked as a research consultant to the College Entrance Examination Board (1970–1972), as a field supervisor for The Psychological Corporation in the development of the Wechsler Intelligence Scale for Children-Revised (WISCOR; 1970–1972), and as staff psychologist at the Rutland Center for Severely Emotionally Disturbed Children (1975–1977). During 1978 and 1979, Kaufman was an assistant professor of early childhood education at the University of Georgia. She also has held faculty positions at DePaul University, the National College of Education, and the California School of Professional Psychology, San Diego, where she also served as director of the Psychoeducational Clinic. Kaufman is now on the faculty of the University of Alabama, where she teaches in the school psychology program.

Kaufman has made a variety of significant contributions to special education and to school psychology. In addition to numerous articles in refereed journals, mostly dealing with assessment of the handicapped and general test use, Kaufman is coauthor of several major works in the field. With Alan S. Kaufman, she coauthored *Clinical Evaluation of Young Children with the McCarthy Scales* (1979) and prepared the case studies for A. S. Kaufman's *Intelligent Testing with the WISC-R.*

In 1983 Kaufman published, again with A. S. Kaufman, the Kaufman Assessment Battery for Children (K-ABC). With Goldsmith and Kaufman, she coauthored the K-SOS, the *Kaufman-Sequential or Simultaneous,* a volume that provides guidelines and insights into the development of individualized educational programs for children. She is also coauthor of the 1985 Kaufman Test of Educational Achievement (K-TEA) and is now working on the development of the Kaufman Adult Intelligence Test.

Kaufman has a variety of honorary listings, including *The World's Who's Who of Women* and *Who's Who in Frontier Science and Technology.* She is a fellow of the Division of School Psychology of the American Psychological Association.

REFERENCES

Kaufman, A. S. (1979). *Intelligence testing with the WISC-R.* New York: Wiley-Interscience.

Kaufman, A. S., & Kaufman, N. L. (1979). *Clinical evaluation of young children with the McCarthy scales.* New York: Grune & Stratton.

Kaufman, A. S., & Kaufman, N. L. (1983). *Kaufman assessment battery for children.* Circle Pine, MN: American Guidance Service.

Kaufman, A. S., & Kaufman, N. L. (1985). *Kaufman test of educational achievement.* Circle Pines, MN: American Guidance Service.

Kaufman, A. S., Kaufman, N. L., & Goldsmith, B. Z. (1984). *K-SOS: Kaufman sequential or simultaneous.* Circle Pines, MN: American Guidance Service.

CECIL R. REYNOLDS
Texas A&M University

KAUFMAN, ALAN S.
KAUFMAN ASSESSMENT BATTERY FOR CHILDREN
KAUFMAN TEST OF EDUCATIONAL ACHIEVEMENT

KAUFFMAN, JAMES M. (1940–   )

James M. Kauffman received his BS degree in elementary education from Goshen College in 1962, his MEd from

James M. Kauffman

Washburn University in Topeka in 1966, and his EdD in special education from the University of Kansas.

He was a founding member of the International Academy for Research in Learning Disabilities. He served as president of the Society for Learning Disabilities and Remedial Education (1980–1981) and is presently senior editor of *Remedial and Special Education*. He is currently professor of special education at the University of Virginia.

Kauffman has authored or coauthored more than 100 journal articles, book chapters, and books on topics relating to special education and psychology. His major interests have been in the definition of and programming for emotionally disturbed and learning-disabled children. He and his colleague, D. P. Hallahan, have been proponents of noncategorical programming for the mildly handicapped. They have collaborated in research on attentional and strategy problems of handicapped children and together authored *Exceptional Children: Introduction to Special Education* (1978). Recently Kauffman's writing has dealt with problems in identification of emotionally disturbed (behaviorally disordered) children and the limits of educability. His most recent work involves training for teachers that makes use of computer simulations of pupils with behavior problems.

REFERENCE

Hallahan, D. P., & Kauffman, J. M. (1978). *Exceptional children: Introduction to special education.* Englewood Cliffs, NJ: Prentice-Hall.

RICK GONZALES
Texas A&M University

KAUFMAN ASSESSMENT BATTERY FOR CHILDREN (K-ABC)

The Kaufman Assessment Battery for Children (K-ABC; Kaufman & Kaufman, 1983) is a measure of the intelligence and achievement of 2½ to 12½ year olds. Haddad and Naglieri (1984) suggested that the K-ABC differs from traditional IQ tests in several ways: (1) it is built from psychological theory with empirical support for its construction. (2) it measures intelligence apart from achievement; (3) it was designed so that the child is allowed ample opportunity to learn how to solve the tasks presented; and (4) it was designed to measure ability (intelligence) on the basis of the processing style required to solve tasks.

The intelligence portion of the K-ABC rests on a convergence of several cognitive and neuropsychological theories. These theories take the perspective that intelligence is comprised of two processes: one that is sequential, analytic, and temporal, and the other, which is holistic, gestalt, and spatial. The authors of the K-ABC identify these two cognitive processes as sequential and simultaneous. The Sequential Processing and Simultaneous Processing scales represent two types of mental functioning that have been identified independently by Luria and his followers, by cerebral specialization researchers, and by cognitive psychologists such as Neisser.

In the Sequential Processing Scale, each task presents a problem that must be solved by arranging the input in sequential or serial order, and in which each idea is linearly or temporally related to the preceding one. The unifying process in this scale is the sequential handling of the stimuli, regardless of content. A Word Order subtest requires the child to point to a series of pictures in the same sequence as the examiner named them; for harder items, the child performs a color interference task before responding (Kaufman & Kaufman, 1983).

The Simultaneous Processing Scale includes problems that are spatial, analogic, and organizational in nature, and that require the input to be integrated and synthesized simultaneously to produce the appropriate solution. This scale is illustrated by the Face Recognition subtest, which involves selecting from a group photograph the one or two faces that were exposed briefly on the preceding page; and by the Gestalt Closure subtest, which requires the child to name an object or scene pictured in a partially completed inkblot drawing (Kaufman & Kaufman, 1983).

The Mental Processing Composite is a unification of the Sequential and Simultaneous Processing Scales and is intended as the measure of total or global intelligence in the assessment battery. The K-ABC intelligence scales avoid measurement of acquired facts and school-related skills in favor of problem-solving tasks that tap more fluid abilities or processes (Kaufman & Kaufman, 1983).

The Achievement Scale assesses factual knowledge and skills usually acquired in a school setting or through alertness to one's environment. This scale includes tasks similar to those in conventional IQ tests (tests of vocabulary, language concepts), traditional achievement tests (reading), or both (general information, arithmetic). For example, the Faces and Places subtest involves naming the well-known person, fictional character, or place pictured

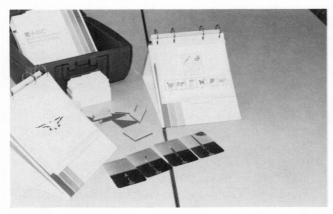

Sample testing materials from the Kaufman Assessment Battery for Children (K-ABC)

in a photograph or drawing. The Riddles subtest requires the child to infer the name of a concrete or abstract concept when given a list of its characteristics (Kaufman & Kaufman, 1983).

The K-ABC provides the teacher and the school psychologist with information about the child's current levels of simultaneous and sequential skills (see figure). This information helps the teacher judge whether the child functions better when instructed in a step-by-step manner or when encouraged to see the entire product before beginning a task. Through the knowledge of these styles, the learning process may be facilitated through direct educational intervention that is geared to capitalize on the child's strong points.

The K-ABC includes a Nonverbal Scale that is composed of selected subtests. This scale, according to the authors, serves as a good estimate of intellectual potential for children in the 4- to 12½-year range who are hearing impaired, who have a receptive or expressive language disorder, or who use English as a second language. All subtests in the K-ABC Nonverbal Scale may be administered in pantomime and are responded to motorically.

The K-ABC uses standard scores with a mean set at 100 and a standard deviation set at 15 in order to permit "direct comparisons of intelligence and achievement for children suspected of learning disabilities and to allow meaningful interpretation of the K-ABC standard score in the context of IQs and standard scores obtained on other major individual tests of intelligence and achievement" (Kaufman & Kaufman, 1983, p. 206).

It is suggested by Vance and Kutsick (1983) that the K-ABC is a more sensitive assessment instrument for minority groups since its standardization is based on 1980 Census data. It includes representative populations of blacks, Hispanics, Native Americans, and Asians in the 2000 American children on which it was standardized. In addition to the stratification variables listed, educational placement was also included to ensure that the sample

would contain proportional representation of exceptional children, e.g., learning disabled, mentally retarded, speech and language delayed, and gifted and talented (Narrett, 1984).

The *K-ABC Interpretive Manual* (Kaufman & Kaufman, 1983) indicates a black-white difference on the Mental Processing Composite of approximately 7 points. A Hispanic-white difference of about 3 points is also reported. Both differences are smaller than those typically reported for IQ tests.

REFERENCES

Haddad, F. A., & Naglieri, J. A. (1984). The Kaufman Assessment Battery for Children: An alternative approach. *Directive Teacher, 6*(1), 12–13.

Kaufman, A. S. (1983). Some questions and answers about the Kaufman Assessment Battery for Children (K-ABC). *Journal of Psychoeducational Assessment, 1,* 205–218.

Kaufman, A. S., & Kaufman, N. L. (1983). *K-ABC Interpretive Manual.* Circle Pines, MN: American Guidance Service.

Narrett, C. M. (1984). Test review: Kaufman Assessment Battery for Children (K-ABC). *Reading Teacher, 37,* 626–631.

Vance, B., & Kutsick, K. (1983). Diagnosing learning disabilities with the K-ABC. *Academic Therapy, 19*(1), 102–112.

ALAN S. KAUFMAN
ANNA H. AVANT
University of Alabama

ASSESSMENT
INTELLIGENCE
INTELLIGENCE QUOTIENT
INTELLIGENCE TESTING
MEASUREMENT

KAUFMAN TEST OF EDUCATIONAL ACHIEVEMENT

Authored by Alan S. and Nadeen L. Kaufman (1985), the Kaufman Test of Educational Achievement is available in two versions, a brief form that delivers global scores for reading, spelling, and mathematics; and a comprehensive form that provides scores in the more specific areas of reading decoding, reading comprehension, spelling, mathematics applications, and mathematics computation. Both tests yield composite scores as well, all scaled to the familiar IQ metric of mean = 100 and standard deviation = 15.

Both versions of the K-TEA are normed for ages 6–0 to 18–11 and both have grade norms ranging from 1.0 through the end of grade 12. Grade norms are available for fall and spring testing.

Average testing time for the comprehensive form is only 20 to 30 minutes in first grade, but it gradually increases to a full hour at grade 12. The brief form takes about 30 minutes or less at every grade.

The K-TEA was standardized on more than 3000 children from 16 states in a stratified sampling, with stratification by grade, sex, geographic region of residence, parent educational level, and ethnicity based on 1980 Bureau of the Census data. The resulting samples closely mimic the U.S. Census statistics. The K-TEA appears to be one of the best, most carefully standardized individual tests of achievement available.

The reliability of the comprehensive form is remarkable. Of the more than 100 internal consistency reliability coefficients reported (by age and subtest) in the test manual, only six are below .90. Most are .95 or higher and the reliability of the composite score is never less than .97. Reliability of the brief form is also excellent. The validity evidence, particularly that regarding content validity, is more extensive than what has been presented in any individual achievement test manual to date.

The coverage of the comprehensive form in reading, math, and spelling is good and gives a detailed view of the child's skills. However, such areas as writing, listening, and language arts are not included and there continues to be a serious need for standardized, objective measures of all academic areas noted in PL 94-142.

A useful interpretive scheme is presented in the K-TEA manual; it incorporates the Kaufmans' "intelligent testing" philosophy, giving examiners the proper statistical/psychometric bases for score interpretation but blending them carefully with observation of the child while he or she is performing. An entire chapter is devoted to clinical analysis of children's errors. The Kaufmans have set a new standard for achievement test manuals with the amount and quality of information in the *K-TEA Comprensive Form Manual*.

REFERENCE

Kaufman, A. S., & Kaufman, N. L. (1985). *Kaufman Test of Educational Achievement*. Circle Pines, MN: American Guidance Service.

CECIL R. REYNOLDS
Texas A&M University

KELLER, HELEN A. (1880–1957)

Helen Adams Keller, blind, deaf, and mute from the age of 18 months, became one of the world's best known examples of victory over a severe handicap. Under the direction of a dedicated and talented teacher and companion, Anne Sullivan Macy, Keller was not only educated; she also became a successful writer, lecturer, and advocate for the handicapped. She graduated cum laude from Radcliff

College in 1904 and began a long career on behalf of the handicapped. She wrote, lectured on the Chatauqua circuit and in vaudeville, served on Massachusetts' State Commission for the Blind, and worked tirelessly for the American Foundation for the Blind from the time it was formed in 1923. Her lobbying for federal legislation for the blind was instrumental in the creation of federal reading services, including talking-book recordings, and the inclusion of federal grant assistance for the blind in the Social Security Act. She involved herself in numerous social causes, including women's suffrage, pacifist movements prior to both world wars, and the antinuclear movement after World War II. Most important, Keller made herself a living symbol of triumph over handicap, and an inspiration to handicapped people everywhere.

REFERENCES

Brooks, V. W. (1956). *Helen Keller: Sketch for a portrait*. New York: Dutton.

Keller, H. (1904). *The story of my life*. New York: Doubleday.

Lash, J. (1980). *Helen and teacher: The story of Helen Keller and Anne Sullivan Macy*. New York: American Foundation for the Blind.

PAUL IRVINE
Katonah, New York

KENNY, SISTER ELIZABETH (1886–1952)

Sister Elizabeth Kenny revolutionized the treatment of poliomyelitis and became an international heroine during the polio epidemics of the 1940s. She began working with polio patients as a nurse in her native Australia—hence the title of "Sister," which is given to nurses in British

Sister Elizabeth Kenny

Commonwealth countries. She developed a method of treatment that, in contrast to the prevailing procedure of immobilizing the muscles with braces or casts, involved stimulating affected muscles to enable them to regain their function. Her success attracted worldwide attention and in 1939 she was invited to the United States by a group of physicians. Her demonstration of her treatment methods to physicians in Minneapolis-St. Paul resulted in a hospital ward dedicated to the Kenny treatment. From this beginning, the world-renowned Kenny Institute was formed, and Sister Kenny's approach became the accepted method of treatment for polio.

REFERENCE

Kenny, E. (1943). *And they shall walk: The life story of Sister Elizabeth Kenny.* New York: Dodd, Mead.

PAUL IRVINE
Katonah, New York

KEOGH, BARBARA (1925–   )

Barbara Keogh received her BA in psychology at Pomona College in 1946. She obtained her MA in psychology at Stanford University in 1947, and her PhD in psychology at the Claremont Graduate School in 1963. She is presently professor of education in the Graduate School of Education at the University of California, Los Angeles.

Keogh's major areas of study are school psychology, psychoeducational evaluation, and special education. She suggests that different models of school psychology should be adopted if services are to be effective for exceptional children. She also contends that schools need a broader view of psychoeducational evaluation to allow a more productive use of school psychology. Keogh believes that as a school psychologist's unique contributions have to do with psychoeducational evaluation (i.e., differential diagnosis, therapeutic planning, and strategies of implementation of findings), the focus of evaluation should be on identification of task-relevant abilities that may be used or developed for learning success.

Keogh's major works include professional articles, research articles, book chapters, and several books. Her books include *Advances in Special Education: Volumes 1–5*; *A System of Marker Variables for the Field of Learning Disabilities*; and *Temperament and Teachability: Individual Differences of Importance in School.*

REFERENCES

Keogh, B. K. (1971). Hyperactivity and learning disorders: Review and speculation. *Exceptional Children, 38,* 101–109.

Keogh, B. K. (1980–1986). *Advances in special education* (Vols. 1–5). Greenwich, CT: JAI.

Keogh, B. K., & Daley, S. (1983). Early identification: One component of comprehensive services for at risk children. *Topics in Early Childhood Special Education, 3*(3), 7–16.

Keogh, B. K., Hewett, F. M., & Becker, L. D. (1973). Research in special education. *UCLA Education, 15*(1), 4–6.

Keogh, B. K., Major-Kingsby, S., Omori-Gordon, L., & Reid, H. P. (1982). *A system of marker variables for the field of learning disabilities.* New York: Syracuse University Press.

Keogh, B. K., & Wilcoxen, A. G. (in press). *Temperament and teachability: Individual differences of importance in school.* Ablex.

ELIZABETH JONES
Texas A&M University

KEPHART, NEWELL C. (1911–1973)

Newell C. Kephart received his PhD from the University of Iowa in 1936. He worked as a mental hygienist at the Wayne County (Michigan) Training School and as a research analyst for the U.S. Employment Service prior to naval service in World War II. In 1946 he joined the faculty of Purdue University, where he served as professor of psychology and education and conducted the Achievement Center for Children, a research and treatment center for handicapped children.

Newell C. Kephart

Kephart, who excelled in presenting classroom procedures in a manner readily understood and accepted by teachers, was a leading contributor to the perceptual-motor training movement of the 1960s. Following retirement from Purdue University in 1968, Kephart served until his death as director of the Glen Haven Achievement

Center in Fort Collins, Colorado, a school devoted to the education of handicapped children and their parents.

REFERENCES

A special tribute. (1973). *Academic Therapy, 8,* 373–374.

Ball, T. S. (1971). *Itard, Seguin, and Kephart: Sensory education—A learning interpretation.* Columbus, OH: Merrill.

Kephart, N. C. (1971). *The slow learner in the classroom* (2nd ed.). Columbus, OH: Merrill.

PAUL IRVINE
Katonah, New York

KERLIN, ISAAC NEWTON (1834–1893)

Isaac Newton Kerlin, a physician, served as superintendent of the Pennsylvania Training School for Feeble-Minded Children (now Elwyn Institute) from 1863 until his death in 1893. An excellent administrator, Kerlin

Isaac Newton Kerlin

made Elwyn a model that influenced the planning of institutions for the mentally retarded throughout the country. Through his efforts the Association of Medical Officers of American Institutions for Idiotic and Feeble-Minded Persons (now the American Association on Mental Deficiency) was formed at Elwyn in 1876. Kerlin, as secretary of the young organization, was responsible for the extension of the membership until it included almost all American physicians interested in mental deficiency.

REFERENCES

Historical notes on institutions for the mentally defective: Elwyn Training School. (1941). *American Journal of Mental Deficiency, 45,* 341–342.

Scheerenberger, R. D. (1983). *A history of mental retardation.* Baltimore, MD: Brookes.

PAUL IRVINE
Katonah, New York

KERNICTERUS

Kernicterus is a form of neonatal brain damage that results from destruction of fetal red blood cells in utero. Excess bilirubin in the blood penetrates the meningeal barrier (blood-brain barrier) and cerebral damage results. This syndrome is usually secondary to RH incompatibility and may be a result of brain lesions. However, it may also occur as a result of drugs, enzyme abnormalities of red blood cells, or liver or other blood infections (Zimmerman & Yannet, 1935). Kernicterus may also manifest athetoid and spastic paralysis in children. It is rarely seen now because it is almost always preventable.

Physically, there is not a consistent picture of kernicterus manifestations with the exception of signs of paralysis in the upper and lower extremities. Some athetoid paralysis, weakness, or muscle rigidity may be seen. Teeth may be yellow and eyes may be hooded. Hearing loss may be present (Lemeshaw, 1982). In newborns, jaundice, poor sucking reflexes, motor delay, and reduced muscle tone may appear. Seizures may be present. Athetoid motor movements such as rigidity and posturing may be present soon after birth.

A broad range of mental retardation can occur, but in many instances it is not seen. Early feeding seems to reduce the depth of jaundice and lower complications (Illingworth, 1983). Several blood problems may occur. Depending on the severity of the athetoid condition and of the motor impairment coupled with speech dysfunction, the child may be placed in multihandicapped educational setting. While these disabilities may make proper assessment and evaluation difficult, it is important to remember that many of these children possess normal intelligence. A multidisciplinary team of evaluators will probably be necessary to accurately assess the child.

Seizures, hearing impairment, and visual and communication problems will require related services, as will motor impairments. Support services may be required to locomote and feed the child. Program placement will necessitate a cohesive effort from a variety of professionals. Settings will vary based on the degree of impairment.

REFERENCES

Illingworth, R. (1983). *Development of the infant and young child: Abnormal and normal* (7th ed.). New York: Churchill, Livingstone.

Lemeshaw, S. (1982). *The handbook of clinical types in mental retardation.* Boston: Allyn & Bacon.

Zimmerman, H., & Yannet, H. (1935). Cerebral sequelae of icterus gravis neonatorum and their relation to kernikterus. *American Journal of Diseases in Children, 49,* 418–423.

SALLY L. FLAGLER
University of Oklahoma

BIRTH INJURIES
NEONATAL BEHAVIORAL ASSESSMENT SCALES

KEYMATH DIAGNOSTIC ARITHMETIC TEST

The KeyMath Diagnostic Arithmetic Scale (Connolly, Nachtman, & Pritchett, 1976) is an individually administered measure of mathematical functioning. It has three major sections: content (numeration, fractions, and geometry/symbols); operations (addition, subtraction, multiplication, division, mental computation, and numerical reasoning); and applications (word problems, missing elements, money, measurement, and time). The test is intended for students in grades K–8. Interpretation is possible based on an examinee's total score, performance on the three major sections, or performance on subtests within the sections. An interpretive guide that permits interpretation by item is also provided in the manual. No special qualifications are required to administer Key-Math, however, the manual must be studied carefully to ensure proper test administration and interpretation.

The Rasch-Wright model (Wright, 1968) was used in the norming of KeyMath. The final norming sample included 1222 children from grades K–8. An item sampling procedure was used so that all subjects did not receive all items. Across the eight grade levels, the total score had internal consistency coefficients of .94 and above. Another indication of reliability were test-retest coefficients of .90 and above for a six-month interval.

REFERENCES

Connolly, A. J., Nachtman, W., & Pritchett, E. M. (1976). *KeyMath Diagnostic Arithmetic Test.* Circle Point, MN: American Guidance Service.

Wright, B. D. (1968). Sample-free test calibration and person meeasurement. *Proceedings of the 1967 Invitational Conference on Testing Problems* (pp. 85–101). Princeton, NJ: Educational Testing Service.

JACK A. CUMMINGS
Indiana University

ACHIEVEMENT TESTS
MATHEMATICS, LEARNING DISABILITIES AND

KEYWORD METHOD

The keyword method is one of several mnemonic (memory-enhancing) techniques used for facilitating the learning and later recall of associative information. First employed by Atkinson (1975) in teaching Russian vocabulary words to college students, the keyword method was first applied to school-age children by Pressley (1977) in the learning of Spanish vocabulary words. Since that time it has been applied in many different content domains with students of several age and ability levels (Pressley, Levin, & Delaney, 1982).

The keyword method employs what Levin (1983) has described as the 3 R's of mnemonic techniques: recoding, relating, and retrieving. For example, in learning the Italian vocabulary word *roccia* (pronounced roach-ia), which means cliff, learners are first provided with (or are asked to generate) a recoded keyword. A keyword is a word that is acoustically similar to the stimulus term, and easily pictured. In this case, *roach* would be a good keyword for *roccia*. In a second step, the keyword is related to the response term via an interactive picture or image. In the *roccia* example, a *roach* could be shown jumping off a cliff. For the final, retrieving step, the learner is asked, when given the stimulus *roccia*, to think back to the keyword *roach*, to think of the picture of the roach, recall what else was in the picture, and respond with the appropriate referent, cliff.

The keyword method has recently been used with learning-disabled (Mastropieri, Scruggs, & Levin, 1985), mentally retarded (Scruggs, Mastropieri, & Levin, 1985), and gifted (Scruggs, Mastropieri, Monson, & Jorgenson, 1985) students. Results to date have suggested that the keyword may be an effective instructional strategy in special education. In addition to simple vocabulary learning instruction, several extensions have been explored in a variety of content-area domains. A combination of a keyword-pegword (rhyming system to teach numbers, e.g., one is bun, two is shoe, etc.) strategy was employed to teach the hardness levels of North American minerals according to Moh's scale. For example, to teach that pyrite is number six on the hardness scale, students were shown an interactive illustration of a pie (keyword for pyrite) on sticks (pegword for six) and taught that when asked for the hardness level of pyrite, they should think of the keyword (pie), remember the picture of the pie on sticks, and respond with the pegword equivalent, six. Since these experiments demonstrated superior performance for mnemonically instructed students, several other studies were conducted to teach multiple attributes mnemonically. These studies not only taught the hardness level of minerals, but also color and common use. For example, to teach that pyrite is six on the hardness scale, yellow in color, and used for making acid, learners were shown an interactive illustration of a yellow (color) pie (keyword for pyrite) resting on sticks (keyword for six) while acid (use) is poured on it. Additionally, similar mnemonic instruction has been adapted to the teaching of classifications in science-related content areas; in all cases, the keyword method has consistently outperformed a variety of control conditions by a wide margin.

Although the keyword method has been proven highly effective in experimental settings, the ultimate practical use of the keyword method for classroom instruction is at present unknown. Recent research by Tolfa-Veit, Scruggs, and Mastropieri (in press), however, has suggested that this technique is effective for long-term instruction of academic units, while McLoone, Zucker, Scruggs, and Mastropieri (in press) has provided evidence that learning-disabled students can be trained to transfer the strategy to independent learning. A review of keyword research efforts with exceptional populations has been provided by Mastropieri et al. (1985).

REFERENCES

Atkinson, R. C. (1975). Mnemotechnics in second language learning. *American Psychologist, 30,* 821–828.

Levin, J. R. (1983). Pictorial strategies for school learning: Practical illustrations. In M. Pressley & J. R. Levin (Eds.), *Cognitive strategy research: Educational applications.* New York: Springer-Verlag.

Mastropieri, M. A., Scruggs, T. E., & Levin, J. R. (1985). Maximizing what exceptional students can learn: A review of research in mnemonic techniques. *Remedial and Special Education, 6,* 39–45.

McLoone, B. B., Zucker, S., Scruggs, T. E., & Mastropieri, M. A. (in press). Mnemonic strategy instruction and training with learning disabled adolescents. *Learning Disabilities Research.*

Pressley, M. (1977). Children's use of the keyword method to learn simple Spanish vocabulary words. *Journal of Educational Psychology, 72,* 575–582.

Pressley, M., Levin, J. R., & Delaney, H. D. (1982). The mnemonic keyword. *Review of Educational Research, 52,* 61–91.

Scruggs, T. E., Mastropieri, M. A., Levin, J. R. (1985). Vocabulary acquisition of retarded students under direct and mnemonic instruction. *American Journal of Mental Deficiency, 89,* 546–551.

Scruggs, T. E., Mastropieri, M. A., Monson, J. A., & Jorgenson, C. (1985). Maximizing what gifted students can learn: Recent findings of learning strategy research. *Gifted Child Quarterly, 29,* 181–185.

Tolfa-Veit, D., Scruggs, T. E., & Mastropieri, M. A. (in press). Extended mnemonic instruction with learning disabled students. *Journal of Educational Psychology.*

THOMAS E. SCRUGGS
MARGO A. MASTROPIERI
Purdue University

MEMORY DISORDERS
MNEMONICS

KHATENA, JOE (1925–   )

Born and raised in Singapore, Joe Khatena was educated in universities both in his native land and in the United States. He obtained a PhD in psychology from the University of Georgia in 1969 and is currently professor and head of the department of educational psychology at Mississippi State University. Khatena has been the recipient of special honors for achievements in psychology and education and cited in numerous listings of outstanding individuals such as the *International Who's Who in Community Services, American Men and Women in Science, Leaders in Education,* and *Who's Who in Frontier Science and Technology.*

Khatena espouses the structure of the intellect model to explain the multidimensionality of giftedness and to suport the six U.S. Office of Education (USOE) categories of giftedness, with the reservation that this model does not explain the emotional and motivational aspects so essential to higher levels of creative intellectual functioning. He emphasizes that creativity in students must be nurtured by parents and teachers, as creativity will be the characteristic that distinguishes the gifted conserver from the gifted extensor of knowledge. His contributions to gifted education have been affirmed with an USOE Office of the Gifted and Talented Certificate of Recognition (1976), presidency of the National Association for Gifted Children (1979), and the Distinguished Scholar Award of that association (1982).

Throughout Khatena's work, he has focused on the perceptional aspects of creativity and the development of measures to identify outstanding abilities in those areas—the Khatena-Torrance Creative Perception Inventory (1976), the Torrance-Khatena-Cunnington Thinking Creatively with Sounds and Images Measure, (1980), and the Khatena-Morse Multitalent Perception Inventory (1985). As author of *Teaching Gifted Children to Use Creative Imagination Imagery* (1979), *Imagery and the Creative Imagination* (1984), and *Educational Psychology of the Gifted* (1982), he also has detailed ways of assisting chil-

Joe Khatena

dren in enhancing their verbal originality and mental imagery.

REFERENCES

Khatena, J. (1979). *Teaching gifted children to use creative imagination imagery.* Starkville, MI: Allan.

Khatena, J. (1982). *Educational psychology of the gifted.* New York: Wiley.

Khatena, J. (1984). *Imagery and creative imagination.* Buffalo, NY: Bearly.

PATRICIA A. HAENSLY
Texas A&M University

KICKLIGHTER, RICHARD H. (1931–)

Richard H. Kicklighter received his PhD in 1962 from the University of Florida, with a major in student personnel services under the direction of Ted Landsman. He is a licensed psychologist and has worked in the schools and institutional and private practice with sensorially, intellectually, and emotionally impaired children and their parents. He is presently the director of the Division of Standards and Assessment in the State Department of Education of Georgia. He has worked as a consultant in the Georgia Program for Exceptional Children.

Kicklighter's areas of interest and research encompass educational test development, statewide student assessment program administration, and coordination of school psychology service programs. He is the coauthor of a psychological test of social competency, the Children's Adaptive Behavior Scale. He is a former president of the Georgia Psychological Association and the Georgia Federation, Council for Exceptional Children, and is a diplomat in school psychology of the American Board of Professional Psychology.

Kicklighter is a coeditor of a standard textbook in the field of school psychology, *Psychological Services in the Schools*, and he authored *Psychological Education in the Elementary School.*

REFERENCES

Kicklighter, R. H. (1975). *Psychological education in the elementary school.* Boston: Houghton Mifflin.

Kicklighter, R. H., & Holt, F. D. (1971). *Psychological services in the schools: Reading in preparation, organization and practice.* Iowa: William C. Brown.

Kicklighter, R. H., & Richmond, B. O. (1980). *Children's Adaptive Behavior Scale* (CABS) Humanics.

ROBERTA C. STOKES
Texas A&M University

KINETIC-FAMILY-DRAWING (KFD)

Family drawings have been used as projective techniques in the diagnosis of children's emotional disorders for many years. Of the various approaches available, the Kinetic-Family-Drawing (KFD), as described by Burns and Kaufman (1970, 1972) is the most popular, particularly among school psychologists. Children are given a blank sheet of paper, a pencil with an eraser, and instructed to "Draw a picture of everyone in your family doing something, including you; try to draw whole people, not cartoon or stick figures, and be sure to have everyone doing something."

The KFDs are analyzed for action, symbols, and style. Action refers to movement of energy among people and/or objects and reflects love, power, and anger. Symbols on the KFD are interpreted according to traditional psychoanalytic theory. For example, the drawing of a bed is associated with sexual and depressive themes. Style on the KFD is reflected in the overall approach to the drawing and may include such characteristics as compartmentalization of figures, underlining, edging figures, lining the bottom of the drawing, and drawing all figures in a small portion of the paper. A quick reference guide to the interpretation of children's KFDs, intended for the already experienced user, has been provided by Reynolds (1978).

REFERENCES

Burns, R. C., & Kaufman, S. H. (1970). *Kinetic Family Drawing (K-F-D): An introduction to understanding children through kinetic drawings.* New York: Brunner/Mazel.

Burns, R. C., & Kaufman, S. H. (1972). *Actions, styles and symbols in Kinetic Family Drawings (K-F-D): An interpretive manual.* New York: Brunner/Mazel.

Reynolds, C. R. (1978). A quick scoring guide to the interpretation of children's Kinetic Family Drawings (KFD). *Psychology in the Schools, 15*, 489–492.

CECIL R. REYNOLDS
Texas A&M University

KIRK, SAMUEL A. (1904–)

Samuel A. Kirk received his BA (1929) and MA (1931) in psychology from the University of Chicago, and his PhD (1935) in physiological and clinical psychology from the University of Michigan. Kirk served as director of the Institute for Research on Exceptional Children and as professor of special education and psychology at the University of Illinois from 1947 to 1967. He has maintained his status as professor emeritus at the University of Illinois and is currently professor of special education at the University of Arizona.

Kirk has guided the developmental course of special education as a field. Like Binet, Kirk was not obsessed with the constancy of the IQ. He believed that intelligence could be changed through educational intervention and has maintained this stance throughout his work. In 1958 results of a study by Kirk (Early Education of the Mentally

Samuel A. Kirk

Retarded) on the effects of preschool education on the social and mental development of young mentally retarded children, together with a study by Harold Skeels (1939), stimulated research on disadvantaged children, influenced the development of Head Start, and persuaded Congress to enact the Early Education Assistance Act of 1968.

In 1968 Kirk published the Illinois Test of Psycholinguistic Abilities, which allowed a comparison of a child's own abilities and disabilities for the purpose of organizing remediation for psycholinguistic deficits. He was also responsible for the development of the term learning disability. Kirk first used the term in a 1962 textbook on educating exceptional children, and later in a speech to several parent groups who were meeting in Chicago in 1963. He used the term to describe a group of children who were not blind, deaf, or mentally retarded, but were still not learning in school. The parent groups used the term and merged to become the Association for Children with Learning Disabilities.

Kirk also served the field of special education at the federal level by heading the Division of Handicapped Children and Youth in the U.S. Office of Education in 1963. In 1967 his testimony to Congress resulted in the establishment of the Bureau for the Education of Handicapped Children. The work of this bureau eventually culminated in PL 94-142, the Education for All Handicapped Children Act of 1975.

Kirk has published approximately 200 blooks, monographs, and articles, and is the recipient of many awards, such as the First International Award in Mental Retardation from the Joseph P. Kennedy Foundation, and a honorary Doctorate of Fellows degree from the University of Illinois. Kirk is currently interested in the transferring of special education and remedial instructional techniques to regular teachers in elementary schools.

REFERENCES

Kirk, S. A. (1958). *Early education of the mentally retarded—An experimental study*. Urbana: University of Illinois Press.

Kirk, S. A. (1963). Behavioral diagnosis and remediation of learning disabilities. In *Proceedings of the Conference on Exploration into the Problems of the Perceptually Handicapped Child* (pp. 1–7). Chicago: Perceptually Handicapped Children.

Kirk, S. A., McCarthy, J. J., & Kirk, W. D. (1968). *The Illinois test of psycholinguistic abilities*. Urbana: University of Illinois Press.

Skeels, H. M. (1966). Adult status of children with contrasting early life experience. *Monographs of the Society for Research in Child Development, 105* (No. 3).

ELAINE FLETCHER-JANZEN
Texas A&M University

KLINEFELTER'S SYNDROME

Klinefelter's syndrome is a chromosomal abnormality occurring in a male who has at least one extra female sex chromosome (i.e., xxy) in contrast to the normal male genotype of xy (Reed, 1975). The extra sex chromosome(s) has been attributed to nondisjunction during meiosis, a process that also results in Down's syndrome, although the precise etiology is unknown (Hoaken, Clarke, & Breslin, 1964). This syndrome is characterized by a generally normal-appearing phenotypical male with small and nonfunctioning testes, gynecomastia (i.e., enlarged breasts), low sex drive, a high-pitched voice, eunuchoid build, obesity, scant facial hair, tallness, and deficiencies of male hormone production. The incidence is reported to vary from 0.15 to 0.3% of the general population or 15 to 30 in every 10,000 males (Lubs & Ruddle, 1970; Reed, 1975). Although it is increasingly being identified during early infancy through genetic screening, Klinefelter's syndrome is typically not diagnosed until after puberty, when the testicles are noted to be abnormally small. It is medically treated with testosterone during adolescence.

Research has consistently indicated that the extra x chromosome(s) material results in proportionately higher risks for a wide variety of developmental and psychological disabilities (Haka-Ikse, Steward, & Cripps, 1979; Money, 1980; Pomeroy, 1980). It has not been established whether the increased vulnerability to disabilities is biological or environmental (Leonard & Rosenberg, 1973). However, abnormal hormones secondary to xxy have been implicated in the impaired functioning of the central nervous system (CNS) that is frequently reported in Klinefelter syndrome patients. Moreover, intellectual functioning was found to decrease with each additional x chromosome (Forssman, 1970). Most males with xxy were found to have low-average intelligence, however, there is no disproportionate severe mental retardation. Wright, Schaefer, and Solomons (1979) reviewed studies that reported on factors typically associated with learning disorders (e.g., early language delay, auditory memory, auditory discrimination). Various types of psychopathology beyond psychosexual difficulties have been reported, including severe disorders such as schizophrenia in addition to such specific symptoms as immaturity, impulsivity, passivity, apathy, and hostility.

Wright et al. (1979) recommended that behavioral practitioners provide comprehensive evaluation of intellectual, academic, and personal-social functioning of xxy persons. They especially recommended that evaluation take place before and after hormone treatment for those first identified during adolescence. Students with Klinefelter's syndrome often require special education placement and counseling. Anticipatory guidance for the child and parents is especially recommended over time regarding such issues as sterility.

REFERENCES

Forssman, H. (1970). Mental implications of sex chromosome aberrations. *British Journal of Psychiatry, 117,* 353–363.

Haka-Ikse, K., Steward, D. A., & Cripps, M. H. (1979). Early development of children with sex chromosome aberrations. *Pediatrics, 62,* 761–766.

Hoaken, P. C. S., Clarke, M., & Breslin, M. (1964). Psychopathology in Klinefelter's syndrome. *Psychosomatic Medicine, 26,* 207–223.

Leonard, M. F., & Rosenberg, L. (1973). Interaction of environmental and genetic factors in Klinefelter's syndrome. *Pediatrics, 52,* 118–120.

Lubs, H. A., & Ruddle, F. H. (1970). Chromosomal abnormality in the human population: Estimates of rates based on New Haven newborn study. *Science, 169,* 495–499.

Money, J. (1980). Human behaior cytogenetics: Review of psychopathology in three syndromes—47, XXY; 47, XYY; and 45, X. In S. I. Harrison & J. F. McDermott (Eds.), *New directions in childhood psychopathology* (pp. 70–84). New York: International Universities Press.

Pomeroy, J. C. (1980). Klinefelter's syndrome and schizophrenia. *British Journal of Psychiatry, 136,* 597–599.

Reed, E. W. (1975). Genetic anomalies in development. In F. D. Horowitz (Ed.), *Review of child development research* (Vol. 4, pp. 283–318). Chicago: University of Chicago Press.

Wright, L., Schaefer, A. B., & Solomons, G. (1979). *Encyclopedia of Pediatric Psychology.* Baltimore, MD: University Park Press.

JOSEPH D. PERRY
Kent State University

GENETIC COUNSELING
GENETIC FACTORS AND BEHAVIOR
GENETIC VARIATIONS
PHYSICAL ANOMALIES

KNIGHT, HENRY M. (1827–1880)

Henry M. Knight, physician and educator, entered the field of mental retardation as a member of the Connecticut

Henry M. Knight

state legislature, when he served on a committee established to ascertain the number of mentally retarded children in that state. Following completion of a census, legislation was proposed for the construction of a school for the retarded. When the legislation failed, Knight gave up his medical practice and, in 1858, established a residential program for retarded children in his home. Through Knight's continuing campaign for public support, the legislature, in 1861, appropriated the necessary funds and Knight's school became the fifth publicly supported institution for the mentally retarded in the United States. Knight served as superintendent until shortly before his death in 1880. The institution was closed in 1917 with the opening of more modern facilities. Knight was one of the founders of the Association of Medical Officers of American Institutions for Idiotic and Feeble-Minded Persons, now the American Association on Mental Deficiency.

REFERENCE

Brown, G. (1964). Memoir of Dr. H. M. Knight. *Association of medical officers of American institutions for idiotic and feeble-minded persons, proceedings, 1876–1886.* New York: Johnson Reprint Corporation.

PAUL IRVINE
Katonah, New York

KOPPITZ, ELIZABETH M. (1919–1983)

Elizabeth M. Koppitz came to the United States from Germany in 1939. She received her PhD from Ohio State University in 1955, and worked as a psychologist in Ohio and in the public schools of New York state until her retire-

Elizabeth M. Koppitz

Emil Kraepelin

ment in 1982. She made major contributions to the field of psychoeducational assessment of children and is best known for the scoring system presented in the *Bender Gestalt Test for Young Children* and her studies of children's human figure drawings.

REFERENCES

In memoriam: Elizabeth M. Koppitz. (1983). *Communique, 12,* 1–3.

Koppitz, E. M. (1964). *The Bender Gestalt Test for young children.* New York: Grune & Stratton.

Koppitz, E. M. (1968). *Psychological evaluation of children's human figure drawings.* New York: Grune & Stratton.

PAUL IRVINE
Katonah, New York

KRAEPELIN, EMIL (1856–1926)

Emil Kraepelin, German psychiatrist, held teaching posts at universities in Dorpat, Heidelberg, and Munich during his long career. Best known for his classification of mental disorders, his descriptions and classifications of the symptoms of mental illness provided a common ground for psychiatric thought; they constitute the basis for the categories in use today. Kraepelin applied the methods of the psychological laboratory to the study of personality, learning, and abnormal behavior. He developed tests to evaluate sensory-motor performance and the psychological deficits of psychiatric patients. He studied the effects of alcohol and tobacco, and was the first to use scientific methods to test the effects of drugs on human behavior. He wrote extensively on the problem of crime, providing

much of the basis for the modern study of the relationship between criminality and mental illness.

REFERENCES

Kahn, E. (1959). The Emil Kraepelin memorial lecture. In B. Pasamanick (ed.) *Epidemiology of mental disorders: A symposium organized by the American Psychiatric Association to commemorate the centennial of the birth of Emil Kraepelin.* Washington, DC: American Association for the Advancement of Science.

Kraepelin, E. (1962). *One hundred years of psychiatry.* New York: Citadel Press.

PAUL IRVINE
Katonah, New York

KUHLMANN, FREDERICK (1876–1941)

Frederick Kuhlmann, psychologist and test developer, obtained his PhD from Clark University in Massachusetts. After holding teaching positions there and at the universities of Wisconsin, Illinois, and Minnesota, he became director of research at the Minnesota School for the Feeble-Minded in Faribault, where he specialized in the assessment and education of mentally retarded children and adults. In 1912 and 1922 Kuhlmann published revisions of the 1908 Binet-Simon Scale, which extended the range of the test down to 3 months and represented one of the earliest efforts to develop a standardized test for infants. In 1927 he and Rose Anderson published a widely used group test of intelligence, the Kuhlmann-Anderson Intelligence Tests. Kuhlmann's individually administered Tests of Mental Development appeared in 1939.

In 1921 Kuhlmann's research department at Faribault became a state office, the Bureau of Mental Examinations, which he headed until his death. Kuhlmann's articles and research reports had widespread influence on other state institutions and on the development of services for mentally retarded students in the public schools of Minnesota. In addition, Kuhlmann was responsible for much of the teaching in the training program for teachers of the mentally retarded at Faribault. Kuhlmann was an active member of the American Association on Mental Deficiency and served as its president in 1940–1941.

REFERENCES

Dayton, N. (1940). President Frederick Kuhlmann. *American Journal of Mental Deficiency, 45,* 3–7.

Maxfield, F. N. (1941). Fred Kuhlmann. *American Journal of Mental Deficiency, 46,* 17–18.

PAUL IRVINE
Katonah, New York

KURZWEIL READING MACHINE

Developed by Raymond Kurzweil in the mid-1960s at the Massachusetts Institute of Technology, the Kurzweil Reading Machine (KRM) is a computer for blind and print-handicapped individuals; it converts printed materials directly into synthesized speech. The KRM converts printed materials from a variety of sources, type sizes, and styles into synthetic, full-word, multilingual speech that is readily understandable after a short period of familiarization. The KRM also functions as a talking calculator and can serve as a full word, voice output computer terminal.

The KRM consists of two principal units: the automatic scanning system and the control panel. The scanning system automatically scans documents up to 11 inches × 14 inches and will read print or type from 6- to 24-point. The push-button control panel activates and directs the system (Kurzweil Computer Products). The development of the KRM offers several important advances over Braille or direct-translation reading machines. Because the output

of the device is speech, it is more easily understood and requires less special training. Relatively high reading speeds (approximately 250 words per minute) are able to be attained (Goodrich et al., 1979).

Users indicate the major advantages of the KRM include providing equal access to entire print collections, immediate availability of materials, and the ability to read at their own pace, on their own schedule, with privacy and independence (Kurzweil Computer Products). Present limitations pertaining to the KRM involve its cost, size, and ability to produce clear speech from poor or elaborate print. As of this writing, the KRM costs approximately $30,000, discouraging purchase by individuals. Generally, the units are placed in schools, libraries, organizations and agencies in an effort to provide access to a larger number of individuals. The size of the scanning system unit, 30 inches × 22 inches × 24 inches, prohibits portability. Poor quality print, unusual type styles, pictures, graphs, complex page formats, and other factors can all make reading and quality speech output difficult for the KRM (McKenzie, 1981).

REFERENCES

Dickman, I. R. (1980). *What can we do about limited vision*? New York: Public Affairs Committee.

Goodrich, G. L., Bennett, R. R., De L'aune, W. R., Lauer, H., & Mowinski, L. (1979). Kurzweil reading machine: A partial evaluation of its optical character recognition error rate. *Journal of Visual Impairment & Blindness, 3,* 389–399.

Kurzweil Computer Products. (1985). Reading Machine Department, Cambridge, MA.

McKenzie, C. (1981). Using the Kurzweil Reading Machine. *Proceedings of the Second National Seminar on Library Services for the Handicapped, National Library of Australia.* (ERIC Document Reproduction Services No. ED 221 211)

HAROLD E. HOFF, JR.
Eastern Pennsylvania Special Education Resources Center, King of Prussia, Pennsylvania

BLIND
ELECTRONIC TRAVEL AIDS
VERSABRAILLE

L

LABELING

Labeling is an imprecise term referring to a series of effects, mostly negative, believed to result from formal classification of students as handicapped. Hobbs (1975) defined classification as "the act of assigning a child or condition to a general category or to a particular position in a classification system" (p. 43). The close relationship of classification and labeling is revealed by Hobbs's (1975) definition of labeling as, "the assignment of a child to a category," which also includes, "the notion of public communication of the way a child is categorized; thus, the connotation of stigma is present" (p. 43).

The somewhat confusing definitions cited are typical of the efforts to separate the effects of classification and labeling. Labeling is the term used to refer to negative effects that are assumed to be associated with the classification of students. These negative effects are most often associated with various mild handicapping classifications, particularly the classification of mild mental retardation (MMR). Labeling effects also are assumed to exist for other classifications such as specific learning disabilities (SLD) and emotionally disturbed (ED), but the negative effects associated with these classifications have not been seen as severe.

Labeling effects depend heavily on social deviance theory (Becker, 1963). Social deviance theory was initiated to explain the effects of the formal justice system on the behavior of persons, often teenagers, who may or may not have been classified as juvenile delinquents. Social deviance theory emphasizes the effects of labels on the behavior of individuals. Formal labels are believed to exert direct influence on behavior through complex processes that, simplified, result in labels creating deviant behavior. The question of whether labels create deviant behavior or whether labels result from significant behavioral deviation is the basic issue in the voluminous professional literature on labeling effects.

One of the strongest statements claiming to show the effects of labels in creating behavior was published by Rosenthal and Jacobson (1968). This widely cited and highly influential study claimed to show the effects of communicating positive information to teachers on the intellectual development of elementary school-aged children. Rosenthal and Jacobson claimed that changes in teachers' beliefs produced by brief statements about children inserted in their educational records led to significant intellectual growth by children, presumably because of subtle changes in how those children were treated by their teachers.

Although the Rosenthal and Jacobson work was severely criticized in the professional literature, and numerous efforts to replicate the findings were unsuccessful, the notion of self-fulfilling prophecy exerted enormous influence on special education in the late 1960s and 1970s, and, to a considerable extent, into the present era. The self-fulfilling prophecy as applied to special education suggests that children and youths acquire deviant behaviors or fail to develop positive behaviors because of the special education classification.

The theme that special education classifications, particularly MMR, have significant negative effects on students was particularly prominent in a widely cited article by Dunn (1968). Dunn argued that MMR special class programs involved stigmatizing labels as well as ineffective interventions. The labeling theme, particularly regarding MMR, was developed further by a 1970 report of the President's Committee on Mental Retardation. This report coined the term six-hour retarded child. Discussions of the labeling effects in the classification/placement process also further developed the theme by (Mercer, 1973, 1979). Although the conclusions of Dunn, Mercer, and the concept of 6-hour retreated child are widely cited, there is little or no evidence showing direct negative effects of special education labels. A continuing problem in the special education literature is the insufficient attention to empirical studies of labeling effects.

Extensive research attempting to identify effects of special education classifications or placements has been conducted. This research is very complex. Perhaps the most serious complication is the fact that labels are not randomly assigned to students (and indeed could not be due to ethical concerns). In the real world, some students are classified and placed; others are not. There are well-known, significant differences separating those who are classified and placed in special education, and therefore potentially vulnerable to labeling effects, and those who are not classified and placed. Thus, an accurate account of the effects of labels in the real world must somehow take into account the differences among students that led to the original referral and then the classification and placement decisions.

Referrals are almost always initiated because of significant learning or behavioral problems in classroom settings. Only a few students are referred, typically under 10%. Students who are referred receive preplacement evaluations in which a multifactored assessment is conducted. The multifactored assessment information is considered by a multidisciplinary team that may or may not recommend classification as handicapped and placement in special education. Thus the students for whom some labeling effect might occur are a highly selected subsample of the general population. Possible effects of labeling, which presumably occur after formal classification and placement, are contaminated with the behavioral characteristics of students that led to their initial referral and eligibility for special education. It is impossible to separate these effects in the real world.

Research attempting to observe developmental changes in self-concept and peer acceptance before and after labeling has been conducted with mixed results. The balance of evidence would appear to suggest that labeling either improves or has no significant effect on self-concept and peer acceptance (Gottlieb, 1980; Guskin, 1978).

The research that shows negative effects of labeling typically uses methodology heavily dependent on simulation. Participants in studies are asked either to imagine their reactions to a labeling circumstance, to read a brief description of a person who has been labeled and then indicate their expectations, or to observe via videotape or film the behavior of a student who they typically have been deceived to believe is handicapped. The results of these studies, which assess the effects of labels on expectations, not on actual behavior, have been mixed. Generally, participants with little or no contact, direct or vicarious, with the person who is supposedly handicapped reveal a significant expectancy effect based on the label. However, participants with more information or prolonged contact, direct or vicarious, with the allegedly handicapped person show reduced and often nonexistent effects of labels on expectations. There is no simple answer to the simple question, "Do labels create expectations?" It would appear that labels do create expectations if there is little contact and limited knowledge. With knowledge and experience, even in simulated studies, the effects of labels are quite limited. Excellent reviews of the labeling and expectancy literature have been provided by MacMillan and colleagues (MacMillan, 1982; MacMillan, Jones, & Aloia, 1974). Persons wishing to draw generalizations about labeling or conduct research on labeling phenomena should consult their work.

The enormously complex labeling literature does yield at least two fairly well established generalizations. First, children and youth classified as mildly handicapped do not like being labeled. Second, many persons, including professionals such as public school teachers, often misunderstand the common special education labels. These two findings provide ample reason to be cautious about the assignment of labels, to exert strong effort to avoid misclassification, to consider alternatives to the current classification system, and to deliver effective programs if labeling is deemed necessary.

Although classification of some kind is generally regarded as absolutely necessary for communication, which in turn affects all aspects of conducting research, developing services, and organizing programs for handicapped students, there is considerable discussion today concerning alternative bases for a classification system. The current system, whereby internal attributes of students form the basis for classification, may be revised in the forseeable future in a number of ways. One possibility is to merge the current categories into a generic mild handicap classification. This combination of specific learning disability, seriously emotionally disturbed, and mild mental retardation, often referred to as cross-categorical, might reduce some of the confusion and misunderstanding, particularly of mild mental retardation. Other reforms of the current classification systems, such as classifying students according to the kinds of services needed rather than according to internal attributes, have been suggested and are being attempted. However, these reforms will not eliminate all possible negative connotations since neutral terms almost inevitably acquire negative connotations when applied to problem behaviors.

Labeling is an enormously complex phenomena about which much distortion, confusion, and misinformation have been communicated. Current works stress the development of alternative approaches to classification that may have fewer negative connotations, as well as the development of classification concepts more directly related to special education programming.

REFERENCES

Becker, H. S. (1963). *Outsiders: Studies in the sociology of deviance.* Glencoe, IL: Free Press.

Dunn, L. (1968). Special education for the mildly retarded: Is much of it justifiable? *Exceptional Children, 35,* 5–22.

Gottlieb, J. (Ed.). (1980). *Educating mentally retarded persons in the mainstream.* Baltimore, MD: University Park Press.

Guskin, S. L. (1978). Theoretical and empirical strategies for the study of the labeling of mentally retarded persons. In N. R. Ellis (Ed.), *International review of research in mental retardation* (Vol. 9, pp. 127–158). New York: Academic.

Hobbs, N. L. (1975). *The futures of children.* San Francisco: Jossey-Bass.

MacMillan, D. (1982). *Mental retardation in school and society* (2nd ed.). Boston: Little, Brown.

MacMillan, D., Jones, R., & Aloia, G. (1974). The mentally retarded label: A theoretical analysis and review of research. *American Journal of Mental Deficiency, 79,* 241–261.

Mercer, J. (1973). *Labeling the mentally retarded.* Berkeley, CA: University of California Press.

Mercer, J. (1979). *System of multicultural pluralistic assessment technical manual.* New York: Psychological Corporation.

Rosenthal, R., & Jacobson, L. (1968). *Pygmalion in the classroom: Teacher expectation and pupils' intellectual development.* New York: Holt, Rinehart, & Winston.

DANIEL J. RESCHLY
Iowa State University

AAMD CLASSIFICATION SYSTEM
SYSTEMS OF CLASSIFICATION
MENTAL RETARDATION
SIX-HOUR RETARDED CHILD

LANGUAGE, ABSENCE OF

The nondevelopment of a language system in several categories of individuals does not preclude the possibility of producing separate sounds or words. For example, it is generally acknowledged that profoundly mentally retarded individuals (with IQs below 20 and marked deficiencies in adaptive behavior) do not develop language. Recent work with nonspeech language systems (Lloyd, 1976; Rondal, 1985) has shown the possibility of equipping such individuals with gestural prosthetic communicative systems that in turn prove helpful in establishing limited functional vocal repertoires. However, one would hardly claim that such systems are truly linguistic in nature. When dealing with problems of this sort, it is useful to recall the distinction between speech and language. The absence of language does not preclude the use of speech sounds and the use of nonspeech communicative systems.

The same distinction between speech and language is relevant when dealing with nonspeech systems such as conventional sign languages (e.g., American Sign Language) with people who cannot resort to vocal communication for reasons of organic insufficiency (either sensory or motoric). Keeping these distinctions in mind, one can propose the following dichotomy for the category absence of language.

There is an absence of language (linguistic capacity) for reasons of severe central organic insufficiency. This category encompasses etiological distinctions such as profound mental retardation, childhood autism, and developmental or congenital aphasia (to be distinguished from acquired aphasia). It is suggested that from 40 to 60% of autistic children are without language (Lotter, 1966; Prior & McMillan, 1973) except for some form of simple echolalia or single-word productions (Rutter, 1965; Wing, 1971). It is not always easy to distinguish between early autism and developmental aphasia. Early autism is generally considered to be a relational or personality syndrome in which interpersonal communication is gravely deficient. The latter syndrome (Benton, 1964; Eisenson, 1963) specifically refers to a deficit affecting the construction and the basic integration of language. An interesting but unexplained cutoff point (in terms of development) for most current authors seems to be 5 or 6 years. If by that age, the child has not developed some primitive form of language, he or she is not likely to initiate language at all in the following years.

There can be an absence of speech without an absence of linguistic capacity, for reasons of severe sensory (e.g., congenital profound deafness) or motoric (e.g., cerebral palsy) handicaps. It is now well known that profoundly deaf individuals are by no means deprived of language capacity. When properly exposed to nonspeech symbolic stimulation (e.g., sign language), they readily develop language capacities much in the way of hearing children learning oral languages (Moores, 1978). In the same way, most individuals suffering from cerebral palsy can be taught to express themselves symbolically and to communicate by the use of various nonvocal and vocal prosthetic devices (Bliss, Rebus systems, Handivoice, Multi-Language Portable, Minspeak, Vocaid, etc.) (Lloyd, 1976; Sylvestre, 1986). Rapid technological advances can be expected in this domain in the coming years.

REFERENCES

Benton, A. L. (1964). Developmental aphasia and brain damage. *Cortex, 1*, 40–52.

Eisenson, J. (1963). Disorders of language in children. *Journal of Pediatrics, 63*, 20–24.

Lloyd, L. (Ed.). (1976). *Communication assessment and intervention strategies.* Baltimore, MD: University Park Press.

Lotter, V. (1966). Epidemiology of autistic conditions in young children. I. Prevalence. *Social Psychiatry, 1*, 124–128.

Moores, D. (1978). *Educating the deaf.* Boston: Houghton Mifflin.

Prior, M., & McMillan, M. (1973). Maintenance of sameness in children with Kanner's syndrome. *Journal of Autism & Childhood Schizophrenia, 3*, 154–167.

Rondal, J. A. (1985). *Langage et communication chez les handicapés mentaux. Théorie, évaluation, intervention,* Brussels: Mardaga.

Rutter, M. (1965). The influence of organic and emotional factors on the origin, nature and outcome of childhood psychosis. *Developmental Medicine & Child Neurology, 7*, 518–528.

Sylvestre, A. (1986). *Education spéciale, multi-handicapés et technologie.* In J. A. Rondal & B. Piérart (Eds.), *Psychopédagogie de l'éducation spécialisée: Aperçu théorique, recherche et perspective.* Brussels: Labor.

Wing, L. (1971). Perceptual and language development in autistic children: A comparative study. In M. Rutter (Ed.), *Infantile autism: Concepts, characteristics and treatment.* London: Churchill Livingstone.

JEAN A. RONDAL
*Laboratory for Language,
Psychology, and Logopedics,
University of Liege, Belgium*

DEAF EDUCATION
LANGUAGE DELAYS
LANGUAGE DEFICIENCIES AND DEFICITS
LANGUAGE DISORDERS

LANGUAGE DEFICIENCIES AND DEFICITS

This article will refer to those cases where language develops and where linguistic retardation maintains itself beyond the temporal limits usually associated with simple delays. Several types of language deficiencies can be distinguished as to their general source although the linguistic signs in the various cases may be comparable.

Specific Language Deficiencies Associated with Impairments of the Central Nervous System

Entities such as dysphasia, acquired and developmental or congenital aphasia, alexias, and dyslexias are in this category. The language disorder may be permanent or transitory as is the case in childhood aphasia.

Dysphasia. The term dysphasia refers to a basic and global deficit in the oral language maintained after 6 years in otherwise normally developing children with adequate sensory and motoric equipment. The problems in the oral language can also affect the acquisition of written language, contributing to a secondary dyslexia/dysorthographia. Dysphasic children are characterized by a low capacity for analyzing words into their phonemic constituents. Sentence repetition is poor but word-by-word reproduction is usually correct. Spontaneous language is often imprecise and lacks grammatical marking and organization. Language comprehension remains inadequate, especially for those words or expressions referring to space, time, and abstract properties of things or events. Dysphasic children have difficulties in learning to read. Reading problems may persist over the entire school period. Text comprehension is often problematic. As a consequence, school work is difficult and failure is frequent.

The various therapeutic options for treating dysphasia can be grouped into two major categories: (1) remediation methods focusing on the specific language difficulties of dysphasic children; (2) the remediation methods with psychotherapeutic orientation (the hypothesis is that language progress will only be made possible to the extent that the children's general relational and interpersonal problems are satisfactorily addressed).

Acquired Aphasia. Acquired aphasia is defined as a language disorder caused by a focal lesion of the central nervous system. Strictly speaking, one should speak of aphasia in only those subjects that have already developed some level of language. Various forms and categories of aphasia have been described—aphasias of Broca, Wernicke, dynamic aphasia of Luria, central aphasia of Goldstein, and nominal aphasia of Head. There appears to be no consensus among authors on the choice of a single classification scheme. Acquired aphasia in children is characterized by the predominance of the expressive disorders (written as well as oral) over the receptive disorders; temporary mutism is not infrequent. When expressive language subsists, utterances are often telegraphic in style, with omission of the functors or grammatical words and morphemes and a marked reduction in the diversity of the lexicon used. Receptive difficulties are not as clear-cut. They may be less prevalent than the expressive problems or they may be marked only in older children (after 6 or 7 years as some studies suggest) (Bay, 1975).

The chronological age variable deserves careful attention in childhood aphasia. Everything else being equal, the younger the child, the better the postlesional evolution until 10 or 12 years of age. After this period, the time needed to restore the language function and the sequelae is similar to that observed in adults (Lenneberg, 1967; Van Hout & Seron, 1983).

Developmental Aphasia (or congenital). McCarthy (1963) defines developmental aphasia as a condition in which language acquisition is prevented in the child owing to a cerebral lesion or an incomplete neurological development before, at, or after birth. To this definition should be added the absence of major sensory motor deficits and intellectual development within normal limits (Leblanc, 1982; Zangwill, 1975). Two major criteria are usually used to diagnose developmental aphasia: the existence of a severe delay in language comprehension and production; a general perceptional dysfunctioning relating to the integration of sequentially presented stimuli. This dysfunctioning may be relatively difficult to identify in the auditory modality where it is sometimes confused with some mild form of auditory deficiency. In addition, developmental aphasic children are often, but not always, emotionally unstable and hyperactive (Eisenson, 1968) and their short-term auditory memory span is short (Hirsch, 1967).

What can cause developmental aphasia? Two hypotheses have been presented: a dysfunctioning or a severe delay in the maturation of the relay systems between the auditory mental pathways and the integration of the vocal stimuli (Benton, 1964); and the existence of early lesions in the temporal and parieto-occipital cortex, particularly in the left cerebral hemisphere (Eisenson, 1968; Landau, Goldstein, & Kleffner, 1960).

An efficient therapeutic approach to developmental aphasia largely depends on the early detection of the pathological entity. Unfortunately, most cases of developmental aphasia are still detected relatively late, for example, around 5 or 6 years (Leblanc, 1979); this prevents or renders more difficult early intervention.

Alexias and Dyslexias. The receptive disorders in written language owing to focal lesions of the central nervous system are commonly labeled *alexias* or *dyslexias*. The latter term also refers to reading problems among children with specific reading disabilities (*developmental dyslexias*). It should be distinguished from so-called agnosic alexia, referring to a major dysfunctioning of the visual perceptual mechanisms, and aphasic alexia, in which the linguistic disorder comes to the forefront (Hecaen, 1967). In agnosic aphasia, the major difficulty for the subjects seems to reside in the primary or literal characteristics of the written message (such as the distinct shapes of the various letters of the alphabet). Cases of pure alexia, or verbal blindness, have been traditionally reported; in them the difficulty in the identification of the letters stands as the only linguistic problem in the patient. In aphasic alexia, global word reading is usually easier than letter deciphering. The major deficit may be located at the level of the identification of single words or at the level of the combination of words in clauses.

Recently this semiology has been markedly modified. Marshall and Newcombe (1973) have proposed regrouping the variety of alexic disorders into three new broad categories: visual dyslexia, surface dyslexia, and deep dyslexia. Visual dyslexia is characterized by reading errors in which the words proposed by the subjects are graphically close to those appearing in the written text. In surface dyslexia, the reading errors mostly result from an incorrect application of the rules pertaining to the grapheme-phoneme correspondance. In deep dyslexia, the correspondence grapheme-phoneme is preserved but the errors are due for the most part to semantic confusions.

The label dyslexia (developmental dyslexia) is also used to refer to children with reading scores considerably below average grade level on tests of reading achievement but within or slightly below the average range on tests of intelligence and tests of achievement in other academic subjects (Manis & Morrison, 1985). There is some consensus among researchers that the principal reading problem manifested by these children is a failure to acquire fluency in word recognition. Comprehension problems noted in disabled readers are generally felt to be secondary, for instance, to derive from the inability to process words with sufficient speed or accuracy (Vellutino, 1979). As to the etiology of developmental dyslexia, there is no general agreement among experts. Neurological, hereditary, affective, sociocultural, and pedagogical factors have been recognized to play a role in the genesis of this reading disability.

Nonspecific Language Deficiencies Associated with Impairments of the Central Nervous System

Permanent albeit evolutive language disorders associated with pathological conditions such as mental retardation and childhood autism are in this category.

Mental Retardation. Mildly to severely mentally retarded children develop speech and language with delays and deficits varying according to the degree of cognitive handicap. There are a large number of pathological conditions affecting the development of the central nervous system and contributing to various degrees of mental handicap (Grossman, 1983, identifies more than 100 such conditions). Among these, Down's syndrome and trisomy 21 have been most studied from a speech and language point of view (Rondal, 1981, 1985). Down's syndrome is a genetic disorder identifiable at birth and before. It leads to moderate or severe mental retardation. In terms of the general characteristics of language development in Down's syndrome, the linguistic problems of these individuals are not necessarily prototypical of the communication and linguistic developments of other mentally retarded people. It is not known at this stage whether the rather extensive knowledge gathered in the recent past on Down's syndrome can be safely generalized to other types of mental retardation.

Phonetics and Phonology. The phonological aspects of babbling (i.e., the types of sounds heard in babbling) are similar in normal and Down's syndrome infants. The same developmental sequences and the same timing are observed regarding the appearance of the various vowels and consonants. Front and central vowels appear first, then back vowels. For the consonants, up to 6 months or so, velar sounds tend to dominate. Then the velars decrease in frequency and alveolar sounds become dominant. Labial consonants remain intermediate in frequency throughout the first year. Reduplicated babbling (repetition of a consonant-vowel syllable a number of times in succession) begins around 8 months in normal infants as well as in Down's syndrome infants. Phonological development is slow and difficult in Down's syndrome children for acoustical, articulatory (motoric), and lexical reasons, but the sequence of development follows much the normal path, for instance, the vowels and the stop consonants (*p, t, k, b, d, g, m, n*) are produced before the fricatives (*f, v, s, z, ch, j, l, r, th*), which are more difficult to articulate. The articulation in Down's syndrome subjects remains generally unclear, with problems associated with the latest phonemes to appear. Even in adults with Down's syndrome, the intelligibility of speech is generally lower than in normal subjects and also lower than in moderately and severely mentally retarded subjects of other etiologies. The articulatory errors, however, are of the same nature in the nonretarded and the retarded subjects. They consist mainly in simplifications of difficult consonants into easier ones, simplifications of consonant clusters, and transformations of consonants.

Lexicon. Vocabulary development is markedly delayed in Down's syndrome children. The onset of meaningful speech (one-word utterances) is delayed by at least 8 or 9 months when compared with normal children. The amount of meaningful speech in the verbal productions of these children is lower than 5%; this figure increases slowly with age up to around 4 years, at which time more meaningful productions appear.

Semantic Structural Basis of Language. When Down's syndrome children begin to combine two or three words in the same utterance, usually not before 4 years, they seem to make use of the same range of relational meanings as those underlying the two- or three-word utterances of younger normal children. It is likely that the semantic relational structure of the language is similar and develops similarly in Down's syndrome as well as in normal children. This is true for production as well as for the understanding of the basic semantic relationships of combinatorial language.

Morpho-Syntax. Rondal's study (1978) indicates that between 4 years and approximatively 10 years, the mean length of utterance (MLU) of Down's syndrome children goes from 1.00 to 3.00. Beyond 10 years, MLU values higher than 3.00 can be obtained (up to 6.00 with a standard deviation of 2.50 for Down's syndrome adolescents and adults).

The understanding and use of grammatical morphemes is one of the areas in which Down's syndrome subjects have particular difficulties. Whereas most grammatical morphemes are understood and used in obligatory contexts by normal children around 9 or 10 years, research indicates that Down's syndrome children are markedly delayed in this respect. Most of them probably never reach a stage where they would correctly use inflexions on verbs to express temporal relationships or subject-verb agreements, or on pronouns to mark them for number and gender, much less use the intricacies of definite-indefinite contrast through the use of articles.

Pragmatics and the Functional Value of Language Despite the severe limitations already mentioned in morphology and syntax, the language of Down's syndrome subjects (particularly the Down's syndrome adults) appears to have functional value. It is informative and the topics introduced are dealt with in such a way as to allow for the necessary continuity of the exchange between interlocutors.

Childhood Autism. What characteristics exhibit the language of those autistic children who eventually develop some linguistic capacity? Autistic children use little speech and their language is abnormal in many respects (Rutter, 1978). Echolalia and pronominal reversal are frequent features. Peculiarities in the form of neologisms and metaphorical usage are common. Defects in the understanding of spoken language are widespread. Although there are some similarities between the language disorder in childhood autism and in developmental dysphasia, the former is markedly more severe, particularly as regards comprehension; it involves both deviant characteristics and an impairment in social usage.

Most current therapeutic programs for autistic children (Rutter & Schopler, 1978) proceed by intensively training the parents to reeducate their own children. Communication and language usually receive high priority, but so do other objectives such as visual and auditory perception, nonverbal cognition, social skills, and positive social habits.

Speech and Language Difficulties Associated with Sensory and/or Motoric Deficits

Entities such as deafness, the language problems associated with blindness, and the speech problems associated with cerebral palsy are in this category.

Deafness. It is customary to range deafness among the language disorders. Actually, deaf subjects are handicapped only to the extent that they use spoken language. Recent research (Hoffmeister, 1982; Moores, 1978) proves that deaf children from deaf parents acquire conventional sign languages (such as Ameslan in the United States) much the same way and according to the same approximate chronology as hearing children from hearing parents. Esoteric sign languages (eg., Ameslan)—not to be confused with standard systems (eg., signed English) borrowing their syntactic organization from the corresponding spoken language—must be considered as the natural language of deaf people. Such languages, as recent linguistic and psycholinguistic work demonstrates, are complete systems exhibiting all the definitional propertiers of true languages (Rondal, Henrot, & Charlier, 1986).

However, 90% of the children with a hearing loss are born to hearing parents. Because of the impact of the total communication movement, the use of a signed system by hearing parents of young deaf children has now been accepted in the United States, but not to the same extent as in other industrialized countries. Studies on the acquisition of a signed system in young deaf children of hearing parents are still rare. Most hearing parents choose a manual coding of the spoken language rather than the esoteric sign language of the deaf community. Developmental data indicate a large variability among the children studied; however, the results generally are encouraging. When they are diagnosed early, properly stimulated, and their hearing parents establish a system of communication as rapidly as possible, the deaf children of hearing parents develop sign language competence that is comparable (though slightly delayed) to that observed in deaf children of deaf parents.

Interesting developments are to be expected in this domain with the advent and generalization of early stimulation programs and total communication principles. Many experts see no reason not to expect quasinormal development and education in deaf children when the communication problems that they face are properly dealt with at the familial and school levels.

Blindness. Blind children at times exhibit transitory delays in lexical development particularly with respect to those vocabulary items associated with visual perception. Such delays are not observed in all cases. This variability has to do with the quality of stimulation in the early environment. Phonological difficulties sometimes reported in blind children do not seem to be more frequent than in the normal population (Warren, 1977). Morpho-syntactical and pragmatical developments also take place within normal limits when the familial milieu is correctly adapting to the special status and functioning of the blind child.

Many blind children seem to have problems in the use of the first-person singular personal pronoun. This may be symptomatic of a specific difficulty in these children to posit themselves explicitly as subjects clearly distinct from other possible subjects and objects in the environment (Fraiberg, 1977). Verbalisms refer to the use of linguistic terms with visual denotations. Previous work had hypothesized that the use of such terms in large amounts by blind subjects leads to increased formality and artificiality in language. However, more recent studies (Demott, 1972) indicate that verbal associations to vocabulary items with visual referents have the same frequency and structural organization in blind and normally sighted people.

Motonic Deficits. It is generally admitted (Bouton, 1976) that cerebral palsied subjects develop language according to the usual progression without exhibiting specific linguistic difficulties. Delays and impairments occur in the area of speech production (deficiencies in sound production, coarticulatory difficulties, rythmic disorders, insufficient respiratory coordination, etc.). The present-day emphasis in the speech education of subjects with cerebral palsy is on the use and development of technical auxiliaries and prostheses in which electronic and computer sciences play a major role.

REFERENCES

Bay, E. (1975). Ontogeny of stable speech areas in the human brain. In E. H. Lenneberg & E. Lenneberg (Eds.), *Foundations of language development*, New York: Academic.

Benton, A. (1964). Developmental aphasia and brain damage. *Cortex, 1*, 40–52.

Bouton, C. (1976). *Le développement du langage. Aspects normaux et pathologiques*. Paris: Masson.

Demott, R. (1972). Verbalism and affective meaning for severely visually impaired and normally sighted children. *New Outlook for the Blind, 66*, 1–8.

Eisenson, J. (1968). Developmental aphasia: A speculative view with therapeutic implications. *Journal of Speech and Hearing Research, 33*, 3–13.

Fraiberg, S. (1977). *Insights from the blind*. New York: Basic Books.

Grossman, H. (Ed.). (1983). *Classification in mental retardation*. Washington, DC: American Association on Mental Deficiency.

Hecaen, H. (1967). Aspects des troubles de la lecture (alexie) au cours des lésions cérébrales en foyer. *Word, 23*, 265–287.

Hirsch, K. (1967). Differential diagnostic between aphasia and schizophrenia language in children. *Journal of Speech & Hearing Research, 32*, 3–10.

Hoffmeister, R. (1982). Acquisition of signed languages by deaf children. In H. Hoeman & R. Wilbur (Eds.), *Communication in two societies*. Washington, DC: Gallaudet College.

Jan, J., Freeman, R., & Scott, E. (1977). *Visual impairment in children and adolescents*. New York: Grune & Stratton.

Landau, W., Goldstein, R., & Kleffner, F. (1960). Congenital aphasia: A clinico-pathologic study. *Neurology, 10*, 915–921.

Leblanc, R. (1979). *Expérience pilote d'enseignement auprès d'enfants souffrant de troubles spécifiques de langage*. Quebec City: Ministry of Education of Quebec.

Leblanc, R. (1982). Aphasie congénitale. In J. A. Rondal & X. Seron (Eds.), *Troubles du langage*. Brussels: Mardaga.

Lenneberg, E. (1967). *Biological basis of language*. New York: Wiley.

Manis, F. R., & Morrison, F. J. (1985). Reading disability: A deficit in rule learning. In L. Siegel & F. Morrison (Eds.), *Cognitive development in atypical children*. New York: Springer-Verlag.

Marshall, J., & Newcombe, F. (1973). Patterns of paralexia: A psycholinguistic approach. *Journal of Psycholinguistic Research, 2*, 175–199.

McCarthy, J. J. (1963). Clinical diagnosis and treatment of aphasia: Aphasia in children. In C. Osgood & M. Miron (Eds.), *Approaches in the study of aphasia*. Urbana, IL: University of Illinois Press.

Moores, D. F. (1978). *Educating the deaf. Psychology, principles, and practices*. Boston: Houghton Mifflin.

Rondal, J. A. (1978). Maternal speech to normal and Down's syndrome children matched for mean length of utterance. In E. Meyers (Eds.), *Quality of life in severely and moderately retarded children: Research foundation for improvement*. Washington, DC: American Association on Mental Deficiency.

Rondal, J. A. (1981). Language acquisition in Down's syndrome children: Recent studies and problems. In *Communication and handicap. Report of EASE 1980*. Helsinki: Finnish Association for Special Education.

Rondal, J. A. (1986). *Le développement du langage chez l'enfant trisomique 21. Manuel pratique d'aide et d'intervention*. Brussels: Mardaga.

Rondal, J. A., Henrot, F., & Charlier, M. (1985). *Le langage des signes*. Brussels: Mardaga.

Rutter, M. (1978). Language disorder in infantile autism. In M. Rutter & E. Schopler (Eds.), *Autism, a reappraisal of concepts and treatment*. New York: Plenum.

Rutter, M., & Schopler, E. (Eds.). (1978). *Autism, a reappraisal of concepts and treatment*. New York: Plenum.

Van Hout, A., & Seron, X. (1983). *L'aphasie de l'enfant*. Brussels: Mardaga.

Vellutino, F. (1979). *Dyslexia: Theory and research*. Cambridge, MA: MIT Press.

Warren, D. (1977). *Blindness and early child development*. New York: American Foundation for the Blind.

Zangwill, O. (1975). The ontogeny of cerebral dominance in man. In E. H. Lenneberg & E. Lenneberg (Eds.), *Foundations of language development*. New York: Academic.

JEAN A. RONDAL
*Laboratory for Language,
Psychology, and Logopedics,
University of Liege, Belgium*

APHASIA
DYSLEXIA
LANGUAGE DELAYS
LANGUAGE DISORDERS
SPEECH, ABSENCE OF

LANGUAGE DELAYS

The first delays in the acquisition of language often announce further complications and developmental difficulties. However, many authors and professionals use the terms language delay and simple language delay to refer to the existence of a marked chronological delay in the acquisition of language by reference to the usual norms in children with average intelligence. There is no criterion that can be used to decide when a delay must be considered to be pathological. The major problem is to distinguish between the language development of the child who is slow but normal and that of the one who is retarded. The term simple language delay is used when the child understands and produces little language between 2 and 5 years (Bouton, 1976). Simple language delays should disappear by 5 or 6 years; otherwise the delay can no longer be considered to be simple and the existence of a serious language deficiency must be acknowledged.

The linguistic signs most clearly associated with language retardation are a marked delay in the onset of the first single- and multiword productions, speech delay (poor articulation and co-articulation of sounds and sequences of sounds, problems in sound discrimination), persistence of overextensions in vocabulary use well beyond the normal time, and persistence of telegraphic speech (absence or low productivity of grammatical words such as articles, pronouns, prepositions, auxiliaries, modals, etc.). Language comprehension may appear to be better than speech, but on careful examination it usually proves unsatisfactory, particularly as to grammatical rules.

The exact etiology of a simple language delay is not known, but most authors see the intervention of the following factors either separately or in conjunction:

1. *Hereditary Background.* A markedly higher proportion of children with language delay than normally developing children have parents or collaterals with language delays or deficiencies (Debray, 1978).
2. *Neurological Factors.* A high proportion of language-delayed children have histories of natal prematurity or perinatal problems and minimal cerebral dysfunction (Debray, 1978).
3. *Affective and Relational Problems.* Stem from the familial context.

REFERENCES

Bouton, C. (1976). *Le développement du langage. Aspects normaux et pathologiques.* Paris: Masson.

Debray-Ritzen, P. (1978). *Lettre ouverte aux parents des petits écoliers.* Paris: Albin Michel.

JEAN A. RONDAL
Laboratory for Language,
Psychology, and Logopedics,
University of Liège, Belgium

EXPRESSIVE LANGUAGE DISORDERS
LANGUAGE DEFICIENCIES AND DEFICITS
LANGUAGE DISORDERS
SPEECH, ABSENCE OF

LANGUAGE DISORDERS

Language has been defined as a code whereby ideas about the world are represented through a conventional system of arbitrary signals for communication (Bloom & Lahey, 1978). A disruption of any of the five major components of this definition (a code, ideas, convention, a system, and communication) would constitute a language disorder. Language disorders can be vastly disruptive to the educational process because nearly all education is transmitted through one form of language or another. Language disorders typically cause a pervasive disruption of one's life. The most significant, unique characteristic that distinguishes humans from other animals is the ability to express thoughts, needs, and wishes through the use of speech and language and to be able to encode and decode sounds quickly in response to the language of others (Tureen & Tureen, 1986).

Language disorders have been differentiated within the larger category of speech disorders. The American Speech-Language and Hearing Association indicates that speech disorders may be characterized as disorders of articulation, language, rhythm, voice, and hearing. Within this context, a language disorder is the inability or decreased ability of the individual to use the words, phrases, or sentences of the language in a meaningful manner. Three broad groupings of language disorders exist: receptive language disorders, expressive language disorders, and a combination of receptive and expressive language difficulties. The relative severity of these disorders varies greatly within disorders and needs to be viewed on a continuum from mild impairment to complete aphasia or mutism. The etiology of language disorders varies tremendously as well.

The speech and language centers of the brain have been well researched and documented beginning more than 150 years ago. Language disorders having neurological origins generally involve the left temporal lobe (especially in the receptive aphasias, also known as Wernicke's aphasia) or a portion of the frontal lobes adjacent to the motor strip on the lower left, a surface known as Broca's area (involved principally in the expressive aphasias, also known as Broca's aphasia). Many other structures of the brain are involved in language, however, and damage or dysfunction to most portions of the left hemisphere will produce at least some minimal disruption of language. Right hemisphere damage can cause language disorders in a small number of cases.

Numerous other factors cause language disorders, including intellectual, psychological, social, genetic, and general maturity factors (Bloom & Lahey 1978; Brown, 1986; Tureen & Tureen, 1986). The assumption of neurological disorders that often accompanies a language disorder may well be in error for a specific case; only through a comprehensive diagnostic assessment can the etiology be determined. Determining the source of the language disorder can be important in developing the correct treatment strategy as well.

Language disorders often are related to more general disorders of auditory processing and occur with high incidence among children with many types of learning disabilities. Language disorders can lead to other forms of speech problems as well, particularly those involved with speech production. The assessment of language disorders involves a careful psychological evaluation of intelligence and personality, formal testing of receptive and expressive language skills, and evaluation of spontaneous speech samples. The latter are particularly useful for determination of sentence structures, lexicon, expressive syntax, grammatical forms, mean length of utterance, comprehension, associative ability, and morphology (Tureen & Tureen, 1986).

Use of the term language disorders is not common among professionals working with an individual child. Language disorders represent a host of problems that may be present in any singular or multiple combination. A child who has a language disorder may have a problem in formulating ideas or conceptualizing information about the world, may develop a code that does not match the conventional code in use, or may simply be delayed in acquiring all of these aspects of language. For clear communication about language disorders, more specific classifications are typically used.

REFERENCES

Bloom, L., & Lahey, M. (1978). *Language development and language disorders*. New York: Wiley.

Brown, R. T. (1986). Etiology of exceptionality. In R. T. Brown & C. R. Reynolds (Eds.), *Psychological perspectives on childhood exceptionality: A handbook*. New York: Wiley-Interscience.

Tureen, P., & Tureen, J. (1986). Childhood speech and language disorders. In R. T. Brown & C. R. Reynolds (Eds.), *Psychological perspectives on childhood exceptionality: A handbook*: New York: Wiley-Interscience.

CECIL R. REYNOLDS
Texas A&M University

CHILDHOOD APHASIA
CLEFT LIP PALATE
DEAF
EXPRESSIVE LANGUAGE DISORDERS
LANGUAGE DEFICIENCIES AND DEFICITS
MUTISM

MUTISM, ELECTIVE
SPEECH, ABSENCE OF
STUTTERING
VOICE DISORDERS

LANGUAGE DISORDERS, EXPRESSIVE

See EXPRESSIVE LANGUAGE DISORDERS.

LANGUAGE THERAPY

Language therapy has undergone significant changes since the 1950s. These changes reflect shifts in perspective on the nature of language and children's acquisition of language skill. Until the mid-1960s, speech-language pathologists primarily sought to determine the etiology (cause) of a child's language problem and to assess, by norm-referenced measures, how "mature" a youngster's speech and language were in relation to the adult model. Emphasis was on classifying children into etiological groupings for remediation, the assumption being that children whose problems stem from similar causes will have the same instructional needs. There was at that time a major focus on speech correction, with grammar correction and vocabulary constituting the remaining concern of both assessment and therapy. In the 1960s language intervention branched in two diverging directions: one devoted to training specific abilities believed to underlie language functioning; the other, an outgrowth of Chomsky's (1957) linguistics revolution, focusing on language itself.

The specific abilities model (Johnson & Myklebust, 1967; Kirk, McCarthy, & Kirk, 1968) attempted to pinpoint separate skills believed crucial as underpinnings for language development and to determine preferred learning modalities. The idea was to generate an individual child's profile of strengths and weaknesses in presumed requisite abilities (e.g., attention, discrimination, sequencing, verbal memory) and to delineate relative strengths and weaknesses among learning modalities (e.g., auditory-vocal, auditory-motor, visual-vocal, and visual-motor) as the basis for planning appropriate intervention goals and methods.

The specific abilities model influenced many practices of language therapists in clinical settings and also spawned a number of language programs used with groups of children in school settings (Bush & Giles, 1977; Dunn, Smith, Dunn, Horton, & Smith, 1981). Working within this framework, clinicians and teachers attempted either to strengthen deficient underlying abilities (attention, sequencing, etc.) and learning modalities (auditory-vocal, visual-motor, etc.) or to harness presumed strengths to compensate for or circumvent presumed weak underlying abilities and learning modalities. While this orientation and its ensuing programs found widespread acceptance through the 1960s and 1970s, both the theoretical base and the practical efficacy have been severely criticized. There is at present no demonstrated validity to the presumption of the specific abilities model that underlying abilities and modality preferences can be identified as separate entities or trained to improve language functioning.

Alternatively, in the 1960s, the linguistic model of language therapy, influenced by Chomsky's (1957) view of language as a linguistic structure with phonemic, semantic, syntactic, and morphologic aspects, stressed analyses of specific features of language, including phonology, vocabulary, syntax, and morphology. Intervention focused largely on training particular syntactic/morphologic forms within highly structured language lessons that often used behavioral shaping techniques.

With the arrival of the 1970s, language therapy expanded the original linguistic model, reorganizing around the central notion of language in context. Increasingly it was realized that the content (semantics) of language is not reducible to vocabulary. It also became evident that the meaningful context and communicative intent of language are inseparable from its form. Intervention began to be designed within naturalistic settings to facilitate children's inducing language rules via natural play contexts (Kretschmer & Kretschmer, 1978; McLean & Snyder-McLean, 1978). Rather than relying primarily on standardized elicitation and imitation tests to determine the goals of intervention, therapists began gathering and analyzing naturally occurring language samples within surroundings familiar to the child.

A dominant paradigm (Bloom & Lahey, 1978) emerged that views language as the interaction of form, content, and use and describes language disorders as problems of form, content, use, or any of their interactions. In addition, the 1970s shifted the language standard from the adult model to the child language model: the sequence that normal children follow in learning language became the model for assessing and guiding the development of children's disordered language. Communication became the pivotal goal of intervention, which meant that language therapy's emphasis shifted from particular aspects of form to facilitating the interaction of content and use.

The 1980s has seen an integration of knowledge garnered over the past 30 years, resulting in a much less fragmented view of children's language and language disorders. Language therapy has approached the child's developing system from a developmental, rather than an adult, model and has attended not only to phonologic and syntactic development, but also to semantic and pragmatic (language use) elaboration. The current challenge has been to more fully understand the dynamic system of form/content/use and to facilitate the development of that system within a communicative context. Increased interest in the language disorders of elementary school children and adolescents has led to two interrelated concerns that have emerged from the more unified and contextual framework of language therapy in the 1980s: concern with the use of language in social contexts, termed pragmatics, and concern with the understanding and production of longer units of language, termed discourse processes.

Concern with pragmatics, initiated in the late 1970s, has expanded in the 1980s (Bryan, Donahue, & Pearl, 1981). Pragmatics has to do with the rules governing language use in social situations, including knowing how to speak in different circumstances to different audiences. Pragmatics encompasses social conventions such as how to open and close conversations, switch speaker/listener roles, initiate conversational topics, maintain topics, and repair breakdowns in communication. Pragmatic content includes the profusion of ways we use language (e.g., to console, to request, to order, to compliment). Language disorders of pragmatic functioning can have severe social and life consequences; thus, when they are present, they are important targets of language therapy. Pragmatic programs for use within classrooms as well as in clinical settings have begun to be available.

Recently, the communicative competence of language-disordered elementary school children and adolescents has been viewed through the pragmatic lens and, additionally, within the framework of discourse processing. Discourse processes have to do with language beyond the sentence level. While including syntax, semantics, and pragmatics, the term also encompasses meaning relationships among sentences, as well as organization of larger language units such as stories. Language therapists have begun to focus on children's understanding and managing of language relations beyond the sentence, focusing on how well children organize their communication to make a point, to explain what happened, to follow the development of a conversation, or to comprehend and remember stories read to them (Feagans, 1983). Means for analyzing and assessing discourse processes and methods for developing these in classrooms and clinical settings represent an emerging theme in language therapy of the 1980s.

The past 30 years have seen major changes in both the focus and the methodology of language therapy, although, as in most fields, some adherents to previous models continue to practice within frameworks abandoned by others. The changes that have shaped practice in the 1980s have cast the language therapist into the role of facilitator who provides appropriate input to the child in meaningful contexts help to the induction of rules of form, content, and use. Communication is considered paramount and the development of communicative competence the focal organizer for language therapy.

REFERENCES

Bryan, T., Donahue, M., & Pearl, R. (1981). Studies of learning disabled children's pragmatic competence. *Topics in Learning & Learning Disabilities, 1*(2), 29–41.

Bush, W. J., & Giles, M. T. (1977). *Aids to psycholinguistic teaching* (2nd ed.). Columbus, OH: Merrill.

Chomsky, N. A. (1957). *Syntactic structures*. The Hague, Netherlands: Mouton.

Dunn, L. M., Smith, J. O., Dunn, L. M., Horton, K. B., & Smith, D. D. (1981). *Peabody language development kits*. Circle Pines, MN: American Guidance Service.

Feagans, L. (1983). Discourse processes in learning disabled children. In J. D. McKinney & L. Feagans (Eds.), *Current topics in learning disabilities*. Norwood, NJ: Ablex.

Johnson, D. J., Myklebust, H. R. (1967). *Learning disabilities: Educational principles and practices*. New York: Grune & Stratton.

Kirk, S. A., McCarthy, J. J., & Kirk, W. D. (1968). *Illinois Test of Psycholinguistic Abilities* (rev. ed.). Urbana: University of Illinois Press.

Kretschmer, R., & Kretschmer, L. (1978). *Language development and intervention with the hearing impaired*. Baltimore, MD: University Park Press.

McLean, J., & Snyder-McLean, L. (1978). *A transactional approach to early language training*. Columbus, OH: Merrill.

KATHERINE GARNETT
*Hunter College, City University
of New York*

LANGUAGE DELAYS
LEARNING DISABILITIES
LANGUAGE DISORDERS

LARGE-PRINT BOOKS

Many low-vision students learn to read using regular-sized print, with or without the use of optical aids. The print selected for low-vision students depends on factors such as the student's motivation and interest, visual acuity and fields of view, reading experience and ability, lighting, and accessibility of print (Jose, 1983).

According to Jose (1983), the advantages of large print are that it is more comfortable and easier to read; it is usually produced on nonglare paper; and it offers a less restricted field of view compared to using regular print with a magnifying lens. However, producing large-type textbooks is expensive. As a result, the number and variety of available books is limited, particularly at the high school and college level. Other disadvantages are that the pictures in these textbooks are usually missing or not as clear as the color pictures in regular print textbooks, and large-print books are large and bulky and look so different

from regular print books that some students are embarrassed to use them (Barraga, 1983).

Decisions regarding print size used should be made by the visually handicapped student, a teacher trained to work with visually handicapped students, parents, and a low-vision team (if available). These decisions should be based on functional assessments comparing the student's performance using many different print sizes, type styles, margin widths, spaces between letters, words, and lines in respect to rate of oral and silent reading, comfort while reading, number of skipped and miscalled words, comprehension, and duration of reading before fatigue (Jose, 1983).

Heward and Orlansky (1984) advise that while size of print is an important variable in instructing low-vision students, other equally important factors to consider are the quality of the printed material, the contrast between print and page, the spacing between lines, and the illumination of the setting in which the student reads. Some low-vision students need to use a variety of media, including several different print sizes, recorded materials, and even braille (depending on the subject matter) to optimize their reading. However, special educators generally agree that a low-vision student should use the smallest print size that he or she can comfortably read (Heward & Orlansky, 1984).

REFERENCES

Barraga, N. (1983). *Visual handicaps and learning*. Austin, TX: Exceptional Resources.

Heward, W. L., & Orlansky, M. D. (1984). *Exceptional children*. Columbus, OH: Merrill.

Jose, R. (1983). *Understanding low vision*. New York: American Foundation for the Blind.

ROSANNE K. SILBERMAN
*Hunter College, City University
of New York*

AMERICAN PRINTING HOUSE FOR THE BLIND
LIBRARIES FOR THE BLIND AND PHYSICALLY
  HANDICAPPED
LIBRARY SERVICES FOR THE HANDICAPPED
LOW VISION

LARRY P.

Larry P. was one of six black children who were plaintiffs in a suit brought in 1971 against Wilson Riles, California state superintendent of public instruction. The suit charged that the IQ tests that were used in determining eligibility for placement in classes for the educable mentally retarded (EMR) were culturally biased. The lawyers for the plaintiffs based their charges of cultural bias on the fact that the average scores for blacks were lower than for whites, and that using the scores resulted in a higher percentage of black children in EMR classes than in regular classes.

As a consequence of the *Larry P* v. *Wilson Riles* suit, the federal district court granted an injunction in 1972 that banned the use of individually administered intelligence tests for black children being considered for placement in EMR classes. This resulted in psychologists having to use alternative methods such as classroom observations, adaptive behavior assessment, and academic achievement measures to determine whether children referred for special education were intellectually retarded and, in turn, eligible for special education services.

In 1976 the case was brought to trial. The plaintiffs were represented by Public Advocates, Inc. and by *pro bono* attorneys from the San Francisco firm of Morrison and Foerster. The state was represented by a deputy attorney general from the state attorney general's office. The plaintiffs' arguments centered on the disproportion of black children in EMR classes as well as the lower average IQs earned by blacks on most standardized tests of intelligence. They contended that the tests were culturally biased because the items were drawn from white middle-class culture to which black pupils were not exposed. This contention was supported, they argued, by the fact that when the six plaintiffs were retested using the WISC-R (the same test that was used to determine their eligibility for the EMR programs), their IQs were higher because black examiners perceived racial, ethnic, or socioeconomic bias and made modifications in the administration of the test such as rewording items, accepting nonstandard responses, or extending time limits. In addition to arguments that the tests were biased against black children, the plaintiffs maintained that the EMR classes did not cover the same subjects as did regular classes, and that the longer the children attended the EMR classes, the greater the performance gap between EMR children and their regular class peers.

The plaintiffs' legal arguments revolved around showing that blacks were overrepresented in EMR classes and that the IQ test was the sole basis for decisions regarding eligibility and placement. If the IQ was the instrument used for placement, and blacks were overrepresented in EMR classes, then, they argued, the tests had to be biased, making the special education classes suspect. Both IQ tests and special education, therefore, discriminated against black children. From a legal standpoint, the burden shifted to the state of California to show that the tests were not biased, and that even though there were more black children in special education classes, the children benefited from the special education programs.

The state's defense rested on data showing that the IQ tests were valid predictors of present and future performance, and that the tests predicted equally well for blacks and whites. Witnesses for the defense testified that the IQ test was administered only after children had a long experience of failing in regular class programs and were referred for evaluation of their eligibility for EMR classes. The state's witnesses also testified that there was a linear relationship between IQs and severity of mental retardation from the mildly (EMR) to the profoundly retarded. The state's witnesses, moreover, rebutted plaintiff testimony that there should be evidence for a biological or metabolic origin of mental retardation; mildly retarded children fall at one end of the normal distribution of intelligence just as gifted children are at the other, higher, end of the continuum. Having to explain why more black than white children were mildly retarded, the state countered with research that showed a relationship between IQs and poverty, poor nutrition, lack of cognitive stimulation, and other environmental factors.

Ultimately, the state had to contend with two factors: one related to the use of IQ tests for special education placement and the second to the benefits of special education. Plaintiffs built their charges against IQ tests on their cultural bias and the contention that they were the sole criterion for placement of certain children in EMR classes. The state showed that the tests were used to determine eligibility for special education and for a diagnosis of the extent of intellectual retardation. The numerous studies of the validity of IQ tests for distinguishing among individuals varying with respect to academic performance, and, therefore, indicative of the construct and criterion validity of IQ tests for both black and white children, were summarized by several witnesses. But the IQ test was not designed to show whether a child would benefit from or improve as a result of special education placement. A showing of a positive or remedial effect on the academic performance or on the level of intelligence of the child resulting from special education placement was necessary to satisfy the court. As the research on EMR programs had not shown this necessary positive effect, the plaintiffs argued that the IQ tests were not valid for EMR placement even though the state showed convincingly that they were valid for making inferences about current level of intellectual functioning, the only psychological inference required for a determination of mild mental retardation and eligibility for special education.

The state's effort to show that a major source of the overrepresentation was attributable more to the process by which the child was referred for psychological evaluation was not successful. Evidence regarding bias in the referral process (i.e., more black boys than black girls and more blacks than whites were referred resulting in overrepresentation of boys over girls and black boys over white boys in EMR classes) did not convince the court that the IQ was not the primary basis for identifying a child for placement in an EMR class. Testimony that only one-fifth (approximately) of referred children were found eligible after IQ testing did not alter the court's opinion that the IQ test was the culprit.

The plaintiffs' evidence that the IQs of blacks were lower than those of whites was the evidence on which the court ultimately relied to judge that the tests were biased. Since IQs were the most frequent piece of information in the case study records of EMR children, the court concluded that the IQ test was the basis for placement in the special education program even though the state had shown that only a portion of all children with IQ scores in the EMR range were ever placed in special education classes. The overrepresentation of black children could have been tolerated if the state had been successful in demonstrating remediation of EMR children's academic deficiencies. The court, therefore, concluded that the tests were biased and the primary basis for placement in dead-end, stigmatizing special education classes.

The court handed down its opinion in 1979 and prohibited schools "from utilizing, permitting the use of, or approving the use of any standardized intelligence tests . . . for the identification of black EMR children or their placement into EMR classes, without securing prior approval of the court." Furthermore the court ruled that any test used for special education purposes should be shown to be valid for the purposes for which they were to be used. The consequences of the *Larry P.* decision in California have been a search for alternative methods, often less reliable and valid, for determining eligibility for special education classes as well as an attempt to select from among those who are eligible, those children who can benefit from special education.

Children who were classified as EMR in 1971, when the suit was filed, were reevaluated by order of the legislature before the trial began in 1976. The reevaluation resulted in a marked reduction in the number of children in special education, but no change in the overrepresentation of minority children in EMR classes. During the trial, the state of California adopted the California Master Plan for Special Education (almost at the same time that Congress passed PL 94-142), eliminating the category of EMR programs and substituting the category of "learning handicapped" to include mildly retarded pupils and those with learning disabilities. There was also a large amount of additional research evidence published during and after the trial on the differential validity of tests of scholastic aptitude, including individual tests of intelligence, using a variety of criterion measures including school grades and adaptive behavior assessments. These data generally have shown that aptitude tests are valid for both blacks and whites.

Have the outcomes of the *Larry P.* case improved the assessment or special education treatment of black children? We have now the burden of showing not only criterion validity, but the validity of IQ tests to identify those who will benefit from special education treatment. Aptitude and IQ tests may be excellent sources of evidence for prediction or diagnosing eligibility, but not necessarily for selecting the children who will profit most from special education. The *Larry P.* decision has not resulted in elimination of minority overrepresentation, only in fewer children being classified as mildly retarded. Some hail this outcome as a beneficial one, while others wonder what will become of children who are categorically denied special education services. Regardless of the psychological tests or procedures used, school psychologists and special education professionals are obligated to show that they are valid and reliable for diagnosing the cause of educational failure, as well as for selecting and placing those who will benefit from special education services.

Throughout this litigation, few concerns were ever raised about the fate of the six black children who were the plaintiffs in the case. Were their futures positively affected by removing them from special education during their elementary school years? Larry P. went to school out of state and was later identified for special education on the basis of his school achievement and classroom performance. By age 19, he still could not pass the test for a driver's license and was not gainfully employed. The one plaintiff who was adapting well in high school had been placed back in special education after leaving San Francisco schools at the request of his mother. If the *Larry P.* decision is to help schools to achieve a better educational outcome for mildly retarded children, educators and school psychologists may have to remain firm in their support of IQ tests as valid diagnostic procedures and turn their attention to the quality of special education interventions and strategies to tailor the specific special educational treatment to the individual needs of the children. Any educational program that separates a group of children from regular class peers can be justified only if it can be shown that there is more benefit in special education placement than in retention in a regular class.

NADINE M. LAMBERT
University of California,
Berkeley

CULTURAL BIAS IN TESTS
INTELLIGENCE
INTELLIGENCE TESTS

LATERALITY

See CEREBRAL DOMINANCE.

LATIN AMERICA AND THE CARIBBEAN, SPECIAL EDUCATION IN

When defining special education in Latin America and the Caribbean it is important to understand that the data on special education in these countries are sparse, outdated, and often represent only a select group of countries. Although general commonalities exist across countries in Latin America and the Caribbean, caution should be taken in overgeneralizing these data to all countries in the region. Countries within this region that are considered developed (e.g., Puerto Rico, Mexico, Argentina, Brazil) are much more advanced in their education services to handicapped students. The issues addressed in this entry will apply only to developing countries (Third World countries) within this region (e.g. Honduras, Costa Rica, Panama, Uruguay, Peru, Barbados, Haiti, Curacao, Dominican Republic). To best understand special education in Latin America and the Caribbean, it is important to discuss the broader, more general context of disabilities in developing countries.

Current data are available that clearly illustrate the dilemma of special education in developing countries. Marfo (1986) estimates that 70% of the world's disabled population are residing in developing countries. Furthermore, it is estimated that only 2% of disabled persons are receiving rehabilitation services (World Health Organization, 1981). Although these statistics are staggering, the reasons for the high numbers are easily explained. Marfo (1986) states that

> poverty and its social manifestations—inadequate nutrition, disease, illiteracy, inequitable distribution of social services, poor housing, poor drinking water, improper hygiene, etc.—are more prevalant in developing than developed countries. (p. 4)

Furthermore, the causes of most childhood disabilities are preventable. For example, malnutrition accounts for an estimated 50% of disabilities in children. Additionally, in pregnant mothers, poor nutrition and starvation have a catastrophic effect on the unborn fetus. Among older children, the inability to combat infections such as cerebral malaria, spinal meningitis, encephalitis, measles, and mumps can lead to serious neurological and sensory impairments (Marfo, 1986). The solution to these problems is clear. Effective health and medical services could provide prevention of many of these disabilities. Unfortunately, curative medicine and not preventive medicine is what is available to the people of these countries. Much of the preventive work occurring in these countries today is sponsored by international organizations such as the World Health Organization (WHO), the United Nations Education, Scientific and Cultural Organization (UNESCO), the United Nations Children's Fund (UNICEF), and the Overseas Assistance Service (OAS).

In the past 20 years, extensive efforts have been made to bring international attention to special education in developing countries. In 1978 the Council for Exceptional Children convened its First World Congress on Future Special Education. Many of the presentations at this historic meeting have been published in the volume *International Perspectives on Future Special Education* (Fink, 1978). In 1979 UNESCO recognized the International Year of the Child, and in 1981, the International Year of the Disabled Child was designated. These events focused needed attention on the problems of disabled children in developing countries. By the year 2000 UNICEF estimated that there would be over 150 million disabled children under 15 years of age in developing countries (Marfo, Walker, & Charles, 1986).

The problems described in the previous section are shared by the majority of countries in Central America, South America, and the Caribbean. Special education in these countries can best be characterized as follows (DeBabra, 1981; Fink, 1978; Hughes, 1986; Thorburn, 1986):

1. Programs are usually sponsored by private or semi-private organizations (e.g., parent groups, advocacy groups, churches, or interested professionals). Only a limited number of countries offer public school education for handicapped children.

2. Most often, paraprofessionals, parents, or volunteers deliver services to disabled children in these countries. There is a severe shortage of trained special education teachers available in Latin America and the Caribbean.

3. Teacher shortages owing to lack of teacher training programs are critical. For example, in 1981, De Babra reported that only 5% of the special education teachers needed are available to serve the handicapped population in Latin America and the Caribbean.

4. Families lack information regarding the nature of their children's handicapping conditions, often leading to continued beliefs in superstitious causes (e.g., evil spirits, taboos, witchcraft).

5. Poorly run institutions, sponsored by government or charitable organizations, provide many disabled children with the only available placement.

6. The few services that are provided to handicapped children are usually centralized in capital cities and few services are available for the scattered rural population.

7. Because of strong cultural and religious beliefs, families often conceal their disabled children from society, making child find efforts extremely difficult.

8. With the instructional and technological advances in special education occurring in developed coun-

tries, it is predicted that the gap in providing special education services to handicapped children will become significantly wider in Latin American and the Caribbean.

9. Traditional teacher-training programs are not adapted to meet the particular and socioeconomic needs of Latin American and Caribbean countries.

10. The high rate of dropouts in Latin America and the Caribbean may indicate a need to focus on diagnosing learning problems as early as possible. In 1965 UNESCO reported that an average of 60% of all children dropped out before they finished grade school.

11. Many countries are battling with compulsory regular education for nonhandicapped children, and the issue of special education as a national priority is extremely low. Education's low priority is due primarily to the emphasis on child labor. Families in Latin America and the Caribbean often depend on children to work in order to assist with the cost of food, shelter, etc.

12. Scarcity of educational materials is often a common characteristic of programs in Latin America and the Caribbean. Special education materials (e.g., assessments, curriculum) available in the United States often are not translated into Spanish. Additionally, the materials may be inappropriate for the geographic and cultural needs of the population.

There are, however, some exemplary programs in Latin America and the Caribbean. In Jamaica in 1975, the Jamaican Early Stimulation Project was developed. Using the Portage model of Wisconsin (Shearer & Shearer, 1972), this project was a great success. Between 1975 and 1983, approximately 1200 children under the age of 6 received services. Most of the teachers had no previous formal training and had not received more than a grade 7 education (Thorburn, 1986). In Barbados the aim of the Barbadian Child Care Project was to train staff for government and private daycare centers. The project trained 69 persons in 2 years and has successfully begun integration of the handicapped preschool program into regular daycare centers on the island (Thorburn, 1986).

Haiti's early intervention program will serve 1.8% of Haiti's 1 million children in the birth to age 6 group. In the first year, 103 daycare centers opened in rural areas. Both handicapped and nonhandicapped preschoolers are being served in order to prevent further disabilities (Thorburn, 1986). In Ecuador teacher training has been the focus of the special education effort. Often regular education teachers find themselves with 50 to 60 students in a primary classroom. Many of those students are learning disabled, mentally retarded, or emotionally disturbed. The goal of the Ecuador project is to train teacher-trainers who will begin to train regular and special education teachers (Pynn, 1978).

In Peru the Escuela Especial Carlos A. Manucci has accomplished much of what is consider state of the art comprehensive education for moderately and severely handicapped students in the area around Trujillo. Although Manucci is a segregated special school, its goals for education are to prepare all its handicapped students for employment and independent life skills. Manucci apparently has high expectations for its special students (Wood, Wood, & Alegria, 1978).

Many more exemplary programs are being established in Latin America and the Caribbean. It is with the help of international organizations and individual commitments that special education services for a majority of disabled children will become a reality. Training skills cannot be imported without adaptations for the cultural, social, and economic status of each country. Organizations such as the Peace Corps and Partners of the Americas provide a unique way to train persons in Latin America and the Caribbean by using special education consultants from the United States (Thorburn, 1977). Continued efforts in research and the dissemination of program effectiveness is needed. Clearly, the task ahead is an enormous one.

REFERENCES

De Babra, M. (1981). *Professional education of the special teacher in Latin America and the Caribbean.* Paper presented at the National Congress on Mental Deficiency, Mexico City, Mexico. (ERIC Document Reproduction Service No. Ed 240 785)

Fink, A. (1978). *International perspectives on future special education.* Reston, VA: Council for Exceptional Children.

Hughes, J. (1986). Educational services for the mentally retarded in developing countries. In K. Marfo, S. Walker, & B. Charles (Eds.), *Childhood disability in developing countries: Issues in habilitation and special education* (pp. 165–176). New York: Praeger.

Marfo, K. (1986). Confronting childhood disability in the developing countries. In K. Marfo, S. Walker, & B. Charles (Eds.), *Childhood disability in developing countries: Issues in habilitation and special education* (pp. 3–26). New York: Praeger.

Marfo, K., Walker, S., & Charles, B. (1986). *Childhood disability in developing countries: Issues in habilitation and special education.* New York: Praeger.

Pynn, M. E. (1978). Special education and developing nations: A proposal for teacher training in Ecuador. In A. H. Fink (Ed.), *International perspective on future special education* (pp. 290–292). Reston, VA: Council for Exceptional Children.

Shearer, M., & Shearer, D. (1972). The Portage Project: A model for early childhood education. *Exceptional Children, 36,* 210–217.

Thorburn, M. (1977). *Small is beautiful.* Paper presented at the meeting of the Partners of the Americas, Santo Domingo, Dominican Republic.

Thorburn, M. (1986). Early intervention for disabled children in the Caribbean. In K. Marfo, S. Walker, & B. Charles (Eds.),

Childhood disability in developing countries: Issues in habilitation and special education (pp. 63–72). New York: Praeger.

Wood, M., Wood, N., & Alegria, A. (1978). The economics of special education in a developing country. In A. H. Fink (Ed.), *International perspective on future special education* (pp. 194–197). Reston, VA: Council for Exceptional Children.

World Health Organization. (1981). *Training the disabled in the community: A manual* (2nd ed.). Geneva, Switzerland.

VIVIAN I. CORREA
University of Florida

CENTRAL AMERICA, SPECIAL EDUCATION IN
MEXICO, SPECIAL EDUCATION IN

LEAD POISONING

The health hazards associated with the use of lead have been known for over 2000 years. Gillfillan (1965) has speculated that lead poisoning may have contributed to the decline of the Roman civilization after the introduction of lead pipes for the supply of drinking water. Mental retardation, sterility, and infant mortality were frequent among influential Romans, and the unearthed bones of wealthy ancient Romans have been found to have high lead content.

Today, much attention is directed toward lead pollution in the environment. Potential health hazards from industrial exposure are created by the use of over 1 million tons of lead each year, by the release of hundreds of thousands of tons of lead into the atmosphere from automobile exhaust emissions, and by the occupational exposure of workers to lead in over 100 different occupations. However, debate continues on whether low levels of lead exposure result in adverse cognitive and behavioral effects (Graham, 1983).

Although not a common element, lead is found in the soil, water, and atmosphere. It occurs more frequently in the natural environment than other heavy metals. Lead is one of the few metals that seems to have toxic effects but no essential function in an organism. Lead can enter the body through diet, eating of lead-based paint (pica), and exposure to an environment containing a high lead content. Foundries, brass works, battery factories, printing operations, and other plants have been shown to increase the amount of lead in the surrounding environment. Needleman (1980) has reported low-level lead intoxication from automobile exhaust fumes.

The most common way of estimating acute levels of lead in the body is by blood test. Chronic lead exposure is determined by measuring the lead content of teeth. However, this estimation technique reveals no significant relationship between body lead and behavior or cognitive performance when socioeconomic status differences are con-

sidered. The analysis of lead in hair samples has been increasingly used to estimate the lead body burden. Marlowe et al. (1984) studied the relationship between hair mineral elements and learning disabilities and found the learning-disabled group had elevated hair lead concentrations.

The mean blood lead levels in urban dwellers range from 10 to 25 mg/100 ml. The mean blood levels of children living in mildly and heavily lead-polluted environments are 26 to 40 mg/100 ml, and 60 mg/100 ml, respectively. At levels of lead absorption in the blood, i.e., 40 mg/100 ml, the body will excrete the majority of the lead intake. At higher levels of absorption, i.e., 50 mg to 120 mg/100 ml of blood, exposure may be reflected by a wide range of clinical symptoms.

The following effects of lead intoxication on the human body systems and organs have been identified:

1. The production of blood cells is impaired (microcytic anemia and increased destruction of red cells).
2. The kidney is impaired (tubular damage in acute intoxication; interstitial-glomerular fibrosis, and tubular atrophy in chronic intoxication).
3. The gastrointestinal tract is affected (colic, constipation, and diarrhea).
4. The bones, liver, immune system, hormonal secretion, and cardiovascular system are affected.
5. The nervous system is damaged (encephalopathy, mainly in children; peripheral neuropathy, mainly in adults).

In spite of a great number of studies and clinical observations, the nature of the neurotropic action of lead still remains unexplained (Beritic, 1984). However, in adults, the usual manifestations of lead poisoning are colic, anemia, and peripheral neuropathy. Acute lead encephalopathy in children results in death in 5 to 20% of the cases; it causes permanent neurological and mental disturbances in over 25% of the survivors. Mentally retarded children who have pica are often found to have elevated blood lead levels. The clinical manifestations of lead poisoning in children develop over a period of 3 to 6 weeks. The child becomes anorexic, less playful, and more irritable. These symptoms may be misinterpreted as a behavior disorder or mental retardation. Intermittent vomiting, vague abdominal pain, clumsiness, and ataxia also may be exhibited, but in a week or less. In the final stages of lead poisoning, vomiting becomes more persistent, apathy progresses to drowsiness and stupor, and periods of hyperirritability, and finally, coma and seizures, are seen. In children under the age of 2, the syndrome evolves rapidly; in older children, recurrent and less severe episodes are more likely to occur.

At blood levels of 50 to 80 mg/100 ml, the symptoms are variable. Some children may have symptoms of severe encephalopathy, whereas others may be asymptomatic; acute encephalopathy may occur abruptly and unpredictably. Children with sickle cell anemia are especially vulnerable to lead neuropathy. In the United States, lead poisoning occurs most often in 1- to 5-year-old children who inhabit slum areas of large cities and ingest leaded paint. However, in recent years, severe forms of encephalopathy have declined owing to better social and medical care. Today there is concern that brain damage also may be caused by subtoxic levels of lead exposure. Long-term subclinical intoxication causes lead neuropathy with decreased reflexes, motor weakness, hypoaesthesia, and reduced nerve conduction velocity (Beritic, 1984).

It is generally accepted that, in children, symptoms of lead poisoning and encephalopathy are associated with blood levels of above 60 mg/100 mls. Subtle behavioral and cognitive effects related to mean blood level of 10 mg/100 ml to 60 mg/100 ml for children exposed to lead have been much debated. It is estimated that 3 to 20% of preschool children have increased lead absorption, i.e., 30 to 80 Pb mg/100 ml. In children living near smelters or in the homes of workers who carry particulate lead home on their clothing, the proportion of increased lead absorption is higher than in their peers. Most cases are asymptomatic, while mild nonspecific symptoms compatible with early plumbism are reported in a few. The range is similar to the area of doubt (45 mg/100 ml) for adult male lead workers. In both cases, the debate concerns the difference between an ideal position of no lead-induced stress on any body system (hematopoietic or nervous) and a practical position that addresses the socioeconomic conditions of, and the cost to, the concerned society (King, 1982).

Blood lead levels below those that produce encephalopathy with severe brain damage have been implicated as a possible cause of more subtle behaviors and learning difficulties (Chisolm & Barltrop, 1979). Sachs et al. (1979) reported no significant relationship between initial blood lead level concentrations of more than 50 mg Pb/100 ml and subsequent mean IQ of children who were treated before an acute episode of severe encephalopathy occurred.

During the postnatal phase of rapid neurodevelopment, which in children extends from birth to 2 or 3 years of age, the brain may be especially vulnerable to nutritional and toxic insults. Even so, most are asymptomatic. Whether such children are at significant risk for subtle, but significant, neurobehavioral impairment has aroused much concern.

Uncertainty concerning the maximum allowable environmental and industrial exposure levels exists because clear relationships among airborne concentrations, biological changes, behavioral and neurological effects, and medical signs and symptoms of lead have not yet been firmly established. However, the literature concerning children exposed to lead shows the most common psychological manifestations are hyperactivity, irritability, and uncooperativeness. Other behavioral characteristics include moodiness, depression, delirium, and occasional mania or psychosis.

Graham (1983) has reviewed the cognitive sequela of mild-to-high lead body burdens and has reached the conclusion that

"at all levels of blood lead from 20 mg/100 ml up to 80 mg/100 ml, there are either small differences on the verge of statistical significance or no differences between high-and low-lead groups, both on a wide range of cognitive measures and in behavioral deficits. . . . Nevertheless, most authorities would now accept that there is a serious possibility that low-level lead exposure may well produce at least a modest deficit in cognitive performance." (pp. 61–62)

REFERENCES

Beritic, T. (1984). Lead neuropathy. *CRC Critical Reviews in Toxicology, 12*(2), 149–213.

Blouin, A. G., Blouin, J. H., & Kelly, T. C. (1983). Lead, trace mineral intake, and behavior of children. *Topics in Early Childhood Special Education, 3*(2), 63–71.

Chisolm, Jr., J. J., & Barltrop, D. (1979). Recognition and management of children with increased lead absorption. *Archives of Disease in Childhood, 54,* 249–262.

Gillfillan, S. C. (1965). Lead poisoning and the fall of Rome. *Journal of Occuupational Medicine, 7,* 53–60.

Graham, P. J. (1983). Poisoning in children. In M. Rutter (Ed.), *Developmental neuropsychiatry* (pp. 52–67). New York: Guilford.

King, E. (1982). Lead poisoning. *Public Health Review, 10*(1), 49–76.

Marlowe, M., Cossairt, A., Welch, K., & Errera, J. (1984). Hair mineral content as a predictor of learning disabilities. *Journal of Learning Disabilities, 17*(7), 418–421.

Needleman, H. (Ed.). (1980). *Low-level lead exposure: The clinical implications of current research.* New York: Raven.

Sachs, A. K., McCaughran, D. A., Krall, V., Rozenfeld, I. H., & Youngsmith, N. (1979). Lead poisoning without encephalopathy. *American Journal of Diseases of Children, 133,* 786–790.

KENNETH A. ZYCH
Walter Reed Army Medical Center, Washington, D.C.

BRAIN DAMAGE
MENTAL RETARDATION
PICA

LEAGUE SCHOOL

The League School, now expanded and known as the League Center, was founded in 1953 by Dr. Carl Fenichel, It is a not-for-profit continuum of care serving multiply mentally handicapped children and adults at four facilities in Brooklyn, New York.

When Fenichel initiated the League School, the children he served were considered uneducable. Their parents, commonly believed to be the root of the problem, often faced the necessity of abandoning their children to mental institutions, since no other options existed. Fenichel maintained that the mind-crippling disorders of severely mentally/emotionally handicapped children resulted from serious learning and language deficits rather than from parental sources. In creating a day school based on this perspective, he pioneered a diagnostic, educational, and treatment program, which was daring and unpopular in the climate of the 1950s. His "reaching and teaching" model proffered the hope that intensive education and treatment would be effective if they included: (1) highly individualized programs based on comprehensive and ongoing assessment; (2) the active participation of parents in educational and treatment partnership with the school; (3) highly organized and structured training to bring order, stability, and direction to the children's disordered minds; and (4) teachers who could limit as well as accept the children.

Today the League Center's continuum of services includes a school-based home training program serving parents of severely disturbed children 18 months to 4 years of age. Both the League School Nursery and the Joan Fenichel Therapeutic Nursery provide day treatment for groups of 2 to 4 year olds. The League School is attended by more than 100 students. Since communication disorders are prevalent and contribute significantly to the students' bizarre behavior, language skills are stressed in the school program. Students with little or no language are in classes staffed by both a language and a special educator; those with some developed communication skills receive language therapy and participate in small-group conversation clinics. There are special programs in physical education, travel training, print shop, crafts, and prevocational training. A six-week summer program extends social and life skills training into a wide range of recreational activities.

The Adult Day Treatment Center serves older adolescents and adults with the goal of developing sufficient self-control and socially acceptable behavior for living independently in the community. Fenichel House is a residence for adults who require continuing supervision in order to live and work in the community. This program is small and operates in a homelike setting.

In addition to providing diagnostic, educational, and treatment programs for hundreds of New Yorkers each year, the League Center serves as a model for special day schools and treatment centers throughout the world. It also serves as a training resource for students and professionals, as a research center, and as a valuable resource for public information, leadership, and advocacy on behalf of mentally handicapped and emotionally disturbed people of all ages (personal communication August 1985).

KATHERINE GARNETT
Hunter College, City University
of New York

LEARNED HELPLESSNESS

The term learned helplessness refers to a theory that has been broadly applied to the study of motivational and emotional problems in recent years. In essence, the theory maintains that the perception that one is helpless, or unable to control or affect significant events in one's life, leads to low self-esteem, undermines goal-oriented motivation, and produces a depressed emotional state. While the theory is now most often applied to human psychology, its historical roots lie in the animal conditioning laboratory (Maier & Seligman, 1976). The work that eventually gave rise to learned helplessness theory was concerned with the impact of uncontrollable aversive stimulation on the conditioning process. The major finding to emerge from this research was that a wide variety of animal species can learn that reinforcements, such as the cessation of aversive stimulation, are uncontrollable or unaffected by any efforts that they might exert. Moreover, such learning experiences were found to have important consequences in regard to motivation, cognition, and emotion. Motivationally, experience with uncontrollable reinforcement was found to lead to a passive, non-goal-oriented state. Cognitively, uncontrollability was found to interfere with the subsequent capacity to learn to control reinforcements that were in fact contingent on the animal's behavior. Emotionally, uncontrollability led to a state that in some ways resembled human depression.

As the theory moved out of the animal laboratory, higher mental processes were accorded a greater role in the events that produce the helpless state. In particular, understanding why one could not control events, called the causal attribution process, became a focus of theoretical activity. According to the most recent version of the theory, it is not mere lack of control, but one's understanding of why one lacks control, that determines the consequences of failing to exert effective control over events (Abramson, Seligman, & Teasdale, 1978). Briefly, the theory maintains that the causes to which uncontrollability is attributable may differ in terms of their perceived stability over time, their generality (i.e., whether the cause influences many areas of life), and their status as internal, personal factors as opposed to external, environmental ones. While other patterns are discussed in the theory, one pattern of causal perceptions that appears to maximize the sense of helplessness consists of the perception that the cause of a set of uncontrollable events is an internal, highly general, and very stable factor.

The theory of learned helpless has received considerable attention from researchers concerned with the nature of children's motivational problems in educational contexts and from persons interested in helplessness as it might relate to clinical depression in both adults and children. The research on motivation has shown that deficits in motivation can be a result of the onset of learned helplessness and that some children are more vulnerable to helplessness than others. Consistent with the theory, those children who tend to overemphasize ability (an internal, general, and stable cause) and underemphasize effort as explanations of lack of control over learning situations have been found to be most vulnerable. Similarly, the onset or maintenance of depression often appears to be associated with a style of causal attribution that overemphasizes stable, general, and personal causes in explanations of controllability.

By definition, most handicapped pupils have some history of academic failure. Teachers are the primary individuals who refer the vast majority of pupils for special education services. While any achievement problem is of concern to teachers, to refer a child for special education services, the pupil must evidence significant problems for a period of time in which various instructional strategies have been attempted. While this practice is necessary to ensure that the child does, in fact, require special education services, it also guarantees that before pupils enter a special education class, they have encountered uncontrollable failure for a substantial portion of their school experience. These failure experiences appear to provide a direct analogue to the conditions that facilitate the development of learned helplessness (Miller & Norman, 1979). Pupils are required to be in school and for some period of time in a classroom setting where there is little chance of success. In light of the emphasis placed on achievement on school tasks by teachers and parents, pupils come to see these activities as important. Despite attempts to complete class assignments, these youngsters are aware that they are failing at tasks that most other classmates can successfully perform and they attribute their problems to their lack of competence.

In view of their achievement history and their attributions for failure, it is not suprising that many handicapped pupils display a variety of behaviors associated with learned helplessness. For example, learning disabled (LD) and mentally retarded (MR) pupils view their failure on academic tasks as being caused primarily by their lack of ability (Licht & Kistner, 1986). Frequently, these pupils express this attribution directly in statements such as, "I'm dumb, I can't do it," despite having the prerequisite skills to accomplish the task. The LD and MR pupils often do not persist on tasks, particularly when they encounter difficulties. Handicapped learners also have problems beginning new activities. Special education teachers find that just getting the child to start a task is a major in-

structional concern. With these self-perceptions, lack of persistence, and failure to initiate learning tasks, youngsters within special education classes evidence not only academic deficits but also motivational problems that can interfere with the acquisition of skills.

With attributions playing a central role in the development and maintenance of learned helplessness, one of the major treatment goals for handicapped children with learning problems is the development of a more adaptive attributional style. In an attempt to remedy motivational problems of handicapped youngsters, special educators frequently recommend a learning environment where children do not encounter failure. Unfortunately, this recommendation fails to bring about changes in the attributional style of these pupils. Rather than learn that their effort plays a critical role in determining their success or failure, these pupils may attribute their successes to easy tasks or to the assistance provided by their special education teachers. Both these perceptions may, in fact, be accurate. In addition, orchestrating a learning environment where the child rarely errs is unrealistic. These experiences do not prepare children to cope with and learn from the failures that all pupils encounter. To alter attributions, teachers must directly teach pupils to ascribe their learning difficulties to factors under their control.

When children fail at a task, Licht and Kistner (1986) suggest that teachers tell their pupils that with effort comes the increased probability of success. For example, investigators have found that teachers' use of the statement "You've been working hard" is more effective in producing performance and self-esteem changes in pupils than use of the statement "You need to work hard." The effectiveness of the former statement may be due to two messages conveyed: the importance of effort and positive feedback concerning the youngster's progress. Researchers also have suggested that attribution retraining procedures be used along with learning strategy training. For example, feedback to pupils concerning the role of effort may be tied directly to the effective use of a strategy ("You looked back at the important information in the text").

While research on classroom application of these procedures is still in its infancy, these attributional retraining procedures hold promise for addressing some of the motivational problems associated with learned helplessness.

REFERENCES

Abramson, L. Y., Seligman, M. E. P., & Teasdale, J. D. (1978). Learned helplessness in humans: Critique and reformulation. *Journal of Abnormal Psychology, 87,* 49–74.

Licht, B. G., & Kistner, J. A. (1986). Motivational problems of learning disabled children: Individual differences and their implications for treatment. In J. K. Torgesen & B. W. L. Wong (Eds.), *Learning disabilities: Some new perspectives.* New York: Academic.

Maier, S. F., & Seligman, M. E. P. (1976). Learned helplessness: Theory and evidence. *Journal of Experimental Psychology, 105*, 3–46.

Miller, I. W., III, & Norman, W. H. (1979). Learned helplessness in humans: A review and attribution-theory model. *Psychological Bulletin, 86*, 93–118.

WILLIAM S. RHOLES
DOUGLAS J. PALMER
Texas A&M University

ANXIETY DISORDERS
ATTITUDES TOWARD THE HANDICAPPED
ATTRIBUTIONAL TRAINING
DEPRESSION
STRESS

LEARNER TAXONOMIES

A taxonomy is any organizational structure that classifies information for some specified purpose. The phrase learner taxonomy refers to the classification of individuals by individual characteristics presumed to represent dimensions of importance to the process of learning. Many learner taxonomies exist in special education; indeed, current learner classification structures (e.g., learning disabilities) represent initial attempts in this vein, though possibly not effective ones.

Several assumptions are implicit in the effort to develop useful learner taxonomies. Among them are the following. Individuals must be viewed as varying on a continuum of individual dimensions that are assumed to be essential to learning. If individuals did not present important individual differences, the need for learner taxonomies would not exist. A second assumption demands that salient individual differences, which are in fact hypothetical constructs, be measurable. Difficulty has traditionally arisen in the validity and reliability associated with such measures. Such difficulty must, in practice, be eliminated. A third prerequisite lies in the presumed capacity of the educator to operate on the elements of the taxonomy. That is, pragmatically, the learner taxonomy must alter the course of instruction in some measurably effective way. If the taxonomy is unable to direct the course of instruction effectively, its purpose, hence activity directed to it, is suspect. Other assumptions are implied; however, the preceding set the initial and important limits for the approach as it is used in education.

Learner taxonomies are inevitably combined with the topic of individual differences. Conceptually, individual differences are thought to emerge within three broad domains of behavior: the cognitive (or thinking) domain, the affective (or emotional) domain, and the psychomotor (the physical activity) domain. Of these, by far the most effort has been directed toward the cognitive domain. However, the cognitive domain limits the definition of learned behaviors. Ultimately, all domains will necessarily receive attention.

Currently, many taxonomies can be described as mostly associated with the cognitive domain; finite, in the sense that some very specific aspect is considered; and heuristic, in the sense that most are based on theoretical models that are as yet unverified. There are exceptions to some of these descriptors however. A widely used taxonomy developed by Krathwohl, Bloom, and Masia (1964) is associated with the affective domain. The taxonomy developed by Bloom et al. (1956) is concerned with a broad realm of cognitive behaviors and learning outcomes. Attempts to qualify children's performance through subscale analysis of tests such as the Wechsler Intelligence Scale for Children-Revised can, in one sense, be seen as an inductive process rather than the more typical deductive process of taxonomy development. That is, the latter represents an attempt to build a model from behaviors rather than predict behaviors from a model.

Despite considerable differences, virtually all learner taxonomies attempt to explain learning behavior and promote an individualized course for instruction. This may be seen in contrast to a behavioral model that emphasizes the relative similarities of the learning process. A task for the educator who accepts the concept of learner taxonomies and related concepts such as cognitive or learning styles is to select the most appropriate model. Comprehensive models generally do not exist and the models now available may offer conflicting recommendations. Because of this and other factors, the actual use of learner taxonomies remains more scarce than the intriguing possibilities the approaches seem to offer.

A vast number of educational taxonomies associated with each domain and more or less oriented toward cognitive or behavioral psychology can be identified. Among the taxonomies that have been influential in the development of special education are those of Bloom et al. (1956), Kagan and Kogan (1970), Kirk and Kirk (1971), Krathwohl, Bloom, and Masia (1964), Piaget (1972), Quay (1964), and Witkin (1969). The recent work of Sternberg (1977) as well as that of Kaufman and Kaufman (1983), the latter based in part on the influential work of Luria (1966), may prove to be fundamental in the development of future learner taxonomies. Interested readers will find the work of Holland (1982), Mann and Sabatino (1985), and Messick (1976) to be valuable.

REFERENCES

Bloom, B. S., Endlehort, M. B., Furst, E. J., Hill, W. H., & Krathwohl, D. R. (1956). *Taxonomy of educational objectives. The classification of educational goals. Handbook I: Cognitive domain.* New York: Longman Green.

Holland, R. P. (1982). Learner characteristics and learner performance: Implications for instructional placement decision. *Journal of Special Education, 16,* 7–10.

Kagan, J., & Kogan, N. (1970). Individual variations in cognitive processes. In P. H. Mussen (Ed.), *Carmichael's manual of child psychology* (Vol. 1). New York: Wiley.

Kaufman, A. S., & Kaufman, N. L. (1983). *The Kaufman Assessment Battery for Children.* Circle Pines, MN: American Guidance Service.

Kirk, S. A., & Kirk, W. D. (1971). *Psycholinguistic learning disabilities: Diagnosis and remediation.* Urbana, IL: University of Illinois Press.

Krathwohl, D. R., Bloom, B. S., & Masia, B. B. (1964). *Taxonomy of educational objectives, Handbook II: Affective domain.* New York: McKay.

Luria, A. R. (1966). *Higher cortical functions in man.* New York: Basic Books.

Mann, L., & Sabatino, D. A. (1985). *Foundations of cognitive process in remedial and special education.* Rockville, MD: Aspen.

Messick, S. (Ed.) (1976). *Individuality in learning: Implications of cognitive styles and creativity for human development.* San Francisco: Jossey-Bass.

Piaget, J. (1972). *The principles of genetic epistemology* (translated by W. Mays). London: Routledge and Kegan Paul.

Quay, H. L. (1964). Dimensions of personality in delinquent boys as inferred from factor analysis of case history data. *Child Development, 35,* 479–484.

Sternberg, R. J. (1977). *Intelligence, information processing, and analytical reasoning: The componential analysis of human abilities.* Hillsdale, NJ: Erlbaum.

Wechsler, D. (1974). *Manual for the Wechsler Intelligence Scale for Children—Revised.* New York: Psychological Corporation.

Witkin, H. A. (1969). Some implications of research on cognitive style for problems of education. In M. Gottsegen & G. Gottsegen (Eds.), *Professional School Psychology* (Vol. 3). New York: Grune & Stratton.

TED L. MILLER
*University of Tennessee,
Chattanooga*

SYSTEMS OF CLASSIFICATION
BLOOM BENJAMIN S.
PIAGET, JEAN

LEARNING DISABILITIES

According to the definition most often used by state departments of education to guide appropriate services, specific learning disabilities afflict

those children who have a disorder in one or more of the basic psychological processes involved in understanding or in using language, spoken or written, which disorder may manifest itself in imperfect ability to listen, think, speak, read, write, spell, or do mathematical calculations. Such disorders include

conditions as perceptual handicaps, brain injury, minimal brain dysfunction, dyslexia, and developmental aphasia. Such term does not include children who have learning problems which are primarily the result of visual, hearing, or motor handicaps, of mental retardation, of emotional disturbance, or environmental, cultural or economic disadvantage (Federal Register, 1977).

A more recent conceptualization by the National Joint Committee on Learning Disabilities stresses the heterogeneity, intrinsicness, and presumed neurological basis of this condition (McLoughlin & Netick, 1983). The Association for Children and Adults with Learning Disabilities adds that learning disabilities can continue into adulthood and can involve socialization skills (Newsbriefs, 1985). Estimates of incidence range from conservative ones of 3 to 5% of the school-age population to as high as 10% (Tucker, Stevens, & Ysseldyke, 1983).

Learning disabilities may occur more often in particular families (Silver, 1971). In families with dyslexics, 88% had other family members with learning disabilities (Hallgren, 1950). Hermann's twin studies (1959) also suggest a genetic basis. Opinions differ as to whether the genetic factor is a recessive, polygenetic, or dominant sex-influenced trait. Certain correlates of learning disorders have been made with nonhereditary genetic defects caused by sex-chromosome aberrations (Wallace & McLoughlin, 1979).

Learning disabilities may also be the result of prenatal, perinatal, and postnatal problems. Maternal health, diet, and lifestyle influence potential for later learning performance problems. Complicated pregnancies (i.e., toxemia, bleeding, prematurity, etc.) are also mentioned frequently (Pasamanick & Knoblock, 1973). Among postnatal factors associated with this condition are head injuries, lead poisoning, and nutritional deficits (Hallahan & Cruickshank, 1973). The central nervous system and brain may be directly and indirectly influenced by malnutrition. Sensory deprivation may also be involved.

Brain damage and minimal brain dysfunction have been related to learning disabilities. Symptoms common to both conditions have been described (Clements, 1966). Neurological comparisons of learning disabled and normal learners were suggestive of neurological problems but not definitive (Myklebust & Boshe, 1969). Results of efforts to distinguish such groups with the EEG have been unclear (Hughes, 1971). Lack of cerebral dominance has been associated with dyslexia, and cerebellar-vestibular dysfunctions with various visual and visual-motor problems (DeQuiros, 1976). While the full significance of a neurological perspective is debated by many (Page-El & Grossman, 1973), some continue to find the approach promising (Gaddes, 1985).

In terms of the immunological system, various types of allergies have been noted in connection with left-handedness and learning disorders, including food allergy with hyperactivity (Feingold, 1975). However controlled, comparative studies debate this connection, except in terms of otitis media and the side effects of allergy medication (McLoughlin, Nall, & Petrosko, 1985). Metabolic and biochemical disorders mentioned are hypoglycemia, an imbalance in acetycholinesterase, hypothyroidism, and a deficiency in inhibitory chemical transducers (Wallace & McLoughlin, 1979). General maturational lag in the development of central nervous system components has also been implicated with this condition (Ames, 1983).

Specific psychological factors connected with this disorder are the comprehension, integration, and use of visual, auditory, and perceptual-motor information (Chalfant & King, 1976). Difficulty with symbols and language are notable (Kirk & Kirk, 1971). The learning-disabled person may be inattentive, too impulsive (Epstein, Hallahan, & Kauffman, 1975), have various types of memory problems (Torgesen, 1985), lack required automated skills (Ackerman & Dykman, 1982), and have poor organizational skills to solve problems (Alley & Deshler, 1979). Problems with various aspects of oral language also differentiate this population from others (Wiig & Semel, 1984).

Environmental factors may be involved in cases of learning disabilities. Poor nutrition, health, and safety can precipitate these problems, as can inadequate linguistic and cognitive models in the home. Sociocultural factors that do not reinforce values for education, regular school attendance, work and study habits, and other supportive skills may create more difficulty for the learning-disabled person. The lack of consistent, appropriate education may also be at fault.

Educational assessment is the systematic process of gathering educationally relevant information to make legal and instructional decisions about the provision of special services (McLoughlin & Lewis, 1986). The data are used to answer such questions as "What are the school learning problems?" "Are they related to having a specific learning disability?" "What are the student's needs?" The data are also used to establish a basis for developing an individualized education plan. The selection and use of appropriate assessment procedures are governed by the principles of PL 94-142 and good practice. Specifically, the assessment is to be a team effort (with the student's parents) that is comprehensive in nature, nondiscriminatory to exceptional and other special groups, and subject to due process procedures. Individual standardized tests and informal procedures concerning intelligence and adaptive behavior, specific learning disabilities, classroom behavior, social-emotional development, reading, mathematics, oral and written language, and career-vocational needs may be used. The informal techniques include observations, work sample analyses, task analyses, informal teacher inventories, criterion-referenced tests, diagnostic teaching, checklists, rating scales, interviews, and questionnaires.

Of particular controversy in the assessment of this con-

dition is the poor quality of procedures to establish the existence of a significant level of discrepancy between a learning-disabled person's ability and actual achievement. All approaches to quantify this gap have been criticized, including the years-below-grade-level procedure and various expectancy formulas based on age, grade level, mental age, etc. (McLoughlin & Lewis, 1986). The use of standard scores and regression analyses are receiving considerable attention (Cone & Wilson, 1981). The following figure shows the various types of scores that have been involved in the statistical analysis of severe discrepancies in learning. Additionally, the tests for visual, auditory, and other information processes are generally considered of questionable validity and reliability, making assessment in these critical areas difficult and reliant on informal techniques (Salvia & Ysseldyke, 1985). Thus, considerable emphasis is being placed on the measurement of cognitive and learning strategies. Other diagnosticians often participate in the assessment, including speech-language-hearing clinicians and counselors; however, full neurological examinations are rare. Many aspects of the assessment process have been criticized, including the disproportionate placement of minorities in learning disability services (Lynch & Lewis, 1982; Ysseldyke et al., 1983). Current trends include renewed interest in informal techniques, curriculum-based assessment, and computer applications.

The Gillingham-Stillman and Fernald approaches to teaching reading and other language arts are based on a psychoneurological orientation (Wallace & McLoughlin, 1979). Numerous materials and activities have been structured around perceptual and information processing assessments such as the Illinois Test of Psycholinquistic Abilities (Kirk, McCarthy, & Kirk, 1968) and others by Frostig and Kephart. The efficacy of these techniques in remediating academic disabilities and their relevance to academic skills are questionable (Hammill, 1982). More language-based programs are exemplified by the language experience approach and linguistically based readers. DISTAR (Englemann & Bruner, 1983) materials in reading and other areas incorporate the principles of applied behavioral analysis. While the choice of actual material by teachers in this area is eclectic, the programming tends to be skill-based; i.e., the objectives for instruction are generated from criterion-referenced or curriculum-based assessment.

There is an increased interest in training specific cognitive learning strategies to acquire and use basic information effectively. Metacognitive approaches are being employed to enhance the understanding and remediation of deficits in attention (Loper, Hallahan, & Ianna, 1982), comprehension (Wong & Jones, 1982), memory (Torgesen, 1985), and other areas. An effort is also made to teach socially appropriate and effective skills (Bryan et al., 1983). The transition into careers and/or higher education is also a basis for secondary school curriculum.

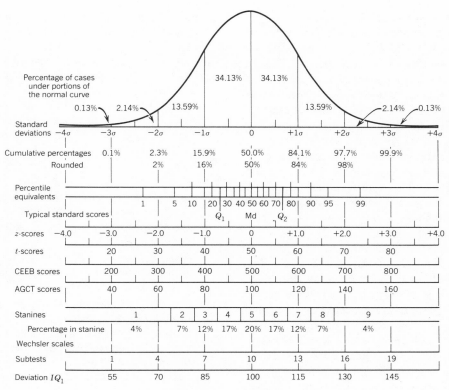

Normal Curve Equivalents.

Some principles of remediation that are prevalent in this field include using concrete-manipulative materials, working from a meaningful context, and providing a consistent structure and routine. Multimodality approaches are often used. Another approach tries to decide how to present material based on the supposed modality preference of the student; current research does not support this approach (Larrivee, 1981). The use of applied behavioral analysis to program materials and to instruct and motivate students is widespread. Peer tutoring and parent involvement have also proven useful. Various psychotropic drugs, such as Ritalin and Dexedrine, have been employed to control hyperactivity with mixed results (Adelman & Compas, 1977); they appear most effective when combined with a cooperative behavior management program (Sprague & Speery, 1974). Megavitamin regimens and various diets have been used with questionable results (Kavale & Forness, 1983).

Preschool programs for learning-disabled children are generally mainstreamed with normal children; they stress speech and language, fine and gross motor, cognitive, self-help, adaptive, and social-emotional development. The multidisciplinary curriculum is structured around developmental and criterion-referenced tests (such as the Learning Accomplishment Profile by Sanford & Zelman, 1981) as well as other procedures.

School-age students with learning disabilities are served in a variety of ways. According to PL 94-142, they should receive their instruction as much as possible with their age-appropriate peers and not be isolated from them

unnecessarily. The appropriateness of a placement is based on the needs of the student as judged by a team of professionals and parents. Most students spend some time in the regular classroom, and their teachers may be supported by a consulting teacher. Such placements are possible with well-designed cooperative learning activities (Smith, Johnson, & Johnson, 1982), peer tutoring, learning centers, behavior management programs (Demers, 1981), and other suitable modifications.

Generally, the students are directly instructed by an itinerant teacher on a regular basis or by a resident resource room teacher for part of each school day. More severely involved students (and perhaps those beginning their remedial programs) are placed in full-time special classes with some mainstreaming activities or in a special day or residential facility. The relative efficacy of one approach over another is unclear because of differences in teacher training, curriculum, instructional procedures, student assignment composition, and research design employed. The practice of assigning children with other diagnosed conditions (e.g., mild mental retardation or behavior disorders) to the same class is becoming more common and is based on the assumption that instructional objectives and methodologies are similar. Parent groups and others are not in full agreement about such modifications of strictly categorical services. Additionally, concern is being expressed over the loss of gains made once these supportive services are discontinued (Ito, 1980).

Reports of secondary and postsecondary school employment indicate generally low-level, low-paying jobs with which learning-disabled persons and their parents are dissatisfied (Association for Children and Adults with Learning Disabilities, 1982; White et al., 1983). Social activities of learning-disabled adults seem typical although limited; there is a tendency for overdependency on others for assistance. Difficulty with law enforcement agencies is reported in some surveys but not others. Some learning-disabled persons intend to or are currently attending vocational schools as well as junior and four-year colleges. Modified testing procedures, study skills training, counseling, and other support services are offered at some universities (Barbaro, 1982). This transition into all aspects of the adult world is an aspect of postschooling servies that is generating considerable creative programming (Garnett & Gerber, 1985).

Families of persons with learning disabilities have a strong influence on them. The families in turn may experience stress as well as other feelings as they move closer to full acceptance of the learning-disabled person (McLoughlin, 1985). Parents are expected to participate fully in various aspects of the remedial program. The Association for Children and Adults with Learning Disabilities is a major parent-support organization. For professionals there are a variety of groups, including the National Council for Learning Disabilities and a division in the Council for Exceptional Children. Teachers are certified to instruct the learning-disabled student after appropriate training at a recognized university; some states have additional teacher competency tests and internship requirements.

REFERENCES

Ackerman, P. T., & Dykman, R. A. (1982). Automatic and effortful information-processing deficits in children with learning and attention disorders. *Topics in Learning & Learning Disabilities, 2,* 12–22.

Adelman, H. S., & Compas, B. E. (1977). Stimulant drugs and learning problems. *Journal of Special Education, 11,* 377–416.

Alley, G., & Deshler, D. (1979). *Teaching the learning disabled adolescent.* Denver, CO: Love.

Ames, L. B. (1983). Learning disability: Truth or trap? *Journal of Learning Disabilities, 16,* 19–20.

Association for Children and Adults with Learning Disabilities. (1982). ACLD Vocational Committee Survey of LD Adults. *ACLD Newsbriefs, 145,* 20–23.

Barbaro, F. (1982). The learning disabled college student: Some considerations in setting objectives. *Journal of Learning Disabilities, 15,* 599–603.

Bryan, T. H., Pearl, R., Donahue, M., Bryan, J., & Pflaum, S. (1983). The Chicago Institute for the Study of Learning Disabilities. *Exceptional Education Quarterly, 4,* 1–22.

Chalfant, J. C., & King, F. S. (1976). An approach to operationalizing the definition of learning disabilities. *Journal of Learning Disabilities, 9,* 228–243.

Clements, S. D. (1966). *Minimal brain dysfunction in children* (NINDS Monograph No. 3, U.S. Publication No. 1415). Washington, DC: U.S. Government Printing Office.

Cone, T. E., & Wilson, L. R. (1981). Quantifying a severe discrepancy: A critical review. *Learning Disability Quarterly, 4,* 359–371.

Demers, L. A. (1981). Effective mainstreaming for the learning disabled students with behavior problems. *Journal of Learning Disabilities, 14,* 179–189.

DeQuiros, J. B. (1976). Diagnosis of vestibular disorders in the learning disabled. *Journal of Learning Disabilities, 9,* 39–47.

Englemann, S., & Bruner, E. C. (1983). *DISTAR Reading 1: An instructional system, teacher's guide.* Chicago: Science Research.

Epstein, M. H., Hallahan, D. P., & Kauffman, J. M. (1975). Implications of the reflectivity-impulsivity dimension of special education. *Journal of Special Education, 9,* 11–26.

Federal Register. (1977, Jan. 19). Washington, DC: U.S. Government Printing Office.

Feingold, B. F. (1975). Hyperkinesis and learning disabilities linked to artifical food flavors and colors. *American Journal of Nursing, 75,* 797–803.

Gaddes, W. (1985). *Learning disabilities and brain function* (2nd ed.). New York: Springer-Verlag.

Garnett, K., & Gerber, P. (Eds.). (1985). Life transitions of learning disabled adults: Perspectives from several countries. *World Rehabilitation Fund, 32.*

Hallahan, D., & Cruickshank, W. (1973). *Psychoeducational foundations of learning disabilities.* Englewood Cliffs, NJ: Prentice-Hall.

Hallgren, B. (1950). Specific dyslexia ('congenital word blindness'): A clinical and genetic study. *Acta Psychiatrica et Neurologica, 65,* 1–279.

Hammill, D. D. (1982). Assessing and training perceptual-motor skills. In D. D. Hammill & N. R. Bartel (Eds.), *Teaching children with learning and behavior problems* (3rd ed., pp. 379–408). Boston: Allyn & Bacon.

Hermann, K. (1959). *Reading disability.* Springfield, IL: Thomas.

Hughes, J. R. (1971). Electroencephalography and learning disabilities. In H. R. Myklebust (Ed.), *Progress in learning disabilities* (Vol. 2). New York: Grune & Stratton.

Ito, R. H. (1980). Long-term effects of resource room programs on learning disabled children's reading. *Journal of Learning Disabilities, 13,* 36–40.

Kavale, K. A., & Forness, S. R. (1983). Hyperactivity and diet treatment: A meta-analysis of the Feingold hypothesis. *Journal of Learning Disabilities, 16,* 324–330.

Kirk, S., & Kirk, W. (1971). *Psycholinquistic learning disabilities.* Urbana, IL: University of Illinois Press.

Kirk, S., McCarthy, J., & Kirk, W. (1968). *Illinois Test of Psycholinquistic Abilities* (revised ed.). Urbana, IL: University of Illinois Press.

Larrivee, B. (1981). Modality preference as a model for differentiating beginning reading instruction: A review of the issues. *Learning Disability Quarterly, 4,* 180–188.

Loper, A., Hallahan, D., & Ianna, S. (1982). Meta-attention in learning disabled and normal students. *Learning Disability Quarterly, 5,* 29–36.

Lynch, E. W., & Lewis, R. B. (1982). Multicultural considerations in assessment and treatment of learning disabilities. *Learning Disabilities, 1,* 93–103.

McLoughlin, J. A. (1985). The families of children with disabilities. In W. H. Berdine & A. E. Blackhurst (Eds.), *An introduction to special education* (2nd ed., pp. 617–660). Boston: Little, Brown.

McLoughlin, J. A., & Lewis, R. B. (1986). *Assessing special students* (2nd ed.). Columbus, OH: Merrill.

McLoughlin, J. A., Nall, M., & Petrosko, J. (1985). Allergies and learning disabilities. *Learning Disability Quarterly, 8,* 255–260.

McLoughlin, J. A., & Netick, A. (1983). Defining learning disabilities: A new and cooperative direction. *Journal of Learning Disabilities, 16,* 21–23.

Myklebust, H., & Boshe, B. (1969). Final reports: Minimal brain damage in children (U.S. Public Service Contract 108-65-142). Evanston, IL: Northwestern University Publications.

Newsbriefs. (1985, Jan./Feb.). Definition of the condition, specific learning disabilities. No. 158, 1.

Page-El, E., & Grossman, H. (1973). Neurologic appraisal in learning disorders. *Pediatric Clinics of North America, 20,* 599–605.

Pasamanick, B., & Knoblock, H. (1973). The epidemiology of reproductive casualty. In S. Sapir & A. Nitzburg (Eds.), *Children with learning problems.* New York: Brunner/Mazel.

Salvia, J., & Ysseldyke, J. E. (1985). *Assessment in special and remedial education* (3rd ed.). Boston: Houghton Mifflin.

Sanford, A., & Zelman, J. (1981). *Learning Accomplishment Profile-Revised.* Winston-Salem, NC: Kaplan Press.

Silver, L. (1971). Familial patterns in children with neurologically based learning disabilities. *Journal of Learning Disabilities, 4,* 349–358.

Smith, K., Johnson, D. W., & Johnson, R. (1982). Effects of cooperative and individualistic instruction on the achievement of handicapped, regular, and gifted students. *Journal of Social Psychology, 116,* 277–283.

Sprague, R. L., & Speery, J. B. (1974). Psychotropic drugs and handicapped children. In L. Mann & D. Sabatino (Eds.), *The review of special education.* Philadelphia: Journal of Special Education Press.

Torgesen, J. K. (1985). Memory processes in reading disabled children. *Journal of Learning Disabilities, 18,* 350–357.

Tucker, J., Stevens, L., & Ysseldyke, J. (1983). Learning disabilities: The experts speak out. *Journal of Learning Disabilities, 16,* 6–13.

Wallace, G., & McLoughlin, J. A. (1979). *Learning disabilities: Concepts and charcteristics* (2nd ed.). Columbus, OH: Merrill.

White, W. J., Deshler, D., Shumaker, J., Warner, M., Alley, G., & Clark, F. C. (1983). The effects of learning disabilities on post-school adjustment. *Journal of Rehabilitation, 49,* 46–50.

Wiig, E. H., & Semel, E. (1984). *Language assessment and intervention for the learning disabled* (2nd ed.). Columbus, OH: Merrill.

Wong, B., & Jones, W. (1982). Increasing metacomprehension in learning disabled and normally achieving students through self-questioning training. *Learning Disability Quarterly, 5,* 228–240.

Ysseldyke, J., Thurlow, M., Graden, J., Wesson, C., Algozzine, B., & Deno, S. (1983). Generalizations from five years of research on assessment and decision-making: The University of Minnesota Institute. *Exceptional Education Quarterly, 4,* 75–95.

JAMES A. MCLOUGHLIN
University of Louisville

LEARNING DISABILITIES, HOLISTIC APPROACH

See HOLISTIC APPROACH AND LEARNING DISABILITIES.

LEARNING DISABILITIES, PROBLEMS IN DEFINITION OF

There are five reasons why educators have difficulty with identifying children with specific learning disabilities. First, many people have equated learning disabilities with any kind of learning problem. This has tended to obscure the target population. Second, there is no single observable characteristic or syndrome of behaviors that is typical of a learning-disabled child because these children present a variety of diverse behavioral symptoms. Third, each child has his or her own unique learning pattern. The behavioral symptoms depend on the kind of disability, its severity, the child's intact abilities, and how the child tries to cope with the problem. Fourth, some of the behavioral symptoms of specific learning disabilities might also arise from visual or hearing impairments, mental retardation, emotional disturbances, social maladjustment, health problems, cultural differences, family problems, or poor instruction. Fifth, when a child is multiply handicapped and has other problems in addition to a specific learning disability, the presence of the learning disability may be overlooked because attention is drawn to the more obvious problems in health, vision, hearing, etc. The more subtle learning disability sometimes remains undetected.

The recognition of specific learning disabilities as a type of handicap is relatively recent. The term became popular in 1963 when representatives of several parent organizations dealing with brain-injured and severely handicapped children met in Chicago to discuss their mutual problems and to establish a national organization.

The concept and label were introduced to include a large group of children who did not fit other categories of handicapping conditions, but who did need help in acquiring school skills.

In the years since 1963, many people have tried to define learning disabilities, but no one has yet developed a definition that is acceptable to everyone. Professionals working with learning-disabled students tended to define learning disabilities from their own professional points of view. Different definitions, therefore, emphasized different aspects of learning disabilities such as neurological damage in the central nervous system, academic failure, visual perceptual disorders, language disorders, psychological process dysfunctions, behavioral symptoms, and impaired learning efficiency.

The literature reflects over 50 items to describe learning-disabled students; Vaughn and Hodges (1973) reported 38 different definitions. At present, state departments of education are using only five terms: learning disabilities; learning disabled; specific learning disabilities; perceptually impaired; and perceptual communication disorders (Chalfant & Pysh, 1984).

The creation of a federal definition of learning disabilities has helped reduce the number of terms and definitions in use, but this definition has serious limitations. The federal definition of learning disabilities included in PL 94-142, the Education for All Handicapped Children Act of 1975, reads:

> The term "children with specific learning disabilities" means those children who have a disorder in one or more of the basic psychological processes involved in understanding or in using language, spoken or written, which disorder may manifest itself in imperfect ability to listen, think, speak, read, write, spell, or do mathematical calculations. Such disorders include such conditions as perceptual handicaps, brain injury, minimal brain dysfunction, dyslexia, and developmental aphasia. Such term does not include children who have learning problems which are primarily the result of visual, hearing, or motor handicaps, of mental retardation, of emotional disturbance, or of environmental, cultural, or economic disadvantage.

Forty-eight states and the District of Columbia define learning disabilities. Two states do not define the learning-disabled population, but serve them through noncategorical programs. Twenty-two states and the District of Columbia use the federal definition verbatim. It is interesting that 26 state educational agencies believed it was necessary to either modify or supplement the federal definition or write their own definition. An analysis of the federal definition, the modified definitions, and the "original" definitions written by states revealed five major components that might be included in a definition of learning disability. These components are (1) failure to achieve; (2) psychological process; (3) exclusionary; (4) significant discrepancy; and (5) etiological (Chalfant & Pysh, 1984).

Academic failure refers to difficulty in learning to read, write, spell, compute arithmetic, acquire receptive and expressive language, or obtain visual-motor coordination in other performance tasks. The federal definition's emphasis on academic failure has included thousands of underachieving, slow-learning, poorly motivated, conduct-disordered, culturally different students in the category of specific learning disabilities. Because these students typically fall further behind academically as they progress through school, their identification in secondary schools increases.

With 46 states including references to achievement failure in their definitions, it is easy to understand how states may fail to recognize gifted students who have a specific learning disability. Gifted students may not have academic failures, but may have a discrepancy between potential and achievement that may require either special education services or the use of special classroom strategies.

There are many factors that could contribute to task failure; this makes it important to identify all children who are failing regardless of cause. This can be done through achievement tests, checklists, screening devices, or teacher referrals. Referrals for individual assessment should not be made, however, until classroom teachers have (1) carefully thought through the child's problems; (2) made special efforts to help the child; (3) sought advice and support from other teachers or child study teams within the building; and (4) failed to help the child.

By trying to teach children individually, teachers often are able to discover whether children are failing to learn academic skills because of poor attendance, frequent moving from school to school, bilingualism, poor instruction, cultural deprivation, or other environmental factors. Thus classroom teachers can begin the process of identification by describing task failure and identifying environmental or instructional factors that may be contributing to the child's problem.

The exclusionary component refers to the handicapping conditions, other than learning disabilities, that cause problems in learning. These include mental retardation; visual impairment; hearing impairment; social-emotional problems; physical problems; poor instruction; cultural or environmental factors; and physical problems.

The student's learning problem must be evaluated to determine whether the difficulty is due to a specific learning disability or to some other handicapping condition. To be eligible for special education services because of a learning disability, the student's primary problem must be a specific learning disability. It is necessary, therefore, to rule out or exclude all other factors that might cause a similar problem.

It is important to understand, however, that learning disabilities sometimes occur in combination with other problems. A visually impaired child, for example, might have difficulty in processing auditory or haptic information; and a hearing-impaired child might have difficulty in processing visual information. Children with multiple handicaps should receive multiple services because the extent and kinds of services needed may be quite different for each handicapping condition.

The specific criteria for the exclusionary impairments varies from state to state. Although guidelines are rather precise about the criteria for visual and hearing impairments, mental retardation, and motor and health impairments, criteria are not clearly delineated for slow learners, social and emotional maladjustment, and cultural, environmental, and economic factors. Variation from one state to another and imprecise criteria result in inappropriate inclusion or exclusion from services for the learning disabled and further confuse the defining of the population in question.

Although the etiology of learning disabilities is included in the definition of learning disabilities by 44 states, its role as a criterion for supporting the identification of a learning disability is minimal. Most state guidelines mention the need to review a student's developmental history and medical information as they relate to the student's daily functioning. Among the etiological factors frequently mentioned as being found among learning disabled students are:

A history of brain injury or neurological problems

Motor coordination problems

Slow speech and language development

Immature social and emotional development

Hyperactivity or hypoactivity

Frequent periods of illness or absenteeism from school

Surgery at an early age

Early symptoms such as infant or early childhood problems in feeding or sleeping, temper tantrums, frequent crying, prenatal or natal difficulties, low birth weight, or premature birth

Information or data concerning the physiological and medical status of a student is in the realm of the physician. However, educators can obtain important information through interviews with parents, reviews of developmental history, and identification of any information that might be a contributing factor to learning disabilities. Cooperation with the medical profession may link the student's classroom behavior to etiological factors that might contribute to a learning disability. This information may not help the teacher address the problems of the learning disabled, but it may help the multidisciplinary team in distinguishing which students are learning disabled (Chalfant, 1984).

One characteristic of the student with a specific learning disability is a severe discrepancy between current achievement and intellectual potential. The finding of a discrepancy between achievement and potential alone, however, does not identify a learning-disabled student, since such a discrepancy also occurs among students whose underachievement is due to frequent absences from school; frequent family relocations; negative attitudes toward school; little motivation; family problems in the home; or instructional discontinuity of any kind. Students with such problems also need help. The basic needs of these students differ from the needs of learning-disabled students. These needs can often be met within the regular classroom or through regular education alternative programs within regular education.

Five major approaches are used to determine discrepancies between achievement and potential. With informal estimates, it is possible to obtain a rough estimate of a discrepancy between a student's level of achievement and his or her intellectual potential. This can be done through observation, by using graded level materials, or by estimating the level of listening comprehension or understanding by asking the student to answer questions that most students of the same chronological age can answer. However, informal procedures for comparing estimated achievement with estimated potential have several disadvantages. They are subjective, arbitrary, and difficult to defend legally, and they need to be confirmed through more accurate standardized procedures.

Grade level discrepancy models allow the comparison of grade level placement and achievement for the purpose of determining whether a discrepancy exists. This can be done by using a constant deviation such as achievement of 1 or 2 years below grade placement. Although this method is easy to use, it does not take into account the number of years a student has been enrolled in school or that a 1-year discrepancy in the eighth grade is not as significant as a 1-year discrepancy in the second grade. A second method for determining deviation from grade level is to increase the magnitude of allowed deviation as grade placement increases. Grade discrepancy models tend to overidentify students who are slow learners or borderline mentally retarded. Many of these students are functioning academically at a level appropriate to their age and intellectual ability. Also, students with high IQs are less likely to be identified as discrepant achievers.

Achievement level expectancy formulas have been used to quantify achievement expectancy level. Unfortunately, each formula emphasizes different kinds of variables, such as number of years in school, grade age, mental age, intelligence quotient, and chronological age, and includes the addition, subtraction, or division of various constant numbers. Achievement level discrepancy models identify severe cases of discrepancies, but are dependent on questionable scores from intelligence tests. These formulas fail to account for the number of years a student has attended school and rely on an arbitrary severity level. Other statistical problems are errors of measurement, norm group comparability, and regression toward the mean (Cone & Wilson, 1981). Students in the dull-normal IQ range of 80 to 90 are more likely to be identified as having a discrepancy than are students scoring 90 or above. Also, students under 8 years of age are more likely to be identified than older students (Danielson & Bauer, 1978).

With standard score discrepancy models, test scores are converted into standard scores with the same mean and standard deviation. The conversion of raw scores to standard scores allows for the comparison of scores across tests, subtests, age, and grade levels (Erickson, 1975). While standard score comparison methods answer many of the statistical criticisms associated with expectancy formulas, they do not take into account the effects of regression of IQ on achievement.

Regression models are used to determine discrepancy between achievement and potential. They take into account the phenomenon of regression toward the mean. It is assumed that regression formulas reduce overidentification of children with IQs over 100, and underidentification of children with IQs below 100 (the opposite of the case for expectancy formulas). In addition, standard score procedures, emphasizing regressive analysis, seem to be more statistically appropriate for quantifying severe discrepancies between aptitude and achievement.

Some of the major concerns about regression analysis follow:

1. "Regression is a precise sophisticated technique being used on tests that are gross measures of behavior" (Lerner, 1984).

2. Regression has an inherent weakness as a way to quantify discrepancy because the intelligence tests that are used have low reliability and fail to meet acceptable psychometric standards (Shepard, 1980; Salvia & Ysseldyke, 1981).

3. There are disagreements among knowledgeable statisticians and psychometrists about certain statistical derivations, concepts, and assumptions with respect to regression. It is not surprising, therefore, that many administrators, special education personnel teachers, and parents do not understand, use, or interpret regression analysis procedures and results.

4. There is failure to account for the number of years a student has been in school.

5. Although the regression procedure makes no assumptions about the appropriateness of a given severity level, selection of an arbitrary severity level is an arbitrary decision.

6. There is lack of teacher preparation for the use of a formula.

7. There is difficulty in determining when special services should be discontinued.

Advocates for the use of regression would take issue with several of these concerns. Regression is not seen as a precise, sophisticated technique, but as a quantitative reflection of what actually occurs in test data. Also, failure

to account for the number of years a student has been in school should not be addressed in a formula; retention is a legitimate regular education intervention and students should not be held accountable for material to which they may not have been exposed.

The presence of a severe discrepancy between achievement and potential is not a sufficient condition for identifying a learning disability. Mellard et al. (1983) point out that a discrepancy yields only statistical information and must be based on more than one simple calculation by formula involving an IQ score. The educational significance of any score must be considered independently of the discrepancy model. For example, discrepancy formulas do not control for cultural bias and are not sufficient to classify a student as learning disabled.

Lerner (1984) points out that eligibility for special education services is and should be a value judgment and should not be made solely by measurement experts. There are many considerations that cannot be placed in a formula that should be considered by administrators, psychologists, special educators, teachers, parents, etc. The decision to determine eligibility should be made by a multidisciplinary team and be based on observation of school performance and behavior, informal assessment, responsiveness to instruction, and standardized test scores. Regression analysis is one small part of the process and should be kept in perspective.

The basic factor in identifying a learning-disabled person is a disorder in one or more of the psychological processes of attention, memory, perceptual ability, thinking, or oral language. Many educators do not have a working knowledge of these psychological processes or how to assess them. It is not possible to observe psychological processes directly. Only inferences about these processes can be made from observation. At present, there is a lack of reliable and valid instruments for assessing and measuring psychological processes. There are three approaches used to determining whether there may be a disorder in one or more of the psychological processes: observing and recording behavioral symptoms; using an informal task-process checklist; and employing standardized tests (Chalfant, 1984).

A list of behavioral characteristics that are symptomatic of possible psychological process disorders is sometimes used. Such lists should be accompanied by criteria for determining a possible process disorder. Another approach is to develop categories of psychological processes believed to be most closely related to school performance. These categories either include detailed behavioral characteristics or are presented in a question format to help direct the diagnostician or teacher to the study of certain behaviors. A task process checklist can be prepared for each academic area. The academic tasks are broken down into subskills. Behaviors are listed for each subskill that might be symptomatic of a processing disability. The teacher checks on whether the student displays these symptoms while performing failed tasks. These screening procedures provide guidelines for observable behaviors that sometimes help educators to recognize students who may be learning disabled. It is necessary, however, to conduct a close evaluation through more extensive assessment procedures.

Informal task-process assessment can be used to determine the possibility of a psychological process disorder. There are five steps. First, select the academic task with which the student is having difficulty. Second, informally assess and rule out other contributing factors such as instructional, cultural, or environmental factors, sensory impairment, intellectual impairment, physical or health problems, or social-emotional maladjustment. Third, break the academic task down into its subtasks. Fourth, determine which psychological processes or developmental abilities are involved in the task. Fifth, assess the processes that are involved in each subtask through informal procedures on several tasks. In this way it is often possible to identify possible process disorders that can be confirmed by the results of standardized tests.

The results of individually administered intelligence tests are analyzed to determine whether a student is learning disabled. An individually administered intelligence test samples many different aspects of verbal and non-verbal mental functioning and provides a measure of general ability. An analysis and grouping of subtest scores can give a clearer interpretation of intraindividual cognitive strengths and weaknesses and provide a measure of general ability.

Specialized abilities tests designed to assess psychological processes are often listed. These tests are in special areas such as language functioning; auditory discrimination; auditory processing; kinesthetic processing; visual processing; and visual-motor integration. Part of the problem with many tests of specialized abilities is that they are not related to a particular academic or school-related task (with the exception of listening tests, comprehension tests, and language tests), and therefore many educators do not know how to relate the results of many specialized tests to day-to-day tasks and behavior in the classroom. For young children, greater reliance should be placed on the developmental scales supported by observation of child behavior at home and at school. Anecdotal records and rating scales also are helpful.

It is not enough to diagnose a disability in a psychological process on the basis of one or two test scores. The presence of a process disability must be validated by having the student perform tasks that require the use of the process in question. If a process disability exists, for example, a student who has difficulty in recalling and repeating what he or she has heard can be expected to have difficulty in remembering names, learning the multiplication tables by rote, or any task that requires auditory recall.

To assure a nonbiased assessment for the culturally or linguistically different student, the multidisciplinary team should include measures of adaptive behavior, criterion-referenced tests, or teacher-made tests suitable for the individual student.

REFERENCES

Chalfant, J. C., & Pysh, M. V. (1984). *Teacher assistance teams* (Workshop materials). Tucson AZ: University of Arizona.

Cone, T. E., & Wilson, L. R. (1981). Quantifying a severe discrepancy: A critical analysis. *Learning Disabilities Quarterly, 4,* 359–371.

Danielson, L. C., & Bauer, J. N. (1978). A formula-based classification of learning disabled children: An examination of the issues. *Journal of Learning Disabilities, 11,* 163–176.

Erickson, M. T. (1975). The Z-score discrepancy method for identifying reading disabled children. *Journal of Learning Disabilities, 8,* 308–312.

Lerner, J. W. (1984). *Learning disabilities: Theories, diagnosis, and teaching strategies* (4th ed.). Boston: Houghton Mifflin.

Mellard, D., Cooley, S., Poggio, J., & Deshler, D. (1983). *A comprehensive analysis of four discrepancy methods* (Research Monograph No. 15). Lawrence KN: University of Kansas Institute for Research in Learning Disabilities.

Salvia, J., & Ysseldyke, J. E. (1981). *Assessment in special and remedial education* (2nd ed.). Boston: Houghton Mifflin.

Shepard, L. (1980). An evaluation of the regression discrepancy method for identifying children with learning disabilities. *Journal of Special Education, 14,* 79–91.

Vaughan, R. W., & Hodges, L. (1973). A statistical survey into a definition of learning disabilities: A search for acceptance. *Journal of Learning Disabilities, 6,* 658–669.

JAMES C. CHALFANT
University of Arizona

KIRK, SAMUEL
LEARNING DISABILITIES
REGRESSION (STATISTICAL)
SEVERE DISCREPANCY ANALYSIS

LEARNING DISABILITIES, SEVERE DISCREPANCY ANALYSIS IN

For many years, the diagnosis and evaluation of learning disabilities have been the subjects of almost constant debate in the professional, scholarly, and lay literature, especially since the passage of PL 94-142. The lack of consensus regarding the definition of learning disabilities is reflected in the day-to-day implementation of PL 94-142; in the absence of a readily acceptable definition, many school districts experience difficulty in deciding who is eligible for services. Both under- and overidentification of learning-disabled (LD) children create significant problems. Undercounting deprives LD children of special services to which they are entitled; overcounting results in the inappropriate placement of students who are not handicapped, the loss of valuable staff time, and the increased expense of operating programs (Chalfant, 1984). Overcounting thus drains resources from other programs and students; if rampant enough, it could result in the demise of LD programs altogether. Errors in LD diagnosis will never be completely eliminated, but the amount of error must be reduced as much as possible while still ensuring that as many LD children as possible receive the special services to which they are entitled.

Two broad factors seem to determine who is LD: (1) the prevailing definition of LD and (2) how that definition is applied on a day-to-day basis. The rules and regulations of implementing PL 94-142 provide a definition of learning disability for use by all states receiving federal funds for special education programs. According to this definition, the diagnosis

> is made based on (1) whether a child does not achieve commensurate with his or her age and ability when provided with appropriate educational experience, and (2) whether the child has a severe discrepancy between achievement and intellectual ability in one or more of seven areas relating to communication skills and mathematical abilities.
>
> These concepts are to be interpreted on a case by case basis by the qualified evaluation team members. The team must decide that the discrepancy is not primarily the result of (1) visual, hearing, or motor handicaps; (2) mental retardation; (3) emotional disturbance; or (4) environmental, cultural, or economic disadvantage. (*Federal Register*, 977, p. 655082)

While this definition gives states some guidance, generally the field has regarded it as vague, subjective, and resulting in diagnosis by exclusion in many cases. Operationalization of the federal definition has varied tremendously across states, resulting in great confusion and disagreement over who should be served. In fact, the probability of LD diagnosis varies by a factor of nearly five purely as a function of the child's state of residence.

Chalfant's (1984) review of state education agency (SEA) definitions across the United States identifies five major components that appear to be reasonably consistent across states. The first is failure to achieve, or, perhaps more aptly, school failure. This represents a lack of adequate levels of academic attainment in one of the principal areas of school learning. It is sometimes seen as relative to grade placement and sometimes as relative to intellectual potential for achievement. The second component, psychological process disorders, refers to disorders in one or more of the basic psychological processes that are believed to underlie school learning. Though never listed or defined in their entirety, such processes include attention and concentration, understanding and use of written and spoken language, conceptualization, and, in general, information processing of all types.

Exclusionary criteria require that the observed symptoms not be due to other factors such as sensory incapacity, mental retardation, emotional disturbance, or educational, economic, or related disadvantages. Etiology, probably the most ill-defined of all factors, typically reflects the need to evaluate a student's medical and developmental histories in order to locate factors believed to be causative of learning disability. These include history of brain injury or substantive neurological problems, motor coordination problems, hyperactivity, general immaturity, delayed speech and language development, and pre- or perinatal difficulties.

The last component, severe discrepancy, is specified in the federal regulations as a child's failure to achieve commensurate with age and ability to the extent that it results in a severe discrepancy between achievement and intellectual ability in one or more of the seven areas listed in the federal regulations. It is important to note that many states seem to ignore the "and ability" component of this definition, focusing only on the mean achievement level of all children of the same age, regardless of ability.

Each of these criteria should have an important role in the diagnosis of learning disabilities and each requires work in terms of definitional and operational clarity. Progress is being made primarily through the impetus of two U.S. Department of Education (USDE) Special Education Programs (SEP) Work Groups and Task Forces: the USDE, SEP Work Group on Critical Measurement Issues in Learning Disabilities, and the SEP National Task Force on Eligibility Criteria for Learning Disabilities Programs.

Although all five components are important, the psychological process component and the severe discrepancy component are the most salient. The severe discrepancy criterion seems a particularly fruitful place to begin in the endeavor to improve methods of diagnosing learning disabilities. The severe discrepancy criterion is the most widely applied across the states. Further, in spite of the fact that severe discrepancy is easily measured relative to other components of the definition of LD, methods of applying the criterion vary widely across states (Reynolds, 1984).

The Federal Work Group on Critical Measurement Issues in Learning Disabilities has recommended a procedure to determine what constitutes a severe discrepancy (Reynolds, 1984); this model seems to be the one preferred by measurement experts (e.g., Willson & Reynolds, 1984).

Objective Determination of a Severe Discrepancy

Clinical judgment has a revered and appropriate place in all diagnostic decision making, even though it has been amply demonstrated that statistical or actuarial approaches are always as good as—and often better than—clinical judgment (Meehl, 1954; Wiggins, 1981). Nevertheless, people should hold the central role of decision making about people. Clinical judgment, however, must be guided by statistical criteria whenever possible. Most states require the demonstration of a severe discrepancy for diagnosis of LD. It is important to note, however, that determining a severe discrepancy does not constitute the diagnosis of a learning disability; it only establishes that the primary symptom of LD exists. A severe discrepancy is a necessary but insufficient condition for a diagnosis of LD.

Two conditions must be met in order to establish that a severe discrepancy exists between two test scores for a particular child. First, the simple difference between the two scores must be reliable enough to yield great confidence that the difference is real and not owed to errors of measurement. Second, the difference must be large enough to be considered unusual among non-LD children.

Formulas (such as those considered by the Bureau of Education for the Handicapped in early proposals for the federal regulations pertaining to learning disabilities diagnosis and placement) that in any way involve the use of grade or age equivalent scores can be quickly rejected as inadequate and misleading. The reasons for this are many; in short, age and grade equivalents do not possess adequate mathematical properties for use in discrepancy analysis (Angoff, 1971; Reynolds, 1981, 1984; Thorndike & Hagen, 1977). In essence, one cannot add, subtract, multiply, or divide age or grade equivalents. In addition, grade equivalents have other problems, including ease of misinterpretation, lack of relevance to curriculum markers (though they appear directly related), and general imprecision. Only standard scores have any real potential for answering the question of severe discrepancy. The following presentations deal only in terms of standardized or scaled scores, mostly of the age-corrected deviation score genre such as those employed by the current Wechsler scales, the Kaufman Assessment Battery for Children, and the Stanford-Binet Intelligence Scale—Fourth Revision.

Reliability of a Discrepancy

As noted, the difference between the scores on the aptitude and achievement measures should be large enough to indicate, with a high degree of confidence (i.e., $p < .05$) that the difference is not due to chance or to errors of measurement. This requires an inferential statistical test of the hypothesis that the aptitude and achievement scores for the child in question are the same. Payne and Jones (1957) first introduced such a test to interpret individual tests of intelligence. More complex methods of calculation involving the reliabilities of the respective scales and the correlation between the two measures have been proffered (Salvia & Ysseldyke, 1981), but the simple computational formula shown is the algebraic equivalent of the more complex formulas (Reynolds & Willson, 1984; Willson & Reynolds, 1984; Zimmerman & Williams, 1982). The test for the significance of the difference of two obtained scores $(X_i - Y_i)$ when the scores are expressed as z-scores is shown in equation 1:

$$z = \frac{X_i - Y_i}{\sqrt{2 - r_{xx} - r_{yy}}} \qquad (1)$$

There is no need to be intimidated by such equations; they are easy to calculate and require no more than beginning high-school algebra. In equation 1, x_i and Y_i represent the child's score on an aptitude measure X and achievement measure Y; r_{xx} and r_{yy} represent the respective internal consistency reliability estimates for the two scales. These reliability estimates should be based on the responses of the standardization sample of each test and should be age appropriate for the child being evaluated; these are most often reported in test manuals. The test statistic is a z-score that is referred to the normal curve. For a one-tailed test with $p = .05$, the critical value of $z = 1.65$. If $z > 1.65$, one can be sufficiently confident that the difference is not due to errors inherent in the two tests. Although a one-tailed test at the .05 level is probably justifiable for evaluating children referred for the possibility of a learning disability, a two-tailed test or a higher level of confidence (e.g., $p = .01$) would provide a more conservative measure of observed differences. For a two-tailed test, the critical value of z at $p = .05$ is 1.96. All other critical values can be determined from any table of values of the normal curve.

After reliability has been established, the frequency of occurrence of a difference score must be evaluated. In the following discussion it will become clear that any discrepancy meeting the recommended criteria for frequency will of necessity also have met the criteria of reliability.

Frequency of a Discrepancy

In evaluating the frequency of a discrepancy score, one must first decide what type of discrepancy score to assess (e.g., a residualized difference between predicted and obtained achievement scores, differences between estimated true scores and residualized true scores, true difference scores). In part, this decision depends on how one interprets the PL 94-142 definition of LD.

To establish that a discrepancy is severe, one must decide which of the following two questions to address:

1. Is there a severe discrepancy between this child's score on the achievement measure and the average achievement score of all other children with the same IQ as this child?
2. Is there a severe discrepancy between this child's measured achievement level and this child's measured level of intellectual functioning?

Both of these questions involve intraindividual variations in test performance (as opposed to purely interindividual norm-referenced comparisons). While this is obvious in the case of the second question, it may not be so evident for the first, which involves an intraindividual comparison because the determination of the average achievement level of all other children with the same IQ is based on the IQ obtained by the individual child in question. Though both are clearly intraindividual difference models, the mathematical models for answering these two questions differ considerably.

The former appears to be the most pressing question for evaluating children with learning problems and is the most consistent with the intent of PL 94-142 because the aptitude or ability we want to define is the aptitude or ability to achieve in academic areas (Reynolds, 1984, 1985). Evaluating the second question is easier in terms of calculation; one can follow Kaufman's (1979) or Reynolds and Gutkin's (1981) recommended methodology for assessing verbal-performance IQ differences on the Wechsler scales. However, this is only the case when no directionality is implied, as in evaluating within test scatter. This is certainly not the case in the diagnosis of learning disabilities, where we are clearly interested in the case in which aptitude exceeds achievement. Thus such models as Linn's Regression Estimates of True Discrepancy Scores, most recently promulgated by the Kansas Institute for Research in Learning Disabilities, that do not account for the regression between aptitude and achievement will be faulty (see Reynolds, 1984, for a review of this model and its problems). An adequate evaluation of the second question, when directionality is known or assumed, is not yet known.

To assess the first question requires a regression model (i.e., a mathematical model that accounts for the imperfect relationship between IQ and achievement). Once regression effects have been assessed, the frequency of occurrence of the difference between the academic performance of the child in question and all other children having the same IQ can be determined. The correct model specifies that a severe discrepancy between aptitude (X) and achievement (Y) exists when, assuming the two tests are scaled to a common metric,

$$\hat{Y} - Y_i \geq SD_y \sqrt{1 - r_{xy}^2}, \qquad (2)$$

where Y_i is the child's achievement score
    X_i is the child's aptitude score
    $\hat{Y}$ is the mean achievement score for all children with IQ = X_i
  SD_y is the standard deviation of Y
    z_a is the point on the normal curve corresponding to the relative frequency needed to denote "severity"
    r_{xy}^2 is the square of the correlation between the aptitude achievement measures

It is necessary to use $\hat{Y} - Y_i$ as the discrepancy score because IQ and achievement are not perfectly correlated.

For example, if the IQ and achievement tests have the same mean and standard deviation ($\overline{X} = 100$; $SD = 15$), and if they correlate at .60, then the average achievement score of all children with IQs of 80 is 88 and of all children with IQs of 120 is 112. Therein lies the need to compare the achievement of the child in question with the achievement of all other children with the same IQ. The term $SD_y 1 - r_{xy}^2$ is the standard deviation of the distribution $\hat{Y} - Y_i$. Since this distribution is normal, we can estimate the frequency of occurrence of any given difference ($\hat{Y} - Y_i$) that corresponds to the point of "severity" on the normal curve. Next, one must establish a value for z_a, a controversial matter in itself.

Establishing A Value for z_a in Discrepancy Models

There are no strictly empirical criteria or research methods for establishing a value for z_a because we have no consensus on a definition of LD. Specifically, we do not have a definition that would allow the generation of a true and globally accepted estimate of the prevalence of the group of disorders subsumed under the term LD. To complicate this issue further, there is no consensus in the LD community regarding whether it is better to risk overidentification (in the hope that nearly all truly LD children will receive services) or to risk underidentification (in order to avoid identifying non-LD children as LD). Taking the second argument to its extreme, the proper procedure would be to identify no children as LD since the proportion of the population exhibiting this disorder is so small (see Schmidt, 1974). Consensus regarding the relative desirability of different diagnostic errors, coupled with valid estimates of prevalence, would provide considerable guidance in establishing a recommended value of z_a. In the absence of such guidance, one can rely only on rational, statistical, and traditional criteria.

It has been argued that a discrepancy should occur relatively infrequently in the normal population of individuals under consideration before being considered severe. Of course, "relatively infrequently" is as open to interpretation as "severe discrepancy." Strong tradition and rational argument in psychology, particularly in the field of mental retardation, argue for a definition of severity as two standard deviations from the mean of the distribution under consideration. With regard to a diagnosis of mental retardation, a score two standard deviations below the mean of an intelligence scale is defined as a severe intellectual problem, which is one of several criteria used for diagnosis. Qualitative descriptions such as mentally or cognitively deficient or lower extreme are common designations below this point in the distribution. At the opposite end of the curve, most definitions of intellectual giftedness refer to IQs falling two or more standard deviations above the mean, with descriptions such as very superior and upper extreme being common. Such practice is widely accepted.

In inferential statistics, confidence levels of .05 in an inference or judgment that a hypothesis can be rejected are the accepted standard. The .05 number corresponds roughly to two standard errors (for a two-tailed test) of the difference being evaluated, or to two standard deviations from the mean of the distribution of the test statistic employed (e.g., z, t, F). There is, thus, considerable precedent in the social as well as physical sciences for using a discrepancy of two standard deviations as a criterion for severity. For a .05 level of confidence, $z = 1.96$; this is close enough to the 2.00 value to support the use of 2.00. The actual 1.96 value is used principally to avoid more fractional alpha levels that may imply an unwarranted level of precision. Thus a value of $z_a = 2.00$ is recommended for determining whether a difference score is severe, though this value needs further qualification.

Since a difference score, whether defined as $\hat{Y} - Y_i$ or as some other value, will be less than perfectly reliable, one must somehow consider this unreliability in defining a severe discrepancy. If one considers underidentification a greater risk than overidentification, then there is a reasonable solution. Otherwise, as mentioned, one would minimize total errors by not identifying any children as LD. While several methods of accounting for potential unreliability in a discrepancy score are possible, the concept of the confidence interval is both popular and applicable. Adopting the traditional .05 confidence level for a one-tailed test, the value of z_a corrected for unreliability can be defined as $z_a - 1.65$ SE (i.e., z_a minus the z corresponding to the one-tailed .05 confidence interval times the standard error of the relevant difference score). A one-tailed value is clearly appropriate here, since we must decide in advance which side to protect; both sides cannot be protected. Under these assumptions, a discrepancy is defined as severe when, substituting 2 for z_a

$$\hat{Y} - Y_i \geq (2\mathrm{SD}_y\sqrt{1 - r_{xy}^2}) - 1.65SE_{\hat{Y}-Y_i}. \quad (3)$$

The calculation of the standard error of $\hat{Y} - Y_i$ is given in Reynolds (1984). Its use is clearly optional, although it does seem advisable to account for error in the process. It is important to note here that this is not the type of measurement error assessed by equation 1. This calculation allows us to identify more children than are likely to be true LD children; on the other hand, it accounts for many possible inaccuracies in the process that might inhibit identification of a truly LD child. The other four components of the most prevalent LD definitions, as previously presented, may then be evaluated to make the final judgment regarding whether or not a child is entitled to and needs services for the learning disabled.

The procedure outlined can objectify determination of a severe discrepancy in LD diagnosis. We may think that with regard to LD diagnosis we "know one when we see one," but if there is no "severe discrepancy," chances are we are wrong, and statistical guidance is necessary to aid human judgment.

The procedure outlined provides guidance for the objective determination of severe discrepancy. A computer program by Reynolds and Stowe (1985) will perform these analyses with all tests in use. It is crucial to bear in mind, however, that mathematical manipulations cannot transform the quality of the initial data.

Quality of the Input Data

The quality of the input or test data used is crucial in assessing a discrepancy. Tests with poor psychometric characteristics can be misleading or can fail to detect a severe discrepancy. The following standards provide guidelines for choosing tests for use in the assessment of a potentially severe discrepancy. Though one will not always be able to choose tests meeting all of these standards, the more that can be met, the better. Of course, the characteristics of the examiner(s), that is, the person(s) gathering the data, are of equal or possibly even greater import.

Tests should meet all requirements stated for assessment devices in the rules and regulations for implementing PL 94-142. This is not only a requirement of law, but is consistent with good professional practice. For example, administering a test in accordance with the instructions provided by the test maker is prerequisite to interpretation of test scores. If a standardized test is not given explicitly according to the instructions provided, inestimable amounts of error are introduced and norm-referenced scores are no longer interpretable. Thus all personnel evaluating children with educational problems must be conversant with the requirements of PL 94-142 and adhere closely to these standards.

Normative data should meet contemporary standards of practice and be provided for a sufficiently large, nationally stratified random sample of children. In practice, this standard is nearly impossible to meet in all respects. Yet it is important to approximate it as closely as possible because standardization samples are crucial to establishing levels of performance for comparison purposes. To know that an individual answers 60 out of 100 questions correctly on an achievement test and 75 out of 100 questions correctly on an intelligence test conveys very little information. On which test did this individual earn the better score? Without knowledge of how a specified referent group would perform on these tests, one cannot answer this question.

Raw scores on a test, such as the number of correct responses or percentage correct, take on meaning only when evaluated against the performance of a normative or reference group. Once the appropriate reference population has been defined, a random sample of this group is tested under as nearly identical procedures as possible with the same administration, scoring, timing rules, etc., for all. This group is known as the standardization sample. Ebel (1972) and Angoff (1971) have discussed a number of the conditions necessary for the appropriate development and use of normative reference group data.

Standardization samples for tests whose scores are being compared must be the same or highly comparable. Under the best of all conditions, the aptitude, achievement, or other tests on which children are being compared to themselves or to others should be conormed; i.e., their standardization samples should consist of precisely the same children. When this is not possible, the norms for each test should be based on comparable samplings of the same population that meet all of the requirements for normative data. Standardization of the scales should have been undertaken in the same general time period, or else equating studies should be done. Scales normed on different samples and at different times are likely not to have the same mean and standard deviation across samples even though they may be scaled to a common metric within their respective samples. This gives the two tests the appearance of actually having the same mean and the same standard deviation across samples even though they may be scaled to a common metric within their respective samples. This gives the two tests the appearance of actually having the same mean and the same standard deviation, even though this may not at all be true. Ample evidence demonstrates that general levels of performance on aptitude and achievement measures vary in the population across time. As just one example, the population mean level of performance on the 1949 WISC is now very close to 110 and the 1974 revision (the WISC-R) now has a mean of nearly 104, though both are scaled within their respective normative samples to a mean of 100. Use of an achievement test normed in 1984 and an intelligence test normed in 1970 would add approximately three or four points to the size of the intelligence-achievement score difference for children with achievement levels below their IQ, purely as an artifact of when the two tests were standardized. In the face of the paucity of conormed scales, using highly similar samples tested at a similar time (or with equating studies completed) is acceptable, but conorming will always be superior provided the sample meets the conditions of normative data mentioned previously.

For diagnostic purposes, individually administered tests should be used. For purely screening purposes (e.g., referral for comprehensive evaluation), group-administered tests may be appropriate, though for young children, individual screening is preferable (Reynolds & Clark, 1983). For all children, but especially for handicapped children, too many uncontrolled and unnoticed factors can affect test performance in an adverse manner. The test administrator is more likely to detect these factors under the conditions of individual assessment, where close observation of the child is possible. Further, individual assessment is more conducive to the use of special adaptations and testing procedures that may be required.

Finally, individual assessment allows for careful clinical observation of the child during performance of a variety of academic and intellectual tasks; this is central to the proper assessment of learning problems for children of all ages (Kaufman, 1979; Reynolds & Clark, 1983). Generally, individual assessment affords better opportunity to maximize the child's performance and provides higher quality data from which to devise interventions.

In the measurement of aptitude, an individually administered test of general intellectual ability should be used. Such a test should sample a variety of intellectual skills; it should be a good measure of what psychologists refer to as "g," the general intellectual ability that permeates performance on all cognitive tasks. If ability tests are too specific, a single strength or weakness in the child's ability spectrum may inordinately influence the overall estimation of aptitude. It is also important to assess multiple abilities in deriving a remedial or instructional plan for a handicapped student and in preventing ethnic bias (Reynolds, 1982). Highly specific ability measures (e.g., Bender-Gestalt, Columbia Mental Maturity Scale, Peabody Picture Vocabulary Test-Revised) constitute a necessary complement to a good assessment, but they are inadequate for estimating the general ability level of handicapped children.

Age-based standard scores should be used for all measures and all should be scaled to a common metric. The formulas for deriving severe discrepancies require the use of at least interval data. Scoring systems such as age or grade equivalents, which are essentially ordinal scales, should be avoided whenever score comparisons are to be made. Such scores may be helpful for purely descriptive purposes, but they are unacceptable for comparing scores of individuals or groups except under special, infrequent, circumstances. Scores that are ratios of age and/or grade equivalents such as an intelligence quotient derived from the traditional formula of (MA/CA) × 100, are also inappropriate. Grade-based standard scores are inappropriate as well. The criteria for LD given in PL 94-142 specifically denote a discrepancy in achievement for age and ability. Age is properly considered in age-based standard scores. The scores should be age corrected at appropriate intervals. Two to six months are reasonable ranges of time in age groupings for the derivation of standard scores, but in no case should groups extend more than 6 months for children below age 6 years or more than 12 months for children above age 6 years.

Age and grade equivalents remain immensely popular despite their serious psychometric deficiencies and misleading nature. In most instances relevant to diagnosis, grade equivalents are abused because they are assumed to have scaled score properties when in fact they represent only an ordinal scale of measurement. Grade equivalents ignore the dispersion of scores about the mean when the dispersion is constantly changing from grade to grade. Under no circumstances do grade equivalents qualify as standard scores. The calculation of a grade equivalent is quite simple. When a test is administered to a group of children, the mean raw score is calculated at each grade level and this mean raw score then is called the grade equivalent score for a raw score of that magnitude. If the mean raw score for beginning fourth graders (grade 4.0) on a reading test is 37, then any person earning a score of 37 on the test is assigned a grade equivalent score of 4.0. If the mean raw score of fifth graders (grade 5.0) is 38, then a score of 38 would receive a grade equivalent of 5.0. A raw score of 37 could represent a grade equivalent of 3.8, 38 could be 4.0, and 39 could be 5.0. Thus, differences will be inconsistent across grades with regard to magnitude of the difference in grade equivalents produced by constant changes in raw scores.

The measures employed should demonstrate a high level of reliability, which should be documented in the technical manual accompanying the test. The specific scores employed in the various discrepancy formulas should have associated internal consistency reliability estimates (where possible) of no less than .80 and preferably of .90 or higher. Coefficient alpha is the recommended procedure for estimating reliability, and should be routinely reported for each age level in the standardization sample of the test at not more than 1-year intervals. It is recognized that alpha will not be appropriate for all measures. Test authors and publishers should routinely use alpha where appropriate and provide other reliability estimates as may be appropriate to the nature of the test. When alpha is not reported, an explanation should be given. Internal consistency reliability (e.g., alpha) will almost always be the most appropriate reliability estimate for intelligence and achievement tests. Internal consistency estimates are the most appropriate of all reliability estimates for these tests because they best determine the accuracy of test scores (Nunnally, 1981).

The validity coefficient, r_{xy}, which represents the relationship between the measures of aptitude and achievement, should be based on an appropriate sample. This sample should consist of a large, stratified, random sample of normally functioning children. A large sample is necessary to reduce the sampling error in r_{xy} to an absolute minimum, since variations in r_{xy} will affect the calculation of a severe discrepancy and affect the difference score distribution the most at the extremes of the distribution, the area of greatest concern. Normally functioning children are preferred for the samples because the definition of severe discrepancy is based in part on the frequency of occurrence of the discrepancy in the normal population. When conorming of aptitude and achievement measures is conducted, this problem is simplified greatly since r_{xy} can be based on the standardization sample of the two measures (which should meet the standards of normative data) without any handicapped children included. Some states use validity coefficients based on estimates derived from research using handicapped children. This practice

is not recommended because the IQ and achievement score distributions of handicapped children are not normal; thus they restrict the range of scores and alter the correlation between IQ and achievement, making it appear artificially smaller than it is in reality.

The validity of test score interpretations should be clearly established. Though clearly stated in the rules and regulations for PL 94-142, this requirement should receive special emphasis, particularly with regard to Cronbach's (1971) discussion of test validation. Validation with normal samples is insufficient for application to diagnosis of handicapping conditions; validity should be demonstrated for exceptional populations (for use of equations (2) and (3), however, r_{xy} should again be based on a normal sample). This requirement is an urgent one, especially in certain areas of achievement where a paucity of adequate scales exists. To determine deviations from normalcy, validation with normal samples should typically be regarded as sufficient. This requirement does not require separate normative data for each handicapping condition. The generalizability of norms and of validity data is in part a function of the question one seeks to answer with the test data and is ultimately an empirical question (Reynolds, 1986; Reynolds, Gutkin, Elliot, & Witt, 1984).

Special technical considerations should be addressed when one uses performance-based measures of achievement (e.g., writing skill). Some measures, such as written expression, involve special problems of reliability and validity. For example, interrater reliability of scoring on any measure calling for judgments by the examiner should be reported and should be .85 to .90 or higher. This would also hold for such tasks as the Wechsler vocabulary and comprehension measures, in which examiners are frequently called on to make fine distinctions between the levels of quality of a response. Highly speeded and primarily memory-based tasks also will pose special technical problems that must be addressed.

Bias studies on the instruments in use should be reported. Criterion-related validity should receive emphasis in this regard, but not to the exclusion of other studies of bias. Bias should be addressed with respect to appropriate demographic variables that may moderate the test's validity. At a minimum, these should include race, sex, and socioeconomic status, though not necessarily simultaneously. In the assessment and diagnosis of LD in particular, sex bias needs to be investigated since boys outnumber girls in classes for the learning disabled by about 3.5 to 1. The procedures for evaluating bias in all aspects of a test are presented in a comprehensive form in Jensen (1980). While measures that exhibit little or no statistical bias are the measures of choice, other measures can be used with the appropriate corrections.

All of the noted points should be considered in the evaluation of test data used for determining a severe discrepancy. It bears repeating that the discrepancy formulas presented here yield results that are only as reliable as the test data used in them. Integrally related to the quality of test data are the characteristics of the examiner; the next section explores this issue.

Who Should Be Diagnosing LD

In one sense, the question of who should be diagnosing LD in the schools has been resolved by PL 94-142. According to the 1977 rules and regulations implementing this law, only the multidisciplinary team is empowered to diagnose handicapping conditions of any type in the schools. It remains legitimate to ask, however, who should be doing the primary assessment of the discrepancy criterion (as well as the psychological process criterion) and interpreting these results to the team? Job titles, education, and certification requirements for any given job in the schools vary greatly from state to state. This variation is troublesome because the quality of the personnel conducting the diagnosis or interpreting it to the team and to the parents is as important to the diagnosis of LD as the quality of the data and the objectivity of the definition.

The task of LD diagnosis is the most difficult of all psychoeducational diagnostic tasks; thus the most highly trained personnel available should be reserved for assignment to evaluating potential LD children.

Although accurate diagnosis of LD in school-aged children is considered the most difficult type of diagnosis mandated by PL 94-142, it is precisely the area of evaluation and diagnosis most often relegated to the least qualified, most poorly trained diagnostic personnel in the schools. Arguments and data (Bennett, 1981; Bennett & Shepherd, 1982) clearly show that the learning disabilities specialists and diagnosticians commonly assigned the task of LD diagnosis do not possess the requisite knowledge of tests and measurements to allow them to interpret test scores adequately. On a test of beginning level measurement concepts, Bennett and Shepherd's (1982) LD specialists answered barely 50% of the questions correctly. A group of first-year graduate students in an introductory measurement class answered more than 70% of the same questions correctly. Using the best trained staff will not solve the problems involved in diagnosis and evaluation of LD children, but it will be a step in the right direction. Who precisely this is will vary from state to state and possibly even from district to district within states; the point is that this subject desperately needs attention.

REFERENCES

Angoff, W. H. (1971). Scales, norms, and equivalent scores. In R. L. Thorndike (Ed.), *Educational measurement* (2nd ed.). Washington, DC: American Council on Education.

Bennett, R. E. (1981). Professional competence and the assessment of exceptional children. *Journal of Special Education, 15,* 437–446.

Bennett, R. E., & Shepherd, M. J. (1982). Basic measurement proficiency of learning disability specialists. *Learning Disability Quarterly, 5,* 177–184.

Chalfant, J. C. (1984). *Identifying learning disabled students: Guidelines for decision making.* Burlington, VT: Northeast Regional Resource Center.

Cronbach, L. J. (1971). Test validation. In R. L. Thorndike (Ed.), *Educational measurement* (2nd ed.). Washington, DC: American Council on Education.

Ebel, R. (1972). *Essentials of educational measurement.* Englewood Cliffs, NJ: Prentice-Hall.

Federal Register. (1977). Rules and regulations for implementing Public Law 94-142, 42. Washington, DC: U.S. Government Printing Office.

Jensen, A. R. (1980). *Bias in mental testing.* New York: Free Press.

Kaufman, A. S. (1979). *Intelligent testing with the WISC-R.* New York: Wiley-Interscience.

Meehl, P. E. (1954). *Clinical versus statistical prediction.* Minneapolis, MN: University of Minnesota Press.

Nunnally, J. (1981). *Psychometric theory* (2nd ed.). New York: McGraw-Hill.

Payne, R. W., & Jones, H. G. (1957). Statistics for the investigation of individual cases. *Journal of Clinical Psychology, 13,* 155–191.

Reynolds, C. R. (1981). The fallacy of "two years below grade level for age" as a diagnostic criterion for reading disorders. *Journal of School Psychology, 19,* 350–358.

Reynolds, C. R. (1982). The problem of bias in psychological assessment. In C. R. Reynolds & T. B. Gutkin (Eds.), *The handbook of school psychology.* New York: Wiley.

Reynolds, C. R. (1984). Critical measurement issues in learning disabilities. *Journal of Special Education, 18,* 451–476.

Reynolds, C. R. (in press). Toward objective diagnosis of learning disabilities. *Special Services in the School.*

Reynolds, C. R. (1986). Assessment of exceptional children. In R. T. Brown & C. R. Reynolds (Eds.), *Psychological perspectives on childhood exceptionality.* New York: Wiley-Interscience.

Reynolds, C. R., & Brown, R. T. (1984). An introduction to the issues. In C. R. Reynolds & R. T. Brown (Eds.), *Perspectives on bias in mental testing.* New York: Plenum.

Reynolds, C. R., & Clark, J. H. (1983). Assessment of cognitive abilities. In K. D. Paget & B. Bracken (Eds.), *Psychological assessment of preschool children.* New York: Grune & Stratton.

Reynolds, C. R., & Gutkin, T. B. (1981). Test scatter on the WPPSI: Normative analyses on the standardization sample. *Journal of Learning Disabilities, 14,* 460–464.

Reynolds, C. R., Gutkin, T. B., Elliot, S. N., & Witt, J. C. (1984). *School psychology: Essentials of theory and practice.* New York: Wiley.

Reynolds, C. R., & Stowe, M. (1985). *Severe discrepancy analysis.* Philadelphia: TRAIN.

Reynolds, C. R., & Willson, V. L. (1984, April). *Another look at aptitude-achievement discrepancies in the evaluation of learning disabilities.* Paper presented at the annual meeting of the National Council on Measurement in Education, New Orleans.

Salvia, J., & Ysseldyke, J. (1981). *Assessment in special and remedial education* (2nd ed.). Boston: Houghton Mifflin.

Schmidt, F. L. (1974). Probability and utility assumptions underlying use of the Strong Vocational Interest Blank. *Journal of Applied Psychology, 4,* 456–464.

Thorndike, R. L., & Hagen, E. (1977). *Measurement and evaluation in education and psychology*. New York: Wiley.

Wiggins, J. S. (1981). Clinical and statistical prediction: Where are we and where do we go from here? *Clinical Psychology Review, 1*, 3–18.

Willson, V. L., & Reynolds, C. R. (1984). Another look at evaluating aptitude-achievement discrepancies in the diagnosis of learning disabilities. *Journal of Special Education, 18*, 477–487.

Zimmerman, D. W., & Williams, R. H. (1982). The relative error magnitude in three measures of change. *Psychometrika, 47*, 141–147.

CECIL R. REYNOLDS
Texas A&M University

DEVIATION IQ
GRADE EQUIVALENTS
INTELLIGENCE TESTING
LEARNING DISABILITIES
LEARNING DISABILITIES, PROBLEMS IN DEFINITION OF
RATIO IQ
SEVERE DISCREPANCY ANALYSIS

LEARNING DISABILITIES AND JUVENILE DELINQUENCY

During the late 1960s and early 1970s, increasing attention and concern had been paid to the possibility of a causal link between learning disabilities and juvenile delinquency (Keiltz & Dunivant, 1986). In response to this concern, the National Institute for Juvenile Justice and Delinquency Prevention (NIJJDP), Office of Juvenile Justice and Delinquency Prevention (OJJDP), commissioned Charles Murray of the American Institute for Research to review empirical evidence of a causal relationship between learning disabilities and juvenile delinquency. After evaluating the empirical evidence, Murray (1976) concluded that while prior research clearly indicated that juvenile delinquents have learning problems, a causal relationship between learning disabilities and juvenile delinquency had not been established. His report recommended that carefully designed research be conducted to assess the effects of learning disabilities on juvenile delinquents and that the efficacy of diagnosing and treating delinquents with learning disabilities be studied.

Over the last 10 years, a number of theories have been advanced to explain the relationship between learning disabilities and juvenile delinquency. Among these, five theories were dominant: (1) the school failure theory, (2) the susceptibility theory, (3) the differential treatment theory, (4) the sociodemographic theory, and (5) the response bias theory (Keiltz & Dunivant, 1986).

The school failure theory holds that a causal relationship between academic failure and delinquent behavior exists (Murray, 1976; Post, 1981). This theory argues that

psychological reactions (such as negative self-concept and frustration) resulting from failure in school contribute to delinquent behavior. The susceptibility theory (Murray, 1976; Post, 1981) holds that the cognitive and behavioral attributes that accompany learning disabilities directly lead to the development of delinquent behavior. Such traits as the inability to anticipate consequences of actions and lack of impulse control increase the likelihood of delinquent behavior.

The differential treatment theory holds that learning-disabled (LD) and non-LD youths participate equally in delinquent activities, but that LD youths are adjudicated more often by the criminal justice system. This theory argues that LD youths are less successful in eluding and avoiding arrests and are more likely to be adjudicated once arrested because they lack certain cognitive and social skills. The theory further contends that LD youths are disposed of more harshly by the juvenile courts because of their social abrasiveness and lack of prior educational success.

The sociodemographic characteristics theory denies that LD and non-LD youths are treated differentially on the basis of cognitive and social characteristics. Instead, differential treatment is attributed to the sociodemographic differences between them. Finally, the response bias theory (Dunivant, 1982) proposes that LD and non-LD youths participate equally in antisocial activities, but when interviewed, LD youths conceal less of their antisocial behavior than their non-LD peers. This theory argues that non-LD youths are more socially astute and create a more favorable impression on the interviewer.

Throughout the late 1970s and early 1980s, in an effort to gather empirical data on the efficacy of diagnosing and treating delinquents with learning disabilities, the Association for Children with Learning Disabilities (ACLD) was funded by the Office of Juvenile Justice and Delinquency Prevention (OJJDP) to design and conduct a remediation program. The National Center for State Courts (NCSC) received a second grant to study the relationship between learning disabilities and juvenile delinquency and to evaluate the effectiveness of the ACLD remediation program. These studies concluded that although the relationship is complex, a learning disabilities-juvenile delinquency link does exist (Keiltz & Dunivant, 1986). Furthermore, empirical evidence indicated that under certain conditions the ACLD remediation program did improve academic deficiencies and reduce future delinquency (Crawford, 1982).

The Foundation for Children with Learning Disabilities provides educational materials to courts and related agencies regarding the relationship between learning disabilities and juvenile delinquency.

REFERENCES

Crawford, D. (1982). *The ACLD-R&D Project: A study investigating the link between learning disabilities and juvenile de-*

linquency, executive summary. Phoenix, AZ: Research and Development Training Institutes.

Dunivant, N. (1982). *A causal analysis of the relationships between learning disabilities and juvenile delinquency.* Williamsburg, VA: National Center for State Courts.

Keiltz, I., & Dunivant, N. (1986). The relationship between learning disability and juvenile delinquency: Current state of knowledge. *Remedial & Special Education, 7,* 18–26.

Murray, C. A. (1976). *The link between learning disabilities and juvenile delinquency* Washington, DC: U.S. Department of Justice.

Post, C. H. (1981). The link between learning disabilities and juvenile delinquency: Cause, effect and "present solutions." *Juvenile & Family Court Journal, 32,* 58–68.

HARRISON C. STANTON
Texas A&M University

ASSOCIATION FOR CHILDREN AND ADULTS WITH LEARNING DISABILITIES
FOUNDATION FOR CHILDREN WITH LEARNING DISABILITIES

LEARNING DISABILITIES MARKER VARIABLES PROJECT

Marker variables reflect the constructs that define and characterize a particular field and provide operational and conceptual organization to that field by allowing readers to assess comparability of research samples (Bell & Hertz, 1979). The purpose of the Marker Variable Project, conducted by Barbara Keogh at the University of California, Los Angeles (UCLA), was to develop and test a set of marker variables in the field of learning disabilities (Keogh, Major, Omori, Gandara, & Reid, 1980).

This UCLA Marker Variable Project sought to identify possible markers from empirical and conceptual perspectives by reviewing the learning disabilities literature to determine the descriptive variables actually used by researchers for defining and selecting subjects, and reviewing various definitions and theoretical orientations to determine which processes and/or abilities were viewed as primary components of learning disabilities. Based on this procedure, a set of marker variables was proposed and then modified by consultants at a series of conferences.

The resulting set of tentative marker variables was organized along three dimensions: (1) descriptive markers, not specific to learning disabilities research but representative of information reasonably expected in any study involving human subjects, including number of subjects, chronological age, grade level, month /year of study, geographic location, community type, race/ethnicity, source of subjects, socioeconomic status, language background, educational history, current educational status, health status, and exclusionary criteria; (2) substantive markers, particularly relevant to the study of learning-disabled children, including general ability, reading and math achievement, and behavioral and emotional adjustment; and (3) topical markers, relating to specific research areas within the learning disabilities field, including activity level, attention, auditory perception, fine motor coordination, gross motor coordination, memory, oral language, and visual perception (Keogh et al., 1980).

Many of the basic issues addressed by the Marker Variable Project continue to be relevant to the field. Learning disabilities research still suffers from inadequate description of study samples, and leaders in learning disabilities research continue to call for a richer description of subjects, the use of topical marker variables, and exploration of subtypes of learning disabilities (Torgeson & Wong, 1986).

REFERENCES

Bell, R. Q., & Hertz, T. W. (1979). Toward more comparability and generalizability of development research. *Child Development, 47,* 6–13.

Keogh, B. K., Major, S. M., Omori, H., Gandara, P., & Reid, H. P. (1980). Proposed markers in learning disabilities research. *Journal of Abnormal Child Psychology, 8,* 21–31.

Torgeson, J., & Wong, B. (Eds.). (1986). *Psychological and educational perspectives on learning disabilities.* Orlando, FL: Academic.

LYNN S. FUCHS
DOUGLAS FUCHS
Peabody College, Vanderbilt University

LEARNING DISABILITIES RESEARCH IN SPECIAL EDUCATION

LEARNING DISABILITY QUARTERLY

Learning Disability Quarterly is the official journal of the Council for Learning Disabilities. The major purpose of the quarterly is to publish educational articles with an applied focus. The main emphasis of each paper is on learning disabilities rather than on topics or studies that incidentally use learning-disabled subjects or only indirectly relate to the field of learning disabilities.

The quarterly seeks papers in categories such as (1) techniques in identification, assessment, remediation, and programming; (2) reviews of literature relating directly to the learning disabled; (3) theory and discussion of pertinent issues; (4) original research with an applied focus; and (5) practices in personnel preparation. *Learning Dis-*

ability Quarterly is published four times a year by the Council for Learning Disabilities. Council dues are $20.

REBECCA BAILEY
Texas A&M University

LEARNING DISABILITY SUBTYPES

According to a survey of professionals in the field of learning disabilities (Adelman & Taylor, 1985), the search for subtypes of specific learning disabilities has emerged in the 1980s as one of the most overriding concerns in the area of practice and related applied research.

Historically, the field has been dominated by single syndrome theories. These theories maintain that there is such a thing as the learning-disabled child (Fisk & Rourke, 1983) and construct appropriate univocal views of major characteristics, etiology, and interventions. Principal among these theories are neurological deficit theories, perceptual deficit theories, and language deficit theories. However, as early as the late 1960s multiple syndrome theories of learning disabilities began to appear in the literature; they have continued to grow in scope and importance. These theories have attempted to deal with the persistently troublesome problem of the heterogeneity of the learning-disabled population by searching for more homogeneous subgroups.

Two basic methods of identifying subgroups have been used: clinical classification and empirical classification. The majority of students in the 1970s used a clinical sorting technique. For instance, Mattis, French, and Rapin (1975) identified three neuropsychological subtypes within a sample identified as dyslexic. The three subtypes were language disorder, articulatory-graphomotor dyscoordination, and visual perceptual disorder. The clinical classification system of Boder (1973) also has been influential. Boder analyzed reading and spelling error patterns to arrive at three subtypes of reading disability: dysphonetic (67%), dyseidetic (10%), and mixed (23%).

More recently investigators have used multivariate classification techniques to group subjects empirically (McKinney, 1984). Empirical subtyping studies have been done using a vast array of factors and across a variety of domains. Within the broader domain of learning disabilities, subtypes of reading, arithmetic, and spelling disability have been developed, as well as behavioral subtypes (Rourke, 1985).

Some of the most advanced work in the area of reading disability, for example, has been done by Lyon (1985). Lyon first identified five subgroups of younger learning-disabled readers and then investigated differential responses to two different teaching methods by one of the subgroups. Results showed that the selected subgroup, which had shown difficulties in morphosyntactic skill, sound blending, receptive language comprehension, and auditory memory and discrimination, did, in fact, respond better to a sight word/analytic phonics method than to a synthetic phonics method.

While still at an early stage, research on learning disability subtypes has shown the feasibility of identifying homogeneous subgroups of learning-disabled students. Developing an adequate taxonomy of learning disability subtypes parallels similar efforts in other areas of exceptionality.

REFERENCES

Adelman, H. S., & Taylor, L. (1985). The future of the LD field: A survey of fundamental concerns. *Journal of Learning Disabilities, 18*, 423–427.

Boder, E. (1973). Developmental dyslexia: A diagnostic approach based on three atypical reading-spelling patterns. *Developmental Medicine & Child Neurology, 15*, 663–687.

Fisk, J. L., & Rourke, B. P. (1983). Neuropsychological subtyping of learning-disabled children: History, methods, implications. *Journal of Learning Disabilities, 16*, 529–531.

Lyon, G. R. (1985). Identification and remediation of learning disability subtypes: Preliminary findings. *Learning Disabilities Focus, 1*, 21–35.

Mattis, S., French, J. H., & Rapin, I. (1975). Dyslexia in children and adults: Three independent neuropsychological syndromes. *Developmental Medicine & Child Neurology, 17*, 150–163.

McKinney, J. D. (1984). The search for subtypes of specific learning disability. *Journal of Learning Disabilities, 17*, 43–50.

Rourke, B. P. (Ed.). (1985). *Neuropsychology of learning disabilities: Essentials of subtype analysis.* New York: Guilford.

TIMOTHY D. LACKAYE
*Hunter College, City University
of New York*

LEARNING DISABILITIES
SEVERE DISCREPANCY ANALYSIS

LEARNING-DISABLED COLLEGE STUDENTS

Since the 1970s learning-disabled students have become increasingly visible on American college campuses. More learning-disabled individuals are choosing the college option (Astin, Hemond, & Richardson, 1982) and increasing numbers are identifying themselves as learning disabled, both prior to and after admission to college. Concomitantly, a few colleges have developed comprehensive support services for their learning-disabled students (Cordoni, 1982). It was not until the 1980s that most colleges began to consider what might be appropriate accommodations and supports beyond those available for all students.

Several factors have contributed to the rise in numbers and visibility of learning-disabled students and to the subsequent response to them at the higher education level. Vogel (1982) noted that increasingly vocal and organized advocacy on the part of learning-disabled adolescents, their parents, learning-disabled adults, and concerned professionals has exerted productive pressure on colleges and universities as well as on graduate and professional schools. Open enrollment policies, particularly significant at the community college level, have encouraged greater numbers of all categories of nontraditional applicants, including learning-disabled students. Probably the most powerful force behind the expanded numbers, increased visibility, and supportive services comes from strong federal and state legislation, particularly PL 94-142, the Education of All Handicapped Children Act of 1975, and Section 504 (especially Subpart E) of PL 93-112, the Rehabilitation Act of 1973. Learning-disabled individuals constitute one of several categories of handicapped people protected under this legislation. These laws prohibit discrimination against qualified handicapped persons in admissions, recruitment, and treatment after admission. They also require that qualified handicapped persons in higher education be provided aids, benefits, and services that afford them equal access to the available opportunities for academic success. In the case of learning-disabled students, such aids and services have included extended time on exams, oral essays to supplement or supplant written exams, exemption from foreign language requirements, readers, tutors, and counseling.

Most descriptions of learning-disabled college students have come from observation and clinical work with students attending support programs within colleges and universities (Barbaro, 1982; Cordoni, 1979; Vogel, 1982). While these descriptions focus on deficits rather than strengths, clearly it is the presence of substantial talent and fortitude that allows learning-disabled adults to succeed in higher education.

Characteristics of learning-disabled college students vary considerably. These students display a variety of different patterns of difficulty that may include one or more of the following: immaturities and disorganization of spoken or written language, perceptual-motor problems, study and time/space organizational difficulties, social discoordination, and weakness in basic reading, spelling, writing, or mathematical skills.

Underlying causes of these difficulties are presumed, though often not proven, to be of neurological or biochemical origin. They represent differences, tendencies, or deficits that may be either inherited or acquired. IQ levels vary as a function of each college program's view of the level needed to succeed, but none are reported to be less than 85 and many are well above average (Mangrum & Strichart, 1984).

While college is not an appropriate avenue for all learning-disabled adults, there is evidence that many can be successful in higher education (Lawrence, Kent, & Henson, 1982). They have enrolled and been successful in a wide variety of college majors. A large number of colleges have acknowledged their learning-disabled student population, but few have organized comprehensive support services such as diagnostic evaluation, remediation, counseling, special focus courses, faculty development, and coordination of services. College policies regarding special support services, as well as modifications in admissions testing, course requirements, and particularly knowledge/skill evaluation are now being addressed by faculty and administrators. The recent influx of greater numbers of identified learning-disabled students has just begun to affect the shape of college programs and policies.

REFERENCES

Astin, A. W., Hemond, M. K., & Richardson, G. T. (1982). *The American freshman: National norms for fall 1982*. Los Angeles: University of California at Los Angeles, Higher Education Research Institute.

Barbaro, F. (1982). The learning disabled college student: Some considerations in setting objectives. *Journal of Learning Disabilities, 15,* 599–603.

Cordoni, B. (1979). Assisting dyslexic college students: An experimental program design at a university. *Bulletin of the Orton Society, 29,* 263–268.

Cordoni, B. (1982). A directory of college LD services. *Journal of Learning Diabilities, 15,* 529–534.

Lawrence, J. K., Kent, L., & Henson, H. W. (1982). *The handicapped student in America's colleges: A longitudinal analysis. Part 3: Disabled 1978 college freshman three years later.* Los Angeles: University of California at Los Angeles, Higher Education Research Institute.

Mangrum, C. T., & Strichart, S. (1984). *College and the learning disabled student: A guide to program selection, development, and implementation.* New York: Grune & Stratton.

Vogel, S. (1982) On developing LD college programs. *Journal of Learning Disabilities, 15,* 518–528.

KATHERINE GARNETT
*Hunter College, City University
of New York*

ADULT PROGRAMS FOR THE DISABLED

LEARNING POTENTIAL

Strategies for the assessment of learning potential have developed as alternatives to standardized norm-referenced assessment. With this method, the student is assessed, coached on assessment tasks, then reassessed. The posttest score is a measure of the student's potential for learning. The objectives of the method are to identify how performance is affected by prior learning experiences, what the processes are by which the student learns, how modifiable the processes are, and how to develop strategies to modify them. The ultimate goal is the prescription of intervention procedures to modify these processes to enhance the efficiency of learning (Haywood, Filler, Shifman, & Chatelanat, 1975).

Although the four most prominent approaches (Budoff, 1968; Feuerstein, 1970; Haywood et al., 1975; Vygotsky, 1978) differ in varying degrees in their theoretical bases and specific techniques, they all operate on the premise that a student's true cognitive ability may be different from what it appears to be from standardized measurement. Investigators view the approach as a way of linking assessment with intervention because the psychologist knows not only what and how much a student needs, but also what instructional strategies work to improve functioning. Although the approach holds potential as an assessment alternative, research is continuing on predictive validity, generalizability of training, and use with a variety of populations.

REFERENCES

Budoff, M. (1968). Learning potential as a supplementary strategy to psychological diagnosis. In J. Hellmuth (Ed.), *Learning disorders* (Vol. 3). Seattle, WA: Special Child Publications.

Feuerstein, R. (1970). A dynamic approach to the causation, prevention, and alleviation of retarded performance. In H. C. Haywood (Ed.), *Social-cultural aspects of mental retardation*. New York: Appleton-Century-Crofts.

Haywood, H. C., Filler, J. W., Shifman, M. A., & Chatelanat, G. (1975). Behavioral assessment in mental retardation. In P. McReynolds (Ed.), *Advances in psychological assessment*. (Vol. 3). San Francisco: Jossey-Bass.

Vygotsky, L. S. (1978). *Mind in society: The development of higher psychological processes*. Cambridge, MA: Harvard University Press.

KATHLEEN D. PAGET
University of South Carolina

**LEARNING POTENTIAL ASSESSMENT DEVICE
VYGOTSKY, LEV S.
ZONE OF PROXIMAL DEVELOPMENT**

LEARNING POTENTIAL ASSESSMENT DEVICE (LPAD)

Developed by Reuven Feuerstein, an Israeli scholar, the Learning Potential Assessment Device (LPAD) is a direct teaching approach for the assessment of learning potential. Representing a dynamic or process approach to assessment, it rests on the ideas that cognitive deficiencies result from faulty adult-child-mediated learning experiences and that cognitive functioning is modifiable (Lidz, 1983). Designed originally for use with low-functioning adolescents, its major purposes are to determine which of a student's cognitive operations are deficient, estimate the

likelihood that the student can master those operations, and design and carry out a modification plan.

The LPAD is not standardized in the manner of conventional tests such as the WISC-R; rather, it involves an interactive process wherein the examiner develops and tests hypotheses about the student's cognitive structures. Most of the test items require nonverbal responses similar to the crystallized general ability tasks described by Cattell (1963). Accordingly, the approach is seen as particularly useful for economically disadvantaged children and adolescents (Haywood, 1982). It is not designed for classification/placement purposes since only informal age comparisons can be made. Thus, it is a supplement to rather than a substitute for other assessment measures. Because the LPAD is a complex assessment process, extensive training is necessary, even for professionals who already have training and experience in individual psychoeducational assessment.

REFERENCES

Cattell, R. B. (1963). Theory of fluid and crystallized intelligence: A critical experiment. *Journal of Educational Psychology, 54*, 1–22.

Haywood, H. C. (1982). Compensatory education. *Peabody Journal of Education, 59*, 272–300.

Lidz, C. S. (1983). Dynamic assessment and the preschool child. *Journal of Psychoeducational Assessment, 1*, 59–72.

KATHLEEN D. PAGET
University of South Carolina

**REMEDIATION, DEFICIT-CENTERED MODELS OF
THEORY OF ACTIVITY
ZONE OF PROXIMAL DEVELOPMENT**

LEARNING STRATEGIES

Learning strategies are strategies used by people to learn or remember things. In contrast, teaching strategies are activities used by teachers to facilitate learning and remembering in students. Teachers may teach a learning strategy to a student so that he or she can use that procedure or strategy as an aid to learning.

Gagne (1970) categorizes eight different kinds of learning: signal; stimulus-response; chaining; verbal association; discrimination; concept; rule; and problem solving. For nonhandicapped students, the first four types are less important for school instruction than the last four. In special education, however, all levels of learning need to be considered by the teacher. Problems associated with learning of all types form the basis of special education programs for most handicapped learners.

Some examples of strategies that are used for the different types of learning may help to explain further the nature of learning strategies. In discrimination learning, which involves acquiring the ability to differentiate among similar inputs in order to respond to those inputs, stimuli need to be presented in order. The critical features of the target stimulus need to be emphasized. Feedback is essential when the correct selection is made, as well as repetition or practice. A mnemonic may be used to assist in discrimination learning. To discriminate between *b* and *p*, the mnemonic that a *b* looks like a boot and is also the first letter of the word might be used. Mnemonics can also be used in verbal association learning (paired associate). Levin et al. (1980) took the learning strategy of a mnemonic and created a teaching strategy to help students learn and remember the states and their capitals.

For concept formation learning, Gagne (1970) has created a sequence that uses several learning strategies. The sequence involves (1) simultaneous presentation of examples of the concept; (2) multiple examples; (3) reinforcement for correct responses; (4) contrasts with nonexamples of the concept; and (5) learner generation of new examples of the concept with reinforcement.

For rule learning, Gagne (1970) suggests informing the learner about the form of the performance expected; asking the learner to recall the concepts that make up the rule; using cues to help the learner to recall, if necessary; and asking the learner to demonstrate one or more concrete instances of a rule.

Other examples of learning strategies besides mnemonics are visualizations, imagery, overt verbalization, rehearsal, spaced review and/or practice, cues, subvocalization, and imitation.

REFERENCES

Gagne, N. E. (1970). *The conditions of learning* (2nd ed.). New York: Holt, Rinehart, & Winston.

Lefrancois, G. R. (1982). *Psychology for teaching* (4th ed.). Belmont, CA: Wadsworth.

Levin, J. R., Shriberg, Z. K., Miller, G. E., McCormick, C. B., & Levin, B. B. (1980). The keyword method in the classroom: How to remember the states and their capitals. *Elementary School Journal, 80,* 185–191.

Robert A. Sedlak
University of Wisconsin, Stout

**BEHAVIOR MODELING
IMAGERY
LEARNING STYLES
MNEMONICS
TEACHING STRATEGIES**

LEARNING STYLES

Learning styles can be defined, in their simplest forms, as ways that students' personal characteristics, including their needs and preferences, stylistically affect their learning (Mann & Sabatino, 1985). However, a variety of different definitional approaches have been taken.

A learning style has been defined by Bennett (1979) as being a "preferred way of learning. It represents a cluster of personality and mental characteristics that influence how a pupil perceives, remembers, thinks, and solves problems" (Holland, 1982, p. 8). According to Hunt (1974), learning styles represent accessibility characteristics, i.e., specific cognitive and motivational characteristics of the learner. Dunn (1983) says learning styles consist of "a combination of physical, psychological, emotional, and widespread elements that affect the ways individuals . . . receive, store, and use knowledge or abilities" (p. 497). Dunn believes that most people have between 6 and 14 learning-style elements that affect them strongly. It should be observed that these definitions and many others emphasize learner preferences as defining learning styles.

Learning styles actually represent subsets of cognitive styles (Mann & Sabatino, 1985). Indeed, inquiry into learning styles often encompasses study of traditional cognitive styles. Nevertheless, learning style constructs tend to be much more classroom and instruction oriented than traditional cognitive style constructs and usually are studied in and applied to instructional contexts. Another characteristic of learning styles that sets them apart from the broader category of cognitive styles is that they tend to be more oriented to environmental events. It may be said at the cost of simplification that cognitive style researchers emphasize the particular ways that individuals respond to and structure their environments, while learning style investigators are more interested in how the environment affects those individuals.

While cognitive styles are currently studied through a variety of paper and pencil methods, they originated in psychological laboratories and have a more rigorous research tradition and deeper data base support than learning styles. The latter are usually dependent on information obtained from behavior checklists, inventories, and questionnaires.

A great variety of learning styles have been identified. Many are applicable to special education (Dunn, 1983), while others are more appropriately applied to higher education (Geogoric, 1979).

Different theorists have taken different theoretical and applied approaches to the study of learning styles. Ausburn and Ausburn (1978) have emphasized the study of learning styles as cognitive styles, and vice versa. Gregoric (1979) has conceptualized learning styles on the basis of students' preferences for particular learning sources and whether students prefer to learn through concrete or abstract means. He thus has been able to distinguish among abstract-sequential, concrete-sequential, abstract-random, and concrete-random learners. Hunt (1974) has proposed a conceptual level (CL) learning style model embodying dimensions of cognitive complexity, maturity, independence, and adaptability to social environments.

Dunn and Dunn, whose work has been particularly school and classroom oriented (1975, 1977, 1979), have identified four major categories of learning-style variables: (1) environmental, (2) emotional, (3) sociological, and (4) physical.

The Dunns' environmental category involves learning style elements relating to students' preferences for learning under different conditions of light, sound, temperature, and design (the last involving preferences for studying under formal or less structured learning conditions). The Dunns' emotional category concerns students' motivation, persistence, responsibility, and need for structure. Their sociological category relates to students' preferences as to learning by themselves or with others. The physical needs category involves modality preferences in learning, which Dunn and Dunn stress heavily, and other physical needs variables they believe are important to learning.

In contrast to cognitive style remedial interventions, which often seek to assist problem and handicapped students by altering or improving their learning styles, intervention efforts in learning style work are less ambitious in demanding change on the students' part. Rather than calling for methods to remediate or change unsatisfactory cognitive styles, learning styles interventionists are more likely to call for modifications in instruction and in the circumstances of learning. Fantini (1980) suggests that we are at a stage in which we should consider designing programs to fit learners rather than attempting to fit learners to standard programs. Dunn and Dunn advise that students' learning styles be matched, in a best fit manner, to teacher styles so as to optimize instruction. Kitson (1982) advises that what might appear to be learning deficits might actually be learning styles that are not being properly addressed in instruction.

In recent years, remedial teachers have been advised to modify their instruction to meet the learning style characteristics of problem readers (Carbo, 1983). Special educators have been similarly advised, for both the gifted and the handicapped (Dunn, 1983; Dunn & Prive, 1980), Smith, 1983). Studies have been carried out to identify the learning styles of handicapped pupils (Thibodeau, 1985); they suggest that mainstreaming approaches should use learning styles as a guide (Jones, 1980). Classroom management and instruction to learning styles also have been recommended as means of meeting the needs of gifted children (Dunn & Prive, 1980; Ricca 1984).

While learning style assessments reveal distinctions between students and their learning preferences, learning style variables may not account for enough learner variances to make them major springboards for educational intervention. Indeed, it is questionable as to how much learning environments can be adjusted to meet particular student needs. In special education, the individualized education plan, which does individualize instruction, conceivably could allow for more adjustment to learning styles than in regular education.

On the positive side, it is both easy and inexpensive to determine students' learning styles through a variety of paper and pencil and observational means. Insight into students' learning styles may provide useful instructional hints for teachers.

REFERENCES

Ausburn, L. J., & Ausburn, F. B. (1978). Cognitive styles: Some information and implications for instructional design. *Educational Communications & Technology Journal, 26*, 337–354.

Bennett, C. I. (1979). Individual differences and how teachers perceive them. *Social Studies, 70*, 56–61.

Blackman, S., & Goldstein, K. M. (1982). Cognitive styles and learning disabilities. *Journal of Learning Disabilities, 15*, 106–113.

Carbo, M. (1983). Research in reading and learning style: Implications for exceptional children. *Exceptional Children, 49*, 486–493.

Dunn, R. (1983). Learning styles and its relations to exceptionality at both ends of the spectrum. *Exceptional Children, 40*, 496–506.

Dunn, R., & Dunn K. (1975). Learning styles, teaching styles. *NASSP Bulletin, 59*, 37–49.

Dunn, R., & Dunn, K. (1977). How to diagnose learning styles *Instructor 87*, 123–124, 126, 128, 130, 132, 134, 136, 140, 142, 144.

Dunn, R., & Dunn, K. (1979). Learning styles, teaching styles: Should they . . . can they . . . be matched. *Educational Leadership, 36*, 238–244.

Geogoric, A. F. (1979). Learning/teaching styles: Potent forces behind them. *Educational Leadership, 36*, 234–236.

Holland, R. P. (1982). Learner characteristics and learner performance: Implications for instructional placement decision. *Journal of Special Education, 15*, 221–238.

Hunt, D. E. (1974). A conceptual level matching model for coordinating learner characteristics with educational approaches. *Interchange, 1*, 68–82.

Hunt, D. E. (1979). The B-P-E paradigm for theory, research, and practice. *Canadian Psychological Review, 16*, 185–197.

Jones, S. (1980). Mainstreaming with reference to learning styles. *Learner in the Process, 2*(2), 52–57.

Kitson, L. (1982). Learning style or learning deficit. *Academic Therapy, 17*, 317–322.

Mann, L., & Sabatino, D. A. (1985). *Foundations of cognitive processes in remedial and special education*. Rockville, MD: Aspen.

Ricca, J. (1984). Learning styles and preferred instructional strategies of gifted students. *Gifted Child Quarterly, 28*, 121–126.

Smith, C. R. (1983, April). *Matching instructional tasks to students' abilities and learning styles*. Paper presented at the annual convention of the association for Children and Adults with Learning Disabilities, Washington, DC.

EMILY WAHLEN
LESTER MANN
*Hunter College, City University
of New York*

COGNITIVE STYLES
DYSPEDAGOGIA
TEACHER EFFECTIVENESS

LEAST RESTRICTIVE ENVIRONMENT (LRE)

The term least restrictive environment (LRE) often has been used synonymously with the term mainstreaming. Although these two terms do refer to the placement of handicapped children, they are not necessarily synonymous. While PL-94-142 specifically guarantees the right to an appropriate education in the least restrictive environment, there is no mention of the term mainstreaming.

There is tacit understanding among professional educators that LRE refers to the placement of a handicapped child in learning situation that most clearly approximates that of a normal child. The ideal conceptualization would be in a regular class. LRE does not necessarily mean that a handicapped child can be placed with normal students for all educational programs.

The inclusion of LRE in PL 94-142 can be traced to the series of articles often referred to as the efficacy studies (Westling, 1986). Although the focus of LRE was originally the mildly retarded, Westling indicates that there is a growing list of authors who are pushing for the inclusion of the lower functioning retarded student in the LRE.

To implement fully the concept of the LRE, a variety of educational environments or alternatives are necessary. The "cascade" of services (Deno, 1970; Reynolds, 1962) provides the framework for such alternatives. Basically, the service alternatives range from the least restrictive (regular classroom with no support) to the most restrictive (residential institution). The concept of LRE dictates movement whenever possible toward the least restrictive environment. It may be that some children will never fully attain the least restrictive environment possible, but it should be the direction in which one should strive to move children.

Sage and Burrello (1986), in their discussion of the acceptance of the LRE principle, indicate that for most types of special education student, the most common placement is the regular class with supplemental services. They note that variations among states, categories served, and services within placements allow only a very rough sense of the nature of services used.

The question of whether the LRE has achieved its intention or provided a better educational environment for the handicapped is still unanswered. There are conflicting results in the area of academics, social adjustment, and self-concept (Westling, 1986).

REFERENCES

Deno, E. (1970). Special education as developmental capital. *Exceptional Children, 87*, 229–237.

Reynolds, M. (1962). A framework for considering some issues in special education. *Exceptional Children, 28*, 367–370.

Sage, D., & Burrello, D. (1986). *Policy and management in special education.* Englewood Cliffs, NJ: Prentice-Hall.

Westling, D. (1986). *Introduction to mental retardation.* Englewood Cliffs, NJ: Prentice-Hall.

PHILIP E. LYON
College of Saint Rose

CASCADE MODEL OF SERVICES

LEFT BRAIN, RIGHT BRAIN

The term left brain, right brain developed from the discovery by neuroscientists that the two cerebral hemispheres in humans are specialized for specific types of information processing. This research has reported that the left cerebral hemisphere, in most persons, processes verbal linguistic stimuli and tends to encode information in a sequential linear manner. Conversely, the right cerebral hemisphere has been shown to be associated with processing visuo-spatial stimuli and to use a holistic, gestalt manner of encoding. While such findings contributed greatly to understanding the unique division of labor of the human brain, most studies employed "split brain patients," people who had had the tissues connecting the two cerebral hemispheres (corpus callosum) severed surgically in an effort to control intractable epilepsy. In normal, non-commissurotimized persons, while cerebral specialization no doubt occurs, the continual exchange of information between the two hemispheres significantly diminishes the concept of the two brains implied by the left brain, right brain schema (Springer & Deutsch, 1981).

Major proponents of the left brain, right brain model have been associated with various aspects of education, particularly special education. Many of the publications, curricula, and study approaches that employ the notion of whole brain teaching, or profess to help teachers use right brain techniques to facilitate children's learning, appear to be, at best, only tangentially related to the hard scientific findings associated with the neurosciences. In an excellent article addressing this concern, Jerre Levy cautions teachers that "it is quite impossible to educate one hemisphere at a time in a normal brain" (1985, p. 44). This caution about the misapplication of findings from hemispheric specialization research should not be interpreted to mean there are no sound educational implications from the neuroscientific literature. One important translation of these scientific findings relates to increased understanding of specific learning disabilities, particularly dyslexia.

Neuroanatomic findings in the 1960s and 1970s revealed the presence of structural asymmetries between the two cerebral hemispheres in persons who had died of non-neurologic causes (Galaburda, LeMay, Kemper, & Geschwind, 1978), a physical attribute that was observed in populations of neonates as well (Witelson & Pallie, 1973). Subsequent studies demonstrated evidence for a reverse asymmetry in children with language disorders, including dyslexia (Hier, LeMay, Rosenberger, & Perlo, 1978; Witelson, 1977), as well as the presence of electroencephalographic (Duffy, Denckla, Bartels, & Sandini, 1980) and cytoarchitectonic abnormalities in the left cerebral hemispheres of dyslexic brains (Galaburda & Kemper, 1979). Studies of the neurospychological processing of children with reading problems, including dyslexia, reveal functional differences that are consistent with relatively superior processing of a sort generally ascribed to the right cerebral hemisphere (Denckla, Rudel, & Broman, 1981; Harness, Epstein, & Gordon, 1984).

REFERENCES

Denckla, M. B., Rudel, R. G., & Broman, M. (1981). Tests that discrimate between dyslexic and other learning disabled boys. *Brain & Language, 13,* 118–129.

Duffy, F. H., Denckla, M. B., Bartels, P. H., & Sandini, G. (1980). Dyslexia: Regional differences in brain electrical activity by topographic mapping. *Annals of Neurology, 7,* 412–420.

Galaburda, A. M., & Kemper, T. L. (1979). Cytoarchitectonic abnormalities in developmental dyslexia: A case study. *Annals of Neurology, 6,* 94–100.

Galaburda, A. M., LeMay, M., Kemper, T. L., & Geschwind, N. (1978). Right-left asymmetries in the brain. *Science, 199,* 852–856.

Harness, B. Z., Epstein, R., & Gordon, H. W. (1984). Cognitive profile of children referred to a clinic for reading disabilities. *Journal of Learning Disabilities, 17,* 346–352.

Hier, D., LeMay, M., Rosenberger, P., & Perlo, V. (1978). Developmental dyslexia: Evidence for a subgroup with a reversal of cerebral asymmetry. *Archives of Neurology, 35,* 90–92.

Levy, J. (1985). Right brain, left brain: Fact and fiction. *Psychology Today, 19*(5), 38–44.

Springer, S. P., & Deutsch, G. (1981). *Left brain, right brain.* San Francisco: Freeman.

Witelson, S. (1977). Developmental dyslexia: Two right hemispheres and none left. *Sciences, 195,* 309–311.

Witelson, S. F., & Pallie, W. (1973). Left hemisphere specialization for language in the newborn. *Brain, 96,* 641–646.

CATHY F. TELZROW
*Cuyahoga Special Education
Service Center, Maple
Heights, Ohio*

CEREBRAL DOMINANCE
HEMISPHERIC FUNCTIONS
INFORMATION PROCESSING

LEFT-HANDEDNESS

Left-handedness, a characteristic of fewer than 10% of humans, is a condition that has generated a tremendous amount of superstition. Negative properties and values have come to be associated with the left, while positive traits are associated with the right. The majority of individuals prefer using their right hands and also are more skilled with their right hands (Corballis & Beale, 1983). Our language also expresses this distinction; for example, a left-handed compliment is an insult, but a right-hand man is a trusted friend. Throughout history the left has represented darkness, evil, demons, death, the Devil, movement, the unlimited, the many, the even, the curved, and the oblong. The left also has been associated traditionally with femaleness and weakness. Since ancient times, left-handedness has implied a substandard subject (Needham, 1974).

Investigators long have been curious about the rarity of left-handedness. However, studies of historical records and artifacts have revealed enough inconsistencies in incidence to preclude any simple choice between culture or biology to explain the origin of handedness. Consequently, combinations of these various nature and nurture explanations have been invoked. Harris (1980) provides an interesting and detailed account of the various theories.

Whether accepting left-handedness as a rare reversal of the biological conditions underlying right-handedness or as a result of resistance to cultural pressure to be right-handed, many investigators have declared left-handedness to be a manifestation of pathology. The pathology theorists of the early 1900s, of whom the Italian criminologist C. Lombroso was the most influential, studied groups of lunatics and various types of criminals. They found that the incidence of left-handedness was greater in these populations and that the incidence among women almost doubled that of men. These findings lent themselves easily to prejudicial views and soon were misconstrued. At the time, it was not uncommon to find reports declaring left-handedness to be more common among blacks, savages, and the poor. These theories of pathology attempted to account for the negative properties associated with left-handedness.

With the growing awareness that the left side of the brain controls the right side of the body, and vice versa, later theorists recognized two different types of left-handedness. Evidence accumulated supporting the fact that left-handedness could result from damage to the left hemisphere of the brain or from anomalous biological or cultural conditions involving no damage to the brain. It was the former type that seemed to predominate in criminals, delinquents, and epileptics (Harris, 1980).

Today, there is no dispute that left-handedness is inherited, at least to a degree. An individual is more likely to be left-handed if one parent is left-handed, and more likely still if both parents are left-handed. However, transmission from one generation to the next is not perfect. Even if both parents are left-handed, there is only a 50% chance that an offspring also will be left-handed, Annett (1964) has devised a theory of handedness that explains this circumstance better than others. She suggests that most people inherit a right shift, or tendency to be right-handed, from two right-handed parents. Most will be right-handed, but a small portion may become left-handed owing to environmental influences or left-side brain damage. Right-handedness also is more marked for females than males since the latter are more susceptible to pathological influences at birth. Annett's alternative to the right shift is not a left shift, but rather a lack of the right shift. A minority of people inherit no genetic predisposition to be either left- or right-handed. Owing to various environmental or pathological influences, half will be left-handed and half will be right-handed, although a good many may be better classified as mixed-handed or ambidextrous.

Recent investigations have revealed a higher incidence of left-handedness in handicapped populations. Fein, Waterhouse, Lucci, Snyder, and Humes (1984) found 18% of a sample of school-age autistic children were left-handed. This figure is consistent with previous studies of autistic children, and is comparable to Satz's (1973) estimate of 83% right-handedness in retarded and epileptic populations. These findings represent an approximate doubling of the left-handedness consistently found in normal populations. Other studies have found markedly greater frequencies of immune disease, migraine, and learning disabilities among left-handers (Geschwind & Behan, 1982). While we can distinguish superstition from fact better than ever before, left-handedness continues to be an elusive phenomenon and a source of fascination and frustration.

REFERENCES

Annett, M. (1964). A model of the inheritance of handedness and cerebral dominance. *Nature, 204,* 59–60.

Corballis, M. C., & Beale, I. L. (1983). *The ambivalent mind.* Chicago: Nelson-Hall.

Fein, D., Waterhouse, L., Lucci, D., Snyder, D., & Humes, M. (1984, Feb.). *Cognitive functions in left and right handed autistic children.* Presentation at the Annual Meeting of the International Neuropsychological Society, Houston, Texas.

Geschwind, N., & Behan, P. (1982). Left-handedness: Association with immune disease, migraine and developmental learning disorder. *Proceedings of the National Academy of Science, USA, 79,* 5097–5100.

Harris, L. J. (1980). Left-handedness: Early theories, facts, and fancies. In J. Herron (Ed.), *Neuropsychology of left-handedness* (pp. 3–78). New York: Academic.

Needham, R. (Ed.). (1974). *Right and left: Essays on dual symbolic classification.* Chicago: University of Chicago Press.

Satz, P. (1973). Left-handedness and early brain insult: An explanation. *Neuropsychologia, 11,* 115–117.

GALE A. HARR
Maple Heights City Schools,
Maple Heights, Ohio

CEREBRAL DOMINANCE
HANDEDNESS AND EXCEPTIONALITY

LEFT-HANDEDNESS, PATHOLOGICAL

An association between left-handedness and some form of abnormality has long been popular (Orton, 1937). The term pathological left-handedness (PLH) is used to refer to an involuntary switch in hand preference (from right to left) in individuals who would otherwise be right-handed. This shift is thought to result from some form of lateralized brain insult.

Research suggests that both genetic and environmental factors may contribute to the determination of hand preference (Annett, 1975; Collins, 1975; Levy & Nagylaki, 1972). Acturarial data are used as evidence in support of a genetic role. For example, the probability of two right-handed parents giving birth to a left-handed child is 0.02. When only one parent is left-handed, the probability is 0.17, but it increases to 0.46 when both parents are left-handed (Chamberlain, 1928). The unknown contribution of environmental factors, however, limits complete acceptance of a genetic hypothesis. Collins (1975), for example, postulates that cultural and environmental biases play a significant role in determining handedness.

Left-handedness is somewhat rare, occurring in approximately 10% of the general population. A higher incidence of left-handedness has been reported in males (Coren & Porac, 1980; Gillberg, Waldenström, & Rasmussen, 1984) and in twins (Howard & Brown, 1970). It is generally thought that these findings reflect an increased susceptibility among these populations to pre- and perinatal complications. A relationship between handedness and birth order also has been reported, by Bakan (1977), who suggests that left-handedness occurs more frequently in the higher risk birth orders (first and fourth or later). Although Bakan's findings are somewhat controversial, they suggest a relationship between neurological insult and complications during pregnancy and/or birth.

A higher incidence of left-handedness has been reported to be associated with a number of conditions including mental retardation, epilepsy, dyslexia, and infantile autism. Evidence is strongest, however, for conditions with a clear neurological basis (Bishop, 1983). Attempts to assess the role of these conditions in left-handedness has resulted in a number of conflicting explanations.

Bakan (1977) maintains an extreme position and postulates that all left-handedness is pathological in origin. According to Bakan, this pathology reflects damage to the particularly vulnerable left hemisphere during the prenatal or infancy stage. This damage is thought to cause the child to favor use of the left hand.

In contrast, Satz (1972) has proposed a model of pathological left-handedness to account for a nearly twofold increase in left-handedness among brain-injured populations (mentally retarded and epileptic). This model includes two groups with distinct etiologies for left-handedness. One group is thought to be comprised of those who are natural left-handers and whose handedness is based on genetic and/or environmental factors. A second group considered in Satz's model is thought to be comprised of those who are pathologically left-handed as a result of early lateralized brain insult. It is hypothesized that early left hemisphere damage causes a shift of handedness from right to left preference.

The model further predicts that early right hemisphere damage would cause natural left-handers to become pathological right-handers (PRH). Given the lower frequency of left-handers in the population, the number of PLH will exceed the number of PRH. Moreover, since the pool of left-handers is relatively small, PLH should make up a significant portion of left-handers.

Satz's model is thought to account for a good deal of the elevated incidence of left-handedness among certain clinical populations. The model appears to be consistent with evidence that the majority of left-handers in the general population are neurologically and cognitively normal.

Although most would acknowledge that some portion of left-handedness is clearly the result of an insult to the brain, few would agree with Bakan's notion that all left-handedness is pathological in origin. Indeed, one must use caution in applying the term pathological left-handedness since there are no proven techniques to distinguish among natural or pathological left-handers.

REFERENCES

Annett, M. (1978). Genetic and non-genetic influences on handedness. *Behavioral Genetics, 8,* 227–249.

Bakan, P. (1977). Left handedness and birth order revisited. *Neuropsychologia, 15,* 837–839.

Bishop, D. V. M. (1983). How sinister is sinistrality? *Journal of the Royal College of Physicians of London, 17,* 161–172.

Chamberlain, H. D. (1928). The inheritance of left handedness. *Journal of Heredity, 19,* 557–559.

Collins, R. L. (1975). When left handed mice live in right handed worlds. *Science, 187,* 181–184.

Coren, S., & Porac, C. (1980). Birth factors and laterality: Effects of birth order, parental age and birth stress or four indices of lateral preference. *Behavioral Genetics, 10,* 123–138.

Gillberg, C., Waldenström, E., & Rasmussen, P. (1984). Handedness in Swedish 10-year-olds: Some background and associated factors. *Journal of Child Psychology and Psychiatry, 25(3),* 421–432.

Howard, R. G., & Brown, A. M. (1970). Twinning: A marker for biological insults. *Child Development, 41,* 519–530.

Levy, J., & Nagylaki, T. (1972). A model for the genetics of handedness. *Genetics, 72,* 117–128.

Orton, S. T. (1937). Specific reading disability-strephosymbolia. *Journal of the American Medical Association, 90,* 1095–1099.

Satz, P. (1972). Pathological left-handedness: An explanatory model. *Cortex, 8,* 121–135.

ARLENE I. RATTAN
Ball State University

RAYMOND S. DEAN
Ball State University
Indiana University School of
Medicine

BRAIN DAMAGE
BIRTH INJURIES
CEREBRAL DOMINANCE
LEFT-HANDEDNESS

LEGAL REGULATIONS OF SPECIAL EDUCATION

See SPECIAL EDUCATION, LEGAL REGULATION OF.

LEGG-CALVÉ-PERTHES DISEASE (LEGG-PERTHES DISEASE)

Legg-Calvé-Perthes disease, named for the physicians who originally described it in the early 1900s, is characterized by destruction of the epiphysis (growth center) of the hip end of the thigh bone. This destruction, which may be partial or complete, is attributed to an unexplained interruption of the blood supply to the epiphysis. It occurs more commonly in males than females, with onset between 4 and 8 years of age (Nagel, 1975; Silberstein, 1975). Early symptoms of Legg-Calvé-Perthes syndrome include moderate knee, thigh, or hip pain; a slight limp; and some restricted range of motion (Magalini, 1971; Nagel, 1975). The syndrome typically is unilateral (Durham, 1969).

Nagel (1975) described three forms of treatment for this condition. Recumbency treatment involves bed rest, perhaps with traction; this traditionally has been the favored treatment (Silberstein, 1975). Resorption of the dead bone and regeneration of the growth center occurs naturally; hence, recumbency treatment permits this natural healing process to occur. However, because regeneration may require 2 to 3 years, recumbency treatment represents a major disruption in a child's life. As an alternative, ambulatory treatment has been developed. This procedure employs a sling, cast, or brace to immobilize the affected leg, permitting the child to walk with crutches. Operative treatment involves drilling or bone grafting the epiphysis or surgically modifying the cup portion of the hip joint. While such procedures have been reported to hasten the repair process, surgery must be followed by several weeks in a body cast, making homebound instruction a necessity (Silberstein, 1975).

During the two- to three-year period of treatment, affected children are significantly impaired and emotional support is essential. Special education and related services may be necessary. A study of long-term outcome suggests the majority of affected children have some residual impairment as adults (Durham, 1969).

REFERENCES

Durham, R. H. (1969). *Encyclopedia of medical syndromes.* New York: Harper & Row.

Magalini, S. (1971). *Dictionary of medical syndromes*. Philadelphia: Lippincott.

Nagel, D. A. (1975). Temporary orthopaedic disabilities in children. In E. E. Bleck & D. A. Nagel (Eds.), *Physically handicapped children: A medical atlas for teachers* (pp. 193–204). New York: Grune & Stratton.

Silberstein, C. E. (1975). In R. H. A. Haslam & P. J. Velletutti (Eds.), *Medical problems in the classroom* (pp. 165–191). Baltimore, MD: University Park Press.

CATHY F. TELZROW
*Cuyahoga Special Education
Service Center, Maple
Heights, Ohio*

PHYSICAL DISORDERS

LEGISLATION REGARDING THE HANDICAPPED

There are dozens (if not hundreds) of federal and state laws concerning individuals with handicaps and as many or more such county or local laws and ordinances. The following is a summary of some of the major pieces of federal legislation regarding persons with disabilities, roughly organized into functional categories. For more comprehensive treatment, the reader is encouraged to seek appropriate sources such as the General Services Administration (1985) and the National Council on the Handicapped (1986) at the federal level.

Accessibility/Affirmative Action/Civil Rights

The Rehabilitation Act of 1973, as amended, is the most important federal legislation in this area. Section 502 of that law authorizes the Architectural and Transportation Barriers Compliance Board to set minimum guidelines and requirements to implement and ensure compliance with the requirements for physical accessibility and use of government buildings outlined in the Architectural Barriers Act of 1968. Section 503 of the Rehabilitation Act requires federal contractors to undertake affirmative action in employment and advancement for persons with disabilities in carrying out contracts of more than $2500. The department of labor is responsible for complaint processing and enforcement of this section. Section 504 of the Rehabilitation Act prohibits discrimination on the basis of handicap in two distinct areas: programs and activities that are recipients of federal financial assistance and programs and activities conducted by government agencies. The department of justice has federal responsibility for this provision.

The Education for All Handicapped Children Act of 1975 (Section III) guarantees a free appropriate public education to all handicapped children. Another relevant statute is the Civil Rights for Institutionalized Persons Act.

Income Maintenance and Health Insurance

Programs authorized by the Social Security Act providing cash payments and health insurance benefits are by far the largest in terms of persons with disabilities served (tens of millions) and dollars expended (tens of billions).

Title II of the Social Security Act authorizes the Disability Insurance program, which replaces in part income lost when a person who has been working in covered employment can no longer work owing to a physical or mental impairment. Once on the disability rolls for 24 months, regardless of age, an individual is eligible for publicly funded health insurance through Medicare (Title XVIII of the act); this generally covers persons over 65. Also authorized by the Social Security Act (Title XVI) is the Supplemental Security Income (SSI) program, which provides income support to indigent aged, blind, or disabled individuals, regardless of prior work history, who meet means and asset tests. In most states, persons eligible for SSI are eligible for the federal-state Medicaid program (Title XIX of the act), which provides medical insurance for low-income individuals. Within the Medicaid program is support for intermediate care facilities for the mentally retarded, residential programs providing care and services. Many disabled individuals also benefit from programs for which they are eligible without regard to disability: Social Security old age and survivors insurance benefits and Medicare (persons over 65).

Four other major programs for special groups of disabled persons deserve mention, two for veterans (Title 38 of the United States Code, various chapters) and two for coal miners. Veterans who have "service-connected" disabilities are eligible for direct monthly payments under the Veterans Compensation Program. Veterans of wartime service with "nonservice connected" disabilities are eligible for a special pension program. Coal miners disabled by black lung disease are eligible for special payments from a program administered by either the Social Security Administration or the Labor Department, depending on when the claim was made.

Education, Rehabilitation, Job Training and Other Services

A variety of services are made available by federal grants or required by federal law. Research, demonstration of model programs, and personnel training authorities are included in several of the following statutes in addition to the major grants discussed in the following paragraphs.

The Education of the Handicapped Act (EHA, which includes the Education for All Handicapped Children Act) requires states to provide all handicapped children with a free appropriate public education consisting of special education and related services. States and localities must adhere to a detailed set of programmatic and procedural requirements. Grants are made to states to help defray the extra costs of providing special education and related services. Separate grants to states are made for preschool handicapped children (under the EHA) and, under Chapter 1 of the Education Consolidation and Improvement Act, for handicapped children in state-operated or state-supported schools.

Title I of the Rehabilitation Act of 1973 provides a grant to states (80% federal, 20% state matching) for the vocational rehabilitation of individuals with mental or physical disabilities, regardless of prior work history. Individuals are eligible for rehabilitative medical, job training, and other services. Title II of the Rehabilitation Act authorizes the National Institute of Handicapped Research; Title VII of that law provides grants to States and non-profit community-based centers to assist severely disabled individuals in improving their capacity for independent living.

Two subsidized housing programs serve individuals with disabilities—Section 8 (of the Housing Act of 1937, as amended), lower income housing assistance of rent subsidies, and Section 202 (of the Housing Act of 1959, as amended), a program of construction of housing for elderly or handicapped persons. One percent of federal gasoline tax revenues are available for transportation projects benefiting disabled individuals. Employers hiring certain disabled individuals are eligible for the Targeted Jobs Tax Credit. Finally, persons with disabilities are eligible for services provided by the Job Training Partnership Act and the Social Services Block Grant (Title XX of the Social Security Act).

REFERENCES

General Services Administration. (1985). *Catalog of federal domestic assistance.* Washington, DC: U.S. Government Printing Office.

National Council on the Handicapped. (1986). *Toward independence: An assessment of federal laws and programs affecting persons with disabilities.* Washington, DC: U.S. Government Printing Office.

JAMES R. RICCIUTI
*United States Office of
Management and Budget*

**ACCESSIBILITY OF PROGRAMS
LEGAL REGULATION OF SPECIAL EDUCATION
SOCIAL SECURITY**

LEHTINEN, LAURA E. (1908–   )

In the 1940s, psychologists and educators often did not know of the existence of brain-injured children. If they did know, they did not do much research into the problems of these children. Laura E. Lehtinen was an exception. She believed that brain-injured children had disorders in per-

ception, concept formation, and mental organization, problems that interfered with the children's learning processes. *Psychopathology and Education of the Brain-injured Child* (Strauss & Lehtinen, 1947) was one of the first books to acknowledge the presence of these children, and to make recommendations to reduce their symptomatic behavior disorders. The book listed criteria for classifying the child who suffered brain damage from other than genetic causes. Lehtinen, who did not believe that brain-injured children had any limitations to their intelligence, suggested a highly structured, directive approach that was mostly kinesthetic. She put her ideas into practice as education director of the Cove School for Brain-Injured Children in Racine, Wisconsin.

Strongly influencing psychologists and educators in the 1950s, Lehtinen believed that motor learning is the necessary basis for subsequent learning. Believing that perceptual difficulties play a major role in learning disabilities, Lehtinen advocated teaching children cursive rather than manuscript writing because in the former, letters are written as units and spacing is less of a problem. Her work helped create interest in, and subsequent research into, the problems of the learning-disabled child. She is best known for her work with A. Strauss.

REFERENCE

Strauss, A. A., & Lehtinen, L. E. (1947). *Psychopathology and education of the brain-injured child.* New York: Grune & Stratton.

E. VALERIE HEWITT
Texas A&M University

LEISURE-TIME ACTIVITIES

Leisure-time activities, or avocations, represent constructive use of leisure time in the pursuit of recreational activities. In addition to providing enjoyment, enhancing the development of skills, and the opportunity for meeting and interacting with individuals who share similar interests, leisure-time activities can help meet certain self-actualization and therapeutic needs.

Leisure-time activities usually involve one of two general focuses. One common focus of leisure time activities involves engagement in activities that are dissimilar to the activities that constitute an individual's vocational or educational experiences. For example, a child whose major activities involve sedentary indoor school attendance might choose outdoor activities such as hiking or horseback riding as a change of pace. The other common focus of leisure-time activities involves those activities that enhance or build on academic or vocational activities that the individual finds enjoyable. For example, a child precocious in mathematics whose school work offers only limited involvement with the subject might engage in leisure-time activities such as doing mathematical puzzles or experimenting with computer simulations.

In special education, leisure-time activities can provide an especially helpful means for ameliorating personal-social and academic handicaps imposed by the educationally limiting condition or conditions. The child receiving special education services, whether physically segregated from peers by special class placement or identified as being different owing to special educational problems, is at risk for developing a sense of isolation or inferiority. Counseling such a child to engage in leisure-time activities in which the educationally limiting conditions or handicaps will not be limiting may represent one approach toward ameliorating these kinds of problems. Leisure-time activities that provide the child with successful experiences can be especially helpful and can aid in the development of feelings of confidence and self-assurance that may not be facilitated in the academic sphere.

Caution may need to be used in encouraging the child with special educational problems to engage in leisure-time activities lest such activities exacerbate feelings of inability to perform. The caution necessary in such cases involves a consideration of how the child's academically limiting condition may relate to given leisure-time activities. The child with attention-deficit disorder, for example, may become frustrated by leisure-time activities such as chess or table games that require extended periods of concentration over time. Similarly, the child with visual perception difficulty may experience difficulty with some craft projects or jigsaw puzzles, but find satisfaction in word games or crossword puzzles. By focusing on the child's strengths, leisure-time activities can be a source of satisfaction and sense of accomplishment rather than a source of further frustration or sense of inadequacy (Hartlage & Telzrow, 1986).

Leisure-time activities can provide supplementary skills training in academically relevant pursuits. Especially for gifted individuals, leisure-time activities can provide the opportunity for enhancing and expanding areas of academic or career interest. Building electronic systems or doing mechanical repairs may be a source of expansion for a child gifted in and interested in physics or mechanics. It can provide an out-of-school opportunity for skill enhancement and development. Even for the exceptional child with academically limiting problems, the opportunity for developing skills in the nonthreatening context of leisure-time activities can have a positive transfer to school settings. For example, the counting in such table games as Monopoly, or the word building skills involved in Scrabble, can be encouraged as an enjoyable approach toward helping the exceptional child with counting or language difficulties.

Consideration of the child's interests, aptitudes, strengths, and weaknesses, matched with leisure-time activities either by formal matching procedures (Hartlage,

1968; Hartlage & Ells, 1983) or intuitively guided counseling, can help transform leisure-time activities into ones that can simultaneously be enjoyable, provide enhancement of existing strengths, and be a source of remediation for academic weakness and a measure of developing personal and social competence and confidence.

REFERENCES

Hartlage, L. C. (1968). *Computer Research Avocational Guidance Test*. Phoenix, AZ: Computer Research.

Hartlage, L. C., & Ells, A. (1983). *Leisure compatability guide*. Scottsdale, AZ: Afterwork.

Hartlage, L. C., & Telzrow, C. F. (1986). *Neuropsychological assessment and intervention with children*. Sarasota, FL: Professional Resource Exchange.

LAWRENCE C. HARTLAGE
Evans, Georgia

ENRICHMENT
MOTIVATION

LEITER INTERNATIONAL PERFORMANCE SCALE (LIPS)

The Leiter International Performance Scale (LIPS) is an individually administered, untimed test used to assess the intelligence of persons ages 2 through 18. LIPS was developed for the purpose of evaluating persons who cannot validly be given conventional intelligence tests such as persons who are deaf or hard of hearing, those who demonstrate speaking or reading difficulties, the bilingual, and those who do not speak English.

The LIPS items are arranged in an age scale format from year 2 to year 18. Each item is administered by placing a stimulus card on a wooden frame and pantomiming directions. The examinee responds by placing a series of blocks into the stalls of the wooden frame (see Figure). The types of tasks found on the LIPS range from perceptually oriented items for preschoolers such as matching color, shape, or number to more conceptually oriented tasks such as the completion of patterns, analogous designs, and classification of objects. Success on all tasks appears to require the use of perceptual organization and visual discrimination abilities and freedom from distractibility. The LIPS raw scores are converted to a mental age (MA), which is used to calculate a ratio IQ.

Reviewers have consistently noted the lack of reliability and validity data available in the LIPS manual, and the inadequate nature of the test's standardization (Matey, 1985; Salvia & Ysseldyke, 1985; Sattler, 1982; Werner, 1965). However, many reviewers and clinicians recognize the usefulness of the LIPS as a diagnostic tool, especially in atypical assessment situations such as the evaluation of preschoolers suspected of having language

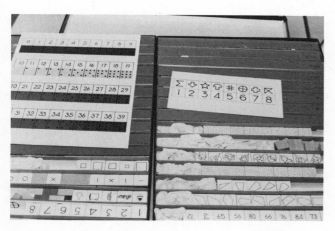

Sample materials for use in assessment with the Leiter International Performance Scale

difficulties. The developmental format of the items from age 2 to age 6 enables the clinician to establish a link between the LIPS assessment results and instructional interventions designed to aid preschool children in the development of cognitive skills.

REFERENCES

Matey, C. (1985). Review of the Leiter International Performance Scale. In D. J. Keyser & R. C. Sweetland (Eds.), *Test critiques* (Vol. 1 pp. 411–420). Kansas City, MO: Test Corporation of America.

Salvia, J., & Ysseldyke, J. E. (1985). *Assessment in special and remedial education* (3rd ed.). Boston, MA: Houghton Mifflin.

Sattler, J. M. (1982). *Assessment of children's intelligence and special abilities* (2nd ed.). Boston, MA: Allyn & Bacon.

Werner, E. E. (1965). Review of the Leiter International Performance Scale. In O. K. Buros (Ed.), *The sixth mental measurements yearbook* (pp. 814–816). Highland Park, NJ: Gryphon Press.

GEORGE MCCLOSKEY
American Guidance Service,
Circle Pines, Minnesota

ASSESSMENT
INTELLIGENCE TESTING

LERNER, JANET WEISS (1926–   )

A native of Milwaukee, Wisconsin, Janet Weiss Lerner received a BA (1947) in special education at the University of Wisconsin, Milwaukee. She received her MEd (1958) in elementary education and reading from the National College of Education, and her PhD (1965) in education administration from New York University. She is currently chair and professor of special education at Northeastern Illinois University.

Lerner's early experiences as an elementary school teacher, and later as an itinerant teacher of brain-injured children and a reading specialist, honed her interest in the areas of reading problems and learning-disabled children. She believes that early, appropriate recognition of a child's academic problem is necessary so that the child can develop the skills needed to function well in school and later in life. Her book *Learning Disabilities: Theories, Diagnosis, and Teaching Strategies* (1985) discusses learning disabilities from a variety of perspectives. She believes in being practical, giving teachers, administrators, and other professionals ideas that they can use in their daily work with children. Lerner also believes that people must have a good grasp of theory to understand the appropriate time and place to use certain techniques and to be effective in the field of special education.

Lerner views reading as a language process, therefore, she sees reading disability as a language disorder (Lerner, 1972). She also advocates the use of trial lessons (to determine how an individual child learns best) and task analysis, breaking a task down into its components and discovering the process necessary to complete the task. She sees these two processes as necessary in special education (Lerner, 1973).

REFERENCES

Lerner, J. (1972, Spring). Reading disability as a language disorder. *Acta Symbolica III*, pp. 39–45.

Lerner, J. (1973). Systems analysis and special education. *Journal of Special Education. 7*, 15–26.

Lerner, J. (1985). *Learning disabilities: Theories, diagnosis, and teaching strategies.* Boston: Houghton Mifflin.

E. VALERIE HEWITT
Texas A&M University

LESCH-NYHAN SYNDROME

The Lesch-Nyhan syndrome is a genetic disorder of purine metabolism first described in depth in 1964 (Nyhan, 1973). It is an autosomal recessive characteristic transmitted from mother to son on the x chromosome. The molecular site of the defect and the primary product of the gene is the enzyme hypoxanthine quanine phosphoribosyl transferase (HGPRT) (Nyhan, 1973).

The syndrome is characterized by increased amounts of uric acid in the bloodstream, and central nervous system disorders consisting of mental retardation, spastic cerebral palsy, choreoathetosis, and a bizarre form of self-mutilating behavior (Lloyd et al., 1981; Nyhan, 1973). Infants appear to be developing normally up until 6 to 8 months, when previously attained motor milestones such as holding the head up or sitting become difficult. The infant eventually becomes hypertrophic, requiring assistance in all aspects of movement. Most individuals with Lesch-Nyhan syndrome will never sit or stand unassisted. Their speech is characterized by athetoid dysarthria. Frequent vomiting, difficulty in swallowing, and pneumonia are also consistent with the syndrome (Nyhan, 1973).

Probably the most striking and troublesome characteristic of the syndrome is aggressive, self-mutilative behavior (Goldstein, Anderson, Reuben, & Dancis, 1985; Nyhan, 1973). It usually begins with the eruption of teeth or shortly thereafter. Unless the primary teeth are removed early on, most individuals with Lesch-Nyhan syndrome bite both their lips and teeth destructively. Individuals are easily recognized by the loss of tissue around the lips (Nyhan, 1973). Unlike other children who may not, owing to sensory neuropathy or congenital indifference to pain, feel any pain during self-mutilating episodes, children with Lesch-Nyhan syndrome scream in pain while they bite themselves. If restrained, they can be cooperative and pleasant. However, if they are not protected from themselves, they will scream and bite all night (Goldstein et al., 1985; Nyhan, 1973). They have also been known to try additional methods of self-injury such as burning with scalding water (Nyhan, 1973). A reason for the self-mutilative behavior is believed to be a distinct biochemical abnormality (Goldstein et al., 1985; Nyhan, 1973). Goldstein et al. (1985) report that the self-mutilative behavior is caused by dopamine sensitivity that can be treated by medication. Further research in this area is indicated.

Lesch-Nyhan syndrome can be determined prenatally by amniocentesis. Nyhan (1973) suggests that pregnancies of those families known to be at risk be closely followed; the ones in which an established normal HGPRT is present should continue to full term.

There is currently no treatment capable of improving the central nervous system characteristics of Lesch-Nyhan syndrome (Nyhan, 1973), although the work done by Goldstein et al. (1985) shows promise for the minimizing of self-mutilating behavior. Aspects of the disease that relate to the overproduction of uric acid (i.e., gout) can be effectively managed by medication. Education of such children would most effectively be carried out in a controlled environment where their medical needs receive top priority.

REFERENCES

Goldstein, M., Anderson, L. T., Reuben, R., Dancis, J. (1985, Feb. 9). Self-mutilation in Lesch-Nyhan disease is caused by dopaminergic denervation. *Lancet*, 338–339.

Lloyd, K. G., Hornykiewicz, O., Davidson, L., Shannak, K., Farley, I., Goldstein, M., Shibuya, M., Kelley, W. N., Fox, I. (1981). Biochemical evidence of dysfunction of brain neurotransmitters in the Lesch-Nyhan syndrome. *New England Journal of Medicine, 305*(19), 1106–1111.

Nyhan, W. L. (1973). The Lesch-Nyhan syndrome. *Annual Review of Medicine, 24,* 41–60.

MARSHA H. LUPI
*Hunter College, City University
of New York*

GENETIC COUNSELING
HEREDITY

LESIONS

The term lesion refers to "an alteration, structural or functional due to a disease" (*Blakiston's*, 1979). Lesions may be acute, subacute, and chronic; these terms are not disease specific. They relate to no specific disease, syndrome, or illness but are only adjectives that describe time of onset and appearance of symptoms.

Acute lesions have a rapid sudden onset, a short course, and pronounced symptoms. The time of onset can range from minutes to a maximum of 36 to 48 hours. Examples of acute central nervous system (CNS) lesions are stroke, head injury, or seizure. Each one of these CNS disorders typically occur suddenly and have observable behavioral symptoms and signs that indicate the need to seek further medical attention.

Subacute lesions fall between the acute and chronic stages. The signs or symptoms usually develop slowly, progressively, or intermittently and become more severe over the course of the illness. Subacute stages of an illness can range from days to a few weeks. An example of a subacute problem would be the reoccurence of a headache, which may indicate a more severe progressing CNS problem.

Chronic lesions are those disorders that present signs or symptoms of illness or dysfunction over a longer time period than the subacute or acute stages. Chronic onset of lesions can range from a period of weeks to months or even years. In many cases, this term has been used to describe something that is only partially treatable or that responds partially to treatment with residual dysfunction. The term does not denote progressive deterioration in any way. In fact, many children with cerebral palsy, which can be a chronic disability, improve with time because of their ability to compensate for the motor dysfunction. Other examples of chronic CNS disorders are Alzheimer's disease, characterized by progressive dementia and diffuse cerebral atrophy, or the effects of a cerebral vascular accident, e.g., a stroke (Gilroy & Meyer, 1969). Cerebral palsy and polio could also be included under a chronic stage disorder.

The terms acute, subacute, and chronic are not mutually exclusive. Each of the three stages can be observed in an individual at certain phases of an illness. Specifically, these terms refer to the initial onset or cause of a CNS lesion and the duration of the assumed outcome of such an injury.

As the observability of an injury increases, so, too, does the potential for systematic development of educational or rehabilitative efforts. Conversely, with less observability there occurs an increasing reliance on unsubstantiated relationships of brain dysfunction and behavior. Thus, with less observable types of brain damage, the decision regarding intervention strategies has often been difficult.

From an educational perspective, children who have observable brain damage owing to injury or illness pose a real challenge for the educator. National statistics estimate that 18,000 children will sustain some form of serious brain insult each year. Hence educators today are seeing a very different population entering and reentering their classrooms. While the effects of a serious insult on a youngster may be unfamiliar to educators, there are similarities in many learning theories that should be familiar to the teacher. Some of the earlier theoretical work, from a developmental perspective, has been used with observable brain-damaged children.

However, because of the diffuse and somewhat undetermined location and function of the brain damage, a teacher may be faced with a child with multiple cognitive, physical, and emotional or affective disorders. Undoubtedly, some educators will see little difference between a brain-injured child and other special needs children. There are, however, three major distinctions that must be addressed: (1) brain injured children do not typically fit existing educational funding categories or definitions; (2) standardized tests used for placement purposes with other special needs children do not accurately predict the level of functioning for these children; and (3) program development for brain-injured children must take into account other factors such as orientation and past experiences to capitalize on the child's already learned behaviors. While the presence of brain-injured children in classrooms may be novel to educators, this special needs population will undoubtedly continue to be placed back into the mainstream of education as recovery from insult permits.

Although the 1960s saw an increase in intervention strategies that originated from an organic disease model (Frostig & Horne, 1964; Roach & Kephart, 1966), the efficacy of such procedures has often been questioned. Even with the assumed best intent of the individuals who have researched this area, to date, medical-neurological technology has been unable to substantiate consistent relationships between inferred lesions and demonstrated learning difficulties. Thus the development of a consistent educational technology for dealing with milder, inferred types of brain damage has often been less than systematic or effective.

Although recent advances in medical technology have increased our understanding of some of the brain-behavior relationships, continued limitations of such technology suggest that many of the educational interventions that have occurred are still in the early stages of development. Until our understanding of the relationship between specific types of brain injuries expands to the degree that we can make specific statements about learning outcomes, we must rely on the presenting behavior of the learner. Reliance on these behaviors does not exclude consideration of brain function or dysfunction, but instead emphasizes that which teachers may change.

REFERENCES

Blakiston's pocket medical dictionary (4th ed.). (1979). New York: McGraw-Hill.

Frostig, W., & Horne, P. (1964). *The Frostig program for the development of visual perception.* Chicago: Follett.

Gilroy, J., & Meyer, J. S. (1964). *Medical neurology.* Toronto: Macmillan.

Roach, E., & Kephart, W. (1966). *The Purdue perceptional-motor-survey.* Columbus, OH: Merrill.

MICHAEL G. BROWN
*Central Wisconsin Center for
the Developmentally Disabled,
Madison, Wisconsin*

J. TODD STEPHENS
*University of Wisconsin,
Madison*

**BRAIN DAMAGE
BRAIN DISORDERS
CENTRAL NERVOUS SYSTEM
LEARNING DISABILITIES**

LEUKEMIC CHILD

Leukemia is a cancer of the white blood cells. In leukemia, normal blood elements are replaced by undifferentiated, i.e., immature cells. These cells are termed blasts (Pendergrass, Chard, & Hartmann, 1985).

In chronic leukemia, there is a malignant proliferation of differentiated or mature cells. In both acute and chronic leukemia, these abnormal cells increase in number and accumulate in the victim's body. The spread can be very rapid if untreated. It will involve bone marrow, lymph nodes, kidney, liver, spleen, lungs, skin, and gonads.

Acute leukemic conditions predominate in children. Ninety-nine percent of leukemic children suffer from acute conditions, 1% from chronic ones. The most common acute leukemia is acute lymphoblastic leukemia (ALL) (Baehner, 1978), which accounts for almost 80% of all childhood leukemic conditions. Acute leukemias of other types are identifiable as acute nonlymphoblastic leukemias (ANLL; Pendergrass, Chard, & Hartmann, 1985).

The incidence and mortality of childhood leukemia have varied over the years, partly because of different reporting procedures and better reporting of causes of death. Reviewed by sex, 30 to 40% higher rates are reported for males (Cutler, Axtell, & Heise, 1967). Some studies have reported a large peak in mortality rates between the ages of two and three, but this has been found true only for white populations of European extraction (Pendergrass, Chard, & Hartmann, 1985).

The treatment of childhood leukemia traditionally has been one of drug therapy. Prednisone, a steroid, has been found to be the best single drug. It is often used with other drugs to optimize treatment. Sometimes bone marrow transplants also are used; they have been found effective even in late-stage anemia. Hopeful expectations have been expressed regarding the use of bone marrow transplants with less advanced leukemic conditions.

The treatment of leukemic conditions has made major strides in recent years, with much longer survival times for leukemic children being reported (Hanson, McKay, & Miller, 1980). As a consequence, leukemia mortality rates are no longer clearly reflective of incidence and new means for establishing the latter have been developed. Data provided by the Third National Cancer Survey (Young & Miller, 1975) and by the Surveillance, Epidemiology, and End Results (SEER) Program of the National Cancer Institute (Silverberg, 1981) show a rise in the incidence for acute lymphoblastic leukemia beginning at approximately 2 years of age with a peaking during the 3- to 4-year age period. The distribution of acute nonlymphoblastic leukemias is fairly flat.

Hereditary factors have been indicated in leukemia. Three or more members of the same generation have been found to be leukemic in some studies, while in others the condition has been found to appear in some families over four generations. If one member of an identical twin pair manifests the disease, the other has about a 25% chance of developing the disease before the age of 10 (Pendergrass, Chard, & Hartmann, 1985).

A variety of other childhood diseases or handicaps manifest higher rates of leukemia. These include immunodeficiency diseases, Fanconi's anemia, ataxia telangiectasia, and Down's syndrome. This suggests that chromosomal abnormalities are related to leukemia. The role of other etiological factors, e.g., chemical exposure and radiation, are as yet unclear; however, increases in leukemia in Japanese populations exposed to atom bomb attacks made it evident that intense exposure to radiation can significantly increase the probability of eventually developing a leukemic condition.

Various stages of improvement in childhood leukemia have been described (Pendergrass, Chard, & Hartman, 1985). Complete remission is established when bone marrow, blood morphology, and physical examination all are found to be normal. An incomplete remission is one in which there are still increased numbers of blast cells to be found in the child's bone marrow, or in which there is persistent anemia, a decrease in platelet count, or abnormalities in the liver, lymph glands, or spleen. Hematologic remission is when the bone marrow is found to be normal even if leukemia persists in other parts of the body. A relapse is considered to occur when blast cells return after

a complete remission was accomplished, either in the bone marrow, the central nervous system, or the testicles.

Through the use of new and more effective medical regimens, both the survival rates and remission rates of children with childhood leukemia have increased dramatically over recent decades. Remission induction rates went from a zero pretreatment level to 60 to 70% during the middle 1960s. By 1978 these rates had reached 90 to 95% for children receiving proper drug therapies. However, the length of complete remission (remission duration) without the use of therapies has not improved. Maintenance therapies must thus be anticipated even for leukemic children who are in complete remission. With maintenance therapies, significantly lengthened remission rates have been achieved.

Along with awareness of the need to continue therapies during remission has come the appreciation that there must be additional treatment to manage the side effects of continued treatment. Thus antibiotics may be given to control infection, and platelet concentrates may be given to treat overt bleeding.

The long-term prognosis for childhood leukemia is still poor. Few individuals who have childhood leukemia survive into adulthood. There are indications that they have a higher risk of manifesting cancer as adults, though there is no clear evidence to indicate that they are susceptible to other diseases.

Of considerable significance to special educators is the fact that central nervous system leukemia has been found to develop in a large percentage of children who have childhood leukemia, even in those who are in states of complete hematologic remission. Research has indicated that this is partly due to the fact that the brain has a protective mechanism that decreases the amount of drugs allowed into brain tissue. The effects of the medications used to treat childhood leukemia thus may be vitiated in respect to their effect on the central nervous system. In attempts to circumvent this problem, medication may be injected directly into the spinal fluid. This procedure has been found to reduce significantly the incidence of central nervous system leukemia and to sustain significantly longer remissions from the disease (Glidewell & Holland, 1973; Pendergrass, Chard, & Hartmann, 1985).

Current medical challenges to the treatment of childhood leukemia include treating the child who fails to achieve a remission after initial therapy or who suffers relapses despite proper maintenance therapies. There are also questions as to how long to treat a child who remains in complete remission, what constitutes the minimal amount of treatment to achieve effective results, and the long-term effects of the disease and its therapies.

The psychological impact on both the child and the family of those having childhood leukemia is of major proportions. The medical management of the condition is arduous and stressful for child, family, and therapists, and often physically painful for the child. The sequelae of treatment as well as the constant knowledge of the consequences of the diseases—learned early by most children—can be overwhelming. The chronicity of the condition and of its medical management and treatment places great stress on family psyches and finances. The leukemic child's social and academic performances can be expected to suffer. The fact that the child, even when surviving into adulthood, can be expected to have lifelong problems also takes its toll. Fortunately, the great strides forward that have been made in the disease's management encourage a positive outlook.

Children who have leukemia are entitled to special education under the provisions of PL 94-142. They are specifically identified as health impaired and entitled to special education under this law (*Federal Register*, 1977, p. 42478).

REFERENCES

Baehner, R. L. (1978). Hematologic malignancies: Leukemia and lymphoma. In C. H. Smith (Ed.), *Blood diseases of infancy and childhood* (4th ed.). St. Louis: Mosby.

Bigge, J., & Sirvis, B. (1986). Physical and health impairments. In N. G. Haring & L. McCormick (Eds.), *Exceptional children and youth* (4th ed.). Columbus, OH: Merrill.

Cutler, S. J., Axtell, L., & Heise, H. (1967). Ten thousand cases of leukemia: 1940–1962. *Journal of the National Cancer Institute, 39*, 993–1026.

Glidewell, O. J., & Holland, J. G. (1973). Clinical trials of the acute leukemia group B in acute lymphocytic leukemia in childhood. *Bibliotheca Haemetologica, 39*, 1053–1067.

Hanson, M. R., McKay, F. W., & Miller, R. W. (1980). Three-dimensional perspective of United States cancer mortality. *Lancet, 2*, 246–247.

Pendergrass, T. W., Chard, R. L., & Hartmann, J. R. (1985). Leukemia. In N. Hobbs & J. M. Perrin (Eds.), *Issues in the care of children with chronic illness*. San Francisco: Jossey-Bass.

Silverberg, E. (1981). Cancer statistics, 1981. *C.A: A Cancer Journal for Clinicians, 31*, 13–28.

Young, J. L., & Miller, R. W. (1975). Incidence of malignant tumors in United States children. *Journal of Pediatrics, 86*, 254–258.

LESTER MANN
*Hunter College, City University
of New York*

CANCER, CHILDHOOD
HEALTH IMPAIRMENTS

LEWIS, MICHAEL (1937–)

A native of Brooklyn, Michael Lewis received his BA (1958) in sociology and his PhD (1962) in psychology from the University of Pennsylvania. He is currently with the

Michael Lewis

department of pediatrics, Division of Child Development, at the College of Medicine and Dentistry at Rutgers University Medical School.

Lewis is deeply involved in studies of infant development. He has challenged the traditional developmental theories that suggest that improving the environment can maximize a child's development. He has emphasized, rather, the concept of co-occurrences: a child's realization that two events that occur close to each other in time can be associated with each other. Lewis sees the co-occurrences of the mother's responsiveness to the child's actions to be more important to the child's development than maternal stimulation (Lewis & Coates, 1980; Lewis & Goldberg, 1969). He does not find these co-occurrences to be causal, but believes that if the mother ignores the child's attempts at interaction with her, the child will be discouraged from future interactions.

Lewis also questions the idea that mothers of handicapped children do not provide their children with appropriate verbal stimulation, thus precluding the appropriate speech development of the children. Lewis (Leifer & Lewis, 1983) found that, contrary to expectations, mothers of handicapped children vary their speech to match their children's language level, providing a facilitative effect on their children's language development.

REFERENCES

Leifer, J. S., & Lewis, M. (1983). Maternal speech to normal and handicapped children: A book at question asking behavior. *Infant Behavior & Development, 6*(2), 175–187.

Lewis, M., & Coates, D. L. (1980). Mother infant interactions and cognitive development in twelve week old infants. *Infant Behavior & Development, 3*, 95–105.

Lewis, M., & Goldberg, S. (1969). Perceptual-cognitive development in infancy: A generalized expectancy model as a function of the mother-infant interaction. *Merrill-Palmer Quarterly, 15*, 81–100.

E. VALERIE HEWITT
Texas A&M University

LEXINGTON SCHOOL FOR THE DEAF

The Lexington School for the Deaf was established in New York City in 1867 to provide oral education for deaf children. There were already more than a dozen schools for deaf students in the United States at that time but all used some form of sign language. The Lexington School was a pioneer in oral education and has remained a strong proponent of speech, speech reading, and aural rehabilitation.

Lexington is a world-renowned leader in the education of deaf infants, children, and adolescents in all levels of educational programs. It offers special programs for multiply handicapped deaf students, including psychiatric and psychological services. Its staff has included such outstanding educators as Mildren Groht, author of *Natural Language for Deaf Children*, Edith Buell, author of *Outline of Language for Deaf Children*, speech teachers Mary New, Eleanor Vorce, and Janet head, and superintendents Clarence D. O'Connor and Leo Connor.

The Lexington School for the Deaf is now located in Queens, New York. In addition to educational programs, it offers a 24-hour information and referral service that provides general information and advocacy services related to hearing impairment. Auxiliary agencies of the school include the Lexington Hearing and Speech Center, the Lexington Center for Mental Health Services, and the Lexington Training Research and Educational Evaluation Service.

REFERENCES

Moores, D. (1982). *Educating the deaf: Psychology, principles and practices*. Boston: Houghton Mifflin.

O'Connor, C. D. (1967). *Lexington School's first century of oral education of the deaf* (Volta Review Reprint 878). Washington, DC: Alexander Graham Bell Association for the Deaf.

ROSEMARY GAFFNEY
Hunter College, City University of New York

LIABILITIES

See LIABILITY OF TEACHERS IN SPECIAL EDUCATION.

LIABILITY OF TEACHERS IN SPECIAL EDUCATION

The concern for teacher effectiveness has focused considerable attention on what happens in the special education classroom. As such, teacher performance is monitored and teachers are held accountable for their actions in the classroom. A byproduct of this is a growing wave of legal action against teachers involving teacher liability.

Teacher liability is usually defined in court as involving negligence or lack of appropriate services for the exceptional student. The result is often a malpractice suit against the teacher (Brady & Dennis, 1984). Alexander (1980) and Brady and Dennis (1984) note that malpractice liability in education usually involves negligence, intentional interference or harm, or constitutional infringement. However, if a liability suit is brought against a teacher, it will likely focus on negligence.

Teacher negligence is affirmed if the court is shown that a teacher (1) owed a duty of care to the student, (2) did not carry out that duty, and (3) the lack of completion of that duty resulted in injury to the student (Brady & Dennis, 1984). To conduct appropriately their duties, it is commonly felt that teachers must provide proper instruction, supervision, and maintenance of equipment. If the lack of these duties results in substantial injury to a student, the teacher may be found liable (Alexander, 1980; Brady & Dennis, 1984; Connors, 1981).

Lack of proper instruction has been defined in many ways. As it pertains to teacher liability, violation of duty seems to be primarily a result of exposing students to physical risk during an instructional period. For example, student injuries in sports or laboratory settings may result in a liability suit. Thus far, the failure of a student to learn has not resulted in teacher liability (Brady & Dennis, 1984).

Connors (1981) notes that proper supervision is usually defined as general supervision; for example, a teacher is responsible for being present and overseeing the activities that take place. In so doing, a teacher must be aware of the situation and the inherent risks involved and take every possible step to see that the potential risks are eliminated. If teacher presence were enough to avoid injury, lack of teacher presence often would result in a finding of liability due to negligence.

Finally, teachers must ensure that equipment used in daily activities is not defective and is in proper working order. Cases have been tried in which defective playground equipment has been the cause of an accident (*District of Columbia* v. *Washington*, 1975). In one case a defective safety guard on a chain saw caused a student to be injured (*South Ripley* v. *Peters*, 1979).

To avoid liability cases, teachers should engage in sound educational practices, consider each child's individual needs, and document the activities that have been conducted.

REFERENCES

Alexander, K. (1980). *School law*. St. Paul, MN: West.

Brady, M. P., & Dennis, H. F. (1984). Integrating severely handicapped learners: Potential teacher liability in community based programs. *Remedial & Special Education, 5*(5), 29–36.

Connors, E. T. (1981). *Educational tort liability and malpractice.* Bloomington, IN: Phi Delta Kappa.

JOHN R. BEATTIE
University of North Carolina,
Charlotte

DYSPEDAGOGIA

LIBRARIES FOR THE BLIND AND PHYSICALLY HANDICAPPED

The National Library Service for the Blind and Physically Handicapped (of the Library of Congress) publishes books and magazines in Braille and in recorded form on disks and cassettes for readers who cannot hold, handle, or see well enough to read conventional print because of a visual or physical handicap. Persons diagnosed as having a reading disability of sufficient severity to prevent their reading printed matter in a normal manner are also eligible for loan services.

Tapes and records of the over 35,000 titles in the National Library Service's collection of best-sellers, biographies, fiction, and how-to and foreign-language books and magazines can be sent free to anyone legally blind, unable to see or focus long enough to read standard print, reading disabled, or physically unable to handle books. They can also be sent free to teachers and librarians in schools with handicapped pupils.

Through a nationwide network of over 160 cooperating libraries, the routine services of the National Library Service include book circulation, outreach, publicity, tape duplication, equipment assignment, publications distribution, reader's advisory, reference assistance, and production of local-interest material. Subscribers to the service receive free playback equipment and the bimonthly *Talking Book Topics* or *Braille Book Review*, which list the latest books and magazines produced by the National Library Service.

In addition to the productions of the National Library Service, the American Foundation for the Blind, the American Printing House for the Blind, and Recording for the Blind also produce a wide variety of taped and recorded materials for disabled readers. While the National Library Service does not produce or distribute textbooks or curriculum materials, the American Printing House for the Blind and Recording for the Blind do.

The following equipment is loaned free of charge to eligible readers as long as Library of Congress materials are being borrowed: talking book machines (for hard and flexible discs), cassette-book machines, headphones, pillow speakers (for handicapped readers who are bedridden), amplifiers (for readers with a significant hearing disability), tone-arm clips (a device attached to talking-book ma- chines for readers who have difficulty grasping the tone arm), and extension levers (for readers who have difficulty operating controls of the cassette-book machine).

The Library of Congress program that evolved into the National Library Service for the Blind and Physically Handicapped was established under President Herbert Hoover in 1931 as an effort to serve blind adults. In 1933 Congress extended the original program of providing Braille texts to include the provision of recorded materials. Congress again extended the program in 1952 to include services to blind children, in 1962 to provide musical instructional materials and scores, and again in 1966 to include individuals with physical handicaps that prevent them from reading standard print material. With over 800,000 subscribers, the National Library Service for the Blind and Physically Handicapped is an expanding enterprise.

REFERENCES

Library of Congress. (1982). *An introduction to the National Service for the Blind and Physically Handicapped.* Washington, DC: Author.

Library of Congress. (1984). *Library resources for the blind and physically handicapped: A directory with FY 1983 statistics on readership, circulation, budget, staff, and collections.* Washington, DC: Author.

Library of Congress. (1984). *Volunteers who produce books.* Washington, DC: Author.

National Library Service for the Blind and Physically Handicapped. *Music services for blind and physically handicapped individuals.* Washington, DC: Author.

National Library Service for the Blind and Physically Handicapped. *Reading is for everyone.* Washington, DC: Author.

Wexler, Henrietta (1981, Jan./Feb.) Books that talk. *American Education, 1*(1), 15–17.

CATHERINE HALL RIKHYE
Hunter College, City University
of New York

LIBRARY SERVICE FOR THE HANDICAPPED

LIBRARY SERVICES FOR THE HANDICAPPED

A free national library program of Braille and recorded materials for blind and physically handicapped persons is administered by the National Library Service for the Blind and Physically Handicapped (NSL), Library of Congress. Established by an act of Congress in 1931 to serve blind adults, the program was expanded in 1952 to include children, in 1962 to provide music materials, and in 1966 to include individuals with other physical impairments that prevent the reading of standard print. The NLS program is funded annually by Congress. The 1985 fiscal appropriation was $36,592,000. Regional and subregional libraries in each state receive funds from local, state, and federal sources, to total an annual expenditure of approximately $60 million.

With the cooperation of authors and publishers who grant permission to use copyrighted materials, NLS selects and produces full-length books and magazines in Braille and on recorded disks and cassettes. Reading materials are distributed to a cooperating network of 56 regional and more than 100 subregional libraries where they are circulated to eligible borrowers. Reading materials and playback machines are sent to borrowers and returned to libraries by postage-free mail.

Books are selected on the basis of their appeal to a wide range of interests. The national book collection currently contains more than 41,000 titles and approximately 10,000,000 copies of Braille and recorded books. Each year, approximately 2000 press-Braille, disk, and cassette titles are mass produced for distribution through network libraries, and an additional 300 Braille titles are produced by volunteers. A limited number of titles are produced in Spanish and other languages. Registered borrowers learn of new books added to the collection through two bimonthly publications.

Seventy magazines on disk and Braille are offered through the program. Current issues are mailed free to readers at approximately the same time the print issues appear. Persons interested in music materials may receive them directly from a collection of over 30,000 items, consisting of scores in Braille and large type; textbooks and books about music in Braille, large type, and recorded forms; and elementary instruction in voice, organ, guitar, recorder, accordian, banjo, and harmonica in recorded form.

Playback equipment is also loaned at no charge for as long as recorded materials provided by NLS and its cooperating libraries are being borrowed. Talking-book machines designed to play disk recorded books and magazines, as well as cassette machines, are available, with such accessories as headphones and pillow phones. Readers with limited mobility may request a remote-control unit, while hearing-impaired readers may be eligible for an auxiliary amplifier for use with headphones.

Free correspondence courses leading to certification in Braille transcribing and proofreading are offered. Voice auditions and informal training are given to volunteer tape narrators affiliated with local recording groups. Thousands of volunteers throughout the United States produce books for libraries and individual readers, and more than 3000 senior or retired telephone industry workers contribute their time and skills in the maintenance and repair of playback equipment.

The NLS also operates a research program directed toward improving the quality of reading materials and equipment, reducing costs, and speeding delivery of services to readers. A consumer relations staff maintains regular contact with consumer groups and individual users of the program to identify service programs and assure that users' needs are being met. Further information may be obtained from local librarians or from the National Library Service for the Blind and Physically Handicapped, Library of Congress, Washington, DC 20542.

JUDY SMITH-DAVIS
*Counterpoint Communications
Company, Reno, Nevada*

BRAILLE
LARGE PRINT BOOKS
**LIBRARY FOR THE BLIND AND PHYSICALLY
  HANDICAPPED**

LIBRIUM

Librium is the tradename for the generic minor tranquilizer chlordiazepoxide. It was the first benzodiazepine to be synthesized; it was marketed in 1960 (Bassuk & Schoonover, 1977). Librium is a less potent muscle relaxant than Valium, but it shares similar antianxiety properties with other benzodiazepines. Librium is recommended for short-term use to deal with psychic discomfort that accompanies unusual situational stress or crisis (Bassuk & Schoonover, 1977). As is the case with all psychotropic medications, such treatment is symptomatic and does not affect the cause of the discomfort. Additional interventions are necessary to assist the individual in crisis to reestablish equilibrium. There is no evidence to support the development of addiction to Librium; however, as with all tranquilizers, psychological dependence can develop (Blum, 1984).

As with all benzodiazepines, sensitivity or overdosage is characterized by drowsiness, fatigue, confusion, and dizziness. Geriatric patients and children are most likely to experience these adverse effects (McEvoy, 1984). A reversible dementia also has been reported among elderly patients after extended administration.

REFERENCES

Bassuk, E. L., & Schoonover, S. C. (1977). *The practitioner's guide to psychoactive drugs.* New York: Plenum Medical.

Blum, K. (1984). *Handbook of abusable drugs.* New York: Gardner.

McEvoy, G. K. (1984). *American hospital formulary service: Drug information 84.* Bethesda, MD: American Society of Hospital Pharmacists.

ROBERT F. SAWICKI
*Lake Erie Institute of
  Rehabilitation, Lake Erie,
  Pennsylvania*

TRANQUILIZERS

LICENSING AND CERTIFICATION OF SCHOOLS, CENTERS, AND FACILITIES

The licensing or certification of schools is under the purview of state governments. The federal government maintains jurisdictition only over the disbursement of federal funds and over the separation of church and state. Many of these functions have been clarified through litigation. The Supreme Court in 1971 ruled that the relationship between the public schools and private parochial schools must not entangle the state in religious affairs. To determine whether a school is religious or sectarian, the court specified a threefold test: whether the school has a secular purpose; whether the school advances or inhibits religion; and whether the school fosters excessive government entanglement with religion (*Lemon* v. *Kurtman*). The Supreme Court has also ruled that it is clearly within the rights of the states to regulate private schools. In *Purce* v. *Society of Sisters* (1925), the court ruled that

> No question is raised concerning the power of the state reasonably to regulate all schools, to inspect, to supervise, and examine them, their teachers, and their pupils, to require that all children of proper age attend some school, that teachers shall be of good moral character and patriotic disposition, that certain studies plainly essential to good citizenship be taught, and that nothing inimical to the public welfare be manifestly taught.

In *State* v. *Williams* (1960), the court ruled that the "exercise of such power must not be arbitrary and must be limited to the preservation of public safety, public health, and morals."

As a result, each state has established rules, regulations, and supervisory procedures for private and parochial schools. These are established through statutes and state education directives and through the regulation of private nonprofit and for-profit business. Each state has its own rules for the physical facilities, health, and welfare of students, the curriculum, and instructional staff of nonpublic schools.

Public Law 94-142 mandates that a free appropriate public education must be made available to each handicapped child by public agencies of the state. Subject to the requirements of the least restrictive environment, this could include placement in or referral to a private school or facility. Subpart D of PL 94-142 deals with handicapped children in private schools. In 121a.401, the state education agency is charged with the responsibility to ensure that a handicapped child placed in a private school or facility by a public agency:

(a) Is provided special education and related services:
  (1) In conformance with an individualized education program which meets the requirements under 121a.340–121a.349 of Subpart C;
  (2) At no cost to parents; and

(3) At a school or facility which meets the standards that apply to State and local educational agencies (including the requirements in this part); and
(b) Has all of the rights of a handicapped child who is served by a public agency.

In a recent court ruling (*Wiley* v. *Scanlon*, 1983) in Pennsylvania, the commissioner of education was found to have acted properly in denying a license to Wiley House for the education of socially maladjusted and emotionally disturbed students. The court ruled that the commissioner had not denied Wiley House due process and that the private school clearly did not meet state standards. In another case (*Language Development Program of W. N. Y., Inc.* v. *Amback*, 1983) a court in New York ruled that a private school can be denied a license without violating the property rights of the owners.

DANIEL R. PAULSON
University of Wisconsin, Stout

CERTIFICATION/LICENSURE ISSUES
PRIVATE SCHOOLS AND SPECIAL EDUCATION

LIFE EXPECTANCY AND THE HANDICAPPED

Researchers indicate that life expectancy of handicapped individuals is increasing (Cunningham, 1985; Dunn, 1973; Hobbs, 1983; Wilson, 1973; Zill, 1985). Factors such as a recent increase in total population; continued research on treatment and etiology of infant disease; better nutrition; improved housing; advanced medical and surgical knowledge; and improved prenatal and neonatal child care practices have contributed to better prognoses for premature infants and to a decrease in the number of infant deaths.

The figures found in the professional literature are frequently based on noneducational frames of reference. An individual may indeed require social or medical services and still be able to function adequately in a school setting. Children with chronic health problems that may affect vision, hearing, or speech nevertheless may function without special education services. In an address to school nurses and school personnel, Cunningham (1985) stated that many diseases that used to be lethal such as renal failure, diabetes, and inflammatory bowel disease now have a 70 to 80% long-term survival. He and others (Pumariegga, 1982) suggest that the goal of the physician and the educator must shift from survival to improving conditions of chronically ill children so that they may grow and develop in a normal fashion. In the past, such children were not expected to survive, much less attend school and engage in extracurricular and athletic activities. A range of appropriate services from hospital settings to general education classrooms must be made available.

Despite these medical advances, children with severe handicapping conditions continue to be born (Batshaw & Perret, 1981; Wolf & Anderson, 1969). The number of children receiving special education services has increased dramatically in the past 10 years. Data from the office of Special Education and Rehabilitation Services indicate the total number of children served under the Education For All Handicapped Children Act (PL 94-142) and Aid to the States for Handicapped Children is well over 4 million (Czajka, 1984). The figures represent 9.2% of the total school-age population (ages 5 to 17). Zill (1985) predicts that by 1995 there could be nearly 6 million special students in public schools.

Friedman and MacQueen (1971) observed that the number of children born with multiple handicapping conditions appears to be increasing. They noted that 25% of all handicapped children have more than one handicapping condition and that another 25% have three or more. The most frequent multiple disabilities reported were mental retardation, behavior disorders, and speech handicaps. Such incidence figures confound statistical information in that some exceptionalities are counted more than once. In other situations they are not reported at all to school officials. Neither physicians nor parents automatically view the school as a resource for the very young severely handicapped child, even though PL 94-142 mandates that schools provide for the identification of all handicapped children from birth through the age of 21.

Health service agencies reported an increase in the number of children with physical impairments. Wilson (1973) suggests the increase reflects the mandate to serve and improve identification procedures. Dunn (1973) found that educators experience great difficulty in determining exact prevalence figures. The number of medically, socially, and legally handicapped individuals exceeds the number within each group that may require special education. Czajka (1984) found similar difficulties. Gaps in the available statistical information regarding the disabled population result from lack of consistent definitions, imprecise survey instruments or reporting methods, and a large variety of groups seeking data, all of which is further complicated by multiple handicapping conditions, combinations of conditions within the same broad condition group, time of onset, and duration of the disability.

In its tenth annual report to Congress, the Department of Health and Human Services Head Start Bureau (1984) reported on the requirement to make available at least 10% of its enrollment opportunities to handicapped children. It noted dramatic growth in numbers in the 10-year period. Until the early 1970s such services to children between ages 3 to 5 were virtually nonexistent. Massive institutionalization was the trend prior to PL 94-142. The report noted the increased need for staff, facilities, coordination with other agencies, services to parents, development of curricular materials, and written agreements.

The implications for parents, physicians, and educators are as dramatic and often as perplexing as the increase in numbers. The implications for services are varied and complex. Before specific questions regarding educational issues can be addressed, there are a variety of fundamental, moral, ethical, and practical questions to be considered. Fuchs (1974) speaks to issues of euthanasia; prenatal diagnoses of disabling diseases; and withholding medical care from seriously impaired newborn infants or seriously impaired young adults. Other questions may deal with where handicapped individuals should live: at home with parents, in group homes in the community, or in institutional settings. Financial questions regarding funding structures, cost-efficient methods of providing adequate services, and agencies payments for services must be sorted out. Hobbs (1983) estimated that the mean cost of care for the first three weeks of life of an infant with spina bifida is $6500, and that the average total cost of care from birth to 2 years was $70,000 (in 1980).

Zill (1985) suggests that it is critical to seek new and better ways to enable handicapped individuals to become economically productive. He indicates it could cost up to $31,000 per year to maintain a handicapped individual in a state-run institution. Opinions regarding institutionalization have changed in recent years. Wolfensberger (1967) found that physicians influenced the choices parents made regarding institutionalization. In a study done in the 1960s, he noted that 40% of general practitioners, 17% of pediatricians, and 11% of obstetricians recommended immediate institutionalization for retarded children. That trend is nearly reversed today. Needed today is a range of services from hospital setting to full-time public school regular education classroom. Such services require a multidisciplinary team approach, including parents as well as medical, agency, and school personnel. A greater number of all types of trained personnel will be called for. Along with more special education teachers, a full range of ancillary personnel such as psychologists, physical, occupational, and speech therapists and a host of other medical and educational specialists, will be needed.

Children who were regularly excluded from public education present problems that may require more and varied related services: assessment; transportation; appropriate technological and educational equipment; media and materials; special classroom aids such as adaptive equipment, communication and feeding devices, and wheelchairs. Vocational education for handicapped individuals must shift from traditional career training to a more intensive, creative K-12 approach to preparing for and matching manpower needs to individual abilities. There is also an increased demand for postsecondary school adjustment and greater assistance with the transition from school to work. There is a healthy new demand to attend to quality-of-life issues that will require that attention be given to quality programming and such things as leisure skill development.

REFERENCES

Batshaw, M. L., & Perret, Y. M. (1981). *Children with handicaps: A medical primer.* Baltimore, MD: Brooks.

Cunningham, R. (1985, Oct.). *The child with chronic disease.* Paper presented at meeting of Health and Disease in the School Foundation, Cleveland, Ohio.

Czajka, J. L. (1984, June). *Digest of data on persons with disabilities.* Prepared under contract to the Congressional Research Service Library of Congress. Washington, DC: Mathematica Policy Research.

Dunn, L. M. (1973). An overview. In L. M. Dunn (Ed.), *Exceptional children in the schools: Special education transition* (pp. 3–62). New York: Holt, Rinehart, & Winston.

Friedman, R. J., & MacQueen, J. C. (1971). Psychoeducational considerations of physically handicapped conditions in children. *Exceptional Children, 37,* 538–539.

Fuchs, V. R. (1974). *Who shall live? Health, economics and social choice.* New York: Basic Books.

Hobbs, N. (1983). *Chronically ill children in America: Background and recommendations.* San Francisco: Jossey-Bass.

Pumariegga, A., (1982). The adolescent with cystic fibrosis: Developmental issues. *Children's Health Care, 2,* 71–81.

U.S. Department of Health and Human Services (1984). The status of handicapped children in Head Start programs. *Tenth annual report of the U.S. Department of Health and Human Services to the Congress of the United States on services provided to handicapped children in project Head Start.* Washington, DC: Author.

Wilson, M. (1973). Children with crippling and health disabilities. In L. M. Dunn (Ed.), *Exceptional children in schools: Special education in transition* (pp. 467–526). New York: Holt, Rinehart, & Winston.

Wolf, J. M., & Anderson, R. M. (1969). *The multiply handicapped child.* Springfield, IL: Thomas.

Wolfensberger, W. (1967). Counseling for the parents of the retarded. In A. A. Baumeister (Ed.), *Mental retardation: Appraisal, education and retardation* (pp. 329–400). Chicago: Aldine.

Zill, N. (1985, June). *How is the number of children with severe handicaps likely to change over time?* Testimony presented for the Subcommittee on Select Education of the Committee on Education and Labor, U.S. House of Representatives.

SALLY E. PISARCHICK
*Cuyahoga Special Education
Service Center, Maple
Heights, Ohio*

ADULT HANDICAPPED
CHRONIC ILLNESS IN CHILDREN
COMMUNITY PLACEMENT
DEINSTITUTIONALIZATION
HANDICAPPING CONDITIONS

LIFE SPACE INTERVIEWING

The life space interview, a form of crisis intervention for emotionally disturbed youngsters, was formulated during the 1950s by Fritz Redl. The term life space refers to events occurring within the child's immediate environment at a specific point in time. Developed in a residential milieu, it is a technique intended for use by classroom teachers and support staff for addressing children's aggressive behavior.

Redl (1966) described the life space interview as a means by which an adult helps a child to mediate an emotionally charged experience. Following a behavioral crisis, the adult and the student engage in an in-depth discussion that focuses on the student's role in the event. The life space interview is viewed as strategically important to the child's therapeutic goals, and themes discussed during the interview may resurface in formal therapy sessions. As behaviorally oriented interventions have gained popularity in schools over the past decade, the life space interview, based in psychoanalytic theory, has gone into decline.

The interviewer, assessing the characteristics of the incident and student, selects one of two goals in conducting the life space interview. Redl (1966) termed the first major goal "the clinical exploitation of the life event." Here the child's awareness of personal responsibility in a given altercation is heightened. The interviewer relates the event to established and recurring behavior problems so that the groundwork for insight is developed. The second general goal is "the administration of an emotional Band-Aid," where an angry and undercontrolled child is helped to disentangle undifferentiated emotions and return to the task at hand. Once the goal is established, several techniques are available.

Redl (1966) discusses five techniques that address the clinical exploitation goal. First is the reality rub-in, where the child is helped to reconcile egocentric perceptions with objective reality. For children who possess adequate defenses but who fail to incorporate critical information into the decision-making process, the interviewer attempts to define and analyze the facts. The child is then helped to recombine factual content in a way that leads to more adaptive behavior. For more disturbed children who actively distort reality, the interviewer may provide the structure necessary for regaining contact with the real world.

The second technique is symptom estrangement. Here the child is helped to disengage from the association that equates the self with the maladaptive behavior. As part of the process, the child learns that secondary gains won through the behavior are not worth the total cost. Massaging numb value areas is the third technique discussed. Here the child is asked to relate the present behavior to long-range survival goals. For example, the juvenile may be prompted to act on a code of fairness or mutual protection. The fourth technique is new tool salesmanship. Here the goal is to teach a response that is more effective than the present maladaptive one. For example, the child might be instructed to seek counseling rather than to fight the next time angry feelings arise. The last technique involves building up resistance. Here the child is helped to break typical behavior patterns by examining the relationship between situations and behaviors. Attention is focused on how the child can exert better behavioral controls and avoid potentially troublesome settings in the future.

Five techniques are listed under the Band-Aid goal. First is draining off frustration acidity, where sympathetic communication about anger or disgust is offered. Second comes support for the management of panic, fury, and guilt. Here the child, recognized as vulnerable and egocentric, is protected from destructive negative feelings. The immediate objective is to help put the event into perspective. The third technique is communication maintenance. Here efforts are made to prevent the deterioration of the therapeutic relationship. Fourth is the regulation of behavior and social traffic technique, which casts the interviewer in the role of a kind police officer reminding the child of rules and consequences without provoking escalation of the maladaptive behavior. Last, Redl (1966) describes umpire services, where the interviewer attempts to maintain vision and balance in a potentially loaded situation. In summary, four factors determine the choice of a technique: the goal of the intervention, the setting in which the event occurred, the individual personality of the child, and the phase of therapeutic treatment within which the child is currently engaged.

Addressing its infrequent use, Heuchert (1983) has recently written that the life space interview is a technique worth reviving. While acknowledging its psychodynamic heritage, Heuchert views the interview as a simple behavioral intervention that can be implemented in the classroom. The teacher knows the child, has observed the behavior, and is in a temporally close position to the event. As such, the teacher can isolate the child and prompt a retelling of the incident. The goal is to improve the child's understanding of the behavior and to develop a workable solution that will reduce future maladaptive behavior.

REFERENCES

Heuchert, C. M. (1983). Can teachers change behavior? Try interviews. *Academic Therapy, 18*(3), 321–328.

Redl, F. (1966). *When we deal with children.* New York: Free Press.

GARY BERKOWITZ
Temple University

PSYCHOANALYSIS
REDL, FRITZ

LIGHTNER WITMER AWARD

Division 16 (School Psychology) of the American Psychological Association presents an annual award in recognition of the production of significant scholarly works within the broad professional domain of school psychology. The award is named for the late Dr. Lightner Witmer, whose early work with school children is considered by many to have originated the field of school psychology. The award is given to young professional and academic school psychologists who have demonstrated scholarship that merits special recognition. Continuing scholarship, rather than completion of a dissertation alone, is the primary consideration in making the award. However, an individual does not need a doctoral degree to be eligible for the award. Nominees must be no older than 35 as of September 1 in the year in which the award is given. The Division of School Psychology gave the first award in 1973.

THOMAS R. KRATOCHWILL
*University of Wisconsin,
Madison*

LINCOLN OSERTESKY TEST

See BRUININKS—OSERTESKY TEST OF MOTOR PROFICIENCY.

LINDSLEY OGDEN R. (1922–   )

Ogden R. Lindsley was born in Providence, Rhode Island, on August 11, 1922. He received his BA and ScM degrees from Brown University in 1948 and 1950. In 1957 he was awarded his Ph.D. in psychology from Harvard University. Lindsley held positions as an assistant psychologist at Brown University from 1948 to 1950 and as an electrophysiologist at Harvard in 1950. He was a fellow during 1951–1952; the assistant principal investigator in psychology for the Atomic Energy Commission Project from 1952 to 1953; the director of the Behavioral Research Laboratory from 1953 to 1965; a research associate from 1956 to 1961; and an associate professor of psychology from 1961 to 1965. In 1965 Lindsley accepted a position as a professor of educational research at the University of Kansas Medical Center. Presently, he is a professor of administration in the Department of Educational Policy and Administration at the University of Kansas in Lawrence.

One of Lindsley's major contributions to the field of special education was his development of a series of standardized procedures for the recording and management of the behavior of children identified as retarded (Lindsley, 1964). The procedures, now commonly known as precision teaching, are based on an application of the principles of operant conditioning and include (1) accurate and precise behavioral definitions, (2) clear delineation of the various stimulus, response, and consequence contingencies, and (3) close study of the behavioral processes. Lindsley (1964) felt that properly designed special education programs should be totally individualized, with all plans subject to constant scrutiny and change if necessary. His premise that "retardation is not the property of a child but of an inadequate child-environment relationship" (Lindsley, 1964, p. 79), and his subsequent work in managing environments, contributed significantly to the development of the technology of special education.

REFERENCE

Lindsley, O. R. (1964). Direct measurement and prosthesis of retarded behavior. *Journal of Education, 147,* 62–81.

ANDREW R. BRULLE
Eastern Illinois University

PRECISION TEACHING

LING METHOD

The Ling method is a systematic procedure for developing and remediating the speech of hearing-impaired children. The first book describing what has become known as the Ling method was written by Daniel Ling (1976). The method relies heavily, but not exclusively, on the optimal use of the hearing-impaired child's residual hearing. Teachers versed in the Ling method emphasize the sequential acquisition of speech skills, the use of acoustic cues, and the automatic coarticulation of sounds in syllables. The model consists of seven developmental stages on both the phonetic and phonologic levels of speech. The phonetic level is the child's capacity to produce the required sound patterns, while the phonologic level is the systematic and meaningful use of those sound patterns.

The initial steps of the Ling method are concerned with the prosodic elements of speech, which are often neglected (Cole & Paterson, 1984). Neglect of these elements results in monotonic, unnatural sounding speech. Prosodic elements in the Ling method include duration, intensity, and pitch.

Abraham and Stokes (1984) found that consistent and systematic practice with meaningful words, as advocated by the Ling method, can improve phoneme production by deaf students, and that speech drill at the syllable level, also advocated by Ling, appears to be a better way to achieve adequate levels of intelligibility for deaf pupils at the phonologic level of speech development. The Ling method is designed to be taught in several brief periods throughout the day rather than in one extended formal speech period.

REFERENCES

Abraham, S., & Stokes, R. (1984). An evaluation of methods used to teach speech to the hearing impaired using a simulation technique. *Volta Review, 86,* 325–335.

Abraham, S., & Weiner, F. (1985). Efficacy of word training vs. syllable training on articulatory generalization by severely hearing impaired children. *Volta Review, 87,* 95–105.

Cole, E., & Paterson, M. (1984). Assessment and treatment of phonologic disorders in the hearing impaired. In J. M. Costello (Ed.), *Speech disorders in children: Recent advances.* San Diego, CA: College Hill.

Ling, D. (1976). *Speech and the hearing-impaired child: Theory and practice.* Washington, DC: Alexander Graham Bell Association for the Deaf.

MARY GRACE FEELY
School for the Deaf,
New York, New York

DEAF
DEAF EDUCATION
SPEECH-LANGUAGE SERVICES

LINGUISTIC-DEFICIT: A CRITIQUE

During the past 50 years, researchers and practitioners have debated whether there is such a thing as a distinct language disorder independent of psychological, neurological, or other considerations. The precursor to the argument for a specific language disability may be found in investigations of adult aphasia during the latter half of the twentieth century. Prior to the 1950s, a few eminent physicians had acknowledged the potential usefulness of linguistics in research on aphasia (Luria in 1947, Goldstein in 1948, and Ombredane in 1951). One major study of phonetic disintegration had been conducted by two physicians collaborating with a linguist (Aljouanine, Ombredane, & Durand, 1939, cited in Lesser, 1978). However, the beginning of the current era of interest in aphasia as a linguistic phenomenon can most likely be dated from the formal proposal of the linguist Jakobson (1955). He argued that aphasia is first and foremost a disintegration of language.

A major contribution from the application of linguistics to aphasiology was the concept that language and linguistic deficits can best be described in terms of different levels of organization. The number of linguistic levels targeted varies according to the theory; but it is common practice to make a working distinction of three main levels: the system of the sounds of speech (phonology), the structural arrangement of sentences (syntax), and the system of meaning (semantics). These linguistic levels are not mutually exclusive. Blumstein (1982) stated:

> Although one can find a fairly selective deficit in components of the grammar, evidence from aphasia does not support the view that the linguistic levels are completely autonomous, nor that deficits occur in only one component of the grammar, while the remainder of the linguistic system remains intact. (p. 207)

With the emergence of the theory of transformational grammar in the early 1960s, linguists speculated that the ability to perceive and acquire certain linguistic relations is innate in the child (Chomsky, 1965). It was argued that the child possesses certain linguistic structures to which he or she attempts to match linguistic input. The brain, in other words, was thought to be "pre-wired" to handle certain types of specifically linguistic input. A further claim was that the study of the linguistic structures of individuals exhibiting damage to the language areas of the brain might provide clues to the nature of the intact "language acquisition device." Some researchers began to examine the language of adult aphasic patients in terms of contemporary linguistic theory, some with the intention of studying the way grammar is actually represented in a speaker's brain. Myerson and Goodglass (1972), for example, attempted to describe the language output of three patients with Broca's (expressive) aphasia by the methods of transformational grammar. The three patients were differentially impaired. The researchers found an inverse correlation between the severity of the aphasia and the number of specific types of distinctions that could be made in the base component, as well as in the number and types of transformational rules used to generate surface structures. They argued that in some cases the limitations seemed to parallel the order of acquisition by the child. However, in reviewing results of research conducted over the past 25 years, one must conclude that language acquisition in children and the dissolution of language in adults do not represent the same process simply reversed (Gleason, 1978).

During the 1960s and 1970s researchers concerned with childhood aphasia began to use the term specific linguistic impairment. They argued that the so-called aphasic child exhibits some type of basic linguistic impairment. "According to this hypothesis, the child is unable to process those basic grammatical relations similar to the type suggested to exist as part of some kind of 'language acquisition device'" (Cromer, 1978, p. 108). However, there has never been a consensus among researchers and practitioners regarding the existence of a distinct language disorder. The views of Piaget have been particularly influential in that language development is seen as dependent on the prior development of cognitive operations (Piaget, 1970). This seems to suggest a causal relationship between a language deficit and some underlying cognitive disturbance.

There is some evidence to indicate that linguistic symptoms may be the result of a generalized deficit in representational behavior (Morehead, 1972). Nevertheless, as Menyuk (1978) has aptly pointed out, "while the notion of a specific language disorder was accepted by some workers, other findings suggested that these children had difficulty in processing incoming information which was not confined to the linguistic sphere" (p. 135)—e.g., nonlinguistic auditory processing and visual-motor memory. Research during the past decade has begun to focus on both the child's linguistic and nonlinguistic deficits in order to find appropriate treatments.

REFERENCES

Blumstein, S. E. (1982). Language dissolution in aphasia: Evidence for linguistic theory. In L. K. Obler & L. Menn (Eds.), *Exceptional language and linguistics*. New York: Academic.

Chomsky, N. (1965). *Aspects of the theory of syntax*. Cambridge, MA: MIT Press.

Cromer, R. F. (1978). The basis of childhood dysphasia: A linguistic approach. In M. A. Wyke (Ed.), *Developmental dysphasia*. New York: Academic.

Gleason, J. B. (1978). The acquisition and dissolution of the English inflectional system. In A. Caramazza & E. Zurif (Eds.), *Language acquisition and language breakdown*. Baltimore, MD: Johns Hopkins University Press.

Jakobson, R. (1955). *Aphasia as a linguistic topic*. Worcester, MA: Clarke University Monographs on Psychology and Related Disciplines.

Lesser, R. (1978). *Linguistic investigations of aphasia*. New York: Elsevier.

Menyuk, P. (1978). Linguistic problems in children with developmental dysphasia. In M. A. Wyke (Ed.), *Developmental dysphasia*. New York: Academic.

Morehead, D. M. (1972). Early grammatical and semantic relations: Some implications for a general representational deficit in linguistically deviant children. *Papers & Reports on Child Language Development, 4*, 1–12.

Myerson, R., & Goodglass, H. (1972). Transformational grammars of aphasic patients. *Language & Speech, 15*, 40–50.

Piaget, J. (1970). Piaget's theory. In P. H. Mussen (Ed.), *Carmichael's manual of child psychology*. New York: Wiley.

PHILIP M. PRINZ
Pennsylvania State University

COMMUNICATION DISORDERS
LINGUISTIC DEVIANCE
LINGUISTIC READERS

LINGUISTIC DEVIANCE

The term linguistic deviance has acquired various meanings in the literature on communicative disorders. The most salient definitions include (1) a general sense in which deviance subsumes all types of linguistic disability (including delay); (2) a more restricted usage where the range of linguistic structures used is comparable to an earlier stage of normal language development, but the frequency of use of specific grammatical forms exceeds normal expectations; and (3) a significantly reduced sense, in which only specific types of structural abnormality are labeled deviant. The last definition of deviance is closest to the general sense of the term in linguistics and in the literature on communicative disorders. Deviance then would include only those utterances that would be both structurally inadmissible in the adult grammar and outside of the expected language development of normal children (Crystal, 1981). For example, if an adult monolingual speaker of English uttered "chicken a," it would be considered deviant on the basis that an adult grammar would reject this construction and that this construction is not a regular feature of normal language development in children.

It should be noted that the term linguistic deviance applies to all components of the psycholinguistic model including phonology, syntax and morphology, semantics, and pragmatics. It has been most widely used in the literature on syntactic language disabilities. Some developmental psycholinguists concerned primarily with syntactic and semantic abnormalities have emphasized the importance of various frequencies of use as a criterion for distinguishing between deviance versus delay (Leonard, 1972; Menyuk, 1964). Most definitions of language delay contain a number of criteria, including slower development of the use of certain structures as well as a reduction in terms of the overall frequency of use of structures. Consonant with the definition of deviance, most definitions of delay contain a number of criteria. Therefore, Ingram (1972) and Morehead and Ingram (1973) conclude that disorder is a function of delayed appearance of a structure, its less frequent and less creative use, and its slower acquisition time.

REFERENCES

Crystal, D. (1981). *Clinical linguistics*. Vienna: Springer-Verlag.

Ingram, D. (1972). The acquisition of the English verbal auxiliary and copula in normal and linguistically deviant children. *Papers & Reports on Child Language Development, 4*, 79–91.

Leonard, L. B. (1972). What is deviant language? *Journal of Speech & Hearing Disorders, 37*, 427–446.

Menyuk, P. (1964). Comparison of grammar with functionally deviant and normal speech. *Journal of Speech & Hearing Research, 7*, 109–121.

Morehead, D. M., & Ingram, D. (1973). The development of base syntax in normal and linguistically deviant children. *Journal of Speech & Hearing Research, 16*, 330–352.

PHILIP M. PRINZ
Pennsylvania State University

COMMUNICATION DISORDERS
LINGUISTIC-DEFICIT, CRITIQUE OF

LINGUISTIC READERS

Linguistic readers, based on the philosophy that the goal of beginning reading instruction should be the automatic recognition of major spelling patterns of the English language, are intended to be used for beginning reading instruction. They have also been used with disadvantaged children who speak nonstandard English (Center for Field Research and School Services, 1970), bilingual children (Digneo & Shaya, 1968), and children with learning disabilities (Myers & Hammill, 1976).

Following the publication of *Why Johnny Can't Read* (Flesch, 1955), in which the linguistic approach to reading was offered as a solution to the national reading problem, Bloomfield and Barnhart (1961) and Fries (1963) developed the first linguistic readers. In these readers several means were used to achieve the goals set forth for linguistic reading programs. First, the vocabulary in beginning material is controlled through phonetic regularity, i.e., only one phonetic value is associated with each letter. For example, beginning materials containing words with *c*, as in *cot*, *cat*, and *cut*, would not contain words in which *c* has a different phonetic value, e.g., *cent*. Likewise, material containing words with *i*, as in *kit*, *zip*, and *dig*, would not include a word like *ride*.

Second, the introduction of spelling patterns is carefully sequenced. For example, in *Let's Read* by Bloomfield and Barnhart (1961), the first 36 lessons concentrate on spelling patterns containing a consonant letter plus a vowel letter plus a consonant letter. Patterns using the vowel *a* as in *cat*, *fat*, *hat*, and *cap*, *lap*, *map* are presented first. Next, patterns using the vowel *i* as in *bit*, *hit*, *sit*, and *fib*, *rib*, *bib* are introduced. These are folllowed by patterns for *u*, *e*, and *o*.

Third, spelling patterns are introduced within the context of whole words, e.g., the words *can*, *fan*, *man*, and *tan* exemplify a particular pattern. Students are guided by the teacher through a process that helps them to discover the pattern. Accompanying reading materials provide practice in applying the knowledge of spelling patterns to the pronunciation of new words and in reading words within the context of phrases and short sentences. Unlike phonics approaches, students are never directed to sound out words or to blend the sounds of individual letters into words.

Fourth, the material is designed to make minimal demands on the child in terms of reading comprehension. The vocabulary is simple. Students are not expected to learn new word meanings. Complex phrases and sentences are avoided. Fifth, oral reading is emphasized as a means of enabling the child to recognize spelling patterns. Finally, the use of pictures and context clues as aids to word recognition are discouraged.

Subsequent authors or linguistic readers modified the approach used by Bloomfield and Barnhart and Fries. Modifications have included the addition of pictures to readers, the introduction of high-frequency, irregularly spelled words such as *the*, the use of color cues, the use of controlled sentence patterns as well as word patterns, and programs that call for sounding and blending vocabularly words controlled for spelling patterns (Chall, 1967).

Chall (1967), in a review of research, concluded that the linguistic approach to teaching reading as defined by linguistic readers is more effective than the sight word approach but less effective than systematic phonics programs. The linguistic readers of the 1960s represented the first attempt to apply linguistics to the field of reading instruction, an effort that has been characterized as superficial and misguided because it was limited to a single aspect of linguistics, for example, phonology (Shuy, 1977).

REFERENCES

Bloomfield, L., & Barnhart, C. L. (1961). *Let's read: A linguistic approach.* Detroit: Wayne State University Press.

Center for Field Research and School Services. (1970). *An evaluation of improving the teaching of English as a second language in poverty area schools.* New York: School of Education, New York University. (ERIC Document Reproduction Service No. ED 058 363).

Chall, J. (1967). *Learning to read: The great debate.* New York: McGraw-Hill.

Digneo, E. H., & Shaya, T. (Eds.). (1968). *The Miami Linguistic Reading Program, 1965–1968.* Santa Fe, NM: New Mexico Western States Small Schools Project. (ERIC Document Reproduction Service No. ED 029 724).

Flesch, R. (1955). *Why Johnny can't read and what you can do about it.* New York: Harper & Brothers.

Fries, C. C. (1963). *Linguistics and reading.* New York: Holt, Rinehart, & Winston.

Myers, P. I., & Hammill, D. D. (1976). *Methods for learning disorders* (2nd ed.). New York: Wiley.

Shuy, R. W. (Ed.). (1977). *Linguistic theory: What can it say about reading?* Newark, DE: International Reading. (ERIC Document Reproduction Service No. ED 133 925)

MARIANNE PRICE
*Montgomery County
Intermediate Unit,
Norristown, Pennsylvania*

**LINGUISTIC DEFICIT
LINGUISTIC DEVIANCE
PHONOLOGY**

LIPREADING/SPEECHREADING

Lipreading is commonly defined as the art of understanding a speaker's thought by watching his or her mouth. Lipreading, or speechreading, as it is more frequently called, is the use of the visual information available in speech to facilitate its comprehension. Speechreading is a difficult skill that not all hearing-impaired persons master. Even the best speechreader cannot see everything that is said, since only about 25% of all speech is visible on the lips. However, a good speechreader can often identify about 75% of a message because speechreading improves when words, phrases, and sentences are used in context (Bishop, 1979).

The ability to speechread depends on many factors, such as visual acuity; the degree of visibility of the articulatory movement ("f" is easy to see, "h" is impossible); the speaker's rate; how well the speaker enunciates; lighting and distance; and the fact that some speech sounds cannot be discriminated from each other. Phonemes that have identical visible aspects of articulation are called homophenes (p,b,m). It has been estimated that approximately 50% of the words in a random sample would constitute homophenes of one or more other words (Sanders, 1982).

Training hearing-impaired students to use their residual hearing in conjunction with speechreading significantly improves their speechreading ability. Profoundly deaf individuals, however, are able to make little use of acoustic cues, and their speechreading performance remains essentially the same whether auditory cues are added or not (Sanders, 1982).

Speechreading is also included in total communication, which involves the simultaneous presentation of information through speech, speechreading, fingerspelling, signing, and other manual forms of communication. Currently, total communication is widely used in schools for deaf students throughout the United States. Recent research into speechreading has emphasized viseme grouping (a viseme is the smallest unit of visible speech); the effectiveness of the use of varying degrees of optical distortion in speechreading training; and the visual intelligibility of deaf speakers themselves (Kanter, 1985).

REFERENCES

Bishop, M. (1979). *Mainstreaming.* Washington, DC: Alexander Graham Bell Association for the Deaf.

Kanter, A. (1985, Summer). Aiming for the best. *N.T.I.D. Focus,* 12–13.

Sanders, D. (1982). *Aural rehabilitation.* Englewood Cliffs, NJ: Prentice-Hall.

ROSEMARY GAFFNEY
*Hunter College, City University
of New York*

TOTAL COMMUNICATION

LITERACY

Literacy is the condition or quality of being able to read and write. The term has been used in a narrow fashion (e.g., ability to sign one's name) and in some cases it has taken on much broader meaning (e.g., computer literacy or economic literacy).

Depending on how literacy is defined and measured, vastly different estimates of the literacy rate are evident.

For example, Clifford (1984) reported that switching from orally administered tests to written tests decreased the number of passing grades by 50% in a 1964 study by the New York Board of Regents. In addition, Chall, Freeman, and Levy (1982) noted that the average (passing) reading ability on a set of eleventh-grade competency tests fell between the seventh and eighth grades. Clifford (1984), using a commonly applied criterion (i.e., adults over 25 years of age who have completed less than 5 years of school), cited the illiteracy rate as 11% in the United States in 1950. Recently, the National Commission on Excellence in Education (1983) reported that the illiteracy rate among 17 year olds in the United States is approximately 13%. In general, illiteracy rates in various studies have ranged from 1 to 20% in the adult population.

The narrow views of literacy were not so much the result of the carefully conceived models as they were the result of necessity. Attempts to estimate the prevalence of literacy among national populations at different times in history forced the use of restricted definitions. For instance, the most common method of estimating the literacy of the populations of Europe during the nineteenth century was the inspection of civil and church records, noting the proportion of documents on which the citizen or supplicant signed his or her name or made a mark. Clearly, the trend in conceptualizing the meaning of literacy in recent times had been toward the expansion of the term. Therefore, we now encounter advocates of computer literacy, television literacy, historical literacy, scientific literacy, civic literacy, functional literacy, technological literacy, and so on.

Literacy has been a controversial concept since its inception, which extends to the time of Socrates. Although the idea of universal literacy (schooling for all citizens) has been received postively by most people, many illustrious individuals have been opponents. For instance, neither Socrates nor Plato viewed the use of books favorably. Each considered them to result in only superficial mastery and poor retention. Modern critics have echoed those complaints and have added to the list. Specifically, the concept of the "six-hour retardate"—i.e., the child who is illiterate in school but functional in the home environment—epitomizes the gap between the literacy requirements of educational institutions and adaptive traditions often found in the home and neighborhood.

With the increase in literacy has come a devaluation that did not exist when illiteracy was the rule rather than the exception. Today, illiterate individuals experience embarrassment and humiliation when their inability to read and write becomes known to others. Critics have decried the power rendered to the political-educational bureaucracies that largely control the delivery of literacy to the masses.

REFERENCES

Chall, J. S., Freeman, A., & Levy, B. (1982). Minimum competency testing of reading: An analysis of eight tests designed for grade 11. In G. Madaus (Ed.), *The courts, validity, and minimum competency testing*. Boston: Kluwer-Nijhoff.

Clifford, G. J. (1984). Buch und lesen: Historical perspectives on literacy and schooling. *Review of Educational Research, 54*, 472–500.

National Commission on Excellence in Education. (1983). *A nation at risk: The imperative for educational reform*. Washington, DC: U.S. Government Printing Office.

RONALD C. EAVES
Auburn University

LITHANE

Lithane (lithium carbonate) is used in the treatment of manic episodes of manic-depressive illness. Its use is not recommended for children under age 12. Adverse reactions may include fine hand tremor, especially during initial days of treatment. Overdose may result in drowsiness and lack of coordination at lower serum levels, with giddiness, ataxia, blurred vision, and ringing in the ears at higher levels. A brand name of Miles Pharmaceuticals, it is available as scored tablets containing 300 mg. Dosage is recommended in the range of 600 mg, three times daily for treatment of acute mania, with approximately half this dosage recommended for long-term control of mania.

REFERENCE

Physicians' desk reference. (1984) (pp. 1368–1369). Oradell, NJ: Medical Economics.

LAWRENCE C. HARTLAGE
Evans, Georgia

DRUG THERAPY

LITHONATE

See LITHANE.

LOCUS OF CONTROL

Locus of control generally refers to the mechanism through which individuals determine or do not determine their actions and behavioral controls. Historically, when behavior was felt to be determined by either person-related or environment-related variables and characteristics, two respective control mechanisms were identified:

internal and external locus of control. Internal locus of control refers to an individual's ability to self-determine actions or behaviors through self-mediation (e.g., self-observation, self-cueing, self-encouragement, self-reinforcement, self-punishment) or specific personal characteristics (e.g., intelligence, persistence, wisdom). External locus of control occurs when an individual's actions or behaviors are actually or perceived to be under the control of external reinforcers or reinforcement schedules in the environment. With this individual, behavioral control is attributed to the environment (i.e., it is outside of the person's control) and to specific contingencies within the environment. Naturally, no individual is fully influenced by either internal or external control mechanisms; some feel, however, that one of these controls has dominance in each person.

Rotter (1966) first proposed the mechanisms of internal and external locus of control. He has developed a personality scale that measures their differential influence within individuals: the Internal-External (I-E) Locus of Control Scale. Through the inventory's items, the clinician can better understand which reinforcers the individual perceives as important in his or her life and to what the individual attributes his or her success or failure (e.g., to skills, hard work, luck, fate, chance, or influential others). Again, it is unlikely that a person would be exclusively internally or externally controlled, yet one dominant locus usually results.

A great deal of research has been done using Rotter's scale and the internal and external locus of control constructs. Internal locus of control individuals tend to attribute achievement or academic success to their own abilities or efforts. For boys, internal locus of control was based on successes that motivated continued achievement. For girls, however, this control was based on feelings of responsibility for their failures and subsequent desires to perform better. Internal locus of control achievers feel pride when successful, yet shame and self-blame when they fail.

External locus of control individuals do not generally experience the range of emotional reactions to success or failure. These individuals attribute success to luck or to external support or instruction. Thus, when successful, they admit only minor responsibility for it; when they fail, they admit again only minor responsibility (i.e., it was someone else's fault that they failed). External locus of control individuals display more learned helplessness. They tend to give up or become immobilized when confronted with difficult situations or situations where they must depend on their own skills or knowledge. At these times, they often show withdrawal, dependency, or anger and frustration (external blaming) reactions.

Sometimes, the close relationship between special educators and students nurtures a dependency that results in external locus of control and/or learned helplessness reactions. Indeed, many studies indicate that mentally re-

tarded persons exhibit external locus of control characteristics, e.g., perceiving events as unrelated to their behavior and personal control, expecting failure in new learning situations, and seeking guidance from others because they do not trust their own problem-solving strategies. Again, an interaction between special students' internal and external control, depending on the situation, appears to be most representative of the true control mechanism.

Rotter (1975), in an updated statement, noted three determinants of behavior: the expectancy of the individual, the value of a reinforcement, and the psychological situation itself. It appears that an understanding of behavior as reciprocally determined by person and environment variables and characteristics is being suggested (Bandura, 1978), with the locus of control construct being further clarified. Clearly, Rotter has identified and operationalized an important psychological construct. Its applications to education and special education have influenced the conceptualization of teaching approaches and reinforcement significantly.

REFERENCES

Bandura, A. (1978). The self system in reciprocal determinism. *American Psychologist, 33,* 344–358.

Rotter, J. B. (1966). Generalized expectancies for internal versus external control of reinforcement. *Psychological Monographs, 80*(609).

Rotter, J. B. (1975). Some problems and misconceptions related to the structure of internal-external control of reinforcement. *Journal of Consulting and Clinical Psychology, 43,* 56–67.

HOWARD M. KNOFF
University of South Florida

COGNITIVE BEHAVIOR THERAPY
DEPRESSION
LEARNED HELPLESSNESS

LOVAAS, O. IVAR (1927–   )

O. Ivar Lovaas earned his BA at Luther College in 1951 and his MS and PhD (1958) from the University of Washington, Seattle. Trained in psychoanalytic theory as well as Pavlovian and Skinnerian learning theory, Lovaas applied the formulations of behaviorism to the treatment of psychotic children. Since 1961 he has served as professor of psychology and as staff psychologist at the Psychology Clinic, and as director of the Psychology Autism Clinic at the University of California, Los Angeles.

Lovaas is recognized as one of the principal leaders in the area of behavioral treatment and teaching of developmentally disabled children. Since 1962 he has researched and developed language, teacher, and parent

O. Ivar Lovaas

training programs that have played a major role in effectively educating and treating autistic, schizophrenic, and other disabled children and youths. His early intervention program for autistic children (begun in 1970) has resulted in major and long lasting improvements in these children. Through his efforts, group homes (or teaching homes) have been established as an alternative to institutionalization; these have allowed handicapped individuals to lead more productive lives. Future research is aimed at the early identification of and intervention for severely handicapped children.

Lovaas's major published works include *The Autistic Child: Language Development Through Behavior Modification Teaching Developmentally Disabled Children: The Me Book* (considered a classic in the field), "Acquisition of Imitative Speech by Schizophrenic Children" (1966), and "Behavioral Treatment and Normal Educational/Intellectual Functioning in Young Autistic Children" (1986). He has published and contributed to over 80 journal articles, books, and related works. He also is a renowned and prolific speaker, presenting addresses, workshops, and lectures throughout the world.

Recipient of a Guggenheim fellowship, a doctor of letters, an honorary degree from Luther College, and numerous research grants, Lovaas also has served on over a dozen journal editorial boards, including the *Journal of Applied Behavior Analysis* as associate editor. He serves as consultant to educational, medical, and research institutions, advisory boards, and public service agencies.

REFERENCES

Lovaas, O. I. (1977). *The autistic child: Language development through behavior modification.* New York: Irvington.

Lovaas, O. I. (in press). Behavioral treatment and normal educational/intellectual functioning in young autistic children. *Journal of Consulting & Clinical Psychology.*

Lovaas, O. I., Ackerman, A., Alexander, D., Firestone, P., Perkins, J., & Young, D. (1980). *Teaching developmentally disabled children: The me book.* Baltimore, MD: University Park Press.

Lovaas, O. I., Berberish, J. P., Perloff, B. F., & Schaeffer, B. (1966). Acquisition of imitative speech by schizophrenic children. *Science, 151,* 705–707.

MARY LEON PEERY
Texas A&M University

LOVITT, THOMAS C. (1930–   )

Thomas C. Lovitt began his professional career as a musician, earning a BA in music education from the University of Kansas in 1952. He subsequently studied at the Eastman School of Music and earned his MA in music education from the University of Kansas in 1960. From 1956 through 1961 he was a musician with the Kansas City Philharmonic, while also holding a variety of positions as a music instructor. Lovitt taught special education for several years while pursuing the EdD in special education, which was awarded by the University of Kansas in 1966.

Lovitt has been a prolific researcher in special education since receiving his doctorate, with just over 100 scholarly publications to his credit. He has worked principally in the area of learning disabilities while spending his academic career within the Experimental Education Unit of the College of Education of the University of Washington. Lovitt joined the University of Washington faculty as an assistant professor in 1966, was promoted to associate rank in 1968, and awarded full professor status in 1972.

Lovitt's early research focused on laboratory studies employing operant conditioning procedures to modify narrative preferences. Later, he coordinated a research classroom at the Experimental Education Unit, where he attempted to employ the principles of applied behavior analysis to the improvement of academic skill in learning-disabled youngsters. Lovitt's more recent research inter-

Thomas C. Lovitt

ests have shifted to the public school classroom and to the development and implementation of precision teaching practices. Lovitt lists as his current primary interests learning disabilities, curriculum development, and techniques for the modification of textbooks in the content areas of secondary school (e.g., science, social studies) so that teachers can instruct slow learners in the classroom more effectively.

Though most of his publishing has been in academic journals (e.g., Lovitt & Curtiss, 1969), Lovitt is perhaps best known for two of his books on children and their relationship to teachers (Lovitt, 1977, 1982).

REFERENCES

Lovitt, T. C. (1977). *In spite of my resistance, I've learned from children*. Columbus, OH: Merrill.

Lovitt, T. C. (1982). *Because of my persistence, I've learned from children*. Columbus, OH: Merrill.

Lovitt, T. C., & Curtiss, H. K. (1969). Academic response rate as a function of teacher- and self-imposed contingencies. *Journal of Applied Behavior Analysis, 2,* 49–53.

CECIL R. REYNOLDS
Texas A&M University

LOW BIRTH WEIGHT INFANTS

Low birth weight infants may be born at term or preterm. Although some sources combine the two categories, they are separate phenomena with separate sequelae. Term low birth weight (TLBW) infants are born between 38 and 42 weeks gestation and show significant deficits in growth relative to some physiologic standards of normal weight newborns. Various criteria have been used. For mild degrees of TLBW, birth weight one standard deviation below the mean for a given gestational age or below the tenth percentile may be used. For severe degrees, birth weight two standard deviations below the mean or below the third percentile is used (Kopp & Parmalee, 1979). Infants meeting the criteria may be diagnosed as small for gestational age (SFGA) or, in the extreme, intrauterine growth retarded (IUGR; Jensen & Bobak, 1985). Some infants meeting a criterion for mild SFGA have parents who are themselves small. Thus the infants demonstrate familial characteristics.

A variety of maternal, placental, and fetal factors are associated with IUGR. The most frequent maternal factor is hypertension; other factors include maternal age less than 17 or greater than 35 years, smoking, ethnicity (more common in blacks), low maternal weight or weight gain during pregnancy, poor general health, and use of certain drugs (including alcohol). Placental factors include antepartum hemorrhage, preterm contractions, and impaired transport of nutrients. Fetal factors include twinning, infections, and congenital malformations (Hobel, 1985; Miller, 1985).

Infants with TLBW are a very heterogeneous group. A small percent show major malformations, which may well correlate with rather than result from low weight. Overall, incidence of mortality and morbidity among IUGR infants is high relative to normal term newborns. Newborns without obvious defects show a characteristic appearance: head relatively large for their undergrown bodies, very little body fat, and dry, parchmentlike skin that appears to hang. They are susceptible to a variety of potentially lethal complications, most commonly asphyxia, but also problems with metabolism and temperature regulation (Kliegman & King, 1983). Infants with TLBW characteristically are hypotonic, unresponsive, inactive, impaired as to neonatal reflexes (Kopp & Parmalee, 1979). These characteristics are particularly apparent in postterm SFGA newborns.

Follow-up studies indicate that the heterogeneity of TLBW infants persists into childhood (Fitghardinge & Steven, 1972a, 1972b). Physically, most are still relatively small. Those whose low birth weight stemmed from placental or uterine insufficiency or nutritional deficit may show accelerated catch-up growth postnatally when placed on an adequate diet, but generally they remain below average in growth (Kliegman & King, 1983). A small percentage show normal growth (Gordon, 1981). Although incidence of mental retardation and seizure disorders is higher than in normal controls, most TLBW children do not show obvious neurological defects. Overall intelligence, except for those with major neurological defects, is in the average range, and somewhat lower in boys than girls. However, educational difficulties are common; in Fitzhardinge and Steven's (1972a, 1972b) sample, some 50% of boys and 36% of girls were having problems in school.

One of the most important variables related to outcome of TLBW infants and children is socioeconomic status (SES) of the parents. Consistently, infants from higher SES, more supportive, environments fare better than those from poorer environments (Kopp & Parmalee, 1979), a relationship that holds for premature and other at-risk infants as well. Hypotonicity, low responsiveness, and weak reflexes make TLBW infants difficult and relatively unresponsive to parenting. As a result, normal parent-child bonding and interaction patterns may suffer, interfering with the child's development and potentiating later abuse. Middle- and upper-class parents appear to be able to compensate for their infants' poor responsiveness. However, low SES parents have much more difficulty in dealing with such infants. Indeed, some of the sensory deficits seen in TLBW infants may result from impaired parent-child interaction (Campbell, 1985). Thus, except in cases involving major defects at birth, outcome is very much the result of a developmental process, with parental social class being perhaps as important as the low birth weight itself.

In sum, most TLBW infants will show more or less normal development. Incidence of problems could be reduced by reducing low birth weight through optimal prenatal care and teaching parents, particularly those from low SES settings, how to cope with their TLBW infant.

REFERENCES

Campbell, L. A. (1985). The very low birth weight infant, sensory experience and development. *Topics in Clinical Nursing, 6,* 19–33.

Fitzhardinge, P. M., & Steven, E. M. (1972a). The small-for-data infant I. Later growth patterns. *Pediatrics, 49,* 671–681.

Fitzhardinge, P. M., & Steven, E. M. (1972b). The small-for-date infant II. Neurological and intellectual sequelae. *Pediatrics, 50,* 50–59.

Gordon, B. A. (1981). *Neonatology, pathophysiology and management of the newborn.* Philadelphia: Lippincott.

Hobel, C. J. (1985). Factors before pregnancy that influence brain development. In J. M. Freeman (Ed.), *Prenatal and perinatal factors associated with brain disorders* (NIH Publication No. 85-1149, pp. 177–195). Bethesda, MD: National Institutes of Health.

Jensen, M. D., & Bobak, I. M. (1985). *Maternity and gynecologic care, the nurse and the family.* St. Louis: Mosby.

Kliegman, R. M., & King, K. C. (1983). Intrauterine growth retardation: Determinants of aberrant fetal growth. In A. A. Fanaroff & R. J. Martin (Eds.), *Behrman's neonatal-perinatal medicine* (3rd ed., pp. 49–80). St. Louis: Mosby.

Kopp, C. B., & Parmalee, A. H. (1979). Prenatal and perinatal influences on infant behavior. In J. D. Osofsky (Ed.), *Handbook of infant development* (pp. 29–75). New York: Wiley.

Miller, H. C. (1985). Prenatal factors affecting intrauterine growth retardation. *Clinics in Perinatology, 12*(2), 307–318.

DORETHA McKNIGHT STONE
ROBERT T. BROWN
University of North Carolina, Wilmington

CONGENITAL DISORDERS
PREMATURITY/PRETERM

LOWENFELD, BERTHOLD (1901–   )

Born in Linz, Austria, Berthold Lowenfeld was a teacher of blind children before he earned his PhD in child psychology from the University of Vienna in 1927. As a Rockefeller research fellow, he studied the education of the blind, and child psychology in the United States from 1930 to 1931. After the Nazi invasion of his homeland in 1938, Lowenfeld emigrated to the United States to become, in 1939, director of educational research for the American Foundation for the Blind in New York City.

Berthold Lowenfeld

In 1949 Lowenfeld made an extensive survey for all Canadian schools for the blind under the auspices of the Canadian National Institute for the Blind. Afterward, he left the East Coast to become superintendent of the California School for the Blind, a position he held until 1964. Since then, he has engaged in research and writing under the sponsorship of the U.S. Office of Education, the California State Department of Education, and the Social and Rehabilitation Service, Department of Health, Education, and Welfare.

Lowenfeld has been a fellow of the American Psychological Association since 1950. Among his honors are the two highest awards in work with the blind in the United States: the Shotwell Memorial Award of the American Association of Workers for the Blind and the Migel Medal for Outstanding Service to the Blind; he also has won the National Accreditation Council Award.

Lowenfeld has over 100 contributions to professional books and journals to his credit., including *Our Blind Children: Growing and Learning with Them, The Changing Status of the Blind: From Separation to Integration,* and *Berthold Lowenfeld on Blindness and Blind People.*

REFERENCES

Lowenfeld, B. (Ed.). (1945). *The blind preschool child.* New York: American Foundation for the Blind.

Lowenfeld, B. (1971). *Our blind children: Growing and learning with them* (3rd ed.). Springfield, IL: Thomas.

Lowenfeld, B. (Ed.). (1973). *The visually handicapped child in school.* New York: Day.

Lowenfeld, B. (1975). *The changing status of the blind: From separation to integration.* Springfield, IL: Thomas.

Lowenfeld, B. (1981). *Berthold Lowenfeld on blindness and blind people.* New York: American Foundation for the Blind.

E. VALERIE HEWITT
Texas A&M University

LOW-INCIDENCE HANDICAPS

Two similar terms are commonly used to describe handicapped populations: prevalence and incidence. Although the terms have similar meanings, and are often used interchangeably, they actually have two distinct meanings. Prevalence indicates the number of people at any given time who exhibit a specific handicap. The prevalence of mental retardation among school-aged individuals may be established by counting all mentally retarded people served by the schools. Incidence refers to the number of people who have been diagnosed as having a handicap anytime during their lives. The prevalence estimate for mental retardation is based on all mentally retarded students, both existing cases and newly diagnosed cases at one point in time. The incidence estimate reflects the number of cases diagnosed at one time or another and does not necessarily reflect active cases.

As may be apparent from these definitions, incidence estimates for a given handicapping condition are typically higher than prevalence estimates. While a large number of people may be affected by learning disabilities at some time in their lives (incidence), the actual number of learning-disabled persons at one time may be relatively small (prevalence). Further, incidence estimates may be substantially more difficult to substantiate than prevalence estimates. Pupil counts may reliably indicate the number of emotionally disturbed youngsters served during a particular school year (prevalence). Conversely, it may be difficult to obtain an accurate count of all students who at any time in their school careers were diagnosed as being emotionally disturbed (incidence).

Because of the relative ease and accuracy with which prevalence data may be obtained, most agencies rely on prevalence estimates when determining the pervasiveness of a handicap. The *Sixth Annual Report to Congress on the Implementation of Public Law 94-142: The Education for All Handicapped Children Act* (U.S. Department of Education, 1984), for example, indicated that 4.4% of all students are learning disabled, 2.86% are speech impaired, 1.92% are mentally retarded. .89% are emotionallly disturbed, .30% are orthopedically handicapped or health impaired, .18% are hearing impaired, .16% are multihandicapped, and .07% are visually impaired.

Children and youths who are orthopedically handicapped or health impaired, hearing impaired, multiply handicapped, or visually impaired represent less than 1% of the entire school population. They also account for under 7% of all handicapped persons. Therefore, these conditions are referred to as low-incidence handicaps. Each of these conditions and the special problems they present will be discussed in the following sections.

Orthopedic impairment is defined by the federal government as "a severe orthopedic impairment which adversely affects a child's educational performance. The term includes impairments caused by congenital anomaly . . . disease . . . and from other causes." Other health impaired individuals are defined as "having an autistic condition which is manifested by severe communication and other developmental and educational problems; or having limited strength, vitality or alertness, due to chronic or acute health problems . . . which adversely affects a child's educational performance" (Federal Register, 1977, pp. 42478–42479).

More so than any other category of exceptionality, children and youths in this group exhibit highly diverse characteristics. Youngsters identified as being orthopedically or otherwise health impaired typically exhibit disorders that affect their mobility or ambulation. These disorders may include cerebral palsy; muscular distrophy, a progressive degeneration of the voluntary muscles; poliomyelitis; spina bifida; multiple sclerosis; and juvenile rheumatoid arthritis (Berdine & Blackhurst, 1985).

Other youngsters included in the general category of orthopedically or otherwise health impaired exhibit disorders that affect vitality. These individuals may have medical disorders that, aside from being life threatening, limit normal and independent school functioning. Disorders that affect vitality include congenital heart defects, cystic fibrosis, diabetes, and asthma (Berdine & Blackhurst, 1985).

A third group of individuals in this general category have convulsive disorders (Berdine & Blackhurst, 1985). These disabilities are commonly referred to as epilepsy. They result from abnormalities in the electrical activity of the brain. Random firing of nerve cells in the cerebral cortex causes uncontrollable motor activity referred to as seizures. Four types of seizures recognized by the Epilepsy Foundation of America (1977) include partial seizures, generalized seizures, unilateral seizures, and unclassified seizures. More frequently used descriptions include petit mal seizures, grand mal seizures, and psychomotor seizures.

The final group of youngsters in this category is labeled autistic. These children and youths exhibit three major characteristics: limited social relationships with parents, family members, and others; severely delayed language and atypical language patterns, including frequent echoing words and phrases; and stereotypic behavior, including finger flicking, body rocking, and an obsession with objects (Rutter, 1978).

The low-incidence category of hearing impairment includes both the deaf and hard of hearing. Deaf persons' hearing impairment is so severe that it limits the aural processing of linguistic information with or without the use of a hearing aid and adversely affects educational performance. Hard of hearing persons' impairment is not sufficiently severe to be included in the definition of deafness, but it does limit individuals' educational performance (Federal Register, 1977). Hearing impairments may be congenital (before birth), adventitious (after birth), prelingual (prior to the development of speech or language), or postlingual (after speech and language are developed). These designations are particularly important to educators because the earlier the onset of the hearing impairment, the more difficult it is for a child to develop language. A final important distinction between hearing impairments is the nature of the loss. Losses resulting from defects in the outer and middle ear often can be treated medically or with amplification. Losses associated with defects in the inner ear and neural pathway are substantially less amenable to correction (Cartwright, Cartwright, & Ward, 1985).

Multihandicapped individuals exhibit two or more handicaps that, in combination, cause educational problems that cannot be remediated through programs designed solely for one of the handicaps (Federal Register, 1977). Multihandicapped youngsters may be deaf and emotionally disturbed, mentally retarded and visually impaired, physically handicapped and learning disabled, or any other combination of disorders. Snell (1978) includes in the population of multiply handicapped individuals all severely and profoundly mentally retarded and emotionally disturbed persons.

The federal government defines visual impairment as limited sight to the extent that "even with correction, adversely affects a child's educational performance. The term includes both partially seeing and blind children" (Federal Register, 1977, p. 42479). A more objective definition, provided by the American Medical Association, distinguishes between blindness and partial vision. Blindness is defined by a visual acuity of 20/200 or less in the better eye following correction, or a field of vision no greater than 20 degrees at the widest diameter. Partial vision is defined by a visual acuity of 20/70 to 20/200 in the better eye (Hatfield, 1975). Visual acuity is the ability of the eye to resolve images at varying distances. A visual acuity of 20/200 means that an individual can resolve images at 20 ft that the general population can identify at 200 ft. The field of vision is the breadth of sight perceptible without changing the point of focus.

Children and youths with low-incidence conditions present one of the greatest challenges for special education agencies and personnel. Low-incidence handicaps are typically the most severe disorders faced by school personnel. Consequently, students with these disorders often require specialized personnel, equipment, and facilities. For example, physically handicapped youngsters often require physical and occupational therapy, mobility and communication aides, and accessible environments. Hearing-impaired students may require amplification, specialized auditory training, and instruction in alternative or augmentative communication systems. Visually impaired learners are likely to need mobility training and instruction in the use of Braille or large print. Finally, multi-

handicapped children and youths commonly require assistance from professionals in multiple disciplines that are matched to the characteristics that define the specific condition.

The small number of students in school districts that require low-incidence services adds additional problems. A rural school district, spanning 20 square miles, may have under 1000 high-school students. Based on the prevalence figures discussed previously, one would expect to find three orthopedically handicapped or health-impaired students, two hearing-impaired students, two multihandicapped students, and only one visually impaired student. It would be impossible, of course, for the hypothetical high school to provide homogeneous classes to serve these youths. Further, it may be difficult for the school district to employ the specialists required to serve the small number of students.

To overcome the preceding problems, special education cooperatives may be formed in which the cost of the low-incidence services is shared by a number of school districts. In the preceding case, the hypothetical school district may join together with nine other school districts. These 10 districts may then employ an itinerant teacher to serve the 10 or so visually impaired youngsters in the cooperative. Two special classes may be formed in central locations, one serving ninth and tenth grade hearing-impaired youths and the other serving eleventh and twelfth grade youths. The costs for staffing and housing these classes would be shared by all of the districts in the cooperative.

In conclusion, low-incidence handicapping conditions include the orthopedically handicapped or health impaired, the hearing impaired, the multihandicapped, and the visually impaired. These students represent less than 1% of the entire school population. Students with low-incidence handicapping conditions typically require the most intense and specialized of all educational services. These services are often shared by special education cooperatives.

REFERENCES

Berdine, W. H., & Blackhurst, A. E. (1985). *An introduction to special education* (2nd ed.). Boston: Little, Brown.

Cartwright, G. P., Cartwright, C. A., & Ward, M. E. (1985). *Educating special learners* (2nd ed.). Belmont, CA: Wadsworth.

Epilepsy Foundation of America. (1977). *Answers to most frequent questions people ask about epilepsy*. Washington: DC: Epilepsy Foundation.

Federal Register. (1977, Aug.). Washington, DC: U.S. Government Printing Office.

Hatfield E. M. (1975). Why are they blind? *Sight Saving Review* 45, (1), 3–22.

Rutter, M. (1978). Diagnosis and definition. In M. Rutter & E. Schopler (Eds.), *Autism: A reappraisal of concepts and treatment*. New York: Plenum.

Sixth Annual Report to Congress on the Implementation of Public Law 94-142: The Education for all Handicapped Children Act. (1984). Washington, DC: U.S. Department of Education.

Snell, M. E. (Ed.). (1978). *Systematic instruction of the moderately and severely handicapped.* Columbus, OH: Merrill.

PATRICK J. SCHLOSS
Pennsylvania State University

AUTISM
EPILEPSY
HIGH INCIDENCE HANDICAPS
ORTHOPEDICALLY IMPAIRED
OTHER HEALTH IMPAIRED

LOW VISION

Historically, the use of various terms related to individuals with visual impairments or those who have no sight has caused great confusion (Barraga, 1983). A committee of the World Health Organization (WHO), chaired by Colenbrander (1977), adopted a classification system of three levels of vision; low vision was identified as a term within the system. This system has allowed medical, optometric, and educational personnel to communicate with each other because the emphasis is on the functioning of the individual and not rigidly focused on exact measurement criteria (Barraga, 1983).

Definitions of low vision still vary. The WHO classification defines the level of disability in someone with severe low vision as "performs visual task at a reduced level of speed, endurance, and precision even with aid." It defines the level of disability in someone with profound low vision as "has difficulty with gross visual tasks; cannot perform most detailed visual tasks" (Colenbrander, 1977); Corn, 1980 defines a person with profound low vision in a practical manner with educational implications: "one who is still severely visually impaired after correction, but who may increase visual functioning through the use of optical aids, nonoptical aids, environmental modifications, and/or techniques." Barraga (1983) further clarifies the term: Low-vision children have limitations in distance vision but are able to see objects and materials when they are within a few inches or at a maximum of a few feet away." Regardless of the definition accepted, these children should not be referred to as "blind".

Low-vision students vary in their visual functioning; some may use their vision more efficiently than others. Some may be able to use their vision for reading, whereas others will need to use braille and other tactile materials to supplement printed materials (Barraga, 1983). A major emphasis in educational programs is to provide vision stimulation and training to low-vision students to help them develop their residual vision as effectively as possible. An excellent resource for helping such students to "learn to see" is the Program to Develop Efficiency in Visual Function developed by Barraga (1980) and the accompanying *Source Book on Low Vision.*

Many low-vision students may benefit from low-vision aids that are characterized as anything that helps people use their vision more efficiently. Optical aids are available for both distance and near vision tasks. They are prescribed by ophthalmologists or optometrists in relation to eye diagnosis, the severity of the condition, the requirements of the particular task, and the individual response of the low-vision student (Faye, 1984). Examples of optical aids are glasses for reading large print, a magnifier stand for reading small print, and a monocular telescope for looking at the blackboard (Heward & Orlansky, 1984). Nonoptical aids are used to improve environmental conditions. They include specific illumination devices such as reading lamps and flashlights; light transmission devices such as absorptive lenses, filters, and lens coatings that reduce glare and increase contrast; reflection control devices such as visors and sideshields; enhanced contrast procedures such as the use of dark colors on a light background and fluorescent strips; and linear magnification aids such as large print books (Faye, 1984). Electronic aids include opaque and transparent projection systems such as slide projectors and closed-circuit television systems (Kelleher, 1982). Regardless of the aids prescribed, the low-vision student must be given intensive follow-up training and support in learning to use them and in evaluating their usefulness in the classroom as well as in other types of indoor and outdoor environments.

Low-vision students also need to develop their auditory skills in order to avail themselves of other valuable resources for accessing knowledge such as cassette tape recorders, computers with synthesized speech output, and electronic reading machines.

REFERENCES

Barraga, N. C. (1980). *Source book on low vision.* Louisville, KY: American Printing House for the Blind.

Barraga, N. C. (1983). *Visual handicaps and learning.* Austin, TX: Exceptional Resources.

Colenbrander, A. (1977). Dimensions of visual performance. *Archives of American Academy of Ophthalmology, 83,* 332–337.

Corn, A. (1980). *Development and assessment of an in-service training program for teachers of the visually handicapped: Optical aids in the classroom.* Unpublished doctoral dissertation, Teachers College, Columbia University, New York.

Faye, E. E. (1984). *Clinical low vision.* Boston: Little, Brown.

Heward, W. L., and Orlansky, M. D. (1984). *Exceptional children.* Columbus, OH: Merrill.

Kelleher, D. K. (1982). Orientation to low vision aids. In S. S. Mangold (Ed.), *A teachers guide to the special educational needs of blind and visually handicapped children* (pp. 45–52). New York: American Foundation for the Blind.

ROSANNE K. SILBERMAN
*Hunter College, City University
of New York*

VISUALLY IMPAIRED
VISUAL TRAINING

LOXITANE

A dibenzoxazepine compound, Loxitane represents a new subclass of tricyclic antipsychotic agent used as a tranquilizer. Its use is indicated for the management of the manifestations of psychotic disorders. Side effects include rigidity (27%), tremor (22%), and drowsiness (11%), with less frequent incidence of confusion, dizziness, and slurred speech. Overdosage results may induce depression and unconsciousness. A brand name of Lederle Laboratories, Loxitane is supplied in capsules of 5, 10, 25, and 50 mg as an oral concentrate and in injectible units of 1 and 10 ml. Dosage levels are recommended in divided doses, two to four times a day, in initial dosage of 10 mg.

REFERENCE

Physicians' desk reference. (1984). (pp. 1078–1080). Oradell, NJ: Medical Economics.

LAWRENCE C. HARTLAGE
Evans, Georgia

DRUG THERAPY

LSD

Lysergic acid diethylamide (LSD) was initially discovered by accident by the Swiss chemist Albert Hoffman. LSD is a psychotominetic drug that elicits vivid hallucinations and intense emotions. Synesthesia, a phenomenon in which perceptions cross modalities may occur (e.g., words are seen and colors heard). The drug is extraordinarily potent and a dosage as low as 50 mg can produce marked psychological effects. Some users report kaleidoscopic imagery that appears before their closed eyes; perceptions are reported to be richer and more intense. There is frequently a distorted perception of body parts. Spatial and temporal distortions are common. Depersonalization may result, and there is almost always a heightened suggestibility. In addition, it is common for users to report an increased awareness of the "true nature of things" and to find special significance in trivial events.

Like other psychotominetic drugs, it is clear that response to LSD is contingent on set and setting. The "bad trip" is perhaps the single most common adverse experience encountered by LSD users. The best treatment during this condition is simply companionship and support from someone who is knowledgeable about the drug and its effects. Even the worst effects typically wear off in 8 to 12 hours.

LSD is a drug that produces rapid tolerance and increasingly larger doses are required to produce an effect over the short run. However, once drug use is discontinued, tolerance rapidly abates. There is no physical dependence on the drug, and there is little evidence of long-term organic brain changes of the sort that are found with the abuse of certain other drugs. However, about 25% of users will experience flashbacks during which they may relive the experience of acute LSD intoxication. Flashbacks rarely occur more than a year after the last use of the drug. Some authors have argued the use of LSD may constitute a risk factor in the development of schizophrenia (Kaplan & Sadock, 1981).

REFERENCE

Kaplan, H. I., and Sadock, D. J. (1981). *Modern synopsis of comprehensive textbook of psychiatry.* Baltimore, MD: Williams & Wilkins.

DANNY WEDDING
Marshall University

DRUG ABUSE
CHILDHOOD SCHIZOPHRENIA

LURIA, ALEXANDER R. (1902–1977)

Alexander Luria was a Russian neuropsychologist. He is best known for his theoretical and practical work on the behavioral consequences associated with focal brain injury. His early work integrated and expanded on the work of other Russian scientists, notably Pavlov and Vygotsky (Hatfield, 1981). Luria incorporated Vygotsky's ideas about the development of the social aspects of speech and Pavlov's neurophysiologic approach to understanding higher cortical processes (Hatfield, 1981).

Luria thought that all higher cortical functions required the concerted and coordinated working of multiple brain areas. His theory is neither a localizationist nor an equipotentialist one. Luria believed that higher cortical functions (e.g., reading) require the operation of functional systems incorporating multiple brain areas. Though specific aspects of the functional system (e.g., movement) are localizable within the brain, the more complex, complete behavior is not localizable. Hence, focal brain damage affects a variety of specific skills because one link in the system is nonfunctional while others are intact (e.g., the brain is not equipotential or homogeneous) (Luria, 1980, 1982). Luria's other contributions include methods for the assessment and treatment of aphasia using his functional systems approach to understanding cortical processes. He also is well known for his seminal work on frontal lobe functions (Pribram, 1978).

REFERENCES

Hatfield, F. N. (1981). Analysis and remediation of aphasia in the USSR: The contribution of A. R. Luria. *Journal of Speech & Hearing Disorders, 46,* 338–347.

Luria, A. R. (1980). *Higher cortical functions in man* (2nd ed.). New York: Basic Books.

Luria, A. R. (1982). *Language and cognition,* New York: Wiley.

Pribram, K. H. (1978). In memory of Alexander Romanovitsch Luria. *Neuropsychologia, 16,* 137–139.

GRETA N. WILKENING
Children's Hospital, Denver, Colorado

LURIA-NEBRASKA NEUROPSYCHOLOGICAL BATTERY
VYGOTSKY, L. S.

LURIA-NEBRASKA NEUROPSYCHOLOGICAL BATTERY

The Luria-Nebraska Neuropsychological Battery (Golden, Hammeke, & Purisch, 1980) is a set of tasks specifically designed for the assessment of brain-damaged individuals. Like other neuropsychological batteries (e.g., Halstead-Reitan Neuropsychological Test Battery), it was developed to provide information regarding the absence or presence of brain damage. The battery also may be used by trained neuropsychologists to assist in rehabilitation planning, to discriminate between functional and organic disorders, to suggest the localization of brain damage, and to make prognostic statements (Moses, Golden, Ariel, & Gustavson, 1983). Based on the theoretical work of A. R. Luria, the battery, though broken into "scales," is really a set of interrelated items that may be evaluated both qualitatively and quantitatively.

The adult version of the battery is composed of 269 items. The children's revision (for children 8 years to 12 years 12 months) is composed of 149 items. Both assess motor functions, pitch and rhythm perception, tactile skills, visual perceptions, receptive and expressive language, motor writing, spelling, reading, arithmetic, memory, and intellectual processes. Intermediate memory is assessed in the adult versions. An estimate, based on demographic data, of premorbid functioning is provided. Validation studies suggest that the batteries can make relevant discriminations at acceptable levels (Golden et al., 1981; Plaisted, Gustavson, Wilkening, & Golden, 1983). There has been much controversy about the battery, however, with some authors critical of developmental methodology and content (Adams, 1980; Golden et al., 1982).

REFERENCES

Adams, K. M. (1980). In search of Luria's battery: A false start. *Journal of Consulting & Clinical Psychology, 48,* 511–516.

Golden, C. J. (1980). In reply to Adams' "In search of Luria's battery: A false start." *Journal of Consulting & Clinical Psychology, 48,* 517–521.

Golden, C. J., Ariel, R. N., McKay, S. E., Wilkening, G. N., Wolf, B. A., & MacInnes, W. D. (1982). The Luria-Nebraska Neuropsychological Battery: Theoretical orientation and comment. *Journal of Consulting and Clinical Psychology, 50,* 291–300.

Golden, C. J., Fishburne, F. J., Lewis, G. P., Conley, F. K., Moses, J. A., Engum E., Wisniewski, A. M., Berg, R. A. (1981). Cross validation of the Luria-Nebraska Neuropsychological Battery for the presence, lateralization, and localization of brain damage. *Journal of Consulting & Clinical Psychology, 49,* 491–507.

Golden, C. J., Hammeke, T. A., & Purisch, A. (1980). *The Luria-Nebraska Neuropsychological Battery.* Los Angeles: Western Psychological Services.

Moses, J. A., Golden, C. J., Ariel, R., Gustavson, J. L. (1983). *Interpretation of the Luria-Nebraska Neuropsychological Battery* (Vol. 1). New York: Grune & Stratton.

Plaisted, J. R., Gustavson, J. L., Wilkening, G. N., & Golden, C. J. (1983). The Luria-Nebraska Neuropsychological Battery—Children's revision: Theory and current research findings. *Journal of Clinical Child Psychology, 12,* 13–21.

Spiers, P. A. (1981). "Have they come to praise Luria or to bury him?" The Luria Nebraska Battery controversy. *Journal of Consulting and Clinical Psychology, 49,* 331–341.

Spiers, P. A. (1982). The Luria-Nebraska Neuropsychological Battery revisited: A theory in practice or just practicing? *Journal of Consulting & Clinical Psychology, 50,* 301–306.

GRETA N. WILKENING
Children's Hospital, Denver, Colorado

HALSTEAD-REITAN NEUROPSYCHOLOGICAL BATTERY
LURIA, A. R.
NEUROPSYCHOLOGY

M

MA

See MENTAL AGE.

MACMILLAN, DONALD L. (1940–   )

A former coach at Laguna Beach High School, Donald L. MacMillan has received widespread acknowledgment for his work in the field of special education generally, but in mental retardation particularly. MacMillan earned his BA degree in education in 1962 from Case Western Reserve University. He then went to the University of California, Los Angeles, (UCLA), where he earned an MA in educational psychology in 1963 followed by an EdD in exceptional children in 1967. MacMillan was graduated with honors and noted for distinction for his dissertation.

In 1968 MacMillan joined the faculty of the University of California, Riverside, where he was promoted to associate rank in 1970. He was made a professor in 1973 and began working as a research psychologist at the UCLA Pacific-Neuropsychiatric Institute the same year. At present, MacMillan is chair of the Developmental and Chronic Disabilities Research Group at the University of California, Riverside.

MacMillan has served the field of mental retardation with distinction in a broad range of roles, including extensive consultantships (e.g., consultant to more than 10 state hospital programs, various public school districts, and federal agencies). He also has served as an editorial reviewer (e.g., as associate editor of the *American Journal of Mental Deficiency* and *Exceptional Children* and as consulting editor to the *Journal of School Psychology*), on the boards of various professional societies, and as a noted teacher and researcher. MacMillan has constantly and effectively researched affective and motivational components of mental retardation (MacMillan, 1969, 1970) as well as related environmental and conditional determinants of mental retardation such as socioeconomic status and ethnicity. MacMillan also has done extensive work on the application of behavioral psychology to the problems of mental retardation (Forness & MacMillan, 1970; MacMillan, 1973).

REFERENCES

Forness, S. R., & MacMillan, D. L. (1970). The origins of behavior modification with exceptional children. *Exceptional Children, 37*, 93–100.

MacMillan, D. L. (1969). Resumption of interrupted tasks by normal and educably mentally retarded subjects. *American Journal of Mental Deficiency, 73*, 657–660.

MacMillan, D. L. (1970). Reactions following interpolated failure by normal and retarded subjects. *American Journal of Mental Deficiency, 74*, 692–696.

MacMillan, D. L. (1973). *Behavior modification in education.* New York: MacMillan.

CECIL R. REYNOLDS
Texas A&M University

MACY, ANNE SULLIVAN (1866–1936)

Anne Sullivan Macy, Helen Keller's teacher, taught the deaf, blind, and mute child from the age of 6, serving as both teacher and companion until her death in 1936.

Helen Keller and Anne Sullivan Macy

Trained at the Perkins Institution for the Blind in Boston, where she resided in the same house as Laura Bridgeman, the first deaf-blind person to be educated, the young teacher developed methods that she successfully used to teach Helen Keller to read, write, and speak, and that enabled Keller to become a well-educated and effective person. In Keller's adult years, Macy, whom Keller always addressed as "teacher," served not only as teacher and interpreter for her, but also managed her extremely busy schedule of writing, lecturing, and personal appearances for many educational and social causes.

REFERENCES

Keller, H. (1955). *Teacher: Anne Sullivan Macy*. New York: Doubleday.

Lash, J. (1980). *Helen and Teacher: The story of Helen Keller and Anne Sullivan Macy*. New York: American Printing House for the Blind.

PAUL IRVINE
Katonah, New York

MAGICAL MODEL

The magical model of exceptionality explains deviance in terms of demonic possession and other supernatural causes. Common beliefs include possession by human and animal spirits and victimization by witches and spell casters (Rosenhan & Seligman, 1984). For centuries the model competed only with the biogenic (organic) model as an explanation of exceptional behavior (Brown, 1986).

The magical model is associated frequently with witch hunts and gruesome persecutions of deviant persons. However, there have also been numerous periods in history when those following a supernatural model offered treatment to the deviant that was far more humane and at least equally effective as that offered by those using naturalistic, biological models (Erickson & Hyerstay, 1980).

Although biological, psychological, and ecological models have displaced magical models in the literature of educational professionals, some residual use of supernaturl explanations occurs in the general culture. The public's attitudes toward the disabled and the disabled's attitudes toward themselves may be partially shaped by these notions of magic.

REFERENCES

Brown, R. T. (1986). Etiology and development of exceptionality. In R. T. Brown & C. R. Reynolds (Eds.), *Psychological perspectives on childhood exceptionality: A handbook* (pp. 181–229). New York: Wiley.

Erickson, R., & Hyerstay, B. (1980). Historical perspectives on treatment of the mentally ill. In M. Gibbs, J. Lachenmeyer, & J. Sigal (Eds.), *Community psychology: Theoretical and empirical approaches* (pp. 29–74). New York: Gardner.

Rosenhan, D., & Seligman, M. (1984). *Abnormal Psychology*. New York: Norton.

LEE ANDERSON JACKSON, JR.
*University of North Carolina,
Wilmington*

HISTORY OF SPECIAL EDUCATION

MAGNESIUM

Magnesium is a light metal that represents an essential body mineral (Ensminger, Ensminger, Konlande, & Robson, 1983; Thomson, 1979). The body contains approximately 20 to 30 g of magnesium, most of which is present in the skeleton (Yudkin, 1985). Magnesium also is found in cell tissue and it represents an essential component of the body's enzyme systems (Yudkin, 1985). The recommended daily allowances of magnesium range from 50 to 70 mg for infants to approximately 300 mg for adults (Ensminger et al., 1983). Dietary sources include a wide variety of foods, including flours, nuts, and spices. The typical western diet supplies ample magnesium (Yudkin, 1985).

While magnesium deficiency is rare under normal circumstances, it may occur in alcoholics and in persons with acute diarrhea or severe kidney disease (Ensminger et al., 1983; Yudkin, 1985). Symptoms of magnesium deficiency include depression; tremors and muscular weakness; confusion and disorientation; dizziness and convulsions; and loss of appetite, nausea, and vomiting (Ensminger et al., 1983; Yudkin, 1985). The salts of magnesium (magnesium sulfate, magnesium carbonate) are used medicinally for their antacid and laxative properties (Malseed, 1983; Parish, 1977). Use in patients with impaired kidney function is contraindicated (Parish, 1977).

REFERENCES

Ensminger, A. H., Ensminger, M. E., Konlande, J. E., & Robson, J. R. K. (1983). *Foods and nutrition encyclopedia* (Vol. 2). Clovis, CA: Pegus.

Malseed, R. (1983). *Quick reference to drug therapy and nursing considerations*. Philadelphia: Lippincott.

Parish, P. (1977). *The doctors' and patients' handbook of medicines and drugs*. New York: Knopf.

Thomson, W. A. R. (1979). *Black's medical dictionary* (32nd ed.). New York: Barnes & Noble.

Yudkin, J. (1985). *The Penguin encyclopedia of nutrition*. Middlesex, England: Penguin.

CATHY F. TELZROW
*Cuyahoga Special Education
Service Center, Maple
Heights, Ohio*

MAGNET SCHOOLS

Magnet schools, also referred to as alternative schools, are established within a school district to allow teachers, students, and parents the right to select specific curricula and/or methods of instruction. Most magnet schools have a well-defined educational goal and provide a superior teaching environment to attract students (Carrison, 1981). These schools offer a choice not only in learning styles, but also in subject specialities designed to match students' talents and interests (Power, 1979). Although magnet schools have been in existence for years as preparation programs for gifted students (e.g., Bronx High School of Science in New York; High School of Performing Arts in New York), the emphasis since the late 1960s has been on creating alternative schools to attract students from outside the immediate neighborhood (Barr, 1982; Power, 1979). This emphasis has altered the entrance requirements for magnet schools from one of stiff competition based on auditions and academic ability to one of volunteerism based on racial quotas.

Vernon Smith, director of the Center for Options in Public Education at Indiana University, listed five ways in which alternative schools may vary from regular school programs: style of instruction, curriculum, clientele, resources, and administrative arrangement (Power, 1979).

Over the years, magnet schools have been developed around many programs. Some of these are science and math, individual guided instruction, environmental education, global education, bilingual or multicultural education, gifted and talented education, health care, marketing, college preparation, performing and visual arts, vocational and work study programs, business and management, human services, law and public administration, transportation, multiple careers for special education, back to basics, and microsociety programs where students design and operate their own democratic society (Clinchy, 1984; Doherty, 1982; Power, 1981). Magnet schools have also used business and industrial resources through special materials, instruction, and/or experiences. This involvement with industry has been called the adopt a school concept (Barr, 1982).

In the 1980s, magnet schools have received much criticism in areas related to changes in the organizational and political processes within the school system (Metz, 1984). Current issues include freedom of choice, educational reform, desegregation and forced busing, and involvement of community leaders (Carrison, 1981). Many of these issues revolve around the area of quality of programming. Are these programs really superior to and different from regular programs? Are the poor really being included? Does integration really occur? Why should there be special programs that are superior to regular programs? What does that mean for the educational programs of the students who are not involved in the magnet programs (Carrison, 1981)? All of these questions will continue to be debated as the success or failure of magnet schools continues to be evaluated in the future.

REFERENCES

Barr, R. D. (1982). Magnet schools: An attractive alternative. *Principal, 61*(3), 37–40.

Carrison, M. P. (1981). Do magnet schools really work. *Principal, 60*(3), 32–35.

Clinchy, E. (1984). Yes, but what about Irving Engelman? *Phi Delta Kappan, 65*(8), 542–545.

Doherty, D. (1982). Flint, Michigan: A case study in magnet schools and desegregation. *Principal, 61*(3), 41.

Metz, M. H. (1984). The life course of magnet schools organization and political influences. *Teachers College Record, 85*(3), 411–430.

Power, J. (1979). Magnet schools, are they the answer? *Today's Education, 68*(3), 68–70.

SUSANNE BLOUGH ABBOTT
Stamford, Connecticut

PRIVATE SCHOOLS AND SPECIAL EDUCATION

MAHLER, MARGARET SCHOENBERGER (1897–)

A native of Sopron, Hungary, Margaret Schoenberger Mahler studied medicine in Germany. She established the first psychoanalytic child guidance clinic in Vienna, then left Europe for the United States in 1938. In 1940 she began to reorganize the children's services for the New York State Psychiatric Institute and Columbia University. She has most recently been a clinical professor of psychiatry at the Albert Einstein College of Medicine in New York.

Mahler was one of the earliest pioneers in the recognition and diagnosis of childhood schizophrenia. She was an early advocate of treatment designs that would include the mother, the child, and the therapist. Her other interests include motility disturbances, particularly symptomatic tics, in both children and adults. She formulated concepts about the process of separation/individuation and how it contributes to identity formation. If this process is disturbed, Mahler believes, a symbiotic psychotic process can develop. Her writings on separation/individuation and infantile psychosis have been translated into several languages.

Mahler has received the Scroll of the New York Psychoanalytic Institute and the Frieda Fromm Reichman Award of the American Academy of Psychoanalysis. She established and developed the child analysis curriculum of the Philadelphia Psychoanalytic Institute.

REFERENCES

Mahler, M. S. (1979a). *The selected papers of Margaret Mahler, M.D.: Infantile psychosis and early contributions* (Vol. 1). New York: Aronson.

Mahler, M. S., (1979b). *The selected papers of Margaret Mahler, M.D.: Separation-individuation* (Vol. 2). New York: Aronson.

E. Valerie Hewitt
Texas A&M University

MAKE-A-PICTURE STORY (MAPS) TEST

The Make-a-Picture Story (MAPS) Test is a variation of other projective storytelling methods used by earlier tests such as the Thematic Apperception Test (TAT) and the Children's Apperception Test (CAT). In the MAPS Test (Shneidman, 1949, 1960), the child selects figures from an array of 67 cutouts in order to make a scene against some 22 background pictures. The child then tells a story for each scene. The MAPS Test was intended to provide greater elicitation of the child's innermost feelings, needs, and desires, enhancing the projective nature of the responding (tests such as the TAT and CAT use ready-made pictures). Since every child responds to different pictures (of their creation), good studies of the reliability and validity of the technique have been nearly impossible to conduct.

The structure of the MAPS Test makes it appealing to elementary and secondary children, however, and it is used periodically in the schools in evaluating seriously emotionally disturbed children (Koppitz, 1982). The MAPS Test stories are scored the same as the TAT stories, except that the number of figures selected by the child for inclusion in the story seems to be of particular significance. There are little data to support the use of the test as other than an adjunct to other clinical methods and in developing a general understanding of a child's general mood and internal drive state. Extensive training is needed to use the MAPS Test appropriately.

REFERENCES

Koppitz, E. M. (1982). Personality testing in the schools. In C. R. Reynolds & T. B. Gutkin (Eds.), *The handbook of school psychology*. New York: Wiley.

Shneidman, E. S. (1949). *The Make-a-Picture Story Test*. New York: Psychological Corporation.

Shneidman, E. S. (1960). The MAPS with children. In A. I. Rubin & M. R. Haworth (Eds.), *Projective techniques with children*. New York: Grune & Stratton.

Cecil R. Reynolds
Texas A&M University

MAKER, C. JUNE (1948–   )

C. June Maker earned her BS degree in education in 1970 from Western Kentucky University, followed by an MS in special education-gifted in 1971 from Southern Illinois University. From 1971 to 1974, she worked as a regional supervisor for the Department of Exceptional Children for the state of Illinois. In 1974 and 1975 she was an administrative intern at the Office of Gifted and Talented for the U.S. Department of Education. She then returned to school, attending the University of Virginia, when she earned her PhD in educational psychology in 1978.

Her major areas of work since that time have centered around curriculum and teaching strategies for the gifted (Maker, 1982), intellect among gifted individuals with handicapping conditions (Whitmore & Maker, 1985), and identifying giftedness in children with other handicaps (Maker, 1976). Maker has attempted to direct her professional activities around the centralizing, general goal of improving the education of gifted individuals, particularly those who may have gone unrecognized. Maker considers her greatest contributions thus far to be (1) emphasizing among educators recognizing and focusing on children's developmental strengths; (2) calling attention to chronically underserved but intellectually talented groups of exceptional children; (3) and disseminating ideas and research in a practical and useful way.

Maker has served the profession in a variety of capacities in addition to that of mentor and researcher. She is presently an associate professor of special education at the University of Arizona, where she coordinates a summer enrichment program for preschool and primary-aged gifted children. She has been an elected member of the board of directors of the National Association for Gifted Children since 1972 and has held various leadership positions in the Association for the Gifted since 1975. She has served as a consultant to programs for the gifted for more than 50 public schools.

REFERENCES

Maker, C. J. (1976). Searching for giftedness and talent in children with handicaps. *School Psychology Digest, 1,* 24–37.

Maker, C. J. (1982). *Curriculum development for the gifted*. Rockville, MD: Aspen.

Whitmore, J. R., & Maker, C. J. (1985). *Intellectually Gifted Persons with Specific Disabilities*. Rockville, MD: Aspen.

Cecil R. Reynolds
Texas A&M University

MAINSTREAMING

Mainstreaming is the popular term used for the legal doctrine of least restrictive environment (LRE). This term and its underlying concept is the product of the civil rights movement of the 1950s and 1960s, during which time courts judged as illegal segregation on the basis of race. Segregation was said to deny some children the opportunity of an education on equal terms with others. This principle was extended to include the handicapped in the cases of *PARC* v. *Commonwealth of Pennsylvania* (1971) and

Mills v. *Board of Education of the District of Columbia* (1972). Educational agencies were encouraged to place students in the most normalized settings possible and discouraged from placing them in stigmatizing or segregated ones. Similarly, the *Larry P.* v. *Riles* (1972) opinion legitimized special educators' concerns about the efficacy of self-contained classes for the educable mentally retarded in increasing the achievement of these types of students. Both the legal and professional arguments were in place for including in legislation the principle of not segregating handicapped students from normal peers except for compelling reasons. Several excellent reviews of this historical period can be found in Gilhool and Stutman (1978) and Weintraub, Abeson, Ballard, and LaVor (1976).

Although the terms mainstreaming and LRE share historical antecedents, they are not equivalent and careless usage of them often leads to confusion about the LRE provisions of PL 94-142. Although the literature has frequently cited this problem (Ballard & Zettel, 1977; Lowenbraun & Affleck, 1978), the terms are still substituted for one another.

LRE mandates (*Federal Register*, 1977, Sections 121a.550–121a.552) that, to the maximum extent appropriate, handicapped children be educated with nonhandicapped children. In cases of severe handicap, the educational agency may remove a student from regular class when instruction in that class with supplementary aids and services such as resource rooms cannot be achieved satisfactorily. To accommodate these students, a continuum of alternative placements must be available to the extent necessary to implement the individualized education program for each handicapped student. The alternative placements include regular classes, special classes, special schools, home instruction, and instruction in hospitals and institutions. Resource room or itinerant instruction, in which a teacher visits classes, is to be provided as a supplementary service to instruction in the regular classroom. Thus, if school personnel or others involved in evaluating and developing individualized educational prorams (IEPs) for students can justify a more restrictive placement than a regular classroom, that placement is acceptable with parental consent.

Mainstreaming has often been interpreted to mean that handicapped students must be instructed in regular classroom settings, which are considered to be the mainstream or the normal environment. According to the U.S. Department of Education (1984), 68% of handicapped students receive most of their education in regular classes while an additional 25% are enrolled in special classes located in buildings with regular education classrooms. Placement in regular classrooms or in school buildings within these classrooms is presumed to give handicapped students more opportunity to be in contact with nonhandicapped peers. Such exposure is thought to present behaviors for handicapped students to emulate. With successful contact, handicapped and nonhandicapped students are likely to achieve acceptance of one another.

The issue of what constitutes successful contact is perhaps the most problematic for mainstreaming. When handicapped students are placed in special classes, they are segregated from normal peers. From the mainstreaming perspective, this situation is unacceptable. Gottlieb (1981) reports that many school districts use the definition that handicapped students must spend at least 50% of their time in a regular class setting for mainstreaming to occur. This arbitrarily fixed amount of time is thought to constitute mainstreaming regardless of the quality of interaction between handicapped and nonhandicapped students or the educational program provided. Placing handicapped students in the same classroom as nonhandicapped students seem to result in desegregation. These students may occupy the same space but they may not be engaged in activities with one another. Gottlieb's (1981) summary of the research literature on educable mentally retarded students indicates their placement in regular classrooms per se does not result in improved achievement or social status.

However, handicapped students' social status has been improved when programs were planned to help incorporate them into the regular class setting (Yoshida, in press). This perspective is represented by two definitions. Kaufman, Gottlieb, Agard, and Kukic (1975) state,

> Mainstreaming refers to the temporal, instructional, and social integration of eligible exceptional children with normal peers. It is based on an ongoing individually determined educational needs assessment requiring classification of responsibility for coordinated planning and programming by regular and special education administrative, instructional, and support personnel. (pp. 40–41)

Similarly, Wang (1981) states that "the term mainstreaming is used here to mean an integration of regular and exceptional children in a school setting where all children share the same resources and opportunities for learning on a full time basis" (p. 196). These definitions clearly point out the responsibility of teachers and administrators to plan and provide an appropriate education program for handicapped students in the regular classroom.

Several excellent reviews of literature have discussed the historical and philosophical underpinnings of mainstreaming and the least restrictive environment and have analyzed research studies conducted on the mainstreaming of handicapped students into regular classroom settings (Leinhardt & Pallay, 1982; Madden & Slavin, 1983; Meisel, 1986; Semmel, Gottlieb & Robinson, 1979).

REFERENCES

Ballard, J., & Zettel, J. (1977). Public Law 94-142 and Section 504: What they say about rights and protections. *Exceptional Children, 44,* 177–184.

Gilhool, T. K., & Stutman, E. A. (1978). Integration of severely handicapped students. In L. G. Morra (Ed.), *Developing criteria for the evaluation of the least restrictive environment provision* (pp. 191–227). Washington, DC: U.S. Office of Education.

Gottlieb, J. (1981). Mainstreaming: Fulfilling the promise? *American Journal of Mental Deficiency, 86,* 115–126.

Kaufman, M. J., Gottlieb, J., Agard, J. A., & Kukic, M. (1975). Mainstreaming: Toward an explication of the construct. In E. L. Meyen, G. A. Vergason, & R. J. Whelan (Eds.), *Alternatives of teaching exceptional children* (pp. 35–54). *Denver: Love.*

Leinhardt, G., & Pallay, A. (1982). Restrictive educational settings: Exile or haven? *Review of Educational Research, 52,* 557–578.

Lowenbraun, S., & Affleck, J. Q. (1978). Least restrictive environment. In L. G. Morra (Ed.), *Developing criteria for the evaluation of the least restrictive environment provision.* (pp. 15–77). Washington, DC: U.S. Office of Education.

Madden, N. A., & Slavin, R. E. (1983). Mainstreaming students with mild handicaps: Academic and social outcomes. *Review of Educational Research, 53,* 519–569.

Meisals, J. (Ed.). (1986). *Mainstreaming: Past and future issues.* Hillsdale, NJ: Erlbaum.

Semmel, M. I., Gottlieb, J., & Robinson, N. M. (1979). Mainstreaming: Perspectives in educating handicapped children in the public school. In D. C. Berliner (Ed.), Review of Research in Education (Vol. 7, pp. 223–279). Washington, DC: American Educational Research Association.

U.S. Department of Education. (1984). *Sixth annual report to Congress on the implementation of Public Law 94-142: The Education for All Handicapped Children Act.* Washington, DC: Author.

U.S. Department of Health, Education, and Welfare. (1977). Education of handicapped children: Implementation of Part B of the Education of the Handicapped Act. *Federal Register, 42*(163), 42474–42518.

Wang, M. C. (1981). Mainstreaming exceptional children: Some instructional design and implementation considerations. *Elementary School Journal, 81,* 195–221.

Weintraub, F. J., Abeson, A., Ballard, J., & LaVor, M. L. (Eds.). (1976). *Public policy and the education of exceptional children.* Reston, VA: Council for Exceptional Children.

Yoshida, R. K. (1986). Setting goals for mainstream programs. In J. Meisel (Ed.), *Mainstreaming: Past and future issues.* (pp. 11–19). Hillsdale, NJ: Erlbaum.

ROLAND K. YOSHIDA
Fordham University

ATTITUDES TOWARD THE HANDICAPPED
EDUCATION FOR ALL HANDICAPPED CHILDREN ACT OF 1975
LEAST RESTRICTIVE ENVIRONMENT
PUBLIC LAW 94–142

MAINTENANCE

The concept of maintenance as it relates to academic school work is that a student can maintain performance with accuracy, even after task-training procedures are no longer employed. Maintenance (as suggested by Alberto & Troutman, 1982) is related to two other concepts: the concept of acquisition, which is antecedent to maintenance; and the concept of generalization, which is subsequent to maintenance.

Acquisition means that the student can do something that he or she could not do before. For example, a student is pretested on the ability to identify the 17 different ways to spell the schwa /ə/ vowel. The pretest result identifies a knowledge of only four ways to spell the schwa sound. After initial training (i.e., 30 minutes per day for 4 weeks using multisensory practice), the student knows 15 of the 17 ways. At this point the student has demonstrated by way of acquisition the initial mastery of a new skill. As the student is called on to use this newly acquired skill, and does so across time without recourse to the original task-training procedures, the student is evidencing a maintenance skill. The attainment of maintenance will probably involve the student in further appropriate practice work that can be identified as overlearning trials and distributed practice.

Overlearning trials are representative of repeated practice or overlearning work that is about half of what is was at the acquisition stage. For example, the initial learning of the 17 ways to spell the sound of schwa /ə/ required 30 minutes of appropriate practice per day for 4 weeks. We can for maintenance purposes, by way of overlearning trials, reduce the time to 15 minutes per day for 2 weeks. Distributed practice is work that is systematically distributed across a designated period of time, such as several weeks. Therefore, the concept of distributed practice as it relates to maintenance is concomitant with the practice suggested for the aspect of overlearning trials, which involve expanded practice relative to some task that the student is assigned to do.

The practical difference is that instead of designating 15 minutes of appropriate practice per day for 2 weeks, the same practice time can be scheduled two times per week for 5 weeks. A major advantage of distributed practice is that it complements long-term memory, and long-term memory is likewise complements the execution of generalization. Generalizing means that a student who was previously handicapped can now perform academic tasks with efficiency and do so independent of assistance. It also means that the student can randomly (or as needed) execute self-directed remedial practices. Thus the concept of generalization and its application represents independence for the learning-disabled (LD) student. When generalization occurs in reference to learning the 17 ways to spell the schwa sound /ə/, the student will spell words with the schwa sound with 96% accuracy across various and random settings that call for the spelling of words with that schwa sound.

What is to be stressed in reviewing the relationship of the continuum of acquisition, maintenance, and generalization is that learning evidenced through correct or corrected work will, under systematic analysis, reveal the interfacing presence of each of the previously mentioned three components. The sequential continuum of learning represented by the three concepts is identified on the following analytical outline developed by Thorpe (1981).

I. Introduction of task by the teacher
II. Acquisition of the skills that the student needs to perform the task.
  A. Instructional techniques
    1. General techniques
      a. Teach to a minimum acquisition level (usually 80% accuracy)
      b. Structure practice sessions
      c. Elicit maximum student response
      d. Use correction and reinforcement
      e. Present multiple activities of short duration
      f. Use distributive practices of short duration
      g. If there are multiple correct responses to a single stimulus, teach each response in isolation
      h. Teach stimuli or responses that have a similar topography in isolation
      i. Develop effective pacing of instructional material
      j. Use challenges to elicit student interest
      k. Use foolers to encourage self-reliance
    2. Group techniques
      a. Develop attention signals
      b. Use task signals to elicit unison responses
    3. Concept teaching
      a. Identify essential discriminations
      b. Present one unknown concept at a time
      c. Use examples and nonexamples
      d. Make examples representative of the concept population
      e. Move from concrete to abstract examples
      f. Irrelevant characteristics are noted and cast out
      g. Move from gross to fine differnces between examples and nonexamples
      h. Use descriptive language when possible
III. Maintenance
  A. Introduction
  B. Appropriate practice activities (usually about 50% of the practice time that was needed at acquisition)
    1. Instructional games
    2. Workbooks
    3. Worksheets
    4. Flashcards
  C. Systematic and regularly scheduled review sessions
  D. Applications of factual material
IV. Generalization
  A. Emphasize similar components
    1. Gather information about regular classroom procedures and expectations
    2. Simplify and fade the reinforcement procedures
      a. Student does not know when and/or for what he is being reinforced
      b. Emphasize behaviors that tend to naturally attract reinforcers
      c. Use some delay feedback procedures

    3. Work on foundational skills and their applications
      a. Emphasize prerequisites to regular classroom expectations
      b. Emphasize working at rate
      c. Emphasize the application of basis facts including using those applications creatively
    4. Work toward similar content procedures and goals
      a. Regular education materials should be introduced and used in conjunction with the special education materials
      b. Emphasize regular classroom social expectations
      c. Introduce extraneous stimuli
      d. Know the minimum level of performance in the regular classroom to which the child is going to be mainstreamed
    5. Progress from individual interactions toward group interactions
    6. Develop independent work skills
      a. Begin to fade teacher support
      b. Develop self-help techniques in the students (pp. 1–2)

Many students who have been and are associated with special education do not initially acquire and thus cannot employ generalization of study habits and skills commonly associated with the successful nonhandicapped student (Kavale, 1985). Thus, maintenance becomes essential. Special education students taught to employ respective concepts associated with maintenance can become independent scholars.

REFERENCES

Alberto, P. A., & Troutman, A. C. (1982). *Applied behavior analysis for teachers*. Columbus, OH: Merrill.

Kavale, K., & Forness, S. (1985). *The science of learning disabilities*. San Diego, CA: College Hill.

Thorpe, H. (1981). *A three-phase instructional strategy for teaching children who have learning difficulties*. Unpublished manuscript, University of Wisconsin, Oshkosh.

ROBERT T. NASH
*University of Wisconsin,
Oshkosh*

GENERALIZATION
MASTERY LEARNING AND SPECIAL EDUCATION

MALADAPTIVE BEHAVIOR

Maladaptive behavior consists of negative behaviors that interfere with normal adaptive functioning. Examples range from swearing and shyness to temper tantrums and theft. Most children exhibit maladaptive behavior at one time or another. Rubin and Balow (1978) indicated that in a study investigating 1586 children, about 60 to 65% were considered to exhibit maladaptive behavior by at least one teacher during a six-year period.

Maladaptive behavior can sometimes be so severe that the normal, everyday activities of children are greatly affected. Children are often placed in special education classes for the emotionally or behaviorally disturbed when there are deficits in classroom learning caused by persistent or unusual maladaptive behavior. In clinical settings, the *Diagnostic and Statistical Manual of Mental Disorders* (3rd edition, American Psychiatric Association, 1980) is used to classify children according to a broad range of behavior disorders, for example, eating disorders, enuresis, hyperactivity, and autism.

Children's maladaptive behavior is seen as quite different from that of adults and, among children, the frequency and severity of maladaptive behavior of boys is significantly greater than that of girls (Sattler, 1982). Quay (1979) distinguished four major patterns of maladaptive behavior in children: conduct disorders consisting of verbally and physically aggressive behavior and problems with interpersonal relationships; anxiety-withdrawal behaviors involving fears, shyness, and general withdrawal from friends, family, and teachers; immaturity, including those behaviors that are inappropriate for the child's age; and socialized-aggressive disorders, typical of delinquent gang behaviors such as stealing, staying out late, and being truant from school with a group of friends.

There are three general methods for assessing maladaptive behavior. Behavior checklists are available for teachers and parents to allow them to rate children's maladaptive behavior on a variety of dimensions. Examples are the Child Behavior Checklist (Achenbach & Edelbrock, 1979), which measures aspects of maladaptive behavior such as delinquency, aggression, cruelty, and hyperactivity, and the Behavior Problem Checklist (Quay & Peterson, 1979), which contains four subscales measuring conduct problems, personality problems, inadequacy, and immaturity. Maladaptive behavior may also be assessed through informal interviews with teachers, parents, peers, and the children being assessed. A final method for the assessment of maladaptive behavior is direct observation of children's behavior in different settings such as the classroom, playground, or home.

Intervention techniques for maladaptive behavior vary, usually according to the severity or frequency of the behavior. For example, behavior modification and structuring of the child's environment is often used by classroom teachers to decrease maladaptive behavior. In special education classrooms for emotionally and behaviorally disturbed children, teachers may implement extensive behavior management programs or cognitive behavior modification (Meichenbaum & Burland, 1979). For severe maladaptive behavior, intensive therapy and drugs may be used.

REFERENCES

Achenbach, T. M., & Edelbrock, C. S. (1979). The Child Behavior Profile II: Boys aged 12–16 and girls 6–11 and 12–16. *Journal of Consulting & Clinical Psychology, 47,* 223–233.

American Psychiatric Association. (1980). *Diagnostic and statistical manual of mental disorders* (3rd ed.). Washington, DC: Author.

Meichenbaum, D., & Burland, S. (1979). Cognitive behavior modification with children. *School Psychology Digest, 8,* 426–433.

Quay, H. C. (1979). Classification. In H. C. Quay & T. S. Werry (Eds.), *Psychopathological disorders of childhood* (2nd ed.). New York: Wiley.

Quay, H. C., & Peterson, D. R. (1979). *Behavior Problem Checklist.* Miami, FL: Authors.

Rubin, R. A., & Balow, B. (1978). Prevalence of teacher identified behavior problems: A longitudinal study. *Exceptional Children, 45,* 102–113.

Sattler, J. M. (1982). *Assessment of children's intelligence and special abilities* (2nd ed.). Boston: Allyn & Bacon.

PATTI L. HARRISON
University of Alabama

CONDUCT DISORDER
DISCIPLINE
INCORRIGIBILITY

MALE TURNER'S SYNDROME

See NOONAN'S SYNDROME.

MALNUTRITION

Malnutrition refers to poor nutritional status and the impairment to health that results from a deficiency, an imbalance, or an excess of one or more of the essential nutrients. Essential nutrients are the constituents or components of foods that must be supplied to the body in adequate amounts to provide energy, promote growth and development of body structures, and maintain and regulate body processes. The nutrients are grouped into six classes: carbohydrates, proteins, fats, minerals, vitamins, and water. For normal, healthy individuals, there is a beneficial range of intake for any nutrient. Continued nutrient intakes above or below the beneficial range are undesirable because this may lead to malnutrition.

Undernutrition refers to inadequate intakes of one or more nutrients and/or the energy from carbohydrates, proteins, or fats as measured in calories. The most extreme form of undernutrition is marasmus.

Overnutrition indicates that one or more nutrients have been consumed in excess, usually involving the intake of more calories (energy value) than the body needs.

The long-term consumption of more energy from food than is needed for the body's internal processes and the individual's daily activities results in obesity.

The impact of nutrient deficiencies on health status is as varied as the degrees of malnutrition. Christian and Greger (1985) chart the progression of consequences of restricted nutrient intake. If all of the essential nutrients are present in the diet but are consumed in less than adequate amounts, the health impact may not be severe. For example, limited growth may occur in children; adults may lose body weight and exhibit poor work capacity. With more limited food intakes, some or all of the essential nutrients may be missing. If this occurs, the body will stop growing, fail to maintain normal metabolic processes, and eventually die.

If the intakes of most nutrients are adequate but one specific nutrient is restricted over time, a nutritional deficiency disease is likely to result. For example, marginal or low levels of vitamin A intake over several years may lead to a lack of visual acuity at night (night blindness). Prolonged inadequate intake of vitamin A leads to a deficiency disease known as xerophthalmia. Although uncommon in developed countries, this disease causes blindness in millions of children around the world (Christian & Greger, 1985).

Nutritional anemia is an example of a deficiency disease resulting from inadequate intakes of the mineral nutrient iron. Anemia is a general term referring to low hemoglobin levels or the low concentration of red blood cells (Christian & Greger, 1985). This condition results in an inadequate supply of oxygen to body cells, causing a person to feel tired and listless.

Anemia can result from loss of blood, genetic conditions, or a complex of other mineral and vitamin deficiencies. However, the most common cause of anemia in the world, including the United States, is iron deficiency (Christian & Greger, 1985). The most vulnerable age groups are preschool children, adolescents, young women, and the elderly.

Cravioto (1981) addresses malnutrition as "a manmade disorder characteristic of the underprivileged segments of society" (p. 4). Usually children who are malnourished have experienced other deprivations such as lack of social and emotional support. As indicated by Cravioto, some intellectual impairment can be overcome with good nutrition and health care coupled with social stimulation. Ricciuti (1981) has indicated that the most effective intervention strategies are likely to be those that are concerned with (1) children's nutritional and health needs; (2) supporting and enhancing the family's capacity to provide developmentally facilitative child care and child-rearing environments; and (3) the provision of increased opportunities for formal and informal educational experiences in daycare centers and schools (p. 119).

Whitney and Sizer (1985) deal with world hunger as a controversial issue demanding the attention of developed nations as well as those of the Third World. Resources cited as urgent needs include education to raise the literacy level, sanitation to assure clean water, and land for food production. Also described are successful interventions such as teaching mothers how to feed their children appropriately with locally produced foods.

Overcoming the adverse effects of widespread malnutrition among the millions of children in developing countries is a challenge requiring more than foreign aid, nutrition education, or one-shot intervention programs (Whitney & Sizer, 1985). Undernutrition in the United States seems to follow poverty and poor overall socioeconomic circumstances. More effective nutrition education approaches and improved access to socioeconomic resources could alleviate some of the health problems associated with poor food practices in the United States.

REFERENCES

Christian, J. L., & Greger, J. L. (1985). *Nutrition for living*, Menlo Park, CA: Benjamin/Cummings.

Cravioto, J. (1981). Nutrition, stimulation, mental development and learning. *Nutrition Today. 16*, 4–14.

Ricciuti, H. N. (1981). Adverse environmental and nutritional influences on mental development: A perspective. *Journal of the American Dietetic Association, 79*, 115–119.

Whitney, E. N., & Sizer, F. S. (1985). *Nutrition: Concepts and controversies*. St. Paul, MN: West.

MaryAnn C. Farthing
*University of North Carolina,
Chapel Hill*

MEGAVITAMIN THERAPY
NUTRITIONAL DISORDERS

MANN, LESTER (1924–   )

Lester Mann is a researcher in special education, currently in the department of special education, Hunter College of the City University of New York, where he serves as department chair. Born January 24, 1924, Mann attended St. John's University in New York (1943–1947), obtaining his BS degree. He then went to New York University, obtaining an MA degree in clinical/experimental psychology in 1948. His PhD degree was obtained from the University of North Carolina in 1953 in clinical/experimental psychology. Mann worked in a number of applied settings after gaining his PhD. He was senior psychologist at the Camden Area Mental Health Clinic, Camden, New Jersey, in 1955–1956, director of child guidance, Montgomery County Public Schools, Norristown, Pennsylvania, from 1957 to 1959, and supervisor of special education classes in 1959–1960. He became director of special education in the Montgomery County Intermediate Unit, Norristown, Pennsylvania, in 1968, a position he held until 1977. During this period, Mann founded the

Journal of Special Education and established one of the few research libraries in special education in the public schools. After a year as adjunct professor at Northern Illinois University (1977–1978), Mann joined the Penn State University King of Prussia Graduate Center as assistant professor of special education, becoming professor of special education there in 1979.

Mann has been editor of the *Journal of Special Education* since 1966 and has been assistant editor of *Diagnostique* since 1980. He also has been consulting editor of *Academic Therapy* since 1967.

Mann is well known for several books, including *The Learning Disabled Adolescent* (1978), with Goodman and Wiederholt. He is also known for his series of reviews of special education, the most recent of which is *The Fourth Review of Special Education* (1980). His 1979 work, *On the Trail of Process*, has received widespread critical acclaim in the United States and Europe; it traces the history of research on cognitive processes and its relationship to special education.

REFERENCES

Mann, L. (1955). Child-physician, patient-therapist: Role and transference problems. *Psychoanalysis, 4*(2), 3–6.

Mann, L. (1971). Perceptual training revisited: The training of nothing at all. *Rehabilitation Literature, 32*, 322–327, 335.

Mann, L. (1979). *On the trail of process.* New York: Grune & Stratton.

Mann, L. (1980). *The fourth review of special education.* New York: Grune & Stratton.

Mann, L., Goodman, L., & Wiederholt, J. L. (Eds.). (1978). *The learning disabled adolescent.* Boston: Houghton Mifflin.

RAND B. EVANS
Texas A&M University

JOURNAL OF SPECIAL EDUCATION

MANUAL COMMUNICATION

Human language is conceived as being primarily produced and perceived in an oral-aural mode (speaking and hearing). Yet all kinds of information is provided by nonvocal means such as facial expressions, gazes (direction, quality), hand movements, gestures, and body movements. Nonvocal communication and manual communication can have an auxiliary function, completing the information provided through the vocal channel, or be the main and often sole channel of communication.

When accompanying vocal communication, nonverbal signs can have a semantic, syntactic, pragmatic, or dialogical function (Scherer, 1980). Examples for manual communication are (1) semantic function, pointing at a person or an object (possibly together with gaze in the same direction; (2) pragmatic function, a hand movement by the listener expressing his or her doubt about the speaker's assertion (possibly together with facial expression, shrugging of shoulders); and (3) dialogical function, the listener lifting his or her hand or forefinger to show an intention to break in (possibly at the same time expressing the same intention through gaze and other body movements).

This kind of manual communication forms a whole with other kinds of nonvocal communication and with vocal communication, whether hand movements occur simultaneously with or between segments of vocal production.

Manual communication independent of vocal communication can be found in various small communities (e.g., that of monks), yet its best known variety is the language of the deaf. The scientific study of sign languages started in the 1960s. It was initiated by the work of W. Stokoe (1960, 1978). Good introductions to these languages are Klima and Bellugi (1979) and Deuchar (1984). Like other natural languages, sign languages have their own phonology, grammar (morphology and syntax), and lexicon.

In the phonology of sign languages (first called cherology, the science of cheremes) each sign has the following features: tabula (location, the place where the sign is made); designator (the shape of the hand); signation (the movement made by the hand); and orientation (of the hand relative to the body). It has been shown that these features can in many ways be compared to the phonemes of spoken languages. Although the iconicity of part of the signs is undeniable, the above features have no meaning. On the other hand, they combine to constitute signs in the same way as phonemes of spoken languages, although they do so simultaneously instead of sequentially.

In the morphology, the categories (gender, number, tense) and the formal processes are not necessarily the same as in spoken languages (e.g., sign languages have compounds, but they have no derivation through affixation). Sign languages express a variety of distinctions such as deixis, reciprocity, number, distributional aspect, and temporal aspect (Klima & Bellugi, 1979).

In the syntax of sign languages, the order in which signs are produced is not arbitrary, i.e., sign languages have their own syntax. Sign languages also have their own lexicon. Lexical differences between sign languages or between a sign language and a spoken language are not fundamentally different from lexical differences between spoken languages (Stokoe et al., 1965).

Since sign languages have existed for centuries. They are acquired as a mother tongue or learned as a second language. Since most deaf people become bilingual (sign and spoken language) and sign languages are used as a medium of communication and interaction within communities, research on sign languages covers all of the domains of spoken languages: linguistics (synchrony and diachrony), psycho- and sociolinguistics, language teaching, etc.

Although hand movements are of primary importance in sign languages, it must be stressed that signers make intensive use of other nonvocal models of expression (gaze, facial expression, movements of head, shoulders, torso, etc.). There are also systems of manual communication, generally called signed languages (e.g., signed French as opposed to the French sign language), that consist of extensions and modifications of a sign language. Most characteristic are the addition of signs for morphological categories that do not exist in the original sign language and a syntax more akin to that of the national spoken language. Signers sometimes use finger spelling, in which one hand–configuration represents one letter in the written version of the spoken language. This is done for most proper names and concepts for which there is no sign or to express a meaning more accurately than a sign allows (e.g., if a sign for poodle does not exist, the sign for dog plus the letters P, O, O, D, L, E would be used).

REFERENCES

Deuchar, M. (1984). *British sign language*. London: Routledge & Kegan Paul.

Klima, E., & Bellugi, U. (1979). *The signs of language*. Cambridge, MA: Harvard University Press.

Scherer, K. (1980). The functions of non-verbal signs in conversation. In R. St. Clair & H. Giles (Eds.), *The social and psychological contexts of language*. Hillsdale, NJ: Erlbaum.

Stokoe, W. C. (1960). *Sign language structure: An outline of the visual communication systems of the american deaf* (Studies in Linguistics, Occasional Papers, 8; reprinted 1978). Silver Spring, MD: Linstok.

Stokoe, W. C., Casterline, D. C., Croneberg, C. G. (1965). *A dictionary of american sign language on linguistic principles*. Silver Spring, MD: Linstok.

S. DE VRIENDT
Vrije Universiteit Brussel,
Belgium

AMERICAN SIGN LANGUAGE
TOTAL COMMUNICATION

MAPS

See MAKE-A-PICTURE STORY TEST.

MARASMUS

Marasmus is a form of severe malnutrition. It results from overall food deprivation from birth or early infancy. It is most common in poverty-level infants who are not breast fed. However, marasmus can occur in children of any age whose diet is grossly inadequate, especially with respect to energy intake (Kreutler, 1980).

Marasmus results in wasting of tissues and severe growth retardation. Loss of muscle mass and subcutaneous fat gives children suffering from this condition a shrunken, old appearance in the face. The rest of the body has the skin and bones appearance typical of starvation. Poor nutritional status lowers resistance to disease, making these children particularly vulnerable to infections such as gastroenteritis, diarrhea, and tuberculosis.

As growth rate declines, both physical stunting and mental and emotional impairment occur if nutrient deprivation continues. Marked retardation in mental development may persist in marasmic children even after physical and biochemical rehabilitation (Cravioto, 1981).

According to Kreutler (1980), when marasmus is combined with protein-energy malnutrition and kwashiorkor resulting from protein deficiency, the incidence of these severe forms of malnutrition is estimated to be from 400 to 500 million. The majority of affected persons are found in developing countries where warfare, civil strife, and drought have produced widespread famine.

Among more affluent societies, marasmic children are usually found in extremely poor socioeconomic and emotionally deprived environments (Williams, 1985). Parents may be ignorant of food values or the importance of providing appropriate food to young infants and children. Parental neglect may also result from complex emotional or mental problems.

Among adults in developed countries, marasmus has occasionally been associated with alcoholism; it is sometimes the result of isolation or hospitalization in elderly people. Self-imposed starvation may also result from an obsession with thinness and a distorted body image as seen in anorexia nervosa (Williams, 1985).

REFERENCES

Cravioto, J. (1981). Nutrition, stimulation, mental development and learning. *Nutrition Today, 16*(5), 4–14.

Kreutler, P. A. (1980). *Nutrition in perspective*. Englewood Cliffs, NJ: Prentice-Hall.

Williams, S. R. (1985). *Nutrition and diet therapy* (5th ed.). St. Louis: Times Mirror/Mosby.

MARYANN C. FARTHING
University of North Carolina,
Chapel Hill

ANOREXIA NERVOSA
EATING DISORDER
MALNUTRITION
NUTRITIONAL DISORDERS
PICA

MARCH OF DIMES

The March of Dimes Foundation was founded by President Franklin D. Roosevelt in 1938 as the National Foundation for Infantile Paralysis to combat the nation's polio epidemic. Basil O'Conner, the President's former law partner, was asked to lead the organization (March of Dimes, 1985). Roosevelt, a victim of polio, recovered partial use of his legs by swimming in the warm spring waters in Georgia and exercising his leg muscles, thereby becoming a national model for polio patients. Later, he purchased the facility at Warm Springs and established the Warm Springs Foundations. Large numbers of individuals with this crippling disease came to the Warm Springs Foundation, making it necessary to build houses and roads and to provide doctors and therapists to develop various exercise programs. Indigent people who came to swim and exercise were welcomed as guests by the President, requiring the foundation to raise additional money. Roosevelt had great compassion for polio patients, many of whom were victims of the nation's economic problems and who could not receive the treatments from which he had so greatly benefited. Moreover, he felt that every city should have hospitals with iron lungs, hot-pack equipment, swimming pools, walking ramps, and lightweight braces. If everyone, Roosevelt reasoned, would give just a little bit, even a dime, a lot of money would be raised for the noble cause. Actor Eddie Cantor named the organization after suggesting that people send their dimes directly to the President at the White House (Sterling, Ehrenberg, & National Foundation for Infantile Paralysis, 1955).

In 1953 Dr. Jonas Salk, a foundation grantee, developed a killed virus vaccine; it was declared in 1955 to be safe, potent, and effective. Before the discovery and licensing of the Sabine oral vaccine in 1962, the National Foundation, assured of its victory over polio, redirected its efforts from treatment to rehabilitation, the prevention of birth defects, and the overall improvement of the outcome of pregnancy. It changed its name to the National Foundation–March of Dimes. The present name, March of Dimes–Birth Defects Foundation, was adopted in 1979 (March of Dimes, 1985). The March of Dimes–Birth Defects Foundation remains the largest voluntary association in America in membership and annual budget. (Sills, 1980). It provides research, professional education, volunteer services, and public health education.

REFERENCES

March of Dimes Birth Defects Foundation. (1985). *All about the March of Dimes.* New York: Author.

Sills, S. T. (1980). *The volunteer: Means and ends in a national organization.* New York: Arno.

Sterling, D., Sterling, P., Ehrenberg, M., & National Foundation for Infantile Paralysis. (1955). *Polio pioneers: The story of the fight against polio.* New York: Doubleday.

FRANCIS T. HARRINGTON
Radford University

MARLAND REPORT

The Marland Report was a response to a mandate from Congress that Commissioner of Education S. P. Marland, Jr., conduct a study to:

1. Determine the extent to which special educational assistance programs are necessary or useful to meet the needs of gifted and talented children.

2. Show which federal education assistance programs are being used to meet the needs of gifted and talented children.

3. Evaluate how existing federal educational assistance programs can more effectively be used to meet these needs.

4. Recommend new programs, if any, needed to meet these needs. (Marland, 1972, VIII).

The report identified the lack of services for gifted and talented youths as well as widespread misunderstandings about this population. Among the major findings were:

1. A conservative estimate of the gifted and talented population ranges between 1.5 and 2.5 million children.

2. Large and significant subpopulations (e.g., minorities and the disadvantaged) are not receiving services and only a small percentage of the gifted and talented population are receiving services.

3. Even where a legal administrative basis exists for providing services, funding priorities, crisis concerns, and a lack of personnel cause programs for the gifted to be impractical.

4. Identification of the gifted is hampered by apathy and even hostility among teachers, administrators, guidance counselors, and psychologists.

5. States and local communities look to the federal government for leadership in the area of education, with or without massive funding.

6. The federal role in delivery of services to the gifted and talented virtually is nonexistent.

These findings, as well as the others, prompted action by the U.S. Office of Education to eliminate the widespread neglect of gifted and talented children. Activities to be initiated included:

1. Identifying a staff member in each of the regional offices of education for gifted and talented education.

2. Creating an Office for the Gifted and Talented under the jurisdiction of the Bureau of Education for the Handicapped.

3. Having the deputy commissioner for school systems was complete a planning report for the commissioner on implementing a federal role in the education of the gifted and talented children by February 1, 1972.

4. Supporting two summer leadership training institutes in 1972 and additional programs in major research and development institutes to work on learning problems and opportunities among minority groups.

5. Using Title V, ESEA, and other authorizations to strengthen state education agencies' capabilities for gifted and talented education.

This report served to focus attention on gifted and talented children. The report's recommendations were important factors in developing state and national programs for the gifted and talented. Moreover, the report was of major significance in involving the federal government in the education of gifted and talented students.

REFERENCE

Marland, S. P., Jr. (1972). *Education of the gifted and talented. Report of the Congress of the United States by the U.S. Commissioner of Education.* Washington, DC: U.S. Government Printing Office.

PHILIP E. LYON
College of St. Rose

MARSHALL v. GEORGIA

Marshall v. *Georgia*, also known as *Georgia State Conference of Branches of NAACP* v. *Georgia*, was a class-action suit filed on behalf of black school-age children in the state of Georgia alleging discrimination in two forms: (1) overrepresentation of black students in the lower, and underrepresentation in the higher, achievement/ability groups within regular education resulting in separation of black and white students; and (2) discrimination in the evaluation and placement of black students resulting in overrepresentation in special education programs for the educable mentally retarded. Both claims were rejected by the trial court in a decision upheld by the Eleventh Circuit Court of Appeals.

Marshall was filed in June 1982 by the Georgia State Conference of NAACP and the Liberty County NAACP on behalf of 45 schoolchildren who were or who might in the future be placed in lower ability tracks within regular education or in special education programs for the educable mentally retarded. Defendants in the case were the state of Georgia and eight local school districts that were generally sparsely populated rural districts with limited economic resources. The trial in *Marshall* was held before Judge V. Avant Edenfield, District Court judge for the Southern District of Georgia, Savannah Division, from October 31 through December 20, 1983.

The allegations of discrimination for both aspects of the case were based on alleged violations in Thirteenth and Fourteenth Amendment rights, Title VI of the Civil Rights Act of 1964, and the Equal Education Opportunity Act. In addition to these provisions, the special education aspect of the case also was filed on the basis of Section 504 of the Rehabilitation Act of 1973. For reasons that are not entirely clear, the plaintiffs' attorneys did not cite the Education for All Handicapped Children Act of 1975 (EHA) as part of their legal basis, perhaps because of the issue of attorneys fees, which, at the time of the trial, were provided under Section 504 but not under EHA. In any event, failure to file under EHA became significant.

The allegations of discrimination against black students who were significantly overrepresented in lower ability/achievement groups, and underrepresented in higher ability/achievement groups, were based on various statistical evidence and expert witness testimony claiming harm to black students as a result of regular education tracking practices. The plaintiffs' expert witness, Martin Shapiro of Emory University, presented data, undisputed by the plaintiffs, that the disproportionality was beyond statistical chance. Another expert witness for the plaintiffs, Robert Calfee, an educational psychologist from Stanford University, argued that the discrepancies in achievement between black and white students were caused, at least in part, by ability/achievement grouping practices. The plaintiffs' attorneys further argued that the ability/achievement grouping disproportionality is related to past discrimination as well as to impermissible practices leading to separation of black and white students.

The plaintiffs argued for imposition of some random assignment plan in which heterogeneous groups of black and white students would be constituted through any method that resulted in classroom proportions reflecting general population percentages. The plaintiffs' expert witness Calfee acknowledged that heterogeneous grouping might harm gifted students and that some grouping by ability or achievement within randomly constituted classrooms would still be necessary.

Curiously, the plaintiffs did not dispute overrepresentation of black students in other educational programs designed for remedial or compensatory purposes. Specifically, black students were known to be significantly overrepresented in the federally funded Chapter 1 program and a state-funded compensatory education program. This overrepresentation, similar in pattern and degree to disproportionality in regular education groups, was apparently acceptable to the plaintiffs, an obvious inconsistency in their case.

The defendants' arguments justifying use of ability/achievement grouping were accepted by the court. The court noted with favor that a combination of methods was used to constitute the groups, that membership in the groups was based on actual performance in the basal curriculum, and that instruction was then based on students' actual performance levels; assignment to ability/achievement groups was flexible with assignments reconsidered periodically and changes made based on performance of students. Defendant districts were able to present data indicating that grouping varied by subject matter and that significant numbers of student assignments were changed based on periodic reviews. The court cited the defendants' expert witness Barbara Learner as arguing persuasively for the use of practices that provide instruction at the student's level. Learner's interpretation of the effective schools literature, and her warning that court intrusion in local district practices in the case of ability/achievement grouping would be a "tragic mistake," were also cited favorably by Edenfield.

The court rejected all claims of the plaintiffs concerning discrimination in the development of ability/achievement groups. The court noted that the remedial instruction provided through the ability/achievement grouping was a positive feature of these practices and the evidence presented indicated these practices benefited, not harmed, black children. The court concluded this aspect of the case with the observation that, "the fact is that students have different levels of ability which must be accommodated."

The special education aspect of the Marshall case involves circumstances similar to those in previous placement bias litigation trials, *Larry P.* v. *Riles* and *PASE* v. *Hannon*. The fundamental issue was overrepresentation of black students in the classification of educable mental retardation (EMR). These students were placed, most often, in self-contained EMR special classes. The plaintiffs also alleged, unlike in previous cases, that black students were suffering discrimination not just because of overrepresentation in EMR, but also because of underrepresentation in programs for the learning-disabled (LD). The plaintiffs' expert witness, Martin Shapiro, presented extensive analyses of data indicating that the disproportionality of black students in EMR and LD programs could not be attributed to statistical chance. Shapiro's finding was about the only result on which the plaintiffs and defendants agreed.

The plaintiffs and the defendants had explanations, sharply differing, for the overrepresentation. The defendants' explanation for the overrepresentation was the association of poverty with mental retardation, a finding reported throughout the twentieth century for various groups in western Europe and North America (Reschly, 1986). In contrast, the plaintiffs attributed the overrepresentation to discrimination in the development and implementation of special education referral, classification, and placement procedures. Unlike previous litigation in this area, the plaintiffs did not focus on alleged biases in intelligence tests per se, but emphasized a variety of other assessment procedures and regulations that they claimed were carried out improperly by state and local defendants.

The alleged improper and inappropriate practices established and implemented by state and local defendants were assumed by the plaintiffs to differentially harm black students. Significantly, the plaintiffs presented no evidence that any of these practices were found more frequently with black than white students, or that revisions in requirements advocated by the plaintiffs would have any differential impact on white or black students. The trial and appellant court verdicts were based at least in part on the fact that the plaintiffs failed to show any evidence of differential impact. In other words, even if the court agreed that the plaintiffs' remedies constituted more appropriate practices, these revised practices may have had little or nothing to do with overrepresentation.

The plaintiffs alleged five areas of improper or inappropriate practices carried out by state and local defendants. The first had to do with the IQ guidelines stated in Georgia regulations and the interpretation and application by local defendants. The Georgia IQ guidelines suggested that significantly subaverage general intellectual functioning had to be two or more standard deviations below the mean. However, some degree of flexibility was common with local defendants and approved by state department officials. The plaintiffs argued for a rigid cutoff score of 70, suggesting that any student with an IQ score of 70 or above was misclassified. They presented several cases in which the full-scale IQ scores of black students in EMR programs was 70 or slightly above. The second issue had to do with the assessment of adaptive behavior, particularly whether a standardized scale must be used in assessing adaptive behavior. The plaintiffs argued for the mandatory use of a standardized scale with a specific, stringent cutoff score.

The third issue also dealt with adaptive behavior, specifically the setting in which adaptive behavior had to be assessed in order to meet state and professional association guidelines. The plaintiffs argued that adaptive behavior assessment should be focused, if not exclusively, at least primarily, on out-of-school adaptive behavior. Further, the plaintiffs' expert witness suggested that for a student to have an adaptive behavior deficit, he or she needed to be performing poorly in all environments. Finally, the plaintiffs argued that various local districts were failing to document properly compliance with all aspects of due process regulations and that there were instances in which triennial reevaluations were not conducted in a timely fashion. As noted earlier, the plaintiffs failed to show that any of the five areas of improper or inappropriate practices occurred more frequently with black EMR students. Thus discrimination was impossible to infer in the view of the court.

The defendants' case was based on explaining overrepresentation owing to the effects of poverty and the use of various professional standards and guidelines. In particular, the American Association on Mental Deficiency (AAMD; Grossman, 1983) manual, *Classification in Mental Retardation*, as well as the National Academcy of Sciences report on special educational overrepresentation (Heller, Holtzman, & Messick, 1982) were relied on heavily by the defendants' expert witnesses, Daniel J. Reschly of Iowa State University and Richard Kicklighter of the Georgia State Department of Education. The defendants' expert witnesses argued that standards for professional practices always have supported viewing results of measures of general intelligence as a range rather than a specific point, and that rigid, inflexible application of numerical guidelines were inappropriate in view of imperfect measurement processes. Specific paragraphs from the AAMD manual were cited as further justification for a flexible IQ guideline.

The question of adaptive behavior assessment was addressed extensively by the defendants' expert witnesses, who noted that none of the available adaptive behavior scales were based on a national standardization sample. Furthermore, adaptive behavior assessment was known to be less precise than intellectual assessment and authoritative sources such as the AAMD classification manual suggested the application of clinical judgment in estimations of adaptive behavior. Clearly, the AAMD manual did not support the application of specific, rigidly applied cutoff scores.

A crucial issue in the case, cited in both the trial and appellate court decisions, was the most appropriate setting for assessing adaptive behavior for school-age children. The plaintiffs argued for exclusive reliance on out-of-school adaptive behavior. The defendants' experts, particularly Reschly, suggested consideration of both settings, but argued that performance in the school setting is probably more important for purposes of classification of children for the EMR program, which is, of course, an educational program. Although the court did not attempt extensive analysis of the setting issue, both the trial and appellate courts cited Reschly's recommendation for reliance on in-school adaptive behavior information for determining deficits in adaptive behavior.

Finally, the state and local defendants had little choice but to acknowledge that violations in proper documentation of due process, performing reevaluations within 3 years for all students, and numerous other regulatory requirements. Local defendants generally cited limitations in resources and the availability of trained personnel as the reasons for these violations. They also noted, with considerable justification, that the violations were nearly always technical, but not substantive.

The court's analysis of the issues noted the plaintiffs' suggested remedies: (1) state and local defendants were to develop and implement rigid cutoff scores for IQ and adaptive behavior; (2) prereferral interventions were to be required prior to referral of students for possible special education classification and placement; (3) adaptive behavior was to be assessed outside of school with an appropriate standardized inventory; (4) the state was to monitor ethnic and racial data by district and cite districts for any misclassifications identified during monitoring activities; (5) all black children in EMR programs in which black children were overrepresented (which would have included nearly every district in the state of Georgia) were to be reevaluated within a short time span using the new state regulations as specified; (6) state and local education agencies were to provide transition programs for any students found to be ineligible under the new rules; and (7) the court was to impose a monitor, independent of the defendants, to ensure compliance with the court-imposed remedies and to report on a timely basis to the court concerning implementation of those remedies.

The court rejected all of plaintiffs' claims concerning discrimination. In addition, all of the plaintiffs' remedies were rejected, including those related to assessment of adaptive behavior, classification criteria for general intellectual functioning and adaptive behavior, mandatory prereferral strategies, and mandatory reevaluation of all black children. The court's basis for rejecting these claims cited various professional association guidelines, particularly the AAMD. The court explicitly endorsed the AAMD: "the court believes the practices as defined and endorsed by the AAMD evidence best professional practices in this regard" (p. 146).

The trial court, as well as the appellate court, was highly critical of the plaintiffs because they failed to provide specific evidence on differential treatment of white and black students. Clearly, overrepresentation as such was not sufficient. The trial court stated pointedly, "The court is somewhat perplexed by plaintiffs' claims in this area. Perhaps the confusion is best explained by failure of proof on the part of plaintiffs." (p. 103). Both trial and the appellate court argued that evidence of discrimination against black students must be presented in order to show that various allegations and remedies presented by the plaintiffs had merit. In the absence of specific evidence, the claims could only be regarded as without proof or foundation.

The trial court did find state and local defendants liable for regulatory violations, but noted that no discrimination was found or implied concerning these findings. State defendants were then ordered to develop a remedial plan whereby local district compliance with various state and federal regulations could be ensured in the future.

The Marshall trial and appeals court decisions established certain clear-cut guidelines concerning allegations of discrimination as well as the development and implementation of programs for the educable mentally retarded. Overrepresentation as such clearly was insufficient to prove discrimination. Overrepresentation had to be accompanied by evidence of discrimination, which both courts suggested needed to be based on comparisons of black and white EMR students. Furthermore, professional association guidelines such as those of the AAMD (Grossman, 1983), and authoritative sources such as the National Academy of Sciences report (Heller, Holtzman, & Messick, 1983), were accorded considerable deference by the courts.

Marshall may well be a landmark decision similar to *Larry P.* in potential impact on classification and placement of EMR students. Both decisions have been based on lengthy trials and upheld by appeals courts. However, the *Marshall* and *Larry P.* courts reached very different conclusions on similar issues. Future developments are therefore impossible to anticipate.

REFERENCES

Grossman, H. J. (Ed.). (1983). *Classification in mental retardation.* Washington, DC: American Association on Mental Deficiency.

Heller, K., Holtzman, W., & Messick, S. (Eds.). (1982). *Placing children in special education: A strategy for equity.* Washington, DC: National Academy.

Reschly, D. J. (1986). Economic and cultural factors in childhood exceptionality. In R. T. Brown & C. R. Reynolds (Eds.), *Psychological perspectives on childhood exceptionality: A handbook* (pp. 423–466). New York: Wiley-Interscience.

DANIEL J. RESCHLY
Iowa State University

**DIANA *v.* STATE BOARD OF EDUCATION
LARRY P.
NONDISCRIMINATORY ASSESSMENT
RACIAL DISCRIMINATION IN SPECIAL EDUCATION**

MASTERY LEARNING AND SPECIAL EDUCATION

"Mastery learning is an optimistic theory about teaching and learning that asserts that any teacher can help virtually all students to learn excellently, swiftly and self confidently" (Bloom cited in Block, 1984, p. 68). Bloom, Hastings and Medaus (1971) believe that both exceptional and nonexceptional learners can benefit from instruction if it is systematic, if the task is broken down into small steps, if goals are clearly stated, students are given sufficient time to achieve mastery, and there is some criterion of what constitutes mastery. From a mastery learning perspective, management of learning requires three basic stages (Block, 1984). The first is the orientation stage, where the teacher clearly states what outcomes are expected from the learner. Grading policy and the standards for mastery are explained, and the learner is oriented to the strategies he or she will be using to master the material.

The second teaching stage is where the instructor uses various approaches for teaching the content. Initially, the whole class is taught the material in a sequence and formatively tested. Subsequently, the students are grouped according to their levels of learning. Corrective procedures are used for those who have not attained a predetermined level and enrichment is provided for those who have. In the third stage, grading stage, which occurs after correctives and enrichment, each student is individually evaluated for mastery. A's are given to students who have reached a predetermined level and I's are awarded to students who score below this standard. Steps are taken to help students replace their I's with A's.

Bloom and his followers (Block & Anderson, 1975) assert that native intelligence matters in learning when instruction is the same for all students. But when instruction is matched to the learners' present level functioning, and other provisions for individualization are made, all students can learn what they are taught. Teachers using mastery learning procedures should find close to 80% of their students attain mastery levels that were previously attained by 20% (Guskey, 1981).

Mastery learning procedures are used successfully in special education programs throughout the United States (Glass, Christiansen, & Christiansen, 1982; Grossman, 1985; Mandell & Gold, 1984; Morsink, 1984). Implicit in PL 94-142 is the mandate that teachers plan educational programs according to the principles of mastery learning. The law requires that each student's individualized educational plan (IEP) includes current levels of performance, annual goals, short-term objectives, evaluation procedures, criteria, and schedules for measuring objectives. Teachers, when preparing IEPs, break the course content into small units, sequence the units hierarchically, and build their objectives around these units. Traditionally, regular classroom instruction has been directed to the group of learners as a whole. Students with mild to moderate learning handicaps are often unable to learn at the same pace as the other students. Exceptional education provides programs for handicapped learners so they can achieve success in school. One of the primary methods used in special education programs to reach that goal is mastery learning, or modification of it.

Some of the most popular commercial materials used in special education classes are based on the principles of mastery learning. DISTAR (Englemann & Bruner, 1969), a reading program for elementary-aged students, breaks reading down into its smallest units, sequences those units in hierarchical order, and teaches each unit to mastery. There are programs that teach thinking skills (Black & Black, 1984) as well as programs that teach social skills (Goldstein, Sprafkin, Gershaw and Klein, 1980) that have been developed with mastery learning in mind. The advantages of mastery learning are consistent with the goals of special education programming. More students accomplish designated objectives and earn higher grades. This, in turn, leads to a positive effect on student self-concept and a heightened interest in subjects where success is achieved (Block & Anderson, 1975).

REFERENCES

Black, S., & Black, H. (1984). *Building thinking skills*. Pacific Grove, CA: Midwest.

Block, J. H. (1984). Making school learning activities more play like: Slow and mastery learning. *Elementary School Journal, 85*(1), 65–75.

Block, J. H. & Anderson, L. (1975). *Mastery learning in classroom instruction*. New York: Macmillan.

Bloom, B. S., Hastings, J., & Medaus, G. (1971). *Handbook on formative and summative evaluation of student learning*. New York: McGraw-Hill.

Englemann, S., & Bruner, E. C. (1969). *DISTAR reading I and II*. Chicago: Science Research.

Glass, R. M., Christiansen, J., & Christiansen, J. L. (1982). *Teaching exceptional students in the regular classroom*. Boston: Little, Brown.

Goldstein, A. P., Sprafkin, R. P., Gershaw, N. J., & Klein, P. (1980). *Skill streaming the adolescent: A structured learning approach to teaching prosocial skills*. Champaign, IL: Research Press.

Grossman, A. S. (1985, January). Mastery learning and peer tutoring in a special program. *Mathematics Teacher*, 24–27.

Guskey, L. (1981). Individualizing instruction in the mainstream classroom: A mastery learning approach. In C. V. Morsink (Ed.), *Teaching special needs students in regular classrooms*. Boston: Little, Brown.

Mandell, C. J., & Gold, V. (1984). *Teaching handicapped students*. New York: West.

Morsink, C. V. (1984). *Teaching special needs students in regular classrooms*. Boston: Little, Brown.

NANCY J. KAUFMAN
University of Wisconsin, Stevens Point

**COMPETENCY EDUCATION
DATA-BASED INSTRUCTION
TEACHING STRATEGIES**

MASTURBATION, COMPULSIVE

Masturbation, or genital stimulation and gratification by oneself, is a common form of sexual behavior that occurs in almost all males and in the majority of females (Taylor, 1970). Young children may handle their genitals, but purposeful masturbation often begins when sexual drives become intense during and after puberty.

Normal adolescence is characterized by a series of developmental phases, which include accommodating the sex drive. These phases are often "long, delayed, and distorted toward passivity" among mentally retarded children (Bernstein, 1985). Such children may engage in masturbation to relieve sexual tension, or simply because it feels good. Gordon (1973) suggested that masturbation is a normal sexual expression no matter how frequently or at what age it occurs, and that all sexual behavior involving the genitals should occur only in private. Motivation for frequent public masturbation, which might be called compulsive masturbation, may be boredom or the lack of anything else interesting to do. In other cases, it may be an attention-getting device.

A recommended approach to the situation is to communicate to the masturbating person that the behavior is not socially acceptable in public. Such an approach gives the person exhibiting the behavior the option to continue in private, and attention-getting behavior is not reinforced. If boredom is the basic problem, it may be possible to substitute some other more socially acceptable activity.

REFERENCES

Bernstein, N. R. (1985). Sexuality in mentally retarded adolescents. *Medical Aspects of Human Sexuality 19*, 50–61.

Gordon, S. (1973). A response to Warren Johnson (on sex education of the retarded). In F. DeLaCruz & G. D. LaBeck (Eds.), *Human sexuality and the mentally retarded*. New York: Brunner/Mazel.

Taylor, D. L. (1970). *Human sexual development: Perspectives in sex education*. Philadelphia: Davis.

P. ALLEN GRAY, JR.
University of North Carolina, Wilmington

**SELF-STIMULATION
SOCIAL SKILLS**

MATERNAL SERUM ALPHA-FETOPROTEIN (AFP) SCREENING

Maternal Serum Alpha-Fetoprotein Screening is a diagnostic blood test performed on pregnant women between the fourteenth and eighteenth weeks of gestation. It determines the presence of alpha-fetoprotein (AFP), a normal protein produced by the fetus that enters the maternal circulatory system early in pregnancy (Jensen & Bobak, 1985).

Elevated levels of maternal AFP have been associated with fetal neural tube defects, the most frequently encountered central nervous system malformations. These defects include anencephaly, encephalocele, and spina bifida (Harrison, Golbus, & Filly, 1984). Anencephaly is the failure of the cerebrum and cerebellum to develop. Encephalocele is the protrusion of the brain through a congenital gap in the skull. Spina bifida is the failure of the lower portion of the spinal column to close, allowing spinal membrane to protrude (Thomas, 1985). Elevated levels indicate the need for the further tests of sonography and amniocentesis to confirm the defect.

REFERENCES

Harrison, M. R., Golbus, M. S., & Filly, R. A. (1984). *The unborn patient, prenatal diagnosis and treatment*. Orlando, FL: Grune & Stratton.

Jensen, M. D., & Bobak, I. M. (1985). *Maternity and gynecologic care, the nurse and the family* (3rd ed.). St. Louis: Mosby.

Thomas, C. L. (Ed.). (1985). *Taber's cyclopedic medical Dictionary* (15th ed.). Philadelphia: Davis.

ELIZABETH R. BAUERSCHMIDT
University of North Carolina, Wilmington

**AMNIOCENTESIS
GENETIC COUNSELING
SPINA BIFIDA**

MATHEMATICS, LEARNING DISABILITIES IN

Learning disabilities in mathematics manifest themselves in at least three different groupings. One of these groups is characterized by an overall deficiency in mathematics such that progress is slow and labored, but steady. A second group displays deficiencies in specific mathematics topics such as fractions, or within a subtopic such as division. A third group is characterized by comprehensive disorders of thinking, reasoning, and problem solving such that performance in both concepts and skills in mathematics is bizarre, distorted, and illogical.

Any discussion of learning disabilities in mathematics must be undertaken with the understanding that the focus is on learning problems and not just classroom failure. Classroom failure may be the result of inappropriate placement; the selection of courses of study that are too difficult; a mismatch between learner needs and teacher practices; or motivational, attitudinal, or behavioral problems that influence performance. Learning disabilities should be attributed to characteristics that are intrinsic to the individual and be of such a quality that progress in ordinary settings is discrepant and below the rate at which nonlearning disabled students progress. These intrinsic characteristics may influence performance in mathematics directly or indirectly. An example of indirect influence would exist with a child who has a reading disability that interferes with mathematics performance. It is not the mathematics per se that is the primary problem. It is just that the child cannot efficiently and effectively interpret the mathematics in order to complete written assignments such as tests, daily work, and homework.

It is important to distinguish between the terms learning and achievement when describing learning disabilities in mathematics. Achievement is that condition in which a child is assessed or taught at a given point in time. That is, the test is given, the number correct are tallied, and some form of score or rank (e.g., grade equivalent) is assigned; or, the lesson is taught, the child either understands or fails to understand, and the teacher proceeds to a new lesson.

Learning, by contrast, is that condition in which a baseline is obtained and the amount of time and number of repetitions or variations in instructional practices that are needed to assist the child to attain the expected standard are determined. The more important consideration is a reduction in the amount of time or repetitions it takes a child to perform to criterion. This may be realized by modifying the instructional procedures or by training the child to be a more efficient learner. The latter may be accomplished by strategy training, metacognitive approaches, or by instruction and practice in learning to learn.

Mathematics is a comprehensive subject in which emphasis must be given to the development of concepts and principles, accuracy and ease in computation, and the use of concepts and principles and computational proficiency to solve problems and make decisions. The great majority of research and programming in mathematics learning disabilities has focused on arithmetical computation. Within this area, the emphasis has been on whole numbers, where efforts have been further subordinated to addition and subtraction. In spite of the fact that teachers have indicated that division is the primary topic with which learning-disabled students have difficulty (McLeod & Armstrong, 1982), there is a paucity of research and instructional development on this topic. By contrast, the literature is replete with work in addition and subtraction (Thorton & Toohey, 1985). The stress on addition and subtraction is understandable when one considers that these are the two computational skills with which children have their initial difficulties. It has yet to be determined whether the early emergence of learning disabilities in addition and subtraction is due to learner deficiencies in concepts and principles, a more cognitive view, or learner deficiencies in attentional factors or memory capabilities, a more behavioral view. Nor has it been fully determined that children who are successful in their introduction to addition and subtraction are the same learning-disabled children who are successful with multiplication and division.

Appraisal in mathematics needs to be comprehensive. There needs to be some reasonable representation of the full range of content at various developmental levels. At the very least, this should include appraisal of concepts and skills, computation, and problem solving across the topics of numbers, fractions, geometry, and measurement. The use of a single topic measure (e.g., a computation test such as the Wide Range Achievement Test [WRAT]; Jastak & Jastak, 1978) suggests that a "g" factor is operating and that performance in one topic of mathematics is sufficient to predict performance in another topic, or that the appraisal is conducted from an interest only perspective where one topic is of primary interest to the examiner. The single topic procedure limits the search for patterns of strengths and weaknesses, but enables one to delve more fully into one area of concern. If the Key-Math Diagnostic Arithmetic Test (Connolly, Nachtman, & Prichett, 1976) is contrasted with WRAT (Jastak & Jastak, 1978), one would note that Key Math covers more topics but does not cover any single topic to the degree that WRAT covers computation. Given these variations, appraisal specialists need to make informed decisions as to the components of their approach.

Instruction and curriculum are interwoven in programs designed to meet the needs of persons having learning disabilities in mathematics. Curriculum choices determine content, the level of the content, and the sequence or sequences in which the content will be presented. With few exceptions (Cawley et al., 1974, 1976) special education has not directed any significant attention to the development of curriculum for mathematics. Two factors tend to influence curriculum choices. One of these is the use of the regular class curriculum, which is largely determined by the textbook in use. The second factor stresses the remedial orientation of computation in whole numbers. This second factor leaves little variation in curriculum.

Instructional choices determine the method by which the content will be presented. It is possible to separate the approaches to instruction into two categories, although it is important to note that more than two categories could be designated and that there is overlap among them. One category of approaches stresses concepts, principles, information processing, and analysis across the topics of mathematics. Another category stresses high rates of correct responses and the habituation of response behavior across a fewer number of mathematics topics, frequently whole number computation and word problem solving.

The first category is influenced by developmentalists such as Piaget (Copeland, 1970; Kamii, 1985; Voyat, 1982) and selected information-processing perspectives (Cawley, 1985; Cherkes-Julkowski, 1985). The second category is influenced by data-based instruction specialists (Blankenship, 1985; Smith & Lovitt, 1976) and direct instructional tacticians (Silbert, Carnine, & Stein, 1981). The orientation selected by teachers is often a function of their training, the amount of preparation required to implement a particular program, their own personal knowledge of mathematics, and the needs of the children. The field is not faced with an either/or conflict. Each approach has its merits, its limitations, and its benefits for children with learning disabilities in mathematics.

A neglected area in all of mathematics is problem solving. Although the National Council of Teachers of Mathematics has designated problem solving as its top priority for the 1980s, special education has yet to make the transition from a computational emphasis to problem solving. This situation exists in spite of the fact that the great majority of children who are learning disabled in mathematics receive the preponderance of their instruction in regular classes. These children are regularly faced with problem solving and some attention must be directed toward this topic. Performance in mathematics requires considerable knowledge, competence in prerequisite skills such as language and reading, and the use of a variety of cognitive acts. Proper programming for the learning disabled requires an approach as comprehensive as the subject itself.

REFERENCES

Blankenship, C. S. (1985). A behavioral view of mathematical learning problems. In J. Cawley (Ed.), *Cognitive strategies and mathematics for the learning disabled* (pp. 49–74). Rockville, MD: Aspen.

Cawley, J. F. (1985). Thinking. In J. Cawley (Ed.), *Cognitive strategies and mathematics for the learning disabled* (pp. 139–162). Rockville, MD: Aspen.

Cawley, J. F., Fitzmaurice, A. M., Goodstein, H. A., Lepore, A., Sedlak, R., & Althaus, V. (1974, 1976). *Project MATH*. Tulsa, OK: Educational Progress Corporation.

Cherkes-Julkowski, M. (1985). Information processing: A cognitive view. In J. Cawley (Ed.), *Cognitive strategies and mathematics for the learning disabled* (pp. 117–138). Rockville, MD: Aspen.

Connolly, A., Nachtman, W., & Prichett, E. M. (1976). *Key Math Diagnostic Arithmetic Test*. Circle Pines, MN: American Guidance Service.

Copeland, R. (1970). *How children learn mathematics*. New York: Macmillan.

Jastak, J. F., & Jastak, S. (1978). *Wide Range Achievement Test*. Wilmington, DE: Jastak Associates.

Kamii, C. (1985). *Young children reinvent arithmetic*. New York: Teachers College Press.

McLeod, T. M., & Armstrong, S. W. (1982). Learning disabilities in mathematics—Skill deficits and remedial aproaches at the intermediate and secondary level. *Learning Disability Quarterly, 5*, 305–311.

Silbert, J., Carnine, D., & Stein, M. (1981). *Direct instruction in mathematics*. Columbus, OH: Merrill.

Smith, D. D., & Lovitt, T. C. (1976). The differential effects of reinforcement contingencies on arithmetic performance. *Journal of Learning Disabilities*, 9, 32–40.

Thornton, C. A., & Toohey, M. A. (1985). Basic math facts: Guidelines for teaching and learning. *Learning Disabilities Focus, 1*, 44–57.

Voyat, G. E. (1982). *Piaget systematized*. Hillsdale, NJ: Erlbaum.

JOHN F. CAWLEY
JAMES H. MILLER
University of New Orleans

ACALCULIA
ARITHMETIC INSTRUCTION
ARITHMETIC REMEDIATION

MATHEMATICS, REMEDIAL

Many normal students encounter difficulties in mathematics. Handicapped students often find the mastery of even rudimentary mathematical skills to be problematic. Concern always has been voiced about these problems, and strides have been taken to improve mathematics instruction in regular education. Yet, relatively little attention has been paid to the improvement of the mathematics skills of children with special needs. There are a variety of reasons for this. One is the availability of inexpensive prosthetics for the mathematically disabled such as inexpensive hand calculators. Through their use a mathematically incapable student can carry out many of the same calculations and solve many of the problems, providing he or she understands their wording, as their more capable peers. Another reason for the less regard attached to mathematics competencies for special learners is that reading is considered more important for basic learning than mathematics. Furthermore, with technology carrying out fundamental mathematics operations for most people, other language arts (still not managed effectively by technology, with spelling a possible exception) also may presume authority over mathematics for students with special needs. Whatever the reasons, schools neglect corrective and remedial efforts directed at handicapped children and youths. There has been relatively little literature devoted to these students with regard to mathematics. The advent of the computer, however, promises to improve this situation because it allows the study of mathematics learning and difficulties in ways that appeal to cognitive scientists.

Among those who have studied the mathematics needs and problems of handicapped students is Cawley (1978, 1984). He points out that failures in mathematics learning may be rooted in mathematics or may grow out of disabilities in other academic skill areas. For example, one student may fail at mathematics because he or she has not mastered its skills and content or has disabilities that prevent such mastery. On the other hand, the student may be capable of such mastery but fail because of poor or impaired cognitive abilities, learning strategies, and study habits (Reisman, 1982). The student also may fail because of inability to master the reading and other language arts required to understand problems and to effectively deploy mathematic applications (Cawley, 1984). Cawley claims that many learning-disabled students would be capable of demonstrating proficiency in mathematics—regardless of the level of content—if their learning disabilities could be removed from their performances. This claim has not been substantiated, mainly because a truly learning-disabled student's disabilities are not readily taken out of the equation. Cawley carefully avoids making extraordinary claims for the approaches that he and his colleagues espouse for improving the mathematics performance of learning-disabled students.

The traditional model of instruction for remedial mathematics has been a diagnostic one, for example, identifying areas of strengths and weaknesses and, traditionally, focusing instructional attention on weak areas, including mathematical skill deficiencies. However, the diagnostic remedial mathematics specialist also might be interested in remediating such dysfunctional learner characteristics as distractibility, inefficient strategies, and poor short- or long-term memory processes (Reisman, 1982). Much of the remedial effort might then go into teaching the mathematically handicapped student strategies appropriate to coping with and overcoming these and other deficiencies related to poor mathematics performance.

In contrast, there are those who recommend a developmental approach, taking the position that good developmental instruction in mathematics represents the best remediation for handicapped learners. Cawley objects that

one of the problems in helping children with learning problems to learn mathematics is that there has been too much emphasis on "how to" to the neglect of the curriculum. He advocates greater emphasis on "what shall we teach, when shall we teach it, and in what sequence is it best taught" (1984, p. ix) in imparting mathematics to learning-disabled children. Nevertheless, he, too recommends that the mathematical instruction of learning-handicapped children be tailored to their particular strengths and weaknesses. Beyond that, he suggests that mathematics instruction for learning-handicapped students should proceed on the premise that the needs of children with learning problems are interrelated and that the activities from skill areas and topics other than mathematics should be used to reinforce positive mathematics behaviors on their part and to encourage application and generalization.

REFERENCES

Cawley, J. F. (1978). An instructional design in mathematics. In L. Mann, L. Goodman, & J. L. Wiederholt (Eds.), *Teaching the learning-disabled adolescent*. Boston: Houghton-Mifflin.

Cawley, J. F. (1984). Preface. In J. F. Cawley (Ed.), *Developmental teaching of mathematics for the learning disabled*. Rockville, MD: Aspens.

Glennon, V., & Cruikshank, W. (1981). Teaching mathematics to children and youth with perceptual and cognitive processing deficits. In V. Glennon (Ed.), *The mathematical education of exceptional children and youth*. Reston, VA: National Council of Teachers of Mathematics.

Reisman, F. (1982). *A guide to the diagnostic teaching of arithmetic*. Columbus, OH: Merrill.

DON BRASWELL
Research Foundation,
City University of New York

MATHEMATICS, LEARNING DISABILITIES IN READING, REMEDIAL

MATHIAS AMENDMENT

During the 97th Congress (1981–1982) in the U.S. Senate, Honorable Charles McC. Mathias, Jr., from Maryland introduced Senate Bill S.604:

> To amend the Communication Act of 1934 to provide that telephone receivers may not be sold in interstate commerce unless they are manufactured in a manner which permits their use by persons with hearing impairments.

On May 6, 1982, Senator Barry Goldwater, chairman of the Subcommittee in Communications, introduced Senator Mathias who testified that the bill required no new research or testing and would "provide great assistance for millions of Americans who have some hearing impairment at a relatively small cost and a relatively small effort by the companies." (Senate Hearing, 1982, p. 14). The bill did not call for retrofitting existing incompatible receivers but affected only new telephone receivers to make them compatible with hearing aids. Senator Mathias recalled that the telephone was a by product of Alexander Graham Bell's search for a device to help the hearing impaired. Ironically for Americans with hearing aids, one of five existing telephones did not produce electromagnetic signals compatible with magnetic telephone pick-ups built into most hearing aids. Thus hearing impaired people were denied an essential part of independent living. The passage of the Mathias Amendment corrected this problem.

REFERENCE

Telephone Service for Hearing Impaired. (1982).

Hearing Before the Subcommittee on Communications of the Committee on Commerce, Science and Transportation, United States Senate, 97th Congress, Second Session on S.604 and S.2355. Serial No. 97-119. Washington, DC: U.S. Government Printing Office.

C. MILDRED TASHMAN
College of St. Rose

MATTIE T. *v.* HOLLADAY

In April 1975, *Mattie T.* v. *Holladay* was filed on behalf of all Mississippi school-age children who were handicapped or regarded by their school as handicapped, for alleged violations or failure to enforce the children's rights under PL 94-142, the Education for All Handicapped Children Act. The plaintiffs were named as either handicapped children excluded from school in segregated special programs or ignored in regular classes, or nonhandicapped minority students who had been misclassified as mentally retarded and hence inappropriately placed.

In 1977 the district court ruled that the defendants were indeed in violation of the plaintiffs' federal rights and ordered a comprehensive compliance plan. On February 22, 1979, the judge approved a comprehensive consent decree, which required that (1) these students be placed in the least restrictive environment (e.g., mainstreamed, put in day programs for institutionalized children, given surrogate parents if parentless); (2) the state redesign its child evaluation procedures so as to be nondiscriminatory; (3) compensatory education be required for those students who had been misclassified and inappropriately placed; (4) school suspensions of longer than 3 days be discontinued; (5) a statewide complaint procedure service be instituted; (6) the state monitoring system be strengthened to ensure local school district compliance

with federal law; and (7) procedural safeguards be put in place as required by the federal statute, to include such features as a parents' rights handbook and community outreach to locate children with special needs.

REFERENCE

Comprehensive consent decree issued to enforce PL 94-142 in Mississippi. (1979, March/April). *Mental Disability Law Reporter, 3*(2), 98–99.

Mattie T. *v.* Holladay 522 F. Supp. 72 (N.D. Mississippi 1981).

MILTON BUDOFF
*Research Institute for
Educational Problems,
Cambridge, Massachusetts*

LARRY P.
MARSHALL *v.* GEORGIA
EDUCATION FOR ALL HANDICAPPED CHILDREN ACT OF 1975

MATURATIONAL LAG

See DEVELOPMENTAL DELAY.

MBD SYNDROME

The MBD syndrome or minimal brain dysfunction syndrome, has for many years been offered as an explanation for and diagnosis of the cluster of behaviors, including hyperactivity, distractibility, and impulsiveness, commonly found in children with academic and behavior problems (Clements, 1966; Cruickshank, 1966, Strauss & Lehtinen, 1947). The rationale for minimal brain dysfunction as an etiological factor in learning problems has some historical support (although somewhat indirect) from nineteenth-century neuroanatomical findings that certain brain areas appear to be necessary for specific language functions (Wernicke, 1874). The twentieth-century translation into academic problems presumably refers to these neuroanatomical substrates (Myklebust, 1954, 1964). Similar neuroanatomic bases for problems in language, information processing, and praxic functions were also recognized in the earlier half of the twentieth century (Nielson, 1948), and the possible role of multimodal central nervous system problems in academic problems represented a popular explanation (Belmont, Birch, & Karp, 1965; Birch & Belmont, 1964). Related findings suggestive of behavioral problems resulting from cerebral lesions (Teuber, 1959) were seen as lending further scientific support to the etiologic role of brain damage in a variety of maladaptive behaviors in children.

The 1960s represented an era when the MBD syndrome was related to many problems of childhood. In light of interest in the subject, the National Institutes of Health sponsored a major review of research. In 1969 their three-phase project was completed (Chalfant & Scheffelin, 1969). The first phase recommended the use of the term minimal brain dysfunction for children of normal overall intelligence who exhibit characteristics of learning or behavior attributable to a dysfunction of the nervous system. The term was chosen to emphasize that it is the child rather than the environment that is different and that all learning and behavior is a reflection of brain function. The second phase analyzed medical and educational services required for children with MDB. The third phase reviewed the state of scientific knowledge regarding the learning disabilities of these children. With more than 3000 references considered, it was concluded that "remedial methods are found to rest on varied and shaky hypotheses, and have rarely been subjected to scientific evaluation even on an empirical basis" (Masland, 1969, iv).

Shortly after publication of the Department of Health, Education, and Welfare report, Reed, Rabe, and Mankinen (1970) reviewed the literature on the subject published during the previous decade. They concluded that the criteria for diagnosing brain damage were generally inadequate or nonexistent, and found little evidence to suggest that children with chronic neurological impairment at the level of the cerebral hemispheres require or benefit from teaching procedures that differ from those used for reading retardates without brain damage.

In recent years there has been comparatively little interest in the use of MBD as either a diagnostic term in medicine or a classificatory term in special education. Recognizing that differential consequences may result from damage to different brain areas, acute versus chronic brain dysfunction can exert different influences on the nature of brain-behavior relationships. The brain contains millions of neurons, with disabilities reflecting both location and numbers of damaged neurons (Hartlage & Hartlage, 1977). It is not surprising, then, that the concept of MBD may be too broad to relate to any meaningful description of a given child or resultant prescription for intervention. Thus the MBD syndrome may represent a term of historic and heuristic value rather than one with specific implications for special education practice.

REFERENCES

Belmont, I., Birch, H. G., & Karp, E. (1965). The disordering of intersensory and intrasensory integration by brain damage. *Journal of Nervous & Mental Diseases, 141,* 410–418.

Birch, H. G., & Belmont, I. (1964). Auditory-visual integration in normal and retarded readers. *American Journal of Orthopsychiatry, 34,* 852–861.

Chalfant, J. C., & Scheffelin, M. A. (1969). *Central processing disorders in children: A review of research.* Bethesda, MD: U.S. Department of Health, Education, & Welfare.

Clements, S. D. (1966, January). *Minimal brain dysfunction in children* (Public Health Service Publication No. 1415). Washington, DC: U.S. Department of Health, Education, and Welfare.

Cruickshank, W. M. (1966). *The teacher of brain injured children.* Syracuse, NY: Syracuse University Press.

Hartlage, L. C., & Hartlage, P. L. (1977). Application of neuropsychological principles in the diagnosis of learning disabilities. In L. Tarnopol & M. Tarnopol (Eds.), *Brain function and reading disabilities* (pp. 111–146). Baltimore, MD: University Park Press.

Masland, R. L. (1969). In J. Chalfant & M. Scheffelin. *Control processing dysfunctions in children: A review of research* (pp. iii–iv). Bethesda, MD: U.S. Department of Health, Education, and Welfare.

Myklebust, H. R. (1954). *Auditory disorders in children: A manual for differential diagnosis.* New York: Grune & Stratton.

Myklebust, H. R. (1964). Learning disorders. Psychoneurological disturbance in children. *Rehabilitation Literature.*

Nielson, J. M. (1948). *Agnosia, aproxia, aphasia: Their value in cerebral localization* (2nd ed.). New York: Hafner.

Reed, J. C., Rabe, E. F., & Mankinen, M. (1970). Teaching reading to brain-damaged children: A review. *Reading Research Quarterly, 5*(3), 379–401.

Strauss, A. A., & Lehtinen, L. U. (1947). *Psychopathology and education of the brain-injured child.* New York: Grune & Stratton.

Teuber, H. L. (1959). Some alterations in behavior after cerebral lesion in man. In *Evolution of Nervous Control.* Washington, DC: American Association for the Advancement of Science.

Wernicke, C. (1874). *Der aphaisiche symptom komplex.* Breslau: Cohn & Weigart.

LAWRENCE C. HARTLAGE
Evans, Georgia

BRAIN DAMAGE
LEARNING DISABILITIES

MCCARTHY, DOROTHEA (1906–1974)

Dorothea McCarthy made her greatest contributions to psychology in the areas of language development and clinical assessment of young children. She earned her PhD in 1928 at the University of Minnesota under the tutelage of Florence Goodenough, who had a strong effect on McCarthy's professional career, convincing her that "cognitive differences among children could be measured at early ages and along several dimensions" (McCarthy, 1972, p. iii). Early in her career, McCarthy contributed two seminal chapters on her pioneering research in the language development of the preschool child and the vocalization of infants; these chapters appeared in Murchison's *Handbook of Child Psychology* and Carmichael's *Manual of Child Psychology*, both prestigious source books at the time.

McCarthy culminated her professional career with the publication in 1972 of the McCarthy Scales of Children's Abilities, a test of the mental and motor abilities of children ages 2½ to 8½ years. This test was developed over a 15-year period and was published one year after her retirement from Fordham University, where she served as associate professor and professor for 40 years (1932–1971).

McCarthy was a fellow of the American Psychological Association (APA), a diplomate in clinical psychology, a former president of both the New York State Psychological Association and APA's Division of Developmental Psychology, and a member of several APA councils and committees. In 1967 she was awarded an honorary degree of doctor of sciences by the College of New Rochelle.

At Fordham University her colleagues considered her most distinctive characteristics to be the soundness and dependability of her research and the high standards she upheld for herself and for the students whose research she directed. Her clinical sense regarding the needs and interests of preschool children is evidenced by the child-oriented tasks she developed for the McCarthy Scales and the clever way these tasks are sequenced within the test to help establish and maintain rapport.

REFERENCE

McCarthy, D. (1972). *Manual for the McCarthy Scales of Children's Abilities*. New York: Psychological Corporation.

ALAN S. KAUFMAN
University of Alabama

MCCARTHY SCALES OF CHILDREN'S ABILITIES

MCCARTHY SCALES OF CHILDREN'S ABILITIES (MSCA)

With an appreciation of the critical need for assessment instruments appropriate for use with young children, the McCarthy Scales of Children's Abilities (MSCA; McCarthy, 1972) was designed to measure both general intellectual level and important special abilities of youngsters between 2½ and 8½ years of age. The MSCA consists of 18 subtests that are grouped into five separate scales: verbal (V), perceptual-performance (P), quantitative (Q), memory, and motor—and a composite scale: general cognitive. The General Cognitive Index (GCI), with a mean of 100 and a standard deviation of 16, is derived from 15 of the 18 subtests and provides a normative indicator of a child's cognitive level. Explaining the use of GCI and the

Sample materials from the McCarthy Scales of Children's Abilities: a test for children ages 2½ to 8½.

avoidance of the term IQ, McCarthy noted the many misinterpretations and unfortunate connotations associated with the latter term (p. 5).

The five MSCA scale indexes each have a mean of 50 and a standard deviation of 10. These scales were chosen primarily on the basis of McCarthy's clinical experience and partially on the results of factor analysis. The following list shows the McCarthy scales with the abilities they are designed to measure:

V—Verbal expression, maturity of verbal concepts

P—Reasoning ability through manipulation of materials

Q—Facility with numbers, understanding of quantitative words

Memory—Short-term memory for visual and auditory stimuli

Motor—Gross and fine motor coordination

The GCI is a composite of V, P, and Q. Since each memory subtest is also included on the V, P, or Q scale, based on the content of its items, the memory scale is also included in the GCI. Kaufman (1982) observes that there is convincing factor-analytic support for the general cognitive, verbal, perceptual-performance, and motor scales; however, the composition of the memory factor fluctuates from group to group, and the quantitative factor frequently fails to emerge at all. Extreme caution is advised in the interpretation of these two scales.

The McCarthy factor structure is similar for different age levels (Kaufman, 1975), for different ethnic or racial groups (Kaufman & DiCuio, 1975; Mishra, 1981), for children having low GCIs (Naglieri, Kaufman, & Harrison, 1981), and for children with school-related problems (Keith & Bolen, 1980). The psychometric quality of the MSCA is further demonstrated by studies indicating its usefulness as a predictor of success in school-related achievement (Massoth, 1985; Massoth & Levenson, 1982). In regard to reliability, a review of MSCA research (Kaufman, 1982) reveals that the internal consistency is well documented. Information on stability, albeit limited to small nonexceptional samples, appears to show adequate test-retest consistency. In addition, the MSCA has been found to correlate with the Wechsler and Binet scales "as highly (.70s and .80s) as these criterion instruments correlate with each other" (p. 163). However, a puzzling but consistent finding shows the GCI to be about one-half standard deviation lower than the WISC-R Full Scale IQ for learning-disabled children; there is also some evidence that the GCI is about one standard deviation below the Stanford-Binet IQ (Form L-M, 1972 norms) for retarded children.

The MSCA has many positive attributes (Kaufman & Kaufman, 1977). It is both psychometrically sound and carefully standardized. A total of 1036 children, with at least 100 children in each of the 10 selected age groups, were included in the standardization group. The sample was stratified to correspond to 1970 estimates from the U.S. Bureau of the Census on several variables—age, sex, color (white or nonwhite), geographic region, father's occupation, and residence (urban or rural). Test directions are clearly written, materials are well-constructed, and tasks are appealing to children. Despite the quality of the instrument and the useful assessment information provided, the McCarthy has a few shortcomings. These include excessive clerical work in scoring, a lack of sufficient ceiling (for unusually gifted students) or bottom (for extremely retarded youngsters), an omission of social comprehension and judgment tasks, and the unavailability of a McCarthy-type battery for use with older children in follow-up evaluations.

Kaufman and Kaufman (1977) state their conviction that the "GCI adequately describes the child's level of functioning in a norm-referenced sense" (p. 117). The Kaufmans suggest that an individualized test interpretation begin with the calculation of a child's own mean scale index on the five separate scales. Relative strengths and weaknesses are then determined by comparing the index for each of the five scales to this mean. They also offer a useful empirical technique for interpreting a child's test score fluctuations on the 18 separate mental and motor subtests. Other considerations in interpretation involve an evaluation of scatter (Kaufman, 1976) and an analysis of strengths and weaknesses on the MSCA in the context of observed behaviors during testing, scores on other tests, and pertinent background information about the child (Kaufman & Kaufman, 1977).

REFERENCES

Kaufman, A. S. (1975). Factor structure of the McCarthy scales at five age levels between 2½ and 8½. *Educational & Psychological Measurement, 35*(3), 641–656.

Kaufman, A. S. (1976). Do normal children have "flat" ability profiles? *Psychology in the Schools, 13,* 284–285.

Kaufman, A. S. (1982). An integrated review of almost a decade of research on the McCarthy scales. In T. R. Kratochwill (Ed.), *Advances in school psychology* (Vol. 2). Hillsdale, NJ: Erlbaum.

Kaufman, A. S., & DiCuio, R. F. (1975). Separate factor analyses of the McCarthy scales for groups of black and white children. *Journal of School Psychology, 13*(1), 10–17.

Kaufman, A. S., & Kaufman, N. L. (1977). *Clinical evaluation of young children with the McCarthy scales.* New York: Grune & Stratton.

Keith, T. Z., & Bolen, L. M. (1980). Factor structure of the McCarthy scales for children experiencing problems in school. *Psychology in the Schools, 17*(3), 320–326.

Massoth, N. A. (1985). The McCarthy Scales of Children's Abilities as a predictor of achievement: A five-year follow-up. *Psychology in the Schools, 22*(1), 10–13.

Massoth, N. A., & Levenson, R. L. (1982). The McCarthy Scales of Children's Abilities as a predictor of reading readiness and reading achievement. *Psychology in the Schools, 19*(3), 293–296.

McCarthy, D. (1972). *Manual for the McCarthy Scales of Children's Abilities.* New York: Psychological Corporation.

Mishra, S. P. (1981). Factor analysis of the McCarthy scales for groups of white and Mexican-American children. *Journal of School Psychology, 19*(2), 178–182.

Naglieri, J. A., Kaufman, A. S., & Harrison, P. L. (1981). Factor structure of the McCarthy scales for school-age children with low GCIs. *Journal of School Psychology, 19*(3), 226–232.

ALAN S. KAUFMAN
MARY E. STINSON
University of Alabama

INTELLIGENCE TESTING
KAUFMAN ASSESSMENT BATTERY FOR CHILDREN
STANFORD BINET INTELLIGENCE SCALE

McDERMOTT MULTIDIMENSIONAL ASSESSMENT OF CHILDREN (M.MAC)

The McDermott Multidimensional Assessment of Children (M.MAC), is a computer guided assessment system for use on microcomputers or through telecommunication networks over phone lines (McDermott, 1986, McDermott & Watkins, 1985, 1986). It has three main purposes: (1) analysis and interpretation of data gathered from psychological and educational tests and standardized interviews and behavioral observations, (2) integration of the data with child demography, a child's unique personal and environmental characteristics, and clinical judgments by a child specialist, and (3) design of individualized educational programs (IEPs) linked directly to foregoing diagnostic information and to objective measures of current

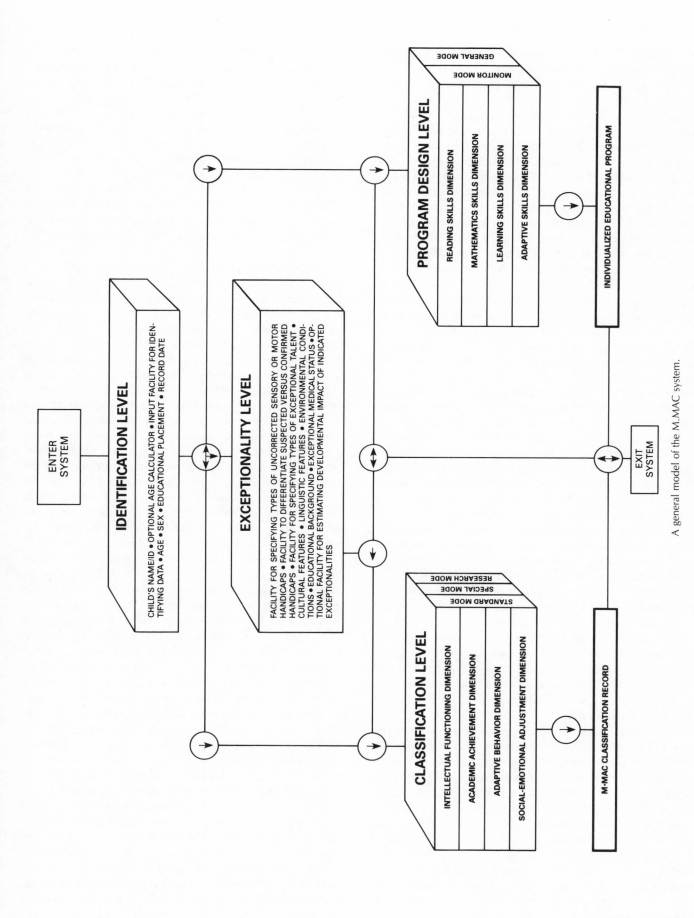

A general model of the M.MAC system.

ENTER SYSTEM

IDENTIFICATION LEVEL

CHILD'S NAME/ID • OPTIONAL AGE CALCULATOR • INPUT FACILITY FOR IDEN-
TIFYING DATA • AGE • SEX • EDUCATIONAL PLACEMENT • RECORD DATE

EXCEPTIONALITY LEVEL

FACILITY FOR SPECIFYING TYPES OF UNCORRECTED SENSORY OR MOTOR
HANDICAPS • FACILITY TO DIFFERENTIATE SUSPECTED VERSUS CONFIRMED
HANDICAPS • FACILITY FOR SPECIFYING TYPES OF EXCEPTIONAL TALENT •
CULTURAL FEATURES • LINGUISTIC FEATURES • ENVIRONMENTAL CONDI-
TIONS • EDUCATIONAL BACKGROUND • EXCEPTIONAL MEDICAL STATUS • OP-
TIONAL FACILITY FOR ESTIMATING DEVELOPMENTAL IMPACT OF INDICATED
EXCEPTIONALITIES

PROGRAM DESIGN LEVEL

GENERAL MODE
MONITOR MODE

READING SKILLS DIMENSION
MATHEMATICS SKILLS DIMENSION
LEARNING SKILLS DIMENSION
ADAPTIVE SKILLS DIMENSION

CLASSIFICATION LEVEL

RESEARCH MODE
SPECIAL MODE
STANDARD MODE

INTELLECTUAL FUNCTIONING DIMENSION
ACADEMIC ACHIEVEMENT DIMENSION
ADAPTIVE BEHAVIOR DIMENSION
SOCIAL-EMOTIONAL ADJUSTMENT DIMENSION

M-MAC CLASSIFICATION RECORD

INDIVIDUALIZED EDUCATIONAL PROGRAM

EXIT SYSTEM

performance. The M.MAC is licensed to qualified specialists by The Psychological Corporation.

The Figure presents a general model of the M.MAC system. As shown, M.MAC has four *levels* corresponding to the four stages of the assessment process. They are the identification level, exceptionality level, classification level, and program design level. A specialist usually enters information for the identification and exceptionality levels and then provides classification data that will result in empirical (objective and reliable) appraisals of abilities and disabilities. The same specialist may continue then to design an IEP through the program design level, the remedial plan that links directly to diagnostic information used to render classifications. Alternatively, IEPs can be developed at a later time or by a different specialist. For example, whereas the classification level may be used by a psychologist or educational diagnostician, the program design level may be used by a special education teacher.

The identification and exceptionality levels are preparatory stages of assessment. Basic demography (age, grade, and gender) collected by the identification level are used to perform high speed searches through M.MAC's memory to locate all of the important statistical data about standardized tests, rating scales, and interview schedules. The M.MAC's memory stores nearly 10,000 statistics (reliability coefficients, special group norms, etc.) that differ for each instrument, age level, grade placement, and gender. Such statistics are required for objective analyses and interpretation. The M.MAC locates and applies in moments what would take an unaided specialist days for a single case study. Through the exceptionality level, the specialist is able to sensitize the assessment process to the influences of children's sensory, motor and speech impairments, cultural and language factors, exceptional talents, educational and environmental background, and general health. This information affects assessment in a variety of ways, e.g., opening special options for including or excluding certain test data, posting warnings about potential threats to the validity of standardized data, and altering the nature of classifications such as learning disabilities and developmental learning disorders. In addition, specialists may indicate the adaptive or developmental "impact" of unusual personal and situational factors in a child's life.

The classification and program design levels are the heart of M.MAC. Each level involves four *dimensions* of child functioning (refer to the Figure); hence the name *multidimensional assessment*. The classification level assesses intellectual functioning, academic achievement, adaptive behavior, and social-emotional adjustment. Users select from the most popular and valid individually administered intelligence and achievement tests, adaptive behavior inventories, and teacher or parent behavior rating scales. As options to this procedure adaptive behavior may be evaluated based on professional judgment (using criteria recommended by the American Association on Mental Deficiency; AAMD; Grossman, 1983) and social-

emotional adjustment may be assessed through projective tests or clinical judgment in accord with standards published in the *Diagnostic and Statistical Manual of Mental Disorders*: DSM-III (American Psychiatric Association, 1980). Data entered for each test are statistically treated and presented in easy to read tables and explained clearly in narrative form. Information across the four classification level dimensions and the identification and exceptionality levels is automatically integrated and multidimensional classifications produced for each child. All information is printed in a 4 to 16 page classification record. Approximately 15 to 20 minutes lapses between the time M.MAC is started and the time the Record has been printed.

The M.MAC produces 148 different classifications: 113 are strictly based on empirical information and 35 on clinical information. Unique among classification systems, M.MAC recognizes variations of *normality* (e.g., good adjustment, commensurate achievement, and normal intellectual functioning) as well as abnormality. The identification of normality is handled with the same rigor applied for identification of exceptionality and psychopathology. Classifications are rendered for intellectual giftedness, areas of exceptional talent, levels of normal intellectual functioning, borderline intellectual functioning, levels of mental retardation, educational and intellectual retardation, areas of commensurate (appropriate) achievement, areas of specific learning disabilities and developmental learning disorders, provisional learning disabilities, areas of possible academic overcompensation, possible visual-motor problems or communication disorders, good or adequate social-emotional adjustment, severity of conduct and anxiety-withdrawal disorders, and types and severity of attention deficit disorders and mixed disturbances of emotions and conduct. Clinical classifications include all childhood disorders recognized by the American Psychiatric Association (APA). For each classification, M.MAC optionally provides code numbers for the major national and international child classification systems (APA, 1980; World Health Organization, 1978).

As represented in the Figure, the classification level has three *operations modes*; standard, special, and research. Operations modes control the quantity and complexity of options that a specialist may wish to apply. Standard mode is like an "auto pilot" making assessment simple and straightforward because all basic decision rules are automatically set according to national and international standard (such as those under PL 94-142, AAMD and APA). For example, general population norms are used for tests, major academic areas such as reading and mathematics are used in detecting learning disabilities, and abnormality is defined by the conventional 3% rule usually associated with mental deficiency and social-emotional maladjustment. The special mode permits users to change such rules for local need and also enables entry, statistical comparison, and combination of data obtained from two teachers or parents in order to enhance the generalization of assessment information. The research mode allows one to alter statistical criteria, to correct test scores for unreliability, and to enter, store, and apply over 3,400 normative statistics unique to a region or school district (e.g., norms developed for special cultural groups or clinical subpopulations).

The M.MAC's program design level has four assessment dimensions (see the Figure); reading, mathematics, learning style, and adaptive behavior. Here, the specialist chooses from a variety of the finest screening and diagnostic tests and observation scales. The IEPs may involve all four dimensions of attainment, although they more often focus on one or two, such as reading and learning style. After criterion referenced or level based information is entered, M.MAC carries out high speed analyses to identify the child's earliest failures and maximum proficiencies. Next, a search commences through several of 54 skills hierarchies and specific behavioral performance objectives are selected from the 1,111 available in memory. These features are unique to M.MAC because, unlike other computerized IEP generators, M.MAC's objectives are keyed *directly* to measured performance; i.e., it is not merely a library entailing the time and error associated with manual selection of remedial objectives. Also, objectives in reading and mathematics are printed with optional reference codes for specific lessons from available computer assisted and computer managed instruction programs. Thus the same computer used for assessment purposes by the specialist can be used for remedial instruction purposes by the child.

The Figure indicates two operations modes for the program design level; monitor and general. When the monitor mode is selected, all recommended objectives are displayed first on the computer screen. The specialist may then tailor an IEP before printing (e.g., reject some recommended objectives and select others based on personal knowledge of the child). In general mode, the IEP is printed directly from assessment data, requiring no preview of recommended objectives. Each IEP is from 4 to 16 pages in length and requires about 15 to 20 minutes to produce.

Although M.MAC is a computer guided assessment system, it is designed for child specialists, not computer specialists. It is driven by menu screens and single keystrokes and requires no prior computer experience. The M.MAC contains thousands of error traps that immediately detect typographical errors, accidental breaches of test norm and score limits and contradictory information, and displays ranges of possible correct responses. The system is accompanied by a 330 page documentation manual that, although not necessary for successful application of the system, provides a host of theoretical and technical information to support M.MAC users.

REFERENCES

American Psychiatric Association. (1980). *Diagnostic and statistical manual of mental disorders* (3rd ed.). Washington, DC: Author.

Grossman, H. J. (Ed.). (1983). *Classification in mental retardation.* Washington, DC: American Association on Mental Deficiency.

McDermott, P. A. (1986). *McDermott Multidimensional Assessment of Children: Telecommunications version.* New York: Psychological Corporation.

McDermott, P. A., & Watkins, M. W. (1985). *McDermott Multidimensional Assessment of Children: Apple II version.* New York: Psychological Corporation.

McDermott, P. A., & Watkins, M. W. (1986). *McDermott Multidimensional Assessment of Children: IBM version.* New York: Psychological Corporation.

World Health Organization. (1978). *Mental disorders: Glossary and guide to their classification in accordance with the ninth revision of the International Classification of Diseases.* Geneva: Author.

PAUL A. McDERMOTT
University of Pennsylvania

ASSESSMENT
ECOLOGICAL ASSESSMENT
TYPOLOGY OF BEHAVIOR PROBLEMS

McGINNIS METHOD

The McGinnis method, also known as the association method, was the recommended teaching approach during the 1950s, 1960s, and early 1970s for children classified as aphasic or diagnosed as suffering from receptive and/or expressive aphasia. Aphasia is defined as an impairment or lesion in the brain causing sensory deprivation.

The association method employs techniques using sight, sound, and kinesthesis as a multisensory teaching approach. The method stresses the importance of attention, recall, and retention. The speech training or oral articulation program emphasizes the kinesthetic sense of movement in the muscular coordination of lip and tongue movements. The student is carefully guided through the training program. The early training establishes the ability to pronounce phonemes in isolation. The memory sequence is established through reading and written form.

The association method further develops language skills through its vertical and horizontal training programs. The vertical program teaches basic language and speech patterns that are to be mastered over a specified period of time. The horizontal training program is the daily teaching paradigm. This program provides for the continuum of grade-level work.

The association method follows seven steps that stress attention, development of specific sounds, the smoothing or combining of sounds into meaningful nouns, the association of appropriate concepts with the noun, the writing of the noun or word using the written word, the development of speech reading, acoustical association, and the association of the meaning of language in both written and oral expression.

REFERENCE

McGinnis, M. A. (1963). *Aphasic children.* Washington, DC: Alexander G. Bell Association for the Deaf.

PAUL C. RICHARDSON
Elwyn Institutes,
Elwyn, Pennsylvania

MEASUREMENT

Measurement is the assignment of numbers to observed behaviors or actions. The observation may be made by humans or by machines. The behaviors may be simple and discrete such as movement of a child's head, or may be complex such as a conversation between a therapist and patient. The measurement of simple or complex behaviors is based on a rule for assigning numbers; the degree of inference is important. Inference is the amount of interpretation used by a human observer in assigning the number associated with the behavior. The rule structure of the assignment may vary from one measurement to another, and the defining characteristic is in the quality of the number.

Two major characteristics of importance to measurement in special education are reliability and validity. Reliability has a technical meaning that is somewhat different from the dictionary meaning. Reliability commonly means trustworthiness. To the extent that we can believe the measurement of a behavior is consistent, we can consider it trustworthy. Consistency is defined in terms of psychometrics (the mathematical modeling of measurement) as maintenance of relative position of a score with respect to other scores. For example, if five people are observed and their scores are 1, 3, 4, 4, 6, high reliability in the observation process would occur if the people were ordered exactly the same on another measurement, say 2, 4, 5, 5, 7, even though the scores are all different. Reliability is consistency of measurement of a score with respect to all other scores. That the two sets of scores all differ by one point is an issue of validity.

Reliability can be examined in three ways. One is to make the same measurement twice. In mental testing this means the same test is given with some interval between; this is termed test-retest reliability. If a test consists of parts that are independently measured, the consistency of the parts with respect to the whole can be examined; this is termed internal consistency. Finally, a complete second test may be constructed that is intended to measure the same thing as the first. Reliability for the two scores is termed parallel forms reliability.

Validity is a concept with several different applications. For the example given previously, one might ask which set of scores better indicates the behavior. In measuring children's school learning, we may be most interested in the content validity of the test: To what extent do the questions represent the topics the children were taught and should have learned? In measuring mental processing we are interested in the construct validity of the intelligence test used: To what extent does the test measure the mental processes it is intended to measure? In measuring a prospective college freshman's achievement as an indicator of future success in college, we are interested in predictive validity. Finally, in measuring how well a screening test indicates learning disabilities in comparison with the diagnoses of trained clinicians, we are interested in concurrent validity. Validity of a test must be associated with purpose for the test.

Inference in observation of behavior is a complex mental process. Reliability of measurement of a human observer typically decreases as the degree of inference necessary to the task increases. It is possible to achieve high reliability for high inference observation at a cost of extensive training and frequent retraining or maintenance practice.

VICTOR L. WILLSON
Texas A&M University

ASSESSMENT
PSYCHOEDUCATIONAL METHODS
RELIABILITY

MEDIATION

Mediation is an intellectual activity that can be used to direct, control, or regulate one's behavior or responses by thinking before acting (Meichenbaum & Aronson, 1979). Mediation is particularly useful during the initial phases of learning, when one is trying to acquire new facts, establish associations, remember information, or learn sequences of action. Mediation can be used to direct motor behavior, to control emotional and social behavior, to remember information, and to learn academically. Mediation may be verbal or visual in nature and its effects increase with meaningfulness (Peterson, Colavita, Sheanan, & Blattner, 1963).

Verbal mediation has application in many situations. Children can analyze their situations or experiences and plan their responses by literally talking to themselves. Verbal mediation can be used to help children learn physical movements. If a teacher simply counts "One, two, three, four," this mediation helps students to perform each movement in sequence at the correct time. Soon the children count aloud for themselves. Later the children can count silently to themselves until the movement patterns become automatic.

Mediation also can be used to control emotional and

social responses. For example, a child who is pushed or knocked down in a lunch line may become very angry. If the child uses verbal mediation, he or she can: (1) focus on the problem—He knocked me down; (2) analyze the emotions—That really makes me mad; (3) analyze the situation—He was playing tag and wasn't looking where he was going; it was accidental. As a result of mediation, the child might conclude that the student should be more careful, but that the situation is not worth getting upset over. The child has controlled his or her own emotions and regulated the social responses. Instead of hitting back, the child might respond by saying, "Hey, be a little more careful." Both Luria (1966) and Vygotsky (1962) suggest that children learn socialization by using language to mediate and regulate their social actions and behaviors.

Mediation has a number of applications in academic learning, as in reading, writing, spelling, and arithmetic. For example, a child might use mediation to remember the steps in computing an addition problem such as

$$\begin{array}{r} 25 \\ +35 \end{array}$$

The child might say, "Five and five are 10. Write the zero and carry the one to the next column. Two and three are five plus the one that was carried—six. Write the six. The answer is 60." In reading, for example, a child who has previously learned to read *cat* and *hat* can use this previous learning to help mediate new but similar words such as *bat* or *fat*. Knowing that the last two letters look alike and sound alike can be used to mediate the rapid learning of the new words.

Mediational strategies can be used for remembering facts, figures, places, and events. For example, a high-school student might use visual mediation to remember a series of errands he or she has to complete on Saturday morning. The student would form a series of visual images of the locations for each errand. The student might visualize going to the post office to mail a package, stopping at the store to buy a bottle of milk, and then mowing the yard and washing the car. This kind of visual mediation is useful in remembering the location of each activity. A student may remember the names of the nine planets and their respective distances from the sun by using a verbal code as a mediating device. For example, "Mary's violet eyes make John stay up night painting." The first letter in each word will help them remember the name, number, and location of the planet from the sun (Mercury, Venus, Earth, Mars, Jupiter, Saturn, Uranus, Neptune, Pluto; Kirk & Chalfant, 1984).

During the initial stages of learning, mediation is usually conscious and overt. The child may verbally say things out loud. In time, mediation becomes covert and the child silently speaks to himself or herself. When learning has occurred and the response is nearly automatic, mediation is no longer necessary.

REFERENCES

Jenkins, J. J. (1963). Mediated associations: Paradigms and situations. In C. N. Cofer & B. S. Musgrave (Eds.), *Verbal behavior and learning* (pp. 210–245). New York: McGraw-Hill.

Kirk, S. A., & Chalfant, J. C. (1984). *Academic and developmental learning disabilities.* Love Publishing.

Luria, A. R. (1966). *Higher cortical functions in man.* New York: Plenum.

Meichenbaum, D., & Asarnow, J. (1979). Cognitive behavior modification and metacognition development: Implications for the classroom. In P. Kendall & S. Hollon (Eds.), *Cognitive behavior interventions: Theory, research, and procedures.* New York: Academic.

Peterson, M. J., Colavita, F. J., Sheanan, III, D. B., & Blattner, K. C. (1964). Verbal mediating chains and response availability as a function of the acquisition paradigm. *Journal of Verbal Learning & Verbal Behavior, 3,* 11–18.

Vygotsky, L. S. (1962). *Thought and language* (E. Hanfmann & G. Vakar, Eds. and Trans.). Cambridge, MA: MIT Press.

JAMES C. CHALFANT
University of Arizona

ATTENTION DEFICIT DISORDER
BEHAVIOR MODIFICATION
LURIA, A. R.
THEORY OF ACTIVITY
VYGOTSKY, L. S.

MEDIATIONAL DEFICIENCY

Mediational deficiency refers to an inability to use verbal mediators to facilitate learning. Luria (1961) proposed that language and thinking are closely related. Progress in one area affects progress in the other. For example, young children use private speech by talking to themselves to direct their activities and formulate their thoughts. This private speech gradually becomes internalized and serves as an effective mediator enabling children to think before they act.

Older children, according to this mediational model, are better learners than young children because they are more likely to use verbal mediators as a learning aid. Consider a concept formation task in which a child is presented with stimuli that combine one of two shapes (triangle, circle) with one of two colors (red, green). The child must choose all instances of the concept, which may be green shapes. Each time the child chooses correctly he or she is reinforced. It has been hypothesized that the older child, using verbal mediators, will label the important features of the situation (in the preceding example, every correct choice is colored green). It has been observed that older children acquire such a concept quicker than younger children. Young children, not using these private labels or mediators, are likely to keep selecting whatever stimulus has been reinforced most often recently.

Younger children have shown that they can perform like older children if they are instructed to use verbal mediators while working on complex concept formation and discrimination problems. (For a review of the role of verbal mediation in discrimination learning, see Kendler & Kendler, 1975.) Because young children are capable of using verbal mediators to improve their performance on learning tasks, they do not have mediational deficiencies. Their difficulty more appropriately reflects a production deficiency. They do not usually produce and use verbal mediators unless instructed to do so.

Mediational research with the mentally retarded began in the early 1960s. Like young children, the retarded were found to have mediational deficiencies. They failed to produce verbal labels that were within their repertoires such as labeling all the responses as instances of a color. A number of studies were carried out to determine whether mentally retarded children and adults could use verbal mediators to facilitate learning if they were instructed to do so. The data indicated that like young children, retarded individuals could use mediational cues to facilitate learning under mediation-prompting conditions. Their problem, then, might be best described as a production deficiency. (For a review of mediational processes in the retarded, see Borkowski and Wanschura, 1974.)

The individual who learns a complex skill and uses it effectively under direct instruction may fail to apply the strategy or skill in other situations. This is especially likely when those situations appropriate for strategy application are not identical to the original situation in which the strategy was learned (Campione & Brown, 1978). Mentally retarded learners experience considerable difficulty when required to transfer their learning to a new situation. After they have been instructed to use mediation and their mediation deficiency has largely disappeared, their performance continues to be characterized by production deficiencies.

The mediational deficiencies so common in the retarded have recently been interpreted in terms of failures of metacognition. Metacognition refers to thinking about one's own thinking. It has two main components. The first is awareness of one's own cognition or thinking (in general, and in relation to the task at hand). The second is regulation of cognition (planning, monitoring, etc.) (Flavell & Wellman, 1971). In metacognitive terms, retarded children have a strategy in their cognitive repertoires that is applicable to the task at hand. However, they lack the knowledge of when, how, and why that strategy might be applied or generalized. Recent intervention studies have been designed to increase metacognition and facilitate generalization in the mentally retarded whose learning is characterized by mediational, or more accurately, production deficiencies.

REFERENCES

Borkowski, J. G., & Wanschura, P. B. (1974). Mediational processes in the retarded. In N. R. Ellis (Ed.), *International review of research in mental retardation* (Vol. 7). New York: Academic.

Campione, J. C., & Brown, A. L. (1978). Toward a theory of intelligence: Contributions from research with retarded children. *Intelligence, 2,* 279–304.

Flavell, J. H., & Wellman, H. M. (1977). Metamemory. In R. V. Kail & J. W. Hagen (Eds.), *Perspectives on the development of memory and cognition.* Hillsdale, NJ: Erlbaum.

Kendler, H. H., & Kendler, T. S. (1975). From discrimination learning to cognitive development: A neobehavioristic oddysey. In W. K. Estes (Ed.), *Handbook of learning and cognitive processes* (Vol. 1). Hillsdale, NJ: Erlbaum.

Luria, A. R. (1961). *The role of speech in the regulation of normal and abnormal behavior.* New York: Liveright.

NANCY L. HUTCHINSON
BERNICE Y. L. WONG
Simon Fraser University

LANGUAGE THERAPY
MEDIATORS
METACOGNITION
THEORY OF ACTIVITY
VERBAL ABILITY OF THE HANDICAPPED

MEDIATIONAL MEDIATORS

See MEDIATORS.

MEDIATION ESSAY

The mediation essay is a series of printed statements that describe specific desirable and undesirable behaviors and the consequences of each. It is used as a behavior change technique that combines the advantages of mild punishment and cognitive intervention (Blackwood, 1970).

The format of a mediation essay is that of a Socratic dialogue, with a question posed and a response detailed. The content is centered around four specific questions and their answers, using the student's own vocabulary. Generally the four questions are as follows: (1) What did I do wrong? (2) Why shouldn't I do _____ (inappropriate behavior)? (3) What should I do? (4) What will happen if I do _____ (appropriate behavior)? (Blackwood, 1970; Morrow & Morrow, 1985). Responses to the first two questions focus on a description of the student's inappropriate behavior and the negative consequences to the child of that

What did I do wrong?

I called out without getting permission. I made funny comments instead of working on my tasks.

Why shouldn't I talk out during work time?

When I talk out I disturb the other students, and they get mad at me. When I talk out it slows me down, and I don't finish my work. When I don't finish my work before recess, I don't get to go outside.

What should I do?

I should raise my hand and ask for permission to talk. I should talk only about the task and if I need help. I should sit quietly until the teacher comes to help me.

What will happen if I sit quietly and get permission to talk?

If I get permission to talk and talk only about the task, I will not disturb the other students. The other students will like me better. Also, if I work quietly I will get my tasks done sooner, and I will get to have free time.

Sample mediation essay.

behavior. Responses to the last two questions present the desirable, alternative behavior and its positive, to the child, consequences. An example of a mediation essay composed for a student exhibiting a high rate of talking out is provided in the Figure.

Mediation essays may be thought of as intermediate management techniques from two perspectives. First, while they act as a form of verbally mediated self-management, imposition of the essay is externally controlled by an adult. This element of external control is more like traditional behavioral interventions; however, the student's exposure to verbal descriptions of behaviors and consequences is similar to the cognitive-behavioral techniques noted by Meichenbaum (1977). Theoretically, through thinking about the essay's dialogue, the student alters his or her behavior to perform in a more appropriate manner. It has been suggested, too, that the student experiences some gratification from this self-control (Henker, Whalen, & Hinshaw, 1980).

Second, according to Marshall (1981), the mediation essay functions as an intermediate step when working with students who have the desired behavior in their repertoire but fail to use the behavior consistently or at the appropriate time. These students may lack the motivation to change, not recognize internal or external cues, not respond positively to simple reinforcement programs. It is this group of students with whom mediation essays are thought to be most effective. The technique not only works to eliminate undesirable behavior, it concurrently presents and encourages more desirable alternative behaviors.

Blackwood (1970) and MacPherson, Candee, and Hohman (1974) offer several suggestions about using the mediation essay. The following are the steps in implementing a mediation essay intervention: (1) identify the target be-

havior, alternative behavior, and consequences for each; (2) compose the essay using vocabulary within the child's repertoire; (3) meet with the student to discuss the need for behavior change, review the essay's content, and explain how the essay will be imposed; and (4) require the student to copy the essay when the student exhibits the target behavior. Marshall (1981) adds that the child should be reinforced for ready compliance with the assignment through a reduction in the number of copies to be made. Furthermore, some backup system is necessary for use in situations of noncompliance.

Research on the efficacy of the mediation essay with both nonhandicapped (Blackwood, 1970; MacPherson et al., 1974) and handicapped (Morrow & Morrow, 1985) students has been promising. The superiority of the mediation essay, with its focus on positive alternative behaviors, over the more traditional punishment essay has been clearly demonstrated in earlier studies.

REFERENCES

Blackwood, R. O. (1970). The operant conditioning of verbally mediated self-control in the classroom. *Journal of School Psychology, 8,* 251–258.

Henker, B., Whalen, C., & Hinshaw, S. (1980)., The attributional contexts of cognitive intervention strategies. *Exceptional Education Quarterly, 1*(1), 17–30.

MacPherson, E. M., Candee, B. L., & Hohman, R. J. (1974). A comparison of three methods for eliminating disruptive lunchroom behavior. *Journal of Applied Behavior Analysis, 7,* 287–297.

Marshall, J. (1981, April). *Mediation essay.* Paper presented at the International Conference of the Council for Exceptional Children, Houston, TX.

Meichenbaum, D. (1977). *Cognitive behavior modification: An integrative approach.* New York: Plenum.

Morrow, L. W., & Morrow, S. A. (1985). Use of verbal mediation procedure to reduce talking-out behaviors. *Teaching: Behaviorally Disordered Youth, 1,* 23–28.

KATHY L. RUHL
Pennsylvania State University

COGNITIVE BEHAVIOR MODIFICATION
CONTINGENCY CONTRACTING
SELF-CONTROL CURRICULUM
SELF-MONITORING

MEDIATORS

A mediator is an event that intervenes between the presentation of a stimulus and the emission of a response. Mediators are postulated to explain differences between learning in children and adults. Specifically, adults appear to use mediators spontaneously whereas children tend not to (Gross, 1985).

Verbal mediators are thought to underlie the more efficient learning or problem solving of older children and college adults in learning experiments (Harlow & Harlow, 1949). It is presumed that older children and college adults who use verbal mediators will label the features of the stimulus array that seem to be important. For example, in an oddity experiment in which the stimulus that differs from the other two stimuli, in say, color, is correctly chosen by the child, the child gets rewarded. The child continues to choose the stimulus with the right color over the next few successive trials/problems and gets rewarded consistently. Underlying the child's successful problem solving is the assumption that he or she uses verbal mediators to label the features of the stimulus array (naming the correct color). On the successive trial in which the child's selection of the stimulus with the correct color fails to net the expected reward, the child should immediately realize that the color mediator is wrong and that picking the odd item is the key to solving oddity problems. Thus children who deploy mediators learn the underlying concepts in oddity problems and in reversal shifts substantially faster. Younger children, being less likely to use verbal mediators, tend to persist in choosing the stimulus that has been rewarded most often (Shaffer, 1985).

Mediators play an important role in children's and adults' learning/problem solving. Compared with younger children, older children, and adults spontaneously use verbal mediators in aid of learning or problem solving. One possible reason for this difference in using verbal mediators pertains to the use of private speech to direct and regulate one's behavior. Private speech is self-talk. Children around 4 to 5 usually accompany their play action or work with verbal descriptions of what they are doing. Luria (1961) and Vygotsky (1962) proposed that young children use private speech as a means of directing or regulating their ongoing activities, making hypotheses, or forming new ideas. Such private speech becomes internalized around ages 5 to 7. There is empirical evidence supporting Luria's and Vygotsky's hypothesized functions of private speech (Goodman, 1981; Tinsley & Waters, 1982). It is pertinent to note that the postulation of mediators reflects the advent of cognitive psychology (Gross, 1985). The notion of mediators would not have been tolerated in the 1950s because behaviorism was the zeitgeist in psychology.

REFERENCES

Goodman, S. H. (1981). The integration of verbal and motor behavior in preschool children. *Child Development, 52*, 280–289.

Gross, T. F. (1985). *Cognitive development*. Monterey, CA: Brooks/Cole.

Harlow, H. F., & Harlow, M. K. (1949). Learning to think. *Scientific American, 181*, 36–39.

Luria, A. R. (1961). *The role of speech in the regulation of normal and abnormal behavior*. New York: Liveright.

Shaffer, D. R. (1985). *Developmental psychology: Theory, research and applications*. Monterey, CA: Brooks/Cole.

Tinsley, V. S., & Waters, H. S. (1982). The development of verbal control over motor behavior: A replication and extension of Luria's findings. *Child Development, 53*, 746–753.

Vygotsky, L. S. (1962). *Thought and language*. Cambridge, MA: M.I.T. Press.

BERNICE Y. L. WONG
Simon Fraser University

COGNITIVE STRATEGIES
LURIA, A. R.
MEDIATIONAL DEFICIENCY
VYGOTSKY, L. S.

MEDICAL CONCERNS OF HANDICAPPED CHILDREN

Current figures from the U.S. Department of Education (1984) indicate that approximately 10% of the 40 million children of school age are handicapped in some way (see Table).

Handicapped Children, U.S. Incidence

Exceptionality	Percent of School Population
Speech impaired	3.5
Mentally retarded	2.3
Emotionally disturbed	2.0
Learning disabled	2.0
Hearing impaired	0.6
Deaf-blind and other multihandicapped	0.6
Crippled and other health impaired	0.5
Visually handicapped	0.1

Exceptionality	Percent Enrolled in Special Education	Number Enrolled in Special Education
Learning disabled	4.40	1,745,871
Speech impaired	2.86	1,134,197
Mentally retarded	1.92	780,831
Behaviorally disordered	0.89	353,431
Other health impaired	0.13	52,026
Multihandicapped	0.16	65,479
Hard of hearing and deaf	0.18	75,337
Orthopedically impaired	0.14	57,506
Visually handicapped	0.07	31,096
Deaf-blind	0.01	2,553
TOTAL	10.76	4,298,327

Five percent, roughly 200,000, are physically disabled. Special education provides for about 150,000 of these children. An increase in certain physical disabilities has been reported in the last two decades (Harkey, 1983; Wilson, 1973). This may be due to improvements in identification, but more likely, medical advances have improved the survival rates of such children. This creates a great need by the schools and its professionals to understand fully the chronically ill, physically handicapped, and sensory-impaired populations, and the problems of these children imposed on the schools. Harkey (1983) feels that at least 1 to 2% of the child population, about 1 million children, have severe enough illnesses to require some kind of additional professional services to function adequately in school. Since 80% of the mildly handicapped are mainstreamed for at least a portion of the day, each teacher's chances of interacting with a handicapped student are very high. Many handicapped children also have concomitant health problems. Thus it is imperative that school professionals become as knowledgeable as possible about handicapping conditions.

One of the most common causes of physical disabilities is the result of damage to the central nervous system (CNS). The CNS involves the brain and spinal cord. Neurological impairment can be congenital (as with spina bifida), inherited (e.g., muscular dystrophy), or acquired later in life as a result of accident or trauma. Anorexia, infectious diseases like meningitis, poisoning, head injury, and strokes are other causes of CNS damage that result in muscular weakness or paralysis.

Cerebral palsy (CP) is the most common of all physical handicaps (about 50% of the physically handicapped have CP). Some CP causes are paralysis, weakness, incoordination in the extremities, and possibly visual and hearing impairment, speech defects, behavior disorders, and perceptual disorders (Denhoff, 1976). Hemiplegic and diplegic CP children may have normal intellectual development, but sensory abilities and emotional responsiveness may be affected by loss of motor control (Nolan & Ashcroft, 1969; Thompson, Rubin, & Bilenker, 1983). Children with CP may be spastic (stiff), ataxic (loose), or atetosic (afflicted by involuntary jerky movements). Hemiplegic and diplegic children may have fairly normal life spans but they will need wheelchairs as they advance in age (Denhoff, 1976).

Spina bifida is a congenital midline defect caused when the bony spinal cord does not close entirely during fetal development. There are many forms of spina bifida and with some (acculta and meningocele) relatively little neurological disability is seen. Paralysis of legs, bladder, and bowel, and hydrocephalus (enlargement of the head) caused by excessive pressure of cerebrospinal fluid are not uncommon. Surgery and shunt implantation are needed and IQ levels may vary depending on the early rectification of hydrocephalus. Spina bifida children as a group have low normal intelligence but relatively good verbal skills (Anderson & Spain, 1977).

Multiple sclerosis usually affects adolescents and adults. It is a CNS disease that causes hardening of myelin sheaths of nerves, sensory problems (visual), tremors, muscle weakness, spasticity, dizziness, and difficulty in walking and speaking. There is no known cure. School-aged children usually remain in public school and receive home instruction when school attendance is impossible (Frankel, 1984).

The muscular dystrophies are actually several different diseases (classic, Duchenne, facioscapulohumeral, myotonic, myasthenia gravis, and progressive atrophy). Most are hereditary (myasthenia gravis is not) and affect the muscle fibers of the body causing weakness and wasting away of muscular tissue. The causes of muscular dystrophies are not known and there is no cure. Symptoms may include swayback postures, waddling walks, propping of extremities, and winging of affected extremities. Muscular dystrophies are more common in boys than in girls. Early death and total disability are common.

Juvenile rheumatoid arthritis (Still's disease) causes muscle and joint pain and stiffness. About 1% of the children under 17 have the disease and more girls than boys are affected. Complications may include atrophy and joint deformity, heart and respiratory problems, and eye infections (Hallahan & Kauffman, 1986).

Seizure disorders affect 1 out of every 320 children. Matthews and Barabas (1985) found that 85% of these children, with the aid of medication, are in ordinary school settings with their disease controlled. About 22%, however, are learning disabled (Dickman, Matthews, & Harley, 1975). Children with epilepsy may have convulsions, loss of consciousness, and loss of motor or sensory functions. Seizures usually fall into three major categories: simple partial, complex partial, and generalized (petit and grand mal). Children with simple petit often have high IQs, while those with mixed type seizures, as a group, have the lowest (Seidenberg, O'Leary, Berent, & Boll, 1981). A wide range of behaviors and inattention can be seen with convulsive disorders. Teachers need to be aware of what to do in situations where seizures occur.

Tic syndromes may effect as many as one out of every four children (American Psychiatric Association, 1980), professionals in an educational setting can expect to encounter them frequently. Tourette syndrome, involving both motor and vocal tics, has been seen with increasing frequency over the past several years. Symptoms may emerge as early as 2 years of age and as late as 15 years. Boys are affected three times more often than girls (Anderson and Abuzzahab, 1976). Training teachers and parents to help the child focus his or her attention and sustain correct responses to situations may help inhibit the behaviors (Golden, 1977). The most effective method for treating tics was developed by Azrin and Nunn (1973).

Congenital defects can include heart and blood vessel damage, as well as abnormalities of the extremities, mouth, and face. These abnormalities can be present at birth (as in the case of Down's syndrome), or they can be acquired through accidents or diseases. They may affect the development of speech, language, and cognition, Clefts of the prepalate and palate are most common, occurring in 1 out of 800 births (Leske, 1981). The teacher will need to work closely with the speech pathologist and physician, who may be involved in corrective surgery as lags in language may be seen over a number of early school years. In addition to his or her unusual appearance, the child may suffer brain damage (as with Down's, Hurler's, Hunter's, and Williams' syndromes).

Hearing losses will appear in about 6% of school-aged children. Only about one-quarter of these children are treated in special education classes (Annals of the Deaf, 1975). The earlier the hearing loss, the more serious the effect, particularly as regards speech development. Meningitis, maternal rubella, and hereditary factors produce the severest deficits. Many hearing-impaired students also have at least one additional handicap. These may include visual problems, mental retardation, CP, epilepsy, heart disorders, and orthopedic disorders (Annuals of the Deaf, 1975).

Children with visual impairment may also appear in regular classrooms. Nearsightedness, farsightedness, and blurred vision are the most common inherited visual problems (Nolan & Ashcroft, 1969). Glaucoma, cataracts, and diabetes also affect vision and if untreated can cause blindness. Coloboma, a congenital degenerative disease, and retinitis pigmentosa cause damage to the retina. Syphilis and rubella also cause visual problems (Hallahan & Kauffman, 1986). Retrolental fibroplasia (RLF) caused by excessive exposure to oxygen concentrations in prenatal infants in incubators has been on the increase partially because medical breakthroughs enable premature children to survive but only with very high concentrations of oxygen (Chase, 1974). With blind children, muscle tone, midline functioning, rotation, balance, and motor movements may be impaired. Imitative abilities are also developmentally delayed. Blind children also lack facial expressions, have delays in smiling and turning, grasping, and speech acquisition, all of which can retard mental and physical development (Adelson & Frailberg, 1976; Jastrzembska, 1976; Warren, 1977).

Other conditions, which are sometimes referred to as handicaps, include cancer, asthma, hemophilia, scoliosis, and sickle cell anemia. It is important that teachers become aware of the different physical and mental characteristics of their handicapped students and be able to establish a good working relationship with the parents and medical and support personnel involved wiith the child. In this way an effective educational program can be planned. Public Law 94-142 requires that handicapped and chronically ill children be served in the least restrictive environment and that they receive an individualized educational program commensurate with their needs. Many of their needed medical accommodations are provided by the school districts in which they reside. These children may need specialized instruction (self-help skills, vocational training, occupational therapy, physical therapy, adaptive physical education), feeding and physical care, and mechanical and manual transportation in addition to regular academic education.

Many teachers have concerns about how best to meet these varied needs in order to provide adequate educational programs for handicapped children. Recent state, federal, and Supreme Court decisions have substantiated the right of these multihandicapped and chronically ill children to be mainstreamed where possible and to have support services provided by the schools (computer-assisted instruction, mechanical interpreters, extended school year, etc.). Given all these mandates, the teacher needs to develop a good interdisciplinary cooperative program with the many specialists involved with handicapped children with medical problems. The teacher must know what other disciplines are involved with the child, and he or she needs to be able to communicate professionally with persons in the medical field about the physical, emotional, cognitive, and social development of the handicapped child. Because of the support services needed, the occupational and physical therapists may be able to give valuable suggestions about working with the child in a regular or resource classroom. Continuing therapeutic management in the classroom will be needed so that the child can have a program that encourages independence and skill development.

Conferences with specialists in prosthetics and orthotics can help the teacher gain a better grasp on the function and operation of devices involved (artificial limbs, mechanical speech devices, life support systems, wheelchairs). Work with the school psychologist, community medical staff, and agencies is necessary to prevent lapses in treatment and to provide vital feedback to medical personnel and parents when new drugs or treatment are initiated. Medical information must be obtained by the teacher regarding the child's condition and the ways in which it may limit his or her participation in the school. Knowledge of hospital school programs needs to be investigated because many of these children will need hospitalization. Cooperative interaction between the sending school and the hospital school is vital if continuity of schooling is to be provided. Itinerant or homebound programs will also be needed and organized augmentation of them should be smooth and timely. Absences are high among these populations and alternative education settings and programs must be available and expediently operated.

Good communication must be maintained with the handicapped child's family. Family cooperation and encouragement is necessary for success in school. The most crucial tool for dealing with illness and disabilities is information; thus parents and teachers need to communicate regularly so that information can be shared. Since these children may have erratic attendance, maladaptive social behavior, severe side effects, and isolation owing to equipment needs and geographic location of care facilities, it is important that parents and school personnel work together to make the various transitions as smooth as possible for the child. Hobbs et al. (1984) have pointed out that chronically ill children are often short-changed educationally because teachers and school professionals develop plans for these children based on existing school services instead of what the child needs. Home and hospital programs, though often necessary, can be sketchy, disjointed, and take place in a diversity of settings.

REFERENCES

Adelson, E., & Frailberg, S. (1976). Sensory deficit and motor development in infants blind from birth. In Z. Jastrzembska (Ed.), *The effects of blindness and other impairments on early development*. New York: American Foundation for the Blind.

American Psychiatric Association. (1980). *Diagnosis and statistical manual of mental disorders* (3rd ed.). Washington, DC: Author.

Anderson, E., & Spain, B. (1977). *The child with spina bifida*. Hampshire, England: Mathuen.

Anderson, F., & Abuzzahab, F. (1976). Current knowledge of the syndrome. In F. Abuzzahab and F. Anderson (Eds.), *Gilles de la Tourette's Syndrome: Vol. 1*. St. Paul, MN: Mason.

Annuals of the Deaf (1975). Demographic studies at Gallaudet College. Silver Springs, MD: Conference of the American Instructors of the Deaf.

Azrin, N. H., & Nunn, R. G. (1973). Habit reversal: A method of eliminating nervous habits and tics. *Behavior Research & Therapy, 2*, 619–628.

Chase, J. (1974). A retrospective study of retrolental fibroplasia. *New Outlook for the Blind, 68*, 61–71.

Denhoff, E. (1976). Medical aspects. In W. Cruickshank (Ed.), *Cerebral palsy: A developmental disability* (3rd revised ed.). Syracuse, NY: Syracuse University Press.

Dickman, S., Matthews, G., & Harley, J. (1975). The effect of early versus late onset of major motor epilepsy upon cognitive-intellectual performance. *Epilepsy, 16*, 73–81.

Frankel, D. (1984). Long term care issues in multiple sclerosis. *Rehabilitation Literature, 45*, 282–285.

Golden, G. (1977). Tourette syndrome: The pediatric perspective. *American Journal of Diseases in Children, 131*, 531–534.

Hallahan, D., & Kauffman, J. (1986). *Exceptional children* (3rd ed.). Englewood Cliffs, NJ: Prentice-Hall.

Harkey, J. (1983). The epidemiology of selected chronic childhood health conditions. *Children's Health Care, 112*, 62–71.

Hobbs, N., Perrin, J., Freys, H., Moynihan, L., & Shayne, M. (1984). Chronically ill children in America. *Rehabilitation Literature, 45*, 206–211.

Jastrzembska, Z. (Ed.). (1976). *The effects of blindness and other impairments on early development*. New York: American Foundation for the Blind.

Leske, M. (1981). Prevalence estimates of communicative disorders in the U.S.: Language, hearing, and vestibular disorders. *ASHA, 23*, 229–237.

Matthews, W., & Barabas, G. (1985). Recent advances in developmental pediatrics related to achievement and social behaviors. *School Psychology Review, 14*(2), 182–189.

Nolan, C., & Ashcroft, S. (1969). The visually handicapped. *Review of Educational Research, 39*, 52–70.

Seidenberg, M., O'Leary, D., Berent, S., & Boll, T. (1981). Changes in seizure frequency and test-retest scores on the Weschler Adult Intelligence Scale. *Epilepsia, 22*, 75–83.

Thompson, G., Rubin, I., & Bilenker, R. (Eds.). (1983). *Comprehensive management of cerebral palsy*. New York: Grune & Stratton.

U.S. Department of Education. (1984). Sixth annual report to Congress on the implementation of Public Law 94-142: The Education of All Handicapped Children Act. Washington, DC: U.S. Government Printing Office.

Warren, D. (1977). *Blindness and early childhood development*. New York: American Foundation for the Blind.

Wilson, M. (1973). Children with crippling and health disabilities. In L. M. Dunn (Ed.), *Exceptional children in the schools* (2nd ed.). New York: Holt, Rinehart, & Winston.

SALLY L. FLAGLER
LOGAN WRIGHT
University of Oklahoma

ABNORMALITIES, NEUROPSYCHOLOGICAL
ADAPTIVE PHYSICAL EDUCATION
MEDICAL HISTORY
MEDICAL MANAGEMENT
PHYSICAL ANOMALIES
PHYSICAL DISABILITIES

MEDICAL HISTORY

When a student has academic or behavioral problems, or does not look physically well, educators often wonder if they should refer the student to a physician or psychologist for further evaluation. There are several areas of inquiry that could help the educator determine the need for one kind of referral or another (Zeltzer & LeBaron, 1984).

An assessment interview with the student should include an inquiry into the student's interests and favorite activities such as hobbies, favorite books, television programs, friends, and pets. The educator should observe whether the student appears unusually shy, defensive, anxious, or depressed. Next, the educator needs to ask about any current academic or interpersonal problems or physical symptoms in general. Questions regarding physical symptoms should include inquiries about pain, fatigue, recent changes in appetite or sleep patterns (including nightmares), activity changes, bodily concerns, or unusual physical sensations. Questions regarding academic and social concerns should include worries about friends, family, teachers, or school performance, or activity in general. Inquiry also should include recent or anticipated problems or changes such as illness in family members, divorce, unemployment, or change of residence.

In obtaining a history of past medical problems such as illnesses, injuries, or hospitalizations special attention should be paid to head injuries, since these may lead to significant changes in school performance, even when minor (Boll, 1983). Bruises or fractures not related to well-documented causes (e.g., automobile accidents or sports injuries) should raise questions in the teacher's mind regarding possible parental abuse. At some point during the interview, the student also should be asked if he or she perceives a problem or wants help. Low self-esteem, fear of parental anger, and other factors may cause a student to be reluctant to volunteer information or ask for help.

The areas of inquiry discussed also should be used in a second interview with parents if no obvious reasons for the problem are immediately evident. Children often are unable to recall important early childhood events that may have a significant impact on them. Also, parents may be willing to talk about family problems that the student feels reluctant to discuss.

A large percentage of visits to general pediatricians are made for nonmedical reasons. In a school setting, one may expect an even greater likelihood that a very large proportion of problems, even when they have a somatic component, are not primarily medical. Somatic complaints are often the manifestation of three types of common problems seen in an educational setting:

1. *Problems Emanating from a Poorly Functioning Family.* Such problems may consist of a poor parent/child relationship, inconsistent parenting, parental discord, physical or sexual abuse, or parental neglect. In problem families, major psychiatric disorders or alcoholism are frequent findings that require serious attention. Suspicion of abuse or neglect should be reported to the Department of Child Welfare.

2. *Anxiety Regarding Change.* Children are often anxious regarding physical or social change. As children and adolescents grow and develop, they are frequently worried about their ability to match perceived standards set by peers, parents, teachers, or themselves. These anxieties may reflect a distorted view of the child's own abilities, but in other cases may represent a realistic self-assessment of the child's own disabilities.

3. *Medical Problems With an Identifiable Organic basis.* If the student is not feeling well physically, he or she may not be able to concentrate on school work, and a decline in the student's academic performance may result.

Any of the problems in these first two categories can be manifested as somatic complaints such as headaches, stomach pains, or fatigue. It is important to note that these symptoms are experienced by the student, are distressing to him or her, and are not made up to gain attention. Such problems also may be accompanied by a drop in school grades, chronic absenteeism, or evidence of anxiety or depressed affect.

In general, any somatic complaints or significant changes in appetite or sleep should be cause for referral to a physician for further evaluation. One exception would be when there is an isolated symptom (e.g., abdominal pain) that is clearly related to a specific source of stress and that disappears when the child no longer has that stress. If the physician is unable to find a cause for the complaints and the problems persist, then the child should be seen by a clinical psychologist or other mental health professional associated with the school. Whether or not a mental health referral is made, maintenance of good physician/educator collaboration can prevent further unnecessary medical work-ups for the child and can facilitate a direct line of medical information when needed (LeBaron & Zeltzer, 1985; Marshall, Wuori, & Carlson, 1984).

REFERENCES

Boll, T. J. (1983). Minor head injury in children—Out of sight but not out of mind. *Journal of Clinical Child Psychology, 12*(1), 74–80.

LeBaron, S., & Zeltzer, L. (1985). Pediatrics and psychology: A collaboration that works. *Journal of Developmental & Behavioral Pediatrics, 6*(3), 157–161.

Marshall, R. M., Wuori, D. F., & Carlson, J. R. (1984). Improving physician/teacher collaboration. *Journal of Developmental & Behavioral Pediatrics, 5*(5), 241–245.

Zeltzer, L. K., & LeBaron, S. (1984). Psychosomatic problems in adolescents. *Postgraduate Medicine, 75*(1), 153–164.

SAMUEL LeBARON
LONNIE K. ZELTZER
*University of Texas Health
Science Center, San Antonio*

MEDICAL MANAGEMENT
PREREFERRAL INTERVENTION
TEACHER EXPECTANCIES

MEDICALLY FRAGILE STUDENT

The medically fragile student requires monitoring by the teacher during the school day in order to ensure that all of the body's physical systems are stable. The student's specific problem may or may not require that the teacher know special intervention techniques in case of emergency.

Medically fragile students are different from each other. They have different needs, energy levels, and potentials. Some children may exhibit a pervasive fragility (a generalized pattern of slow growth and development) but require no specific intervention. More likely, the child will have a chronic illness or experience an acute episode of a condition that requires that specific procedures be available when needed or that the daily routine be modified in order for the child to participate in school activities.

One of the most frequently observed types of medically fragile student is one who requires the use of a ventilator to facilitate breathing. The child may need the ventilator at all times during the school day or for part of the day. Once the medical team has decided the child is stable and no longer requires daily monitoring by medical personnel, the student may attend school. Often the child will be served in a program for physically and health-impaired students.

The teacher has two additional roles in providing education for the child if no health care professional is available. The teacher must be taught to monitor the child and the equipment and must learn about preventing of the spread of infection to the child. Any bacteria or virus may be a potential threat to the well being of the child on a ventilator. School board written policy should be followed as to best practice for the teacher to follow if another child in the room has cytomegalovirus or is a known carrier or exhibitor of any communicable disease.

For each medically fragile child the teacher and school administration should be trained to handle specific procedures that the child may need. For instance, if the student has life-threatening seizures, school personnel need to know exactly what procedures the child's parents and physicians want followed. All directions must be written in detail, signed, and dated and discussed with the principal and teacher before the child attends school.

Other health problems that may label a child medically fragile include chronic diseases, terminal conditions, post-surgery recovery, apnea, severe depression, cardiovascular problems, and kidney dysfunction. For some medically fragile children there are periods when they will be hospitalized for a long time, thus requiring hospital-based educational services.

REFERENCES

Ashcroft, S. (1984, Winter). Education and chronically ill children. *Peabody Journal of Education, 61,* 2.

Dykes, M. K., & Venn, J. (1983). Using health, physical and medical data in the classroom. In J. Umbreit (Ed.), *Physical disabilities and health impairments: An introduction.* Columbus, OH: Merrill.

Kleinberg, S. (1982). Educating the chronically ill child. Rockville, MD: Aspen.

MARY K. DYKES
University of Florida

HEALTH MAINTENANCE PROCEDURES
HOSPITAL SCHOOLS

MEDICAL MANAGEMENT

Because of advances made during the past 10 to 15 years in medical diagnosis and treatment, many childhood diseases formerly considered fatal have now become chronic illnesses such as cystic fibrosis and cancer (Zeltzer, 1978). Because of improved medical management, many children who would have been bedridden are now able to attend school. Examples include those with cyanotic heart disease, chronic renal disease, and rheumatologic diseases such as systemic lupus erythematosis and rheumatoid arthritis. Asthma and diabetes mellitus are the most common chronic illness of childhood. These and others are discussed in a text by Blum (1984) and a volume edited by Haggerty (1984).

Medical management of these illnesses for some children involves frequent physician visits, daily medication, and self-monitoring. Some illnesses result in multiple absences or restrictions from normal school-related activities. Some illnesses are associated with pain such as the joint pain found in lupus erythematosis, rheumatoid arthritis, hemophilia, or sickle cell disease. Many children who need repeated blood tests or treatment-related injections experience pain and anxiety associated with the needles. Chronic disease also may cause delayed physical growth and development.

When a chronic illness flares up, children often feel anxious or depressed about having to miss out on planned activities. Some children worry about the possibility of dying. Although chronic illness per se does not invariably lead to increased anxiety or poor self-esteem, such feelings, when they do occur, can lead to chronic school absenteeism and poor relationships with peers. The medications that are required to manage most illnesses often have side effects with psychological consequences. For example, some of the medications taken by children with asthma can lead to hyperactivity or periods of irritability and short attention span.

Chronic illness can restrict the child's independence to varying degrees. Parents usually monitor their ill child's activities more closely than they otherwise would; the child also may be dependent on parents for help with treatment. The achievement of developmental milestones, especially independence, is therefore difficult. The adolescent may try to achieve independence in ways that are destructive and inappropriate such as being noncompliant with medications. Some adolescents engage in risk-taking behaviors or ignore symptoms of the illness. Denial of the chronic illness is not necessarily maladaptive and may help children to engage in age-appropriate activities as long as treatment requirements are met.

The role of the educator in managing such children in an academic setting is to become as well informed as possible about the particular illness and its treatment. The educator needs to discuss the illness and the treatment with the student and his or her parents and, if possible, with the physician. The educator needs to develop an educational plan that is flexible and highly individualized. This plan needs to be reviewed frequently as the student's needs may change because of variations in the course of the disease. Chronically ill children usually respond well to educators who are personally supportive and interested in them as individuals. It is important for educators to recognize that most children and adolescents are remarkably resilient and that they cope well with illness and its treatment. The most important contribution the educator can make is to become well acquainted with the ill student and to encourage a normal life as much as possible while responding to the child's individual needs.

REFERENCES

Blum, R. (Ed.). (1984). *Chronic illness and disabilities in childhood and adolescence*. Orlando, FL: Grune & Stratton.

Haggerty, R. (Ed.). (1984). Chronic disease in children. *Pediatric Clinics of North America, 31*(1), 1–275.

Johnson, I. J., Zeltzer, L., & LeBaron, S. (1981). Chronic disease during adolescence. *Seminars in Family Medicine, 2*(3), 197–200.

Weitzman, M. (1984). School and peer relations. *Pediatric Clinics of North America, 31*(1), 59–69.

Zeltzer, L. (1978). Chronic illness in the adolescent. In I. R. Shenker (Ed.), *Topics in adolescent medicine* (pp. 226–253). New York: Stratton Intercontinental Medical.

SAMUEL LeBARON
LONNIE K. ZELTZER
*University of Texas Health
Science Center, San Antonio*

CHEMOTHERAPY
DIABETES
MEDICAL HISTORY

MEDICAL MODEL, DEFENSE OF

The medical model describes a theoretical orientation that focuses on the underlying, frequently physical cause of an observed problem, impairment, or disorder (Davis, 1980). Synonyms for the medical model include the disease model and the pathological model. The medical model has its origin in the field of medicine, where the identification of pathology within the individual is an important emphasis. Mercer (1973) describes the medical model as inherently evaluative, in that behaviors or symptoms that disrupt the individual's functioning are negative while those that enhance functioning are positive. In addition, the medical model is bipolar, associated either with sickness or "wellness." In applying the medical model, clinicians use conservative criteria when making diagnostic decisions, since failure to identify pathology when it is present is considered a serious error (Helton, Workman, & Mutuszek, 1982).

Within the field of special education, the medical model is most clearly applicable in cases of physical impairment such as visual, hearing, or orthopedic handicaps. Assessment techniques are designed to identify signs of such physical disability. Mass screenings in schools for vision or hearing problems, scoliosis, or tuberculosis are conducted within the framework of the medical model. Consistent with the ethical standards of this orientation, conservative decision rules are employed. Children identified as at risk for the disorder as a result of the screening procedure are referred for additional assessment and, if necessary, appropriate treatment (Helton et al., 1982). Application of the medical model in other areas of special education, particularly with the mildly handicapped, has been criticized. Mercer (1973), for example, stated that "the medical model for conceptualizing mental retardation in the community was inadequate" (pp. 20–21). Mercer does note, however, that the use of the medical model is more defensible in cases of mental retardation syndromes where there is "clear evidence of biological dysfunction" (p. 8).

In a detailed discussion of the application of the medical model in the interpretation of specific learning disabilities, Gaddes (1985) indicates that many of the most frequent criticisms of the medical model (e.g., that it does not promote change or growth and minimizes the role of psychoeducational intervention) are not inherent in the model itself, but are a result of abuses in its application. Gaddes indicates that use of a neuropsychological model, which is a special orientation within the generic medical model, has a number of important advantages. Neuropsychology, he argues, is a respected, established scientific field. Because all behavior is a byproduct of brain and central nervous system functioning, understanding brain-behavior relationships is critical to knowledge of children's learning and behavior. A neuropsychological diagnostic model helps identify the cause of observed disorders, which in turn leads to the development of more effective interventions.

REFERENCES

Davis, W. E. (1980). *Educator's resource guide to special education*. Boston: Allyn & Bacon.

Gaddes, W. H. (1985). *Learning disabilities and brain function: A neuropsychological approach* (2nd ed.). New York: Springer-Verlag.

Helton, G. B., Workman, E. A., & Matuszek, P. A. (1982). *Psychoeducational assessment*. New York: Grune & Stratton.

Mercer, J. R. (1973). *Labeling the mentally retarded*. Berkeley: University of California Press.

CATHY F. TELZROW
*Cuyahoga Special Education
Service Center, Maple
Heights, Ohio*

BIOGENIC MODELS
NEUROPSYCHOLOGY
PSYCHOGENIC MODELS

MEDICATION

See SPECIFIC MEDICATION.

MEGAVITAMIN THERAPY

Megavitamin therapy may be defined as treatment with quantities of one or more vitamins in amounts 10 or more times the recommended dietary allowance (Haslam, Dalby, & Rademaker, 1984). Hoffer, Osmond, and Pauling, pioneers in the field of megavitamin therapy, have indicated that such treatment (also known as orthomolecular treatment) can have desirable effects on many schizophrenics, emotionally disturbed children, and children with various learning and behavior problems. Pauling (1968) suggests that molecular concentrations normally present in the brain affect brain functioning. The ideal concentrations for an individual may differ from those that would result from normal diet and genetic factors. In such cases, the provision of additional concentrations of vitamins and minerals may be required to correct inbalances. In his work with schizophrenic and autistic children, Cott (1974) noted a decrease of hyperactivity and improved concentration and attention span following megavitamin therapy.

Megavitamin therapy has been the focus of considerable controversy. Critics point out that there are no conclusive large-scale studies that indicate long-term benefits from massive doses of vitamins; in fact, there may be harmful side effects from extended use of these vitamins in large quantities (Shaywitz, Siegel, & Pearson, 1977). A study conducted by Haslam et al. (1984) concludes that megavitamins are ineffective in the management of attention deficit disorders, and should not be used because of their potential toxicity.

REFERENCES

Cott, A. (1974). Treatment of learning disabilities. *Orthomolecular Psychiatry, 3,* 343–355.

Haslam, R. H. A., Dalby, J. T., & Rademaker, A. W. (1984). Effects of megavitamin therapy on children with attention deficit disorders. *Pediatrics, 74*(1), 103–111.

Pauling, L. (1968). Orthomolecular psychiatry. *Science, 160,* 265–271.

Shaywitz, B. A., Siegel, N. J., & Pearson, H. A. (1977). Megavitamins for minimal brain dysfunction: A potentially danger-

ous therapy. *Journal of the American Medical Association, 238,* 1749–1750.

BARBARA S. SPEER
*Shaker Heights City School
District, Shaker Heights,
Ohio*

MALNUTRITION
NUTRITIONAL DISORDERS

MEICHENBAUM, DONALD (1940–)

Donald Meichenbaum earned his BA at the City College of New York in 1962 and his MA and PhD in 1966 from the University of Illinois, Urbana. Meichenbaum is noted as one of the founders of cognitive behavior modification. Since 1966, he has served as professor of psychology at the University of Waterloo, Ontario, Canada, and as a clinical psychologist in private practice.

Meichenbaum's major fields of interest include psychopathology, cognitive-affective development, and stress and coping. His research centers on the role of cognitive factors in mediating behavior and on the development of assessment and therapeutic procedures studying the relationship of emotion and behavior. Treatment procedures such as stress inoculation training with adults and self-instruction training with impulsive, aggressive children reflect his influential contributions as a researcher and as a psychotherapist, as well as his multidimensional study of cognition and emotion.

Meichenbaum's major publications include *Cognitive-Behavior Modification: An Integrative Approach* (considered a classic in the field), *Stress-Inoculation Training, Stress Reduction and Prevention,* and *The Unconscious Reconsidered.* He has published over 80 journal articles, books, and associated works. In addition, he is an active speaker, presenting workshops and lectures throughout the United States, Canada, Europe, Israel, and the Soviet Union.

Recipient in 1974 of the Consulting Psychology Research Award given by Division 13 of the American Psychological Association, Meichenbaum also serves on the editorial board of a dozen journals and is associate editor of *Cognitive Therapy and Research.* He has received numerous research grants and serves as a consultant to medical, educational, psychiatric, correctional, and business institutions.

REFERENCES

Meichenbaum, D. (1977). *Cognitive-behavior modification: An integrative approach.* New York: Plenum.

Meichenbaum, D. (1983). *Stress reduction and prevention.* New York: Plenum.

Meichenbaum, D. (1985). *Stress-inoculation training.* New York: Pergamon.

Meichenbaum, D., & Bowers, K. (1984). *The unconscious reconsidered*. New York: Wiley.

MARY LEON PEERY
Texas A&M University

MELLARIL

Mellaril is the trade name for the generic phenothiazine, thioridazine. In addition to its general applications for symptomatic relief in psychotic disorders, Mellaril also appears to show some efficacy in psychotic disorders with depressive components. It also has been used in short-term, symptomatic treatment of agitation, depression, sleep disturbance, and fears in elderly patients, and for the short-term symptomatic treatment of hyperactivity, combativeness, attention problems, mood lability, and poor frustration tolerance in children (McEvoy, 1984).

Mellaril has similar dose effectiveness ratios as Thorazine, another phenothiazine that is used in the management of psychotic symptoms (Seiden & Dykstra, 1977). Like all phenothiazines, Mellaril produces some sedation, especially during early administration. In addition, anticholinergic effects (dry mouth, urinary retention, motor incoordination), extrapyramidal symptoms, dystonic reactions, motor restlessness, and parkinsonlike symptoms are among the adverse effects that may be experienced early in treatment or from overdosage. Tardive dyskinesia, which is characterized by rhythmic involuntary movements of the oral musculature and face, and sometimes of the extremities, is also a possible side effect. This is of some concern because tardive dyskinesia is resistant to treatment.

REFERENCES

McEvoy, G. K. (1984). *American hospital formulary service: Drug information 84*. Bethesda, MD: American Society of Hospital Pharmacists.

Seiden, L. S., & Dykstra, L. A. (1977). *Psychopharmacology: A biochemical and behavioral approach*. New York: Van Nostrand Reinhold.

ROBERT F. SAWICKI
*Lake Erie Institute of
Rehabilitation, Lake Erie,
Pennsylvania*

STELLAZINE
THORAZINE
TRANQUILIZERS

MEMORY DISORDERS

Neuropsychological research suggests that memory disorders may occur with brain injury or neurological disease. Generally speaking, a memory disorder refers to a deficiency in the storage and/or retrieval of information. Impaired memory functioning is one of the most common symptoms of generalized cerebral damage (Strub & Black, 1977).

An understanding of memory disorders is facilitated by an appreciation of the basic memory components. Although a number of memory modals have been proposed, three distinct yet interactive memory stores are generally implicated (Shallice, 1979). Incoming sensory information is thought to be held briefly and selected for future processing in a sensory register. Research in this area suggests that information in the sensory register is either transferred to short-term memory or is rapidly replaced by incoming information.

Short-term store, or immediate memory, is portrayed as a temporary working memory of limited capacity. Information in the short-term store has been shown to be accessible for 20 to 30 seconds (Norman, 1973) and limited to approximately five to nine items (Miller, 1956). Information in the short-term memory is rehearsed and subsequently stored in long-term memory or is displaced by incoming information. Thus rehearsal serves to prolong the memory trace as well as to facilitate permanent storage. In sum, information in short-term memory appears to be unstable and lost or inaccessible unless transferred into the more enduring long-term store.

Long-term memory refers to the relatively permanent storage of information. Seen as the result of repeated presentations of information or very salient stimuli, long-term storage involves a relatively permanent structural or biochemical change in the brain (Hillgard & Bower, 1975). The long-term storage of information involves both transfer and consolidation of sensory inputs. Simply stated, transfer refers to the transmission of information from short-term memory to long-term memory or directly to long-term memory from the sensory register. A much more complex process, consolidation involves the progressive strengthening of memory traces over time. Disruption of the consolidation process may impair the ability to learn.

Much of the information in long-term memory has been shown to be stored on the basis of abstract conceptual properties of the stimulus (Craik & Lockhart, 1972). However, a recent investigation by Dean, Gray, and Yekovich (under review) indicates that more superficial stimulus attributes (i.e., visual or auditory components) may also play a prominent role in the storage process. Consistent with the notion of a relatively permanent memory trace, these investigators suggest that under some conditions stimuli may be stored in long-term memory as "literal copy."

Retrieval of a memory trace from the long-term store is seen to involve the reactivation of the same physical structure or biochemical conditions that were responsible for the initial storage or encoding process (Bloch & Laroche, 1984). This reactivation process appears to be triggered by stimuli that are the same or similar to the original encoding event.

The brain has been clearly linked to memory processing. Indeed, convincing data have been offered that closely tie the temporal area of the brain to memory functioning. Primarily involved in audition, the temporal lobe appears to be instrumental in triggering complex memories. In addition, a substantial amount of research has shown that damage to the hippocampus (structure within the limbic system lying just under the temporal flap) serves in the consolidation and transfer of information to long-term store. It has also been shown that bilateral damage to the hippocampus results in the inability to learn other than simple rudimentary motor skills (Barbizet, 1963). On the basis of such data, it has been concluded that the temporal lobe and specifically the limbic system may be the underlying anatomical substrates of the memory system.

Damage to the temporal lobe or its related structures (e.g., hippocampus, fornix, mammillary bodies, thalamus) often results in memory dysfunction. The most prevalent disorder, retrograde amnesia, refers to an impairment in the ability to retrieve information from the period prior to brain pathology. While most often affecting memories stored up to 30 minutes preceding the damage (Lezak, 1983), retrograde amnesia relates to the disturbance of memories from several months to many years prior to onset. However, older, well-ingrained memories are rarely permanently disrupted.

Anterograde amnesia, a much more serious memory disturbance, is characterized by a profound deficit in the ability to retain new information. While immediate (short-term) memory functioning may be intact, the ability to recall day-to-day events over hours is severely impaired. Thus learning new material is difficult, if not impossible. Interestingly, however, a number of investigators have shown that patients suffering from chronic anterograde amnesia generally are able to retrieve information learned prior to the neuropathology (Squire & Slater, 1978). These data suggest that anterograde amnesia stems from a problem in encoding new information rather than from difficulty in retrieving previously stored information.

In addition to affecting memory processes in circumscribed ways, cerebral pathology may also differentially affect the storage and retrieval of specific types of material. For example, depending on the location of the brain dysfunction, a memory deficit may be limited to either verbal or nonverbal material. So, too, a specific memory deficit may be isolated to previously learned motor behaviors (Corkin, 1968).

A further distinction in memory disorders can be made between episodic and semantic memory. As proposed by Tulving (1972), episodic memory refers to the storage of specific temporally dependent information. This type of memory includes contextual information about day-to-day events (e.g., memory for the events of one's day). Semantic memories do not seem dependent on such temporal events, but rather are stored on the basis of abstract conceptual properties. Semantic memory consists of an organized store of symbols, concepts, language, and rules (e.g., the conceptualization that baseball is a game).

Transient global amnesia, a relatively common memory disorder, is characterized by a sudden, seemingly unprovoked onset of anterograde amnesia. In such cases, the individual is temporarily unable to store episodic information. However, there appears to be no loss in other cognitive functions. Interestingly, memories stored hours or even days prior to the attack may also be inaccessible, but retrieval of more remote memories seems to be intact. Typically lasting only several hours, transient global amnesia does not cause permanent memory deficits. Indeed, aside from an inability to remember events that occurred during the amnesic episode, memory functioning is completely restored. Although the etiology is not clear, transient global amnesia has been associated with cerebral vascular problems in the elderly and temporal lobe epilepsy in younger adults (Barbizet, 1970).

Traumatic brain injuries often produce memory impairments (traumatic amnesia). Typically, postconcussion memory loss includes both retrograde and anterograde amnesia. Following a traumatic loss of consciousness, individuals often experience a temporary inability to store and retrieve incoming information. During the posttraumatic period, the individual may appear to behave normally, but may later have little recollection of specific behaviors. A number of investigators have concluded that posttraumatic amnesia is significantly related to the length of coma as well as the severity of the cerebral insult (Evans, 1975).

Older memories usually remain intact after the trauma, however, memories involving the minutes or several hours prior to the cerebral trauma may be inaccessible. Moreover, if the coma lasts for several days or weeks, the retrograde amnesia may be much more pervasive. Over time, however, many of the well-ingrained memories are again accessible. While a number of memory disturbances seem to be concomitant with traumatic head injuries, the specific effects of such trauma are dependent on the severity, age, and site of the damage (Lezak, 1983).

One of the most common memory disorders is dementia. Dementia is characterized by deficits in memory, judgment, abstract reasoning, and cognition in general. Personality disturbances may also be concomitant with dementia. While dementia is often associated with older individuals, it may develop at any age. Although minor memory problems may be concomitant with normal aging, they do not characteristically impede daily functioning. However, the memory deficiencies that accompany dementia may lead to the inability to acquire new information or to use previously stored information. While the etiology of these memory disturbances is not always clear, a number of investigations with demented patients have found reduced cholinesterase levels in those areas of the brain typically associated with memory (Perry et al., 1978).

Characterized by progressive cognitive, social, and behavioral deterioration, Alzheimer's disease has been classified as a primary degenerative dementia. One of the earliest signs of Alzheimer's disease is an impaired ability to recall temporally dated events. Increasing difficulty in the retrieval of words (dysnomia) from long-term memory may continue to limit social interaction. For the most part, however, immediate (short-term) memory seems to be much less impaired. While more well-ingrained memories may persist, retrieval of past memories becomes progressively more difficult. Indeed, those past memories that are most relevant to the individual appear to be the least disrupted (Barbizet, 1970). With time, the impaired ability to store new information and to use previously stored information makes learning virtually impossible. As the disease progresses the individual may be unable to function independently.

Pick's disease, a relatively rare disorder, is similar to Alzheimer's. Indeed, aside from postmortem cortical differences, the only observable difference between the two conditions is the onset of memory loss. While memory deficits are one of the earliest symptoms of Alzheimer's disease, personality disturbances precede memory impairment in Pick's disease. Alzheimer's disease is often confused with depression soon after onset.

Although Korsakoff's syndrome appears to be closely linked with alcohol abuse, it is more closely associated with a chronic vitamin B^1 (thiamine) deficiency and as such may occur for other reasons. The major symptom associated with this syndrome is anterograde amnesia. Indeed, individuals suffering from Korsakoff's syndrome are typically incapable of learning new information, and may have no recall of material presented to them minutes before. Consistent with this pervasive impairment in learning, severe disruption of the consolidation and retrieval processes have been implicated (Butters & Cermak, 1980).

Neuropsychological data on Korsakoff's patients suggest that these individuals typically experience deficiencies in episodic memory (Barbizet, 1970). However, these patients may have spotty memories, in that bits and chunks of their past histories may be recalled. Thus when communicating with others, they often attempt to fill in the missing information with elaborate fabrications (confabulations). While a number of investigators have argued that immediate (short-term) memory is within normal limits for the Korsakoff's patient (Baddeley & Warrington, 1970), more recent data (Ryan, Butters, & Montgomery, 1979) suggest that short-term memory functioning is also impaired.

Congenital anomalies may also lead to problems of memory and learning. Clearly, such congenital abnormalities as cerebral palsy, meningitis, and hydrocephalus have been associated with severe learning and memory difficulties. The memory disorders associated with these congenital conditions tend to be pervasive and may make learning difficult at best. Consistent with this pervasive impairment in learning, severe disruption of the storage and retrieval processes have been shown to be characteristic. Because of this diffuse impairment, patients often require special education services or custodial care.

In conclusion, a number of memory disorders have been shown to be concomitant with cerebral pathology. Indeed, damage to the temporal portion of the brain often leads to memory dysfunction. While this article has reviewed the basic memory disorders, Hécaen and Albert (1978) should be consulted for a more thorough discussion of this topic.

REFERENCES

Baddeley, A. D., & Warrington, E. K. (1970). Amnesia and the distinction between long and short term memory. *Journal of Verbal Learning & Verbal Behavior, 9*, 176–189.

Barbizet, J. (1963). Defect of memorizing of hippocampal-mammillary origin: A review. *Journal of Neurology, Neurosurgery, & Psychiatry, 26*, 127–135.

Barbizet, J. (1970). *Human memory and its pathology.* San Francisco: Freeman.

Bloch, V., & Laroche, S. (1984). Facts and hypotheses related to the search for the engram. In G. Lynch, J. L. McGaugh, & N. M. Weinberger (Eds.), *Neurobiology of learning and memory* (pp. 249–260). New York: Guilford.

Butters, N., & Cermak, L. S. (1980). *Alcoholic Korsakoff's syndrome.* New York: Academic.

Corkin, S. (1968). Acquisition of motor skills after bilateral medial temporal lobe excision. *Neuropsychologia, 6*, 255–266.

Craik, F. I. M., & Lockhart, R. S. (1972). Levels of processing: A framework for memory research. *Journal of Verbal Learning & Verbal Behavior, 11*, 671–684.

Dean, R. S., Gray, J. W., Yekovich, F. R. (under review). *Modality effects in long-term memory.*

Evans, M. (1975). Discussion of the clinical problem. *In Ciba Foundation Symposium, No. 34 (new series). Symposium on the outcome of severe damage to the CNS.* Amsterdam: Elsevier-Excerpta Medica.

Hécaen, H., & Albert, M. L. (1978). *Human neuropsychology.* New York: Wiley.

Hillgard, E. R., & Bower, G. H. (1975). *Theories of learning.* Englewood Cliffs, NJ: Prentice-Hall.

Lezak, M. D. (1983). *Neuropsychological assessment.* New York: Oxford University Press.

Miller, G. A. (1956). The magical number seven, plus or minus two: Some limits on our capacity for processing information. *Psychological Review, 63*, 81–97.

Norman, D. A. (1973). What have the animal experiments told us about human memory? In J. A. Deutsch (Ed.), *The physiological basis of memory* (pp. 248–260). New York: Academic.

Perry, E. K., Tomlinson, B. E., Blessed, G., Bergmann, K., Gibson, P. H., & Perry, R. H. (1978). Correlation of cholinertic abnormalities with senile plaques and mental test scores in senile dementia. *British Medical Journal, 2*, 1457–1459.

Ryan, C., Butters, N., & Montgomery, K. (1979). Memory deficits in chronic alcoholics: Continuities between the "intact" alcoholic and the alcoholic Korsakoff patient. In H. Begleiter & B. Kissin (Eds.), *Alcohol intoxication and withdrawal* (pp. 180–196). New York: Plenum.

Shallice, T. (1979). Neuropsychological research and the fractionation of memory systems. In L. G. Nilsson (Ed.), *Perspectives on memory research* (pp. 218–236). Hillsdale, NJ: Erlbaum.

Squire, L. R., & Slater, P. L. (1978). Anterograde and retrograde memory impairment in chronic amnesia. *Neuropsychologia, 16,* 313–322.

Straub, R. L., & Black, F. W. (1977). *The mental status examination in neurology.* Philadelphia: Davis.

Tulving, E. (1972). Episode and semantic memory. In E. Tulving & W. Donaldson (Eds.), *Organization of memory* (pp. 205–218). New York: Academic.

JEFFREY W. GRAY
Ball State University

RAYMOND S. DEAN
*Ball State University
Indiana University School of
Medicine*

AMNESIA
CHOLINESTERASE
DYSNOMIA

MENINGITIS

Meningitis is an infection or inflammation of the membranes covering the brain and spinal cord. It may affect the arachnoid, the pia mater, and the cerebrospinal fluid in the subarachnoid space. The infection resulting in meningitis may occur via spinal fluid pathways, directly from a local infection or the bloodstream, or via retrograde thrombophlebitis (*Melloni's*, 1985). Meningitis is classified by the causative agent, and may include bacterial meningitis, meningococcal meningitis, and viral meningitis. A lumbar puncture is conducted to obtain a sample of cerebrospinal fluid in which the causative agent can be identified (Thomson, 1979).

Seventy percent of the cases of bacterial meningitis are caused by Streptococcus pneumoniae, Neisseria meningitidis, and Homophilus influenza type b, collectively (Swartz, 1979). There is a strong age component associated with the etiologic agent in cases of bacterial meningitis. In neonates, gram-negative bacilli are the major bacterial cause of meningitis, with H. influenza type b the most common agent in children under the age of 5 (Swartz, 1979). Neisseria meningitidis is the offending bacterium in meningococcal meningitis, a common form of the disease. Transmission may occur from person to person via hand to hand, hand to mouth, or mouth to mouth contact

(Feldman, 1979). Epidemics of meningococcal meningitis may occur in heavily populated areas such as military bases or urban centers (Swartz, 1979).

Bacterial meningitis is characterized by an acute onset of fever, headache, vomiting, and stiff neck. Prior history of upper respiratory infection, acute otitis, or pneumonia may be identified (Swartz, 1979). Drowsiness and lethargy may be evident. Seizures may be present in 20 to 30% of affected individuals. Partial or complete sensorineural hearing loss may occur in patients over 3 years of age, and may persist (Swartz, 1979). While rapid recovery from bacterial meningitis typically follows prompt treatment with antibiotics, residual neurologic impairment may be identified in 10 to 20% of recovered individuals (Swartz, 1979).

Viral meningitis, in contrast to the bacterial form, is described as "a benign, self-limited illness" (Johnson, 1979, p. 817). The coxsackie and echoviruses are associated with approximately 50% of the cases of viral meningitis (Johnson, 1979). Symptoms develop rapidly, and include headache, fever, stiff neck, sore throat, nausea, and vomiting; symptoms may persist from 3 to 14 days. Full recovery is typically within 1 to 2 weeks (Johnson, 1979).

Some children with a history of bacterial meningitis may require special education and related services. Hearing loss may be a residual impairment in some individuals, and generalized intellectual deficiency resulting from high fever or seizures may be identified. A multifactored evaluation is essential in planning an educational program for affected children.

REFERENCES

Feldman, H. A. (1979). Meningococcal disease. In P. B. Beeson, W. McDermott, & J. B. Wyngaarden (Eds.), *Cecil textbook of medicine* (pp. 417–423). Philadelphia: Saunders.

Johnson, R. T. (1979). Viral meningitis and encephalitis. In P.B. Beeson, W. McDermott, & J. B. Wyngaarden (Eds.), *Cecil textbook of medicine* (pp. 817–821). Philadelphia: Saunders.

Melloni's illustrated medical dictionary (2nd ed.). (1985). Baltimore, MD: Williams & Wilkins.

Swartz, M. N. (1979). Bacterial meningitis. In P. B. Beeson, W. McDermott, & J. B. Wyngaarden (Eds.), *Cecil textbook of medicine* (pp. 411–416). Philadelphia: Saunders.

Thomson, W. A. R. (1979). *Black's medical dictionary* (32nd ed.). New York: Barnes & Noble.

CATHY F. TELZROW
*Cuyahoga Special Education
Service Center, Maple
Heights, Ohio*

MENINGOMYELOCELE

Meningomyelocele is an abnormal outpouching of the spinal cord through an opening in the back of the spine. The term is synonymous with myelomeningocele and is a more common form of spina bifida than a meningocele (an outpouching that includes only the protective membranes but not the spinal cord). The outpouching of the spinal cord and its nerve roots into the meningomyelocele causes a flaccid paralysis and loss of sensation in the lower extremities or trunk. This loss of function depends on the level of the spinal cord defect and the number of nerve roots involved.

The cause of a meningomyelocele is essentially unknown. It occurs when the neural tube (the cells that form the spine and spinal cord) fails to develop and close completely in the first few weeks of pregnancy. A meningomyelocele may be detected using several intrauterine tests, most commonly amniocentesis or ultrasound. Early treatment includes closure of the open sack to prevent infection, a procedure that often requires the removal of some neural elements. Additional surgery also may be required subsequently to repair other conditions that are frequently associated with meningomyelocele. These secondary conditions may include hydrocephalus and orthopedic abnormalities in the legs or spine such as club foot or scoliosis.

Loss of bowel and bladder control is common for persons with a meningomyelocele. Management of bowel and bladder function may include a combination of suppositories, diet, medication, and clean intermittent catheterization. Physical and occupational therapy, bracing, wheelchairs, and other assistive devices often promote increased functional independence and permit a productive and rewarding life.

REFERENCES

Bleck, E. E. (1985). Myelomeningocele, meningocele, spina bifida. In E. E. Bleck, & D. A. Nagel (Eds.), *Physically handicapped children—A medical atlas for teachers* (pp. 181–192). New York: Grune & Stratton.

Burr, H. C. (1970). Classification of myelomeningocele and congenital spinal defects. In *American Academy of Orthopedic Surgeon's Symposium on myelomeningocele* (pp. 1–18). St. Louis: Mosby.

Long, C. (1971). Congenital and traumatic lesions of the spinal cord. In G. H. Krusen, F. J. Kottke, & P. M. Ellwood (Eds.), *Handbook of physical medicine and rehabilitation* (2nd ed., pp. 475–516). Philadelphia: Saunders.

DANIEL D. LIPKA
Lincoln Way Special Education
Regional Resource Center,
Louisville, Ohio

PHYSICAL HANDICAPS
SPINA BIFIDA

MENTAL AGE

Mental age is an age-equivalent score derived from a general test of intellectual skill or aptitude. The mathematical derivation is the same as for other types of age-equivalent scores. A mental age represents the mean level of performance or a group of children at a particular chronological age on the test in question. For example, if the average number of questions answered correctly by children aged 8 years, 2 months on an intelligence test was 33, then, in future administrations of the same test, all children who answer 33 questions correctly would be assigned a mental age of 8 years, 2 months.

This type of score has been often misinterpreted in intelligence and aptitude testing. The mental age does not take into account the dispersion of children's scores about the mean and has a standard deviation that varies considerably across age. Thus a child who is 2 years below chronological age in mental age, may or may not have a significant problem. For a 5 year old, a mental age of 3 years represents serious retardation in the development of intellectual skills. A 16 year old with a mental age of 14 will fall within the average range of intelligence. It is not true that a 6 year old with a mental age of 9 years has the same intellectual skills or thinks and reasons like a 12 year old with a mental age of 9 years.

Mental ages have been popular for some time and are necessary in the calculation of ratio IQs, a type of IQ scale abandoned many years ago by all major tests of intelligence. Mental ages are regarded by most psychologists and psychometricians as a poor method of score reporting; standard scores are considered superior in all instances (Reynolds, Gutkin, Elliott, & Witt, 1984).

Mental age is usually abbreviated as MA and reported as the year followed by a decimal and the number of months (or in some cases, fraction of a year, though this option is usually confusing), as in MA = 9.4, which means that the child's mental age is 9 years, 4 months.

REFERENCES

Reynolds, C. R., Gutkin, T. B., Elliott, S. N., & Witt, J. C. (1984). *School psychology: Essentials of theory and practice.* New York: Wiley.

CECIL R. REYNOLDS
Texas A&M University

CENTRAL TENDENCY
DEVIATION IQ
GRADE EQUIVALENTS
RATIO IQ
STANDARD DEVIATION

MENTAL DEFICIENCY

See MENTAL RETARDATION.

MENTAL ILLNESS

Mental illness is a disease or condition that is manifested in disruptions of an individual's behavior, thinking, perception, or emotions. Other terms used synonomously are mental, psychiatric, and psychological disorder or disease. The single most important concept in determining whether or not someone is mentally ill is his/her level of adaptive functioning. One area of adaptive functioning, indeed the most critical, is the person's social relations.

Problems in social relations can be viewed in terms of quantity and quality. Does the person shun social contact or the development of close relationships? Social isolation and withdrawal are cardinal manifestations of mental disorder. However, the person's motives for social avoidance must be considered. A motive of intense anxiety or gross indifference, for example, is indicative of a mental disorder. However, social withdrawal may be considered normal under some conditions such as while writing a dissertation or acclimating to a foreign culture.

The quality of social relationships is another dimension of social adaptiveness. Here a diagnostician assesses the degree to which the person manipulates others for his or her own selfish purposes, shows a lack of empathy, or is unable to establish or maintain intimate relationships. Involvements predominately characterized by excessive hostility, suspiciousness, jealousy, dominance, or undue submissiveness and dependency may also serve as markers of mental disorder. In addition to social adaptation, occupational or academic functioning may also reveal evidence of mental illness.

When evaluating a person's school or job performance, several questions are important. Has there been a decline in functioning? Do emotions, thoughts, or behaviors interfere with performance? Does the person obsessively focus on details to the neglect of the broader perspective? Does the individual report a lack of energy, fatigue, bodily complaints, and pessimism? Is the person's work history characterized by absenteeism, frequent job changes and arguments with bosses and coworkers? Problems in any one of these areas may indicate a psychological disorder.

Use of leisure time may be of concern when it involves excessive drug use, stealing, dangerous impulsive activity, or gambling that disrupts social relations. In the case of children or adolescents, vandalism, unusually premature sexual activity, fighting, delinquency, or arson are all examples of maladaption.

The final area of adaptive functioning that is assessed is self-care. This consists of the basic necessities of feeding, grooming, and hygiene, and are judged within the context of the person's social reference group. One overt manifestation of a mental disorder is a deterioration in self-care, as is found, for example, in chronic schizophrenia.

It is important to note that no single behavior can be used to diagnose mental illness. The circumstances leading to the behavior or cluster of behaviors and their severity in compromising adaptive functioning are taken into account when making a diagnosis of mental disorder.

When a patient complains about his or her behavior, thoughts, perceptions, or emotions, he or she is stating a symptom. Often symptoms are found to cluster together and the term syndrome is applied. For example, sadness, lack of energy, pessimism, and changes in appetite and sleeping are a few of the symptoms that make up the depressive syndrome. The beginning of a syndrome is its onset and the manner in which it unfolds is its course. The individual's level of functioning prior to the onset of the disorder is called premorbid adjustment and is designated along a continuum of good to bad. Just before the onset of the disorder, there may be a transition period that presages the syndrome. This is known as the prodrome or prodromal phase. For example, people who suffer from epilepsy or migraine headaches will notice feeling "different," (called an aura); this feeling signals the seizure or headache. The phase of the disorder that persists after the syndrome has abated but during which problems still exist is called the residual phase. Some disorders seem to develop rapidly and are called acute. If the syndrome persists, the term chronic phase is applicable. Not all disorders show this sequential pattern. For example, simple phobias may be chronic but they have no prodromal or residual phase. Schizophrenia, in contrast, can be meaningfully discussed using all of the mentioned definitions. Clinicians have also found it useful to distinguish disorders based on their cause or etiology. Those disorders having a biological dysfunction as a basis are referred to as organic. When no known biological cause can be identified, psychological factors are considered the cause and the term functional is applied. One clear example of an organically based mental disorder is delirium. Dependent personality disorder represents an example of a functional disorder. The organic/functional dichotomy is not always clear (e.g., schizophrenia), and indeed organic and functional factors may coexist in a single individual (e.g., psychophysiological disorders).

No other term in psychiatry has prompted more heated debate than mental illness. It has been used as a vehicle for politically based, interprofessional fighting, as well as a means of focusing on differences in theoretical approaches to abnormal behavior. Although the current controversies about the usefulness of the concept of mental illness are recent, the term has a long history.

Several arguments have been offered to the effect that the sickness model, embodied in the term mental illness, has outlived its usefulness. One implication of this model is that physician-psychiatrists should hold primary, if not sole, responsibility for the treatment of people labeled as mentally ill. The terms illness, cure, psychiatric hospital, treatment, remission, and relapse are all borrowed from medicine and applied to the psychotherapeutic endeavor. And who best to administer the treatment but someone trained within the medical profession? Thus, some authors have argued that psychiatry is endorsing a view of abnormal behavior that strengthens their professional territorial boundary (Mowrer, 1960).

Other attacks aimed at the sickness model are rooted in alternate theoretical approaches to mental illness such as replacing the term with the phrase "problems in living" (Kanfer & Phillips, 1970; Szasz, 1961). This learning-based framework holds that abnormal behavior is not a manifestation of an underlying psychic disorder, but is a result of a reciprocal interaction between behavior and environment (Bandura, 1969; Davison & Neale, 1982). Within this framework, terms such as mental illness, disease, symptoms, and cure have little meaning. Symptoms are not the outgrowth of an underlying psychic disease process but are the client's problems. They are learned, maladaptive strategies that may have several purposes such as anxiety reduction, avoiding negative social consequences, or evoking positive consequences from others. The implications for diagnosis and treatment are accordingly different from the traditional sickness model (Kanfer & Grimm, 1977, 1980). Recently the debate has become less political, and paradigmatic demarcations are beginning to blur as clinicians strive for a theoretical rapprochement (Wachtel, 1977).

The purpose of psychological testing is to gather information concerning a person's personality characteristics, psychopathology, strengths, deficits, and interactions with his or her environment. Sometimes testing is conducted to answer a specific question: Does the patient have a thought disorder? At other times, extensive testing is carried out to provide a broad, yet in-depth, picture of the person's functioning. There are virtually hundreds of psychological tests, most of which are used in research settings. The most commonly employed instruments are the Mental Status Exam, the Rorschach Inkblot Test, and the Minnesota Multiphasic Personality Inventory (MMPI).

The Mental Status Exam is administered within an interview format and is qualitative in nature in that no test score is obtained. It provides a general picture of several areas of functioning and is most often used during an intake interview. Some of the dimensions of concern are the person's insight, content of thought, emotional reactions, sensorium, and judgment. The mental status report should address at least the following questions: Is emotional response appropriate? Does the patient comprehend his or her current situation? Is there evidence of delusions or hallucinations? Is there any impairment of retention or recall of information? Is the patient oriented to time, place, and person? What is the patient's physical appearance? Based on the results of the mental status exam, any number of dispositional recommendations follow, including medication, hospitalization, further testing, out-patient therapy, etc. The mental status examination for children focuses on some of the same areas of functioning as does the exam for adults—appearance, thinking, perception, and emotional reaction. In addition, however, the clinician

evaluates the child's activity level and attention span, coordination, speech comprehension and expression, manner of relating, and intellectual functioning (Goodman and Sours, 1967). With younger children, the behavioral facets can be evaluated indirectly through games and role playing. The results of this examination may suggest the need for more formal testing, family therapy, or hospitalization.

The Rorschach is but one of several, albeit the most popular, projective techniques. These projective tests present unstructured or ambiguous stimuli and require the person to identify a picture, tell a story, or complete a sentence, depending on the test. It is assumed that the individual will project or reveal important aspects of his or her personality, such as needs, conflicts, motives, and fears. The Rorschach Test was created in 1911 and consists of 10 inkblots, each of which the person is asked to identify. Several scoring systems are available that code the individual's responses in terms of, e.g., level of detail, originality of responses, number of responses to each card, whether or not texture (e.g., "furry") was seen, and reaction to the few cards with color.

Projective tests have been adapted for use with children. They often employ cartoon figures. The Blacky Pictures depict a small dog and his parents and siblings in various scenes for which the child must relate a story. Projective techniques are the subject of controversy because of their questionable reliability and validity. The subjective quality of test interpretation, the high level of inference used in making statements about cognitive and affective functioning, as well as the expense in time needed for administration and scoring have lead many psychologists to abandon their use. However, even though the popularity of projectives has waned in the last 20 years, they are still commonly used as part of a diagnostician's battery of tests.

The MMPI is known as an objective test since it yields quantitative measures of psychopathology. It is rivaled only by the Rorschach in the number of research articles and books concerning the instrument (over 6000). While there are numerous objective measures of personality and mental disorders, none has achieved the degree of popularity afforded the MMPI. The test is comprised of over 500 true-false items that assess several types of disorders, including schizophrenia, depression, hysteria, mania, hypochondriasis, and anxiety, to name a few. The test was first validated in the 1940s on several groups of patients who were in treatment for various mental disorders. An individual scoring high, for instance, on the depression scale is answering the test items in a manner similar to the way in which the original sample of diagnosed depressives responded on the test. The MMPI has been criticized for adopting a trait view of behavior that fails to consider the manner in which situational variables modulate the expression of abnormality. Nonetheless, the MMPI remains a favorite instrument among psychologists, particularly in psychiatric hospital settings.

The recent edition of the *Diagnostic and Statistical Manual* (DSM-III) lists over 30 disorders under the heading "Disorders Usually First Evident in Infancy, Childhood, or Adolescence." The disorders range in severity from infantile autism to developmental arithmetic disorder.

It is not uncommon for parents to voice concern when their children exhibit what appears to be deviant behavior. Fortunately, most children's problems are time limited. It is typical for 2 year olds to fear strangers, 4 year olds to fear the dark, and 5 year olds to fear dreams and robbers (Gray, 1971). Symptoms occurring before the age of six have little predictive significance for later problems. There are, of course, notable exceptions. A child with many symptoms at one age is likely to have several symptoms at a later age (Robins, 1972). Mental retardation and Infantile Autism are usually evident at an early age and persist through subsequent developmental periods.

An example of a childhood disorder is attention deficit disorder with hyperactivity. This disorder is also referred to as hyperkinesis or hyperactivity. The main features are short attention span, impulsivity, and excessive motor activity. These children give the impression of not listening and have difficulty in carrying tasks through to completion. Their school work is often sloppy, unorganized, and replete with careless errors of omissions and insertions. Their attention deficit is exaggerated in the classroom and when performing in loosely structured settings. They appear to be perpetually in motion as they run and climb excessively. The disorder is usually evident by age three but may go undiagnosed until the child enters school. It is typical that the child's behavior fluctuates across situations and time. Thus, the disorder is not invariant and periods of well-organized behavior are to be expected. The child may show personality characteristics of stubborness, bullying, low frustration tolerance, and outbursts of anger. The disorder may persist into adulthood, disappear at puberty, or show a diminution of excessive motor activity while still revealing attentional deficits. Approximately 3% of children have this problem and 90% of them are boys.

Another common childhood disorder is separation anxiety disorder. The essential aspect of this disorder is excessive anxiety surrounding separation from major attachment figures, home, or familiar surroundings. The child may become anxious to the point of panic and refuse to sleep at friends' homes, go to school, or play a few blocks from home. Anticipated separation may evoke physical complaints such as headaches or stomach aches. These children are often preoccupied by thoughts of death and horrible fears of harm befalling the family. The ill-defined fears of the younger child may become more focused in later years and center on potential dangers such as kidnapping, burglars, or car accidents. Adolescent boys may deny feeling anxious when away from their mothers, but their propensity to stay at home, and discomfort when forced to leave the house for a day or two, reflect their separation anxiety. Children with this disorder often fear the dark and prefer to sleep with their parents, even if it requires sleeping on the floor outside their mother and father's bedroom door. These children may be described as clinging, demanding, and in need of constant reassurance. The disorder typically begins after some trauma such as a move, death of a pet, illness, or loss of a friend or relative. The disorder may persist for several years with exacerbations and remissions. Further, separation anxiety may continue into adulthood and manifest itself in a person's reluctance to move out of the house or excessive dependency on a spouse.

REFERENCES

Bandura, A. (1969). *Principles of behavior modification.* New York: Holt, Rinehart, and Winston.

Davison, G. C., & Neale, J. M. (1982). *Abnormal psychology.* New York: Wiley.

Goodman, J. D., & Sours, J. A. (1967). *The child mental status examination.* New York: Basic Books.

Gray, J. (1971). *The psychology of fear and stress.* New York: McGraw-Hill.

Harris, M. (1974). *Cows, pigs, wars, and witches: The riddles of culture.* New York: Random House.

Kanfer, F. H., & Grimm, L. G. (1977). Behavior analysis: Selecting target behaviors in the interview. *Behavior Modification, 1,* 7–28.

Kanfer, F. H., & Grimm, L. G. (1980). Managing clinical change: A process model of therapy. *Behavior Modification, 4,* 419–444.

Kanfer, F. H., & Phillips, J. S. (1970). *Learning foundations of behavior therapy.* New York: Wiley.

Mowrer, O. H. (1960). "Sin," the lesser of two evils. *American Psychologist, 15,* 301–304.

Robins, L. N. (1972). Follow-up studies of behavior disorders in children. In H. C. Quay & J. S. Werry (Eds.), *Psychopathological disorders in childhood.* New York: Wiley.

Sarbin, T. R. (1967). On the futility of the proposition that some people be labeled "mentally ill." *Journal of Consulting Psychology, 31,* 447–453.

Szasz, T. S. (1961). *The myth of mental illness: Foundations of a theory of personal conduct.* New York: Hoeber-Harper.

Wachtel, P. (1977). *Psychoanalysis and behavior therapy: Toward an integration.* New York: Basic Books.

LAURENCE C. GRIMM
University of Illinois, Chicago

PROJECTIVE TECHNIQUES
SOCIOPATHY

MENTALLY RETARDED, EDUCABLE

See EDUCABLE MENTALLY RETARDED.

MENTAL RETARDATION

Mental retardation has been known for centuries and different terms have been used by professional workers to refer to individuals having the condition. Among terms used centuries ago are naturals, idiots, and natural fools. Early in the twentieth century, the terms moron, imbecile, and idiot referred to three levels of retardation (from highest to lowest). Until about 1940, the term feebleminded was used. Other terms in recent use include mental subnormality and developmental disability, the latter inferring a long-term severe disability.

Until the twentieth century, when intelligence tests became available, retardation was defined in terms of an individual's inability to meet minimal demands of the culture. Around the turn of the century, Alfred Binet was commissioned by the French minister of public instruction to develop a method of identifying Parisian students who could be expected to fail in the regular school curriculum and who therefore required a special instructional program (MacMillan, 1982). The French test was translated and used in America by Henry Herbert Goddard at the Vineland Training School; later it was revised, and norms were provided by Lewis Terman. Terman's 1916 edition of the Stanford Binet Intelligence Scale was quickly adopted as a standardized, objective, norm-referenced way of identifying retarded children. The IQ became a standard for classification. Through experience in testing, large numbers of individuals were identified as retarded on the basis of extensive clinical observations: the IQ of 70 was established as the common cutoff score for retardation. State laws concerning retardation used IQs no more than 70 or 75 (or occasionally 79) as the criterion for eligibility for special education classes. Prominent psychologists such as David Wechsler, who devised a series of intelligence tests, consistently warned against the rigid use of intelligence test scores as a sole criterion for diagnosing retardation. It was not until 1959 that a formal change was made by the leading professional organization concerned with retardation, the American Association on Mental Deficiency (AAMD). The AAMD Committee on Classification and Terminology provided a definition that included criteria of both measured intelligence and adaptive behavior (Grossman, 1983). The AAMD definition has been adopted, sometimes in slightly modified wording, in the classification systems of the American Psychiatric Association (*Diagnostic and Statistical Manual-III*) and the World Health Organization (International Classification of Diseases-9). The 1983 wording of the AAMD definition reads:

> Mental retardation refers to significantly subaverage general intellectual functioning existing concurrently with deficits in adaptive behavior and manifested during the developmental period.

The developmental period is defined as the time between conception and the eighteenth birthday. Deficits may be manifested by slow, incomplete, or arrested development.

General intellectual functioning is defined as the results obtained after individual administration of a general intelligence test such as the Stanford-Binet Intelligence Scale or the age-appropriate Wechsler scale. Group tests, brief tests, and tests measuring only one or two factors are considered insufficient for identification of retardation.

Significantly subaverage is defined as full-scale IQ of no more than approximately 70. The criterion of approximately 70 allows for consideration of the standard deviation and reliability of tests. Depending on test characteristics and other available data, a student with an IQ of 75, or even 79, could be classified as retarded if there are also deficits in adaptive behavior.

Adaptive behavior refers to the effectiveness of the individual, or the degree to which one meets the standards of personal independence and social responsibility expected for one's age and cultural group. Expectations differ for different ages. Deficits are reflected during infancy and preschool years in the areas of sensorimotor skills development, basic communication skills (including speech and language), self-help skills, and early socialization skills. During early school and adolescent years, adaptive behavior deficits are reflected in the application of academic skills to activities of daily living, the use of appropriate reasoning and judgment in mastery of the environment, and the use of social skills appropriate for age or for younger children. During late adolescence and adulthood, adaptive behavior deficits may be reflected in any of the skills cited for younger persons or in deficits of social responsibilities and performance or vocational activities such as competitive employment.

In schools it is important to differentiate students who are mentally retarded from those who have emotional disturbances or behavior problems because different educational provisions are needed. Although it is reported that a higher proportion of retarded persons have emotional and behavioral problems than would be found in the general population, sometimes the behavior that is viewed as problem behavior is consistent with the mental age rather than the chronological age of the retarded individual; in such cases, most educators and psychologists would not call the student disturbed. A small minority, particularly when the disability is severe, is both retarded and disturbed. Generally, it appears that retarded persons have difficulty in learning, reasoning, and performing tasks that are easy for others of their age, whereas emotionally disturbed or behavior-disordered children may be able to learn and reason, but perform inappropriately. Both groups may have difficulty in regular classrooms.

Retarded persons have in common their difficulty in mastering school work and coping with environmental demands. As a group, they are characterized by delayed language development, problems in attending to relevant stimuli, short-term memory deficits, deficient memory strategies, and restrictions on the level of attainment possible. They are, however, not all alike. In addition to individual differences within the population, there are identifiable subgroups with characteristics in common. One system of subclassification is related to causality, or medical diagnoses associated with the retardation. For the majority of cases, no precise etiology can be determined. These cases are generally classified in medical systems as environmental influences or cultural-familial retardation.

Another large group includes those classified as unknown prenatal influence. The subgroup of chromosomal abnormalities, including Down's sydnrome, is the largest medical subgroup for whom firm evidence is available. Other subgroups are infections and intoxications (including rubella, viral infections, and maternal disorders), trauma or physical agent (including prenatal injury and hypoxia at birth), metabolism or nutrition (including phenylketonuria [PKU] and hypothryoidism), gross brain disease, and perinatal conditions (such as extreme immaturity and fetal and/or maternal nutritional disorders). Medical classification systems are very useful for medical treatments, prevention programs, and research on prevention and treatment, but available psychoeducational research suggests that they offer little aid in the development of educational plans.

Educational planning is aided by a subgroup classification system of levels of retardation. Retarded students who function at different levels of retardation have different long-term prognoses and require different educational programs, curricula, methods, and materials. Originally, three levels were differentiated. In recent years, differences observed led to the use of four levels: mild, moderate, severe, and profound. The mild group, which makes up approximately 75 to 85% of the total retardation population, is called educable mentally retarded (EMR) in school settings. Those individuals are in the IQ range of about 55 to 70. Most students in the EMR range are capable of learning basic academic skills of reading, writing, and arithmetic. Most can learn vocational skills needed for competitive employment, although the work is likely to be semiskilled or unskilled.

These students enter school at the usual age, but formal reading and writing instruction may be delayed until about age 8 or 9. During the earliest school years, they may be given instruction in simple arithmetical concepts, understanding of the home and community, and early development of good work habits. School activities throughout their program have heavy emphasis on experience rather than abstraction. Curricula are designed to provide basic skills for coping with the environment as children and adults. Thus a curriculum would include the rights and responsibilities of citizenship, occupational training, home management, and such areas as personal health and lifestyles as well as basic academic skills. Educable children usually develop language skills that are needed for conducting everyday life activities. For the majority of the EMR students, etiology is uncertain, although most are classified as cultural-familial, a designation suggesting that a combination of environment and polygenic inheritance is involved. After the school years, a majority of EMR students are employed (especially during a good economy). They are likely to be more in need of social and support services than the general population, but with such services, they tend to function with relative independence in society as adults. For these students it is especially important for educators to help them to develop their interpersonal and social skills and good work habits.

The moderate level of retardation (IQ range about 35 to 55) includes essentially the same group as those called trainable mentally retarded (TMR) in schools. Until the 1950s, this group was usually excused from public schools. Then parent groups began private schools. Gradually classes were moved under public school auspices. The curricula for TMR students differs from EMR curricula because TMR students are considered to be unlikely to develop independence as adults. They have sometimes been referred to as semidependent because most develop skills needed to take care of their personal needs, occupational skills that make sheltered workshop employment possible, and some household skills. They are unlikely to learn to handle finances beyond simple purchases and usually need some supervisory help throughout life. Well-designed school programs emphasize the use of concrete lesson materials (e.g., real objects rather than two-dimensional representations on paper, careful modeling rather than heavy emphasis on verbalized directions). Good programs for these students usually do not begin instruction in basic academics until early adolescence. The academic skills taught are generally those appropriate for survival in the community and include learning to recognize signs and common symbols, learning to recognize and use coins, and telling time to the half- or quarter-hour. A word recognition approach rather than phonics is appropriate for instruction in reading.

It is rare for a TMR student to develop reading comprehension skills sufficient for mastering prose material or to manipulate numbers with real understanding. In addition to development of skills of self-care and simple occupational skills, it is especially important for the curriculum to include leisure skills. Most TMR students eventually develop language skills, but articulation problems are more common than in the EMR group, and both vocabulary and syntax are likely to be somewhat limited. In addition to using actual experiences, educators have relied heavily on principles from reinforcement theory in teaching TMR students. Thus token economy, contingency management, and other concepts from behavior modification are used extensively.

Neither severely retarded (IQ range about 20 to 35) nor profoundly retarded (IQ below 20 or 25) students were generally considered public school responsibility until after the passage of PL 94-142 in 1975. Educators usually referred to all retarded children below the TMR level as custodial; it was assumed that all such children would be in residential facilities. Although it is true that today about 80% of individuals who are in residential facilities are severely or profoundly retarded, many others have always remained at home. With the deinstitutionalization movement, many others have returned to towns and cities and are provided education through public schools.

After experimenting with several terms, educators seem to have settled on the designation of severe/profound or developmentally disabled to identify these two subgroups. Some special educators have proposed the term severely handicapped, but the research reports using that term suggest that severely handicapped is a general, hetereogeneous term that includes a substantial proportion of TMR individuals. Severely retarded children tend to differ from profoundly retarded ones in their speech/language development, likelihood of concomitant medical and physical problems, maximal level of cognitive development, need for additional services, and probable length of life. Both groups are likely to have more physical problems than other retarded children, but the profoundly retarded are less likely to learn to walk, talk, and attain other skills. Educational programs for these two groups have strong emphasis on self-help skills such as self-feeding and dressing. Applications of reinforcement theory are by far the most common method of instruction and almost always provided by using real objects and situations. The prevalence of severe and profound retardation is very low and so many school districts have formed collaboratives in which students can be grouped according to educational needs. Collaboratives offer an effective way to provide physical and occupational therapy and other special services needed in programs for these students.

Some students who have severe degrees of retardation also have serious behavioral problems. Some of those are diagnosed as having autism and some have autisticlike behavior. Such children pose great challenges to educators because of their deficits in understanding and using language. Extensive training is needed by those who provide educational services to these children.

Teachers tend to be wary of using the term retarded. Some believe that the label is stigmatizing. Available research suggests that the label itself is unlikely to stigmatize when teachers have opportunities to interact with children. However, it seems to be true that in our society, retarded persons are disvalued, so any term that identifies the condition tends to become perjorative. As we learn to value others for what they are, rather than for what they are not, the label can become less onerous.

In summary, mental retardation, one of the largest of the special education categories, including several subgroups for whom educational programs differ. Retarded students can be subgrouped in ways that facilitate education for them. Although they have difficulty in learning, to a greater or lesser degree, all can be taught and profit from well designed educational programs.

REFERENCES

Grossman, H. G. (Ed.). (1983). *Classification in mental retardation*. Washington, DC: American Association on Mental Deficiency.

MacMillan, D. L. (1982). *Mental retardation in school and society* (2nd ed.). Boston: Little, Brown.

SUE ALLEN WARREN
Boston University

AAMD ADAPTIVE BEHAVIOR SCALES
ADAPTIVE BEHAVIOR
EDUCABLE MENTALLY RETARDED
LABELING
TRAINABLE MENTALLY RETARDED
VINELAND ADAPTED BEHAVIOR SCALES

MENTAL RETARDATION, JOURNAL OF

The journal of *Mental Retardation* was first published in 1963 by the Boyd Publishing Company. In 1986 it is currently up to volume 23, the aim of the journal remains the same since its inception. *Mental Retardation* is a multidisciplinary professional journal devoted to meeting the needs of and supplying information about effective ways to help people who are retarded and their families. Thus new teaching approaches, administrative tools, program evaluation studies, new program developments, service utilization studies, community surveys public policy issues, training studies, and case studies are welcome as are research studies that emphasize the application of new methods.

Manuscripts are reviewed by the editor, sent to peer reviewers, and sent back to the editor for a final selection of the articles to be published. The journal recieves about 175 manuscripts a year, but only about 34 are actually published. The journal is published bimonthly and in addition there are two to three special issues yearly. The total circulation is 10,000.

The editor is Louis Rowitz from the University of Illinois, Chicago. He was appointed by the American Association on Mental Deficiency (AAMD) after a "search." Rowitz in turn appointed his editorial assistants and the board of consulting editors, approximately 35 persons who must be members of the association and who are subject to consideration of the AAMD before final approval is made.

TERESA K. RICE
Texas A&M University

MENTAL RETARDATION, SEVERE

The label of severe mental retardation is used to describe persons who receive intelligence testing scores of more than four and up to five standard deviations below the norm (IQ = 20 to 35 on the Stanford-Binet and 25 to 39 on the Wechsler scales). Also, deficits in adaptive behavior (i.e., a lack of behaviors necessary to meet the standards of personal and social responsibility expected for a given chronological age) are considered in the labeling process according to the classification system of the American Association of Mental Deficiency (AAMD; Grossman, 1977). Adaptive behavior is typically assessed through the administration of the Adaptive Behavior Scale of the AAMD, or a similar instrument that provides a profile of skill levels that can be used to compare an individual's adaptive behavior profile with that of the group of persons who are mentally retarded.

This system of labeling provides a descriptive assessment of the level of functioning that is used for classification of persons; hence it is used for placement into categorical programs. The use of such a categorical approach to labeling emphasizes deviations from a normal developmental sequence and degree of impairment, but it does not reveal the heterogeneity among persons who are labeled severely mentally retarded, or provide prescriptive information pertinent to the development or implementation of individualized habilitative or training programs (Sailor & Guess, 1983).

The inability to perform basic skills suggests a need for labeling that is based on the level and extent of systematic instruction and environmental modification that are required to establish functional skills (Sailor & Guess, 1983). Such an instructional approach to the definition of mental retardation changes the emphasis from that of the limits of learning that are possible to the level of assistance needed in the habilitative or training process (Gold, 1980).

Historically, the care and treatment of persons with severe retardation has largely emphasized deficits in ability. The consequences of such negative attitudes have been neglect, ridicule, segregation in institutional settings, and pessimism regarding habilitative efforts. Kauffman (1981) provides an accounting of the history of mental retardation in the United States since the beginning of the nineteenth century. In the early nineteenth century there was a period of optimism regarding the education of the handicapped. At this time it was assumed that all handicapped persons could be provided with residential care that would make them contributing members of society, or at least greatly improve their skill levels and the conditions under which they lived. This was the period when Dorthea Dix led the movement to institutionalize the handicapped to protect them from abuse, and when successes in teaching the severely retarded were being reported by Samuel Howe and Edouard Seguins. The size of

institutions rapidly increased in the late nineteenth century without a corresponding increase in resources. The effect of the cutback in resources relative to the number of persons who were institutionalized resulted in a decline in the quality of care. The focus of institutions changed from that of providing training to that of providing custodial care and permanent segregation from society as pessimism grew in the face of lack of success in curing the condition of mental retardation.

The change from optimism to pessimism regarding educability and the need for segregation in institutional settings continued into the twentieth century and was maintained by H. H. Goddard's theory of eugenics. Goddard believed that mental retardation and criminality were linked together by genetic influences; however, these conclusions were based on the faulty interpretation of family genealogical studies.

In the 1950s an early event was significant for the change in the care of the mentally retarded. That event was the formation of the National Association of Parents and Friends of Retarded Children (which later became the National Association for Retarded Citizens). This organization was influential as an active lobby in securing publicly supported educational programs. Professional organizations such as the American Association for Mental Deficiency and the Council for Exceptional Children also were involved in lobbying for the provision of educational services.

In the 1960s and 1970s there was a shift to a more optimistic outlook regarding the provision of services to individuals labeled severely mentally retarded. These persons began to receive skill training services in institutional settings in the 1960s and, to a limited extent, educational services in the public schools in the 1970s. The beginning of deinstitutionalization and the provision of community-based services also appeared. This stands in stark contrast to the preceding decades, in which severely retarded persons were provided food, shelter, and medical care in large institutions.

In the 1960s and 1970s several events were responsible for a change to the provision of habilitative programming. These events included (1) continued advocacy by parents' groups; (2) the enactment of legislation such as PL 94-142, the Education Act for All Handicapped Children of 1975, PL 94-103, the Developmentally Disabled Assistance and Bill of Rights Act of 1975, and PL 93-112, Section 504 of the Rehabilitation Act of 1973, which mandated services and guaranteed the rights of persons with handicaps; (3) litigation such as *Brown* v. *the Board of Education* in 1954, in which the Supreme Court struck down segregated education systems, *Wyatt* v. *Stickney* in 1974, in which the Supreme Court decided for a constitutional right to treatment, and the *Pennsylvania Association for Retarded Citizens* v. *Commonwealth of Pennsylvania*, which guaranteed due process in educational placements to prevent exclusion from a free public education; (4) advances in instructional technology by behavioral researchers (Whitman, Sciback, & Reid, 1983); and (5) advocacy for the normalization principle (Wolfensberger, 1969).

During the 1960s and 1970s a number of changes occurred in habilitative programming. The focus of instructional technology changed from basic self-care skills and reduction of inappropriate behaviors in institutional settings to a focus on community living skills for persons working and living in a variety of residential options in the community. These changes were strongly reflective of the instructional approach to the definition of mental retardation (Gold, 1980).

The reforms in treatment models and improvements in instructional technology continued into the 1980s. Models have been developed for the training of vocational and independent living skills. These models actively involve persons with severe retardation in all aspects of community life (Cuvo & Davis, 1983; Rusch, 1986) and represent an optimistic viewpoint that persons with severe retardation can participate more fully in their home communities with appropriate training and support services. To achieve this goal of participation in community life to the fullest extent possible, increased service options in vocational, residential, and community programs need to be developed and expanded to accommodate the needs of persons labeled severely mentally retarded. The Association for Persons with Severe Handicaps has emerged as a dynamic coalition of parents and professionals with the purpose of ensuring full integration of people labeled as severely mentally retarded in school, residential, vocational, and other community environments.

REFERENCES

Cuvo, A. J., & Davis, P. K. (1983). Behavior therapy of community skills. In M. Hersen, R. M. Eisler, & P. M. Miller (Eds.), *Progress in behavior modification* (Vol. 14). New York: Academic.

Gold, M. W. (1980). *Try another way training manual.* Champaign, IL: Research.

Grossman, H. J. (1977). *Manual of terminology and classification in mental retardation.* Washington, DC: American Association on Mental Deficiency.

Kauffman, J. M. (1981). Historical trends and contemporary issues in special education in the United States. In J. M. Kauffman & D. P. Hallahan (Eds.), *Handbook of special education.* Englewood Cliffs, NJ: Prentice-Hall.

Rusch, F. R. (Ed.). (1986). *Competitive employment: Issues and strategies.* Baltimore, MD: Brookes.

Sailor, W., & Guess, D. (1983). *Severely handicapped students: An instructional design.* Boston: Houghton Mifflin.

Whitman, T. L., Sciback, J. W., & Reid, D. H. (1983). *Behavior modification with the severely and profoundly retarded: Research and application.* New York: Academic.

Wolfensberger, W. (1969). *Changing patterns in residential services for the mentally retarded.* Washington, DC: President's Commission on Mental Retardation.

HAROLD HANSON
PAUL BATES
Southern Illinois University

MENTAL RETARDATION
PROFOUNDLY RETARDED

MENTAL STATUS EXAMS

The mental status examination is an attempt to integrate qualitative observation with standardized assessment in a brief form. An examiner attempts to sample a broad enough representation of mental processes and behavioral performance to decide whether a disorder is present. Additionally, a brief examination also allows hypothesis building in the sense that the pattern of findings may be related to a specific syndrome. Historically, the majority of brief examinations were developed with an eye toward psychopathology; currently, more attention is being placed on the efficient identification of neuropsychological disorders, specifically dementia among the elderly.

In a review of mental state tests, Weintraub and Mesulam (1985) include the following general areas for consideration within an examination:

Wakefulness, arousal, and attention

Mood and emotional responsiveness

Learning and recall

Aspects of language and communication, including pragmatics

Arithmetic manipulation/calculation

Complex perceptual tasks

Constructional tasks

Spatial distribution of attention

Conceptual reasoning

Synthetic reasoning (i.e., translating a problem into plans and action)

Unlike a standardized battery (e.g., Wechsler scales, Halstead-Reitan Neuropsychological Battery, Luria-Nebraska Neuropsychological Battery), mental status evaluation was intended as a flexible approach that could be modified to the needs of a clinical issue. Thus all areas listed generally will not be included in every examination; if all areas are included, the weight given a particular area in terms of the depth of observation is likely to vary with both preliminary findings and the focus of the particular question. The preceding list is more of a menu than a constant procedure. One of the obvious limitations of such a qualitative approach is the expertise of the examiner. Novices are more likely to attend to areas and rely on techniques with which they are familiar than be led by the needs of the question and insightful hypothesis testing.

When selecting procedures and organizing an assessment, the clinician must be prepared to allow assessment items to vary along several dimensions. Assessment techniques must permit observation of both complex performance and very simple performance. Procedures need to vary input and output modalities while attempting to maintain a focus on targeted mental processes. Lateralized performance also must be observed. In creating such an examination, a clinician must not sacrifice depth of observation for brevity. (For applications of mental status examinations, see Weintraub & Mesulam, 1985; Strubb & Black, 1983.) Though these goals sound sensible in terms of a brief diagnostic procedure, the usual mental status exam is a finite set of tasks whose performance generates a score that may be compared with a norm-referenced criterion.

It is interesting to note that if one reviews the development of successive mental status examinations, the usual stimulus for development of a new procedure is that the preceding technique was not extensive enough (Turner, Kreutzer, Lent, & Brockett, 1984). In such an evolutionary process, the distinction between a standardized battery and a brief mental status examination is notably blurred. The following are examples of brief examination procedures.

The Mini Mental State (Folstein, Folstein, & McHugh, 1975) was originally intended to assess the cognitive integrity of psychiatric patients. Cutoff scores have been developed for normal, elderly, demented patients, and psychiatrically disturbed persons (Weintraub & Mesulam, 1985). Traditional assessments of persistent, directed reasoning (serial 7's), and immediate recall are included.

The Cognitive Capacity Screening Examination (CCSE; Jacobs et al., 1977) is a 30-item questionnaire intended to discriminate brain impairment from a functional behavior disorder. Validational study by Jacobs et al. suggests that scores of 19 or less identify cognitively impaired persons. Techniques similar to those of the Mini Mental State are used.

Strubb and Black (1983) have produced what is probably the most extensive short-form examination. The Mental Status Examination in Neurology offers not only a wide variety of procedures, but also provides an extensive interpretive guide. Unlike preceding examples, the Strubb and Black method attempts to discover the pattern among an individual's strengths and weaknesses and to relate the findings to likely brain dysfunction. It addresses a wide variety of cognitive processes and relies on clinical interpretation rather than cutoff scores.

Turner et al. (1984) have recently developed the Brief Neuropsychological Mental Status Exam (BNMSE). The procedure was intended to produce a functional description of basic mental processes, including concentration, sustained attention, global language functions, and oral memory. Individual items were drawn from a variety of standard procedures (e.g., WAIS: Digit Span, Arithmetic; Babcock Story Recall; Wechsler Memory Scale, etc.). A manual is available to assist in interpretation. The procedure is intended to serve as a guide for rehabilitation planning.

REFERENCES

Folstein, M. F., Folstein, S. E., & McHugh, P. R. (1975). Mini-mental state. *Journal of Psychiatric Research, 12*, 189–198.

Jacobs, J. W., Bernhard, M. R., Delgado, A., & Strain, J. J. (1977). Screening for organic mental syndrome in the medically ill, *Annals of Internal Medicine, 86*, 40–46.

Strubb, R. L., & Black, F. W. (1983). *The mental status examination in neurology.* Philadelphia: Davis.

Turner, H. B., Kreutzer, J. S., Lent, B., & Brockett, C. A. (1984). Developing a brief neuropsychological mental status exam: A pilot study. *Journal of Neurosurgical Nursing, 16*, 257–261.

Weintraub, S., & Mesulam, M. (1985). Mental state assessment of young and elderly adults in behavioral neurology. In M. Mesulam (Ed.), *Principles of behavioral neurology* (pp. 71–124). Philadelphia: Davis.

ROBERT F. SAWICKI
*Lake Erie Institute of
Rehabilitation, Lake Erie,
Pennsylvania*

ASSESSMENT
CLINICAL INTERVIEW

MERCER, CECIL D. (1943–   )

Cecil D. Mercer was educated at the University of Virginia, where he received the EdD in special education in 1974. He is currently professor of education at the University of Florida and also codirector of the University of Florida Multidisciplinary Diagnostic and Training Program. Mercer's principal special education interest is in the area of learning disabilities. He is perhaps best known for his two basic texts, *Students With Learning Disabilities* and *Teaching Students with Learning Problems.* Mercer maintains direct contact with learning-disabled students primarily through his involvement with the learning disabilities program at Shands Teaching Hospital in Gainesville, Florida.

REFERENCES

Mercer, C. D. (1983). *Students with learning disabilities.* Columbus, OH: Merrill.

Mercer, C. D., & Mercer, A. R. (1985). *Teaching students with learning problems* (2nd ed.). Columbus, OH: Merrill.

STAFF

MERCER, JANE R.

See SYSTEM OF MULTICULTURAL PLURALISTIC ASSESSMENT.

MERRILL, MAUD AMANDA (1888–   )

Maud Amanda Merrill earned her PhD in psychology at Stanford University in 1923 and served on the faculty there until 1947. She was coauthor, with Lewis M. Terman, of the 1937 revision of the Stanford-Binet Tests of Intelligence.

REFERENCE

Terman, L. M., & Merrill, M. A. (1977). *Measuring intelligence.* Cambridge, MA: Riverside.

PAUL IRVINE
Katonah, New York

MERRILL-PALMER SCALE

The Merrill-Palmer Scale is an individually administered intelligence test for children ages 18 months to 6 years. The scale was developed by Stutsman in 1931 as an alternative to, or supplement for, the Stanford-Binet. It consists primarily of performance tests measuring fine motor skills, although a few verbal items are included. The specific number and type of items administered varies depending on the age of the child (from 3 to 14 items are administered at each 6-month age period). Each item is scored as a success, a failure, an omission, or a refusal, and the total score can be converted into a mental age, a sigma value, and a percentile rank.

The test is particularly useful for assessing children lacking verbal skills (e.g., very young, developmentally delayed, or handicapped). Two excellent reviews of the scale (Honzik, 1975; Loeb, 1985) have identified several problem areas, including an excessive number of timed tests that penalize the slow-moving, thoughtful child and inadequate standardization. In addition, the test is difficult to interpret because the standard deviations of the mental age do not increase in proportion to advancing chronological age beyond 54 months. The test is published by Stoelting Company, Chicago.

REFERENCES

Honzik, M. P. (1975). The Merrill-Palmer Scale of Mental Tests. In O. K. Buros (Ed.), *Intelligence tests and reviews.* Highland Park, NJ: Gryphon Press.

Loeb, H. W. (1985). Merrill-Palmer Scale. In D. J. Keyser & R. C. Sweetland (Eds.), *Test critiques* (Vol. 2). Kansas City, MO; Test Corporation of America.

Stutsman, R. (1931). *Mental measurement of preschool children.* New York: World Book.

ROBERT G. BRUBAKER
Eastern Kentucky University

INTELLIGENCE
INTELLIGENCE TESTING

METABOLIC DISORDERS

Metabolic disorders are inherited defects of highly complex disease entities of which there are several general types with more specific and typically rare subtypes. The study of metabolic disorders is expanding rapidly and more than 2000 different types of inborn errors of metabolism and morphology have been identified (Ampola, 1982). Most of these diseases are single recessive gene defects that result in impaired metabolism of fat, protein, amino acids, or carbohydrates because of a deficiency in essential enzymes. Some of the more commonly known of these diseases are cystic fibrosis, diabetes, galactosemia, phenylketonuria (PKU), and Tay-Sachs disease.

Metabolic disorders are of relevance to special education practitioners because of the developmental and behavioral sequelae of these diseases. For example, they have been found to be associated with intellectual deficits (Kanner, 1979), social-behavioral problems (Allen et al., 1984), and childhood psychiatric disorders (Nyhan, 1974). Moreover, the siblings of a child with metabolic disorders may experience psychosocial sequelae (Langdell, 1979). The impact of metabolic diseases on development and behavior varies with such factors as the specific type of medical disorder, age of onset, type and efficacy of medical treatment, social support systems, and premorbid level of functioning (Lehr, 1984). Recent medical advances have resulted in a decline in the morbidity and mortality caused by metabolic disorders with a concomitant rise in the percentage of childhood disabilities attributable to these.

The more common metabolic disorders with known developmental and behavioral sequelae are Cushing's disease, cystic fibrosis, diabetes, galactosemia, and PKU. While cognitive functioning does not appear to be impaired in such diseases as cystic fibrosis, social-emotional adjustment is typically affected owing to associated stressors. There is much still unknown regarding the long-term sequelae of metabolic disorders. For example, while recent advances in the medical treatment of PKU has resulted in decreased mental retardation, hyperactivity, epilepsy, and microcephaly, there is evidence of continued but less severe learning and behavioral problems.

Amniocentesis is effective for identifying only certain metabolic disorders. For example, Tay-Sachs disease can be detected by testing the amniotic fluid, but this is not true for galactosemia and PKU. Genetic counseling, regular education in schools, public education, and planned pregnancy programs are recommended to prevent and minimize developmental disabilities from metabolic disorders (Langdell, 1979). Beyond this, Langdell also recommends legislation to ensure that every newborn receives medical examination through 1 month of age to identify and treat metabolic disorders. There is presently a lack of effective treatment for most metabolic diseases; the most relevant current emphasis should be directed at prevention through genetic screening and planned parenthood. Practitioners might refer parents to the following two national organizations for reliable information concerning metabolic disorders: Science Information Division, National Foundation—March of Dimes, Box 2000, White Plains, NY, 10602; and National Genetics Foundation, 9 West 57th Street, New York, NY 10019.

REFERENCES

Allen, D. A., Affleck, G., Tennen, H., McGrade, B. J., & Ratzan, S. (1984). Concerns of children with a chronic illness: A cognitive-developmental study of juvenile diabetes. *Child Care, Health, & Development, 10*, 211–218.

Ampola, M. G. (1982). *Metabolic diseases in pediatric practice*, Boston: Little, Brown.

Kanner, L. (1979). *Child psychiatry*. Springfield, IL: Thomas.

Langdell, J. I. (1979). Working with parents to discover and treat inherited metabolic diseases. In J. D. Nosphitz (Ed.), *Basic handbook of child psychiatry*. (Vol. IV, pp. 86–90). New York: Basic Books.

Lehr, E. (1984). Cognitive effects of acute and chronic pediatric medical conditions. In P. R. Magrab (Ed.), *Psychological and behavioral assessment: Impact on pediatric care* (pp. 235–278). New York: Plenum.

Nyhan, W. L. (1974). *Heritable disorders of amino acid metabolism: Patterns of clinical expression and genetic variation*. New York: Wiley.

JOSEPH D. PERRY
Kent State University

GENETIC COUNSELING
INBORN ERRORS OF METABOLISM

METACOGNITION

Metacognition refers to individuals' knowledge "about knowing and about how to know" (Brown, 1975). With this knowledge, learners allocate and orchestrate their cognitive resources effectively to meet task demands. Metacognition may be viewed as one of many potential domains of knowledge and skill that children may acquire; however, in this case, the domain is not reading or arithmetic, it is thinking. Recent investigations by cognitive psychologists, developmental psychologists, and special educators indicate that youngsters' metacognitive knowledge and skill may play a critical role in school achievement (Brown, Bransford, Ferrara, & Campione,

1983). Many handicapped pupils with learning problems evidence metacognitive deficiencies.

Educators' and psychologists' interest in metacognition reflects the view that human behavior is the outcome of a variety of mental events and processes. That is, students do not merely react to environmental demands. Rather, they interpret their world. It is these thoughts and perceptions that subsequently guide their behavior. A central tenet of this viewpoint is that individuals actively attempt to understand their environment. While motivational factors may interfere with this problem-solving activity and some learners may not understand task demands or how to perform a task, most students attempt to understand what the task requires and then initiate problem-solving activities.

In view of the myriad of thoughts that learners may have when approaching a task, coordination of these various thoughts and strategies is critical. For example, a pupil may see himself or herself as poor in math; however, doing practice problems at the end of the chapter seems to improve performance on math tests. While other pupils may choose not to do the practice problems, this student decides, in view of his or her limited competence in math, to complete these practice assignments. It is this monitoring and coordination of individuals' thoughts about their own abilities, the nature of task requirements, and the strategies used to accomplish learning goals that is metacognition.

An area that has received substantial attention within the metacognitive research literature is reading comprehension. A metacognitive analysis of reading stresses the active role of the reader, who allocates attention to critical information in the text, accurately monitors comprehension of text, and strategically employs strategies for remediating detected comprehension failures. Consistently, younger and less competent readers differ in their metacognitive knowledge and functioning when compared to older and more competent readers (Baker & Brown, 1984). Poor readers tend to view reading primarily as a decoding task. In contrast, good readers perceive reading as a means to gaining information and understanding. Poor readers also have greater difficulty in identifying important text information and determining when they have failed to understand the text. For example, asking poor readers if they have read and understood their assignments may elicit a positive response. However, when asked what the story was about and who the main characters in the story were, these pupils frequently have no idea. These responses, which are common in the experiences of many parents and teachers of handicapped pupils, indicate youngsters' lack of metacognitive awareness concerning what reading and understanding entails.

As a result of this deficiency in metacognitive knowledge, these pupils do not attempt strategies to remediate their comprehension failures. Failing to understand text material is a common experience for both poor and good readers. The major difference is that good readers recognize when and why they do not understand the information. As a consequence, they can effectively select and use strategies such as rereading or relating the text information to prior knowledge in an attempt to ameliorate their lack of understanding. Unfortunately, even when poor readers recognize that they are having difficulty understanding, many do not have adequate knowledge of or skills in the effective use of learning strategies.

These metacognitive characteristics of poor readers have been identified in handicapped pupils in the performance of a variety of academic, problem-solving, and memory tasks (Brown et al., 1983). Identification of these characteristics has resulted not only in a better understanding of human learning but in the development of instructional interventions for these pupils. Since the latter part of the 1970s, a variety of metacognitive training programs have been developed. In the area of reading, one training approach that has received considerable attention is the reciprocal teaching program developed by Brown and Palinscar (1982). In this program, pupils and a teacher take turns leading a dialogue on a segment of text that they are jointly attempting to understand. The purpose of this dialogue is to get the child to be aware of and use metacognitive skills that are related to effective reading comprehension. These skills include self-review, self-questioning, clarifying important text information, and predicting events in the text. As pupils' competence to perform these metacognitive tasks increases the teacher decreases his or her level of guidance. This intervention results not only in pupils' increased ability to paraphrase, ask meaningful questions, and predict text materials, but pupils also improve on a variety of comprehension tests immediately after the training and on follow-up assessments several months later.

While many handicapped pupils with learning problems may evidence specific deficits in rudimentary skills such as letter and number identification, it has become clear that teaching these individuals to be literate will require instruction in how to think and solve problems. Research in metacognition has helped educators to identify knowledge and skill deficits that may limit handicapped pupils' ability to learn and to design instructional programs that will meet their learning needs.

REFERENCES

Baker, L., & Brown, A. L. (1984). Metacognitive skills in reading. In D. P. Pearson (Ed.), *Handbook of reading research* (pp. 353–394). New York: Longman.

Brown, A. L. (1975). The development of memory: Knowing about knowing, and knowing how to know. In H. W. Reese (Ed.), *Advances in child development and behavior* (Vol. 10, pp. 103–152). New York: Academic.

Brown, A. L., Bransford, J. D., Ferrara, R. A., & Campione, J. C. (1983). Learning, remembering, and understanding. In J. H. Flavell & E. M. Markman (Eds.), *Handbook of child psychology: Vol. 1. Cognitive development* (pp. 77–166). New York: Wiley.

Brown, A. L., & Palinscar, A. S. (1982). Inducing strategic learning from texts by means of informed, self-control training. *Topics in Learning & Learning Disabilities*, 2, 1–17.

Douglas J. Palmer
Texas A&M University

READING DISORDERS
RECIPROCAL DETERMINISM

MEXICO, SPECIAL EDUCATION IN

Official efforts to serve handicapped students in Mexico began during the administration of President Benito Juarez. A school for the deaf was set up in 1866 and one for the blind in 1870. Today, by law, educational services must be provided to all children between the ages of 6 and 14 who have special needs. To meet this legal mandate, a wide variety of services have been established. They are managed by the Ministry of Public Education, the Ministry of Public Health, and the services of social welfare. They include 7 schools for the blind, 549 special education and rehabilitation centers, 22 psychological clinics, 44 speech therapy clinics, 121 centers for the mentally retarded, 40 clinics for auditory and language problems, and 8 centers for learning-disabled children (Kent, 1981; Nieto Herrera, 1981). Although the majority of government-sponsored services are clustered in the most populous states, other schools originally set up with private funds can win financial support from the Mexican government once they demonstrate effectiveness and stability. A special organization, the Instituto Mexicano para la Proteccion de Infancia (IMPI), was established to help improve services to all children, including the handicapped. It is supervised at the national level by the president's wife with governors' wives coordinating efforts on the state level.

As important as these accomplishments are, they have fallen far short of meeting the letter of the law. A look at the larger demographic context reveals the magnitude of the problem faced by Mexican educators. De Babra (1981) estimates that 97% of the exceptional children in Latin America have no services available to them, and the state of general education itself is a matter of concern. Of the region's population as a whole, 60% drop out before finishing grade school. In Mexico, the statistics appear to be somewhat better, with an overall school attendance rate of 76% and a grade school dropout rate of 43% (Nieto Herrera, 1981).

In many rural villages, schooling is not available or not taken advantage of. Although public education is free, families are expected to pay for uniforms, supplies, and, in some cases, to contribute to the maintenance of the school buildings. Student-teacher ratios in the public schools are commonly 50 to 1, discouraging strict enforcement of compulsory attendance laws and decreasing the likelihood that children with special needs will be given the extra attention they require in integrated settings.

Precise statistics on the proportion of children actually receiving special educational services are difficult to pin down. Reliable numbers on children with specific needs are unavailable owing to the lack of surveys. There is also a tendency for families to hide handicapped children as a protective measure or from a sense of shame. Even in more densely populated areas, where services are more plentiful, handicapped children are often expected to help with household chores and the care of siblings, or to contribute to the family income by begging on the streets rather than receiving educational services.

The problem of identifying and counting the handicapped is even more vexing when trying to reach beyond the most profoundly disabled to those whose handicaps are less obvious such as the learning disabled. Here the indications from sample groups are chilling. Nieto Herrera (1981) reports that in 1974, 1200 children entering first grade in the Federal District were examined. Fully 35% of those children were found to have some sort of learning disability.

In view of such widespread need, teacher training becomes an issue of high priority. During the 1970s, most of the existing training programs were established. The original approach was to look to countries with better developed systems of special education. Crowner (1978) described three training alternatives that emerged from international cooperation. The first was study abroad for Mexican special educators. The problem with this approach was that both the degree requirements and in many cases the instruction itself were inappropriate to the needs of students from Mexico.

The second approach was consultation and advisement on site in Mexico arranged by the government or some philanthropic organization. This kind of technical assistance could take any number of forms, from informal visits lasting 2 to 3 days, to 1-day workshops, to extended teacher training at institutes. Generally, the needs were too great to be addressed adequately in these activities, but such training had the strength of being conducted in and responsive to the real situation. The third approach was to use visiting professors to work with Mexican educators for a more extended period of time. This approach has been successful in establishing and refining some permanent training programs.

There are now emerging three types of training intended for different professional levels. The goal of one is to train university graduates to develop special educational approaches and techniques that are of high quality and appropriate for Mexican students. A simplified form of training is offered to paraprofessionals in the hope of preparing large numbers of personnel to help relieve the acute shortage of specialists in the field.

The third approach, sponsored by the government, focuses on upgrading the skills and knowledge of primary school teachers with regard to special education. The training is conducted in two stages. In the first, the teachers are introduced to basic information about recognizing and teaching children with various types of special needs. In the second stage, teachers take a series of classes leading to competence in one of three fields of specialization: speech and hearing; mental retardation; or learning disabilities. There are six centers in various Mexican states offering this kind of training. Approximately 150 teachers complete the program each year, and the government hires and places every successful graduate (Farha, 1981).

REFERENCES

Crowner, J. M. (1978, June) *A U.S./Mexican cooperative training program to serve Spanish speaking handicapped children.* Paper presented at the First World Congress on Future Special Education, Stirling, Scotland. (ERIC Document Reproduction Service No. ED 158 548).

De Barbra, M. G. (1981, September). *Professional education of the special teacher in Latin America and the Caribbean.* Paper presented at the First National Congress on Mental Deficiency, Mexico City, Mexico. (ERIC Document Reproduction Service No. ED 240 785).

Farha, I. (1981, December). Mexico. *Proceedings of the International Symposium on Services for Young Disabled Children, Their Parents, and Families, Washington, DC* (ERIC Document Reproduction Service No. Ed 221 002).

Kent, D. (1981). A school for exceptional children in San Miguel de Allende, Mexico. *Journal of Visual Impairment & Blindness, 75*(7), 292–296.

JANET S. BRAND
Hunter College, City University of New York

LATIN AMERICA, SPECIAL EDUCATION IN

MEYERS, C. EDWARD (1912–   )

C. Edward Meyers, born in Chicago, has been a consistent, longstanding contributor to special education and the psychology of exceptional children. He earned his BS in education at the University of Illinois in 1937 and his MA in

C. Edward Meyers

educational psychology in 1939 also from the University of Illinois. His formal education was completed with the awarding of the PhD in educational psychology by the University of Iowa. Meyers is now Professor Emeritus at the University of Southern California in the Division of Educational Psychology, which he formerly chaired, and serves as a research psychologist at the University of California, Los Angeles, Mental Retardation Research Center. He held many positions in areas related to special education over the years, including in service delivery (e.g., psychologist, State Hospital of Iowa, 1941–1944; psychologist, University of Denver Clinic, 1942–1945) and in academic research (mostly in various positions at the University of Southern California).

For 10 years Meyers was editor of the *Monographs of the American Association on Mental Deficiency* (1972–1982). He has served on the editorial boards of most major journals in mental retardation at some time in his career. His academic, scholarly awards are numerous and include the Education Award of the American Association of Mental Deficiency (1977), the Distinguished Service Award of the Division of School Psychology of the American Psychiatric Association (1982), and special citations for research from Phi Delta Kappa in 1965 and 1974.

Meyers is best known and respected for his research in the field of mental retardation. Over his productive career (Meyers directed over 100 doctoral dissertations and has more than 100 journal publications to his credit), Meyers focused on the impact of family and related environmental factors on the cognitive and emotional development of children, particularly those with general cognitive impairments (Meyers et al., 1964; Yoshida & Meyers, 1978). Most recently, Meyers undertook extensive investigation of the outcomes for children affected by the California "decertification" experience. This work (Meyers, MacMillan, & Yoshida, 1978, 1980) turned out to be one of the largest studies of mainstreaming ever conducted. Meyers is now directing research into the lives of severely impaired children.

REFERENCES

Meyers, C. E., Dingham, H. F., Orpet, R. E., Sitkei, E. G., & Watts, C. A. (1964). Four ability factor hypotheses at three preliterate levels in normal and retarded children. *Monographs of the Society for Research in Child Development, 29* (No. 56).

Meyers, C. E., MacMillan, D. L., & Yoshida, R. K. (1978). Validity of school psychologists' work in the light of the California decertification experience. *Journal of School Psychology, 16*, 3–13.

Meyers, C. E., MacMillan, D. L., & Yoshida, R. K. (1980). Regular class education of EMR students: From efficacy to mainstreaming. In J. Gottlieb (Ed.), *Perspectives on handicapping conditions*. Baltimore, MD: University Park Press.

Yoshida, R. K., & Meyers, C. E. (1975). Effects of labeling as EMR

on teachers' expectancies for change in a student's performance. *Journal of School Psychology, 67*, 521–527.

CECIL R. REYNOLDS
Texas A&M University

ADAPTIVE BEHAVIOR SCALE
MAINSTREAMING
MENTAL RETARDATION

MICROCEPHALY

Microcephaly, a congenital anomaly, is characterized by an abnormally small head in relationship to the rest of the body and by an underdeveloped brain resulting in some degree of mental retardation. The condition is described by Udang and Swallow (1983) as one in which the cranium of the affected individual is less than two standard deviations below the average circumference size for age, sex, race, and period of gestation. The primary or inherited form of microcephaly is transmitted by a single recessive gene, while the secondary form is the result of environmental factors (Gerald, 1982; Robinson & Robinson, 1965; Telford & Sawrey, 1977; Udang & Swallow, 1983). Factors associated with microcephaly include maternal infections; trauma, especially during the third trimester of pregnancy or in early infancy; anoxia at birth; massive irradiation or indiscriminate use of X-ray; and chemical agents.

Individuals who have the primary form of the disorder are generally more seriously affected (Robinson & Robinson, 1965). In addition to the small, conical-shaped skull, the scalp may be loose and wrinkled. The forehead generally is narrow and receding; the back of the skull is flattened; the facial features can be normal, although frequently the lower jaw recedes. The stature of the affected individual is very small with a curved spine and stooping posture, flexed knees, and disproportionately long arms and legs. Such individuals almost always are severely retarded and may not develop speech or primary self-help skills.

Individuals with the secondary form of microcephaly are not as severely affected. Although the skull is small, other symptoms are less visible or may not be present at all. The degree of mental retardation is less severe. Occasionally such individuals may be found in day classes for the moderately retarded (Dunn, 1973). There is no treatment for microcephaly. Medical care is primarily supportive and educational. A full range of custodial and educational services is needed (Udang & Swallow, 1983).

REFERENCES

Dunn, L. M. (1973). Children with moderate, severe and general learning disabilities. In L. M. Dunn (Ed.), *Exceptional children in the schools: Special education transition* (pp. 65–123). New York: Holt, Rinehart, & Winston.

Gerald, P. (1982). Chromosomes and their disorders. In J. Wyngaarden & L. Smith (Eds.), *Cecil 16th edition textbook of medicine* (pp. 17–22) Philadelphia: Saunders.

Robinson, H., & Robinson, N. (1965). *The mentally retarded child: A psychological approach.* New York: McGraw-Hill.

Telford, C., & Sawrey, J. (1977). *The exceptional individual.* Englewood Cliffs, NJ: Prentice-Hall.

Udang, L., & Swallow, H. (Eds.). (1983). *Mosby's medical and nursing dictionary.* St. Louis: Mosby.

SALLY E. PISARCHICK
*Cuyahoga Special Education
Service Center, Maple
Heights, Ohio*

CHROMOSOMAL ABNORMALITIES
CONGENITAL DISORDERS
PHYSICAL ANOMALIES

MICROTRAINING

Microtraining is a practice teaching method used in a majority of teacher education programs. Teacher trainees involved in microtraining typically prepare a brief lesson, present the lesson to a small group of students, observe a videotape of the lesson, modify the lesson based on their own critique or the critique of a supervisor, and reteach the lesson. As is apparent from these procedures, microtraining emphasizes the use of objective feedback in improving the teacher's future performance. The term microtraining is used because the teacher trainee is involved in a simulated teaching experience that minimizes the complexities of actual teaching. Specifically, only a few students are involved in a brief and highly structured lesson (Gregory, 1972).

Microtraining was introduced in the Secondary Teacher Education Program at Stanford University in the early 1960s. Keith Acheson, then a graduate student at Stanford, is frequently credited with its development as a preservice teacher training method. One decade after the inception of microtraining, over 100 research articles evaluating its effectiveness had been reported and over half of the teacher education programs in the United States had incorporated it as a required preservice clinical experience (Turney, Clift, Durkin, & Traill, 1973).

Allen and Ryan (1969) conceptualized microtraining as including five essential elements. First, although microtraining is conducted in a laboratory setting, and both the students and teacher are aware that the instructional context is fabricated, real teaching and learning take place. Second, as mentioned earlier, the complexities of actual classroom instruction are reduced. From one to five students may be involved in the lesson; the lesson is limited to a single concept or skill; and the length of the lesson may be limited from 5 to 20 minutes. Third, microtraining targets specific instructional competencies. These may include the use of specific materials, teaching procedures, or motivational techniques. Fourth, instructional variables including time, students, feedback, and supervision are controlled to enhance the effectiveness of the practice ex-

ercise. Finally, feedback to the teacher is emphasized. In typical microtraining experiences, the teacher observes a videotape of the lesson immediately after the session. He or she, with the assistance of a supervisor, critiques the lesson and identifies objectives for the next microlesson.

Beyond these basic elements, there are a number of variations of the basic microtraining methodology. Jensen (1974) has suggested 24 basic alterations. These result from various combinations of feedback options (e.g., videotapes, audiotapes, peers, critiquer), critique options (e.g., others, self), and reteach options (e.g., teach only, systematic reteach, trials-to-criterion). In addition to these options, microtraining may be conducted with peers versus actual pupils, and with various combinations of feedback modes (e.g., peers using videotape, critiquer using audiotapes, etc.).

REFERENCES

Allen, D. W., & Ryan, K. A. (1969). *Microteaching.* Cambridge, MA: Addison-Wesley.

Jensen, R. N. (1974). *Microteaching: Planning and implementing a competency-based training program.* Springfield, IL: Charles Thomas.

Gregory, T. B. (1972). *Encounters with teaching: A microteaching manual.* Englewood Cliffs, NJ: Prentice-Hall.

Turney, C., Clift, J. C., Dunkin, M. J., & Traill, R. D. (1973). *Microteaching: Research theory and practice.* Sydney, Australia: Sydney University Press.

PATRICK J. SCHLOSS
Pennsylvania State University

TEACHER EFFECTIVENESS
TEACHING STRATEGIES

MIDDLE EAST, SPECIAL EDUCATION IN THE

Perhaps no other Third World region has made as much progress over the last decade as the Middle East in the area of special education. With the rapid development of the oil and travel industries, money became readily available to many countries and their individual universities could develop and expand their program offerings in the areas of teacher training rehabilitation services and institutional care for the handicapped. The two countries that led in this movement were Egypt and Israel. Arab countries such as Kuwait, Jordan, and Saudi Arabia have also made significant gains in the programming for and treatment of handicapped youngsters. However, the cutback in oil prices, declining tourism, and the increase in terrorist activities may well affect the continued development of special education programs in the Middle East.

Egypt. The purpose of educational services and programs in the area of special education in Egypt is assessment of abilities and aptitudes to aid the handicapped in developing an independent lifestyle. Basically, there are three major handicapping conditions that the schools in Egypt focus on. Visual education is for those individuals who are classified as blind or visually impaired. These individuals are entitled to 6 years of elementary schooling, 3 years of intermediate and secondary level schooling, and college based on their abilities (visually and intellectually).

The deaf and hearing impaired are entitled to auditory education. This education consists of 8 years of elementary school and 3 years of intermediate vocational school (As-hawal, 1986).

Education for the mentally retarded consists of two separate programs. Children and youths who score between 50 and 70 on Egyptian IQ tests can be enrolled in an elementary education program for 8 years. The first 2 years of schooling concentrate on academic skills, the following years on vocational/career opportunities. Education is handled through the Ministry of Education. For children and youths who score below 50 on an IQ test, education consists of vocational training with few academic skills emphasized. These programs are handled through the Social Affairs Ministry. There are hospitals for the more severely and profoundly retarded.

Perhaps the leading university focusing on the education of teachers for the handicapped is Ain Shams University in Roxy-Cairo. This university's training program is under the auspices of a special branch of the Ministry of Education that is responsible for special education. A teacher who plans to teach in the area of special education must be a graduate of a university that has a faculty of education and have at least one additional year of course work within one of the specialized areas. The teacher training programs are weak in practicum experience but strong on the theoretical and philosophical aspects of education.

Saudia Arabia, Rahrain, Kuwait, and Jordan. Perhaps in no area has the influence of the Egyptian scholars in special education been more evident than in Saudia Arabia, Bahrain, Kuwait, and Jordan. These Middle Eastern countries often use Egypt's university personnel to develop their individual special education teacher training programs and service delivery models. Basically, we see the same structure in these countries for teacher education and services for exceptional children as we do in Egypt. When faculty members from Egyptian universities are called on to develop special education programs in their neighboring countries, they use the Egyptian model, administrative structure, and governing procedures and adapt them to the individual country.

In countries such as Saudia Arabia, where the *Koran* is interpreted strictly and the Moslem faith is strongly adhered to, there is a separation of boys and girls, not only at the elementary level but also the university level in terms of education programs, treatment facilities, and, to a lesser degree, opportunities. Special education in most of the Middle East is developing at a rapid pace but it still has a long way to go. However, each government has made a commitment at the program level to develop effective special education programs to meet the needs of their handicapped children and youths.

Israel. Hebrew University is the leader in terms of preparing professionals for the area of special education. Teacher training programs at Israeli universities rival many of those found at the leading American universities. A major difference between Israel and other Middle Eastern countries regarding programs for exceptional students is the emphasis Israel gives to preschool experiences. Much preschool education in the areas of academics and social skills comes from the kibbutz, where one can usually find a qualified special education teacher. In addition, emphasis is given to parent education in terms of programs available and treatment of their handicapped child. Another major difference between the special education teacher preparation programs of Israel and other Middle Eastern countries is the amount of emphasis given to practice experience by the universities in Israel. However, treatment facilities such as hospitals for the mentally retarded and emotionally disturbed are scarce and have limited staff.

An attempt needs to be made to integrate theories and effective practice in special education throughout the Middle East. In addition, ways in which practices can be adopted to areas with severe economic and social problems must be developed. Mba (1983) indicates that only a small percentage of handicapped children receive schooling and that opportunities for training special educators are limited in the African countries. However, most Middle Eastern countries demonstrate a high interest in the areas of gifted education and retardation.

REFERENCES

El-Ashawal, A., & Vance, H. (1986, April). *Special education in Egypt and the Middle East.* Paper presented at the meeting of the Council for Exceptional Children, New Orleans, LA.

Mba, P. O. (1983). Trends in education of handicapped children in developing countries with particular reference to Africa. *Journal of Special Education, 7,* 273–278.

HUBERT B. VANCE
East Tennesse State University

ADEL E. ASHAWAL
Ain Shams University

MIGRANT HANDICAPPED

Migratory farmworkers are those individuals who must move their home bases and travel to other locations, usually hundreds of miles away, in search of seasonal farmwork. This mass movement of migratory farmworkers takes place every year during periods that coincide with the planting and/or harvesting of agricultural products; it is commonly referred to as the migrant stream.

There are three major identifiable migrant streams within three broad geographical areas. One stream is found within California, Oregon, and Washington. The other stream begins in the Lower Rio Grande Valley of Texas and farms out into the Midwest, Rocky Mountains, and Red River Valley. The third major stream originates in southern Florida and moves northward along the Atlantic coast as far as New York State (Stoops-King, 1980).

Migrant farmworker families are usually comprised of low socioeconomic ethnic minorities that include Mexicans, Mexican-Americans, blacks, Native Americans, Indians, and Central and South Americans. The heaviest concentrations of migratory farmworker children reside in the states of Texas, California, Washington, Arizona, Colorado. Florida, and New Mexico (Goldfarb, 1981).

The nature of seasonal migratory labor causes most of the migrant farmworkers to experience considerable deprivation in the basic human needs of nutrition, health, housing, and education. The typical migrant family lives below the poverty level, experiences high infant mortalities, is exposed to the hazards of chemical insecticides and pesticides, and has a low educational level. The average life span of a migrant farmworker is thought to be 47 years (Thedinger, 1982). The critical needs of migrant children prompted Congress to amend Title I of the Elementary and Secondary Education Act of 1965 (currently identified as Chapter I of the Consolidated and Improvement Act of 1981) to address the educational and health needs of these children (U.S. Government Accounting Office, 1983).

The federally funded Migrant Education Program was initiated on the premise that migrant children suffer educational interruptions when forced to move into different school districts. This program provides federal aid for supplementary instructional services, medical and health services, and parent training services provided that the children meet the following specified criteria:

> migratory means a child whose parent or guardian is a migratory agricultural worker or a migratory fisher; and who has moved within the past 12 months from one school district to another to enable the child, the child's guardian or a member of the immediate family to obtain temporary or seasonal employment in an agricultural or fishing activity.

Over 500,000 migratory children have been counted as eligible in approximately 3100 projects (U.S. Government Accounting Office, 1983). In addition, early childhood education and nutrition intervention efforts are available through selected programs in several states.

Characteristically, migrant children are mobile within the educational systems and, as such, pose unique information management concerns. One of the features of the federal migrant education program is an automated telecommunication system, the Migrant Student Record Transfer System (MSRTS), which transmits data regarding the children. This system, headquartered in Little Rock, Arkansas, enables participating school districts to obtain and forward via computer pertinent educational,

medical, and demographic information. This system makes it possible to notify a receiving school that a certain migrant student was enrolled in a special education program in the sending school.

While states generally do not have accurate data on numbers of migrant handicapped pupils, migrant children tend to be underrepresented in special education (U.S. Government Accounting Office, 1981). With the national average of 10 to 12% of school-aged children identified as handicapped, surveys indicate that less than 6% of the migrant pupils are identified as handicapped. These children are underrepresented despite the presence of a variety of conditions that place this population at risk.

The reasons for this potential underrepresentation of migrant pupils are varied and complex. Many migrant parents have limited information regarding the nature of various handicapping conditions and the variety of special education services that are potentially available. They may view their child's learning or behavior problems as normal adjustment problems or may be completely unaware that the child is experiencing serious learning problems. In addition, as with many parents, they may deny the presence of a problem because of their own perceived guilt that they may have done something that caused the child's problem. These parents may also deny the existence of a handicapping condition if they think that the child will have to be placed in a special residential facility away from the family. The family also may view their child's participation in an elaborate educational system requiring parental involvement as economically disruptive. Most migrants are employed at daily rates and are not reimbursed for justifiable absences. Typically, all of the adult members in the family are members of the labor crew.

A critical feature of recent legislation pertaining to the education of handicapped pupils is that the child's parent or guardian is to be informed about the educational rights and services available. Unfortunately, few migrant parents evidence the knowledge and sophistication required to seek appropriate services for their disabled children. Migrant and special education programs rarely coordinate efforts to guarantee that migrant parents are adequately informed to advocate for the most appropriate interventions for their handicapped children.

Because of the cultural, economic, and linguistic backgrounds of many migrant pupils, teachers may be hesitant to refer these children for learning or behavioral problems. Teachers may think that the child's severe academic difficulties are due to poverty or the fact that the child's primary language is not English. As a result, teachers may not refer these pupils for special education services. Teachers or administrators may also believe that the child will not remain enrolled long enough to warrant the initiation of costly referral and assessment procedures.

With recent legislation and litigation, there has been increased concern for the appropriateness of assessment procedures for determining special education eligibility of minority pupils. Since many migrant youngsters are from ethnic minorities, there is some reluctance on the part of school administrators and diagnostic staff to assess and place these children in special education instructional settings.

Providing special education and related services to handicapped pupils is also an expensive activity. The majority of the costs for special education are covered primarily by local school district and state revenues. Migrant pupils are generally enrolled in small rural school districts with a limited tax base. As a consequence, these schools may have limited financial resources for special education personnel, space, supplies, and other required services for migrant handicapped pupils. While school districts are required to provide the services the child needs, not merely the services already available in the schools, the quality and range of special education services are, in fact, determined by the financial resources of the schools. Unfortunately, large numbers of migrant handicapped youngsters may not be served because of the lack of funds that are available within the schools they attend.

Finally, children of migrant workers may not receive special education services because of established bureaucratic policies. For example, migrant handicapped pupils may receive services for educationally disadvantaged pupils or for limited English-speaking youngsters and as a result of school policy or practices not be eligible for any additional compensatory training programs such as special education. In addition, while there have been efforts such as the MSRTS to more effectively monitor these migrant youngsters as they move from district to district, surveys indicate that when migrant handicapped children move, only 80% of these pupils are provided special education services by receiving schools (U.S. Government Accounting Office, 1981).

Addressing this issue of underrepresentation of handicapped migrant youngsters in special education will require better informed parents, teachers, and assessment personnel, and closer coordination and monitoring of services by local school districts and state and federal agencies. Reflecting on the history of special education, complex problems such as those associated with migrant handicapped children may be resolved only through the political and advocacy activities of migrant farmworker organizations.

REFERENCES

Goldfarb, R. L. (1981). *A caste of despair*. Ames IA: Iowa State University Press.

Stoops-King, J. (1980). *Migrant education: Teaching the wandering ones*. Bloomington, IN: Educational Foundation.

Thedinger, B. (1982, September 14). Testimony in citing U.S. Public Health Service. Subcommittee on Labor Standards of the Committee on Education and Labor, House of Representative, 97th Congress, HR 7102.

U.S. Government Accounting Office. (1981, September 30). *Disparities still exist in who gets special education*. Report to Sub-

committee on Select Education, Committee on Education and Labor, House of Representatives.

U.S. Government Accounting Office. (1983, May). *Analysis of migration characteristics of children served under the migrant education program*. Report to the Congress of the United States.

DIEGO GALLEGOS
San Antonio Independent
School District, San Antonio,
Texas

DOUGLAS J. PALMER
Texas A&M University

BILINGUAL EDUCATION
CULTURAL BIAS IN TESTS

MILDLY HANDICAPPED, COMPETENCIES OF TEACHERS OF

Current emphasis on teacher competencies and accountability in education have resulted in efforts to determine what teachers do, what impact their actions have on learners, and what teachers need to know in order to perform as professionals. The development of professional standards and teacher competencies has been the focus of many studies during the past several decades. Since the mildly handicapped compose the largest segment of exceptional learners and since their needs appear to have so much in common, it is natural that many of the searches for generic competencies have targeted this group.

During the past decade the search for common and specialized competencies for the mildly handicapped has received the attention of researchers. However, the pursuit of competency statements is not new and can be chronicled over a period of several decades. During the 1950s competency-based instruction became an issue in teacher education and some of the first studies were conducted. The U.S. Department of Health, Education, and Welfare supported a study to determine specific competencies needed by maladjusted children served as part of the mildly handicapped population (Mackie, Kvaraceus, & Williams, 1957).

Throughout the 1960s and 1970s a number of studies examined and outlined competencies appropriate for teachers of the mildly handicapped, including those students categorized as learning disabled (LD), behaviorally disordered (BD), and educably mentally handicapped (EMH). Most of these studies focused a specific categorical area rather than on the common needs of the students and then on the common needs of their teachers. Teacher competencies examined by Rabinow (1960), Dorward (1963), Hewett (1966), Adelman (1972), and Bullock and Whelan (1971) represent examples of these studies. It is apparent from recent teacher competency studies such as those compiled by the Division for Children wtih Learning Disabilities (1978), Pattavina (1983), Keegan (1981), Davis (1983), and Dugoff, Ives, and Shotel (1985) that most of the competency studies continue to focus on the categorical areas. In 1967 Schwartz presented a proposal for a noncategorical approach to the mildly handicapped. A 5-year study resulted from this proposal. It described specific competencies that all teachers of the mildly handicapped should have (Schwartz & Oseroff, 1975). Other projects were described by Schwartz, Oseroff, Drucker, and Schwartz (1972) in a report on a conference focusing on innovative noncategorical projects in the education of the handicapped. Most recently, Bursuck and Epstein (1986) studied generic competencies needed by teachers of the mildly handicapped.

Progress has been made recently in determining how competency statements have been derived. In early studies, researchers relied on author opinion (Shores, Cegelka, & Nelson, 1973) and validation by professional consensus or a historical study of the nature of teaching the handicapped (Schwartz & Oseroff, 1975). Recently, researchers have attempted to validate competencies by demonstrating a causal relationship between competency and student achievement. Student academic and social gain is a desired educational outcome. A competency statement is truly valid if the skill, knowledge, or behavior described by the competency is demonstrated by successful teachers, discriminates between successful and unsuccessful teachers, and results in improved student performance (Shores et al., 1973).

An issue pertinent to studies that discuss competencies needed by teachers of the mildly handicapped is whether the same competencies are essential for teachers in all three areas: LD, BD, and EMH. Although the literature clearly addresses the categorical versus noncategorical approach for training teachers of the mildly handicapped, the debate continues. Whether teachers of behaviorally disordered children need the same skills as teachers of children who experience academic problems, such as those categorized as LD or EMH, is still unresolved.

Carri (1985) examined what teachers of the mildly handicapped perceived as the important competencies, and found that while there were no marked differences between teachers of EMH and LD students, teachers of BD students reported distinct differences. These differences were perceived in the areas of assessing and evaluating student behavior, curriculum design and use, and professional information. Additionally, Chandler and Jones (1983) note that although conditions that exist in most special education settings such as structure, consistency, and individualized programmed instruction are essential in teaching both LD and BD children, students with emotional problems need more behavior management and affective development than is traditionally provided in the standard LD setting.

Gable, Hendrickson, Shores & Young (1983) examined teacher-student interaction through direct observation. Their study revealed no significant differences among teachers of LD, ED, and EMH regarding antecedent behaviors such as modeling. Questioning instructional approach, Gable et al. reported that findings of this study supported the notion that teacher competencies should directly relate to students' specific needs rather than categorical labels.

In a review of the current competency listings, a number of key components can be noted. These include topics such as direct instruction (Poplin, 1983; Stainback & Stainback, 1980), computer literacy skills (Bursuck & Epstein, 1986), consultation skills for resource teachers (D'Alonzo & Wiseman, 1978; Davis, 1983; Dugoff et al., 1985; Friend, 1984), and an emerging emphasis on secondary programs (Bursuck & Epstein, 1986; Pattavina, 1983; Zigmond, 1978).

Knowledge of specific competencies can be applied to the field in a number of ways. They can be used as guidelines for the development or modification of programs for teacher preparation, for establishing certification requirements; criteria for employment; and standards for monitoring ongoing professional practices (Newcomer, 1978). It is evident that these competency statements should be used for a variety of purposes, but student gain should be the criterion for determining which statements are valid. This can only be achieved through continued application and experimentation.

Student gain is the ultimate measure for competency validation, and current and future studies will focus sophisticated measurement techniques on the use of competency statements in teacher preparation across the three mildly handicapped categorical areas.

REFERENCES

Adelman, H. S. (1972). Teacher education and youngsters with learning problems: Part III: The problem pupil and the specialist teacher. *Journal of Learning Disabilities, 5,* 13–24.

Bullock, L. M., & Whelan, R. J. (1971). Competencies needed by teachers of the emotionally disturbed and socially maladjusted: A comparison. *Exceptional Children, 37,* 485–489.

Bursuck, W. D., & Epstein, M. H. (1986). A survey of training programs for teachers of mildly handicapped adolescents. *Teacher Education and Special Education, 9,* 3–8.

Carri, L. (1985). Inservice teachers' assessed needs in behavioral disorders, mental retardation, and learning disabilities: Are they similar? *Exceptional Children, 51,* 411–416.

Chandler, H. N., & Jones, K. E. (1983). Learning disabled or emotionally disturbed: Does it make any difference? Part II. *Journal of Learning Disabilities, 16,* 561–564.

D'Alonzo B. J., & Wiseman, D. E. (1978). Actural and desired role of the high school learning disability resource teacher. *Journal of Learning Disabilities, 11,* 63–70.

Davis, W. E. (1983). Competencies and skills required to be an effective resource teacher. *Journal of Learning Disabilities, 16,* 596–598.

Division for Children with Learning Disabilities. (1978). *Code of ethics and competencies for teachers of learning disabled children and youth.* Reston, VA: Author.

Dorwood, B. (1963). A comparison of the competencies for regular classroom teachers and teachers of emotionally disturbed children. *Exceptional Children, 30*, 67–73.

Dugoff, S. K., Ives, R. K., & Shotel, J. R. (1985). Public school and university staff perceptions of the role of the resource teacher. *Teacher Education & Special Education, 8*, 75–82.

Friend, M. (1984). Consultation skills for resource teachers. *Learning Disabilities Quarterly, 7*, 246–250.

Gable, R. A., Hendrickson, J. M., Shores, R. E., & Young, C. C. (1983). Teacher-handicapped child classroom interactions. *Teacher Education & Special Education, 6*, 88–95.

Hewett, F. W. (1966). A hierarchy of competencies for teachers of emotionally handicapped children. *Exceptional Children, 33*, 7–11.

Keegan, W. (1981). *Competencies for teachers who instruct children with learning disabilities. Project I.O.U.* (Report No. OEG-073-2850). Washington, DC: U.S. Department of Education.

Mackie, R. P., Kvaraceus, W., & Williams, H. (1957). *Teachers of children who are socially and emotionally handicapped.* Washington, DC: U.S. Government Printing Office.

Newcomer, P. L. (1978). Competencies for professionals in learning disabilities. *Learning Disabilities Quarterly, 1*, 69–77.

Pattavina, P. (1983). *Generic affective competencies: A model for teaching socially and emotionally disturbed adolescents.* Washington, DC: U.S. Department of Education.

Poplin, M. (1983). Professional growth and the LD specialist. *Learning Disabilities Quarterly, 6*, 102–106.

Rabinow, B. (1960). A training program for teachers of the emotionally disturbed and socially maladjusted. *Exceptional Children, 26*, 287–293.

Schwartz, L. (1967). Preparation of the clinical teacher for special education: 1866–1966. *Exceptional Children, 34*, 117–124.

Schwartz, L., & Oseroff, A. (1975). *The clinical teacher for special education.* Tallahassee, FL: Florida State University, College of Education, Educational Research Institute.

Schwartz, L., Oseroff, A., Drucker, H., & Schwartz, R. (1972). *Innovative non-categorical and interrelated projects in the education of the handicapped.* Tallahassee, FL: Florida State University, College of Education, Department of Habilitative Sciences.

Shores, R. E., Cegelka, P. T., & Nelson, C. M. (1973). Competency based special education teacher training. *Exceptional Children, 40*, 192–197.

Stainback, S., & Stainback, W. (1980). Some trends in the education of children labeled behaviorally disordered. *Behaviorially Disordered, 5*, 240–249.

Zigmond, N. (1978). A prototype of comprehensive services for secondary students with learning disabilities. *Learning Disabilities Quarterly, 1*, 39–49.

ANDREW OSEROFF
LISA MONDA
CYNTHIA VAIL
Florida State University

COMPETENCY TESTING OF TEACHERS
PROFOUNDLY HANDICAPPED, COMPETENCIES FOR TEACHERS OF

MILDLY HANDICAPPED, TEST-TAKING SKILLS AND THE

Test-taking skills, or test-wiseness, has been defined by Millman, Bishop, and Ebel (1965) as "a subject's capacity to utilize the characteristics and formats of the test and/or the test-taking situation to receive a high score" (p. 707). Additionally, they state test-wiseness to be "logically independent of the knowledge of the subject matter for which the items are supposedly measured" (p. 707). Test-taking skills can therefore be seen as a set of abilities that can be applied to a variety of tests regardless of their content.

Currently, most mildly handicapped students spend the largest portion of the school day in mainstream classrooms (Friend & McNutt, 1984; Heller, 1981). Therefore, they are expected to cope with the same academic demands as nonhandicapped students. A frequent and important demand in the mainstream class is taking teacher-made, objective (e.g., true-false, multiple-choice, matching) tests. Indeed, academic success is largely measured by how well students perform on these tests (Cuthbertson, 1979; Schumaker & Deshler, 1983). For example, Cuthbertson found that 60% of a student's grade depends solely on test scores. Apart from prior knowledge and amount of studying, a source of variance affecting test scores is the test-taking skills or test-wiseness of the individual taking the test.

Unfortunately, evidence exists that, when compared as a group with nonhandicapped peers, mildly handicapped students lack test-wiseness (Forness & Duorak, 1982; Keogh, 1971; Scruggs, Bennion, & Lifson, 1985). Some general behaviors considered characteristic of the mildly handicapped that may account for poor test-taking ability include distractibility, impulsivity, and anxiety. Specific behaviors noted by researchers include attending to the wrong part of test directions, making an answer choice before reading all available choices, not reading questions carefully, and not using cues when guessing.

While most related research has investigated the test-taking characteristics of handicapped students, little research exists on the effectiveness of teaching these students skills or strategies for taking tests. In fact, most available studies have not used handicapped subjects. Hughes (1985) analyzed test-taking instruction research and noted the most frequently taught skills used in these studies. They are, in order of frequency, efficient use of time, reading directions thoroughly, skipping items when unsure, marking answers appropriately, using available cues when guessing (e.g., choosing the longest options, avoiding absolute words such as always and never), reviewing work, and reading all answer options in a multiple choice question before marking an answer.

Two commercial test-taking programs have been used with mildly handicapped adolescents (i.e., learning disabled and behaviorally disordered) with some positive effects on test scores. Both programs, SCORER (Carman & Adams, 1972) and PIRATES (Hughes, Schumaker, &

Deshler, in press) include all of the frequently taught skills noted. Additionally, a federally funded project to investigate the effectiveness of teaching learning-disabled elementary students test-taking skills is currently under way (Scruggs, Bennion, & Lifson, 1985).

REFERENCES

Carman, R. A., & Adams, W. R. (1972). *Study skills: A student's guide for survival.* New York: Wiley.

Cutherbertson, E. B. (1979). *An analysis of secondary testing and grading procedures.* Unpublished master's thesis, University of Kansas, Lawrence.

Forness, S. R., & Duorak, R. (1982). Effects of test time limits on achievement scores of behaviorally disordered adolescents. *Behavioral Disorders, 7*(4), 207–212.

Friend, M., & McNutt, G. (1984). Resource room programs: Where are we now? *Exceptional Children, 51*(2), 150–155.

Heller, H. W. (1981). Secondary education for handicapped students: In search of a solution. *Exceptional Children, 47*, 582–583.

Hughes, C. (1985). *A test-taking strategy for emotionally handicapped and learning disabled adolescents.* Unpublished doctoral dissertation, Gainesville: University of Florida.

Hughes, C., Schumaker, J. B., & Deshler, D. D. (in press). *The test-taking strategy.* Lawrence, KS: EXCEL.

Keogh, B. (1971). Hyperactivity and learning disorders: Review and research paradigm. *Developmental Psychology, 10*, 590–600.

Millman, J., Bishop, C. H., & Ebel, R. (1965). An analysis of test-wiseness. *Educational & Psychological Measurement, 25*, 707–726.

Schumaker, J. B., & Deshler, D. D. (1983). *Setting demand variables: A major factor in program planning for the LD adolescent.* Lawrence: University of Kansas, Institute for Research in Learning Disabilities.

Scruggs, T. E., Bennion, K., & Lifson, S. (1985) Learning disabled students' spontaneous use of test-taking skills on reading achievement tests. *Learning Disabilities Quarterly, 8*(3), 205–210.

CHARLES A. HUGHES
Pennsylvania State University

MEASUREMENT
TEST ANXIETY

MILLS v. BOARD OF EDUCATION OF THE DISTRICT OF COLUMBIA (1972)

In 1972 a class-action suit was brought against the District of Columbia Board of Education by the parents of seven school-aged handicapped children for failure to provide all handicapped children with a publicly supported education. In December 1971 the court issued a stipulated agreement, and order that required that the plaintiffs be provided a publicly supported education; that the District of Columbia Board of Education provide a list of every school-aged child not receiving a publicly supported education; and that the Board of Education attempt to identify other handicapped children not previously identified.

In January 1972 the U.S. District Court issued an order establishing the right of all handicapped children to a publicly supported education. It indicated that the exclusion of children from public school without the provision of a prior hearing and review of placement procedures denied handicapped children the rights of due process and equal protection of the law.

JAMES BUTTON
United States Department of Education

MILWAUKEE PROJECT

The term Milwaukee Project is the popular title of a widely publicized program begun in the mid-1960s as one of many Great Society efforts to improve the intellectual development of low-achieving groups. It was headed by Rick Heber of the University of Wisconsin (UW), Madison, who was also director of the generously funded Waisman Institute in Madison. The Milwaukee Project was a small study with some 20 experimental subjects and 20 control subjects. It was not reported on by the investigators in any refereed scientific journals, yet its cost was some $14 million, mostly in federal funds, and its fame was international, since it claimed to have moved the IQs of its subject children from the dull-normal range of intelligence to the superior range of intelligence.

Enthusiasm, controversy, and scandal subsequently surrounded the history of the project. Its claimed success was hailed by famous psychologists and by the popular media. Later in the project, Heber, the principal investigator, was discharged from UW, Madison and convicted and imprisoned for large-scale abuse of federal funding for private gain. Two of his colleagues were also convicted of violations of federal laws in connection with misuse of project funds. Almost two decades after the beginning of the project, the scientific world had not yet seen the long-promised final report. However, the project has received uncritical acceptance in many college textbooks in psychology and education. For this reason, it is an important study to understand.

The first formal report of the Milwaukee Project appears to have been a short oral paper delivered at a conference in Warsaw (Heber & Garber, 1970). The sampling process for selection of children to be studied was later described as follows:

> We surveyed a residential area of the city of Milwaukee characterized by 1960 census data as having the lowest median family income, the greatest rate of dilapidated housing, and the greatest population density per living unit. Over a six-

month period, all families residing in this area with a newborn infant, and at least one other child . . . , were selected for study. (Heber et al., 1972, p. 4)

The purpose was to identify families with a high probability of producing retarded offspring. According to reports, among 88 located families, 40 had maternal IQs of 80 or higher, and 48 were below 80.

Earlier work showed an association between child and mother retardation. The Milwaukee Project was designed to treat the whole family to improve the chances for normal child intelligence. The treatment was to consist of two components: (1) the infant, early childhood stimulation program and (2) a maternal rehabilitation program. "Intervention . . . began as soon as was feasible after birth (within 6 months)" (Garber, 1975, p. 289).

According to the experimenters, just 20 children were randomly assigned to the E group and 20 to the C group. Then tests were given frequently to both groups, but only the experimental children received the double treatment of child stimulation and maternal rehabilitation.

From the first reports, there were remarkable claims of treatment effects. A spectacular graphic was displayed: a series of IQ test results beginning at 12 months with scores every 3 to 6 months until the age of 6 years. Both groups, experimental and control, began at about 115 IQ. The control group plummeted to the 90s by 24 months and stayed low throughout the period. But the experimental group actually rose from its high beginning and stayed high. According to Heber et al. (1972):

The mean IQ of the Experimental group at 66 months is 124 (s.d. = 8.6), compared to the Control group's mean IQ of 94 (s.d. = 10.7): a difference of thirty points. (pp. 48–50)

With such claimed results, the project was widely publicized in the popular press. The President's Commission on Mental Retardation wrote that the intelligence of the parent was indeed "a vital factor in the intelligence of children—mainly because of the environment that the parents create for the young child." And *Time* magazine, apparently taking its cue from the commission, stated flatly that such retardation was environmental in origin. On inquiry, a *Time* staffer explained that this had been proved by the Milwaukee Project (Page, 1972, p. 9). Nor was there more skepticism in the official publications of organized scientific psychology. A former American Psychological Association president described the project as "very exciting" (Trotter, 1976, p. 46).

Furthermore, the message was picked up by writers everywhere. As one scientist later noted:

Who can forget the great days of the early 1970s when the first reports emerged. . . . The news spread beyond America to the whole English-speaking world. . . . Heber's results quickly found their way into the textbooks: [One] was typical with its references to this 'exciting' study, its 'most encour-

aging' results, its 'impressive' findings—not the usual language of a text. (Flynn, 1984, p. 40)

The textbook treatment was reviewed by others (Sommer & Sommer, 1983) who saw an actual increase in references (but always in obscure publications) to the project from 1977 to 1982. Their analysis, they noted:

Yields a picture of research findings becoming widespread in textbooks . . . without ever having been subjected to journal review. Our experience is that textbooks are regarded as authoritative by the students who read them and the faculty who adopt them. (p. 983)

Since the project has not been substantially described in refereed journals (at least in its first 17 years), and technical reports have been of limited circulation, the project has not received extensive technical criticism. Yet there have been sharp exceptions taken to its methodology. There is internal evidence that the randomization was flawed, that replacements in the children were unreported, that the treatments were contaminated by the IQ test material, that the treatments had never been adequately described, and that the IQ testing itself, carried out by friendly project personnel, was cast in doubt by the one outside examiner (Page, 1972; Page, 1986; Page & Grandon, 1981). At no time have project personnel published responses to these criticisms.

Others have written of the violation of scientific practice in the fugitive, unrefereed publications (Sommer & Sommer, 1983, 1984). Flynn (1984) reexamined the data and presented adjusted results that showed a real decline for the experimental group of 16 IQ points (p. 40).

One of the questions remaining is how the experimental children have performed in their later schooling, once away from the control of the project. The goal of such intensive training had been, of course, to prepare them for satisfactory accomplishment in later schooling and life. Reports from the project itself are again cryptic and difficult to find or to interpret. But one source of information (Clarke & Clarke, 1976, pp. 224–225) reported that there was no longer a difference between experimental and control children in measured reading ability. Of course, reading ability is the first goal of elementary education, and comprehension is highly correlated with intelligence tests.

When a study of such symbolic importance deviates so much from any past results and is so inconsistent with other evidence, then it must rely on the reputation of its personnel, or on society's desire to believe in the results. It is therefore relevant that reputations have been severely damaged in federal court. The project's director, Heber, was sentenced and imprisoned for his misuse of federal funds, and two others were also convicted, and one imprisoned (see news stories by Rob Fixmer, *Capital Times*, Madison, Wisconsin, January 1981). Perhaps most relevant has been the project's failure, long before the trials, to bring its sampling, procedures, and data into the light of public scrutiny even after its international publicity and the expenditure of some $14 million, most of it federal, for 20 experimental children and their controls.

REFERENCES

Clarke, A. M., & Clarke, A. D. B. (1979). *Early experience: Myth and evidence*. New York: Free Press.

Flynn, J. R. (1984). The mean IQ of Americans: Massive gains 1932 to 1978. *Psychological Bulletin, 95*(1), 29–51.

Garber, H. (1975). Intervention in infancy: A developmental approach. In M. Begab & S. Richardson (Eds.), *The mentally retarded and society*. Baltimore, MD: University Park Press.

Heber, R., & Garber, H. (1970). An experiment in the prevention of cultural-familial retardation. In D. A. Primrose (Ed.), *Proceedings of the Third Congress of the International Association for the Scientific Study of Mental Deficiency*. (Vol. 1, pp. 34–43). Warsaw: Polish Medical Publishers.

Heber, R., Garber, H., Harrington, S., Hoffman, C., & Falender, C. (Dec. 1972). *Rehabilitation of families at risk for mental retardation: Progress report*. Madison: University of Wisconsin, Rehabilitation Research and Training Center in Mental Retardation.

Page, E. B. (1972). Miracle in Milwaukee: Raising the I.Q. *Educational Researcher, 1*(10), 8–15.

Page, E. B. (1986). The disturbing case of the Milwaukee Project. In H. H. Spitz (Ed.), *The raising of intelligence*. Hillsdale, NJ: Erlbaum.

Page, E. B., & Grandon, G. M. (1981). Massive intervention and child intelligence: The Milwaukee Project in critical perspective. *Journal of Special Education, 15*(2), 239–256.

Sommer, R., & Sommer, B. A. (1983). Mystery in Milwaukee: Early intervention, IQ, and psychology textbooks. *American Psychologist, 38*, 982–985.

Sommer, R., & Sommer, B. (1984). Reply from Sommer and Sommer. *American Psychologist, 39*, 1318–1319.

Trotter, R. (1976). Environment and behavior: Intensive intervention program prevents retardation. *APA Monitor, 7*, 4–6, 19, 46.

ELLIS B. PAGE
Duke University

HEBER, R. F.
INTELLIGENCE
MENTAL RETARDATION

MINIMAL BRAIN DYSFUNCTION

See MBD SYNDROME.

MINIMUM COMPETENCY TESTING

Minimum competency testing is assessment to determine whether students possess skills that have been designated as prerequisites for either grade promotion or graduation with a high-school diploma. Minimum competency testing enjoys widespread public and political support as it is seen as a means of raising academic standards and increasing educational achievement (Haney & Madaus, 1978). A majority of the states have instituted minimum competency testing requirements (Pipho, 1978), however, there is no unanimity as to the purpose and content of the tests, which are determined at the state or local school district level.

The inclusion of handicapped students in minimum competency testing programs is problematic. Some educators are totally opposed to minimum competency testing of the handicapped (Chandler, 1982). However, the tide of opinion favors inclusion provided appropriate accommodations are made to ensure fairness and nondiscrimination in the testing process.

Minimum competency testing of the handicapped has been challenged on the basis of the Education of All Handicapped Children Act (PL 94-142), Section 504 of the Rehabilitation Act of 1973, and constitutional grounds. The constitutionally based objection involves issues of due process and equal protection as set forth in the Fourteenth Amendment. Thus far, the courts have upheld the right of states to establish minimal competency standards. The courts have intervened on behalf of handicapped students only when academic standards have been clearly arbitrary and unfair, when criteria have been applied in a discriminatory manner, or when students have not been provided with sufficient notice of requirements prior to the imposition of sanctions (McCarthy, 1983).

Section 504 of the Rehabilitation Act of 1973 prohibits discrimination against an "otherwise qualified individual" in any program or activity supported wholly or in part by federal funds. Opponents of minimum competency testing of the handicapped have argued that denial of a diploma to a handicapped student is a violation of Section 504. The courts have not concurred. The courts accept the allegation of discrimination only if a handicapped individual who is able to meet all requirements of a given program "in spite of his handicap" is denied the benefits of that program. There is no inherent right to a diploma in the absence of the ability to meet academic standards. However, the courts have recognized that Section 504 entitles physically handicapped students to accommodations of the testing situation (e.g., format, environment, response mode, etc.).

A third challenge to the minimum competency testing stems from the PL 94-142 provision for "appropriate" educational programs for the handicapped. Opponents of minimum competency testing have challenged the appropriateness of special education programs that do not prepare handicapped students to pass minimum competency tests. The Supreme Court addressed the issue in *Board of Education of the Hendrick Hudson Central School District* v. *Rowley* (1982). The majority opinion stated that the entitlement of handicapped children in PL 94-142 did not guarantee maximization of student potential or guaranteed outcomes. Rather, the student is entitled to an individualized educational program "with sufficient supportive services to permit the child to benefit from the instruction" (McCarthy, 1983). Therefore, students who have received special instruction to address their unique deficiency, but were not prepared for minimum competency testing, cannot claim that these programs were "inappropriate" (McCarthy, 1983).

Special educators who condone minimum competency testing for the handicapped still face decisions on inclusion and exclusion. Ewing and Smith (1981) found that three general practices prevail: (1) inclusion of all handicapped, (2) exclusion of all handicapped, and (3) selective inclusion or exclusion based on handicapping condition. They suggest that inclusion or exclusionary decisions can be facilitated by dichotomizing the handicapped into two groups: students who require modification of the learning environment and students who require modified curriculum and instructional goals. Minimum competency testing would be appropriate for the former group as they share essentially the same educational and curricular goals with nonhandicapped students. Minimum competency testing would not be appropriate for the latter group, which is characterized by lower achievement potential and strives for lower levels of skill development removed from the curriculum of regular education (Ewing & Smith, 1981).

The exclusion of severely/profoundly impaired students will give rise to few if any objections. The appropriate decision for the educable mentally retarded student is less clear-cut. Negative consequences as a result of minimum competency testing despite testing accommodations have been reported in at least two studies to date (McKinney, 1983; Serow & O'Brien, 1983). In contrast, specific modifications in format and presentation reportedly enhanced the performance of learning-disabled students (Beattie, Grise, & Algozzine, 1983; Grise, Beattie, & Algozzine, 1982).

The prudent approach is to decide the appropriateness of minimum competency testing on a case-by-case basis as part of the development of the student's individualized educational program (IEP). The IEP can be used as the vehicle for connecting competency testing with the student's overall instructional program (Cressey & Padilla, 1981; Olson, 1980; Schenk, 1981). The minimum competency requirements for which the student will be held accountable and the accommodations to be made can be documented in the IEP, thus ensuring a shared understanding between the school and the family.

Accommodations in minimum competency testing to meet the needs of the handicapped can address standards or particulars of the testing situation. Modification of standards involve "differential" standards for graduation, which can take the form of special competency tests, lowered performance standards, or modifications of testing procedures. Differential standards (with the exception of passage of the regular test with modified procedures) result in the issuance of a special diploma or certificate other than the regular diploma to the handicapped student at the time of graduation (Cressey & Padilla, 1981).

A variety of possible modifications of testing procedures have been discussed by numerous special educators (Fox & Weaver, 1981; Morrisey, 1980) and the list of recommendations is extensive. The essential consideration is to enable the handicapped individual to demonstrate his or her knowledge and accomplishments despite physical or sensory handicap.

REFERENCES

Beattie, S., Grise, P., & Algozzine, B. (1983). Effects of test modification of the minimum competency performance of learning disabled students. *Learning Disabilities Quarterly*, 6(1), 75–76.

Chandler, H. N. (1982). A modest proposal. *Journal of Learning Disabilities*, 15(5), 306–308.

Cressey, J., & Padilla, C. (1981). *Minimal competency testing and special education students: A technical assistance guide.* Menlo Park, CA: SRI International.

Ewing, N. J., & Smith, J. (1981). Minimum competency testing and the handicapped. Reston, VA: Council for Exceptional Children.

Fox, C. L., & Weaver, F. L. (1981). Minimal competency testing: Issues and options. *Academic Therapy*, 16(4), 425–435.

Grise, P., Beattie, S., & Algozzine, B. (1982). Assessment of minimum competency in fifth grade learning disabled students: Test modifications make a difference. *Journal of Educational Research*, 76(1), 35–40.

Haney, W., & Madaus, G. F. (1978). Making sense of the competency testing movement. *Harvard Educational Review*, 48(4), 462–484.

McCarthy, M. M. (1983). The application of competency testing mandates to handicapped children. *Harvard Educational Review*, 53(2), 146–164.

McKinney, J. D. (1983). Performance of handicapped students on the North Carolina minimum competency test. *Exceptional Children*, 49(6), 547–550.

Morrissey, P. (1978). Adaptive testing: How and when should handicapped students be accommodated in competency testing programs? In R. M. Jaeger & C. K. Tittle (Eds.), *Minimum competency achievement testing.* Berkeley, CA: McCutchan.

Olsen, K. R. (1980). Minimum competency testing and the IEP process. *Exceptional Children*, 47(3), 176–183.

Pipho, C. (1978). Minimum competency testing in 1978: A look at state standards. *Phi Delta Kappan*, 59(9), 585–588.

Schenk, S. J. (1981, April). *Ramifications of the minimum competency movement for special education.* Paper presented at the annual meeting of the American Educational Research Association, Los Angeles, CA.

Serow, R. C., & O'Brien, K. (1983). Performance of handicapped students in a competency testing program. *Journal of Special Education*, 17(2), 149–155.

LIBBY GOODMAN
Pennsylvania State University

ACHIEVEMENT TESTS
COMPETENCY TESTING

MINNESOTA MULTIPHASIC PERSONALITY INVENTORY (MMPI)

The Minnesota Multiphasic Personality Inventory (MMPI) is a structured, global, and standardized test of personality used extensively in the United States and many other countries to assess mental or psychological functioning within both the normal and abnormal ranges. A wide range of personality is assessed by a self-report questionnaire containing in excess of 500 true–false items. In form, this assessment instrument is usually presented as a booklet of printed questions with a separate answer sheet. Computerized administration of the MMPI presents items on the computer screen; this format is growing in popularity. Computer scoring and interpretation of the MMPI has become highly advanced.

Originally developed in the 1940s at the University of Minnesota as an aid in the diagnosis of mental disorders, the MMPI has experienced prodigious growth both in frequency and range of use. Today it is among the most often administered of all psychological tests. In addition to its continued use in psychopathology, the MMPI is widely employed with normal populations from college students to nuclear plant operators. It is the most frequently used test for selection of police officers in the United States. The test questions or item pool has been used as the basis for hundreds of additional tests, some having been added to the original 14 MMPI scales.

The MMPI has also inspired an enormous amount of literature. Research reports, interpretive manuals, descriptions, and criticism, along with a variety of short forms of the inventory, are among the publications. The most comprehensive source of information regarding the development and interpretation of this assessment instrument is *An MMPI Handbook, Volume 1: Clinical Interpretation* (Dahlstrom, Welsh, & Dahlstrom, 1972). Dahlstrom and Dahlstrom (1980) have also edited a selection of readings on the MMPI.

REFERENCES

Dahlstrom, W. G., & Dahlstrom, L. E. (Eds.). (1980). *Readings on the MMPI: A new selection on personality measurement.* Minneapolis: University of Minnesota Press.

Dahlstrom, W. G., Welsh, G. S., & Dahlstrom, L. E. (1972). *An MMPI handbook, Vol. I: Clinical interpretation.* Minneapolis: University of Minnesota Press.

ROBERT R. REILLEY
Texas A&M University

PERSONALITY ASSESSMENT

MINOR PHYSICAL ANOMALIES

A set of minor physical anomalies (MPAs) frequently occurs with Down's syndrome and is apparently linked with a variety of behavioral abnormalities. Examples of MPAs are soft and pliable ears, tongue with rough and smooth spots, fine electric hair, high-steepled palate, head circumference larger or smaller than normal, curved fifth finger, single crease across the palm of the hand, epicanthus, and a gap between the first and second toe. Most children show a few of these characteristics (Waldrop & Halverson, 1971).

A higher than normal number of MPAs is correlated with conditions such as mental retardation, autism, learning disabilities, schizophrenia, and attentional deficit disorder (Krouse & Kauffman, 1982). However, the relationship between MPAs and behavioral abnormalities appears to hold reliably only in boys. Within-group variability in MPAs is such that MPA scores of disordered boys only are higher than those of normals. However intriguing they are as correlates, MPA scores should not be used clinically to diagnose individual children. Such use would yield a large number of false positives (Firestone & Peters, 1983).

REFERENCES

Firestone, P., & Peters, S. (1983). Minor physical anomalies and behavior in children: A review. *Journal of Autism & Developmental Disorders, 13,* 411–425.

Krouse, J. P., & Kauffman, J. M. (1982). Minor physical anomalies in exceptional children: A review and critique of research. *Journal of Abnormal Child Psychology, 10,* 247–264.

Waldrop, M. F., & Halverson, C. F. (1971). Minor physical anomalies and hyperactive behavior in young children. In J. Hellmuth (Ed.), *Exceptional infant: Studies in abnormalities.* (Vol. 2, pp. 343–380). New York: Brunner/Mazel.

ROBERT T. BROWN
ELLEN B. MARRIOTT
University of North Carolina, Wilmington

DOWN'S SYNDROME
PHYSICAL ANOMALIES
PHYSICAL HANDICAPS
DYSMORPHIC FEATURES

MISCUE ANALYSIS

Miscue analysis is a research technique developed by Kenneth Goodman in 1970 to describe the language and thought processes involved in the act of reading. Based on psycholinguistic theory, Goodman described reading as an interaction between the language of the reader and the language of the author (Goodman & Burke, 1972). To discover how both language and thought processes are involved in reading, children's oral miscues were analyzed as they read unrehearsed passages of text. Miscues were defined as unexpected responses that deviated from the expected responses in the text. Specifically, miscue analysis is used as a means of identifying and evaluating the strategies employed by skilled and unskilled readers as they attempt to construct meaning from written text.

The procedures used in miscue analysis have been simplified for classroom use in a diagnostic instrument called the Reading Miscue Inventory (Goodman & Burke, 1972). Burke (1974) cites procedures that include recording children's oral reading errors and classifying the errors based on the following questions:

1. *Graphic Similarity.* How much does the miscue *look* like the expected response?

2. *Sound Similarity.* How much does the miscue *sound* like the expected response?

3. *Grammatical Function.* Is the grammatical function of the reader's word the same as the grammatical function of the text word?

4. *Syntactic Acceptability.* Is the sentence involving the miscue grammatically acceptable?

5. *Semantic Acceptability.* Is the sentence involving the miscue semantically acceptable?

6. *Meaning Change.* Is there a change in meaning involved in the sentence?

7. *Correction and Semantic Acceptability.* Do corrections by the reader make the sentence semantically acceptable? (p. 23)

These questions are applied to each miscue to determine how readers process three kinds of information from the printed page: grapho-phonic, syntactic, and semantic (Goodman, 1969).

First, grapho-phonic information enables readers to recognize the letters in the text and convert them to sounds. Phonics is the term commonly used to describe this letter-sound matching. Second, syntactic information brings to the act of reading an implicit knowledge of the grammatical rules of the language. With this information readers have the ability to predict linguistic patterns in written materials. Third, semantic information makes it possible for readers to draw on their own experiences and knowledge as they interpret the author's message. This semantic information is crucial as readers attempt to understand the relationship between their personal experiences and the experiences of the author.

Research on miscue analysis is inconclusive because of inconsistencies in classifying and interpreting specific reading miscues. Wixson (1979) points out that miscue procedures are not designed to account for variables such as instructional methods, type of text, passage length and difficulty, and reader's purpose. It has been suggested (Leu, 1982; Wixson, 1979) that miscue patterns may be a function of these variables rather than a reflection of a particular reader's processing strategies.

One of the most significant findings of miscue analysis research is that the reading strategies of proficient readers are different from those of less skilled readers. Because proficient readers have greater language competency, they tend to make errors that are more syntactically and semantically acceptable than less proficient readers (Goodman, 1969; Goodman & Burke, 1972). Readers with a strong language background have already acquired enough semantic and syntactic information to predict the language structures found in many reading materials; they need only a minimal amount of grapho-phonic information to complete the reading process. Conversely, children with deficient language backgrounds or competencies lack the semantic and syntactic information to predict meaningful language patterns in many reading materials. Such children produce miscues that result in meaning changes and alter or obscure the author's message. Lacking the highly developed syntactic and semantic competencies of good readers, poor readers become too dependent on grapho-phonic information.

Teachers can use the results of miscue analysis to improve their instructional strategies. After classifying and interpreting students' miscues, teachers should provide the appropriate language experiences necessary to develop the conceptual understandings needed to comprehend the author's message. Once teachers know the type of miscues children make, they can provide experiences that build bridges from the language and thought of the child to the language and thought of the author.

REFERENCES

Burke, C. (1974). Preparing elementary teachers to teach reading. In K. S. Goodman (Ed.), *Miscue analysis: Applications to reading instruction.* Urbana, IL: National Council of Teachers of English.

Goodman, K. S. (1969). Analysis of reading miscues: Applied psycholinguistics. *Reading Research Quarterly, 5*(1), 9–30.

Goodman, Y. M., & Burke, C. L. (1972). *Reading miscue inventory: Procedures for diagnosis and evaluation.* New York: Macmillan.

Leu, D. J., Jr. (1982). Oral reading error analysis: A critical review of research and application. *Reading Research Quarterly, 17*(3), 420–437.

Wixson, K. L. (1979). Miscue analysis: A critical review. *Journal of Reading Behavior, 11*(2), 163–175.

CHRIS CHERRINGTON
Lycoming College

LINGUISTIC READERS
READING DISORDERS
READING REMEDIATION

MNEMONICS

Mnemonics are among the oldest strategies used to enhance recall of information such as facts, names, sequences, and concepts. In recent years they have been helpful to students labeled learning disabled and mildly handicapped (Mastropieri, Scruggs, & Levin, 1985; Rose, Cundick, & Higbee, 1983). Examples of tasks taught by such strategies include reading comprehension and concept formation.

One frequently used mnemonic with learning-disabled students is the rhyming or pegword technique. It consists of remembering a simple rhyme pairing a number and an object such as "one-bun, two-shoe, three-tree." The learner then pairs the new information with each object in the rhyme. Another strategy requires the learner to visually imagine a set of loci in which he or she can place the new information. The keyword method combines a special word for the information (e.g., box for "bauxite") with a pegword.

REFERENCES

Mastropieri, M. A., Scruggs, T. E., & Levin, J. R. (1985). Mnemonic strategy instruction with learning disabled adolescents. *Journal of Learning Disabilities*, *18*, 94–100.

Rose, M. C., Cundick, B. P., & Higbee, K. L. (1983). Verbal rehearsal and visual imagery: Mnemonic aids for learning disabled children. *Journal of Learning Disabilities*, *16*, 352–354.

THOMAS ZANE
Johns Hopkins University

AMNESIA
MEMORY DISORDERS

MOBAN

Moban is the proprietary name of molindine, a white crystalline powder used as a tranquilizer (Modell, 1985). The drug acts on the ascending reticular activating system to reduce depression, aggressiveness, and spontaneous locomotion. Tranquilizing effects reportedly are achieved without such negative concomitants as incoordination or muscle relaxation. Moban typically is used in the management of schizophrenia.

Common side effects associated with Moban include initial drowsiness, depression, and hyperactivity. Moban has been associated with seizure activity on occasion. Increased activity may occur in some individuals, and hence protective environments may be necessary. Tardive dyskinesia is a possible side effect. Moban has not been shown to be effective in the management of behavior problems associated with mental retardation. Use of Moban in children under 12 years of age is not recommended.

REFERENCES

Modell, W. (Ed.). (1985). *Drugs in current use and new drugs* (31st ed.). New York: Springer-Verlag.

Physician's desk reference (37th ed.). (1983). Oradell, NJ: Medical Economics.

CATHY F. TELZROW
*Cuyahoga Special Education
Service Center, Maple
Heights, Ohio*

THORAZINE
TRANQUILIZERS
STELAZINE

MOBILE EDUCATION UNITS

As the name implies, mobile education units are vans, buses, recreational vehicles, or trailers that have been converted to house specialized materials, media, and testing equipment to serve handicapped children and youths. They are in use in rural areas primarily, where geographic distances and learner sparsity make the units an efficient means of making special materials and services available to teachers and learners. These units are usually owned by the administrative unit that is responsible for supportive special education services (e.g., BOCES, CESA, Intermediaate Unit).

The term mobile special education unit is a generic category of vehicle. The size and purpose of the unit is dependent on the needs of the region being served. Some units are used exclusively for testing. Space is at a premium in many schools and even if space is available, it may not be appropriate for services such as psychological testing or auditory assessments because of noise or distractions. Mobile units that are designed for these purposes have special lighting and noise reduction materials to improve the environment for testing. The unit travels around a geographic region on a schedule and is parked adjacent to a school for an extended period. The psychologist or audiologist may double as the driver of such a unit.

Sometimes a mobile unit will change locations daily and will house an itinerant specialist such as a speech and language specialist, occupational therapist, or physical therapist. Again, because schools may not have the available appropriate space or equipment, these units can become an efficient means of providing services in rural areas. Finally, there are mobile units that move from school to school on a weekly or biweekly schedule. They act like lending libraries, as an extension of a materials resource center. Materials are checked out for a 1- to 2-week period. By using a mobile library, the special education district need not purchase many expensive items for each of its special education classes. Use can be maximized by this system of sharing.

ROBERT A. SEDLAK
University of Wisconsin, Stout

HOMEBOUND INSTRUCTION
ITINERANT SERVICES

MOBILITY INSTRUCTION (GENERAL)

Mobility instruction is a term used to represent specific daily functional living skills that are incorporated into educational programs for moderate and severely handicapped populations. The purpose of this instruction is to allow individuals to safely engage in planned movement from one location to another (Merbler & Wood, 1984).

Included in this group of functional skills are activities that promote independent travel within the immediate home environment as well as the local community. Instruction in toileting and meal preparation, and travel training for shopping, employment, or community recreation are examples of the activities included in mobility instruction.

Historically, mobility training has been part of the curriculum for the visually impaired. Only recently has this aspect of instruction been addressed in the curriculum for the mentally retarded. This relatively new focus on mobility training for mentally retarded individuals has resulted from the growing number of handicapped persons who are living and working within local communities. These populations must obtain skills that will allow them to function as independently as possible within their communities (Wheeler et al., 1980).

Within the last 10 years there has been growing support for systematically incorporating functional skills into the existing curriculum for the mentally retarded. A variety of programs have been recently developed that focus on the direct teaching of these skills. Mobility training programs such as those reviewed by Martin, Rusch, and Heal (1982), include activities that engage individuals in real-life experiences as well simulated travel activities conducted within a classroom setting. Basic to any program is the need to provide direct practical instruction in travel as well as related skill development. For example, while it is essential to provide individuals with simulated and real-life experiences in locating and boarding a bus, mobility instruction must also include the development of such related skills as decision making and the ability to adapt to changes in routines. These skills are essential because changes in the environment, as in a bus schedule, are common.

Other considerations for the development of curriculum in this area include the need to analyze the variety of sub-skills that lead to successful travel. To teach bus travel, it is necessary to teach individuals how to safely cross intersections, locate a bus stop, use a bus ticket, and board a bus.

While there is a need for additional research that will evaluate the effectiveness of mobility instruction, there are preliminary indicators that reveal that real-life experiences are more effective than simulation activities for training mobility skills.

Regardless of how simulation and real-life experiences are combined, it is important that the mobility instruction be systematic. Equally important is that parents and group-home workers allow handicapped individuals opportunities to practice these skills independently (Certo, Schwartz, & Brown, 1977).

REFERENCES

Certo, N., Schwartz, R., & Brown, L. (1977). Community transportation: Teaching severely handicapped students to ride a public bus system. In N. G. Haring, & L. J. Brown (Eds.), *Teaching the severely handicapped* (Vol. 2, pp. 147–232). New York: Grune & Stratton.

Martin, J., Rusch, F., & Heal, L. (1982). Teaching community survival skills to mentally retarded adults: A review and analysis. *Journal of Special Education, 16*(3), 243–267.

Merbler, J. B., & Wood, T. A. (1984). Predicting orientation and mobility proficiency in mentally retarded visually impaired children. *Education & Training of the Mentally Retarded, 19*(3), 228–230.

Wheeler, J., Ford, A., Nietupski, J., Loomis, R., & Brown, L. (1980). Teaching moderately and severely handicapped adolescents to shop in supermarkets using pocket calculators. *Education & Training of the Mentally Retarded, 15*(2), 105–112.

FRANCINE TOMPKINS
University of Cincinnati

ELECTRONIC TRAVEL AIDS
TRAVEL AIDS FOR THE HANDICAPPED

MOBILITY TRAINING

Formal training of the blind to help them move independently had its beginnings in the United States with the founding of the first dog guide school, Seeing Eye, Inc. of Morristown, New Jersey (Bledsoe, 1980). Although many blind individuals had traveled independently for centuries, it was not until the founding of this dog guide school that efforts were made to formalize a sequential approach to independent travel.

However, the formal curriculum for mobility training owes its roots to the cane rather than the dog. Over the years, mobility training for the blind has had many names. Sir Francis Campbell, an American who was naturalized and knighted in Britain, wrote extensively in the 1860s about the need for formal mobility training under the broad term "foot travel." Father Thomas Carroll, founder of the Catholic Guide for All the Blind, coined the term peripatology, which could be loosely defined as the study of travel. The most common term today is orientation and mobility. Orientation in this context is the acquisition of knowledge about one's environment; mobility means one's ability to move freely and safely from one place to another. The individual who teaches orientation and mobility is commonly referred to as a mobility specialist, although the terms peripatologist or orientator are also used.

Richard Hoover, who started his career as a physical education instructor at the Maryland School for the Blind, developed a technique and a cane while he was a sergeant in 1944 with the Army Medical Corps attached to a blind rehabilitation program at Valley Forge Army General Hospital. Hoover recognized the inadequacies of the commonly used white cane, which was in reality an orthopedic aid; he developed a much longer and lighter cane.

The need for teachers to instruct the blind in the use of this new cane and techniques became obvious. Valley Forge Army Hospital, Avon Old Farms Rehabilitation Center, and later Hines Veterans Hospital, trained their own mobility specialists for the instruction of blinded veterans. When the Hoover concept was more widely accepted and applied to the young civilian population, university degree programs were developed, first at Boston College in 1960 and a year later at Western Michigan University.

The 22nd edition of the American Foundation for the Blind *Directory of Agencies Serving the Visually Handicapped in the United States* (1984) lists 16 colleges or universities that offer degree programs that prepare orientation and mobility specialists.

The training, either at the bachelor's or master's level, consists of course work in the nature and needs of the blind, training in the specific skills and techniques of teaching independence, and a block of hours working under a blindfold. The formal course work is followed by a term of practicum supervised by a qualified mobility specialist. The Mobility Interest Group of the Association for the Education and Rehabilitation of the Blind and Visually Impaired certifies graduates of university training programs.

A sizable number of mobility specialists work in larger school systems, where they provide training to blind students. In addition to direct training of children and youths, they also consult with teachers of younger children in the development of concepts that will later enhance travel independence.

REFERENCES

American Foundation for the Blind. (1984). *Directory of agencies serving the visually handicapped in the U.S.* (22nd ed.). New York: Author.

Bledsoe, C. W. (1980). Originators of orientation and mobility training. In R. L. Welsh & B. B. Blasch (Eds.), *Foundation of orientation and mobility*. New York: American Foundation for the Blind.

Muldoon, J. F. (1986, March). Carroll revisited: Inductions in rehabilitation, 1938–1971. *Journal of Visual Impairment & Blindness, 80*(3), 617–626.

GIDEON JONES
Florida State University

BLIND LEARNING APTITUDE TEST
DOG GUIDES FOR THE BLIND
VISUAL TRAINING

MOBILITY TRAINING AND THE HANDICAPPED

See MOBILITY INSTRUCTION (GENERAL); See also MOBILITY TRAINING.

MODEL PROGRAMS FOR SEVERELY AND PROFOUNDLY HANDICAPPED INDIVIDUALS

The purpose of model education programs for individuals with severe to profound handicaps is to look at the state of the art in the instruction of such individuals and to continue to innovate by investigating current practices in a variety of ways. Typically receiving funding from outside sources (e.g., Office of Special Education and Rehabilitative Services at the federal level), model programs may include demonstration projects in local school systems, work with nonschool personnel such as parents via parent training projects, or adult vocational and independent living skills training programs.

Common features in model programs use an empirical base to draw conclusions about techniques and services. This data base enables investigators to draw accurate conclusions about the best practices for instruction and services for individuals with severe or profound handicaps. In addition, model programs have a consumer orientation in that they involve outcomes that will be of use to service programs, parents, guardians, or advocates who have an interest in the needs of severely and profoundly handicapped persons. A variety of research methods are generally used in model programs, including single-subject studies, survey research, and ethnographic investigation (Paine, 1984). Evaluation components of model programs are developed to ensure that all administrative and direct service goals are completed in a timely and satisfactory manner. Finally, dissemination of final products (e.g., specific examples of training programs, assessment manuals, in-service training kits) takes place at the end of the model program's final funding year as well as throughout the years the project is in place. Typically, model programs are funded for 3 to 5 years at the federal level.

Two examples of model programs are the Community-Based Instruction Program (CBIP) in Albemarle County, Virginia (project director, Adelle Renzaglia) and the Specialized Training Program (STP) in Eugene, Oregon (program director, G. Thomas Bellamy). The CBIP (Snell & Renzaglia, 1986) was a federally funded 3-year project that was established to serve school-age students with severe and profound handicaps. Prior to the start of the program, these students were being served inappropriately in preschool classes, in classes for students with mild to moderate handicaps, or in homebound instruction. Three classes were established in integrated settings: a high-school class serving individuals ages 16 to 21 years of age located in a high school that serves approximately 2000 nonhandicapped students; a middle-school class serving students ages 12 to 15 years that was located in a middle school housing approximately 375 nonhandicapped sixth through eighth grade students; and an elementary classroom serving students ages 6 to 11 years in an elementary school with approximately 225 nonhandicapped kindergarten through fifth-grade students.

Students in the CBIP classrooms had a variety of handicapping conditions. Some had limited expressive language, vision, or hearing impairments. Several students were severely motorically impaired (e.g., severe hypertonic cerebral palsy). Other students exhibited major behavior problems (e.g., aggression, self-stimulation, noncompliance).

Students in the high-school class spent most of their day outside of the classroom in vocational, community, leisure/recreational, and domestic skills training. For students ages 20 to 21 years, the major emphasis was on vocational training for future competitive employment. Younger, less skilled students received vocational training in community training sites or in the community sheltered workshops.

Domestic skills training for high-school students took place in two sites: a group home in which two students lived and a home in the community where skills could be trained and practiced on a daily basis. Community skill training took place on location (e.g., pedestrian skills taught on a public street, grocery shopping skills taught in grocery stores) or in the classroom (e.g., using vending machines, purchasing food at a restaurant) with generalization assessed and trained at the actual community site. Leisure/recreation skills training also took place in community sites (e.g., using a video machine at a video arcade) as well as in the classroom (e.g., social phone conversations) with generalization assessed and trained in community environments.

Classroom programming in the middle school empha-

sized (1) providing vocational training on real jobs in a school setting; (2) teaching domestic skills in a school-based apartment setting; (3) teaching community mobility skills; (4) teaching hygienic and grooming skills in the gym locker room before and after physical education class; (5) teaching functional academic skills (e.g., time telling, money skills); and (6) teaching appropriate leisure/recreational activities in the classroom and the community. In addition, behavior management programs were implemented to decrease maladaptive behaviors as needed.

At the elementary level, students received instruction in basic self-care skills (e.g., toileting), appropriate mealtime behaviors, dressing, receptive and expressive language skills, motor skills in the context of functional activities, and appropriate use of leisure time. Several students at this level were taught to partially participate in activities because of severe motor limitations. All elementary students participated in a physical education program daily in which they had a chance to interact with their nonhandicapped peers.

Extensive contact with parents and ancillary staff (i.e., domestic/home living skills specialist, adaptive physical education instructor) took place in planning educational programs for individual students. A transdisciplinary approach was taken in the CBIP. In addition, trainers looked at the current and future needs of students to ensure the smooth functioning of program goals and to maximize instructional time and student progress.

The STP (Boles, Bellamy, Horner, & Mank, 1984) was implemented to develop, field test, and disseminate a structured employment model emphasizing benchwork assembly tasks for adults with severe handicaps. Initially developed within a university center as an on-campus vocational program for severely and profoundly mentally retarded individuals, the program moved into a field test phase in which community vocational training was offered in three states using the STP model. Currently, the program is in a model implementation phase in which a work support center is being developed to assist localities throughout the nation in developing STP sites.

The STP provides employment in the area of small parts assembly (e.g., electronic units). Work is procured from local industries and workers are trained on a one-to-one basis until they are able to enter a supported production setting. Applied behavior analysis procedures are used for training and areas of instruction include personal competence in the surrounding community as well as in the work place. Each model site operates as a small not-for-profit business and follows well-defined procedures for management, finance, and commercial operation.

Through careful planning of the site activities and training, as well as support for groups wishing to start replication sites, the STP model has provided multiple work sites for severely to profoundly handicapped individuals. Systematic instruction has enabled these individuals, heretofore unserved in competitive employment sites, to have a viable alternative to sheltered work or no-work options.

The two models described indicate the types of programming that are being investigated and disseminated following demonstration of innovative practices. In general, model programs for individuals with severe or profound handicaps should include the following: data-based assessment of current and future needs; ongoing data-based evaluation of progress; integration of severely handicapped students/adults with their nonhandicapped peers; transdisciplinary programming; home-school interaction; chronological age-appropriate programs; objectives that are functional for students'/adults' current or future needs; and systematic instruction in specific domains such as the domestic (e.g., grooming, household chores), leisure/recreation, community (e.g., restaurant use, pedestrian skills, grocery shopping), and vocational (Snell & Renzaglia, 1986).

REFERENCES

Boles, S. M., Bellamy, G. T., Horner, R. H., & Mark, D. M. (1984). Specialized training program: The structured employment model. In S. C. Paine, G. T. Bellamy, & B. Wilcox (Eds.), *Human services that work* (pp. 181–205). Baltimore, MD: Brookes.

Paine, S. C. (1984). Models revisited. In S. C. Paine, G. T. Bellamy, & B. Wilcox (Eds.), *Human services that work* (pp. 269–276). Baltimore, MD: Brookes.

Snell, M. E., & Renzaglia, A. (1986). Moderate, severe, and profound handicaps. In N. G. Haring & L. McCormick (Eds.), *Exceptional Children and Youth* (4th ed.). Columbus, OH: Merrill.

CORNELIA LIVELY
University of Illinois,
Urbana-Champaign

APPLIED BEHAVIOR ANALYSIS
FUNCTIONAL INSTRUCTION
TRANSFER OF LEARNING
TRANSFER OF TRAINING
VOCATIONAL TRAINING OF THE HANDICAPPED

MONOGRAPHS OF THE SOCIETY FOR RESEARCH IN CHILD DEVELOPMENT

Monographs of the Society for Research in Child Development is one of three publications of the Society for Research in Child Development. Published irregularly by the University of Chicago Press, the *Monographs* series is perhaps the longest continuous publication in the field of child development.

In general, the series is intended for the publication of significant research articles that are longer than those normally published in journals. Of particular interest are longitudinal studies and research that appeals to a large number of developmentalists from a variety of fields.

Recent topics for the *Monographs* have been children's friendships, children at risk for developmental disorders, and the lasting effects of early education. In addition to monographs concerning normal child development, the *Monographs* also publish research on special or atypical children, including the hearing and visually impaired. The *Monographs* series is read by psychologists, pediatricians, special educators, anthropologists, social workers, and others, particularly in North America.

MICHAEL J. ASH
JOSE LUIS TORRES
Texas A&M University

MONTESSORI, MARIA (1870–1952)

Maria Montessori, who was Italy's first woman physician, originated the educational system known as the Montessori method. The major features of her method were a non-graded classroom, individualization of instruction, sequential ordering of learning tasks, sensory and motor training, use of concrete materials, abolition of punishment, discovery learning, and freedom of activity and choice. First used in 1899 for the instruction of mentally retarded children, Montessori soon found that her approach was equally effective with nonhandicapped children. Her influence is evident today in both special classes and preschool and lower elementary programs. Montessori taught and lectured in many countries and her schools sprang up throughout the world. A visit to the United States in 1914 led to the formation of the American Montessori Society, with Alexander Graham Bell as president.

REFERENCES

Goodman, L. (1974). Montessori education for the handicapped: The methods—the research. In L. Mann & D. A. Sabatino (Eds.), *The second review of special education* (pp. 153–191). Philadelphia: JSE.

Montessori, M. (1964). *The Montessori method.* New York: Schocken.

Orem, R. C. (Ed.). (1970). *Montessori and the special child.* New York: Capricorn.

Standing, E. M. (1962). *Maria Montessori: Her life and work.* New York: New American Library.

PAUL IRVINE
Katonah, New York

MONTESSORI METHOD

MONTESSORI METHOD

Maria Montessori was born in Chiavalle, Italy, in 1870; after receiving her doctorate she visited asylums, which spurred her interest in retarded children. Using some of the work of Itard and Seguin, she designed materials and an instructional method that was so successful that after one year of instruction, the retarded children had learned enough to pass the state examination given to normal children after one year of schooling. Montessori felt that if a retarded child could accomplish so much through her methods, a normal child should be able to accomplish even more. Gradually she devised materials and equipment to realize her goals and formulated an underlying philosophy based on the dignity and spiritual worth of the child. Between 1912 and 1917 she put her ideas into five key books: *The Montessori Method, Pedagogy and Anthropology, Dr. Montessori's Own Handbook,* and *The Advanced Montessori Method, Volumes I and II* (Gitter, 1970).

Montessori's method has many aspects of relevance to special educators. Because of her background as a physician, Montessori was concerned with the whole child's total development and physical well-being. She believed that children are possessed of an instinctive motivation and potential for psychological development, and that children's natural striving toward intellectual fulfillment is so great that, given the opportunity, they will willingly work toward development of the mind and body (Goodman, 1974).

If the child's role changes in the classroom, the teacher's role also changes. The teacher, or directress, the term Montessori preferred, became a guiding and supporting person in Montessori's classroom. Responsibilities included preparation of the environment, the introduction and demonstration of new materials, the maintenance of order, and the keeping of developmental and anecdotal records on each child (Goodman, 1974). Observation is fundamental to the method; the teacher is trained to observe carefully, so that the classroom becomes a diagnostic environment. The teacher checks the child's physical, perceptual-motor, and speech development, and takes appropriate action when a problem is noted.

The Montessori classroom provides a prepared environment, organized by ground rules, in which the child is able to move and work constructively in relative freedom, without disruption from other children. The engineered classroom resembles this prepared environment, which is organized around activity centers designed to produce order. The centers include the mastery center, where academic tasks are offered; the exploratory center, which contains an array of manipulative materials for the pursuit of scientific exploration; and the order center, which is reserved for specialized supportive one-to-one instruction (Kottler, 1977). The child can work directly with the didactic material he or she has chosen, for as long as desired, creating an individual curriculum paced at an individual rate. This makes it more likely that the child will experience a pattern of success, rather than failure (Orem, 1969).

Montessori believed that the areas in which the child needs assistance are motor function, where balance is secured, walking is learned, and movements are coordinated; and sensory function, from the environment, where the foundations of intelligence are laid for the continued exercise of observation, comparison, and judgment (Livingston-Dunn, 1982). Her curriculum emphasized sensory education, motor education, and language training. The program was, by design, preacademic, and early academic work was included for children only after the more basic skills, gross and fine-motor coordination, and perceptual abilities had been fully developed (Goodman, 1974).

Many educators have turned toward Montessori as a possible solution to the educational problems of handicapped children. Individuation is central to special education and is attainable using the Montessori system. The nondemanding atmosphere is appropriate for children who cannot deal with pressure, and many children with sensory and perceptual deficits can benefit from the Montessori materials and methods. By applying several senses to a learning task, one sense can substitute for deficits in another sensory channel.

The early entrance age, as young as 3 years, is important in early intervention programs for children who need a head start. However the program's merits are not corroborated by results of objective evaluation, which offer little evidence to support the educational value of the Montessori method (Goodman, 1974). It is indicated that the Montessori environment may help handicapped children by its nongroup structure to feel more accepted by peers, a prime factor in the development of self-image (Krogh, 1982). However, Montessori does not emphasize transformational thinking, or acknowledge the importance of broad experiences. She does not make use of the unplanned as well as the planned environment and events. She does not place a high value on the early development of symbolic behavior, including language. These are important aspects in childhood development and present serious criticisms of Montessori's method (Bruce, 1984).

REFERENCES

Bruce, T. (1984). A Froebelian looks at Montessori's work. *Early Child Development and Care, 14*(1–2), 75–83.

Gitter, L. L. (1970). *The Montessori way.* Seattle, WA: Special Child.

Goodman, L. (1974). Montessori education for the handicapped: the methods—The research. In L. Mann & D. A. Sabitino (Eds.), *The second review of special education.* Philadelphia: O.S.E. Press.

Kottler, S. B. (1977, April). *The Montessori approach to the education of the exceptional child—Early childhood through high school.* Paper presented at the Annual International Convention, The Council for Exceptional Children, Atlanta, GA.

Krogh, S. L. (1982, April). Affective and social development: Some ideas from Montessori's prepared environment. *Topics in Early Childhood Special Education. 2*(1), 55–62.

Livingston-Dunn, C. (1982, Dec.). *Functional art therapy for the severely handicapped.* Master's thesis ED229947. Northern Illinois University.

Montessori, M. (1964). *The Montessori method.* New York: Schocken.

Orem, R. C. (1969). *Montessori and the special child.* New York: Putman.

Taylor-Hershel, D., and Webster, R. (1983, Jan./Feb.). Mainstreaming: A case in point. *Childhood Education, 59* 175–179.

CATHERINE O. BRUCE
Hunter College, City University of New York

ECOLOGICAL EDUCATION FOR THE HANDICAPPED
HUMANISTIC SPECIAL EDUCATION
MONTESSORI, MARIA

MOORES, DONALD F. (1935–   )

Donald F. Moores received his BA (1958) in psychology from Amherst College, his MS (1959) in deaf education from Gallaudet College, his MA (1963) in school administration from California State University, Northridge, and his PhD (1967) in educational psychology and psycholinguistics from the University of Illinois. Currently, he is director of the Center for Studies in Education and Human Development, Gallaudet Research Institute, and a professor of education and research at Gallaudet College.

Since his early experiences as a teacher of the deaf, Moores' professional life has been spent trying to improve educational services to the deaf. Moores (1976) found that a child's deafness limits his or her capabilities to manipulate and react to the environment. If nothing is done to help compensate for these difficulties, the child's communication skills deteriorate, and the child's overall development is delayed or impoverished.

Similarly, he has found that deafness has little direct effect on intellectual and motor development, at least through age eight (Moores, Weiss, & Goodwin, 1978). What is harmful is the delay of either cognitive-academic training or the use of manual communication. Those children who do not receive such training early in life do not catch up with their peers, at least by age 8. The least beneficial method of instruction is the aural-only method within the traditional nursery school framework.

REFERENCES

Moores, D. (1976). Early childhood special education for the hearing handicapped. In H. Spicker, R. Hodges, & N. Anastasiow (Eds.), *Early education for the handicapped.* Minneapolis: University of Minnesota Press.

Moores, D. F., Weiss, K. L., & Goodwin, M. W. (1978). Early education programs for hearing-impaired children: Major findings. *American Annals of the Deaf, 123*(8), 925–936.

E. VALERIE HEWITT
Texas A&M University

MORAL REASONING

Moral reasoning refers to the manner in which a person cognitively processes information to arrive at a judgment as to whether an act is right or wrong. The research emphasis in this area is not on the factors that influence moral behavior, but rather how increasingly complex levels of moral reasoning evolve within the context of cognitive development. The prevailing theory of moral judgment is Kohlberg's (1969); it has as its underpinnings the work of Jean Piaget (Piaget & Inhelder, 1968).

Piaget and Kohlberg hold that the development of moral reasoning rests on the elaboration of general cognitive development, including, for instance, decreasing egocentrism and the use of concrete and formal operations. It is believed that a child is incapable of reasoning through a moral dilemma at a level more advanced than the overall level of cognitive development at which he or she is functioning.

Kohlberg (1976) proposes three levels of moral reasoning, each with two stages. At the preconventional stage, the child cannot help but solve ethical dilemmas from an egocentric perspective. Thus what is wrong is anything that leads to punishment; the effects of one's actions on others is unappreciated. As egocentrism declines, the child is able to assume the viewpoint of another person, albeit in a concrete, individualistic way. Now an act may be considered right if it is based on an agreement, a deal, or some kind of fair exchange. During the conventional stage, the child begins to consider the perspective of society, yet still within a rather concrete framework. Moral reasoning has an authoritarian flavor in that the child is heavily influenced by adherence to interpersonal expectations and social standards. Notions of "good girl–nice boy" and "law and order" operate as justifications for the resolutions of moral dilemmas. At the postconventional or principled level, the individual is able to engage in more abstract thinking about ethical matters, evidencing the emergence of formal operational thinking. A moral perspective is able to develop that recognizes universal ethical principles that are self-chosen. Laws or social agreements are usually viewed as valid because they are derived from universal principles. If a law is at variance with a principle, behavior should follow the principle. It must be emphasized that the level of moral reasoning displayed is not based on the final answer as to how one should behave or, for that matter, actual conduct. Rather, it is based on the rationale used to justify an action.

Kohlberg has been criticized on a number of accounts. His belief that his system represents a hierarchy of moral reasoning and is constant across cultures is seen by some as ethnocentric (Baumrind, 1978). Other investigators believe he underestimates the moral knowledge of young children because of their rudimentary use of language (Schweder, Turiel, & Much, 1981). Recent findings have shown that many people operate at the preconventional level well into adolescence and most adults score at the conventional level (Rest, 1983). More research is needed to provide information about the relationships among cognitive development and level of moral reasoning, the universality of moral principles, the value of higher stages (postconventional), and how they all relate to moral behavior.

The research on moral reasoning and mental retardation has emerged only within the last 10 years: only a handful of studies exist. They represent a convergence of Kohlberg's theory on moral reasoning with differing perspectives on the cognitive development of socioculturally retarded individuals (Zigler, 1969). According to Weisz and Zigler (1979), retarded persons represent the low end of the normal distribution of intelligence but they "traverse the same stages of development in the same order" (p. 846). Further, a nonretarded and retarded child with similar mental ages (MA) should exhibit the same levels of moral reasoning. Research seems to support this position. In studies by Taylor and Achenbach (1975) and Kahn (1976), nonretarded children compared with older retarded children with the same average MAs evidenced no difference in their levels of moral reasoning. However, a recent study by Kahn (1985) suggests that the etiology of the retardation may affect the level of moral reasoning. Four groups of subjects were matched on MA: nonretarded, socioculturally mildly retarded, organically impaired mildly retarded, and organically impaired moderately retarded. Moral reasoning scores were similar between the nonretarded and socioculturally mildly retarded subjects and between the organically based groups. However, the organically impaired groups both scored lower than the nonretarded and socioculturally retarded groups. Moreover, the basis for the organic impairment seemed to be inconsequential with respect to moral reasoning. In summary, it appears that nonretarded and retarded individuals, equated for MA, show the same levels of moral reasoning. When the etiology of the retardation is known to be organic, then moral reasoning appears to fall below what would be expected given the level of MA. The reasons for this are unclear and await further research.

REFERENCES

Baumrind, D. A. (1978). A dialectical materialist's perspective on knowing social reality. In W. Damon (Ed.), *New directions in child development: Moral development.* San Francisco: Jossey-Bass.

Kahn, J. V. (1976). Moral and cognitive development of moderately retarded, mildly retarded, and nonretarded individuals. *American Journal of Mental Deficiency, 81*, 209–214.

Kahn, J. V. (1985). Evidence of the similar-structure hypothesis controlling for organicity. *American Journal of Mental Deficiency, 89*, 372–378.

Kohlberg, L. (1976). Moral stages and moralization: The cognitive-developmental approach. In T. Lickona (Ed.), *Moral development and behavior.* New York: Holt, Rinehart, & Winston.

Piaget, J., & Inhelder, B. (1968). *The psychology of the child.* New York: Basic Books.

Rest, J. R. (1983). Morality. In P. Mussen, J. Flavell, & E. Markman (Eds.), *Handbook of child psychology. Vol. 3: Cognitive development* (4th ed.). New York: Wiley.

Schweder, R., Turiel, E., & Much, N. (1981). The moral intuitions of the child. In J. H. Flavell & L. Ross (Eds.), Social cognitive development: Frontiers and possible futures. New York: Cambridge University Press.

Taylor, J. J., & Achenbach, T. M. (1975). Moral and cognitive development in retarded and nonretarded children. *American Journal of Mental Deficiency, 80*, 43–50.

Weisz, J. R., & Zigler, E. (1979). Cognitive development in retarded and nonretarded persons: Piagetian tests of the similar-sequence hypotheses. *Psychological Bulletin, 86*, 831–851.

Zigler, E. (1969). Developmental versus difference theories of mental retardation and the problem of motivation. *American Journal of Mental Deficiency, 73*, 536–556.

Laurence C. Grimm
University of Illinois, Chicago

CONSCIENCE, LACK OF
PIAGET, JEAN
SOCIAL SKILLS TRAINING

MORSE, WILLIAM C. (1915–   )

William Morse received his MA in 1939 and his PhD in 1947 in educational psychology from the University of Michigan. From 1945 to 1961, he was the director of the University of Michigan Fresh Air Camp, a group therapy program for disturbed boys and graduate training program for university students. It was here that Morse became an advocate of qualitative and participant-observation methods of research. In addition, with the leadership of Fritz Redl, he worked out a philosophy of residential treatment emphasizing life space interviewing and group dynamics. He has a sustained interest in the training of teachers of the emotionally disturbed.

In 1965 Morse became chairman of the Combined Program in Education and Psychology of the University of Michigan. He is currently professor emeritus of educational psychology and psychology. His principal publications include *Conflict in the Classroom: The Education of*

Emotionally Disturbed Children, The Education and Treatment of Socio-Emotionally Disturbed Children and Youth, Affective Education for Special Children and Youth, and Humanistic Teaching for Exceptional Children.

REFERENCES

Morse, W. C. (Ed.). (1979). *Humanistic teaching for exceptional children: An introduction to special education.* Syracuse, NY: Syracuse University Press.

Morse, W. C. (1985). *The education and treatment of socio-emotionally disturbed children and youth.* Syracuse, NY: Syracuse University Press.

Morse, W. C., Avdizzone, J., Macdonald, C., & Pasick, P. (1980). *Affective education for special children and youth: What research and experience say to the teacher of exceptional children.* Reston, VA: Council for Exceptional Children.

Morse, W. C., Long, N., & Newmar, R. (1980). *Conflict in the classroom: The education of emotionally disturbed children.* Belmont, CA: Wadsworth.

ELAINE FLETCHER-JANZEN
Texas A&M University

MORSINK, CATHERINE V. (1937–   )

Catherine V. Morsink began her education career in 1959 when she received her BA in elementary education from Western Michigan University. For the next 10 years, she held a variety of teaching positions, in classes for the gifted, remedial reading programs, and the regular classroom. During this period, she also attended Rockford College (Illinois), where she was awarded the MAT in the teaching of reading in 1968. Morsink then went to the University of Kentucky where, while working as a materials specialist and later as training director at the University of Kentucky Regional Special Education Instructional Materials Center, she earned the EdD in special education in 1974.

Catherine V. Morsink

Morsink began her career with an interest in direct service delivery to children. During her various teaching stints, she developed a variety of ideas and materials for working with exceptional children in the context of the regular classroom, long before mainstreaming became popular. Her interests gradually shifted throughout the course of her graduate education, moving toward interests in special education personnel preparation and the evaluation of the various materials and methods she had developed over the years.

Morsink's best known and perhaps most influential work, *Teaching Special Needs Students in Regular Classrooms* (Morsink, 1984a), was an outgrowth of her shifting emphasis. This work reflects Morsink's academic preparation as well as her many years of experience as a front line special education teacher; it came on the heels of a return to the classroom as a grade 3 teacher during a sabbatical leave in 1980.

Since earling her PhD in 1974, Morsink's academic ascension has been swift. In 1974 she became an assistant professor of special education at the University of Kentucky. She was promoted to associate rank in 1977, and quickly became chair of the department of special education in 1978. In 1980 Morsink moved to the University of Florida, where she became professor and chair of the department of special education, a position she still holds.

Morsink is the author of the DELTA system for teaching decoding skills in reading (Morsink, 1984b). She serves on the editorial board of the *Journal of Teacher Education*, and is currently completing a volume on the effectiveness of women in educational administration.

REFERENCES

Morsink, C. V. (1984a). *Teaching special needs students in regular classrooms.* Boston: Little, Brown.

Morsink, C. V. (1984b). *DELTA: A design for word attack* (2nd ed.). Madison, WI: Learning Multi-Systems.

CECIL R. REYNOLDS
Texas A&M University

MOSAICISM

Mosaicism is a rare type of Down's syndrome in which an error in cell division occurs at an early stage of mitosis (cell division). It is the coexistence of cells with different chromosomal counts in one individual. This chromosomal anomaly is not present at conception (Robinson & Robinson, 1965). Individuals who exhibit mosaicism appear to have less pronounced physical features of Down's syndrome and their intellectual performance generally is not as impaired. Pueschel (1982) details the three major types of Down's syndrome. In all cases of Down's syndrome, there is the presence of additional genetic material in the cell. Instead of the usual 46 chromosomes in each cell, an individual with Down's syndrome has 47. The extra chromsome may derive from either the egg or the sperm. Nondisjunction, found in 95% of individuals with Down's syndrome, is rarely familial. In this type of Down's syndrome, the two number 21 chromosomes (of the sperm or the egg) do not separate properly during cell division. Thus one cell will have an extra 21 chromosome. When united with a normal cell, trisomy 21 will result. The very first cell at conception will have 47 chromosomes. Translocation, a much less common type of Down's syndrome, is inherited. It occurs in only 3 to 4% of all Down's syndrome cases. It occurs when the additional number 21 chromosome material becomes attached or translocated to another chromosome.

Mosaicism, the least common form of Down's syndrome, is found in about 1% of all cases. Mosaicism is not familial. Rather, it is thought to be due to an error in early cell division following conception. The first cell resulting from fertilization has the normal number of chromosomes. At some point after the egg is fertilized, the extra chromosome appears. At birth the child has some cells with 46 chromosomes and others with 47, thereby creating a mosaiclike pattern. Cells with 45 or fewer chromosomes usually do not survive.

The extra chromosome 21 is always associated with mental retardation and specific physical characteristics. Gibson and Frank (1961) list the most common features: large fissured tongue; short stubby hands; epicanthal fold at inner corner of the eye; single transverse crease across palm; inward curving little finger; flattened nose; fused ear lobules; cleft between big and second toe; small, flattened skull; short fifth finger; smooth simple outer earlobe; congenital heart problems; and a little finger with one lateral crease rather than two. All traits may not occur in any one individual with Down's syndrome. Mosaics may exhibit few if any visible signs. They may have normal intelligence (Koch & Koch, 1974). The number of symptoms present is thought to be dependent on the age of the embryo when the error of cell division occurs. The earlier the division, the more severe the effect.

The reasons that chromosomes do not divide properly are not clearly understood (Smith & Wilson, 1973). Suspect are radiation and X-ray exposure; viral infections; misuse of drugs; or problems of hormone or immunological balance. Mosaics can transmit Down's syndrome to the next generation. Some may not know they are mosaics until they produce a child with mosaicism or until cytogenetics reveals their condition. Amniocentesis can be performed during the first 12 to 16 weeks of pregnancy to determine if such chromosomal abnormalities exist (Dorfman, 1972).

REFERENCES

Dorfman, A. (Ed.). (1972). *Antenatal diagnosis*. Chicago: University of Chicago Press.

Gibson, D., & Frank, H. F. (1961). Dimensions of mongolism: I. Age limits for cardinal mongol stigmata. *American Journal of Mental Deficiency, 66,* 30–34.

Koch, R., & Koch, K. (1974). *Understanding the mentally retarded child: A new approach.* New York: Random House.

Pueschel, S. M. (1982). *A study of the young child with Down syndrome.* New York: Human Science.

Robinson, H. B., & Robinson, N. M. (1965). *The mentally retarded child: A psychological approach.* New York: McGraw-Hill.

Smith, W. D., & Wilson, A. A. (1973). *The child with Down's syndrome: Causes, characteristics and acceptance.* Philadelphia: Saunders.

SALLY E. PISARCHICK
*Cuyahoga Special Education
Service Center, Maple
Heights, Ohio*

CHROMOSOMAL ANOMALIES
CONGENITAL DISORDERS
DOWN'S SYNDROME
HEREDITY
MINOR PHYSICAL ANOMALIES

MOSS, JAMES W. (1926–   )

Born in Wilmar, California, James W. Moss received his BA (1952) in psychology, with a minor in sociology, and his MA (1953) in psychology at San Jose State College. He received his PhD (1958) with a major in clinical psychology and a minor in special education from George Peabody College. He is currently the director of the Employment Training Program and Research Associate, College of Education, Child Development and Mental Retardation Center, University of Washington.

Moss has invested most of his career in research relating to improving education for exceptional children. He does not believe that children should be given a diagnostic label unless that label applies exactly. Otherwise, he finds that labels are more harmful than helpful to children (Moss, 1973). Most of his published works have involved training and education programs for the mentally retarded (Moss, 1974; Moss & Chalfant, 1965; Tisdall & Moss, 1962).

Moss has been listed in *Who's Who in the South and Southwest, Who's Who in the West,* and *American Men and Women of Science.* He has been a National Institute of Mental Health fellow. During 1985–1986, he was the associate commissioner of the Office of Developmental Programs, Rehabilitation Services Administration, Office of Special Education and Rehabilitation Services, U.S. Department of Education.

REFERENCES

Moss, J. W. (1973). Disabled or disadvantaged: What's the difference? *Journal of Special Education, 7*(4).

Moss, J. W. (1974). Trends and issues in special education. In N. G. Harding (Ed.), *Behavior of exceptional children: An introduction to special education*. Columbus, OH: Merrill.

Moss, J. W., & Chalfant, J. (1965, November). Research and demonstration programs for handicapped children and youth. *Exceptional Children*.

Tisdall, W., & Moss, J. W. (1962, September). A total program for the severely mentally retarded. *Exceptional Children*.

E. VALERIE HEWITT
Texas A&M University

MOTIVATION

Motivation is generally believed to consist of two components, drive and incentive. Drive is something that invigorates activity without necessarily determining the type of activity. For example, a splinter in a finger may lead to a variety of energetic behaviors until the splinter is removed, even though it does not mandate any one specific behavior. Incentive is a stimulus that evokes approach or avoidance behaviors. For example, the availability of a tasty dessert may arouse approach behaviors even by people who are not hungry.

Many biologically determined motivations are described as homeostatic processes. A homeostatic process is one that tends to maintain constancy of some variable. For example, we use both physiological and behavioral means to maintain a nearly constant body temperature. Drinking enables us to maintain a nearly constant concentration of solutes in the cells and a nearly constant volume of blood. Eating enables us to maintain a steady supply of nutrients to the cells and a fairly steady body weight.

Many social motivations, however, are not homeostatic. Humans experience a need for affiliation and a need for achievement. Such motivations may remain at a high level over long periods of time. Fulfilling our affiliation or achievement needs does not weaken the motivation for further affiliation or achievement, however. In that way, such activities differ from drinking and eating.

A child's need for achievement is related in large part to the behavior of his or her parents. The parents of children with a strong need for achievement are highly sensitive to both the capacities and the limitations of their children. They tend to set stricter rules than most parents when their children are young and more lenient rules when their children are older. They set high but realistic expectations for their children and reward them strongly for each achievement (Winterbottom, 1958).

It is well known that Sigmund Freud emphasized the importance of the sexual motivation in human behavior. Adler (1927, 1964) proposed that the most central human motive is the striving for a feeling of superiority. Different people may seek such a feeling in different ways. Some do so simply by seeking excellence on the job or at home or in their volunteer work. Others may attempt to excel in their self-discipline and in their ability to deprive themselves of pleasure. For example, anorexia nervosa may be described in such terms. Still other people obtain public attention and some feeling of being special through their criminal activities, a luxurious lifestyle, public drunkenness, or other unproductive behavior. To understand someone's behavior, it is often helpful to analyze the ways in which the person may be trying to achieve a sense of superiority. For example, a disruptive child may simply be seeking attention.

Goals that people set for themselves can become highly effective motivations (Locke, Shaw, Saari, & Latham, 1981). Clear and specific goals lead to enhanced performance in many settings; vague goals such as "do your best" are ineffective. Generally, very high goals lead to the best performance, so long as the goals remain realistic. For a goal to influence behavior, the individual must make a commitment, preferably in public, to achieving the goal and must receive periodic feedback on progress toward the goal. It is also important to receive a reward for reaching the goal; otherwise, people become indifferent toward further goals.

Goals lead to enhanced performance in several ways. They focus attention and thereby reduce distraction. They increase persistence. They also motivate people to develop new strategies to achieve the goal, even at the expense of other worthwhile ends. For example, someone who sets a goal of increased quantity of output may decrease quality.

REFERENCES

Adler, A. (1927). *Understanding human nature*. New York: Greenberg.

Adler, A. (1964). *Superiority and social interest*. Evanston, IL: Northwestern University Press.

Locke, E. A., Shaw, K. N., Saari, L. M., & Latham, G. P. (1981). Goal setting and task performance: 1969–1980. *Psychological Bulletin, 90,* 125–152.

Winterbottom, M. R. (1958). The relation of need for achievement to learning experiences in independence and mastery. In J. W. Atkinson (Ed.), *Motives in fantasy, action and society* (pp. 453–478). New York: Van Nostrand.

JAMES W. KALAT
North Carolina State University

ACHIEVEMENT NEED
APPLIED BEHAVIOR ANALYSIS
POSITIVE REINFORCEMENT

MOTOR-FREE VISUAL PERCEPTION TEST (MVPT)

The Motor-Free Visual Perception Test (MVPT; Colarusso & Hammill, 1972 is a test of visual perception that avoids

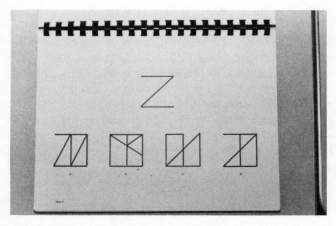

An example of an item from the motor-free Visual Perception Test; can you find the hidden Z?

REFERENCE

Colarusso, R. P., & Hammill, D. P. (1972). *Motor-free visual perception test.* Novato, CA: Academic Therapy.

CECIL R. REYNOLDS
Texas A&M University

BENDER-GESTALT TEST
DEVELOPMENTAL TEST OF VISUAL-MOTOR
    INTEGRATION
VISUAL-MOTOR AND VISUAL PERCEPTION PROBLEMS

motor involvement. It is designed for use by psychologists, educational diagnosticians, and others trained in individual assessment. The MVPT is easily administered in 15 to 20 minutes to children ages 4 through 8 years. It is divided into five item types intended to measure the following components of visual perception: spatial relationships, visual discrimination, figure-ground, visual closure, and visual memory. The Figure illustrates an item from the figure-ground grouping.

As the authors (Colarusso & Hammill, 1972) note, most of the tests used to assess visual perception (e.g., Bender Gestalt Test, Developmental Test of Visual-Motor Integration, and the drawing subtests of the McCarthy Scales of Children's Abilities) are actually measures of visual-motor integration skills, which require visual perceptual ability but make major demands on the child's fine motor skills. Children are frequently misdiagnosed as having visual-perceptual disorders on the basis of poor performance on tests requiring extensive motor performance. The MVPT avoids the confounding of visual perception with motor skills in its assessment.

A good, solid assessment of visual perception independent of motor ability is a useful tool to those who must evaluate handicapped children. However, the MVPT is one of few such scales available and the manual lacks the necessary information for a proper evaluation of the quality of the scale. The description of the standardization sample is severely limited, giving little more than the sample size (which at 881 is credibly large). Much of the psychometric data on the MVPT as reported in the manual are incomplete and reflect naivete regarding principles of test construction. Reliability of the scale is moderate (high .70s and low .80s for internal consistency estimates). The MVPT is useful principally because of the lack of other instruments from which to choose; however, it is easy to administer and score and has considerable intuitive appeal.

MOTOR LEARNING

Motor learning is necessary to acquire the skills required for effective movement of the body. Although some authors have distinguished between motor and movement activities, the terms are often interchangeable (Harrow, 1972). Oxendine (1984) has noted three types of motor (or perceptual motor) learning. First is the maturationally related behavior that typically is developed early in life. Walking, speaking, and general body coordination are in this category. The second group of skills is high in perceptual components and includes communicative behaviors such as handwriting. These activities are necessary for continued educational progress. A final set of motor behaviors is learned because the performance of these activities results in direct benefits to the actor. Much of vocational and recreational accomplishment is built on motor learning.

The motor learning process involves progress from a cognitive phase, where the learner tries to understand the process involved, to an associative or practice phase, where the learner perfects the skill. Finally, the learner enters an autonomous phase, where the activity becomes habitual (Oxendine, 1984). Once the activity is habitual, it does not require conscious control and may operate under a different memory system from that used for other activities (Tulving, 1985). It is difficult for individuals for whom many motor tasks are routine to separate and verbally label the components of these activities. An individual who has reached the autonomous phase may thus find it difficult to communicate with someone in the cognitive phase of motor learning. Many special education students may be in the cognitive phase on tasks that most people have mastered and take as a matter of course.

The sensorimotor deficits faced by many special education students make the issue of motor performance objectives particularly central in the design of education for those students. Motor learning is not only important for its own sake, but as a component of cognitive and affective development. Activities learned in physical-education programs for the handicapped increase self-esteem and allow for social interaction in games (Moon & Renzaglia, 1982). Basic motor skills are necessary for the activities of daily living. Learning the motor behaviors required for communication is crucial for cognitive development.

Harrow (1972) has developed a taxonomy of tasks in the psychomotor domain. As with classification systems in the cognitive and affective domains, this taxonomy is designed to allow the teacher to specify educational objectives. Often the special education teacher must produce objectives aimed at needs of a given disability group. Motor learning behavioral objectives typically include motor skills of daily living and fine and gross motor performance (Fredericks et al., 1976; Hawkins et al., 1983).

Motor learning objectives for moderately and severely disabled students may involve behaviors that can be taught to most nondisabled individuals without any carefully constructed plan or method. The Hawkins et al. (1983) project is an example of the use of motor performance objectives to produce detailed activity programs for an enriched home and school environment. Such planning may be necessary to produce desired levels of simple motor learning.

REFERENCES

Fredericks, H. D., Riggs, C., Furey, J., Grove, D., Moore, W., McDonnell, J., Jordan, E., Hanson, W., Baldwin, V., & Wadlow, M. (1976). *The teaching research curriculum for moderately and severely handicapped.* Springfield, IL: Thomas.

Harrow, A. J. (1972). *Taxonomy of the psychomotor domain.* New York: McKay.

Hawkins, R. P., McGinnis, L. D., Bieniek, B. J., Timmons, D. M., Eddy, D. B., & Cone, J. D. (1983). *The school and home enrichment program for severely handicapped children.* Champaign, IL: Research.

Moon, M. S., & Renzaglia, A. (1982). Physical fitness and the mentally retarded: A critical review of the literature. *Journal of Special Education, 16,* 269–287.

Oxendine, J. B. (1984). *Motor learning* (2nd ed.). Englewood Cliffs, NJ: Prentice-Hall.

Tulving, E. (1985). How many memory systems are there? *American Psychologist, 40,* 385–398.

LEE ANDERSON JACKSON, JR.
University of North Carolina,
Wilmington

MOVEMENT DISORDERS
MOVEMENT THERAPY
PERCEPTUAL TRAINING
VISUAL MOTOR PROBLEMS

MOVEMENT THERAPY

Movement therapy, creative movement therapy, body movement therapy, and dance therapy are all terms used interchangeably in the literature to describe a psychoanalytic, therapeutic approach that assists the disabled individual in the expression of his or her feelings and emotions in an acceptable manner through movement. Body movement therapy was described by Weisbrod (1972) as "the planned use of any aspect of dance, movement, and sensory experience to further the physical and psychic integration of the individual" (p. 66). It has been used successfully with the learning disabled, emotionally disturbed (e.g., schizophrenics and inhibited neurotics), deaf or hearing impaired, blind, aphasic, and retarded, as well as normal children and adults, to assist in language development and/or nonverbal communication skills (Chace, 1971; Weisbrod, 1972; Zumberg & Zumberg, 1979).

Movement therapy was greatly influenced by the psychoanalytic theories of Reich (1942), Jung (Hochheimer, 1969), and Sullivan (1953). Their contributions related to the expressiveness of body language, the therapeutic value of artistic experiences, and the interactive nature of personality. Influence was also exhibited by Laban's (1950) analysis of movement behaviors, Burton's (1974) improvision techniques, and Jacobson's (1958) and Schultz and Luthe's (1959) relaxation techniques.

The goal of movement therapy for childhood schizophrenics, who may be nonverbal or confused verbally, is to assist them to communicate and relate through movement. The goal for inhibited neurotics, who may be verbal but unable to express clearly certain ideas, notions, or convictions about themselves, the world, or others, is to confront blocked areas through the use of the body (Long, Morse, & Newman, 1971). The goal for all individuals is to present experiences that have underlying value to assist them in confronting their emotions (Weisbrod, 1972). This can be accomplished through activities that include imitation of nature or animals, expression of past, present, or future feelings of self or others, and use of music, voice, hand clapping, feet stamping, or environmental sounds in rhythm instruments (Shea, 1978). For example, having the child demonstrate the movement related to the loss of a toy, may help him or her to express sadness or pain. Emotions such as anger, joy, and depression may be expressed by having the child perform the rhythm attached to rhythmic bases.

Chace (1971) described differences between goals for normal children and disturbed individuals. For normal children, who are constantly, conscientiously, reaching out for knowledge, and using movement to explore the world, movement goals are established that allow them to develop a heightened awareness of body coordination, a sensitivity to musical tones and rhythms, and an alertness to new ways of using the body in dance patterns. For disturbed adults, on the other hand, the goals must be to reeducate them to use their bodies for more than expressing immediate emotions. They must learn to reach out to the world around them. "With both children and mental patients, it is important to remember that dance (movement) sessions . . . are for the purpose of building sufficient awareness of self through expressive movement" (Chace, 1971, p. 218). The final goal of all movement therapy is the development of more confidence in functioning in the world of reality.

Although movement therapeutic techniques must have defined limits of expected behavior and organized instruction in the use of the body, they must also be structured to allow for experimentation and the development of self-confidence. Chace (1971) stated that with children, this is accomplished by holding firm limits while allowing the child to widen them as he or she develops naturally, but with mental patients, the limits must not only be clearly defined, but often help must be given to the patient to expand and push outward from the limits into the real world. "Demonstration followed by guided exploration facilitates the development of creative movement" (Weisbrod, 1972, p. 68).

REFERENCES

Burton, C. (1974). Movement as group therapy in the psychiatric hospital. In *Dance therapy—Focus on dance*. Washington, DC: American Association for Health, Physical Education and Recreation.

Chace, M. (1971). Dance in growth or treatment settings. In N. J. Long, W. C. Morse, & R. G. Newman (Eds.), *Conflict in the classroom: The education of children with problems* (2nd ed.). Belmont, CA: Wadsworth.

Hochheimer, W. (1969). *The psychotherapy of C. G. Jung*. New York: Putnam.

Jacobson, E. (1958). *Progressive relaxation*. Chicago, IL: University of Chicago Press.

Laban, R. (1950). *The mastery of movement*. London: MacDonald & Evans.

Long, N. J., Morse, W. C., & Newman, R. G. (Eds.). (1971). *Conflict in the classroom: The education of children with problems* (2nd ed.). Belmont, CA: Wadsworth.

Reich, W. (1942). *Character analysis*. New York: Farrar, Straus & Giroux.

Schultz, J. H., & Luthe, W. (1959). *Autogenic training: A psychophysiological approach in psychotherapy*. New York: Grune & Stratton.

Shea, T. M. (1978). *Teaching children and youth with behavior disorders*. St. Louis: Mosby.

Siegel, E. V. (1984). *Dance-movement therapy: The mirror of ourselves: A psychoanalytic approach*. New York: Human Services.

Sullivan, H. S. (1953). *The interpersonal theory of psychiatry*. New York: Norton.

Weisbrod, J. A. (1972). Shaping a body image through movement therapy. *Musical Education Journal, 58*(8), 66–69.

Zumberg, C., & Zumberg, M. (1979). Movement: A therapeutic technique for use with the learning disabled. *Academic Therapy, 14*(3), 347–352.

SUSANNE BLOUGH ABBOTT
*Bedford Central School District,
Mt. Kisco, New York*

DANCE THERAPY

MOVIGENICS

Movigenics is a theory of learning disabilities developed by Raymond H. Barsch (1965, 1967), in which he postulated that learning difficulties are related to an individual's inability to interact effectively with space. The word movigenics was derived from two Latin words, *movere*, meaning to move, and *genesis*, meaning origin and development. "It is, therefore, the study of the origin and development of patterns of movement in man and the relationship of these movements to his learning efficiency" (Barsch, 1967, p. 33). The theory is based on Barsch's premise that human learning is related to movement efficiency. As a child adapts to his or her environment and learns to move effectively through it, he or she also develops language as a means of defining experience in connection with space (Lerner, 1971). Movigenics is based on 10 constructs of human behavior (Barsch, 1967, pp. 35–64):

1. The fundamental principle underlying the design of the human organism is movement efficiency.
2. The primary objective of movement efficiency is to economically promote the survival of the organism.
3. Movement efficiency is derived from the information the organism is able to process from an energy surround.
4. The human mechanism for transducing energy forms into information is the percepto-cognitive system.
5. The terrain of movement is space.
6. Developmental momentum provides a constant forward thrust toward maturity and demands an equilibrium to maintain direction.
7. Movement efficiency is developed in a climate of stress.
8. The adequacy of the feedback system is critical in the development of movement efficiency.
9. Development of movement efficiency occurs in segments of sequential expansion.
10. Movement efficiency is symbolically communicated through the visual-spatial phenomenon called language.

These constructs form the theory from which Barsch developed a curriculum that allows a child to explore and experience himself or herself in space. The classroom stimuli is well structured and kept to a minimum; there are no desks or books, lighting is artifically controlled, and a designated space is carpeted for crawling. Although activities are well planned, they are presented randomly to assist children in becoming less rigid (McCarthy & McCarthy, 1969). Hart and Jones (1968) describe the way in which Barsch's curriculum can be used as a social model for guiding parents in child-rearing practices.

Barsch was highly influenced by Werner, Strauss, and Getman. He is one of the four main perceptual-motor theorists who are well known for their work with learning-disabled children. The other three theorists are Kephart, Getman, and Frostig (Hallahan & Cruickshank, 1973).

REFERENCES

Barsch, R. H. (1965). *A movigenic curriculum.* Madison, WI: Bureau for Handicapped Children.

Barsch, R. H. (1967). *Achieving perceptual-motor efficiency. A space-oriented approach to learning,* (Vol. 1). Seattle, WA: Special Child Publications.

Hallahan, D. P., & Cruickshank, W. M. (1973). *Psycho-educational foundations of learning disabilities.* Englewood Cliffs, NJ: Prentice-Hall.

Hart, J., & Jones, B. (1968). *Where's Hannah? A handbook for parents and teachers of children with learning disorders.* New York: Hart.

Lerner, J. W. (1971). *Children with learning disabilities* (2nd ed.). New York: Houghton Mifflin.

McCarthy, J. J., & McCarthy, J. F. (1969). *Learning disabilities.* Boston, MA: Allyn & Bacon.

SUSANNE BLOUGH ABBOTT
Bedford Central School district,
Mt. Kisco, New York

BARSCH, RAYMOND H.
PERCEPTUAL MOTOR DIFFICULTIES
SENSORY INTEGRATIVE THERAPY

MULTICULTURAL SPECIAL EDUCATION

Poplin and Wright (1983) served as guest editors for a special issue of the *Learning Disability Quarterly* (Volume 6) that focused on cultural pluralism. They indicated that the topic of cultural pluralism was necessary to the special education literature for three reasons: (1) many minority-culture children are placed in special education because of cultural, linguistic, or racial differences; (2) of those minority-culture students who do not have handicaps, some have specific learning disabilities, and (3) special educators are often vanguards of new ideas in the schools. In addition, there appears to exist a continued overrepresentation of minority students in special education programs.

The concept of multicultural special education abounds with controversies, one of which is the issue of overrepresentation of minority children in special education classes. However, there are other issues that demand even greater attention such as linguistic differences versus linguistic difficulties, minority-culture norms versus expected classroom behavior, and biases on assessment procedures as well in instrumentation.

Plata and Santos (1981) state that the purpose of bilingual special education "is to meet the academic, sociocultural, and psychological needs of non-English speaking handicapped pupils who cannot meet performance standards normally expected of a comparable group of English speaking handicapped pupils" (p. 98). Chan and Rueda (1979) refer to a "hidden curriculum" that interferes with learning and social adaptations by many children who come from a culturally deprived environment. Cartwright, Cartwright, and Ward (1984) suggest that educators must address the role of the school in socializing culturally different students in terms of expectation and accommodate greater diversity within the schools.

In addition to the hidden curriculum (Chan & Ruedu, 1979), consideration should be given to the language variables sometimes referred to as a double handicap (Megan, 1982). Many times the language used by minority children is somewhat different; this should not to be perceived as negative but should be appreciated and respected. In fact, most experts suggest that schools should not try to change a child's dialect in the hopes of improving academic skills. Curriculum materials currently available for minority children and youths are either culturally or historically irrelevant according to Rodriguez (1981).

The concept of nondiscriminatory testing is a major concern regarding multicultural special education. Assessment of students referred for special education services, especially the mentally retarded and learning disabled, has been an intensely debated topic; a major issue is the fairness and usefulness of conventional practices (Reschly, 1982). However, this issue is far from simple. As Sattler (1984) points out, there are many different types of biases in assessment. Reschly (1982) indicates that there are many different ways to define the concept of test biases. Compounded by strong emotional feelings and the complexity of the assessment process, Reynolds (1982) suggests that the controversy over nondiscriminatory assessment will probably continue. Test developers, test authors, and test users (teachers, psychologists) must be sensitive to the many differences children from various cultures bring to assessment procedures. These factors, along with a commitment to interpreting test scores cautiously and objectively and in accordance with economic and cultural factors, may enhance efforts to meet the educational needs of multicultural students. Adequate assessment instruments that can fairly assess children of different linguistic or cultural backgrounds have not been developed.

The issues concerning multicultural education have received serious consideration by those in special education because of the overrepresentation of minorities in classes for the mildly handicapped. The major challenge faced by educators is the ability to appreciate and understand the abilities of minority children. Multicultural education and mainstreaming share a common goal: integrating the handicapped and the culturally different student and adult into the mainstream of school and society. We must insist on sound and effective instructional programs that are relevant to the students who come from a different culture.

REFERENCES

Cartwright, G. P., Cartwright, C. A., & Ward, M. E. (1984). *Educating special learners* (2nd ed.). Belmont, CA: Wadsworth.

Chan, K. S., & Rueda, R. (1979). Poverty and children in education: Separate but equal. *Exceptional Children, 45*(6), 422–428.

Megen, E. L. (1982). *Exceptional children in today's schools: An alternative resource book.* Denver: Love.

Plata, M., & Santos, S. L. (1981). Bilingual special education: A challenge for the future. *Teaching Exceptional Children, 14*(3), 97–100.

Poplin, M. S., & Wright, P. W. (1983). The concept of cultural pluralism: Issues in special education. *Learning Disability Quarterly, 6*(4), 267–272.

Reschly, D. J. (1982). Assessing mild mental retardation: The influence of adaptive behavior, sociocultural status, and prospects for nonbiased assessment. In C. R. Reynolds & T. B. Gutkin (Eds.), *The handbook of school psychology.* New York. Wiley.

Reynolds, C. R. (1982). The problem of bias in psychological assessment. C. R. Reynolds & T. B. Gutkin (Eds.), *The handbook of school psychology.* New York: Wiley.

Rodriguez, F. (1981, February.). *Mainstreaming a multicultural concept into special education guidelines for teacher trainers.* Paper presented at the Council for Exceptional Children Conference on the Exceptional Bilingual Child, New Orleans, LA.

Sattler, J. M. (1948). *The assessment of children's intelligence and special abilities* (2nd ed.). Boston: Allyn & Bacon.

HUBERT R. VANCE
University of Maryland, Eastern Shore

CULTURE FAIR TESTS
MAINSTREAMING
NONDISCRIMINATORY ASSESSMENT

MULTIDISCIPLINARY TEAM (MDT)

Multidisciplinary team (MDT) is defined by Golin and Ducanis (1981) as "a functioning unit composed of individuals with varied and specialized training who coordinate their activites to provide services to children" (p. 2). The MDT is often used interchangeably with the term interdisciplinary team. Teamwork in child guidance has been prominent since the early 1900s; it became even more evident in education in the 1950s. The use of the MDT with exceptional children increased because of the whole child concept and because of the legislative mandates passed by various states and then by the federal government. The whole child concept was developed by Whitehouse in 1951, when he described a human being as an "interacting, integrated, whole" (p. 45). Problems of exceptional children are interrelated and cannot be adequately treated in isolation. The various services needed by the exceptional child must be coordinated; therefore, the team approach was developed.

In 1975 PL 94-142, the Education For All Handicapped Children Act, was passed. It required that all handicapped children be provided with an appropriate educational program in the least restrictive environment. The Bureau of Education for the Handicapped Office of Education wrote regulations for PL 94-142 stating that the team includes "at least one teacher or other specialist with knowledge in the area of suspected disability" (Golin & Ducanis, 1981, p. 86). "The child is assessed in all areas related to the suspected disability, including where appropriate, health, vision, hearing, social and emotional status, general intelligence, academic performance, communicative status, and motor abilities" (Golin & Ducanis, 1981, pp. 86–87).

Possible team members include school administrators, school psychologists, special educators, physicians, parents, social workers, teachers, student teachers, diagnosticians, speech therapists, physical therapists, occupational therapists, audiologists, nurse counselors, curriculum specialists, optometrists, and vocational rehabilitation counselors (Jones, 1978). The role of the school psychologist can be augmented or supplemented by a psychiatrist or an ophthalmologist. This will depend on the needs of the student and school experiences with local professionals. The physician, in many instances, will be either the family physician or the student's pediatrician. An occupational therapist can provide insight as to needed therapy concerning fine motor control. The student's regular classroom teacher will probably be the most reliable reference for components of the student's classroom performance beyond that indicated by formal tests.

The MDT is responsible for the individual evaluation and educational planning for public school handicapped children. The team decides if the student is eligible for special services. Through the individual education plan (IEP) conference, a written program is developed for the student. The IEP should include:

Statements of the child's present levels of educational performance

Statements of short-term objectives and long-range goals

Statements of specific services and special education to be provided

Statements indicating beginning dates and duration of service

Statements describing evaluation procedures and time frames to determine whether instructional objectives are being met

The intervention of the MDT must be evaluated periodically so the program can be adjusted if necessary for the child's best interests. The service can be only as good as the composition and functioning of the team.

Communication, both written and oral, is essential for understanding and for progress within the parameters of the IEP. Teams function within and among organizations. For example, members to serve one client might represent a group home, a mental health center, or a vocational school. Roles of team members are usually defined by the professional roles they have in the school system. Diverse knowledge and skills are combined to provide solutions to specific problems. This is the basic reason for involving a MDT. The child is the center, the focus of the team. If the team is sidetracked or weakened by conflicts and misunderstandings, the child will suffer. One of the major problems according to Ysseldyke and Regan (1980) is false identification and subsequent assignment in an alternative educational program outside of the regular classroom. Their recommendation for obviating such a happening is "that no child . . . should be relegated to a given level in the continuum based on his or her performance on norm referenced tests. Rather, service should be provided on the basis of demonstrated and documented intervention effectiveness" (p. 466). Professionals who would follow this advice would probably be more apt to employ the concept of criterion instruction as advocated by Popham and Baker (1970).

The parents are important members of the team, yet many researchers report a breakdown of communication between parents and professionals. Professionals complain that parents are overprotective, interfering, and not understanding. Parents complain that professionals are intimidating and do not allow them to be active in the decision-making process (Golin & Ducanis, 1981). Recently the "hand of the parent" was given a strong vote of support by the U.S. Supreme Court. The decision of School Committee of the Town of Burlington versus Department of Education of Massachusetts (1985) stated that courts may now order schools to reimburse tuition to parents who have made private school placements so as to obtain appropriate instruction for their academically deficient children where the school is unwilling or unable to provide that instruction.

Determining professional structure of the MDT is often easier than determining the best course of study for the handicapped student. The purpose of the MDT is to develop a plan of instructional remediation to obviate a given child's academic deficits, and thereby assist the handicapped learner to succeed in school. Kavale and Forness (1985) states, "The basic nature of LD intervention has proven to be an elusive and vexing problem for the field. The many proposed hypotheses regarding the essence of LD have generally failed to provide a comprehensive and definitive statement regarding its essence" (p. 138).

The MDT is seriously impacted by the individual team member's functional knowledge of current programs and techniques for academic remediation. Many recent studies on reading, e.g., the Report of the Commission on Reading (1984), strongly recommends that teachers of beginning reading and spelling should present well-designed phonics instruction. Yet, in actual practice today, many elementary teachers and reading specialists continue to downplay the importance of didactic phonic remediation. This reference also highlights the responsibilities that the school's teachers and administrators have in assuring their patrons that language literacy for all students is the highest of instructional priorities. Being as literate as possible is critical for the special education student whether he or she is educable mentally retarded (EMR), learning disabled (LD), dyslexic, or emotionally disturbed (ED). The Coalition for Literacy (1984) advocates that educators return to the use of a phonics-based methodology for both developmental and remedial reading and spelling instruction so that productivity and quality of life are improved. The MDTs bear a heavy responsibility to the children they affect.

If MDTs are to serve the purpose for which they are intended, there must be a concerted effort by all members of the MDT to keep communication and participation at the highest possible level.

REFERENCES

Coalition for Literacy. (1984). *Volunteer against illiteracy.* New York: Advertising Council.

Commission on Reading. (1984). *Becoming a nation of readers.* Washington, DC: U.S. Department of Education.

Golin, A. D., & Ducanis, A. J. (1981). *The interdisciplinary team; A handbook for the education of exceptional children.* Rockville, MD: Aspen.

Jones, R. L. (1978). Protection in evaluation procedures criteria and recommendation. In *Developing criteria for evaluation of the protection in evaluation procedure provisions of Public Law 94-142.* Washington, DC: U.S. Office of Education, Bureau of Education for the Handicapped.

Kavale, K., & Forness, S. (1985). *Science of learning disabilities.* San Diego: College Hill Press.

Kirk, S. A., & Chalfant, J. C. (1984). *Academic and developmental learning disabilities.* Denver, CO: Love.

Popham, W. J., & Baker, E. (1970). *Systematic instruction.* Englewood Cliffs, NJ: Prentice-Hall.

School Committee of the Town of Burlington v. *Department of Education of Massachusetts*. (1985, May 1). *Education for the Handicapped Law Report* (Suppl. 144).

Whitehouse, F. A. (1951, Nov.). *Teamwork: A democracy of professions. Exceptional Children, 18*, 45–52.

Ysseldyke, J. E., & Regan, R. R. (1980, March). Nondiscriminatory assessment: A formative model. *Exceptional Children 46*, 465–466.

ROBERT T. NASH
University of Wisconsin,
Oshkosh

EDUCATION FOR ALL HANDICAPPED CHILDREN ACT OF 1975
INDIVIDUAL EDUCATION PLAN

MULTIHANDICAPPED HEARING IMPAIRED (MHHI)

The Multihandicapped Hearing Impaired (MHHI) are individuals with a hearing loss greater than 90 dB who have an additional handicapping condition secondary to their deafness. The Office of Demographic Studies at Gallaudet College defines additional handicapping conditions as any physical, mental, emotional, or behavioral disorder that significantly adds to the complexity of educating a hearing-impaired student. The most common secondary impairments are emotional disturbance, learning disability, and mental retardation (D'Zamko & Hampton, 1985). Approximately one third of hearing-impaired students can be classified as MHHI.

It is important to note that the educational effects of the multiple handicaps are not additive. The educational planning for multiply handicapped students does not merely involve combining teaching strategies for the hearing impaired with those for the other handicap. Rather, the resulting educational needs are unique because the learning characteristics and educational needs vary widely. Additionally, educators cannot assume that medical conditions equal educational needs (Jones, 1986).

REFERENCES

D'Zamko, M., & Hampton, I. (1985). Personnel preparation for MHHI students. *American Annals of the Deaf, 130*, 9–14.

Jones, T. (1984). A framework of identification, classification and placement of multihandicapped hearing impaired students. *Volta Review, 86*, 142–151.

MARY GRACE FEELY
School for the Deaf, New York,
New York

DEAF
DEAF-BLIND
MULTIPLY HANDICAPPED

MULTIPLE BASELINE DESIGN

The multiple baseline design is one of several single-subject applied behavior analysis research designs for evaluating the effects of interventions on the behaviors of handicapped children and youths. While intervention withdrawal or reversal designs are the most frequently used of the single-subject designs, there are instances in behavioral research where a return to baseline phase is not an appropriate alternative for evaluation purposes. Zucker, Rutherford, and Prieto (1978), Kazdin (1982), and Barlow and Hersen (1984) identify several situations where a return to baseline is not appropriate for either ethical or scientific reasons.

First, once some behaviors are acquired, they may no longer be dependent on the intervention and thus will be maintained by naturally occurring reinforcers in the environment. For example, if an intervention is initiated to increase an isolate child's cooperative behavior with peers on the playground, the child may continue cooperative behavior through acquired peer social reinforcement despite the fact that the teacher intervention is reversed.

A second situation where the reversal design may be inappropriate occurs with behaviors that, once they are acquired, are essentially nonreversible. For example, if a behavioral intervention program is initiated to teach a child the letters of the alphabet, once the child has acquired this skill, it is unlikely that withdrawal or reversal of the intervention will result in a loss of ability to repeat the alphabet. Rate of response may decrease, but probably not the basic skill itself.

A third instance is when the teacher cannot accurately reverse the intervention procedures to return to baseline levels of functioning. For example, if the intervention involves systematic attention to student on-task behavior and ignoring of off-task behavior, the teacher may find it impossible to replicate baseline rates of attention and ignoring during the reversal phase.

The fourth situation involves children's behaviors that may be so dangerous or noxious that further instances of the behavior cannot be tolerated, even for a brief reversal period. If, for example, an intervention is effective in stopping a child's self-destructive behaviors, few teachers would want to withdraw the intervention and count the number of self-destructive behaviors.

The multiple baseline design (see Figure) is used in situations where the reversal design may not be appropriate for evaluating intervention effects. This design involves establishing baselines on several different behaviors concurrently, and then systematically applying the intervention to one of the targeted behaviors. If this behavior changes in the desired direction, then the same intervention is applied to the second behavior. If the second behavior also changes in the direction desired, the intervention is than applied to the third target behavior, and so on. If each behavior changes when, and only when, in-

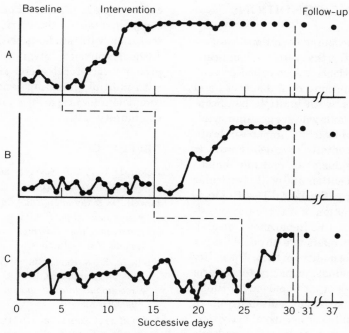

Baseline   Intervention   Follow-up

Successive days

Sample multiple baseline graph.

tervention is applied to it, experimental control is demonstrated.

There are three types of multiple baseline designs. The first of these involves evaluating the effects of the intervention on the same behavior of the same child in two or more settings. For example, the teacher may be interested in stopping a child's hitting other students during recess, lunchtime, and classtime. Response contingent time-out may be applied to hitting during recess; if successful, then during lunchtime; if successful, then during classtime.

The second type of multiple baseline design involves measuring and evaluating the effects of a particular intervention on two or more behaviors of the same child in the same setting. For example, an overcorrection procedure might be made contingent on various self-stimulatory behaviors of an autistic student. Following a period of baseline on finger flicking, clapping, and hand gazing episodes, overcorrection would be made contingent on finger flicking while baseline was continued on clapping and hand gazing. If finger flicking decreased significantly, the overcorrection precedure would then be applied to clapping and so on.

The third variation of the baseline design involves evaluating intervention effects across several children who exhibit a similar behavior in the same setting. The example here might be to begin simultaneous baselines on the rate per minute of two or more children's summing of two-digit addition facts. Intervention, perhaps in the form of a contract for increased rate, would be initiated first with one child while baseline data were continued to be collected for the other two children. If the first child's rate increased contingent on the intervention, a contract would then be initiated with the second child and so on.

The most important factors in research using multiple baseline designs are that baselines for all behaviors are begun at the same time and that ongoing measurement and recording of all behaviors is continuous throughout the procedure. Subsequent applications of the intervention are determined by their effects on the immediately preceding behavior. The most powerful conclusions regarding the effectiveness of the interventions can be drawn when there are closely related or functional behavior changes following repeated applications of the intervention across settings, behaviors, or subjects.

REFERENCES

Barlow, D. H., & Hersen, M. (1984). *Singlecase experimental designs: Strategies for studying behavior change.* New York: Pergamon.

Kazdin, A. E. (1982). *Single-case research design: Methods for clinical and applied settings.* New York: Oxford University Press.

Zucker, S. H., Rutherford, R. B., & Prieto, A. G. (1979). Teacher directed interventions with behaviorally disordered children. In R. B. Rutherford & A. G. Prieto (Eds.), *Monograph in behavior disorders: Severe behavior disorders of children and youth* (Vol. 2, pp. 49–61). Reston, VA: CCBD.

ROBERT B. RUTHERFORD, JR.
Arizona State University

BEHAVIORAL OBJECTIVES
BEHAVIORAL OBSERVATION
BEHAVIOR MODIFICATION

MULTIPLE HANDICAPPING CONDITIONS

Students with multiple handicapping conditions are persons with two or more disabilities that result in handicaps within functional living experiences. Also called persons with severe handicapping conditions, dual diagnosis, and orthopedic disabilities, persons with multiple handicapping conditions include individuals who are deaf-blind, autistic, cerebral palsied, neurologically impaired, brain damaged, schizophrenic, or mentally retarded (Fewell & Cone, 1983). Labeling individuals as multiply handicapped should be done with caution and with particular focus on outcomes. Accordingly, the World Health Organization (1978) urges the adoption of a three-tier classification system including the terms impairment, disability, and handicap. Impairment refers to a physiological or anatomical loss or other abnormality or both. Disability is the limitation of an individual's capacity to perform some key life function because of an impairment. Handicap describes the limitation imposed by a disability on an individual's ability to carry on his or her usual activities.

According to these definitions, a student with multiple handicapping conditions would have limitations in educational development as a result of two or more disabilities. Thus the definition of children with severe handicaps of the U.S. Office of Education describes children

> who, because of the intensity of their physical, mental, or emotional problems, need educational, social, psychological, and medical service, beyond those which are traditionally offered by regular and special education programs, in order to maximize their full potential for useful and meaningful participation in society and for self-fulfillment. (U.S. Office of Education, 1974)

From another perspective, Baker (1979) provides a definition that includes an individual

> whose ability to provide for his or her own basic life-sustaining and safety needs is so limited, relative to the proficiency expected on the basis of chronological age, that it could pose a serious threat to his or her survival.

Numerous specialists are involved in educational programming for students with multiple handicaps, including therapists in speech, language, communication, occupational, physical, adapted physical education, and recreation areas. Together these specialists form a multidisciplinary team for the development of an individualized education plan. A sharing of roles should be emphasized, with the classroom teacher assuming the position of coordinator. The educational curriculum focuses on chronological-age-appropriate programs, functional activities, implementation of precise daily schedules, and the development of curricular domains within domestic living, general community functioning, recreation/leisure, and vocational areas (Snell & Renzaglia, 1986). An important component within the curriculum is the provision for integration with students without identifiable handicaps. Although physical integration is a first step, strategies to promote reciprocal social interactions among students with multiple handicaps and their peers is an essential component for preparing students to function within home community settings.

REFERENCES

Baker, D. B. (1979). Severely handicapped: Toward an inclusive definition. *AAESPH Review, 4*, 52–65.

Fewell, D., & Cone, J. (1983). Identification and placement of severely handicapped children. In M. Snell (Ed.), *Systematic instruction of the moderately and severely handicapped* (2nd ed.) (pp. 46–73). Columbus, OH: Merrill.

Snell, M. E., & Renzaglia, A. M. (1986). Moderate, severe, and profound handicaps. In N. G. Haring & L. McCormick (Eds.), *Exceptional children and youth* (4th ed., pp. 271–310). Columbus, OH: Merrill.

U.S. Office of Education. (1974). *Code of federal regulations, Title 45, Section 121.2*. Washington, DC: Bureau of Education for the Handicapped.

World Health Organization. (1978). *International classification of diseases*. (9th rev.). Washington, DC: Author.

ERNEST L. PANCSOFAR
University of Connecticut

DEAF-BLIND
LABELING
MENTAL RETARDATION
OTHER HEALTH IMPAIRED
CHILDHOOD SCHIZOPHRENIA

MULTIPLE REGRESSION

Multiple regression is a statistical procedure in which a single continuous dependent variable is regressed on several continuous independent variables. Typical purposes are to predict dependent variable scores from the independent variables, model real world variable relationships, and explain dependent variable variation concisely.

There are two conditions in multiple regression that determine analysis and interpretation. In the first condition, all independent variables are statistically independent of each other. While this does not occur naturally very often, it can be occasionally obtained from theory or from judicious selection of independent variables. In this case, each independent variable is related to the dependent variable in magnitude equal to Pearson's correlation; the Pearson correlation squared equals the proportion of dependent variable variance accounted for. The sum of all the squared correlations for independent variables is equal to the squared multiple correlation, a measure of the total variance proportion accounted for by all independent variables. In a Venn diagram of these circles, the two independent variables intersect the dependent variable circle but do not intersect each other between independent variables.

The more usually observed condition is one in which one or more of the independent variables are not statistically independent of each other. This implies that the independent variables will be correlated with each other and with the dependent variable. In this case, there is overlap in the amount of variance accounted for in the dependent variable by two or more independent variables. In a Venn diagram, the circles representing independent variables intersect each other as well as the circle representing the dependent variable. The squared multiple correlation is still defined as the total proportion of variance in dependent variable accounted for. However, now the contributions of the individual independent variables are more difficult to discern because they overlap. The partial correlation between an independent variable $X1$ and dependent variable Y is defined as the Pearson correlation between two errors of regression. $X1$ is regressed on all the other independent variables and for each subject a predicted score is subtracted from the observed score to create one error score, $E1$. Similarly, the dependent variable is regressed on the other independent variables and an error score Ey is computed. The partial correlation is the correlation between $E1$ and Ey. Its square represents the unique or independent contribution of $X1$ to the variance in Y. The total squared multiple correlation is a function of the partial correlations but it cannot be simply stated (Darlington, 1978).

Uses of multiple regression in prediction are usually to make decisions based on past performance. For example, colleges make first-year selection decisions based on high-school percentile rank and Scholastic Aptitude Test (SAT) scores' prediction of the first year's college grade point average (GPA). High-school rank and SAT score are independent variables, termed predictors; college GPA is the dependent variables. Typical multiple correlation is about .5, with about 25% of freshman GPAs predictable. The SAT score might add about 5% to the prediction based on high-school rank alone.

The use of multiple regression in modeling or theory building is based on specifying the order of including independent variables in the multiple regression. Thus contributions of the independent variables to dependent variable variance is dependent on the order of entry. This is sometimes called hierarchical regression or ordered regression. A special case is termed path analysis, in which the partial correlations are computed in specified order. They are interpreted as path coefficients, the direct influence of one variable on another (Pedhazur, 1982).

Often the purpose for multiple regression is parsimonious prediction when there are many possible predictors or independent variables. Not all are necessary or desirable owing to the expense of data collection, so a smaller subset of predictors that will perform nearly as well as all predictors available is sought. There are several strategies available to find this parsimonious subset: forward, backward, and stepwise regression. There are several variants available with each. Forward multiple regression begins with the best single predictor, the greatest magnitude Pearson correlation with the dependent variable. It adds new predictors according to some criteria for improving prediction or increasing squared multiple correlation with the dependent variable. When there is little change after adding a new variable, the procedure ends. Backward regression begins with all predictors and drops them out until there are large drops in the predictive criteria. For example, with both forward and backward regression, a criterion might be used that additional predictors must improve the squared multiple correlation by .05 (Draper & Smith, 1982). Stepwise multiple regression is a variant on either forward or backward regression in which variables previously entered are tested to see whether they are no longer needed after new variables have been included. This means that a new combination of predictors are now able to predict along with the previous set. Thus the first predictor entered might eventually be dropped. Multiple regression is widely used in the behavioral sciences. In its most general form, it encompasses most statistical techniques, including the analysis of variance, as the general linear model.

REFERENCES

Darlington, R. B. (1978). Reduced variance regression. *Psychological Bulletin, 85,* 1238–1255.

Draper, N. R., & Smith, H. (1982). *Applied regression analysis* (2nd ed.). New York: Wiley.

Pedhazur, E. (1982). *Multiple regression in behavioral research* (2nd ed.). New York: Holt, Rinehart, Winston.

VICTOR L. WILLSON
Texas A&M University

DISCRIMINANT ANALYSIS
RESEARCH IN SPECIAL EDUCATION

MULTIPLE SCLEROSIS (MS)

Multiple sclerosis (MS) is a progressive neurologic disease affecting the brain and spinal cord. It generally is considered a disease of young adults, with symptoms rarely occurring before adolescence or after age 40 (Brown, 1971); mean age of onset is 30 years (Kaufman, 1981). Females are affected more than males (Kaufman, 1981; Magalini, 1971), and although no clear-cut hereditary component has been identified, the incidence is much higher in close relatives of afflicted persons (Kaufman, 1981; Thomson, 1979).

Multiple sclerosis is considered a demyelinating disease, in that the myelin (fatty sheaths surrounding nerve fibers) in the central nervous system is disseminated. Plaques or hardened patches of scarred nerve fibers are evident in the central nervous system of MS patients. The name multiple sclerosis derives from these scarred (sclerosed) masses, together with the multiple episodic nature of the disease (Kaufman, 1981; *Melloni's*, 1985). Multiple sclerosis is also known as *disseminated sclerosis* (Brown, 1971; Magalini, 1971).

Early symptoms of MS may be mild and vague, and hence may be dismissed by affected individuals or their families. Such symptoms include blurred vision, tingling or numbness in the trunk or extremities, vertigo, intention tremor, and clumsiness. Episodes of symptoms characteristically are followed by periods of remission, a pattern that may persist for several years. Despite the intermittent nature of the disease, MS is a progressive condition, and afflicted individuals demonstrate increasing neurologic impairment. Advanced symptoms of MS include ataxia (a gait disturbance characterized by a broad-based stance and lurching movements), scanning speech (evidenced by monotonous, staccato speech with slurring adjacent sounds), and nystagmus (tremor of eye movements). Other signs associated with the disease include bladder and bowel disturbances, partial or complete blindness (retrobulbar neuritis), and hyperreflexive movements (e.g., Babinski sign). While a number of experts report affective disturbances in MS patients, particularly emotional lability and euphoria (Kaufman, 1981; Magalini, 1971; *Mosby's*, 1983), Lechtenberg (1982) takes issue with such reports. He cites studies that indicate a high incidence of depression in MS patients, and suggests the symptom of euphoria may be better described as "a masked depression manifested by unrealistic or excessively optimistic attitudes" (p. 216).

The cause of MS is unknown, although commonalities have been identified among afflicted patients. Multiple sclerosis is considered a disease of temperate climates (Brown, 1971; Kaufman, 1981). While their role in transmission of the disease is unknown, many MS patients had small, indoor pets as children (Kaufman, 1981). Toxic viral and allergic metabolic etiologies have been hypothesized (Magalini, 1971). Diagnosis of MS relies largely on clinical symptoms and the multiple episodic nature of the disease. Few laboratory tests are pathognomonic of MS, although elevated gamma globulin in conjunction with normal protein levels in cerebrospinal fluid may suggest the presence of the disease (Kaufman, 1981). Numerous medical and psychological conditions may mimic MS, including Guillain-Barre syndrome, tumors of the brain or spinal cord, and hysteria.

Few beneficial therapeutic interventions have been identified in the treatment of MS. Physical or occupational therapy may facilitate optimal range of motion and may provide for environmental adaptations when necessary. Corticosteroid treatments may shorten symptomatic episodes (Kaufman, 1981). Diets designed to reduce exposure to allergy-related foods reportedly have been associated with remissions of symptoms in some MS patients (*MS and diet*, 1984).

REFERENCES

Brown, J. A. C. (1971). *The Stein and Day international medical encyclopedia*. New York: Stein & Day.

Kaufman, D. M. (1981). *Clinical neurology for psychiatrists*. New York: Grune & Stratton.

Lechtenberg, R. (1982). *The psychiatrist's guide to diseases of the nervous system*. New York: Wiley.

Magalini, S. (1971). *Dictionary of medical syndromes*. Philadelphia: Lippincott.

Melloni's illustrated medical dictionary (2nd ed.). (1985). Baltimore, MD: Williams & Wilkins.

Mosby's medical and nursing dictionary. (1983). St. Louis: Mosby.

MS and diet. (1984). *Programs for the handicapped* (ISSN 0565-2804), *5*, 12.

Thompson, W. A. R. (1979). *Black's medical dictionary*. (32 ed.). New York: Barnes & Noble.

CATHY F. TELZROW
*Cuyahoga Special Education
Service Center, Maple
Heights, Ohio*

**GAIT DISTURBANCES
PHYSICAL DISABILITY**

MULTISENSORY INSTRUCTION

A multisensory approach to instruction involves presenting instructional content through several modalities such as the visual, auditory, kinesetic, and tactile modalities. The rationale underlying this instructional approach is that learning may be enhanced if the content to be learned is presented through several sensory modalities. The Fernald (1943) method and the Gillingham-Stillman (1960) method typify the multisensory approach to teaching reading. However, the two methods differ in emphasis. While the Fernald method emphasizes whole-word learning, the Gillingham-Stillman method emphasizes the teaching of phonics, specifically individual phonemes and sound blending.

The Fernald method originated from Grace Fernald's attempts at teaching reading to the severely disabled and to children who had normal intelligence but were severely reading disabled. The method involves the child's own selection of a word to learn, regardless of length. The child traces the word, saying the word out loud while tracing it. This procedure is repeated until the child can write the traced word from memory. The word is to be learned and written as a unit rather than by sounds or syllables. If the child fails to write the word after tracing it, the teacher swiftly removes the erroneously written or half-written word from the child and has the child start afresh tracing and rewriting the word. The Fernald method does not permit copying the traced word because Grace Fernald believed the copying process in which the child looks back and forth between copy and the word being written disrupts the child's learning of the word.

Gillingham and Stillman developed their instructional method for reading-disabled children through their association with Orton (Myers & Hammill, 1982), whose theory that reading disability stems from deficient establishment of cerebral dominance is well-known. The Gillingham-Stillman method revolves around teaching individual letter-sound associations and then blending these letter sounds into words. Specifically, the child is presented with a letter on a card. The child learns the name of the letter and its sound. Subsequent activities include tracing and copying the letter and writing it from memory. In this multisensory way, the child progresses in learning individual letter-sound associations and in blending these letter sounds into words (Bryan & Bryan, 1979).

Although Fernald's method and Gillingham-Stillman's method have reported clinical success with reading-disabled individuals, there is no conclusive empirical data to date on the superiority of their instructional efficacy when compared with other remedial approaches (Silberberg, Iverson, & Goins, 1973). Hence evaluative research on their instructional efficacy appears to be called for. Moreover, research is needed to understand why these remedial methods work with particular reading-disabled individuals.

REFERENCES

Bryan, T. H., & Bryan, J. H. (1979). *Understanding learning disabilities* (2nd ed.). Sherman Oaks, CA: Alfred.

Fernald, G. M. (1943). *Remedial techniques in school subject.* New York: McGraw-Hill.

Gillingham, A., & Stillman, B. (1960). *Remedial training for children with specific disability in reading, spelling, penmanship.* Cambridge MA: Educators Publishing Service.

Myers, P. I., & Hammill, D. D. (1982). *Learning disabilities: Basic concepts, assessment practices, and instructional strategies.* Austin, TX: PRO-ED.

Silberberg, N., Iverson, I., & Goins, J. (1973). Which remedial method works best? *Journal of Learning Disabilities, 6,* 547–556.

BERNICE Y. L. WONG
Simon Fraser University

READING
READING REMEDIATION
TEACHING STRATEGIES

MUNSON, GRACE E. (1883–1980)

Born in a sod house near Orleans, Nebraska, Grace Munson believed in self-growth and advancement through educational attainment. From one-room schools on the prairie, she moved through Peru (Nebraska) Normal School (1905) and the University of Nebraska (Phi Beta Kappa) for a BA (1911) and a PhD (1916) with time out for a MA from Wellesley College (1912), where she was an alumnae fellow.

Professionally, she was a rural Nebraska teacher near Geneva, (1899–1903), teacher and principal in Harlan County (1905–1909), and instructor in education at the University of Nebraska (1912–1918) before moving to Chicago, where she was a school psychologist and teacher (1918–1935), director of the Bureau of Child Study (1935–1946), and assistant superintendent in charge of special education (1946–1949).

While she was director of the bureau, the staff moved beyond serving the mentally retarded to improving programs and services for the gifted, maladjusted, truants, and others whose achievement was not as expected on the basis of their intellectual ability. As a psychologist and educator, her work was guided by an interpretation of Rousseau's *Emile* in light of contemporary child study methods. She continually sought ways of moving children through the basic skills at their own rates regardless of grade placement. As bureau director she initiated throughout Chicago an adjustment teacher program, which involved releasing teachers from classroom duties to work with individuals needing help, a reading readiness program for children in first grade who were not ready to read, a reading improvement program for students entering high school, and self-appraisal and careers courses for juniors in high school. In addition, she expanded and standardized the citywide testing program in reading readiness, achievement, and intellectual assessment.

An innovative leader who welcomed suggestions, her criticism of others and of ideas was both trenchant and effective. Although her professional activity and leadership was usually limited to greater Chicago, she helped organize the Chicago Psychological Club in 1924 for psychologists in the bureau and the Institute for Juvenile Research, a group serving mental health needs. Through the club she was instrumental in brining some of the great names from across the United States into dialogue with Chicago professionals.

JOSEPH L. FRENCH
Pennsylvania State University

MUSCULAR DYSTROPHY (MD)

Muscular dystrophy (MD) describes a group of inherited disorders characterized by severe, progressive weakness associated with atrophy of the skeletal muscles bilaterally. The most common forms of the disease typically have an early onset and produce increased wasting and eventual death. Because of the shortened life of afflicted persons, approximately two-thirds of muscular dystrophy patients are children ages 3 to 15 (Weiner, 1973).

Although classification systems for muscular dystrophy vary, there is general agreement that Duchenne's dystrophy (pseudohypertrophic type) is the most common variant. Other categories include faciocapulohumoral dystrophy (affects facial and shoulder muscles; onset in second decade) and limb-girdle muscular dystrophy (typically does not affect children) (Bleck, 1975; Buda, 1981; Rowland, 1979). Incidence figures vary widely by type, from 5 per million births for faciocapulohumoral type to 250 per million births for Duchenne's (Rowland, 1979). Duchenne's dystrophy is inherited via an x-linked mode of transmission, although spontaneous genetic mutation is reported to be fairly common, with perhaps two-thirds of afflicted children having no family history of the disorder (Rowland, 1979). It is by definition a condition that affects males exclusively, although female carriers have been reported to show mild clinical symptoms (Buda, 1981). In late 1985, researchers reported the ability to identify carriers of the Duchenne's gene with 98% accuracy; significant progress was also being made in the effort to identify the exact location of the gene (Kolata, 1985). Other forms of muscular dystrophy are transmitted as autosomal dominant or recessive traits (Rowland, 1985).

The onset of Duchenne's dystrophy generally occurs during the preschool period. Walking may be delayed, and early signs of the disorder may include difficulty in raising from a supine or sitting position or difficulty in climbing stairs. As the disease progresses and muscles in the pelvic girdle become affected, a characteristic waddling gait, with a sway back and protruding pelvis, may be observed (Bleck, 1975). Progressive weakness is characteristic of Duchenne's dystrophy, and children may be wheelchair bound by age 10 or 12 (Bleck, 1975; Kolata, 1985). Death typically occurs in the third decade, as a result of respiratory failure or involvement of the heart muscles (Weiner, 1973).

A number of early studies reported an increased incidence of mental retardation in boys afflicted with Duchenne's dystrophy; the mean IQ was reported to be approximately one standard deviation below the mean. Other studies have revealed a verbal < nonverbal discrepancy in boys with Duchenne's dystrophy, although there is no consensus among the experts (Mearig, 1983). A recent study of older and younger Duchenne's victims reported an age effect, with younger boys exhibiting greater deficits in verbal and attentional-organizational skills than older subjects (Sollee, Latham, Kindlon, & Bresnan, 1985).

Children with MD may require special education and related services. Adaptive equipment, attendant services, and appropriate therapies may be necessary for MD children. While a typical profile of neuropsychological strengths and weaknesses has not been established for boys with Duchenne's dystrophy, converging data suggest individual differences may be present that warrant a modified instructional program.

REFERENCES

Bleck, E. E. (1975). Muscular dystrophy-Duchenne type. In E. E. Bleck & D. A. Nagel (Eds.), *Physically handicapped children: A medical atlas for teachers* (pp. 173–179). New York: Grune & Stratton.

Buda, F. B. (1981). *The neurology of developmental disabilities.* Springfield, IL: Thomas.

Kolata, G. (1985). Closing in on the muscular dystrophy gene. *Science, 230,* 307–308.

Mearig, J. S. (1983). Evaluation of cognitive functioning in children with neuromuscular and related physical disabilities. In C. R. Reynolds & J. H. Clark (Eds.), *Assessment and programming for young children with low-incidence handicaps* (pp. 157–199). New York: Plenum.

Rowland, L. P. (1979). Diseases of muscle and neuromuscular junction. In P. B. Beeson, W. McDermott, & J. B. Wyngaarden (Eds.), *Cecil textbook of medicine* (15th ed., pp. 914–930). Philadelphia: Saunders.

Sollee, N. D., Latham, E. E., Kindlon, D. J., & Bresnan, M. J. (1985). Neuropsychological impairment in Duchenne muscular dystrophy. *Journal of Clinical & Experimental Neuropsychology, 7,* 486–496.

Weiner, F. (1973). *Help for the handicapped child.* New York: McGraw-Hill.

CATHY F. TELZROW
*Cuyahoga Special Education
Service Center, Maple
Heights, Ohio*

ADAPTED PHYSICAL EDUCATION
MUSCULAR DISTROPHY ASSOCIATION
PHYSICAL HANDICAPS

MUSCULAR DYSTROPHY ASSOCIATION (MDA)

The Muscular Dystrophy Association (MDA) (810 7th Avenue, New York, NY 10019, [212] 586-0808) was formed in 1950 by a small group of parents whose children were victims of muscular dystrophy (Weiner, 1973). It is a voluntary health agency of parents and science professionals designed to combat neuromuscular disorders. The national headquarters provides information and referral services, media campaigns; it also sponsors research conferences of a national and international scope. The MDA has established 85 outpatient clinics that provide diagnostic and follow-up services for afflicted persons. There are over 300 local chapters of the Muscular Dystrophy Association in the 50 states, Washington, DC, Guam, and Puerto Rico (Foster, Szoke, Kapisovsky, & Kriger, 1977). Local affiliates provide financial aide for a wide variety of authorized services, including purchase and repair of orthopedic appliances, physical therapy, and transportation to and from clinics. Some chapters sponsor summer camps or recreational activities.

REFERENCES

Foster, J. C., Szoke, C. O., Kapisovsky, P. M., & Kriger, L. S. (1977). *Guidance, counseling, and support services for high school students with physical disabilities.* Cambridge, MA: Technical Education Research Centers.

Weiner, F. (1973). *Help for the handicapped child.* New York: McGraw-Hill.

CATHY F. TELZROW
*Cuyahoga Special Education
Service Center, Maple
Heights, Ohio*

MUSCULAR IMBALANCE

Muscular imbalance occurs when there is difficulty or lack of integration in the interaction of opposing muscle groups. Normally there is a finely graded interaction of opposing muscle groups facilitated by reciprocal innervation of the muscles. Paralysis, weakness, or interruption in innervation may result in an imbalance. Depending on the location and severity of the muscle imbalance, the individual may not be able to remain upright, extend the arm, focus the eyes, or hop on one foot. Motor skills performance may be severely impaired or minimally effected. A muscle imbalance may lead to fatigue, difficulty in respiration, impaired oral-motor skills, pain, impaired visual focus, or numerous other conditions depending on the nature, location, and pervasiveness of the imbalance.

Signs of muscle imbalance may be observed in the classroom. Actions such as tilting the head to read, leaning to one side after being seated for a period of time, slumping, or significant deterioration of handwriting toward the end of a writing period may all be signs of a muscle imbalance or weakness.

REFERENCES

Fraser, B., & Hensinger, R. *Managing physical handicaps.* Baltimore, MD: Brookes.

Heiniger, M., & Randolph, S. (1981). *Neurophysiological concepts of human behavior.* St. Louis: Mosby.

Ward, D. (1984). *Positioning the handicapped child for functions.* St. Louis, Phoenix.

MARY K. DYKES
University of Florida

MOVEMENT THERAPY
MUSCULAR DYSTROPHY

PHYSICAL DISABILITIES
VISUAL MOTOR PROBLEMS

MUSEUMS AND THE HANDICAPPED

Access of the handicapped not only to museums but to fuller appreciation of art itself was vastly extended with the passing of the Vocational Rehabilitation Act of 1973. Section 504 of that law prohibits discrimination against the disabled by government-funded organizations; this has had a significant impact on the way museums plan and implement their exhibits and educational programs. This is not to say that there were no programs for the handicapped prior to Section 504. The Mary Duke Biddle Gallery in Raleigh, North Carolina, pioneered the tactile approach for blind and visually impaired patrons as early as 1966, and the Lions Gallery of the Senses was established in Hartford, Connecticut, in 1972. These early efforts were exceptional, however, and they were not without their critics (Kenny, 1983). One important criticism stemmed from the fact that galleries and museums specifically for the handicapped, while admirable in their motivation, were unintentionally segregationist in their effect.

Museums responded in a variety of ways. To avoid segregation, the efforts generally revolved around an expansion of services and multisensory experiences for all visitors. But the museums had little experience with nonvisual efforts. Steiner (1983) points out some of the misapprehensions that surfaced as sighted curators began to plan for the visually impaired: that the legally blind have no sight at all; that most blind people read braille; and that the blind are automatically more sensitive to touch and sound than the sighted. Without conscious effort, it is also very easy to underestimate (or overlook altogether) the amount of background knowledge that the sighted pick up unconsciously from their environment and apply to the appreciation of art. In an effort to avoid mistakes that might easily result from such misunderstandings, museums across the country began organizing advisory boards made up of the handicapped to help guide and plan the new efforts.

Since then, tactile exhibits have become much more common. Conservation experts found ways to avoid some of the worst dangers of human touch: coating objects with lacquer or wax, for example, or requiring that visitors wear gloves or wash their hands and remove jewelry before enjoying the exhibit. Sometimes, when objects are too valuable or perhaps too large for touching, reproductions are created. There have been cases in which the reproductions were constructed so that they could be taken apart to show their inner structure as well. Occasionally, paintings have been specially reproduced with a variety of textures replacing the colors of the original. Black and white photographs often accompany objects on display.

This has helped the partially sighted by enlarging details, simplifying the visual information by reducing it to two dimensions, and increasing contrast for better comprehension (Smithsonian Institute, 1977).

Museums have also become much more sensitive to the special problems handicapped people face when trying to move through exhibit areas (Hunt, 1979). Barriers have been removed for those in wheelchairs. Tactile maps, three-dimensional models of exhibit spaces, and specially designed carpet trails help the visually impaired find their way around. Staff training has helped museum personnel be sensitive to those patrons who need extra help and those who prefer more independence. Training has also been aimed at improving the clarity and precision of oral directions. Other services geared specifically to the handicapped have also been introduced (Mims, 1982). These include regularly scheduled tours conducted by staff and volunteers who can communicate with the deaf, braille and large-print labels, subtitled and captioned films, large-print newsletters and announcements of coming attractions, and the inclusion of art education and special tours on radio reading services and in talking-book projects. For those who are institutionalized or homebound, there are suitcase exhibits that can be borrowed from museums. These often include slides and audio tapes, along with reproductions of art objects.

Some museums across the country have been able to implement exemplary programs, maintaining continuous gallery experiences for the handicapped and interweaving them with other aspects of the art education program. The New York Metropolitan Museum in New York City, the De Young Memorial Museum in San Francisco, the Plimouth Plantation, a living history museum in Plymouth, Massachusetts, the Smithsonian Institute in Washington, DC, and the Wadsworth Antheneum in Hartford, Connecticut, are only a few examples. Horizons for the Blind of Chicago is a good source of further information on accessibility and special programs for the handicapped in museums, galleries, and art and science centers.

REFERENCES

Hunt, S. (1979). An exhibit for touching. *Journal of Visual Impairment & Blindness, 73*(9), 364–366.

Kenny, A. P. (1983). A range of vision: Museum accommodations for visually impaired people. *Journal of Visual Impairment & Blindness, 77*(7), 325–329.

Mims, S. K. (1982). Art museums and special audiences. *School Arts, 81*(7), 32–33.

Smithsonian Institute National Air and Space Museum. (1977). *Museums and handicapped students: Guidelines for educators.* (ERIC Document Reproduction Service No. ED 152 062) Washington, DC: Smithsonian Institute.

Steiner, C. (1983). Art museums and the visually handicapped consumer: Some issues in approach and design. *Journal of Visual Impairment & Blindness, 77*(7), 330–333.

JANET S. BRAND
*Hunter College, City University
of New York*

MUSIC THERAPY

Music therapy is the use of music in all of its forms to modify nonmusical behavior (Lathom & Eagle, 1982) and to promote mental health, social development and adjustment, and motor coordination. At times it is used as a therapeutic tool in rehabilitation and for recreational or educational purposes. Perhaps the most important contribution of music to special education is that it can promote learning through activities that are enjoyable.

Therapeutically, music has been known to have a significant psychological and physiological effect on handicapped students' personality (Nordoff & Robbins, 1971). Behaviorists have used music to alter overt behavior (Warren, 1984). Freudians have recommended the use of music to reduce anxiety, catharsis, and sublimation, and to change affective states. Humanists view the use of music as a vehicle to stimulate the process of self-actualization (Harvey, 1980).

Music therapy in a variety of applications has been practiced in hospitals, schools, institutions, and private settings in a one-to-one or group approach. It includes moving to music, playing instruments, presenting musicals, attending concerts, dancing, creating music, singing, and listening.

The role of the music therapy should be distinguished from the role of music education in special education. Music therapy has remedial goals. Music education teaches the knowledge and skills of music as an aesthetic, enriching, and pleasurable experience for all children, including the handicapped (Alley, 1979). In special education, music therapy has been used to increase handicapped students' ability to follow directions and to attend to and respond to logical sequences of movement, voice, and music. Task analysis has assisted in these purposes (Alley, 1979). It is advised that in special education, the music therapist select musical activities that are within the students' skill levels thus tasks may be as simple as listening to rock music or playing in the school orchestra.

Lathom and Eagle (1982) found that the majority of music therapists focus on improving gross and motor skills. This is accomplished by movement activities to music and the coordinated use of the hands, arms, and body while playing a musical instrument. Music therapists have sought to encourage cooperation between handicapped children and adults in producing musical effects. They have also used music to reinforce correct performance in group behavior.

After the passage of PL 94-142, music educators turned to music therapists, who had already established a tradition of success in teaching music to handicapped populations. As a result, many of the music materials and teaching procedures for the handicapped have their basis in music therapy. From 1975 to 1985, music education and music therapy for the handicapped have spread from private or residential programs to all aspects of special education under the aegis of PL 94-142 (Alley, 1979).

REFERENCES

Alley, J. (1979). Music in the IEP: Therapy education. *Journal of Music Therapy, 16*(3), 111–127.

Boxill, E. (1985). *Music therapy for the developmentally disabled.* Rockville, MD: Aspen.

Harvey, P. (1980). The therapeutic role of music in special education: Historical perspectives. *Creative Child & Adult Quarterly, 5*(3), 196–203.

Lathom, W., & Eagle, C. (1982). Music for the severely disabled child. *Music Education Journal, 38*(49), 30–31.

Nordoff, P., & Robbins, C. (1971). *Therapy in music for handicapped children.* New York: St. Martins.

Warren, B. (Ed.). (1984). *Using the creative arts in therapy.* Cambridge MA: Brookline.

THOMAS BURKE
Hunter College, City University of New York

DANCE THERAPY
GAMES FOR THE HANDICAPPED
RECREATIONAL THERAPY

MUTISM

Mutism is defined as the lack of articulate speech (Kanner, 1975). According to Kolvin and Fundudis (1981), there are many forms of mutism. They may be divided into those with a presumed biological basis and those considered psychological in nature. Mutism with a biological basis is typically associated with profound deafness, serious mental handicap, infantile autism, or akinetic mutism. As a symptom of psychological disturbance, two further types are delineated. Traumatic mutism is identified as having a sudden onset immediately following a psychological or physical shock and is thus considered a hysterical reaction. Elective mutism is a condition in which speech is confined to a familiar situation or a small group of select others.

Kanner (1948) was among the first to discuss mutism in the psychiatric literature. He identified lack of sound perception as the most frequent cause and differentiated deaf mutism into congenital and acquired forms. Deafness existing at birth or acquired at a very early age usually prevents the development of speech. Congenital mutism can be due to physical anomalies of speech or auditory mechanisms; acquired mutism may be the result of illnesses such as meningitis or congenital syphilis. The congenital form is more common in boys than girls. Kanner estimated approximately .07% deaf mutes in the population.

Other forms of mutism are also described by Kanner. Mutism without deafness may be identified in cases of severe and profound mental retardation when the capacity for verbal expression and comprehension is severely delayed. Mutism as a symptom of childhood schizophrenia and early infantile autism is also common. Temporary mutism as an occasional symptom of hysteria was suggested by Kanner as a result of emotional conflict.

Kanner also described cases of voluntary silence associated with aphasia. "Comprehension of language and motor ability are intact. Some of the patients speak to certain people and on certain occasions only. Their responses in areas other than speech are adequate" (p. 492). This description is strikingly similar to current conceptions of elective or selective mutism.

A variety of terms can be found in traditional classifications of childhood mutism. For example, speech avoidance (Lerea & Ward, 1965), speech inhibition (Treuper, 1897), speech phobia (Mora, Devault, & Schopler, 1962), thymogenic mutism (Waternik & Vedder, 1936), and traumatic mutism (Hayden, 1980) are among the terms used to describe and classify children displaying similar symptomatology.

Early writers commonly defined mutism by exclusion (Kratochwill, 1981). Tramer (1934) distinguished selective mutism from language retardation and schizophrenic mutism. Some writers perceived mutism as being closely tied to other forms of intrapsychic personality patterns. Weber (1950) stressed a specific disposition to reactions of stupor and depression in mute children. An abnormal dependence on the mother was noted, which was hypothesized to be related to oral dependency needs and a regression to early infantile social relations. Heuger and Morgenstern (1927) related a case in which partial mutism developed into total mutism. The authors reported that the child continued to communicate through drawings, and they proposed that the disorder was caused by castration anxiety.

In an extensive discussion of mutism among psychotic children, Etemad and Szurek (1973) reported that 30% of the 264 psychotic children seen at the Langley Porter Neuropsychiatric Institute Children's Service between 1946 and 1961 were totally mute or showed a marked paucity of verbal expression relative to expected age norms. The terms hysterical aphonia, childhood aphasia, and developmental aphasia have been used to describe failure to develop or extreme difficulty in using language and speech as symptomatic of psychoses (Schroeder, Gordon, & Hawk, 1983). Other writers suggest that mutism occurs in childhood schizophrenia and early infantile autism (Kanner, 1975; Shirley, 1963).

Differential diagnosis is important in distinguishing between elective mutism and mutism owed to other disorders. In severe and profound mental retardation there may be a general inability to speak reflective of a pervasive developmental disorder and developmental language disorder. Rutter (1977) notes that where elective mutism is typically a "pure" emotional disorder, mutism may develop as a reaction to an underlying speech or language handicap. Kolvin and Fundudis (1981) report that 50% of the elective mute children identified in the Newcastle Epidemiological Study displayed immaturities of speech or other speech difficulties.

Several considerations are important in distinguishing elective mutism from the mutism of the child with a language disorder. The chronicity of the symptom and premorbid verbal facility are important in the differential diagnosis. The child with a developmental or congenital language disorder is more likely to have a history of atypical speech and language development, whereas the elective mute child frequently has normal speech and language development during preschool years (Richman & Eliason, 1983).

Another group of children who may appear to be elective mutes are children of families who have emigrated to a new country and who refuse to speak the new language (Bradley & Sloman, 1975). Elective mutism should usually be diagnosed only in those cases where comprehension of the new language is adequate but the refusal to speak persists.

According to the third edition of the *Diagnostic and Statistical Manual of Mental Disorders* (DSM-III; 1980), only in elective mutism is lack of speaking the predominant disturbance. General refusal to speak, as seen in some cases of major depression, avoidant disorder of childhood or adolescence, overanxious disorder, oppositional disorder, and social phobia, should not be diagnosed as such.

Elective or selective mutism as a childhood disorder was first described by Kussmaul in 1877 and later formally identified by Tramer (1934). The disorder is currently conceptualized as having the following features by the American Psychiatric Association (DSM-III, 1980):

1. The child continuously refuses to speak in almost all social situations, including school.

2. The child has the ability to speak and the ability to comprehend spoken language.

3. The problem is not due to another mental or physical disorder.

Hayden (1980) created four diagnostic categories of elective mutism based on a study of 68 children. These types include (1) symbiotic, characterized by a symbiotic relationship with a caretaker and a submissive but manipulative relationship with others; (2) speech phobia, characterized by fear of hearing one's own voice often accompanied by ritualistic behaviors; (3) reactive, characterized by withdrawal and depression possibly resulting from trauma; and (4) passive aggressive, characterized by hostile use of silence as a weapon. Although the information obtained in this study was not well standardized, an important finding was that there was a high prevalence of child physical and sexual abuse in all four groups.

Although there are few prevalence studies of this childhood disorder, some data currently available suggest that it is relatively rare. Morris (1963) reported an incidence of .4% of clinic cases and Salfield (1950) reported 1%. Existing incidence studies are not of the highest quality and these reported data cannot be trusted at this time. The number of treatment reports in the applied and clinical literature suggest that the disorder may be more prevalent than incidence data suggest. For example, Hayden (1980) and Sanok and Ascione (1979) suggest that many cases of elective mutism may go unreported because of the self-isolating nature of families of elective mute children, lack of acknowledgment of its severity, and general occurrence only in school situations. There is agreement that the disorder occurs most often in early childhood (5–7 years of age), is difficult to treat, and tends to be intractible over time (Kratochwill, 1981; Labbe & Williamson, 1984). The disorder is often accompanied by social withdrawal and even social skill deficits, but little research has focused on this aspect of the disorder.

There is a good deal of clinical literature in which there are reports of successful treatment; these studies have been reviewed in detail elsewhere (Friedman & Karagon, 1973; Kratochwill, 1981; Kratochwill, Brody, & Piersel, 1979; Labbe & Williamson, 1984; Sanok & Ascione, 1979). Both traditional dynamic therapy and behavior therapy treatment procedures have been employed with elective mute children.

Dynamic therapies have concentrated on the neurotic characteristics of elective mutism and usually involve insight-oriented therapy focusing on the child's personality structure. Traditional research and treatment programs have been in the form of descriptive and/or treatment case studies; they generally suggest a heterogeneous group of children (Koch & Goodlund, 1973). Common features include neurotic behaviors related to trauma experienced at critical times during speech development, with fixation occurring within the oral stage (Parker, Olsen, & Throckmorton, 1960; Salfield, 1950). Anxiety-related reactions to unfamiliar people or situations, including school and separation, suggest a fear-reduction function of mutism (Von Misch, 1952). Negative, insecure home environments also appear highly related to mutism, with the child engaged in a highly controlling, ambivalent, dependent relationship with his or her mother (Wright, 1968).

Diverse psychodynamic therapeutic interventions have been employed with electively mute children. Unfortunately, lack of specificity in treatment content and long-term therapeutic effectiveness make conclusive statements impossible. Clinically based individual therapies are documented in the literature with varying degrees of success (Arajarvi, 1965; Chethnik, 1973). Adams and Glasner (1954) described separate treatments using play and speech therapy with some concomitant psychotherapy. However, the course of treatment and follow-up were nonspecific and appeared ineffective.

In general, dynamically oriented therapists view mutism as symptomatic of family conflict (Von Misch, 1952; Weber, 1950). Long-term family therapies have been employed with some success (Browne, Wilson, & Laybourne, 1963; Elson, Pearson, Jones, & Schumacher, 1965; Pustrom & Speers, 1964). Similarly, individual psychotherapy with concurrent parental counseling has been the focus of treatment (Mora, Devault, & Schopler, 1962; Koch & Goodlund, 1973).

Although it remains difficult to identify the specific psychodynamic strategies that appear most effective in the treatment of elective mutism, a consistently identified theme is difficulty in treatment. This is especially reflected in the overall length of treatment (several months to several years), lack of generalization from the treatment setting (e.g., clinic) to the problem areas in the nat-ural environment where the mutism occurs (e.g., school), and lack of consistent follow-up and maintenance of results (Kratochwill, 1981; Kratochwill, Brody, & Piersel, 1979).

Behavior therapy treatment procedures have been divided into neomediational S-R or applied behavior analytic techniques. Although neomediational S-R procedures (e.g., systematic desensitization) have focused on purported anxiety components of the disorder, most specific treatment components within this area are operant treatment techniques (Kratochwill, 1981; Labbe & Williamson, 1984). The operant procedures can be broken down into the following categories: contingency management, stimulus fading with positive reinforcement, response initiation procedures including shaping, response cost, escape avoidance, and reinforcer sampling. Most studies have involved treatment packages in which several of these independent treatment techniques have been used in combination or successively across a treatment program.

Behavioral interventions used in the treatment of elective mutism generally have been shown to have positive results. However, a number of conceptual and methodological issues have been raised in the empirical research literature in this area. First, there has typically been little work focusing on the systematic link between assessment tactics and development of a treatment program. Second, there have been few standardized (in the procedural rather

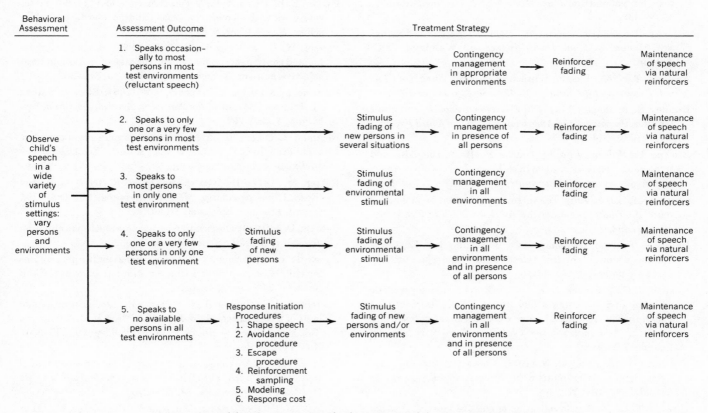

Assessment and therapeutic strategies for the treatment of elective mutism in children.

than psychometric sense) assessment and treatment procedures for dealing with elective mutism. In addition, many of the clinical outcome studies have a number of methodological limitations including inadequate experimental controls, definition of outcomes, and criteria that meet contemporary standards of good clinical research (Kratochwill, 1981).

Labbe and Williamson (1984) developed a conceptual framework for linking assessment and treatment (see Figure). Assessment involves direct measures of the child's speech in numerous settings (e.g., school, home, community) in the presence of various individuals (parents, teachers, peers). Treatment procedures are then linked to a possible assessment outcome. Five outcomes are possible: (1) the child speaks to most people in most situations, but with low frequency; (2) the child speaks to at least one person in all situations; (3) the child speaks to most persons, but only in one environment, (4) the child speaks to only one or a very few persons in only one environment: and (5) the child speaks to no one who is available for participation in a treatment program. As noted in the figure, various treatment procedures that have been developed in the operant literature are matched to the assessment outcomes that characterize the disorder.

REFERENCES

Adams, H. M., & Glasner, P. J. (1954). Emotional involvement in some form of mutism. *Journal of Speech & Hearing Disorders, 19,* 59–69.

American Psychiatric Association. (1980). *Diagnostic and Statistical Manual of Mental Disorders* (3rd ed.). Washington, DC: Author.

Arajarvi, T. (1965). Elective mutism in children. *Annals of Clinical Research of the Finnish Medical Society, 11,* 46–52.

Bradley, S., & Sloman, L. (1975). Elective mutism in immigrant families. *Journal of the American Academy of Child Psychiatry, 14,* 510–514.

Browne, E., Wilson, V., & Laybourne, P. (1963). Diagnosis and treatment of elective mutism in children. *Journal of the American Academy of Child Psychiatry, 2,* 605–617.

Chethik, M. (1973). Amy: The intensive treatment of an elective mute. *Journal of the American Academy of Child Psychiatry, 12,* 482–498.

Elson, A., Pearson, C., Jones, C. D., & Schumacher, E. (1965). Follow-up study of childhood elective mutism. *Archives of General Psychiatry, 13,* 182–187.

Etemad, J. G., & Szurek, S. A. (1973). Mutism among psychotic children. In S. A. Szurek & I. N. Berlin (Eds.), *Clinical studies in childhood psychoses: 25 years in collaborative treatment and research, the Langley Porter Children's Service.* New York: Brunner/Mazel.

Friedman, R., & Karagon, N. (1973). Characteristics and management of elective mutism in children. *Psychology in the Schools, 10,* 249–252.

Hayden, T. L. (1980). Classification of elective mutism. *Journal of the American Academy of Child Psychiatry, 19,* 118–133.

Heuger, M. G., & Morgenstern, M. (1927). Un cas to mutisme chez un enfant myopathique ancieu convulsif. Gverion dn. muttisme par la psychoanalyse. *L'Encephale, 22,* 478–481.

Kanner, L. (1975). *Child psychiatry.* (3rd. ed.) Springfield, IL: Thomas.

Koch, M., & Goodlund, L. (1973). Children who refuse to talk: A follow-up study. *Bulletin of the Bell Museum of Pathology, 2,* 30–32.

Kolvin, I., & Fundudis, T. (1981). Elective mute children: Psychological development and background factors. *Journal of Child Psychology & Psychiatry, 22,* 219–232.

Kratochwill, T. R. (1981). *Selective mutism: Implications for research and treatment.* Hillsdale, NJ: Erlbaum.

Kratochwill, T. R., Brody, G. H., & Piersel, W. C. (1979). Elective mutism in children: A review of treatment and research. In B. B. Lahey & A. E. Kazdin (Eds.), *Advances in clinical child psychology* (Vol. 2, pp. 193–240). New York: Plenum.

Labbe, E. E., & Williamson, D. A. (1984). Behavioral treatment of elective mutism: A review of the literature. *Clinical Psychology Review, 4,* 273–292.

Lerea, L., & Ward, B. (1965). Speech avoidance among children with oral-communication defects. *Journal of Psychology, 60,* 265–270.

Mora, G., Devault, S., & Schopler, E. (1962). Dynamics and psychotherapy of identical twins with elective mutism. *Journal of Child Psychology & Psychiatry, 3,* 41–52.

Morris, J. V. (1963). Cases of elective mutism. *American Journal of Mental Deficiency, 57,* 661–668.

Parker, E. B., Olsen, T. F., & Throckmorton, M. C. (1960). Social case work with elementary school children who do not talk in school. *Social Work, 5,* 64–70.

Piersel, W. C., & Kratochwill, T. R. (1981). A teacher-implemented contingency management package to assess and treat selective mutism. *Behavioral Assessment, 3,* 371–382.

Pustrom, E., & Pustrom, E., Spears, R. W. (1964). Elective mutism in children. *Journal of the American Academy of Child Psychiatry, 3,* 287–297.

Richman, L. C., & Eliason, M. (1983). Communication disorders of children. In C. E. Walker & M. C. Roberts (Eds.), *Handbook of clinical child psychology* (pp. 697–722). New York: Wiley.

Rutter, M. (1977). Delayed speech. In M. Rutter & L. Hersov (Eds.), *Child psychiatry: Modern approaches* (pp. 688–716). Oxford, England: Blackwell Scientific.

Salfield, D. J. (1950). Observations in elective mutism in children. *Journal of Mental Science, 96,* 1024–1032.

Sanok, R. L., & Ascione, F. R. (1979). Behavioral interventions for childhood elective mutism: An evaluative review. *Child Behavior Therapy, 1,* 49–68.

Schroeder, C. S., Gordon, B. N., & Hawk, B. (1983). Clinical problems of the preschool child. In C. E. Walker & M. C. Roberts, (Eds.), *Handbook of clinical child psychology* (pp. 296–334). New York: Wiley.

Scott, E. (1977). A desensitization program for the treatment of mutism in a 7-year-old girl: A case report. *Journal of Child Psychology & Psychiatry, 18,* 263–270.

Shirley, H. F. (1963). *Pediatric psychiatry.* Cambridge, MA: Harvard University Press.

Tramer, M. (1934). Electiver mutismus bei Kindern. Z. *Kinderpsychiatric, 1*, 30–55. In E. Postrum & R. W. Speers (1964). Elective mutism in children. *Journal of American Academy of Child Psychiatry, 3*, 287–297.

Treuper, J. (1897). Ein knabe mit sprechhemmunger auf psychopathischer grundlage. *Zeitschrift fur Kinderfehler, 5*, 138–143.

Von Misch, A. (1952). Elektiver mutismus in kindersalter. *Zietschrift fuer Kinderpsychiatrie, 19*, 49–87.

Waternik, J., & Vedder, R. (1936). Einige faelle von thymogenem nutismus bu sehr jungen kindern und seine behandlung. *Zeitschrift Kinderforsch. 45*(Suppl.), 368–369.

Weber, A. (1950). Zum elektiven mutisums der kinder. *Zietschrift fuer Kinderpsychiatrie, 17*, 1–15.

Wright, H. L. (1968). A clinical study of children who refuse to talk in school. *Journal of the American Academy of Child Psychiatry, 7*, 603–617.

Thomas R. Kratochwill
Sylvia Z. Ramirez
Susan M. Sheridan
*University of Wisconsin,
Madison*

**ELECTIVE MUTISM
LANGUAGE DEFICIENCIES AND DEFICITS
SPEECH, ABSENCE OF**

MUTISM, ELECTIVE

See ELECTIVE MUTISM.

MYKLEBUST, HELMER R. (1910–   )

Helmer Myklebust received his BA in 1933 from Augusta College, MA in the psychology of deafness in 1935 from Gallaudet College, and a MA in clinical psychology in 1942 from Temple University in Philadelphia. He then went on to receive his EdD in psychology and guidance in 1945 from Rutgers University. Myklebust also completed several postdoctoral studies in mental retardation and clinical psychology, neurology, and psychoanalysis.

In 1948 Myklebust developed the Institute for Language Disorders at Northwestern University. With an interdisciplinary staff of ophthalmologists, pediatricians, neurologists, and otolaryngologists, research was conducted on the diagnosis and definition of language disorders in children. Myklebust coined the term language pathology, which gave emphasis to the aphasias and dyslexias, which, in turn, served as a foundation for the development of the concept of learning disabilities.

Myklebust also developed the first graduate training program in learning disabilities and organized a systematic approach to observing the behavioral impact (behavioral symptomatology) of deafness, brain dysfunction, mental retardation, and emotional disturbance.

Helmer R. Myklebust

His principal publications include *Auditory Disorders in Children, A Manual for Differential Diagnosis* (1954) (the most complete statement of his behavioral symptomatological approach to the differential diagnosis of handicaps in young children) and *The Psychology of Deafness: Sensory Deprivation, Learning and Adjustment* (1960), which addressed evidence of the psychological consequences of early life deafness (cognitive, personality, social, language, and motor).

Myklebust was editor of and contributor to *Progress in Learning Disabilities* (1968–1983), five volumes that address the relationship between brain dysfunctions and learning—neurologic, psychologic, and educational. He has written numerous book chapters and over 130 journal articles, and has received many awards and honorary degrees. He continues to work on a third volume on development and disorders of writing in children because he believes "that we have only begun to think about the importance of ability to write, normal and abnormal, and its role in intellectual development, illiteracy, and in all aspects of special education" (personal communication, August 1985).

REFERENCES

Myklebust, H. R. (1954). *Auditory disorders in children, A manual for differential diagnosis* New York: Grune & Stratton.

Myklebust, H. R. (1967). *Psychology of deafness: Sensory deprivation, learning and adjustment.* New York: Grune & Stratton.

Myklebust, H. R. (Ed.). (1968–1983). *Progress in learning disabilities* (Vols. 1–5). New York: Grune & Stratton.

Elaine Fletcher-Janzen
Texas A&M University

MYOPIA

See VISUAL IMPAIRMENT.

N

NARCOLEPSY

Narcolepsy is a psychiatric disorder characterized by an abnormal need to sleep during the day along with pathological episodic attacks of REM sleep. Symptoms include sleep paralysis, cataplexy, and hypnogogic hallucinations. In the past, this disorder also has been referred to as Friedmann's disease and as Gelineau syndrome.

Narcoleptic attacks typically come at predictable times during the day; e.g., postprandial drowsiness is especially common among narcoleptics after they have ingested meals high in protein. The narcoleptic attacks are typically irresistible. The patient with narcolepsy is an individual who will usually be able to fall asleep easily at night but who may have trouble remaining asleep.

Age of onset for narcolepsy is typically in the late teens or early twenties. The symptoms may be controlled with medication, but the condition usually persists throughout adult life. The prevalence of the disorder is estimated to be 4/10,000, with males and females equally affected (Kaplan & Sadock, 1981).

Cataplexy occurs in the majority of cases of narcolepsy. Cataplexy refers to sudden transient loss of muscle tone in the trunk or extremities. It is often triggered by strong emotions, either positive or negative. During cataplexy, the afflicted individual is still conscious but is rendered totally immobile. Most narcoleptics can remember the events that occurred during the period of cataplexy.

Sleep paralysis also occurs in many cases of narcolepsy. It is somewhat rarer than cataplexy and typically occurs as the narcoleptic individual falls off to sleep or just as he or she is emerging from sleep. It is a frightening experience in which the individual finds himself or herself awake but unable to move.

The diagnosis of narcolepsy is typically established by documenting sleep-onset REM periods in an all-night polysomnogram or by multiple sleep latency testing. The polysomnograms of some narcoleptics will reveal significant sleep apnea and sleep related myoclonus (Gregory & Smeltzer, 1983).

Genetic studies have demonstrated a strong genetic loading for this disorder. The etiology is still not fully understood. Treatment with tricyclic antidepressants may sometimes be useful. Imipramine is the tricyclic that has been most studied. In addition, amphetamines and methylphenidate have been used in the treatment of narcolepsy.

REFERENCES

Gregory, I., & Smeltzer, D. J. (1983). *Psychiatry*. Boston; Little, Brown.

Kaplan, H. I., & Sadock, D. J. (1981). *Modern synoposis of comprehensive textbook of psychiatry*. Baltimore, MD: Williams & Wilkins.

DANNY WEDDING
Marshall University

NASH, CHARLES E. (1875–1953)

Charles Emerson (Ted) Nash served as a teacher at the Training School at Vineland, New Jersey, from 1898 to 1923, and as the institution's superintendent from 1923 until his death in 1953. A talented teacher and inspirational leader, Nash was a mainstay of the Training School during the years of growth to its preeminent position in the field of mental retardation.

Charles E. Nash

REFERENCES

Commemorative issue: Charles Emerson Nash. (1948). *Training School Bulletin, 45*, 134–153.

Honoring Charles Emerson Nash. (1953). *Training School Bulletin, 50*, 31–37.

PAUL IRVINE
Katonah, New York

NASH, WILLIAM R. (1943–   )

William R. Nash, a native of Cincinnati, earned his BA in psychology (1965) and MEd in education (1967) at Georgia Southern College. He went on to the University of Georgia, where his mentor was E. Paul Torrance, earning the EdD in educational psychology in 1971. He joined the faculty of the Department of Educational Psychology at Texas A&M University (TAMU) in 1972. Nash is now a professor in that department, where he also serves as director of the TAMU Institute for the Gifted and Talented.

Nash's professional interests and most significant writings have centered around education for the gifted and talented and creative thinking skills. Most recently, he contributed to a major work that attempts to provide more conceptual guidance to the field (Haensly, Reynolds, & Nash, 1986). Of greater significance has been Nash's contribution to advocacy and political activity on behalf of gifted children. Nash has served the National Association for Gifted Children (NAGC) in nearly every available elective office including each of the vice presidencies and the presidency. He also has served as a consultant to numerous school districts on matters related to educational programs for the gifted and talented and also to other noteworthy organizations such as the Sid W. Richardson Foundation and the Texas Scottish Rite Hospital. Nash is a frequently sought speaker for state meetings and conferences on the gifted.

In addition to these activities, Nash has acted as mentor to a number of gifted adolescents. Many of his doctoral students have gone on to become leaders in their fields, often aspiring to leadership positions in NAGC, taking faculty positions at a variety of universities, and establishing other institutes for the gifted and talented throughout the country.

REFERENCE

Haensly, P., Reynolds, C. R., & Nash, W. R. (1986). Giftedness: Coalescence, context, conflict, and commitment. In R. J. Sternberg & J. Davidson (Eds.), *Conceptions of giftedness*. New York: Cambridge University Press.

CECIL R. REYNOLDS
Texas A&M University

NATIONAL ASSOCIATION FOR GIFTED CHILDREN
TORRANCE, E. PAUL

NATIONAL ADVISORY COMMITTEE ON HANDICAPPED CHILDREN AND YOUTH

The National Advisory Committee on Handicapped Children and Youth was authorized in Section 604 of Public Law 98-199:

> Amendments with respect to the Advisory Committee on the Education of Handicapped Children and Youth, National Advisory Committee on Handicapped Children and Youth
>
> Sec., 4. Section 604 of the act is amended to read as follows: National Advisory Committee on the Education of Handicapped Children and Youth.
>
> Sec. 604.(a) The secretary shall establish in the Department of Education a national advisory committee on the education of handicapped children and youth, consisting of 15 members, appointed by the secretary. Not less than five such members shall be parents of handicapped children and the remainder shall be handicapped persons (including students), persons affiliated with education, training, or research programs for the handicapped, and those having demonstrated a commitment to the education of handicapped children.
>
> (b) The advisory committee shall review the administration and operation of the programs authorized by this act and other provisions of the law administered by the secretary with respect to handicapped children (including the effect of such programs on improving the educational attainment of such children) and make recommendations for the improvement of such programs. Such recommendations shall take into consideration experience gained under this and other federal programs for handicapped children and, to the extent appropriate, experience gained under other public and private programs for handicapped children. The advisory committee may make such recommendations to the secretary as the committee considers appropriate and shall make an annual report of its findings and recommendations to the secretary not later than June 30 of each year. The Secretary shall transmit each such report,

William R. Nash

together with comments and recommendations, to the Congress.

(c) There are authorized to be appropriated for the purpose of this section $200,000 for fiscal year 1984, and for each of the two succeeding fiscal years.

Although funds were authorized to provide for the establishment of this committee, funds have never been appropriated. Consequently, this committee has never met and its membership has not been noted. It is possible that the administration has not used existing funds to create this committee out of concern that the committee would assume oversight responsibility for the programs operated by the department.

MARTY ABRAMSON
University of Wisconsin, Stout

NATIONAL ASSOCIATION FOR GIFTED CHILDREN (NAGC)

The National Association for Gifted Children (NAGC) was founded in 1954. It is comprised of 5000 members with 20 regional groups. The NAGC caters to teachers, librarians, university personnel, administrators, and parents. Through these and other interested individuals, the NAGC pursues the further education of the gifted. Through its efforts, the NAGC hopes to enhance children's potential for creativity and individual thought.

The NAGC provides teachers and parents with information focusing on the development of the gifted child through such publications as *Gifted Child, Quarterly*. The NAGC usually holds its annual convention in October or November.

MARY LEON PEERY
Texas A&M University

NATIONAL ASSOCIATION FOR RETARDED CITIZENS

The National Association for Retarded Citizens, commonly referred to as the ARC, is the largest volunteer organization solely devoted to improving the welfare of all children and adults with mental retardation. The association also provides services to parents and other individuals, organizations, and communities for jointly solving problems related to retardation.

Founded in 1950, and currently structured around 1300 state and local member affiliates (units), the ARC maintains a national organizational membership of 160,000 individuals. Created essentially as a grass roots organiza-

tion, the ARC's membership is comprised of people with mental retardation, parents and other family members, and advocates and professionals who work with this population.

The ARC's mission is to provide the more than 6 million Americans who are mentally retarded or who may possess other disabilities with services, employment, training, education, and opportunities for independent living. Prominent among the association's goals are:

Allowing greater numbers of people with mental retardation to live in the community through group homes and an improved social service system.

Advocating increased funding of public programs and services needed by individuals with mental retardation.

Reducing the incidence of mental retardation through the implementation of known methods of prevention.

Establishing effective advocacy systems throughout the country to ensure that the legal rights of all persons with mental retardation are protected.

Achieving appropriate, free public educational opportunities, including preschool, continuing education, and compensatory and transitional programming for mentally retarded children, youths, and adults.

Increasing employment opportunities for persons who are mentally retarded.

Improving public understanding and acceptance of mental retardation.

A nonprofit organization largely supported by individual memberships and corporate contributions, the ARC's national headquarters are located in Arlington, Texas.

REFERENCE

Association for Retarded Citizens. (1985). *ARCFACTS*. Arlington, TX: Author.

GEORGE JAMES HAGERTY
Stonehill College

NATIONAL ASSOCIATION FOR THE DEAF (NAD)

The National Association for the Deaf (NAD) was founded in 1880. It has 18,000 members and 50 state groups. The NAD is open to all deaf adults and interested individuals. The objectives of the organization are the promotion of legislation and the protection of civil rights for the deaf in the areas of employment, communications, and citizenship.

In addition to maintaining a speaker's bureau and a legal defense fund, NAD conducts and supports programs offering educational opportunities, vocational training, rehabilitative services, mental health services, and research. It serves as a clearinghouse for information on deafness and acts as a liaison for other handicapped people and organizations. Programs include communications skills, nationwide professional training for instructors of manual communication, and training of the undereducated and disadvantaged deaf in the Washington area.

Publications include *Broadcast* (a newspaper), *Deaf American* (a magazine), and various textbooks concerning American Sign Language, manual communication systems, and all other aspects of deafness. The NAD is affiliated with the World Federation of the Deaf.

RICK GONZALES
Texas A&M University

NATIONAL ASSOCIATION OF SCHOOL PSYCHOLOGISTS (NASP)

Formed in 1969, the National Association of School Psychologists (NASP) is a 9000-member strong professional association. The NASP was formed because many practicing school psychologists saw a need for uniform credentialing of school psychologists, a national identity for the profession of school psychology, a vehicle for communication among school psychologists, and a means for influencing legislation and regulations related to the delivery of school psychological services. The founding members of NASP believed the American Psychological Association (APA) to be unresponsive to the needs of practicing school psychologists, most of whom possessed degrees beneath the doctoral level and who were, therefore, not eligible for membership in APA. In addition, the NASP members believed APA emphasized scientific/academic issues and wanted a national organization that emphasized issues of more immediate concern to practitioners. The four stated purposes of the new organization were (1) to actively promote the interests of school psychology; (2) to advance the standards of the profession; (3) to help secure the conditions necessary to the greatest effectiveness of its practice; and (4) to serve the mental health and educational interests of all children and youths (Farling & Agner, 1979).

The NASP showed phenomenal growth during its first 15 years. True to its name, membership today is overwhelmingly comprised of practicing school psychologists. Approximately 70% of its practitioner members received training at the specialist level (60 semester hours) or higher, with 20% holding doctoral degrees. Approximately 90% of the practitioner members are employed by public schools (Reschly & Genshaft, 1986).

The NASP has been at the forefront of many issues affecting handicapped students. Its input has shaped numerous federal and state laws, including PL 94-142 (Rights of All Handicapped Children Act of 1975). It works in partnership with national education and special education groups to influence legislation and regulations affecting schoolchildren. The NASP has published position papers and adopted resolutions relating to nondiscriminatory assessment, parental rights in child evaluations, corporal punishment, and other issues relevant to the education of all students. The organization has a governmental and professional relations committee that provides information and technical assistance to a network of affiliated state school psychology associations. Its Social Issues Committee vigorously advocates for children's rights, cosponsoring a major international conference on the psychological abuse of children in 1983.

A primary objective of the NASP has been the promotion of high-quality professional practice. Toward this objective, the NASP, as a constituent member of the National Council for Accreditation of Teacher Education (NCATE), accredits school psychology training programs at the specialist and doctoral levels. Also, the NASP strives to meet its members' professional development needs. Members receive a monthly newsletter, the *Communique*, as well as an excellent, highly regarded professional journal, *School Psychology Review*. The NASP's Publication Committee is responsible for disseminating many additional NASP publications, including textbooks and reference books. Approximately 2000 persons attended the 1986 annual NASP convention, an important continuing education opportunity provided to school psychologists.

To accommodate and support members' special interets,the NASP sponsors the following active interest groups: urban, rural, preschool, vocational, social-emotional assessment and intervention, and families. These groups publish their own newsletters and hold symposiums at the annual convention.

In its short history, the NASP has had a large impact on the delivery of school psychology services. In partnership with other professional groups, including the Council for Exceptional Children and APA, it strives to improve the mental health and learning of school-age children.

REFERENCES

Farling, W. H., & Agner, J. (1979). History of the National Association of School Psychologists: The first decade. *School Psychology Digest, 8*, 140–152.

Reschly, D. J., & Genshaft, J. (1986, April). *Preliminary report: Survey of NASP leadership and practitioner members on selected issues.* Ames: Iowa State University.

JAN N. HUGHES
Texas A&M University

AMERICAN PSYCHOLOGICAL ASSOCIATION

NATIONAL ASSOCIATION OF STATE BOARDS OF EDUCATION (NASBE)

The National Association of State Boards of Education, popularly recognized as NASBE, is a nonprofit membership organization dedicated to providing programs and services for the leadership development of members of state boards of education. Throughout the 50 states and 7 U.S. territories, over 600 citizen-volunteers provide policy direction to public education through their appointment to the state board. These officials set standards for instruction, student performance, textbook content, high-school graduation, and teacher training and certification. As important state decision makers, they affect the educational experiences of America's 40 million students.

Founded in 1959, NASBE's principal objectives are state leadership in education policy making; promoting excellence in education for all students; advocating equality of access to educational opportunity; and ensuring the responsible lay governance of public education.

NASBE serves as a national voice, professional forum, and direct-service provider for its membership of state policy makers. Through a diversity of association activities, the NASBE offers state board members skill training in policy formulation and organizational management; research, information, and technical assistance pertinent to current and emerging national education issues; and liaison with federal and state officials (including executive and legislative branch representatives) and a broad spectrum of other national education organizations.

Located in Alexandria, Virginia, NASBE has two affiliated bodies that serve the unique informational and training needs of related professionals who serve state board members: the Conference of State Board Attorneys and the Association of Executive Secretaries to State Boards of Education.

REFERENCE

National Association of State Boards of Education. (1985). *Policy making for excellence and equity*. Alexandria, VA: Author.

GEORGE JAMES HAGERTY
Stonehill College

NATIONAL ASSOCIATION OF STATE DIRECTORS OF SPECIAL EDUCATION (NASDSE)

The National Association of State Directors of Special Education (NASDSE) is an independent, nonprofit membership organization designed to serve the informational and professional needs of the chief administrators of special education at the state level.

Founded in 1938, NASDSE provides state directors of special education and related state education agency staff with information on national trends and activities; in-service training in program administration and policy development; and technical assistance in implementing programs at the state and local levels. Additionally, the association serves as the national representative for state directors of special education and their state agency colleagues, advocating on behalf of NASDSE membership before federal and state-level deliberative bodies and decision makers (including legislative and executive branch officials and commissions). NASDSE maintains a close affiliation with other national professional and advocacy organizations in order to effectively represent the positions and interests of the association members and to address the broader needs and interests of the special education community.

NASDSE is governed by a board of directors elected from the general membership of 57 state directors of special education (representing all 50 states and 7 U.S. territories). With its offices located in Washington, DC, NASDSE serves as an important resource for improving state capabilities in administering the array of federal special education program and funding requirements. The organization also serves as a central vehicle for state administrators of special education programs to identify collectively and address, in a national forum, current and emerging issues and concerns.

REFERENCE

National Association of State Directors of Special Education. (1986). *NASDSE: Its mission, programs and activities*. Washington, DC: Author.

GEORGE JAMES HAGERTY
Stonehill College

**ADMINISTRATION OF SPECIAL EDUCATION
SUPERVISION IN SPECIAL EDUCATION**

NATIONAL CENTER, EDUCATIONAL MEDIA AND MATERIALS FOR THE HANDICAPPED

The National Center, Educational Media and Materials for the Handicapped facilitated the production and distribution of instructional media and materials designed for use in the special education of handicapped students. The center was founded in 1972 and had a staff of seven under the direction of Thomas M. Stephens. The center developed instructional management systems; conducted in-service training workshops and conferences; and provided individualized instruction to teachers on media and materials for handicapped students. The center published the journal *The Directive Teacher* semiannually along with texts, teacher materials, and bibliographies. This project's funding was discontinued. Materials can be obtained from National Center, Educational Media and Materials for the Handicapped, 354 Arps Hall, 1945 W. High Street, Ohio State University, Columbus, OH 43210.

DANIEL R. PAULSON
University of Wisconsin, Stout

NATIONAL COUNCIL FOR ACCREDITATION OF TEACHER EDUCATION (NCATE)

The National Council for Accreditation of Teacher Education (NCATE) was founded in 1954 to establish a national body for uniform application of standards in teacher preparation. The primary activities of the NCATE are at present the development and promulgation of standards for and review and accreditation of college and university programs for the preparation of all teachers and other professional school personnel at the elementary and secondary levels. The NCATE is the only appropriately credentialed organization to conduct such activities on a national level. It is authorized by the Council on Postsecondary Accreditation (COPA) to adopt standards and procedures for accreditation and to determine the accreditation status of institutional programs engaged in the basic and advanced preparation of professional school personnel. The NCATE is also recognized as the appropriate accrediting body in educational preparation by the U.S. Department of Education.

Controversy occasionally arises in some areas of professional preparation. In the field of school psychology, for example, there is an apparent dual responsibility for accreditation. The American Psychological Association is authorized to accredit doctoral training programs in the recognized professional specialty areas of psychology, including clinical, counseling, and school psychology. The NCATE also accredits such programs whenever they are housed in a college of education, as is typically the case in a department of educational psychology. An interorganizational committee is currently working to resolve these and related issues.

The purpose of NCATE accreditation is fourfold:

1. To assure the public that particular institutions offer programs for teachers and professional school personnel that meet national standards of quality.
2. To ensure that children and youths attending school are served by well and appropriately trained personnel.
3. To advance the teaching profession through the improvement of preparation programs.
4. To provide a practical basis for reciprocity among

the states in certifying professional school personnel.

The NCATE's efforts have been largely successful to this point. Most major institutions of higher learning that offer teacher and related personnel programs adhere to the NCATE standards.

The NCATE offers accreditation in special education and in most of the related service categories as well, including school psychology, educational diagnosis, and school counseling. Any school that offers a 4-year or more degree in education or a related field is eligible for an evaluation for accreditation by the NCATE provided the school is approved by its appropriate state agency, has obtained the appropriate regional accreditation, is an equal opportunity, nondiscriminatory employer, and has graduated a sufficient number of students from its program to allow for an evaluation of the quality of the preparation. The specific standards for NCATE accreditations are revised frequently as are application procedures. Institutions, associations, societies, or individuals seeking to obtain more detailed information about the NCATE, its standards, or the accreditation process should contact the Director, NCATE, 1919 Pennsylvania Avenue, NW, Suite 202, Washington, DC 20006.

CECIL R. REYNOLDS
Texas A&M University

NATIONAL EASTER SEAL SOCIETY

Founded in 1919 by a concerned Ohio businessman in cooperation with Rotary Clubs, this voluntary health care agency has also been known as the National Society for Crippled Children and Adults. Societies at the national, state (multistate), and local level are administered by volunteer boards of directors. The society is the oldest and largest organization providing direct services to people with disabilities. Research grants are awarded by the society.

Direct services are available to any person with a disability resulting from any cause including disease, illness, injury, or accident. Services are provided on an ability to pay basis but no individual is refused service because of financial limitation. Services include physical, occupational, and speech-language therapies; vocational evaluation and training; camping and recreation; and psychological counseling to gain maximum independence. Services to children include preschool training, health screening, and speech-language therapies. The society serves in an advocacy role to obtain equal rights for all disabled persons. Contacts with federal, state, and local governments focus on the elimination of environmental barriers, the creation of positive attitudes, and an increased recognition of individual abilities. A governmental affairs office is maintained in Washington, DC, for lobbying activities on behalf of the disabled. National headquarters is located at 2023 West Ogden Avenue, Chicago, IL 60612.

PHILIP R. JONES
*Virginia Polytechnic Institute
and State University*

NATIONAL EDUCATION ASSOCIATION (NEA)

Founded in 1857 as the National Teacher Association, the current name, National Education Association (NEA), was adopted in 1876. The NEA is the largest professional organization or union of teachers; it has a membership in excess of 1.6 million. Membership includes elementary and secondary school teachers, college and university professors, counselors, and others concerned with education. Administrative and supervisory personnel may or may not be included in membership depending on the nature of employee relations and the labor laws of a given state. Over 10,000 local units are organized into 53 state groups.

The organization, while advocating for improved education for all children and young adults, including the handicapped has a primary interest in the rights and welfare of teachers. A strong governmental relations unit maintains constant vigilance in promoting education in Congress. A strong political action network supports congressional efforts. The association also endorses candidates for national office. Interest in professional development results in a variety of in-service training activities and materials. A number of constituent divisions and affiliates include classroom teachers, college and university personnel, junior college personnel, and a student NEA. The NEA holds a large annual convention and publishes a journal and other relevant publications. The NEA headquarters is located at 1201 Sixteenth Street, NW, Washington, DC 20036.

PHILIP R. JONES
*Virginia Polytechnic Institute
and State University*

NATIONAL ENDOWMENT FOR THE HUMANITIES (NEH)

In 1965 Congress put forth the National Foundation on the Arts and Humanities Act for the advancement of scholarship and progress in the arts and humanities in the United States. This act created the National Endowment for the Humanities (NEH) as a grant-making agency of the federal government that supports research, education, scholarship, and public programs in the humanities. According to the 1965 act, the term humanities includes many disciplines: archaeology; comparative religion; the theory, history, and criticism of the arts; modern and classical languages; literature; linguistics; history; philosophy; jurisprudence; ethics; social sciences (those aspects that include humanistic content and use humanistic methods); and areas that study and apply the humanities to the present conditions of national life. Thus the National Endowment for the Humanities supports work that promotes knowledge in all the subject areas encompassing the humanities, complementing local and private efforts by increasing nonfederal aid for high-quality projects.

The NEH poses as its two requirements for funding that works be significant to learning in the humanities and that theory and concept be exemplary and likely to succeed. Support is expressed in many forms: fellowships and stipends for research and study; opportunities for individuals to share and discuss research; summer seminar programs and institutes for high-school and college teachers in their subject areas; radio and television programs; reading and discussion groups in libraries; interpretive museum exhibitions; panels and symposiums composed of humanities scholars addressing general audiences about important works in their respective fields; scholarly publications such as bibliographies, dictionaries, atlases, encyclopedias, translations, and editions of major texts; archaeological explorations in the United States and abroad; and courses and materials necessary for the promotion of liberal arts in undergraduate education. The NEH does not fund projects or research outside the aforementioned fields, study or research in pursuit of an academic degree (except the Faculty Graduate Study Program for Historically Black Colleges and Universities), political, ideological, religious, or partisan works, training in the arts, or works of art. Currently, the Endowment is requesting proposals for projects involving the bicentennial of the U.S. Constitution and the 500th anniversary of Christopher Columbus's arrival in the New World.

To help support the financial base of national museums, libraries, cultural organizations, and other institutions, grants are made through five divisions—Education Programs, Fellowships and Seminars, General Programs, Research Programs, and State Programs—and two offices, the office of Challenge Grants and the Office of Preservation. Two additional agencies provide assistance to American art and artists and to museums; respectively, the National Endowment for the Arts and the Institute of Museum Services. To apply, an organization or individual submits a project proposal to any of the Endowment's programs. The application is assessed by persons outside the Endowment, any of 1000 scholars and professionals in the humanities who serve on 150 panels, for quality. After peer review, the endowment staff selects the projects that will be recommended for funding. The chairman of the Endowment, who is appointed by the president of the United States for a 4-year term, is responsible for the final designation of awards. He or she is advised by a board of 26 private citizens who serve 6-year terms (also nominated by the president), the National Council on the Humanities. This council also recognizes yearly the highest official honor the federal government bestows for intellectual achievement in the humanities, the Jefferson Lecture. Established by the Endowment in 1972, the lecture is delivered in the spring and provides an opportunity for an outstanding scholar to present issues of concern in the humanities. This forum is open to professionals, scholars, and the general public. Past Jefferson lecturers have include Saul Bellow, Erik Eriksen, John Hope Franklin, Paul Freund, Gerald Holton, Edward Shils, Barbara Tuchman, Jaroslav Pelikan, Lionel Trilling, Townsend Bermeule, Robert Penn Warren, and C. Vann Woodward.

Through its Public Affairs Office, the NEH publishes a variety of materials. A bimonthly review of current work and theory in the humanities is offered in *Humanities*, available from the U.S. Government Printing Office. The NEH also publishes an *Annual Report, The Columbian Quincentenary, The Bicentennial of the U.S. Constitution, Special Programs for Historically Black Colleges and Universities*, and *Support for Museums and Historical Organizations*, all available at no cost from the Public Affairs Office.

MARY LEON PEERY
Texas A&M University

NATIONAL FEDERATION OF THE BLIND (NFB)

Founded in 1940, the National Federation of the Blind (NFB) is the largest organization of the blind in America; it claims over 10% of the blind as members. Sighted persons may also join. State level units exist in every state, and local chapters are organized in larger communities. Members not able to affiliate with a local chapter are considered at large. Membership levels include associate, contributing, supporting, sponsoring, sustaining, and president's club, based on amount of dues paid.

The major purpose of NFB is the complete integration of the blind into society on the basis of equality. Objectives include removal of legal, economic, and social discrimination; education of the public; and achievement by all blind individuals of the right to exercise to the fullest their talents and capacities. The organization provides for joint action by the blind and provides an avenue for the blind to advocate on behalf of themselves.

The NFB serves as an information center and referral service on blindness for the blind, the newly blinded, and the public at large. Legislative affairs receive major attention at the state and federal level both in lobbying and subsequent dissemination of information programs and services available to the blind. Major emphasis is also devoted to job opportunities and protection of rights for the

constituency. A monthly news and issues publication is produced in braille and record form and is available to all blind individuals without cost. The annual convention is the largest gathering of the blind in the world, with over 2500 in attendance. The NFB offices are located at 1800 Johnson Street, Baltimore, MD 21230.

PHILIP R. JONES
*Virginia Polytechnic Institute
and State University*

NATIONAL HEAD INJURY FOUNDATION (NHIF)

The National Head Injury Foundation (NHIF) was founded in 1980, it was the first national organization to advocate for head-injured persons and their families. Annually 700,000 persons with head injuries require hospitalization. Between 50,000 and 90,000 of these suffer intellectual or behavioral deficits that preclude return to normal life. Approximately two-thirds of these individuals are under 30 years of age. While most head injuries result from accidents (mostly automobile), similar abnormalities arise from encephalitis, cerebral hemorrhage, and oxygen deprivation to the brain (NHIF, 1980).

Foundation concerns cover a broad spectrum of services. Specific goals are to serve disabled individuals who were normal prior to injury; foster research in treatment; provide legal information and resources; list facilities for acute, intermediate, and long-term care; develop support networks; and institute hot line contact for persons in need. Additionally, the foundation seeks financial support for patients; cognitive, behavioral, and vocational retraining; appropriate residential facilities; and recreational/social support (Gruber & Cloyd, 1985). Services offered include training seminars for professionals; grants to chapters; clinicians' awards; speaker's bureau; media library; and phone information for head-injured families and professionals.

There are 21 state groups totaling 10,000 members. Subcommittees are Acute Neurotrauma Task Force; Insurance Task Force; Legal and Financial Planning; Prevention Study Groups; and Special Education Task Force. Publications include a newsletter, an annual report, and a resource directory for head injury rehabilitation services. Headquarters are 18A Vernon Street, Framingham, MA 01701.

REFERENCES

Gruber, K., & Cloyd, I. (Eds.). (1985). *Encyclopedia of associations. Vol. 1. National Organizations of the U.S.* (20th ed.) Detroit, MI: Gale Research.

National Head Injury Foundation. (1980). *Pamphlet*. Framingham, MA: Author.

C. MILDRED TASHMAN
College of St. Rose

NATIONAL INFORMATION CENTER FOR HANDICAPPED CHILDREN AND YOUTH (NICHCY)

The National Information Center for Handicapped Children and Youth (NICHCY) is a project for the development and dissemination of free information relating to educational rights of and special services available to the handicapped. The NICHCY also provides technical assistance to parents, educators, advocates, and others. It answers individual questions, provides advice to groups, and connects people with available services and agencies for improving the lives of the handicapped (National Information Center for Handicapped Children and Youth, undated).

The NICHCY publishes *News Digest* four times a year and *Transition Summary* twice a year to share the experiences of individuals in resolving problems facing the handicapped. It also distributes timely fact sheets.

The organization was founded in 1970 as the National Special Education Information Center. It was later known as the National Information Center for the Handicapped and, in 1982, as Closer Look—Parents' Campaign for Handicapped Children and Youth. The organization's current status was established as part of the Education of the Handicapped Act (PL 94-142 as amended by PL 98-199). It is funded by the U.S. Department of Education, Office of Special Education and Rehabilitative Services, Special Education Programs.

REFERENCE

National Information Center for Handicapped Children and Youth. (Undated brochure). *National Information Center for Handicapped Children and Youth.* Washington, DC: Author.

DOUGLAS L. FRIEDMAN
Fordham University

SPECIAL NET

NATIONAL INSTITUTE OF EDUCATION (NIE)

Founded in 1972, the National Institute of Education's mission was to promote educational equity and to improve the quality of educational practice. In carrying out this mission, the NIE supported research and dissemination activities that were designed to help individuals regardless of race, age, sex, economic status, ethnic origin, or handicapping condition, and to realize their full potential through education.

Support for research was organized in three main program areas: (1) teaching and learning, (2) educational policy and organization, and (3) dissemination and improvement of practice. The NIE was charged by the U.S. Congress with critically examining such features of the educational system as vocational education, the benefits of supportive programs for failing low income students, and sex equity issues. Another major activity of the NIE was funding the efforts in research and development of improved practices. The NIE also provided support for, and monitored the activities of, a number of independent educational research laboratories and centers located throughout the United States.

MILTON BUDOFF
*Research Institute for
Educational Problems,
Cambridge, Massachusetts*

NATIONAL INSTITUTE OF MENTAL HEALTH

The National Institute of Mental Health provides a national focus for the federal effort to increase knowledge and advance effective strategies to deal with health problems and issues in the promotion of mental health and the prevention and treatment of mental illness. In carrying out these responsibilities, the institute conducts and supports research and research training on the biological, psychological, behavioral, epidemiological, and social science aspects of mental health and illness; conducts and supports research on the development and improvement of mental health services and prevention programs and on their administration and financing; collaborates with and provides technical assistance and data to state and local authorities to assist them in providing and evaluating more effective mental health programs; supports other federal agencies and national, foreign, state, and local organizations, hospitals, professional associations, and volunteer groups to promote mental health and to provide for the care, treatment, and rehabilitation of mentally ill persons; collects, analyzes, and disseminates scientific findings and data on the treatment of mental illness; carries out administrative and financial management, policy development, planning and evaluation, and public information functions that are required to implement such programs; and exercises administrative and policy oversight for the operation of Saint Elizabeth's Hospital.

MILTON BUDOFF
*Research Institute for
Educational Problems,
Cambridge, Massachusetts*

NATIONAL INSTITUTE OF NEUROLOGICAL AND COMMUNICATIVE DISORDERS AND STROKE

The National Institute of Neurological and Communicative Disorders and Stroke conducts and supports fundamental and applied research on human neurological and communicative disorders such as Parkinson's disease, epilepsy, multiple sclerosis, muscular dystrophy, head and spinal cord injuries, stroke, deafness, disorders of speech, and language development problems. The institute also conducts and supports research on the development and function of the normal brain and nervous system in order to better understand normal processes relating to disease states.

MILTON BUDOFF
Research Institute for
Educational Problems,
Cambridge, Massachusetts

NATIONAL JOINT COMMITTEE ON LEARNING DISABILITIES (NJCLD)

The National Joint Committee on Learning Disabilities (NJCLD) is a committee of representatives of organizations concerned with individuals with learning disabilities. The member organizations that support the NJCLD and its activities are the American Speech-Language-Hearing Association, the Association for Children and Adults with Learning Disabilities, the Council for Learning Disabilities, the Division for Children with Communication Disorders—Council for Exceptional Children, the International Reading Association, and the Orton Dyslexia Society.

The NJCLD held its first official meeting in 1975. Along with providing an interdisciplinary forum for the review of national issues relating to learning disabilities, the NJCLD serves to facilitate cooperation and communication among the member organizations and to identify research and service delivery needs in this area.

The NJCLD position papers on issues relating to learning disabilities are available through the Orton Dyslexia Society, 724 York Road, Baltimore, MD 21204.

SHIRLEY A. JONES
Virginia Polytechnic Institute
and State University

NATIONAL LEARNING DISABILITIES ASSISTANCE PROGRAM

Public Law 91-230, the Elementary and Secondary Education Act Amendments of 1970, repealed Title VI of the Elementary and Secondary Education Act as of July 1, 1971. The act consolidated a number of previously separate federal grant programs relating to handicapped children under a new authority, the Education of the Handicapped Act (EHA). The 1970 EHA also added Part G, a new authorization for funding programs for children with specific learning disabilities.

The purpose of the program under Part G of the EHA was to assist states in identifying, diagnosing, and serving children with specific learning disabilities. This discretionary grant program provided support for research efforts, training for teachers and supervisors of teachers of children with specific learning disabilities, and model demonstration service centers aimed at stimulating increased statewide services for the target population.

Public Law 94-142 amended the definition of handicapped children to include the category of specific learning disabilities. With that statutory change, funds under any of the other EHA programs could be used for children with specific learning disabilities. Part G was repealed in 1983 by PL 98-199.

SHIRLEY A. JONES
Virginia Polytechnic Institute
and State University

NATIONAL MERIT SCHOLARSHIP CORPORATION

Founded in 1955, this independent organization is devoted to scholarship activities for intellectually talented young people. Organizations and businesses are solicited to support scholarships through the merit program. Annual testing by some 18,000 high schools for eligible juniors results in the naming of semifinalists. Semifinalists represent the top half of 1% tested in each state. Semifinalists compete for nonrenewable and renewable awards ranging from $1000 to $8000. Approximately 6000 awards are made annually.

Over 600 corporate foundations, professional associations, unions, trusts, and universities underwrite grants to support the program. Recipients must be U.S. citizens. The corporation has also administered since 1964 the Achievement Scholarship Program for Outstanding Negro Students. This separate program is devoted to increasing educational opportunities for promising black students. Over 650 black undergraduate scholarships are awarded annually. The corporation publishes booklets and other information for secondary students and interested individuals. Headquarters are located at One American Plaza, Evanston, IL 60201.

PHILIP R. JONES
Virginia Polytechnic Institute
and State University

NATIONAL REHABILITATION ASSOCIATION (NRA)

The National Rehabilitation Association (NRA) was founded in 1925. It consists of 18,000 members constituting 70 local groups. With its headquarters in Alexander, Virginia, the NRA is a consolidation of counselors, therapists, physicians, disability examiners, vocational evaluators, and other individuals interested in the rehabilitation of disabled people.

Among its activities, the NRA sponsors the Graduate Literary Award Contest, is involved in legislation, develops accessibility guidelines, and offers specialized education. Its newsletter is published six times annually; its *Journal of Rehabilitation* is published quarterly; and there is a Monograph of the Annual Mary E. Surtzer Memorial Seminar.

The NRA holds its annual convention in the fall, usually during the period of August to October.

MARY LEON PEERY
Texas A&M University

NATIONAL SOCIETY FOR AUTISTIC CHILDREN (NSAC)

The National Society for Autistic Children (NSAC) is an organization of parents, professionals, and other interested people who promote legislation, educational programming, and research that benefits autistic children as well as those children with severe behavior disorders. The primary focus of the organization is the improvement of educational services for autistic individuals at local, state, and national levels. The NSAC sponsors a job exchange that includes the matching of qualified professionals with available openings. Local chapters support and operate various direct-service programs such as group homes or recreational programs.

The NSAC makes available a vast array of informational pamphlets on topics such as management techniques and the definition of autism. The NSAC has an information and referral service that has specific information on the availability of programs, organizing community services, legislation, training institutions, taxation, facilities, funding sources, organizations, contacts in other countries, and research projects.

The NSAC publishes three newsletters: one for lay readers, one for teachers of autistic children, and one for organizations and local chapters. More information can be obtained from the National Society for Autistic Children (NSAC), 1234 Massachusetts Avenue, SW, Suite 1017, Washington, DC 20005.

PHILIP E. LYON
College of St. Rose

NATIONAL SOCIETY FOR CHILDREN AND ADULTS WITH AUTISM

The National Society for Children and Adults with Autism was founded in 1965. It consists of 6500 members in 157 local groups. The society caters to parents, teachers,

speech therapists, pediatricians, psychologists, neurologists, and others interested in children's severe disorders of communication and behavior. The society's major purpose is to inform the public of the symptoms and problems of autistic individuals, thereby providing a better understanding of the condition in general. Through greater awareness of the disorder and its symptomatology, the society hopes to ensure early and accurate diagnosis.

Among the services the society provides to the public is a National Information and Referral Service in Washington DC, a data bank on information and services available for autistic children, adults, and their families. The society also publishes a bimonthly newsletter and the *National Directory of Services and Programs for Autistic Children*. The society holds four to six regional meetings yearly, and its annual convention meets in June or July.

MARY LEON PEERY
Texas A&M University

NATIONAL SOCIETY FOR CRIPPLED CHILDREN AND ADULTS

See NATIONAL EASTER SEAL SOCIETY.

NATIONAL SOCIETY FOR THE PREVENTION OF BLINDNESS (NSPB)

Founded in 1908, the National Society for the Prevention of Blindness (NSPB) has as its primary purpose preventing blindness and conserving sight. This purpose is addressed through nationwide programs of public and professional education, research, and industrial and community services. Services include promotion and support of local glaucoma screening, preschool vision testing, industrial eye safety, and collection of data on the nature and extent of the causes of blindness and defective vision. Funding is entirely from contributions, memorial gifts, bequests, and legacies. Corporate and foundation support is extensive.

Grants for medical research and research fellowships in ophthalmology are available through NSPB. The society publishes a quarterly journal and a newsletter. Pamphlets on eye diseases, children's eye care, and industrial, sports, and school eye safety are available. The NSPB distributes home eye tests for preschoolers and adults and issues testing charts, posters, films, and radio/TV material. A major thrust of the organization has been the promotion of safety eyewear for various occupations and athletics. Offices are located at 500 E. Remington Road, Schaumburg, Illinois, 60173.

PHILIP R. JONES
*Virginia Polytechnic Institute
and State University*

NATIONAL TECHNICAL INSTITUTE FOR THE DEAF (NTID)

The National Technical Institute for the Deaf (NTID) was established in June 1965 by Congress and signed into law (PL 89-36) by President Lyndon B. Johnson. The law specifically included provisions relating to program size, program objectives, location, administration, curriculum, admission standards, duration of course study, and research. The bill also mandated that a national advisory board on the establishment of NTID be appointed. This board consisted of 12 members with the commissioner of education and the commissioner of vocational rehabilitation specified as ex officio members.

The board was to review proposals from institutions of higher education for the construction and operation of NTID. Further, the board was to make sure other recommendations to the secretary of health, education, and welfare as appropriate regarding the establishment and operation of NTID. Under PL 89-36, the board ceased to exist once the secretary entered into an agreement with an institution of higher education.

In November 1966 the Rochester Institute of Technology (RIT) in Rochester, New York, was announced as the site for the NTID. The following January, D. Robert Frisina was selected to head NTID with the title of RIT vice president for NTID. A pilot group of students enrolled in September 1968.

Today NTID is the only technological college for deaf people in the world. There are more than 1000 deaf students at NTID. Students can earn certificates in 1½ years of study or masters' degrees in 6 or more years. Students can choose from programs offered at NTID or at the other colleges of RIT. Students at NTID must have good high-school grades, at least an overall grade 8 achievement level on a standardized test, and a hearing loss of about 70 dBs or greater (without a hearing aid) in the better ear. Appropriate support services are available for students who need them. Further information may be obtained by writing NTID, PO Box 9887, Rochester, NY 14623.

REFERENCES

Brill, R. G. (1974). *The education of the deaf.* Washington, DC: Gallaudet College Press.

National Technical Institute for the Deaf. (*undated*). *Your college for careers.* Rochester, NY: Rochester Institute of Technology.

PHILIP E. LYON
College of Saint Rose

NATURE VERSUS NURTURE

The source of various traits has been debated throughout history. Some attribute honesty to genetic inheritance while others emphasize the modeling of family members, the influence of peers, or perhaps the mores held within a sector of society (Weinberg, 1983).

No area of human achievement has spurred greater controversy concerning the contributions of heredity and environment than the study of intelligence (Hallahan & Kauffman, 1986). Owing to the longstanding controversy and its social and political ramifications, it is vital that key issues be kept clear. Two issues are disputed: the validity of intelligence tests and the extent to which intelligence can be attributed to genetic inheritance. Intelligence tests, in particular the IQ test, contain items that probe an individual's ability to solve problems, comprehend words and passages, complete puzzles, and so forth. Such tests have been used in Europe and the United States for years, but have been under attack for being culturally biased. That is, the knowledge needed to do well on these tests is of value in some sections of society but not others.

The second major issue, the degree to which intelligence is inherited, is even more controversial. Some authorities (e.g., Jensen, 1969; Scarr & McCartney, 1983) have held that most of a person's intelligence is genetically determined. A majority of scholars in the field, however, have taken the position that intelligence is influenced mostly by environmental factors, or that the relative contributions of the two factors cannot be separated. (Block & Dworkin, 1976; Bouchard & McGue, 1981).

Nature does provide a promising method for evaluating the relative effects of heredity and environment. The crucial factor is to keep heredity constant. To study the offspring of the same parents is not sufficient, for each child has his or her own unique genetic makeup. It is only identical or monozygotic twins who share identical heredity; consequently, differences between these twins can be safely attributed to environmental factors.

In order to control for the effects of the environment, a number of comparisons need to be made. One comparison can be made between identical twins and between identical twins and their siblings. Another comparison can be made between the degree of difference between fraternal or dizygotic twins. Although fraternal twins are products of separate ova and sperm, they should otherwise be treated similarly to identical twins. Studies reveal that identical twins are consistently similar across a variety of measures. It is therefore reasonable to conclude that heredity does significantly influence children's development (Weinberg, 1983). However, the influence differs across traits: identical as well as fraternal twins resemble each other most in their physical traits, somewhat less in intelligence, and still less in personality and emotions.

Research on identical twins raised in different environments studies the extent of the contribution of the environment. A review of the literature on this topic by Farber (1981) reveals that identical twins who were separated but raised in similar environments had negligible differences in intelligence. However, identical twins' performances on intelligence tests could differ markedly if their environments were very different.

It is not possible to directly assess hereditary factors where there are no twins. Because some people have made unsubstantiated inferences about racial differences in intelligence, many psychologists are extremely cautious about speculating on the inheritability of intelligence (Block & Dworkin, 1976). Consequently, psychologists have favored the study of environmental factors, trying to determine how family factors, as well as the persons, institutions, and norms of the larger society, influence children's behavior, and how children themselves may affect their environments.

Most socialization studies take a broad view of the context in which the human develops. Research into the effects of malnutrition on intelligence is difficult to conduct for ethical reasons, yet evidence does exist, from animal and human studies, to lead to the conclusion that early malnutrition contributes to the incidence of mental retardation. Offspring of high socioeconomic groups, on the average, earn higher IQs than those of low socioeconomic parents. Poor performance on infant developmental scales are more likely to result in poor intellectual performance at later ages (4 and 10 years) in the context of low socioeconomic status than in the context of high socioeconomic status (Scarr & Weinberg, 1981).

The research clearly reveals that intelligence is influenced by both hereditary and environmental factors. Environmental influences come from birth weight, nutrition, and various familial sources. Consequently, hereditary and environmental factors continually interact to influence the child's development.

REFERENCES

Block, N., & Dworkin, G. (Eds.). (1976). *The IQ controversy.* New York: Pantheon.

Bouchard, T. J., Jr. (1983). Do environmental similarities explain the similarity in intelligence of identical twins reared apart? *Intelligence, 7,* 175–184.

Bouchard, T. J., Jr., & McGue, M. (1981). Familial studies of intelligence: A review. *Science, 212,* 1055–1059.

Farber, S. L. (1981). *Identical twins reared apart: A reanalysis.* New York: Basic Books.

Hallahan, D. P., & Kauffman, J. M. (1986). *Exceptional Children,* Englewood Cliffs, NJ: Prentice-Hall.

Jensen, A. R. (1969). How much can we boost I.Q. and scholastic achievement? *Harvard Educational Review, 39,* 1–123.

Scarr, S., & McCartney, K. (1983). How people make their own environments: A theory of genotype-environmental effects. *Child Development, 54,* 424–435.

Scarr, S., & Weinberg, R. A. (1981). The transmission of authoritarianism in families: Genetic resemblance in social-political attitudes? In S. Scarr (Ed.), *Race, social class, and individual differences in I.Q.* Hillsdale, NJ: Erlbaum.

Weinberg, R. A. (1983). A case of a misplaced conjunction: Nature or nuture? *Journal of School Psychology, 21,* 9–12.

JOSEPH M. RUSSO
Hunter College, City University of New York

ASSESSMENT
INTELLIGENCE
INTELLIGENCE TESTING
SOCIOECONOMIC STATUS

NAVANE

Navane (thiothixene hydrochloride) is a psychotropic drug used in the management of manifestations of psychotic disorders. It is not recommended for use in children under 12 years of age. Side effects can include drowsiness, especially on initiation of drug therapy, as well as agitation, restlessness, insomnia, and occasional instances of seizures and paradoxical exacerbation of psychotic symptoms. Overdosage symptoms can include muscular twitching, drowsiness, and dizziness, with gross overdose potentially resulting in gait disturbance and coma.

A brand name of Roerig Pharmaceuticals, Navane is available in capsules containing 1, 2, 5, and 10 mg, as a concentrate, and as an injection (intramuscular) vial. Dosages are individually adjusted, generally beginning with small doses of 2 mg three times a day, with increases up to 60 mg per day as needed.

REFERENCE

Physicians' desk reference. (1984) (pp. 1685–1688). Oradell, NJ: Medical Economics.

LAWRENCE C. HARTLAGE
Evans, Georgia

ATARAX
BENADRYL
COMPAZINE
DRUG THERAPY

NCATE

See NATIONAL COUNCIL FOR ACCREDITATION OF TEACHER EDUCATION.

NEGATIVE PUNISHMENT

The removal of a stimulus to decrease inappropriate/interferring behaviors is referred to as negative punishment. Time-out from positive reinforcement and response cost procedures are commonly employed strategies for decreasing the future probability of targeted behaviors. When employing these strategies, the obtrusiveness with which the environment is altered deserves special attention. For example, a tantrum during a meal can be handled by removing the child from the room, removing the child to a short distance from the table so direct observation of peers is still present, or removing the food from the child for a specified number of minutes. A recommendation for teachers is to provide the least amount of change in the environment that is most effective in reducing future occurrences of inappropriate behaviors. In a similar manner, the removal of previously earned points/tokens (response cost) can vary in intensity relative to the severity of the targeted activity to be decreased. For further information and examples the references below may be consulted.

REFERENCES

Bellack, A. S., & Hersen, M. (Eds.). (1985). *Dictionary of behavior therapy techniques* (p. 155). New York: Pergamon.

Kazdin, A. E. (1984). *Behavior modification in applied settings* (3rd ed., pp. 125–153). Homewood, IL: Dorsey.

ERNEST L. PANCSOFAR
Bowling Green State University

NEGATIVE REINFORCEMENT

Negative reinforcement is the removal or avoidance of an aversive stimulus from the environment that increases the future occurrence of the behavior immediately preceding the removal. Examples from everyday situations include buckling a seat belt to remove the aversive sound of the buzzer, bringing an umbrella outside on a rainy day to escape being wet, and ingesting a pain reliever to reduce the intensity of a headache. Negative reinforcement includes both escape and avoidance components. In a classroom situation, escape from the loud sound of a fire alarm increases the future likelihood of vacating a room during a fire drill. Similarly, avoiding a verbal reprimand from a teacher by remaining on task during a math assignment is an example of negative reinforcement.

Negative reinforcement is often confused with and mislabeled as punishment. In negative reinforcement, the future probability of a behavior that is followed by the removal of an aversive stimulus increases. However, the future probability of the occurrence of a behavior followed by the removal of a positive stimulus (negative punishment) or the presentation of an aversive event (positive punishment) decreases. Further reading references are cited below.

REFERENCES

Kazdin, A. E. (1984). *Behavior modification in applied settings* (3rd ed., pp. 31–33). Homewood, IL: Dorsey.

Sulzer-Azaroff, B., & Mayer, G. R. (1977). *Applying behavior-analysis procedures with children and youth* (pp. 140–141). New York: Holt, Rinehart, & Winston.

ERNEST L. PANCSOFAR
Bowling Green State University

BEHAVIOR ANALYSIS, APPLIED
BEHAVIOR MODIFICATION
NEGATIVE PUNISHMENT

NEISWORTH, JOHN T. (1937–   )

Born in Pittsburgh, Pennsylvania, John T. Neisworth received his BS (1959) in psychology, his MEd (1961) in special education, and his PhD (1967) in special education and educational psychology from the University of Pittsburgh. He is currently a professor of special education in the Division of Special Education and Communication disorders, Pennsylvania State University.

Neisworth has advocated abandoning the use of an IQ label, believing that the label of mentally retarded is more likely to harm a child than it is likely to help obtain appropriate services for the child (Neisworth, 1969). He feels that most problems of exceptional children are developmental in nature. In *The Exceptional Child: A Functional Approach* (Smith & Neisworth, 1983), the response of parents to the news that their child is impaired is considered. Neisworth believes that parents' responses to their child can determine how well the child will eventually function.

Retardation: Issues, Assessment, and Intervention (Neisworth & Smith, 1978) covers multidisciplinary concerns of mental retardation, specifically for the educator of the retarded pupil. It addresses such issues as what retardation is, how it is caused, and what should be done to help retarded individuals. Neisworth strongly believes that most retarded persons can accomplish more than most people think possible.

Currently, Neisworth is working on a student-setting correspondence instrument that would help school personnel make more appropriate child placement decisions.

REFERENCES

Neisworth, J. T. (1969). Educational irrelevance of "intelligence." In R. M. Smith (Ed.), *Diagnosis of Educational Differences.* Columbus, OH: Merrill.

Neisworth, J. T., & Smith, R. M. (Eds.). (1978). *Retardation: Issues, assessment, and intervention.* New York: McGraw-Hill.

Smith, R. M., & Neisworth, J. T. (1983). *The exceptional child: A functional approach.* New York: McGraw-Hill.

E. VALERIE HEWITT
Texas A&M University

NEONATAL BEHAVIORAL ASSESSMENT SCALE (NBAS)

The Neonatal Behavioral Assessment Scale (NBAS) was initially published in 1973 (Brazelton, 1973). Recently, revisions were made and the experiences of 10 years were summarized (Brazelton, 1984). Four NBAS training centers and eight authors contributed to the revised edition. The scale is in use in over 400 locations; six training centers have been established in the United States, six in Europe, and one in Israel; over 125 published studies have appeared within the United States and in cross-cultural contexts.

Behavioral evaluation of the newborn infant has concerned many who are interested in understanding the relative contribution of the infant to the nature-nurture equation. Many researchers feel that the individuality of the infant may be a powerful influence in shaping the way in which his or her relationship with the caretaker develops. Hence, there are many reasons for evaluating behavior as early as possible.

Early evaluation of infant behavior is of use in cross-cultural studies. Differences in groups of neonates such as those described by Geber and Dean (1957) and Brazelton et al. (1976), identify the kinds of neonatal behaviors that may contribute to the perpetuation of child-rearing practices that preserve cross-cultural differences among adults.

The neonate's behavior cannot be assumed to be purely of genetic origin, although genetic endowments do lead to important differences in neonatal behavior. Intrauterine nutrition and infection (Klein, Habicht, & Yarbrough, 1971; Lester, Als, & Brazelton, 1982) and drugs (Sepkoski, Garcia-Coll, & Lester, 1982), to name but a few possible influences, affect the fetus for 9 months, interacting with genetic endowment. There is rapidly accumulating evidence that the newborn infant is powerfully shaped before delivery. Routine perinatal events such as maternal medication and anesthesia, further influence the infant's reactions (Brazelton & Robey, 1965).

When the NBAS was conceived (Brazelton, 1962), the neonate was still thought of as a passive recipient of environmental stimuli. The infant's ability to shut out or handle stimuli by changing to a habituated or sleep state was a revelation (Brazelton, 1962). By the same token, an infant who had too low a threshold for intake of stimuli (hypersensitivity), or too disorganized a response to stimuli, might be at the mercy of the environment. Learning to handle internal psychophysiological reactions and to control motor overreactions may be a long and costly task for a very sensitive baby.

The revised NBAS assesses the newborn's repertoire on 28 behavioral items (e.g., lability of skin color, hand-mouth facility, orientation to face and voice), each scored on a 9-point scale. The scale measures the coping capacities and the adaptive strategies of the infant; these emerge as the baby recovers from the stresses of labor and delivery and adjusts to the demands of the extrauterine environment. This process of adaptation can be measured by studying patterns of change, called profile or recovery curves (Lester, 1984).

To assess these patterns of change, at least two but preferably three or more examinations are needed for each infant. The first should be done on day two or three, when the immediate stresses of labor and delivery have begun to wear off. The next examination is best done at 7 to 10 days, while the third may be done at 14 days or at 1 month. Scores from these successive exams establish a behavioral pattern of change over the first weeks of life. This pattern, in turn, might become an important measure of prediction of later developmental outcome (Lester, 1984; Lester, Hoffman, & Brazelton, submitted manuscript).

The NBAS also includes an assessment of 20 of the newborn's neurological responses (e.g., hand grasp, sucking, passive movement of arms and legs). Each reflex is scored on a four-point scale, from 0 to 3. The reflex items identify gross neurological abnormalities by deviant scores; they are not designed to provide a neurological evaluation.

In the second edition of the NBAS (Brazelton, 1984), nine supplementary items have been added, to be used with the NBAS in the assessment of high-risk infants. These items attempt to summarize the quality of the baby's responsiveness, the physiological cost to the infant of such responses, and the amount of input from the examiner necessary to organize the responses. Only examiners trained specifically to work with high-risk infants should use the NBAS.

Currently, the NBAS is being used as a form of intervention with parents of newborns. Among the categories being studied with the NBAS are the following:

High-risk infants
The effects of obstetric medication
The effects of maternal substance abuse
Cross-cultural comparisons of newborn behavior
Prediction
NBAS as a form of intervention

Goals for the future include establishing the value of the NBAS as a clinical instrument for all newborns with a more systems-oriented approach; evaluating the constantly changing but interactive aspects of the systems within the baby as they represent genetic endowment and intrauterine experience; and establishing newborns' interactions with perinatal variables and experiential influences. To understand the use of NBAS as a communicative system between parents and concerned professionals in order to provide intervention to enhance the parent-infant interaction may be the most important goal of all.

REFERENCES

Brazelton, T. B. (1962). Observations of the neonate. *Journal of the American Academy of Child Psychiatry*, 1, 38–58.

Brazelton, T. B. (1973). *Neonatal Behavioral Assessment Scale.* Philadelphia: Lippincott.

Brazelton, T. B. (1984). *Neonatal Behavioral Assessment Scale* (2nd ed.). Philadelphia: Lippincott.

Brazelton, T. B., & Robey, J. S. (1965). Observations of neonatal behavior: The effects of perinatal variables in particular that of maternal medication. *Journal of the American Academy of Child Psychiatry*, 4, 613–637.

Geber, M., & Dean, R. F. A. (1957). The state of development of newborn African children, *Lancet*, 1, 1216–1219.

Klein, R. B., Habicht, J. P., & Yarbrough, C. (1971). *Effect of protein caloric malnutrition on mental development.* In Cap Publication No 1–571.

Lester, B. M. (1984). Data analysis and prediction. In T. B. Brazelton (Ed.), *Neonatal Behavioral Assessment Scale* (2nd ed.). (pp. 85–96). Philadelphia: Lippincott.

Lester, B. M., Als, H., & Brazelton, T. B. (1982). Regional obstetric anesthesia and newborn behavior: A reanalysis toward synergistic effects. *Child Development*, 53, 687–692.

Lester, B. M., Hoffman, J., & Brazelton, T. B. *A longitudinal study of term and preterm infants: Evidence for the predictive validity of the Neonatal Behavioral Assessment Scale.* Manuscript submitted for publication.

Sepkoski, C., Garcia-Coll, C., & Lester, B. M. (1982). The cumulative effects of obstetric risk variables on newborn behavior. In L. P. Lipsitt & T. M. Field (Eds.), *Infant behavior and development: Perinatal risk and newborn behavior* (pp. 33–39). Norwood, NJ: Ablex.

T. Berry Brazelton
*Children's Hospital, Boston,
Massachusetts*

INFANT ASSESSMENT

NETHERLANDS, SPECIAL EDUCATION IN

In the Netherlands, as in other European countries, the first schools for special education were founded to meet the pedagogical needs of sensory disabled and severely mentally retarded children. In 1790 a school for deaf children was started in Groningen, followed by several schools for deaf or blind children during the nineteenth century. In 1855 the first school for severely mentally retarded children was founded. These schools were supported by funds raised in churches and by other charitable contributions. In 1901 the Compulsory Education Act was put into effect to give all children the opportunity to attend school and to fight analphabetism. In the following years it became clear that elementary school was not suitable for certain categories of children who were not severely disabled but nevertheless needed special education. As a result, the Act

on Special Education made it possible in 1920 to found separate schools for children with different kinds of sensory, physical, and mental handicaps. Over the next 60 years the total number and the amount of different types of schools increased. In the Netherlands, schools can be public or denominational; as a result, a large and diverse system of schools for special education was created. The schools are financed, like public schools, by public sources. Because the Netherlands is a smalll country, transport from home to school and vice versa is relatively easy to carry out.

The Table represents the situation in 1984 in terms of numbers of schools, children, boys, and girls.

There are three educational levels. The level for the very young (3 to 6 years of age) is the smallest of the three (comprising approximately 4000 children). Most children attend special elementary schools (ages 6 to 12, approximately 66,000) or a school for continued special education (age 12 and up, approximately 27,000). In 1984, 11,500 children left special education (most of them went to schools for continued regular education) and 400,700 visited regular nursery schools, while 1,094,400 went to elementary schools and 1,207,000 to schools for continued regular education.

In 1985, as a consequence of changes in basic educational concepts in the late 1960s and 1970s, nursery and elementary schools were legally integrated to form the Basis school (ages 5 to 12). Several arguments were advanced to justify this change. First, education is thought to

Special Education in the Netherlands

Category of Children	Schools	Children	Boys	Girls
1. Severely mentally retarded	116	7,799	4,504	3,274
2. Educable mentally retarded	297	32,133	20,048	12,085
3. 1 and 2 combined	26	—	—	—[a]
4. Primary learning disabled	310	38,433	29,536	8,897
5. Emotionally disturbed	66	4,704	3,842	862
6. Deaf	10	990	498	492
7. Hearing-impaired	6	696	437	259
8. Speech-impaired	1	174	114	60
9. 7 and 8 combined	24	3,182	2,113	1,069
10. Blind	5	239	152	87
11. Nearsighted	5	371	233	138
12. Physically handicapped	30	3,412	2,064	1,348
13. Multihandicapped	19	1,373	863	510
14. Admitted to hospital	27	1,632	1,030	602
15. Suffering from long illnesses	17	1,548	1,034	514
16. Visiting pedilogical institute	10	949	726	223
Total	969	97615	67195	30410

[a] Numbers of children, boys and girls incuded, in 1 and 2.
Source: Centraal Bureau voor de Statistiek.

be a continuous process not to be hindered by arbitrary thresholds like the transition from nursery to elementary school. Second, the concept of individual progress is stressed and with it the concept of individualized education instead of the more traditional concept of education in classes. This development can be of consequence for some parts of the special education system, which, as the counterpart of the regular system, has also met with criticism. The main criticisms are (1) the continuous increase in the number of children depending on special education, (2) the placement of categories of children who have many psychological characteristics and pedagogical needs in common in different types of schools (e.g., for the educable mentally retarded and for the primary learning disabled), (3) the difficulties children encounter when going back from the special to the regular system, and (4) the quality of the special education itself.

Along with the Basisschool Act, the Interim Act on Special Education was put into effect. After a 10-year period of development supported by the government, this act makes it possible to integrate certain types of special schools and to tighten the relations between schools for special and regular education. At the same time, conditions are changed in the Basisschool to meet the needs of some of the less severely disabled children and to try to stop the growing outflow of children to schools for special education. Today there already are a few integrated schools for special education. With respect to some categories of children (e.g., the blind and nearsighted), regular schools occasionally profit from the services of schools of special education. In the schools for special education, individual educational plans are used more and more frequently as a means to direct instruction and pedagogical measures for individual children. In 1995 the results of these processes of development will be taken into account when the definitive Act on Special Education is formulated.

ARYAN VAN DER LEIJ
*Free University, Amsterdam,
The Netherlands*

NEURAL EFFICIENCY ANALYZER (NEA)

During the past 20 years, a number of psychologists have argued that traditional intelligence tests (e.g., Stanford-Binet, Wechsler) are often inappropriate because they are culturally biased. In response to such criticism, many attempts have been made to develop measures of cognitive functioning that are both objective and culturally free.

A unique approach to culture-free assessment of cognitive functioning came in the late 1960s and early 1970s with Ertl's (1968) work with the Neural Efficiency Analyzer (NEA) (Tracy, 1972). Seen as providing an unbiased view of intelligence, the NEA was purported to measure the efficiency and speed of neuronal transmission. Specifically, the instrument measures the latency in milliseconds from the onset of a flash of light to the appropriate change in electrical activity in the brain. Ertl (1968) argued that tachistoscopically presented light flashes evoke a change in the electrical activity in the brain that could be detected by an electroencephalogram (EEG). Following the presentation of 100 flashes of light (presented at random intervals), the latency data were subjected to a computer analysis that provided both an average evoked potential and a predicted intelligence quotient (Ertl Index).

Although Ertl and Douglas (1970) reported that scores on the NEA correlate significantly with a number of standardized intelligence tests (e.g., Wechsler Intelligence Scale for Children, Primary Mental Abilities Test), more recent investigations have failed to replicate Ertl's claims (Sturgis, Lemke, & Johnson, 1977). Indeed, contrary to the earlier investigation by Ertl and Douglas (1970), NEA scores have not proven useful in discriminating among children with different levels of academic abilities (Evans, Martin, & Hatchette, 1976).

While the NEA appeared to be an innovative attempt to minimize the cultural bias in intelligence testing, little empirical evidence exists to support the use of this measure on a clinical basis. Moreover, with the major goals of intellectual assessment being to portray an individual's functioning in a number of separate yet related cognitive areas as well as to predict potential for future development, any unitary measure of cognitive functioning would have questionable use.

REFERENCES

Ertl, J. (1968). Evoked potential and human intelligence. Final Report, VSOE, Project No. 6-1454.

Ertl, J., & Douglas, V. (1970). Evoked potentials and dyslexia. Internal Report No. 32, Neural Modals, LTD.

Evans, J. R., Martin, D., & Hatchette, R. (1976). Neural Efficiency Analyzer scores of reading disabled, normally reading and academically superior children. *Perceptual & Motor Skills, 43,* 1248–1250.

Sturgis, R., Lemke, E. A., & Johnson, J. J. (1977). A validity study of the Neural Efficiency Analyzer in relation to selected measures of intelligence. *Perceptual & Motor Skills, 45,* 475–478.

Tracy, W. (1972). Goodbye IQ, hello EI (Ertl Index). *Phi Delta Kappan, 54,* 89–94.

JEFFREY W. GRAY
Ball State University

RAYMOND S. DEAN
*Ball State University
Indiana University School of
Medicine*

**ERTL INDEX
INTELLIGENCE**

NEURODEVELOPMENTAL THERAPY (NDT)

Neurodevelopmental therapy (NDT) is an approach toward working with individuals who have cerebral palsy and other neuromuscular disorders. Originating in England with the work of Berta and Karl Bobath in the 1940s (Bobath, 1980), NDT was presented to professionals in the United States in 1959 (Campbell, 1982). A number of basic and advanced courses in principles and techniques of NDT are offered in the United States; they lead to certification in neurodevelopmental therapy for teachers and therapists (speech, occupational, and physical). These courses are presented by the Neurodevelopmental Treatment Association, headquartered in Chicago, Illinois.

Several key aspects are considered to be important when providing NDT. Children with movement disorders may have an underlying basis of atypical postural tone (e.g., hypertonia, hypotonia) that needs to be normalized. Failure to develop normal tone may lead to an abnormal sequence of motor development that could result in postural fixations or blocks and compensatory movement patterns. This abnormal sequence may ultimately lead to contractures and orthopedic deformities (Campbell, 1983). A problem-oriented approach is used in NDT, and assessment of tone and movement patterns is completed prior to intervention. Intervention includes providing support at key points of control (i.e., head/neck, shoulders, hips/pelvis) and normalizing tone through positioning and handling techniques that sometimes make use of adaptive equipment (Finnie, 1975). Major emphasis in this treatment technique is on goal-directed movement leading to normalized movement patterns within the context of functional activities.

The main goals for NDT in the classroom are to analyze movement dysfunction accurately, to implement facilitation/inhibition procedures (to increase normal movement), to teach others necessary procedures for consistent management of the motor-impaired student across people and situations, to use adaptive equipment to the extent that equipment replaces unattainable functions, and to prevent the sequence of abnormal motor development from progressing to the point of formation of contractures and orthopedic deformities (Campbell, 1982).

REFERENCES

Bobath, K. (1980). *A neurophysiological basis for treatment of cerebral palsy*. London: Heinemann.

Campbell, P. H. (1982). *Introduction to neurodevelopmental treatment*. Akron, OH: Children's Hospital Medical Center.

Campbell, P. H. (1983). Students with movement difficulties. In M. E. Snell (Ed.), *Systematic instruction of the moderately and severely handicapped* (pp. 169–202). Columbus, OH: Merrill.

Finnie, N. (1975). *Handling the young cerebral palsied child at home*. New York: Dutton.

CORNELIA LIVELY
University of Illinois,
Urbana-Champaign

CEREBRAL PALSY
PHYSICAL THERAPY

NEUROFIBROMATOSIS

Neurofibromatosis, also known as Von Recklinghausen's disease, is a congenital neurologic disorder transmitted as an autosomal dominant trait (*Mosby's*, 1983). Early signs of the disorder include the presence of six or more café au lait spots larger than 1.5 cm, generally present at birth. Multiple skin-colored tumors, called neurofibromas, develop along nerve sheaths during childhood or early adulthood. Freckles evident in the axillae (armpits) represent the Crowe's sign of neurofibromatosis (Johnson, 1979).

These apparently benign early signs of neurofibromatosis may signal serious neurologic complications. Multiple tumors of the spinal nerves or cranial nerves may occur, with increased incidence of intracranial meningiomas, cystic lung disease, scoliosis, and hypertension in young victims (Rosenberg, 1979). Cranial nerves may be affected, leading to impaired hearing or deafness, impaired vision or blindness, and facial weakness. Risk of malignancy in tumors has been reported (Johnson, 1979). A proliferation of the soft tissue neurofibromas may result in serious cosmetic disfigurement, as illustrated in the film *Elephant Man*. Other serious neurologic disorders, including spina bifida, meningocele, or epilepsy, have been associated with neurofibromatosis (*Mosby's*, 1983).

Although intelligence of affected individuals may be normal, there is evidence of increased incidence of mental retardation (Johnson, 1979; Rosenberg, 1979). Studies have reported brain pathology in affected individuals, including histologic abnormalities in the cerebral cortex (Rosenberg, 1979). Neurofibromatosis occurs in one of 2500 to 3000 live births, with a prevalence of 0.04% (Johnson, 1979; *Mosby's*, 1983). Approximately 100,000 persons in the United States are estimated to have the disorder (*Fact Sheet*, 1983). Although serious handicaps are associated with neurofibromatosis, the disease rarely is considered life threatening, and prognosis for survival is reported to be good.

Treatment of the patient with neurofibromatosis generally consists of management of the various sequelae of the disease. Scoliosis may be treated with surgery or braces. Painful or disfiguring skin tumors may be removed, although there is some evidence to suggest these may recur (*Fact Sheet*, 1983). Management of hypertension is necessary for affected individuals. For the child with neurofibromatosis, school officials should be cognizant of the potential effects of this condition on physical, mental, and social development. Multifactored evaluation is advisable for affected children who exhibit school difficulties, with appropriate special education or related services, as indicated. Information about neurofibromatosis is available to affected persons, their families, and professionals from the National Neurofibromatosis Foundation, 70 W. 40th Street, 4th Floor, New York, NY 10018.

REFERENCES

Fact sheet: Neurofibromatosis (pamphlet). (1983, May). Bethesda, MD: Office of Scientific and Health Reports, NINCDS.

Johnson, M. (1979). Certain cutaneous diseases with significant systemic manifestations. In P. B. Beeson, W. McDermott, & J. B. Wyngaarden (Eds.), *Cecil textbook of medicine* (15th ed., pp. 2266–2312). Philadelphia: Saunders.

Mosby's medical and nursing dictionary. (1983). St. Louis: Mosby.

Rosenberg, R. N. (1979). Inherited degenerative diseases of the nervous system. In P. B. Beeson, W. McDermott, & J. B. Wyngaarden (Eds.), *Cecil textbook of medicine* (15th ed., pp. 764–772). Philadelphia: Saunders.

CATHY F. TELZROW
*Cuyahoga Special Education
Service Center, Maple
Heights, Ohio*

CAFÉ AU LAIT SPOTS
PHYSICAL DISABILITIES
SPINA BIFIDA

NEUROLINGUISTIC PROGRAMMING (NLP)

Neurolinguistic programming (NLP) is a model for effective interpersonal communication introduced by Bandler and Grinder (1975, 1976) for use in counseling and psychotherapy. The model is based on the belief that humans receive, store, and process information through their senses, or representational systems. Each individual has a preferred or primary representational system (PRS), either visual, auditory, or kinesthetic, through which information is most effectively processed. Interpersonal communication is enhanced, according to the theory of NLP, when dialogue reflects a match of preferred representational systems.

According to Bandler and Grinder, there are three ways PRS can be identified. One method is through analysis of language patterns. The predicates used in natural language (verbs, adjectives, and adverbs) relate to the three representational systems. One person "sees" the point; another "hears" what is meant; still another "grasps" a situation. Lankton (1980) found that matched predicates between counselor and client resulted in greater therapeutic rapport.

Observation of eye movements is another method proposed by Bandler and Grinder (1979) for determining PRS. They suggest that the direction of eye movements indicates the specific part of the brain in which information is stored, and, therefore, the representational system being used. For most right-handed people, upward eye movements indicate visual images, lateral movements indicate auditory images, downward movements to the left show internal dialogue or auditory representation, and downward movements to the right reflect kinesthetic representation. The third method proposed is direct questioning regarding preferred modality.

In addition to matching speech patterns, Bandler and Grinder highlight other nonverbal behaviors that result in enhanced rapport and communication. These include matching of body postures, facial expressions, hand gestures, and speech rate. Once rapport is established, leading is employed: the counselor slowly changes the language and gestures used in an effort to move the client to a more productive state. Anchoring refers to the use of a verbal or kinesthetic signal to return the client to a productive state.

The NLP has recently been applied to the field of education. Torres and Katz (1983) suggest that if teachers are aware of their own PRS and the PRS of their students, and if the channels of communication are matched, learning is facilitated. Teachers who are aware of the multiplicity of receptive modes present within a group may develop greater flexibility and teach more effectively through a variety of communication channels.

Neurolinguistic programming and the implications derived from it remain controversial. Studies have shown that neither predicate analysis nor eye movement observations are reliable methods of determining PRS (Dorn, Atwater, Jereb, & Russell, 1983; Shaw, 1977). Further evaluation in classrooms and clinics will be necessary to determine the full value of these theories.

REFERENCES

Bandler, R., & Grinder, J. (1975). *The structure of magic I.* Palo Alto, CA: Science and Behavior.

Bandler, R., & Grinder, J. (1976). *The structure of magic II.* Palo Alto, CA: Science and Behavior.

Bandler, R., & Grinder, J. (1979). *Frogs into princes: Neurolinguistic programming.* Moab, Utah: Real People Press.

Dorn, F. J., Atwater, M., Jereb, R., & Russell, R. (1983). Determining the reliability of the NLP eye-movement procedure. *American Mental Health Counselors Association Journal,* 5(3), 105–110.

Lankton, S. (1980). *Practical magic.* Cupertino, CA: Meta Publications.

Shaw, D. L. (1977). *Recall as effected by the interaction of presentation representational system and primary representational system.* Unpublished doctoral dissertation, Ball State University.

Torres, C., & Katz, J. (1983). Neuro-linguistic programming: Developing effective communication in the classroom. *Teacher Educator, 19*(2), 25–32.

BARBARA S. SPEER
*Shaker Heights City School
District, Shaker Heights,
Ohio*

ABILITY TRAINING
CEREBRAL DOMINANCE
HYPNOSIS
PSYCHOTHERAPY
TEACHING STRATEGIES

NEUROLOGICAL IMPRESS METHOD

The neurological impress method was developed to facilitate reading among children with severe reading disabilities (Hecklman, 1969; Langford, Slade, & Barnett, 1974). It may be most effective with students beyond 10 years of age. In this approach, teacher and student read aloud at a rapid pace, with the teacher sitting slightly behind and directing his or her voice into the student's ear. At first, the teacher may read somewhat louder and faster, encouraging the student to maintain pace and not to worry about faltering or misreading. The teacher's finger slides along the print, underscoring the words as they are read. As the student becomes more comfortable, he or she may assume the vocal and pointing lead. Continuing through the passage, teacher and student alternate leading and following.

While initially easier material is selected, the level of difficulty is gradually increased. Other than this selection process, there is no particular preparation of material prior to the oral unison reading. The approach is not specifically concerned with word recognition, word analysis, or comprehension; its focus is on fluency and on phrasing. The aim is to develop and maintain reading fluency over as many pages as possible, stopping before fatigue sets in.

In a study using the neurological impress method, Lorenz and Vockell (1979) found no significant gains in either word recognition or reading comprehension. On the other hand, improvement was noted in reading expressiveness, in fluency, and in students' confidence in their reading ability. Kann (1983) has suggested that the neurological impress method may be profitably combined with repeated readings, another approach that promotes fluency and syntactic competence (Samuels, 1979). Clearly, the neurological impress method does not represent a full reading program for disabled readers. It may, however, provide a valuable adjunct to other approaches. It may facilitate the chunking of phrases and the smoothing out of slow or choppy reading habits in some poor readers.

REFERENCES

Hecklman, R. G. (1969). The neurological impress method of remedial reading instruction. *Academic Therapy, 4,* 277–282.

Kann, R. (1983). The method of repeated readings: Expanding the neurological impress method for use with disabled readers. *Journal of Learning Disabilities, 16,* 90–92.

Langford, K., Slade, K., & Barnett, A. (1974). An explanation of impress techniques in remedial reading. *Academic Therapy, 9,* 309–319.

Lorenz, L. & Vockell, E. (1979). Using the neurological impress method with learning disabled readers. *Journal of Learning Disabilities, 12,* 420–422.

Samuels, S. J. (1979). The method of repeated readings. *Reading Teacher, 32,* 403–408.

KATHERINE GARNETT
*Hunter College, City University
of New York*

NEUROLOGICAL ORGANIZATION

Used generically, neurological organization refers to the functional organization of the brain, including the brain stem, the midbrain, and the neocortex. It is frequently encountered in neuropsychological research, a large portion of which is devoted to the investigation of individual differences in neurological organization and to the development of comprehensive theories of the functional organization of the brain. The term also has a more specific usage, as it is most often encountered in special education.

Special education and related services personnel are most likely to see the term used in the context of the Doman and Delacato approach to remediation of learning disorders. The Doman and Delacato theory and the subsequently derived treatment methods rely on a systematic vertical and horizontal development and organization of function within the human brain. The neuropsychological theory that underlies the work of Doman and Delacato is based on the biogenetic principle that "ontogeny recapitulates phylogeny;" this principle contends that if an individual does not follow this sequential continuum of development, as prescribed by Doman and Delacato, problems of mobility and/or communication will develop. The therapeutic methods of Doman and Delacato are designed to overcome early deficiencies in development and to restore proper neurological organization.

Doman and Delacato maintain that there are six major functional attainments of humans: motor skills, speech, writing, reading, understanding, and stereognosis (recognition of objects by touch). The attainment of these skills is believed to be dependent on the uninterrupted and successful neuroanatomical progress toward neurological organization. Delacato (1959) defines neurological organization as:

that physiologically optimum condition which (sic) exists uniquely and most completely in man and is the result of a total uninterrupted ontogenetic neural development. This development recapitulates the phylogenetic neural development of man and begins during the first trimester of gestation and ends at about six and one-half years of age in normal humans. This orderly development progresses *vertically* through the spinal cord and all other areas of the cortex, as it does with all mammals. Man's final and unique developmental progression takes place at the level of the cortex and is *lateral* (from left to right of from right to left). (p. 19)

Each higher level of functioning is dependent on successful movement through each of the lower levels of development. Doman and Delacato argue that if the highest level of function (cerebral dominance) is incomplete or unfunctioning, then a lower level of neurological organization will dominate the individual's intellectual behavior. The highest level of neurological organization, complete cerebral dominance, is, according to the theories of Doman and Delacato, what gives humans their great capacity for communication and sets them apart from other animals.

Unfortunately, there has been virtually no research supportive of either the Doman and Delacato theory of neurological organization or its derived treatment programs. The developmental milestones appear to have been misplaced as well. Forty percent of normal five to nine year olds have mixed dominance (eye-hand preference), showing that complete dominance is not typically established by age six and one-half, as Doman and Delacato claim. The treatment programs of Doman and Delacato have been condemned by resolution by many major health organizations in the United States and Canada. It is unlikely that the Doman and Delacato concept of neurological organization will prove useful in working with the handicapped. A longer review of the approach is available in Reynolds (1981).

REFERENCES

Delacato, C. H. (1959). *The treatment and prevention of reading problems: The neuropsychological approach.* Springfield, IL: Thomas.

Reynolds, C. R. (1981). The neuropsychological basis of intelligence. In G. Hynd & J. Obrzut (Eds.), *Neuropsychological assessment and the school age child: Issues and procedures.* New York: Grune & Stratton.

CECIL R. REYNOLDS
Texas A&M University

DELACATO, C. H.
DOMAN, G.
PATTERNING
READING DISORDERS

NEUROPSYCHOLOGY

Neuropsychology is the study of the relationships between behavior and the brain. Its emphasis is on understanding the mechanisms of the brain responsible for both simple and complex patterns of functioning (e.g., auditory discrimination, reading, memory). Since the mid-twentieth century, a good deal of professional attention has been directed to the understanding of specific loci of functioning in the brain. Indeed, Broca (1861) and Jackson (1874) observed a relationship between patients' behavior and specific areas of damage to the brain. In fact, some credit these observations of brain-behavior relationships as the birth of neuropsychology (Dean, 1986).

The clinical neuropsychologist's role has both diagnostic and therapeutic elements. Diagnosis concerns the identification of impaired neurological processes and the area of the brain implicated. Through therapeutic interventions, the neuropsychologist often works to structure experiences that maximize strengths and minimize weaknesses in an attempt to remediate processing disorders (Pfeiffer, Dean, & Shellenberger, 1986). In child neuropsychology, an increasing interest has been shown in the use of neuropsychological methods that use children's cognitive strengths to structure educational experiences for the remediation of learning and behavior problems.

Clinical neuropsychology continues to be concerned with functional assessments and the mapping of specific behaviors to areas of the brain. A number of assessment measures have been specifically designed by neuropsychologists to make inferences about the brain. These measures provide information concerning the integrity of patients' brain functioning in both cognitive processing and affective dimensions of behavior. The assessment of cognitive processing may include measures of general ability, verbal and nonverbal functions, perceptual-motor functioning, and academic achievement. Affective dimensions of behavior may include measures of personality, emotional functioning, and interpersonal/social skills. These measures allow one to describe brain functioning on a continuum, ranging from brain damage involving trauma to the brain (e.g., head injury or stroke) to the opposite end of the continuum, in which the individual is neurologically intact with no signs of dysfunction. Moreover, the search for a single measure of brain damage or organicity (e.g., Bender-Gestalt Test) has been abandoned by most neuropsychologists because of the complex nature of brain functioning (Dean, 1986).

The hemispheres of the brain can be viewed as processing information using different modes. The right hemisphere seems to use a more visual, spatial, simultaneous processing style whereas the left seems to use a more analytical, verbal, sequential style. The application of these processing differences recently has been attempted with some success in both educational assessment and remediation (Dean, 1981, 1984; Reynolds, 1984).

A number of neuropsychologists have begun to isolate the biological or organic factors involved in many of the emotional (behavioral) disorders (e.g., some forms of depression, hyperactivity, schizophrenia) that previously were thought to be functionally related to stress in the environment (Dean, 1985). These findings are important because they begin to tie brain functioning more clearly to human emotions and psychopathology. Additionally, these findings indicate that some disorders, or even subgroups of certain disorders, once considered environmentally caused actually may be biologically based. Therefore, in school remedial planning, an evaluation of the neuropsychological components of functioning may be as important as an evaluation of the child's current environment. In sum, neuropsychology has made significant contributions in the understanding of brain-behavior relationships and in providing distinct direction for the education and rehabilitation of children and adults with brain dysfunctions. Clearly, neuropsychology has the potential for becoming a major link between medicine, education, and the psychological sciences.

REFERENCES

Broca, P. (1861/1960). Remarks on the seat of the faculty of articulate language, followed by an observation of aphasia. In G. von Bonin (Trans.), *Some papers on the cerebral cortex.* Springfield, IL: Thomas.

Dean, R. S. (1981). Cerebral dominance and childhood learning disorders: Theoretical perspectives. *School Psychology Review, 10,* 373–388.

Dean, R. S. (1984). Functional lateralization of the brain. *Journal of Special Education, 18,* 239–256.

Dean, R. S. (1985). Neuropsychological assessment. In J. D. Cavenar, R. Michels, H. K. H. Brodie, A. M. Cooper, S. B. Guze, L. L. Judd, G. L. Klerman, & A. J. Solnit (Eds.), *Psychiatry* (pp. 1–16). Philadelphia, Lippincott.

Dean, R. S. (1986). Perspectives on the future of neuropsychological assessment. In B. S. Plake & J. C. Witt (Eds.), *Buros— Nebraska series on measurement and testing: Future of testing and measurement.* Hillsdale, NJ: Erlbaum (pp. 203–244).

Jackson, J. H. (1874/1932). On the duality of the brain. In J. Taylor (Ed.), *Selected writings of John Hughlings Jackson* (Vol. 2). London: Hodder & Stoughton.

Pfeiffer, S. I., Dean, R. S., & Shellenberger, S. (1986). The school psychologists in medical settings: Neurology section. In T. Kratochwill (Ed.), *Advances in school psychology* (Vol. 5). Hillsdale, NJ: Erlbaum (177–202).

Reynolds, C. R. (Ed.). (1984). The Kaufman Assessment Battery for Children. *Journal of Special Education, 18*(3).

RIK CARL D'AMATO
Ball State University

RAYMOND S. DEAN
Ball State University
Indiana University School of Medicine

CEREBRAL DOMINANCE
HEMISPHERIC FUNCTIONING
LEFT BRAIN, RIGHT BRAIN
NEUROLOGICAL ORGANIZATION
SPLIT-BRAIN RESEARCH

NEWLAND, T. ERNEST (1903–)

T. Ernest Newland earned his BA from Wittenberg College in 1925 and his PhD under Sidney Pressey at Ohio State in 1931. After 7 years at Bucknell University, Newland became chief of the Division of Special Education in the Pennsylvania Department of Public Instruction; he served from 1938 to 1942, while services to exceptional children were rapidly developing in both number of children served and quality of programming. For 20 years he was a professor in the College of Education at the University of Illinois.

Newland is the author of over 200 articles, editorials, reviews, and abstracts, most on topics relevant to special education. He is most noted for furthering educators' understanding of testing as one part of the assessment process, furthering psychologists' understanding of intelligence as involving both product and process, developing the Blind Learning Aptitude Test (1969), and writing *The Gifted in Socioeducational Perspective* (1976).

T. Ernest Newland

In addition, Newland is responsible for many "firsts" in the field of special education. He implemented the first statewide county supervisor of special education program; inaugurated the first mandated state hearing test program for public school children; caused the first legal state definition of exceptional children to include the gifted; and facilitated the establishment and functioning of the first fully committed doctoral program in school psychology at the University of Illinois (Urbana).

Newland has chaired committees of the Council for Exceptional Children (and its predecessor) and the American Psychological Association. He has been honored with awards from the Association for the Gifted, the Illinois Psychological Association, and the Division of School Psychology of the American Psychological Association.

REFERENCES

Newland, T. E. (1969). *Blind Learning Aptitude Test.* Urbana: University of Illinois Press.

Newland, T. E. (1976). *The gifted in socioeducational perspective.* Englewood Cliffs, NJ: Prentice-Hall.

JOSEPH L. FRENCH
Pennsylvania State University

NEW YORK STATE ASSOCIATION FOR RETARDED CHILDREN v. CAREY

See WILLOWBROOK CASE.

NEW ZEALAND, SPECIAL EDUCATION IN

Special education in New Zealand has a long and rich history of development throughout the twentieth century. The New Zealand Crippled Children Society was founded in 1935 and soon thereafter the government extended its help to children who suffered physical, mental, or social handicaps. In the 1940s the number of small special classes for mentally retarded children was increased, residential schools were opened, and services were developed for blind children and for children with speech impairments. Public and educational concern regarding underachievement among culturally disadvantaged Maori and European children heightened in the following decades (Mitchell, 1973). Presently, a variety of handicapping conditions are recognized for special education service provision in New Zealand; these include mental retardation, learning disability, emotional/social maladjustment, speech/language impairment, hearing handicap, visual handicap, physical handicap/health impairment, and multiple handicap.

Recent epidemiological research in New Zealand has yielded prevalence estimates almost identical with estimates obtained in major studies in the United States, Europe, and Australia. While a sizable number of disabled children are currently receiving special educational services in New Zealand, little information is available on the extent or effectiveness of these services. Services for deaf-blind children are well developed, but there is concern that only a small proportion of children within other categories of handicapping conditions are receiving special education provisions (Wilton, 1984).

Perhaps because most of the special services for handicapped children are provided in segregated settings, the majority of students with disabilities attend regular schools without participating in special programs (Wilton,

1984). Off-site centers for disruptive secondary school pupils are an example of segregated service delivery. Initially formed on a voluntary basis by concerned community members, the off-site centers are now administered by the New Zealand Department of Education and are seen as a reflection on the failure of the schools to cater adequately to Maori and Polynesian students (Galloway & Barrett, 1984). There are presently seven off-site centers that are completely separated from mainstream facilities for disruptive secondary-level students.

REFERENCES

Galloway, D., & Barrett, C. (1984). Off-site centers for disruptive secondary school pupils in New Zealand. *Educational Research* 26(2), 106–110.

Mitchell, D. R. (1973). Education of the disadvantaged child. In G. H. Robinson & B. T. O'Rourke (Eds.), *Schools in New Zealand society* (pp. 285–298). New York: Wiley.

Wilton, K. (1984). Handicapped children of preschool- and school-age in New Zealand: Special educational needs and available services. *Exceptional Child. 31.* 173–184.

GREG VALCANTE
University of Florida

AUSTRALIA, SPECIAL EDUCATION IN
CHINA, SPECIAL EDUCATION IN
CENTRAL AMERICA, SPECIAL EDUCATION IN

NIE

See NATIONAL INSTITUTE OF EDUCATION.

NIGERIA, SPECIAL EDUCATION IN

Educational services for handicapped children have been slow to develop in Nigeria. As of 1977, there were 26 special educational services focused primarily on the physically handicapped or mentally retarded primary school-aged child (UNESCO, 1981). These schools enrolled 2072 students and were made up of five schools for the blind and visually handicapped, seven schools for the deaf and hearing impaired, and eight schools for the physically handicapped. There were six homes for the mentally retarded. Little attention has been paid to the handicapped preschool child.

Because early detection and intervention programs are scarce, handicapped children are usually not seen until they enroll for primary school at age 6. The health departments try to provide prevention services. They operate antenatal clinics that give expectant mothers some education as to the care of themselves and their unborn children. For example, education is given on proper diet, the dangers of self-medication, and infectious diseases. Immunizations against tetanus are given, but there is a high incidence of malaria, meningitis, polio, and sickle cell disease (UNESCO, 1981). These clinics compete with tribal clinics run by herbalists. There are 299 baby clinics for both handicapped and nonhandicapped babies. These clinics are understaffed and lack personnel trained to recognize abnormalities. The impact of these clinics is minimal in a country that is 73% rural and has a population that more than tripled from 1970 to 1980 to 74 million (UNESCO, 1982). There is no central registry for handicapped children and the number of children who are not receiving medical and educational services is unknown. The government has proposed a health plan that would establish a teaching hospital in each of the 19 states of the federation. It is hoped that these hospitals would provide screening and treatment for handicapped children and education for their families.

There is a lack of qualified special education teachers. Of the teachers staffing the 26 special educational facilities, only 52 out of 134 are trained to work with the handicapped (UNESCO, 1981). Governmental efforts have gone toward alleviating these shortages by training special education teachers for the handicapped and expanding the number of qualified teachers. In 1974 a Special Educational Unit was established under the Teacher Training Section of the Federal Ministry of Education. There is a Federal Advanced Teacher Training College for Special Education in Ibadan offering a 3-year training course (UNESCO, 1981). It is hoped that 100 students per year will graduate. Both the government and voluntary agencies have provided subsidies for students who wish to study special education abroad.

Obstacles to the growth of special education services to handicapped children are many. The country is trying to expand general primary education and secondary education. This goal is made difficult not only because of the rural nature of the country, the large population, poverty, and a 70 to 79% illiteracy rate, but also because of cultural diversity. There are 250 ethnic language groups in 19 states of the federation. These cultural variations result in superstition and taboos regarding the birth of a handicapped child and whether or not educational services should be given.

REFERENCES

UNESCO. (1981). *Handicapped children: Early detection, intervention and education in selected case studies from Argentina, Canada, Denmark, Jamaica, Jordan, Nigeria, Sri Lanka, Thailand, and the United Kingdom* (Report No. ED/MD/63). Paris: Author.

UNESCO. (1982). *Conference of ministers of education and those responsible for economic planning in African member states in Harare: Development of education in Africa: A statistical review* (Report No. ED-82/MINEDAF/REF. 2). Paris: Author.

KAREN F. WYCHE
*Hunter College, City University
of New York*

AFRICA, SPECIAL EDUCATION IN

NIMH

See NATIONAL INSTITUTE OF MENTAL HEALTH.

NIND

See NATIONAL INSTITUTE OF NEUROLOGICAL AND COMMUNICATIVE DISORDERS AND STROKE.

NMR

See NUCLEAR MAGNETIC RESONANCE.

NONCOMPLIANT CHILDREN

Noncompliant children are those who fail to comply with the desires, rules, or policies established by others. They are norm-violating and frequently chronically disruptive. The term noncompliant is used in some states to describe youths who have come to the attention of the courts or the authorities. A noncompliant child is not necessarily emotionally disturbed or behaviorally disordered. Frequently, noncompliant children are socially different but not necessarily socially deviant.

What can be done to assist noncompliant children in the classroom? Unfortunately, special educators often neglect to inform their pupils of what is expected of them in terms of acceptable classroom behavior. Initial class periods should be used to orient students to student/teacher (jointly established) classroom rules that will provide a solid learning atmosphere. If the teacher permits a loose structure to being with, it will become more difficult to establish rules later. Time should be allowed in the classroom to regularly rehearse and review the rules. Students should be reminded of the rules periodically. The teacher and the students can identify which rules are not working or need further clarification.

Pupils should become part of the rule-making process. If the teacher and students cooperate in developing rules, students will learn courtesy, respect for authority, and acceptance of responsibility in the process. The teacher must actively involve students, requesting input and providing feedback about classroom procedures and policies as they are developed and administered. The purpose is to create a healthy climate in the classroom. Such a climate exists when there are known and shared expectations for both teachers and students as they work cooperatively to help students with the learning of social skills.

A first step in selecting appropriate classroom rules is to ask what students need to accomplish in social learning to create an effective teaching/learning environment. Thus the rules focus on social learning and not discipline, facilitating instruction and learning. This point is particularly important for children placed in least restrictive environments.

The second step in developing rules is to identify and explicitly state them (Canter & Canter, 1979). The rules need to be precise, practical, and understood by all. Rules should be clear to all teachers working with a child, to the child, and to any observers. It is useful to post rules so that children will see them, use them, and not forget them. It should be made clear when a rule has been observed or broken, especially with mentally retarded and behaviorally disordered students.

Students should be given a clear rationale for the rules to help them understand that good behavior generates a positive classroom environment. Inappropriate behavior, on the other hand, disrupts the classroom, causes tension, and makes learning and development difficult or even impossible. Mainstreamed students may be tempted to act out frustrations if they fail to understand the reasons for their frustrations.

It is also important to establish an appropriate learning climate. A number of teacher role behaviors are prerequisite to the elimination of noncompliant behaviors. Pupils seem to respect a teacher who is firm, decisive, and at the same time kind and patient. Through consistency, the child learns that certain behaviors are not acceptable and that others must be learned. Inconsistency, however, leaves a student unable to predict what will happen as the consequence of an act.

A positive attitude is necessary to project an atmosphere of optimism regarding students' academic accomplishments. A planned instructional approach is required if the teacher is to enable the students to learn academic material. Flexibility in teacher expectations and resulting student behavior is needed in the classroom; without it, there is the possibility that students will become stereotyped by the teacher. Consistency is necessary if students are to accurately identify and predict the important rules of the classroom. Understanding between human beings (i.e., empathy, concern, or appreciation) goes a long way in promoting preventive discipline with handicapped students.

Pupils may become dissatisfied with poor learning conditions in the classroom and frustrated because of pressure stemming from inappropriate teacher control techniques. How we teach is critical to maintaining preventive discipline. Teaching behaviors that enhance achievement tend to reduce deviant behaviors and vice versa. Teaching behaviors that do not promote achievement, positive attitudes, or student involvement are linked with higher rates of deviant behavior.

Teachers should seek to provide meaningful learning experiences. If learning is to be meaningful, it must be related to an individual's concerns, meet social and personal needs, and promote interaction with the environment.

Even adults respond to the requests of authority figures readily and willingly when the task appears meaningful to them personally. Certainly, meaningfulness is important to youngsters who may have difficulty in understanding long-term reinforcements of successful memory exercises, rote learning, and busy work.

Traditional disciplinary practices require school officials to make rules; students are to obey them. School officials enforce rules; students are the recipients of that enforcement. School officials establish punishment; students are to accept the punishment. In short, historic punishment practices place teacher and student into adversarial relationships. Positive discipline brings the student and teacher into a planned social learning environment where the classroom, the playground, the corridor, the bus, or the walk to and from school become the curriculum. This social learning curriculum is just as important as any academic, vocational, or remedial instruction.

The quality of teacher/student interactions is a useful indicator of behavior control in the classroom. These interactions can be either positive or negative. In an ideal classroom, positive interactions should be a major goal and should be achieved frequently.

Teacher-initiated interactions generally require compliance from the student. If the student complies, the teacher provides positive consequences. If the student does not comply, the teacher provides negative consequences first and then repeats the original direction. If the student then complies, the teacher provides positive consequences. If the student does not comply again, the teacher provides stronger negative consequences and the cycle continues until the student complies. The teacher then provides positive consequences.

Student-initiated interactions can be either appropriate or inappropriate behaviors. If behavior is appropriate, the teacher provides positive consequences. If behavior is inappropriate, the teacher provides negative consequences first and directs the student toward appropriate behavior. If the student then exhibits appropriate behavior, the teacher provides positive consequences. In all cases of teacher/student interactions, the end result should be the teacher's providing positive consequences.

REFERENCE

Canter, L., & Canter, M. (1979). *Assertive discipline workbook: Competency based guidelines and resource materials.* Los Angeles: Lee Carter Associates.

STAN KARCZ
University of Wisconsin, Stout

APPLIED BEHAVIOR ANALYSIS
CLASSROOM MANAGEMENT
CONDUCT DISORDERS
ENGINEERED CLASSROOM

NONDISCRIMINATORY ASSESSMENT

Millions of tests are used yearly in schools for many purposes (e.g., grading, screening, placement, guidance, diagnosis, advancement, retention, formative and summative evaluation). While the public's attitudes toward testing are positive (Lerner, 1981), a number of authors (Black, 1963; Gross, 1963; Kamin, 1974; Mercer, 1972) have criticized testing generally; criticisms directed toward the uses of tests with minority students have identified additional abuses (Williams, 1974). These abuses include assessing students in their nondominant language; using tests that reflect only white middle-class values and abilities; using inadequately prepared and culturally insensitive assessment personnel; overidentifying and placing minority students in mentally retarded classes and lower ability groups; allowing minority students to remain in inferior classes for years; restricting minorities' educational opportunities; not informing parents when important educational decisions are made; basing important educational decisions on meager and unvalidated information; and denigrating the dignity of racial groups in light of low test performance (Oakland, 1977; Oakland & Parmalee, 1985).

Once aware of these issues, educators, psychologists (Reynolds, 1982), politicians (Bersoff, 1981), judges (Sattler, 1981), and others sought different but often complementary ways of clarifying the issues and improving the assessment of minority children. For example, in their quest to obtain suitable measures, psychologists have developed culture-fair and culture-specific measures, criterion-referenced measures, and behavioral assessment devices; translated tests from English to other languages; normed tests to include more minority children, developed ethnic and pluralistic norms; and developed statistical models to use tests fairly (Oakland & Parmalee, 1985; Jensen, 1980).

Attempts to resolve questions of test bias are confused by differing definitions of bias. Some of the more prominent definitions are follow. Readers are encouraged to see Reynolds (1982), Scheuneman (1981), Jensen (1980, 1981), Flaugher (1978), Humphreys (1973), Darlington (1971), Lord (1980), and Berk (1982) for extensive reviews of methods to detect test bias.

Traditional definitions of bias rely largely on the three conceptions of validity: content, criterion related (including concurrent and predictive), and construct (including internal and external). Statisticians seemingly favor those methods that combine judgment and statistics. For example, logical analysis may be employed to establish the relevance of items to the trait being assessed and to identify items that may offend members of particular groups. Statistical techniques then can be used to identify aberrant items—those operating inconsistent with other items presumably measuring the same trait. Judgment again may be used to examine possible patterns among the statistically biased items and to further refine one's understanding of the trait (Shepard, 1982). Methods using item bias (as opposed to criterion-related validity) may be preferred because they can be incorporated into the first stages of test construction, thus leading to the early elimination of biases that may eventually compromise the test's validity. Furthermore, regression methods to detect criterion-related bias and factor-analytic methods to detect construct bias may be employed later with greater ease and confidence following the use of item methods.

Psychometrists often define bias through definitions that emphasize the relation between test items and the total test (e.g., item-total correlations). However, others prefer definitions that emphasize the entire test and focus on possible bias in selection or placement decisions.

Three definitions of bias appear prominently. The regression approach holds that bias is present when a test predicts differently for one group than another. Thus, bias is defined in terms of differences in the regression of a criterion measure on an independent variable (Cleary, 1968).

A second model frequently used is the quota system. Using this model, persons are selected in the same proportion as they are found in the population. If a community's population is 80% white and 20% black, one black will be selected for every four whites. Two separate cutoff scores are set to allow this selection ratio when between-group differences in mean scores exist.

A third model, the corrected-criterion model (Darlington, 1971), allows social and political implications using various culture-fair models to be weighed. A choice of models depends on the relative importance attributed to selecting persons with the highest scores versus giving members of minority groups more opportunities to be selected. A practical effect of this model is to add bonus points to scores of members of certain groups to help ensure a larger selection ratio for them.

In terms of a functional definition of bias, the testing process with students typically has two major activities: the collection and interpretation of information and the use of it. Oakland (1981) has suggested that a definition of bias should address both components and proposed the following broad definition for nonbiased assessment:

Nonbiased assessment provides a quality assessment that eliminates, minimizes, or at least recognizes the presence of biasing conditions. Bias is apparent from predilections and procedures that prevent or obscure either (1) the full and accurate appraisal of conditions influencing a child's development or (2) the use of information to help maximize a child's development. (Oakland, 1981, p. 2)

Thus multiple sources of bias need to be considered without focusing attention exclusively on narrow psychometric issues.

Biases can emanate from many sources: children, parents, educational personnel, assessment and intervention processes, and school system policies and practices. Possible child-related characteristics that can contribute to bias include linguistic dominance and competence, test-taking skills and attitudes, motivations, expectations, cultural values, lifestyles, and personality characteristics. Parental characteristics that can contribute to bias include attentiveness to factors important to their children's growth and development, interest in and support for educators and education, use of time and motivation to attend to children's needs, adequate information about their children's school and social activities, values, lifestyles, and linguistic and communication abilities. Characteristics of educational personnel that can contribute to bias include attitudes toward persons based on age, gender, race, social class, and religion, language and dialects, commitments and values, and professional competence. Assessment and intervention strategies that can affect bias include the validity and comprehensiveness of information acquired, the technical adequacy of the measures used, the attitudes and competencies of the appraisal staff, the standards used to evaluate pupil performance, and the availability of viable interventions. Policies and practices of school systems that can contribute to bias includes willingness to use financial and professional resources appropriately, responsiveness to the needs of individual pupils, commitment to high professional standards, compliance with state and national legislation and litigation, diversity and quality of personnel and services, and morale of the staff. Each of these areas can affect the accuracy of the appraisal and the use of appraisal information to maximize a child's development.

Numerous sets of guidelines exist for designing and delivering nonbiased assessment programs. Professional associations together with federal and state agencies have proposed strategies intended to be both professionally sound and educationally relevant.

National associations such as the American Personnel and Guidance Association (APGA) and the American Psychological Association (APA) have tried to steer a steady course by providing guidelines for the development and use of tests (e.g., APA's Standards for Educational and Psychological Testing, 1985) and position papers that address specific issues.

The federal government has responded in various ways (Oakland, 1977). Public Law 94-142 has had the most sig-

nificant and far-reaching influence on determining non-biased assessment policies and practices in the schools. The legislation contains six key features that affect assessment.

An individual educational plan (IEP) is written annually and specifies desirable educational goals and methods. Parents are encouraged to participate on the team that develops the IEP and to exercise their right to receive and consider all pertinent information the school has about their child. Due process provisions of the bill help to ensure that parents may examine all documents concerning their child, receive written notices in their native language when their child is being evaluated, question and object to information they think is incorrect or injurious, submit evidence and obtain legal council and other professional advice, request that their case be reviewed by an impartial hearing officer, and appeal any decision through other courts.

Tests are described as being culturally nondiscriminatory when they have been validated for the specific purposes for which they are being used, are administered by trained and competent examiners using standardized procedures, and assess multiple yet specific areas of education need. Information about the pupil's medical, social, psychological, and educational development should be collected and interpreted by trained professionals. When assessing pupils with sensory or other physical impairments, the tests must assess their capabilities unattenuated by their impairments. Submitting all information to a multidisciplinary team for evaluation and decisions constitutes a key feature of a nonbiased program. Specialists also are encouraged to propose helpful interventions (Heller, Holtzman, & Messick, 1982). School systems must fully reassess pupils every 3 years in order to note progress toward goals specified in the IEP and to determine continued eligibility for special education.

REFERENCES

American Personnel and Guidance Association. (1972). The responsible use of tests: A position paper of MEG, APGA, and NCME. *Measurement and Evaluation in Guidance, 5,* 385–388.

American Psychological Association. (1985). *Standards for Educational and Psychological Testing,* Washington, DC. Author.

Berk, R. A. (Ed.) (1982). *Handbook of methods for detecting test bias.* Baltimore, MD: Johns Hopkins University Press.

Bersoff, D. (1981). Legal principles in the nondiscriminatory assessment of minority children. In T. Oakland (Ed.), *Nonbiased assessment.* Minneapolis: University of Minnesota.

Black, H. (1963). *They shall not pass.* New York: Morrow.

Cleary, T. A. (1968). Test bias: Prediction of grades of Negro and white students in integrated colleges. *Journal of Educational Measurement, 5,* 115–124.

Darlington, R. B. (1971). Another look at "culture fairness." *Journal of Educational Measurement, 8,* 71–72.

Flaugher, R. L. (1978). The many definitions of test bias. *American Psychologist, 33,* 671–679.

Gross, M. (1963). *The brain watchers*. New York: New American Library.

Heller, K. A., Holtzman, W. H., & Messick, S. (Eds.). (1982). *Placing children in special education: A strategy for equity*. Washington, DC: National Academy.

Humphreys, L. G. (1973). Statistical definitions of test validity for minority groups. *Journal of Applied Psychology, 58*(1), 1–4.

Jensen, A. R. (1980). *Bias in mental testing*. New York: Free Press.

Jensen, A. R. (1981). *Straight talk about mental tests*. New York: Free Press.

Kamin, L. (1974). *The science and politics of IQ*. Hillsdale, NJ: Erlbaum.

Lerner, B. (1981). Representative democracy, "men of zeal," and testing legislation. *American Psychologist, 36*, 270–275.

Lord, F. M. (1980). *Application of item response theory to practical testing problems*. Hillsdale, NJ: Erlbaum.

Mercer, J. R. (1972). IQ: The lethal label. *Psychology Today, 6*, 44–47, 95–97.

Oakland, T. D. (Ed.). (1977). *Psychological and educational assessment of minority children*. New York: Brunner/Mazel.

Oakland, T. D. (Ed.). (1981). *Nonbiased assessment* (a project of the National School Psychology Inservice Training Network). Minneapolis, MN: Upper Midwest Regional Resource Center.

Oakland, T., & Parmalee, R. (1985). Mental measurement of minority-group children. In B. Wolman (Ed.), *Handbook of intelligence*. New York: Wiley.

Reynolds, C. R. (1982). The problem of bias in psychological assessment. In C. R. Reynolds & T. B. Gutkin (Eds.), *The handbook of school psychology*. New York: Wiley.

Sattler, J. M. (1981). Intelligence tests on trial: An "interview" with judges Robert F. Peckham and John F. Grady. *Journal of School Psychology. 19*(4), 359–369.

Scheuneman, J. D. (1981). A new look at bias in aptitude tests. In P. Merrifield (Ed.), *Measuring human abilities* (*New Directions in Testing and Measurement*, No. 12). San Francisco: Jossey-Bass.

Shepard, L. A. (1982). Definitions of bias. In R. A. Berk (Ed.), *Handbook of methods for detecting test bias*. Baltimore, MD: Johns Hopkins University Press.

Williams, R. L. (1974). Scientific racism and IQ: The silent mugging of the black community. *Psychology Today, 7*(12), 32–41.

THOMAS OAKLAND
University of Texas, Austin

CULTURAL BIAS IN TESTING
INDIVIDUAL EDUCATION PLAN
RACIAL DISCRIMINATION IN SPECIAL EDUCATION

NONSHELTERED EMPLOYMENT

Diverse employment options are available for graduates of special education programs. In the past, sheltered employment was a highly probable adult work setting for individuals with mental retardation. Today, several al-

ternative employment options provide graduates with opportunities to experience work conditions in the mainstream of society. Nonsheltered employment comprises a range of work situations, including mobile work crews, enclaves within industry, competitive employment, and a supported work approach. These outcomes are enhanced through a commitment to a longitudinal progression of functional vocational curricular activities. The activities provide the mentally retarded with the requisite skills to function within integrated, community employment settings. The sequence of activities that follows results in nonsheltered employment options for individuals graduating from special education programs.

The first of these activities is a survey of nonsheltered community employment opportunities. Local market conditions, as well as future trends in employment, are carefully analyzed by vocational development specialists. Advisory committees comprised of representatives from the chamber of commerce, local manufacturing companies, government agencies, industries, nonprofit agencies, and other major sources of employment in the local community convene to provide feedback relative to local community employment opportunities.

The second step is to analyze requisite skills from targeted employment opportunities. Detailed job skill inventories are collected by a job development specialists as they observe currently employed workers performing activities within selected occupations. Socialization, academic, strength/stamina, transportation, orientation, and other critical skills are detailed. Two outcomes emerge from this analysis. First, for transition plans, priority individual educational plan objectives are directly related to requisite skills within anticipated future work settings. Second, a longitudinal sequence of activities is integrated into the curriculum to provide ample exposure and opportunities for acquiring requisite skills.

A criterion-referenced assessment of the trainee is the third step in the sequence of activities. Once the requisite employment skills have been delineated through local job skill inventories, students/adults are assessed in natural, community work environments to evaluate current proficiencies relative to job demands. Norm-referenced, simulated assessments should be deemphasized when readying individuals for nonsheltered employment. The focus of assessment is to match as closely as possible currently available jobs with proficiency strengths of individuals. When deficiencies occur, trainers use systematic training strategies to teach new skills.

With systematic training strategies, trainers are paired with students/adults at an employment site and act as job coaches for the trainees. Acquisition strategies include varying the intensity of prompts prior to the occurrence of a behavior or providing varying intensities of feedback/reinforcement. Additionally, modification of the task itself may include altering the sequence of steps, modifying the physical nature of the materials, allowing the trainee to independently complete parts of the task, and rearranging duties of the trainee so that coworkers complete the more difficult steps of an activity.

Follow-along services are supplied in the final activity of the nonsheltered employment options. A critical dimension of nonsheltered employment is the fading of assistance from the trainer to allow the site supervisor of nondisabled workers to assume the same duties with the trainee. This fading process includes the analysis of supervisory feedback forms, the collection of data for rate and quality of work, the interviewing of parents to clarify incentives for long-term employment, and the willingness of a school/agency to be on call for crisis situations that, if not immediately handled, could result in termination of the trainee.

REFERENCES

Rusch, F. R. (Ed.). (1986). *Competitive employment: Service delivery models, methods, and issues.* Baltimore, MD: Brookes.

Wehman, P., & Hill, J. (1985). *Competitive employment for persons with mental retardation: From research to practice.* Richmond, VA: Commonwealth University, Research Training Center.

Wehman, P., Kregel, J., & Barcus, J. M. (1985). From school to work: A vocational transition model for handicapped students. *Exceptional Children, 52,* 25–37.

ERNEST PANCSOFAR
Bowling Green State University

SHELTERED WORKSHOPS
VOCATIONAL REHABILITATION
VOCATIONAL TRAINING OF THE HANDICAPPED

NOONAN'S SYNDROME (MALE TURNER'S SYNDROME)

Noonan's syndrome, which closely resembles Turner's syndrome phenotypically, primarily affects males; it may be a sex-linked chromosomal abnormality, but the specific cause is uncertain. Characteristics are similar to those of females with Turner's syndrome (Bergsma, 1979). Children with Noonan's syndrome usually are short in stature, have webbed necks or short broad necks with excessive skin folds, and swelling and puffiness of the extremities, especially the hands and feet. Swelling, present at birth, may disappear as the child develops. Testicular underdevelopment and missing secondary sexual development are often seen. Eyes are widely spaced, may slant, squint, or have epicanthal folds, and nearsightedness is often noted (Collins & Turner, 1973). Low-set ears are prominent and slanted. Hair is coarse and teeth may be misshapen. Fingers and toes may be shortened and nails will be short and poorly developed. Occasionally loss of muscle tone may be reported, as will visual and hearing deficits.

Congenital heart disease is a common finding. Mild mental retardation is fairly common, although some children with Noonan's syndrome will have normal intelligence (Lemeshaw, 1982).

Educational placement should consider the degree of cognitive developmental disability that exists in the child although educable or trainable classes may often be necessary because of additional handicaps that may accompany this syndrome. Related services will be necessary if hearing and vision losses are documented. Since secondary sexual characteristics may be lacking, psychological and guidance counseling may be necessary to remediate for self-image and adjustment conflicts that may arise as the male reaches puberty. This will be more necessary if the child is mainstreamed. Medical care may often be necessary because of heart problems, as well as an adaptive physical education program.

REFERENCES

Bergsma, D. (1979). *Birth defects compendium* (2nd ed.). New York: National Foundation, March of Dimes.

Collins, E., & Turner, G. (1973). The Noonan syndrome: A review of the clinical and genetic features of 27 cases. *Journal of Pediatrics, 83,* 941–950.

Lemeshaw, S. (1982). *The handbook of clinical types in mental retardation.* Boston: Allyn & Bacon.

SALLY L. FLAGLER
University of Oklahoma

CROUZON'S SYNDROME
HUNTER'S SYNDROME
MENTAL RETARDATION
PHYSICAL ANOMALIES

NORMAL CURVE EQUIVALENT (NCE)

Normal curve equivalents (NCEs) are an esoteric score system designed specifically for use in evaluating federal Chapter 1 programs (Tallmadge, Wood, & Gamel, 1981). The NCEs are standard scores that have been scaled to a mean of 50 and a standard deviation of 21.06 (Mehrens & Lehman, 1984). This unusual choice of metrics was made so that a score system would exist that has normalized standard scores, has equal intervals, and has the same mean and range as percentile scores (1 to 99). Many users apparently believe that NCEs are thus in direct correspondence with a percentile rank scale, however, this occurs only at three points on the NCE scale; scores of 1, 50, and 99 coincide with the percentile rank scale. This direct correspondence does not occur at other points on the scale because of the equal interval nature of NCEs (as with most other standard score systems) where the distance between scores of 20 and 30, 45 and 55, and 70 and 80 is the same.

On a percentile scale, these distances are decidedly unequal. A gain in scores on a percentile rank score from the 90th to the 95th percentile is approximately twice as great as the gain in scores from the 80th to the 85th percentile.

Many achievement tests are now providing conversion tables for the derivation of NCEs expressly to make the tests eligible for use in Chapter 1 evaluations and reporting schemes. Outside of this use, NCEs have little purpose. More familiar systems, including percentile ranks and the familiar IQ-type scale, are more readily understood and accessible. The NCEs are easily confused with percentile scores.

REFERENCES

Mehrens, W. A., & Lehman, I. J. (1984). *Measurement and evaluation in guidance* (3rd ed.). New York: Holt, Rinehart, & Winston.

Tallmadge, G. K., Wood, C. T., & Gamel, N. (1981). *Users' guide: Title 1 evaluation and reporting system* (Vol. 1). Washington, DC: U.S. Department of Education.

VICTOR L. WILLSON
CECIL R. REYNOLDS
Texas A&M University

NORMAL CURVE
PERCENTILE SCORES
Z-SCORES, DETERMINATION OF DISCREPANCIES IN

NORMALIZATION

The strong belief of parents and advocates that the mentally retarded have a right to live and function in what is considered a normal environment led to the concept of normalization. These advocates stressed the fact that the handicapped are citizens and should be provided with opportunities and programs similar to those provided to normal children and adults. The term normalization originated in Denmark and was first implemented successfully in Scandinavian countries (Wolfensberger, 1972). Nerje (1979) introduced the term to America and defined it as "making available to all mentally retarded people patterns of life and conditions of everyday living which are close as possible to the regular circumstances of society" (p. 173).

During the 1970s there were many publications that listed suggestions for implementing the normalization principles. A collection of some popular comments were made by Bruininks and Warfield (1978), including the following:

Planning and managing for retarded people services that require attention to normative cultural patterns.

Allowing retarded people to experience normal routines of the day (e.g., dressing, eating in normal-sized groups) and normal routines of the life cycle (e.g., activities appropriate to one's age) that generally accompany increasing maturity.

Respecting choices and desires, and providing normal economic and civic privileges.

Providing education, training, care, and residential living facilities of normal size and appearance.

Using generic services whenever possible rather than separate ones. (pp. 191–192)

Recently, the term has been used to refer not only to the mentally retarded but to all handicapped individuals. Regardless of the type of disability, the individual should be included as much as possible in the community and society. This involves participation in what is considered normal daily living activities such as attending school (education), working at a job or sheltered workshop (employment), and attending movies and participating in activities at parks and YMCAs (recreation and leisure activities). Hallahan and Kauffman (1986) state that there are three major ways professionals have tried to implement the normalization principle. They are antilabeling, mainstreaming, and deinstitutionalization. The antilabeling movement focuses on eliminating labels and categories such as mental retardation, emotionally disturbed, and learning disabled. There are many disadvantages to labeling, which numerous educators believe strongly outnumber the advantages. It has been suggested and supported by research that labels bias expectations and views of the handicapped. The mainstreaming movement involves placing a handicapped child in an educational setting that is in the least restrictive environment; this means that based on educational and related service needs, the child should be placed with nonhandicapped children as much as possible. Deinstitutionalization is the process of removing handicapped individuals from the institution to community-based living quarters. During the late 1960s, there was a great deal of attention placed on the inadequate care provided by many institutions. The institution was considered the dumping ground for the helpless individuals regardless of the level of severity of the handicapping condition. The current trend is to place the handicapped closer to their families and communities. These environments include community residential facilities, group homes, and halfway houses.

REFERENCES

Bruininks, R. H., & Warfield, G. (1978). The mentally retarded. In E. L. Meyen (Ed.), *Exceptional children and youth: An introduction*. Denver: Love.

Hallahan, D. P., & Kauffman, J. M. (1986). *Exceptional children: Introduction to special education*. Englewood Cliffs, NJ: Prentice-Hall.

Nirje, B. (1979). Changing patterns in residential services for the mentally retarded. In E. L. Meyen (Ed.), *Exceptional children and youth: An introduction*. Denver: Love.

Wolfensberger, W. (1972). *The principle of normalization in human services*. Toronto, Canada: National Institute on Mental Retardation.

JANICE HARPER
*North Carolina Central
University*

CASCADE OF SERVICES
DEINSTITUTIONALIZATION
INDEPENDENT LIVING

NORM-REFERENCED TESTING

Norm-referenced tests (NRT) refer to a broad array of standardized tests, the results of which are interpreted by comparing the performance of examinees with that of a specified population of individuals, or norm group. In a broader sense, NRT often refers to a type of test frequently defined by contrasting it with criterion-referenced tests (CRT), where test results are referenced to a particular content domain and provide information about the skills an examinee has acquired, not the rank of an examinee in a norm group (Anastasi, 1982).

Most standardized tests are norm referenced. They are designed to be administered under standard conditions, according to carefully specified directions, and scored in an objective manner so that the results may be referenced to norms based on a representative sample of the population who took the test under similar conditions during standardization. The normative frame of reference for most standardized tests used in schools is usually a national (U.S.) age or grade group such as eight-year-old children, sixth-grade pupils, or college-bound high-school seniors.

A variety of norm-referenced tests are used in psychology and education. Intelligence tests, aptitude tests, achievement tests, and interest and personality tests all rely mainly on norm group comparisons for their interpretation. The contrast between NRT and CRT refers specifically to achievement tests and, even more specifically, to those at the elementary school level that assess basic reading, arithmetic, and language skills (Anastasi, 1982; Mehrens & Lehmann, 1984). Even though the items used in NRT and CRT may appear to be indistinguishable, norm-referenced tests are almost always broader in their content coverage than the narrowly focused criterion-referenced tests.

With NRT, the interpretive process typically consists of consulting various types of norms, of which standard scores and percentile ranks have the greatest utility. Intelligence and scholastic aptitude test results are usually reported in terms of age-based standard scores and percentile ranks, while achievement test results are commonly reported in terms of grade-based standard scores and percentile ranks. Grade equivalents are also frequently reported for achievement tests despite the fact that there are logical and statistical problems that obfuscate their meaning (Thorndike & Hagen, 1977). A typical norm-referenced interpretation for a 10-year-old child who obtained a standard score of 110 and a percentile rank of 74 on a verbal intelligence test would emphasize the fact that this child's standard score in verbal intelligence of 110 equaled or exceeded 74% of 10-year-old children tested in the norming sample. Standard scores frequently reference performance to the curve of normal distribution, a mathematical function that underlies much of NRT test construction and norming procedures.

The current pedagogic emphasis on individualized instruction, especially computer-assisted instruction, with its reliance on mastery of a carefully sequenced curriculum, has advanced the cause of CRT. In fact, Cronbach (1984) has observed that the current enthusiasm for criterion reference and domain reference is chiefly a reaction against a competitive, comparative emphasis in education: an emphasis fostered by NRT.

Measurement experts seem to agree that too much attention has been focused on the apparent differences between norm-referenced and criterion-referenced tests, while too little attention has been given to their similarities, especially the fact that a normative frame of reference is implicit in all testing regardless of the interpretive system used to reference the scores. The construction of criterion-referenced tests requires information about the skills and capabilities of the intended examinees. In addition, normative information of a sort is needed when criterion-referenced mastery tests are used to regulate progress through a curriculum. In the latter instance, questions inevitably arise about the typical, or expected, rate of progress through the sequenced curricular units or content strands (Anastasi, 1982; Thorndike & Hagen, 1977).

The ultimate justification for any test is the use to be made of the results. While at one time a considerable difference of opinion existed between proponents of NRT and CRT, the chasm seems to have been narrowed by the recognition that both types of measures provide useful information. Choice of one or the other depends on the decisions that need to be made by the test user. The NRT is most appropriate for educational and employment selection. As stated earlier, aptitude, interest, and personality assessment are all norm-referenced because an external, comparative frame of reference provides the most useful sort of interpretation. Achievement testing may employ both NRT and CRT. If information is needed, for example, about which curriculum objectives a student has mastered, then CRT will provide the most useful information. If, on the other hand, a survey of pupil achievement in several areas is needed, or if a school district wants to know how its pupils compare with those in other districts, then NRT provides more useful information (Mehrens & Lehmann, 1984). Current elementary achievement batteries, which provide both norm-referenced and criterion-referenced interpretive data, attest to the utility of having both types of information available. Such tests frequently provide standard norm-referenced information for broad content domains such as reading, mathematics, and language. They also provide information on content objectives, or clusters, and sometimes on the test items.

Benefits of both NRT and CRT come closest to realization when users exercise caution and sound judgment in the selection and interpretation of either type of measure. Since its introduction around 1920, NRT has undergone periodic episodes of both unrestrained use and enthusiasm followed by disenchantment and disillusionment. When introduced in mastery testing in the 1920s, CRT was subsequently abandoned because of its narrow focus and inability to capture the full extent of individual differences. Readers are urged to keep this historical perspective in mind when assessing the merits of NRT and CRT. A balanced view of both types of measurement procedures will undoubtedly yield the most benefits to test users and test takers.

REFERENCES

Anastasi, A. (1982). *Psychological testing*. New York: Macmillan.

Cronbach, L. J. (1984). *Essentials of psychological testing*. New York: Harper & Row.

Mehrens, W. A., & Lehmann, I. J. (1984). *Measurement and evaluation in education and psychology*. New York: CBS College.

Thorndike, R. L., & Hagen, E. P. (1977). *Measurement and evaluation in psychology and education*. New York: Wiley.

GARY J. ROBERTSON
American Guidance Service,
Circle Pines, Minnesota

ASSESSMENT
CRITERION REFERENCE TESTING
MEASUREMENT

NORTHWESTERN SYNTAX SCREENING TEST

The Northwestern Syntax Screening Test, developed by Laura L. Lee, is purported to measure the syntactical language structure of students ages 3 to 8. This instrument was developed as a screening device and was not intended to be used as a measure of a student's overall language skills. It consists of 20 identical linguistic structures that compose the instrument's receptive and expressive portions (Lee, 1979).

The developers suggest that when using the test as a screening device for a kindergarten class, the examiner cease testing when it is determined that the student is at or above the 10% level for his or her age group. If the instrument is being used to obtain supplemental information on a student's syntactical language ability, it is suggested that the test be completed. Although the paired sentences are ordered by increasing difficulty, the test is too short to establish basal or ceiling scores (Lee, 1979).

This test has been criticized because of a lack of reliability data. Klein (1980) attempted to establish reliability data, but the time period between test-retest was 7 months. Based on this extended time period and the lack of reliability data, Pearson and Stick (1985) concluded that a need for these data still exists.

In addition, researchers have expressed concern over the lack of validity data. Most researchers reported that this screening instrument has been effective in identifying students with delayed syntactical language abilities, but there have also been reports of false positives (Pearson & Stick, 1985).

Normative data have been criticized based on the limitations of geographic area, economic class, and age intervals of 1 year. Norms were established on 344 students between the ages of 3-0 and 7-11. These students attended nursery or public school, were from middle- or upper-income families in which standard American dialect was spoken and were judged by their teachers as not having handicapping conditions that would inhibit normal language development (Pearson & Stick, 1985).

Lee acknowledges these criticisms and recommends that the clinician use the instrument for its intended purpose, as a screening device for students speaking standard English. Lee also recommends that clinicians establish their own norms dependent on their local population (Lee, 1979).

REFERENCES

Klein, A. E. (1980). Test-retest reliability and predictive validity of the Northwestern Syntax Screening Test. *Educational & Psychological Measurement, 40,* 1167–1172.

Lee, L. L. (1979). *Northwestern Syntax Screening Test.* Evanston, IL: Northwestern University Press.

Pearson, M. E., & Stick, S. L. (1985). Review of Northwestern Syntax Screening Test. In J. V. Mitchell, Jr. (Ed.), *The ninth mental measurements yearbook* (pp. 1059–1063). Lincoln: University of Nebraska Press.

ETTA LEE NURICK
Montgomery County
Intermediate Unit,
Norristown, Pennsylvania

NUCLEAR MAGNETIC RESONANCE (NMR) OR MAGNETIC RESONANCE IMAGING (MRI)

Nuclear magnetic resonance (NMR) or magnetic resonance imaging (MRI) is a technique for imaging the brain and body parts. This technique is based on the premise that atomic nuclei with odd numbers of either protons or neutrons possess a small magnetic field that is dependent on the spin of these nuclear particles. With the application of a strong external magnetic source, there is a weak torque that is exerted on the nuclei; the nuclear particles orient to the applied magnetic field. During this alignment process, the nuclei oscillate about the magnetic field like a compass needle aligning with Earth's magnetic field. The degree of oscillation is directly related to the strength of the magnetic field. The degree of magnetic field resonance emitted can be detected by measuring the magnetic field changes, which in turn relate to the density of the tissue or structure being examined. At this point, the process becomes similar to computerized axial tomography (CAT scanning) in that a density coding system is used to create the image. In CAT scanning this is based on the number of X-ray particles that pass through tissue. In NMR or MRI the density is dependent on the resonance of atomic nuclear particles to different magnetic fields. The physics of this procedure are outlined in the works by Bottomley (1984) and Pykett, Newhouse, and Buonanno (1982).

The NMR technique provides an image that approximates anatomical appearance of the structure being imaged (see Figure). In comparison with CAT scanning, there are some major advantages. Since no ionizing radiation is used, there is no hazard from X-ray irradiation. The NMR image better differentiates certain tissue differences so that in NMR brain sections there is a clearer image between brain and bone and white and gray matter (see Figure 1). The NMR also allows the detection of subtle

tissue changes that cannot be detected with CAT scanning and permits the topographic demonstration of the anatomic changes underlying neurobehavioral syndromes (DeMyer, Hendrie, Gilmor, & DeMyer, 1985; DeWitt, Grek, Buonanno, Levine, & Kistler, 1985). Current drawbacks to NMR include its cost, the fact that it is a new procedure and clinical studies are lacking, and the inability to scan patients with any type of metallic implants (i.e., pacemakers, artificial joints, aneurysm clips, etc.) because of the strength of the magnetic field.

REFERENCES

Bottomley, P. A. (1984). NMR in medicine. *Computerized Radiology, 8,* 57–77.

DeMyer, M. K., Hendrie, H. C., Gilmor, R. L., & DeMyer, W. E. (1985). Magnetic resonance imaging in psychiatry. *Psychiatric Annals, 15,* 262–267.

DeWitt, L. D., Grek, A. J., Buonanno, F. S., Levine, D. N., and Kistler, J. P. (1985). MRI and the study of aphasia. *Neurology 35,* 861–865.

Pykett, I. L., Newhouse, J. H., Buonanno, F. S. (1982). Principles of nuclear magnetic resonance imaging. *Radiology, 143,* 157–163.

ERIN D. BIGLER
*Austin Neurological Clinic
University of Texas, Austin*

CAT SCAN
X-RAY AND HANDICAPPING CONDITIONS
X-RAY SCANNING TECHNIQUES

Sagittal section demonstrating NMR-MRI technique in visualizing cerebral structures. The detailed obtained with NMR-MRI techniques approaches what would be observed with an actual anatomic specimen.

NUTRITIONAL DISORDERS

Nutritional disorders has been used as an umbrella term to cover the full range of eating (anorexia nervosa, bulimia, and pica), metabolic, and nutritional disorders. Those looking for a good overall general review of the major nutrition-related health problems in children and methods of preventing them should see Fomon (1977).

REFERENCE

Fomon, S. J. (1977). Nutritional disorders of children: Prevention, screening, and followup (publication number (HSA) 77-5104). Rockville, MD: Department of Health, Education, and Welfare.

MARY ANN C. FARTHING
*University of North Carolina,
Chapel Hill*

ANOREXIA NERVOSA
EATING DISORDERS
METABOLIC DISORDERS

O

OBESITY

Obesity is the most common nutrition-related problem in the United States today. Data from health and nutrition surveys indicate that the prevalence of obesity among adults ranges from 25 to 30% in various population groups. It is estimated that from 5 to 10% of school-age children and 10 to 15% of adolescents are obese (Pipes, 1985). The prevalence of obesity appears to be lower among low-income preschool children, but the trend is reversed for adolescents (Peck & Ullrich, 1985).

Obesity is defined most simply as excess body fat (Bray, 1979). It is characterized by an excessive deposition of adipose tissue. One criterion that is commonly used to indicate obesity is 20% above the recommended standard weight for height, age, and sex. Obesity is also classified by various authorities in relation to fat cell size and number, age when obesity first occurs, psychosocial factors, and degree of severity (Peck & Ullrich, 1985).

Overweight is a term that is often used interchangeably with obesity in the literature. However, overweight can refer to any degree of weight that is above the accepted standard for height. It can result from increased lean body mass, adipose tissue, or both (Pipes, 1985).

Gross obesity is easy to recognize by visual inspection. However, the use of weight for height standards aids in measuring the degree of overweight or obesity. The adult height-weight tables are based on the extensive records maintained by life insurance companies over the years. The standards used for children are growth grids prepared in 1978 by an expert panel for the National Center for Health Statistics (NCHS) (Pipes, 1985). Standards for tricep fatfold measurements with calipers have also been published by NCHS. Careful use of these standards with children as they grow can aid in identifying those for whom intervention measures should be initiated to prevent inappropriate weight gains.

A large body of data now exists that documents the health hazards that obesity poses for adults. Obese individuals are at higher risk for hypertension, cardiovascular disease, adult onset diabetes, and gallbladder disease. They may also be discriminated against in job placement and advancement.

Peck and Ullrich (1985) cite psychological and social problems as the greatest health hazards for the obese child. Such problems include a poor self-image, sense of failure, and a passive approach to life. These authors point out that although health risks associated with childhood obesity are not so clear-cut, studies indicate that rigid weight control measures for children can interfere with normal growth and development, mental functioning, and reproductive capacity. The increase in disturbed eating behaviors such as anorexia nervosa and bulimia may be related to extreme and persistent weight reduction measures.

The fact that many obese children become obese adolescents and obese adults is cause for concern. Early onset obesity is usually more severe and resistant to treatment than adult onset obesity (Pipes, 1985).

Detailed descriptions of appropriate measures for intervention with childhood or adult obesity are beyond the scope of this discussion. Peck and Ullrich (1985) offer guidance for health professionals working with obese children. They suggest a progression of activities based on the magnitude and complexity of the problem. Any approach should be planned after assessment of the circumstances and needs of the person involved.

Sound weight management programs also exist for working with adolescents and adults. Most authorities recommend a multidisciplinary approach to intervention. Sound programs include behavior modification, lifestyle changes to increase activity levels, and appropriate changes in food practices.

Prevention of obesity requires careful attention to its causes. Genetic factors such as body build and individual variations in fat storage patterns are important in the etiology of obesity (Peck & Ullrich, 1985). Environmental influences such as familial food practices and parenting skills should not be overlooked. A sedentary lifestyle with little exercise on a daily basis contributes to both childhood and adult obesity.

Regardless of other factors involved, excess weight results when more food energy is taken over time than is required for the growth, maintenance, and activity of the body. Preventive measures should be directed toward positive changes in attitude, lifestyle, and eating patterns in all segments of the population at risk of obesity.

REFERENCES

Bray, G. A. (Ed.). (1979). *Obesity in America*. Washington, DC: National Institutes of Health.

Peck, E. B., & Ullrich, H. D. (1985). *Children and weight: A changing perspective.* Berkeley, CA: Nutrition Communications Associates.

Pipes, P. L. (1985). *Nutrition in infancy and childhood* (3rd ed.). St. Louis: Times/Mirror Mosby.

MaryAnn C. Farthing
University of North Carolina, Chapel Hill

**ANOREXIA NERVOSA
EATING DISORDERS**

OBJECTIVE PERSONALITY TESTS

See PERSONALITY TESTS, OBJECTIVE.

OBSERVATIONAL LEARNING

Observational learning, the currently preferred term for imitation, is a basic process in the development of normal and abnormal behavior. As Bandura (1986) has said, "Through the years, modeling has always been acknowledged to be one of the most powerful means of transmitting values, attitudes, and patterns of thought and behavior" (p. 47). But that acknowledgment has not been explicit in many theories of learning, and only in recent decades has observational learning itself been extensively studied. The current status of observational learning is due in large part to the pioneering work of two groups of researchers. Miller and Dollard (1941) emphasized the role of imitation in both the acquisition of new behaviors and the facilitation or disinhibition of previously learned behaviors. Bandura (1962) and Bandura and Walters (1963) provided evidence on the way in which imitation influences the development of behavior, the role of imitation in identification, and the extent to which children imitate behavior modeled by others. Observational learning is a basic concept in social learning theory. Further, imitation, particularly delayed imitation, is for Piaget an important aspect of development during the sensorimotor period.

Although behaviorists (Gewirtz, 1971) have attempted to explain imitation on the basis of reinforcement of stimulus-response associations, such an explanation appears unable to handle easily a variety of phenomena, including initial imitation and delayed imitation. Therefore, this entry will generally follow the cognitive model of observational learning proposed by Bandura (1986).

Types of Modeling Effects

A model can affect an observer's behavior in a variety of ways.

Acquisition of Novel Responses. Strictly speaking, observational learning refers to the acquisition of novel responses. Indeed, observing a model can result in a child's performing a response that had virtually zero probability before the observation. For example, to evaluate different theories of identificatory learning, Bandura, Ross, and Ross (1963) exposed nursery-school children to adult models who exhibited a number of novel—and bizarre—behaviors such as exclaiming "A stickero" on picking up a sticker picture and "Weto-smacko" on licking it. The children later imitated a number of these behaviors. Further, children exposed to aggressive models tended to imitate the specific aggressive responses displayed.

Inhibition and Disinhibition. Modeling may also decrease (inhibit) or increase (disinhibit) previously learned responses. In many studies of modeled aggression, subjects emit a variety of aggressive behaviors, not just those modeled, in testing (Steuer, Applefield, & Smith, 1971). Further, the consequences to models of their behavior may influence observers. In one study, children who saw a model punished for aggressive behavior subsequently showed lower aggression than those who saw a model who received no consequences. In that particular study, however, children who saw a model rewarded for aggressive behavior did not show higher aggression (Bandura, 1965). Thus disinhibition may occur when observers see models perform prohibited responses without suffering adverse consequences, and inhibition may occur when observers see models punished for their behavior (Bandura, 1986).

Response Facilitation. Response, or social, facilitation occurs when models cue particular behaviors. Thus models can activate, channel, or support the behavior of others (Bandura, 1986). A common example is looking up when one sees a group of people looking up.

Environmental Enhancement. In this case, the model's behavior directs the observer to specific stimuli rather than specific responses. Thus a child watching a group of children eating a particular food may start eating that food instead of another food.

Arousal Effects. Models who express emotional reactions may arouse those emotions in observers. In some studies of modeling of aggressive behavior, the observers not only showed more aggressive behavior, but appeared to be experiencing a heightened state of aggression.

Processes in Observational Learning

In Bandura's (1986) social cognitive analysis of observational learning, modeling is presumed to operate mainly by providing information. Bandura (1986) proposes a four-component model to account for observational learning. Because these processes become more sophisticated with age, observational learning shows important developmental trends. The processes may be briefly summarized.

Attentional Processes. In order to learn, one must attend to the modeled activities. Given the variety of models and other stimuli generally available, a child will selectively attend to relatively few. Observer factors that influence attention include perceptual capabilities and arousal level. Characteristics of the modeled activity such as conspicuousness and functional value also influence attention. Model characteristics and past experiences of the observer with the model are additional factors.

Retention. For delayed imitation to occur, the observer must be able to remember the modeled activity. Retention entails symbolic transformation into images and words. As with verbal material, transformation into meaningful terms and elaborated rehearsal facilitate retention of observed activities. Bandura (1986) stresses the importance of immediate and intermittent actual and cognitive rehearsal of observed activities.

Production Processes. Bandura (1986) suggests that "most modeled activities are abstractly represented as conceptions and rules of action which specify what to do" (p. 63). To produce the activity, responses must be organized in accordance with those conceptions and rules. A variety of evidence using verbal reports and recognition tests indicate that both children and adults can learn modeled activities without actually having performed them. Motor deficits may limit accurate imitation, and improvement may result from improvement in motor skills. Feedback is important in improving such skills. In complex motor skills such as those involved in playing a musical instrument, corrective modeling may be the most valuable. In corrective feedback, a skilled individual models the activity correctly; students then attempt to match it.

Motivational Processes. Behavior may be acquired through observational learning but not performed in the absence of appropriate incentive. Direct, vicarious, and self-produced rewards are all important in the actual production of learned responses, as is the observer's own motivation.

Reducing Children's Fears

Exposure to a fearless model is an effective way of reducing severe fears and anxiety in both children and adults. The general procedure involves having the anxious or fearful person observe a model (sometimes multiple models) coping with a situation that arouses anxiety in the observer. After several such observations, reduction in fear or anxiety frequently occurs.

To consider one classic example, Bandura, Grusec, and Menlove (1967) randomly assigned nursery-school children who were severely afraid of dogs to watch one of several films. Two treatment films showed a 4 year old coming into increasingly close contact with a dog. Across eight brief sessions, the child went from initially standing near the dog while it was in a pen to finally being in the pen playing with the dog. The two films differed only in that one was conducted in a party atmosphere and the other in a neutral atmosphere. Control groups watched films that showed the dog and the party, but no model, in order to control for effects of mere exposure to the feared object or a playful setting. In a series of graded tests, the children were asked to approach and pet a novel dog and even to climb into a pen and remain alone with a dog. Children who had watched either treatment film showed less fear of and more interaction with the dogs in testing relative both to pretest scores and the control groups. Follow-up tests showed that the reduction in fear lasted at least 1 month.

Modeling techniques, using live, filmed, or even cognitive (imagined) models, have been used to reduce fears of a variety of settings, including the dentist's office and the hospital (Bandura, 1986).

Modeled information can be acquired and retained without being immediately performed in the absence of appropriate incentives. For example, Bandura (1965) had groups of children watch a film in which a model displayed a high level of aggressive behavior toward another character. Different groups of children saw different endings to the film; the model was rewarded, punished, or suffered no consequences for aggressive behavior. In immediate testing, children who saw the model punished showed much less agressive behavior; girls were less aggressive than boys. However, when offered reinforcement for producing the modeled aggressive behavior, both boys and girls who saw all films reproduced a large number of the modeled behaviors. Thus, consequences to a model influence performance of modeled behaviors much more than learning of the behaviors.

Different models induce different degrees of imitation. Two factors that consistently appear as important in both experimental (Bandura, Ross, & Ross, 1963) and correlational (Hetherington & Frankie, 1967) research are power and warmth. Models are particularly likely to be imitated if they behave in an authoritative way, exerting control but showing care and concern.

An observer who is reinforced for imitating some modeled responses will also imitate other responses of the same model; this is important for the application of modeling techniques (Baer & Sherman, 1964). Thus a child who does not initially show high levels of imitation may be conditioned by appropriate reinforcement techniques to imitate in general.

Imitation begins to develop in infancy and becomes more exact during early childhood, with imitation of some responses developing earlier than others. For example, imitation of simple motor and social behaviors increases regularly from 12 to 24 months, whereas imitation of more complicated sequences may begin to occur only at 24 months or later (McCall, Parke, & Kavanaugh, 1977).

Although most theories suggest that infants should not begin to imitate until several months of age, Meltzoff and Moore (1977) have reported that 12- to 20-day-old infants imitate simple facial expressions such as sticking out the tongue and gaping. Some subsequent studies failed to find any evidence for newborn imitation (McKenzie & Over, 1982), while others reported imitation in even younger infants (Field et al., 1982), leaving the phenomenon in considerable doubt.

Television has a variety of effects on children. Considerable experimental and correlational evidence indicates that televised violence increases the aggressive behavior of some children, particularly boys and those who were already aggressive. On the other hand, viewing of programs such as "Mr. Rogers' Neighborhood" increases prosocial behavior. The research literature is voluminous (Liebert, Sprakin, & Davidson, 1982).

A common recommendation to parents and teachers is to avoid using physical punishment with children because the punisher is providing a model of aggressive behavior that may be imitated by the child. Laboratory research (Gelfand et al., 1974) supports this recommendation. Young children imitate both punitive and reward control techniques, and the imitation persists over time.

Most children do imitate; others can be trained to imitate. Formal observational learning and reinforcement programs can be used to increase a variety of prosocial behaviors and to decrease antisocial or maladaptive ones. Additionally, children will imitate under informal circumstances. Teachers should remember that they generally have the characteristics that further imitation. If their behaviors are discrepant with their words, children are likely to follow the behaviors. "Do as I say and not as I do" is not likely to be successful. Finally, all who work with children would do well to remember that power and warmth, not power alone, are important characteristics of successful models.

REFERENCES

Baer, D. M., & Sherman, J. A. (1964). Reinforcement control of generalized imitation in young children. *Journal of Experimental Child Psychology, 1*, 37–49.

Bandura, A. (1962). Social learning through imitation. In M. R. Jones (Ed.), *Nebraska symposium on motivation* (Vol. 10, pp. 211–274). Lincoln: University of Nebraska Press.

Bandura, A., & Walters, R. H. (1963). *Social Learning and Personality Development.* New York: Holt, Rinehart, & Winston.

Bandura, A. (1965). Influence of models' reinforcement contingencies on the acquisition of imitative responses. *Journal of Personality & Social Psychology 1*, 589–595.

Bandura, A. (1986). *Social foundations of thought and action: A social cognitive theory.* Englewood Cliffs, NJ: Prentice-Hall.

Bandura, A., Grusec, J. E., & Menlove, F. L. (1967). Vicarious extinction of avoidance behavior. *Journal of Personality & Social Psychology, 5*, 16–23.

Bandura, A., Ross, D., & Ross, S. A. (1963). A comparative test of the status envy, social power, and secondary reinforcement theories of identificatory learning. *Journal of Abnormal & Social Psychology, 67*, 527–534.

Field, T. M., Goodson, R., Greenberg, R., & Cohen, D. (1982). Discrimination and imitation of facial expressions by neonates. *Science, 28*, 179–181.

Gelfano, D. M., Hartmann, D. P., Lamb, A. K., Smith, C. L., Mahan, M. A., & Paul, S. C. (1974). The effects of adult models and described alternatives on children's choice of behavior management techniques. *Child Development, 45*, 585–593.

Gewirtz, J. L. (1971). Conditioned responding as a paradigm for observational, imitative learning and vicarious reinforcement. In H. W. Reese (Ed.), *Advances in child development and behavior* (Vol. 6, pp. 273–304). New York: Academic.

Hetherington, E. M., & Frankie, G. (1967). Effects of parental dominance, warmth, and conflict on imitation in children. *Journal of Personality & Social Psychology, 6*, 119–125.

Liebert, R. M., Sprakin, J. N., & Davidson, E. S. (1982). *The early window: Effects of television on children and youth* (2nd ed.). Elmsford, NY: Pergamon.

McCall, R. B., Parke, R. D., & Kavanaugh, R. D. (1977). Imitation of live and televised models by children one to three years of age. *Monographs of the Society for Research in Child Development, 42*(5, Serial No. 173).

McKenzie, B., & Over, R. (1982). Young infants fail to imitate facial and manual gestures. *Infant Behavior & Development, 6*, 85–95.

Meltzoff, A., & Moore, M. K. (1977). Imitation of facile and manual gestures by human neonates. *Science, 198*, 75–78.

Miller, N. E., & Dollard, J. (1941). *Social learning and imitation.* New Haven, CT: Yale University Press.

Steuer, F. B., Applefield, J. M., & Smith, R. (1971). Televised aggression and the interpersonal aggression of preschool children. *Journal of Experimental Child Psychology, 11*, 442–447.

ROBERT T. BROWN
University of North Carolina,
Wilmington

ACTIVITY, THEORY OF
BEHAVIOR MODELING
LEARNING STYLES
PHOBIAS AND FEARS
SOCIAL LEARNING THEORY

OBSESSIVE COMPULSIVE DISORDERS

Obsession is defined by the American Psychiatric Association (1980) as, "A persistent, unwanted idea or impulse that cannot be eliminated by logic or reasoning" (p. 98). A compulsion is, "An insistent, repetitive, intrusive, and unwanted urge to perform an act that is contrary to one's ordinary wishes or standards. . . . Failure to perform the compulsive act leads to overt anxiety. Compulsions are obsessions that are still felt as impulses" (American Psychiatric Association, 1980, p. 20). In addition to the major attributes of obsession and compulsion, a number of additional responses are often present. Yaryura-Tobias and Nezirogly (1983) report that individuals who exhibit obsessive compulsive responses are also likely to be depressed (94%), anxious (90%), aggressive (65%), and dysperceptive (60%). Though occurring less frequently, individuals with obsessive compulsive disorders may also have sleep disorders (49%), family disturbances (45%), sexual dysfunctions (34%), or appetite disorders (33%); they may also be self-abusive (16%).

The disorder has an extensive history in the psychological literature, with reports of obsessive compulsive behavior even appearing in ancient writings (Yaryura-Tobias & Nezirogly, 1983). It has also produced a substantial body of applied treatment research as illustrated in a review by Foa and Steketee (1980). Despite substantial professional interest, the incidence of obsessive-compulsive disorders is relatively low. Beech and Vaughan (1978) report that the incidence in psychiatric patient populations is between 0.1 and 4%. Among the general population, an incidence of approximately .05% has been reported (Black, 1974).

Although there is some disagreement, many authorities believe that individuals are constitutionally predisposed to developing obsessive compulsive behavior and that life events eventually trigger the responses (Vila & Beech, 1978). Supporting this view is an increased rate of occurrence among relatives of people with obsessional disorder (Kringlen, 1965). Also, onset of the disorder typically occurs in association with difficult events occurring in the teens or early twenties (Lo, 1967).

Obsessive compulsive reactions have been described as conforming to four major courses: progressive deterioration, variable severity but never symptom free, phasic with remissions, and constant. Regardless of the course, the disorder is typically considered to be serious and the prognosis for a majority of affected persons is poor (Kringlen, 1965). Common treatments have included psychotherapy, behavior therapy, pharmacological intervention, vitamin and diet therapy, and psychosurgery. Each approach has been demonstrated to be variably effective, and is more likely to be prescribed based on the orientation of the therapist rather than the clinical features of the individual.

REFERENCES

American Psychiatric Association. (1980). *A psychiatric glossary* (5th ed.). New York: Author.

Beech, H. R., & Vaughan, M. (1978). *Behavioral treatment of obsessional states.* New York: Wiley.

Black, A. (1974). The natural history of obsessional neurosis. In H. R. Beech (Ed.), *Obsessional states* (pp. 19–54). London: Methuen.

Foa, E. B., & Steketee, G. S. (1980). Obsessive compulsives: Conceptual issues and treatment interventions. In M. Hersen, R. M. Eisler, & P. M. Miller (Eds.), *Progress in behavior modification* (Vol. 8). New York: Academic.

Kringlen, E. (1965). Obsessional neurotics. *British Journal of Psychiatry, 11,* 709–722.

Lo, W. H. (1967). A follow-up study of obsessional neurotics in Hong Kong Chinese. *British Journal of Psychiatry, 113,* 823–832.

Vila, J., & Beech, H. R. (1978). Vulnerability and defensive reactions in relation to the human menstrual cycle. *British Journal of Social & Clinical Psychology, 16,* 69–75.

Yaryura-Tobias, J. A., & Nezirogly, F. A. (1983). *Obsessive-compulsive disorders.* New York: Marcel Dekker.

PATRICK J. SCHLOSS
Pennsylvania State University

EMOTIONAL DISORDERS
MENTAL ILLNESS

OCCUPATIONAL THERAPY

Occupational therapy is the art and science of directing man's participation in selected tasks to restore, reinforce, and enhance performance, facilitate learning those skills and functions essential for adaptation and productivity, diminish or correct pathology, and to promote and maintain health. p. 204–205 (Council on Standards, 1972)

The primary concern of occupational therapy is response to activity. Special activities reather than exercise are used to increase function. These activities are purposeful and often medically prescribed. They may include manual, creative, or industrial arts. Occupational therapy activities are often part of the treatment plans for persons with physical, mental, and/or psychiatric disorders or disabilities. Although functional activity is the primary goal, the occupational therapist is equally concerned with the social, psychological, and communicative development of the patient.

In the early years, occupational therapy was primarily a service-oriented field with practice occurring mainly in hospitals and rehabilitation facilities. Today, occupational therapists have added research and the investigation and perfection of improved treatment methodology to their professional obligations. The field has broadened dramatically. Occupational therapists are members of multidisciplinary teams wherever their services are needed, as consultants, supervisors, or direct-service givers.

Along with the implementation of PL 94-142 came the critical need for occupational therapists in public school settings. Here they became involved in direct services (e.g., screening, referral, evaluation, program planning and implementation, reevaluation, and formulation of individual education plans) and indirect services (e.g., administration and management and consultation) (American Occupational Therapy Association, 1980). Many services that are critical to the development of severely handicapped children are provided by occupational therapists. The most important of these include the improvement of sensory integration, handling, and positioning. In many instances, it is necessary for the occupational therapist to adapt equipment for individuals. It is not uncommon for the occupational therapist to work with the physical therapist to provide services.

Increasing patients' daily living is another area for which occupational therapists assume responsibility. Patients may be physically disabled or developmentally delayed, young or old. Occupational therapists also may work with speech and language pathologists to develop strategies for improving oral motor functioning, thereby improving feeding and eating skills.

In 1984 W. L. West reaffirmed the philosophy and practice of occupational therapy today. A few of the important points follow:

Activity is the essence of living and is significantly interrelated with high morale.

To some degree, life itself is seen as purposeful occupation.

It is the purposefulness of behavior and activity that gives human life order.

Occupational therapy's body of knowledge lies in human behavior and activity as well as in the effect of pathology on behavior and the effect of activity on pathology (p. 16).

These statements reiterate the importance of functionality within the field of occupational therapy. The occupational therapist's task is to help each individual served achieve the fullest potential for a productive, satisfying, and self-sufficient life.

Two levels of assistants are available to work under the supervision of a registered occupational therapist: the certified occupational therapy assistant (COTA) and the occupational therapy aide (OTA).

REFERENCES

American Occupational Therapy Association. (1980). Standards of practice for occupational therapists in schools. *American Journal of Occupational Therapy, 34*, 900–905.

Council on Standards, American Occupational Therapy Association. (1972). Occupational therapy: Its definition and functions. *American Journal of Occupational Therapy, 26*, 204–205.

West, W. L. (1984). A reaffirmed philosophy and practice of occupational therapy for the 1980s. *American Journal of Occupational Therapy, 38*, 15–24.

ANNE CAMPBELL
Purdue University

**CAREER EDUCATION FOR THE HANDICAPPED
PHYSICAL THERAPY
REHABILITATION**

OFFICE OF SPECIAL EDUCATION (OSE)

When the U.S. Department of Education was created in 1980, the Office of Special Education (OSE) succeeded the Bureau of Education for the Handicapped. It had the same mission as the bureau, to help implement federal initiatives relative to the education of the handicapped. The OSE's organizational structure and functions were essentially unchanged. The OSE was one of three agencies, including the Rehabilitative Services Administration and the National Institute of Handicapped Research, that formed the Office of Special Education and Rehabilitative Services. In 1982 the U.S. Department of Education changed the name of the organization to Special Education Programs.

EMILIA C. LOPEZ
Fordham University

SPECIAL EDUCATION PROGRAMS

OLYMPICS, SPECIAL

The Special Olympics is the world's largest training and sports competition for the mentally retarded (Cipriano, 1980). Since its inception in 1968, over 2 million participants and volunteers have been involved in its local, regional, national, and international programs.

The development of the Special Olympics can be traced to the establishment of the Joseph P. Kennedy, Jr., Foundation in 1946. The foundation's goal was "to seek the prevention of mental retardation by identifying its causes and to improve the means by which society deals with its citizens who are mentally retarded" (Fact Sheet). The foundation subsequently sought to develop programs that foster public awareness of mental retardation. The Special Olympics is one of these.

The goal of the Special Olympics is to train its participants to compete in individual and team sports. The Olympics emphasizes sportsmanship, skill development, cooperation through teamwork, working toward achieving athletic goals, competing for self-fullment.

As is the case in the other Olympic Games, the importance of the Special Olympics lies in the training and preparation of individuals to compete, not in the games themselves. The games are intended to demonstrate the results of training progress (Henroid, 1979).

The first International Special Olympics was held in Chicago in 1968. There were 1000 competitors from 20 states and Canada on that occasion. By 1985 every state and 33 countries had organized Special Olympics training and competition programs. In the United States, over one million persons with mental retardation participate each year in local and state training and competition efforts in over 20,000 communities.

The International Special Olympic Games are held every 4 years. There are 16 different sports conducted during the summer and winter phases of the games. These include track and field, pentathlon, frisbee, swimming, diving, bowling, floor hockey, poly hockey, volleyball, team basketball, cheerleading, run-dribble and shoot, cross-country, soccer, equestrian, race walking, figure skating, alpine skiing, Nordic skiing, and snowshoeing.

A significant feature of the Special Olympics program is the large (now over 450,000 in number) volunteer force that organizes and administers the training and conditioning programs from local to international levels. The volunteers' tasks include fund-raising at the local and regional levels, transportation, and administrating local training clubs, as well as coaching and conducting competitions. Special Olympics volunteers come from schools, colleges, churches, social groups, and civil organizations such as the Rotary Club. They also come from the National Basketball and National Hockey professional sports leagues.

The International Special Olympic Games are fully sponsored by the Joseph P. Kennedy, Jr., Foundation. Local and regional programs and competitions preparing participants for the Special Olympics are funded through fund-raising efforts by the volunteer force. Contributions are secured from individual, group, and sources. The funds so raised are administered by a professional staff at regional and state Special Olympics offices.

State Special Olympics organizations conduct Special Olympics training schools in 16 sports. They use volunteer coaches that are certified by the training schools to coach mentally retarded participants. A participant must belong to a local training club for a specified period of time and be trained by the certified coaches.

An evaluation conducted by Orelove, Wahman, and Wood (1982) indicates the following advantages derived from participation in the Special Olympics program: development of sports skills; participation in activities endorsed and supported by society; a high degree of parental involvement and relationships with school and community groups; and the opportunity for mentally retarded persons to engage in age-, sex-, and ability-related competition. Nevertheless, Orelove, Wahman, and Wood (1982) state that the Special Olympics program does not espouse the principle of normalization. The program is only for handicapped individuals. In contrast, proponents of normalization advise that athletic competition should be integrated so as to include both handicapped and nonhandicapped persons. They also advise that the Special Olympics be expanded to include recreational activities and to minimize the overemphasis on competition and athletic training (Orelove, Wahman, & Wood, 1982).

REFERENCES

Cipriano, R. (1980). *Readings in Special Olympics.* Guilford, CT: Special Learning Corporation.

Fact sheet. (Undated). Washington DC: Joseph P. Kennedy, Jr., Foundation.

Henroid, L. (1979). *Special Olympics and Paraolympics.* New York: Watts.

Orelove, F., Wahman, T., & Wood, J. (1982). An evaluative review of Special Olympics: Implications for community recreation. *Education & Training for the Mentally Retarded, 17*(5), 325–329.

THOMAS BURKE
Hunter College, City University of New York

EQUINE THERAPY
RECREATION FOR THE HANDICAPPED
THERAPEUTIC RECREATION

ON-LINE DATA BASE FOR SPECIAL EDUCATION

Computerized storage of text and numeric data has made large collections of information more easily retrievable than ever before. Educators who have access to terminals or personal computers outfitted with a modem and the necessary software can tap into an increasing number of data bases in all fields and disciplines. With regard to research in special education, it is best to remember that every data base dealing with educational concerns in general will contain information useful to special educators. The largest educational data base is maintained by the Educational Resources Information Center (ERIC). Its scope is inclusive, and thousands of documents and journal articles on topics in special education have been indexed. When preparing to search either the online or print versions of ERIC, be sure to check the *Thesaurus of ERIC Descriptors* for the plethora of terms related to special education and disabilities. The Council for Exceptional Children has built an on-line data base that also uses ERIC descriptors. Its name is Exceptional Child Education Resources. Begun in 1966, this data base was developed specifically to aid all those studying and working in the field of special education. It is the on-line counterpart to a quarterly print document of the same name. It contains over 50,000 records culled from a variety of sources, including conference proceedings, doctoral dissertations, research reports, journal articles, teaching guides, and other instructional materials (Woodbury, 1982).

For instructional methods and materials appropriate to specific disabilities, there are two on-line data bases to consider. The first, produced by the National Information Center for Special Education Materials between 1974 and 1977, contains approximately 36,000 records of instructional materials and special equipment for use with handicapped learners. This data base has not been updated since its compilation, however, so recent innovations and new materials are not included. Another source for information on computer-based instructional materials is the Special Education Software Center run by LINC Resources of Columbus, Ohio. LINC will provide clients with a printout from its in-house data base of software programs designed for handicapped students. The records include information on required hardware, publisher, age, reading level, and type of disability. While the center does not conduct evaluations of the software, staff members can refer users to other sources of evaluation information.

The National Rehabilitation Information Center (NARIC), located at Catholic University of America, offers two useful on-line resources. Abledata describes commercial products for the disabled. It provides information on brand name, manufacturer, cost, and use. Although not geared specifically to education, it contains some information on educational products as well as on devices that may increase access of the handicapped to education. The second resource, called by the same name as the center, provides information on both print and audiovisual materials pertaining to the rehabilitation of people with physical, mental, and emotional disabilities. The documents range from research reports and training manuals to resource guides and directories.

Those interested in information pertaining to emotional disabilities should consult the NIMH (National Institute for Mental Health) data base, maintained by the National Clearinghouse for Mental Health Information in Rockville, Maryland. Citations in this data base come from over 1000 journals world wide and cover virtually every aspect of mental health. Also included are citations of books, research reports, conference proceedings, and nonprint materials. Updated monthly with the addition of approximately 3500 citations, this data base is accessible only on line.

SpecialNet, a new on-line service, is managed by the National Association of State Directors of Special Edu-

cation in Washington, DC. Although not a bibliographic data base, it provides a wealth of information of all sorts for special educators. It is a computer-based communications network designed to provide the latest information on educational services and programs and to deliver that information instantly. It does this in two ways. First, SpecialNet offers a wide variety of electronic bulletin boards. Some of these focus on specific disabilities such as VISION for those interested in the visually impaired, DEAFNESS for hearing impairments, or MULTIHANDICAPPED for severe or multiple disorders. Others deal with news from associations such as the Council for Exceptional Children (CEC) or the American Speech-Language-Hearing Association (ASHA). Still others serve as directories of one sort or another. CONSULTANT, for example, lists those willing to consult in various areas of education, and RPF tracks grants and contracts issued by various federal agencies. Member groups or organizations are also able to set up and maintain a bulletin board of their own. SpecialNet also serves as a vehicle for electronic mail. With this utility, members can send messages to each other, or send information to a list of individuals and groups. The state education agency of every state participates in this network, as well as other state and federal offices, universities, and special projects.

REFERENCES

Bulford, S. (1985, June). Special education software center database operable. *School Microcomputing Bulletin*, p. 80.

National Association of State Directors of Special Education. (n.d.). *Questions & answers about SpecialNet special education communication network*. Washington, DC: Author.

Woodbury, M. (1982). *A guide to sources of educational information* (pp. 186, 256). Arlington, VA: Information Resources Press.

JANET S. BRAND
Hunter College, City University of New York

INSTRUCTIONAL MEDIA/MATERIALS CENTER SPECIALNET

OPERANT CONDITIONING

As conceived by Skinner (1938), operant conditioning is essentially learning in which behavior is affected by its consequences, as in the simple paradigm for positive reinforcement:

$$R \rightarrow S^R$$

A contingency exists such that reinforcement (S^R) occurs only if a particular response (R) has occurred. The contingent relationship between response and reinforcement is one of the factors that most differentiates operant from Pavlovian conditioning. The response becomes more frequent (increases in probability) when followed by a reinforcing stimulus. The paradigm is clearly related to Thorndike's (1911) Law of Effect, which says, in essence, that responses followed by satisfying consequences become more firmly connected to the situation. The classic example of operant conditioning is a rat in an operant chamber containing a lever. If the rat is deprived of food, presses the lever, and is reinforced with food, then lever presses increase. If the response is reinforced only in the presence of a specific stimulus, S^D or discriminative stimulus, then the paradigm becomes:

$$S^D \rightarrow R \rightarrow S^R$$

For example, the rat may be reinforced (S^R) for bar pressing (R) only when a light (S^D) is on.

Skinner has proposed that the main task of psychology should be the functional analysis of behavior. That is, psychologists should determine of what antecedents and consequences behavior is a function. This approach has led to a model of behavior widely used by those who apply the operant approach to human behavior:

$$A \rightarrow B \rightarrow C$$

(Antecedents) (Behavior) (Consequences)

Operant conditioning is an important factor in the development of a wide variety of children's social and play behavior and also is important in the development of self-esteem and self-control (Bijou & Baer, 1967). Skinner has applied operant concepts to an understanding of everyday life (1953) and the development of a utopian society (1948).

Basic Aspects

The basics of operant conditioning can be briefly described.

Acquisition. As more responses are followed by reinforcement and response strength increases up to some maximum.

Extinction Occurs. If the response is no longer followed by reinforcement, its probability decreases, and it occurs less often.

Spontaneous Recovery. When put in the situation some time after extinction, the organism responds again, but at a lower rate.

Generalization and Discrimination. When responses are conditioned to occur to one discriminative stimulus, the child or animal will respond to similar stimuli; but if ex-plicitly nonreinforced for responding to a second stimulus, the organism generally will learn to respond only to the first.

Punishment. A response will become less likely if followed by either presentation of an aversive stimulus (positive punishment) or removal of a desired stimulus (negative punishment). Because punishment, particularly positive punishment, may have a variety of undesirable consequences, operant psychologists generally recommend other means of behavioral control.

Important Issues and Concepts

Nature of the Operant. Although we frequently talk about responses, Skinner's (1938) concept of the operant emphasizes a specified outcome rather than an actual response in terms of specific muscle movements. Thus if a child is reinforced for pushing a panel, panel-pushing is the operant. It does not matter whether the child presses with his or her left or right hand, left or right foot, or even the nose. The effects of behavior rather than the structure of the response itself are stressed.

Timing of Reinforcement and Punishment. Generally, reinforcing and punishing stimuli affect performance most if presented as soon as possible after the specified response. A reinforcing stimulus reinforces whatever response it immediately follows, such that a response that occurs between the target response and the reinforcement will be most reinforced. Punishment is actually most effective if delivered as the child just begins to make the undesirable response (Aronfreed, 1968).

In older children, time between response and reinforcement or punishment can be bridged by verbal mediators. At the time reinforcement or punishment is presented, words are used to reinstate the original situation where the child's behavior occurred. Aronfreed (1968) has demonstrated that such mediators increase the effectiveness of delayed punishment in inhibiting children's undesirable behavior.

Schedules of Reinforcement. Responses can be reinforced only intermittently rather then continuously (e.g., after every fourth response rather than after every response). One of Skinner's most important discoveries was that these partially reinforced responses are far more resistant to extinction than are 100% reinforced responses. Thus intermittent and unsystematic reinforcement increases the persistence of behavior. More detail on schedules and partial reinforcement can be found in most introductory or child psychology texts.

Primary vs. Conditioned (Secondary) Reinforcers. Primary reinforcers are stimuli that are intrinsically reinforcing such as food, water, and some kinds of tactile stimulation. Conditioned reinforcers are those stimuli that have acquired reinforcing power by being paired with another reinforcer. Thus money, grades, praise, and recognition are conditioned reinforcers. Conditioned reinforcers such as money can be very powerful because they are generalized reinforcers—they can be used to obtain a variety of other reinforcers.

Reinforcement History and Hierarchy. Different stimuli are reinforcing for different children and adults, making universal reinforcements hard to identify. Children will, partly as a result of their own histories, have different hierarchies of preferred reinforcers, although some items such as bubble gum are highly preferred by many young children. Further, reinforcement hierarchy generally changes with age: young children prefer tangible rewards, older children prefer social approval, and still older children prefer the intrinsic reinforcement from being correct (Witryol, 1971). However, tangible rewards may be more important for older low socioeconomic status children and for retarded children (Zigler, 1984), indicating that individual reinforcement hierarchies need to be considered in working with children.

Idiosyncrasies in reinforcer value led Premack (1965) to formulate a heuristic principle: preferred activities may be used to reinforce nonpreferred activities.

Positive and Negative Reinforcement. Reinforcement, by definition, increases behavior. Positive reinforcement occurs when a response is followed by presentation of a preferred event; negative reinforcement occurs when a response is followed by termination of an aversive event.

Shaping. Occasionally, a desired response may not be in the child's behavioral repertoire, in which case no response occurs that can be reinforced. In such cases, operant psychologists use shaping, or the method of successive approximations, to reinforce behaviors that increasingly resemble the target response. For example, Harris, Wolf, and Baer (1964) observed that a young boy spent virtually all of his time playing alone. Concerned about the child's subsequent social development, they established a target behavior of interactive play with other children and instructed the boy's preschool teacher to reinforce, with attention and approval, successive approximations to interactive play. The teacher ignored the boy when he played alone, but reinforced him initially when he just looked at other children playing, then when be began to move toward other children, and finally only when he interacted with other children. In a limited number of sessions, interactive play was successfully shaped.

Implications for Educators

Educators and others working with children should be sensitive to the effects of their behavior on children with whom they interact. Their behavior will frequently reinforce or punish children, sometimes inadvertently. Further, the child's perception determines whether a given event is rewarding or punishing. Using a common example, a teacher who yells at a misbehaving child views the yelling as a punisher, but to the child the attention may be reinforcing. On the other hand, to a very shy child, public recognition may be punishing. Of concern also is the possibility that adults will intermittently reinforce a child's undesirable response, therefore increasing its persistence and resistance to extinction.

In dealing with handicapped, particularly retarded, children, we need to consider that more tangible reinforcers and praise may be required to maintain performance than is the case with normal children.

REFERENCES

Aronfreed, J. (1968). Aversive control of socialization. In W. J. Arnold (Ed.), *Nebraska symposium on motivation* (pp. 271–320). Lincoln: University of Nebraska Press.

Bijou, S. W., & Baer, D. M. (Eds.). (1967). *Child development: Readings in experimental analysis*. New York: Appleton-Century-Crofts.

Bijou, S. W., & Baer, D. M. (1978). *Behavior analysis of child development*. Englewood-Cliffs, NJ: Prentice-Hall.

Harris, F. R., Wolf, M. M., & Baer, D. M. (1964). Effects of adult social reinforcement on child behavior. *Young Children, 20*, 8–17.

Premack, D. (1965). Reinforcement theory. In D. Levine (Ed.), *Nebraska symposium on motivation* (pp. 123–180). Lincoln: University of Nebraska Press.

Skinner, B. F. (1938). *The behavior of organisms: An experimental analysis*. New York: Appleton-Century-Crofts.

Skinner, B. F. (1948). *Walden two*. New York: Macmillan.

Skinner, B. F. (1953). *Science and human behavior*. New York: Macmillan.

Thorndike, A. E. L. (1911). *Animal intelligence*. New York: Macmillan.

Witryol, S. I. (1971). Incentives and learning in children. In H. W. Reese (Ed.), *Advances in child development and behavior* (Vol. 6). New York: Academic.

Zigler, E. (1984). A developmental theory on mental retardation. In B. Blatt & R. J. Morris (Eds.), *Perspectives in special education: Personal orientations* (pp. 173–209). Glenview, IL: Scott, Foresman.

ROBERT T. BROWN
*University of North Carolina,
Wilmington*

**BEHAVIOR MODIFICATION
CONDITIONING
GENERALIZATION
SKINNER, B. F.**

OPHTHALMOLOGIST

An ophthalmologist, sometimes called an oculist, is a medical doctor who specializes in the diagnosis and treatment of defects and diseases of the eye by prescribing lenses and, in some cases, drugs, performing eye surgery, and carrying out other types of medical treatment (Cartwright, Cartwright, & Ward, 1981, p. 71). Ocular disorders are of special significance because they often provide clues to the presence of systemic diseases and to other congenital malformations present in many handicapped children. Congenital rubella, Down's syndrome, and Marfan's syndrome are three conditions that are commonly associated with or are causes of visual impairments. Lists of ocular diseases and disorders are available in several resources (Goble, 1984; Jose, 1983; Nelson, 1984).

An important responsibility of the ophthalmologist related to serving visually impaired children and youths (which can also be performed by the optometrist) is a complete eye examination. This should include the following: developmental history, distance visual acuity, inspection of the eyes for evident physical problems, evaluation of ocular motility, determination of basic refractive status of the eyes, evaluation of accommodation of the eyes for near vision; visual field studies; testing of intraocular pressure; testing of color vision; and examination of the interior of the eye including the retina and vitreous (Goble, 1984; Nelson, 1984).

One of the subspecialists within the field of ophthalmology is a pediatric ophthalmologist, who focuses on the recognition, understanding, early treatment, and ultimately, prevention of ocular disease in childhood. This specialist is particularly skilled in areas such as visual development in the preverbal child, ocular genetics, amblyopia, and congenital cataracts (Nelson, 1984). He or she may be of particular value on multidisciplinary teams with special educators and parents to provide resources to meet the visually impaired child's developmental and educational needs.

REFERENCES

Cartwright, G. P., Cartwright, C. A., & Ward, M. E. (1981). *Educating special learners*. Belmont, CA: Wadsworth.

Goble, J. L. (1984). *Visual disorders in the handicapped child*. New York: Marcel Dekker.

Jose, R. (1983). *Understanding low vision*. New York: American Foundation for the Blind.

Nelson, L. B. (1984). *Pediatric ophthalmology*. Philadelphia: Saunders.

ROSANNE K. SILBERMAN
*Hunter College, City University
of New York*

DEVELOPMENT OPTOMETRY
MULTIDISCIPLINARY TEAMS
OPTOMETRIST
VISUAL ACUITY
VISUALLY IMPAIRED

OPTACON

The optacon (optical-to-tactile converter) is a small electronic device that converts regular print into a readable vibrating form for blind people. When its tiny camera containing a transistorized retina lens module moves over print symbols, the image is converted to a tactual representation of the letter shape through vibrating pins. The machine is divided into three subsystems: the camera, which converts images of print into corresponding electrical impulses; the electronics section, which processes the electrical impulses; and the tactile array, which displays in vibrating form the information transmitted by the electronics from the camera. The blind person tracks the printed material using the camera with his or her right hand and reads the tactile image with the forefinger of the left hand, which is resting on the tactile array (Telesensory Systems, 1977).

Learning to read with the optacon requires extensive training, practice, and motivation. The blind learner is taught letter recognition through associating tactile sensations with letter shapes and their corresponding names. To recognize a letter, the student must be able to discriminate the characteristics or critical features of the letter from a moving image, and then match the features to the correct name of the letter. In addition to good tactile discrimination, the successful user has to have excellent language skills and knowledge of spelling rules (orthography), grammar rules (syntax), and sentence meaning (semantics).

Reading with the optacon is a slow process because the machine displays only one letter of a word at a time. It is not intended to replace braille. However, it provides the blind reader with instant access to printed matter such as personal mail, greeting cards, recipes, catalogs, applications for college or jobs, banking statements, bills, musical notation, and phone numbers. It also enables the blind student to read graphs and charts. In addition, there are special lens attachments that enable the blind user to read cathode-ray tubes and find employment using computers. Optacon use is not being taught in school programs as extensively as possible because of the time required and the wide variety of other skills needed by the visually handicapped student. However, the intellectual blind reader should be given the opportunity to learn this valuable specialized skill.

REFERENCES

Howell, M. (1984). A tingle of print. *New Beacon, 63*, 208–210.

Telesensory Systems. (1977). *Optacon training: Teaching guidelines.* Palo Alto, CA: Author.

ROSANNE K. SILBERMAN
*Hunter College, City University
of New York*

**BLIND
BRAILLE
VISUALLY IMPAIRED
VISUAL TRAINING**

REFERENCES

Chalkley, T. (1982). *Your eyes* (2nd ed.). Springfield, IL: Thomas.

Jose, R. (1983). *Understanding low vision.* New York: American Foundation for the Blind.

ROSANNE K. SILBERMAN
*Hunter College, City University
of New York*

**DEVELOPMENTAL OPTOMETRY
LOW VISION
MULTIDISCIPLINARY TEAMS
OPHTHALMOLOGIST
VISUALLY IMPAIRED
VISION TRAINING**

OPTOMETRIST (OD)

An optometrist (OD) is a licensed doctor of optometry who is trained to measure the refractive errors of the human eye and prescribe lenses to correct those refractive errors (Chalkley, 1982). Some optometrists specialize in prescribing lenses and other types of optical aids for low-vision students and spend a major portion of their professional time in low-vision clinics. These eye specialists work closely with special educators and base their decisions on information given and recommendations made by parents and other professionals on a multidisciplinary team. It is critical for the special educator and the optometrist to establish good communication to be sure that the student's corrective lenses are providing maximum vision for school activities. The aid of choice will vary, depending on the strength of the power needed, the visual fields and working distances required, and the low-vision student's motivation (Jose, 1983).

The categories of low-vision aids that can be prescribed by the optometrist are:

Telescopes (including binoculars), which assist with distance tasks

Telemicroscopes (near-point telescopes), which incorporate a reading cap into the front lens for near tasks

Microscopes (any spectacle-mounted device such as a reading lens, a loupe, or a clip-on), to increase magnification for long-term near-distance tasks

Magnifiers (stand and hand-held), to assist in short-term spotting tasks at near distance

Field-utilization aides (prisms, minification), to assist in increasing field of vision (Jose, 1983)

Some optometrists are involved in doing perceptual-motor training. The appropriateness of this role for the optometrist is questioned by many special educators.

ORAL FACIAL DIGITAL SYNDROME (OFDS)

Oral facial digital syndrome (OFDS) appears to be a result of an X-linked chromosome that affects both males and females but that is said to be lethal in males. It is characterized by a midline cleft of the face with visibly abnormal structural defects of the mouth, teeth, tongue, and hands. Prominent clefting of the lips and palate and a marked lobulated tongue are highly visible; these may result in speech dysfunction. Teeth are abnormal. The nose tends to be broad and lacks demarcation from the skull. Growths may appear on the face and scalp hair may be sparse (Goodman & Gorlin, 1977). Fingers are broad, fused, and abnormal and extra fingers are often seen. Extremities may also have abnormal growth. No significant posture or neurological or motor problems are noted, although finger abnormalities may be apparent in fine motor development. In half of the cases, mild mental retardation is reported. No significant health problems are seen with this syndrome (Katzman, 1979; Lemeshaw, 1982).

In nearly half of the cases of OFDS, mental retardation will probably result in placement in an educable class. Speech may be affected by clefting and related services will probably be necessary. Digital abnormalities will definitely affect fine motor development so special training and materials will be required to help the child develop appropriate skills. Physical and occupational therapy may be required, as will adaptive physical education. Because deficits are so visible, counseling may be required and long-term emotional problems (particularly poor self-image) may be a result of this syndrome. For this reason, mainstreamed settings, while cognitively appropriate, may not be the optimal setting for a child with this syndrome. Team management of this child's educational plan will be necessary.

REFERENCES

Goodman, R., & Gorlin, R. (1977). *Medical aspects of mental retardation* (2nd ed.). Springfield, IL: Thomas.

Katzman, R. (Ed.). (1979). *Congenital and acquired cognitive disorders.* New York: Power.

Lemeshaw, S. (1982). *The handbook of clinical types in mental retardation.* Boston: Allyn & Bacon.

SALLY L. FLAGLER
University of Oklahoma

HURLER'S SYNDROME
MENTAL RETARDATION
PHYSICAL ANOMALIES

ORAL LANGUAGE OF THE HANDICAPPED

Language is defined as a coded set of rule-governed, arbitrary symbols, universally understood by a particular set of people and used to catalog or express ideas, objects, and events. There are five distinct but interlinked components of language: phonology, morphology, semantics, syntax, and pragmatics. Phonology refers to the rules associated with the ordering of phonemes. Phonemes are speech sounds that distinguish meaning in a language. For example, /m/ and /p/ are phonemes in English; if they are interchanged in words, there is a corresponding change in meaning. Morphology refers to the rules governing morphemes, the smallest meaningful units in language. There are free morphemes that can stand by themselves such as "happy" and "the," and bound morphemes that carry meaning but cannot stand by themselves. Prefixes such as un- and suffixes such as -ly are bound morphemes.

Semantics refers to the meaning of words in a language. Syntax describes the manner in which words are arranged in sentences. Pragmatics refers to the rules of communication in social interactions. The basic unit of pragmatics is a speech act; a behavior that communicates a single message. Speech acts include a locutionary act, an illocutionary act, and a perlocutionary act. A locutionary act is the actual surface form of the utterance and includes syntax, semantics, and phonology. The illocutionary act is the actual intent of the utterance. The perlocutionary act is the effect of the utterance on the listener.

While much is known about the components of language, researchers are less sure how children acquire language. However, numerous investigators have established major milestones in the development of language in children (Eisenson, 1972; Menyuk, 1972). Although the rate of acquisition varies from child to child, major changes occur between the ages of 2 and 4 years, with development continuing through the elementary school years (Carrow-

Woolfolk & Lynch, 1982). Between birth and 2 months of age, the infant's cry is similar to an animal sound and represents an instinctive means of expressing cold, hunger, discomfort, and other physical sensations. Babbling begins around 2 months, and continues until the baby is approximately 6 months old. The baby produces playful sounds with his or her speech organs, using the upper foodways for secondary, expressive purposes rather than for the primary purpose of food intake. Much of this babbling occurs when the baby is alone.

Around the age of 6 months, the baby begins to use vocalizations to get attention or express demands. Inflection becomes prominent around 8 months of age, giving the baby's vocal play the tonal characteristics of adult speech. Somewhere between 10 and 18 months of age, the child's first true words appear, although gestures are very important in stabilizing their meaning. Talking continues to be largely a form of play or an accompaniment to action. Spoken words gradually assume communication functions between 18 months and 24 months. During this time, vocalizations increase in variety and inflection, assuming a conversational character so strongly marked that the child seems to be conducting a long, meaningful conversation in a foreign language.

Between 24 and 30 months, the child begins to display holophrastic speech. Holophrastic speech refers to the possibility that a single word utterance expresses a complex idea. For example, the word "milk" may mean, "I want some milk," "the milk is gone," or "I spilled the milk." Often, a child's one-word utterance is closely linked with action, emotion, or things and their names. During this time, longer and more varied combinations of words develop. Earliest combinations are verbs with nouns such as "Daddy go" followed by adjective-noun combinations. First- and second-person pronouns are also common. The speaking vocabulary shows a sharp increase and ranges from between 200 and 300 words.

By approximately 3 years of age, the child's vocabulary is extensive and sentences are longer and more complex. Language behavior progresses toward a functional integration with the total behavior of the child. At 4 years of age, the child talks about everything, playing with words and questioning persistently. By 5 years of age, the child has acquired the rules of grammar and syntax governing tense, mood, number, word order, and construction of compound and complex sentences. In addition, the child has learned intonation patterns. Language continues to develop throughout the elementary school years, with some aspects such as vocabulary expanding throughout life.

Although normal children vary in their acquisition of language structure, they typically speak and comprehend standard English by the time they enter first grade. However, children displaying a handicapping condition may be at risk for delayed or deviant language development. A language disability may be concomitant in children displaying any of the following handicapping conditions: learning disability, mental retardation, hearing impairment, autism, or emotional disturbance.

Children with learning disabilities may display deficits in one or more of the following areas: oral expression, listening comprehension, written expression, basic reading skills, reading comprehension, mathematics calculation, or mathematics reasoning (Federal Register, 1977). Although language is one of many areas in which a child may evidence a learning disability, the ramifications are tremendous with language, as they may be associated with problems in reading, spelling, writing, and arithmetic. Preschool learning-disabled children are frequently not interested in verbal activities and may be delayed in their language development. Their syntax is primitive and may be accompanied by delays in the acquisition of morphological patterns. They may be unable to name pictures rapidly or identify colors, letters of the alphabet, days of the week, months of the year, and seasons (Bryen, 1981). School-aged learning-disabled children have an overall vocabulary that is within normal limits; however, they may have difficulty understanding that one object can be represented by several symbols. In addition, they may be unable to comprehend pronouns and the passive voice or to express comparative, spatial, and temporal relationships (Wiig & Semel, 1976).

Language impairment in an individual who is mentally retarded may reflect the degree of retardation. Investigators report that 45% of the mildly retarded, 90% of the severely retarded, and nearly 100% of the profoundly retarded have a language disability (Gomez & Podhajski, 1978; Schlanger, 1973; Spreen, 1965). Investigations of the language of the mentally retarded have yielded conflicting results. Lackner (1968) reported that retardation does not result in a different form of language; rather, language develops more slowly and terminates at a stage below that of a nonhandicapped child. Coggins (1979) and Miller and Yoder (1974) report similar findings. In contrast, Menyuk (1971) and Schiefelbusch (1972) report that retarded individuals use morphemes differently than their nonhandicapped peers. They do not generate rules of inflection; rather, they use only those inflections they have memorized through repeated use. Bliss, Allen, and Walker (1978) report limited use of the future tense, embedded sentences, and double-adjectival noun phrases.

Many researchers have demonstrated that hearing-impaired individuals are delayed in language acquisition (Goda, 1959; Myklebust, 1960; Pugh, 1946). However, it is still not clear whether hearing-impaired individuals develop language at a slower rate or whether their language is deviant. Investigators report that deaf children have smaller vocabularies than hearing peers and have difficulty with analogies, synonyms, and multiple meanings (Templin, 1963). Deaf children use more nouns and verbs but fewer conjunctions and auxiliaries than hearing peers (Goda, 1964; Simmons, 1962). Results of studies of grammatical structure indicate difficulty with use of the passive voice (Power & Quigley, 1973), gerunds and infinitives (Quigley, Wilbur, & Montanelli, 1976), relative pronouns (Wilbur, Montanelli, & Quigley, 1976), and verb constructions (Swisher, 1976). Pragmatic growth is also affected by hearing impairment. Deaf children have difficulty understanding how to communicate information to others, interact less frequently, and are less comfortable in social interchanges (Hoemann, 1972).

Although very little descriptive data exist, emotionally disturbed children are often characterized as having problems in language (Lovaas, 1968; Werry, 1979). In fact, a child's inability to use language is often a factor in the diagnosis of emotional disturbance. Rich, Beck, and Coleman (1982) noted sporadic and usually inappropriate imitation of words and phrases by behaviorally disordered children. The language of children suffering from infantile psychosis has been described as lacking true meaningful verbal interaction (Lovaas, 1977). Schizophrenic children exhibit wide variations in the meaningfulness of the language they display (Swanson & Reinert, 1984). More extensive research has been conducted on the language displayed by children diagnosed as autistic. Almost half of all autistic children are mute (Rutter, 1965), while those who are verbal display atypical language. Many are echolalic, repeating the last word of a phrase or an entire sentence spoken to them with no apparent comprehension of their meaning (Baltaxe & Simmons, 1975; Fay, 1969). Autistic children sometimes display delayed echolalia, repeating utterances in new, inappropriate contexts. Vocabulary acquired by some autistic children may consist of memorized lists (such as capital cities) or may focus on a single topic (such as dates); however, this vocabulary is rarely used to communicate in a functional manner (Fay, 1980). In addition to unusual vocabulary development, verbal autistic children may display pronoun reversal, using you instead of I to refer to themselves. They may also omit prepositions and conjunctions from phrases (Wing, 1969). Verbal autistic children may display pragmatic errors. They are unaware of the rules of conversation, do not judge the appropriateness of their comments, and may talk about topics of interest only to themselves (Ricks & Wing, 1976).

It is important to consider the interaction between the handicapping condition and delayed or deviant language development. For example, a child who evidences a language disorder may be unable to express feelings and concerns in a socially acceptable manner and may resort to disruptive and violent behaviors. Such a child may subsequently be labeled emotionally disturbed when, in fact, the language disability may be the primary handicapping condition. Conversely, a child evidencing Down's syndrome may be unable to respond appropriately to parental overtures of love and affection. Parents may find a lack of smiling and cooing discouraging and may inadvertently provide less verbal stimulation to their child. The child may subsequently be labeled mentally retarded but may also evidence a language disability. Educators are advised to consider the relationship between a handicap and a language disability when designing and implementing intervention strategies for handicapped children.

REFERENCES

Baltaxe, C., & Simmons, J. (1975). Language in childhood psychosis: A review. *Journal of Speech & Hearing Disorders, 40,* 439–458.

Bliss, L., Allen, D., & Walker, G. (1978). Sentence structures of trainable and educable mentally retarded subjects. *Journal of Speech & Hearing Research, 20,* 722–731.

Bryen, D. N. (1981). Language and language problems. In A. Gerber & D. N. Bryen (Eds.), *Language and learning disabilities* (pp. 27–60). Baltimore, MD: University Park Press.

Carrow-Woolfolk, E., & Lynch, J. I. (1982). *An integrative approach to language disorders in children.* New York: Grune & Stratton.

Coggins, T. (1979). Relationship meaning encoded in the two-word utterance of Stage I Down's syndrome children. *Journal of Speech & Hearing Research, 22,* 166–178.

Eisenson, J. (1972). *Aphasia in children.* New York: Harper & Row.

Fay, W. H. (1969). On the basis of autistic echolalia. *Journal of Communication Disorders, 2,* 38–47.

Fay, W. H. (1980). Aspects of language. In W. H. Fay & A. L. Schuler (Eds.), *Emerging language in autistic children* (pp. 21–50). Baltimore, MD: University Park Press.

Federal Register (1977, Dec. 29). (65082–65085.) Washington, DC.

Goda, S. (1959). Language skills of profoundly deaf adolescent children. *Journal of Speech & Hearing Research, 2,* 369–376.

Goda, S. (1964). Spoken syntax of normal, deaf, and retarded adolescents. *Journal of Verbal Learning & Verbal Behavior, 3,* 401–405.

Gomez, A., & Podhajski, B. (1978). Language and mental retardation. In C. H. Carter (Ed.), *Medical aspects of mental retardation* (pp. 51–65). Springfield, IL: Thomas.

Hoemann, H. (1972). The development of communication skills in deaf and hearing children. *Child Development, 43,* 990–1103.

Lackner, J. R. (1968). A developmental study of language behavior in retarded children. *Neuropsychologia, 6,* 301–320.

Lovaas, O. (1968). A program for the establishment of speech in psychotic children. In H. Sloan & B. MacAulay (Eds.), *Operant procedures in remedial speech and language training* (pp. 125–156). Boston: Houghton Mifflin.

Lovaas, O. (1977). *The autistic child.* New York: Halsted.

Menyuk, P. (1971). *The acquisition and development of language.* Englewood Cliffs, NJ: Prentice-Hall.

Menyuk, P. (1972). *The development of speech.* New York: Bobbs-Merrill.

Miller, J. F., & Yoder, D. E. (1974). An orthogenetic language teaching strategy for retarded children. In R. L. Schiefelbusch & L. L. Lloyd (Eds.), *Language perspectives-acquisition retar-*

dation, and intervention (pp. 505–528). Baltimore, MD: University Park Press.

Myklebust, H. (1960). *The psychology of deafness.* New York: Grune & Stratton.

Power, D. J., & Quigley, S. P. (1973). Deaf children's acquisition of the passive voice. *Journal of Speech & Hearing Research, 16,* 5–11.

Pugh, G. (1946). Appraisal of the silent reading abilities of acoustically handicapped children. *American Annals of the Deaf, 91,* 331–335.

Quigley, S. P., Wilbur, R. B., & Montanelli, D. S. (1976). Complement structures in the language of deaf students. *Journal of Speech & Hearing Research, 19,* 448–466.

Rich, H., Beck, M., & Coleman, T. (1982). Behavior management: The psychoeducational model. In R. McDowell, G. Adamson, & F. Wood (Ed.), *Teaching emotionally disturbed children* (pp. 131–166). Boston: Little, Brown.

Ricks, D. M., & Wing, L. (1976). Language communication and the use of symbols in normal and autistic children. In L. Wing (Ed.), *Early childhood autism* (pp. 93–134). Oxford, England: Pergamon.

Rutter, M. (1965). Speech disorders in a series of autistic children. In A. W. Franklin (Ed.), *Children with communication problems.* London: Pitman.

Schiefelbusch, R. L. (1972). Language disabilities of cognitively involved children. In J. Irwin & M. Marge (Eds.), *Principles of childhood language disabilities.* Englewood, NJ: Prentice-Hall.

Schlanger, B. S. (1973). *Mental retardation.* Indianapolis, IN: Bobbs-Merrill.

Simmons, A. A. (1962). A comparison of the type-token ratio of spoken and written language of deaf children. *Volta Review, 64,* 417–421.

Spreen, O. (1965). Language function in mental retardation. *Journal of Mental Deficiency, 69,* 482–489.

Swanson, H. L., & Reinert, H. R. (1984). *Teaching strategies for children in conflict* (2nd ed.). St. Louis: Times Mirror/Mosby.

Swisher, L. P. (1976). The language performance of the oral deaf. In H. Whitaker & H. A. Whitaker (Eds.), *Studies in neurolinguistics* (pp. 53–93). New York: Academic.

Templin, M. C. (1963). Vocabulary knowledge and usage among deaf and learning children. *Proceedings of the International Congress on Education of the Deaf.* Washington, DC: U.S. Government Printing Office.

Werry, J. (1979). The childhood psychoses. In H. Quay & J. Werry (Eds.), *Psychopathological disorders of childhood* (pp. 43–89). New York: Wiley.

Wiig, E., & Semel, E. M. (1976). *Language disabilities in children and adolescents.* Columbus, OH: Merrill.

Wilbur, R. B., Montanelli, D. S., & Quigley, S. P. (1976). Pronominalization in the language of deaf students. *Journal of Speech & Hearing Research, 19,* 120–140.

Wing, L. (1969). The handicaps of autistic children: A comparative study. *Journal of Child Psychology and Psychiatry, 10,* 1–40.

MAUREEN A. SMITH
Pennsylvania State University

EXPRESSIVE LANGUAGE DISORDERS
LANGUAGE DEFICIENCIES AND DEFICITS
LANGUAGE DELAYS
LANGUAGE DISORDERS

ORAL READING

Oral reading, or reading aloud, is a technique that is used frequently during reading instruction, especially in the early elementary school grades. Oral reading often occurs in small groups in which each child takes a turn reading aloud sections of text. Allington (1984) reports a general decline in the amount of oral reading across grade levels. The decline is more dramatic for good reader groups; poor readers spend proportionately more time reading orally than do good readers.

Oral reading has been used both as a technique for reading practice and as an assessment technique. Errors in reading aloud can be analyzed to determine what kind of instruction is needed. Much attention also has been given to the best procedures for handling oral reading errors.

Several error correction procedures have been associated with greater than average reading gains (Anderson, Hiebert, Scott & Wilkinson, 1985). Most research suggests that if large numbers of errors are made, the selection may be too difficult and an easier one should be provided. Generally, errors should be ignored unless they disrupt the meaning of the text; frequent corrections will interrupt the child's train of thought and comprehension and may encourage the child to wait passively for help. For errors that affect meaning, an initial strategy is to see whether the child self-corrects without help. If that does not happen, the teacher should direct the child to clues about the word's meaning or pronunciation, depending on the error made. Once the correct word has been identified, the child should reread the sentence to help preserve the meaning.

As an assessment technique, oral reading in small groups is largely impressionistic, since teachers rarely make written records of oral reading strategies and behaviors (Allington, 1984). Both qualitative and quantitive systems for noting the nature and number of errors have been developed. Yet an analysis of oral reading errors may have limited generalizability to errors in other contexts, i.e., errors in isolation may not be comparable to those in context or to silent reading.

Much debate has occurred over the relative merits and disadvantages of oral and silent reading. Some studies have suggested that the merits and disadvantages may vary as a function of the child's skill level. For example, Miller and Smith (1985) found that poor readers had higher comprehension scores when reading grade-level passages orally than when reading them silently, although performance levels were relatively low for both reading formats. Readers at a medium level of competence had higher comprehension scores when reading silently than orally; no differences were found for the best readers in the study. The researchers hypothesized that oral reading may improve the performance of poor readers by demanding attention to individual words.

Oral reading has been used frequently with handicapped children exhibiting difficulties. It provides practice for students who might otherwise not read; a method for teachers to determine the effects of their instruction; and a diagnostic function that indicates sources of difficulty for particular students (Jenkins, Larson, & Fleisher, 1983).

Several studies have been conducted on the effects of error correction procedures with handicapped students. In an investigation of the effects of two such procedures (word supply and phonic analysis) on elementary learning-disabled (LD) students' oral reading rates, Rose, McEntire, and Dowdy (1982) found both procedures generally more effective than no error corrections. The word supply procedure was found to be relatively more effective than the phonic analysis procedure. In contrast, delayed teacher attention to oral reading errors was more effective than immediate attention or no attention in reducing the number of uncorrected oral reading errors and increasing the number of self-corrections by moderately mentally retarded children (Singh, Winton, & Singh, 1985).

Allington (1984) notes that poor readers tend to receive instruction emphasizing accuracy over rate, fluency, or sensitivity to syntactic elements. Poor readers are corrected more quickly and more often than good readers, and are more often directed to surface level features of text. Poor readers have been found to make fewer self-corrections than good readers.

One way to diminish the problem of poor fluency or comprehension with oral reading by small groups of poor readers is to have the children repeatedly read the same passage until attaining an acceptable level of fluency. Repeated reading can occur with the assistance of a tape recorder, a teacher aide, or peers.

Another method to improve oral reading fluency is to have children read a passage silently before reading it aloud. However, classroom observations indicate that previewing is the exception, rather than the rule (Anderson, Hiebert, Scott, & Wilkinson, 1985).

Rose (1984; Rose & Sherry, 1984) found previewing procedures (allowing the learner to read or listen to a passage prior to instruction and/or testing) to be effective in increasing oral reading rates of both elementary and secondary LD students.

REFERENCES

Allington, R. L. (1984). Oral reading. In P. D. Pearson (Ed.), *Handbook of reading research* (pp. 829–864). New York: Longman.

Anderson, R. C., Hiebert, E. H., Scott, J. A., & Wilkinson, I. A. G. (1985). *Becoming a nation of readers: The report of the Commission on Reading.* Champaign, IL: Center for the Study of Reading.

Jenkins, J. R., Larson, K., & Fleisher, L. (1983). Effects of error correction on word recognition and reading comprehension. *Learning Disability Quarterly, 6*(2), 139–145.

Miller, S. D., & Smith, D. E. P. (1985). Differences in literal and inferential comprehension after reading orally and silently. *Journal of Educational Psychology, 77*(3), 341–348.

Rose, T. L. (1984). The effects of two prepractice procedures on oral reading. *Journal of Learning Disabilities, 17*(9), 544–548.

Rose, T. L., McEntire, E., & Dowdy, C. (1982). Effects of two error-correction procedures on oral reading. *Learning Disability Quarterly, 5*(2), 100–105.

Rose, T. L., & Sherry, L. (1984). Relative effects of two previewing procedures on LD adolescents' oral reading performance. *Learning Disability Quarterly, 7*(1), 39–44.

Singh, N. N., Winton, A. S. W., & Singh, J. (1985). Effects of delayed versus immediate attention to oral reading errors on the reading proficiency of mentally retarded children. *Applied Research in Mental Retardation, 6*(3), 283–293.

LINDA J. STEVENS
University of Minnesota

READING
READING IN THE CONTENT AREAS
READING REMEDIATION

ORAL VERSUS MANUAL COMMUNICATION

Oral versus manual communication refers to the debate surrounding the methodology used to educate individuals with hearing impairments. The oral method consists of speech reading, auditory training, speech, written expression, reading, and the use of common gestures (Chasen & Zuckerman, 1976). This method emphasizes maximum use of audition to develop the oral communication skills necessary for successful integration of hearing-impaired persons into society. The oral method has also been referred to as the auditory-oral, acoupedic, natural, and unisensory method (Bender, 1981). Strictly interpreted, the manual method includes the use of sign language, finger spelling, and common gestures. Rarely, however, do supporters of manual communication advocate exclusion of speech and speech reading; rather, they encourage simultaneous use of these methods (Pahz & Pahz, 1978).

Manual communication has been used interchangeably with total communication, a phrase coined in the late 1960s and formally adopted in 1976. Total communication actually refers to a philosophy of communication with and among hearing-impaired people. Deaf individuals select communication methods from a variety of options including speech, speech reading, audition, finger spelling, sign language, reading, and written expression (Convention of Executives of American Schools for the Deaf, 1976).

Much of the debate surrounding oral and manual communication has focused on the merits of each. Advocates of oral communication express the following beliefs:

1. Maximum development of speech and speech-reading skills can be achieved only through maximum dependence on speech and speech reading. Using sign language interferes with the development of these skills.
2. Oral communication enhances integration into the mainstream of society. Use of sign language separates the child from family and friends (Berger, 1972).
3. A deaf child should be exclusively oral until it is established through repeated attempts that he or she cannot progress without some means of manual communication.

In contrast, advocates of manual communication express the following beliefs:

1. Oral communication gives the development of language a low priority after speech, speech reading, and auditory training.
2. Use of manual communication facilitates the development of language and other concepts and knowledge vital to normal mental development. Use of oral communication to learn language is a painfully slow process for most children and may waste many of the formative years necessary for language acquisition.
3. Reliance on speech reading to gain information is unreasonable as many speech sounds are not visible on the lips. Use of manual communication provides complete, accurate information that requires no educated guesses to fill in gaps.

Each of these methods has enjoyed a period of popularity only to be discarded in favor of the other in light of changes in public opinion or medical and technological advances. Participants in the oral/manual controversy have debated these methods for over 200 years. The first debate occurred between Abbe Charles Michel de l'Epée, the "father of sign language," and Samuel Heinicke, the "father of oralism."

In 1760 de l'Epée opened a school in Paris, France, the first school anywhere in which deaf children could receive an education. Epée believed deaf people could communicate more effectively by using visual symbols rather than speech. Therefore, students attending the school were instructed by teachers communicating with signs collected by de l'Epée from populations large enough to include deaf people. He believed these signs constituted a mother tongue for the deaf and supplemented them with grammatical markers to indicate gender, tense, and number. Eighteen years later, in 1798, Heinicke opened Germany's first school for the deaf, in which students were educated through speech and lip reading. Heinicke maintained his approach facilitated integration of the deaf into general society. Word of de l'Epée's success reached Heinicke and in 1782 both men asked scholars at the Zurich Academy to settle their dispute. Although academy members found in favor of de l'Epée's methods, Heinicke and his supporters remained unconvinced and continued to argue vigorously for the oral method.

de l'Epée's method of manual communication was brought to the United States by Thomas Hopkins Gallaudet. Gallaudet had been sent to Europe by Mason Cogswell and a group of influential friends to study techniques for educating hearing-impaired individuals. Gallaudet traveled to Paris to study the manual methods of Abbe Roch Ambrose Cucurron Sicard, who had trained as a teacher under Epée. He returned to America in 1816 and, in 1817, assisted in the establishment of the American Asylum for the Deaf in Hartford, Connecticut. Assisted by Larent Clerc, a former pupil of Sicard, Gallaudet succeeded in adapting French sign language in order to teach English. Thus, manual communication was established as a method for educating hearing-impaired students in America.

By the middle of the nineteenth century, prominent educators had become dissatisfied with manual communication. In 1843 Horace Mann and Samuel Gridley Howe traveled to Germany to visit the oral schools there and returned to the United States convinced of the superiority of oral communication. Interest in this method of communication led to the establishment of the New York Institute for Impaired Instruction (now the Lexington School) in 1874 and the Clarke School for the Deaf in Chelmsford, Massachusetts, in 1867. Thus proponents of each method of communication had firmly established schools for hearing-impaired students that used their preferred methods.

By the end of the nineteenth century, each side of the oral/manual controversy was represented by prominent, highly educated men. Edward Miner Gallaudet, president of the National College for the Deaf and Dumb (predecessor to Gallaudet College), sided with advocates of manual communication. Alexander Graham Bell, an oral teacher of the deaf and future inventor of the telephone, sided with advocates of oral communication. Both were strong-willed and opinionated and disagreed over the goals of educating hearing-impaired people as well as the methods by which to accomplish those goals (Benderly, 1980). Gallaudet believed manual communication encouraged the development of a deaf culture and community. Bell maintained that deaf people should be absorbed into the mainstream of society and that oral communication was the best way to ensure this process. His position received far-reaching support. In 1880 delegates to the Congress of Teachers of the Deaf in Milan voted overwhelmingly in favor of oral communication as the preferred method of educating hearing-impaired children. By the close of the nineteenth century, every country except the United States made the oral method a national policy. Although still used in the United States, manual communication was reserved for use with slower students in upper grades.

During the twentieth century, interest in the oral method continued as a result of technological advances. Improvements in hearing-aid technology and the development of auditory training programs allowed many deaf children to use their residual hearing and maximize the benefits received from an oral education. However, many improvements also occurred in medicine during the twentieth century. Widespread use of antibiotics and vaccinations eliminated many of the causes of hearing impairments. These medical advances saved the lives of children born prematurely or suffering from infections but at the same time left many of these children hearing impaired. Thus during the 1940s and 1950s, hearing-impaired students being served in programs for the deaf were more likely to be suffering from prelingual losses and multiple handicaps (Benderly, 1980). By the 1960s, professionals' concern for the welfare of these students, coupled with an increased sensitivity to minority groups and an appreciation of their distinct characteristics, resulted in a revived interest in the use of manual communication (Pahz & Pahz, 1978). Schools in Louisiana, North Carolina, and California began experimenting with manual methods of communication (Benderly, 1980). Once again, the controversy between supporters of each method surfaced. To settle the issue once and for all, supporters on each side began to gather empirical data to demonstrate the superiority of their methods. Unfortunately, the evidence failed to decide definitively in favor of either oral or manual communication.

Berger (1972) reported orally trained deaf students demonstrated speech-reading skills superior to those demonstrated by manually trained deaf students. Lavos (1944), in an early study, reported that orally trained students scored higher than their manually trained peers on language usage, arithmetic reasoning, and computation. Other studies have supported the use of manual communication. Manually trained deaf students have demonstrated superior performance on measures of word recognition (DiCarlo, 1964), reading (Delaney, Stuckless, & Walter, 1984; DiCarlo, 1964; Meadow, 1968; Orwid, 1970), speech reading (Delaney, Stuckless, & Walter, 1984; DiCarlo, 1964; Orwid, 1971), written language (Meadow, 1978; Orwid, 1971), and math (Chasen & Zuckerman, 1976; Delaney, Stuckless, & Walter, 1981; Meadow, 1968). It should be noted, however, that many of the manually trained students included in those investigations were educated in programs incorporating a philosophy of total communication. Therefore, they were encouraged to develop speech and speech-reading skills and to use any residual hearing.

It is apparent that no clear winner of the oral/manual debate has emerged as supporters on either side can easily document the superiority of their methods. This has led some school systems to offer a choice of communication options to hearing-impaired students. The trend appears to be toward manual methods as provided in programs embracing a philosophy of total communication. Jordan, Gustason, and Rosen (1979) report that 4774 classrooms incorporated some form of manual communication to educate hearing-impaired students while 2370 classrooms incorporated the oral method.

REFERENCES

Bender, R. (1981). *Conquest of deafness* (3rd ed.). Danville, IL: Interstate Printers.

Benderly, B. L. (1980). *Dancing without music: Deafness in America.* Garden City, NY: Anchor/Doubleday.

Berger, K. (1972). *Speechreading: Principals and methods.* Baltimore, MD: National Education Press.

Chasen, B., & Zuckerman, W. (1976). The effects of total communication and oralism in deaf third-grade "rubella" students. *American Annals of the Deaf, 121,* 394–402.

Convention of Executives of American Schools for the Deaf (1976). *Defining total communication.* Rochester, NY.

Delaney, M., Stuckless, E. R., & Walter, G. G. (1984). Total communication effects—A longitudinal study of a school for the deaf in transition. *American Annals of the Deaf, 129,* 481–486.

DiCarlo, L. (1964). *The deaf.* Englewood Cliffs, NJ: Prentice-Hall.

Jordan, I. K., Gustason, G., & Rosen, R. (1979). An update on communication trends at programs for the deaf. *American Annals of the Deaf, 124,* 350–357.

Lavos, G. (1944). The reliability of an educational achieved test administered to the deaf. *American Annals of the Deaf, 89,* 226–232.

Meadow, E. (1968). Early manual communication in relation to the deaf child's intellectual, social, and communication functioning. *American Annals of the Deaf, 113,* 29–41.

Orwid, H. L. (1971). Studies in manual communication with hearing impaired children. *Volta Review, 73,* 428–438.

Pahz, J. A., & Pahz, S. P. (1978). *Total communication.* Springfield, IL: Thomas.

MAUREEN A. SMITH
Pennsylvania State University

DEAF EDUCATION
SIGN LANGUAGE TRAINING
TOTAL COMMUNICATION

ORDINAL SCALES OF PSYCHOLOGICAL DEVELOPMENT

The Ordinal Scales of Psychological Development (Uzgirus & Hunt, 1975) were designed to assess developmental abilities in infants up to 2 years of age. The scales were developed from a Piagetian principle that there is an invariant sequence of developmental landmarks, not linked to a specific age, that are characteristic of an infant's ability to manipulate and organize interactions with the environment (Gorrell, 1985). There are six basic abilities measured: (1) the development of visual pursuit, (2) the development of means for obtaining desired environmental events, (3) the development of vocal and gestural imitation, (4) the development of operational causality, (5) the construction of object relations in space, and (6) the development of schemes for relating to others.

Scoring is done by checking possible actions from a sample list. Interpretation is objective; therefore, for more reliable results, the tester should be familiar with the test procedure. The obtained information is compared in terms of the developmental advancement or retardation exhibited by the testee. Rosenthal (1985) has found the ordinal scales to have good reliabilities. Percentage of interrater agreement was found to be 96.1%, and agreement between sessions was 79.9%. The test was praised because it narrowed its focus for assessment, unlike its broad-ranged predecessors.

REFERENCES

Gorrell, J. (1985). *Test critiques* (Vol. 2). Kansas City: Test Corporation of America.

Rosenthal, A. C. (1985). Review of assessment in infancy: Ordinal Scales of Psychological Development. In J. H. Mitchell, Jr. (Ed.), *The ninth mental measurements yearbook* (Vol. 2). Lincoln: University of Nebraska Press.

Uzgirus, T. C., & Hunt, J. (1975). *Assessment in infancy: Ordinal Scales of Psychological Development.* Urbana: University of Illinois Press.

LISA J. SAMPSON
Eastern Kentucky University

ORGANIZATIONAL CHANGE

During the remainder of this century, organizational change will be an important issue in special education. Organizational change refers to the process that any organizational unit (e.g., work group, department, school, school district) adapts to client needs, rules, regulations, and other factors. Organizational change acknowledges the fact that all organizational units are in flux and that they adapt to demands in either functional or dysfunctional ways. Currently, concern exists nationwide for effective, efficient, and responsive service delivery systems (National Coalition of Advocates for Students, 1985). Furthermore, it is important for special education systems to be compatible and well-coordinated with regular education systems. Functional organizational change in special education, therefore, should take into account these important issues.

To accomplish functional organizational change, it is fundamental that a planned, systematic approach be employed by local level professionals. A planned, systematic approach is one that includes the following phases and constituent activities (Maher & Bennett, 1984):

Clarifying the Organizational Problem

1. Assessing the organizational problem
2. Assessing organizational readiness for change
3. Defining the problem in measurable terms

Designing the Organizational Intervention

1. Describing purpose, goals, and objectives
2. Generating and selecting interventions to implement
3. Developing a written intervention design

Implementing the Organizational Intervention

1. Maximizing the degree to which the intervention is implemented in technically adequate, ethical, useful, and practical ways

Assessing the Organizational Intervention

1. Assessing the extent to which design elements were implemented
2. Assessing the extent to which goals of the interventions were attained

The first phase, clarifying the organizational problem, is an often neglected but important activity. It assesses an organization's readiness for change. One framework that has seemed useful for assessing organizational readiness for change is Davis and Salasin's (1975) A-VICTORY framework. The A-VICTORY is an acronym of eight factors believed to be related to organizational readiness for change (see Illback & Hargan, 1984 for an example of how the A-VICTORY framework can be used in special education). These eight factors are:

*A*bility. Resources available to carry out implementation of the intervention, including human, financial, material, technological, and physical ones.

*V*alues. Attitudes and beliefs of organizational members concerning what comprises acceptable organizational behaviors.

*I*dea. Degree to which organizational members have a clear and comprehensive understanding of a proposed intervention.

*C*ircumstances. Current organizational factors that may either inhibit or facilitate an organization's accommodation of an intervention.

*T*iming. Degree that implementation of intervention is compatible with important events occurring within the organization.

*O*bligation. Organizational members' perceptions of the extent to which an intervention is needed.

*R*esistance. Extent that organizational members have misgivings or concerns about adopting the intervention.

*Y*ield. Extent that organizational members believe that there will be important benefits from the intervention.

In regard to the second phase, designing the organizational intervention, five criteria can be used in developing the intervention's design. These criteria have been adapted from Provus (1972). The first criterion, clarity, refers to the degree to which the design is understandable and clear. Comprehensiveness, the second criterion, concerns the extent to which the design includes details relative to the purpose, implementation, and expected outcomes of the intervention. The third criterion, internal consistency, denotes the extent that components of the design are logically interrelated. Compatibility is the fourth criterion and refers to the degree to which the design is compatible with both the need for the intervention and with ongoing routines within the organization. The final criterion, theoretical soundness, denotes the extent that the components of the design are consistent with good professional practice as indicated by expert opinion and empirical research.

An often neglected aspect of the third phase, implementing the organizational intervention, is systematically facilitating the implementation of the intervention. Recent research (e.g., Maher, 1984) identified six activities that appear to be related to facilitating the implementation of organizational interventions. First, implementors of the intervention should discuss with one another the purpose, implementation, and expected outcomes of the intervention. Second, intervention implementors should have the opportunity to understand each other's concerns and misgivings about the intervention. Third, intervention implementors should be encouraged, given positive, feedback and otherwise reinforced for their contributions. Fourth, the intervention should be adapted as a result from feedback from relevant organization members. Fifth, positive expectations about the intervention's success should be fostered and maintained among the intervention's implementors. Finally, learning should occur about potential obstacles to implementing the intervention.

During the fourth phase, assessing the organizational intervention, at least two types of assessment questions should be addressed: (1) what components of the intervention were implemented? and (2) Were the stated goals of the intervention attained? These two questions seem to be particularly germane to developing and improving special education service delivery systems (Maher & Bennett, 1984). However, other assessment questions can also be addressed: (1) did the intervention cause the observed outcomes? (2) What were the related or unintended effects (either positive or negative) of the intervention? (3) What were an individual's reactions to the intervention?

Beer (1980) has identified four general categories of approaches to organizational change. They are diagnostic, process, technostructural, and individual. The purpose of a diagnostic intervention is to collect information that might help define the nature and scope of the organizational problem. Often, a diagnostic intervention is followed by other organizational interventions. One or more of four data collection methods can be used in diagnostic intervention: direct observation, review of permanent products or written records, interviews, and questionnaires or rating forms.

Process approaches to organizational intervention target relationships among organizational members for change. One approach to process intervention, survey feedback, encompasses both the collection of survey data and the communication of the survey's results to selected organizational members. Another process approach, team development, involves team members in a collaborative effort to improve their teams' effectiveness and efficiency. The system development process approach is intended to improve relationships between interdependent work teams. The final process approach is process consultation. Though process consultation can overlap with the other process approaches, it is chiefly concerned with a consultant helping selected organizational members to understand and change problematic organizational processes.

Technostructural approaches to organizational change entail altering organizational structures as a means to improving worker satisfaction or productivity. One technostructural approach involves altering systems of reward, such as the manner in which wages or verbal praise are delivered to staff. The second technostructural approach is managing job performance. This approach may involve management by objectives (MBO), goal setting, performance appraisal, or performance review and development. Job design, also a technostructural approach, entails altering characteristics of work tasks or working conditions so that workers are more satisfied or productive. The fourth technostructural approach to intervention, organizational design, concerns making global structural changes such as decentralizing the decision-making process within an organization.

The fourth category of approaches to organizational change focuses on the individual staff. An example of this approach, recruitment and selection, is concerned with matching the job role demands with abilities and skills of the individual. Another individual approach attempts to further organizational change by engaging individuals in continuing professional development activities. Finally, individual counseling can be used to reduce or alleviate interpersonal or personal problems that may be interfering with a staff's productivity (for a more extensive dis-

cussion of approaches to changing school organizations, see Maher, Illback, & Zins, 1984).

REFERENCES

Beer, M. (1980). *Organization change and development: A systems view.* Santa Monica, CA: Goodyear.

Davis, H. T., & Salasin, S. E. (1975). The utilization of evaluation. In E. L. Struening & M. Guttentag (Eds.), *Handbook of evaluation research* (Vol. 1). Beverly Hills, CA: Sage.

Illback, R. J., & Hargan, L. (1984). Assessing and facilitating school readiness for microcomputers. *Special Services in the Schools, 1,* 91–105.

Maher, C. A. (1984). Implementing programs and systems in organizational settings: The DURABLE approach. *Journal of Organizational Behavior Management, 6,* 69–98.

Maher, C. A., & Bennett, R. E. (1984). *Planning and evaluating special education services.* Englewood Cliffs, NJ: Prentice-Hall.

Maher, C. A., Illback, R. J., & Zins, J. E. (1984). *Organizational psychology in the schools: A handbook for professionals.* Springfield, IL: Thomas.

National Coalition of Advocates for Students. (1985). *Barriers to excellence: Our children at risk.* Boston: Author.

Provus, M. (1972). *Discrepancy evaluation.* Berkeley, CA: McCutchan.

CHARLES A. MAHER
Rutgers University

LOUIS A. KRUGER
Tufts University

HUMAN RESOURCE DEVELOPMENT SUPERVISION IN SPECIAL EDUCATION

ORTHOGENIC SCHOOL

The Orthogenic School was established by Bettelheim (1950) to promote the application of Freudian principles of psychoanalysis to the treatment of behaviorally disordered children and youths. Adherents to psychoanalysis and the Orthogenic School approach believe that each individual's thoughts and behaviors are determined by unconscious motivations, formed during earlier stages of development. Disorders of behavior (overt and covert) are the result of early conflicts left primarily unresolved; these conflicts can result in a fixation of development at a particular Freudian stage. In the Orthogenic School of Bettelheim, teachers would create a permissive environment in which children could act on their impulses. Rather than correct behavior problems, teachers would work to help students achieve insight into their behavior through interpreting the symbolism of their actions. The Orthogenic School created a therapeutic milieu where the intrapsychic anxieties of troubled youths need not be contained.

The Orthogenic School movement did not achieve widespread acceptance or implementation in special education circles although psychodynamic thought has influenced the development of various psychoeducational models of treatment in the schools.

REFERENCE

Bettelheim, B. (1950). *Love is not enough.* New York: Macmillan.

CECIL R. REYNOLDS
Texas A&M University

ORTHOPEDICALLY HANDICAPPED

With advances in legislation for handicapped individuals (e.g., PL 94-142, Section 504 of the Rehabilitation Act), a greater number of orthopedically handicapped students are being mainstreamed into classes with their nonhandicapped peers. In addition, students with multiple disabilities (e.g., severe mental retardation and cerebral palsy) are being served in public school settings with increasing frequency. The classroom teacher must take into account the specific needs of orthopedically handicapped students when planning instruction. An awareness of the types of orthopedic disabilities as well as intervention methods is useful for teachers of students with such disabilities.

Orthopedic handicaps may be congenital (present from birth) or acquired (from trauma or injury). Certain conditions such as cerebral palsy involve one or all of the extremities. Cerebral palsy is a nonprogressive disorder caused by damage to the brain that results in disturbance of voluntary motor function. Individuals with cerebral palsy may be affected in one (monoplegia) to all of their limbs (quadriplegia; Jones, 1983). Other students may have disabilities in just one area of the body (Fraser & Hensinger, 1983). Common spinal deformities that affect voluntary movement include scoliosis (curvature of the spine) and spina bifida. Spina bifida may have associated hydrocephalus (fluid accumulation in or around the brain) and may cause various levels of disturbance of voluntary limb function depending on the degree and location of the spinal deformity.

Common disabilities in the legs and feet include hip dislocation or subluxation (separation of the femur and acetabulum that does not entail complete dislocation), knee flexion and extension deformities, and foot deformities such as equinus (foot pointed down) and calcaneus (foot pointed up). Wrist, hand, and arm deformities may include contractures of the elbow flexors (in which the elbow stays stiffly bent), ulnar deviation of the wrist (in which the wrist is flexed and the hand deviates to one side), thumb-in-hand deformity, or finger flexion deformity.

Surgical treatment of these deformities is sometimes the option chosen by parents or guardians, specialists, or the physically disabled person. In addition, various types of braces, prosthetic, and orthotic devices may be used prior to the decision to have surgery or following surgery as a method of preventing further deformities. The classroom teacher should be familiar with prosthetic and orthotic devices and positioning equipment (e.g., adapted wheelchairs) that are used by students with orthopedic handicaps. Close consultation with ancillary staff (e.g., occupational therapists, physical therapists) should occur on a regular basis to facilitate appropriate management techniques.

Because the classroom teacher often has orthopedically handicapped students in class for most of the day, carry over of techniques used in special therapy sessions should occur in the classroom (Dykes & Venn, 1983). Classroom teachers should closely observe the general health and changes in health status of their students and make referrals as needed. Knowledge of physical adaptations through consultations with specialists and attendance at in-service or preservice classes on management of the orthopedically handicapped will be necessary for the classroom teacher. Modification of instructional strategies and materials may be required to meet students' physical needs. Finally, awareness of the psychosocial aspects of physical disabilities (Carpignano, Sirvis, & Bigge, 1982) will be necessary in order to address the social and emotional needs of students with orthopedic handicaps.

As technological advances in electronics and microcomputers continue, increased adaptation of seating, communication devices, and replacements for bracing equipment (e.g., the use of electronic stimulation) will be seen. Advances in medical care (e.g., computerized tomography [CT] scanners, position emission tomography [PET] scanners, computerized gait laboratories) will continue to allow doctors and physical therapists to make better use of their resources in managing neuromuscular problems in persons with handicaps. In addition, advances in surgical care will allow for more sophisticated analyses of pre- and postoperative conditions. In addition, prevention of deformities through surgery will continue to have successful results in coming years (Fraser & Hensinger, 1983). These advances will surely have an effect on students with orthopedic disabilities entering public school classrooms.

The teacher of students with orthopedic handicaps can provide appropriate instruction by working closely with specialists and providing carry over of techniques and adaptations suggested by specialists into the classroom. With a team approach in which all members of the staff, as well as the student where appropriate, have a share in program planning, education for students with orthopedic handicaps will allow such students to function as independently as possible.

REFERENCES

Carpignano, J., Sirvis, B., & Bigge, J. (1982). Psychosocial aspects of physical disability. In J. L. Bigge (Ed.), *Teaching individuals with physical and multiple disabilities* (2nd ed., pp. 110–137). Columbus, OH: Merrill.

Dykes, M. K., & Venn, J. (1983). Using health, physical, and medical data in the classroom. In J. Umbreit (Ed.), *Physical disabilities and health impairments: An introduction* (pp. 259–280). Columbus, OH: Merrill.

Fraser, B. A., & Hensinger, R. N. (1983). *Managing physical handicaps: A practical guide for parents, care providers, and educators.* Baltimore, MD: Brookes.

Jones, M. H. (1983). Cerebral palsy. In J. Umbreit (Ed.), *Physical disabilities and health impairments: An introduction* (pp. 41–58). Columbus, OH: Merrill.

CORNELIA LIVELY
*University of Illinois,
Urbana-Champaign*

CEREBRAL PALSY
MULTIPLY HANDICAPPED
SPINA BIFIDA

ORTHOPEDIC IMPAIRMENTS

Public Law 94-142 divided the classification of physical handicaps into the two categories of orthopedic impairments and health impairments for special education purposes. Orthopedic impairments include physical disabilities primarily related to skeletal, joint, and muscular disorders such as congenital anomalies, club foot, or the absence of a limb; and impairments owed to bone tuberculosis or poliomyelitis, cerebral palsy, amputations, and contractures (i.e., shortening of some limb as a consequence of some other condition). Cerebral palsy represents the highest number in this group. Muscular dystrophy, spina bifida, spinal cord injury, spinal cord atrophy, ostegenesis imperfecta, Legg-Calve-Perthes disease, and juvenile rheumatoid arthritis are other physically handicapping conditions within the orthopedically handicapped category (Bigge & Sirvis, 1986).

Data collected by the federal government regarding children and youths receiving special education and related services under PLs 94-142 and 89-313 found that 56,209 children are orthopedically impaired (U.S. Office of Education, 1985). This does not include children who may have been orthopedically impaired but were counted, because of other handicapping conditions, as multiply handicapped.

REFERENCES

Bigge, J., & Sirvis, B. (1986). Physical and health impairments. In N. G. Haring & McCormick (Eds.), *Exceptional children and youth* (4th ed., pp. 313–354). Columbus, OH: Merrill.

U.S. Office of Education. (1985). *Seventh annual report to Congress on the implementation of Public Law 94-142: The Education of All Handicapped Children Act.* Washington, DC: U.S. Government Printing Office.

LESTER MANN
*Hunter College, City University
of New York*

HEALTH IMPAIRMENTS

ORTHOPSYCHIATRY

Orthopsychiatry is perhaps best described as a collaborative or interdisciplinary approach to the promotion of mental health and the study of human development. Psychiatrists, psychologists, educators, social workers, pediatricians, nurses, lawyers, and other professionals constitute the American Orthopsychiatric Association, founded in 1924. From its earliest years, orthopsychiatry as a field has served as a forum for uniting the contributions from many disciplines and attacking mental health problems with a unified approach (Levy, 1931). Orthopsychiatry addresses issues affecting adolescents, adults, families, and, especially, children. Based on the assumption that an individual's problems are the result of the interplay of one's psychic and organic capabilities with the social milieu, orthopsychiatry focuses on both prevention and treatment of the individual in societal and environmental contexts. Extending the scope of health care beyond the consultation room and clinic has also been an historical emphasis in orthopsychiatry.

In recent years, orthopsychiatry has become widely known as the field where the roles of professionals from numerous disciplines are integrated in the prevention of illness and the promotion of mental health. The American Orthopsychiatric Association has actively promoted the elimination of rivalries and competition among professionals, and has become involved with issues of civil liberty, behavioral illnesses, fetal mental health, and genetic engineering (Pierce, 1984).

Membership in the American Orthopsychiatric Association is open to all those working in the mental health fields who meet certain educational, or employment criteria. The association publishes the *American Journal of Orthopsychiatry*, a quarterly publication of selected theoretical, research, administrative and clinical articles; *Readings*, a journal of reviews and commentary; and the *Ortho Newsletter*. The American Orthopsychiatric Association is headquartered in New York City; it sponsors an annual meeting each spring.

REFERENCES

Levy, D. M. (1931). Psychiatry, and orthopsychiatry. *American Journal of Orthopsychiatry, 1,* 239–244.

Pierce, C. M. (1984). Twenty-first century orthopsychiatry. *American Journal of Orthopsychiatry, 54,* 364–368.

GREG VALCANTE
University of Florida

ECOLOGICAL ASSESSMENT PSYCHOLOGICAL CLINICS, THE PSYCHOLOGY IN THE SCHOOLS

ORTHOPSYCHIATRY MOVEMENT

Orthopsychiatry is a term that was adopted by a group of nine psychiatrists who first met in January 1924. The prefix ortho is a derivation of the Greek word for straight. Orthopsychiatry, therefore, literally means straight psychiatry. It was originally defined by the founding members as the "endeavor to obtain straightness of mind and spirt" (*American Orthopsychiatric Association,* 1985). By 1949 the American Orthopsychiatric Association (AOA) stated that "Orthopsychiatry connotes a philosophy . . . of interrelationships of various professions interested in learning about and shaping human behavior" (AOA, 1985). Since that time, it has "evolved to include the concepts of a preventive interdisciplinary approach and the interrelationship of social policy and mental health" (AOA, 1985).

The impetus to found the orthopsychiatry movement came from a group of psychiatrists, but it quickly moved to include psychologists and social workers (Lowrey, 1957). The initial meeting of the American Orthopsychiatric Association, held in Chicago in June 1924, had the topic of prevention as its major theme (Mohr, 1938). This interest in prevention became a primary focus of the movement, and was expanded on to include three types of prevention. "Primary prevention refers to preventing the disease before it begins. Secondary prevention involves diagnosing the disease and instituting immediate treatment. Tertiary prevention concerns itself with treatment efforts to prevent or minimize further progression of a chronic condition" (Wolman, 1977, p. 161). From the standpoint of prevention as well as of treatment, it soon became apparent that a need existed for services from more than one specialty or discipline. This need for teamwork among professionals was recognized and encouraged by the orthopsychiatry movement. Initially this teamwork was seen as being the strict domain of psychiatrists, psychologists, and social workers. The anticipated roles were for the psychiatrist to see the child, the social worker to counsel the parent, and the psychologist to perform needed testing. During the 1960s, as other disciplines became more involved in the counseling field, the movement expanded to include many other professionals.

In 1985 the AOA had over 10,000 members, including psychiatrists, psychologists, social workers, nurses, educators, pediatricians, sociologists, lawyers, anthropologists, and other mental health professionals and paraprofessionals.

The AOA has published the *American Journal of Orthopsychiatry* since 1930. The goal of the journal is to synthesize and apply the

knowledge base of psychiatry, psychology, social work, and related medical, behavioral, educational, and social sciences. The relationship of clinical concerns to broader issues—environmental, familial, societal—that affect individual development . . . as well as the journal's dedication to promoting a preventive approach to problems of mental illness

have been consistent themes since its inception (AOA, 1985).

Membership in the organization as of 1985 is open to anyone working in the mental health or a related field who meets one of the following conditions: has a master's degree, a postgraduate degree, 2 years' employment in a mental health setting, 2 years in private practice, 4 years of active involvement in community mental health work, or full-time graduate work.

Members of the organization receive the *American Journal of Orthopsychiatry*; are exempt from general registration fees at the annual meeting; have priority registration for all meetings and workshops; are encouraged to submit proposals for presentation at meetings; receive *Ortho Newsletter*; participate in the association's governance, committees, and task forces; receive annual book discounts; are listed in and receive the *Ortho Membership Directory*; and have free use of the employment services at the annual meeting. As membership expanded, the movement's emphasis also began to change from one of concern about theoretical constructs and techniques of therapy to one of broader sociological and political problems and their relationship to mental health. The orthopsychiatry movement led the way for the concept of child guidance clinics and the subsequent passage by Congress of the Community Mental Retardation and Mental Health Centers Act of 1963. It also assisted in assuring that the educational system provide appropriate educational services to children in the area of mental health (Trippe, 1958). An excellent compilation of articles related to orthopsychiatry and education demonstrated the diversity of the roles of members of the movement (Krugman & Gardner, 1958).

The orthopsychiatric movement was a leader in the interdisciplinary approach to clinical practice, theory, research, and the study of social factors as they affect mental health.

Ortho has applied an interdisciplinary perspective to a wide range of issues affecting children, adolescents, adults, families, schools, and community mental health. Since the beginning, orthopsychiatry's philosophy has included an emphasis on prevention as well as treatment and has focused on the individual within the context of society. This broad-based interdisciplinary concept best characterizes orthopsychiatry and distinguishes it from the more specifically focused professional membership organization. (*Ortho: Interdisciplinary approaches to mental health*, 1985, p. 4)

REFERENCES

American Orthopsychiatric Association. (1985). Membership pamphlet. New York: Author.

Krugman, M., & Gardner, G. E. (Eds.). (1958). *Orthopsychiatry and the schools.* New York: American Orthopsychiatric Association.

Lowrey, L. G. (1957). Historical perspective. *American Journal of Orthopsychiatry, 27*, 223.

Mohr, G. J. (1938). Orthopsychiatry—fifteenth year. *American Journal of Orthopsychiatry, 8*, 185.

Ortho: Interdisciplinary approaches to mental health (1985, April). Paper presented at 62nd annual meeting of the American Orthopsychiatric Association, New York.

Trippe, M. J. (1958). Mental health and the education of the exceptional child. In M. Krugman & G. E. Gardner (Eds.) *Orthopsychiatry and the schools*, New York: American Orthopsychiatry Association.

Wolman, B. B. (Eds.). (1977). *International encyclopedia of psychiatry, psychology, psychoanalysis, and neurology* (Vol. 8). New York: Aesculapius.

SUSANNE BLOUGH ABBOTT
Stamford, Connecticut

CHILD PSYCHIATRY
CLINICAL PSYCHOLOGY

ORTON, SAMUEL T. (1879–1948)

Samuel T. Orton, a physician, is best known for his studies of children with severe reading disabilities. The children

Samuel T. Orton

with whom he worked, although not otherwise handicapped, experienced extreme difficulty in acquiring the skills of reading, writing, spelling, or speech. Orton found that these language difficulties were constitutional and were often associated with confusion in direction, time, and sequence. Orton called this syndrome word blindness and set forth principles for its remediation. Teaching procedures developed by his associates, Anna Gillingham and Bessie W. Stillman, are widely used today in special education. The Orton Society, formed a year after Orton's death, carries forward the work that be began.

REFERENCES

Bulletin of the Orton Society. Pomfret, CT: Orton Society.

Orton, S. T. (1937). *Reading, writing and speech problems in children.* New York: Norton.

PAUL IRVINE
Katonah, New York

ORTON DYSLEXIA SOCIETY

The Orton Dyslexia Society, founded in 1949 as the Orton Society, Inc., is the only international, scientific, and educational association concerned exclusively with the widespread problem of specific written language disability or specific developmental dyslexia. The society's membership includes all persons interested in the diagnosis and treatment of children and adults who have experienced difficulty in learning the skills of written language. The society was named in honor of Samuel T. Orton, a well-known neurologist who was an American pioneer in the study of dyslexia.

The Orton Dyslexia Society has members in every state of the United States and in many foreign countries; there are over 30 branches. It holds a national conference each fall, and interim meetings are held by branches. It publishes a quarterly newsletter, "Perspectives on Dyslexia," and the annual *Annals of the Orton Society*, a professional journal about specific language disabilities that is sent free to members and is also available for purchase or subscription.

The society issues books, monographs, a cumulative index of the *Annals* (earlier called the *Bulletin*), reprints, and conference tapes. It also promotes public information on the subject of dyslexia through other media of communication. The Anna Gillingham Fund has been established as a loan fund to assist teachers in training for work in this field.

The society's Division of Research is actively concerned with biological, cognitive, and educational research. It sponsors the brain research in the neuroanatomical laboratory of the Neurological Unit, Beth Israel Hospital, Boston, Massachusettes. The purpose of the division is to expand the frontiers of knowledge regarding the causes, nature, prevention, treatment, and remediation of dyslexia. Inquiries will be answered by the International Office of the ODS, 724 York Road, Baltimore, MD 21204.

SYLVIA O. RICHARDSON
University of South Florida

ORTON-GILLINGHAM METHOD
ORTON, SAMUEL T.

ORTON-GILLINGHAM METHOD

The Orton-Gillingham method of teaching reading was developed by Anna Gillingham (Gillingham & Stillman, 1968) and is based on the theoretical work of the American neurologist Samuel Orton. Orton (1937) cultivated a special interest in dyslexic children (children of normal intelligence with a severe reading disability). He believed that weak associative power was central to these children's difficulties, stemming from incomplete suppression of the nondominant cerebral hemisphere. Gillingham translated these theories into a highly structured reading method that stresses the repeated association of individual phonemes with their sound, name, and cursive formation.

Initially, individual letters are taught using drill cards and a carefully structured question-answer format focused on the letter sound (introduced by key words), the letter name, and the letter formation (first traced, then copied, and finally written from memory). After mastering all these aspects of the first group of letters (a, b, h, i, j, k, m, p, t), the student is taught to blend them into simple consonant-vowel-consonant words (e.g., map, hit, Tim). Instruction then focuses on the spelling of these same simple words, again in a structured format that requires repeating the word, naming and simultaneously writing the letters, and reading the word after it is written.

The similarly structured introduction of subsequent single letters, blends (e.g., st, cl, tr) and other letter combinations (e.g., sh, ea, tion) is meticulously sequenced. Later stages in the sequence include sentence and story writing, syllabification, dictionary skills, and advanced spelling rules.

Often referred to as a multisensory approach, the Orton-Gillingham method is one of several reading methods that emphasizes the phonetic regularities of English in its instructional sequence. It differs from other code-emphasis approaches by teaching letter sounds in isolation and requiring a considerable amount of individual letter blending (e.g., m-a-p = map). Its instructional format is highly repetitious. Within this method the teacher repeatedly combines reading with writing activities and relies heavily on drill techniques. The instructional materials include phoneme drill cards, phonetically regular

word cards, syllable concept cards, little stories, and a detailed manual (Gillingham & Stillman, 1968).

The Orton-Gillingham method assumes a tutorial setting. Two adaptations of the method, which are conceived for small groups and classrooms as well as a tutorial arrangement, are *Recipe for Reading* (Traub & Bloom, 1970) and *Multisensory Approach to Language Arts* (Slingerland, 1974).

REFERENCES

Gillingham, A., & Stillman, B. (1968). *Remedial teaching for children with disability in reading, spelling, and penmanship.* Cambridge, MA: Educator's Publishing Service.

Orton, S. T. (1937). *Reading, writing, and speech problems in children.* New York: Norton.

Slingerland, B. H. (1974). *A multisensory approach to language arts for specific language disability children.* Cambridge, MA: Educator's Publishing Service.

Traub, N., & Bloom, F. (1970). *Recipe for reading.* Cambridge, MA: Educator's Publishing Service.

KATHERINE GARNETT
*Hunter College, City University
of New York*

OSBORN, ALEXANDER FAICKNEY (1888–1966)

Alexander Faickney Osborn, an advertising executive, financier, civic leader, author, and educator, was widely known for his emphasis on creativity as a teachable skill. He has been described as "a seminal thinker and gifted writer, whose clear and practical explanation of the basic concepts of creative thinking and problem solving would influence the thinking, teaching, and research of tens of thousands of others over at least a half-century" (Isaksen & Treffinger, 1985, p. 4). Among Osborn's accomplishments are his introduction and promotion of a technique of organized ideation called brainstorming and the development of a system for teaching creative problem solving.

He has authored several books on creativity including *How to Think Up* (1942), *Your Creative Power* (1948), and *Wake Up Your Mind* (1952). His most popular book, *Applied Imagination: Principles and Procedures of Creative Thinking* (1953), now in its third revision and eighteenth printing, is a classic. Osborn's dedication to the power of imagination has had a significant impact on the development and training of creative potential. His firm belief in the idea that people can be taught to become better creative thinkers led to the establishment of the Creative Education Foundation in Buffalo, New York (1954). The foundation was developed to disseminate information on the development of creative thinking skills and to sponsor the annual week-long Creative Problem Solving Institute. In 1967 the first issue of the *Journal of Creative Behavior*, a quarterly on creative development, was published by the foundation.

REFERENCES

Dodge, E. N. (Ed.). (1968). *Encyclopedia of American biography.* (Vol. 38). New York: American Historical.

Isaksen, S. G., & Treffinger, D. J. (1985). *Creative problem solving: The basic course.* New York: Bearly.

Osborn, A. F. (1957). *Applied imagination: Principles and procedures of creative thinking.* New York: Scribner.

Staff. (1971). *The national cyclopedia of American biography.* (Vol. 53). New York: James T. White.

MARY M. FRASIER
University of Georgia

CREATIVE PROBLEM SOLVING INSTITUTE

OSGOOD, CHARLES E. (1916–   )

Charles Osgood was born in Brookline, Massachusetts, on November 20, 1916. He is a noted linguist and researcher and a Guggenheim fellow. He obtained his BA at Darthmouth College in 1939 and his PhD in psychology at Yale 1945. Osgood was an instructor at Yale from 1942 to 1945, conducted psychological research for the U.S. Air Force and Navy from 1946 to 1947, and was an assistant professor from 1946 to 1949. Since 1950 Osgood has been associated with the University of Illinois, Urbana as an associate professor (1950–1955), professor (1955–1981), and professor emeritus (since 1981). From 1955 until 1965, Osgood was director of the Institute of Communication Research, University of Illinois, Urbana. Osgood's model of verbal interaction has provided the theoretical basis for the construction of ITPA (Illinois Test of Psycholinguistic Abilities), which was widely used in the late 1960s and 1970s for the assessment of children with learning disabilities. Osgood is the author and coauthor of numerous publications, including *Method and Theory of Experimental Psychology* (1953); the *Measurement of Meaning* (1957); and *Cross-cultural Universals of Affective Meanings* (1975).

REFERENCES

Osgood, C. E. (1953). *Method and theory of experimental psychology.* New York: Oxford University Press.

Osgood, C. E., May, W. H., & Miron, M. S. (1975). *Cross-cultural universals of affective meanings.* Urbana: University of Illinois Press.

Osgood, C. E., Suci, G. J., & Tannenbaum, P. (1975). *Measurement of meaning.* Urbana: University of Illinois Press.

Who's who in the Midwest. (1984). (19th ed.). Chicago: Marquis Who's Who.

IVAN Z. HOLOWINSKY
Rutgers University

OSTEOPOROSIS

Osteoporosis is the manifestation of the disorder known as osteopenia, meaning a reduction of bone mass (Behrman & Vaughan, 1983). Primary osteoporosis is most common in elderly postmenopausal women. Secondary osteoporosis is more common in inactive younger people such as hemiplegics, alcoholics, or those suffering from malnutrition. Treatment with steroids and heparin may also cause the condition. It is generally asymptomatic until a fracture or cracking of a vertebrae has occured while lifting a heavy object or from an unexpected jolt (Wandel, 1981).

Treatment of the condition may include dietary alteration, administration of sex hormones, and minerals to aid in calcification (Cooley, 1977; Rubin, 1985). Safeguards must be taught to both the individual and the family, including instruction on how to lift heavy objects safely. First-aid instruction for fractures is also essential (Wandel, 1981).

REFERENCES

Behrman, R., & Vaughan, V. (1983). *Nelson textbook of pediatrics* (12th ed.). Philadelphia: Saunders.

Cooley, D. (Ed.). (1977). *Family medical guide* New York: Better Homes and Gardens.

Rubin, K. (1985). *Osteoporosis in Prader-Willi syndrome.* Presentation at Prader-Willi Association National Conference, Windsor Locks, CT.

Wandel, C. (1981). *Diseases, the nurses' reference library series* Philadelphia: Informed Communications.

JOHN E. PORCELLA
*Rhinebeck Country School,
Rhinebeck, New York*

BRITTLE BONE DISEASE
PRADER-WILLI SYNDROME

OTHER HEALTH IMPAIRED

Other health-impaired children include those pupils whose health problems severely affect learning. Federal law designates this group as including children with severe orthopedic impairments, illnesses of a chronic or acute nature that require a prolonged convalescence or that limit that child's vitality and strength, congenital anomalies (e.g., spina bifida or clubfoot), other physical causes (e.g., amputation or cerebral palsy), and other health problems including, but not limited to, hemophilia, asthma, severe anemia, and diabetes. This category constitutes about 4% of those children classified as handicapped (Ysseldyke & Algozzine, 1984). Unfortunately, the terminology used for children suffering other health impairments does not indicate any commonality in student need as the categorization is based on recognizable differences in condition and not on necessary educational interventions (Reynolds & Birch, 1982).

Other health impairments may be the result of congenital defects or adventitious (acquired) disabilities. The tremendous heterogeneity associated with the term requires attention to the one obvious common factor of such children, a physical condition that interferes with normal functioning by limiting the child's opportunity to participate fully in learning activities by affecting the body's supply of strength and energy or the removal of wastes; by reducing mobility; and by creating severe problems in growth and development (Kneedler, Hallahan, & Kauffman, 1984).

Although the continuum may range from mild to severe impairments, educational principles for other health-impaired children include:

1. Placement and education within the mainstream of the public school to the maximum capability of the child. For those children requiring special classes, special schools, or home/hospital instruction, direct efforts to return them as soon as possible to regular education (Heron & Harris, 1982).

2. Architectural modifications including the removal of all architectural barriers to full school integration and the modification of classroom structure and environment to allow optimal mobility and exploration.

3. Parent and family education (assumed by the school) to provide for coordination of effort, resources, and services.

4. Trained teachers and paraprofessionals who will assist other health-impaired children within the school setting.

5. Coordination and use of all necessary support and resource personnel by school districts serving such children, including transportation modifications, physical and occupational therapy, adaptive physical education, and vocational education and counseling (Gearheart & Weishahn, 1980).

REFERENCES

Gearheart, B. R., & Weishahn, M. W. (1980). *The handicapped child in the regular classroom* (2nd ed.). St. Louis: Mosby.

Heron, T. E., & Harris, K. C. (1982). *The educational consultant: Helping professionals, parents, and mainstreamed students.* Boston: Allyn & Bacon.

Kneedler, R. D., Hallahan, D. P., & Kauffman, J. M. (1984). *Special education for today.* Englewood Cliffs, NJ: Prentice-Hall.

Reynolds, M. C., & Birch, J. W. (1982). *Teaching exceptional children in all america's schools.* Reston, VA: Council for Exceptional Children.

Ysseldyke, J. E., & Algozzine, B. (1984). *Introduction to special education.* Boston: Houghton Mifflin.

RONALD S. LENKOWSKY
*Hunter College, City University
of New York*

DIABETES
EDUCATION FOR "OTHER HEALTH IMPAIRED" CHILDREN
PHYSICAL DISABILITIES
SPINAL BIFIDA

OTIS-LENNON SCHOOL ABILITY TEST (OLSAT)

The Otis-Lennon School Ability Test (OLSAT) is described as a power measure of abstract thinking and reasoning ability (Otis & Lennon, 1979). It is claimed to predict reliably success in cognitive and school-related activities. Test items employ verbal, figural, and numerical stimuli. The OLSAT has five levels covering grades 1 through 12. Fall and spring norms are available by age or grade. The age-based school ability index has the same statistical properties as the deviation IQ. No special attention was provided in the norming to include special education pupils. The OLSAT, when administered with the Stanford Achievement Test or the Metropolitan Achievement Test, yields an achievement/ability comparison. The rationale for using a measure of school ability or intelligence to predict achievement results could be questioned. Why not use previous achievement as the predictor? No educational interventions are proposed that make use of the information contained in OLSAT. Perhaps a subsequent edition will make use of the processing or learning style employed by pupils.

REFERENCE

Otis, A. S., & Lennon, R. T. (1979). *Otis-Lennon School Ability Test.* New York: Psychological Corporation.

THOMAS F. HOPKINS
*Center for Behavioral
Psychotherapy,
White Plains, New York*

ACHIEVEMENT TESTS
DEVIATION IQ
INTELLIGENCE TESTING

OTITIS MEDIA

Otitis media is an inflammation or infection of the middle ear. Nasal secretions back up and infect the Eustachian tube so that the air pressure in the middle ear is no longer equalized and a partial vacuum is created, causing an impairment in hearing. The infection can also be caused by the puncturing of the eardrum. There are three types of otitis media—acute, serous, and chronic.

Acute otitis media and serous otitis media are the most prominent causes of conductive hearing loss in children. The symptoms of acute otitis media include ear pain, hearing loss, aural discharge, and a sensation of fullness in the ear. While commonly occurring in infants and children, it may occur at any age. The onset usually follows an upper respiratory tract infection. Fever is usually present. The common treatment is bed rest, analgesics, and antibiotics. Ear drops are usually of limited value but local heat is helpful. Oral decongestants may also hasten relief. Acute otitis media, if properly treated with antibiotics, usually is resolved. If treatment is terminated prematurely, resolution of the infection may be incomplete and a conductive hearing loss may persist.

Serous otitis media is characterized by the accumulation of fluid in the middle ear that results in a temporary hearing loss. The absence of fever and pain distinguish it from acute otitis media. The hearing loss is characterized by a plugged feeling in the ear and a reverberation of the patient's voice. Treatment consists of nasal decongestants. Antihistamines may be given if a nasal allergy is suspected as the cause. Tonsillectomy and adenoidectomy may be necessary to permanently correct the condition (Bluestone, 1982).

Chronic otitis media is nearly always associated with perforation of the eardrum. There are two types of chronic otitis media: benign and that which is associated with mastoid disease (Shaffer, 1978). The latter is more serious by far and is characterized by a foul smelling drainage from the ear as well as impaired hearing. If chronic mastoiditis occurs in infancy, the mastoid bone does not develop a good cellular structure. Antibiotic drugs are usually of limited use in combatting the infection, but they may be useful in treating complications. Local cleansing of the ear with antibiotic powders and solutions is one method of treatment. Surgery may be needed in other cases. The complications of chronic otitis media and mastoiditis may be meningitis and sinus thrombosis.

REFERENCES

Bluestone, C. D. (1982). Otitis media in children: To treat or not to treat? *New England Journal of Medicine, 306,* 1399.

Shaffer, H. L. (1978). Acute mastoiditis and cholesteatoma. *Otolaryngology, 86,* 394.

ROBERT A. SEDLAK
University of Wisconsin, Stout

DEAF
EXPRESSIVE LANGUAGE DISORDERS
LANGUAGE DELAYS

OTOLARYNGOLOGIST

An otolaryngologist is a specialist who can treat diseases of and perform surgery on the ear, nose, and throat. An otolaryngologist may be consulted for disorders that might manifest themselves as speech or hearing disorders. An examination by an otolaryngologist will require an inspection of the nose, neck, throat, head, and ears. The otolaryngologist will locally anesthetize the area of the nose and use a series of probes to check for blockages and mucus. The Eustachian tubes are then checked for their functional efficiency. The physician checks for thick bands of adhesions or growths of adenoid tissue in the fossae of Rosenmueller behind the tubal openings. Using a tongue depressor and a mirror these can be seen by looking up the nasopharynx. The entire interior of the mouth is examined, including the teeth and tongue. Finally, the ears are examined using an otoscope (Sataloff, 1966).

The otolaryngologist may work in cooperation with other specialists. An audiologist may be consulted to do a hearing examination and consider nonsurgical remedies for a hearing problem or postsurgical services. A speech pathologist may work with an otolaryngologist for nonsurgical remedies for speech difficulties or for postsurgical services (Northern & Downs, 1974).

REFERENCES

Northern, J. L., & Downs, M. P. (1974). *Hearing in children.* Baltimore, MD: Williams & Wilkins.

Sataloff, J. (1966). *Hearing loss.* Philadelphia: Lippincott.

ROBERT A. SEDLAK
University of Wisconsin, Stout

DEAF
OTITIS MEDIA
SPEECH PATHOLOGIST

OTOLOGY

Otology is the study of diseases of the ear. This includes deafness and other hearing defects as well as ear aches, discharges, and infections of the mastoid. An otologist is a medical doctor who specializes in the treatment of these diseases and problems. An otologist can diagnose causes of hearing problems and recommend medical and surgical treatments. An otologist may have an MD (doctor of medicine) or a DO (doctor of osteopathy) degree.

An otologic examination will involve far more than just an examination of the ear because the cause of some symptoms may lie in the nose, neck, or throat. An initial examination begins with a case history. Surgery for correction of otosclerosis and ossicular defects leaves no detectable scars; therefore questions regarding such surgery are necessary in taking a health history. Since otology deals with diseases of the ear, an otologist may call in an otolaryngologist to assist with a case when the source of the condition might originate in the nose or throat. An otolaryngologist deals with symptoms and diseases in which there is some relationship among the ear, nose, and throat.

ROBERT A. SEDLAK
University of Wisconsin, Stout

DEAF
OTITIS MEDIA
OTOLARYNGOLOGIST

OTOSCLEROSIS

Otosclerosis is a common conductive hearing loss that occurs with the onset of middle age. The eardrum and middle ear appear to be normal through an otoscope. What develops, however, is the formation of spongy bone in the cochlear bone. The cause is unknown. The name otosclerosis is misleading for the process is really not a sclerotic one but more like a vascularization in the bone. There are more people with otosclerosis than have sought medical attention for the condition. Evidence of this fact is the result of autopsies that have been done on persons without any known history of hearing impairment. Otosclerosis can occur without a resultant hearing loss. This occurs when otosclerotic changes affect areas of the bony labyrinth other than the oval window. When a hearing loss is associated with otosclerosis, it is referred to as clinical otosclerosis. The condition develops over a period of months or even years. The hearing gradually diminishes as the footplate becomes more fixed. In some cases, the hearing loss stops after reaching only a mild level. More frequently, the hearing loss stabilizes at 50 to 60 dB. The hearing deficit starts in the lower frequencies and progresses to the higher ones (Davis & Silverman, 1974).

Otosclerosis is a condition more common in females than in males and the symptoms may be aggravated by pregnancy. The condition is often found in several people in the same family. While there may be a genetic linkage to the condition in some cases, prediction based on genetic theory is not refined. Offspring of two people with otosclerosis have been found to have normal hearing. The condition could occur in just one ear. Surgery may help to restore some of the hearing loss (Sataloff, 1966).

REFERENCES

Davis, H., & Silverman, S. R. (1974). *Hearing and deafness*. New York: Holt, Rinehart, & Winston.
Sataloff, J. (1966). *Hearing loss*. Philadelphia: Lippincott.

ROBERT A. SEDLAK
University of Wisconsin, Stout

DEAF
DEAF EDUCATION
OTITIS MEDIA

OVERACHIEVEMENT AND SPECIAL EDUCATION

Typically, overachievement is not an area considered in association with special education. However, there are areas within special education where children exhibit superior abilities. For example, gifted and talented children possess skills or abilities that are considered to be superior to those found in the normal population. This is the area of special education where overachievement is prevalent. Another example of a group of children who exhibit extraordinary abilities are idiot savants. These children are markedly retarded except for some highly developed skill that is grossly discrepant with their functioning in other areas (Knopf, 1984). These unusual abilities within the context of delayed development are also found in autistic children (Rimland, 1964). There is no satisfactory explanation for these rare occurrences of isolated areas of outstanding abilities in individuals who show delayed development in all other areas. Nevertheless, idiot savants have been noted with special abilities that are, by far, superior to those found in the normal population in art, music, mechanics, calculation, mental calendar manipulation, and memory (Rimland, 1964).

Aside from those areas where children possess superior skills or abilities, overachievment would not usually be considered associated with special education. Achievement below normal performance, or underachievement, is more common, and most areas of special education focus on the inability to learn. For example, the mentally retarded, learning disabled, and emotionally disturbed manifest conditions that adversely affect educational performance; children with speech and language problems who are unable to comprehend language or express themselves adequately have difficulties in learning; and the physically impaired (e.g., those with hearing impairments, visual impairments, and health impairments) exhibit handicaps that affect achievement.

Special education has generally focused on these children's deficiencies, but in addition to weaknesses, these children also have strengths. It is these strengths that allow the special child to overachieve in some areas. For example, moderately retarded children generally do not learn to read beyond a first-grade level (Kirk & Gallagher, 1983). However, some of these children do read at higher levels. This ability to read at higher levels is probably owed to individual strengths in reading ability. In all likelihood, this reading ability would not demonstrate overachievement when compared with the normal population, but when compared with these children's other abilities, it may well demonstrate overachievement. Therefore, overachievement in special education must be considered in relation to each child's abilities and disabilities.

It appears that the key to understanding overachievement in special education is to focus on intraindividual differences (i.e., differences within individual children). If we focus on the individual strengths of each child, it then becomes possible to discover areas of skill development where the child is overachieving. By considering overachievement in this manner, it becomes clear that a child in any area of special education can demonstrate overachievement in a wide variety of skills. Furthermore, in many instances these children can also demonstrate overachievement in those areas restricted by their handicaps if some compensation or modification is made to the learning environment that will allow them the opportunity to learn and/or display those skills.

REFERENCES

Kirk, S. A., & Gallagher, J. J. (1983). *Educating exceptional children* (4th ed.). Boston: Houghton Mifflin.

Knopf, I. J. (1984). *Childhood psychopathology: A developmental approach* (2nd ed.). Englewood Cliffs, NJ: Prentice-Hall.

Rimland, B. (1964). *Infantile autism*. Englewood Cliffs, NJ: Prentice-Hall.

LARRY J. WHEELER
*Southwest Texas State
University*

UNDERACHIEVEMENT

OVERACHIEVEMENT AND THE GIFTED

While considerable attention had been given to the problems of the underachieving gifted student, overachievement in the gifted remains poorly defined. Generally, a discrepancy criterion is used to categorize students where a gap between expectation (as measured by aptitude and intelligence tests) and performance (as measured by achievement tests) indicates that a student is under or overachieving. Lack of uniformity in the measurement criteria makes it difficult to establish clear categories, and a child who may qualify as overachieving according to one system may be excluded when a different system is used (Tannenbaum, 1983).

Some reviewers identify psychosocial factors that may contribute to discrepancies between expectation and performance. Whitmore (1980) suggests that the overachieving gifted student is more able to control feelings of academic anxiety, feels more adequate and confident, and has feelings of greater self-value than an underachieving counterpart. Furthermore, the overachieving gifted student tends to be more interested in academic pursuits than in social activities. Asbury (1974) found no consistent psychosocial factors underlying discrepant achievement. In-

terestingly, Tannenbaum (1983) proposes that any discrepancy between expectation and performance in the direction of overachievement points to an error in the measurements determining expectations. Overachievement is thus an "illusion resulting quite clearly from underprediction." Inasmuch as measures of expectation purport to indicate a child's capacity, it would seem that overachievement places a student in the absurd position of performing beyond his own capacity.

REFERENCES

Asbury, C. A. (1974). Selected factors influencing over- and underachievement in young school-age children. *Review of Educational Research, 44*, 409–428.

Tannenbaum, A. J. (1983). *Gifted children: Psychological and educational perspectives*. New York: Macmillan.

Whitmore, J. R. (1980). *Giftedness, conflict and underachievement*. Boston: Allyn & Bacon.

BERNICE ARRICALE
*Hunter College, City University
of New York*

OVERCORRECTION

Overcorrection refers to a punishment procedure and includes the systematic application of prescribed strategies to decrease the future occurrence of targeted behaviors. An overcorrection package may include verbal reprimands, time-out from positive reinforcement, short verbal instructions, and graduated guidance. The two major procedures of overcorrection are restitution and positive practice. Restitution means restoring the environment or oneself to a state that is vastly improved relative to the prior condition. Positive practice involves the repeated practice of certain forms of behaviors relevant to the content in which the behavior occurred (Hobbs, 1985).

Foxx (1982) describes three characteristics of overcorrection acts, including the existence of a direct relationship to the student's misbehavior; implementation immediately following the misbehavior; and rapid administration of overcorrection acts. While administering overcorrection acts, the teacher employs a full or partial graduated guidance form of assistance followed by a shadowing procedure as the program develops. In a full graduated guidance technique, the teacher maintains full contact with the student's hands. In partial graduated guidance, the teacher uses a thumb and forefinger to gently guide the movements of the student. Eventually, the teacher shadows the student by placing a hand in close proximity to the student's hand and initiating contact only when the student fails to complete the movements of the overcorrection act.

A sample behavior that could result in an overcorrection consequence is excessive spillage of food during meals.

A simple correction procedure would require the student to clean only the immediate area of the spillage. Overcorrection would extend this requirement to cleaning additional areas in the cafeteria as well. Additionally, the teacher may require the student to overly clean designated areas even though these areas may not need attention.

In a review of behaviors that have been targeted for overcorrection acts, Ferretti and Cavalier (1983) summarized the reported effectiveness with eating skills, toileting skills, aggressive-disruptive behaviors, stereotype behaviors, and self-injurious behaviors. In these research reports, the individual components of each overcorrection package of strategies were not evaluated. However, general observations of the effectiveness of overcorrection procedures were favorable. Overcorrection acts have been successfully implemented with individuals with mental retardation, autism, emotional handicaps, and behavioral disorders.

Caution must be exercised during the formulation and implementation of the components of an overcorrection package. A minimum intensity level of intrusiveness should be maintained that affects the desired behavioral reduction of the targeted behavior. From a practical standpoint, overcorrection requires the investment of close teacher to student contact throughout the implementation of the procedures. Additionally, the physical strength of a strong student must be considered relative to a teacher's ability to guide the movements of the overcorrection acts. A different reductive procedure may be necessary if the teacher is unable to complete the required full graduated guidance.

The appeal of overcorrection is the educative component of teaching the student a correct way of behaving to replace the targeted negative behavior. The implementation of aversive consequences that resemble overcorrection acts, but fail to include this educative component, are mislabeled as overcorrection. Careful monitoring of all aspects of this reductive procedure needs to be included to provide adequate safeguards against potentially abusive situations. As a punishment alternative, overcorrection requires additional investigations to substantiate previous claims of rapid reduction of undesirable behaviors.

REFERENCES

Axelrod, S., Brantner, J. P., & Meddock, T. D. (1978). Overcorrection: A review and critical analysis. *Journal of Special Education, 12,* 367–391.

Ferretti, R. P., & Cavalier, A. R. (1983). A critical assessment of overcorrection procedures with mentally retarded persons. In J. L. Matson & F. Andrasik (Eds.), *Treatment issues and innovations in mental retardation* (pp. 241–301). New York: Plenum.

Foxx, R. M. (1982). *Decreasing behaviors of severely retarded and autistic persons* (pp. 91–111). Champaign, IL: Research Press.

Hobbs, S. A. (1985). Overcorrection. In A. S. Bellack & M. Hersen (Eds.), *Dictionary of behavior therapy techniques* (pp. 158–160). New York: Pergamon.

Kazdin, A. E. (1984). *Behavior modification in applied settings* (3rd ed.) (pp. 136–139). Homewood, IL: Dorsey.

Ollendick, T. H., & Matson, J. L. (1978). Overcorrection: An overview. *Behavior Therapy, 9,* 830–842.

ERNEST L. PANCSOFAR
University of Connecticut

BEHAVIOR MODELING
BEHAVIOR MODIFICATION
DESTRUCTIVE BEHAVIOR

P

PALMAR CREASE

Human palms are covered by creases of different depths, lengths, and directions. The flexion creases are formed during early intrauterine life and are thought to be influenced by factors causing anomalies in the embryo. Variations in appearance of the palmar creases have been linked to certain medical disorders. Therefore, alterations have medical diagnostic value and usually are included in dermatoglyphic analysis. The three main creases have been the primary focus of most investigations. They are the radial longitudinal or thenar crease, the proximal transverse, and the distal transverse. Alter (1970) measured differences in the space between palmar creases, noted abnormalities, and described variations in a normal population.

A single crease across the palm of the hand frequently is described as characteristic of Down's syndrome (Robinson & Robinson, 1965; Telford & Sawery, 1977). The proximal and distal transverse creases are replaced or joined into a single crease that transverses the entire palm. This has been referred to as a single palmar crease, single transverse fold, four finger line, or simian crease. The term simian crease, although frequently used, is not appropriate. The frequency of the single palmar crease ranges between 1 and 15% in controlled populations and possibly higher in groups with developmental defects (Schaumann & Alter, 1976). Researchers noted that the variability in appearance makes determination difficult and may partially account for the wide range in reported frequency.

REFERENCES

Alter, M. (1970). Variation in palmar creases. *American Journal of Diseases of Children, 20*, 424.

Robinson, H. B., & Robinson, N. M. (1965). *The mentally retarded child: A psychological approach.* New York: McGraw-Hill.

Schaumann, B., & Alter, M. (1976). *Dermatoglyphics in medical disorders.* Heidelberg, Germany: Springer-Verlag.

Telford, C. W., & Sawery, J. M. (1977). *The exceptional individual.* Englewood Cliffs, NJ: Prentice-Hall.

SALLY E. PISARCHICK
*Cuyahoga Special Education
Service Center, Maple
Heights, Ohio*

**DOWN'S SYNDROME
PHYSICAL ANOMALIES**

PARAPLEGIA

Paraplegia is a term used to describe a physical condition in which the individual is unable to functionally use the lower extremities of the body. The term describes the topography of the impairment and does not suggest the etiology of the physical limitations, which may be of varied origin (Best, 1978).

Paraplegia results from many disorders that interfere with the brain or spinal cord's ability to transmit stimuli to the motor effectors (muscles) of the legs, or from the inability of the larger muscles of the legs themselves to act in a functional manner. It may result from cerebral palsy, which is a nonprogressive disorder of the central nervous system where the brain is involved, or from orthopedic disorders that involve the musculoskeletal system such as muscular dystrophy. In the former condition, the neurological input to the muscles may be impeded at the level of the brain. The latter involves an asymmetrical deterioration of muscle fibers, depriving the legs of the necessary activity for gross muscular action. Conditions such as spina bifida, in which there is often a physical interruption in the continuity of the spinal cord, may also cause impairment of the body's function below the level of the lesion (injury). The origin of the paraplegia can be congenital (either the disorder or predisposition is present from birth) or adventitiously (accidentally) acquired. The former may include genetically transmitted disorders such as Werdnig-Hofmann disease, where the anterior horn cells (those cells of the spinal cord having motor function) deteriorate and lose function early in the child's development, or traumatic injury, which can occur at anytime in life.

While the disease underlying the paraplegia often suggests additional concerns for management, many of these diseases are more of a concern for medical intervention than for educational. Educational management and teaching, however, must take into consideration the limitations imposed on the individual with paraplegia, as well as safety and health considerations. When paraplegia results from neurological impairment, sensory deficits to the lower segments of the body may also be sustained as well as functional deficits (Capildeo & Maxwell, 1984). These deficits, which may include bowel and bladder incontinence (Staas & LaMantina, 1984a), also require assistance from both a psychological and hygienic perspective. The paraplegic who manifests sensory deficits and maintains a sitting posture for most of the day should avoid remaining in one position in school, at home, or in other settings for a prolonged period of time. Since sensitivity to pain may be impaired, prolonged placement in one position may increase skin irritation that goes unrecognized by the individual until sores or descubiti develop (Kottke et al., 1982; Kosiak, 1982).

In the nonsensorily impaired individual, discomfort usually accompanying skin erosion allows for the independent shift in positioning that facilitates, avoiding injury. If the primary means of movement is accomplished by use of a wheelchair, a firm seat or wheelchair insert providing a firm seat and lateral support should be used. Reliance on the webbed or sling seat often found in portable folding chairs does not allow for adequate uniform support. The paraplegic may begin to favor one side of the supportive webbed seat, asymmetrically tipping the body. To regain a vertical perspective to the environment, compensation of the spine in the opposite direction is likely to be forced, resulting in a scoliosis (lateral curvature of the spine) over time. Aside from orthopedic implications, infringement on the diaphragm may reduce vital capacities by reducing pulmonary (lung) function. This can result in shallow, rapid cycles of breathing that increase tendencies toward respiratory problems. These shallow, rapid cycles further impede reducing body noise, making localization of low-amplitude sounds more difficult and interfering with the controlled expiration necessary to speech production.

Management must also include an understanding of the nutritional needs of the individual with paraplegia. Since activities may be circumscribed, caloric intake for the active nonparaplegic is not an accurate gauge for determining diet. Such a diet would provide excess nutritive support resulting in weight gain. Diet should, therefore, be provided on an individual basis, taking into consideration the specific activity level of the individual.

The environmental experience, is regarded as part of the educational process, will be impaired if provision for available alternatives to independent ambulation are not provided. The younger child with paraplegia who is deprived of free exploration of the environment may be impeded in concept development (Connor et al., 1978). For the toddler, a device such as a scooter board or crawl-a-gator may assist in active environmental exploration. This device consists of a board on which casters are mounted. The child lies prone on the device and propels himself or herself around the floor by pushing the ground with the upper extremities. The older child may begin to use a wheelchair or a parapodium. The latter device allows the child and preadolescent with paraplegia to ambulate in an upright position to more freely explore and learn. Training in donning (putting on) and duffing (removing) the parapodium is essential to increasing the independent functioning of the individual. With developed upper extremities, the parapodium can also be used to climb stairs.

Within the classroom, a standing table may be used to support the child in an upright position, freeing the upper extremities for manual exploration of learning materials, and concomitantly avoiding static positioning. This table is ideal for use in the classroom where academics may require writing and other skills requiring hand use and lower body support. Thus for the special educator to accommodate the needs for education and management of the individual with paraplegia, a comprehensive understanding of methods and materials necessary to circumvent the functional impairedness becomes essential. This management includes positioning, locomotion, and the ability to attend in a learning situation, free from the distraction imposed by the disability.

REFERENCES

Best, G. A. (1978). *Individuals with physical disabilities: An introduction for educators.* Saint Louis: Mosby.

Capildeo, R., & Maxwell, A. (Eds.). (1984). *Progress in rehabilitation: Paraplegia.* London: Macmillan.

Connor, F. P., Williamson, G. G., & Siepp, J. M. (1978). *Program guide for infants and toddlers with neuromotor and other developmental disabilities.* New York: Teacher's College Press.

Kosiak, M. (1982). Prevention and rehabilitation of ischemic ulcers. In F. J. Kottke, G. K. Stillwell, & J. F. Lehman (Eds.), *Krusen's handbook of physical medicine and rehabilitation.* Philadelphia: Saunders.

Kottke, F. J., Stillwell, G. K., & Lehman, J. F. (Eds.) (1982). *Krusen's handbook of physical medicine and rehabilitation.* Philadelphia: Saunders.

Rushkin, A. P. (Ed.). (1984). *Current therapy in physiatry.* Philadelphia: Saunders.

Staas, W. E., & La Mantina, J. (1984a). The neurogenic bladder: Physiologic mechanisms and clinical problems of bladder control. In A. P. Ruskin (Ed.), *Current therapy in physiatry* (pp. 396–410). Philadelphia: Saunders.

Staas, W. E., & La Mantina, J. (1984b). Descubitus ulcers. In A. P. Ruskin (Ed.), *Current therapy in physiatry* (pp. 410–419). Philadelphia: Saunders.

ELLIS I. BAROWSKY
*Hunter College, City University
of New York*

CEREBRAL PALSY
MUSCULAR DYSTROPHY
SPINA BIFIDA

PARAPROFESSIONALS

Various descriptors have been used to identify the paraprofessional in special education. MacMillan (1973) has identified as potential paraprofessionals, nonprofessional adults, older children in the role of tutor, and parents. Tucker and Horner (1977) identify a paraprofessional as any person other than the teacher who is engaged in providing educational opportunities for handicapped children. While not considered a fully trained professional, the paraprofessional is one who is expected to possess certain competencies that will promote a higher quality and more effective educational program for the handicapped.

Interest in the use of paraprofessionals in special education programs has largely been based on three issues: relieving the special education teacher from nonprofessional duties; increasing the quality of the instructional program; and meeting the needs of a burgeoning number of special education programs.

The use of paraprofessionals in the special education classroom was first reported in the 1950s (Cruickshank & Haring, 1957). The conclusions drawn from this investigation were that the teachers who had paraprofessionals assigned to their classrooms felt that they were able to do a better job of teaching. The administrators of these programs concurred with this opinion, as did the parents of the children, who felt their children had profited from the presence of a paraprofessional in the classroom. In the 1960s, as a result of professional and legislative efforts, there emerged an increased interest in the establishment of a number and variety of educational services for the handicapped. As a result of this, there was an immediate critical shortage of professional personnel to meet the rapid expansion of special education programs (President's Panel on Mental Retardation, 1962). The paraprofessional was viewed as a potential solution to this problem (Blessing, 1967).

In the ensuing years, the concept of paraprofessionals as an answer to manpower problems and improved quality of classroom instruction gained considerable acceptance. Roos (1970) recognized the need for less sophisticated trained personnel as an answer to the shortage of trained special educators. MacMillan (1973) also felt that the use of paraprofessionals in special education programs was an appropriate means for closing the manpower gap. In addition, various authors (Hanson, 1969; Karnes, Teska, & Hodgins, 1970) concluded that the instructional program in the special classroom was enhanced by the presence of paraprofessionals. Karnes and Teska (1975) determined that the use of paraprofessionals was not only effective, but that in some instances, paraprofessionals were as capable as professional teachers in carrying out instructional programs. The available evidence supported the concept that paraprofessionals can and do serve a meaningful and significant role in special education programs. However, there emerged a further concern relative to the type of training that is necessary to produce effective paraprofessionals, and their role in the classroom remains an issue for discussion.

Competency to function as an effective paraprofessional is, in many ways, directly related to the perceived role of the paraprofessional in the program. Competencies have been identified at various levels of sophistication. Tucker and Horner (1977) feel that training should be directly related to skills that would assist the paraprofessional in changing student behavior. They feel that this should include training in areas such as curriculum, task analysis, and even parent counseling. Greer and Simpson (1977) take a somewhat more generic approach by defining the paraprofessional as a tutor. In training for this role, they enumerate a number of competencies that are indigenous to a variety of teaching functions (e.g., assessment, programming, scheduling and teaching). Other authors (Fimian, Fafard, & Howell, 1984; Gartner, 1972) have been more specific in the identification of areas or topics that they feel are necessary to produce a competent paraprofessional. These topics entail many of the traditional child development and curriculum/method sequences, as well as characteristics, behavior management techniques, and routine clerical skills. In summary, the training program for paraprofessionals may vary depending on the individual's qualifications and experience as well as the perceived role of the paraprofessional in the assigned special education program.

The position of the paraprofessional in special education programs has usually been one of a subordinate. The paraprofessional is expected to carry out his or her assigned duties in tandem with the fully trained professional. The assumption is that while paraprofessionals may be a valuable addition to the overall program, the teacher must be regarded as the one ultimately responsible for the teaching function. However, paraprofessionals have been used in a variety of ways in the educational setting. Their duties have usually encompassed activities such as clerical work, supervision of nonacademic activities, housekeeping, acting as parent surrogates, and sometimes even as active teachers engaged in the instructional process under the supervision of the trained teacher (Blessing, 1967; Greer & Simpson, 1977; MacMillan, 1973).

Recent concerns for the extension of educational programs to a population of handicapped that has been unserved in an educational setting (e.g., the severely and profoundly handicapped) has created a potential new role for the less than baccalaureate trained (paraprofessional) teacher. Although Sontag, Burke, and York (1976) feel that teachers working with the severely handicapped should be rigorously trained and possess a number of specific and precise competencies, Burton and Hirshoren (1979) view the use of well-trained paraprofessionals as teachers as a resolution of problems that are indigenous to this level of programming (e.g., available manpower, individualization of instruction, and teacher burnout). Tucker and Horner (1977) have acknowledged the need for well-trained paraprofessionals in programs for the severely handicapped and agree that it is impractical to rely on fully trained teachers to provide the individualized instruction that is necessary in these programs.

While enjoying considerable discussion, the paraprofessional role in special education has not been clearly defined. However, it appears that the paraprofessional currently enjoys a higher level of acceptance in programs that serve the more severely handicapped. While there is some theoretical and practical evidence of their success in other levels of programs, the paraprofessional is still not a universally accepted concept in all special education programs.

REFERENCES

Blessing, K. R. (1967). Use of teacher aides in special education: A review and possible application. *Exceptional Children, 34,* 107–113.

Burton, T. A., & Hirshoren, A., (1979). The education of the severely and profoundly retarded: Are we sacrificing the child to the concept? *Exceptional Children, 45,* 598–602.

Cruickshank, W., & Haring, N. (1957). *A demonstration: Assistants for teachers of exceptional children.* Syracuse, NY: Syracuse University Press.

Fimian, M. J., Fafard, M., & Howell, K. W. (1984). *A teacher's guide to human resources in special education.* Boston: Allyn & Bacon.

Gartner, A. (1972). The curriculum: Issues in combining theory and practice in training teacher aids. *Journal of Research & Development in Education, 5,* 57–68.

Greer, B. B., & Simpson, G. A. (1977). A demonstration model for training noncertified personnel in special education. *Education & Training of the Mentally Retarded, 12,* 266–271.

Hanson, F. M. (1969). Aides for the trainable mentally retarded. *Journal of the California Teachers Association, 65,* 23–26.

Karnes, M. B., & Teska, J. (1975). Children's response to intervention programs. In J. J. Gallagher (Ed.), *The application of child development research to exceptional children.* Reston, VA: Council for Exceptional Children.

Karnes, M. B., Teska, J. A., & Hodgins, A. S. (1970). The successful implementation of a highly specific preschool instructional program by paraprofessional teachers. *Journal of Special Education, 4,* 69–80.

MacMillan, D. L. (1973). Issues and trends in special education. *Mental Retardation, 11,* 3–8.

President's Panel on Mental Retardation. (1962). *A proposed program for national action to combat mental retardation* . Washington, DC: U.S. Government Printing Office.

Roos, P. (1970). Trends and issues in special education for the mentally retarded. *Education & Training of the Mentally Retarded, 5,* 51–61.

Sontag, E., Burke, P. J., & York, R. (1976). Considerations for serving the severely handicapped in the public schools. In R. M. Anderson & J. G. Greer (Eds.), *Educating the severely and profoundly retarded.* Baltimore, MD: University Park Press.

Tucker, P. J., & Horner, R. D. (1977). Competency based training of paraprofessionals training associates for education of the severely and profoundly handicapped. In E. Sontag, J. Smith, & N. Certo (Eds.), *Educational programming for the severely and profoundly handicapped.* Reston, VA: Council for Exceptional Children.

THOMAS A. BURTON
University of Georgia

TEACHER BURNOUT
TEACHER EFFECTIVENESS

PARENTAL COUNSELING

Counseling parents of handicapped children has taken a number of different forms. Variations in counseling strategies reflect diverse professional orientations as well as differing family dynamics and needs. Because new challenges often arise as the child's disability interacts with increased demands at different developmental stages, counseling is frequently a recurrent need in families with handicapped children.

Parental counselors include teachers, guidance counselors, educational evaluators, social workers, psychologists, physicians, and other parents. Counseling can range from informal and infrequent teacher/parent exchanges to long-term programs that involve all family members. Counseling approaches can be grouped into three broad categories: those providing information about the nature of the child's disability, those offering psychotherapeutic insight into the often conflicting emotions that accompany recognition of the disability, and those providing training to improve parent/child interactions and to manage the child's behavior.

Counseling aimed at educating parents about the nature of their child's disability is probably the most common. In order for parents confronted with a handicapped child to make appropriate and realistic adjustments, they need various sources of accurate and pragmatic information. The information-focused counseling provided by physician, psychologist, and/or evaluator when the child's handicap is first identified is clearly crucial for parents. Information-centered counseling is also provided when teachers share their insights, goals, and expectations and when parent organizations (e.g., ACLD, ARC, Closer Look) offer pamphlets, telephone hotlines, and parent support groups.

Psychotherapeutic approaches to parent counseling focus on helping parents to work through and resolve emotional stresses and conflicts often precipitated by the presence of a disabled child in the family. Such counseling can occur with parents and counselor alone, jointly with the handicapped child, or with all active family members, including siblings and even caretaking grandparents. With advances in the understanding of the complex interrelations within families, the trend has been in the direction of including more family members in psychotherapeutic counseling (Foster & Berger, 1979). Sibling relationships represent one of those significant complexities that recently has spawned nationwide sibling support groups as well as greater consideration of siblings within the context of counseling (Grossman, 1972).

A third category of counseling is parent training programs. Through such programs, parents learn more effective means of communicating with their children and methods for better managing their children's problem behaviors. Parent training programs teach techniques such as active listening and problem solving (Gordon 1975), ways to function as filial therapists (Guerney, 1969), methods for becoming behavioral change agents (McDowell, 1974). Numerous research studies demonstrate that parents can be effective in working with and modifying their children's behavior and that such parent involvement is generally positive (McDowell, 1976).

Increasingly, two theoretical notions, or frameworks, have informed many of the counseling approaches available to parents of handicapped children: stages of grief theory and family systems theory. Regardless of the particular approach (educational, psychotherapeutic, or parent training), many of those who counsel parents have been guided by, or at least sensitized by, one or both of these frameworks. The first reflects the prevalent view that many, if not all, parents of handicapped children undergo some version of a mourning process in reaction to their child's disability. To varying degrees, this represents a loss of the hoped for intact, healthy child. Variations on Kubler-Ross's (1969) stages of grief theory have been proposed to explain parents' emotional journey toward productive adjustment to their child's handicapping condition (Seligman, 1979). These mourning stages include denial of the existence, the degree, or the implications of the disability; bargaining, often evident in the pursuit of magical cures or highly questionable treatments; anger, often projected outward onto the spouse or the helping professional or projected inward, causing feelings of guilt and shame; depression, manifest in withdrawal and expressions of helplessness and inadequacy; and acceptance, the stage in which productive actions can be taken and positive family balances maintained. It is commonly believed that any of the earlier stages can be reactivated by crises or in response to the child's or the family's transitions from one developmental stage to another.

Family systems theory, particularly Minuchin's structural analysis (Minuchin, Rosman, & Baker, 1978) and Haley's (1973, 1976, 1980) strategic approach provides another highly valued conceptual framework for counseling. Within this framework, families are seen as interdependent systems whose problems are relational. This view offers concepts and techniques for considering the effects on all parts of the family of intervention with one member or with one subsystem. By focusing on the dynamics of a family's structure, hierarchy, and stage in the family life cycle, family systems theory offers a more complex, and therefore more accurate, understanding of the functioning, development, and needs of a particular family with a handicapped child (Foster, Berger, & McLean, 1981).

Both family systems theory and stages of grief theory are widely applicable conceptual influences within family counseling. Neither of these frameworks mitigates against using any of a wide variety of other educational, psychotherapeutic, or parent training methods to promote growth in families with handicapped children.

REFERENCES

Foster, M., & Berger, M. (1979). Structural family therapy: Applications in programs for preschool handicapped children. *Journal of the Division for Early Childhood, 1*, 52–58.

Foster, M., Berger, M., & McLean, M. (1981). Rethinking a good idea: A reassessment of parent involvement. *Topics in Early Childhood Special Education, 1*(3), 55–65.

Gordon, T. (1975). *Parent effectiveness training.* New York: Plume.

Grossman, P. (1972). *Brothers and sisters of retarded children.* Syracuse, NY: Syracuse University Press.

Guerney, B. G. (1969). Filial therapy: Description and rationale. *Journal of Consulting Psychology, 28*, 304–310.

Haley, J. (1973). *Uncommon therapy.* New York: Norton.

Haley, J. (1976). *Problem-solving therapy.* San-Francisco: Jossey-Bass.

Haley, J. (1980). *Leaving home.* New York: McGraw-Hill.

Kubler-Ross, E. (1969). *On death and dying.* New York: Macmillan.

McDowell, R. L. (1974). *Managing behavior: A program for parent involvement.* Torrance, CA: Winch.

McDowell, R. L. (1976). Parent counseling: The state of the art. *Journal of Learning Disabilities, 9*(10), 48–53.

Minuchin, S., Rosman, B., & Baker, L. (1978). *Psychosomatic families.* Cambridge, MA: Harvard University Press.

Seligman, M. (1979). *Strategies for helping parents of exceptional children.* New York: Free Press.

KATHERINE GARNETT
*Hunter College, City University
of New York*

FAMILY COUNSELING
PARENT EFFECTIVENESS TRAINING
PSYCHOTHERAPY

PARENT EDUCATION

Parents rarely receive direct instruction in how to parent. For many, such knowledge comes from their own personal experience of being parented, and from the advice of grandparents, friends, and neighbors. Parents of abused and neglected children are often reported to lack both effective parenting skills (Wolfe, 1985) and a social network of friends and neighbors who could be helpful with child rearing (Polansky, Gaudin, Ammons, & Davis, 1985).

The purposes of parent education programs are to help parents develop greater self-awareness, use effective discipline methods, improve parent-child communication, make family life more enjoyable, and provide general information on child development (Fine, 1980). Parent education is distinguished from parent therapy in that parent education is time-limited and has behavior change as a goal rather than personality change (Dembo, Sweitzer, & Lauritzen, 1985). Approaches have been developed from a wide variety of theoretical orientations, including behavioral (Becker, 1971; Patterson & Gullison, 1971), Adlerian

(Dreikurs & Soltz, 1964), systematic training for effective parenting (Dinkmeyer & McKay, 1976), transactional analysis (James, 1974), humanistic (Ginott, 1965, 1968) and parent effectiveness training (Gordon, 1975). Each of these programs is delivered in a group format; all include reading materials for parents, demonstrations of techniques, and discussions of technique applications.

Given the variety of education programs available, program evaluation is essential. Dembo, Sweitzer, and Lauritzen (1985) recently published an extensive review of 48 evaluation studies. In each of these studies, children with severe developmental or behavioral problems were excluded. Behavioral approaches were evaluated in 15 studies, Adlerian in 10 studies, and parent effectiveness training (PET) in 18. Only five studies compared one training program with another (Adlerian with behavioral and PET with behavioral).

Behavioral training programs are less homologous than Adlerian or PET programs, and therefore more difficult to evaluate. Most programs attempt to teach an overview of behavioral concepts, use of social and nonsocial reinforcers, techniques for strengthening and weakening behavior chains, observation and recording procedures, and parent awareness of the ways in which their behavior is shaped by their children. Behavioral approaches were evaluated in 15 studies. "The typical program included middle class parents trained by a PhD or Master's level psychologist for a period of 18 to 20 hours to deal with their male acting-out children ranging in age from 3 to 10 years" (Dembo, et al., 1985, p. 174). About three-quarters of the studies reporting follow-up data reported significantly improved child behavior compared with controls. Follow-up periods for those studies using random assignment of subjects ranged from 1 to 4 months. Studies without random assignment to training groups reported improved child behavior at 12 months' follow-up.

The goals of Adlerian approaches are to help parents understand what motivates their children's behavior and how family dynamics affect child behavior; to improve family communication through the use of the family council; and to help children develop responsibility through the use of logical consequences and democratic problem-solving (Dreikurs & Soltz, 1964). Ten studies provided evaluation data regarding the effectiveness of Adlerian approaches relative to no training. Most of the subject in these studies were mothers only; little data were provided in these studies regarding the trainers. Sessions varied from 6 to 10 weekly 1- to 1½-hour sessions. One study used random assignment with a child management discussion group as a placebo (Freeman, 1975); this study found no significant difference between the treatment group that studied the Dreikurs & Soltz (1963) test and the unstructured discussion group. Studies reporting data on parents' child-rearing attitudes generally reported positive changes, although no changes in child behavior were reported. No study included generalization or follow-up data.

Parent effectiveness training emphasizes learning human relations strategies that include the use of active listening, I-messages (e.g., "I want you to clean up your room now"), and democratic problem solving. The PET groups were evaluated in 18 studies. The training program consists of 8 weekly 3-hour sessions led by a trainer certified by Effectiveness Training Associates. Only five studies used random assignment to treatment groups. None of these studies indicated significant changes in child behavior. Only one out of four studies found significant differences in parent attitudes at follow-up; this change was in increased empathy.

Only five studies comparing different educational approaches were identified in the Dembo et al. review, one comparing Adlerian and behavioral approaches, the other four comparing behavioral and PET approaches. These studies failed to find any significant differences between approaches. Each of these approaches focuses on changing parent behaviors and attidues toward their children. They were developed prior to the current child-effects Zeitgeist in child development research (Bell, 1979); their effectiveness could possibly be improved by consideration of children's effects on their parents and by treating the family as a unit. Other concerns raised by Dembo et al. in their review involve the effectiveness of these programs with differing cultural groups, the lack of attention by researchers and program developers to differing needs of parents, the assessment of aptitude-treatment interactions, and the lack of methodological rigor in the majority of studies.

REFERENCES

Becker, W. C. (1971). *Parents are teachers*. Champaign, IL: Research Press.

Bell, R. Q. (1979). Parent, child, and reciprocal influences. *American Psychologist, 34*, 821–826.

Dembo, M. H., Sweitzer, M., & Lauritzen, P. (1985). An evaluation of group parent education: Behavioral, PET, and Adlerian programs. *Review of Educational Research, 55*, 155–200.

Dinkmeyer, D., & McKay, G. (1976). *Systematic training for effective parenting*. Circle Pines, MN: American Guidance Service.

Dreikurs, R., & Soltz, V. (1964). *Children: The challenge*. New York: Hawthorn.

Fine, M. J. (1980). The parent education movement: An introduction. In M. J. Fine (Ed.), *Handbook on parent education*. New York: Academic.

Freeman, C. W. (1975). Adlerian mother study groups: Effects on attitudes and behavior. *Journal of Individual Psychology, 31*, 37–50.

Ginott, H. G. (1965). *Between parent and child*. New York: Macmillan.

Ginott, H. G. (1968). *Between parent and teenagers*. New York: Macmillan.

Gordon, T. (1975). *P.E.T.: Parent effectiveness training*. New York: American Library.

James, M. (1974). *Transactional analysis for moms and dads.* Reading, MA: Addison-Wesley.

Patterson, G. R., & Gullison, M. E. (1971). *Living with children.* Champaign, IL: Research Press.

Polansky, N. A., Gaudin, J. M., Ammons, P. W., & Davis, K. B. (1985). The psychological ecology of the neglectful mother. *Child Abuse & Neglect, 9,* 265–275.

Wolfe, D. A. (1985). Child-abusive parents: An empirical review and analysis. *Psychological Bulletin, 97,* 462–482.

JOHN MacDONALD
Eastern Kentucky University

PARENT COUNSELING
PARENT EFFECTIVENESS TRAINING
FAMILY RESPONSE TO A HANDICAPPED CHILD
FAMILY THERAPY

PARENT EFFECTIVENESS TRAINING

See PARENT EDUCATION.

PARENTING SKILLS

Parents of students with disabilities are faced with needs not apparent to parents of students without identifiable disabilities. They are no longer passive recipients of services but assume a strong advocacy role on behalf of their children. Specifically, skills to be developed include learning to reduce stress, being involved in the individualized education plan (IEP), following through on home programming, helping the child to interact with friends and siblings, and managing behavior.

According to Wikler (1983), the "various stresses experienced by families of mentally retarded children are exacerbated over time by unexpected discrepancies between what might have been and what is." Reactions to normal life experiences from birth through adulthood occur with varying intensities and resolutions. The term chronic sorrow refers to the experiences of parents when they compare their child with peers without handicaps at developmental milestones, including when peers begin walking, talking, and entering public schools, begin puberty, graduate from school, and leave home. Available support comes through local associations for retarded citizens, family therapists, and other groups that provide outlets for sharing information and receiving nonjudgmental feedback concerning the unique experiences of family members.

Active participation by parents is an encouraged and mandated aspect of the IEP. This participation occurs through systematic contact with school personnel regarding rights and responsibilities of home and school representatives. At the basic level, identification, evaluation, and placement decisions involve a due process component to ensure that decision outcomes are acceptable to all involved parties. Increasingly, teachers are assuming the role of consultant to parents and viewing the parents as the real experts in their child's life. With this perspective, teachers are initiating extensive questionnaires for parents to complete prior to the IEP conference. Included in these questionnaires are activities that are pinpointed as having the highest value to the parents for their child's development. Thus communication skills between home and school environments are essential for optimum development of the IEP.

A common characteristic of students with handicapping conditions is the lack of generalization from school to community-based settings without active planning. Accordingly, parents are increasingly solicited to continue teaching their child in the skills being addressed at school. Principles of applied behavior analysis common to many school-based programs can be acquired by parents to ensure continuity of instruction. These instructional strategies may include prompting hierarchies, reinforcement schedules, and task modifications. Increasingly, parents are provided training in these areas when the child is very young (Hanson, 1977).

Parents express concern about the impact of a child with handicaps on siblings and peers in the neighborhood (Powell & Ogle, 1985). Developing friendships, participating in community activities, and interacting with family members are activities that contribute to a quality of life for individuals with disabilities. Parents are obtaining information and support to foster these relationships through peer support groups, journals such as *Exceptional Parent*, peer tutors, community integration specialists, and parent training seminars.

Understanding the relationships among antecedents, consequences, and a targeted child behavior is of prime concern when attempting to decrease undesirable behaviors. Antecedents involve events that immediately precede a behavior of concern to the parent and that may have a precipitating effect on the behavior. Consequences are events following the behavior of concern that may serve to reinforce and maintain an undesirable activity by the child. Finally, the undesirable behavior itself needs to be precisely defined for determining the exact parameters of attention. Numerous strategies are employed, including positive and negative reinforcement, shaping, token economy, time out, punishment, and overcorrection.

REFERENCES

Ehly, S. W., Conoley, J. C., & Rosenthal, D. (1985). *Working with parents of exceptional children.* St. Louis: Time Mirror/Mosby.

Gallagher, J. J., & Vietze, P. M. (Eds.). (1986). *Families of handicapped persons: Research, programs, and policy issues.* Baltimore, MD: Brookes.

Hanson, M. J. (1977). *Teaching your Down's syndrome infant: A guide for parents.* Baltimore, MD: University Park Press.

Powell, T. H., & Ogle, P. A. (1985). *Brothers and sisters: A special part of exceptional families.* Baltimore, MD: Brookes.

Turnbull, H. R., & Turnbull, A. P. (Eds.) (1985). *Parents speak out: Then and now (2nd ed.).* Columbus, OH: Merrill.

Wikler, L. (1983). Chronic stresses of families of mentally retarded children. In L. Wikler & M. P. Keenan (Eds.), *Developmental disabilities: No longer a private tragedy* (pp. 102–110). Washington, DC: American Association on Mental Deficiency.

ERNEST L. PANCSOFAR
University of Connecticut

FAMILY RESPONSE TO A HANDICAPPED CHILD
INDIVIDUAL EDUCATION PLAN (IEP)
SIBLINGS OF THE HANDICAPPED

PARENTS OF THE HANDICAPPED

Parents of handicapped children and youths have been one of the most influential factors in the education of and the delivery of services to handicapped younsters throughout the history of special education. Over the past decade, groups organized by parents have been described as trailblazers in the crusade to win full acceptance of children with handicaps as human beings. These organizations have gained strength through painstaking and often self-sacrificing efforts. Parents have helped other parents, started schools, collected funds, collected facts and figures for unmet needs, lobbied for reforms, and initiated community services (Closer Look, 1978).

As early as 1930, parents began to unite efforts and band together to share problems and to seek answers regarding the education and care of exceptional children (Sarason & Doris, 1969). The first parent group to organize on behalf of handicapped children were the parents of children with cerebral palsy. A mother of a cerebral palsied child in New York ran an advertisement in *The New York Times* soliciting other parents who had children with cerebral palsy. Through this effort, the National Society of Crippled Children was formed. Subsequently, the United Cerebral Palsy Association was organized in 1948. Shortly thereafter, the National Association of Retarded Citizens was organized in 1950. This trend toward unity among parents with similar interests continued. Recently, organizations of parents of the learning disabled and parents of the gifted and talented have formed (Barsh, 1961; Fortier, 1968; Gallagher, 1983; Orlansky, 1984).

The crippling effects of World War II among prewar professionals, businesspeople, or otherwise respected citizens, along with an increasing number of handicapped children born into middle- and upper-income families, provided new directions for the parent movement. Parents rejected the concept of institutionalization and insisted that schools provide an education for their children in their respective communities. At the same time, parents persistently encouraged educators to recognize their rights as parents to seek relief for their children and to pass laws that would meet the needs of handicapped children (Webster, 1976). The most noteworthy legislation of recent years, PL 94-142, mandates parental rights and involvement in the education of handicapped children and youths. Martin (1979) summarized these rights, as follows.

Handicapped children are entitled to an independent educational evaluation that will be considered when placement and program decisions are made. Parents have the right to be told where an independent evaluation may be obtained at no expense or low expense, to have the agency pay for the independent evaluation if the agency's evaluation is not appropriate, and to be informed of the procedures for obtaining an independent evaluation at public expense and the conditions under which such an evaluation may be obtained.

Parents have the right to notice before the agency initiates, or changes (or refuses to initiate or change), the identification, evaluation, or placement of the child; to have that notice in writing, in their native language, or other principal mode of communication, at a level understandable to the general public; to have the notice describe the proposed action and explain why those other options were rejected; and to be notified of each evaluation procedure, test, record, or report the agency will use as a basis for any proposed action. Parents also have the right to give or withhold consent before an evaluation is conducted and before initial placement is made in special education; to revoke consent at any time; and to forfeit to the agency to proceed in the absence of consent to a hearing to determine if the child should be initially placed.

Parents are entitled to request an impartial due process hearing to question the agency's identification, evaluation, or placement of the child, or to question the agency's provision of a free appropriate public education; to be told of any free or low-cost legal or other relevant services available (e.g., experts on handicapping conditions who may be a witness at the hearing); to have the hearing chaired by a person not employed by a public agency involved in the education of the child or otherwise having any personal or professional interest in the hearing; to see a statement of the qualifications of the hearing officer; to be advised and accompanied at the hearing by counsel and to be accompanied by individuals with special knowledge or training in problems of the handicapped; to have the child present; to have the hearing open to the public; to present evidence and confront, cross-examine, and compel the attendance of witnesses; to prohibit the introduction of any evidence at the hearing that has not been disclosed at least five days before the hearing; to have a record of the hearing; to obtain written findings of fact and a written decision within 45 days after the initial request for the hearing; to appeal to the State Board of Education and receive a decision within 30 days of filing of an appeal; to have a hearing and an appeal set at a time reasonably convenient to the parent; to appeal a decision from the State Board of Education in court; and to have the child remain in his or her present educational placement during the pending of the administrative proceeding, unless parent and agency agree otherwise.

Parents also have the right to have a full and individual evaluation of the child's educational needs; have more than one criterion used in determining an appropriate educational program; have the evaluation performed by a multidisciplinary team; have child assessed in all areas related to the suspected disability; have a reevaluation every 3 years or more often if conditions warrant or if the parent or the child's teacher requests it.

Parents of handicapped children are entitled to have their child educated with nonhandicapped children to the maximum extent possible; have their child removed from the regular educational environment only after supplementary aids and services are tried and found unsatisfactory; have a continuum of alternate placements so that removal from the regular educational environment can be the least necessary deviation; have available supplementary services such as a resource room or itinerant instruction to make it possible for their child to remain in regular class placement; have their child placed within the school that he or she would attend if nonhandicapped unless the individual education plan requires some other arrangement; have their child participate with nonhandicapped children in nonacademic and extracurricular services and activities such as meals, recess, counseling, clubs, athletics, and special interest groups.

It is important that parents restrict access to their child's records by withholding consent to disclose records; be informed before information in their child's file is to be destroyed; and be told to whom information has been disclosed. In addition, the law stipulates that parents or guardians must be involved in developing the individualized education program (Turnbull & Schulz, 1979).

The roles of parents of handicapped children have been outlined as advocates, resources, teachers, and counselors by Knoblock (1983), Heyward & Orlansky (1984), Brown and Moersch (1982), and Nowland (1971). Parents may obtain information and listings of state and local agencies serving handicapped individuals from Closer Look: A Project of the Parents' Campaign for Handicapped Children and Youth, Box 1492, Washington, DC 20013. This national information center for handicapped children and youths will provide information at no cost to parents. The November, 1985 issue of *News Digest* provides information for both parents and teachers of handicapped children.

REFERENCES

Barsh, R. (1976). *The parents of the handicapped child.* Springfield, IL: Thomas.

Berdine, W., & Blackhurst, A. (1985). *An introduction to special education* (2nd ed.). Boston: Little, Brown.

Brown, S., & Moersch, M. (1982). *Parents on the team.* Ann Arbor: University of Michigan Press.

Bubolz, M., & Whiren, A. (1984). The family of the handicapped: An ecological model for policy and practice. *Family Relations, 33,* 5–12.

Department of Health, Education and Welfare Office of Education. (1977, Aug. 23). Education of handicapped children. *Federal Register, 42*(163).

Farber, B. (1968). *Mental retardation: Its social context and social consequences.* Boston: Houghton Mifflin.

Fortier, L., & Wanless, R. (1984). Family crisis following the diagnosis of a handicapped child. *Family Relation, 33,* 13–24.

Hallahan, D., & Kauffman, J. *Exceptional children: Introduction to special education* Englewood Cliffs, NJ: Prentice-Hall.

Heyward, W., & Orlansky, M. (1984). *Exceptional children: An introductory survey of special education* (2nd ed.). Columbus, OH: Merrill.

Kazak, A., & Marvin, R. (1984). Differences, difficulties and adaptation: Stress and social networks in families with a handicapped child. *Family Relations, 33,* 66–77.

Kirk, S., & Gallagher, J. (1983). *Educating exceptional children* (4th ed.). Boston: Houghton Mifflin.

Knoblock, P. (1983). *Teaching emotionally disturbed children.* Boston: Houghton Mifflin.

Martin, R. (1979). *Educating handicapped children: The legal mandate.* Champaign, IL: Research Press.

National Information Center for Handicapped Children and Youth. (1978) *Closer look.* Rosslyn, VA: Interstate Research.

National Information Center for Handicapped Children and Youth. (1985). *News digest.* Rosslyn, VA: Interstate Research.

Nowland, R. (1971). *Counseling parents of the ill and handicapped.* Springfield, IL: Thomas.

Sarason, S. A., & Doris, J. (1969). *Psychological problems in mental deficiency* (4th ed.). New York: Harper & Row.

Turnbull, A., & Dixon, J. (1980). Preschool mainstreaming: Impact on parents. In J. J. Gallagher (Ed.), *New directions for exceptional children: Ecology of exceptional children,* (Vol. 1). San Francisco: Jossey-Bass.

Turnbull, A., & Schulz, J. (1979). *Mainstreaming handicapped students: A guide for the classroom teacher.* Boston: Allyn & Bacon.

Turnbull, A., & Turnbull, H. (1978). *Parents speak out.* Columbus, OH: Merrill.

Webster, E. (1976). *Professional approaches with parents of handicapped children.* Springfield, IL: Thomas.

FRANCES T. HARRINGTON
Radford University

BUCKLEY AMENDMENT
EDUCATION FOR ALL HANDICAPPED CHILDREN ACT OF 1975
FAMILY COUNSELING
FAMILY RESPONSE TO A HANDICAPPED CHILD
SPECIAL EDUCATION, LEGAL REGULATION OF

PARKHURST, HELEN (1887–1973)

Helen Parkhurst devised the Dalton Plan and founded the Dalton School in New York City. The essence of the Dalton Plan, based on Parkhurst's concept of the school as a laboratory where students are experimenters and not just participants, was individualization of instruction through student contracts, with each student working individually at his or her own pace to carry out contracted assignments.

Early in her career, Parkhurst studied with Maria Montessori in Italy; from 1915 to 1918 she supervised the development of Montessori programs in the United States. She left the Montessori movement to put her own educational plan into practice at schools in Pittsfield and Dalton, Massachusetts. She founded the Dalton School in 1920 and served as its director until her retirement in 1942. Parkhurst lectured throughout the world and established Dalton schools in England, Japan, and China. Her book, *Education on the Dalton Plan*, was published in 58 languages. After retiring from the Dalton School, Parkhurst produced radio and television programs for children and conducted a discussion program in which she gave advice on family life.

REFERENCES

Parkhurst, H. (1922). *Education on the Dalton Plan.* New York: Dutton.

Parkhurst, H. (1951). *Exploring the child's world.* New York: Appleton-Century-Crofts.

PAUL IRVINE
Katonah, New York

PARTIALLY SIGHTED

The term partially sighted was used to classify and place students in special classes whose distance visual acuity was between 20/70 and 20/200 in the better eye after correction (Hatfield, 1975). In 1977 the classifications of levels of vision adopted by the World Health Organization omitted the use of partially sighted in its system. (Colenbrander, 1977). As a result, this term has virtually disappeared from the recent literature (Barraga, 1983).

REFERENCES

Barraga, N. C. (1983). *Visual handicaps and learning.* Austin, TX: Exceptional Resources.

Colenbrander, A. (1977). Dimensions of visual performance. *Archives of Ophthalmology, 83,* 332–337.

Hatfield, E. M. (1975). Why are they blind? *Sight Saving Review, 45,* 3–22.

ROSANNE K. SILBERMAN
Hunter College, City University of New York

BLIND
LOW VISION
VISUALLY IMPAIRED
VISUAL TRAINING

PARTIAL PARTICIPATION

The principle of partial participation entails the position that all students with severe handicaps (including the profoundly mentally retarded and the severely physically disabled) can acquire a number of skills that will enable them to function at least partially in a variety of least restrictive school and nonschool environments or activities (Baumgart et al., 1980). Because of the severity of their sensory or motor impairments as well as deficits in attentional and learning processes, some severely handicapped students have difficulty in learning skills needed to function independently in current and subsequent least restrictive environments. Rather than denying access to these environments, proponents of the principle of partial participation believe adaptations can be implemented that will allow students to participate in a wide range of activities.

Adaptations via modes of partial participation can take on a variety of dimensions in the activities of severely handicapped learners (Baumgart et al., 1982; Wehman, Schleien, & Kiernan, 1980). Materials and devices can be used or created in an effort to adapt tasks (e.g., using an enlarged adaptive switch to operate kitchen appliances, using picture communication cards to communicate needs in a restaurant, using a bus pass instead of coins when a student is unable to count coins for bus fare, using frozen waffles rather than a waffle iron and batter when preparing breakfast). The sequence of steps in skills being taught can be modified (e.g., dress in a bathing suit before going to community pool if extra time is needed to manipulate clothing; sit on the toilet first, then pull pants down if unsteady on feet in the bathroom). Personal assistance can be provided for part or all of a task (e.g., peers push wheelchair to help deliver attendance records to office, teacher takes bread out of bag and places it in toaster prior to having student press lever on toaster). Rules can be changed or adapted to meet the needs of individual students (e.g., allow student to eat lunch in two lunch periods in cafeteria if he or she is a slow eater owing to physical disabilities). Societal or attitudinal as well as physical environments can be adapted (e.g., installing wheelchair ramps in public places, installing electronic doors in public buildings to make them more accessible for wheelchair users).

The classroom teacher willl need to follow a number of steps to implement partial participation strategies successfully. These include: (1) taking a nonhandicapped person's inventory of steps/skills used in a particular task; (2) taking a severely handicapped student's inventory of steps used or skills exhibited for the same task; (3) determining the skills that the handicapped student probably can acquire; (4) determining the skills the handicapped student probably cannot acquire; (5) generating an adaptation hypothesis; (6) conducting an inventory of adaptations currently available for use; (7) determining individualized adaptations to be used; and (8) determining skills that can probably be acquired using individualized adaptations (Baumgart, et al., 1982).

Several considerations are recommended when using individualized adaptations for severely handicapped students. These include: (1) empirically verifying the appropriateness and effectiveness of adaptations in the criterion or natural environment; (2) avoiding allowing students to become overly dependent on adaptations; and (3) carefully selecting adaptations to meet needs of individual students in critically functional environments (Baumgart et al., 1980). Appropriate applications of the principle of partial participation will enhance the access of severely handicapped individuals to integrated environments available to the nonhandicapped population at large (Brown et al., 1979).

REFERENCES

Baumgart, D., Brown, L., Pumpian, I., Nisbet, J., Ford, A., Sweet, M., Messina, R., & Schroeder, J. (1982). Principle of partial participation and individualized adaptations in education programs for severely handicapped students. *Journal of the Association for Persons with Severe Handicaps, 7*(2), 17–27.

Baumgart, D., Brown, L., Pumpian, I., Nisbet, J., Ford, A., Sweet, M., Ranieri, L., Hansen, L., & Schroeder, J. (1980). The principle of partial participation and individualized adaptations in education programs for severely handicapped students. In L. Brown, M. Falvey, I. Pumpian, D. Baumgart, J. Nisbet, A. Ford, J. Schroeder, & R. Loomis (Eds.), *Curricular strategies for teaching severely handicapped students functional skills in school and nonschool environments.* (Vol. 10). Madison, WI: Madison Public Schools and the University of Wisconsin.

Brown, L., Branston-McClean, M. B., Baumgart, D., Vincent, L., Falvey, M., & Schroeder, J. (1979). Using the characteristics of current and subsequent least restrictive environments in the development of curricular content for severely handicapped students. *Journal of the Association for Persons with Severe Handicaps, 4*, 407–424.

Wehman, P., Schleien, S., & Kiernan, J. (1980). Age appropriate recreation programs for severely handicapped youth and adults. *Journal of the Association for Persons with Severe Handicaps, 5*, 395–407.

CORNELIA LIVELY
*University of Illinois,
Urbana-Champaign*

HUMANISTIC SPECIAL EDUCATION
LEAST RESTRICTIVE ENVIRONMENT

PASAMANICK, BENJAMIN (1914–   )

Benjamin Pasamanick began his professional studies at Cornell University, where he received his BA in 1936.

Benjamin Pasamanick

During this period he began studying physiology and biochemistry and was accepted as the only undergraduate advisee of Nobel Laureate James Sumner. In 1937 Pasamanick went to the University of Maryland School of Medicine, earning his MD in 1941. His psychiatric internship was completed at Brooklyn State Hospital and Harlem Hospital, both in New York City. Following his psychiatric residency at the New York State Psychiatric Institute in 1943, Pasamanick became an assistant at the Yale Clinic of Child Development, where he was the only psychiatrist ever accepted to study under Arnold Gesell. Pasamanick subsequently held numerous faculty, research, and clinical positions at medical schools and clinics throughout the northeastern United States. He presently holds two positions. Pasamanick is the Sir Aubrey and Lady Hilda Lewis Professor of Social Psychiatry at the New York School of Psychiatry. He also holds the position of professor of psychiatry at the New York University College of Medicine.

Throughout his illustrious career as a mentor-scholar-clinician in child psychiatry, Pasamanick has maintained an interest in exceptional children, particularly the mentally retarded. He has always challenged conventional practices, promoting change and innovation at all levels. Pasamanick particularly sought a melding of basic research in child development with practice and the promotion of a clear conceptual framework for treatment.

Though a prolific writer and researcher throughout his career, Pasamanick is perhaps best known for his massive, longitudinal studies of the development of black infants (Granich, 1970). Pasamanick was the first to demonstrate that the behavioral development of black infants, as an indicator of intellectual maturity, was indistinguishable from that of white infants. In 1949 the American Psychiatric Association awarded Pasamanick its Hofheimer Prize for his work. This longitudinal study was one of many as Pasamanick tried to tease out the multidimensional, multifactorial influences on children's development. He eventually came to believe that early in life, intelligence and related cognitive skills are primarily biologically determined, but they become increasingly psychologically and socially determined with age, ultimately being driven by socioeconomic factors.

Pasamanick extensively studied the continuum of reproductive casualty and epidemiology. He reported on this work in detail during 1961, when he held the prestigious Cutter Lectureship at Harvard, the first psychiatrist to hold this position. Pasamanick has had a substantial influence on service delivery to handicapped children in a variety of settings. He served as president of the American Orthopsychiatric Association during 1970–1971 and as president of the American Psychopathological Association (1967) and the Theobald Smith Society (1984). He has authored or edited 17 books and has more than 300 scholarly publications to his credit. He has served on the editorial boards of *Child Development, American Journal of Mental Deficiency, Merrill-Palmer Quarterly*, and the *Journal of Biological Psychiatry*, among others.

REFERENCE

Granich, B. (1970). Benjamin Pasamanick. *American Journal of Orthopsychiatry, 40*, 368–372.

CECIL R. REYNOLDS
Texas A&M University

AMERICAN ORTHOPSYCHIATRIC ASSOCIATION

PASE v. HANNON

PASE (Parents in Action on Special Education) v. *Hannon* (Joseph P. Hannon, superintendent of the Chicago public schools at the time this case was filed) was a class-action suit on behalf of black students who were or who might be classified as educable mentally retarded (EMR) and placed in self-contained special classes. PASE was established by a parent advocacy group assisted by the Northwestern School of Law Legal Assistance Clinic and the Legal Assistance Foundation in Chicago. The U.S. Department of Justice filed a friend of court brief on behalf of the plaintiffs. Defendants in the case were various officials employed by the Chicago Board of Education as well as the Board of Education of the State of Illinois. *PASE* resulted in a 3-week trial conducted by Judge Grady, who issued an opinion deciding the case on July 7, 1980.

The issues and expert witness testimony in *PASE* were virtually identical to the testimony in *Larry P.* v. *Riles*, heard by Federal District Court Judge Peckham in California in a trial concluded in May 1978. The fundamental allegations were that overrepresentation of black students in EMR special class programs constituted discrimination, and that overrepresentation was caused by the defendants' use of biased IQ tests. The plaintiffs claimed the overrepresentation from biased IQ tests violated constitutional and statutory protections, particularly the Equal Protec-

tion Clause of the Fourteenth Amendment and the nondiscrimination protections in the Education for All Handicapped Children Act of 1975 and Section 504 of the Rehabilitation Act of 1973. The plaintiffs and defendants agreed that black students constituted about 62% of the total school population in Chicago, but 82% of the EMR population. The actual percentage of black students classified as EMR was 3.7%; in contrast, 1.3% of white students were classified as EMR.

In a 3-week trial in 1979, the plaintiffs relied heavily on several of the witnesses who appeared just under 2 years earlier in the *Larry P.* trial in California. In particular, the plaintiffs relied on Leon Kamin's analysis of the historical pattern of racist attitudes and beliefs among early developers of intelligence tests in the United States (Kamin, 1974). Robert Williams, a prominent black psychologist, provided testimony concerning the differences in the cultures of white and black students and identified a few examples of biased items. Although other witnesses appeared for the plaintiffs, the testimony of Kamin and Williams was noted prominently in Grady's decision.

Witnesses for the defendants contended overrepresentation reflected the genuine needs of black students, who were claimed to have a higher EMR incidence owing to the effects of poverty. This emphasis on socioeconomic status as an explanation for overrepresentation was also relied on by *Larry P.* defendants, though unsuccessfully. The association of EMR with poverty has been reported for many decades throughout the western world for diverse racial and ethnic groups. The defendants also contended that any biases that might exist in IQ tests were neutralized in the placement process through the use of procedural protections such as parental informed consent, the development of a multifactored assessment that focused on educational needs, and decision making by a multidisciplinary team.

Judge Grady clearly was dissatisfied with the evidence presented by both the plaintiffs and the defendants. He noted, somewhat testily, that only cursory information on the testing question was presented in the evidence. He questioned attorneys for both sides and learned that no one relied heavily on careful analysis of each of the test items in preparing for the case. He then concluded that an analysis of each of the items on the three tests in question, the Wechsler Intelligence Scale for Children, the Wechsler Intelligence Scale for Children-Revised, and the Stanford Binet, was required for him to decide on claims of bias. Judge Grady then undertook an item-by-item analysis of the questions on the three tests.

Approximately two thirds of the space in Judge Grady's lengthy opinion was devoted to his analyses of the intelligence test items. Judge Grady provided the exact wording of the item, the correct answer, and the scoring criterion, where appropriate, for determining whether a response was awarded one or two points. This unprecedented breach of test security was initially shocking to many professionals, but no known harm or serious threat to normative standards has been reported.

Judge Grady concluded from his personal analysis of the IQ test items that only eight of several hundred items were biased. He noted that four of those eight items were not on current versions of the tests, and that those that were generally appeared at the upper limits of the test. Items that appeared at the upper limits of the test typically would not be given to students who might be considered for classification as EMR. Grady concluded that any biases that existed on the test exerted a very small influence on classification and placement decisions, and agreed with the defendants that other safeguards, mentioned earlier, compensated for these negligible biases.

The sharply different opinions in *PASE* and *Larry P.* did not go unnoticed in the professional literature (Bersoff, 1982; Sattler 1980). The trial opinions were markedly different despite virtually identical issues and similar evidence. The reason different conclusions were reached can best be understood from an analysis of the different approaches taken by the federal court judges. Judge Grady required that a direct connection be established between biased items and misclassification of black students as EMR. He found no such connection in Kamin's testimony about historical patterns of racism, in Robert Williams' descriptions of differences in cultural backgrounds of white and black students, and in his own analyses of items. Grady then ruled that the absence of a clear connection between biased items and misclassification prevented the plaintiffs from prevailing. In contrast, Judge Peckham in *Larry P.* accepted allegations of item bias and concluded that the other protections in the referral, classification, and placement process were insufficient to overcome these biases. Both decisions have been criticized; *PASE* because of the method used by Judge Grady (Bersoff, 1982) and *Larry P.* because of conclusions concerning item biases that did not reflect available evidence (Reschly, 1980; Sandoval, 1979).

The plaintiffs appealed the *PASE* trial decision. However, before the appellate court ruled, the issues in the case were rendered moot by the decision of the Board of Education in Chicago to ban the use of traditional IQ tests with black students being considered for classification and placement as EMR. This ban was part of a negotiated settlement in still another court case concerning the desegregation of the Chicago public schools. The appeal was then withdrawn by the plaintiffs.

The *PASE* decision is an interesting contrast to that in *Larry P.*, but it does not have the impact of *Larry P.* for a variety of reasons. Other decisions from later in the 1980s such as *Marshall* v. *Georgia*, (1984, 1985), are expected to have greater influence in the future.

REFERENCES

Bersoff, D. (1982). Larry P., and PASE; Judicial report cards of the validity of individual intelligence tests. In T. Kratochwill (Ed.), *Advances in school psychology* (Vol. 11), (pp. 61–95). Hillsdale, NJ: Erlbaum.

Kamin, L. J. (1974). *The science and politics of IQ*. New York: Halsted.

Reschly, D. (1980). Psychological evidence in the *Larry P.* opinion: A case of right problem-wrong solution. *School Psychology Review*, 9, 123–135.

Sandoval, J. (1979). The WISC-R and internal evidence of test bias with minority groups. *Journal of Consulting & Clinical Psychology*, 47, 919–927.

Sattler, J. (1980, November). In the opinion of . . . . *Monitor*, pp. 7–8.

DANIEL J. RESCHLY
Iowa State University

**DIANA v. STATE BOARD OF EDUCATION
LARRY P.
MARSHALL v. GEORGIA
NONDISCRIMINATORY ASSESSMENT**

PATH ANALYSIS

Path analysis is a technique developed in the 1930s by Sewell Wright (1934) for the purpose of studying causal relationships among variables. Path analysis provides mathematical models expressing the direct and indirect effects of variables assumed to have causal status on variables assumed to be affected by the causal variables. A direct effect occurs when one variable influences another in the absence of mediation by a third variable. For example, one might assume that a particular educational intervention had a direct effect on student achievement. An indirect effect exists when a causal variable affects a dependent variable by influencing a third variable, which in turn affects the dependent variable directly. For example, teacher training might be assumed to affect teaching behavior, which would influence student achievement. Under these conditions, teacher training would have an indirect effect on student achievement. Its influence on achievement would occur through its effect on teaching behavior.

The mathematical models used to express causation in path analysis have their origins in regression analysis. The simplest path model is one involving the regression of a dependent variable on one or more variables assumed to explain variation in the dependent variable. For instance, student achievement might be regressed on an educational intervention assumed to affect achievement. Under this model, the intervention would have a direct effect on achievement. The residual term in the regression equation would also be included in the model. It is assumed to be uncorrelated with other variables in the equation. The residual would be treated as a causal variable indicating the effects of variables not explicitly included in the model on achievement. For instance, intelligence is a variable not explicitly identified in the model that might account for part of the variation in achievement. Many other variables that might affect achievement could be identified.

Models involving indirect effects require more than one regression equation. For instance, the example given involving the indirect effect of teacher training on achievement would require two regression equations. The first would include the regression of achievement on teacher training and teacher behavior; the second would include the regression of teacher behavior on teacher training. The general rule governing the number of equations is that one equation is needed for each dependent variable.

The two models discussed to this point assume unidirectional causation. For instance, in the indirect effects model, teacher behavior is assumed to affect achievement, but achievement is not assumed to affect teacher behavior. Models assuming unidirectional causation are called recursive. Ordinary least squares (OLS) regression can be used with recursive models. Nonrecursive models assuming bidirectional causation between one or more pairs of variables require procedures that go beyond OLS regression. Duncan (1975) provides an excellent discussion of nonrecursive models.

Causal relations may be expressed in path analysis not only through mathematical models, but also through path diagrams such as the one shown in the following Figure. Variables A and B in the diagram are called exogenous variables. An exogenous variable is a variable whose variation is explained by factors outside of the causal model. The curved double-headed arrow indicates that variables A and B are related and that no assumption is made regarding the direction of the relationship. Variables C and D are endogenous variables. Endogenous variables are affected by exogenous variables and/or other endogenous variables.

The Ps in the model represent path coefficients. In a recursive model, these are standardized regression weights. Each path coefficient is interpreted as that fraction of the standard deviation in the dependent variable for which the causal variable is directly responsible. For instance, P_{da} indicates that fraction of the standard deviation in variable D for which variable A is directly responsible. The standardized regression weights functioning as path coefficients in path models are no longer widely used in causal modeling. The assumption that all variables in a causal model should be placed on the same scale has been challenged. Unstandardized weights are now typically used. See Duncan (1975) for a discussion of the problems associated with standardized weights.

Path analysis may be regarded as a special case of a more general technique called structural equation modeling (Bentler, 1980; Joreskog & Sorbom, 1979). The major difference between path analysis as it was developed by Wright and structural equation models is that structural equation models may include latent as well as manifest variables. A latent variable is a variable that is not observed directly, but rather is inferred from two or more manifest indicators. For example, student achievement could be treated as a latent variable to be inferred from scores on two or more achievement tests. A structural equation model expresses the effects of one set of variables on another set of variables. The variables in the model may include both latent variables and manifest variables. For instance, a model might include the effects of sex on student achievement in mathematics. Sex would be a manifest variable in this model and mathematics achievement could be a latent variable inferred from two or more test scores. Structural equation modeling represents a powerful extension of Wright's pioneering work in path analysis. With structural equation techniques, it is possible not only to represent a broad range of causal relations among variables, but also to represent a wide variety of latent variables that may be of concern in educational and psychological research.

REFERENCES

Bentler, P. M. (1980). Multivariate analysis with latent variables. In M. R. Rozenweig & L. W. Porter (Eds.), *Annual review of psychology* (Vol. 31). Palo Alto, CA: Annual Review.

Duncan, O. D. (1975). *Introduction to structural equation models*. New York: Academic.

Joreskog, K. G., & Sorbom, D. (1979). *Advances in factor analysis and structural equation models*. Cambridge, MA: Abt.

Wright, S. (1934). The method of path coefficients. *Annals of Mathematical Statistics, 5,* 161–215.

JOHN BERGAN
University of Arizona

MULTIPLE REGRESSION
REGRESSION (STATISTICAL)

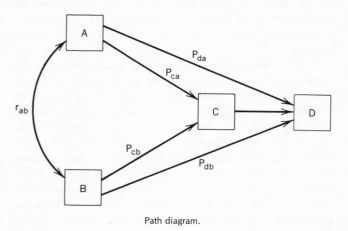

Path diagram.

PATHOLOGICAL LEFT-HANDEDNESS

See LEFT-HANDEDNESS, PATHOLOGICAL.

PATH-REFERENCED ASSESSMENT

Path-referenced assessment (Bergan, 1981, in press; Bergan, Stone, & Feld, 1985) is a new approach that references ability to position in a developmental sequence. The path-referenced approach has recently been applied in the Head Start Measures Battery (Bergan & Smith, 1984), a set of six cognitive scales designed to assist in planning learning experiences to promote the development of Head Start children. Within the path-referenced framework, ability is defined as a latent (unobserved) variable estimated from overt performance on test items. The ordering of skills in a developmental sequence is indicated by variations in item difficulty. Items of low difficulty reflect tasks related to lower levels of development, whereas items of high difficulty are associated with higher levels of development. The examinee taking a path-referenced test obtains a latent ability score referred to position in a developmental sequence and used to indicate the probability of performing the various tasks in the sequence correctly. For example, a child taking the math scale of the Head Start Measure Battery might receive a latent ability score indicating high probabilities of performing simple counting tasks correctly and low probabilities of performing more complex addition tasks correctly.

The path-referenced approach applies latent trait models (Bock & Aitkin, 1981; Lord, 1980) to the problem of referencing ability to position in a developmental sequence. The general latent trait model asserts that the probability of performing a test item correctly is a function of latent ability and certain item parameters. Item parameters that may be reflected in a latent trait model include item difficulty, item discrimination (which gives the strength of the relationship of the item to the underlying latent ability), and a guessing parameter. Latent ability and item difficulty are placed on the same scale in the latent trait model. The path-referenced approach uses the latent ability parameter to estimate an individual's ability, described as his or her developmental level. Item difficulty parameters are used to quantify developmental sequences. The fact that latent ability and item difficulty are on the same scale is used to reference developmental level to position in a developmental sequence. For example, suppose that a child taking a math test including a set of counting items receives a developmental level score of 50. Assume that the difficulty of counting to 5 was 48 and the difficulty of counting to 10 was 52. The child's position in the counting sequence would lie between counting to 5 and counting to 10.

The construction of path-referenced tests requires the testing of hypotheses about the developmental sequencing of skills constituting an ability. The hypothesis testing orientation links path-referenced assessment to cognitive research and theory. Embretson (1985) has pointed out that psychometric practice generally is far removed from the hypothesis testing tradition of cognitive psychology. Hypothesis testing is typically restricted to studies of test validity and does not include the testing of hypotheses about items based on assumptions about underlying cognitive processes. The construction of developmental sequences in path-referenced tests requires that hypotheses be advanced related to the cognitive processes associated with tasks in a sequence. In particular, the demands associated with the processes involved in task performance must be identified so that the hypothesized ordering of skills in a sequence can be established. The sequence must then be empirically validated. Cognitive theory and research provide the basis for forming hypotheses about sequencing.

Path-referenced assessment differs in significant ways from both norm-referenced assessment and criterion-referenced assessment. Norm-referenced assessment references test performance to position in a norm group. An ability score is given indicating where the individual stands in the group. Ability is defined in terms of group position. In the path-referenced approach, ability is estimated from test performance using a latent trait model. Latent ability is then referenced to position in a developmental sequence. Path referencing indicates where the individual is in a sequence and in so doing specifies the competencies that have been mastered in the past and those that lie ahead as development progresses.

Criterion-referenced assessment references test performance to the mastery of objectives (Glaser, 1963; Nitko, 1980). The objectives may or may not reflect tasks that are sequenced (Nitko, 1980). Although latent trait models have been used in criterion-referenced assessment (Nitko, 1980), they have not been integrated into the theory underlying criterion-referenced tests. The criterion-referenced approach ignores the ability construct altogether. Overt test performance is linked directly to the mastery of objectives. In path-referenced assessment, overt performance is used to estimate ability. Ability is then related to position in a developmental sequence and used to establish the probability of correct performance of tasks in the sequence. Use of the ability construct requires that individual skills be part of an empirically validated system of knowledge. Each skill in the system contributes to ability. When one teaches a set of skills that are part of a knowledge system, ability is affected. The educator operating from a path-referenced perspective is concerned with teaching ability. The mastery of specific objectives is related to ability. The educator operating from a criterion-referenced framework is concerned with the mastery of objectives. No assumptions are made about the relationship of objectives to ability.

Path-referenced tests may be used in a number of ways. One major use has to do with the management of instruction. Information on path position can be used in establishing individualized learning experiences in educational settings. For example, the Head Start Measures Battery is used by teachers in the Head Start program to provide individualized learning experiences for children. Teachers use planning guides reflecting skills measured by the battery to plan learning experiences appropriate to each child's developmental level in each of the content areas measured by the battery.

A second use of path-referenced assessment involves placement in a special program. Norm-referenced instruments are typically used in making placement decisions. However, path-referenced instruments also may make a useful contribution in determining placement. The major goal of placement is typically to provide a program that is appropriate to the learning needs of the student. To assist the decision-making process, information associated with path position can be related to information about the kinds of learning opportunities available in a special program. A decision to place would imply that learning opportunities congruent with path position can be provided better in the special program than in other available alternatives.

A third use of path-referenced instruments involves evaluating learner progress. Path-referenced instruments provide quantitative ability scores reflecting a continuous ability scale. Gains can be described in terms of the difference between pretest and posttest ability. Path-referenced instruments are better suited to measuring gains than frequently used norm-referenced technology because path-referenced scores do not depend on group position (Bergan, in press). Moreover, since path-referenced ability scores are linked to path position, it is possible to determine changes in the performance of specific skills that accompany progress.

A fourth important use of path-referenced instruments has to do with curriculum design. Path-referenced instruments can provide information about the structure of knowledge in specific content areas. For example, a path-referenced math scale may provide information on the developmental sequencing of math skills. Information on the sequencing of skills can be used in formulating curriculum sequences in math. It should be noted that this does not imply that the sequence of instruction should be the same as the sequence of development.

Because the path-referenced approach is new, it is too early to specify the full variety of applications that it may find in assessment. However, it is worth noting that the need for assessment providing information related to skill sequences has been recognized for many years. This need

was thoroughly articulated in Gagne's (1962, 1970, 1977) work. Unfortunately, until recently the technology for building assessment devices associated with skill sequences has been lacking (Bergan, 1980). Latent trait technology affords a practical approach to the construction of assessment instruments that are developmental in character. Latent trait technology has been widely used in assessment in recent years (Hambleton, 1983), and it is reasonable to expect that it will find increasing application in the assessment of development.

REFERENCES

Bergan, J. R. (1980). The structural analysis of behavior: An alternative to the learning hierarchy model. *Review of Educational Research, 50,* 225–246.

Bergan, J. R. (1981). Path-referenced assessment in school psychology. In T. R. Kratochwill (Ed.), *Advances in school psychology* (Vol. 1). Hillsdale, NJ: Erlbaum.

Bergan, J. R. (in press). Path-referenced assessment: A guide for instructional management. In C. A. Maher (Ed.), *Special services in the schools.* New York: Haworth.

Bergan, J. R., & Smith, A. N. (Eds.). (1984). *Head Start Measures Battery.* Washington, DC: Department of Health and Human Services.

Bergan, J. R., Stone, C. A., & Feld, J. K. (1985). Path-referenced evaluation of individual differences. In C. R. Reynolds & V. L. Willson (Eds.), *Methodological and statistical advances in the study of individual differences.* New York: Plenum.

Bock, R. D., & Aitkin, M. (1981). Marginal maximum likelihood estimation of item parameters: Application of an algorithm. *Psychometrika, 46,* 443–459.

Embretson, S. E. (Ed.). (1985). *Test-design: Developments in psychology and psychometrics.* Orlando, FL: Academic.

Gagne, R. M. (1962). The acquisition of knowledge. *Psychological Review, 69,* 355–365.

Gagne, R. M. (1970). *The conditions of learning* (2nd ed.). New York: Holt, Rinehart, & Winston.

Gagne, R. M. (1977). *The conditions of learning* (3rd ed.). New York: Holt, Rinehart, & Winston.

Glaser, R. (1963). Instructional technology and the measurement of learning outcomes: Some questions. *American Psychologist, 18,* 519–521.

Hambleton, R. K. (Ed.). (1983). *Applications of item response theory.* Vancouver, British Columbia: Educational Research Institute of British Columbia.

Hambleton, R. K., & Eignor, D. R. (1979). *A practitoner's guide to criterion referenced test development, validation, and test score usage. Washington, DC: National Institute of Education and Department of Health, Education, and Welfare.*

Lord, F. M. (1980). Applications of item response theory to practical testing problems. Hillsdale, NJ: Erlbaum.

Nitko, A. J. (1980). Distinguishing the many varieties of criterion-referenced tests. *Review of Educational Research, 50,* 461–485.

JOHN R. BERGAN
University of Arizona

ASSESSMENT
DEVELOPMENTAL DELAYS
HEAD START

PATTERNING

Patterning is also known as the Doman-Delacato treatment method for children with neurological disabilities. The center for the treatment program is located in Philadelphia under the name Institutes for the Achievement of Human Potential. The central theory of the Doman–Delacato treatment method is the neurological organization of the individual. The theory posits that the individual progresses through four neurological developmental stages: medulla and spinal cord, pons, midbrain, and cortex. The stages finalize in hemispheric dominance. The theory further proposes that mankind develops in an orderly manner. The rationale stresses that an individual's development in mobility, vision, audition, and language follows specific neurological stages that are correlated with anatomical progress. In this treatment method, a specific program of patterning is developed for each client. The patterning features definite time sequences for selective exercises that can be imposed either actively or passively on the nervous system. It is claimed that these exercises lead to improvement in the sensory motor functions of the individual.

The Doman-Delacato treatment was popular during the 1960s. Advocates of the treatment program have reported success with a wide range of disabilities, including mental retardation, brain damage, learning disabilities, physical handicaps, aphasia, language disorders, and dyslexia. Numerous reports from professionals, paraprofessionals, and parents have confirmed the success of the treatment program. The widespread acceptance of neurological exercises was enhanced through articles published in popular magazines such as *Good Housekeeping* and *Reader's Digest.*

Medical terms, educators, and persons serving in the human services field have studied, evaluated, and researched the claims of the advocates of neurological organization theories. The numerous studies and carefully controlled research reviews do not support the purported achievements of the patterning approach.

REFERENCES

Bower, G. (1966). *Neurophysiology of learning* (3rd ed.). New York: Appleton-Century-Crofts.

Doman, G. (1966). *Neurological organization and reading.* Springfield, IL: Thomas.

Glass, G., & Robbins, M. (1967). A critique of experiments on the role of neurological organizations in reading performance. *Reading Research Quarterly, 3,* 5–51.

Money, J. (Ed.). (1962). *Reading disabilities: Progress and research needs in dyslexia.* Baltimore, MD: Johns Hopkins Press.

Robbins, M. (1966). A study of the validity of Delacato's theory of neurological organization. *Exceptional Children, 32*(8), 517–523.

Paul C. Richardson
Elwyn Institutes,
Elwyn, Pennsylvania

NEURODEVELOPMENTAL THERAPY
NEUROLOGICAL ORGANIZATION
NEUROPSYCHOLOGY

PDR

See PHYSICIANS' DESK REFERENCE.

PEABODY INDIVIDUAL ACHIEVEMENT TEST (PIAT)

The Peabody Individual Achievement Test (PIAT; Dunn & Markwardt, 1970) is an individually administered, wide range (K–12), norm-referenced measure of scholastic achievement. There are five subtests: mathematics, reading recognition, reading comprehension, spelling, and general information. The PIAT was standardized on a representative sample of 2889 schoolchildren based on grade, sex, race, parental occupation, geographical region, and community size.

The PIAT is untimed, therefore examinees are not pressured to complete their answers in a hurried manner. Generally, it takes 30 to 40 minutes to administer. No formal training is required for the examiner, but the manual should be carefully studied to ensure proper administration and scoring. Percentiles, standard scores, grade equivalents, and age equivalents may be generated for the five subtests and for the combined total score. The appropriate cautions for use of age and grade scores are included in the manual.

Data on the reliability of the subtests and total score are presented in terms of test-retest stability coefficients in the manual. These coefficients range from a low of .42 for spelling at the kindergarten level to .94 for reading recognition at the third-grade level. In general, the stability data reveal that the total test score is reliable, but caution must be exercised in the interpretation of scores of kindergarten children.

A multiple-choice format is used on all but the general information and reading recognition subtests. For instance, on the spelling subtest, the examiner pronounces a word and the examinee is expected to select the correct word from four options. This format is particularly well suited to students with physical limitations that impair their ability to write. However, a problem with the approach is that guessing may artificially inflate a student's score.

REFERENCE

Dunn, L. M., & Markwardt, F. C. (1970). *Peabody Individual Achievement Test: Manual*. Circle Pines, MN: American Guidance Service.

JACK A. CUMMINGS
Indiana University

ACHIEVEMENT TESTS
ASSESSMENT

PEABODY LANGUAGE DEVELOPMENT KITS— REVISED (PLDK-R)

The Peabody Language Development Kits—Revised (PLDK-R) are multilevel programs designed to facilitate development of the receptive, associative, and expressive components of oral language development and cognitive skills in young children. The PLDK-R program has two main purposes: to stimulate overall language skills in standard English and to advance children's cognitive skills about 1 year per level (Dunn, Smith, Dunn, Horton, Smith, 1981). An overall language development program is stressed rather than specific training in selected psycholinguistic processes. The PLDK-R contains four levels of various activities emphasizing the skills of reception through sight, hearing, and touch; conceptualization through divergent, convergent, and associative thinking; and expression through vocal and motor behavior. Target populations with which the program may be employed include children with limited proficiency in standard English, children in preschool through third grade, children from non-English speaking backgrounds, and children with a variety of cognitive and linguistic disabilities, including mild to moderate mental retardation, hearing impairments, learning disabilities, and central nervous system disorders.

Twelve major changes have been made from the original program edition:

1. The difficulty of the lessons has been increased to challenge today's more sophisticated children and to make the activities more appropriate for children with standard English backgrounds.
2. Variations have been frequently suggested at the end of the activities to make the tasks easier or harder so that a wider range of individual differences can be accommodated.
3. Virtually all the activities are new or extensively revised; only about half are based on original activities.
4. Lesson content has been spelled out in greater detail so that aides can use the kits more easily than before.
5. Each activity is introduced with a focus statement that briefly summarizes its content.
6. All the activities have been classified in the appendixes by skill and subject so that users can select specific types of activities to teach.
7. A concerted effort was made to remove sexual, racial, ethnic, and age biases from the lessons, art, and recordings.
8. Many materials have been added or changed including puppets, posters, and stories.
9. Nearly all the picture cards are new, with photography and art that is up to date and realistic.
10. Duplication of picture cards with other levels has dramatically been reduced; only a handful of cards are used in more than one level.
11. Most written language and nationalistic content has been removed from the pictures to make the program more suitable for use in other countries.
12. All the packaging is new, including the roomy, attractive plastic cases that make the materials more accessible (Dunn et al., p. 2–3).

The activities of PLDK-R level P provide practice in syntactical and grammatical structure, logical thinking, and the labeling of language; they are designed primarily for 4 and 5 year olds. The two lesson manuals, containing 360 lessons with two activities each, and the teacher's guide, comprise the core program of level P. Two puppets, the popular P. Mooney and the independent Zoey, are major characters who encourage participation and focus attention on the activities. P. Mooney appears regularly in lessons that involve describing, naming, talking, and following directions, while Zoey is used in lessons that involve thinking, imagining, and problem-solving activities.

A balanced program of oral language and cognitive development activities, including brainstorming and problem solving, is presented at level 1, designed for use with groups of children 6 years of age. The central puppet character Peabella, a world-famous bloodhound detective, teaches problem-solving skills and is assisted by Shiner, a black-eyed puppy who is frequently confused but capable of learning. The children are able both to teach him and learn from his mistakes.

The PLDK-R level 2, designed primarily for 7 year olds, emphasizes further stimulation of cognitive processes through various problem-solving and brainstorming activities. Two space-age puppets, Pippa and Ariel, encourage creative thinking and reasoning.

Stimulation of all aspects of the thinking and reasoning

process is emphasized at level 3. Activities highlight the formulation of ideas and concepts fostered through opportunities for creativity. Jayoh and Debya are central characters who, by means of a magical microphone, travel forward and backward in time. Level 3 is designed primarily for 8 year olds.

The PLDK-R is an excellent self-contained, comprehensive program designed to stimulate oral language and cognitive development skills for a diversity of children. Classroom teachers, special-education teachers, speech-language pathologists, and teachers of English as a second language will find the program beneficial.

REFERENCE

Dunn, L., Smith, J., Dunn, L., Horton, K., & Smith, D. (1981). *Peabody Language Development Kits-Revised Manuals Level P, 1, 2, and 3.* Circle Pines, MN: American Guidance Service.

SUSAN MAHANNA-BODEN
TRACY CALPIN CASTLE
Eastern Kentucky University

ORAL LANGUAGE OF THE HANDICAPPED
ORAL VERSUS MANUAL COMMUNICATION

PEABODY PICTURE VOCABULARY TEST– REVISED (PPVT-R)

The Peabody Picture Vocabulary Test–Revised (PPVT-R) (see Figure) is designed as a measure of receptive vocabulary for persons 2½ to 40 years of age (Dunn & Dunn, 1981). Administration of the PPVT-R requires some formal training, and it is imperative that stimulus words be pronounced according to *Webster's New Collegiate Dictionary*. Interpretation of the PPVT-R requires training in psychological testing. Two parallel or alternate forms are available. Items are dichotomously scored with raw scores converted to standard scores, age equivalents, percentile ranks, and stanines. The estimated time for administration of the PPVT-R (usually 35 to 45 items per child) is 10 to 20 minutes.

Principal uses of the PPVT-R in special education are as a screening measure of intelligence and in the evaluation of language functions. It is virtually never used as a sole criterion for placement or diagnosis, nor should it be, as it lacks adequate technical properties and breadth of assessment of language. It remains useful as an adjunct to other instruments as part of a comprehensive battery of tests.

REFERENCE

Dunn, L., & Dunn, L. (1981). *Peabody Picture Vocabulary Test Revised.* Circle Pines, MN: American Guidance Service.

STAFF

A training item from the Peabody Picture Vocabulary Test Revised. The examiner says a word corresponding to one of the four pictures, and the child points to the appropriate picture of successful.

PEABODY REBUS READING PROGRAM

The Peabody Rebus Reading Program is a representational symbol system designed to teach early reading skills to children. A basic vocabulary of pictographic symbols known as rebuses represent entire words or parts of words; they provide a foundation for developing reading and comprehension skills. Rebus symbols may be classified into four basic categories: combination symbols, which primarily depict objects or actions (e.g., ball = ⊘); relational symbols, which depict locations or directions (e.g., in = ⊙, on = ⌂); and abstract symbols, which are primarily arbitrary symbols representing ideas such as "at" = ↓ and "too" = ↘). The fourth category combines symbols with alphabet letters, affixes (e.g., doing = ↯), and other rebuses (e.g., into = ⊙ ↘).

The Peabody Rebus Reading Program includes two levels. The reading level is designed as an alternative, complementary, or supplementary program for traditional readiness programs (Woodcock, Clark, & Davies, 1969). Two workbooks each containing 384 exercise frames are introduced to children. As a student marks an answer using a moistened pencil eraser, a special "invisible ink" indicates the accuracy of the selection. On completion of this level, a child will have developed several prereading skills such as matching spoken words to printed words, reading in a left-to right direction, and comprehending rebus words and sentences. At the second level, the transition level, students progress from reading rebuses to reading spelled words. Teaching materials include one workbook and two rebus readers, emphasizing systematic substitution of spelled words for rebuses. Initially, the spelled words are paired with their corresponding rebus symbols. The symbols are gradually faded to effect transition to standard orthography. On completion of the transition level, a student will be able to read 122 spelled words, sound out words, recognize punctuation, and read stories.

The Peabody Rebus Reading Program is designed to introduce children to reading by first having them learn a vocabulary of rebuses in the place of spelled words. The program has additional application for facilitating the development of language skills.

REFERENCE

Woodcock, R. W., Clark, C. R., & Davies, C. O. (1969). *The Peabody Rebus Reading Program*. Circle Pines, MN: American Guidance Service.

SUSAN MAHANNA-BODEN
TRACY CALPIN CASTLE
Eastern Kentucky University

PEACE CORPS, SPECIAL EDUCATION IN

The Peace Corps is a volunteer program that was established in 1961 by President John Kennedy. Its goal is to help the people of interested countries and areas of the world in meeting their needs for trained manpower through the help of American volunteers. The promotion of a better understanding of Americans on the part of the people served, and a better understanding of other people on the part of Americans, are also basic goals of the program (Shute, 1986). During the 1960s, goodwill among nations was advocated by early Peace Corps participants. During the 1970s, individuals in both the host countries and the United States recognized the need for technically skilled individuals familiar with local needs in food, job, health, and schooling areas. Thus in recent years, programs for volunteers cover such diverse assignments as work in agriculture, industrial arts/skilled trades, and health and education (Peace Corps, 1986). Over 5200 volunteers in 63 countries now offer their services in three major world regions: Africa (Sub-Saharan Africa), Inter-America (Central and South America), and NANEAP (North Africa, Near East, Asia, and the Pacific). Training is provided to the volunteers in the language, history, customs and social-political systems of the host country.

The Peace Corps offers a program for individuals interested in special education. Volunteers can be assigned specific placements working with children displaying mental retardation, learning disabilities, emotional disturbances, blindness or visual impairments, deafness or hearing impairments, multihandicaps, or speech problems. Assignments in special education cover teacher training and direct classroom teaching. Volunteers in the teacher-training program conduct needs assessments, organize and implement workshops and seminars, develop teaching aids using locally available materials, give demonstration lessons, establish criteria for evaluation, observe teachers, and monitor teachers' progress. Those participating in the direct-teaching program help to screen and assess the special child's abilities and progress; teach classes in academics, extracurricula areas, and self-help skills; and structure activities to facilitate interactions of the special child with the family and community.

To qualify as a special education volunteer, an individual must be a U.S. citizen and be at least 18 years of age. There are also medical and legal criteria. Finally, the special education volunteer should possess a four-year degree with some preservice teaching in special education (actual teaching experience is preferred but not obligatory). All volunteers receive a monthly allowance to cover housing, food, and spending money. On completion of the two-year service commitment required of all volunteers, an allotment for every month served is provided as a readjustment allowance on return to the United States (Shute, 1986).

REFERENCES

Peace Corps, (1986). *The toughest job you'll ever love*. Washington, DC: ACTION.

Shute, N. (1986). *After a turbulent youth, the Peace Corps comes of age*. Washington, DC: ACTION.

LAWRENCE O'SHEA
University of Florida

COMMUNITY BASED SERVICES
VOLUNTARY AGENCIES

PEDIATRICIAN

A pediatrician is a medical doctor or osteopathic physician who has completed a residency in pediatrics. In addition to the medical care of the newborn, infant, child, and adolescent, the pediatrician is trained in many areas important to the overall growth and development of the child: motor development and coordination, sensory development, psychosocial maturation, and moral and cognitive development.

A wide variety of medical conditions may handicap a child's ability to learn. Some may be due to hereditary factors. Others may be prenatal and relate to the health of the mother or to direct dangers to the fetus such as infections or drugs. Some may be perinatal, occurring during or immediately following the birth process. This group includes complications resulting from the mechanics of labor and delivery. Some conditions may occur or be diagnosed only after the infant has gone home. Thus it is clear that the pediatrician has an important role in special education.

First, the pediatrician may be able to diagnose a condition that could have an adverse effect on the child's ability to learn and estimate the approximate extent of the handicap. Based on this and other relevant information, a plan for intervention and education can be developed. Second, school performance may be the first valid indication that a child is not developing normally. A comprehensive pediatric examination is a vital part of the overall assessment of such developmental problems so as to identify or rule out contributing medical factors, such as visual problems. If needed, detailed remedial measures may then be implemented (Berlin, 1976).

When necessary, the pediatrician can help by referral of the child to other specialists whose expertise may be needed to identify or treat the precise problems in question. Examples of medical specialists to whom such referral may be made include ophthlamologists for disorders of the eyes, neurologists for conditions related to the brain or other parts of the central nervous system, and ear, nose, and throat specialists for children with hearing impairments. Children's health problems may manifest themselves at school. If there is a medication or other treatment program in force, teachers can both monitor and encourage compliance with this program. Over 50% of all American parents have sought help from a pediatrician for school-related problems (American Academy of Pediatrics, 1978). For this reason, it is important that pediatricians and teachers maintain open lines of communication so that they may assist one another in helping children with both school-related and health problems.

REFERENCES

American Academy of Pediatrics (1978). *The future of pediatric education*. Washington, DC: Author.

Berlin, C. M. (1975). Medical bases of exceptional conditions. In R. M. Smith & J. T. Neisworth, (Eds.), *The exceptional child: A functional approach*. New York: McGraw-Hill.

WILLIAM J. SHAW
LOGAN WRIGHT
University of Oklahoma

PEDIATRIC PSYCHOLOGIST

The past two decades have been a period of significant professional growth for pediatric psychology. In general, the number of psychologists in medical settings has increased rapidly and the scope of their activities has widened enormously. Wright (1967) first used the term pediatric psychologist to refer to "any psychologist who finds himself dealing with children in a medical setting which is nonpsychiatric in nature" (p. 323). A year later, in 1968,

the Society of Pediatric Psychology was founded; it eventually became a section of the Division of Clinical Psychology of the American Psychological Association. The *Journal of Pediatric Psychology* was established by the society in 1976; it has since become a major source of clinical and research publication for the field.

There are three major types of pediatric settings in which pediatric psychologists work: (1) the pediatric hospital or multispecialty general hospital inpatient unit, (2) the ambulatory care facility (outpatient clinic or private pediatric office), and (3) the comprehensive care center (e.g., kidney dialysis center, burn hospital) for chronic illnesses or chronic medical conditions, which may provide outpatient and/or inpatient services. The primary clinical responsibilities of the pediatric psychologist in these settings are basically twofold: to provide direct psychological services to patients and to consult to a variety of pediatric medical subspecialties including nephrology, cardiology, hematology-oncology, endocrinology, neurology, genetics, and surgery.

The longest history of association between psychology and primary health care is that between psychologists and pediatricians. This association has been strengthened recently by several groups involved in the training and certification of pediatricians. First, the educational role of pediatric psychologists has been highlighted by recommendations of the Task Force on Pediatric Education (American Academy of Pediatrics, 1978), which placed an increasing emphasis on training in the area of behavioral pediatrics. Second, the Committee on Psychosocial Aspects of Child and Family Health of the American Academy of Pediatrics (1982) noted the important role of the pediatrician in the evaluation and treatment of common behavioral and developmental disorders as well as somatic disorders with psychosocial etiology. This committee also stressed the value of a collaborative relationship between pediatricians and clinical psychologists in the treatment of these problems. Therefore, an increasing recognition of the role of health-related behaviors in the prevention, development, and maintenance or exacerbation of illness has helped to foster the expansion of pediatric psychology as a subspecialty within clinical psychology.

Pediatric psychologists work with a wide range of health-related and developmental problems in children and adolescents (Magrab, 1978; Varni, 1983). They are called on to deal with many common childhood problems and issues of child-rearing that are presented frequently to the pediatrician. Among these common problem areas are eating and sleeping difficulties, toilet training and bed wetting, learning and developmental disorders, and problems in child management.

Over the past 20 years, pediatricians have increasingly focused on the prevention of disease and the management of chronic childhood illnesses for which there are no known cures, such as cystic fibrosis, sickle cell disease, and juvenile diabetes. This shift in the practice of pediatrics has placed a new emphasis on patients' problems of daily living, issues of quality of life, and problems related to compliance with therapeutic regimens. It has further supported the active involvement of pediatric psychologists in the comprehensive delivery of health care to children.

Many children present in medical settings with physical symptoms of unclear origin or with symptoms having significant psychosocial components, including headaches, chronic abdominal pain, and failure to thrive. The psychosocial concomitants of physical illness in children represent a major source of referrals to pediatric psychologists.

Behavioral treatment procedures have shown considerable promise as an approach to alleviating or reducing the symptomatic behaviors associated with a number of somatic disorders in children (Siegel, 1983). Pediatric psychologists have used a variety of behavioral techniques such as biofeedback, relaxation training, and various operant conditioning procedures to successfully modify the symptoms associated with such disorders as asthma, ruminative vomiting, and enuresis.

Pediatric psychologists have also been concerned with the prevention of health-related problems. Among the problems that have received considerable attention in this area are the reduction of stress associated with hospitalization and painful medical procedures and the management of behaviors (e.g., overeating) that are associated with the development of physical disorders such as high blood pressure.

Finally, pediatric psychologists who work in hospital settings are often called upon to provide emotional support to health-care personnel who deal with children having life-threatening conditions. Professional burnout is a significant problem with staff who provide medical care to terminally ill children. The pediatric psychologist may consult with the staff to help them cope with the emotionally draining experiences that they encounter in these settings.

REFERENCES

American Academy of Pediatrics, Committee on Psychosocial Aspects of Child and Family Health. (1982). Pediatrics and the psychosocial aspects of child and family health. *Pediatrics, 79,* 126–127.

American Academy of Pediatrics, Task Force on Pediatric Education. (1978). *The future of pediatric education.* Evanston, IL: American Academy of Pediatrics.

Magrab, P. R. (1978). *Psychological management of pediatric problems.* Baltimore, MD: University Park Press.

Siegel, L. J. (1983). Psychosomatic and psychophysiological disorders. In R. J. Morris & T. R. Kratochwill (Eds.), *The practice of child therapy.* New York: Pergamon.

Varni, J. W. (1983). *Clinical behavioral pediatrics: An interdisciplinary biobehavioral approach.* New York: Pergamon.

Wright, L. (1967). The pediatric psychologist: A role model. *American Psychologist, 22,* 323–325.

LAWRENCE J. SIEGEL
*University of Texas Medical
Branch, Galveston*

PARENT EDUCATION
PEDIATRICIAN
PSYCHOSOCIAL ADJUSTMENT
PSYCHOSOMATIC DISORDERS

PEDRO DE PONCE

See PONCE DE LEON, PEDRO DE.

PEER RELATIONSHIPS

When the topic of peer relationships is discussed in the literature, it is usually characterized as the interaction of handicapped students with their nonhandicapped classmates. This is an important and relevant topic in light of the impact PL 94-142 has had in ensuring that handicapped students be educated in the regular classroom whenever appropriate.

Current research suggests that handicapped students are often not included in many activities in the regular classroom. It has been shown that the classroom teacher sometimes fails to include the handicapped child into many typical academic activities. For example, one study (Brophy & Good, 1974) found that regular classroom teachers tended to initiate more negative interactions with low-status, learning-disabled students than with high-status, nonlearning-disabled students. Other researchers have demonstrated that this type of nonproductive negative interchange between the classroom teacher and the handicapped student will have a significant impact on the relationship between the handicapped child and his or her regular class peers (Weinstein, Marshall, Brattesani, & Middlestadt, 1982). The negative interaction between the handicapped student and the teacher seems to solidify the low status of the low-performing student.

The relationship between handicapped students and their peers is a complex phenomenon that is molded by many factors. Several of the more noteworthy factors are age of the handicapped child, attitudes and behavior of the classroom teacher, type of handicapping condition affecting the student, self-concept and skill level of the handicapped student, and whether or not the regular class students have been prepared to understand the specific needs of some mainstreamed students. For example, it has been suggested that beginning in the early elementary grades, the influence of the peer group increases as the handicapped child gets older. In other words, during the early years of a handicapped child's school experience, parent and teacher acceptance are more important than peer approval or acceptance.

Methods to improve the peer relationships of the handicapped child can be found in the literature. As an example of one such approach, Schwartz (1984) provides a checklist for regular class teachers to follow when preparing for the arrival of a mainstreamed handicapped child. Among other activities, teachers are asked to give regular class peers information about handicapping conditions and allow for any questions students might have. Such procedures help increase the frequency of positive interaction between the handicapped child and his or her peers. This approach is particularly important with physically handicapped students. Some research suggests that the physically handicapped child is the least likely to be accepted by his or her nonhandicapped peers.

REFERENCES

Brophy, J., & Good, T. (1974). *Teacher-student relationships: Causes and consequences.* New York: Holt, Rinehart, & Winston.

Schwartz, L. L. (1984). *Exceptional students in the mainstream.* Belmont, CA: Wadsworth.

Weinstein, R. S., Marshall, H. H., Brattaseni, K., & Middlestedt, S. E. (1982). Student perceptions of differential treatment in open and traditional classrooms. *Journal of Educational Psychology, 74,* 679–692.

CRAIG DARCH
Auburn University

MAINSTREAMING
PEER TUTORING

PEER TUTORING

Peer and cross-age tutoring procedures have been identified in the literature as having success in the instruction of handicapped children. Tutoring programs have been successful in improving a wide variety of academic skills. Peer tutors have been effective in teaching math (Johnson & Bailey, 1974) and spelling (Harris, 1973), but have most often been applied for reading skills (Chaing, Thorpe, & Darch, 1980). Many authors identify the need to carefully prepare children before they perform as tutors (Schloss & Sedlak, 1986). Procedures for preparing children to function as tutors have not been extensively discussed in the

literature. There are few sources readily available for a comprehensive description of tutor preparation techniques that have been successfully implemented.

Although there is little research that has been conducted on particular training procedures, anecdotal information leads to the conclusion that carefully designed interactions and tutor preparation are important for the success of a tutoring program. If peer tutoring programs are to be beneficial to everyone involved, the teacher must invest time in the development, implementation, and evaluation of these instructional sessions.

One issue that designers of tutoring programs should consider is the identification of potential peer tutors. This is difficult because research has not given teachers definitive answers as to the characteristics of good peer tutors.

Some studies in special education that have shown tutoring to be effective have older students tutoring younger students (Parson & Heward, 1979). Other reports indicate that large age differences are not critical to an effective peer tutoring program (Dineen, Clark, & Risley, 1977). In fact, one peer tutoring study demonstrated that learning-disabled (LD) elementary-age students were effective in teaching other elementary LD students placed in the same resource room (Chiang, Thorpe, & Darch, 1981). Therefore, based on information currently available, it is safe to conclude that tutor-tutee age difference is not in itself critical to the success of a peer tutorial program.

It appears that tutors can be selected from most special education programs. Research has demonstrated that effective peer tutors can come from either able or less able students. While studies within regular classrooms are common, low-achieving and special classroom students have also been effective tutors (Paine et al., 1983). Several studies have shown higher functioning LD students to be effective tutors for lower functioning LD classmates.

For several reasons, student assignments as tutors can be justified. Tutoring can improve self-concept, be used as a means of practicing previously learned skills, and reinforce academic or social performance. The peer tutoring program can be instrumental in helping special education students develop a more positive attitude and self-image. The success that tutees achieve in these carefully designed programs can contribute to important changes in previously unmotivated students.

REFERENCES

Chaing, B., Thorpe, H., & Darch, C. (1980). Effects of cross age tutoring on word recognition performance of learning disabled students. *Learning Disability Quarterly, 3,* 11–19.

Dineen, J. P., Clark, H. B., & Risley, T. R. (1977). Peer tutoring among elementary students: Educational benefits to the tutor. *Journal of Applied Behavior Analysis, 10,* 231–238.

Harris, V. W. (1973). Effects of peer tutoring, homework, and consequences upon the academic performance of elementary school children (Doctoral dissertation, University of Kansas, 1972). *Dissertation Abstracts International, 33*, 11-A, 6175.

Johnson, M., & Bailey, J. S. (1974). Cross-age tutoring: Fifth graders as arithmetic tutors for kindergarten children. *Journal of Applied Behavior Analysis, 7*, 223–232.

Maher, C. A. (1984). Handicapped adolescents as cross age tutors: Program description and evaluation. *Exceptional Children, 51*, 56–63.

Paine, S., Radicchi, J., Rosellini, L., Deutchman, L., & Darch, C. (1983). *Structuring your classroom for academic success.* Champaign, IL: Research.

Parson, L. R., & Heward, W. L. (1979). Training peers to tutor: Evaluation of a tutor training package for primary learning disabled students. *Journal of Applied Behavior Analysis, 12*, 309–310.

Schloss, P., & Sedlak, R. (1986). *Instructional methods for students with learning and behavior problems.* Boston: Allyn & Bacon.

CRAIG DARCH
Auburn University

DIRECT INSTRUCTION
PEER RELATIONSHIPS
SOCIAL SKILLS TRAINING
TEACHER EFFECTIVENESS

PENNSYLVANIA ASSOCIATION FOR RETARDED CITIZENS v. PENNSYLVANIA (1972)

Commonly known as the *PARC* decision, the case of the *Pennsylvania Association for Retarded Citizens* v. *Pennsylvania* is one of two landmark court decisions granting educational rights to the handicapped (the other is *Mills* v. *Board of Education of Washington, DC.*) *PARC* and *Mills* were instrumental in the passage of state and federal laws guaranteeing equal access for the handicapped to all educational programs.

The *PARC* case was a class-action suit (the suit was certified by the court as representing all similarly situated individuals in Pennsylvania) brought by the Pennsylvania Association for Retarded Citizens and 13 mentally retarded students. The suit was brought because three students had been denied attendance in the public schools of Pennsylvania. The case was brought under the equal protection and due process clauses of the Fourteenth Amendment to the U.S. Constitution. In *PARC*, the plaintiffs argued that allowing the state to provide a free public education to some of its citizens while denying other of its citizens the right to attend the same schools or to receive an appropriate education at state expense was unfair and denied equal protection of the law. They also argued that handicapped children were excluded from public education without access to due process. (The Fourteenth Amendment does not deny the ability of a state to deprive a citizen of any fundamental right; however, before a right

can be violated, the state must demonstrate a compelling interest and must grant the citizen a hearing and other such protection as may be deemed necessary under the due process clause.)

In deciding for the plaintiffs, the court clearly acknowledged that admitting seriously disturbing, profoundly retarded, physically handicapped children would be difficult and expensive at all levels; however, the court ruled that the interests of the handicapped were protected by the Fourteenth Amendment and that this protection outweighed the difficulties created by providing an education to the handicapped. The decision was extensive in its requirements and many of its provisions are routinely included in present statutes. The *PARC* decision required the state to provide a free, appropriate education to all handicapped children regardless of the nature or extent of their handicaps; to educate handicapped children alongside nonhandicapped children to the extent possible; to conduct an annual census to locate and serve handicapped children; to cease and desist from applying school exclusion laws, including prohibition of serial suspension practices; to notify parents before assessing a child to determine the presence of a handicap and prior to placement in a special education program; to establish procedures to meet the due process requirements of the Fourteenth Amendment should disagreements arise regarding the school's decision about a handicapped child's educational placement or program; to reevaluate handicapped children on a systematic basis; and to pay private school tuition if the school refers a child to a private school or cannot reasonably meet the needs of a handicapped child in a public setting. Later interpretations of the *PARC* decision by other courts have concluded that the schools must also use proven, state-of-the-art teaching methods with the handicapped (under the requirement of providing an appropriate education).

Following the *PARC* decision and the subsequent ruling in *Mills*, a flood of suits came forth arguing for the rights of the handicapped to equal educational opportunities. Few of these cases were even litigated, however, as most states during the period 1972 to 1974 passed and funded legislation requiring local school districts to provide special education programs for the handicapped.

The *PARC* decision and related cases had a profound effect on special education as currently practiced. *PARC* fostered a rapid change in American schools, bringing into local schools, for the first time in many cases, children with severe disabilities, including profound levels of mental retardation, deafness, blindness, multiple handicaps, and the severe orthopedic impairment.

CECIL R. REYNOLDS
Texas A&M University

CONSENT DECREE
EQUAL EDUCATIONAL OPPORTUNITY

EQUAL PROTECTION
LEAST RESTRICTIVE ENVIRONMENT
MAINSTREAMING
MILLS *v.* BOARD OF EDUCATION OF DISTRICT OF
COLUMBIA

PEOPLE FIRST

People First is a self-advocacy organization run by and for people with mental retardation. It has the dual purpose of assuring the availability of the services, training, and support needed to maintain and increase the capabilities of people with developmental disabilities for leading independent and normal lives; and of demonstrating to society that the disabled are people first and handicapped second (People First, 1984). Groups of mentally retarded people are taught to organize their affairs, run meetings, and make decisions and carry them through. All of this is accomplished with minimal help from nonhandicapped advisers. To a large extent, these groups are not only concerned with the needs and problems of mentally retarded people, but also the needs and problems of all handicapped people. Statewide and national conventions of self-advocacy groups have been held and an international self-advocacy movement of People First groups is emerging.

One of the first self-advocacy groups was Project Two, which operated in Nebraska. In 1968 many institutionalized mentally retarded individuals were moved to community-based facilities; hence Project One was deinstitutionalization. Deinstitutionalized people felt they needed a sounding board—a self-help group; hence Project Two. Similar developments occurred in Oregon, where there were self-help groups. Three mentally retarded members and two nonhandicapped advisers attended a conference for mentally handicapped people in British Columbia, Canada. They returned inspired with the idea of starting an organization of people with mental retardation who would put together such conferences. This was the beginning of the People First movement in America. What is interesting is that the movement started up 2 years after Project Two but was unaware of the other group's existence.

Self-advocacy groups have sprung up in America and Britain. Such groups are challenging traditional views of mental handicaps, handicapped people, and mentally retarded persons who can speak for themselves. Self-advocacy groups stretch nonhandicapped people's expectations and attitudes, thereby helping to create a new independence for mentally handicapped persons. In California, People First was contracted by the State Council of Developmental Disabilities to critique the current service system for the developmentally disabled. The unique aspect of this project is that it was entirely conducted by the consumers of the services and was not the work of professionals.

REFERENCES

People First of California. (1984). *Surviving the system: Mental retardation and the retarding environment.* Sacramento, CA: State Council on Developmental Disabilities.

Williams, P., & Shoultz, B. (1982). *We can speak for ourselves.* Bloomington, IN: Indiana University Press.

MILTON BUDOFF
*Research Institute for
Educational Problems,
Cambridge, Massachusetts*

ADVOCACY FOR HANDICAPPED CHILDREN
ADVOCACY ORGANIZATIONS

PERCENTILE SCORES

A percentile score is a score derived from the relative position of a raw score in the entire distribution of raw scores. The raw score must possess at least rank information; i.e., raw scores must be able to be ranked. Usually we assume at least intervals for the raw scores, so that a one-point difference has the same meaning for all possible scores. Percentile scores lose this interval quality.

The calculation of a percentile score is based on the number of scores lower than the raw score being changed or transformed. A percentile score of 50 means that half (50%) of the scores in the raw score distribution fall below the score under consideration. This percentile score is also called the median. A percentile score of 10 means 10% of the scores are lower, and a percentile score of 90 means 90% of the scores are lower.

Percentile scores are not equal intervals. That is, a 10 percentile point difference has a different meaning when examined for a score of 10 or 50. The difference between percentile scores of 10 and 20 may represent many raw score points, while the difference between 50 and 60 may represent only a few. This is because raw score distributions typically have most scores clustered around the average score, perhaps two thirds of the scores within one standard deviation, so that 10% of the scores will occur within a few points of each other. At the extremes of the score distribution there are few people, and 10% may represent a large raw score range. Percentile scores should not be treated as interval scores. They cannot be routinely added, subtracted, divided, or multiplied to obtain anything sensible. Their primary use is to inform the user of the relative position of a raw score with respect to all other raw scores. In standardized testing, in which a norm sample has been carefully sampled, the percentile score tells us how an observed raw score compares with the norm group distribution of raw scores.

VICTOR L. WILLSON
Texas A&M University

GRADE EQUIVALENTS
MEASUREMENT

PERCEPTUAL AND MOTOR SKILLS

Perceptual and Motor Skills (titled *Perceptual and Motor Skills Research Exchange* in 1949) is published bimonthly. Two volumes a year total between 2000 and 3000 pages. About 30% of the articles are submitted from outside the United States. The purpose of this journal is to encourage scientific originality and creativity from an interdisciplinary perspective including such fields as anthropology, physical education, physical therapy, orthopedics, anesthesiology, and time and motion study. Articles are experimental, theoretical, and speculative. Special reviews and lists of new books received are carried. Controversial material of scientific merit is welcome. Submissions are examined by multiple referees, and critical editing is balanced by specific suggestions as to changes required to meet standards.

A recent survey made in the 35th year of publication showed that *Perceptual and Motor Skills* was listed for the preceding decade in the top 5% of psychology journals for numbers of citations elsewhere of its articles and total numbers published of refereed, selected archival articles. For more than 30 years this journal has consistently maintained a policy of being highly experimental, open to all defensible points of view, encouraging of new and often unpopular ways of approaching problems, and protective of authors by careful but open-minded refereeing and editing.

REFERENCES

Ammons, C. H., & Ammons, R. B. (1962). Permanent or temporary journals: PR and PMS become stable. *Psychological Reports*, *10*, 537.

Ammons, R. B., & Ammons, C. H. (1962). Permanent or temporary journals: Are PR and PMS stable? *Perceptual & Motor Skills*, *14*, 281.

C. H. AMMONS
*Psychological Reports/
Perceptual and Motor Skills,
Missoula, Montana*

PERCEPTUAL CONSTANCY

Perceptual constancy refers to the ability to perceive objects possessing invariant properties such as size, shape, and position in spite of changes in the impression on the sensory surface. Essentially, this means that one recognizes a chair as not only a chair but as the same chair regardless of the viewing angle. Even though an object may have been seen only from a single point of view, we are often able to recognize that object from different distances and from nearly any angle of view.

Perceptual constancy seems to be largely an innate skill (Martindale, 1981). For example, when we observe from a great distance a man who is 6 feet in height, he may appear to be only an inch tall; however, he will be perceived as roughly his correct height nevertheless. Normal individuals can easily perform such tasks with objects not previously seen whenever any other environmental cues are present.

Perceptual constancy is an integral part of overall visual perception and is involved heavily in the early reading process. Disorders of perceptual constancy are relatively rare, but they do occur and can wreak havoc with early learning. Children learn to recognize letters and words even though they see them printed in a variety of orthographic representations. Much variability of printing by children and their teachers occurs during the early learning stages as well, yet children master these various representations with relative ease. The generalization necessary to performing such tasks of visual pattern recognition requires perceptual constancy. Children with mild disturbances of perceptual constancy or higher order visual pattern recognition will have great difficulty with many school tasks, but especially with reading. The disorder is low enough in incidence, however, that accurate estimates of its prevalence are unavailable.

REFERENCE

Martindale, C. (1981). *Cognition and consciousness.* Homewood, IL: Dorsey.

CECIL R. REYNOLDS
Texas A&M University

DEVELOPMENTAL TEST OF VISUAL PERCEPTION
PERCEPTUAL DEVELOPMENT (LAG IN)
PERCEPTUAL TRAINING

PERCEPTUAL DEFICIT HYPOTHESIS

The perceptual deficit hypothesis, a once widely accepted view of learning disabilities, exerted a dominant influence on special education teaching and evaluation practices from the early 1960s to the mid-1970s. While the perceptual deficit hypothesis encompasses a number of variants, its central notion is that learning disabilities arise from perceptual-motor dysfunction of neurological origin (Cruickshank, 1972). Learning-disabled children are viewed as having deficient form perception and/or visual analysis, and these deficiencies are believed to be the central feature of their difficulties in learning to read.

This view of learning disabilities widely influenced special education practice through the writings and programs of Kephart (1960), Getman (1962), Barsch (1965), and Frostig (1961). Remedial programs reflected this orientation by emphasizing gross and fine-motor training, ocular exercises, spatial orientation, balance board training, visual discrimination, sequencing, closure exercises, etc., as necessary prerequisites to more direct teaching of academics. It was believed that such foundation training in sensory-motor functions would remediate underlying processing deficits and was a required prerequisite to higher order, conceptual, or symbolic learning.

Proponents of the perceptual deficit hypothesis were influenced by Piaget's theories concerning the role of maturation and motor functioning in perception, by gestalt psychology's emphasis on perceptual development, and by Strauss and Lehtinen's (1947) work with brain-injured children. In their programs for learning-disabled children, these pioneers of special education translated stage theories of learning literally into hierarchies of preacademic remediation activities that sought to develop motor, visual, and visual-motor skills prior to focusing on academic learning. In theory, the development of academic skills required mastery of these lower-level functions.

By the mid 1970s, the perceptual deficit hypothesis and its concomitant remedial programs began to receive severe and substantial criticism. Aspects of the underlying theory were questioned and fault was found with the early foundation research. The overly simplified and literal translation of theory into practice was decried as an essential misinterpretation of the concept of perception. New research indicated that learning disabilities, and reading disabilities in particular, were attributable more to problems in the verbal realm than to perceptual deficits (Vellutino et al., 1977).

Tests used to diagnose specific aspects of perceptual deficit came under particularly heavy fire. The most commonly used, the Frostig Developmental Test of Visual Perception (DTVP; Frostig, 1961), was criticized for its weak theoretical foundation. In addition, the DTVP was found to have insufficient factorial validity, meaning that its subtests do not actually tap distinct and separate perceptual functions and therefore cannot be validly used to specify different remedial activities. Thus the widespread use of this test for diagnostic/prescriptive purposes was resoundingly invalidated. Additionally, perceptual training based on the Frostig test was found to have no relation to academic progress and only a negligible effect on DTVP performance itself (Hammill, Goodman, & Wiederhold, 1974). There arose the ethical issue of spending children's limited classroom time on pseudo prerequisite exercises with no validated relationship to academic achievement.

Remediation based on the perceptual deficit hypothesis, along with remediation based on the Illinois Test of Psycholinguistic Abilities (ITPA), continues to be debated under the broader rubric of underlying process training. Underlying process training has come to represent a genre of emphasis within special education in general, and

within the study of learning disabilities in particular. Proponents of one or another of the process orientations seek to psychologically parse special students into a variety of processing strength/weakness categories in order to pinpoint areas of underlying need. While this effort has had appeal to many special educators because of the puzzling performance discrepancies of learning-disabled students, its basic assumptions have been seriously questioned.

The assumptions of a process orientation are that human performance can, in fact, be parsed into psychologically distinct categories, that any given parsing categories are valid compartments, that valid tests exist with which to parse, and that remediation based on underlying processing profiles will transfer to functional and academic learning. Currently, the state of the art in psychology and special education does not support any of these assumptions.

REFERENCES

Barsch, R. H. (1965). *A movigenic curriculum* (Publication No. 25). Madison: Wisconsin State Department of Instruction.

Cruickshank, W. M. (1972). Some issues facing the field of learning disability. *Journal of Learning Disabilities, 5,* 380–383.

Frostig, M. (1961). *The Marianne Frostig Developmental Test of Visual Perception.* Palo Alto, CA: Consulting Psychologists.

Getman, G. (1962). *How to develop your child's intelligence.* Luverne, MN: Announcer.

Hammill, D., Goodman, L., & Wiederholt, J. L. (1974). Visual-motor processes: Can we train them? *Reading Teacher, 27,* 469–480.

Kephart, N. (1960). *The slow learner in the classroom.* Columbus, OH: Merrill.

Strauss, A. A., & Lehtinen, L. E. (1947). *Psychopathology and education of the brain-injured child.* New York: Grune & Stratton.

Vellutino, F. R., Steger, B. M., Moyer, S. C., Harding, C. J., & Niles, J. A. (1977). Has the perceptual deficit hypothesis led us astray? *Journal of Learning Disabilities, 10,* 54–64.

KATHERINE GARNETT
*Hunter College, City University
of New York*

PERCEPTUAL DEVELOPMENT
PERCEPTUAL REMEDIATION

PERCEPTUAL DEVELOPMENT, LAG IN

Lag in perceptual development has been hypothesized as a major cause of learning difficulties in children by Kephart, Delacato, and Getman, among others. In general, these theorists believe there is a sequential series of strategies children use to process information from the environment; if learned incompletely at any stage, these strategies will cause learning difficulties at higher levels. These theorists maintain that proficiency in perceptual functioning provides an essential foundation for academic learning. Furthermore, they presume children experience academic failure because of developmental lags in these perceptual systems, lags that can and must be ameliorated before academic learning can occur. Although varying somewhat in theoretical orientation, these researchers, as well as Frostig, Barsch, Ayres, Doman, S. Kirk, and W. Kirk, advocate perceptual training to both establish the necessary foundation for and enhance the acquisition of academic learning. Their research provides much of the foundation for current work in the field of learning disabilities (Smith, 1984).

An early proponent of perceptual-motor training, Kephart (1971) believed that motor learning underlies all learning. Basing his theory on works of Hebb, Strauss, Werner, Piaget, and Montessori, Kephart hypothesizes that perceptual development occurs through motor activity and corresponding sensory feedback. Once developed, the perceptual system functions without sole reliance on motor response. It is only through completion of this developmental sequence that the child can readily acquire concepts necessary for academic learning. To ameliorate the underlying developmental limitations and distortions that Kephart believed result in academic failure, he developed a training program based on gross motor activities such as posturing and balancing, locomotion, and throwing and catching balls.

Delacato believes training specific locomotor tasks will influence various centers in the brain and other perceptual and cognitive functions controlled by these centers. One critical aspect of his theory is the establishment of hemispheric dominance to improve speech and other sensory functions. He advocates training the child in unilateral hand use and monocular activities and removing music from the child's environment (Cratty, 1979). Maintaining that unmastered stages of neurological development result in reading and other academic difficulties, Doman and Delacato (Ayres, 1975) emphasize remedial activities designed to recapitulate their hypothesized sequence of neurological developmental. In an effort to establish the unilateral cerebral dominance believed critical in treating reading difficulties, they prescribe training to attain sleep posturing, crawling, and activities that foster unilateral hand, eye, and foot dominance.

Getman holds a position similar to Kephart. Like Kephart he proposes movement as a prerequisite to learning. Unlike Kephart, he emphasizes the importance of vision in the learning process and uses vision in a global sense. He hypothesizes that deficiencies in some visual components will lead to learning difficulties (Cratty, 1979). Designed to enhance academic success, particularly reading, Getman's training program includes locomotor and balancing activities as well as eye-hand coordination and other tasks to enhance ocular function.

Frostig (1964) maintains that poor perceptual development precludes conceptual learning, resulting in academic difficulties. Focusing on visual-perceptual learning, training in gross motor activities and paper and pencil tasks follows assessments using Frostig's Developmental Test of Visual Perception (DTVP). According to Frostig, when integrated with regular academic tasks, these activities promote sensorimotor development, ameliorating dysfunctional perceptual processes and enhancing academic performance.

Barsch's (1967) movigenics curriculum emphasizes the academic value of efficient cognitive and physical movement. Like previous theorists, Barsch views the child as a perceptual-motor being whose successful development depends on proper spatial orientation. Movigenics emphasizes activities that enhance visual-perceptual and motor development.

Ayres' (1975) sensorimotor integration theory posits that the foundations to learning are established through the integration of sensory feedback to the brain. Maintaining that perception and movement are dependent on proper sensory integration, Ayres postulates numerous deficits resulting in poor perceptual-motor functioning. To increase integration and facilitate academic learning, Ayres advocates sensory stimulation through activities such as rolling, spinning, and swinging exercises.

Kirk and Kirk (1971) advocate a different approach to the diagnosis and remediation of learning difficulties. Focusing on the communication abilities of the child, Kirk and Kirk provide psycholinguistic evaluation and training to facilitate academic learning. Although training focuses on auditory and visual perception, Kirk and Kirk advocate training focusing on the individual's weak areas.

Although numerous perceptual-motor theories and training programs exist, research findings to support the theories on which they are based or validate their efficacy have not been found. Hammill, Goodman, and Wiederholt (1974) reviewed studies investigating the effects of the perceptual training programs of Frostig, Kephart, and Getman on readiness skills, intelligence, and academic achievement. Of the studies reviewed, positive effects of training on intelligence and academic achievement were not demonstrated and readiness skills improved in only a few cases. In a study of the effects of Delacato's training method on reading ability and visual-motor integration, O'Donnell and Eisenson (1969) found no improvements in either visual-motor integration or reading ability. Further, a number of researchers, professional groups, and parent groups have severely criticized Delacato's theory and program (Aaron & Poostay, 1982).

Finally, in an evaluation of 38 studies employing Kirk and Kirk's psycholinguistic training model, Hammill and Larsen (1978) found only six demonstrating positive results and concluded that the efficacy of psycholinguistic training remains nonvalidated. Although perceptual and psycholinguistic training theorists maintain the efficacy of their treatment programs, others question the large amounts of time and money expended on these unsubstantiated perceptual-training programs (Hammill et al., 1974). Research may validate their value in certain cases, but general use appears unwarranted. In summarizing on perceptual and motor training, Mann (1979, p. 358–359), tells us that "The new scientific pedagogy was going to revitalize education, provide individual prescriptive correctives for learning problems, reclaim the cognitively impaired. Down with models of general intellectual incompetency! Down with medical models of noneducational etiology! The promised land was at hand. Alas, neither Moses nor we ever crossed to the other side" (pp. 538–539). Little has changed.

REFERENCES

Aaron, I. E., & Poostay, E. J. (1982). Strategies for reading disorders. In C. R. Reynolds & T. B. Gutkin (Eds.), *The handbook of school psychology* (pp. 410–435). New York: Wiley.

Ayres, A. J. (1975). Sensorimotor foundations of academic ability. In W. M. Cruickshank & D. P. Hallahan (Eds.), *Perceptual and learning disabilities in children* (Vol. 2, pp. 301–360). Syracuse, NY: Syracuse University Press.

Barsch, R. H. (1967). *Achieving perceptual motor efficiency.* Seattle, WA: Special Child.

Cratty, B. J. (1979). *Perceptual and motor development in infants and children.* New York: Macmillan.

Frostig, M., & Horne, D. (1964). *The Frostig program for the development of visual perception: a teacher's guide.* Chicago: Follett.

Hammill, D., Goodman, L., & Wiederholt, J. L. (1974). Visual-motor processes: Can we train them? *Reading Teacher, 27,* 469–478.

Hammill, D., & Larsen, S. (1978). The effectiveness of psycholinguistic training: A reaffirmation of position. *Exceptional Children, 44,* 402–414.

Kephart, N. C. (1971). *The slow learner in the classroom* (2nd ed.). Columbus, OH: Merrill.

Kirk, S. A., & Kirk, W. D. (1971). *Psycholinguistic learning disabilities: Diagnosis and remediation.* Chicago: University of Illinois Press.

Mann, L. A. (1979). *On the trail of process.* New York: Grune & Stratton.

O'Donnell, P. A., & Eisenson, J. (1969). Delacato training for reading achievement and visual-motor integration. *Journal of Learning Disabilities, 2,* 441–447.

Smith, C. R. (1984). *Learning disabilities: The interaction of learner, task, and setting.* Boston: Little, Brown.

SHIRLEY PARKER WELLS
ELEANOR BOYD WRIGHT
*University of North Carolina,
Wilmington*

NEUROLOGICAL ORGANIZATION
REMEDIATION, DEFICIT-CENTERED MODEL OF

PERCEPTUAL DISTORTIONS

Perceptual distortion is a clinical term referring to aberrant reception and interpretation of stimuli by one or more of the five basic senses: vision, hearing, smell, taste, and touch. Perceptual distortion typically occurs in conjunction with schizophrenia, severe depression, and psychomotor and ideopathic epilepsies. Schizophrenics are particularly susceptible to perceptual distortion and often process incoming sensory information abnormally via attenuation or reduction. Schizophrenics traditionally have been thought to underestimate tactile, auditory, and visual stimuli in particular. Related to perceptual distortion is evidence that schizophrenics have a defective sensory-filtering mechanism that does not allow them to focus on the most relevant of stimuli at any given time (Pincus & Tucker, 1978). Perceptual distortions that mimic the schizophrenic's perceptual distortions also may be induced by various psychoactive drugs. Prolonged sensory deprivation can also produce perceptual distortions and full-blown hallucinations.

In contrast to schizophrenics, depressed and epileptic individuals exaggerate the intensity of incoming stimuli. Psychomotor seizures produce the most specific of the perceptual distortions but they tend to be ideopathic. Perceptual distortions may also be considered a soft sign of neurological impairment and may occur with learning disabilities, though the latter is far less frequent than commonly believed.

REFERENCE

Pincus, J. H., & Tucker, G. J. (1978). *Behavioral neurology* (2nd ed.). New York: Oxford University Press.

CECIL R. REYNOLDS
Texas A&M University

CHILDHOOD SCHIZOPHRENIA
EPILEPSY
PERCEPTUAL DEVELOPMENT, LAG IN

PERCEPTUAL-MOTOR DIFFICULTIES

Perceptual-motor development is recognized as a basic foundation for later learning. The perceptual deficit hypothesis holds that academic difficulties underlie perceptual deficits (Daves, 1980) and that improving the perceptual processes will bring about improvement in academic achievement. Frequently, children with serious learning disorders have difficulty with spatial orientation, eye-hand coordination, and body image. The early work of Strauss and Lehtinen (1947) described such disorders using the term brain-injured, but later such disorders were labeled the Strauss syndrome by Stevens and Birch (1957).

They described the child with perceptual-motor difficulties as one who showed disturbances (separately or in combination) in perception, thinking, and emotional behavior.

Kinsbourne (1968) drew an analogy between the developmental syndrome of cognitive deficits and the acquired Gerstmann syndrome in some adults with parietal lesions in the dominant hemisphere. In both syndromes, he noted selective delay in the ability to recall and use information regarding relative position of items in spatial or temporal sequence; selective difficulty in learning to read and write; spelling errors characterized by errors of letter order and script malorientation; delayed acquisition of finger order sense; inability to discriminate between right and left; and difficulty in arithmetic. He concluded that the developmental syndrome probably represented a developmental lag rather than an indication of localized or lateralized cerebral damage.

There is little question regarding the importance of the development of perceptual-motor skills. Cratty (1975) notes that a child with perceptual-motor difficulties cannot translate thoughts into written and printed form with the same precision as a normally developing child. Such a child also may possess various perceptual deficits within one or more modalities (touch, kinesthesia, vision, audition) that may combine as evidence of a defective nervous system and lead to learning problems. Cruickshank (1979) also emphasized that perceptual processing deficits or neurological dysfunction underlie learning problems. Such problems are related to receiving, processing, and responding to information from outside the environment and from inside the child's own body. The ability to understand, remember, think, and perform perceptual-motor skills all precede the ability to read, write, or master arithmetic. Strategies to assist children in the overall learning process were developed (Kephart, 1963) based on the notion that perceptual-motor deficits are primarily organic in nature, and further, that they can be remediated by the development of specific skills such as form perception, eye-hand coordination, and temporal-spatial relationships.

Both Frostig (1975) and Kephart (1975) emphasized the need to develop skills in their natural order. They stressed the effect of motor processes on perception and the effects of perception on cognitive processes (i.e., the use of vision and motor skills or activities in the formation of a concept). In a similar manner Barsh (1963) developed a curriculum, movigenics, involving a progressively more complex sequence of activities in which children explore and orient themselves in space. Barsh's emphasis was on the development of muscular strength, dynamics, balance, space, body awareness, and rhythmics.

Controversy exists regarding the efficacy of such programs. Much of the research to replicate beneficial results linking perceptual motor training to academic achievement (Balow, 1971; Goodman & Hammill, 1973; Zigler & Seitz, 1975) suggests that the claims are unwarranted. Little evidence has been found to support the use of percep-

tual-motor activities in the treatment or prevention of disabilities in reading or other specific school subjects. However, other research tends to confirm earlier claims (Ayres, 1972; Gregory, 1978; Masland, 1976; Neman, 1974). There is continued interest in and support for determining the benefits of specific sensory-motor training.

REFERENCES

Ayres, A. (1972). *Sensory integration and learning disorders*, Los Angeles, Western Psychological Services.

Balow, B. (1971). Perceptual-motor activities in the treatment of severe reading disabilities. *Reading Teacher, 24*, 513–525.

Barsh, R. H. (1963). *Enriching perception and cognition: Techniques for teachers* (Vol. 2). Seattle, WA: Special Child.

Cratty, B. J. (1975). *Remedial motor activities for children*. Philadelphia: Febiger.

Cruickshank, W. M. (1979). Learning disabilities: Perceptual or other? *Association for Children with Learning Disabilities Newsbriefs, 125*, 7–10.

Daves, W. E. (1980). *Educator's resource guide to special education: Terms-laws-tests-organizations*. Boston: Allyn & Bacon.

Frostig, M. (1975). The role of perception in the integration of psychological functions. In W. Cruickshank & D. Hallahan (Eds.), *Perceptual and learning disabilities in children* (Vol. 1, pp. 115–146). Syracuse: Syracuse University Press.

Goodman, L., & Hammill, D. (1973). The effectiveness of the Kephart-Getman activities in developing perceptual-motor and cognitive skills. *Focus on Exceptional Children, 4*(9), 19.

Gregory, R. L. (1978). Illusions and hallucinations. In E. C. Carterette & M. P. Friedman (Eds.), *Handbook of Perception: Vol. 9. Perceptual Processing* (pp. 337–358). New York: Academic.

Kephart, N. C. (1963). *The brain injured child in the classroom*. Chicago: National Society for Crippled Children and Adults.

Kephart, N. C. (1975). The perceptual-motor match. In W. Cruickshank & D. Hallahan (Eds.), *Perceptual and learning disabilities in children* (Vol. 1, pp. 63–70). Syracuse: Syracuse University Press.

Kinsbourne, M. (1968). Developmental Gerstmann syndrome. *Pediatric Clinics in North America, 15*(3), 771–778.

Masland, R. (1976). The advantages of being dyslexic. *Bulletin of the Orton Society, 26*, 10–18.

Neman, R. (1974). A reply to Zigler & Seitz. *American Journal of Mental Deficiency, 79*, 493–505.

Stevens, G. D., & Birch, J. W. (1957). A proposal of clarification of the terminology and a description of brain-injured children. *Exceptional Children, 23*, 346–349.

Strauss, A. A., & Lehtinen, L. E. (1947). *Psychopathology and education of the brain-injured child* (Vol. I). New York: Grune & Stratton.

Zigler, E., & Seitz, V. (1975). On an experimental evaluation of sensory motor patterning: A critique. *American Journal of Mental Deficiency, 79*, 483–492.

SALLY E. PISARCHICK
*Cuyahoga Special Education
Service Center, Maple
Heights, Ohio*

MOVIGENICS
VISUAL-MOTOR AND VISUAL-PERCEPTUAL PROBLEMS
VISUAL PERCEPTION AND DISCRIMINATION

PERCEPTUAL REMEDIATION

Perceptual disabilities have received much attention in the field of learning disabilities. Strauss and Werner (1942) and Strauss and Lehtinen (1947) focused their work on perceptual disabilities; many others also believed perceptual difficulties to be one of the main problems of many learning disabled individuals (Mercer, 1979).

Students with perceptual difficulties have a variety of problems. For example, some do not attend to the relevant dimensions of stimuli, but rather, focus on unimportant details and ignore the crucial parts. Others might not be able to distinguish between hard or soft objects by touch, or may not be able to differentiate between selected sounds (Mercer, 1979). There are many remedial programs that are designed to help children with these types of perceptual problems function better.

Many of these programs emphasize a perceptual modality approach; this is based on the assumption that students' strengths and weaknesses in learning are related to their preferred modalities. It is felt that some children learn best using visual input, while others may use auditory or tactile input more efficiently. There are several ways remedial programs can be structured to assist children with these problems. First, teaching can be done using the child's strongest modality; second, emphasis can be placed on the weak modality to try to strengthen it; third, all modalities can be considered in the teaching process by both emphasizing the strong sense and strengthening the weak one. However, some children have problems integrating information from several modalities. Programs for them should avoid multisensory instruction and focus on limited stimulation that stresses primarily one modality (Mercer, 1979).

This approach to learning disabilities stresses psychological processing abilities and related motor functioning. While there are many who disagree with this orientation (Vellutino, 1978), supporters of this approach state that underlying receptive, integrative, and expressive dysfunctions affect such areas as perception, memory, and linguistic and motor functioning. Problems in these areas are viewed as interfering with reading, oral and written language, mathematics, and other aspects of learning (Adelman & Taylor, 1983).

Applications of this theory is referred to as diagnostic prescriptive teaching or as a diagnostic remedial approach. Remedial programs develop from psychoeducational evaluations that examine the child's specific strengths and weakness; commonly used tests include the Developmental Test of Visual Perception, the Develop-

mental Test of Visual Motor Integration, the Illinois Test of Psycholinguistic Abilities, the Wepman Auditory Discrimination Test, the Weschler Scales of Intelligence for Children–Revised, and standardized achievement tests (Adelman & Taylor, 1983).

Advocates of the perceptual-motor approach such as Kephart, Frostig, Barsch, and Cratty have developed perceptual-motor training programs designed to remediate diagnosed deficiencies. The methods used in these programs are generally developmental in nature and stress the importance of early motor learning and visual spatial development in children. While there may be different rationales for these programs, the basic orientation and training activities are similar, and provide suggestions about how to use movement, exercises, games, and other activities to improve children's learning (Myers & Hammill, 1969).

A controversial remedial program was proposed by Doman and Delacato (Delacato, 1966) based on their view of neurological organization. They proposed a patterning approach for neural retraining in which the child is passively moved through early stages of movement patterns or is taught the acceptable pattern to use in exercises. There are many critics of this approach (Gearheart, 1973), although milder versions of some of the activities have been proposed by others. For example, Ayres (1973) also emphasized neural retraining, and stated that intersensory integration of visual, tactile, and kinesthetic perceptions is essential for reading. The methods she proposed are designed to integrate sensory systems by controlling sensory input through vestibular and somatosensory systems.

Cruickshank (Cruickshank, Bentzen, Ratzeburg, & Tannhauser, 1961) focused his suggestions for remedial programs on children who had difficulties with figure-ground perception, distractibility, and hyperactivity. He provided activities and methods that reduced environmental stimuli, provided multisensory experiences, heightened the value of the important stimuli, and, in general, provided highly structured educational activities.

Another perceptual remediation approach is based on work by Kirk and Kirk (1971) on psycholinguistic learning disabilities. This work led to the development and use of the Illinois Test of Psycholinguistic Abilities (ITPA). The test is based on Osgood's model of communication, and consists of 12 subtests that evaluate abilities in the major channels of communication: visual-motor and auditory-vocal. In addition, the ITPA also examines three types of psycholinguistic processes: receptive, organizing, and expressive; and two levels of organization: representational and automatic (Gearheart, 1973). The results of this test provide a psycholinguistic age and a profile of abilities for the child being diagnosed. It is the profile of abilities that identifies the child's strengths and weaknesses for remedial program planning. Several books have been published that provide specific remedial materials, activities, and suggestions for teaching; *Aids to Psycholinguistic Teaching* (Bush & Giles, 1969) and *Psycholinguistic Learning Disabilities: Diagnosis and Remediation* (Kirk & Kirk, 1971) are both sources for remedial programs.

Johnson and Myklebust (1967) were interested in the diagnosis and remediation of auditory disorders. They proposed a theory of sequential levels of language acquisition and developed specific remedial procedures designed to strengthen deficit areas and to teach through the intact modalities.

Several others proposed remedial programs that emphasized multisensory approaches to the teaching of reading and other academic subjects. Orton (1937) viewed reading problems as a result of mixed cerebral dominance, and advocated right-handed and right-sided practice to establish dominance. His remedial approach to reading was an individually paced phonics approach supplemented with kinesthetic aids. Fernald (1943) focused on the remediation of basic academic skills by stressing that learning could be improved by enhancing the vividness of stimuli. She advocated multisensory methods as well as meaningful content and high-interest activities. Similar techniques were also developed by Gillingham and Stillman (1966), who stressed language development through visual, auditory, and kinesthetic stimulation in the dominant hemisphere. Their activities emphasized phonics, multisensory techniques, repetition, and drill.

There are many other perceptual remediation programs. Those that have been described are representative of the majority of approaches that have been developed to try to remediate the perceptual problems of learning-disabled and brain-injured children.

REFERENCES

Adelman, H., & Taylor, L. (1983). *Learning disabilities in perspective.* Glenview, IL: Scott, Foresman.

Ayres, J. (1973). *Sensory integration and learning disorders.* Los Angeles: Western Psychological Services.

Bush, W., & Giles, M. (1969). *Aids to psycholinguistic teaching.* Columbus, OH: Merrill.

Cruickshank, W., Bentzen, F., Ratzeburg, F., & Tannhauser, M. (1961). *A teaching method for brain-injured and hyperactive children.* Syracuse, NY: Syracuse University Press.

Delacato, C. (1966). *Neurological organization and reading.* Springfield, IL: Thomas.

Fernald, G. (1943). *Remedial techniques in basic school subjects.* New York: McGraw-Hill.

Gearheart, B. (1973). *Learning disabilities—educational strategies.* St. Louis: Mosby.

Gillingham, A., & Stillman, B. (1966). *Remedial training for children with specific disability in reading, spelling, and penmanship* (7th ed.). Cambridge, Mass: Educators Publishing Service.

Johnson, D., & Myklebust, H. (1967). *Learning disabilities: Educational principles and practices.* New York: Grune & Stratton.

Kirk, S., & Kirk, W. (1971). *Psycholinguistic learning disabilities: Diagnosis and remediation.* Urbana IL: University of Illinois Press.

Mercer, C. (1979). *Children and adults with learning disabilities.* Columbus, OH: Merrill.

Myers, P., & Hammill, D. (1969). *Methods for learning disorders.* New York: Wiley.

Orton, S. (1937). *Reading, writing, and speech problems of children.* New York: Norton.

Strauss, A., & Lehtinen, L. (1947). *Psychopathology and education of the brain-injured child.* New York: Grune & Stratton.

Strauss, A., & Werner, H. (1942). Disorders of conceptual thinking in the brain-injured child. *Journal of Nervous Mental Diseases, 96,* 153–172.

Vellutino, F. (1978). Toward an understanding of dyslexia: Psychological factors in specific reading disability. In A. Benton & D. Pearl (Eds.), *Dyslexia* (pp. 63–111). New York: Oxford University Press.

DEBORAH C. MAY
*State University of New York,
Albany*

PATTERNING
PERCEPTUAL DEFICIT HYPOTHESIS
PERCEPTUAL TRAINING
PSYCHOLINGUISTICS

PERCEPTUAL SPAN

Perceptual span is a term encountered in the study of reading. It refers principally to the amount of visual information useful to a reader during a single fixation. Readers are able to apprehend only a limited amount of information during the fixation of the eye's journey across a line of print; however, it has been long noted that skilled readers are also able to recognize words that are a short distance to the right and to the left of the fixation (Woodworth, 1938). This perceptual span (or span of apprehension) is useful to the skilled reader, increasing speed and comprehension of reading. Specifying the nature and extent of this span and its relationship to disorders of reading has been a controversial process (Pirrozzolo, 1979). Pirrozzolo (1979) has described the four major methods of measuring perceptual span, another controversial topic.

The first primary method described by Pirrozzolo is the technique of dividing the number of eye movement fixations into the number of characters appearing on a line or in a passage of text. A second technique for assessing perceptual span requires the tachistoscopic exposure of letters and words and a verbal report on the material seen during these brief exposures. A third method involves visual fixation at a measured point, identification of visible stimuli that are then displaced, and gathering of new data. The fourth method of measurement requires the provision of a fixed span (or window) of information that can be manipulated by the experimenter to determine the reader's perceptual span. Sophisticated computer presentations have been devised for the last method.

Over the last century, researchers and clinicians have hypothesized that disabled readers have a less efficient or possibly a dysfunctional application of their perceptual span. Frank and Levinson (1976) have recently suggested, as one example, that disabled readers have a lower blurring speed than nondisabled readers. This is believed to be due to a cerebellar-vestibular dysfunction that adversely affects the reading process by reducing clear vision and making correct orientation more difficult.

There is sizable evidence (overwhelming in Pirrozzolo's view) from studies of visual function in reading disabilities to indicate that visual-perceptual defects are unrelated to reading disabilities. Problems in occulomotor scanning, sensory and perceptual skills, and perceptual span are clearly not causative in the vast majority of cases of reading disorders, but these areas may appear abnormal as a result of the reading disability.

REFERENCES

Frank, J., & Levinson, F. (1976). C-V dysfunction in dysmetric dyslexia. *Academic Therapy, 12*, 251–283.

Pirrozzolo, F. J. (1979). *The neuropsychology of developmental reading disorders*. New York: Praeger.

Woodworth, R. S. (1938). *Experimental psychology*. New York: Holt.

CECIL R. REYNOLDS
Texas A&M University

PERCEPTUAL DEVELOPMENTS, LAG IN
PERCEPTUAL TRAINING
READING DISORDERS
SENSORY-INTEGRATIVE THERAPY
VISUAL PERCEPTION AND DISCRIMINATION
VISUAL TRAINING

PERCEPTUAL TRAINING

Since many theorists believe that perception is a learned skill, it is assumed that teaching or training can have an effect on a child's perceptual skills (Lerner, 1971). Once perceptual abilities have been assessed, there are various teaching procedures and programs that can be used to improve perceptual skills.

Some of the most frequently used educational programs for children with learning disabilities have focused on perceptual training activities. While many of these perceptual training programs have emphasized visual or visual-motor training, there are also perceptual training activities in the areas of auditory perception, haptic and kinesthetic perception, and social perception. In spite of all the available material on these perceptual training programs, many researchers have questioned their effectiveness as a way to improve school learning (Hallahan & Cruickshank, 1973; Hammill & Larsen, 1974).

Since similar perceptual training activities have been used in many different programs, it is often unclear who first used them (Hallahan & Kauffman, 1976). However, most of these training activities are based on theories that began with the work of Werner and Strauss (1939). The following descriptions of some of these perceptual training programs provide an overview of these theories and activities.

Newell Kephart worked closely with Werner and Strauss and derived many of his educational techniques from them. This perceptual-motor theory of learning disabilities stresses that perceptual-motor development helps the child establish a solid concept of his or her environment and that perceptual data only become meaningful when they are connected with previously learned motor information (in Kephart's terms, when a perceptual motor match occurs). Children with learning problems are viewed as having inadequate perceptual-motor development, manifested by motor, perceptual, and cognitive disorganization. Kephart argues that these children are unable to benefit from standard school curricula (Lerner, 1971).

The book *The Slow Learner in the Classroom* (Kephart, 1971) presented Kephart's perceptual-motor training program, which included activities involving chalkboard training, sensory-motor training, ocular-motor training, and form-perception training. The chalkboard training activities were recommended for promoting directionality, crossing the midline, orientation, tracing, copying, and eye-hand coordination. The activities presented in the sensory-motor training portion of the program were designed to help the child coordinate the movements of his or her body. Balance beams, balance boards, "angels in the snow" exercises, and trampolines are used to develop total body coordination in the gross motor systems. Ocular-motor training was proposed to help children gain control over their eye movements; it includes activities for ocular pursuit in which the child follows objects visually. Because of Kephart's belief that motor activities influence visual development, the activities in the form-perception training include assembling puzzles, constructing designs from matchsticks, and putting pegs in pegboards (Hallahan & Kauffman, 1976).

Getman (1965) also proposed a model that attempts to illustrate the sequences of children's development of motor- and visual-perceptual skills. This model, called the visuomotor complex, is applied in a manual of training activities, *The Physiology of Readiness: An Action Program for the Development of Perception in Children* (Getman, Kane, Halgren & McKee, 1964). The program described in this model has activities in the following six areas: general coordination, balance, eye-hand coordination, eye movements, form perception, and visual memory. The exercises in the general coordination section deal mainly with movements of the head, arms, and legs; they are designed to provide children with practice in total body movement. A balance beam is used for most of the activities in the balance section; the activities emphasize the use of visual perception for the acquisition of better balance.

The eye-hand coordination program involves the children in chalkboard exercises that are designed to increase their ability to coordinate eyes and hands. Activities in the eye-movement program are aimed at increasing children's ability to move their eyes rapidly and accurately from one object to another, while the form-perception program has children using templates to trace shapes on the chalkboard and on paper, eventually leading to the drawing of the figures without templates. The final part of the program, the visual-memory activities, uses a tachistoscope or slide projector to flash slides of figures for children to name, trace in the air, circle, trace on worksheets, or draw. The purpose is to develop children's visual imagery skill by showing more complex figures for shorter periods of time as the children become more proficient.

Frostig and Horne (1964) have a visual-perception training program designed for remediation or readiness training. The Frostig Program for the Development of Visual Perception has activities in the areas of eye-motor coordination, figure ground, perceptual constancy, position in space, and spatial relations. Each of these areas has worksheets for the teacher to use with the children. The eye-hand exercises focus on coordinating eye and hand movements by having the children draw lines between boundaries. The figure-ground exercises have the children find and trace figures embedded within other lines and figures. Perceptual generalization is emphasized in the perceptual constancy exercises; the children are trained to recognize that objects remain the same even if presented in different forms, colors, sizes, or contexts. The position in space exercises have the children place themselves in various positions (e.g., over or under) in relation to objects in the room; worksheets are also provided that require the children to discriminate objects in various positions. Finally, the spatial-relations exercises have the children do worksheets to observe spatial relationships.

Barsch's movigenic theory proposes that difficulties in learning are related to the learner's inefficient interaction with space. The training program that evolved from this theory has a series of activities that are a planned developmental motor program (Barsch, 1965). There are three main components to this curriculum: postural-transport orientations, which include muscular strength, dynamic balance, body awareness, spatial awareness, and temporal awareness; percepto-cognitive modes of gustatory, olfactory, tactual, kinesthetic, auditory, and visual activities;

and degrees of freedom of bilaterality, rhythm, flexibility, and motor planning. Chapters on each of these aspects of the program are included in the curriculum along with exercises to use with learning-disabled children.

Several books and training manuals that focused on training motor skills were written and developed by Cratty (1973). These materials present exercises similar to those found in physical education programs for the purpose of enhancing motor skills and improving a child's cognitive abilities.

REFERENCES

Barsch, R. (1965). *A movigenic curriculum* (Bulletin No. 25). Madison, WI: Department of Instruction, Bureau for the Handicapped.

Cratty, B. (1973). *Teaching motor skills.* Englewood Cliffs, NJ: Prentice-Hall.

Frostig, M., & Horne, D. (1964). *The Frostig program for the development of visual perception.* Chicago: Follett.

Getman, G. (1985). The visuomotor complex in the acquisition of learning skills. In J. Hellmuth (Ed.), *Learning disorders,* (Vol. 1). Seattle, WA: Special Child.

Getman, G., Kane, E., Halgren, M. & McKee, G. (1964). The physiology of readiness: An action program for the development of perception in children. Minneapolis: Programs to Accelerate School Success.

Hallahan, D., & Cruickshank, W. (1973). *Psychoeducational foundations of learning disabilities.* Englewood Cliffs, NJ: Prentice-Hall.

Hallahan, D., & Kauffman, J. (1976). *Introduction to learning disabilities.* Englewood Cliffs, NJ: Prentice-Hall.

Hammill, D., & Larsen, S. (1974). The relationship of selected auditory perceptual skills and reading ability. *Journal of Learning Disabilities, 7,* 429–436.

Kephart, N. (1971). *The slow learner in the classroom* (2nd ed.). Columbus, OH: Merrill.

Lerner, J. (1971). *Children with learning disabilities.* Boston: Houghton Mifflin.

Werner, H., & Strauss, A. (1939). Types of visuo-motor activity and their relation to low and high performance ages. *Proceedings of the American Association of Mental Deficiency, 44,* 163–168.

DEBORAH C. MAY
State University of New York,
Albany

MOVIGENICS
PERCEPTUAL REMEDIATION

PEREIRE, JACOB R. (1715–1780)

Jacob R. Pereire, an early educator of the deaf, was the originator of lip reading and the creator of the first manual alphabet for the deaf that required the use of only one hand. Pereire also demonstrated that speech can be understood by using the tactile sense to perceive the vibrations and muscular movements produced by the voice mechanism.

Pereire conducted schools for the deaf in Paris and Bordeaux, and his methods were further developed by de l'Epée and Sicard at the National Institution for Deaf-Mutes in Paris. In recognition of his work, Pereire received an official commendation of the Parisian Academy of Science, was made a member of the Royal Society of London, and was awarded a pension by King Louis XV.

REFERENCE

Lane, H. (1984). *When the mind hears.* New York: Random House.

PAUL IRVINE
Katonah, New York

PERFORMANCE INSTABILITY

Performance instability refers to inconsistent functioning on a given task across time. As a characteristic of handicapped children, performance instability often is confused with a second type of variability referred to by O'Donnell (1980) as intraindividual discrepancy. Whereas performance instability denotes changeability within a single domain across time, intraindividual discrepancy refers to variability across different performance areas within a similar time frame.

Historically, performance instability has been viewed as a distinctive characteristic of learning-disabled children. Strauss and Lehtinen (1947) reported dramatically unstable performance among their pupils. Similarly, Ebersole, Kephart, and Ebersole (1968) indicated that learning-disabled children inconsistently retained previously learned materials. More recently, Swanson (1982) typified the learning-disabled population as performing in a fragmented, inconsistent manner. In addition, performance instability is included explicitly and implicitly in well-known classification schemes for identifying learning-disabled students, such as the Strauss syndrome (Stevens & Birch, 1957), Clements' symptoms of minimal brain dysfunction (Clements, 1966) and attention deficit disorders (American Psychiatric Association, 1980). Moreover, learning disabilities teachers appear to agree on the importance of performance instability as a descriptor of their students (Aviezer & Simpson, 1980).

Nevertheless, the validity and usefulness of performance instability as a salient learning disabilities characteristic is weakened by at least two facts. First, work in two areas that are conceptually related to performance instability—attention disorders and impulsivity—demonstrates that learning-disabled children do not behave distinctively when compared with pupils with different la-

bels of exceptionality. Second, research exploring performance instability among normal and mildly handicapped learning-disabled and behavior-disordered students indicates that the three groups are essentially comparable in the extent to which they manifest performance instability on academic tasks (Fuchs, Fuchs, & Deno, 1985; Fuchs, Fuchs, Tindal, & Deno, 1986).

REFERENCES

American Psychiatric Association. (1980). *Diagnostic and statistical manual of mental disorders* (3rd ed.). Washington, DC: Author.

Aviezer, Y., & Simpson, S. (1980). Variability and instability in perceptual and reading functions of brain injured children. *Journal of Learning Disabilities, 13,* 41–47.

Clements, S. D. (1966). *Minimal brain dysfunction in children: Terminology and identification* (NINDS Monograph No. 3, U.S. Public Health Service Publication No. 1415). Washington, DC: U.S. Government Printing Office.

Ebersole, M., Kephart, N. C., & Ebersole, J. B.. (1968). *Steps to achievement for the slow learner.* Columbus, OH: Merrill.

Fuchs, D., Fuchs, L. S., & Deno, S. L. (1985). Performance instability: An identifying characteristic of learning disabled children? *Learning Disability Quarterly, 8,* 19–26.

Fuchs, D., Fuchs, L. S., Tindal, G., & Deno, S. L. (1986). Performance instability of learning disabled, emotionally handicapped, and nonhandicapped children. *Learning Disability Quarterly, 9,* 84–88.

O'Donnell, L. G. (1980). Intra-individual discrepancy in diagnosing specific learning disabilities. *Learning Disability Quarterly, 3,* 10–18.

Stevens, G. D., & Birch, J. W. (1957). A proposal for clarification of the terminology used to describe brain-injured children. *Exceptional Children, 23,* 346–349.

Strauss, A., & Lehtinen, L. (1947). *Psychopathology and education of the brain-injured child.* New York: Grune & Stratton.

Swanson, H. S. (1982). In the beginning was a strategy: Or was it a constraint? *Topics in Learning & Learning Disabilities, 2,* x–xiv.

DOUGLAS FUCHS
LYNN S. FUCHS
Peabody College, Vanderbilt University

ATTENTION DEFICIT DISORDER
IMPULSE CONTROL

PERINATAL FACTORS IN HANDICAPPING CONDITIONS

A number of perinatal factors increase the risk of handicapping conditions in the newborn. Social factors include lack of prenatal care, maternal age, inadequate maternal nutrition, use of alcohol, tobacco, or drugs, stress, work, and fatigue. Maternal disease factors such as hypertension, diabetes, and heart disease may also affect fetal condition at birth. However, alterations in the birth process itself may contribute to the development of fetal handicapping conditions. Preterm labor, postterm labor, premature rupture of membranes, multiple births, antepartum hemorrhage, breech presentations, Caesarean sections, and forceps deliveries all add to the risk of unfavorable fetal outcomes and handicapping conditions (Avery & Taeusch, 1984).

The purpose of prenatal care is to provide ongoing education and evaluation during pregnancy. Serial evaluations permit the physician or midwife to uncover actual or potential morbid states and institute timely interventions with the potential for improved fetal outcome. Early detection of urinary tract infections, hypertension, heart murmurs, protein or sugar in the urine, too little or too rapid uterine growth, or swelling of extremities provides the health-care team with the opportunity to arrest the development of the more serious maternal cardiac or renal disease, hypertension, premature labor, or complications of unexpected multiple births. Therefore, lack of good prenatal care can and often is associated with poor fetal and/or maternal outcome (Harrison, Golbus, & Filly, 1984).

Maternal age represents a nonspecific influence on fetal outcome at birth. Adolescent women 15 years and younger have increased incidences of newborns with neurologic disorders and low birth weights. Women 40 years and older are at increased risk for stillborns or infants with chromosomal abnormalities (Avery & Taeusch, 1984).

Inadequate maternal nutrition and insufficient maternal weight gain of less than 14 pounds have been associated with low infant birth weight. The heavy use of alcohol during pregnancy increases the newborn's risk for growth retardation, microencephaly, cardiac anomalies, and renal anomalies. Tobacco use during pregnancy increases the newborn's risk for low birth weight, prematurity, and even stillbirth. Prescribed, over-the-counter, or recreational drugs may have an adverse effect on the neonate. The probability of a drug causing harm is dependent on the drug itself, the dose, route of administration, stage of gestation, and the genetic makeup of the mother and fetus. Drugs increase the risk of low birth weight, chromosomal abnormalities, organ anomalies, and even fetal death. Further, drugs can create problems with resuscitation and potential withdrawal phenomenon in the newborn (Hobel, 1985).

Stress, work, and fatigue have been associated with an increased risk for poor fetal outcome. The association between stress, work, fatigue, and pregnancy complications is not clear, but it is related to growth retardation and/or low birth weight of the neonate (Creasy, 1984).

Maternal disease factors associated with poor fetal outcome and handicapping conditions include hypertension, diabetes, and heart disease. Hypertension is the most frequently identified maternal problem associated with growth retardation. Hypertension is also associated with preterm labor, low birth weight, cerebral palsy, mental retardation, and fetal death (Avery & Taeusch, 1984).

Poorly controlled maternal diabetes with associated high blood sugars is related to poor fetal outcome. The risk for growth retardation, congenital defects, and brain damage is increased by the complications of diabetes. Maternal heart disease with associated reduced cardiac output is also associated with the increased risk of prematurity and low birth weight. (Hobel, 1985).

Prematurity with its complications is associated with many handicapping conditions. Postterm pregnancy refers to pregnancy lasting longer than 42 weeks. Postterm pregnancy is associated with an increased risk for growth retardation, distress, and even death of the neonate (Hobel, 1985).

The premature rupture of membranes is associated with an increased risk of premature birth and an increased risk for neonatal infection (Oxorn, 1986). Multiple births, antepartum hemorrhage, breech presentation, Caesarean section, and forcep deliveries also increase the risk of handicapping conditions to the newborn. These alterations in the birth process increase the risk for neonatal mortality, central nervous system hemorrhage, asphyxia, and long-term neurologic disability (Avery & Taeusch, 1984).

REFERENCES

Avery, M. E., & Taeusch, H. W. (Eds.). (1984). *Schaffer's diseases of the newborn* (5th ed.). Philadelphia: Saunders.

Creasy, R. K. (1984). Preterm labor and delivery. In R. K. Creasy, & R. Resnik (Eds.), *Maternal-fetal medicine, principles and practice* (pp. 415–443). Philadelphia: Saunders.

Harrison, M. R., Golbus, M. S., & Filly, R. A. (1984). *The unborn patient, prenatal diagnosis and treatment.* Orlando, FL: Grune & Stratton.

Hobel, C. J. (1985). Factors during pregnancy that influence brain development. In J. M. Freeman (Ed.), *Prenatal and perinatal factors associated with brain disorders* (NIH Publication No. 85-1149, pp. 197–236). Bethesda, MD: U.S. Department of Health and Human Services.

Oxorn, H. (1986). *Human labor and birth* (5th ed.). Norwalk, CT: Appleton-Century-Crofts.

ELIZABETH R. BAUERSCHMIDT
University of North Carolina, Wilmington

MICHAEL BAUERSCHMIDT
Brunswick Hospital, Wilmington, North Carolina

ETIOLOGY
NEONATAL BEHAVIOR ASSESSMENT SCALES
PREMATURITY/PRETERM

PERKINS-BINET TESTS OF INTELLIGENCE FOR THE BLIND

The Perkins-Binet Tests of Intelligence for the Blind (Davis, 1980) were designed to assess the intellectual functioning (verbal and performance) of visually handicapped children. Shortly after their appearance it became evident that there were a number of significant flaws in the tests. Reviewers (e.g., Genshaft & Ward, 1982) found the test manual lacking in technical information. Instructions for administering were vague, and in some instances, incomplete. The tests were lengthy and difficult to administer, and scoring criteria were unclear. There were also concerns about psychometric adequacy and the lack of reliability and validity data (Gutterman, Ward, & Genshaft, 1985). The tests have since been withdrawn from the market.

REFERENCES

Davis, C. J. (1980). *The Perkins-Binet Tests of Intelligence for the Blind.* Watertown, MA: Perkins School for the Blind.

Genshaft, J., & Ward, M. (1982). A review of the Perkins-Binet Tests for the Blind with suggestions for administration. *School Psychology Review, 11*(3), 338–341.

Gutterman, J. E., Ward, M., & Genshaft, J. (1985). Correlations of scores of low vision children on the Perkins-Binet Tests of Intelligence for the Blind, the WISCR-R and the WRAT. *Journal of Visual Impairment & Blindness, 79,* 55–58.

ROBERT G. BRUBAKER
Eastern Kentucky University

BLIND
VISUALLY IMPAIRED

PERKINS SCHOOL FOR THE BLIND

The Perkins School for the Blind was the first private residential school for the blind chartered in the United States. It was founded by Samuel Gridley Howe in 1832 to serve two blind students and was originally called the New England Asylum for the Blind. At that time asylum was all that even the most fortunate blind person could expect out of life. However, Howe, a strong believer in education, changed the name to the New England Institution for the Education of the Blind. Today, it is known as the Perkins School for the Blind, after Thomas Perkins, a prominent Boston merchant and one of the school's early benefactors. Probably one of its most well-known students was Helen Keller, who attended Perkins from 1887–1892.

The Perkins programs are comprehensive and serve a wide variety of blind, visually impaired, deaf-blind, and multiimpaired children, teenagers, and adults. The pro-grams include preschool services, ages 0–5; primary and intermediate services, ages 6–15; secondary services, ages 15–22; deaf-blind program, ages 5–22; severely impaired program, ages 16–22; adult services, ages 18 and up; and community residence and independent living services, ages 18 and up. The philosophy is to prepare students and clients to meet everyday life to the best of their abilities emotionally, socially, physically, vocationally, and avocationally (Annual Report, 1984).

Perkins also provides other services besides direct care, including the Samuel P. Hayes Research Library, which collects print material about the nonmedical aspects of blindness and deaf-blindness. In addition, it houses a museum on the history of blind and deaf-blind and a historic collection of embossed books for the blind. The Howe Press is located at Perkins. It is the developer and manufacturer of the Perkins Brailler, used throughout the world. The Howe Press also distributes children's books, brailling accessories, and other aids and materials for blind and low-vision students.

REFERENCE

Perkins School for the Blind Annual Report. (1984). Watertown, MA: Author.

ROSANNE K. SILBERMAN
*Hunter College, City University
of New York*

BLIND
VISUALLY IMPAIRED

PERSEVERATION

Perseveration is used in special education to describe behavior that is continued by a child beyond the normal end point of the behavior and that is accompanied by difficulty in changing tasks. Perseveration is considered to be a soft neurologically sign and is believed to be most common among learning-disabled and brain-injured children. Lerner (1971) discusses perseverative behavior as one of the four major behavioral characteristics of learning-disabled children.

In formal assessment, perseveration is often noted on such tasks as the Bender-Gestalt, in which the child is required to reproduce a series of nine drawings. Figures one, two, and six of this series require lines or rows of circles, dots, and repeating curves. Once started on the task of making dots, circles, or repeating curves, some children have great difficulty in stopping and subsequently distort their drawings greatly. Such children seem to get carried away by a specific activity, repeating it over and over, unable to stop. Perseveration is most commonly seen in motor tasks, but it can also be present in verbal behavior and even in thought patterns.

On intelligence tests such as the Wechsler Intelligence Scale for Children-Revised, children may display verbal or ideational perseveration. Although not formally scored as perseveration, this behavior lowers children's intelligence test scores significantly. On tasks such as telling how two everyday, common objects are alike (the similarities subtest of the WISC-R), some children will give the same fundamental answer to each pair of items; they seem unable to alter their mental set once established. Anxiety may also promote perseverative behavior.

Levine, Brooks, and Shonkoff (1980) have presented an interesting, useful view of perseveration and have provided some excellent clinical examples. They note that transitional events, or even minor changes in routine, constitute common impediments to many children with learning disorders, many of whom are perseverative. At the same time, some of these children are impersistent at academic or other tasks, a finding that seems paradoxical on the surface. However, as Levine, Brooks, and Shonkoff (1980) note, there may be a fine line between impersistence and perseveration, and the two traits coexist in some children.

Difficulties with adaptability may be a component of a general biological predisposition to inefficient attentional strategies. Children who cannot shift tasks, activities, or mental sets may be reflecting anxiety linked to issues of loss or fear of failure, or may be demonstrating neurological abnormalities associated with frontal lobe or possibly reticular function. Koppitz (1963, 1975) has reviewed a number of studies in which children with brain damage demonstrate higher levels of perseverative behavior than do normal children of the same age. Perseveration is one of the best indicators of neurological impairment on the Bender-Gestalt Test (Koppitz, 1963, 1975) and is one of the least subjective scoring categories.

The following clinical illustrations from Levine, Brooks, and Shonkoff (1979) are useful in understanding the different features of perseveration as well as its relationship to impersistence.

1. A child may find the daily progression of routines difficult to manage. Getting up in the morning, dressing, eating breakfast, and preparing for school may present problems. The youngster may linger over each activity. The same pattern may appear when the youngster returns from school; there may be problems initiating routines, coming in from play, disengaging from the television set, and preparing for sleep. Parental efforts to induce a shift of activities may result in severe temper tantrums and unbridled anger.

2. A child may persist at an activity, wishing to sustain it beyond a reasonable period. Such a youngster has difficulty in suspending a project for continuation. Sometimes the behavior reflects a child's wish to pursue some enterprise that is likely to yield success rather than to move on to a riskier endeavor that might culminate in failure; such tenacity may be an avoidance response. At other times perseveration may be a consequence of cognitive inertia with regard to shifting sets. For example, some children with memory deficits or difficulties in establishing object constancy may experience change as overwhelming.

3. A child may resist any changes in daily routine. His or her behavior may deteriorate at the prospect of an unexpected visit to a relative. The youngster may be upset by the arrival of cousins for an overnight visit or by having to give up his or her own bed for the night. Some children crave consistency, or a sameness that helps provide order in a world that seems chaotic. They do not appreciate surprises and instead insist on knowing exactly what is going to happen each day (pp. 240–241).

Painting (1979) has commented, appropriately, that perseveration may occur because a particular response is so gratifying to a child that it is repeated primarily for the pleasure involved. A child with learning problems who gets a test item correct or who has mastered a particular activity may perseverate in the behavior because it promotes feelings of success and aids the child's self-esteem.

Perseveration may occur for a variety of reasons. Good diagnosis must go beyond designation of the presence of perseveration to explaining why the child perseverates. Treatment choices are likely to be impacted significantly by etiology in the case of perseverative behavior.

REFERENCES

Lerner, J. (1971). *Children with learning disabilities*. Boston: Houghton Mifflin.

Levine, M. D., Brooks, R., & Shonkoff, J. P. (1980). *A pediatric approach to learning disorders*. New York: Wiley.

Koppitz, E. M. (1963). *The Bender Gestalt Test for Young Children*. New York: Grune & Stratton.

Koppitz, E. M. (1975). *The Bender Gestalt Test for Young Children. Vol. II. Research and application, 1963–1973*. New York: Grune & Stratton.

Painting, D. H. (1979). Cognitive assessment of children with SLD. In W. Adamson & K. Adamson (Eds.), *A handbook for specific learning disabilities*. New York: Halsted.

CECIL R. REYNOLDS
Texas A&M University

BENDER-GESTALT TEST

PERSONALITY ASSESSMENT

Personality assessment, defined as the description and measurement of individual characteristics, has traditionally been divided into four distinct types: interview, objective, projective, and behavioral. Clinicians frequently use one or more of these assessment methods as an integral component of psychological evaluations.

The interview, which has historical precedence over other methods, was formerly seen as unreliable and subjective. Interviewees are often unwilling to reveal negative things about themselves, and may present different information depending on the style and personal characteristics of the interviewer. On the positive side, an interview can be one of the most direct methods of obtaining information. Structured instruments such as the Schedule for Affective Disorders and Schizophrenia (SADS; Endicott & Spitzer, 1978) and the Diagnostic Interview Schedule (DIS; Robins, Helzer, Craughan & Ratcliff, 1981) have demonstrated empirical validity and adequate reliability and thus reflect a resurgence of the interview method.

Objective personality assessment, which includes questionnaires such as self-report measures and inventories, is typically the most standardized and structured method of assessing personality. Questionnaires can be scored quickly and used for group administrations; however, they are prone to poor validity when people do not give truthful answers. The most common objective instrument is the Minnesota Multiphasic Personality Inventory (MMPI; Hathaway and McKinley, 1943), which contains 10 clinical scales used in identifying specific psychological disorders. Other frequently used instruments include Gough's California Psychological Inventory (Gough, 1957), the Sixteen Personality Factor Questionnaire (16PF; Cattell & Stice, 1957), and the Guilford-Zimmerman Temperament Survey (Guilford & Zimmerman, 1949).

Projective techniques, which are less standardized, require good clinical judgment in interpretation. They include the Rorschach Test (Rorschach, 1942), the Thematic Apperception Test (TAT; McClelland, Atkinson, Clark, & Lowell, 1953), figure drawings, word association, and sentence completion tests. The Rorschach has enjoyed the most widespread use in clinical settings. The rationale behind the test is that unconscious desires, coping styles, and other personality features are projected through interpretation of the inkblots. As there are no right or wrong answers, it is believed that projective techniques are better able to assess an individual's actual personality characteristics. Critics of these techniques argue that interpretation is subjective and highly dependent on the skills of the interpreter. Exner (1974) has developed a structured, comprehensive scoring system for the Rorschach in an attempt to increase the scientific validity of this measure.

Behavioral assessment examines present behavior, with the expectation that such observation aids in the prediction of future actions. Methods include naturalistic observation, analogue observation, self-monitoring, and participant observation.

Although personality assessment has been a widely used and valuable clinical tool, the validity has been problematic. Objective criteria for diagnosis has been provided by the DSM-III (the *Diagnostic and Statistical manual of Mental Disorders*), but prediction of DSM-III diagnosis via personality assessment is still a controversial issue. Ongoing research is therefore aimed at increasing predictive validity and reliability and the DSM-III diagnostic compatibility with personality assessment.

REFERENCES

Cattell, R. B., & Stice, G. F. (1957). *Handbook for the Sixteen Personality Factor Questionnaire*. Champaign, IL: Institute for Personality and Ability Testing.

Edwards, A. L. (1959). *Edwards personal preference schedule*. New York: Psychological Corporation.

Endicott, J., & Spitzer, R. L. (1978). A diagnostic interview: The schedule for affective disorders and schizophrenia. *Archives of General Psychiatry, 35*, 837–844.

Exner, J. E. (1974). *The Rorschach: A comprehensive system* (Vol. I). New York: Wiley.

Gough, H. G. (1957). *California Psychological Inventory: Manual*. Palo Alto, CA: Consulting Psychologists Press.

Guilford, J. P., & Zimmerman, W. S. (1949). *The Guilford Zimmerman Temperament Survey: Manual of instructions and interpretations*. Beverly Hills, CA: Sheridan Supply.

Hathaway, S. R., & McKinley, J. C. (1943). *MMPI manual*. New York: Psychological Corporation.

McClelland, D. C., Atkinson, J. W., Clark, R. A., & Lowell, E. I. (1953). *The achievement motive*. New York: Appleton-Century-Crofts.

Robins, L. N., Helzer, J. E., Croughan, J., & Ratcliff, K. S. (1981). The NIMH diagnostic interview schedule: Its history, characteristics, and validity. *Archives of General Psychiatry, 38*, 381–389.

Rorschach, H. (1942). *Psychodiagnostics*. Berne, Switzerland: Huber.

CONSTANCE Y. CELAYA
FRANCES F. WORCHEL
Texas A&M University

DIAGNOSTIC AND STATISTICAL MANUAL OF NEURAL DISORDERS (DSM III)
MENTAL ILLNESS
MENTAL STATUS

PERSONALITY INVENTORY FOR CHILDREN (PIC)

The Personality Inventory for Children (PIC) was developed over approximately a 20-year period, primarily by

Robert Wirt and William Broen. With its 600 items, 33 subscales (3 validity scales, 1 general screening scale, 12 primary clinical scales, and 17 supplemental scales), point of origin, and emphasis on profiling of scores for interpretation, it is similar in many ways to the Minnesota Multiphasic Personality Inventory (MMPI). At least one reviewer has characterized the PIC as a junior MMPI (Achenbach, 1981).

The PIC originated with the efforts of Wirt and Broen to create an objective personality scale for children that could serve many of the same purposes with this population as the MMPI serves with adults and older adolescents. Primarily from an atheoretical, purely rational basis (though previous empirical work has apparently been consulted), Wirt and Broen initially wrote 550 test items, 50 for each of 11 content scales. The original scales included withdrawal, excitement, reality, distortion, aggression, somatic concern, anxiety, social skills, family relations, physical development, intellectual development, and asocial behavior. As with the items, the various scales of the PIC were developed largely from a logical, rational basis and retained on a purely empirical basis with no attention to theories of personality (though some individual scales have an implicit theoretical basis, many of a Freudian or psychoanalytic nature).

As opposed to virtually all other objective personality scales, the PIC is not a self-report inventory. Rather, it is completed by an informant, recommended strongly by the authors to be the child's mother, although the father or any significant other knowledgeable of the child's behavior and preferences is acceptable. Instructions to the respondent on the administration booklet are simple, straightforward, and easy to understand. No other instructions are provided. The respondent indicates true or false in response to each of the 600 declarative test items. The scale is unquestionably too lengthy for practical application in the school, but this should not affect its use in clinics or private practice setting. School personnel may see information based on the PIC from outside referral sources, particularly when clinical child psychologists are used to evaluate emotionally disturbed children.

The PIC is normed on 2390 children ages $5\frac{1}{2}$ to $16\frac{1}{2}$ years, with about 100 boys and 100 girls at each year interval. The PIC was normed between 1958 and 1962; 81.5% of the children included were from a single school district and the majority of the remainder from a single medical clinic. Current practice dictates large, nationally stratified random samples of children for major assessment devices. At a minimum, the sample should be carefully stratified according to traditional demographic characteristics, even for a local sampling. Sampling essentially only from the Minneapolis area seems inexcusable for a scale published in the late 1970s. The sample is also outdated, being more than 25 years old. How parents perceive and respond to their children may well have changed over this lengthy period and a complete renorming is in order. At present,

normative data for the PIC are best described as inadequate despite its positive attributes (i.e., using a large sample and normal children). The PIC provides traditional T-scores (mean = 50, standard deviation = 10) for interpretive purposes. This is a typical approach to personality inventory scores and perfectly acceptable.

The PIC is a lengthy personality scale for children that is hard to understand. It has serious psychometric deficiencies with standardization, norming, and reliability and serious problems with the construct validity of the scale. As a research tool, however, it is ready for widespread but careful use in a variety of areas. As a clinical tool, it holds promise, but its widespread use in diagnosis and decision making is premature and must await, at a minimum, a complete renorming of the scale. Better interpretive scoring systems are also needed as an aid to clinicians. The present computerized scoring and interpretive system does little more than group statements checked by the respondent into coherent paragraphs, giving little new information. Though its use is growing in clinical settings, it has not been widely adopted in schools. An extensive critique of the PIC can be found in Reynolds (1985).

REFERENCES

Achenbach, T. M. (1981). A junior MMPI? *Journal of Personality*, 45, 332–333.

Reynolds, C. R. (1985). Review of Personality Inventory for Children. In J. V. Mitchell (Eds.), *Ninth mental measurements yearbook*, Lincoln: Buros Institute.

CECIL R. REYNOLDS
Texas A&M University

PERSONALITY ASSESSMENT

PERSONALITY TESTS, OBJECTIVE

An objective test of personality is one in which the subject is required to make forced choices in response to questions or statements. The scale is objectively scored using templates to organize responses according to the factors measured by the scale. In objective tests of personality, the test items are likely to be interpreted as asking or stating the same thing by most respondents. In most instances, those items are constructed in a manner that avoids ambiguity. The possible alternatives are "yes" or "no" or "true" or "false." In other instances, they may be in a multiple choice format with up to five options.

The validity of the test is established by analyzing the responses and response patterns of persons who have been clinically identified as deviant and comparing the responses to those selected by nondeviant (control) groups. The Minnesota Multiphasic Personality Inventory

(MMPI) is probably the best known and most widely regarded personality inventory of this kind. In contrast to a projective test of personality such as the Rorschach Test an objective personality test allows for psychometric manipulation and profile analysis.

Another widely used objective personality test is the California Psychological Inventory (CPI). It is a pencil and paper inventory that contains 18 scales and 480 items. These scales were developed using an empirical model in much the same way as the MMPI. Other approaches used to construct objective personality tests are through factor analysis, intuitive-theoretical or intuitive-rational models. Studies of the different methods used for establishing the validity of objective personality tests found the methods to be comparable.

The Eysenck Personality Inventory (EPI) is a two-scale test that measures introversion-extroversion and neuroticism-stability. The scale contains 57 items and takes less time to administer than many scales. It contains a lie scale as a part of its organization; however, this aspect of the scale is not viewed as being reliable.

Objective personality assessment procedures are used by clinicians and researchers interested in identifying psychological problems. The results are used to help them better understand the individual and to help them resolve problems. There is some concern that the use of the scales for excluding persons from employment or educational opportunities is inappropriate and may carry some legal liabilities. In the future, their use in clinical settings may be more applicable than for purposes of employment screening.

ROBERT A. SEDLAK
University of Wisconsin, Stout

MMPI
PERSONALITY ASSESSMENT
REVISED CHILDREN'S MANIFEST ANXIETY SCALE
RORSCHACH

PERSONNEL TRAINING IN SPECIAL EDUCATION

See SPECIAL EDUCATION, TEACHER TRAINING IN.

PESTALOZZI, JOHANN HEINRICH (1746–1827)

Johann Heinrich Pestalozzi, a Swiss educator, greatly influenced education in Europe and the United States. Believing that ideas have meaning only as related to concrete

Johann Heinrich Pestalozzi

things and that learning must therefore proceed from the concrete to the abstract, he developed a system of education through object lessons that were designed to help the child develop abstract concepts from concrete experience.

Pestalozzi operated a number of orphanages and schools, the most notable being his boarding school at Yverdon, founded in 1805. His school demonstrated concepts such as readiness, individual differences, ability grouping, and group instruction, and contributed to the inclusion in the curriculum of the practical subjects of geography, nature, art, music, and manual training. Large numbers of educators visited Yverdon and hundreds of Pestalozzian schools were established in Europe. Pestalozzi's object method was first used in the United States in the schools of Oswego, New York; the Oswego Normal School trained teachers in Pestalozzi's methods. Of his numerous publications, Pestalozzi's *How Gertrude Teaches Her Children* best sets forth his educational principles.

REFERENCES

Pestalozzi, J. H. (1978). *How Gertrude teaches her children.* New York: Gordon.

Silber, K. (1973). *Pestalozzi: The man and his work.* New York: Schocken.

PAUL IRVINE
Katonah, New York

PETS IN SPECIAL EDUCATION

Animals have long been used in classrooms throughout the world. The classic goldfish and gerbils have been used to teach basic animal facts. Teachers have also used pets to foster responsibility in their students. Animals can provide valuable classroom or instructional assistance far beyond the traditional expectations. Sustenance instruction, responsible behavior training, and abstract concepts development can be enhanced by involving special education students with animals. These animals may be provided in the classroom or they may be pets from home.

Any pet (fish, dog, cat, bird, etc.) may be used for sustenance instruction. Special education students can better learn the basic needs of animals through active participation in the pet's care. The students identify the need for food, water, shelter, and love. Instruction may include concepts such as appropriate food for different species, appropriate quantities of food and water, how climate affects the need for shelter, and how animals exhibit and respond to affection.

Teaching responsibility is a multifaceted, often difficult task. Whenever special education students have the responsibility for pets in the classroom or at home, the teacher should be attempting to develop various components of responsible behavior. Students should learn to create feeding, watering, bathing, walking, etc., schedules. In creating schedules for their pets, students may learn to develop schedules for their own lives. Caring for pets also aids in developing task commitment, as well as relationship commitment. Another facet of responsibility, self-initiation, is readily taught when students must care, without reminders from the teacher, for classroom animals.

Students may also develop observation skills through involvement with pets. Because pets are basically nonverbal, students must watch for changes in the animals' appearance or mannerisms to detect illness or injury.

Many special education students have difficulty in understanding abstract concepts such as life, death, and love. The birth or death of a classroom pet may be used to teach the rudiments and sentiments of such abstract concepts. The emotions of love, caring, and affection may be developed or more objectively understood by special education students when pets are used.

JONI J. GLEASON
University of West Florida

EQUINE THERAPY
RECREATION

PEVZNER, MARIA SEMENOVNA (1901–   )

As a physician-psychiatrist and doctor of pedagogical sciences, Maria Pevzner is known for her work on oligophrenia (mental deficiency). Her research has been concentrated in the areas of child psychopathology and clinical assessment of atypical children. She suggested classification of oligophrenics into five groups: (1) with dif-

fuse maldevelopment of the cortical hemispheres without serious neurological implications; (2) with cortical deficits and impaired perceptual abilities; (3) with various sensory, perceptual, and motor deficits; (4) with psychopathological behavior; and (5) with maldevelopment of the frontal lobes (Pevzner, 1970). Well-known publications of Pevzner are *Children Psychopaths* (1941), *Children Oligophrenics* (1960), *Developmental Assessment and Education of Oligophrenic Children* (1963), and *Children with Atypical Development* (1966).

REFERENCE

Pevzner, M. S. (1970). Etiopathogenesis and classification of oligophrenia (translated by G. Malashko). *Szkola Specjalna, 4,* 289–293.

IVAN Z. HOLOWINSKY
Rutgers University

PHENOBARBITAL

Of the many available anticonvulsant medications, phenobarbital is the least expensive, most effective, best known, and most widely used barbiturate. It is the drug of choice for tonic-clonic (grand mal) epilepsy, neonatal fits, and febrile convulsions (Maheshwari, 1981), and may be viewed as the drug of choice for childhood epilepsy except in cases of absence (petit mal) attacks (Swanson, 1979). It even may be used as an effective agent in pure petit mal epilepsy as a measure against the development of grand mal epilepsy (Livingston, Pruce, & Pauli, 1979).

All anticonvulsant medications have side effects and the extent and severity of such side effects often influence medication choice. Unlike many anticonvulsant drugs, phenobarbital has few somatic side effects; however, it appears to have more pronounced effects on mental or cognitive functions in children (National Institutes of Health, 1980). Sedation or drowsiness is the chief side effect of phenobarbital in children. This initial effect of mental slowing is most pronounced when the drug is first administered. The effect generally declines within several weeks (Livingston, Pauli, Pruce, & Kramer, 1980; Schain, 1979) and appears to be dose related (Livingston, et al., 1980; Livingston, Pruce, Pauli, & Livingston, 1979; Swanson, 1979; Wolf, 1979). Common behavioral side effects include hyperactivity, extreme irritability, and aggression (Fishman, 1979; Livingston, et al., 1980; Nelson, 1983; Wilensky, Ojemann, Temkin, Troupin, & Dodrill, 1981). Other side effects involving cognitive or higher cortical functions include impaired attention, short-term memory deficits, defects in general comprehension, dysarthria, ataxia, and, in some cases, poor language development (Levenstein, 1984).

Fortunately, the side effects do not appear to be permanent, and withdrawal or replacement with other medications often produces significant amelioration of these deficits. For example, withdrawal may lead to dramatic improvements in personality patterns and learning skills (Schain, 1979). Continuous monitoring of possible side effects and appropriate adjustment of anticonvulsant medication is therefore of the utmost importance in effective management of seizure disorders.

REFERENCES

Fishman, M. A. (1979). Febrile seizures: One treatment controversy. *Journal of Pediatrics, 94*, 177–184.

Levenstein, D. (1984). Phenobarbital side effects: Hyperactivity with speech delay. *Pediatrics, 74*, 1133.

Livingston, S., Pauli, L. L., Pruce, I., & Kramer, I. I., (1980). Phenobarbital vs. phenytoin for grand mal epilepsy. *American Family Physician, 22*, 123–127.

Livingston, S., Pruce, I., & Pauli, L. L. (1979). The medical treatment of epilepsy: Initiation of drug therapy. *Pediatrics Annals, 8*, 213–231.

Livingston, S., Pruce, I., Pauli, L. L., & Livingston, H. L. (1979). The medical treatment of epilepsy: Managing side effects of antiepileptic drugs. *Pediatrics Annals, 8*, 261–266.

Maheshwari, M. C. (1981). Choice of anticonvulsants in epilepsy. *Indian Pediatrics, 18*, 331–346.

National Institutes of Health. (1980). Febrile seizures: Long-term management of children with fever-associated seizures. *British Medical Journal, 281*, 277–279.

Nelson, K. B. (1983). The natural history of febrile seizures. *Annual Review of Medicine, 34*, 453–471.

Schain, R. J. (1979). Problems with the use of conventional anticonvulsant drugs in mentally retarded individuals. *Brain & Development, 1*, 77–82.

Swanson, P. D. (1979). Anticonvulsant therapy: Approaches to some common clinical problems. *Postgraduate Medicine, 65*, 147–154.

Wilensky, A. J., Ojemann, L. M., Temkin, N. R., Troupin, A. S., & Dodrill, C. B. (1981). Clorazepate and phenobarbital as antiepileptic drugs: A double-blind study. *Neurology, 31*, 1271–1276.

Wolf, H. S., (1979). Controversies in the treatment for febrile convulsion. *Neurology, 29*, 287–290.

CHARLES J. LONG
University of Tennessee,
Memphis
Memphis State University

ABSENCE SEIZURES
ANTICONVULSANTS
GRAND MAL SEIZURES
MEDICAL MANAGEMENT

PHENOTHIAZINES

Phenothiazine is the class of drugs that historically has been most often prescribed in the treatment of psychotic disorders. This class of medications, which provides symptomatic relief from many of the disturbing symptoms of disorders like schizophrenia; has replaced the more radical methods of symptom control (e.g., psychosurgery). In addition, the significant behavioral changes that occur when medication regimens are optimally effective allow patients to be treated in outpatient clinics rather than be chronically hospitalized. There are three major classes of phenothiazines that are relatively similar in their overall actions but different in their dose/response ratios and the overall amount of sedation produced (Bassuk & Schoonover, 1977). The subgroups include

Aliphatic
    Chlorpromazine   (Thorazine)
    Promazine   (Sparine)

Piperidine
    Thioridazine   (Mellaril)
    Piperacetazine   (Quide)
    Mesoridazine   (Serentil)

Piperazine
    Trifluoperazine   (Stelazine)
    Perphenazine   (Trilafon)
    Fluphenazine   (Prolixin)

The major criticisms of phenothiazines revolve around the exclusive, long-term use of these drugs to control observable symptoms without an attempt to deal with etiology or overall adaptiveness (Marholin & Phillips, 1976). Crane (1973) provides an additional criticism indicating that phenothiazines also have been used within long-term treatment centers to control reactions to institutionalization and enforced restrictions: i.e., punitively.

Phenothiazines produce side effects that may be grouped into four classes: involuntary muscular contractions, especially in the area of the face; motor restlessness; parkinsonlike symptoms such as rigidity, motor slowing, excess salivation, slurred speech, flat facial expression, and gait disturbance; and tardive dyskinesia, a syndrome that consists of stereotyped, repetitive involuntary movements and persists even after medication is discontinued (Bassuk & Schoonover, 1977). Side effects in children are similar to those of adults; however, parents additionally should be aware of sun sensitivity, when children are outside for extended periods of time, and learning/concentration difficulties, especially during onset of treatment (Bassuk & Schoonover, 1977).

REFERENCES

Bassuk, E. L., & Schoonover, S. C. (1977). *The practitioner's guide to psychoactive drugs.* New York: Plenum Medical.

Crane, G. (1973). Clinical pharmacology in its 20th year. *Science, 181*, 124–128.

Marholin, D., & Phillips, D. (1976), Methodological issues in psychopharmacological research: Chlorpromazine—a case in point. *American Journal of Orthopsychiatry, 46,* 477–495.

ROBERT F. SAWICKI
*Lake Erie Institute of
Rehabilitation, Lake Erie,
Pennsylvania*

MELLARIL
STELAZINE
THORAZINE
TRANQUILIZERS

PHENYLKETONURIA (PKU)

Phenylketonuria (PKU) was one of the earliest biochemical irregularities associated with mental retardation. Folling noted in 1934 that a few institutionalized retardates had urine with a peculiar "mousy" odor, which was found to arise from the excretion of phenylacetic acid. Classic PKU results from the absence of the enzyme phenylalanine hydroxylase, which normally converts phenylalanine, an essential amino acid common to most proteins and many other foods, into tyrosine and its constituent components. The resulting high levels of phenylalanine damage developing brain tissue. Since brain damage is irreversible, permanent and severe mental retardation is a predictable outcome, as are seizures, tremors, and hypopigmentation of skin (Smith, 1985).

An autosomal recessive inborn error of amino-acid metabolism, PKU is expressed only in those homozygotic for the defective gene. Incidence is about 1 in 10,000 births in whites and Orientals, but much lower in blacks. Heterozygotes typically produce enough enzymes for normal metabolism. Affected homozygotes are usually normal at birth since prenatally they received already metabolized nutrients through the umbilical cord. If the disorder is undiagnosed and untreated, progressive brain damage begins. Until the 1950s, prognosis was poor; most affected individuals had IQs of about 30 and were institutionalized.

Neonatal screening is now universal. Although a urine test was originally used, diagnosis is now through the Guthrie test, which reveals excess phenylalanine through a blood test 24 to 48 hours after birth. If PKU is diagnosed, the infant is placed on a low phenylalanine diet, which is synthetic because of the ubiquitous presence of phenylalanine in protein. Dietary treatment must begin within a few days of birth for maximal effectiveness. Adult IQ of early treated PKU individuals is about 90; IQ becomes lower with delay of treatment so that by about 3 years of age, maximal damage has occurred. The diet is the sole nutrient fed in infancy. Some (e.g., Berkow, 1977) suggest that thereafter low-protein foods such as fruits and vegetables may be tolerated, whereas others (e.g., Smith, 1985) recommend strict adherence to the diet. The taste of the diet is aversive, and maintaining the child on it while the rest of the family eats regular food can be an increasingly serious problem as the child grows.

Since phenylalanine is toxic only to developing brain tissue, treatment can cease or be relaxed when brain development is complete. Authorities disagree on when the diet can be terminated, but common practice has been to return the child to normal food at about age eight. However, research suggests that longer dietary treatment may be advisable. Dietary treatment for PKU is a classic example of genetic-environmental interaction. On a normal diet, individuals with PKU genotype will develop phenotypic IQ of about 30; dietary intervention alters the predicted developmental pathway, resulting in nearly normal phenotypic IQ (Brown, 1986).

However, treated PKU children may show specific def-

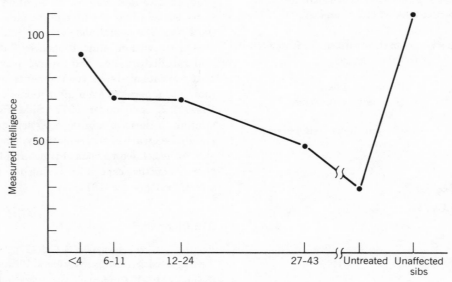

Mean IQ of PKU children as a function of the age at which dietary treatment began.

icits in perceptual motor functioning and arithmetic achievements that are more serious than would be expected on the basis of their slightly below average IQs. They appear to have neuropsychological deficits similar to those of brain-damaged children (Brunner, Jordon, & Berry, 1983; Pennington, von Doorninck, McCabe, & McCabe, 1985), and have particular deficits in visuospatial and conceptual skills, which may partially account for their problems with mathematics. Pennington et al. (1985) suggest that the deficits may occur because the children are taken off of the diet before the completion of relevant brain development. Although the number of subjects in these studies was small and the findings need confirmation, those working with treated PKU children should be aware that such children may have some specific learning deficits.

The effectiveness of the diet has had one tragic and unexpected effect. In the late 1960s, it became clear that children born to PKU women who had eaten normal food during pregnancy suffered prenatal growth retardation, microcephaly, and brain damage, even though the children did not have the PKU genotype. Although the effects were variable, many of the children died early or became severely retarded. The problems may have been more serious than in untreated PKU itself (Lenke & Levy, 1980). The pregnant women had transmitted unmetabolized phenylalanine to their embryos and fetuses at the prenatal critical period for adverse influences on brain development. A common recommendation now is for PKU women to return to the diet throughout the time they may become pregnant. But regulation of optimal phenylalanine levels is difficult, and no dietary program is completely effective. The safest recommendation is for PKU women not to have children. Thus treated women have an additional responsibility during childbearing years, and some who are at a marginal level of functioning may need some social service assistance (Brown, 1986).

REFERENCES

Berkow, R. (Ed.). (1977). *The Merck manual* (13th ed.). Rahway, NJ: Merck, Sharpe, & Dohme.

Brown, R. T. (1986). Etiology and development of exceptionality. In R. T. Brown & C. R. Reynolds (Eds.), *Psychological perspectives on childhood exceptionality* (pp. 181–229). New York: Wiley.

Brunner, R. L., Jordon, M. K. & Berry, H. K. (1983). Early treated PKU: Neuropsychologic consequences. *Journal of Pediatrics*, *102*, 381–385.

Lenke, R. R., & Levy, H. (1980). Maternal phenylketonuria and hyperphenylalaninia: An international survey of untreated and treated pregnancies. *New England Journal of Medicine*, *303*, 1202–1208.

Pennington, B. F., von Doorninck, W. J., McCabe, L. L., & McCabe, E. R. B. (1985). Neuropsychological deficits in early treated phenylketonuric children. *American Journal of Mental Deficiency*, *89*, 467–474.

Smith, L. H., Jr. (1985). The hyperphenylalaninemias. In J. B. Wyngaarden & L. H. Smith, Jr. (Eds.), *Cecil textbook of medicine* (17th ed., pp. 1126–1128). Philadelphia: Saunders.

ROBERT T. BROWN
University of North Carolina, Wilmington

BIOCHEMICAL IRREGULARITIES
INBORN ERRORS OF METABOLISM

PHILLIPS, BEEMAN N. (1927–)

A mathematics and physics major, Beeman N. Phillips completed his BA degree at Evansville College in 1949. He pursued graduate training at Indiana University, earning both his MS (1950) and EdD (1954) in educational psychology. Immediately following the completion of his doctoral degree, Phillips served as director of the Division of Research of the Indiana State Department of Public Instruction. In 1956 Phillips joined the faculty of the Department of Educational Psychology at the University of Texas, Austin, where he has remained.

At the University of Texas, Austin, Phillips founded one of the first doctoral training programs in school psychology, a program considered by many in the field to be the leading program in the country. Though its focus has changed in recent years, the program was particularly successful in pioneering and promoting consultation models for indirect service delivery in the provision of school psychological services. As the director and only continuous faculty member of the program, Phillips has been a key element in the development of the profession of school psychology. Among other professional leadership roles, Phillips has served as president of the Division of School Psychology of the American Psychological Association and was the editor of the *Journal of School Psychology* from 1972 to 1980. In 1978 Phillips was given the Division of School Psychology Distinguished Service Award.

Beeman N. Phillips

Applied educational and psychological research has been the consistent focus of Phillips's research program. He has also been concerned with developing conceptual and methodological rigor in school psychological research, the latter perhaps best exemplified in a 1982 chapter in the *Handbook of School Psychology*. For the past 15 years, Phillips has researched school stress and anxiety and their relationship to school adjustment and learning (Phillips, 1978). Phillips's work as a whole reflects a strong educational orientation to psychological research coupled with a concern for theoretical relevance and practical applications of research. Phillips has emphasized the need for a better interface between psychology and schooling and the means to achieve this interface.

REFERENCES

Phillips, B. N. (1978). *School stress and anxiety: Theory, research and intervention*. New York: Human Sciences.

Phillips, B. N. (1982). Reading and evaluating research in school psychology. In C. R. Reynolds & T. B. Gutkin (Eds.), *The handbook of school psychology*. New York: Wiley.

CECIL R. REYNOLDS
Texas A&M University

JOURNAL OF SCHOOL PSYCHOLOGY
SCHOOL STRESS

PHILOSOPHY OF EDUCATION FOR THE HANDICAPPED

The philosophical beliefs and values that underlie special education are diverse, dynamic, and interrelated. They reflect broad social issues such as attitudes toward individuals with handicaps as well as specific educational concerns. Three key issues are access to education, placement, and instruction.

Issues of access to education involve questions relating to which children have a right to education and whether all children can benefit from instruction. Questions of access and educability were first raised with respect to individuals with severe and obvious handicaps—the blind, deaf, mentally retarded, and seriously emotionally disturbed. Concern for these individuals prompted the earliest intervention efforts, beginning in the United States as early as 1817. The achievements of educators such as Edouard Seguin gave rise to optimism that education could cure or ameliorate severe handicapping conditions and resulted in an expansion in the number of available treatment programs for these populations (Kauffman, 1981).

The enactment of compulsory school attendance laws in the early twentieth century brought a wider range of students to the public schools. As a result, the special educational needs of moderately handicapped students became apparent. Special classes were instituted, providing these students with some measure of access to education, but few programs were designed to deliver the type of instructional program necessary to ensure that these students could profit from their schooling. (See Kauffman, 1981, Reynolds & Birch, 1982 for a detailed chronology of major historical influences in special education.)

The beginnings of the civil rights movement in the 1950s set the stage for further changes in philosophies of educational access. Equal educational opportunity became a focus for the efforts of increasingly active parent groups and professionals in special education. A body of case law, beginning with the *Brown* v. *Board of Education* decision, eventually developed and affirmed the principle of handicapped children's right to education.

With the passage of the Education for All Handicapped Children Act (PL 94-142) in 1975, access to education became a formally recognized right for all handicapped children. However, unresolved philosophical issues are raised by this legal guarantee. For example, are there children who are so severely handicapped that they cannot benefit from the extensive (and costly) efforts necessary to "educate" them? Such questions will undoubtedly be a focus of continuing debate and litigation.

The question of what organizational setting, or placement, is most appropriate for handicapped students has been answered differently through the history of special education. Beginning with residential institutions, the range of placement options has gradually increased to include special schools, special classes within public schools, and, finally, integration into regular public school classes (mainstreaming). Public Law 94-142 requires that handicapped students be placed, to the maximum extent appropriate, in regular educational environments with their nonhandicapped peers. This mandate is known as placement in the least restrictive environment. Mainstreaming and least restrictive placement are outgrowths of the broader philosophical concept of normalization—the belief that handicapped persons should, to the greatest extent possible, be integrated into society.

Without appropriate instructional strategies, any mainstreaming or least restrictive placement efforts are unlikely to succeed. Individualized instruction, first advocated by nineteenth-century educators such as Itard and Seguin, has been formalized through PL 94-142's requirement that an individualized education program be developed and its execution monitored for each child placed in special education.

The philosophical issues that have shaped special education have evolved and changed significantly over the past two centuries. A contemporary philosophy of education for the handicapped incorporates a diversity of complex issues that include those related to access to education, educability, placement, and instruction.

REFERENCES

Hallahan, D. P., & Kauffman, J. M. (1982). *Exceptional children: Introduction to special education.* Englewood Cliffs, NJ: Prentice-Hall.

Kauffman, J. M. (1981). Historical trends and contemporary issues in special education in the United States. In J. M. Kauffman & D. P. Hallahan (Eds.), *Handbook of special education* (pp. 3–24). Englewood Cliffs, NJ: Prentice-Hall.

Paul, J. L. (1981). Service delivery models for special education. In J. M. Kauffman & D. P. Hallahan (Eds.), *Handbook of special education* (pp. 291–310). Englewood Cliffs, NJ: Prentice-Hall.

Reynolds, M. C., & Birch, J. W. (1982). *Teaching exceptional children in all America's schools.* Reston, VA: Council for Exceptional Children.

MARY LOUISE LENNON
RANDY ELLIOT BENNETT
*Educational Testing Service,
Princeton, New Jersey*

EDUCATION FOR ALL HANDICAPPED CHILDREN ACT OF 1975

PHOBIAS AND FEARS

Fear in children and youths is a very strong emotion and is associated with behavioral, cognitive, and physiological indicators of anxiety. When a handicapped child or youth experiences fear that is not age-related in a setting where there is no obvious external danger, the fear is irrational, and the person is said to have a phobia. When the person begins to avoid the nondangerous feared situation, even while maintaining that such action is foolish, the phobia is commonly referred to as a phobic reaction (Morris & Kratochwill, 1983). Fear, on the other hand, is an integral part of normal child development. Many children's fears are transitory, appear in children of similar age, and generally do not interfere with everyday functioning. In fact, some fears that occur during development provide children with a means of adapting to various life stressors.

Those fears observed in infancy typically occur as a reaction to something taking place in the child's environment (e.g., the presence of strangers or loud noises). As the child grows into the toddler and preschool years, the fears broaden and involve the dark, ghosts and other supernatural figures, parent separation, and fears of particular events, objects, or persons. With growth into the early to middle school years, developmental fears continue to broaden and include such stimuli as animals, thunder and lightning, the dark, parent separation, bodily injury, and sleeping alone. As the child enters preadolescence and adolescence, the normative fears turn more toward school performance, physical appearance, bodily injury, peer acceptance, death, and imaginary figures (Morris & Kratochwill, 1983).

Separating the meaning of fear from the meaning of phobia has been discussed by Marks (1969). He suggests that phobia is a subcategory of fear that "(1) is out of proportion to the demands of the situation, (2) cannot be explained or reasoned away, (3) is beyond voluntary control, and (4) leads to avoidance of the feared situations" (p. 3). In addition, Miller, Barrett, and Hampe (1974) have stated that a phobia "persists over an extended period of time . . . is unadaptive . . . [and] is not age or stage specific" (p. 90).

Although a fair amount of research has been conducted on the incidence and prevalence of children's fears, less research has been published on children's phobias. Miller et al. (1974), for example, report that the incidence of intense fears (phobias) was about 5% of their sample of 7- to 12-year-old children. Similarly, Marks (1969) reported that the percentage of children having phobias who were referred to a British clinic was only 4%. Other studies estimated the prevalence of phobias among children to be less than 8% of the number of child referrals to a clinic or in the general child population.

With respect to developmental or normative fears, studies have shown that young children, 24 to 71 months of age, experience on the average 4.6 fears (Jersild & Holmes, 1935). Forty-three percent of children who are 6 to 12 years of age experience at least seven or more fears (Lapouse & Monk, 1959). In preadolescent and adolescent youths, 66% of those sampled reported fears of violence (Orton, 1982). Although girls tend to be more fearful than boys in the early years, this difference does not seem to appear on a regular basis in pre- and early adolescence. No literature exists on the incidence or prevalence of phobias and fears in handicapped children and youths.

Numerous studies have been published over the past several years on intervention approaches for reducing fears and phobias. The assumptions underlying these approaches have generally followed a behavioral orientation. There are five major behavior therapy approaches for fear or phobia reduction in children and youths: systematic desensitization (including variations of this procedure); flooding-related therapies; contingency management procedures; modeling; and self-control procedures. Of these methods, the one that has been used primarily in research is systematic desensitization or variations of this method. With regard to handicapped children and youths, few research studies have been published on the treatment of fears and phobias; however, of those studies that have been published, the majority have used a procedure that is based on systematic desensitization.

REFERENCES

Jersild, A. T., & Holmes, F. B. (1935). Methods of overcoming children's fears. *Journal of Psychology, 1,* 75–104.

Lapouse, R., & Monk, M. A. (1959). Fears and worries in a representative sample of children. *American Journal of Orthopsychiatry, 29,* 803–818.

Marks, I. M. (1969). *Fears and phobias.* New York: Academic.

Miller, L. C., Barrett, C. L., & Hampe, E. (1974). Phobias in childhood in a prescientific era. In A. Davids (Ed.), *Child personality and psychopathology: Current topics* (pp. 84–120). New York: Wiley.

Morris, R. J., & Kratochwill, T. R. (1983). *Treating children's fears and phobias: A behavioral approach.* New York: Pergamon.

Orton, G. L. (1982). A comparative study of children's worries. *Journal of Psychology, 110,* 153–162.

RICHARD J. MORRIS
University of Arizona

THOMAS R. KRATOCHWILL
*University of Wisconsin,
Madison*

**ANXIETY DISORDERS
EMOTIONAL DISORDERS**

PHONOLOGY

Phonology is the study of the linguistic rules of grammar as they relate to speech sounds and the structure within the language. As children learn their native language, they internalize the phonological rules that govern how sounds are perceived and produced in spoken language. By age 6, most children have generally mastered the phonological system of their native language (Gibson & Levine, 1975).

In the grammatical structure of each language there is a phonological component that governs acceptable and unacceptable sound sequences within words. Although the phonological level of language is abstract, the rules describe the acceptable sound sequences that represent underlying meanings. One of these rules, for example, explains why the phonetic interpretation of *sign* is modified in the word *signature*. Sometimes these rules can be explicitly stated; other times they are part of the tacit knowledge of the speaker (Carroll, 1986).

Before children develop an oral language system, they use gestures and prelinguistic sounds such as crying and babbling to communicate. As children experiment with the phonological patterns of speech, they develop an internal structure for perceiving and producing sounds of their native language. Even though young children may not accurately produce a word like elephant, they have the ability to understand when the word is pronounced correctly.

Preschool children are also capable of distinguishing words that are phonetically acceptable in the English language. This implicit knowledge of the phonological rules of English was documented in a study by Messer (1967) in which he pronounced two pseudowords and asked 4 year olds to choose which sounded more like a word. The children consistently chose words that were allowable within the English phonological rule system (for instance "klek" was preferred to "dlek"). This implicit knowledge of English phonology can also be observed when children automatically alter the pronunciation of "s" in such words as bugs, bats, and badges or "ed" in words like jumped, graded, and glowed. While at first these variations may appear irregular and random, they are in fact based on regular phonological rules.

Regularities and consistencies within the English phonological language system have also been studied. Chomsky and Halle (1968) present a comprehensive analysis of the English phonological rule system in *The Sound Pattern of English*. This study of English phonology reveals that phonological rules govern how the stress patterns and sounds of words vary according to their grammatical functions within sentences. For instance, the /k/–/s/ phonetic variation appears consistently in words such as medicate–medicine, critical–criticize, and romantic–romanticize. Within the rules of phonology described by Chomsky and Halle (1968), these phonetic variations are systematic and predictable. Speakers of the English language automatically and unconsciously vary these pronunciations according to their internal knowledge of English phonology.

Some children exhibit phonological disorders that cause incorrect articulation of sounds. Since these phonological disorders result in faulty speech sounds, the speaker has difficulty in communicating with the listener. Hallahan and Kaufman (1986) identify three types of errors in phoneme production that interfere with communication between speakers and listeners: omissions, substitutions, and distortions. Omission errors occur when only parts of words are pronounced ("I oss my oat" for "I lost my coat"). Substitution errors are observed when incorrect phonemes are substituted for correct phonemes ("wed" for "red"). Distortion errors refer to productions that approximate target sounds yet are not quite correct.

While 2 to 3% of the children in elementary school show signs of such phonological disorders, these same children show dramatic improvement in articulatory skills as they reach middle school age (Hallahan & Kaufman, 1986). These improvements can be expected to occur even in the absence of speech therapy (Shriberg, 1980).

REFERENCES

Carroll, D. W. (1986). *Psychology of language.* Monterey, CA: Brooks/Cole.

Chomsky, N., & Halle, M. (1968). *The sound pattern of English.* New York: Harper & Row.

Gibson, E., & Levine, H. (1975). *The psychology of reading.* Cambridge, MA: MIT Press.

Hallahan, D. P., & Kaufman, J. M. (1986). *Exceptional children: Introduction to special education* (3rd ed.). Englewood Cliffs, NJ: Prentice-Hall.

Messer, S. (1967). Implicit phonology in children. *Journal of Verbal Learning & Verbal Behavior, 6,* 609–613.

Shriberg, L. D. (1980). Developmental phonological disorders. In J. Hixon, L. D. Shriberg, & J. H. Saxman (Eds.), *Introduction to communication disorders.* Englewood Cliffs, NJ: Prentice-Hall.

CHRIS CHERRINGTON
Lycoming College

LINGUISTIC READERS
READING DISORDERS
READING REMEDIATION

PHYSICAL ANOMALIES

A physical anomaly is any bodily attribute that deviates significantly from normal variation. Technically, physical anomalies need not be disabling or handicapping though, as will be noted, they often occur concomitant to a variety of handicapping conditions. For instance, prematurely gray-haired individuals exhibit a physical anomaly, yet, the anomaly is unlikely to be viewed as an impairment (i.e., a disability). It is also unlikely to serve as a disadvantage that makes achievement in particular circumstances exceptionally difficult (i.e., a handicap).

Special educators are most directly concerned with physical anomalies that limit an individual's success in typical life activities (e.g., occupational, familial, and social activities). Such physical anomalies may be found in virtually all of the traditional exceptionalities. However, they are most clearly apparent in the following categories: visual, hearing, and physical handicaps, health problems, and mental retardation.

Physical anomalies can impose handicaps in one or many important domains (e.g., cognition, affect, and motor). Functionally, the individual may have difficulty in academic achievement (e.g., reading, mathematics), in social/emotional adjustment (e.g., making and sustaining friendships, attaining a positive self-concept), and in physical activities (e.g., locomotion, orientation).

Visual anomalies, depending on the age at onset, may be classified as congenital (present at birth) or adventitious acquired sometime after birth). Generally, the impairment concerns visual acuity, field of vision, ocular motility, accommodation, color vision, or corneal opacity.

Like visual anomalies, hearing problems may be classified in different ways. For instance, classification may depend on age of onset (congenital vs. adventitious). Distinctions are also based on the degree of hearing loss (i.e., deaf or hard of hearing). Finally, hearing problems may be conductive or sensorineural in nature. A conductive hearing loss results from interference with the physical transmission of sound waves from the outer ear to the inner ear. On the other hand, a sensorineural hearing loss, as suggested by the name, is caused by neurological damage to nerve tissue in the inner ear. Sound may be grossly distorted to the listener or may not be transmitted at all. In general, sensorineural hearing losses have the more pessimistic prognosis.

Physical handicaps are varied but are commonly categorized as neurological or orthopedic in origin. The former results from injuries, congenital defects, or the progressive deterioration of portions of the central nervous system (CNS). Because most human functions are heavily dependent on an intact CNS, neurological disorders may present particular difficulty for the child and the educator. For instance, it is often difficult to determine a child's true intellectual ability because a motoric handicap may prevent the child from exhibiting it. Cerebral palsy, spina bifida, convulsive disorders, and poliomyelitis are common neurological disorders.

Orthopedic, or musculoskeletal, disorders may be congenital or adventitious. They affect the bones (including joints) and muscles. Accidents, diseases, and hereditary anomalies cause most of the orthopedic disorders. Some of the more common of these conditions are muscular dystrophy, amputations, osteogenesis imperfecta, scoliosis, arthritis, and Legg-Perthes disease.

Other children have conditions in which physical health is poor either permanently of intermittently. Although their conditions are frequently less visually apparent than neurological or orthopedic disorders, they may well face handicapping circumstances in many functional areas (e.g., academic performance, social acceptance). Among the most common of these conditions are epilepsy, cystic fibrosis, juvenile diabetes mellitus, sickle cell anemia, and hemophilia.

The physical anomalies that exist among the mentally retarded population are extensive. Over 250 have been classified so far. Even so, these represent no more than about 25% of the diagnosed cases of mental retardation in the United States. The American Association on Mental Deficiency (Grossman, 1973) has classified the known causal agents of mental retardation as follows: (1) infections and intoxication; (2) trauma and physical agents; (3) metabolism and nutrition; (4) gross brain disease; (5) prenatal influence; (6) chromosomal abnormality; (7) gestational disorders; (8) psychiatric disorders. As with other physical anomalies, individuals with mental retardation suffer from a wide array of affective and motor problems. However, it is their difficulty in cognition and adaptive behavior that best characterizes these children.

Physical anomaly is a term also used to describe a variety of physical aberrations that accompany a host of medical syndromes that typically require special education. Many of these syndromes are genetic disorders that are diagnosed by the specific constellation of physical anomalies apparent to the trained eye. In cases where only one or two minor physical anomalies are present (e.g., hair whorls and a palmar crease), they are often considered to be "soft signs" indicative of neurological problems. Observable minor physical anomalies are often related to neurological problems through coincidental development. The same initial tissue that develops during the embryonic stage into the central nervous system (the neural tube) also forms the epidermis, the outer covering of the body. Also, human chromosomes control more than one aspect of physical development and where one abnormality occurs, others are likely to be present.

Minor physical anomalies occur in many forms and in conjunction with a host of disorders. In Down's syndrome (trisomy 21) one finds a broad flat face, pronounced epicanthal folds, a small palate, and malformed ears. Trisomy 13 will result in microcephaly, physical cardiac defects, polydactyly, cleft lip and palate, and malformation of the eyes and ears. Both of these syndromes frequently result in mental retardation ranging from mild to profound. Marfan's syndrome, most often associated with learning disabilities, though occasionally resulting in mild retardation, occurs with elongated arms and legs, arachnodactyly (long, spiderlike fingers), and malformations of the eyes and heart.

REFERENCES

Abuelo, D. N. (1983). Genetic disorders. In J. L. Matson & J. A. Mulick (Eds.), *Handbook of mental retardation*. New York: Pergamon.

Brown, R. T. (1986). Etiology and development of exceptionality. In R. T. Brown & C. R. Reynolds (Eds.), *Psychological perspectives on childhood exceptionality: A handbook*. New York: Wiley-Interscience.

Grossman, H. J. (Ed.). (1973). *Manual on terminology and classification in mental retardation*. Washington, DC: American Association on Mental Deficiency.

RONALD C. EAVES
Auburn University

CECIL R. REYNOLDS
Texas A&M University

DOWN'S SYNDROME
GENETIC FACTORS AND BEHAVIOR
MENTAL RETARDATION

PHYSICAL EDUCATION AND EDUCATION OF THE HANDICAPPED

See ADAPTED PHYSICAL EDUCATION.

PHYSICAL EDUCATION FOR THE HANDICAPPED

Physical education is a means of developing motor and sports skills and physical fitness with handicapped populations. Recently, physical education programs for the handicapped have been emerging throughout the United States in residential, private, and public educational institutions (American Association of Health, Physical Education and Recreation, 1981).

The federal government's concern for disabled veterans during and after World War II and its provisions to mainstream and rehabilitate them played a seminal role in the development of adapted physical education. Adapted physical education is the commonly accepted term to designate physical education instruction to handicapped persons in a public or private school setting. Veterans Administration hospitals use corrective, occupational, and physical therapists to help the veterans get back into the mainstream of society and to lead productive lives. Also, innovations developed through federally supported research have found their way in adapted physical education programs across the country (Sherrill, 1985).

From 1950, owing to a variety of political and legal means used by advocacy groups, programs for other handicapped populations began to grow as the rights of handicapped persons with congenital disorders advanced across a broad front. Evidence from numerous research studies began to indicate the positive value of sports participation for all handicapped populations. Programs such as wheelchair sports and the Special Olympics focused on promoting athletic participation among handicapped populations. From 1952 to 1979 the American Association for Health, Physical Education and Recreation (AAHPER) published a series of monographs on curriculum training of staff and guidelines for adapted physical education for schools (Adams, 1981).

It was not until the late 1960s and early 1970s that the federal government began to play a vital role in spurring the growth of adapted physical education programs in the public schools. Large sums of money were allocated for staff training of adapted physical education teachers, and for research and demonstration projects (Adams, 1981). The focus of these federally supported projects was to place more adapted physical education teachers in the field and to use special demonstration centers as models for others looking to upgrade their programs.

During the mid-1970s the federal government enacted the Rehabilitation Act of 1973 (PL 93-112) and the Education for All Handicapped Children Act of 1975 (PL 94-142). The most far-reaching part of PL 93-112 was section 504. It stated that "no qualified person . . . shall be excluded from participation or denied the benefits . . . under any program receiving federal assistance" (Sherrill, 1985). This nondiscriminatory clause indicated physical education was an important concern.

Until the enactment of PL 94-142, there were very few physical education programs in the public schools for handicapped children. The new law, however, stated that education for the handicapped shall include instruction in physical education. Also, the regulations called for equal opportunities for the handicapped to intramural and interscholastic sports competition. As a result, all handicapped children were accorded rights to physical education instruction to the same extent as the nonhandicapped (Auxter & Pyer, 1985).

Since 1975 more and more handicapped persons are being identified and placed in adapted physical education programs. About 12% of the school-age population is handicapped and receiving appropriate instruction. According to PL 93-380 (Education Amendment of 1974), handicapped children must be placed in the least restricted school environment with an individualized educational program prepared by the appropriate personnel. This law provided the impetus for the use of individualized education plans (IEP) in physical education and the opportunity for the handicapped to participate with nonhandicapped children in actual physical activity.

Because of the need to collaborate with other professionals regarding each handicapped student's activity needs and educational goals, adapted physical educators may serve as part of a multidisciplinary team with occupational and physical therapists and the special education teacher.

Many terms have been applied to programs of physical activity for the handicapped. Each of these terms represents a specific approach to improving motor and physical performance. Terms such as corrective, developmental, modified, therapeutic, or special physical education are representative of aspects of adapted physical education.

Corrective physical education is a means of remediating structural and functional dysfunctions through physical exercise or motor activities. The dysfunctions, although impairing, are generally correctable. Developmental physical education focuses on improving delayed motor and physical development through exercise and motor skill activities. Modified physical education has activities that are adapted to the learning levels of the handicapped regardless of individual differences. Therapeutic physical education denotes the use of physical education activities under the prescription of a medical doctor. Special physical education is a selected program of developmental activities designed to meet the limitations of those who cannot participate in unrestricted and regular physical education. This term has not gained nationwide acceptance owing to its controversial connotation.

Adapted physical education is a "diversified program of developmental activities, games, sports, and rhythms suited to the interests, capacities, and limitations of students with disabilities who may not safely and successfully engage in unrestricted participation in vigorous activities of the general physical education program" (AAHPER, 1952).

By definition, adapted physical education includes activities:

Planned for persons with learning problems owed to motor, mental, or emotional impairment, disability, or dysfunction.

Planned for the purpose of rehabilitation, remediation, prevention, or physical development.

Modified so the impaired, disabled, or handicapped can participate.

Designed for modifying movement capabilities.

Planned to promote optimum motor development.

Occurring in a school setting or within a clinic, hospital, residence facility, daycare center or other locale where the primary intent is to influence learning and movement potential through motor activity.

Adapted physical education differs from regular physical education in that it has a federally mandated base and a multidisciplinary approach to individual program planning, covers an age spectrum from early childhood to adulthood, has educational accountability through the individualized education plan (IEP), and emphasizes cooperative service among the school, community, and the home to enhance a handicapped person's capabilities (Sherrill, 1985).

The aim of physical education for the handicapped is to aid in achieving physical, social, and emotional growth commensurate with their potential. Objectives of adapted physical education programs vary from program to program depending on population characteristics, instructional expertise, facilities, and equipment. Some of the commonly accepted objectives of most programs are

To help students correct physical conditions that can be improved.

To help students protect themselves from any conditions that would be aggravated through physical activity.

To provide students with opportunities to learn about and participate in a number of appropriate recreational leisure time sports and activities.

To help students to become self-sufficient in the community.

To help students to understand their physical and mental limitations.

To help students to understand and appreciate a variety of sports that they can enjoy as spectators.

Prior to participation in a physical education program conducted by a public school, the handicapped student must have a thorough physical examination. Abnormalities are identified by the physician and suggestions for management are made to school personnel. The physician's suggestions usually include follow-through procedures to ensure proper class placement and appropriate educational placement based on the extent of physical activity needs and limitations. The adapted physical education teacher must be aware of the physician's guidelines and interpret them into an appropriate physical activity program.

Often, identification of the student needing special help is made by teacher observation in the regular physical education class or in the student's regular classroom. Sometimes the student is not making adequate progress or is frustrated by his or her present involvement in games and sports. The student may not be classified as needing special help because he or she passed the medical examination by the physician. In this case, the physical education program is adapted to suit the capabilities of the student.

Handicapped students are required to take a battery of motor, physical fitness, and perceptual-motor tests for the making of the yearly IEP (AAHPER, 1981). Short- and long-term goals for the academic year are developed from the test results along with the specific activities recommended for each goal.

After being identified as needing special help, a handicapped student, depending on the size of the school, may be assigned to one of the following types classes. The first is a segregated program in which all of the students are in need of adapted physical education. The student receives individual attention, is accepted, and is protected from unlimited competition. The disadvantage of a segregated program is that the class fosters isolation and non-acceptance from peers. In the second type, a student may be placed in an integrated class participating with able-bodied students in the least restricted environment in terms of physical activity.

A third type of physical education program for the handicapped is the dual class, in which the student is placed one day in the segregated class and one day in the integrated class. With this approach, individual attention may be given for special needs. At the same time, the student is able to interact with peers in the regular physical education class.

Once a handicapped pupil is given an appropriate physical education class placement, it is the role of the physical education instructor to provide a program of physical activity throughout the school year. In addition to planning and implementing the IEP, the physical education instructor acts as a counselor to aid the student in:

Setting reasonable physical activity goals

Transferring class skills and habits to other environments

Promoting healthful practices

Coordinating program goals with the student's family and related services within the school and community

Providing a framework that fosters socialization skills in the least restrictive environment

Recording progress and continually evaluating needs and interests through physical activity

The aim of a physical education curriculum for the handicapped is to develop physical fitness and motor skills through exercise and sports. For effective learning to take place, it is necessary to know the different levels of functioning in motor learning that affect a student's performance in class. There are three levels of functioning in motor skill acquisition: (1) input functions, (2) abilities, and (3) motor skill.

Basic input functions include the equilibrium reflexes, the vestibular system, vision, audition, and tactile and the kinesthetic senses. Their role is to provide sensory information to the central nervous system. If all systems are intact, the person will have a coordinated sense of movement and motion. If one or more are not intact, as is the case in many handicaps, it is important for the instructor to adapt activities that either develop or compensate for that input function.

The second level of functioning includes abilities that are perceptual-motor and physical in nature. Perceptual-motor abilities include balance, laterality, directionality, body image, spatial awareness and cross-lateral integration. Physical fitness parameters consist of strength, muscle and cardiovascular endurance, and flexibility. Motor fitness includes speed, power, agility, and motor coordination. If the sensory input functions are intact, the abilities develop through developmental motor and fitness experiences. If all of the abilities are intact, their use and development provide the groundwork for learning motor and sports skills.

The highest level of functioning is motor and sport skill acquisition. Motor skills are fundamental movement patterns of daily activity such as walking, running, hopping, etc. Sports skills are motor in nature but are specific to learning a particular sport. Examples of sports skills are throwing a ball, doing the crawl stroke, and riding a bike. If the input systems and the abilities are intact, then skill acquisition occurs through movement and sports experiences. This means instruction, practice, and instructional feedback in sport and movement activities.

Activities to develop motor, sports, and physical fitness are classified according to the number of participants and the level of skill acquisition. Individual activities include swimming, self-defense, tennis, bowling, dancing, weight training, and karate. Team sports include such activities as wheelchair basketball, soccer, frisbee, and softball. The third type are activities that enhance physical and motor development such as aerobics, dance, and weight training. In many schools, classes may be subdivided according to skill levels within the particular activity. In swimming, for instance, there may be classes or subdivisions within a class for beginners, intermediates, and advanced swimmers.

For the handicapped student to meaningfully participate in a sport, it is often necessary to modify some aspect of the sport to suit the capabilities of the student. For instance, wheelchair basketball is an adaptation of regular basketball in which the participants wheel around and pass the ball as opposed to dribbling and running. General guidelines followed by most instructors who teach adapted physical education state that the activity must be adaptable for effective learning to occur. This means that equipment, rules, or the manner of play may need to be modified for the participants. For instance, to accommodate the limited motor capabilities of a developmentally delayed group, the soccer field could be smaller and the ball could be lighter for it to be kicked farther and more accurately. In addition, activities could be designed to suit the students' abilities and not their disabilities. For example, a student with spina bifida is capable of learning how to swim because of intact upper body coordination. Finally, the instructor should be able to sequence and time learning experiences according to the students' capabilities.

REFERENCES

Adams, R. C. (1981). Adapted physical education. In J. Kauffman & D. Hallahan (Eds.), *Handbook of special education* (pp. 1–27). Englewood Cliffs, NJ: Prentice-Hall.

American Association of Health, Physical Education and Recreation. (1981). Resource guide in adapted physical education. Reston, VA: Author.

Auxter, D., & Pyer, J. (1985). *Adapted physical education.* St. Louis: Mosby.

Guiding principles for adapted physical education. (1952). *Journal of Health, Physical Education & Recreation, 35,* 15–16.

Sherrill, C. (1985). *Adapted physical education and recreation* (3rd ed.). Dubque, IA: Brown.

THOMAS R. BURKE
*Hunter College, City University
of New York*

ADAPTED PHYSICAL EDUCATION
ADAPTIVE BEHAVIOR
OLYMPICS, SPECIAL
RECREATION FOR THE HANDICAPPED

PHYSICAL HANDICAPS

Children with physically handicapping conditions are often designated by such terms as crippled and other health impaired (COH), or as physically handicapped or physically disabled (Bigge & Sirvis, 1986). Sometimes such terms are used interchangeably and are confusedly applied to individuals with visual or hearing impairments. It is true that children with physical handicaps frequently have other handicaps as well, e.g., language and speech problems, vision and hearing impairments, and behavioral problems.

According to Section 504 of the Rehabilitation Act of 1973, a person is physically handicapped if that person has a physical impairment that significantly limits participation in any of life's activities. Public Law 94-142 attempted to resolve definitional ambiguities in the conceptualization of physical handicaps by dividing the general category of physical handicaps into two broad categories: (1) orthopedic impairments, which are disabilities primarily related to skeletal, joint, and muscular disorders; and (2) health impairments, which are comprised of physical conditions that affect children's educational performance (*Federal Register*, 1977).

Regarding the educational needs of physical handicapped children, Wald (1977) has observed that the general category includes individuals who, "as a result of permanent, temporary, or intermittent medical disabilities, require modifications in curriculum and instructional strategies" (p. 95).

Data collected by the federal government regarding children and youths receiving special education and related services under PL 94-142 and 89-313 revealed that 56,209 children were orthopedically impaired and 54,621 were other health impaired, a total of .27% of the entire U.S. school-age population (U.S. Office of Education, 1985). The greatest percentage of those identified as physically disabled were individuals who had cerebral palsy. Not necessarily included in the federal count were children and youths identified as multiply handicapped, many of whom also have physical disabilities.

REFERENCES

Bigge, J., & Sirvis, B. (1986). Physical and health impairments. In N. G. Haring & L. McCormick (Eds.), *Exceptional Children and youth* (4th ed., pp. 313–354). Columbus, OH: Merrill.

U.S. Office of Education. (1985). *Seventh annual report to congress on the implementation of Public Law 94-142: The Education of All Handicapped Children Act.* Washington, DC: U.S. Government Printing Office.

Wald, J. R. (1977). Crippled and other health impaired and their education. In F. P. Connor, J. R. Wald & M. J. Cohen (Eds.), *Professional preparation for educators of crippled children.* New York: Teachers College Press.

DON BRASWELL
*Research Foundation, City
University of New York*

HEALTH IMPAIRMENTS

PHYSICALLY HANDICAPPED

A variety of interchangeable terms have been used to describe persons with physical handicaps. For example, these individuals will often be categorized as physically disabled, physically impaired, crippled, orthopedically impaired, other health impaired, or multiply handicapped. The legal definition for orthopedically impaired is a severe orthopedic impairment that adversely affects a child's education performance (*Federal Register*, 1977). The term includes impairments caused by a congenital anomaly (e.g., clubfoot, absence of some member, etc.), impairments caused by disease (e.g., poliomyelitis, bone tuberculosis, etc.), and impairments from other causes (e.g., cerebral palsy, amputations, and fractures or burns that cause contractures). The legal definition for other health impaired is having an autistic condition that is manifested by severe communication and other developmental and educational problems; or having limited strength, vitality, or alertness because of chronic or acute health problems (e.g., a heart condition, tuberculosis, rheumatic fever, nephritis, asthma, sickle cell anemia, hemophilia, epilepsy, lead poisoning, leukemia, or diabetes) that adversely affect a child's educational performance (*Federal Register*, 1981).

The range of disability varies from mild to profound physical impairment. Nonetheless, it is current practice to categorize physically handicapped students as having average to above average intelligence, and physically handicapped/multiply handicapped students as having additional impairments such as mental retardation, blindness, or deafness. Additionally, mild to moderate learning disabilities often are found with students whose only handicapping condition is physical.

It is estimated that the incidence of physical handicaps is 2% (Smith, 1984). In the school year 1984–1985, 73,292 multihandicapped, 58,924 orthopedically impaired, and 69,688 other health-impaired students received special education services (Office of Special Education and Rehabilitation, 1985). The most common physical impairments found in schools are cerebral palsy, myelomeningocele (spina bifida), and muscular dystrophy. Although children with communicable diseases such as cytomeglavirous, herpes, hepatitis, and acquired immune deficiency syndrome (AIDS) are being denied entry into some schools (Dykes, 1984–1985), the incidence of these diseases is on the rise and will have to be addressed within the public school system.

Most physically handicapped and health-impaired students are served in a combination of regular and special programs (Walker & Jacobs, 1984). Nevertheless, Dykes (1984–1985) suggests that 85% of health-impaired and 35% of orthopedically impaired children should be served solely in regular classrooms. Physically and multiply handicapped students are usually served in special education classrooms, separate facilities, or hospital/homebound programs.

The educational needs of physically handicapped students vary as widely as the definitions, etiologies, and educational placements. For most physically handicapped students, the regular academic curriculum is most appropriate. In addition, an emphasis is placed on helping the students to gain independent living skills such as grooming, dressing, and food preparation. Perhaps the greatest needs of these students are in the areas of adaptive equipment (Campbell, 1983) and technology (Vanderheiden & Walstead, 1982). Often physically handicapped students require wheelchairs, crutches, head pointers, arm and leg braces, etc. It is common for the physically handicapped child to use a nonverbal/augmentative communication system (e.g., Zygo 100, Tetra-Scan II, Omni) or use microcomputers for a variety of instructional purposes (Rushakoff & Lombardino, 1983). Technological advances have narrowed the gap in providing adequate educational instruction to students who cannot speak, move, or use their hands.

Another major area for intervention with physically handicapped students is in social and self-concept development. Often the physically impaired student is characterized as passive, less persistent, having a shorter attention span, engaging in less exploration, and displaying less motivation (Jennings et al., 1985). Additionally, physically handicapped students are found to be more dependent on adults and to interact less with their peers. Programs serving these students must consider socialization and independence. Parents as well as teachers need to find ways to facilitate independence and build self-esteem.

The education of physically handicapped students requires a transdisciplinary team effort. Because the students have a variety of medical needs, educational program planning often will include pediatricians, neurologists, physical therapists, occupational therapists, speech clinicians, nurses, orthopedic surgeons, vision specialists, and most important, the families of these students. Often, families of physically handicapped children must be the central focus of the educational process. It is with their support that programs in daily living and social skills training can actually work. Likewise, it is team support that enables families to more easily adjust to the demands of raising a child with physical or other health impairments.

REFERENCES

Campbell, P. (1983). Basic considerations in programming for students with movement difficulties. In M. Snell (Ed.), *Systematic instruction of the moderately and severely handicapped* (2nd ed., pp. 168–102). Columbus, OH: Merrill.

Dykes, M. K. (1984–1985). Assessment of students who are physically or health impaired. *Diagnostique, 10,* 128–143.

Jennings, K., Connors, R., Stegman, C., Sankaranarayan, P., & Mendelson, S. (1985). Mastery motivation in young preschoolers: Effect of a physical handicap and implications for educational programming. *Journal of the Division for Early Childhood, 9,* 162–169.

Office of Special Education and Rehabilitation. (1985). *School year 1984–85 report of services by category.* Washington, DC: U.S. Department of Education.

Rushakoff, G., & Lombardino, L. (1983). Comprehensive microcomputer applications for severely physically handicapped children. *Teaching Exceptional Children, 16,* 18–22.

Smith, O. S. (1984). Severely and profoundly physically handicapped students. In P. Valletutti & B. Sims-Tucker (Eds.), *Severely and profoundly handicapped students: Their nature and needs* (pp. 85–152). Baltimore, MD: Brookes.

Vanderheiden, G., & Walstead, L. (1982). *Trace Center international software/hardware registry.* Madison: University of Wisconsin, Trace Center.

Walker, D. K., & Jacobs, F. H. (1984). Chronically ill children in school. *Peabody Journal of Education, 61*(2), 28–74.

VIVIAN I. CORREA
University of Florida

ACCESSIBILITY OF BUILDINGS
AUGMENTATIVE COMMUNICATION DEVICES
MULTIPLY HANDICAPPED
OTHER HEALTH IMPAIRED

PHYSICAL RESTRAINT

A punishment procedure that involves the immobilization of limbs or the entire body is referred to as physical restraint. The intent of physical restraint is to decrease or eliminate the unacceptable behavior immediately preceding the onset of the physical restraint procedure. Physical restraint should be employed only after ample documentation is obtained that lesser intrusive interventions were ineffective.

Immobilization methods vary and may range from holding a student's hands by the side of the body to applying a mechanical arm restraint at the elbows to prevent self-injurious blows to the face. Several recommendations have been offered for implementing physical restraint procedures. Bitgood, Peters, Jones, and Hathorn (1982) recommend that the teacher be positioned behind the student and firmly grasp the student's shoulders to hold them against the back of the seat. A second method of physical restraint involves holding the shoulders while the student is in a bent-over position in a chair (Reid, Tombaugh, & Heuvel, 1981). A third method is holding both of the student's hands behind the back of a chair (Rapoff, Altman, & Christopherson, 1980). The exact method of restraint will vary along several lines, including the size of the student; the size of the teacher; the alternative activity to be taught to the student to replace previously observed unacceptable behaviors; and the position of the student relative to the activity being taught.

In addition to actively immobilizing parts of a student's body, mechanical restraints can be employed. These restraints can restrict the student's movements to strike parts of the body, or materials (e.g., elbow pads, helmets, face masks) can be worn over injured areas to prevent future injuries.

The duration of time during which each instance of physical restraint is employed has varied from 3 seconds to 15 minutes, with most reported studies containing recommendations of 10 seconds to 1 minute. That is, following the occurrence of an unacceptable behavior, the teacher would employ a restraint procedure for a pre-established time interval. If the student is calm and nonaggressive at the end of the time interval, the restraint is removed. However, if the student continues to struggle as the time expires, an additional duration of time must elapse during which the student is calm prior to removing the physical restraint.

Applying physical restraint as a behavioral intervention should not automatically be associated with punishment. Researchers have observed that physical restraint may act as a reinforcer for continued maladaptive behaviors. Favell, McGimsey, and Jones (1978) evaluated situations in which physical restraint actually resulted in increased frequencies of aggressive behaviors. Similarly, Singh, Winton, and Ball (1984) documented an increase in out-of-seat behavior when followed by contingent physical restraint. Finally, Foxx and Dufrense (1984) evaluated the reinforcing effects of hinged metal splints on the self-injurious behavior of a mentally retarded resident within a large residential facility. Interestingly, the authors were able to fade a self-restraint of a preferred object (large plastic glass) to a socially accepted form of self-restraint in the form of a wristwatch and eyeglasses.

Reasons cited for the reinforcing properties of physical restraint include a relaxing feeling of being immobile and resultant drowsiness; physical contact from a reinforcing adult; reduction in demands placed on the student who escapes from disliked activities by engaging in unacceptable behaviors resulting in physical restraint procedures.

When physical restraint results in a decrease or elimination of unacceptable behavior, several potential advantages may occur: undue physical strength or endurance by the teacher may not be required; little staff training is required; no verbal instruction is necessary, although some teachers include a verbalization of the unacceptable behavior prior to the physical restraint; minimum level of discomfort is afforded the student; the student cannot engage in unacceptable behaviors while being restrained; long-lasting effects are observed; and few side effects are noted.

Potential disadvantages that need to be considered prior to the implementation of a physical restraint procedure include an inability of small-frame teachers to restrain physically stronger students; the association of restraint with close physical contact and attention from the teacher; time lost from educational activities while the student is restrained; restraint itself may be reinforcing for the student; procedures have the potential to be highly aversive and intrusive; the student's physical strength may be increased through isometric type of exercising while resisting the restraint; an inexperienced teacher may use physical restraint in an arbitrary, capricious manner; physical restraint has the potential for injury.

Guidelines have been offered for the judicious application of physical restraint procedures, and teachers need to safeguard the rights of each student by adhering to at least the following:

1. Obtain informed consent from the student's guardian

2. Closely monitor the procedure to prevent intentional or unintentional abuse

3. Positively reinforce appropriate behaviors

4. Consider less restrictive alternatives prior to physical restraint

5. Use minimum physical force

6. Document length of time and frequency of instances of physical restraint

7. Administer physical restraint only in a contingent manner

8. Train all individuals in all environments frequented by the student

9. Maintain a resource file of successful documentations of the use of physical restraint to guide the development of the parameters for a targeted student

10. Fade the intensity of restraint materials to socially acceptable, nondebilitating materials (Foxx & Dufrense, 1984)

11. Identify functional, life skill activities to replace self-injurious or stereotypic behaviors when decreasing unacceptable behaviors via physical restraint

REFERENCES

Bitgood, S. C., Peters, R. D., Jones, M. L., & Hathorn, N. (1982). Reducing out-of-seat behaviors in developmentally disabled children through brief immobilization. *Education & Treatment of Children, 5,* 249–260.

Favell, J. E., McGimsey, J. F., & Jones, M. L. (1978). The use of physical restraint in the treatment of self-injury and as positive reinforcement. *Journal of Applied Behavior Analysis, 11,* 225–241.

Foxx, R. M. (1982). *Decreasing behaviors of severely retarded and autistic persons* (pp. 51–60). Champaign, IL: Research Press.

Foxx, R. M., & Dufrense, D. (1984). "Harry": The use of physical restraint as a reinforcer, timeout from restraint, and fading restraint in treating a self-injurious man. *Analysis & Intervention in Developmental Disabilities, 4,* 1–13.

LaGraw, S. J., & Repp, A. C. (1984). Stereotypic responding: A review of intervention research. *American Journal of Mental Deficiency, 88,* 595–609.

Rapoff, M. A., Altman, K., & Christophersen, R. (1980). Elimination of a retarded blind child's self-hitting by response-contingent brief restraint. *Education & Treatment of Children, 3,* 231–237.

Reid, J. G., Tombaugh, T. N., & Heuvel, K. V. (1981). Application of contingent physical restraint to suppress stereotyped body rocking of profoundly mentally retarded persons. *American Journal of Mental Deficiency, 86,* 78–85.

Shapiro, E. S., Barrett, R. P., & Ollendick, T. H. (1980). A comparison of physical restraint and positive practice overcorrection in treating stereotypic behaviors. *Behavior Therapy, 11,* 227–233.

Singh, N. N., Winton, A. S. W., & Ball, P. M. (1984). Effects of physical restraint on the behavior of hyperactive mentally retarded persons. *American Journal of Mental Deficiency, 89,* 16–22.

Waddell, P. A., Singh, N. N., & Beale, I. L. (1984). Conditioned punishment of self-injurious behavior. In S. E. Breuning, J. L. Matson, & R. P. Barrett (Eds.), *Advances in mental retardation and developmental disabilities* (pp. 85–134). Greenwich, CT: JAI.

ERNEST L. PANCSOFAR
University of Connecticut

PHYSICAL THERAPY

Physical therapists are responsible for physical restoration. Employing a variety of equipment, they use massage and regulated exercise to improve coordination and balance, reeducate muscles, restore joint motion, and increase the patient's tolerance for activity.

Occupational therapists help the patient to develop skills associated with daily living such as dressing, eating, and grooming. After carefully assessing the patient's needs, they design techniques and use adaptive equipment to enhance abilities. Facilities often include a model bathroom and kitchen in which patients can practice daily living skills. In addition, these therapists work with families and employers to suggest modifications in the patient's home and work environment.

Physiatrists are doctors who have specialized in physical medicine and rehabilitation; they usually direct the treatment program in a rehabilitation facility if the patient is severely disabled and requires many services. The American Hospital Association classifies these facilities into four types: completely independent rehabilitation hospitals; self-contained rehabilitation hospitals within large medical centers; defined rehabilitation units within hospitals; and hospitals that provide rehabilitation services but have no formalized units.

The purpose of a rehabilitation facility determines its services and staff; programs for treating patients with spinal cord injuries are different from those that help deaf people. In general, most facilities employ a team of physiatrists, therapists, psychologists, social workers, nurses, and other professionally trained personnel.

A physical therapist employs mechanical and muscle strengthening exercises to assist patients who will benefit from these activities to improve their quality of life. Physical therapists are frequently members of interdisciplinary teams, where they contribute to the overall management of the patient. The goal of most client service is to obtain entry into independent living and competitive employment. An example of services might include deep heat, paraffin baths, hydrotherapy, mild stretching, or strengthening exercises for a person with a crippling arthritis; strengthening and coordinating exercises for a person with a cerebral palsy; development, frequently in concert with an occupational therapist, of exercises for mobility through walking, leg braces, a wheelchair, or some combination; and the appropriate use of any prosthetic devices. Braces, wheelchairs, and other appliances require instruction in their use and care. Physical therapists generally teach these skills. They also join with occupational, speech, hearing, or other therapists in assisting the patient in the use of the prosthetic device to accomplish independent living or vocational skills.

Physical therapy, then, is the act of teaching motor strengthening, motor control, balance, and other skills to handicapped persons. It combines these motoric trainings with prosthetic devices to help the patient to accomplish needed goals by reducing the effects of disability. Physical therapy is one aspect of the total training needed to reduce the effects of disability to enable the handicapped person to profit from residual (normal) bodily functions. Frequently, both the general public and the handicapped person, particularly the newly handicapped person, become overwhelmed at the presence of a handicapping condition. What frequently is not seen is the amount of usable function that remains. The principle involved is to provide the handicapped person with training of muscle groups, motor control, balance, etc., to promote the use of the residual, nonhandicapped functions.

A few of the categories and types of skills taught in physical therapy as they apply to special education are listed.

1. Health (severity of problem health behaviors)
2. Attendance and promptness (degree of presence in school and time-telling behaviors)
3. Feeding/eating (degree of competency in eating skills)
4. Drinking (degree of competency in drinking skills)
5. Toileting (degree of competency in toilet skills)
6. Grooming (degree of competency in washing, showering, and personal hygiene skills)
7. Dressing (degree of competency in independent dressing skills)
8. Undressing (degree of competency in independent undressing skills)
9. Nasal hygiene (degree of competency in maintaining hygienic and socially acceptable conditions of the nose)
10. Oral hygiene (degree of competency in toothbrushing behavior)
11. Self-identification (degree of competency in pointing to body parts, knowing family members, and information about self)
12. Sensory perception (degree of competency in discriminating among stimuli on the basis of touch, taste, smell)
13. Auditory perception (degree of competency in discriminating among stimuli on the basis of auditory cues)
14. Visual Motor I (degree of competency in interpreting simple fine-visual motor skills)
15. Visual Motor II (degree of competency in integrating complex visual motor skills)
16. Gross Motor I (degree of competency in demonstrating simple mobility, eye-hand coordination, and gross motor skills)
17. Gross Motor II (degree of competency in demonstrating complex gross motor skills, motor sports)
18. Prearticulation (degree of competency in controlling mouth parts)
19. Articulation (degree of competency in making vowel and consonant sounds)
20. Language comprehension (degree of competency in understanding communication)
21. Language development (degree of competency in using gestures, sounds, and words to communicate)
22. Listening (degree of competency in attending and reacting to verbal communication)
23. Adaptive behaviors (degree of competency involving exploratory play and problem-solving skills)
24. Impulse control (degree of competency in controlling disruptive behaviors and accepting criticism)
25. Interpersonal relations (degree of competency in cooperating and interacting with others in social situations)
26. Responsible behaviors (degree of competency in accepting rules, obeying authorities, and demonstrating socially approved behaviors)
27. Personal welfare (degree of competency in demonstrating safe behaviors in hazardous conditions)

DAVID A. SABATINO
*West Virginia College of
Graduate Studies*

OCCUPATIONAL THERAPY
PHYSICAL DISABILITY

PHYSICIANS' DESK REFERENCE (PDR)

The *Physicians' Desk Reference*, known popularly as the PDR, is an annual publication of Medical Economics Company. It reports information on more than 2500 drugs. The information is supplied entirely by the drug's manufacturer but is edited and approved by medical personnel employed by the publisher. The PDR contains descriptions of drugs (with pictures in many cases of the most common form), indications for use, recommendations regarding dosage levels, and antidotes for some drugs. Management information for overdosage developed by the Institute for Clinical Toxicology is also presented. The *PDR* is intended primarily for use by physicians and was developed to make readily available essential information on major pharmaceutical products. The *PDR* is useful to allied health professionals and to special educational personnel. It is particularly useful to the latter because of the high incidence of medication usage by handicapped children. The *PDR* is likely to be available in the reference library of any special education program.

CECIL R. REYNOLDS
Texas A&M University

PHYSIOTHERAPY

Physiotherapy or physiatry is the treatment of disease with the aid of physical agents such as light, heat, cold, water, and electricity, or with mechanical apparatus. The person responsible for physiotherapy is a physiatrist: a physician who specializes in physiotherapeutics or physiotherapy. Physical therapy, or the application of physiotherapy as practiced by physical therapists or occupational therapists, is supervised by the physiatrist responsible for the physical therapy unit.

The primary purpose of physiotherapy is to provide for the controlled movement of the extremities and for the other muscle and joint articulation necessary for the activities of daily living or competitive employment. Muscles are strengthened, coordination exercises are offered, and mechanical (nonchemical) applications to increase the range of motion and strength for each joint are provided.

The range of patients includes those suffering from damage to either the central or peripheral nervous systems; those suffering from any disease or mechanical injury; and those afflicted with a birth defect affecting muscle and bone. Two primary systems treated are the skeletal and nervous systems. Some of the more common conditions treated are strokes (cerebral vascular accidents), cerebral palsy, head trauma, spinal cord injuries, arthritis, polio, and a number of inherited and acquired bone, joint, or muscle problems.

Dorland's Medical Dictionary fails to define physical handicaps for an obvious reason: the term is too broad to define in direct reference to a pathogenesis (disease entity). Educators have traditionally used the term physically handicapped to categorize those children and youths who, because of bodily disability, require specialized education. Under such a rubric, physical handicap equates with bodily disability; therefore, practically all handicapping conditions are physical (e.g., vision and hearing impairments, forms of mental retardation, and brain injury).

Generally, a physical handicap can contain four char-

acteristics: (1) a neuromuscular disability resulting from damage to the central nervous system; (2) a disability related to a lower common neural pathway (nerves and muscles outside of the central nervous system); (3) a disability resulting from an injury or disease that destroys nerves, muscles, or bone peripheral to the central nervous system; or (4) a health impairment that reduces vitality and thereby results in a weakened physical condition.

Diagnostically the two major groups are orthopedically handicapped and other health impaired. The orthopedically handicapped constitute the group that is neuromuscularly handicapped as a result of insult or trauma to the central nervous system or as a result of lower common neural-muscular-orthopedic (skeleton system) damage peripheral to the central nervous system. Other health-impaired conditions have numerous etiologies but have in common a condition that so weakens the individual that he or she must limit or modify the activities and therefore participate in physiotherapy to obtain relief.

DAVID A. SABATINO
*West Virginia College of
Graduate Studies*

ORTHOPEDICALLY IMPAIRED
OTHER HEALTH IMPAIRED

PIAGETIAN APPROACH TO SPECIAL EDUCATION

Jean Piaget (1950, 1952, 1977), Switzerland's noted genetic epistemologist, proposed a developmental and constructivist model of human cognition from birth to adolescence based on biological processes. Although his theory has been applied to regular education for several decades, fewer efforts have been made to apply his work to exceptional populations (Gallagher & Reid, 1981; Reid, 1981; Wachs & Furth, 1980). One reason for this apparent lack of interest is Piaget's derivation of theoretical principles from observations of essentially normal children, with the consequent assumption of lack of applicability to handicapped individuals. A second obstacle has been an assumed lack of fit between more holistic instructional goals and strategies compatible with Piagetian theory and the specific, step-by-step goals and methods typically prescribed for handicapped learners. Nevertheless, Piaget's cognitive-development theory provides a useful means of understanding and teaching children with exceptional needs.

Concepts integral to Piaget's theory include structures, adaptation, stages of development, conservation, equilibration, and egocentrism. According to his theory, cognitive development consists of progression through an invariant sequence of stages, with the child incorporating the structures (organized patterns for dealing with the environment) acquired at each stage into qualitatively different, higher order structures at each succeeding stage. The child's progression from stage to stage results from adaptation, which describes the process of interaction between the child's current maturational level and environmental stimuli. Two complementary processes constitute adaptation: assimilation and accommodation. Assimilation refers to the child's incorporation of features of the environment into his or her existing structures. Accommodation is the modifying of one's structures in response to environmental demands. To illustrate, when an infant desires to touch a new mobile dangling from the crib, the infant must accommodate his or her vision and movements to the distance. Simultaneously, the infant assimilates the mobile into already existing patterns of behavior: structures for reaching and grasping.

As a result of adaptation, the developing child continually creates new structures out of previously acquired structures to better interact with the environment. Piaget describes the development of these structures in terms of a series of stages: sensorimotor, preoperational, concrete operational, and formal operational. The sensorimotor stage (birth to $1\frac{1}{2}$ years) describes the infant and prelinguistic child. The infant manifests cognition through actions on objects, such as jiggling the crib to set a mobile in motion. The preoperational stage ($1\frac{1}{2}$ to 7 years) is characterized by use of language, symbolic behavior, and lack of conservational logic. The 2-year-old child demonstrates symbolic behavior by pretending that a broom is a horse and "riding" it. The preoperational child has not yet acquired the structures necessary for conservation: the ability to recognize that matter is conserved despite superficial changes in shape or form. For example, when a 3 year old is presented with two identical balls of clay, one of which is subsequently rolled into a cigar shape, the child perceives the remaining ball and the cigar as being unequal in size. When asked which is larger (or "has more"), the child may attend only to length and select the cigar, or only to width, and choose the ball. The child does not consider the two dimensions simultaneously.

Children in the stage of concrete operations (7 to 12 years) have acquired the rules of conservation as well as an understanding of relational concepts. The fourth state, formal operations (12 and above) describes children who can use abstract rules in problem solving and conceptualize in hypothetical terms.

Piaget's theory postulates that although children vary in the age at which they reach a given stage, all follow the same sequence. Progression from stage to stage occurs through equilibration, or the reorganization of structures through assimilation and accommodation, resulting in higher order structures. Disequilibrium, or a state of conflict, occurs when the child's current structures are applied (assimilation) and found insufficient to the task. According to Piaget, the child is inherently motivated toward equilibrium and therefore toward resolving the conflict. For example, the child entering the stage of concrete operations recognizes that the cigar-shaped clay is longer than the ball and yet was an equivalent ball in its original form. To resolve the conflict, the child reorganizes (accommodates) his or her structures; new structures for the simultaneous consideration of the two dimensions of length and width and for conservation result. The child thus reaches a new state of equilibrium.

Piaget's constructivist model has been used to explain social cognition, or children's logical understanding of themselves and other individuals in interaction. Children's development of social cognition parallels their intellectual development, progressing through a sequence of stages from egocentric to sociocentric thought. The infant is egocentric, or centered around the self. As children mature and gain experience with the environment, they become decentered; they learn that the self is separate from other people, that other people have thoughts and feelings, and that other people's thoughts and feelings may differ from their own. Development of social cognition in several areas parallels stages of cognitive development. These areas include referential communication, role taking, moral judgment, and rule implementation.

Referential communication refers to one's ability to describe a stimulus such that the listener can correctly locate the same stimulus out of an array of similar items, and is examined using speaker-listener pairs or dyads. Young children's referential communication is often termed egocentric in that they usually fail to consider the listener's perspective. For example, a 2 year old requesting a favorite cup may ask a listener to bring the "cup Grandpa gave me," not recognizing that the listener is not privy to Grandpa's gift. Role or perspective taking refers to the ability to consider other people's point of view: their thoughts, feelings, or, literally, what is in their range of vision. Children progress from a lack of separation between self and environment (early infancy) to simultaneous consideration of multiple perspectives.

Three stages characterize children's development of moral judgment: objective morality, subjective morality, and interpretation of the act (Piaget, 1932). Children in the stage of objective morality base their judgments of good and bad behavior on objective criteria such as the amount of damage incurred, for example, when someone breaks a lamp while trying to clean the table. In subjective morality, good or bad intentions become a prime criterion for judging behavior. At the highest level, children simultaneously consider intent and outcome and develop a sense of moral responsibility for the own actions.

Children's play and use of rules in play follow a similar developmental pattern. In parallel play, young children share materials and physical proximity but act independently, without a common set of rules. At a later stage (incipient cooperation), they know the rules and attempt to win at games. Finally, children together develop and elaborate rules appropriate for the situation (genuine co-operation).

Much of the research on Piaget's theory has addressed the invariance of the sequence of stages: the impact of specific training on development, especially on acquisition of conservation; the relationship of social cognition to cognitive development; and the relationship between social cognition and social behavior. For a more comprehensive discussion of the research, the reader is referred to Flavell (1971, 1972) on invariant sequence, Klein and Safford (1977) on training, and Shantz (1975) on social cognition.

In general, the research in all four areas has produced somewhat inconsistent results interpretable in a variety of ways depending on the researcher's theoretical orientation. Moreover, attempts to measure level of cognitive development have been criticized as producing merely another assessment of general intelligence. Studies of cognitive development in young children have questioned preschoolers' apparent egocentricity and inability to conserve as artifacts of task difficulty (Gelman, 1979). On the other hand, inconsistent findings regarding stage invariance, training of conservation concepts, and correlation between stages of cognitive and social cognitive development may be interpreted within a Piagetian framework as reflective of the fact that a given child may simultaneously be at different stages of development for different concepts (e.g., conservation of quantity, conservation of mass, role taking, moral judgment). Inconsistencies may result from investigators' use of different measures to assess levels of cognitive development. In addition, procedures may fail to discriminate between children who have already attained a given stage and children who are in transition between stages.

Because cognitive development results from an interaction between child structures and environmental stimuli, differences in quantity and quality of experience may affect acquisition of concepts. For example, a mentally handicapped child with a chronological age of 10 and a mental age of 7 might be expected to perform at approximately the same level as an intellectually average child with a chronological and mental age of 7 and a gifted child with a chronological age of 5 and a mental age of 7. However, differences among these children in years of experience would impact on acquisition of cognitive concepts. In short, although more definitive research is needed, Piaget's theory of cognitive development has contributed significantly to thinking about the learning process.

Piaget himself made little reference to the application of his theory to educational practice. However, psychologists and educators have derived from Piaget's work several principles for instruction appropriate for both academic and social learning. Piaget's theory, applied to special populations, assumes that all children, handicapped and nonhandicapped, proceed through the same invariant sequence of stages using the same processes of assimilation, accommodation, and equilibration. Thus, while the rate of development may differ for exceptional learners, the instructional principles continue to be applicable. Experimental attempts to propel children (exceptional and nonexceptional) to a higher level of development through training generally have been unsuccessful (Gallagher & Reid, 1981), theoretically because children's stage progression depends on maturation as well as environment. The instructional principles that follow are directed at the teaching of concepts, generalizations, and thinking processes rather than at increasing the level of cognitive development.

1. Because children's thinking is qualitatively different at the various stages of development, teaching objectives should be matched to children's level of development.

2. Learning is the acquisition of higher order structures transformed from and built on previous structures. Thus, learning involves the acquisition of broad, general rules or frameworks rather than particular, isolated facts. As such, learning proceeds through understanding rather than through incorporation of rote responses.

3. Children are internally motivated by a desire for achieving equilibrium. Thus, learning is facilitated by the presentation of optimally challenging tasks and discrepant events that predispose the child to disequilibrium.

4. Children learn best through interacting with and manipulating environmental stimuli.

5. Group interactions may present children with ideas that challenge their own, leading to disequilibrium, reorganization, and new structures.

These principles have been translated into more specific guidelines for teaching learning-disabled students (Moses, 1981). These guidelines are appropriate for other special needs children:

1. Begin with an encountering stage that permits children to interact with the materials before a problem is posed. Present concrete materials that permit children to experience and impose many kinds of change.

2. Allow children to set goals before they deal with transformations.

3. Present problems that involve puzzling transformations. Create situations that stimulate children to infer and reason spontaneously.

4. Permit children's creation and use of alternative methods of problem solving.

5. Accept children's methods of problem solving, even if they lead to failure.

6. Create a nonthreatening, nonexternally evaluating atmosphere. Avoid praise, criticism, or other an-

nouncements that label children's responses, since external evaluation reinforces dependence on the environment.

7. Require children to anticipate or predict the results of their actions, observe outcomes, and compare their hypothesized outcomes with results.

8. Be responsive to the children: listen, accept all responses, and respond with appropriate feedback.

Teaching methods consistent with these principles and guidelines include cooperative learning, hypothesis testing, discovery learning, inquiry, and other approaches that encourage inductive thinking. Cooperative learning is an instructional strategy whereby students work together in small groups to complete academic tasks. Potential benefits include gains in academic content, basic skill development, problem solving, and socialization. More research is needed on the efficacy of cooperative learning with exceptional students (Pullis & Smith, 1981). Gallagher and Reid (1981) describe hypothesis testing approaches for teaching exceptional students as another method consonant with Piagetian theory.

The inductive approaches developed by Taba and her colleagues (Taba et al., 1971), and Suchman's problem-solving methods (Kitano & Kirby, 1986), provide step-by-step information for developing teaching activities consistent with Piagetian theory and applicable to mildly handicapped and gifted students. Taba's inductive approaches include methods for developing concepts, attaining concepts, applying generalizations, exploring feelings, and solving interpersonal problems. For example, a concept attainment strategy for the concept "square" requires teacher presentation of examples and nonexamples of squares and children's induction of a definition for square. Teachers may use the developing concepts strategy for assessing children's current ideas about a subject and for encouraging classification of concepts related to the subject. Suchman's problem-solving approach provides a concrete method for children's attainment of such objectives as letter, numeral, color, and shape names, vocabulary, sight words, and arithmetic facts.

A federally funded research project (Kitano et al., 1982) provides preliminary data supporting the use of inductive methods based on Suchman's problem-solving approach with mildly mentally retarded and learning-disabled elementary-age students. Results indicated that learning-disabled children who received instruction in language arts using inductive methods showed gains similar to those achieved by learning-disabled controls who received instruction with traditional didactic and behavioral approaches. As a group, the educable mentally handicapped children demonstrated greater achievement in language arts objectives with inductive approaches than matched peers in the control condition. These results suggest that inductive methods may constitute a viable addition to traditional approaches to instruction with mildly handi-

capped learners. While more research is needed to validate the efficacy of such approaches for special populations, the approaches have theoretical merit and provide alternatives to traditional deductive methods.

Piaget's theory of cognitive development has had specific application to mild and severe/profound mental retardation, learning disabilities, gifted, and other categories.

Mental Retardation

Although Piaget's writings reflect little interest in individual differences, his ideas have been used to interpret the cognitive behavior of exceptional individuals. For example, Inhelder (1968) noted that the level of cognitive development ultimately achieved by mentally retarded individuals depended on their degree of impairment, with the severe-profound fixated at the sensorimotor level, the moderately retarded at the preoperational stage, and the mildly retarded rarely advancing beyond the level of concrete operations.

During the 1960s and 1970s, Piaget's theory sparked a new view on the field of mental retardation. The developmental approach to mild, familial mental retardation provided a positive alternative to deficit approaches, which assume that mentally handicapped individuals by definition possess deficits (e.g., in processes such as attention, memory, organization, or in neurological structures) that require remediation. The developmental view, articulated by Zigler (1967; Zigler & Balla, 1982) and Iano (1971), suggests instead that the familial educable mentally retarded constitute the lower end of the normal curve and differ from the intellectually average only in terms of rate of development and final level achieved. Mental age serves as an indicator of current developmental level.

In general, proponents of developmental theory as applied to the mildly mentally retarded suggest that this approach enables teachers to view retarded children in terms of normal stages achieved at a slower rate. Klein and Safford (1977) concluded from their review of research literature that stages of development in the mentally retarded population parallel those described by Piaget for nonhandicapped children, but appear at later chronological periods. Hence, the mildly retarded can be expected to perform according to their mental ages. The implication for educators is that methods applied to normal children can be used effectively with mildly retarded students of similar mental age. Thus, these individuals can profit from many regular instructional techniques and a broader curriculum appropriate to normally achieving children. Iano (1971) noted that educators too often assume that the mentally retarded have deficiencies in learning rate, retention, and the ability to generalize and abstract. As a result, teachers emphasize great amounts of repetition, structure, concrete presentation, and slow, step-by-step introduction of new material. He asks whether the retarded child's failure to reason and problem solve is due to an inability to understand or to an emphasis in teaching on the rote and mechanical.

Although the developmental approach as applied to mental retardation has received serious criticism (e.g., Spitz, 1983), research has neither disproved the developmental approach nor proved the deficit position, and probably never will (Spitz, 1983). In the meantime, the application of Piagetian instructional methods with the mildly retarded merits serious investigation and offers an exciting alternative to teachers wishing to broaden their instructional repertoire. Most important, application of Piagetian approaches to instruction may provide variety and challenge to the children themselves.

Piaget's descriptions of the sensorimotor stage, normally covering birth to 18 months, have served as a basis for interpreting the behavior of the severely/profoundly handicapped, assessing their level of cognitive development, and developing appropriate curricula. The six substages of the sensorimotor period can be summarized as follows (Stephens, 1977), together with sample instructional tasks appropriate to each.

Reflexive (birth–1 month). This phase is initially characterized by reflex actions (e.g., hand waving, kicking, crying, sucking, grasping) and visual tracking of objects. These actions become more coordinated and generalized. Sample task: To encourage visual tracking, hold a bright moving object 10 inches from the subject's eyes and move the object slowly across the subject's field of vision. If visual tracking fails to occur spontaneously, physically turn the subject's head to follow the object.

Primary Circular Reactions (1–4.5 months). Reflexive behavior becomes elaborated and coordinated. The infant becomes interested in movement itself, as in observing his or her own hand waving. Repeated as ends in themselves, these actions are "circular" responses. Sample task: Move a colorful, sound-producing object from side to side and up and down to encourage coordination of visual tracking and touching of the object with the hand. If visual tracking coordinated with touching the object does not occur spontaneously, physically guide the behavior.

Secondary Circular Reactions (4.5–9 months). The infant intentionally repeats chance movements that produce a desirable effect (e.g., shaking a rattle to produce a sound). Sample task: Demonstrate a squeeze toy and hand it to the subject. Guide the squeezing behavior to elicit the sound if the behavior does not occur spontaneously.

Coordination of Secondary Schema (9–12 months). The infant begins to discriminate between self and environment, to imitate speech sounds and movements of others, and to differentiate means and ends. Sample task: Demonstrate

and guide a means-ends activity such as dropping an object into water to create a splash.

Tertiary Circular Reactions (12–18 months). The infant actively experiments and discovers new means to ends, such as pulling a blanket to reach a toy that is resting on it. Sample task: Provide opportunities for (and guidance as necessary) discovering a means-ends activity such as obtaining an unreachable object using a stick.

Invention of New Means Through Mental Combinations (18–24 months). The infant considers alternatives, solves problems, and completes development of object permanence. Sample task: Demonstrate and permit experimentation with fitting objects of different sizes and shapes into slots of various size and shape.

Based on her earlier work with severely retarded individuals, Woodward (1963) concluded that many of the seemingly inappropriate behaviors of this population are explainable within a Piagetian framework. Given that profoundly handicapped individuals operate at a sensorimotor level, mannerisms such as hand flapping in front of the eyes can be interpreted as sensorimotor patterns developed in the course of coordinating vision and grasping, as in the subphase of primary circular reactions.

Uzgiris and Hunt (1975) developed an assessment procedure for charting infant development founded on major areas of cognitive functioning during the sensorimotor period. Such an assessment procedure can be adapted for use with severely/profoundly handicapped individuals of various chronological ages. Areas of functioning assessed by Uzgiris and Hunt include visual pursuit and object permanence; means for achieving desired environmental events; gestural and vocal imitation; operational causality; object relations in space; and development of schemas in relation to objects.

Because severely/profoundly handicapped individuals generally do not proceed beyond the preoperational stage, curricula can be derived for this population based on the sensorimotor subphases and adapted according to chronological age. Development of appropriate curricula of a Piagetian nature for the severely/profoundly handicapped requires matching objectives to the individual's present level of development; active involvement of the individual; opportunity for the individual to proceed at his or her own pace; opportunities for exploration and manipulation; opportunities for repetition and practice; and adaptation for any associated sensory or motor impairments.

Learning Disabilities

By most definitions, learning-disabled students possess average to superior intellectual potential but manifest academic and social achievement at levels significantly lower than this potential would predict. Delays in cognitive and social-cognitive development have been explored through research as possible factors in explaining the discrepancy between potential and achievement in academic and social areas. Suggestions for teaching interventions based on Piagetian theory have also been offered in the literature.

Research. In general, the research suggests that learning-disabled (LD) children demonstrate performance inferior to that of nondisabled (NLD) children on tasks designed to measure cognitive development and social cognition. Speece, McKinney, and Appelbaum (1986) found a developmental delay in LD children's attainment of concrete operations compared with nondisabled (NLD) controls over a 3-year-period. However, their results also suggested that when the LD children attained the concrete operational stage, they acquired specific concepts in the same sequence and at the same rate as did NLD children. Moreover, for the LD but not the NLD group, Piagetian measures of cognitive development (conservation scores) and age better predicted academic achievement than did verbal intelligence. Most important was the finding that while the LD children as a group improved over the 3-year period, they failed to catch up with their NLD peers. Speece et al. (1986) concluded that delayed cognitive development may constitute an important explanatory factor for continued academic underachievement experienced by LD children despite intervention.

Dickstein and Warren (1980) reported similar delays in LD children's role-taking ability compared with NLD children in cognitive, affective, and perceptual tasks. Their analysis of the performance of children from 5 to 10 years of age suggested that larger differences in scores occurred in the younger age groups and that performance among LD children improved little between ages 8 and 10. Horowitz (1981) also found lower performance for LD children on an interpersonal role-taking task, but no significant differences between the two groups on a perceptual role-taking measure. However, as indicated by Horowitz, results were confounded by differences between the two groups in intelligence. Wong and Wong (1980) found significant differences between LD and NLD children in role taking, with LD girls demonstrating much poorer skills than LD boys.

Finally, investigations of LD children's referential communication skills corroborate the findings on role taking that LD children possess deficits in social cognition relative to their NLD peers. Noel (1980) found LD students less effective in providing descriptive information about objects than NLD controls because of the LD children's tendency to describe objects by shape rather than by label or name. Spekman (1981) further reported that LD speakers tended to give more unproductive, irrelevant, or repetitious messages than did NLD children on communication tasks. These findings suggest that LD children communicate less effectively than do NLD children.

As a whole, results of investigations on role taking and

communication suggest that deficits in these skills may be one source of social problems evidenced by some LD children. Having difficulty in anticipating other people's views and accommodating their messages to others' needs reduces LD children's chances for successful social interactions.

Teaching. The literature has suggested Piagetian-derived instructional strategies for LD students both as tools for presenting academic content and for remediating deficits in social-cognitive skills. Gallagher and Quandt (1981) presented questioning strategies consistent with Piagetian theory for improving reading comprehension of LD students. They suggest, for example, the use of inference questions that require students go beyond the information given. Such questioning strategies present puzzling problems that stimulate equilibration. Moses (1981) offers examples of arithmetic instruction to illustrate the use of Piagetian guidelines for teaching LD students. Role-taking training through each child's sequential adoption of the various roles in a story also has been suggested (Chandler, 1971) as a vehicle for improving role-taking skills and social behavior.

Gifted

As with other areas of exceptionality, Piaget's theory as applied to the gifted has implications for research and practice.

Research. Piaget's theory would predict that the intellectually gifted, like the intellectually handicapped, follow the same sequence of stages as average children but differ in rate of progression. Carter and Ormrod (1982) found through their review of research that mentally retarded, average, and gifted children follow the same sequence of stages, supporting Piaget's view of sequence invariance. However, studies investigating differences between gifted and nongifted learners in rate of progression have yielded conflicting results. Carter and Ormrod suggest that discrepant findings might be due in part to differences in age groups studied. For example, young gifted children may not show superiority over average children in rate of cognitive development because such development, according to Piaget, is limited by maturity and experience, which may not differ significantly in quantity or quality in the early years.

There is some evidence to suggest that gifted children progress more rapidly than average children within a stage but achieve transitions to concrete and formal operations at approximately the same age as their peers. However, research by Carter (1985) and Carter and Ormrod (1982) indicates that gifted children both progress more rapidly than average children within a stage and demonstrate earlier transition to succeeding stages. In a study of 125 gifted and 98 average children aged 10 through 15, Carter and Ormrod (1982) found that the gifted outperformed controls at each age level and achieved formal operations at earlier ages. Specifically, the gifted students appeared to enter formal operations by age 12 or 13, while the average students, including 15 year olds, had not yet attained formal operations. Carter (1985) compared the cognitive development of 180 intellectually gifted, 325 bright average, and 168 average children ages 10 to 16. Major findings were that the gifted children outperformed intellectually average children at all age levels and outperformed bright average children at the lower age levels (10 to 14). Data were interpreted as indicating that gifted children establish their cognitive advantage as early as age 10. These studies suggest that intellectually gifted children may achieve higher stages of cognitive development at earlier ages than their average peers.

Despite common observations that gifted children express earlier concerns about morals and values, research on gifted children's social-cognitive development does not provide clear evidence that gifted children are advanced in this area relative to their average peers. Moral reasoning has some relationship to verbal intelligence. However, while some intellectually gifted students demonstrate advanced levels of moral judgment development, this is not true of all gifted students.

Teaching. Gifted children who are advanced in cognitive development compared with their intellectually average peers may require special interventions to prevent boredom and accompanying frustration. However, educators should not assume that all gifted children function at an advanced stage of cognitive development relative to their chronological age. Rather, every child should be assessed to determine level of cognitive development.

The process of concept acquisition through equilibration described by Piaget has relevance to instruction for the gifted. Guidelines for instruction consistent with Piaget's theory, described earlier, appear highly appropriate for gifted students because of their consistency with goals for the gifted, including optimum use of intellectual abilities, development of self-direction, and practice in higher level thinking skills (e.g., analysis, synthesis, evaluation). Kitano and Kirby (1986) describe specific methods for teaching the gifted consistent with Piagetian guidelines.

Other Categories

A few investigators have examined the application of Piagetian principles to children with other types of exceptionalities: cerebral palsy, hearing handicaps, visual impairments, and emotional disturbance. A review of these studies by Gallagher and Reid (1981) suggests that (1) intellectually normal children who have cerebral palsy progress at approximately the same rate as nonhandicapped children, although the former are slower to per-

form on tasks requiring manipulation, need more trials and encouragement, and have a lower frustration tolerance; (2) deaf children and blind children display minor or no delays in attainment of conservation compared with normal peers when accommodations are made for language and sensory differences and subjects are carefully matched; and (3) seriously emotionally disturbed children show deviations from normal developmental patterns.

In conclusion, the available research on cognitive development of exceptional learners suggests, for the most part, that exceptional individuals progress through the same sequence of stages described by Piaget for normal children, although they vary in rate of development and level ultimately attained. Application of Piagetian theory to practice suggests use of strategies that engage children in active problem solving appropriate to their current level of development. Additional research is required to demonstrate the efficacy of Piagetian-derived instructional strategies for handicapped and gifted learners. Such strategies have potential as additions to the instructional repertoire of special education teachers.

REFERENCES

Carter, K. R. (1985). Cognitive development of intellectually gifted: A Piagetian perspective. *Roeper Review, 7*(3), 180–184.

Carter, K. R., & Ormrod, J. E. (1982). Acquisition of formal operations by intellectually gifted children. *Gifted Child Quarterly, 26*(3), 110–115.

Chandler, M. J. (1973). Egocentrism and antisocial behavior: The assessment and training of social perspective-taking skills. *Developmental Psychology, 9*(3), 326–332.

Dickstein, E. B., & Warren, D. R. (1980). Role-taking deficits in learning disabled children. *Journal of Learning Disabilities, 13*(7), 378–382.

Flavell, J. (1971). Stage-related properties of cognitive development. *Cognitive Psychology, 2,* 421–453.

Flavell, J. (1972). An analysis of cognitive developmental sequences. *Genetic Psychology Monographs, 86,* 279–350.

Gallagher, J. M., & Quandt, I. J. (1981). Piaget's theory of cognitive development and reading comprehension: A new look at questioning. *Topics in Learning & Learning Disabilities, 1*(1), 21–30.

Gallagher, J. M., & Reid, D. K. (1981). *The learning theory of Piaget and Inhelder.* Austin, TX: Pro-Ed.

Gelman, R. (1979). Preschool thought. *American Psychologist, 34*(10), 900–905.

Horowitz, E. C. (1981). Popularity, decentering ability, and role-taking skills in learning disabled and normal children. *Learning Disability Quarterly, 4*(1), 23–30.

Iano, R. P. (1971). Learning deficiency versus developmental conceptions of mental retardation. *Exceptional Children, 58,* 301–311.

Inhelder, B. (1968). *The diagnosis of reasoning in the mentally retarded.* New York: John Day.

Kitano, M. K., Julian, N., Shoji, C., Trujillo, R., & Padilla, E.

(1982). *Heuristic methods for the mildly handicapped: Research report and manual for teaching language arts and reading*. Las Cruces, NM: New Mexico State University.

Kitano, M. K., & Kirby, D. F. (1986). *Gifted education: A comprehensive view*. Boston: Little, Brown.

Klein, N. K., & Safford, P. L. (1977). Application of Piaget's theory to the study of thinking of the mentally retarded: A review of research. *Journal of Special Education*, *11*(2), 201–216.

Moses, N. (1981). Using Piaget principles to guide instruction of the learning disabled. *Topics in Learning and Learning Disabilities*, *1*(1), 11–19.

Noel, M. M. (1980). Referential communication abilities of learning disabled children. *Learning Disability Quarterly*, *3*(3), 70–75.

Piaget, J. (1932). *The moral judgment of the child* (M. Gabain, Trans.). New York: Harcourt, Brace & World.

Piaget, J. (1950). *The psychology of intelligence* (M. Percy & D. E. Berlyne, Trans.). London: Routledge & Kegan Paul.

Piaget, J. (1952). *The origins of intelligence in children.* (M. Cook, Trans.). New York: International University.

Piaget, J. (1977). *The development of thoughts: Equilibration of cognitive structures*. New York: Viking.

Pullis, M., & Smith, D. C. (1981). Social cognitive development of learning disabled children: Implications of Piaget's theory for research and intervention. *Topics in Learning & Learning Disabilities*, *1*(1), 43–55.

Reid, D. K. (Ed.). (1981). Piaget learning and learning disabilities. *Topics in Learning & Learning Disabilities*, *1*(1).

Shantz, C. U. (1975). The development of social cognition. In E. M. Heatherington (Ed.), *Review of child development research* (Vol. 5, pp. 257–323). Chicago: University of Chicago Press.

Speece, D. L., McKinney, J. D., & Appelbaum, M. I. (1986). Longitudinal development of conservation skills in learning disabled children. *Journal of Learning Disabilities*, *19*(5), 302–307.

Spekman, N. J. (1981). Dyadic verbal communication abilities of learning disabled and normally achieving fourth- and fifth-grade boys. *Learning Disability Quarterly*, *4*(2), 139–151.

Spitz, H. H. (1983). Critique of the developmental position in mental-retardation research. *Journal of Special Education*, *17*(3), 261–294.

Stephens, B. (1977). A Piagetian approach to curriculum development for the severely, profoundly, and multiply handicapped. In E. Sontag (Ed.), *Educational programming for the severely and profoundly handicapped* (pp. 237–249). Reston, VA: Council for Exceptional Children, Division on Mental Retardation.

Taba, H., Durkin, M. C., Fraenkel, J. R., & McNaughton, A. H. (1971). *A teacher's handbook to elementary social studies. An inductive approach* (2nd ed.). Menlo Park, CA: Addison-Wesley.

Uzgiris, I. C., & Hunt, J. M. (1975). *Assessment in infancy ordinal scales of psychological development*. Urbana, IL: University of Illinois Press.

Wachs, H., & Furth, H. (1980). Piaget's theory and special education. In B. K. Keogh (Ed.), *Advances in special education* (Vol. 2, pp. 51–78). Greenwich, CT: JAI.

Wong, B. Y. L., & Wong, R. (1980). Role-taking skills in normal achieving and learning disabled children. *Learning Disability Quarterly*, *3*(2), 11–18.

Woodward, M. (1963). The application of Piaget's theory to research in mental deficiency. In N. Ellis (Ed.), *Handbook of mental deficiency: Psychological theory and research*. New York: McGraw-Hill.

Zigler, E. (1967). Familial mental retardation: A continuing dilemma. *Science*, *155*, 292–298.

Zigler, E., & Balla, D. (Eds.). (1982). *Mental retardation: The developmental-difference controversy*. Hillsdale, NJ: Erlbaum.

MARGIE K. KITANO
New Mexico State University

COGNITIVE DEVELOPMENT
DIRECT INSTRUCTION
INDIVIDUALIZATION OF INSTRUCTION
INTELLIGENCE
PIAGET, JEAN

PIAGET, JEAN (1896–1980)

Jean Piaget was a Swiss psychologist whose explorations of the cognitive development of children helped to revolutionize education in the twentieth century. He described the sequence of mental development in three phases: (1) the sensory-motor phase, from birth to about age 2, during which children obtain a basic knowledge of objects; (2) the phase of concrete operations, from about 2 to 11, characterized by concrete thinking and the development of simple concepts; and (3) the formal operations phase, from about age 11, emphasizing abstract thinking, reasoning, and logical thought. Piaget's theories and descriptions of developmental sequences have encouraged teaching methods that emphasize the child's discovery of knowledge through the presentation of developmentally appropriate problems to be solved.

Born in Neuchatel, Switzerland, Piaget was educated at the university there, was director of the Jean Jacques Rousseau Institute in Geneva, and professor at the University of Geneva. In 1955 he established in Geneva the International Center of Genetic Epistomology, where he and his associates published voluminously on child development.

REFERENCES

Furth, H. G. (1969). *Piaget and knowledge*. Englewood Cliffs, Prentice-Hall.

Piaget, J. (1926). *The language and thought of the child*. New York: Humanities.

PAUL IRVINE
Katonah, New York

PIC

See PERSONALITY INVENTORY FOR CHILDREN.

PICA

Pica refers to the consumption of dirt, clay, laundry starch, paint chips, chalk, and other nonfood items. The practice is most common among pregnant women and seems to result from strong compulsions or cravings for a wide variety of unsuitable substances having little or no nutritional value.

Lackey (1983) has summarized the major theories put forward to explain the cause of pica. Explanations include psychological determinants such as bizarre cravings described as the female's response to pregnancy. A cultural basis for pica stems from the fact that certain forms of the practice are passed along as family traditions in some cultures or regions of the world.

Among the physiological reasons proposed to explain pica are the altered taste and smell occurring during pregnancy. Nonfood substances may also be used to cope with nausea, hunger, and excess salivation when food supplies are scarce.

Pica is also common among young children in families for whom the practice is culturally acceptable. Beal (1980) reports that the highest incidence is among low-income children between the ages of 18 months and 2 years, but it is also found among 4 to 6 year olds. The nonfood items ingested by these children include dirt, paint chips, plaster, paper, and crayons.

Pica can have a number of adverse effects on the nutritional and health status of the people involved. Lackey (1983) cites several health hazards for pregnant women. The nonfood items may displace foods, causing a deficiency of calories or nutrients. If starch is ingested, it provides excess calories and promotes undesirable weight gain. Ingested substances may be toxic or interfere with mineral absorption. In the case of iron, poor absorption can lead to nutritional anemia.

The highest incidence of pica among children also occurs at ages when iron deficiency is common (Beal, 1980). However, a greater hazard posed for young children is related to the ingestion of lead-based paint chips (Christian & Greger, 1985). The resulting lead toxicity can lead to brain damage. Hence, screening for lead toxicity includes campaigns to identify children with pica.

REFERENCES

Beal, V. A. (1980). *Nutrition in the life span.* New York: Wiley.

Christian, J. L., & Greger, J. L. (1985). *Nutrition for living.* Menlo Park, CA: Benjamin/Cummings.

Lackey, C. J. (1983). Pica during pregnancy. *Contemporary Nutrition* 8(11).

MARYANN C. FARTHING
University of North Carolina,
Chapel Hill

ANOREXIA NERVOSA
EATING DISORDERS
LEAD POISONING
OBESITY

PIERS-HARRIS CHILDREN'S SELF-CONCEPT SCALE

The Piers-Harris Children's Self-Concept Scale (Piers, 1969) is a self-report inventory designed to measure self-concept in children ages 9 through 16. The 80-item scale consists of short statements reflecting concerns children have about themselves. There are 36 positive statements and 44 negative statements written at a third-grade reading level. Responses (yes or no) indicative of a favorable self-concept are worth one point and total scores (also expressed in percentile and stanine score form) can range from 0 through 80. Scores are also obtained on six subscales: behavior, intellectual and school status, physical appearance and attributes, anxiety, popularity, and happiness and satisfaction. The test takes 15 to 20 minutes to complete and may be self- or group-administered. Reported test-retest reliability has ranged from r = .62–.75 (2 to 7 months) and r = .80–.96 (3 to 9 weeks) with KR20 coefficients ranging from .88–.93 (Hughes, 1984). Evidence of construct validity was reviewed by Piers (1977).

REFERENCES

Hughes, H. M. (1984). Measures of self-concept and self-esteem for children ages 3–12 years: Review and recommendations. *Clinical Psychology Review, 4,* 657–692.

Piers, E. V. (1969). *The Piers Harris Children's Self-Concept Scale.* Nashville, TN: Western Psychological Services.

Piers, E. V. (1977). *The Piers-Harris Self-Concept Scale, research monograph No. 1.* Nashville, TN: Western Psychological Services.

ROBERT G. BRUBAKER
Eastern Kentucky University

CHILDREN'S MANIFEST ANXIETY SCALE
SELF-CONCEPT

PINEL, PHILIPPE (1745–1826)

Phillipe Pinel, French physician and pioneer in the humane treatment of the mentally ill, served as chief physician at two famous mental hospitals in France, the Bicêtre and the Salpêtrière. Convinced that mental illness was not a result of demoniacal possession, as was commonly believed, but of brain dysfunction, Pinel released his patients from the chains that were used to restrain them and replaced deleterious remedies such as bleeding and purging with psychological treatment by physicians.

Through publications in which he set forth his methods for the care and treatment of the mentally ill, Pinel's ideas gained wide acceptance throughout the western world. France, through Pinel's efforts, became the first country to attempt the provision of adequate care for the mentally ill.

REFERENCE

Pinel, P. (1801). *Traité médico-philosophique sur l'aliénation mentale*. Paris: Richard, Caille & Revier.

PAUL IRVINE
Katonah, New York

PITUITARY GLAND

The pituitary is a small gland located at the base of the brain immediately beneath the hypothalamus, above the roof of the mouth, and behind the optic chiasma. The pituitary lies in a bony depression called the sella turcia. The pituitary is also sometimes referred to as the hypothysis.

The pituitary regulates the secretions of a number of other endocrine glands and often is referred to as the master gland. However, its function is closely linked to the hypothalamus, and the pituitary and hypothalamus must be thought of as a system rather than independent entities. The hypothalamus and the pituitary are connected by a rich supply of nerves called the infundibulum.

Morphologically, the pituitary is a small gland. It weighs less than a gram and is only about a centimeter in diameter. It consists of two major lobes, the anterior pituitary (adenohypophysis) and the posterior pituitary (neurohypophysis). These two lobes are connected by a much smaller pars intermedia. The anterior pituitary manufactures a number of hormones that serve to trigger the release of still others. The hormones directly secreted by the anterior pituitary include growth hormone, thyroid-stimulating hormone (TSH), adrenocorticotrophic hormone (ACTH), and gonadotrophic hormones such as follicle-stimulating hormone (FSH), luteinizing hormone (LH), and lactogenic hormone (prolactin).

Adrenocorticotrophic hormone (ACTH) is intimately involved in stress reactions. Release of this hormone by the pituitary causes the adrenal cortex to produce cortisol and other steroid hormones that help prepare the body for fight or flight. Gonadotrophic hormones (e.g., follicle-stim-

ulating hormone and luteinizing hormone) activate the ovaries and testes so that estrogen and testosterone, respectively, are produced.

Prolactin is a hormone that affects the mammary glands and that appears to be involved in the regulation of maternal behavior in vertebrates. Somatotropin (STH or growth hormone) is a hormone necessary for normal growth. Excesses of somatotropin result in the clinical condition of acromegaly.

It is useful to view the pituitary as a link in a complex chain of events that tie the hypothalamus to other glands. However, the hypothalamus lacks direct neural connection with the anterior pituitary, and instead influence is exerted by release factors transported through a complex system of blood vessels called the hypothalamic-hypophyseal portal system.

The posterior pituitary (neurohypophysis) secretes antidiuretic hormone (ADH) and oxytocin. Release of these hormones is triggered by complex connections with other parts of the nervous system. The cells of the posterior pituitary do not produce hormones themselves but instead serve as storage sites for hormones produced by the anterior hypothalamus. When blood pressure falls, the secretion of ADH stimulates the kidneys to reduce their excretion of water into the urine. Lack of ADH can produce diabetes insipidus. Oxytocin plays an important role in inducing contractions during labor, and it is necessary for the contraction of the smooth muscles of the mammary glands, which are needed to produce milk in response to sucking.

REFERENCES

Asterita, M. F. (1985). *The physiology of stress*. New York: Human Sciences.

Groves, P., & Schlesinger, K. (1979). *Biological psychology*. Dubuque, IA: Brown.

DANNY WEDDING
Marshall University

DIABETES

PKU

See PHENYLKETONURIA.

PLACEBOS

Placebos are substances or therapeutic interventions that produce their effects as a result of the expectations of the recipient and the therapist. As originally applied in medicine, placebo therapies improved patients' conditions despite the fact that the placebos had no direct physiological action. Placebos, therefore, became an aid to physicians who lacked a specific therapy and a nuisance variable to researchers studying therapeutic effectiveness.

The placebo effect is most powerful in social situations where an experimental approach produces high hopes for success (Orne, 1969). To differentiate between placebo and direct therapeutic physiological effects, it has become commonplace in drug research to use a double-blind procedure. In such a design, both the person administering the therapy and the subject are unaware (blind) as to whether a given dose contains the experimental substance or a physiologically inert placebo. If the placebo and treatment interventions result in similar effects, the value of the new therapy is called into question. Practical or ethical considerations often limit the applicability of double-blind studies, and the existence of potential placebo effects remains a problem in a variety of areas of research.

Although placebos may be physiologically inert, recent research has indicated that they may have a biological effect. For example, Levine, Gordon, and Fields (1978) have provided some evidence that placebos that were supposedly analgesics activated the endorphins that are the body's internal painkillers.

There has been great controversy concerning the use of the placebo concept in understanding behavioral change interventions. Critelli and Neumann (1984) have argued that the placebo effect is more than a nuisance variable and the display of empathy, nonpossessive warmth, etc., that may occur in a placebo intervention may be an important part of the therapy. In the classroom, the expectations of teachers and students about the probabilities of high student performance during an educational intervention may play a significant role in its effectiveness (Zanna, Sheras, Cooper & Shaw, 1975).

Thus both the special education researcher and classroom teacher may need to take placebos into account. The researcher may wish to provide a placebo control group where subjects receive a treatment that is irrelevant to the planned intervention. Such a treatment allows control subjects to experience the attention that goes to those undergoing the treatment of interest (Cook & Campbell, 1979). The classroom teacher should be aware of the combination of placebo and direct effect of interventions and, therefore, foster expectations of success.

REFERENCES

Cook, T., & Campbell, D. (1979). *Quasi-experimentation: Design and analysis issues in field settings.* Boston: Houghton Mifflin.

Critelli, J., & Neumann, K. N. (1984). The placebo: Conceptual analysis of a construct in transition. *American Psychologist, 39,* 32–39.

Levine, J., Gordon, N., & Fields, H. (1978). The mechanism of placebo analgesia, *Lancet, 2,* 654–657.

Orne, M. (1969). Demand characteristics and the concept of quasi-
controls. In R. Rosenthal & R. Rosnow (Eds.), *Artifact in behavioral research* (pp. 147–181). New York: Academic.

Zanna, M., Sheras, P., Cooper, J., & Shaw, C. (1975). Pygmalion and Galatea: The interactive effect of teacher and student expectancies. *Journal of Experimental Social Psychology, 11,* 279–287.

LEE ANDERSON JACKSON, JR.
*University of North Carolina,
Wilmington*

DOUBLE-BLIND DESIGN
TEACHER EXPECTANCIES

PLACENTA

The placenta (Latin for "cake") transfers life-sustaining supplies from the mother to the prenate, disposes of the prenate's wastes, and protects the prenate from some harmful substances. It begins to form during the germinal period and becomes differentiated as a separate disk-shaped organ during the embryonic phase (Annis, 1978). The umbilical cord extends from the center of the smooth fetal surface. The maternal surface is composed of many convoluted branches, creating a surface area of about 13 m^2, which provides maximum exposure to blood vessels in the uterine lining. At term the placenta is about 18 cm in diameter and weighs about 570 g.

The placenta includes two completely separate sets of blood vessels—one fetal and one maternal. Only small, light molecules may pass through the placental barrier; maternal and fetal blood never mix. Although the exact mechanisms of transfer of nutrients and wastes between the two systems are not completely understood, transfer of gases and water is accomplished by simple diffusion (Hytten & Leitch, 1964). The placenta protects the prenate from overexposure to elements in the mother's blood (e.g., hormones and cholesterol) by reducing their concentration in the fetal blood; it also prevents some teratogens from reaching the fetus.

In a small percentage of pregnancies, impairments involving the placenta create serious consequences. In about 10% of pregnancies the placenta fails to produce progesterone in the early weeks, resulting in spontaneous abortion. Infrequently, the placenta is small or malformed, causing retarded fetal growth or possibly stillbirth. When the placenta partially or entirely covers the cervical opening (placenta previa), the membranes usually rupture early in the third trimester, leading to a premature delivery.

Even during normal functioning, the placenta is an imperfect filter. As the fetus matures, placental blood vessels enlarge and stretch the placental barrier more thinly, thus decreasing its ability to filter larger molecules. Many harmful agents (e.g., bacteria) are kept out during the early prenatal stages, when teratogens are potentially most dangerous. For example, syphilis cannot cross until after the twentieth week. Viruses (including rubella), because they are so small, are able to pass through during this critical period. Many chemicals that the mother ingests that are potentially harmful (e.g., alcohol, caffeine, and carbon monoxide) pass through in ever-increasing dose levels as the placental barrier thins.

Technical details on the structure and function of the placenta may be found in Wynn (1968) and Assali et al. (1968).

REFERENCES

Annis, L. F. (1978). *The child before birth*. Ithaca, NY: Cornell University Press.

Assali, N. S., Ditts, P. V., Jr., Plentl, A. A., Kirschbaum, T. H., & Gross, S. J. (1968). Physiology of the placenta. In N. S. Assali (Ed.), *Biology of gestation*. New York: Academic.

Hytten, F. E., & Leitch, I. (1964). *The physiology of human pregnancy*. Oxford, England: Blackwell.

Wynn, R. M. (1968). Morphology of the placenta. In N. S. Assali (Ed.), *Biology of gestation*. New York: Academic.

PAULINE F. APPLEFIELD
*University of North Carolina,
Wilmington*

CONGENITAL DISORDERS
PREMATURITY/PRETERM

PLASTICITY

Plasticity in the human sciences is the absence in an individual of predetermined developmental characteristics and a concomitant modifiability by organismic or environmental influences. The concept is not limited to the capacity to change in accord with outside pressure. It includes the power to learn from experience and modify behavior while retaining predisposing genetic inheritance. Educator John Dewey (1916) emphasized the characteristic plasticity of the immature child as a specific adaptability for growth. Basic to this concept is a person's power to modify actions on the basis of the results of prior experiences. In addition, plasticity implies the development of definite dispositions or habits. Habits, Dewey wrote, give control over the environment and power to use it for human purposes.

As a feature of the young child, plasticity is often most evident in exceptional children where deviation from the norm is significant. It has been seen frequently in gifted children, in schizophrenic children, and in some children with organic brain disorders (Bender, 1952). Many such children show prodigious accomplishments or become late bloomers and manage to make up for what they might have missed in earlier years both in educational and social development.

A study by Chess, Korn, and Fernandez (1971) of 235 victims of a 1964 worldwide rubella epidemic began when the youngsters were 2 years old. Development showed an overall delay during the first years of life, with characteristic impairment in language and motor sensorimotor functions. One-third of the children were diagnosed as showing varying degrees of mental retardation during the preschool period, while only one-fourth showed evidence of mental retardation at ages eight and nine. The IQs of the nonretarded children also showed progressive increases as they entered the school-age period. Detailed case studies of a number of the children who showed such improvement demonstrated that they came through a diverse and roundabout pattern to normal school functioning. Often they pioneered new territory in the acquisition of language, social development, and learning—thereby affirming the inherent plasticity of human brain function in the young child.

Similar individual-specific roads to cognitive language and social functioning have been demonstrated for children with congenital heart disease who had corrective surgery, children who contracted polio before the days of the Salk vaccine, children with rheumatic fever, and children with chronic kidney disease. Recently, studies of blind children have demonstrated similar plasticity (Fraiberg, 1977).

Plasticity takes on a negative connotation as applied by Bender (1953) to the concept of childhood schizophrenia. According to Bender, a physiological crisis may interfere with the maturation of the child in every area of functioning. The disturbance has a plastic quality that gives a primitive pattern to all behavior and renders the child incapable of satisfactorily dealing with autonomic responses, motility, perceptions, symbol formation, language, ideation, and interpersonal relationships. This causes anxiety and elicits defense mechanisms. Because of the plastic quality of the disorder, any function or area of behavior can be retarded, regressed, fixated, or accelerated. In *Principles of Education*, Bolton (1910) stated, "Where there is evolution, there is plasticity" (p. 8). Biological plasticity underlies the adaptive physiological process primary to organic evolution. Psychological plasticity underlies the adaptive behavior process primary to education and social evolution.

REFERENCES

Bender, L. (1952). *Child psychiatric techniques*. Springfield, IL: Thomas.

Bender, L. (1953). *Aggression, hostility and anxiety in children*. Springfield, IL: Thomas.

Bolton, F. E. (1910). *Principles of education*. New York: Scribner.

Chess, S., Korn, S., & Fernandez, P. (1971). *Psychiatric disorders of children with congenital rubella*. New York: Brunner/Mazel.

Dewey, J. (1916). *Democracy and education.* New York: Macmillan.

Fraiberg, S. (1977). *Insights from the blind.* New York: International Universities Press.

WARNER H. BRITTON
Auburn University

INTELLIGENCE
ZONE OF PROXIMAL DEVELOPMENT

PLATO AND THE GIFTED

Plato was among the earliest philosophers to formulate a classification of students within three levels of public education. Plato wanted to separate "men with hearts and intellects of gold" to train and educate them for the highest functions of the state as kings, rulers, or executives. Without proper nurture, the brightest student would not be likely to be willing to serve the state's citizens (Burt, 1975).

Plato's three levels of public education included common elementary school, secondary school with selective admission, and a state university with admission still more selective. On the elementary level, the curriculum covered literature, music, and civics. On the secondary level, students were prepared for future military and civil service posts by studying in the curriculum areas of mathematics, arithmetic, plane and solid geometry, astronomy, and harmonics. In higher education there were 5 years of "dialectic" learning followed by 15 years of practical experience for those chosen to be the leaders of the ideal state (Brumbaugh, 1962).

These rulers or guardians were trained and later employed for external warfare and internal police work. The 15 years of rigorous intellectual training prepared the select few for lives as philosophers. Plato's ideal state depended on its kings being philosophers or its philosophers being kings (Plato, 1973/393BC).

The republic of Plato required education for both men and women. This was thought to be revolutionary at the time. Women received the same educational opportunities and training for the mind and body; they were also instructed in the art of war. If a woman possessed the right natural gifts, she shared the highest of public duties equally with men. Every occupation was open to her, but it understoood that she was physically weaker. A man's nature was thought to be suited for majesty and valor and a woman's for orderliness and temperance (Morrow, 1960).

The idea of gifted students within the educational system was especially evident in the republic during the open discussions on mathematics. Plato believed that all students should be introduced to mathematics and discussed how this subject had an effect on the mental powers of a student; he believed it sharpened a student's wits and helped to fix attention. The skills of higher mathematics were seen as needed by the chosen few future rulers. These gifted students would study with systematic thoroughness and exactness (Morrow, 1960). Students were chosen for this advanced curriculum if they demonstrated that they understood the general connection of the various curriculum areas. If a student successfully grasped both a practical and theoretical connection, at the age of 30 the student would be admitted to the highest and most complete of all possible studies—philosophy.

REFERENCES

Bosanquet, B. (1908). *The education of the young in the republic of Plato.* Cambridge, England: Cambridge University Press.

Brumbaugh, R. S. (1962). *Plato for the modern age.* New York: Crowell-Collier.

Burt, C. (1975). *The gifted child.* New York: Wiley.

Morrow, G. R. (1960). *Plato's Cretan city: A historical interpretation of the laws.* Princeton, NJ: Princeton University Press.

Plato. (1972). *The republic of Plato* (F. M. Cornford, Trans.). New York: Oxford University Press. (Original work published 370 BC)

Plato. (1973). *Plato: Laches and charmides* (R. E. Sprague, Trans.). Indianapolis: Bobbs-Merrill. (Original work published 393 BC)

DEBORAH A. SHANLEY
*Medgar Evers College, City
University of New York*

GIFTED CHILDREN
HISTORY OF SPECIAL EDUCATION

PLAY

Play among humans can be described as an attitude rather than a category of behaviors (Damon, 1983). Play is often regarded as the opposite of work in so far as attitude is concerned. A child who is having fun with an activity (as evidenced by laughing and smiling) is playing. Conversely, a child who is practicing his game skills to perfection is working. In fact, it has been suggested that the word play is most effectively used as an adverb, as in "the child stacked the blocks playfully" (Miller, 1968).

Regardless of its seemingly nonserious origins, play is a critical developmental activity. Many aspects of our social, motor, and cognitive lives have their origins in childhood play. The famous Russian psychologist Lev Vygotsky argued throughout his short, albeit brilliant career, that play creates the conditions for the child's acquisition of new competence in imaginative, social, and intellectual skills.

One method of classifying children's play is based on interactions with other children. Five categories of play can be distinguished (Parten, 1932). The first type, solitary play, involves no interaction at all with other children. In onlooker play, the second type, the child simply observes other children at play. This is thought to be the first phase of a preschooler's interaction with other children.

When children begin to engage in the same activity side by side without taking much notice of each other, parallel play is said to occur. Associative play, the fourth type, occurs in older preschoolers; in this type, play becomes much more interactive. During this phase, two or more children partake in the same activity doing basically the same thing; however, there is no attempt to organize the activity or take turns.

Cooperative play, an organized activity in which individual children cooperate to achieve some sort of group goal, usually does not appear until age 3. At this stage children become more able and eager to participate in social forms of play. Solitary play does not ever disappear. Most children are capable of playing alone if a companion is not available. Onlooker behavior persists even into adulthood.

The symbolic nature of play is vital to the development of the child; it performs several functions in that development. First, children can use their symbolic skills, like language, in new and different ways, in a sense testing the limits of those skills. Second, children can, through play, do and say things that are normally difficult to express or taboo. Third, as children exit infancy they can use play in a cooperative, social fashion. "Make believe" allows children to explore social roles, work in cooperation with others, and experiment with social roles and rules (Damon, 1983).

Children who are handicapped may be less able to use play effectively and therefore may lose out on some of the important outcomes of play. For example, a physically handicapped child may not be able to engage in normal social play with other children. Hence, that child needs special arrangements or interventions to make sure that he or she has access to normal opportunities for play.

REFERENCES

Damon, W. (1983). *Social and personality development: Infancy through adolescence*. New York: Norton.

Miller, S. (1968). *The psychology of play*. Middlesex, England: Penguin.

Parten, M. B. (1932). Social participation among preschool children. *Journal of Abnormal & Social Psychology, 27,* 243–269.

MICHAEL J. ASH
JOSE LUIS TORRES
Texas A&M University

PLAYTEST

The PLAYTEST procedure is currently recognized as one possible approach to screening and direct assessment of an infant's auditory functioning (Butterfield, 1982). The PLAYTEST system was originally developed by B. Z. Friedlander as a research tool for measuring infants' selective listening and receptive voice discrimination abilities within the home environment (Friedlander, 1968).

The system consists of a simple, portable, automated toy apparatus that attaches to the infant's crib or playpen. An audio or video-audio recorder and response recorder complete the equipment. The apparatii are attached at different locations on the crib or playpen. When the infant attends to either device, the responses activate the accompanying stereophonic tape recorder. The tape recorder is fitted with an endless loop audio tape. Certain systems are equipped to provide video-audio feedback instead of just audio feedback. Separate channels on the device carry different prerecorded sound samples.

The infant's frequency and duration of response to the various sources of auditory stimuli are used to infer the current level of auditory discrimination and selective listening abilities. Both the audio and the video-audio PLAYTEST systems use a response recorder to register the infant's differential response to the various auditory stimuli.

The PLAYTEST system has proven a valuable research tool in the investigation of auditory functioning in infants (Friedlander, 1968, 1970, 1971, 1975). One interesting finding is that very young infants show a clear preference for the mother's voice as opposed to a simple musical score.

It appears that the PLAYTEST system also provides an invaluable means of identifying infants at high risk for developing significant language disorders later in life (Butterfield, 1982; Friedlander, 1975). Butterfield (1982) envisions the PLAYTEST procedure as an instrumental screening and assessment procedure in the very early detection of auditory processing and/or discrimination problems in infants. He has described modifications of the existing system that would enable professionals to assess infants less than 6 months of age for possible auditory dysfunctions (Butterfield, 1982).

REFERENCES

Butterfield, E. C. (1982). Behavioral assessment of infants' hearing. In M. Lewis & L. T. Taft (Eds.), *Developmental disabilities: Theory, assessment, and intervention*. New York: SP Medical & Scientific.

Friedlander, B. Z. (1968). The effect of speaker identity, voice inflection, vocabulary, and message redundancy on infants' selection of vocal reinforcement. *Journal of Experimental Child Psychology, 6,* 443–459.

Freidlander, B. Z. (1970). Receptive language development in infancy: Issues and problems. *Merrill Quarterly of Behavior & Development, 16*, 7–51.

Friedlander, B. Z. (1971). Listening, language, and the auditory environment: Automated evaluation and intervention. In J. Hellmuth (Ed.), *The exceptional infant* (Vol. 2). New York: Brunner/Mazel.

Friedlander, B. Z. (1975). Automated evaluation of selective listening in language impaired and normal infants and young children. In B. Z. Friedlander, G. M. Sterritt, & G. E. Kirk (Eds.), *The exceptional infant* (Vol. 3). New York: Brunner/Mazel.

JULIA A. HICKMAN
University of Texas, Austin

AUDITORY DISCRIMINATION
DEAF
LANGUAGE DISORDERS

PLAY THERAPY

Play therapy is a therapeutic technique used with children that emphasizes the medium of play as a substitute for the traditional verbal interchange between therapists and adult clients. The roots of play therapy can be traced back to the psychoanalytic work of Sigmund Freud (1909), and the classic case of Little Hans, in which Freud directed the child's father in techniques used to treat the child's severe phobia. Direct work with a child was first initiated by Hug-Hellmuth (Gumaer, 1984), who applied Freudian analysis to children under age 7. It soon became apparent that children lacked the verbal ability, interest, and patience to talk with a therapist for an extended period of time. Thus in the late 1920s, both Melanie Klein and Anna Freud developed therapeutic methods that used play as the child's primary mode of expression (see Figure). Anna Freud stressed the importance of play in building the therapeutic relationship, deemphasizing the need for inter-

Small furniture, a pleasant atmosphere, and a caring therapist, all prerequisite to successful play therapy.

pretation. Klein, however, approached play therapy much like traditional adult psychoanalytic work, with free play becoming a direct substitution for free associations, and insights and interpretation retaining primary importance.

In the following decade, Otto Rank was an important contributor with his notion of relationship therapy. Rank stressed the importance of the emotional attachment between the child and the therapist, focusing mainly on present feelings and actions of the child. In the 1940s and 1950s, Carl Rogers client-centered therapy was modified by Virginia Axline (1947) into a nondirective play therapy. Axline's work, which has remained one of the cornerstones of current play therapy, is predicated on the belief that the child has within himself or herself the ability to solve emotional conflicts. According to Axline, it is the job of the play therapist to provide the optimal conditions under which the child's natural growth and development will occur. The basic rules of Axline's approach have become the standard for nondirective play therapy. They include the development of a warm relationship, acceptance, permissiveness with a minimum of limits, reflection of feelings, and giving the child responsibility for directing the sessions, making choices, and implementing change.

The effectiveness of play therapy has been attributed to its direct relevance to the child's developmental level and abilities. Woltmann (1964) stresses that play allows the child to act out situations that are disturbing, conflicting, and confusing and, in so doing, to clarify his or her own position in relation to the world around. Inherent to the success of play therapy is the make-believe element. Through fantasy and play, children are able to master tasks (drive a car, fly a spaceship), reverse roles (become parent or teacher), or express overt hostility without being punished. Woltmann believes that play therapy allows the child to "eliminate guilt and become victorious over forces otherwise above his reach and capabilities." Caplan and Caplan (1974) provide a further rationale for the effectiveness of play therapy. They contend that the voluntary nature of play makes it intrinsically interesting to the child and reduces the occurrence of resistance. The child is free to express himself or herself without fear of evaluation or retaliation. Through fantasy, the child can gain a sense of control over the environment without direct competition from others. Finally, play therapy is seen as developing both the child's physical and mental abilities.

The selection of the play media is an important part of the therapy. Gumaer (1984) notes that toys should be durable, inexpensive, and safe. They should be versatile (e.g., clay, paints) so that children may use them in a number of ways. Toys should encourage communication between the child and therapist (e.g., telephones, puppets). Some toys should be selected for their ability to elicit aggression such as a toy gun or a soldier doll. Finally, toys should be relatively unstructured; items such as board games or books leave little room for creativity. In addition to the toys already mentioned, Axline (1947) commonly employs a set of family dolls, a nursing bottle, trucks and cars, and, if possible, a sandbox and water.

In recent years, play therapy has expanded to include a number of settings, participants, and techniques. Ginott (1961) has developed a method that provides a specific rationale for toy selection and that emphasizes the importance of limit setting. Dreikurs and Soltz (1964) use play therapy that emphasizes the natural and logical consequences of a child's behavior. Myrick and Haldin (1971) describe a play process that is therapist directed and shorter in duration than Axlinian therapy, thus making it more practical for use in school settings. For further study, the reader is directed to *The Handbook of Play Therapy* (Schaefer & O'Conner, 1983), which describes specific techniques such as family play and art therapy, as well as play therapy directly tailored to such childhood disturbances as abuse and neglect, divorced parents, aggression, learning disability, and mental retardation.

REFERENCES

Axline, Virginia (1947). *Play therapy.* Boston: Houghton Mifflin.

Caplan, F., & Caplan, T. (1974). *The power of play.* New York: Anchor.

Dreikurs, R., & Soltz, V. (1964). *Children: The challenge.* New York: Hawthorne.

Freud, S. (1909). Analysis of a phobia in a five-year-old boy. In *Standard Edition.* (Vol. 10). London: Hogarth.

Ginott, H. (1961). *Group psychotherapy with children.* New York: McGraw-Hill.

Gumaer, J. (1984). *Counseling and therapy for children.* New York: Free Press.

Myrick, R., & Haldin, W. (1971). A study of play process in counseling. *Elementary School Guidance and Counseling.* 5(4), 256–263.

Schaefer, C., & O'Conner, K. (1983). *The handbook of play therapy.* New York: Wiley.

Woltmann, A. (1964). Concepts of play therapy techniques. In M. Haworth (Ed.), *Child psychotherapy* (pp. 20–31). New York: Basic Books.

FRANCES F. WORCHEL
Texas A&M University

FAMILY THERAPY
PLAY
PSYCHOTHERAPY

PLURALISM, CULTURAL

Cultural pluralism is a sociological concept that refers to the dual enterprise of acceptance and mobility within the mainstream, majority culture while preserving the minority cultural heritage. Cultural pluralism is seen by many as the most desirable cultural milieu and has been promoted in a variety of settings, including education and employment.

The term is best recognized in special education in relation to the work of Mercer et al. (Mercer & Lewis, 1979) in the assessment of mental retardation. Mercer has argued that past efforts in assessment and placement in special education programs for mildly mentally retarded children have failed to recognize the pluralistic nature of American society. In addition to the mainstream Anglo cultural, Mercer has proposed that black, Hispanic, and other cultures need to be recognized and their norms and mores accepted as equivalent to Anglo norms and mores. Mercer attempts to equate these groups' performance on intelligence tests by developing pluralistic norms. According to Mercer (Mercer & Lewis, 1979), traditional intelligence tests developed and normed on the white majority only measure the degree of Anglocentrism (i.e., relative adherence to white middle-class values) in the home when used with minorities. To accommodate other cultures, principally black and Hispanic, Mercer developed a set of regression equations to equate the IQ distributions of each ethnic group. Mercer hopes to promote cultural pluralism in special education by equating the relative proportions of each ethnic group in special education programs. Mercer believes that by equating these distributions, the stigma associated with special education placement will be evenly distributed, leading to greater tolerance and acceptance of alternative cultures.

REFERENCE

Mercer, J. R., & Lewis, J. (1979). *System of multicultural pluralistic assessment.* New York: Psychological Association.

CECIL R. REYNOLDS
Texas A&M University

CULTURAL BIAS IN TESTING
DISPROPORTIONALITY
SYSTEM OF MULTICULTURAL PLURALISTIC ASSESSMENT

POLAND, SPECIAL EDUCATION IN

Special education in Poland has a long history. In 1817, the Institute of Deaf-Mute and Blind was established in Warsaw. In 1922 Maria Grzegorzewska (1888–1967) established the Institute of Special Education, which conducted research and trained teachers. In 1924 a special education section of the Polish Teachers Association was established (Kirejczyk, 1975). In 1976 the National Institute of Special Education was reorganized into the Graduate School of Special Education.

In the 1950s programs for the mentally retarded were segregated into 120 self-contained schools. In the 1960s there were 331 special classes within elementary schools with an enrollment of over 5000 youngsters. By the 1970s the number of such classes increased to 698, with an enrollment of nearly 11,000. Currently, there are over 250 special schools in Poland, in addition to a considerable number of special classes within public schools.

Handicapped pupils in Poland are educated in special preschool facilities, special elementary schools, special vocational schools, residential boarding schools, and rehabilitation and therapeutic facilities; they also receive home instruction (Belcerek, 1977). Various levels of interaction of exceptional children within the mainstream of education are also provided (Hulek, 1979), e.g., regular programs with some supplemental instruction, special classes within regular schools (there are presently over 1100 such classes for the mildly handicapped within the Polish public schools and 57 within the vocational schools), selected activities within regular schools, and special schools in the vicinity of regular schools, with cooperative programs.

The intellectually subnormal population in Poland has been estimated to range from 1.3 to 1.87% of the general population. Polish psychologists are using IQs in their classification of the mentally retarded. The ranges of the levels of classification are similar to the AAMD classification system. In addition to health examinations, psychological and social-developmental examinations are also given. An evaluation for the purpose of special class placement consists of a detailed classroom observation, educational evaluation, and psychological and medical evaluation. Structural classroom observation usually lasts 1 school year. Additionally, a detailed anecdotal record of the child's activities is maintained. The record includes a description of the role of the parents and the extent of their cooperation with the school. Detailed records with samples of the child's performance are sent to the child study team as additional information. Slow learners and children who do not show good educational progress are directed to prevocational classes at 14 or 15 years of age. Curriculum in Polish special schools consists of the study of the Polish language, geography, music, history, and nature.

Special educators in Poland prefer the term therapeutic pedagogy, or special pedagogy, rather than defectology, a term widely used in the Soviet Union. The mildly retarded attend 8 years of basic special school, followed by 3 years of specialized vocational training. A new 10-year curriculum for the mentally retarded recommends the following areas of training and education: adaptation and social living, language stimulation, arithmetic, visual-motor tasks, music, physical exercise, technical-practical activities, and prevocational training. Training goals and objectives for the severely handicapped include physical development and acquisition of manual skills, development of self-help and everyday activity skills, development of basic information, appropriate interpersonal relationships, and prevocational training.

Elska (1985) reported that vocational curriculum for the mildly handicapped consists of two periods per week in grades 1 through 4, four periods in grade 4, and six periods in grades 5 through 8.

Within the system of special education exist numerous vocational schools, e.g., 248 schools with a 3-year curriculum, 5 with a 4-year, and 6 with a 5-year.

Special education teachers in Poland are prepared at 4-year teacher's training institutions which they enter after graduation from high school. Some experienced teachers of subjects enter universities that have a special education teachers' training program. Since 1973, in addition to the National Institute of Special Education, special education teachers are also prepared at 11 universities (Belcerek, 1977). In 1977 the Polish Ministry of Education opened postgraduate studies in special education at the Graduate School of Special Education in Warsaw. The areas of study at the school include diagnosis and assessment of exceptionalities and the study of deaf, hard-of-hearing, chronically ill, and socially maladaptive children. Special educators are also trained at the Graduate School of Education in Krakow.

Guidelines for the training of special educators have been developed by the special education team of the Pedagogical Science Committee of the Polish Academy of Sciences (Hulek, 1978). Guidelines recommend that a student in special education become familiar with teaching nonhandicapped and subsequently handicapped children; teachers should cooperate with various agencies and institutions outside the school; and teachers should continuously be upgrading their education after graduation by attending in-service classes.

Special education studies in Poland are published in *Informator Szkolnictwa Specjalnego* (Bulletin of Special Education), *Nowa Szkola* (New School), *Szkola Specjalna* (Special School), and *Educacja* (Education; formerly *Badania Os'wiatowe*, Educational Research).

REFERENCES

Belcerek, M. (1977). Organization of special education in Poland. In A. Hulek (Ed.), *Therapeutic pedogogy*. Warsaw: State Scientific Publication.

Elska, V. (1985). Organization of vocational training of abnormal children in special schools in Polish Peoples Republic. *Defectologia* (Defectology), *1*, 62.

Holowinsky, I. Z. (1980). Special education in Poland and the Soviet Union: Current developments. In L. Mann & D. Sabatino (Eds.), *The fourth review of special education*. New York: Grune & Stratton.

Hulek, A. (1978, June). *Personnel preparation: International comparison*. Paper presented at the First World Congress on Future Special Education, Sterling, Scotland.

Hulek, A. (1979). Basic assumptions of mainstreaming exceptional children and youth. *Badania Oswiatowe* (Educational Research), *3*(15), 99–112.

Kirejczyk, K. (1975). Half-century of activity of the Special Education Section of the Polish Teacher's Association. *Szkola Specjalna* (Special School), *1*, 7–18.

IVAN Z. HOLOWINSKY
Rutgers University

POLITICS AND SPECIAL EDUCATION

Through the middle of the twentieth century, the politics surrounding special education can be characterized as the politics of exclusion. The primary decision makers were school officials who excluded from the public schools students with special needs requiring services not provided to the majority of students (Copeland, 1983). The grounds for exclusion tended to be observably inappropriate or disruptive behavior, rather than rigorous identification of the nature of students' needs or impediments to learning. Parents typically acquiesced in such decisions without questioning the denial of public school resources to their children.

A minority of the excluded students were kept at home, while the majority were referred to publicly or charitably supported residential institutions, often at some distance from their homes. There is little evidence to suggest that either local government authorities or school officials sought to establish locally situated residential institutions. Presumably, they sought to avoid the tax burden that might be incurred owing to the high costs of providing for severely impaired students.

By the beginning of the twentieth century, state-supported systems of residential institutions had emerged, with annual budgets and bureaucracies to administer them and ensure implementation of state regulations (Lynn, 1983). The institutions tended to specialize in one particular type of handicap. Funding formulas varied according to labeled disabilities. Children and youths with special needs were often improperly classified and placed because of inadequate evaluation and subjective if not prejudicial stereotypes (Kirp & Yudof, 1974). Few handicapped students transferred from one institution to another, and few permanently exited the institutions of initial placement to enter public schools. There was little coordination among different institutions. Many were, in fact, in competition with each other for scarce state resources.

Organized advocacy groups tended to lobby state legislatures individually on behalf of their particular clients (Lynn, 1983). Public policies were differentiated by type of handicap and servicing institution, advocates and clients, and implementing bureaucracies. They also varied from state to state. The overall pattern, however, was for the major portion of special needs students, funds, and service delivery systems to be located outside the public school systems.

Around the turn of the century, forces began to emerge that would contribute toward the inclusion rather than the exclusion of special needs students from public school systems (Sarason & Doris, 1979). Refinements in evaluation technology facilitated the identification of the special needs of handicapped students and suggested management and instructional methods appropriate to them. As a result, there was a widespread increase in the number of special classes within public schools (though outside the mainstream of regular students). State and federal legislative bodies enacted programs and provided funds for such classes. Parent advocacy groups and associations of special educators pressed for increased outlays to meet the needs of specific categories of handicapped children and youths.

Since services for different disabilities incurred different costs, there are indications that various funding formulas may have had a significant effect on local school policies and practices (Lynn, 1983). The proportion of students labeled as having particular disabilities varied from district to district and among states, often in relation to variations in the amounts of funds that could be obtained for specific handicaps. It also varied in relation to the type of diagnostic instruments used, the type of specialists in the school, and the type of specialized services already provided. The politics of inclusion were thus influenced by local practices and political configurations and maneuverings of special education interest groups, legislators, and bureaucracies.

Although emerging special education policies, funds, programs, and practices may not have always matched the needs of special education students, their legitimacy was increasingly accepted, and they provided the leverage for progressively including special needs students within the public schools. By 1975 mandatory legislation that provided for the education of special needs students had been passed in all but two states. By that time, the states' financial contribution had risen to more than half the total revenues allocated to special education. By 1979 approximately 140 different federal programs serving the handicapped had been enacted. By the early 1980s, localities and special districts were contributing a total of $5.8 billion; states $3.4 billion; and the federal government a total of $804 million (Lynn, 1983).

However, it became clear as support for special education advanced, that two separate systems had developed: one outside the public schools, the other inside. Parent advocates now moved to expand the one that had been established within the public schools by pressing for geographic, social, and educational inclusion of special needs students within the system. These efforts contributed to the exodus of the majority of special education students from state-run residential institutions into the public schools, and to considerable cost shifting from the former to the latter.

The legal basis for this shift came from landmark court decisions establishing the rights of special education students to free and appropriate public schooling (*Watt* v. *Stickney*, 1970; *Diana* v. *State Board of Education*, 1970 and 1973; *PARC* v. *Pennsylvania*, 1972.) The Fourteenth Amendment guarantees of due process and equal protection were invoked to affirm the rights of special needs children to the free public schooling offered to other children. The U.S. Constitution was applied to protect these students from discriminatory public school practices in the same manner in which it had been applied to protect minority group students in such decisions as *Brown* v. *Board of Education* in 1954.

While court action gave significant impetus to recognition of the rights of access of students with special needs to public schools, it did so by declaring prior school policies and practices unconstitutional. Yet such determinations tended not to specify what was or would be judged constitutional. Rather, the courts began to act as umpires, ordering plaintiffs and defendants to negotiate compromises that would be acceptable to both and not unconstitutional (Kirp, 1981). Their role was to set up a structured, adversarial process within state and local school systems in which the courts would act as mediators rather than lawgivers. The process would thus be open-ended in terms of its duration, given the lengthiness of legal proceedings, and unpredictable in terms of its possible outcomes.

The debates and conflicts as to placement of handicapped students, as well as services to be provided them, spread to the federal arena as well, where advocates sought to apply the inclusionary principles of court decisions to congressional enactments. These advocates rode on the coattails of the civil rights movement and the Civil Rights Act of 1964. They encountered countervailing forces similar to those that hampered civil rights activists in their efforts to obtain federal enactments and implement them through the federal system. The movement and the act and its numerous amendments sought to eliminate discriminatory practices by public schools that had denied students geographic, social, and educational inclusion because of their ethnicity, national origin, sex, or impoverishment (Bordier, 1983).

They provided the U.S. Congress with a model for a major legislative enactment designed to protect the rights of special needs students. Passed in 1975, the Education for All Handicapped Children Act, PL 94-142, affirmed their right to a free, appropriate public education in the least restrictive environment; required the identification, evaluation, and placement of students with special needs according to an individual educational plan (IEP); and guaranteed parental rights of participation in educational decisions concerning their children.

Under PL 94-142, the federal government was to pay a graduated percentage of average per pupil expenditures by public elementary and secondary schools, starting with 5% in 1979 and culminating in 40% by 1982. Implementation of the legislature was nominally nonmandatory. However, most school districts followed suit, presumably because they would have been hard pressed by the parents of special needs students if they did not seek to obtain available federal funds. Furthermore, an earlier law, Section 504 of the Vocational Rehabilitation Act of 1973, forbade discrimination against handicapped students in programs receiving federal financial assistance. Under 504, school districts were routinely required to sign compliance statements affirming that they did not discriminate against students on the basis of race, national origin, sex, or handicap. Since the law was initially interpreted to mean that failure to sign compliance statements could jeopardize receipt of federal financial assistance, compliance (at least on paper) via these statements became the norm.

Program guidelines and regulations of federal implementing agencies such as the Department of Health, Education, and Welfare reflected court decisions and congressional enactments and established compliance machinery within the department (later the Department of Education) and the Justice Department. The Office of Civil Rights was established to coordinate the compliance activities of the federal agencies involved. While this machinery has not been shown to have had a significant impact on educational practices, it provided an institutional and legal context for the politics of inclusion at state and local levels.

By the middle 1980s, at the end of the first Reagan presidency and at the beginning of the second term, funding for implementation of PL 94-142 was curtailed. The law and its regulations were weakened by congressional interventions and Department of Education actions designed to lessen the federal role in education and to devolve social sector responsibilities (including education in general and special education in particular) to the states.

However, because PL 94-142 had assigned significant responsibilities and funds for implementation to state authorities, by the early 1980s, the latter had already adopted laws and regulations reflective of the principles and the delivery system the federal government had mandated earlier. Such legal frameworks, created at state levels, remained in force even after the federal law itself was weakened in the 1980s. Furthermore, state and local authorities had voted to increase expenditures in order to comply with PL 94-142.

When cutbacks in funding occurred at the federal level, and signs of backlash against rapidly increasing expenditures for previously underserved groups appeared at local and state levels, advocates seeking to protect the rights of special needs students used these policies and funding allocations as precedents to justify continuing aid to special education. The role and responsibilities of state and local authorities became established independent of federal laws and regulations. Local school systems followed suit, and the progressive inclusion of special education students proceeded, at least geographically and socially if not educationally.

The enrollment of special needs students increased significantly. Schools formalized their identification, evaluation, and referral procedures, and included new participants in the process. These included committees on the handicapped, appointed by local school boards; parents and their counsels; new categories of special educators and clinicians; "regular" teachers, administrators, and ancillary personnel who had not previously had responsibility for special needs students; and multidisciplinary evaluation teams. The earlier politics of inclusion that affected the federal court system and the federal government had thus significantly increased the number of participants in the politics of inclusion at the local level. Their participation was focused on the legally specified, formalized procedures that court decisions and legislative enactments had established to improve educational services provided to students with special needs.

In the meantime, the signs of a new movement in the field of special education appeared; this would engender new policy approaches designed to integrate a whole spectrum of institutions providing services to handicapped students, including but not limited to school systems (Copeland, 1983). The needs of special education students for services beyond those provided by public schools had became increasingly apparent, and new service providers outside the schools had emerged. The institutions that provided these services, and the funding sources on which they drew, were separate from the public schools.

Interinstitutional cooperation and coordination was needed, but it would require the development of policies, regulations, and funding formulas that were complementary. For example, agencies dealing with public welfare (e.g., social services, aid for dependent children, foster care, Medicaid), health (e.g., maternal and child health), mental health/retardation/developmental disabilities, vocational rehabilitation, and corrections needed to work more closely. As the public schools incorporated the major portion of the children and youths who had previously been assigned to residential institutions, it became clear that the schools could not provide all the collateral services that these students would require.

Linking these services required interagency cooperation and the development of coalitions of advocacy groups to formulate legislation and programs to link their budgets, staffs, and services into an integrated delivery system of which the public schools would be a part. It also required intricate planning that would continue to promote the inclusion of special needs students within the educational mainstream while at the same time requiring the differentiation of these students according to their needs for external services. This blueprint for the 1990s would re-quire interagency policy making, programming, and budgeting. It would provide an ambitious and complex political agenda for the advocates of special and general education, as well as external social services for children and youths.

REFERENCES

Bordier, J. (1983). Governance and management of special education. *The Forum 4*(3), 4–13.

Copeland, W. C. (1983, January). Strategies for special education in the 1980s. *Policy Studies Review, 2* (Special Issue 1), 242–260.

Kirp, D. (1981). The bounded politics of school desegregation litigation. *Harvard Educational Review, 51*(3), 395–414.

Kirp, D., & Yudof, M. (1974). *Education and the law.* Berkeley, CA: McCutchan.

Lynn, L., Jr. (1983). The emerging system for educating handicapped children [Special issue]. *Policy Studies Review, 2*, 21–58.

Sarason, S., & Doris, J. (1979). *Educational handicap, public policy, and social history.* New York: Free Press.

NANCY BORDIER
*Hunter College, City University
of New York*

**EDUCATION FOR ALL HANDICAPPED CHILDREN ACT OF 1975
HISTORY OF SPECIAL EDUCATION
MAINSTREAMING**

POLYDIPSIA

Polydipsia is excessive drinking of water. It is often associated with water intoxication and polyuria (excessive urination). It is essential to distinguish polydipsia that is biologically based from psychogenic polydipsia (Singh, Padi, Bullard, & Freeman 1985). Most cases of polydipsia are not due to psychogenic factors (Wright, Schaefer, & Solomons, 1979). Psychogenic polydipsia involves the consumption of excessive quantities of water over a brief time period that is often associated with water intoxication. Water intoxication symptoms include headache, excessive perspiration, and vomiting, as well as more severe symptoms such as convulsions and even death (Blum, Tempey, & Lynch, 1983). Psychogenic polydipsia in children is reported to be rare and there is a lack of epidemiological studies available reporting reliable incidence. Among psychiatric patients, the incident is reported to range from 6.6 to 17.5% (Singh et al., 1985).

Biological determinants of abnormal thirst and polydipsia include diabetes, hypercalcemia, congestive heart failure, intracranial disease, potassium deficiency associated with renal disease, and meningitis (Chevalier, 1984). Another physical form of polydipsia during infancy occurs when infants are fed on demand with an overly diluted formula (Wright et al., 1979).

Psychogenic polydipsia is associated with a wide spectrum of psychopathology ranging from mild personality disorders to severe psychosis (Singh et al., 1985). Various explanations for psychogenic polydipsia have been provided including the psychodynamic concept of an oral personality (Singh et al., 1985) or an obsessive-compulsive personality (Wright et al., 1979). It may also result from a behavioral condition such as a conditioned response (Linshaw, Hipp, & Gruskin, 1974).

There is presently no single treatment recommended in the literature for psychogenic polydipsia. The treatment would depend on the aspects of the aspects of the condition relative to a particular case. Polydipsic children with central nervous system (CNS) involvement would be at risk for learning disorders and possibly special education services. Those with more severe psychological disorders may be in need of special programs for behavioral handicaps.

REFERENCES

Blum, A., Tempey, F. W., & Lynch, W. J. (1983). Somatic findings in patients with psychogenic polydipsia. *Journal of Clinical Psychiatry, 44,* 55–56.

Chevalier, R. L. (1984). Polydipsia and enuresis in childhood renin-dependent hypertension. *Journal of Pediatrics, 104,* 591–593.

Linshaw, M. A., Hipp, T., & Gruskin, A. (1974). Infantile psychogenic water drinking. *Journal of Pediatrics, 85,* 520–522.

Singh, S., Padi, M. H., Bullard, H., & Freeman, H. (1985). Water intoxication in psychiatric patients. *British Journal of Psychiatry, 146,* 127–131.

Wright, L., Schaefer, A. B., Solomons, G. (1979). *Encyclopedia of pediatric psychology.* Baltimore, MD: University Park Press.

JOSEPH D. PERRY
Kent State University

MEDICAL HISTORY
MEDICAL MANAGEMENT

PONCE DE LEON, PEDRO DE (1520–1584)

Pedro de Ponce de Leon, a Spanish Benedictine monk, is credited with creating the art of teaching the deaf. His method, as described by early historians, consisted of teaching the student to write the names of objects and then drilling the student in the production of the corresponding sounds. Whether lip reading was taught is not known, nor from the surviving accounts of his work can it be ascertained whether Ponce de Leon used any signs in teaching his students. It is known that his methods were successful with a number of children.

After Ponce de Leon's death in 1584, no one continued his work, but it is probable that his success, which received much publicity, influenced the development of methods to educate the deaf in Spain in the early seventeenth century.

REFERENCE

Bender, R. E. (1970). *The conquest of deafness.* Cleveland, OH: Case Western Reserve University Press.

PAUL IRVINE
Katonah, New York

PORCH INDEX OF COMMUNICATIVE ABILITIES (PICA)

The Porch Index of Communicative Ability (PICA) is designed to assess and quantify gestural, verbal, and graphic abilities of aphasic patients. As a reliable standardized instrument, the PICA provides quantitative information about a patient's change in communicative function and enables the examiner to make predictive judgments relative to amount of recovery (Porch, 1971).

The PICA is a battery of 18 subtests; 4 verbal subtests ranging from object naming to sentence completion; 8 gestural ranging from demonstrating object function to matching identical objects; and 6 graphic on a continiuum from writing complete sentences to copying geometric forms. For consistency, 10 common objects are used within each subtest (e.g., toothbrush, cigarette, fork, pencil). A multidimensntional binary choice 16-point scoring system is used to determine the degrees of correctness of a patient's response. The scoring system judges responses according to their accuracy, responsiveness, completeness, promptness, and efficiency. Administration time is variable, usually averaging approximately 60 minutes.

Prior to administering the PICA, participation in a 40-hour workshop for test administration, scoring, and interpretation is required. Examiners must complete a rigid testing protocol to insure a high degree of reliability. The PICA is a valuable clinical tool for providing valid and accountable descriptions of an aphasic patient's current and future level of communicative performance.

REFERENCE

Porch, B. (1971). Porch Index of Communicative Ability. Vol. 2. Administration, scoring, and interpretation (revised ed.). Palo Alto, CA: Consulting Psychologists.

SUSAN MAHANNA-BODEN
TRACY CALPIN CASTLE
Eastern Kentucky University

APHASIA
DEVELOPMENTAL APHASIA